INDIANA
UNIVERSITY

Midwestern Pioneer

Volume IV | Historical Documents Since 1816

INDIANA UNIVERSITY

Midwestern Pioneer

Volume IV / Historical Documents Since 1816

THOMAS D. CLARK

INDIANA UNIVERSITY

Bloomington

Copyright © 1977 by Indiana University

All rights reserved

*No part of this book may be reproduced or utilized in any form
or by any means, electronic or mechanical, including photocopying
and recording, or by any information storage and retrieval system,
without permission in writing from the publisher.*

Library of Congress catalog card number: 74-126207

ISBN: 0-253-37501-0

Manufactured in the United States of America

To my grandson
Edwin Hemphill Clark

CONTENTS

Preface

The history of a university of necessity has to deal with the central facts of change. No institution worth its salt remains static for any length of time. Personalities come and go, some leaving deep impressions upon the university, and others tending to level it to the quality of their personalities. Every change involves the making of decisions in context of contemporary times. The impulses and methods of arriving at decisions become collectively the heart of university growth. It can be said generally that professors and administrators have had limited prophetic powers, and too few of them have bothered to turn back to the past to learn whether or not problems which seem so original and urgent have not been discussed and dealt with by earlier generations of decision-makers.

This has been especially true when faculties and administrations have dealt with problems of curriculum, promotions, tenure, number and arrangements of credits for graduation, length of class periods, student relations, and grading systems. No statistician could even hazard an educated guess as to the time and energy professors have spent discussing these subjects, especially those of length of class periods and grading systems. It would tax a historian to say precisely how much change has taken place in these areas over the century and a half of Indiana University history covered by this documentary collection.

No facts in the operation of a university are more important than maintenance of quality standards of instruction, the learning process, research, and the assurance of academic freedom. Throughout its history, Indiana University professors and administrators have concerned themselves deeply with these questions. It has ever been a relatively simple matter to state instructional and research aims and objectives, but nearly always impossible to define and apply them. The degree of originality and freshness of a university program lies in the diversity of approaches and points of view involved in both teaching and research. It has been so easy for university decision-makers to talk about quality instruction in general terms, even to speak of it in the flowery rhetoric of academia, but it is almost impossible to define either a good teacher or good teaching in terms of the student in the classroom. The discussions go on with new deans and presidents paying tribute to "good" professors in ritualistic fidelity, but never resolving the eternal issue of adequate teaching.

Curricula content and organization have involved Indiana University professors and administrators in an almost perpetual debate since the day Andrew Wylie arrived in Bloomington to become the first president.

Even before him John Hopkins Harney and Baynard Rush Hall and the Board of Trustees had been concerned with matters of curriculum. The conflicting forces of tradition and progress have ever brought into issue the holding onto the verities while surrendering to the pressures of timeliness. Every age has made its demands upon Indiana University to be current in its offerings. In this respect, much of the history of the institution has reflected that of the state and the nation. In the twentieth century it has reflected the main forces of world history.

Maintenance of academic freedom with all its subtleties and human nuances has been historically a never ending subject of discussion and policy-making. In its most elementary human terms, academic freedom has meant the adjustments which have been made by both individual professors and the academic in order for each to function with a maximum amount of productivity and creativity. Beyond this, professors and their institutions have ever assumed the obligation to generate a common spirit of intellectualism and eternal questioning and investigation in such a manner as not to stifle individual opinions and values.

The outward thrust of Indiana University has always been optimistic. Presidents from Andrew Wylie to Elvis J. Stahr, Jr. have marched to the university podium with vibrant blueprints for the future in their inaugural addresses. They have expressed educational philosophies, beliefs that under their administration the future would be brighter, and they have pleaded for support. They have challenged the university community and its constituency to live up to the glowing ideals of public higher education in terms of their ages. In less than subtle words, the presidents have left the impression in their addresses and annual reports that things would be better in the future than in the past. For Indiana University, in its lean years, better times were bound to arrive. At least presidents and professors could always look forward to the next biennial session of the Indiana General Assembly with something approaching a childish hope.

Nowhere in the historical files of Indiana University is there a document which undertakes to delineate the Indiana legislative mind, or describes with a degree of certainty the lack of primary vision on the part of the average legislator and governor for the great potentials to the state of higher public education. There no doubt were, over a century and a half, literally hundreds of anti-intellectual legislators, but to give this as a fundamental reason for failure to provide adequate support for Indiana University from one biennium to another would be too simple an answer. There was no doubt some failure to translate in applicable terms the practicality and overall importance of an educated and cultivated Hoosier society, to lower the bars of state provincialism, to destroy prejudices of all sorts, to reduce religious and political bigotry, and to give a predominantly rural agrarian society the assurances it so actively demanded to safeguard its mores and folk culture. Too, Indiana University was from the outset involved in burdensome competition, first with church-related schools, and then with rising state-supported colleges and universities. In a fiscal sense it is doubtful that the State of Indiana at any time during the University's existence had devised a system of public revenue adequate to make possible effective appropriations to any branch of its public services. Reflected in this compilation of university documents is a long and urgent supplication for financial support. Sometimes these pleas reached a crescendo of hysterical outcries. There perhaps was never a truly good time in the University's history in terms of a fulfilled adequacy; some times were better than others.

Efforts have been made in this volume to delineate the rise of Indiana University against a full enough documentary background to give insight into the long range of its history. This has necessitated the inclusion of some documents which may appear to a reader to be ephemeral, and they are, but a university is as human as its most casual professor or student. Elements of change are hard to bring into full focus within the restrictive limitations of either formal or casual documentation. Many of them are subtle and interrelated to many other facts of university operation and growth. Nevertheless the development of a focus on change has been a primary objective in the preparation of this volume. For instance, attention has been centered upon those periods in the University's history when discernible transitions were made from one stage of operation to another. In areas of student relationships, the record is full, and at best no selection of documents can bring these into full focus. The intellectual and social impacts of students in all eras of the institution's history are reflected in youthful responses to the University, in their frustrations and dissatisfactions, and in their sentimental attachments. They too have had academic rights and defined domains of freedom to which they have often reasserted claims.

Again, this compilation of documents has of intellectual and physical necessity had to be highly selective. It is the hope of the editor, however, that a dependable historical profile of Indiana University emerges from the documents included. Of broader concern is the hope that included here is a substantial enough volume of primary materials to give both a sense of historical background and of continuity to reflect the rise of Indiana as a major public university.

So far as there is a centralizing theme aside from the basic chronological historical thread, it is that of the nurturing and expanding of the cardinal concepts of public higher education in Indiana as a cultural and pragmatic force in an open democratic society. Traceable throughout Indiana University's history are the central concepts of the founders, who themselves were influenced by the stirrings of the age in which the institution was conceived and chartered.

Documents published in this volume represent some of the sources consulted in the preparation of my three-volume history of the University. In these volumes, I undertook to narrate and interpret the history of the institution over its rather broad scope of existence and as it underwent changes and expansions. Even in so extensive a work, I of necessity had to be selective in the presentation of the subject. In neither the history nor in the compilation of this documentary collection has it been my desire to preclude further searches into the voluminous collection of materials which have been accumulated in the University's archives. It has, however, been my desire to prepare in collective form enough documentation to give everyone who becomes concerned about the past of Indiana University a concept of the processes by which changes and evolutions have occurred. Fundamentally it seems important for every person having a voice in decision-making, professors and administrators, to have at hand a source of information describing the processes of past changes. A university in which people are uninformed about its past is one without spirit or a sense of its continuity; it is an institution set afloat on a sea of confusion and needless repetition of mistakes and outmoded experiences. This volume is designed to give the staff and constituents of Indiana University some sense of the past by delineating the hopes, challenges, and realities of a century and a half of nurturing the basic concepts of public higher education within the broad concepts of the Jeffersonian dream of an informed and functional American intellectual democracy.

I am under deep obligation to Pamela Bennett and Eileen Walters, who assisted materially in the organization of this rather large body of materials. I alone am responsible for the final selection and inclusion of the published documents, and for their introduction and identification.

THOMAS D. CLARK

November 18, 1976

[I]

The Founding Years
1816–1830

The years 1816–1830 were of basic importance in the history of American higher education. In these years Thomas Jefferson's University of Virginia was founded, in the northwest two public institutions in Ohio were in operation, and in 1816 delegates to the Indiana Constitutional Convention in Corydon made education a public responsibility in the state's first Constitution. The Indiana provision for education, however, was significant in the fact that the framers of the Constitution, and later legislators, conceived the state's concern for education to cover the entire field from the most elementary one-room school to the maintenance of a seminary or college at the apex of the pyramid.

Indiana University was chartered by legislative act in 1820, but it was not until 1825 that classes were actually taught. This latter date, it must be said, is in some dispute, but evidence seems to be strong in favor of April 1825. There were men in Indiana in that year who had a somewhat developed notion of what such an institution should be, but there were few or no men who had actual experience either as teachers or as college graduates which would enable them to open the doors of a seminary and start it on the road to maturity. Baynard Rush Hall was both able and colorful, but even he was inexperienced in the field of teaching and educational administration. This was also true of John Hopkins Harney, who was subsequently added to the faculty.

An even greater lack for that of knowing precisely what the central objectives of the Seminary were, and how they might be achieved with the students and instructors already at hand. Almost immediately it became apparent to the Board of Trustees, the Board of Visitors, and the Governor of Indiana that two steps should be taken to improve the struggling little institution tucked away in the backwoods at Bloomington. First, the institution had to be administered by a man with education experience, and, second, the Seminary should be raised to college status in order more clearly to define its ultimate objective. After a search,

1

which within itself reflected the inexperience of the Trustees, the Board elected Andrew Wylie to the presidency. Wylie revealed in his inaugural address that he was a man with a vision, maybe not entirely in keeping with the more practical one of David H. Maxwell and other Hoosiers, but a vision nevertheless.

In accepting the presidency of Indiana University Andrew Wylie had to deal with three problems. First was that of organizing a new faculty, because he did not seem to get along with Hall and Harney, and second was to enlarge the seminary curriculum to more nearly reflect its new college status. Finally, the new President was called upon, along with the Board of Trustees, to operate a college from the limited resources which three townships of public lands returned to the institution.

The documents included in this section reflect clearly the nature of Indiana University during the foundation first decade of its corporate existence. Still, in 1830 Indiana College must be considered as no more than the chrysallis stage of what in time was to become a major American public university realizing in most ways the ultimate dream of a peoples' university.

Document 1

The Constitution Origin

Delegates to the Constitutional Convention at Corydon began discussion of the educational article of the Constitution on June 12, 1816, and continued the discussion intermittently until June 27, just two days before the document was finally adopted. James Scott, later to become a member of the Supreme Court, William Polke, John Boone, Dan Lynn, and John Badollet were members of the educational committee. Back of this discussion was an interesting chapter of educational concern in the Indiana Territory, revolving particularly about Vincennes University and the federal grant of public land. The general philosophy embodied in the constitutional article, however, seems to have come largely from the 1792 Constitution of New Hampshire. Whatever its sources of origin, Article 9 has remained a viable constitutional force in the history of Indiana University.

*   *   *

Knowledge and learning generally diffused through a community, being essential to the preservation of a free government, and spreading the opportunities and advantages of education through the various parts of the country being highly conducive to this end, it shall be the duty of the general assembly to provide by law for the improvement of such lands as are, or hereafter may be granted by the United States to this state, for the use of schools and to supply any funds which may be raised from such lands, or from any other quarter, to the accomplishment of the grand object for which they are or may be intended. But no lands granted for the use of schools or seminaries of learning shall be sold by authority of this state, prior to the year eighteen hundred and twenty; and the monies which may be raised out of the sale of any such lands, or otherwise obtained for the purpose aforesaid, shall be and remain a fund for the exclusive purpose of promoting the interest of literature and the sciences, and for the support of seminaries and the public schools. The general assembly shall from time to time, pass such laws as shall be calculated to encourage intellectual, scientifical, and agricultural improvement, by allowing rewards and immunities for promotion and improvement of arts, sciences, commerce, manufactures, and natural history; and to countenance and encourage the principles of humanity, industry, and morality.

It shall be the duty of the general assembly, as soon as circumstances will permit, to provide by law for a general system of education, ascending in a regular gradation from township school to a state university, wherein tuition shall be gratis, and equally open to all.

And for the promotion of such salutary end, the money, which shall be paid as an equivalent, by such persons exempt from military duty, except in times of war, shall be exclusively, and in equal proportions, applied to the support of county seminaries; also, all fines assessed for any breach of the penal laws, shall be applied to said seminaries, in the counties wherein they shall be assessed.

Article 9, sections 1, 2, and 3 Indiana Constitution, June 29, 1816.

Document 2

The Legislative Mandate

On December 7, 1819, Governor Jonathan Jennings informed the Indiana General Assembly that the time had arrived to enact legislation which would establish both public schools and the Seminary. After 1820 the Assembly could authorize the sale of the township lands. The bill creating the Seminary was read the second time on January 15, 1820, and was passed by the Legislature on January 19. The law was signed by Governor Jennings January 20, 1820, and the way was cleared for the location and organization of Indiana Seminary in the Perry Township in Monroe County.

*   *   *

CHAPTER XLVIII
AN ACT to establish a State Seminary, and for other purposes.
APPROVED, JANUARY 20, 1820

SEC. 1. BE *it enacted by the General Assembly of the State of Indiana,* That Charles Dewey, Jonathan Lindley, David H. Maxwell, John M. Jenkins, Jonathan Nichols, and William Lowe, be, and they are hereby appointed trustees of the state seminary, for the state of Indiana, and shall be known by the name and style of the trustees of the state seminary, of the state of Indiana, and they, and their successors in office, shall have perpetual succession, and by the name and style aforesaid, shall be able and capable in law, to sue and be sued, plead, and be impleaded, answer, and be answered unto, as a body corporate and politic, in any court of justice; and the trustees hereby appointed, shall continue in office, until the first day of January, one thousand eight hundred and twenty-one, and until their successors are chosen and qualified.

SEC. 2. The trustees aforesaid, or a majority of them, shall meet at Blooming-ton, in the county of Monroe, on the first Monday in June next, or so soon thereafter, as may be convenient, and being first duly sworn to discharge the duties of their office, shall repair to the reserved township of land in said county, which was granted by Congress to this state, for the use of a seminary of learning, and proceed to select an eligible and convenient site for a state seminary.

SEC. 3. It shall be lawful for the trustees hereby appointed, to appoint an agent, who shall give bond with security to be approved of by the trustees afore-said, payable to the Governor and his successors in office, for the use of the state seminary aforesaid, in the sum of twenty thousand dollars, conditioned for the faithful performance of the duties of his office; and it shall be the duty of the agent aforesaid, after taking an oath of office, to proceed to lay off, and expose to sale, under the sanction of the trustees aforesaid, any number of lots, or quantity of land, within the reserved township, aforesaid, and contiguous to Bloomington, not exceeding one section, or six hundred and forty acres thereof.

SEC. 4. It shall be the duty of the agent aforesaid, first to expose to sale, such lots as may be selected most contiguous to the site which may be selected for the seminary aforesaid, and take of the purchasers of any lots or lands which he may sell, under the provisions of this act, such payments and security therefor, as may be directed by the trustees aforesaid.

SEC. 5. The trustees aforesaid, shall so soon as they deem it expedient, proceed to the erection of a suitable building for a state seminary, as also a suitable and commodious house for a Professor, on the site which may be selected by them for that purpose.

SEC. 6. The trustees aforesaid, shall within ten days after the meeting of the next General Assembly, lay before them a true and perfect statement of their proceedings so far as they have progressed under the provisions of this act, and a plat of the lots or lands laid off and sold, and the amount of the proceeds of such sales, and also a plan of buildings, by them erected, or proposed to be erected.

SEC. 7. The trustees hereby appointed, shall before they enter upon the duties of their office, give bond and security, to be approved of by the Governor, in the sum of five thousand dollars, payable to the Governor and his successors in office, for the use of the state seminary, conditioned for the faithful performance of the duties of their office; and if any vacancy shall happen in the office of trustees, the governor shall fill such vacancy, by an appointment which shall ex-pire on the first day of January next.

The Laws of the State of Indiana, 4th Session, 1819, pp. 82–83.

Document 3

Opening the Seminary Doors

Many of the historical sources dealing with the actual beginnings of Indiana Seminary accept May 1, 1824, as the correct date. There is, however, sufficient vagueness about this date to bring it under question. John Hopkins Harney wrote on July 4, 1828, that "This institution formerly called the State Seminary was commenced at this place little more than three years ago under favorable circumstances." Earlier the Indiana *Gazette,* January 8, and April 3, 1825, reported that the Seminary had just opened. It seems that evidence is substantial enough to accept April 3, 1825, as the opening date. The brief statement by *Amator Scientiae,* August 4, 1825, seems to substantiate the April opening.

*   *   *

Communication.
Indiana State Seminary.—Classical instruction has now been carried on in the state Seminary at Bloomington, since the first Monday of last April.—The teacher, the Rev. Raynard [*sic*] R. Hall, is a graduate of Union college, N. York, is a thorough and accomplished scholar—and is most assiduous in his attention to the instruction of the scholars, and to the interests of the institution.

The progress of the pupils has been good—the first session of the present year will soon close, and the second commence near the 20th of September. It may be important for persons desirous of the advantages of the institution to know this.— The present prospect of the institution is encouraging to its friends, and the friends of literature.

AMATOR SCIENTIAE

Vincennes; Aug. 4, 1825.

Vincennes *Western Sun,* August 13, 1825.

Document 4

The Public Land Legacy

The Enabling Act of April 19, 1816, which responded to the Indiana territorial petition for statehood added an extra township to the one granted in 1785 in the Northwest Land Ordinance, and subsequently provided for on March 26, 1804, by an Act of Congress. The Constitution of 1816, and the legislative act of January 19, 1820 creating the Indiana Seminary reserved the lands to the Seminary. Perry Township was located in 1820, and in July of that year the school was permanently located in Bloomington. Governor Ray's report is a description of the utilization of this township land down to 1825.

*   *   *

By a grant of Congress, a section of land in each township in this state, has been invested in the inhabitants of such townships for the use of Common Schools; two entire townships have been invested in the Legislature for the use of a State Seminary, and by a provision of our constitution; all fines assessed for a breach of the penal laws, and all commutations for militia services, are appropriated to the use of County Seminaries. The common school lands are estimated at six hundred and eight thousand, two hundred and seven acres, which, at two dollars per acre, would produce a fund of one million two hundred and sixteen thousand four hundred and forty-four dollars. This sum at interest at six per centum per annum, would produce seventy-two thousand nine hundred and eighty-six dollars yearly. There is now forty thousand nine hundred and sixty acres of college lands granted to the state; all of which will show that we are furnished *with means*. It still remains for the Legislature to improve and increase these several funds, so as to carry this general scheme of education into complete effect. For further and better information on this subject in detail, permit me to refer you to the able and lucid report of a committee raised by a joint resolution of the General Assembly, approved January 9th, 1821, which was made at the ensuing session, and is now on file in the office of the Secretary of State. This report is worthy an attentive examination. I will remark, however, that this report is predicated upon a supposition that the Legislature can legally sell the lands for the use of township schools. Upon this point much doubt and great diversity of opinion exists, and it is believed that upon an attentive examination of the terms of the compact granting the sale of these lands, the right to sell will at least appear questionable, and the reasoning to support that position loose and unsatisfactory, unless the consent of the landholders in each township can be obtained. It may be noticed that section No. 16, in each township is *granted to the inhabitants of such township for the use of schools;* and they may view it as an incident to their purchase. There can be no doubt as to the right of the Legislature to sell the seminary lands, for they are by the terms of the grant *"vested in the Legislature,"* to be appropriated solely to the use of a Seminary by the Legislature; and the 1st section, 9th article of the constitution wisely intimates the propriety of a sale of these lands after the year 1820. It may well be worth your attention to enquire whether they are not daily diminishing in value under the existing mode of leasing them.

The Seminary at Bloomington, supported in part by one of these townships, is in as flourishing a condition as could have been anticipated. Tuition is comparatively cheap, and no pains are spared to make the institution respectable. It cannot, I think, fail to receive our patronage. It has been suggested, that it would be serviceable to the Seminary, to place it under a directory remote from the place of its location.

The Secretary of State will lay before you the result of the enumeration of the free white male inhabitants of this state, authorized by an act of the last General Assembly, to a conformity with which the rates of representation are at this session to be reduced. In noticing the present strength of the state it may not be uninteresting to take a review of its *unparalleled increase* for the last twenty-five years. In the year 1800, it is supposed the territory contained 5,000 souls; in 1805, the population is estimated at 11,000; in 1810, at 24,000; in 1815, at 68,780; in 1820, when a census was taken under a law of the United States, at 147,178; in 1825, on a fair computation, at 250,000. Thus we perceive that our increase since 1800, proceeding in geometrical ratio, has amounted almost to a duplication every five years. Calculating upon a multiplication of inducements to settle our domains, and the continued expansion of our territory, by the year 1830 we will appear respectable in the councils of the federal government. To know that at this time we can number forty thousand citizen soldiers, give us a presentiment of our glorious destiny.

Indiana *Senate Journal,* 1825–26, p. 29.

Document 5

The Professor and the Seminary

This news story from the Vincennes *Western Sun* seems to substantiate the "first Monday of April (1825) next" as the correct date for the opening of the Seminary. Baynard R. Hall, a Presbyterian minister and graduate of Union College and Princeton Theological Seminary, was the first professor.

*   *   *

STATE SEMINARY OF INDIANA
NOTICE

The Trustees of this institution are authorized to inform the public that the Seminary buildings are now in a state of preparation, and will be ready for the reception of Students by the *first Monday of April next;* at which time the first session will commence under the superintendance of the Rev'd. BAYNARD R. HALL, whom the trustees have engaged as a teacher. Mr. Hall is a gentleman, whose classical attainments are perhaps not inferior to any in the western country; and whose acquaintance with the most approved methods of instruction in some of the best universities in the U. States, and whose morals, manners, and address, render him every way qualified to give dignity and character to the institution.

There will be two sessions of five months, in the year.

The admission fee for each scholar at the commencement of every session will be two dollars and fifty cents, making the expense of tuition for a year the sum of five dollars.

Good boarding can be had in respectable families, either in town, or country, at convenient distances, and on moderate terms, not exceeding $1 25 cents per week.

The institution will for the present be strictly classical, and each scholar will be required to furnish himself with a supply of classical books, of which the following are recommended, and will be needed from term to term.

Ross's Latin Grammar, latest edition.
Colloquies of Corderius. Latin.
Selectae e Veteri, do.
Selectae e Profanis, do.
Cæsar, do do.
Virgil, and Mairs' introduction, do.
Valpy's Grammar—latest edition. Greek.
Testament, do.
Graeca minora, do. do.

None of these books are to be accompanied with an English translation, but this remark is not intended to extend to such editions as have notes in English; which indeed for beginners are preferable.

The choice of Lexicons in either language is left discretionary with the student: Ainsworth's in Latin and Schrevelius' in Greek, are however recommended. Other books than these specified, as progress in the languages is made, will hereafter be necessary; but these only at present need be procured[.] The whole number of students according to the different degrees of improvement, will be distributed into several classes in which the books just enumerated are to be employed.

The Seminary buildings are erected on an elevated situation, affording a handsome view of Bloomington the county seat of Monroe county, and also a commanding prospect of the adjacent country which is altogether pleasant and well calculated for rural retreats; and as it regards the healthiness of its situation, we hazard nothing in the assertion, that it cannot be excelled by any in the western country.

JOSHUA O. HOWE.
JOHN KETCHAM.
JONATHAN NICHOLS.
SAMUEL DODDS.
WILLIAM LOWE.
D. H. MAXWELL.
Trustees.

Bloomington, January 7, 1825.

Vincennes *Western Sun,* February 19, 1825 and *General Advertiser.*

Document 6

A Vein of Gubernatorial Optimism

In this message to the Indiana General Assembly on December 8, 1826, Governor Ray struck at the very heart of the problem of managing public institutional lands in the land-hungry early decades of the nineteenth century on the American frontier. Management of the lands governed the fate of the Indiana Seminary itself, and the Governor knew how careless and indifferent the public could be in a matter of this sort.

*   *   *

But, while our best energies are exerted, to improve the natural advantages and to bring into active and useful exertion, the various resources of the state, shall we leave to neglect, the culture of the mind, the education of our youth, and the advancement of science and intelligence amongst our fellow-citizens? The reflection, that we are deeply responsible to our successors and to posterity, for a march of intellect co-equal with the flowing increase of our population—with the regenerated spirit of the age—and for a diffusion of light and knowledge in proportion to the brightening rays which daily beam new lustre on our falling forests, forbid it. The awakened zeal of the world in the cause of mind, and the golden opportunity which *we* possess, to shine in the republic of letters forbid it. The pride of our state, aroused by the noble examples of her sisters, calls on us to be no longer indebted to them for the progress of knowledge and science. And the time has fully come, when our prospects and circumstances will permit this heart-cheering subject to receive the fostering attention and countenance of the legislature. Those governments that exist through their usurpation, frauds and force, and whose principle is fear, require an ignorant populace; but in one like ours, where virtue is the principle, and *reason* alone moves the great machinery, intelligence is the rock on which all hope is reposed. I would therefore, earnestly suggest the propriety of extending the means of the state to the furtherance of the object, with such liberality as our combined means will justify. With the control of the available donation in lands, which has been vested in *you*, for the use of a seminary of learning, and of the section reserved to the *inhabitants* of the several congressional townships for the use of *common schools*, a treasury filled beyond the correspondent charges against it, and a people anxious for the dissemination of useful knowledge to applaud you, I have every confidence that the subject of education from its *first* principles to its more *advanced* and liberal summits, will receive your unreserved sanction and effectual encouragement. It must be admitted, that these lands subject to our use for the best of purposes, although intrinsically valuable, are at present in a great degree, either wild, and covered with nature's rank, rich, uncultivated growth, (as is to be feared are the minds of too many of our rising youth) or only so partially improved and tenanted, as to be of but trifling avail now, and of little promise to the future. The propriety is therefore respectfully submitted, of giving such permanency to the management or disposal of these various tracts, as will leave an *immediate* aid and spring to the high objects they were designed to advance. The public Seminary at Bloomington, with the exertions of its directors, and of the scientific professor under whose immediate charge the institution, with every propriety is placed, is advancing in usefulness and character. It is presented as deserving your paternal care, and as requiring only your favorable countenance and support, to ensure its permanency and respectability. If the judicious intimation in our constitution as to a sale of the seminary lands after the year 1820, should be repulsed by your views of policy, and our state institutions are left solely to rely upon the proceeds of those lands for support, you can then, easily be made sensible of the necessity of appropriating something from the treasury towards the improvement of this rising seminary. Books, apparatus for the illustration of the sciences, and a decent compensation to the professor are indispensible pre-requisites to the success of the college. With such ample resources in land as we possess for building up and patronizing a great state institution of learning, in Indiana, she should no longer indulge herself in a state of passivity on this subject, but at once admit the truism, that letters and intelligence are the precursors of power. Education made the Greeks good members of the commonwealth by enabling them to acquire such arts and habits, as rendered their services available, in peace or war. In the most flourishing period of the Roman republic, literature had a patron in every great man; and instruction prepared all orders of their youth for the senate, the bar, or the field. But here in this land of freedom more than any where else, knowledge is our sword and shield—hence let us gird upon posterity this formidable panoply, and the republic is safe.

That section of land in each congressional township, for the use of common schools requires your particular notice. The laws regulating these lands are susceptible of improvement. Something should be done to prevent the commission of waste upon them. To find the most effectual preventive there is some difficulty. What strikes me as most likely to succeed, under the present mode of disposing of them, is to give long leases for a certain and determinate term of years, on a yearly ground rent, and to subject tresspassers to an indictment in the circuit court. In this way you may create such an interest in the lessee as to induce him to preserve the soil and timber; whilst on the other hand you threaten him and all others with the terrors of a public prosecution. You will find that the law regulating these sections, is extremely loose, having no vindicatory clause. The example, however, which Ohio has set in getting an act of Congress passed for the sale of similar lands, may influence your decision, and induce you to embrace that course. Whatever plan you may devise, let it have uniformity in view. There are already leases given in this state on these lands for almost every term, from five to ninety nine years. This will present great confusion, to the future legislator, if he ever concludes to dispose of the right of soil.

Indiana *Senate Journal*, 1826–27, pp. 31–34.

Document 7

Disposition of the Lands in Three Townships

This act of the Indiana General Assembly, January 25, 1827, was a response to Governor Ray's request for the establishment of administrative procedure to authorize oversight of the public lands appropriated to Indiana Seminary. The Act outlines the terms by which the lands should be divided and sold.

*   *   *

CHAPTER C.
An Act concerning the Seminary Townships of land in
Gibson and Monroe Counties.
(APPROVED—JANUARY 25, 1827)

SEC. 1. *Be it enacted by the General Assembly of the State of Indiana,* That James Smith of Gibson county be, and he is hereby appointed commissioner on behalf of this state, and authorized to sell the reserved townships of Seminary lands in Gibson county; and that James Borland of Monroe county be, and he is hereby appointed commissioner as aforesaid, and authorized to make sale of the reserved township of Seminary lands in Monroe county, in manner and form as hereinafter directed.

SEC. 2. That before entering upon the duties enjoined by this act, the commissioners aforesaid shall severally be sworn by some authorized person, faithfully to perform their duty as herein required, and moreover give bond with approved sureties in the penalty of fifty thousand dollars each, payable to the state of Indiana, and to be approved of by the Governor, and conditioned for the faithful performance of the duties of the office aforesaid; which bond shall be filed in the office of the auditor of public accounts, and shall from its date, be a lien on the lands and tenements of the obligors.

SEC. 3. That said commissioners shall severally proceed to divide the lands in the several townships by half quarter sections, from north to south, into first, second and third rate, and severally shall make out and deposit a map or plat thereof, with the recorders of Gibson and Monroe counties severally, who shall forward transcripts thereof to the treasurer of state: And it is hereby enacted, that the minimum price of the said first rate land shall be three dollars and fifty cents, or the second rate land two dollars and twenty-five cents, and of the third rate land, one dollar and twenty-five cents per acre; and no sale of any of said lands shall be for a less sum than the minimum price aforesaid.

SEC. 4. That the said commissioner of the Gibson reserved township, shall proceed on the first Monday of September next, to sell the lands in his township; and the said commissioner of the Monroe reserved township, shall proceed to sell the lands in his township on the first Monday of October next; of which sales notice shall be given by the treasurer of this state, in the newspapers published at the seat of government, and such other places as he may deem advisable, for a reasonable time prior thereto; which sales shall severally continue not exceeding two weeks.

SEC. 5. That the said lands shall be sold at public auction, in half quarter sections, and one fourth of the purchase money shall be paid at the time of sale, and the balance due to remain at interest, at the option of the purchaser, his heirs and assigns, for ten years, and thereafter at the option of the state commissioners for that purpose, under the direction of the General Assembly: *Provided,* That the interest shall be punctually paid in advance, at the commencement of each year, and a failure to pay the interest of two years successively, for ninety days after the second years interest becomes due, shall forfeit to the state, for the use of said seminary, the tract of land on which such interest may be due, also the benefit of the contract by which it is held, and the state shall forthwith have right to hold and possess such lands; and all purchasers, their heirs or assigns, after a failure to pay the first interest due in advance as aforesaid, shall from thenceforth be considered as tenants at will only; and if he, she or they shall after that time, commit any unnecessary waste upon the premises occupied, and upon which the interest has not been paid as aforesaid, it shall be the duty of the commissioner of the proper township, to commence in his own name, for the use of the seminary fund, an action of trespass before some justice of the peace in the county where the land lies; on the trial of which a jury may be summoned, and if the jury return a verdict of guilty, the justice shall render a judgment thereon, which verdict and judgment shall justify and authorize the said commissioner to take immediate possession of the tract of land in question, by calling to his assistance, if necessary, a posse comitatus of his county; and from that time the state shall of right hold and possess such land. And whenever full payment shall be made for any tract of land sold as aforesaid, the purchaser, his heirs and assigns, shall be entitled to a patent therefor from the state of Indiana, under the seal thereof, signed by the Governor, and countersigned by the Treasurer of state.

SEC. 6. That the commissioners aforesaid shall severally receive the moneys arising from the sales of land in their respective townships, and shall give to purchaser certificates specifying the amount by them paid, the tract of land purchased and the balance due thereon; which certificates shall be presented to the recorder of the county in which such township is situate; and it is hereby made the duty of said recorder to record such certificate at full length in a book to be by him kept for that purpose, and afterwards to return such certificate to the proper owner; and whenever other payments may be made the said commissioner shall receipt therefor, and such receipt shall be presented as aforesaid to the proper recorder, who shall record the same as herein before directed, and also endorse the amount so paid on the back of the original certificate; and when final payment shall be made, a final certificate shall be given by the said recorder to the purchaser, his heirs or assigns; and on presentation thereof, and filing the same with the treasurer of state, the purchaser, his heirs or assigns, shall be entitled to receive a patent as aforesaid.

SEC. 7. That the said commissioners and recorders shall severally keep proper books of accounts, and shall make quarterly reports to the treasurer of state for their transactions under this act; and it is hereby made the duty of said treasurer, to devise the forms of receipts and certificates, and direct the mode of keeping accounts and making quarterly reports as aforesaid, previous to the day of sale.

SEC. 8. That it shall be the duty of said commissioners to pay over to the state treasurer, or his order, all moneys which may come into their hands from the sale of the lands aforesaid, at such times as may be directed by said treasurer, and to take his receipt therefor.

SEC. 9. That the treasurer of state shall, under the direction of the General Assembly, direct a public sale of all tracts of land authorized by this act to be sold, and which may remain unsold at the sales herein provided for, in like form and upon like conditions as heretofore prescribed.

SEC. 10. That three sections of the seminary lands in Monroe county, viz: one on the east, one on the south, and one on the west, the most contiguous to the section heretofore sold, and on which the state seminary buildings are now erected, shall be and the same are hereby reserved from sale.

SEC. 11. That the treasurer of state shall keep an account current with the state seminary, of and concerning the monied transactions provided for by this act, and with the commissioners aforesaid; and the said treasurer shall be subject, in relation to the trust, duties and liabilities by this act created, to the provisions of the revenue laws of this state so far as they are applicable.

SEC. 12. That it shall be the duty of the treasurer of state to pay quarter yearly, to the president of the board of trustees of the state seminary, who may reside in Monroe county, or to the order of said president signed by himself and countersigned by the secretary of said board, any interest of money in his hands that may heretofore have accrued, or that may hereafter accrue from the sales of the seminary townships aforesaid: *Provided however,* That the treasurer shall in no case pay over as aforesaid, any greater sum than shall be allowed yearly, as a salary to the teacher or teachers of the state seminary, by the trustees authorized by law to make such allowances.

SEC. 13. That it shall be the duty of the commissioners of Gibson and Monroe counties, severally to give yearly leases on any improved unsold land within their respective townships, for the greatest sum they can obtain, and the moneys arising from such leases when collected, shall be paid over by said commissioners to the state treasurer, as herein before directed.

SEC. 14. That the said commissioners shall severally receive two per centum upon all moneys by them paid over to the state treasurer as aforesaid, in full for all services required by this act; and the recorders of Gibson and Monroe counties, for their services, shall severally receive such compensation as may hereafter be allowed by law.

SEC. 15. If the appointment of both, or either of said commissioners, shall become vacated by death, removal, or resignation, the Governor shall fill such vacancy until an election shall be made by a subsequent legislature, who shall give the same bond and security, and be subject to the same liabilities as the commissioners appointed under this act are or may be.

SEC. 16. That all laws and parts of laws heretofore in force, on the subject of leasing said reserved townships of land, be and the same are hereby repealed.

CHAPTER CI.

An Act appointing a Board of Visitors to the State Seminary at Bloomington, and for advancing the interests of said institution.

[APPROVED—JANUARY 26, 1827.]

SEC. 1. *Be it enacted by the General Assembly of the State of Indiana,* That the Governor and Lieutenant Governor, for the time being, the judges of the Supreme Court of this state, the judge of the District Court of the United States, for the district of Indiana, the District Attorney of said district, Moses Tabbs,

John E. Hubbs, Samuel Hall, Samuel Gwathney, Jeremiah Rowland, Reuben W. Nelson, Jeremiah Sullivan, Samuel Merrill, John Test, William B. Laughlin, William M'Clure, William S. Cornett, Beaumont Parkes, Henry Way, Jeremiah Cash, Samuel Scott and George H. Dunn, be, and they are hereby appointed a board of visitors to the state seminary at Bloomington; to continue as such for three years from the date of this act, and until successors are appointed, who, or any five of whom are authorized and requested to act as visitors aforesaid in the manner hereinafter specified.

SEC. 2. The board of visitors aforesaid are hereby authorized semi-annually, on the Thursdays preceding the session of the supreme court at Indianapolis, to assemble in the town of Bloomington, and proceed to visit and inspect the seminary aforesaid; whenever any five of the above named visitors shall convene in pursuance of this act, they shall appoint from their number, a president and secretary of said board; the president so appointed shall, as soon as convenient, notify the president or some one of the trustees of said state seminary, of their attendance at said place, and readiness to proceed in visiting and inspecting the said seminary; whose duty it shall be forthwith to call a meeting of said trustees, who are hereby required to attend at the place of meeting of said board of visitors, with the records of the corporation, and submit the same to the inspection and examination of said board of visitors, and also to give such verbal explanation of the past proceedings of said trustees as may be called for, or which the said trustees may deem necessary or proper. It shall further be the duty of said trustees, at the same time to exhibit in writing to said visitors, a detailed report of the finances of the seminary; the number of teachers and students belonging to said seminary; the various branches of science and literature taught; the course of tuition and discipline adopted; the by-laws and regulations enacted, as well for the teachers as the students, and the progress made by the students; noting particularly in said report, the names of those students who have distinguished themselves in any or all the branches of education, and also those who have been exemplary for their good conduct.

SEC. 3. After the examination of the records aforesaid, together with the report of said trustees, which shall be retained and preserved by the said visitors, it shall be the duty of the said trustees to conduct the said visitors to the hall or building in which the students are assembled, for the purpose of personally inspecting their studies and progress; during which inspection, it shall be the duty of the principal and assistant teachers to call on the several students for such exhibition of their scholarship as may be in their power to give; and to invite the said board of visitors individually or collectively, to propound any question to the students, or to suggest any course of examination they may think proper; and at the close of said examination, the visitors aforesaid by their president or some member of the board, shall deliver such address to the students as to them shall seem proper.

SEC. 4. The said board of visitors are hereby authorized to recommend the repeal of any by-laws, rules or regulations adopted by the trustees of the state seminary, which to them may seen inexpedient, improper, or contrary to the interests of the institution.

SEC. 5. It shall be the duty of the visitors to make an annual report of their proceedings to the General Assembly, which shall be addressed to the speaker of the house of representatives, and which shall contain the report of the trustees in the second section provided for, their own acts and opinions, and also any recommendations they may think proper to make, of such measures, within the competency of the legislature, as may tend to sustain, foster and improve the seminary aforesaid.

Laws of Indiana, 1826–27, pp. 95–99, 99–100.

Document 8

The Seminary in Operation, the First Report

The Board of Visitors, November 1, 1827, made a favorable report on the character of instruction, the professors, and student responses in the Indiana Seminary. In two years the infant institution had made genuine progress, and Professors Baynard Rush Hall and John Hopkins Harney had given a good account of their stewardship.

*　　*　　*

The examination of the students at the State Seminary in Bloomington, took place on Thursday last in the presence of the trustees of the institution, the board of visitors appointed by the legislature, and a respectable assemblage of private citizens. The exercises were commenced at 9 o'clock in the morning and continued until nearly sunset except a short intermission at noon. Different classes were critically examined in the Latin and Greek Grammars, the Introduction to making Latin and Greek, Caesar, Virgil, Graeca Minora, Geography, Geometry and Algebra. The performances were highly creditable both to the scholars and the professors, and there appeared to be but one opinion amongst those present, on the propriety of proceeding immediately to a course of collegiate studies, and giving the institution the rank and dignity of a College. The materials for commencing respectably are already on the spot. The two professors, MR. HALL of the languages and MR. HARNEY of the mathematics, if we may judge from the late examination, would do honor to any of the colleges of our country. Students for forming two respectable classes are now there, and nothing within ordinary calculation to ensure success appears to be wanting, but the approbation of the legislature, the appointment of a President who shall be worthy of public confidence, and the commencement of a Library and Philosophical Apparatus. Sufficient funds for these objects are under the control of the state. The late sales of the Seminary Township in Monroe amounted to about $23,000, those of the township in Gibson, to about $7,000. These sums, with $2,300 previously in the treasury and the rents of land yet unsold, will yield not less than $2,000 annually. A capatious building for recitations and a house for one of the Professors are already erected. The other building might be erected from further sales of land or be dispensed with for the present.

The central, healthy and delightful situation of Bloomington, the low price of tuition and boarding; both of which will not exceed twenty four dollars for a session of five months—and the character of the Professors employed there, can scarcely fail of producing results not less useful than honorable to the state. That the best plan which could possibly be devised for a Literary Institution will, in the present case, be adopted, or that the Trustees or Professors will be persons against whom, no one will take exceptions, cannot reasonably be expected. But one plan can be followed and but one set of men employed. There may have been other measures that would have ensured success and other men of equal merit, but it is not certain that those measures would have been pursued as perseveringly or those men have united as harmoniously as in the present case. It is not the part of wisdom to make changes without necessity, nor of patriotism to oppose the design because the favorite means to promote it are not used.

Indianapolis *Indiana Journal,* November 6, 1827.

Document 9

Governor Ray Looks Ahead

The optimistic report of the Board of Visitors which reached Governor Ray early in November, 1827 was reflected in his message to the General Assembly, December 4, 1827, in which he transmitted the Board's enthusiasm. This message was of major importance because it contained the recommendation that Indiana Seminary be transformed into Indiana College.

*   *   *

The board of visitors to the Bloomington Seminary, sat there, for the first time, on the first Thursday of the last month. They witnessed, with special satisfaction, the examination of the students, in the various branches of science and literature, to which their attention had been devoted by their able instructors. The proficiency to which many scholars had attained in the Latin and Greek languages, and in the Mathematics, presented both students and professors in the most favorable light. That portion of Seminary lands, which was sold in Monroe and Gibson counties, brought a fair price, producing near thirty thousand dollars. The interest upon this sum, together with the amount due the institution from the state, will produce an interest of two thousand dollars for its support. All unite in supposing, that the interest on the fund is now sufficient to justify the institution in taking the rank of a college, and to employ a President and other Professors; leaving a sum to be appropriated, each year, to purchase a library and apparatus. Your body is respectfully requested to give the institution a college charter. When all this shall have been accomplished, but little doubt is entertained, that the youth of Indiana can obtain their education at home, without performing an unnatural journey to another state for it. Proper regulations will follow, as a matter of course, so as to enable the poor to enjoy its advantages, as well as the rich.

Indiana *Senate Journal,* 1827–28, p. 23.

Document 10

The Report of the Board of Visitors

This was the third stage of the Report of the Board of Visitors in which the creation of an institution of collegiate rank in Bloomington neared realization.

*   *   *

The Speaker laid before the house the following communication, to wit:
To the Speaker of the House of Representatives:

In compliance with the "act appointed a Board of Visitors to the State Seminary at Bloomington," approved January 26, 1827, the following persons, viz. James B. Ray, James Scott, R. W. Nelson, Samuel Hall and Samuel Merrill convened at Bloomington on Thursday the 1st day of November, 1827.—The Board was organised by appointing James Scott President, and Samuel Hall Secretary. The duty prescribed to the Visitors of "personally inspecting the studies and progress of the students," was carefully attended to, for the principal part of the day, during which every scholar was critically examined in the different branches of education, in which he had been engaged. It is with much pleasure that the Board express their full approbation of the manner in which both teachers and scholars, acquitted themselves on this subject; there was but one opinion among the Visitors; that more ability to teach, was exhibited by the Professors, and more apparent proficiency by the scholars, than they had ever before witnessed on a similar occasion.

The Board afterwards proceeded to examine the records of the corporation, the proceedings of the trustees and the by-laws of the institution, which were submitted to them, and they found with much satisfaction, that every requisite provision had been made to advance the interests of science, to preserve morality and good order, and to guard against sectarian influence.

At the request of the trustees, the board also examined their proceedings in relation to the appointment of the last professor, and on this subject, the Visitors were unanimous in their approbation.

In conclusion, the Visitors conceive, that they should not fully perform their duty, were they not to suggest to the Legislature, the propriety of giving collegiate powers to the institution at Bloomington.

The time they think has arrived, when the liberal donation by Congress for a state University should be made to realize some of the benefits for which it was designed. The sale of the Seminary lands has produced the necessary funds— suitable Professors are already engaged—students too are there, anxious to obtain at home what they must otherwise seek from abroad. The buildings immediately wanted have been erected, and Bloomington from its healthy and central situation, and its cheap and abundant markets affords, it is believed, facilities for promoting the interests of literature which should not be neglected.

Respectfully submitted,
JAMES SCOTT, *President.*

SAMUEL HALL, *Sec'ry.*

The above report was read and referred to the committee on Education.

Indiana *House Journal,* 1827–28, pp. 64–65.

Document 11

Indiana College

The result of the Report of the Board of Visitors and Governor Ray's supportive message was the enactment, January 24, 1828, of the law transforming Indiana Seminary into "a College, adjacent to the town of Bloomington in the County of Monroe." The law set forth the purposes of the college and the conditions for managing its instructional and fiscal affairs.

*   *   *

An act to establish a College in the State of Indiana.

SEC. 1. Be it enacted by the General Assembly of the State of Indiana, That there shall be, and hereby is created and established, a College, adjacent to the town of Bloomington in the County of Monroe, for the education of youth in the American, learned, and foreign languages, the useful arts, Sciences, and literature, to be known by the name and style of the Indiana College, and to be governed and regulated as hereinafter directed.

SEC. 2. There shall be a board of Trustees appointed consisting of fifteen persons residents of this state, who shall be, and hereby are constituted a body corperate and polatic, by the name of "the Trustees of the Indiana College," and in their said corperate name and capacity may sue, and be sued, plead and be impleaded in any court of record, and by that name shall have perpetual succession.

SEC. 3. The said Trustees shall fill all vacancies which may happen in their own body, elect a president of the Board, Secretary, Treasurer, and such other officers as may be necessary for the good order and government of said corporation, and shall be competent at law and in equity to take to themselves and their successors in their said corperate name, any estate, real, personal or mixed, by the gift, grant, bargain, sale, conveyance, will, devise or bequest of any person or persons whomsoever, and the same estate, whether real or personal, to grant, bargain, sell, convey, demise, let, place out on interest, or otherwise dispose of, for the use of the said College, in such manner as to them shall seem most beneficial to the institution, and to receive the rents, issues, profits, income and interest thereon, and apply the same to the proper use and support of the said College and generally in their said corperate name, shall have full power to do and transact all and every the business, touching or concerning the premises, or which shall be incidently necessary thereto, as fully and effectually as any natural person, body politic or corperate may or can do, in the management of their own concerns, and to hold, enjoy, exercise and use the rights, powers and privileges incident to bodies politic or corperate, in law and in equity.

SEC. 4. The said Trustees shall cause to be made for their use, one common seal with such devices and inscriptions thereon as they shall think proper, under, and by which all deeds, diplomas, certificates and acts of the said corporation shall pass and be authenticated.

SEC. 5. The said Trustees or a majority of them shall meet at Bloomington in the County of Monroe on the first Monday in May next, and after severally taking an oath or affirmation faithfully and impartially to discharge the duties by this act enjoined, shall proceed to organize a board by electing one of their members as President, and the board when so formed, shall appoint a Secretary and Treasurer, who shall severally before entering upon the duties of their respective offices, take an oath or affirmation faithfully and impartially to perform the duties appertaining to their respective offices; and the Treasurer shall give bond with three or more securities, to be approved by said Trustees, in the sum of twenty thousand dollars payable to the State of Indiana, and conditioned for the faithful discharge of the duties of his office of Treasurer to said corporation, and which bond executed and approved as aforesaid shall be deposited in the office of the Treasurer of State.

SEC. 6. The said board of Trustees when organized in manner aforesaid, shall forever thereafter determine the time of their future meetings, the manner of notifying the same, and act on their own adjourments [*sic*] as to them shall seem most expedient, and shall from time to time as occasion may require, make and ordain reasonable rules, ordinances and by laws, with reasonable penalties for the good government of the College, and the regulation of their own body, not repugnant to the laws and constitution of this State.

SEC. 7. The said board of Trustees shall from time to time, as the interest of the institution may require, elect a President of said College, and such Professors, Tutors, Instructors and other officers of the same, as they may judge necessary for the interest thereof, and shall determine the duties, salaries, emoluments, responsibilities and tenures of their several offices, and designate the course of instruction in said College.

SEC. 8. The said board of Trustees shall have full power to remove any one of their own body, for misconduct, breach of the by laws, or gross immorality, and may at any time they may deem it necessary for the good of the institution, remove any of the officers of said College or corporation, and others appoint in their stead.

SEC. 9. The President, Professors and Tutors shall be styled the Faculty of said College, which faculty shall have the power of enforceing the rules and regulations adopted by the said Trustees for the Government of the students, by rewarding or censuring them, and finally by suspending such as after repeated admonition, shall continue refractory, until a determination of a quorum of the Trustees can be had thereon, and of granting and conferring, by and with the approbation and consent of the board of Trustees, such degrees in the liberal arts and sciences, as are usually granted and conferred in other Colleges in America, to the students of the College, or others who by their proficiency in learning or other meritorious distinction, may be entitled to the same, and to grant unto such graduates, diplomas, or certificates under their common seal and signed by the Faculty to authenticate and perpetuate the memory of such graduations.

SEC. 10. No President, Professor or other officer of the College shall, whilst acting in that capacity be a Trustee, nor shall any President, Professor, Tutor, Instructor or other officers of the College, ever be required by the Trustees to profess any particular religious opinions, and no student shall be denied admission, or refused any of the privileges, honors or degrees of the College, on account of the religious opinions he may entertain, nor shall any sectarian tenets or principles be taught, instructed or inculcated at said College by any President, Professor, Tutor or instructor thereof.

SEC. 11. That Edward Borland, Samuel Dodds, Leroy Mayfie[l]d, Jonathan Nichols, James Blair, David H. Maxwell, William Bannister and William Lowe of the County of Monroe, George H. Dunn of the County of Dearborn, Christopher Harrison of the County of Washington, Seth M. Levenworth of the County of Crawford, John Law of the County of Knox, Williamson Dunn of the County of Montgomery, Ovid Butler of the County of Shelby, and Bethuel F. Morris of the County of Marion, shall be and hereby are appointed Trustees agreeably to the provisions of this act, and shall hold their first meeting as herein before directed, and should a majority of them, (who shall at all times be necessary to constitute a quorum for the transaction of business,) fail to meet on the said first monday in May, the Governor of this State is hereby authorized and required to appoint some subsequent day for the meeting of said Trustees, giving to each of them twenty days notice thereof in writing, and said Trustees or a majority of them when convened in pursuance of such notice shall proceed to organize the board in manner herein before directed; and the President of the College shall be empowered to call occasional meetings of the Trustees, in such manner as the board of Trustees may by their by-laws direct.

SEC. 12. That all monies arising from the sale of the Seminary townships, in the Counties of Monroe and Gibson, shall be and forever remain a permanent fund for the support of said College, and the interest arising from the amount of said sales together with the three reserved sections in the Seminary Townships, situate in the county of Monroe, and all the buildings which have been erected adjacent to the town of Blomington in said County of Monroe for the use of the State Seminary, with all the real and personal property of every description belonging to or connected with said State Seminary, as the property of the State, and all gifts, grants and donations which have been or hereafter may be made, for the support of the College, shall be and hereby are forever vested in the aforesaid Trustees and their successors, to be controlled, regulated and appropriated by them in such manner as they shall deem most conducive to the best interest and prosperity of the institution: Provided, That the said Trustees shall conform to the will of any donor or donors in the application of any estate which may be given, devised or bequeathed for any particular object connected with the institution, and that the real estate hereby vested in the said Trustees and their successors, shall be by them held forever for the use of said College, and shall not be sold or converted by them to any other use whatsoever.

SEC. 13. That Benjamin Parke of the County of Washington, James Scott of the County of Clark, Jesse L. Holman of the County of Dearborn, Isaac Blackford of the County of Knox, and George Bush of the County of Marion, shall be and hereby are appointed a board of Visitors, any three of whom shall constitute a quorum for the transaction of business, whose duty it shall be annually to visit said College, examine the situation of the property both real and personal of said College, inspect the course of instruction adopted by the said Trustees and practised by the Faculty of said College, also the proceedings of said board of Trustees and their by-laws, and recommend to said Board of Trustees such alterations and amendments as they may deem necessary for the good of the institution, and also to enquire into the financial concerns of said corporation by examining the books of the Treasurer thereof, and make a report of their examination, inspections and inquiries to the Governor of this State to be by him laid before the General Assembly thereof. The above named persons shall constitute the Board of Visitors of said College, until the General Assembly by a joint resolution of both houses shall appoint other persons in their stead.

SEC. 14. That it shall be the duty of the Secretary of said corporation, to keep a true and faithful record of all the proceedings of said Board of Trustees in a suitable book to be procured by them for that purpose, and make such copies and transcripts of the orders and proceedings of said Board of Trustees as may from time to time be required, and the same duly certify, under the seal of the corporation, and for his servises he shall receive such compensation as said Trustees may from time to time allow, to be paid out of any funds in the Treasury of said corporation not otherwise appropriated.

SEC. 15. That it shall be the duty of the Treasurer of said corporation to keep a full, true and faithful account of all monies by him received by virtue of his said office, in suitable books to be for that purpose provided, and pay such monies out from time to time as may be required by and upon the order of said Board of Trustees, duly certified by their Secretary, and keep a similar account of such disbursements, and furnish the said board of Trustees whenever they may require the same, a full, true and complete statement of such receipts and disbursements, and exhibit to them for their inspection, his original books of entry, and also submit his books to the inspection and examination of the Board of Visitors of the College, and shall moreover annually transmit to the Governor of this State, to be by him laid before the General Assembly thereof, a true and complete statement of the annual receipts and expenditures of said corporation; and should said corporation ever be dissolved by Legislative enactments or otherwise, it shall in such case be the duty of said Treasurer, to pay over and deliver to the Treasurer of State, for the use of this State, all monies and funds in his hands belonging to said corporation at the time of such dissolution, and should any Treasurer of said Corporation at any time be guilty of any defalcation in the discharge of the duties of his said office, the said Trustees shall have the right of an action therefor against said Treasurer and his sureties on his official bond, in the name of the State of Indiana, for the use of said Trustees, and of prosecuting the same to final judgment and recovery, or in case of dissolution of said corporation, such action shall be sustained for the use of the State.

SEC. 16. That the constitution of the said College herein and hereby declared and established, shall be and remain the inviolate constitution of said College, and the same shall not be changed, altered or amended by any law or ordinance of the said Trustees, nor in any other manner than by the Legislature of this State.

This act to take effect and be in force from and after its passage.

H[arbin] H. Moore
Speaker of the House of Representatives
John H. Thompson
President of the senate

Approved January 24th A. D. 1828
J. Brown Ray
Gov. of Inda

_____

From copy provided by Secretary of State.

Document 12

Andrew Wylie Elected President

The law creating Indiana College provided for a Board of Trustees of fifteen self-perpetuating members to have almost complete freedom in the operation of the College. One of its first acts, after organizing itself, was the election of Andrew Wylie of Washington College, Pennsylvania, as President. This report which appeared in the Indiana *Journal,* May 22, 1828, indicates that Wylie was elected President at that time. There is some question of this fact. It was not until October 5, 1828, that he was actually elected by the Board as the record indicates. This news story no doubt refers to the submission of Wylie's name to the Board.

*   *   *

A majority of the Trustees of the College met at Bloomington, and organized themselves into a Board, on Monday, the 5th inst. They have elected Doctor Andrew Wilie, at this time President of Washington College, Pennsylvania, as President of the Indiana College.

As to general qualifications it is believed that there is no man in the United State of the same age, better calculated to stand at the head of an institution of this kind. He is profound in all the various branches collegiate of literature, and possesses an extensive fund of general knowledge.

As a disciplinarian, he is capable of managing with dignity and energy, the internal government of any College. In short, if extensive literary acquirements, affability of manners, and dignified deportment, may be considered qualifications, Dr. Wilie is eminently fitted for the Presidency of an institution of the highest literary character.

The first session of the Indiana College will commence on the first Monday of June next.

The price of tuition will be $5.00 per semester, or $10.00 per year.

Indianapolis *Indiana Journal,* May 22, 1828.

Document 13

The "Poor Man's Child"

Governor Ray's Message to the Indiana General Assembly, December 2, 1828, reflects both a democracy and a liberality unusual for the times. His reference to the education of women is an interesting one indeed. The rest of the message is a recitation of the Jeffersonian philosophy of public higher education.

*　　*　　*

Nor, can I suppose that female education, will escape the attention of my honorable auditory. It is *that* better half of creation, who teach the most lasting moral, political and social lessons, and write them upon an ever-living recollection.

The State Seminary, at Bloomington, has, at length, taken the rank of a College, and President Wiley, from Pennsylvania, a very accomplished and scientific gentleman, has taken it in charge. The interest and success of this institution, call for an enlargement of the buildings, a library and such necessary apparatus as our pecuniary ability will enable us, at this time, to procure. The earlier we endow it with a liberal hand, the sooner may we expect to see it flourish, and rise to that elevated rank and reputation, which will tender a guarantee to the youth of the state, that they can receive an education as complete and useful at home, as in other states. This necessary pre-requisite effected, the low price at which children are instructed and boarded at Bloomington, and the healthiness of its situation, will offer an additional inducement for giving this college the preference. And we should continually feel a lively solicitude to adopt the most effectual plans, from time to time, to bring the privileges of this institution, as much within the reach of the *poor man's child*, as practicable. As the money of the wealthy will secure to their offspring its advantages, it is the indigent who have the strongest claim upon your deliberations. A portion of the waste lands adjoining the institution, laid out and enclosed in *fields* and *gardens,* attached to it, and offered *free* of rent, to the industrious youth, without resources, who desires to enter college, would enable many a poor young man, gratified with such an opportunity, to acquire for himself, the rich blessings of a good education, by the labor of his own hands. Neither would a correct knowledge of either agriculture or horticulture, do the slightest injury to even those, who might not be forced to necessity, to till the ground, to improve the head. It ought not to be supposed too readily, that whilst the mind is treasuring up the weighty masses of science and literature, which are crowded upon it, that the healthful action and vigor of the body, can be neglected, without doing an irreparable injury to the health of the student.—Let us aim to improve rather than impair all of the parts that constitute the *man*, the *head*, the *heart*, and *body*.

Indiana *Senate Journal*, 1828–29, pp. 17–18.

Document 14

Hall, Harney, and the Classics with some Mathematics

The Board of Visitors in its first report on Indiana College, January 1, 1829, was comprehensive in its description of both the academic and fiscal status of the institution. Andrew Wylie had not yet arrived in Bloomington.

*   *   *

The President laid before the senate the following communication from the Governor, with the following report from the board of visitors and the treasurer of the Indiana college:

EXECUTIVE DEPARTMENT
Indianapolis, Ind.
Jan. 10, 1829.

HON. M. STAPP,
    President of the Senate:
Sir:—Accompanying this message, you will find the report of the board of visitors, of the Indiana college, of the last October meeting at Bloomington; together with a report from the agent of the late trustees, of the state seminary of Indiana, which you are respectfully requested to lay before the honorable senate.
Your most ob't. servant,
J. BROWN RAY.

To his Excellency James B. Ray, Governor of the State of Indiana.
The undersigned, being a majority of the board of visitors of the Indiana college, have the honor to inform you, that, in conformity to the act of the legislature, we visited Bloomington in October last, at the time fixed by the laws of the institution for the annual meeting of the board of trustees, and for the public examination, and other collegiate performances of the students. The examination was conducted by the Rev. Mr. Hall, professor of languages, and Mr. Harney, professor of mathematics. In the languages, the classes were examined on Ross's Latin Grammar, Mair's Introduction, Selectæ Veteri, Sallust, Valpy's Greek Grammar, Author's Exercises, Græca Minora, and the first volume of Græca Majora. In Mathematics, the examination was on Algebra, Geometry, the application of the former to the latter, the nature of irrational quantities, including the Diaphantine Analysis, Anylitical plane Trigenometry, the construction of Mathe-

matical tables, the doctrine of Fluxions, &c. The number of students was thirty-five; as many, certainly, as could have been expected at so early a period of the institution; the first year of its establishment not having yet expired. Except in one or two branches, none had advanced beyond the studies usually pursued in a Freshman class; and the most of them were only in the preparatory department.

We had the pleasure to be present at several meetings of the board of trustees, subsequent to the examination. Some important amendments were made by them to the by-laws, which, however, are still considered somewhat defective. A committee was appointed to investigate this subject, and form a complete system of rules for the government of the college, to be presented to the board of trustees at their next annual meeting. The four regular classes usual in similar institutions, are now organized, and also a preparatory department; the studies of the latter, being in the languages, those already mentioned, together with Kirkham's English Grammar, Woodbridge's Geography, Colburn's Arithmetic—first lessons and sequel. The studies of the Freshman class are, Cicero's Orations, Virgil, Graeca Majora, 1st volume, Adam's Roman Antiquities, Murray's English Grammar, Colburn's Algebra, American Geography, Compositions in English and Latin, Hutton's Geometry. Those of the Sophomore class are Walker's Rhetorical Grammar, Horace, Eastern Geography, Hedge's Logic, Blair's Lectures, Graeca Majora, continued, Tytler's Elements of History, Cicero de Oratore, Potter's Grecian Antiquities. The course of studies for the Junior and Senior classes have not yet been established. The great importance of these higher studies suggested the propriety of not fixing them for the present. The subject is referred to the consideration of the committee on the by-laws, whose report will contain their matured opinion relative to these studies. By the time that report is made, the president elect will, no doubt, have removed to Bloomington, and taken charge of the institution, which will secure to the board of trustees the advice and assistance of that experienced and intelligent gentleman, in further digesting the whole course of instruction, and in perfecting the by-laws.

Every possible care appears to be taken of the college edifice, and its appurtenances. The rooms of the building are appropriated to the purposes of recitation, excepting one in the second story, which is occupied by a literary society of the more advanced students; the village of Bloomington furnishing every convenience as to boarding and private rooms for study.

With respect to the financial concerns of the institution, the visitors beg leave to refer your excellency to the report of the treasurer, herewith transmitted, and to the report of the superintendant of the loan office, made to the legislature during the present session; which reports will be found to contain the necessary information on this subject.

The above statements, with the papers referred to, embrace, it is believed, every thing relative to the college, which the law makes it the duty of the visitors to transmit annually to the Governor of the state. In closing this communication, the undersigned take great pleasure in saying, that the regulations of the institution, the proceedings of the board of trustees, the qualifications and deportment of the faculty, and progress of the students, were calculated to excite our highest hopes for the prosperity of the college.

JESSE L. HOLMAN,
ISAAC BLACKFORD,
GEORGE BUSH.

Indianapolis, January 1, 1829.

The agent for the late trustees of the state seminary of Indiana, respectfully reports:

That the seminary section (sold in the year 1820,)

for the sum of	$4822 00	
Received one year's rent for the seminary	16 00	
Received of J. Robinson for clay and cabin	15 00	
do. D. Rowlings for rails	7 00	
Interest received	316 80	
When added makes		$5176 80
Of which there has been expended	4409 53	
Agent's 5 per cent. on the same	220 47	
		4630 00
Leave due of said fund		546 80
Tuition fees received prior to May 1828	143 50	
Tuition fees received since	99 62	
		243 50
		790 30
Of which there has been paid to orders		152 50
Leaves due the institution		637 80

JAMES BORLAND, *Treasurer.*

Honorable Board of Visitors Indiana College.
October 31, 1828.

Which were read; and
   On motion by Mr. Gregory,
Ordered, That they be spread on the journals.

Indiana *Senate Journal,* 1828–29, pp. 228–231.

Document 15

Land Sales

In December 1829 Andrew Wylie was in Bloomington, and Indiana College was ready to begin not only its second session, but a new era in higher education in Indiana. It was evident to Governor Ray that funds had to be forthcoming to finance the expansion of the College. He gave the legislators a fatherly admonition about the sale of the college's lands.

*   *   *

INDIANA COLLEGE

It is supposed that this institution will commence its first session, with about fifty scholars, under the charge of the Rev. Mr. Wiley, its president. Additional sales of the college lands, are called for, to create a fund for the purchase of a library and the necessary apparatus for the professorships. The plan of sales recommended for the disposition of the canal and road grants of land, would, if applied, to those lands, create a handsome fund annually for the gradual increase of a library and other essential college appendages. If any abuses have existed in the institution, they should be promptly exposed; and if on the other hand, its professors have been unrighteously assailed, it will be your pleasing task, to forthwith announce their innocence that confidence in the college, may be more fully confirmed.

Indiana *Senate Journal,* 1829–30, p. 37.

Document 16

Andrew Wylie's Vision

President Andrew Wylie regarded higher education as a serious fact in American life. He arrived in Bloomington with both a philosophy of education and a will to apply it. In an extensive inaugural address he set forth the objectives of higher education in the context of the age and of his idealism. This address left no uncertainty as to the ambitions, ideals, and perspectives of the man who had been elected to the presidency of the struggling backwoods college. The main challenge was to find the necessary financial support to sustain it.

*   *   *

ADDRESS.

GENTLEMEN OF THE BOARD, AND
      RESPECTED AUDIENCE:

Of what advantage is a College to the community? To this question it is reasonably expected that, on an occasion like the present, a plain and satisfactory answer should be given. Institutions of this kind depend for their prosperity upon public favor, which, without the prospect of reciprocal advantage, it cannot be expected the public should bestow. On this principle, then, let the question be placed; and let us approach it, laying aside all prejudice on either side.

That colleges are necessary to furnish young men destined for the liberal professions with a general acquaintance with literature and science and to train them to habits of mental discipline, as preparatory to their entering upon those studies which are strictly professional, has been, for centuries, the prevailing opinion; an opinion, therefore, which ought not, but upon good and sufficient reasons, to be discarded. But, not to rest the matter upon authority, since the prevalence of an opinion is no certain evidence of its correctness, it may not be amiss, on the present occasion; to bestow some remarks on this view of the subject.

And to begin with the profession of medicine. Health, it will be readily admitted, by all especially who have ever been deprived of it, is among the most valuable of earthly blessings. Yet how precarious is the possession of it. The diseases by which it is liable to be impaired make up a list of frightful magnitude. Now, for all these, or nearly all, nature has provided a preventive, a remedy, or a palliative. These, however, are not obvious. Science is necessary to find them out, and skill, to apply them. But how are this science and skill to be acquired? They are stored away in books and in the minds of men who are eminent in medical knowledge; and thence they cannot be drawn without the help of those acquisitions which it is the intention of a college education to impart. A medical lecture, whether delivered or printed in a book, is Arabic to the mere English scholar. Let such an one attend a thorough course in any of the most respectable of our halls of medical science, and let him, while there, make the best use of his opportunities, and yet he shall return home with little more advantage from the instructions which have been delivered, than if he had spent the same time in feeding cattle upon a farm. And the reason is, he does not understand the terms employed. The analysis, the classification, the discrimination—the whole method of instruction, is beyond his reach. He is in a new world. Strange objects are made to pass in succession before his eyes; but they are, to his view, enveloped in mist. He sees nothing distinctly, and what he does see he is incapable of reducing to any orderly arrangement; so that, in the end, he retains nothing more of all that has engaged his attention than a kind of confused recollection that there were wonderful things told him, of which he can give no further account.

But, it has been asked, why could not the lecturer make his instructions plain, so that the mere English scholar might understand them. He could: but he would have to go back to elementary principles and extend his course accordingly. That is to say, he must do the very same thing for his pupil that is now done for him in college—and at ten times the expense.

People complain of public instructors in the arts and sciences for writing and speaking a language which nobody but the learned can understand; whereas, in truth, the difficulty lies in the things to be taught, not in the terms by which a knowledge of them is communicated. The ideas are uncommon: they lie beyond the range of ordinary thought, and the terms by which they are indicated must lie, consequently, out of the compass of ordinary language. Philosophy, which, in its most extensive signification, means all kinds of knowledge that are valuable, except that which pertains to the common concerns of life and which nobody has any occasion to learn, has, and must have, a language of its own. If the appropriate terms in which it is now taught were laid aside, others must be invented to fill their place, or ordinary words must be used in a new signification. Such a mode of communication would be tedious, doubtful, and embarrassing to the learner in a much higher degree than that which adopts the beautiful, terse, and comprehensive language in which philosophy delights. To use learned terms on common topics is pendantry. But learned themes it is next to impossible to discuss in colloquial style. An example, taken from one of the plainest and most useful theorems of geometry, will illustrate, at once, the truth of these remarks. When I say, "In any right-angled triangle the square of the hypothenuse is equal to the squares of the remaining sides," I express a proposition in philosophical language; and the unlearned do not understand either the words, or the proposition. Again; I express the same thing in familiar language: thus, "In any three-sided straight-lined figure, one of whose sides is perpendicular to another side; if squares be drawn on its three sides, the large square upon the slanting side opposite the two perpendiculars is exactly equal to the two smaller squares taken together; and this is absolutely true, whatever be the size of the three-sided figure, or the proportion of its sides to each other." Now, the unlearned reader, or hearer, understands the words, taken separately, but he knows no more of the doctrine which they express—the nature of the proposition, nor its uses—than he did before. The only difference is, that, in the one case he may be imposed upon—be induced to think that he understands the subject when he does not; but in the other, he is not so liable to be deceived, because the words as well as the things are strange to him, and as soon as he understands the former the latter will need no explanation.

No man, who is not utterly unacquainted with the history of science, needs to be informed that the knowledge of things is intimately complicated with the knowledge of words. Language is not only the vehicle, but the instrument of thought. Hence an additional reason why a knowledge of those languages from which medical terms have been derived should facilitate the acquisition of the science itself.

But, to say that the physician should be well acquainted with the Latin and

Greek languages, is saying but little. He should be profoundly versed in mental philosophy, a much nobler branch of learning: for, such is the influence of the mind upon the body, that he who would prescribe for the maladies of the one should understand the operations of the other.

It is almost too obvious to need mention that Chymistry, which lies at the foundation of the Materia Medica, is all-important to the physician.

As for the other branches of science and literature which compose the college course, they may not be so intimately connected with the science of medicine. But as a professional man the physician ought not be a mere retailer of drugs. His intercourse with society requires that he should be a man of refinement and general intelligence.

So important, in these respect, is a college education, that without it the professional of medicine would sink at once, and, along with it, whatever knowledge the experience of past ages has been collecting, from the results of innumerable cases and applications, for the purpose of alleviating the sufferings which accident and disease are inflicting upon the human race.

What would be the consequences may be readily conjectured from what we see occasionally taking place in neighborhoods where men are permitted to take up the profession, as they would a trade, without having gone through a course of preparatory studies. When sickness or calamity enters one of the families of such a village or neighborhood, seized with alarm and not knowing what to do, they send for "the doctor." He receives his unhappy patient, as the essayer would a piece of untested ore, as a subject on which experiments are to be tried. Suffering nature may indicate the malady and suggest the cure by the plainest symptoms. The case may have occurred, in the history of nosology ten thousand times, and scientific men may have defined it as often, and prescribed the treatment. It matters not. The empiric knows nothing of it all: and to shew that he at least has confidence enough in his own skill, he goes instantly to work, pursues a bold practice, and stays not his hand, till his patient has made good his escape from all experiments, and life together. Or, if a strong constitution, bidding defiance at once to the disease and the doctor, should set the sick man upon his feet again, the credit of the cure is denied to kind nature and ascribed to the man of pills or the man of steam—as the case may be; and life prolonged in one becomes the occasion of its being shortened to many more. For the name of the "successful physician" is trumpeted to the winds, and he operates, for the future, upon a greater number of subjects, with greater confidence, and more terrible effect.

Far be it from me to deal, on this or any other subject, in indiscriminate censure. I honor the medical profession and desire that those whose talents and virtues have adorned it should be held, as they will be, in everlasting veneration. Their services have cheered the dark hour of affliction, and brought solace and comfort to the anxious and the desponding. Some, too, it is freely admitted, have, by a superior native sagacity, and by unwearied application to study in a more private way, and without enjoying the advantages of a regular education, rendered important services to mankind in the medical profession. Such instances, however, are comparatively rare; and their attainments and success form no apology for such as, presumptuously, and without the requisite qualifications, thrust themselves into a calling where they aggravate the sufferings which they profess to remove, and mock the hopes which their noisy pretensions sometimes unhappily excite.

But though it should be granted that the student of medicine might acquire, in a given time, as much knowledge in the art which he intends to practice, without a previous acquaintance with the learned languages as with it—a supposition which never can be verified in fact—yet, let it be remembered that the knowledge which he thus acquires is not general. It belongs to one subject alone, and does not facilitate the acquisition of ideas on any other. He may, therefore become a physician; but he will be a mere physician, and cannot expect to rise above mediocrity in his profession, or to contribute any thing to the stock of medical knowledge which the world already possesses. He, on the contrary, who takes "the good old way" and devotes himself, in the first place, to the acquisition of general science and literature, is exercising his mind in a way which gives vigor and activity to all its faculties, and the knowledge which he is acquiring has the additional advantage over those studies which are directed toward a particular profession that it renders his future progress, in all other kinds of knowledge, pleasant and easy.

Let us, in the next place, view the question now under consideration as it stands connected with the legislation and jurisprudence of the community.

There can scarcely be presented an object of contemplation more delightful than that of a community in which peace and good order prevail;—where the boundaries of individual rights are fixed by law, and fortified by the certain application of proper penalties. Where this is the case the operations of the whole society go on undisturbed; every man pursuing his own occupation, laying by his gains and making provision for his family; and as he trains them to habits of virtue, and sees them going out and coming in under his paternal supervision, he feels secure in the confidence that the tranquillity of this lovely scene is not to be broken up by any "son of mischief;" because every son of mischief knows that, the moment he transgresses those boundaries which the law makes sacred, the force of its vengeance will be turned upon him. Needs it be demonstrated that this tranquillity and good order depend upon the just administration of wise and wholesome laws, or that wise and wholesome laws can neither be enacted nor properly administered by ignorant men?

The questions litigated in courts of justice are often of deep importance to the parties concerned: and the whole community has an interest in their being justly decided. Such questions, affecting property, liberty, and life itself, could not with safety be left to the adjudication of men drawn on the emergency from the common walks of life. What security could there be in such cases to the rights of individuals, during those excitements of popular feeling which take place so frequently and rise so high in all free government, if those great landmarks were removed or disregarded which the care and experience of past ages have set up to direct the course of justice. What bulwark against the oppression of the opulent and powerful could be found for the weak and the helpless, if society should have its Verres and its Hastings, but not a Cicero or a Burke? As matters now are, it is often hard for the honest and unsuspecting part of the community to pass unmolested. But how much more so would it be, if villany, lurking in his den of rapine, were left to make inroads upon the happiness of society, secure of a retreat? And secure he would be, but for those who by their skill in law are qualified, and from professional interest and pride are disposed to pursue him to his last resort, and drag him forth to suffer the frowns of public indignation and the penalty of injured justice. But on these topics I need not enlarge, since the necessity of making the study and application of the law the business of a separate profession, has been felt and acknowledged in the usages of all civilized nations. Permit me only to ask, by whom this profession, so noble in itself and so conducive to the public good, ought to be filled. By sophomores of slender intellect and scanty knowledge and boundless impudence, who, having no merit on which to rely, will have recourse to every base art for the purpose of advancing themselves or reducing others to their own level? Or, by men of respectable attainments in literature and science, who are qualified to do justice to the cause of their client, and who would scorn to prostitute their powers by patronizing fraud and injustice, and whom the country might, without disgrace, employ in the legislative or the judiciary departments? It is a characteristic of our nature to be always aspiring after something higher or more perfect than that to which we have already attained; and that is a wise provision in the government of any community which gives scope for the exercise of this disposition on the part of its citizens, in ways conducive to the general good. And it seems natural and reasonable, that the skill and experience which have been gained in the profession of explaining and declaring the law, should be transferred to the higher office of enacting it, and to that of adjudicating under it. During the revolution, at the formation of the general and state governments, and at every subsequent period of our history, this practice has obtained. Hence an additional reason why a thorough and substantial education should be required in those who aim at the legal profession.

There is scarcely any species of knowledge which the duty of a legislator does not put in requisition. He should be profoundly acquainted with the science of morals, that he may be able justly to appreciate virtue as tending above all things else to promote the public good, and clearly to discern what measures to adopt to prevent destructive vices from taking root in the community. He should be well versed in the science of human nature, that he may distinguish between those cases in which the civil authority may properly interpose, and those which ought to be left to the control of public opinion and individual interest. He should understand those natural and artificial relations which constitute the framework of human society, and those points of contact at which the different interests and pursuits of men press upon each other, that he may not, in his zeal to protect the rights of one class of citizens, expose those of another class to injury. He should be extensively read in the history of legislation; that he may be able to compare one constitution and code of laws with another, the genius and institutions of one people with those of another, theoretical principles with practical results; that he may in all his deliberations call in the aid of experience, and, at the same time, correct and modify the results of a limited experience, by those extensive analogies which are discoverable upon a comprehensive survey of the course of human actions and events. He should have attentively examined the peculiarities of our situation, government and genius as a people; that the legal enactments which he may have a hand in forming, may accord with the nature of our free institutions, and not with those which grew out of the feudal systems of the old world.

Now, let me ask, whether such qualifications as these can reasonably be expected in a man whose mind has never been trained to the habit of accurate and connected thinking, in the process of literary and scientific investigations? That these qualifications are indispensible to every man who aspires to a seat in our halls of legislation is not pretended, but they are highly desirable must surely be granted.

The interests of each particular state, as involved in its relation to the Union, and of the Union, itself as connected with the other nations of the earth, it is reasonable to suppose, will be maintained and promoted in proportion to the competency of the men to whom they are intrusted. The time was, when the power of nations depended upon the number and discipline of their armies. The progress of science and arts has transferred it now to different hands, and intellect has become more important than muscular strength, and the pen a mightier instrument than the sword. The truth of this remark has often been exemplified in the history of modern nations, who have frequently lost in negotiation what, at an immense expenditure of blood and treasure, they had gained by their prowess in arms.

But, if it is necessary that men of cultivated talent should be employed in enacting and interpreting our laws, in presiding in our courts of justice, in negotiating our treaties, and in managing our public business generally, it is certainly not less so that none but those of this character should aspire to the office of giving public instruction on the great matters of morality and religion. Were this office of human institution merely, there never had existed, probably, any difference of opinion on this subject. But because those who first filled it were qualified for the exercise of its important functions in a supernatural manner, and because divine grace is justly considered an indispensible qualification for it, some seem to imagine that the necessity of literary attainments is entirely superseded. To those who hold this opinion it is sufficient, for the present, to reply that miracles have long since ceased, and that the power of working them, while that power was enjoyed, constituted no part of those qualifications which fitted the primitive teachers "of the way of righteousness" for the discharge of their office, but was a mere appendage to it. The disciples of Christ received instructions from him in the ordinary way. Paul's remarks, as to the qualifications of those who were by him thought worthy of the sacred office, shew that he did not think didactic powers unnecessary. Grace does not supersede the necessity of human efforts, nor suspend the laws of nature. The nature of the office shews the necessity of extensive learning in those who would discharge its duties. The Bible must be explained, which, as to the matter of it, is the most comprehensive book that ever was written, and, as to the style, so peculiar and idiomatic, that no mere English scholar can possibly interpret its meaning. It gives a view of the world throughout its whole duration from the creation to the general judgment. We find in it every species of writing, whether of prose or of poetry. It embraces all kinds of subjects, and draws illustrations from every thing on earth and in heaven. It relates to things visible and invisible, time and eternity, providence, grace, redemption—the moral government of God, and the agency of man. In short, there is not a subject relating to man, either in his individual or social character, which does not occupy a place in the sacred pages. Such is the text book prepared by the spirit of inspiration for the use of the public teacher of religion. And will any offer, without the key of knowledge, to open this immense magazine of instruction? I pity that minister of religion who enters the sacred office without grace. If he thinks that grace without knowledge is sufficient, though not so much to be pitied, he is surely neither to be encouraged nor commended.

The warmth of feeling and the evidence of knowledge, like heat and light in the rays of the sun, are blended in religion. The attempt to separate them is both foolish and wicked. Monkish teachers once took away the light; and a night of superstition followed, in which imposture played off its tricks, undetected, before the ignorant multitude. The neologists, more recently, have taken away the warmth, and have given, for day, moonshine, in which no glow of holy feeling can be experienced, nor any great and noble enterprise performed. The philosophers of the last century attempted at once to put out both the light and heat of religion, and to supply their place by the fire of their torches; and, after they had "encompassed" themselves with sparks of their own kindling, and "walked" for awhile in the light of their unhallowed fires, they and their followers sunk down together in the shame and sorrow of an everlasting disappointment. Let no man think of repeating these, or any of these experiments.

It is most deplorable that persons should be found, in this age of the world and of the church, to decry human learning, as they call it, as unnecessary in him who undertakes to deliver instructions publicly on the subject of religion; and more deplorable still, that they should be kept in countenance by the extravagance of those who run into the opposite extreme, and, in examining the pretensions of candidates for the sacred office, require evidence of human learning by none of the grace of God. With the latter, however, I have no concern at present. To the former I would say, If your object is to preserve the purity of religion by preventing men under the influence of unhallowed motives from intruding into its most sacred functions, why favor the pretensions of the weak and ignorant? Are not they the most ambitious, and fond of display, as well as most liable to be imposed upon by their feelings? What sacrifice do they make, what prospects of advancement in the world do they renounce, what humiliating services do they undertake, from love to the souls of men? Is not God the God of order? What kind of order is that where ignorance teaches and weakness rules? Is it reason, or is it madness, to suppose that the author of those beautiful and magnificent arrangements, which we every where behold in the works of nature, should connect the supernatural influxes of the Divine Spirit with the hallucinations of idiocy? Who can endure, that the magnificent conceptions and idiomatic phrases of Paul, or Isaiah, or of Asaph, should come under the examination of a critic, who, one while, mistakes a piece of irony for direct affirmation, and, another, substantiates a proof from the fancied analogies of a parable?

If colleges were of no further use than merely to apply the test of its duties, as so many prelusory trials to be performed by such as have in view the office of the gospel ministry, they ought to be regarded as highly important. But, besides this advantage, the studies which employ the attention of the student at college not only furnish a various and salutary exercise to all his mental faculties, and thus tend to develope whatever talent he may possess, but furnish him with those ideas and impressions which will enable him with greater ability afterwards to discharge the duties of the sacred office. Of these studies we shall select those that belong to Natural Science, because none seem so little connected with religion as they; and accordingly, none are so little valued, usually, by the theological student. In systems of theology they are seldom even referred to. The sacred scriptures, however, do not slight the discoveries of natural science. They conduct us at once to the work of nature in the account they give of the genesis of the world, and refer us, in almost every page, to the same source for suitable impressions of the Divine Majesty. This fact deserves to be profoundly considered by those who would confine the enquiries of the theologican, and the scope of his public instructions, to the narrow circle of a few articles of faith. Particularly does it deserve to be remarked, that those portions of scripture which are purely devotional tend to direct the mind, in admiring contemplation, to those scenes of grandeur which are exhibited in the earth, the air, the sky, the ocean. And every attentive reader of the Evangelists has observed with what frequency and inimitable tenderness, He who teaches as never man taught, there refers to those parts of nature which are near us, with which, of course, we are best acquainted, and which are principally employed in administering to our comfort and gratification, as affording illustrations of the care and goodness of our Father in Heaven. How immensely superior are those ideas which we thus derive from the works of nature over those which are to be met with in the dry and vapid speculations of the mystical divine. They present to our view God as he is. They bring Him near us, place Him in contact with our spirits, and almost within the apprehension of our very senses. We feel his kindness flowing out, from the inexhaustible exuberance of nature, by a thousand channels. In the benign aspect of his creation we behold the light of his countenance: and we are filled with awe and delight. "Whoever will consider aright," says the father of modern philosophy, "will acknowledge that, next to the word of God, the most certain cure of superstition, and the best aliment of faith, is the knowledge of nature. Therefore philosophy is given to religion as her most faithful handmaid; the one manifesting the will, the other the power, of God: nor did he mistake who said, 'ye err, not knowing the scriptures nor the power of God,' thus inseparably blending and joining together the knowledge of his will, and the contemplation of his power."

No emotion of the soul approaches so near the nature of pure devotion, or blends so readily with it, as that which arises in the mind on contemplating the grandeur and beauty of the material universe; and there is no better way of preserving the mind from low and unworthy conceptions of the Great Supreme, than by frequently exercising its contemplative powers upon the glory of his works. Now surely it may be reasonably demanded of the public teacher of religion, that he should conduct the minds of his hearers in those sublime contemplations. But where shall he acquire the ability, if not at college? At a theological seminary he cannot; for natural science is not taught there; and, without a competent knowledge in this and other branches taught in our most respectable college, no young man, whatever may be his capacity, is prepared for receiving that kind of instruction which is communicated in a theological seminary, any more than one could be prepared for entering college, without having first obtained a knowledge of the preparatory branches of an English education. And, if either the college course or the theological were to be dispensed with in the case of a candidate for the sacred office, I should unhesitatingly say, let it be the latter. For, when the student has advanced to a certain point in mental improvement, he becomes his own best instructor. The quarry is before him, uncovered. His tools are prepared, and he is possessed of strength and skill to use them. His success, now, will depend more upon the vigor and perseverance of his exertions than upon the directions of a by-stander.

It is the tendency of all studies merely professional to produce an effect upon the mind similar to that which, it has been observed, particular employments have upon certain parts of the body. The part that is most exercised becomes the strongest, as the arms of the smith and the legs of the porter, while the parts not exercised continue in a state of relative weakness. So it is with the mind. If its thoughts be long confined to one channel they cannot, at length, be drawn into any other; and thus a peculiar way of thinking is produced; and not unfrequently, owing perhaps to the influence of concurrent causes, an illiberal cast is given to the whole mind. Religion has suffered greatly from teachers whose disposition, taste, and character have been vitiated in this way. To this source in part may be traced fierce disputes about trifles, bigotry, hypocrisy, persecution, fanaticism, and infidelity; evils which have always been found to prevail, wherever the office of giving instruction in religion has fallen into the hands of men whose minds have not been enlightened, purged, and liberalized by the influence of general science. Where, on the contrary, the character of the clergy is respectable for talents, knowledge, and virtue, the influence which they exert is happy, thrice happy, for the community. Allow me to give an instance out of many; one which I am induced to select on the present occasion, because, if I mistake not, it deserves, at this moment, the special attention of the West. I refer to the cause of temperance. That great and glorious reformation which, on this subject, is now pervading the United States, had its origin in the influence of the clergy; their eloquence and zeal urged it on, and by their efforts an impulse has been given to the public mind which, it is hoped, will not cease, till we, as a nation, shall become as remarkable for our temperance as we had been infamous for its contrary. The great and salutary change, in this respect, which has already taken place in the public morals, has been owing to learning, animated by piety, exerting itself in collecting facts from every quarter, and presenting them, in glowing colors, before the view of an awakened community. And thus it has ever been, in the case of every great and permanent reformation which has taken place in the world. But what has ignorance effected? Nothing but mischief. What has zeal in religion, without knowledge, effected? Again, I say, nothing but mischief.

No one of this respectable audience, it is hoped, will do so much injustice to the feelings and views of the speaker as to entertain the suspicion that it has been his aim, in the remarks that have been just made, to question the motives, or disparage the labors of those very worthy men who, though destitute of the advantages of a liberal education, have felt themselves conscientiously bound to engage in the self-denying labors of the gospel ministry. He has known more than one of this description who have been "burning and shining lights" in the church of God. He would be understood as speaking of things generally. All cannot be equally learned. Allowance must be made for circumstances, and especially for the wants of a poor and scattered population. But still, it is important that those who aspire to the office of teaching others on the subject of religion, should themselves be as well instructed as possible. And it is, at this moment, a matter of congratulation, among the friends of knowledge and virtue, that the different denominations of professing Christians in our land are beginning to manifest a zeal and an emulation, on the subject of education, worthy of the glorious cause which, notwithstanding minor differences, all are honestly laboring to promote. Methodists, Baptists, Episcopalians, Presbyterians—all sects and parties, forgetting their differences and unmeaning and unprofitable disputes, seem to vie with each other in efforts for furnishing candidates among them for the sacred office with the best means of instruction in literature, science and religion, which their means and circumstances can afford. "Such contention," in the language of Hesiod, "is good for mortals." May success crown their efforts!

But yet, as there remains much to be accomplished, and as some still continue to doubt and to lag behind on this subject, it is important that it be constantly held up to view and urged upon the public attention.

Colleges are necessary, I would observe in the next place, to furnish for the community a sufficient number of teachers for academies and common schools. In many parts of our country the business of communicating elementary instruction is committed to teachers who are shamefully incompetent; and sometimes, to persons who are not merely incompetent, but degraded and vicious; whose characters are a disgusting compound of stupidity and sin; who have nothing in them to engage the attention or command the respect of their pupils, and who are actually despised both by parents and children, but nevertheless employed, because others more respectable cannot be obtained at so cheap a rate! The consequences are such as might be expected. The children, whose misfortune it is to be committed to the tuition of such masters have their faculties benumbed. They contract a dislike for books and learning. Their taste is vitiated, and they fall into gross and vulgar habits. And the best part of their lives is thrown away, and, not unfrequently, their characters and prospects forever ruined, for the want of proper instruction and discipline.

When it is considered, how important is that period of life which passes away while our youth are attending inferior schools, and what a controuling influence, over the whole tenor of their future course, the habits which they contract while there, are likely to exert, we can scarcely require too high a grade of qualifications in those who are intrusted with the early part of their education. It is commonly supposed that he who knows but little can as readily teach others that little, as one who knows more. This is a great mistake. A person of uncultivated mind cannot even direct the road to a stranger which he may have travelled a thousand times. The superiority of a well instructed mind is manifest even in little things, and a philosopher, should he condescend to take charge of an elementary school, would communicate a knowledge of the simplest rudiments to a child, in a shorter time, and to much better purpose than a person of inferior attainments. For, to teach any thing effectually, a man must possess not only a knowledge of what is to be communicated, but of the mind that is to receive it; as the physician must understand not only the nature of medicine but of the human constitution, and the state of his patient. But to acquire a knowledge of the mind and its modes and laws of operation, without an acquaintance with the general circle of literature, is impossible. It lies deep in the recesses of the temple of science, and can be approached only through the outer apartments. Yet, unless it be gained, a talent for communicating instruction, even of the humblest kind, cannot be acquired. For, if our modes of instruction are not in conformity with the modes of thinking which nature has established in the constitution of the mind, our teaching will be vain. On these principles only can we account for the fact that some schools have been remarkable for producing eminent men; while, from others, dunces only have gone forth. This difference in the result cannot be owing, entirely, to an original difference in the capacity of the pupils; though, in part, it may; for the same system which tends to send out dunces, at the conclusion, is calculated, in the first instance, to allure them. A boy of vigorous intellect will surmount the difficulties which lie in the road to knowledge, whatever may be the talents and capacity of his guide: but, surely, it must make a difference, as to the pleasure and speed of his progress, whether his feet be encumbered with clogs, or equipped with the wings of Mercury. In the same period of time that, under an ordinary teacher, he would spend in learning to read and write indifferently, and in gaining a mere smattering of Arithmetic, he might, with competent instruction, become not only a respectable proficient in these branches, but in Grammar, Geography, and the elements of Natural Philosophy. Were, therefore, the number of those who have completed a liberal course of study, increased to such a degree as to justify the practice of employing none others in the capacity of instructors in our common schools, every family in our land would reap no inconsiderable advantage; and our colleges, should they yield no further benefit to the public than that of furnishing a sufficient supply of such teachers, would richly deserve its patronage.

But the majority of this nation must ever be devoted to other employments than those for which we have, in the preceding remarks, attempted to shew that a liberal education is necessary. They are, and will, principally, continue to be, farmers. That they should all enjoy the advantages of a liberal education, is not in the nature of things possible. But, that a considerable number of them should, is not impossible. And certainly, as it respects both themselves and the community, it is highly desirable. They are, now, the most respectable class in society. If they were better educated they would be still more so. Every farmer, whose mind should be expanded by the influence of science, would become a centre of light and of influence in his neighborhood. The improvements, which his superior knowledge and taste would enable him to introduce into his condition, would be observed and imitated by others. This whole class of citizens would thus, at length, be enabled to avail themselves of the many advantages which the Author of nature has afforded them, and which, if improved, would render them the happiest of mortals.

> "O fortunatos nimium, sua si bona norint,
> Agricolas!"
> ("O happy, if he knew his happy state,
> The swain.")

The control of all other classes of men in society is with the farmers. The government is theirs. How important, then, that they be enlightened. An ignorant people cannot long be free. They will vilify their benefactors and caress their enemies—I mean those who flatter them.—They will oppose their own best interests. They will forge chains for themselves. A people who undertake to maintain their liberties, without fostering institutions of learning, undertake to make war against those laws which the Governor of the universe has fixed for the management of his dominion over his intelligent creatures, laws which are settled as the foundations of the earth, and strong as the "pillars of heaven." Vice and ignorance are inseparable. Ignorance cannot direct, and vice must be kept under the strong hand of power. The good of the universe requires it: God has decreed it: earth and hell prove it. That education tends to promote knowledge and virtue needs no proof. An educated man cannot exist without throwing light around him. He cannot be a vicious man.

I am a believer in the omnipotence of education. I do not mean without the grace of God. But the only book that tells me of the grace of God, informs me also that if I "train up a child in the way he should go, when he is old he will not depart from it." There does, indeed, come forth, now and then, from the walls of a college, an individual with the reputation of having completed an entire course of education, who is, nevertheless, prepared to be a burden to himself and a nuisance to society. Such an instance, however frequently it may occur, makes nothing against the position I have taken. For that, after all is the least important part of an education which is obtained at college. I must go into the house where this youth was reared up from the cradle, and see whether the fear of God is there,—whether the parents observe the Sabbath, and read the bible, and offer up the morning and the evening sacrifice, and attend upon that other ordinance of divine institution which the wise of this world call "the foolishness of preaching,"—whether they, in bringing up their children, add example to precept, and discipline to example, using assiduously caution, reproof, admonition, yes, and, in early life, that old-fashioned, puritanical instrument, the rod of correction. For you must not take a boy from the bosom of a family where he has been nurtured in indolence and vice, where, perhaps, he had learned to lie, to curse and swear, and to spurn at authority, before he could speak distinctly, and to drink and gamble and so on, before he has reached the age of puberty,—you must not put such an one into a college and ask the professors to work a miracle upon him. For, the truth is, he is formed already, and all the colleges and all the means in the world cannot re-form him. Nor must you take, as a fair experiment, a youth who has been blessed with a good and pious education at home, and afterwards put to a seminary under the superintendence of an unprincipled teacher,—where he will have grimace for religion and flattery for friendship, and where all his former good principles will fall under the corrupting influence of a system which is hollow and deceptive throughout, and which addresses itself to the vanity of the pupils, and other corrupt propensities of human nature—for such seminaries and such teachers there are;—I say you must not do this; and then, should your boy, once so lovely and so promising, be spoiled, cast the blame upon institutions of a different character or upon education in general. When I say that education is omnipotent, I mean an education which is good—good throughout; that part which is obtained in the nursery and at the paternal fireside; that part which is obtained at the college. I mean, too, that, through all these parts, it should comprise instruction, training, and government;—instruction communicated in such ways as to render it interesting, and in such an order and method as are in conformity to the arrangement of faculties which nature has set up in the constitution of a rational soul;—training in the exercise of these dispositions, and in the performance of these acts, which constitute a truly noble and amiable character;—and government firm but paternal, founded on such principles and conducted in such a manner, tempered with such kindness, and directing all things pertaining to the whole matter of the pupil's education with so manifest and zealous a regard to his best interest, that, without doing violence to reason and conscience and gratitude, he cannot make light of it. Let the child go through such a course of education as this, and if, when he arrives at mature age, he does not turn out to be a sound and ripe scholar, learned, and wise, and good, it will be a case without a precedent.

In the remarks already made, our attention has been chiefly directed to the influence which education is calculated to exert upon the general mass of the community; and if they have been founded in truth, this influence must be acknowledged to be, in the highest degree, salutary. Whether it tends to promote the individual happiness of those who are engaged in literary and scientific pursuits may not be so evident. If happiness consisted in the accumulation of riches, the question would be easily decided. The talents and habits which are employed in the investigation of truth, are of a very different order from those which are requisite in the pursuit of wealth; and those works of genius which have procured for their authors immortality after death, added but little to their means of subsistence while living. It cannot be denied, also, that the labors of the mind are less conducive to health, and have a more exhausting effect upon the spirits, than those of the body. So that "he who increaseth knowledge increaseth sorrow." These considerations, however, affect the question of man's happiness only as it respects his animal nature; and so far as the pleasures of the body are concerned, the advantage is clearly on the side of him who is devoted to active pursuits, with as little application to intense and continued thinking as possible. He, therefore, in whose constitution there is more of the animal than of the rational, consults badly for himself when he resolves to make himself a scholar. An honest teacher would forbid pupils of this description to prosecute the hopeless attempt, and direct their attention to some of those useful employments in which muscular, rather than mental, energy is required. But this faithful office is seldom performed and seldomer thankfully received. The opinion is that the eminence of a teacher is to be estimated according to the number of his pupils. The name of an "invita Minerva"-student appears as large on the roll as any other; and so he is retained, and perhaps flattered into the belief that he is making great and rapid advances, and is infallibly destined to cut a figure in the world! But, however happy he may feel, in the mean time while indulging those visionary prospects, the stern reality of things will teach him at length that his choice has been exceedingly unhappy. I make these remarks, because I believe that the number of such students, in different seminaries in the United States, is, somehow or other, increasing out of all reasonable proportion.

But, though a liberal education, bestowed on an inferior mind, is more likely to diminish than enhance the happiness of the person, as the armour of a giant would crush the body of a pigmy; yet, where there exists a respectable degree of native talent, the opposite result may be expected. Much of that dissatisfaction in which so many spend their lives, proceeds from the want of a capacity to discover and appreciate the advantages which nature has placed within their reach. And, as this capacity belongs to the mind, he that improves his mind improves his condition. He now finds access to sources of enjoyment unknown to him before. He can converse with "the mighty dead," through the medium of their works. His soul harmonizes with the beautiful and the sublime which scenes of nature exhibit. The glory spread over creation his eye beholds with rapture. The intimate acquaintance which he has with those wonderful contrivances, which, like the secret springs of a machine, lie concealed in the structure and composition of things, furnishes him with unceasing occasion for admiration. His thoughts take a wider range, in proportion as the sphere of his knowledge is enlarged, and consequently meet with entertainment in a greater variety of objects. His soul is awakened to a consciousness of its own native dignity by the contemplation of those magnificent arrangements, which the wisdom of the Creator has set up in those vast regions of space where planets, comets, suns and systems perform their revolutions. The Universe, to his view, is a temple, filled with the august presence of HIM who formed it, inspiring into his soul elevated conceptions with their corresponding emotions of awe and delight.

How much more exalted and pure are pleasures such as these, than those which are to be found in the ways of low sensuality, sordid avarice, or restless ambition! "Let any man," says a writer in one of the most respectable periodicals of the day, "pass an evening in vacant idleness, or even in reading some silly tale, and compare the state of his mind when he goes to sleep or gets up next morning with its state some other day when he has passed a few hours in going through the proofs, by facts and reasoning, of some of the great doctrines in Natural Science, learning truths wholly new to him, and satisfying himself by careful examinations of the grounds on which known truths rest, so as to be not only acquainted with the doctrines themselves, but able to shew why he believes them, and to prove before others that they are true—he will find as great a difference as can exist in the same being; the difference between looking back upon time unprofitably wasted, and time spent in self-improvement: he will feel himself in the one case listless and dissatisfied, in the other comfortable and happy; in the one case, if he do not appear to himself humbled, at least he will not have earned any claim to his own respect; in the other case he will enjoy a proud consciousness of having, by his own exertions, become a wiser and therefore a more exalted creature."

The pleasures of literature, it has been often and justly remarked, are less dependant on circumstances than any other. "They strengthen the mind in youth," says Cicero, "and afford comfort in old age: they impart an ornament to prosperity, and a refuge and solace in adversity: they delight at home, and are no encumbrance abroad: by night, on a journey, in the country, they are most faithful and agreeable companions." To gain the countenance and support of these "companions," no base compliances are necessary; nor are any hypocritical arts, or senseless forms requisite to secure their friendship; nor need we fear lest, on a reverse of fortune, they should refuse to acknowledge our acquaintance. Disgusted with the vices and follies of a treacherous race of beings, who cannot enter into his views, because they can form no conception of what is great and noble in the human character, the man of science, though possessed of but a moderate fortune, may retire, at pleasure, within the resources of his own mind, and there enjoy the banquet of intellectual delight, free from the annoyance of those harpies which infest, with their noise, stench and pollution, the entertainments of ordinary life. It is surely a satisfaction worthy of a magnanimous spirit, to reflect that there is, at least, one sphere of enjoyment, over the goods of which fortune has no control, and of which the arrogance of all-absorbing wealth can claim no monopoly, and which, like the treasures of heaven itself, "moth and rust cannot corrupt, nor thieves break through and steal."

From the tenor of the remarks which have been made, it will readily be perceived, what are the views of the speaker on the important subject of education in general, and, consequently, what course he will endeavour to pursue in the very responsible and arduous station to which he is about to be introduced. Yet, an additional remark or two may be necessary to prevent mistakes.

And, in the first place, it is intended that classical learning shall hold its place—a grade of equal importance with any other kind of learning—in the course of literature to be pursued. The objections to this need not now be mentioned, or refuted. They are mostly frivolous. To a correct knowledge of the English language the shortest road is through the Latin; and this once gone over, any other modern language of Europe, except the German, can be learned in about a fourth part of the time which would otherwise be requisite. Exercises in classical literature afford the best mental discipline; they strengthen the memory, give a readiness of perception and utterance, a power of discrimination and of tracing analogies; they store the fancy with pleasant images, and furnish the means of forming the taste upon the most perfect models. And if, as Lord Bacon has intimated, two languages are as necessary to a scholar as two wings to a bird, that time must surely be well spent which enables a young student to balance his native language by the acquisition of one so noble in itself as that which was spoken by the masters of the world. Of the Greek I need say nothing; for no one ever learned the Latin who could afterwards rest contented without this.

As to the mode of giving instruction which we intent to pursue, it would be difficult to speak particularly, at present. I shall only therefore say, in the general, that, after full and frequent conversations on the subject, we are of one mind, (I speak of the Faculty,) and resolved to pursue such methods as shall tend to exercise and improve the understanding rather than burden the memory. We shall build on first principles, and aim at laying the foundation broad and deep, leaving it to our pupils to go on with the superstructure, in after life, as they may find leisure and opportunity.

As it respects the management of the discipline and government of the Institution, no means of producing unnatural excitements shall be resorted to. It is with the mind as with the body: the less stimulus the better. False praise, especially, shall never be used for this purpose; much less for popularity. A propensity to flatter is the character of a base mind. The thing itself is contrary to truth, and corrupting in its tendency. The great principles of government, by which we shall hope to maintain our authority, will be, truth, reason, honor, interest, religion.

Purity of morals shall be made a primary object. Whenever any student shall shew symptoms of sloth, or of any other vice, commencing upon him, he shall be addressed on the subject; and, if admonition prove ineffectual, he shall be sent away. No indolent or dissipated youth need ask for admission, even for a day, within these walls. Let none think hard of this. Colleges were intended, not to reform the vicious, but to instruct those who wish to learn. They are schools, not penitentiaries. Yet, our government shall be paternal, just, kind and tender to the obedient, severe only where necessity requires.

On the subject of religion, as on all others, the utmost freedom of opinion and remark shall be allowed. Lectures on the Evidences of Christianity will constitute a part of our course; and while the utmost care and delicacy shall be observed in touching upon any of those points with respect to which difference of opinion exists between different sects of professing Christians, and even upon those wherein professing Christians of all denominations differ from the Deist, care will be taken to "vindicate the ways of God" by inculcating suitable sentiments respecting his character and government, as indicated to us in his works as well as in his word. Our honest endeavour, for ourselves and for our pupils, so far as they may be influenced by our instructions and example, shall be to serve and worship the Author of Nature, the God of the Bible.

On his blessing we will rely, (with the assistance of our respectable colleagues and the support and co-operation of the Board and other friends of the infant Institution,) for success in the undertaking which we are now about to commence,—that of rearing up an Institution, which shall become, before long, the pride and glory of the State, the loved and revered spot to which her sons shall resort, to enjoy advantages, equal, at least, to those of any other seat of learning west of the Alleghanies. Whatever industry and zeal on our part can effect, we here pledge for the accomplishment of this object; and if we should not meet with success we shall, at least, try to deserve it.

THE END.

The Changing Image by Title
1832–1840

It was difficult indeed for even the most optimistic supporter of Indiana Seminary to read into its story the realization of an ultimate dream of a functionally important institution. The objectives of the tiny institution were stated in vague generalities in both the constitutional mandate and the subsequent legislative act creating the school. It was easy enough to visualize the challenge, but applying the practical processes of meeting it was another matter. Classes which Baynard Rush Hall and John Hopkins Harney had conducted were purely within the context of the theological academy of the times. They reflected little or nothing in their teaching of the political rhetoric which had been so generously uttered about the need and potential services of a public institution.

In changing the title of the institution from "Seminary" to "College," the promoters of the idea no doubt felt it would have greater latitude to develop into a broadly-based public institution of service as well as learning. The decade 1828 to 1838 was an exciting one, if not in terms of growth for Indiana College, then in the efforts to establish the school's missions. Election of a man to the presidency with Andrew Wylie's strong notions of what an education should be and how it should be accomplished was bound to produce both personal frictions and some growing pains. The organization of a college staff at any time boils down to a matter of bringing divergent personalities into a single system and of trying to persuade them to seek the accomplishment of a common objective. In the 1830s this task was made extremely difficult because there was not an abundance of professorial talent in America for a new institution to draw from, and the difficulties were made even greater when prospective instructors were invited to go to the backwoods of southern Indiana to teach in a struggling frontier college. Governor Noah Noble promoted the change of title from Indiana College to Indiana University, again in the belief that the more inclusive and prestigious title would be a step in the direction of broader accomplishments by the institution. The new title of "University" required re-examination of the internal structures of the school, a higher projection for it, and a considerable re-consideration of its financial support.

The decade of college status had not been an unusually happy one. Personalities of conflicting views marred the opening of the decade, and later there were deterrent individuals who would have declared even the purchase of books by the president an illegal act. Perhaps the most significant facts in this decade were the attempts to broaden the University's curriculum to include law, pedagogy, and agriculture. Too, there were some serious reconsiderations of the Board of Trustees and of the school's financial conditions.

Basically, the people of Indiana and their political leaders had not fully informed themselves on the obligations which their society had assumed in chartering and organizing, first a seminary, then a college, and finally taking the long step toward the creation of a university. Almost every document in this section reveals limitations of vision, conditions of the time, and a lack of sophistication on the part of leadership at all levels, especially in the Governor's office.

Document 17

Men Approaching a Common Mountain from Opposite Directions

All was not smooth sailing in Indiana College. Differences between Andrew Wylie and his two professors, Baynard Rush Hall and John Hopkins Harney resulted in the latter's dismissal. This dispute had arisen out of a comedy of errors started by President Wylie when he overlooked a promise to a student, Samuel Givens, to place him at the end of an oratorical program. Too, President Wylie accused John Hopkins Harney of threatening to attack him with a knife. Nevertheless the trustees reported the College in a fairly stable condition.

*   *   *

Mr. Morgan presented the following report from the trustees of Indiana College:

The board of trustees of the Indiana College, in compliance with a joint resolution of the General Assembly of the state of Indiana, concerning the said College, approved Jan. 25th, 1830, respectfully report:

The first subject that claimed the attention of the board, was a difficulty that had taken place, among the faculty, of no recent date. In consequence of this difficulty, professor Hall had withdrawn his services, two weeks before the close of the session, and professor Harney, had assumed an attitude towards Dr. Wylie, which rendered his services of little avail. Both parties were prepared with ample documents for a judicial contest. But the board, after deliberating on the subject of those difficulties, and the relation which they sustained to the institution, which they believed to be that of guardians, rather than that of a judicial tribunal, declined to investigate those difficulties, and by a unanimous vote, removed professor Harney. After removing these professors, the board proceeded to fill their places, by electing Beaumont Park, of Madison, to supply the place occupied by professor Hall, and Jesse Elliott, of Rising Sun, who had the most ample recommendation, to supply the place occupied by professor Harney. With Mr. Park, one member of the board had been acquainted for the last ten years, and had no doubt his qualifications or his peculiar adaptation for the situation for which he was appointed. So that, upon the whole, the board anticipate the most favorable result to the institution, from the present organization of the faculty.

The number of students, in consequence of the derangement hitherto alluded to, could not be ascertained. A number of those that belonged to professor Hall's department, had withdrawn. The number was, however, between fifty and sixty. There is a new College edifice erected, the construction of which is highly creditable to the individuals by whom it was erected, and is every way suitable for all the purposes of a College. The length of this edifice, so far as the board now recollects, is 65 feet long and 50 feet wide. The foundation of stone, dressed and laid in the most substantial manner. This building is enclosed, and the lower floor is laid in a very substantial manner, with oak plank and the upper floor wtih poplar plank. The walls above the foundation, are of brick, which appear to be of the best quality.

The college has a library, consisting of 175 volumes as reported. They consist of History, Geography, Belles Lettres and treaties on Chemistry and mental and moral Philosophy. The books are all new, and by an estimate, considered very reasonable, and valued at $600. These books were procured by Dr. Wylie, while on a tour previous to his taking charge of the institution; and have not cost the institution one cent. The faculty of the College, consists of a President, Andrew Wylie, and the two before mentioned. The salary of the first is $1000 and the one third of the tuition fees, in the whole not to exceed $1300; of the others, $400 and not exceed $650: but the aggregate of these sums has not been reached in any case. Besides these, a tutor has been employed, William H. Stockville, who receives no compensation for his services, but an exemption from the payment of the tuition fee, which is $7 50 per session.

The board proceed now to the last requirement of the joint resolution of the General Assembly, to wit: whether the 10th section has been complied with. This section forbids the introduction into College, of sectarian tests. The board do not know of any, even the slightest abuses of the kind; nor do they apprehend that any difficulty can arise at any time, from this source, when the religious complexion of the board is considered. The members, of the board are of different religious tenets.

The members present, the last session of the board, were David H. Maxwell, of Monroe, William Hendricks, of Jefferson, Seth M. Levenworth, of Crawford, Jonathan Nichols, of Monroe, William Banister, of Monroe, Leroy Mayfield, of Monroe, James Blair of Monroe and William B. Laughlin, of Rush.

All of which is most respectfully submitted,

DAVID H. MAXWELL, Pres.
W. B. LAUGHLIN, Ch'r. Com.
appointed for this purpose.

December 1, 1832.
On motion of Mr. Whitcomb, said report was laid on the table.

Document 18

A Reach for "Harmony and unanimity"

By December 1834, the Indiana College enrollment had increased to one hundred students. The faculty still consisted of the president, two professors, and a tutor. The curriculum might well have been copied from the famous Yale Report of 1828. Wylie was fundamentally a classicist.

*   *   *

The Speaker laid before the House the following report of the Trustees of the Indiana College, with an accompanying document:

The Board of Trustees of Indiana College, in compliance with a joint resolution of the General Assembly of the State of Indiana, concerning said College, approved Jan. 25, 1830, respectfully report—

That in consequence of the non-attendance of a quorum of the Board of Trustees last year, owing to the prevalence of cholera in this place, no report was made to your honorable body at that time. In 1832, when the board last met, they were under the necessity of re-organizing the Faculty of the College, by the appointment of Messrs. Parks and Elliott; the former in the place of Mr. Hall, Professor of Languages, and the latter gentleman in lieu of Mr. Harney, Professor of Mathematics. Since that period, harmony and unanimity of sentiment exist among the gentlemen composing the Faculty of the College, and it is truly gratifying to the Board, that they can bear ample testimony, not only to the talents and acquirements of the President and Professors, but to the industry and assiduity of those gentlemen in their several departments. When the last report was made, the number of students was between fifty and sixty; that number has considerably increased, and they at this time amount to eighty-three,* as per catalogue accompanying this report, which also contains the names and places of residence of the students; by which it will be perceived that a large majority of them are inhabitants, and many of them natives of this State. The new college edifice is not yet entirely completed, but hopes are entertained that it will be so, at an early period; the board conceiving it to be their duty to husband the resources of the institution as much as possible; therefore but a small portion of its funds is annually appropriated for this purpose.

The college library contains at this time, as per report, between four and five hundred volumes. These consist of history, geography, chemistry, philosophy, belles lettres, and a number of miscellaneous works, a considerable portion of which were presented by individuals to Doctor Wylie, for the use of the college.

An appropriation of seventy-five dollars per annum has been made for the gradual increase of the library, and the Faculty have been instructed to make a code of by-laws, on the principle of keeping it up, and see the same executed.

An appropriation, also, has been made of one thousand dollars, to be expended under the direction of the President and Professor of Mathematics, for procuring a chemical and Philosophical apparatus, in addition to the instruments already on hand.

* Since this Report was made, the number of students has increased to nearly a hundred.

The Faculty of the college consists at present of a President, Andrew Wylie, D. D., and the two before named gentlemen, namely:—Messrs. Parks and Elliott; the former receives a salary of $1,300, and the latter $725, each per annum; also a Tutor, for the preparatory department has been employed, at a salary not exceeding three hundred dollars per year.

Heretofore part of the salary of the Faculty was contingent on the tuition fees, but it is now made permanent, in consequence of the comparatively large increase of the number of students.

An act of your honorable body was some time since passed, authorizing the sale of one of the reserved sections of land belonging to the college, lying immediately south of the edifice—part of the section was sold, and the commissioner did not feel authorizied to offer the remainder, without a renewal of the act, as the limitation had expired. The board would therefore respectfully suggest the propriety of the Legislature renewing the act, for the sale of the balance of the south section.

In proceeding to the last requirement of the joint resolution of the General Assembly, namely; whether the 10th section has been complied with. This section forbids the introduction into the college of sectarian tests, or the inculcation of sectarian principles. The Board takes great pleasure in assuring the General Assembly, that they are unacquainted with the slighest abuses of the kind, nor do they apprehend any difficulty on this score can arise at any time, when it is recollected that the members of this board belong to different religious denominations of christians.

The members present at the last session of the board, were, David H. Maxwell, Jonathan Nichols, Leroy Mayfield, James Blair, Joshua O. Howe, and Wm. C. Foster, of Monroe county, Wm. Hendricks, of Jefferson, Dennis Pennington, of Harrison, Seth M. Levenworth, of Crawford, and Allen Wiley, of Dearborn county.

WM. C. FOSTER
*Chairman of the Committee
appointed for this purpose.*

Bloomington, Sept. 30, 1834.

COURSE OF STUDIES.

The preparatory department.—Arithmetics, English grammar, geography, Latin grammar, historae sacrae, Viri Homae, Caesar, Sallust, Cicero's select orations, and English compositions.

COLLEGE PROPER.

Freshman class. 1st Session.—Ovid, Virgil, (Bucolics, Georgics, and Aeneid,) Horace, (odes, satires, epistles, Carmen Seculare, de arte poetica,) and Valpy's Greek grammar, compositions.

2d Session.—Greek grammar, Delectus, Greek testament, collectanea Graeca Minora, Graeca majora commenced, compositions, and Themes.

Sophomore class. 1st Session.—Graeca majora, (first and second volumes,) Herodotus, Thucydides, Xenophon, Polybius, Lysias, Isocrates, Demosthenes, Plato, Aristotle, Dionysius, Halicarnassus, Longinus, Homer, Hesiod, Sophocles, Euripides, Theocritus, Bion, Moschus, Sappho and Anacreon.

2d Session.—Cambridge mathematics, algebra, with the formation and application of Logarithms, geometry, plane, spherical and descriptive.

Junior class. 1st Session.—Cambridge mathematics, plane trigonometry, spherical trigonometry, application of algebra to geometry. Projections, dialling, mensuration, plane and trigonometrical surveying, differential and integral calculus, with practical exercises.

2d Session.— (Cambridge mathematics, physics, and optics,) statics, dynamics, hydrostatics, hydrodynamics, hydraulics, acoustics, optics, Mitchel's chemistry, with a course of experimental lectures, by Prof. Elliott, and lectures on grammar and philology, by Dr. Wylie.

Senior class. Mental and moral philosophy, evidences of Christianity, in connection with natural religion. Rhetoric, with a review of select portions of the Greek, Latin, and English classics, logic, political economy, constitution of the U. S. Cicero de Oratore and Homer.

REMARKS.

The Faculty, to whom is entrusted the government, and instruction of the students, consists of the President, who is also professor of mental and moral science—a Professor of mathematics, natural philosophy and chemistry, and a Professor of languages—a Teacher of the preparatory department, and such other tutors as may from time to time be found necessary. The course occupies four years: the first three sessions, (after entering college,) are spent in Professor Parks' department; the second three in Professor Elliott's, and the last two in Dr. Wylie's.

All the members of the college are engaged on Saturdays, in exercises in oratory, elocution, and composition, under the superintendance of the President, and professor of languages.

No young man will be suffered to remain in connection with the institution, who does not give evidence of a mind worthy of cultivation, and a disposition to improve all his opportunities.

The course of studies pursued in Indiana College is intended to make thorough scholars and practical men. The attention of the students is directed to but one primary object at a time, and his whole force and energies required to be concentrated on that object, and in this way it is found that more can be acquired, and more thoroughly understood, than by distracting the mind by a multiplicity of pursuits.

COMMENCEMENT. The commencement for conferring degrees, is held annually, on the last Wednesday of September.

The meeting of the board of trustees and visitors is held annually, on the Monday preceding the commencement.

Stated meetings of the Faculty are held on Saturdays at eleven o'clock, A. M.

Expenses. The tuition fee is $7 50 per session, or $15 per annum, and the contingent fee for wood, sweeping, &c., $1. Board, lodging, &c. can be had at from $1 25 to $1 50 per week.

Arrangements are now making, in preparing rooms in the college buildings for the accommodation of students, which will materially diminish their expenses and promote their improvement.

Which was read and referred to the committee on Education.

On motion of Mr. Vawter,

Ordered, That 300 copies of said report be printed, for the use of the members of this House.

Indiana *House Journal,* 1834–38, pp. 45–48.

Document 19

The Cause of Education among Competing Philosophies

The success of Indiana College and the rise of two private colleges inspired Governor Noah Noble to think in terms of higher things. No doubt he too had an "enlarged benevolence of heart" and here expressed for the first time the notion that the Seminary, now turned College, should now prepare to take the third step by turning itself into a university.

A year later the Governor was more specific in his recommendation that the Board of Trustees and the General Assembly create a state university. The College was hardly as far advanced as Governor Noble seemed to believe. It had less than $5,000 capital in hand, and a $70,000 endowment. The nation was caught in the panic of 1837, and the College was in debt.

*   *   *

The condition of the State College at Bloomington, has much improved during the present year, while every thing seems to indicate for it, a continued and increasing prosperity. It is indeed gratifying to observe that the cause of education is in the fostering care of the same spirit which is now prompting the people of Indiana, to put forth their energies in behalf of internal improvements. The institution at Crawfordsville in the north-west, and the one at Hanover in the south-east part of the state, built up and supported as they are by private capital, furnishes, in their unusual growth and advancement, the proudest commentary on that enlarged benevolence of heart which must exist in the bosoms of their founders. The success of these institutions has suggested to my mind the propriety of your complying with that requisite of the constitution, which provides for the establishment of a university. This can be easily accomplished by clothing the Bloomington college with that charter. By so doing you will withdraw the state institution from all competition with the private constitutions named, or with those that may hereafter be established; you will allay the jealousy and put down the spirit of opposition which probably exists or may exist among them; and on the contrary create a reciprocity of interests mutually beneficial to all. These views, however, are submitted with great deference to the better and more matured consideration of the legislature.

Governor Noble to General Assembly, December 8, 1835; Indiana *House Journal*, 1835–36, pp. 16–17.

Document 20

Meeting Public Expectations

Governor Noah Noble, in public expression at least, was a friend of Indiana College. He expressed genuine optimism for its future and promoted with some considerable zeal the changing of the institution's title to that of "University."

* * *

In its usefulness and in the high reputation it is rapidly acquiring, the State College at Bloomington is meeting the expectations of the public, and is achieving all that was promised by its ardent friends and advocates. Its patronage from our citizens and from those of other states is increasing, which is the best evidence of its merits. Reared as it has been, as a favorite institution, and partaking as it does of State character, nothing should be omitted that is calculated to elevate its standing, increase its prospertiy, and extend its usefulness. With that view I suggested at our last annual meeting the propriety of bestowing upon it the character and endowments of a State University; and as time and reflection have confirmed the opinion then advanced, I now renew the recommendation.

Governor Noble to General Assembly, December 6, 1836 (delivered); Indiana *House Journal,* 1836–37, pp. 23–24.

Document 21

The Pangs of Growth

At the moment the Governor of Indiana was recommending the elevation of the College to university status, the outlook for staffing the school with desirable faculty was grim. There was, however, one ray of hope; the Trustees believed they could sell the Perry Township lands for a profit.

* * *

To the Honorable the members of the Senate, and House of Representatives of the State of Indiana:

In compliance with the requisition, expressed in the charter of the State College of Indiana, the Trustees of said college beg leave respectfully to submit the following

REPORT:

Having for the last two years entered into a detailed report of the concerns of the college, and nothing of a new or interesting character having occurred in the interim, the Trustees would merely state for the information of the General Assembly, that the College continues to increase in prosperity, the number of students annually augmenting, and the reputation of the institution being considerably enhanced both at home and abroad. The Professor of Mathematics, Mr. Elliott, has resigned his situation in the College, and accepted the Presidency of the State College of Mississippi. Mr. Maxwell, the tutor in the Preparatory Department, having received an invitation to act as Professor of Languages in the above College, the places of those gentlemen have consequently become vacant, and been temporarily supplied by the Faculty.

The Board would respectfully solicit the attention of the legislature, to the propriety of selling the two reserved sections of land lying immediately east and west of the College, particularly the former. Land is at present selling at an exorbitant price in the vicinity of Bloomington, and it is believed advantageous sales may be made of those sections by paying one-fourth in hand, and the balance in three or four years, with interest from the date. As an additional inducement we would remark, that those sections of land would deteriorate in value, if not sold immediately, from the fact that the timber on them is liable to be continually pillaged. Messrs. Morris, McLaughlin, & Dunn not having complied with the act of the legislature in attending regularly the sessions of the Board, their places have been supplied by the appointment of Messrs. West, Ballard, and Turner.

All of which is respectfully submitted.

WM. C. FOSTER,
Chairman of Committee.

December 15th, 1836.

Trustees to General Assembly; Indiana *Senate Journal,* 1836–37, p. 130.

Document 22

An Expression of Trustee Optimism

This annual report of the Board of Trustees for 1837 is more oratorical than realistic. An uninformed reader of Paris C. Dunning's eloquent prose would get the notion that Indiana College had already fulfilled the mission set for it by the framers of Indiana's first Constitution. Though the school was in debt, its financial resources limited, and its faculty weakened by resignations, the trustees were expectant of a "perpetuity of those inestimable blessings of civil and religious liberty, arising from our present happy republican form of government."

*   *   *

To the General Assembly of the State of Indiana:

In compliance with the provisions of the charter of the Indiana College, the Trustees of said Institution respectfully submit their annual report:

In presenting this report, the Trustees cannot refrain from an expression of their deep felt satisfaction, at the increasing prospects and success of the institution. It still continues to gain a firmer hold upon the confidence and affections of the community, in the midst of which it is located, nor does this confidence, which has been so justly inspired in the public mind, from the expanding usefulness and success of the institution, appear to be confined to the immediate vicinity of the college, or to the limits of our own State, it has spread throughout the whole extent (or nearly so) of the valley of the Mississippi. By a reference to the annual catalogue of the officers and students of this institution, it will appear, that the number of the students in attendance upon the exercises of the college, has been gradually, and steadily increasing since its organization, the causes of which the Trustees are confidently induced to believe, may be found, not alone in the peculiar healthfulness of Bloomington, (the place of its location,) the morality of her citizens, or the cheapness of board: but the high and well earned literary reputation of the *President* and *Professors* of Indiana College.

The Trustees would (as evidence of the flourishing condition of the college) direct the attention of the Legislature to the cheering fact, that the number of students who are in attendance at the institution, who contemplate prosecuting a regular collegiate course of studies, is much greater than it has been at any previous period since its organization, which fact alone is sufficient to satisfy the most incredulous mind in community, of the salutary influence which this institution has exerted, and is yet exerting upon the public mind, both in reference to the ability of the Faculty to impart instruction to those who have capacity to receive it; but likewise in reference to the indispensable necessity of a thorough training and preparation of the youthful mind, preparatory to the successful entrance of an individual upon the broad, active and expanding theatre of human life. The number of students from distant States has rapidly increased within the last two years, and it is an undeniable, though gratifying fact, that many young gentlemen, who have pursued their regular collegiate course of studies in the colleges of adjoining States, until the time of their entrance into the last year of the senior class have abandoned those colleges and have and are availing themselves of the advantages, deriveable from the instruction of the learned President of this Institution.

The number of students who were in attendance during the last collegiate year, was one hundred and thirty seven. At the present session there are in attendance considerably upwards of one hundred, and many more who intend returning have not yet arrived. The Trustees would here remark that the number in attendance during the winter session is never so great as in the summer session, for which they are unable ao assign any particular reasons.

The Trustees of the college, have within the past year, (owing to the great increase in the number of students who desire to prosecute a regular collegiate course of studies, as well as to provide for the proper accommodation of those who are classed as irregulars,) been induced to add to the Faculty, two professorships, one of mixed mathematics and chemistry, which has been filled by the election of Mr. Theophilus A. Wylie, a graduate of the Pennsylvania University, (at Philadelphia,) a gentleman eminently qualified for the station. The other of Greek and French Languages, necessary branches of English Literature, Arithmetic, Grammer, Book Keeping, &c., which is filled by Mr. Augustus W. Ruter, a gentleman of a high order of talents, who is in past assisted by Professor Parks, whose urbane manners, age, experience and talents eminently qualify him for the discharge of all the duties incumbent on him, in this department, but also as the regular Professor of Languages. The other studies heretofore pursued, are yet rigorously enforced by the Faculty. The Government adopted in the institution is in its character parental, imitating as far as practicable, the government of a father over his family. Experience has in part confirmed the Trustees in the belief of the propriety of this plan of governing the students, more particularly the older class of them. It is believed that no more effectual plan for forming a good moral character in youth, and habits of industry and attention to any department of business, can be adopted, than that which appeals directly to the interest, duty, reason and virtuous emulation of an individual, which are deemed to be the most correct principles upon which young gentlemen can base their character and regulate their intercourse with the community; in furtherance of this most desirable object, the Board of Trustees have, in addition to the preceding form of government, made it the duty of the President of the Faculty (commencing sometime anterior to the present time) to deliver a public discourse or lecture, on some moral or religious subject, on each Sabbath day in the college chapel to the students, who are recommended to attend. It is not however made an imperative duty on them to do so; the President understanding the views of the Board of Trustees on this subject, carefully abstains from the inculcation of any sectarian principles or doctrines. This course in connection with other measures which have been adopted, has produced, and is producing upon the students the happiest effects in forming a character for correct moral deportment, and a rigid attention to study, in which particulars, it is confidently asserted that the students in this institution are not *excelled,* if *equalled,* by those of any other in the union.

The charter of the College clearly prohibits the teaching, or inculcation either directly or indirectly, of any religious sectarian principles, this provision has been strictly complied with. Sectarianism in the remotest degree, being excluded from the public or private instructions and discourses of the Faculty; the public discourses and private sentiments of the President in particular, will, it is believed, shield him from any imputation of the kind, the hatred which all *bigots* bear to him, being the best testimonial in his behalf in this matter.

The Trustees would here remark, that the public discourses delivered by the President to the students, on each Sabbath day, are numerously attended by the members of other denominations of christians in Bloomington and its vicinity, whenever it is convenient for them to attend; and that no complaint has ever yet reached them in relation to the manner in which the President discharges his duty in reference to this particular provision of the charter: upon the contrary, the Trustees are induced to believe that it is one of the strongest evidences of the propriety of the course which they have adopted; nor would they have been thus minute on this subject, but for the fact that prejudices have heretofore existed in the public mind against Indiana College, in relation to this particular subject, in view of this they deem it their imperious duty to defend the character of the Institution from the malign influence which such prejudices are calculated to exert over its growing prospects and usefulness.

It is a source of great pleasure to the Board of Trustees that they are enabled to announce to the public, and especially to the patrons of the College, the pleasing intelligence that the College Library is at this time quite respectable. In addition to many valuable works which were previously on hand, there are added many more; during the past year fifteen hundred dollars was appropriated to the enlargement of the College Library and Apparatus. By the agency of the President, an addition has been made of books selected with great care in the Eastern cities, of a character admirably suited to stimulate and gratify a taste for the solid standard works of Literature and Science.

In addition to the regular course of studies pursued in the College, the students are divided for the performance of what are usually called "Saturday exercises," into three departments: the more advanced students in the department immediately under the tuition of the President, engaged in composition, declamation, delivering extempore, (or by the aid of premeditation only) original speeches, debating and rhetorical reading. There are also two literary societies, each composed of about thirty members (students) of the more advanced character, who spend one evening of each week in exercises similar to the "Saturday exercise:" each society has furnished itself a very handsome library of choice and select books, the exercises of the respective societies have had an astonishing effect in eliciting a laudable ambition amongst the members and other students, to excel in the improvement and cultivation of their intellectual powers. The Board of Trustees have appointed a committee composed of members of their own body, whose duty it is (in connection with such other members of the Board as may see cause) to attend the semi-annual examinations and other exercises of the students of the College, it was thought by the Board that such a course would not only operate as a stimulus to the students to excel in their studies, but likewise enable them to ascertain the proficiency of Professors and Students in their various departments; the Board would further state that they cannot let the present opportunity pass, without bearing their testimony to the honorable manner in which the students underwent their examinations at the last annual College commencement: it would have been particularly gratifying to the true patriot, and more especially to every Indianian, could he have been present and heard the classical and eloquent speeches delivered by the young gentlemen who graduated upon that occasion, many of whom were the sons of citizens of Indiana.

From the liberal legislation extended to the College by the General Assembly of the State, within the last two or three years, the Board of Trustees have been enabled to secure an available fund, (accruing from the sales of certain sections of the reserve lands) equivalent to twenty-five or thirty thousand dollars, which fund is exclusive of what has usually been termed the permanent College fund, which is in the hands of the Treasurer of State, who is the superintendent of the loan office, and the interest of which alone was applicable to the use of the College, by a special resolution adopted at the last September session of the Board of Trustees: it was determined by said Board not to use any of the interest accruing on the permanent fund of the College until the principal and accruing interest should amont of one hundred thousand dollars; this desirable object we think may be accomplished within five years, and still leave at the command of the Board a fund sufficient with the small tuition fees paid by the students, to pay the President and Professor of the College their usual salaries, erect the necessary buildings which may be needed, and enlarge the Library and College Apparatus.

Boarding can be obtained in moral and respectable families in the town of Bloomington, and the vicinity, at a price varying from one dollar fifty to two dollars per week, in view however of the increasing number of students and fearing some difficulty might in future arise in obtaining comfortable boarding, the Board of Trustees have caused to be erected a large two story brick building sufficient (when finished) to accommodate forty or fifty persons, the building will be completed in May next, and the necessary arrangements have been made for the reception at that time of such as may desire to avail themselves of its advantages, the adoption of this plan it is believed will prevent any difficulty, either in obtaining the necessary accommodations for students, or increase in the prices of the same.

The health of the students has been excellent, not a solitary case of severe indisposition having occurred within the past year.   .

Congress (ever mindful of the interests of the great body of the people) being desirous to diffuse the genial influence of education throughout the community, did by the second proposition of the sixth section of an act of Congress, approved April 19th, 1816, entitled "an act to enable the people of the Indiana Territory, to form a Constitution and State Government, and for the admission of such State into the union, on an equal footing with the original states; *Provided,* that all the salt springs, within the said Territory, and the lands reserved for the use of the same, together with such other lands as may be the President of the United States, be deemed necessary and proper, for the working of said salt springs, not exceeding in the whole, the quantity contained in thirty six entire sections shall be granted, to the said State, for the use of the people of said State, and the same to be used under such terms, conditions, and regulation, as the Legislature of the said State shall direct, and whereas Congress did, subsequently by an act of said body, approved July 3rd, 1832, authorize the Legislature of the said State to dispose of said lands, and apply the proceeds thereof to the purposes of education in said State, and whereas, the Legislature of the State did by an act approved February 2nd, 1833, appoint Commissioners clothed with authority to sell said lands, with a view to raise funds for the purposes contemplated by the original donors, and whereas said lands have been sold and the funds accruing from said sale have not by any act of the Legislature of said State been definitely appropriated to any specific object, the Board of Trustees would most respectfully suggest to your honorable body, the propriety of appropriating said funds to the endowment, and establishing of a permanent Professorship in the Indiana College, with the view of educating and preparing young men free of any tuition, fee, to become teachers in the primary schools of the State, the Board of Trustees are aware that they may by this recommendation subject themselves to the charge of cupidity, in the estimation of some portions of the community who may feel some jealously towards this institutions, they nevertheless confidently believe that the fund could not be disposed of in any manner, so well calculated to carry out so effectually the liberal views and intention of Congress, and the act of the State Legislature, as the one herein suggested: if arguments were needed to prove the correctness of the foregoing position they can be adduced, it is a fact which cannot be successfully controverted, that the foundation of a good education must be early laid in the youthful mind, and that this object is as a general rule to be accomplished, or missed in the incipient stage of instruction, which first commences in the primary schools of the country, how important then is it to lay well the foundation, if you desire the super-structure which is to be erected thereon, to be durable. If this recommendation of the Board, should meet with the favorable consideration of the Legislature, the Board do most confidently believe; that within the short space of ten years, the State of Indiana will be furnished with a sufficient number of competent teachers, for all the primary schools of the State, than which a more gratifying and useful object cannot be attained.

In concluding this report which has already been protracted and minute, and the only apology for which is an earnest desire on the part of the Board to place within the knowledge of the Legislature, a true and faithful exposition of the condition of that institution, which we ardently hope and believe will, with prudent management, become the ornament of the State, and prove a lasting monument of the wisdom of its founders,) we cannot without a dereliction of duty fail to recommend to your honorable body, the propriety of granting a charter incorporating it as a State University: this measure we deem of importance, not from the consideration alone, that we believe it was contemplated by the framers of our most *excellent Constitution*, that the Legislature should at as early a time as convenient, establish a State University; but from the fact of the tendency of such a measure, to diffuse information over every portion of our community; to extend the sphere of its usefulness, and to improve the moral and intellectual condition of the human family, by which means more than all others combined, are we to expect a perpetuity of those inestimable blessings of civil and religious liberty, arising from our present happy republican form of government.

PARIS C. DUNNING,
Chairman of the Committee
of the Board.

Indiana Documentary Journal, 1837.

Document 23

"A Broader Diffusion of the Lights of Science"

Governor Noble was determined not to let the idea of transforming Indiana College into a university die a-borning. One can easily detect his anxiety over the indifference of members of the General Assembly to the idea.

*   *   *

The present is the last opportunity I shall have of appealing to you in behalf of the State College at Bloomington, and I cannot, without disregarding the suggestions of duty, pass it by in silence. A high standard of proficiency is required from the candidates for its honors, a wholesome discipline is enforced, and every effort is made by the faculty to ensure the promised objects of its establishment. They have succeeded thus far in advancing with the progress of our growth and resources. The wants of the age now demand a broader diffusion of the lights of science and of the principles of sound morality and virtue, and deeming this a propitious time for carrying into effect the provision of the constitution of Indiana, with regard to the establishment of a State University, I beg you to indulge me in repeating the recommendation, that you shall bestow on the institution that distinction and the necessary endowments.

Indiana *House Journal*, 1837–38, p. 20.

Document 24

A University by Legislative Fiat

The Indiana General Assembly, February 15, 1838, enacted the law that elevated Indiana College to university status. Legislators, by accepting the recommendation of the Committee on Education, believed they were enlarging the sphere of the institution's usefulness, and were offering to young Hoosiers in the future the means of better qualifying themselves for practical pursuits in life.

*   *   *

Mr. Dunning from the committee on Education, reports.
MR. PRESIDENT—

The committee on education to whom were referred so much of the governor's message, as relates to the State college at Bloomington, a resolution of the Senate upon the subject of changing the character of the institution from that of a college to a State University, endowing it with powers and privileges commensurate with the dignity and importance of the State, and also that part of the annual report of the board of trustees of the college, which recommends to the General Assembly of the State, the propriety of establishing it a State University, have had those several matters under consideration, and after bestowing upon them the attention which the important interests therein involved, demands, have directed me to report, that in their opinion the prosperity and character of the institution and of the State at large, would be greatly enhanced in a literary point of view, by changing the character of the institution, in the manner proposed in those several communications, believing as they do, that the sphere of its usefulness would be much enhanced by so enlarging its operations as to establish the requisite number of professorships in which might be taught, not only a full and complete course of collegiate studies but also so much only as might be necessary to qualify young gentlemen for the ordinary pursuits of life in a profitable manner. They deem it proper here to state, that they conceive it was the intention of the framers of the constitution to establish at as early a period as convenient a State University in which should be taught such branches of the useful arts and sciences as would not only qualify the youth of the State for the various learned professions, but also so much only as might enable that portion of our youth, who desire to pursue the highly useful avocations of agriculture and the mechanic arts, thereby extending to every interest in the community, all those inestimable blessings, which arise from the diffusion of science through every department of business. The committee deem it unnecessary to enter into a minute exposition of the advantages resulting to the community at large, from the adopting of the measures proposed, and the more fully to carry into effect those views, the committee have unanimously instructed me to report the following bill, to wit:

No. 144—a bill to establish a university in the State of Indiana;—which being read, was,

On motion of Mr. Dunning,

The rules being suspended, read a second time and referred to a committee of the whole, and made the special order of the day for Monday next.

Indiana *Senate Journal*, 1837–38, pp. 519–520.

Document 25

The Legislative Blueprint for a University

The Legislature defined the purposes of the rising Indiana University within the somewhat narrow limits of teaching languages, the useful arts and sciences, serving the professions, and literature. There is no hint in this legislation as what legislators believed "the useful arts and sciences" to be. Did they also have in mind the practical arts and applied sciences?

*   *   *

An Act to establish a University in the State of Indiana

SECT. 1. Be it enacted by the General Assembly of the State of Indiana. That there shall be and hereby is created and established a University adjacant to the town of Bloomington in the County of Monroe for the education of youth in the American learned and foreign languages, the useful arts, Sciences, (including Law and Medicine) and Literature, to be known by the name and style of the "Indiana University" and to be governed and regulated as hereinafter directed.

SEC. 2. There shall be a board of trustees appointed consisting of twenty one persons residents of this State who shall be and hereby are constituted a body corporate and politic by the name of the trustees of the Indiana University and in their corporate name and capacity may sue and be sued plead and be impleaded in any court of record and by that name shall have perpetual succession.

SEC. 3. The said trustees shall fill all vacancies which may occur in their own body elect a President of the board Secretary treasurer and such other officers as may be necessary for the good order and government of said corporation and shall be competent in law and in equity to take to themselves and their successors in their said corporate name any estate real personal or mixed by the gift grant bargain sale conveyance will devise or bequest of any person or persons whomsoever and the same estate whether real personal or mixed to grant bargain sell convey demise let, place, out on interest or otherwise dispose of for the use of the said University in such manner as to them shall seem most beneficial to the institution and to receive the rents issues profits income and interest thereon and apply the same to the proper use and support of the said University and generally, in their said corporate name shall have full power to do and transact all and every the business touching or concerning the premises or which shall be incidentally necessary thereto as fully and effectually as any natural person body politic or corporate may or can do in the management of their own concerns and to hold enjoy exercise and use the rights powers and privileges incident to bodies politic or corporate in law and equity

SEC. 4. The said trustees shall cause to be made for their use one common seal with such devises and inscription thereon as they shall think proper under and by which all deeds diplomas and certificates and acts of the said corporation shall pass and be authenticated.

SEC. 5. The said trustees or any ten of them shall meet at Bloomington in the County of Monroe on the last Monday of September next in the year (1838) and after severally taking an oath or affirmation faithfully and impartially to discharge the duties by this act enjoined shall proceed to organize a board, by electing one of their members as President and the board when so formed shall appoint a Secretary and treasurer who shall severally before entering upon the duties of their respective offices take an oath or affirmation faithfully and impartially to perform the duties appertaining to their respective offices and the treasurer shall give bond with three or more securities to be approved by said trustees, in the sum of twenty thousand dollars payable to the State of Indiana and conditioned for the faithful discharge of the duties of his office of Treasurer to the said corporation and which bond executed and approved as aforesaid shall be deposited in the office of the Treasurer of State

SEC. 6. The said board of trustees when organized in manner aforesaid shall forever thereafter determine the time of their future meetings, the manner of notifying the same and act on their own adjournments as to them shall seem most expedient and shall from time to time, as occasion may require make and ordain reasonable rules ordinences and by laws—with reasonable penalties for the good government of the University and the regulations of their own body not repugnant to the laws and constitution of this State

SEC 7. The said board of trustees shall from time to time as the interest of the institution may require elect a President of said University and such Professors tutors instructors and other officers of the same as they may judge necessary for the interest thereof and shall determine the duties salaries emoluments responsibilities and tenures of their several offices and designate the course of instruction in said University

SEC. 8. The said board of trustees shall have full power to remove any one of their own body for misconduct breach of the bye laws or gross immorallity and may at any time they may deem it necessary for the good of the institution remove any of the officers of said University or corporation and others appoint in their stead

SEC. 9. The President professors and tutors shall be styled the faculty of said University which faculty shall have the power of enforcing the rules and regulations adopted by the said trustees for the government of the students by rewarding or censuring them and finally by suspending such as after the necessary admonition shall continue refractory untill a determination of a quorum of the trustees can be had thereon and of granting and confering by and with the aprobation and consent of the board of trustees such degrees in the liberal arts and Sciences including those of Law and Medicine as are usually granted and confered in other Universities in America to the students of the university or to others who by their proficiency in learning or by other meritorious distinction may be entitlled to the same and to grant unto such graduates diplomas or certificates under their common seal and signed by the faculty, to authenticate and perpetuate the memory of such graduation.

SEC. 10. No President professor or other officer of the University shall whilst acting in that capacity be a trustee nor shall any President professor tutor instructor or other officer of the University ever be required by the trustees to profess any particular religious opinions and no student shall be denied admission or refused any of the privileges honors or degrees of the University on account of the religious opinions he may entertain, nor shall any sectarian tenets or principles be taught instructed or inculcated at said University by any President professor tutor or instructor thereof provided however that if at any meeting of the board of trustees of the University there should be one wanting to make a quorum then and in that case the President of the faculty of said University shall for the time being be considered as a member of said board and have power to act as such but so soon as a quorum of the said board shall be present, then the President shall no longer sit as a member of said board

SEC. 11. His Excellency David Wallace Governor of the State of Indiana (who shall be ex officio vice President of the board and his successors in officer forever) William Hendricks of the County of Jefferson Seth. M. Leavenworth of the County of Crawford David. G. Mitchell of the County of Harrison James M. Farrington of the County of Vigo John Law of the County of Knox Rev. Allen Wiley of the County of Montgomery Nathaniel West and Isaac Blackford of the County of Marion Jesse L. Holman of the County of Dearborn, Robert Dale Owen of the County of Posey Richard W. Thompson of the County of Lawrence Samuel K. Hoshour of the County of Wayne George. W. Ewing of the County of Cass Hiram A Hunter of the County of Gibson Jonathan Nichols Paris C Dunning James Blair Chester G Ballard Joshua O. Howe Leroy Mayfield and William Turner of the County of Monroe shall be and hereby are appointed trustees of said University agreeably to the provisons of this act and shall hold their first meeting as herein before directed; and should any ten of them (who shall at all times be necessary to constitute a quorum for the transaction of business) provided however that a deficiency of one may be supplied in the manner heretofore prescribed in the tenth section of this act) fail to meet on the said last Monday of September next, the Gove[r]nor of this State is hereby authorized and required to appoint some subsequent day for the meeting of said trustees giving to each of them twenty days notice thereof in writing and said trustees or a quorum of them when convened in pursuance of such notice shall proceed to organize the board in manner hereinbefore directed and the President of the University shall be empowered to call occasional meetings of the trustees in such manner as the board of trustees may by their bye laws direct.

SEC. 12. That all monies which have heretofore or which may hereafter arrise from the sales of the Seminary townships of land in the Counties of Monroe and Gibson shall be and forever remain a permanent fund for the support of said University and the interest arising from the amount of said sales together with the amount of the sales of the three reserve sections in the seminary township situated in the County of Monroe, the residue of the unsold sections aforesaid and all the buildings which have been erected adjacent to the town of Bloomington, in the said County of Monroe and which are now used by and belong to the Indiana College together with all the estate either real personal or of any discription whatever, belonging to or in anywise connected with the Indiana College as the property of the State and all gifts grants and donations which have been or hereafter may be made previous to the taking effect of this act, for the support of the Indiana College shall be and hereby are forever vested in the aforesaid trustees and their successors, to be controlled, regulated and appropriated by them in such manner as they shall deem most conducive to the best interest and prosperity of the institution *Provided* that the said trustees shall conform to the will of any donor or donors in the application of any estate which may be given, devised or bequeathed for any particular object connected with the institution and that the real estate hereby vested in the said trustees and their successors, shall be by them held forever for the use of said University, and shall not be sold or converted by them to any other use whatsoever

SEC. 13. That it shall be the duty of the secretary of said Corporation, to keep a true, and faithful record of all the proceedings of said board of trustees in a suitable book to be procured by them for that purpose, and make such copies and transcripts of the orders and proceedings of the said board of trustees as may from time to time be required, and the same duly certify under the seal of the corporation and for his services he shall receive such compensation as said trustees may from time to time, allow, to be paid out of any funds in the treasury of said corporation not otherwise appropriated

SEC. 14. That it shall be the duty of the treasurer of said corporation to keep a full true and faithful account of all monies by him received by virtue of his said office, in suitable books to be for that purpose provided and pay such monies out from time to time as may be required by and upon the order of said board of trustees duly certified by the secretary and keep a similar account of all such disbursements, and furnish said board of trustees whenever they may require the same a full true and complete statement of such receipts and disbursements and exhibit to them for their inspection his original books of entry, and also submit his books to the inspection and examination of the board of visitors of said University; which may at any time hereafter be appointed by the General Assembly of this State and shall moreover annually transmit to the Gove[r]nor of this State to be by him laid before the General Assembly thereof, a true and complete statement of the annual receipts and expenditures of said corporation, and should said corporation ever be dissolved by Legislative enactment or otherwise, it shall in such case be the duty of said Treasurer to pay over and deliver to the treasurer of the State for the use of this State all monies and funds in his hands derived from the State, belonging to said corporation at the time of such dissolution and should any treasurer of said corporation at any time be guilty of any defalcation in the discharge of the duties of his said office, the said trustees shall have the right of an action therefor against said treasurer and his surities on his official bond, in the name of the State of Indiana, for the use of said trustees and of prosecuting the same to final judgement and recovery, or in case of dissolution of said corporation such action shall be sustained for the use of the State

SEC. 15. That the power and authority of the present trustees of the Indiana College over and concerning the said institution the funds, estate, property, rights, and demands thereof, shall forever cease and determine from and after the organization of the board of trustees of Indiana University named in this act: and all the funds estate, property rights demands privileges & immunities of what kind or nature soever belonging or in any wise appertaining to said Indiana College shall be and the same are hereby invested in the trustees of the Indiana University appointed by this act and their successors in office for the uses and purposes only of the said University; and the said trustees and their successors in office, shall have, hold, possess, and exercise, all the power and authority over the said institution and the estate and concerns thereof in the manner herein before prescribed

SEC. 16. That The Constitution of the said University herein and hereby declared and established shall be subject to be changed, altered or amended by the legislature of this State, all laws or parts of laws coming within the purview of this act are hereby repealed. This act to take effect and be in force from and after its passage

Th[omas] J Evans
Speaker of the H. R.
Amz [Amaziah] Morgan
President of the Senate

Approved Feby. 15 1838   President of the Senate
David Wallace   Protem

Document 26

"The Prospering Cause of Education"

Governor David Wallace, like Governor Noah Noble before him, was optimistic that Indiana University would enjoy "the glorious destiny that awaits it." He, however, did not define that destiny.

*   *   *

. . . .

The cause of education, I am happy to state, is prospering. A new and imposing character has been given to the state institution at Bloomington. It has put on the habil[i]aments and assumed the dignity of a university. Its splendid endowments, its able and devoted professors, its healthful location—all claim for it even though in infancy a distinguished place among the great literary lights of the nation. This generation may indeed be proud of it, but above all, they should be proud of the glorious destiny that awaits it; that of becoming the intellectual nursing mother of the future sons of Indiana. . . .

. . . .

Indiana *Senate Journal,* 1838–39, p. 23.

Document 27

Mrs. Theophilus Wylie's View

Mrs. Theophilus A. Wylie, wife of the Professor of Natural Philosophy, gave an *Indiana Daily Student* reporter a view of what Bloomington and the newly named Indiana University were like when she arrived in the town. Changing of the title of the institution had no bearing upon the frontier conditions of the community.

*   *   *

The Daily Student January 19, 1905
"Has Watched Growth of University for Period of More than Half a Century"
"Mrs. Wylie, Widow of the Late Professor Wylie Relates Some Experiences which Happened When Monroe County was Wild Frontier"
There is probably no one now living who has been so long and intimately associated with Indiana University as Mrs. Wylie, the widow of the late Professor T. A. Wylie. In her more than sixty-five years residence in Bloomington Mrs. Wylie has watched the growth of the little village to a city and the college to a great University.
In an interview with a Daily Student reporter, Mrs. Wylie said:
"When I came here in 1838 things were in a rather primitive state. There were no railroads then in this part of the country and the National road was just being built. We came from Pittsburgh to New Albany by boat and the rest of the way to Bloomington in a stage coach drawn by four horses. The roads were very bad; the stumps of the recently cut trees sticking up in the middle of the roadway and grazing the coach at every turn.
About five miles from Bloomington the stage upset and I had to be rescued through a window by my husband.
As we approached the town I noticed a large brick building.
"What do you think that is?" asked my husband.
"I think it must be a cotton factory," I answered, thinking of the mills we had passed on our way.
"No," my husband replied with a laugh, "that is a factory for educating young men. That is the College."
"There were three large buildings close together, the Latin and Grammar schools as well as the College. There was also a long wooden building at First and Railroad streets. This was a kind of co-operative students' club kept by a Mr. and Mrs. Russel. Not very far away was a log house, the home of the president of the college.
"We drove on up the street to the Orchard House, where a number of people were assembled to meet us. This Orchard house was on the site now occupied by Benckert's bakery, and was a great curiosity to many in those days on account of its great size. It was three stories high.
"Yes, it was a pretty wild place when I first came. The farmers made almost everything at home. The houses were lighted by tallow "dips" and the farmers' wives went to church in their sun-bonnets and wove their own linsey-woolsey. My own dresses came from Philadelphia, but they were nearly worn out before I could wear them. When the women heard that a new dress had come from the

East they would send miles and miles for the pattern and there was nothing to do but pack up the pretty silk dresses in a saddle-bag and let them go. I did not always like to see my nice dresses carried around the country in that way, but my husband comforted me by telling me we had come west to educate the people and that this was part of the education.

"Once a year the farmers loaded their wagons and went to New Albany on a trading trip. One of the things they brought back with them was loaf-sugar in big blue paper cones. We afterwards broke the sugar with a hammer and a knife and crushed it with a rolling-pin. This sugar was used when we had "company"—the common brown homemade variety being thought good enough for the children.

"It was pleasanter socially in those days. There were few servants and when there was a large party everybody helped. When there was a sickness in a professor's family the students acted more like our own children than like strangers."

In spite of her many years, Mrs. Wylie's memory yet retains numberless anecdotes and stories of the early days.

There is one of a big black bear who paid an early morning call upon the wife of one of the settlers and of the Indian pow-wows held in Dunn's Woods[.] Another is of a physician who so far disbelieved in co-education, as to have his house built with two front doors and two separate stair-cases; one to be used by the boys and the other by the girls.

Perhaps the most interesting story is about an early student "strike." One of the Professors had gone to a party and as there were no roads and a good deal of mud had left his shoes together with his cane outside his host's door. Some prowling undergraduates found the shoes and cane and proceeded to hold a general jollification. When the Professor claimed his property, the students refused to give up the shoes except in exchange for a liberal supply of the good things intended for the party. There was nothing for it, but to ransom the shoes at any price. The next day, however, the offending students were called up by the President and requested to leave town. This they did but they did not go alone. The whole student body turned out as a guard of honor and "galanted" them as far as Gosport.

Indiana *Daily Student*, January 19, 1905.

Document 28

The Weed of Bigotry

The evil weed bigotry grew abundantly in the Hoosier social and intellectual garden. Denominationalism was always near the surface. Indiana University on the one hand was expected to teach a highly moralistic philosophy of life, but at the same time do so in the narrow context of non-sectarianism, which in the 1830s was almost an impossibility. Although the Board of Trustees and the university faculty fitted into the moralistic pattern, and their religious or denominational affiliations were varied enough to maintain a fairly even balance in this area, members of the Committee on Education of the General Assembly were still in doubt.

This was only one of the attempted in-roads on academic freedom in Indiana University in these early years.

* * *

Doc. No. 18. H. of Reps.

Mr. Kinney's Report
from the
Committee on Education
in Relation to
the Indiana College.
January 9, 1839.
Five hundred copies ordered to be printed.

The committee on education, to whom was referred a resolution of this House, directing it "to inquire into the practicability and expediency of establishing a law which shall more effectually prevent our public institutions of education from fostering and cherishing one religious sect to the exclusion of another,"

Report:

That from the terms of the resolution, they have had some difficulty in determining the precise nature of the inquiry directed. We have many public institutions devoted to literary purposes, but as they are all governed either by authority given by charters, and supported by private funds, or are under the direct or indirect government of the people, except the State University at Bloomington, it is supposed this last institution is meant by the resolution. Your committee is deeply impressed with the conviction that this institution should be governed upon liberal principles, that the citizens of the state may be able to point to it with pride, and repose the most unlimited confidence in the integrity, capacity and liberal views of those who have the immediate charge of its affairs; and would feel themselves guilty of a gross dereliction of duty were they to fail in the disclosure of any fact tending to show a different management of its affairs. Your committee, from a desire to learn the whole truth, have considered the characters of the trustees of this college; and certainly, if talents, experience, and well known public services can furnish any assurance of enlightened liberal policy in the government of the college, we have this assurance in the gentlemen who constitute the board of trustees. And we should not lose sight of the fact that the board is appointed by the representatives of the people of the whole state. They are at present Paris. C. Dunning, Robert Dale Owen, Isaac Blackford, Nathaniel West, William Hendricks, Jesse L. Holman, S. R. Houshour, John Law, Tilghman A. Howard, James Farrington, James Blair, Wm. Turner, C. G. Ballard, Allen Wiley, Joshua D. How, Leroy Mayfield, David Wallace, Hiram A. Hunter, David G. Mitchell, Richard W. Thompson and Seth M. Levenworth. Eight of these gentlemen are believed to be members of no church, four, members of the Methodist E. Church, two of the Presbyterian, two of the Campbellite, two of the Baptist, one a Covenanter, one of the Associate Reform, and one of the Cumberland Presbyterian. If, therefore, we had no confidence in the integrity, patriotism and enlarged views of these gentlemen, we should hardly suspect them of combining together to favor any one religious sect to the exclusion of all others or of any other. But as any suspicion in the public mind (however unfounded) would lessen the usefulness of this institution, it has been thought proper to push the inquiry a little further, and ascertain if possible, whether in any other department of the college, sectarian principles have been inculcated; and whether one sect has in fact been favored to the exclusion of others. The united testimony of those who have enjoyed the benefits of the institution, of citizens who have been conversant with its management, and of others whose duty it has been to inform themselves of the nature of the instruction imparted in its halls, is, that the president and professors have carefully avoided the discussion or inculcation of sectarian doctrines, and that students have in no instance been persuaded in the least to change their religious course, nor has any effort been made to produce on their minds the slightest sectarian bias. There are no legal restraints in religious matters upon the the trustees of this state institution; they are left entirely untrammelled in the conduct of its affairs. In the selection of those who shall be the lights of these halls of science, the trustees are confined to no sect, party or country, nor should they be. And if in the choice heretofore made, a majority of its professors and the president have been of the same faith (and it is admitted to be so) there can be no suspicion from the character of those who made these selections, that it has been the result of design. Your committee, however, notwithstanding these expressions of confidence, feel constrained to say that in their opinion, some prompt and decisive action on the part of the trustees of the college is necessary to give it that rank which, from its liberal endowment, the people have a right to expect. But it is believed that this end cannot be attained by legislative enactment, without furher light as to the causes which have retarded its prosperity. The adoption of the following resolution is therefore recommended.

Indiana *Documentary Journal,* 1838.

Document 29

The President under Carping Fire of a Jealous Colleague

President Wylie was criticized by Cornelius Pering for overstepping his authority in various ways, one of which was purchasing books and scientific instruments when the Board of Trustees had only authorized the purchase of United States and Indiana maps. Involved in this complaint was William C. Foster of the Board of Trustees. Wylie had to defend himself before a kangaroo court inquiry into his actions. Governor David Wallace's statement to the General Assembly, December 3, 1839, was the concluding act of the dispute. The plain truth was that Wylie was too advanced for most backwoodsmen in Indiana in the late Jacksonian era.

*   *   *

At the request of Doctor Wylie, President of the University at Bloomington, against whom it will be remembered, charges of mal conduct, in the administration of the affairs of that institution had been preferred, and widely circulated through the medium of newspapers and other channels, a meeting of the board of trustees was called, which I attended, in the month of April last. At this meeting the board entered into quite a labored and patient examination of all the charges, which resulted in the entire acquittal of the accused by the unanimous vote of the members present. Indeed the testimony so far from implicating

President Wylie in the smallest degree triumphantly vindicated his conduct throughout, and placed him in point of firmness and integrity as an officer, on higher ground, than the malice or envy of foes had before permitted him to occupy. I regret to say, however, that a majority of the board, after mature consideration, deemed it essential to the peace, harmony, and prosperity of the University, to vacate three of the Professorships; two of these are still vacant—one having been filled, as I have since been informed, at the September session of the board of trustees.

The subject of education is one of paramount interest, and merits the first and last consideration of an American legislator. Heretofore, preparatory steps only, have been taken to bring about the establishment of the common school system in Indiana. The newness of the country, the sparseness of the population, and the demand for all the time and labor of the settler to prepare him a comfortable home, have, thus far, forbid any successful attempt toward accomplishing this desirable object. But the period has at length arrived when this field may be advantageously occupied; when the wants and circumstances of a vast majority of the people, are such as to justify, and even require immediate action. If we take the census of 1830 as a criterion, we have within the limits of the state about 272,000 minors over the age of five, and under the ages of eighteen and twenty-one years. This number, we know, is constantly and rapidly increasing, by means of immigration, and with it, as a matter of course, the necessity of devising some speedy and efficient plan to ensure instruction to them all.

To effect this object the creation of a board of public instruction would probably be the most successful,—a board whose duty it should be to superintend the establishment of schools in every county; to see that the funds are carefully husbanded and equitably distributed; to provide competent teachers; and by public addresses, or otherwise, to wake up and encourage the people to lend a helping and sustaining hand in forwarding so noble an undertaking.

That we have abundant means already provided, with which to operate successfully and profitably on this plan, cannot, I think, be rationally denied. According to the very able and interesting report of Judge Kinney, prepared with great care and labor, as chairman of the committee on education, of the last house of representatives, we will have by 1850, in the saline fund, the tax on bank stock, the surplus revenue, the reserved sixteenth sections of land, the sinking fund or bank stock, the unsold saline lands, the lands returned as delinquent to the school commissioners, a capital rising four millions of dollars—two millions of which are now within the absolute control, and may be applied at any moment, by the legislature. The latter sum, therefore, judiciously invested, may be made productive of a revenue of at least one hundred and fifty thousand dollars per annum; enough certainly to answer present purposes, and to ensure a safe and prosperous beginning.

One of the great difficulties we have at present to encounter, is the scarcity of competent and qualified school teachers. To remedy which, a scheme something like this has been suggested; namely, to authorize a separate department in the State University, under the control of its president, devoted exclusively to preparing and qualifying young men for the duties of professional teachers. To the attainment of this object, the proceeds of the saline fund, amounting to some two thousand dollars per annum, might be profitably applied. This would enable the state to provide that the necessary books and tuition should be furnished free of expense, and that each county should be entitled to send one or more of their most deserving and promising young men. Imperfect as is this skeleton of the plan proposed, still I flatter myself, that it will be sufficient to direct your attention to the subject, and to call from your more matured and deliberate consideration a better.

Indiana *House Journal*, 1839–40, pp. 25–26.

Document 30

A Concerned Legislature, but not Financially Concerned

This curious resolution submitted by the Chairman of the Legislative Education Committee is characteristic of public feeling of oversight responsibility for education, but without financial involvement. This resolution falls just short of being a bumptious charge of mismanagement of a starved institution.

*   *   *

Mr. Bowen from the committee on education, made the following report:
MR. PRESIDENT—

The committee on education, to whom was referred a resolution of the Senate, instructing said committee on inquire into and report the condition of the State University; whether or not it is in a flourishing condition; and if not, what is the cause, and what means should be adopted to secure its prosperity? with a view to make it in point of fact, what it purports to be, a State University, have had the same under consideration, and a majority of the committee than present directed me to report a resolution to the Senate, asking for a joint committee of both houses, with power to send for persons and papers.

In obedience thereto I have herewith submitted the following resolution:

Resolved, By the Senate, the House concurring therein, That a joint committee of two from the Senate and three from the House, be appointed by the President of the Senate and Speaker of the House respectively, with power to send for persons and papers, to inquire into the condition of the State University, whether or not it is in a flourishing condition; and if not, what is the cause, and what means should be adopted to secure its prosperity? with a view to make it in point of fact, what it purports to be, a State University, and report the result of their investigation to the legislature;

Which report was concurred in, and the resolution laid upon the table.

Indiana *Senate Journal*, 1839–40, p. 165.

Document 31

Building an Infant Library

This joint resolution of the Indiana General Assembly, December 31, 1830, marks the beginning of the documentary collection in the Indiana University Library.

*   *   *

CHAPTER CXXIII.

A Joint Resolution of the General Assembly of the State of Indiana, directing ing the secretary of state to deliver certain public documents to the board of trustees of Indiana College.

[APPROVED, DECEMBER 31, 1820.]

Resolved, by the General Assembly of the state of Indiana, That the Secretary of State, be directed to inform the board of trustees of Indiana college, that there are in his office certain boxes containing public documents, which through the munificence of the General Government, are to be presented to the trustees, by the legislature, as additions to the library of the college, and say that they are now subject to the order of the board of trustees.

Resolved, That the secretary of state be further directed, to present to the executive committee of the Historical Society of Indiana, for the use of said society, the boxes of public documents addressed to his office, or the governor of the state, and marked for the "Historical Society of Indiana," and also such further documents as may be addressed to his office or the executive of this state, and addressed to the said society.

Laws of Indiana (special), 1830–31, p. 172.

Document 32

Mr. Clay's Reply

Indiana College students no doubt had whiggish leanings and looked south of the Ohio to a perennial presidential candidate to grace their first commencement. Too, they recalled the cry of the Warhawk, and associated Henry Clay with the heroics of William Henry Harrison at Tippecanoe. These letters in a sense represent a contest between students and politician as to which one could be most gracious in phraseology and flattering sentiment.

* * *

We copy, from the last Bloomington paper, the following correspondence, which has lately taken place between the students of the Indiana College and Mr. Clay. It is no doubt a source of regret to the young gentlemen who entertain so much regard for that distinguished individual, that circumstances should render it inconvenient for him to visit the institution at the time desired.

BLOOMINGTON, Sept. 17th, 1830.

To the Hon. Henry Clay:

Sir:—At a meeting of the students of Indiana college we were appointed a committee to solicit the pleasure of your company at the first commencement of our State College, which will take place on Wednesday the 27th Oct.

Having understood that it was your determination to visit our state in Nov., and attend a celebration of the battle of Tipacanoe in connexion with the Hero who distinguished himself upon that occasion, and as our village is nearly on your route, we would do injustice to our feelings, we would be dishonoring to cause of literature if we permitted one of her devoted sons, and able advocates to pass, without exhibiting to him that testimony of respect which has distinguished service and zealous labor so highly and justly merit. But permit us to tell you, sir, that it is not only your devotedness to the promulation of science and literature, that has attracted our attention, and deserves our notice. In casting our eyes over the political annals of our country, we behold the name of *Clay*, first—in the cause of Liberty; first—in the cause of Humanity; and first—in promoting the prosperity and honor of our happy country. Your presence, sir, on that occasion, if convenient to yourself, will really be pleasing and interesting to us. The minds of our youth will be inspired with a love of just fame, and honorable distinction, in associating themselves with the man who has arisen, by his own exertions, from indigence and obscurity, to the first rank among the authors and statesmen of the age in which he lives; in congratulating and interchanging sentiments of friendship with him who has "filled the measure of his country's glory!" him whom two great continents hail as the bold champion and successful promoter of their best interests, their dearest privileges and most invaluable blessings. Please sir, let us know as soon as convenient whether you can attend with us; and accept for yourself sentiments of the highest respect and esteem.

Yours, &c.

JAMES S. ROLLINS,
LEWIS BOLLMAN,   *Committee.*
JAMES W. DUNN,
W. S. STOCKWELL.

ASHLAND, 25th Sept. 1830.

Gentlemen:—I have much satisfaction in acknowledging the receipt of your polite letter of the 17th instant, as a committee of students of Indiana College, wishing my attendance at its first commencement, on the 27th proximo. Although I had no design, as you had understood, of visiting Indiana for the purpose of celebrating the battle of Tippecanoe, I had wished to view some land which I own near Terre-Haute, with the intention of establishing a stock farm, and for that purpose had contemplated an excursion this fall; but I now apprehend that I shall not be able to execute it. I must, therefore express my regret at not being able to be present on an occasion so interesting to the state and to the youth of Indiana. Although not personally among you, I beg you and the rest of the students of the college to accept my fervent wishes for the complete success of their endeavors to improve their minds and acquire knowledge. May they fulfil the fondest hopes of their parents and relatives, and by their exemplary conduct and literary and scientific attainments, render the infant college worthy of the state whose name it bears.

I request also, gentlemen, your acceptance of my grateful acknowledgments for the flatering manner in which you have been pleased to speak of my public services and career. I should be glad to interchange friendly salutations with you, and be most happy if I thought that I could, either by personal intercourse, or by example, animate you in the pursuit of just fame and honorable distinction and strengthen your attachment to the liberties and interest of our common country.

With great respect,
I am, your ob't serv't.
H. CLAY.

Messrs. James S. Rollings, Lewis Bollman, Jas. W. Dunn & W. H. Stockwell.

Madison *Indiana Republican,* October 28, 1830, quoting *Indiana Journal.*

Document 33

In Bold Relief

David H. Maxwell on October 28, 1830, presented a full picture of Indiana College in that year. There was lack of space for all the college's functions. The library was indeed meager, and there were fifty-seven students, thirty-four of whom were Hoosiers. By any standards of cost, the main building had been constructed at a ridiculously cheap figure as were the other structures. Student expenses were indeed minimal, and so were professorial and presidential salaries.

*   *   *

The Speaker laid before the House, a communication from D. H. Maxwell, President of the Board of Trustees of Indiana College, accompanied by the following report of said trustees, which was read and referred to the committee on Education, viz:

"The Board of Trustees of the Indiana College, in compliance with a joint resolution of the General Assembly of the state of Indiana, concerning said college, approved, Jan. 25, 1830, respectfully report,

That the college edifices consist of one brick building, sixty feet long, and thirty-one wide; of two stories high, containing six rooms, which have been arranged by the faculty and occupied as recitation rooms, hall, library room, and by the Library Society established among the students. This building was erected by the trustees of the late State Seminary in the years of 1823 and 4, and cost about 2,400 dollars. There is also a brick dwelling house thirty-one feet long, and eighteen feet wide, containing four rooms and having a small kitchen attached thereto. This house was likewise built by the trustees of the State Seminary in the year 1823 and 4, and cost 891 dollars, and is at present occupied by Mr. Hall, one of the professors of the college, who at his own expense has built several other necessary out-houses upon the premises. These buildings were erected in compliance with legislative acts upon that subject: there has also been erected within the last two years, a large brick building seventy-five feet long, fifty feet wide, and three stories high; the exterior walls are only constructed and the roof put on, and the windows and doors of which will be enclosed immediately so as to prevent the building from being injured by the weather. There are 300,000 bricks in the walls of this edifice, and the estimated expense of the materials and work thus far is 4,333 dollars and 66 cents: in this estimate is included the dome or cupala, the sash for the windowns, and painting the cornice, dome and deck roof. Of the foregoing sum, there has been paid 3,117 dollars and 19 cents, the balance not being due until next summer. When the funds of the institution will admit of further progress, it is contemplated by the Board to finish the building, as it is imperiously called for by existing circumstances, viz: The increasing number of students; the diversified nature of their studies; the indispensible necessity in some instances for different appartments for the inculcation of different sciences; the need of appropriate rooms for chemical, philosophical and astronomical apparatus when they can be obtained, (for the present there is no place for them) also the pressing necessity for a large hall, or chapel, so called, for the use of the students on *commencement* days and for the accommodation of the public on those occasions, and lastly the use of rooms in both the college buildings as commons, or lodging rooms for the students. Boarding although it is obtained very low at Bloomington, is the most expensive item in the education of a young man.

In some of the most respectable colleges in the United States, it has become the practice for ten or twelve young men to unite, and from time to time purchase articles of diet in market, and hire some person to cook, and keep a table for them, and in this way, their boarding does not cost them more than 50 or 62½ cents per week. To do this, however, they must have lodgings in the college buildings, and to provide such at as early a day as practicable, has been one main object with the Board of trustees, in erecting the present large college edifice. These are all the improvements on the college premises, which are in other respects entirely naked and unimproved, not having around them an enclosure of any kind, the determination being to expend upon no object but what will have a tendency to add to the usefulness and character of the institution. The college has a library containing 235 volumes, so assorted as to embrace History, Geography, Belles Lettres, and treatises on Chemistry, and mental and moral Philosophy.

The books are all new, and of the most approved authors, and estimated as being very low at 600 dollars. These books were obtained for the college by the instrumentality of Mr. Wylie, the president, whilst on a tour preparatory to his taking charge of it, and have not cost the state or the institution a solitary cent, having been gratuitously presented to him in his official capacity by various donors in the middle and eastern states; one gentleman alone, Arthur Tappan, of N. York, make a present of 100 dollars, an act of liberality entitled to, as it has received especial thanks of the Board. There are two globes, one terrestrial and the other celestial, purchased by the Board for 31 dollars, but it is painful to the Board to be compelled to state that the college has no Philosophical apparatus.

The professors cannot discharge their duties as they would wish, indeed they can with but great difficulty get along without the apparatus, and as the funds at the disposal of the Board will not at present warrant the required expenditures, it is hoped that the General Assembly will aid by an appropriation. What is there more calculated to expand the mind and enlighten it, than the study and developments of experimental philosophy? Nature cannot be comprehended without its aid; and will the General Assembly, the guardians of this institution, who are bound as they love and respect the state, to protect, foster and exalt it; will they stand still whilst strangers at the distance of a thousand miles are generously giving it an impulse on its march onward? This Board will continue to entertain a very different expectation. The faculty of the college consists of a President, Andrew Wylie, two other professors, Baynard R. Hall, and John H. Harney; and besides these, a tutor, William H. Stockwell, who has been employed from time to time.

The compensation of the President is 1000 dollars, and one third of the tuition fees, not to exceed 1,300 dollars, of the other professors 400 dollars each, and one-third of the tuition fees, not to exceed 650 dollars each, but the aggregate of these sums has never been reached in any case. The tutor receives nothing for his services but an exemption from the payment of the tuition fee (which is 7 dollars 50 cents per session) and an equal participation with the students in the means of acquiring information.

The number of students in college is 57; 34 of whom reside in Indiana, 10 in Kentucky, 8 in Pennsylvania, one in Tennessee, one in Mississippi, 1 in Louisiana, 1 in Illinois, and 1 in Missouri. This time a year ago, the whole number of students was only 30.

The Board have now to report on the next requirement of the joint resolution of the General Assembly, to wit: whether the 10th section of the act establishing the college, has been complied with, which section forbids the introduction into the college of sectarian tests, and the inculcation of sectarian principles. The Board disclaim the slightest knowledge of any such abuses.

The Board do not sustain the present faculty on account of any religious opinions they may profess, but for their literary attainments, their exalted qualifications, their particular adaptation to the stations which they fill.

They know of no cause of complaint against the faculty, but on the contrary believe that they have faithfully discharged their respective duties. If at any time the Board should find that the faculty or any member of it has been faithless to the important trusts confided to him, more especially if the attempt should be made in violation of the constitution of the college to teach 'sectarian tenets or principles,' to the students, the Board will promptly and fearlessly remove them. In addition to the obligation which the Board are under to their families, to the state, and by the oaths they have taken, to support the constitution or charter of the college, to prevent the introduction of sectarian tests and qualifications, it will be perceived by the General Assembly, that the institution at this time derives a further guarantee from the religious complexion of the Board of Trustees, the members where of are as follows:

David H. Maxwell, Pres't. Monroe	co.	
William Hendricks, Jefferson	co.	
Williamson Dunn	do.	co.
Rev. John Strange	do.	do.
George H. Dunn, Dearborn,	do.	
John Law, Knox	do.	
Thomas H. Blake, Vigo	do.	
Seth M. Levenworth, Crawford	do.	
Ratliff Boone, Warrick	do.	
Jonathan Nichols, Monroe	do.	
James Blair,	do.	do.
William Banister,	do.	do.
Rev. Leroy Mayfield, do.	do.	
Ovid Butler, Shelby,	do.	
B. F. Morris, Marion,	do.	

Of this Board it is believed 4 are Presbyterians, or at least were so educated; 4 Protestant Episcopalians; 3 Baptists; 2 Methodists; 1 Covenanter, and 1 member of the *Christian* society or church. Out of such a mixture of religious opinion, it cannot reasonably be supposed that a majority could be prevailed upon to establish, or in any respect to countenance a sectarian domination;

All which is respectfully submitted.

The foregoing report was presented to the Board by Messrs. Blake, Hendricks and Dunn, of Dearborn, being a committee appointed to draft the same, and adopted by the Board *nem con.*—

Whereupon it was

Ordered, That the President of the Board do transmit copies of the same,

directed to the President of the Senate, and Speaker of the House of Representatives, at the ensuing session of the General Assembly, with a request that
they lay the same before the Houses over which they respectively preside.

D. H. MAXWELL, *Pres't*
of the Board Trust's Ind. Coll.

Bloomington, Oct. 28, 1830.

Indiana *House Journal,* 1830–31 (15th Session), October 28, 1830.

Document 34

The First Step up to University Status

If the legislative educational committee was serious in its request for
information as to whether or not Indiana University was making a proper
transition to a higher status, all it had to do was read the Minutes of the
Board of Trustees, September 24, 1838. They reveal a detailed picture of
the struggling school's affairs. These minutes eloquently reflect the fact
learned many times over in America, that a mere change of title did not
in fact mean a significant change in conditions of education.

*   *   *

Journal

Of the proceedings of the Board of Trustees of Indiana University, at their
first session, begun and held in the University Building, adjacent the town of
Bloomington on Monday the 24th day of September in the year of our Lord
1838, being the day appointed by law for the meeting of the said Board of the
University

The following persons, named in the eleventh Section of an Act entitled
"an Act to establish a University in the State of Indiana, Approved February
15th 1838." Viz John Law of the County of Knox, Robt Dale Owen of the County
of Posey, Richd W Thompson of the County of Lawrence Saml K. Hoshour of
the county of Wayne, Paul C. Dunning, Jas Blair Joshua O. Howe, Chester D.
Ballard, Wm Turner & Leroy Mayfield from the County of Monroe, appeared in
conformity with the 5th Section of said Act, and after having severally taken an
affirmation, faithfully and impartially to discharge their duties as trustees of
Indiana University; proceeded to organize, by calling John Law to the Chair

On Motion of Mr Owen   The Board now proceeded to the election of a
President and Secretary, which resulted in the choice of P. C. Dunning Esq
President and James D. Maxwell Secretary. The Pres. elect in the chair

On Motion of Mr Law   Resolved That there be and hereby are appointed
five standing Committees of this Board Viz A Committee of Ways and Means,
Library Committee, Examining Committee, A Building Committee and a Committee on Claims, whose duty it shall be to consult and report on the various
maters [sic] refered to them, affecting the interest of the University. Whereupon
the chair announced the appointment of the following standing Committees and
order of business

Committee of Ways & Means	{	Thompson Hoshour & Mayfield
Library Committee	{	Owen Thompson & Blair
Examining Committee	{	Law Turner & Howe
Building Committee	{	Turner Ballard & Howe
Committee on Claims	{	Thompson Blair & Mayfield

Mr Ballard moved the adoption of the following resolution

Resolved That this Board now proceed to the election of a Trustee, of Ind University, to fill the vacancy occasioned by the decease of Johnathan Nichols Esq., which motion after some discussion was laid on the table, with notice that it would be called up on to morrow.

On motion of Mr Ballard the Board adjourned to meet to morrow Morning at 8 Oclock

Tuesday Sept. 25

Board met pursuant to adjournment. Members present same as yesterday. His Excellency Gov. Wallace, (Ex Officio Vice President of this Board) having appeared in the Hall of Trustees, took his seat as a member of this Board. According to previous notice, the motion to go into an election for a Trustee, to fill the vacancy occassioned by the decease of Johnathan Nichols was called up from the table, and upon the question of its adoption was decided in the affirmative. Whereupon the Bd proceeded to the election Messrs Thompson and Hoshour acting as Tellers On counting the ballots T. A Howard, having received a majority of all the votes given, was declared duly elected

On Motion of Mr Law   Resolved That report of the committee of "Ways & Means" of Ind College, made through Mr West, their chairman, at the annual session of sd College Sept. 25th 1837 be and is hereby refered to the Committee of "Ways & Means" of Ind. University, with leave to report upon the same

On Motion of Mr Law   Resolved That the bills of Messrs Wright and King & Ballard, presented to this Bd, be refered to the Committee on Claims, and also that said Committee report to this Board the *Liabilities* of Indiana University as nearly as practicable

On Motion of Mr Dunning   Resolved That the Secretary of this Board be authorized to procure stationary, for the convenience of the members, and also to procure sunitable books for recording the proceedings thereof

On Motion of Mr Owen The Board now proceeded to the election of a President of Ind. University, when upon counting the ballots, the vote stood as follows Viz

For Prest of Ind. University	{	Dr Wylie	9
			2

Whereupon the Chair declared Dr Wylie duly elected

On Motion of Mr Thompson   Resolvd That a Committee of three be appointed, to wait on Dr Wylie, and inform him of his election and the chair appoints Messrs Thompson Law & Owen said Committee

On Motion of Mr Owen   Resolved That a committee of three be appointed to arrange in conjunction with the President of Ind. University, the Proffessorships of said University, Whereupon the chair appointed Owen, Law & Thompson said Committee

Mr Thompson, Chairman of the committee of "ways and means" to which was refered the last report of the committee of "ways and means" of Indiana College, on leave submitted the following report *Viz*

Report

Mr President. The committee of "Ways and means," have in the discharge of their duty, called upon the agent of the College Fund for a statement of the balance of monies in his hands, and have received a report from him of his receipts and expenditures up to this time, which report although not final, for the want of vouchers for some three hundred dollars, affords such evidence as may be relied on, of the amount in his hands. It exhibits the amount received by him since his last report to the Board as $2592,93¾ of which amount he has expended and paid out $1557,98¾ leaving a balance in his hands of $1034,94¼ out of which is to be deducted an allowance to said Commissioner, for surveys of the east and West Sections, and for his services in laying out the same, which will probaly [*sic*] amount to $150,00, leaving a balance of $884,94¼ which the committee do not report as the actual sum, but so near thereto, as they can now arrive at, in consequence of their not being an adjustment and settlement of the actual balance in the hands of Mr Alexander, in accordance with a resolution of this Board, at its last meeting, which required *that* settlement and the reception of the amount by the Treasurer. To ascertain the available means of the University The Committee have learned from the Commissioner, that there will be due and payable on the 1st of the ensuing month of November the sum of (about) $1050,00 from the sale of the west Section. This amount added to the balance of $884.94¼ makes the aggregate sum of $1934.94¼ available on the first of Nov. 1838.

The committee found much difficulty in arriving accurately at the Amount of monies in the Treasurer's hand, in consequence of his absence from home. They however suppose from such information as they have received that there is about $1900.00. This amount added to the balance on Nov. 1st will make at that time an aggregate balance of $3834.94¼ This Amount or a great portion thereof in the hands of the Treasurer, may have been loaned by the Treasurer since the last meeting of the Board, as at that meeting a resolution was adopted authorizing the loaning any surplus in the hands of the Treasurer, if it should be deemed expedient, by the Prest of the Board. The death of the late President and the absence of the Treasurer, render it impossible to ascertain these facts.   Upon this view of the means of the Institution, the Committee have reflected much upon the course which the Board should pursue to meet the number of claims now due the University. They have no means of arriving at the exact amount, but it must be, from the fact there have been no recent payments and much work done lately, very large. They are aware, that at the last meeting, the Board adopted a resolution, expressing it as their opinion, that under no circumstances, ought the funds now in the hands of the Treasurer of State, to be touched. This resolution meets the concurrence of the Committee, and good policy would dictate, that the seventy odd thousand dollars, now in his hands, be suffered to remain, until at least, amounts to the sum of $100000. Admitting therefore the policy of that resolution, they have some difficulty, in determining, what course the Board ought to pursue. The funds loaned by the Treasurer of State, are producing eight per cent, and if the funds now in the hands of the commissioner and treasurer cannot be made *immediately* available, it is the opinion of the Committee, that a loan had better be effected, of such amt. as may be deemed necessary, at the rate of six per cent interest, which arrangement will make a nett saving of two per cent. This Loan can be easily obtained and the interest promptly met, out of the funds now on hands Under this view of the condition of the University, the Committee recomend [*sic*] the adoption of the following resolution   Resolved That the Board do hereby authorize the borrowing of the sum of $5000.00 from some branch of the State Bank of Indiana and that the President of the Board is authorized to carry this resolution into effect

On Motion of Mr Law The above report and accompanying resolution were concurred in

SEPTEMBER SESSION 1838
Tuesday Evening 2 Oclock

Members present as in the morning. The President upon taking the chair laid before the Board, a communication from the students of Indiana College which on motion was laid on the table.

Mr Owens, from the select committee, to arrange Proffessorships in Indiana University, reported as follows Viz

Report

The Committee to which was refered the arrangement in conjunction with the President of the University, Report that in their opinion, these should remain in the University, as last year, they were arranged in the College Viz. One Prof. of Latin and teacher of English Literature One Prof. of Nat. Philosophy & Chemistry—One Prof of Mathematics & One Tutor & Principal of the preparatory department, & that in addition thereto, there be established a Proffessorship of Law. Which report on motion was concurred in

On Motion of Mr Ballard   The Board now proceeded to fill the different Proffessorships, embraced in the above report, when on counting the ballots, it appeared that the following named gentlemen were unanimously elected to the Proffessorships to which their names are severally annexed viz:

Professorship of Nat. Phil & Chemistry	Theophilus A. Wylie
" " " " Pure Mathematics	Jas F. Dodds
" " " " Greek & French	Augustus W. Ruter
" " Latin & English Literature	Beaumont Parks

The Board were about to proceed to the election of a teacher and Principal in the Preparatory Department, where upon the President of the University having made some remarks upon the propriety of abolishing Sd department Mr Owen moved the adoption of the following resolution   Resolved That the Chair of the Preparatory Department in Ind University be made vacant.

Mr. Thompson moved to amend said resolution by striking out from the Resolving clause and inserting as follows Viz. That a descretionary power be given to the Faculty, to vacate this department or not, as to them may seem best and as circumstances may require. Which Amendment was adopted.

The President of the University on leave being granted, submitted to the Board the following communication Viz

"The Library is of vital importance to the Institution, and were the funds such as to justify, the appropriation of $5000. annually, as is done at Cambridge Mass. for its increase, it would be desirable. In the nature of things, rules are required in the management of a Library, otherwise it must quickly go to By the operation of one of these rules—one adopted as necessary in all Libraries, a certain individual has become liable to be charged with the price of the entire set of Shirley's Works, he having taken out and lost one of the volumes. Not feeling myself at liberty to grant a dispensation of exemption from the rule in this case, or in any other, I submit the matter to your higher authority, with the hope that such a precedent may be set in this case as may serve as a rule of interpretation in all similar cases hereafter

All of Which is respectfully submitted

by Your &c

A. Wylie

Which communication, on motion was laid on the table

On Motion of Mr Law the Board now proceeded to the election of some suitable person to fill the Proffessorship of Law in Ind University, when upon counting the ballots it appeared that the Hon. Miles G. Eggliston was unanimously elected. On Motion of Mr. Thompson   Resolved that a committee be appointed to inform the Hon. Miles G. Eggliston of his election to the Proffessorship of Law in Ind. University, and to ascertain, whether or not he will accept the same, & that said Committee be authorized to employ some suitable and qualified person, in the event of the refusal of Judge Eggliston, to fill said Proffessorship, during the ensuing Session of the University. Wherupon [sic] the chair announced Messrs Thompson, Law, & Wallace said committee

On motion of Mr Ballard the Board adjourned to meet to morrow morning at 8 Oclock A. M.

26th Sep. Wednesday Morning

Board met. Members present as on yesterday. This being the day of Commencement Exercises; the Board adjourned to meet on to morrow morning at 8 Oclock A. M.

Sep. 27.

Thursday Morning

Board met according to adjournment. Members present as on yesterday. Judge Blackford, having taken the necessary obligation faithfully & impartially to perform his duties as trustee of Ind University, took his seat on this Board. The President of the University also took an oath of Office to act as trustee in the case and emergency as provided in the charter. The Secretary elect, not having been previously sworn, also took an Oath of Office administered by W. A. Gorman Esq. Mr Turner from the Committee on Claims to which was referred the Bill of Wright & King, contractors for building Boarding house here asks for instructions from the Board as to what course the committee should pursue on the subject of a difficulty in setling [sic] with Wright & King when

On Motion of Mr Owen   Resolved That the difficulty with the contractors of New Building, be refered back to the Building Committee, with this expression of the Board "That in order to ascertain, what should be deducted from the amount due, for the entire house as originally contracted for, in order to come at the sum due, by a subsequent contract for an additional upper story, that the deductions be made at the rates which the parts to be deducted, *are to cost the Board* In other words, That a duly proportioned estimate, of the work as originally contracted for, be obtained, in which estimate, the various items to be deducted as above, shall be seperately [*sic*] estimated of the proportionate accuracy of which the Committee shall be satisfied; and which estimate shall amt. in all to sixteen hundred and fifty dollars. And by the seperate amounts as ascertained, in such an estimate, and at no other rates, shall the above deductions be made

On Motion of Mr Law   Resolved That there be allowed the sum of one hundred and fifty dollars, to be appropriated as follows Viz. Thirty dollars to Mr McCrea—the leadr of the Band—Twenty dollars to the Band, and the remaining sum of one hundred dollars, to be applied by Mr McCrea, in the purchase of instruments and music, for the use of the Band

Resolved furthermore, that the instruments of music, heretofore purchased by the Board, and those now directed, to be purchased, be placed under the care of Mr McCrea, as leader of the Band and in the care of his successor in Office, hereafter being leader of said band

Resolved That Mr McCrea, if possible form a Band out of the students of the University, giving them such instruction as may be necessary, and that he be allowed therefor, such sum as may be deemed right & proper for his services.

Resolved That the President of the Board be authorized to draw on the treasurer for the funds necessary to carry said resolutions into effect

The President laid before the Board the following communication from Prof. Wylie Viz

To the Board of Trustees Ind University

In presenting this paper to the Board of Trustees, it is taken for granted that it is their desire, to do all in their power to facilitate the imparting of instruction to the students of the University. The expense to which the Board has already gone in procuring books and apparatus is a suffcent proof of the assumption made, but as there are some things connected with the use and keeping of the apparatus, which may have been overlooked, it has been thought proper, to present this paper, not in the spirit of dictation, but to make some suggestions which, if they are attended to, will certainly enable your memorialist, to discharge his duties with more satisfaction to himself & advantage to his class. For the purpose of instruction in Natural Philosophy, the board have provided some excellent pieces of apparatus. It is not however sufficient, merely to have the apparatus, but there should also be provided, a convenient place for keeping and displaying it. Untill lately, all the apparatus was collected together in the floor of a small room. It is now placed in a room somewhat larger and more convenient, but still this is not its proper place It is at a distance from the recitation room. There is a risk in conveying some of the instruments from one room to another, to say nothing about the loss of time and other inconveniences. The apparatus too is exposed to dust and injury from other sources. It would be proper to have suitable cases made in the recitation room in which the apparatus might be safely and conveniently Kept

As regards the using and displaying the apparatus we labor under still greater disadvantages. Fire and water are constantly used by the chemist. But there is no way at present in the College of using conveniently either of these agents. The stove used in heating the room can be applied to very few chemical operations. Besides this a risk is run of setting fire to the building by the accidental falling of some combustible, on the floor, as there is no hearth over which all operations with fire ought to be conducted. Water is constantly used in the Laboratory, in making gasses, for cleansing and making solutions To carry from the nearest spring, which is at a considerable distance from the Building is exceedingly inconvenient, especially in winter, and if all that ought to be used were carried it would occasion a great loss of time. Unless some means be provided for having a supply of water, it will be almost impracticable, to use the fine hydro-pneumatic apparatus, which has lately been procured. The proper arrangement for Chemical instruction, could hardly be made in the College Building. There should be a small building erected, especially approp[r]iated to this purpose, in which the apparatus could be conveniently managed and the proper fixtures made. Whether or not the Board should find it convenient to attend to all the suggestions made, it would be gratifying, if they would make provisions to remedy some of the inconveniences mentioned or at least to think favorably of the hints thrown out in this paper, now presented for their consideration

T. A. Wylie

On motion of Mr Law   The above communication was laid on the table The president laid before the board, a letter from Mr Merill to Dr Wylie informing the Board of a remission of $5.00 premium on Eastward draft which letter was laid on the table and on motion of Mr Owen, the following resolution was adopted   Resolved that the thanks of this Board be presented to Mr Merrill, for the Work presented by him to the Library and his liberality in liquidating a portion of a draft on the Eastward procured by Mr Merrill, and that the Secretary send to Mr Merrill a copy of this resolution

Mr Owen from the Library Committee offered the following report

Report

The Committee on the Library report that they have examined the Library of the University and find the same in good order and preservation. While your Committee were pleased to find in the Library many interesting and useful and some rare and curious works, they regretted to perceive, that many others of a standard character, and some especially useful to us as American citizens, were still deficient. In looking over the works on the Shelves, they noticed one (the Thesauris) which however valuable in itself, and however essential as a work of reference, in a very extensive and complete library did not seem to your committee as useful, in the present stage of the institution as its prise ($300) expended in other, less costly works would be. They recommend therefore, that if the said works can be sold (as your Committee have been informed it can be) for the same it cost; the president of the University be empowered and instructed so to sell it, and to invest the proceeds chiefly in works connected with the early history of our country—in voyages and travels, and in other standard English Works. They would especially reco[m]mend the following Smiths History of Virginia 1624 Cotten Mather's Magnalia Belknaps American Biography Hillard's Life and Adventures of Capt. John Smith Pinchas His Pilgrimes (if not too expensive) Charlevoix's Journal Historique Volney's View of the Soil and Climate of the United States Hickwelder's Historical Account of the Indians [Thomas] Jefferson's Notes on Virginia Bloome's "State of his Majesty's Isles & Territories in America History of the Five Nations (By Colden London 1758) De Lasalle Expedition and Discovery in N. A. 1678 Graham's United States Lewis and Clarks' Travels to the Rock[y] Mountains Long's Expedition [to the Rocky Mountains] Franklins Voyage to the North River Parry's Voyage in Search of a North West passage Peronsee's [Voyage in Search of a North West passage] Bruces Travels to Abysinia Mungo Park's Travels in Africa Dobrizhoffer's History of the Abipones Les oevrues de Las Casas (Las Casas was Bishop of Chiapa—Work not to be had Short of Paris) Sismondis Italian Republic Carvers travels up the Mississippi River Manner's Tonga Islands Edgeworths Complete

Works Todd's Johnstons Dictionary Mosheims Ecclesiastical History Spark's Life of John Gay Debates in the convention for forming the constitution of the U. S. Sparks Life and writings of Govern[or] Morris Rollins Ancient History Last Days of Pompeii By Bulwer Rise and Fall of Athens By Bulwer Burke's Works Jacqueline of Holland Mary of Burgundy Attila [Samuel Johnson] Rambler [Sir Richard Steele] Tatler [Samuel Johnson] Idler [Addison and Steele] Spectator [Adam] Smiths Wealth of Nations Say's Political Economy Ricardo's [Political Economy] [John Stuart] Mills Elements of Political Economy [Thomas] Jefferson's Memoirs (Edited by his Grandson) 4 vols. Campbells Pleasures of Hope Pleasures of the Imagination ([Mark] Akenside) Roger's Italy Mrs Barbauld's Works [Edmund] Spencer's Fairy Queen Arnott's Physics Irving's Columbus Irvings Companions of Columbus Arabian Nights Pleasures of Memory (Rogers) Or as many of the same as may not be in the Library of the University
On Motion of Judge Blackford the Above Report was laid on the table

On Motion of Mr. Ballard The Communication of the Prest. of the University relative to the loss to the College of one volume of Shirley's Works; was called up from the table and refered to the Committee on the Library Mr Law offered to the consideration of the Board the following resolution Resolved That the building Committee be directed in the course of ensuing year, to cause to be erected, a suitable building for the delivery of Chemical and Philosophical Lectures & for the reception of the necessary Chemical and Philosophical Apparatus, including a furnace, Labratory &c. and that in the erection and arrangement of said building, said Committee confer and consult with the Prof. Chemistry and Natural Philosop[h]y of the University. Which resolution on Motion of Judge Blackford was laid on the table

Mr Blair from the Committee on Claims to which was refered the duty of ascertaining as nearly as practicable the liabilities of Indiana University begged leave to submit the following report

Report

The Committee on claims begs leave to submit the following. Having no report from the Treasurer your Committee have [had] great trouble in collecting the different items, and our report must necessarily be very imperfect, but as far as we can ascertain the Liabilities of the University are as follow

Salary of Prof Parks		$400.00	
" " " Prof Kuter $435.00 or		535 00	935.00
" " " Prof Wylie's		511 37½	
Paid of Pittsburgh by Prof Wylie $12 46 on a/c of College			
Recd on this account	3.39		
Leaving a balance against University of	8.07	8.07	
Acct. in McCalla's Store for Articles necessary in Prof Wylie's Department		4.75	
A Seward's a/c for work done		3.37½	
Total of Wylie's A/at			527.57
C. G. Ballard's A/c for services on Building Committee fifteen days (at $1.50 per day)		22.50	
Mr Turner's A/c. for Services on Bulg Comt., 4 days		6.00	
Prof Dodds Salary (Suppose to be)		375.00	403.50

Balance due to Pres Wylie on Library A/c. &c.	740 00	
Salary of Prest. Wylie Supposed to be	700.00	1440.00
Joshua O. Howe's A/c on Book $4.75		
Also A/c for Services on Builg Comty 4 days 6.00	10.75	10.75
Amt due Wm S. Wright (supposed to be) on New College Building $1500.00 & Book A/c $19 00	1519.00	1519.00
Total of Liabilities		$4835 82

There are no doubt some small items, which your committee have not been able to collect, but the above exhibit is beleived [sic] to be within a small amount of the claims now against the University. Your committee in the conclusion of their report would beg leave to recommend to the Board, the adoption of the following resolution   Resolved That the Board allow the payment of the above A/cts as they appear on the Books or when a settlement can be made. Which report with the accompanying resolution were concurred in.

On Motion of Mr Owen   Resolved That the various By Laws and other resolutions and regulations, heretofore adopted and not rescinded by the Board of Ind College, and not rescinded or modified by any by Law or resolution of the Board of Trustees of Indiana University, be adopted by Said Board, as their By Laws resolutions and regulations, and that the Secretary copy the Same into the book, in which are recorded the minutes and proceedings of the Said Board of the University

On Motion of Mr Law   Resolved That the By Laws embraced in the pre-ceeding resolution, be refered to a committee of two   Whereupon the Chair appointed Messrs Law & Blackford said Committee

On Motion of Mr Law   Resolved that Messrs Blair Turner and the Presi-dent of the University be authorized to make such arrangements as are necessary in order to obtain a suitable steward of the common-hall—to make a contract with him for the board of the Students—to have the building prepared for the reception of students—and to determine the price to be paid by students for the use of the dormitories, for each session—and to make all such regulations for using said building as may be necessary to carry into effect the object for which said building was erected at as early a period as practicable

Mr Hoshour now asks and obtains leave of absence for the remainder of the session of the Board.

On Motion of Mr Law   Resolved That the President of this Board and Messrs Howe and Mayfield, be and they are hereby directed, as early as prac-ticable, to make a full and complete settlement of the A/cts of the Treasurer and Commissioner, with the Ind. University, and if necessary to take such steps, legal or otherwise, as may be deemed necessary to enforce said settlement. On Motion of Mr. Owen—Resolved that the fees of Jas Blair, who was compelled by failure of eyesight to leave Cole. during its last session after a few days attend-ance be remitted

On motion of Mr Owen   Resolved That Prof Dodds be appointed Li-brarian of the University to serve one year from this date.

On Motion of Mr Turner   Resolved That a reduplicate of the certificate recd by the students from the treasurer, be by them handed to the President of the University & by him to the Committee on Claims, and that he be requested to hand in to said Committee an account of all delinquencies in paying admittance fees, that come under his observation

On Motion of Mr Law   Resolved That the Faculty of the University appoint a janitor, whose duty it shall be to ring the Bell—attend to making the fires and to keeping the University Buildings and campus in order and generally to do and perform all the duties required of the janitor of a College and that his compensation be one hundred dollars per annum

On Motion of Mr Law   Resolved That the President of the Board of Trustees of Ind University be directed previous to the next session of the Board, to procure and fit up some room of the University Buildings for the use and occupation of the Board of Trustees at their regular sessions   Resolved That the Prest of the Board be directed to make out a report to the state of the University, to be submitted at its next session

On Motion the Board adjourned to meet at 2 Oclock P. M.

Thursday Sepr. 27th 2 Oclock P.M.

Board met pursuant to adjournment. Members present as in the morning except Mr Hoshour who obtained leave of absence. Mr. Turner from the Building Committee, submitted the following report

Report

The Building Committee beg leave to report, that after examination they find that the whole cost of the Boarding House has been $3147.00 instead of $3383.00, the first bill, making a difference in favor of the Board of $236.00 and further that by an order formerly obtained $1500.00 have been paid and that $1647 is yet due to King and Wright (the undertakers) Which report was concurred in

On Motion of Mr Ballard   Resolved That Prest. Wylie be requested to procure a Seal for the University, with such engravings and devices as he may think appropriate, and also a plate for Diplomas

On Motion of Mr Blair   Resolved That Austin W. Morris Esq be appointed an agent on the part of the Board of Trustees of Ind University to examine the accounts of the Treasurer and Commissioner with the College— examining them fully so as to ascertain the exact balances due on their books, and comparing the several items of their accounts with the vouchers—noting any discrepancies in the same if any exist and state an account current showing the present situation of the funds in these officers hands

Secondly To report the manner in which said accounts are kept on the books; and if any difficulty arise from the present mode of keeping the books, that the same be suggested and the remedy proposed

Thirdly To report whether any and if any, what changes are necessary in rendering an accurate statement of the A/cts of said officers, preserving the proper checks and balances—and whether the further action of the Legislature or of this Board is necessary in order to remedy any evil, in the present mode of stating and keeping said accounts. That said report when made, shall be presented to the President of the Board if said Board be adjourned when said report is prepared and that the President of the Board shall take such action on the same as he may think necessary—That the President of the Board, be authorized to allow Mr Morris such sum as may be deemed right and proper for his services in the examination aforesaid.

Mr Blackford now moved to take up from the table, the report of the Committee on the Library, and upon the question, shall the report be so taken up it was decided in the negative.

On Motion of Mr Turner   Resolved That the president of the Board be authorized to give to Wright & King, an order on the Commissioner of the College Lands for $1647.00 to liquidate a balance due said Wright and King for the Building of the College Boarding house, which order is to be paid in notes recd said Commissioner for Lands sold.

The President laid before the Board the Claims of Hassell Hunt which was refered to the Committee on Claims

On Motion of Mr Owen   Resolved that the President of the Board be empowered to insure the University Buildings against fire in the Indiana Mutual insurance company: *Provided* They can there be insured at a rate not higher than that of common Brick dwelling houses, it being specified in the policy of insurance that Chemical Lectures and experiments are permitted within the building erected for that purpose

On Motion of Mr Law   The resolution authorizing the Building Committee to take measures for erecting suitable buildings for the reception of a furnace and Labratory was taken up from the table and adopted

Mr Owen from the Library Committee to which was refered the case of "loss to the University of one volume of Shirley's Work,["] submitted the following report

Report

The Committee on the Library to which was refered a case of loss of one of a series of volumes belonging to the Library; the said volume being borrowed by one of the Board, and while in his possession destroyed by fire Report That among the By Laws, now in force for the regulation of the Library, they find one requiring any individual who borrows a book and looses or destroys the same; to take the imperfect series and pay for the complete series. Your Committee are of opinion, that if a dispensation is to be given in this particular case of hardship, to one of their own members, that the responsibility ought to fall on the entire Board, and not on one of its Committees. They do not feel it their duty as a committee to recommmend the setting aside the regulation, though they are individualy of opinion, that the case is one of so much hardship that if in any instance the rules are to be departed from such departure would be justified in this.

Mr Blackford moved that the above report be recd which was decided in the negative, when Mr Law moved, that it be recommitted to the Committee on the Library, which was also decided in the negative. The report therefore lays upon the table

On Motion of Mr Law   Resolved that the Board will not henceforth either allow adjust, settle or pay any account hereafter, unless the same be made out with the proper items, sighned [sic] by the parties and vouchers if necessary, and presented to the Committee on Claims whose duty it shall be receive no account unless thus stated and sighned with the necessary vouchers

On Motion of Mr Turner   Resolved That as the Committee on Claims, cannot now accurately report on some of the Claims made against the board; that such claimants be required to go before said committee and satisfy them of the correctness of their claims and that then the president of the Board be authorized to grant order

On Motion of Mr Law   Resolved That the Secretary of the Board be authorized, to procure such books as are necessary in order to record—1st The Reports of Treasurer and Comr and all papers and documents presented by them, and which should be recorded

Secondly All accounts audited and passed upon by the Board in an Alphabetical order Showing the ammount of Acct, when made and upon whom drawn in seperate Colum[n]s, commencing at the present session of the Board

On Motion of Mr Law   Resolved That the Building Committee be directed to remove the Privy, now in the Campus from its present situation, and have a new one with good vaults in some more convenient and private situation. Resolved further that the building Committee be directed to improve the campus, by making gravel walks, and planting out ornamental trees, and that be authorized to employ some suitable person to make such improvements the expense when estimated to be paid out of the College fund on the order of the President

On Motion of Mr Law   The Board now proceeded to the election of a treasurer of Ind University, Messrs Blackford and Ballard acting as tellers. Upon the first ballotting the vote stood as follows Viz

For Treasurer   Joseph M Howe   recd 7 votes
                                 Thos McCalla   "   3. "

Joseph M. Howe having recd a majority of the votes given was declared duly elected

On Motion of Mr Law: Resolved That the Secretary receive a per diem allowance of three dollars and fifty cents, for services during the present session of the Board. On Motion the Board adjourned to meet to night at Mr Orchards at 7 Oclock

Thursday Night

Board met members present as in the morning. Joseph M. Howe through his brother, having presented the names of Messrs John Orchard Michael Buskirk and Joshua O Howe, as his sufficient securities for the faithful performance of his duties as Treasurer of Ind University, they were duly recognized as such by the Board.

Mr Law from the Committee to which were refered the By Laws &c of Ind College reported verbally that they be and hereby are adopted as the ByLaws of Ind University Mr Blair moved that the report of Committee on the Library relative to the loss of one volume of Shirleys works be now taken up which motion being lost

On Motion of Mr Owen   Resolved That Mr Ballard be excused from taking the whole set of Shirley's Works upon paying $2.00 for the lost volume.

Whereupon the Board adjourned to meet on the Monday previous to the last Wednesday in *September 1839*   James D. Maxwell Sec.

First Board meeting, September 24, 1838; from Minutes of Board of Trustees, pp. 7–23.

Document 35

The Applied Science of Agriculture

Within two years after the passage of legislation creating Indiana University, there was a demand that the institution give courses in agriculture. This reflected an awareness on the part of legislators that Indiana as an expanding farming state needed scientifically trained men to help guide its economic destiny. This suggestion for the creation of a professorship in agriculture was stimulated partly by the boom in agricultural knowledge in the 1840s. The idea of teaching the science of farming, and the operation of a "pattern farm," is an interesting forerunner of the general movement to create agricultural colleges as outlined in the subsequent Morrill Act of 1862.

*   *   *

The subject of an agricultural school or college, is one of vital importance, and one that should receive the mature and deliberate action of this General Assembly. It has occurred to your committee, that a distinct professorship, in our present State University, might be advantageously appropriated to the instruction of such as might attend, in the theory as well as practice, of rural economy in its various branches.

To the due success of agriculture, as of all other arts, both theory and practice are necessary—they reflect light on each other. If the former, without the latter, be a vain science, the latter, without the enlightening precepts of the former, is generally enslaved to ancient modes, however erroneous; or is, at best, too tardy and partial, in adopting salutary changes. In no instance, perhaps, is habit more unyielding, or irrational practice more prevalent, than among those who cultivate the soil. Hence agriculture is far below the attainments to which it ought to aspire.

A professorship of agriculture might derive great advantage from the chair of chemistry, in that institution. This science is every day penetrating some of the hidden laws of nature, and tracing the useful purposes to which they may be made subservient. Agriculture is a field on which it has already begun to shed its rays, and on which it promises to do much towards unveiling the processes of nature, to which the principles of agriculture are related. The professional lectures on chemistry, which are to embrace these principles, could not fail to be auxiliary to a professorship, having lessons on agriculture for its essential charge. It would also greatly assist this plan of agricultural instruction, to place under the superintendence of the professor a small farm, to be cultivated as a pattern farm, illustrating a system at once profitable and improving; not only bringing to the test new modes of culture and management, but introducing new plants and animals deemed worthy of experiment. In obtaining these, much aid might be found in the patriotic exertions of our foreign ministers, consuls, and naval officers, who are, by a circular of the Treasury Department, required to collect and transmit to this country, valuable plants and seeds, which may come under their observation abroad; and it might well happen, that occasional success, in rearing new species or varieties of peculiar value, would yield in seeds and stocks, a profit defraying all expenses incurred, aside from the immense advantage that would accrue to the State at large.

A farm, exhibiting an instructive model, observed as it would be by every visiter, and understood as it would be, in its principles and plans, by students returning to their dispersed homes, could not fail to spread some information on the subject of agriculture, and to cherish that spirit of imitation and emulation which is the source of improvement in every art and enterprize.

Your committee are therefore of opinion that the most munificent policy should be pursued to change the present order of thing. That such laws should be passed as will induce the creation of values at home, for the supply of our home necessities. And that this may be done understandingly, and as agriculture is the grand basis upon which the manufacturing and commercial interests are founded, that such appropriations should be made as will enable the Indiana State Board of Agriculture to carry into effect the duties assigned them by the law authorizing their organization. That in addition to this, an agricultural department and an experimental farm be annexed to our State University—that further and adequate appropriations be made to enable agricultural associations to award suitable premiums for agricultural products and manufactured articles—that our geological survey be continued; a bounty on salt, iron, sugar from the sugar beet, and silk manufactured from cocoons the product of this State, be awarded.

Indiana *House Journal*, 1839–40, pp. 451–452.

Document 36

The Science of Pedagogy

It is to be doubted that the framers of the First Indiana Constitution in 1816 had any concept whatever of what constituted either a good teacher or a good school. Though public schools were provided for, there were no provisions for the training of teachers. As in the case of agriculture, Indiana legislators and private friends of education felt the pressures being exerted in the 1840s for the establishment of public schools on a more modern basis, and the recognition of the fact that teaching was an art with which the colleges and universities should concern themselves.

*   *   *

FRIDAY MORNING, FEB. 21 [1840]

The Senate assembled.

The President laid before the Senate the following communication from the President of the State University at Bloomington;

Which was read and laid upon the table.

To the General Assembly of the State of Indiana:

In compliance with a resolution, adopted by the board of trustees of Indiana University, at the Sept. session thereof in the year 1839, directing the President of the board to memorialize the legislature on behalf of the board, for an appropriation of the saline funds to the endowment of a separate professorship in Indiana University for the education of teachers of common schools in Indiana, the undersigned respectfully presents the following memorial:

By the second proposition of the 6th section of an act of Congress, approved April 19, 1816, entitled "an act to enable the people of the Indiana Territory to form a constitution and state government and for the admission of such state into the Union on equal footing with the original states," it is provided that all the salt springs within the said territory, and the lands reserved for the use of the same, together with such other lands as may by the President of the U. States be deemed necessary and proper for the working of the said salt springs not exceeding in the whole the quantity contained in thirty six entire sections, shall be granted to the said state, for the use of the people of said state, and the same to be used, under such terms, conditions and regulations as the legislature of the said state shall direct; and whereas, Congress did subsequently by an act of said body, approved July 3, 1832, authorize the legislature of the said state, to dispose of said lands and apply the proceeds thereof, to the purposes of education in said state; and whereas, the legislature of this state, did by an act, approved February 2, 1833, appoint commissioners, clothed with full authority and power to sell said land with a view to raise funds for the purposes of education, in accordance with the true meaning and spirit of the acts of Congress, and the clear and unequivocal intention of the original donors; and whereas, a considerable fund, (now amounting to nearly twenty thousand dollars, as appears by the report of the Treasurer of State) has been raised by the sale of said lands, and the interest accruing on the money since said sale, and which now is and has for years past been lying dormant, so far as regards the promotion of the cause of education, it is deemed proper and expedient by the board of trustees of Indiana University, to call the attention of the legislature to this important subject, and to earnestly request them to appropriate the money arising from the sales of said lands to the endowment of a permanent and separate professorship in said institution, for the education, free of tuition fee, a competent number of teachers of common schools, said professorship to be filled by the board of trustees of the University, yet to be under the direction and control of the President of the University, as the other professorships are now (to a certain extent.) The board feel confident that in making this recommendation, they are representing the best interests of the people of Indiana, and more especially the rising generation of children, those who are to be our successors as citizens and officers; those who are to assume upon themselves the weighty responsibilities of the faithful management of the destinies of the greatest and happiest nation on the face of the globe. They deem it unnecessary to say to a body so enlightened as the legislature of Indiana, that upon the virtue and intelligence of the people, depend more than on any other cause, the permanency and stability of our happy institutions; that the foundation of that virtue and intelligence are laid, first, and the deepest in the common schools of our country; it is there the minds of our youth are first moulded and fashioned. It is in the primary schools of the country where the first and most lasting impressions are made upon the tender mind for weal or for woe. How important then is it that the teachers of common schools, should be men of well cultivated minds, men whose morals are pure and unsullied; and what is so apt to accomplish both of those very important objects so effectually, as to educate them well, improve their minds, and their morals will, to a great extent, necessarily be good. It is certainly very important to the legislature, that some action should be had upon this subject. Some steps should be taken, and that speedily, for the accomplishment of that object, which of all others, in a free and enlightened community is most to be desired. Your honorable body have directed your attention with much laudable zeal, to the improvement of our natural resources and our physical condition, and the board would respectfully suggest the propriety of prompt and energetic action upon this important subject; indeed the board would respectfully suggest to your honorable body, that the true meaning and spirit of the acts of Congress, and our state legislature, have been violated by the non-action of the legislature heretofore in regard to this fund, and that the undoubted intention and laudable exertions of the original donors of this fund, have been neglected and contemned by a failure of a previous legislature to act upon this matter. The board would further suggest the propriety as an auxiliary in carrying out this great enterprise, to wit: the improvement of the condition of our common schools, the appointment of an officer similar to that of a superintendent of common schools for the state. The plan has been adopted in several of the states of this union. Ohio, Kentucky, Tennessee, and the young state of Michigan, with others, have all engaged successfully in this grand project.

Shall Indiana longer remain indifferent to this important subject? Will she not expend a portion of her energies in the improvement of the intellectual powers of her citizens? The board confidently entertains the opinion that she will. We know the patriotism that actuates her legislators, will impel them to speedy and definite action upon this subject. The board will not attempt to conceal the fact, that a contrariety of opinion exists in other states as to the most effectual and speedy plan of bringing about this great result, to wit: the improvement of the condition of our common schools by the education of teachers, yet they cannot forbear an opinion of their settled conviction, as to the propriety of the plan heretofore pointed out. The fact that the associations of those engaged in this department of science, would be with others whose exclusive attention is directed to the acquisition of knowledge would operate upon them as a great incentive to persevere in the laudable and interesting vocation in which they were embarked. It would be the mingling together of congenial minds, for their mutual improvement.

In addition to this the pleasure to be derived from the literary societies of Indiana University, their extensive library of choice books of science and history, the information to be derived incidentally (if the expression is allowed) from the intercourse with her professors, and the university exhibitions, and lastly, but not least, the advantages derivable from the University library itself, to the lover of, and seeker after science are incalculable. Here we have extensive buildings, and every other necessary preparation for the accommodation of a school of that character. Many other important advantages might here be mentioned (were it necessary) and the time of the undersigned would permit of their enumeration. In conclusion, if the wisdom of the legislature of Indiana, should impel them to adopt a plan different from the one suggested in this imperfect memorial, the board will still have left to them the pleasing reflection, that indirectly at least, they may have been instrumental in effecting some good to the community. Believing, as they most confidently do, that some such plan as has been proposed, must and soon will be adopted, and that the adoption of that plan will conduce greatly to the peace and harmony of our growing community and to the prosperity of our beloved institutions.

PARIS C. DUNNING,
Pres't. B. T. Ind. U.

Indiana *Senate Journal*, 1839–40, pp. 453–455.

[III]

Years of Transformations
1835–1851

No one in the 1830s could have taken seriously the fact that an elevation in name alone would bring significant improvements to Indiana University. In the same vein it was not possible to orate or report a university into being. First of all, the public hand lay heavily upon the institution without extending to it the necessary support to grow up to either its immediate possibilities or to fulfill the publicly expressed dreams for the institution. Tucked away in Bloomington with a tiny faculty and a small student body, it was indeed difficult for Indiana University and its friends to undertake a dramatic enough program to attract widespread public attention.

In this age of Jacksonian politics in Indiana, it was difficult to present a really progressive case for higher education. As one Hoosier was reported to have said, "General Jackson did not have much education, and no one else needed any more than the President of the United States." In this age which prided itself on being so down to earth in the consideration of human and public problems, there was a need for a greatly expanded curriculum in which the applied sciences could be introduced. Notions were not really lacking about the kinds of programs which would best serve the Indiana public, but initiating them took both ingenuity and increased financial support. Clearly the state's public school system needed teachers, its courts needed the services of professionally trained lawyers, and its farms needed the services of plant specialists, agricultural engineers, chemists, and informed dirt farmers. In the years when American technology was becoming a fact in the expansion of the farm, the administration of Indiana University understood in part at least that the institution stood challenged in this area. The struggle to broaden the curriculum constituted one of the basic chapters in the University's history, and the documents pertaining to it reveal the kinds of forces and handicaps which kept it from becoming as important in the antebellum years as it might have been.

Two major problems in the early 1850s virtually defeated the University. The first of these was the search for a staunch successor to Andrew Wylie. Although the names of John H. Lathrop and Alfred Ryors appear in the presidential list, neither of these men made any really discernible contribution to the University. In fact the struggle to find good presidential leadership acted as a demoralizing influence. The curriculum was not expanded, the faculty was a mere holding body, and the University was allowed to languish in every other way when the challenge seemed so urgent. A second problem was the failure of the Second Indiana Constitutional Convention in 1851 to recognize the existence of the University. What had been so bright an idea in 1816, on the face of documentary evidence, had faded by mid-century. There was no constitutional indication that Indiana University was to become a major financial responsibility of the state, or that its offerings would be strengthened and broadened. Tragically there was lacking that single strong and dedicated voice in the convention which could have reminded constitution-makers of their broader commitments.

Document 37

Andrew Wylie's Intimate Views of the University

The four letters reproduced here were written by President Wylie between 1835 and 1847. They express views, aspirations, and frustrations which his formal reports could not convey. These letters, in the possession of Mrs. Thana Wylie of Bloomington, and edited by Donald F. Carmony, Professor of History in the University and Editor of the *Indiana Magazine of History*, reveal a human being far beyond that of his public image.

*   *   *

FAMILY LETTERS OF ANDREW WYLIE,
PRESIDENT OF INDIANA UNIVERSITY
Edited by Donald F. Carmony
Contributed by Mrs. Thana Wylie*

The four letters which follow[1] are personal and family letters from the pen of Andrew Wylie, the first president of Indiana University, 1829–1851. Wylie's letter to his wife, Margaret, was written in 1835, while she was visiting in Cannonsburg, western Pennsylvania, where they had lived before he became president of Indiana University or Indiana College as it was known from 1828 to 1838. It alludes to difficulties in the construction of "the building"—presumably the residence now known as Wylie House which was erected during the 1830s. In a very human way it evidences Andrew Wylie's concern for his wife, how much she was missed, and the problem of managing household and family affairs in her long absence. It also pictures some of the common perils and hardships of travel in pioneer days. Moreover, the letter to Mrs. Wylie, like those to sons Craig and Sam, reveals the considerable hold which religious faith and views had on Dr. Wylie.

The three remaining letters from President Wylie to his sons Craig and Sam suggest much regarding the mingled hopes and doubts, aspirations and frustrations, and promises and setbacks which he faced as president of Indiana University. President Wylie not only administered the internal affairs of the infant university, but he also did some of the teaching and spent much time ironing out thorny problems with trustees, placating legislators, and giving addresses at meetings of importance. Within the institution there was frequent turmoil among faculty members, between the professors and students, and in relations between town and gown. Faced with a multiplicity of duties, Wylie, as the letters amply illustrate, was vulnerable to attack on several fronts.

These three letters also indicate an abiding paternal interest in what his sons were doing and in the kind of men he hoped they would become. His comments to Sam about health and exercise now seem a bit amusing; but they, and his emphasis on the even greater importance of the "health of the soul," indicate a father's deep concern for his children.

Andrew Wylie, born on April 12, 1789, grew up on a farm in western Pennsylvania and performed the usual hard work typical of rural life of that day. Of Scotch-Irish extraction, the family was Presbyterian. Wylie himself was licensed as a Presbyterian minister in 1812 and was ordained an Episcopal minister in 1841. In 1810 Wylie graduated from Jefferson College, in western Pennsylvania; two years later, when only about twenty-three years old, he was elected president of the college. In 1817 Wylie became president of nearby Washington College and in 1829 he moved to Bloomington, Indiana, to assume the presidency of Indiana College.

As a farm boy Wylie had learned how to swing the ax in chopping and felling trees. While president of Indiana University, he at times performed such labor for exercise. In 1851 while so doing, he cut his foot; the resulting complications led to his early death from pneumonia.

Bloomington June 24th, 1835[2]

My Dear Margaret.

Through the great goodness of God our lives & health are still preserved. Last week we received your letter by Eliza which gave us the very welcome account of your safe arrival at Wheeling & of the welfare of our friends generally. It is here, as yet, a time of general health: though we have had almost incessant rains & tremendous floods since within a few days after you left us till this week which has been fair. But now it thunders, the sky is overcast & we expect rain again. Mrs Nichols departed this life last monday week. This was, you know, not an unexpected event. You would, doubtless, like to know how we make out to get along without you. And I am afriad & almost ashamed to tell. The amount of it is, we do the best we can, & that is bad enough. We have Nancy Swift, without whose assistance we could not get along at all. In the house things are broken & lost at a sad rate. The building is at a stand. I am distracted & ready to sink under the burden of so many cares. I wish a thousand times every hour that you were safe at home with us. I feel lost & miserable without you & am so much reduced in flesh & spirits that you would hardly know me. I count the hours as months till you return. I say not this to urge your return. For I tremble to think of the danger by the way. The cholera, as you have, no doubt, heard, has lately broken out with fatal violence at Madison, where as many as from 12 to 20 have been buried in a day. And rumor says it is also at Louisville & other places along the river. I have sometimes the most melancholy foreboding.—this, you know is my besetting sin, & I strive against it as well as I can. The death of our lamented William, presses harder on me also since you left us, so that my spirts are sometimes quite sunk. Then "I chide my heart that sinks so low" & look around to count the many & unmerited blessings which Our Heavenly Father—blessed be his Holy Name!—still allows us to enjoy—& then again I reproach myself with ingratitude & unprofitableness. Thus wretchedly do I waste my life & strength. Most fervently to I pray, & try to hope, that your life may be preserved, & that you may be kept in health & peace & restored to us once more. But I know & *feel* that the time will be long. For I cannot think of advising you to come so long as the cholera continues on the river: & to come through in the stage as I did last year, would be, *for you*, out of the question, unless you had some kind & intimate friend for a protector. Even then, I should hardly advise it, for the road, unless greatly improved since last year, is, towards this end of it, scarcely passible. So that, on the whole, I must try & content myself the best I can, till frost comes in the fall, when, if you live, you can descend the river without danger from cholera. But what shall take place, or what shall become of us before that time, God only knows. Our duty, in the mean time, is meekly to resign ourselves to his most holy will, making it our great & main concern to commit the keeping of *our souls* to Him, in well-doing as to a merciful Creator, seeking his face & favor with our whole hearts, & encouraging ourselves in the cheerful hope, that *whenever* & *wherever* & *by whatever* means "our earthly house of this tabernacle may be dissolved we may have a building of God an house not made with hands eternal in the heavens." There, my dear Margaret, might it please our gracious God, that *you* & *I* & *all our dear children* should meet at last—after all our crosses, trials & sorrows in this short life—O the transporting thought! it is too much—my unbelieving heart will not let me entertain it. This—alas! alas! is my infirmity. God strengthen my faith & hope! God, of his boundless mercy & grace grant us this great & amazing blessing for Christ's sake! Amen! Amen! Amen! O were *his* Amen to it, how would my burdened soul bound, exult & triumph. Well, let me say, "Thy will be done"! But *I* have something to do for the attainment of this end! O what responsibility!—I never yet in all my life engaged in any thing with so little spirit as this *building;* & nothing to which I ever put my [hands?] dragged so heavily. But yet it seems to have been forced upon me by necessity.—Things, too, seem to go against in the undertaking. At this moment the rain descends in torrents. Craig, poor fellow, is, likely, out in it; for he went with the waggon, this morning to the mill, for boards to cover a lime kiln which the rains have nearly spoiled. Three days ago, John went a black berry-gathering on the old mare without my knowledge. The mare threw him & only came home this morning. Yesterday the luckless fellow (John) fell off the sawpit & hurt his head against a log. He is well enough now; but I was sadly frightened for a while lest he had sustained some serious or perhaps fatal injury. I see, from these escapes, how easy it would be, did a guardian Providence intermit his care, for us to have sorrow upon sorrow. How thankful should we be for safety, health, *reason* & all Gods other precious gifts & mercies!—Anderson continues to enjoy pretty good health. If the weather permitted him to be taken out, he would not be any thing the loser by his weaning.

All join me in live to you & all our friends.

Your ever loving & affectionate husband
Andrew Wylie

Mrs. M. Wylie
P. S. Should the cholera cease, & good company offer & should *you wish so to do*, we, particularly *I*, would be *very, very* desirous how soon you could get away from dear friends, at Cannonsburg & Wheeling to meet once more *a dearer friend* in this miserable Bloomington. Yours as ever A. W.

N. B. Should any of our married ladies be disposed to make themselves merry & witty at my expense, now that I am left in the sad predicament of a lonely lover whose dearest jewel is so far away, you can tell them—I trust from your own experience—but I know not how that may [be?]—that 20 years acquaintanceship in the marriage life [m]akes the parties, if they love each other, only the more [ne]cessary to their mutual happiness. A. W. So with one thing & another, I have let my pen run on till my space is all filled. Remember me *specially* to our dear mother.

Bloomington July 1st 1840

Dr. Craig.
If you get but few letters from us, do not think we forget you but only that we are busy. I am particularly so. Dodds & Mary have come back from Spencer to which they had removed—not being pleased with things & prospects there. Mary is still in ill-health. They talk of going up to Pennsylvania. *If* they go—for it is yet doubtful—Elizth will probably go with them.

As to the University I cannot say very confidently. Ammen proves to be a most efficient teacher.[3] If Morrison who will be here in the fall should do his part as well the Faculty will be second to none this side Yale[4] Foster seems to be sunk—though still not so low as he ought & would were the community high toned in their feelings—He introduced among his charges *one* too atrocious to mention: it related to William & aimed at fixing a black stain on his memory[5] Bennet was summoned to prove the unutterable thing—but did not give testimony: the committee having resolved to adjourn to meet again the week before the meeting of the Board. In this matter my patience has been severely tryed & I have need to pray "lead me not into temptation"—that of doing to Foster what, for my own sake I ought not.

I receive letters from Columbia Mo. from which as well as from other sourses I *suppose* that they will elect me to the presidency of the University to be established there. But I do not much fancy the idea of another removal—especially westward.[6] There are many signs of the tide turning in my favor in this state. But there is no dependence to be put in what we call tides of popular favor—nor indeed in many in any shape.

I find it difficult to get money—So, if my pamphlets are sold I wish you to take the money & with it pay Fetter. I hope to be able shortly to pay him off intirely. Mary's journey will cost me something, & there are many ways to take away, & but one to bring in money. *You* will have to be frugal & depend on yourself chiefly.—We expect to receive the Equator shortly under better auspices I trust. A periodical is I think indispensible to us.—The family are in tolerably go[od] health. John has had a slight chill [which?] seems what the Irish people call   Dr. Leatherman wrote me lately. He still has some notion of moving to Missouri.

Give my best respects to Mr. & Mrs. Miller & Bayless & family. Shew respect to the latter they have always been our friends. Of the former I need say nothing. Render yourself as useful as you can: shun vice & the vicious: cultivate the virtues & piety. Study the Bible & pray to God to direct you in all your ways.—

"Trust in the Lord & be doing good: so shalt thou dwell in the land & verily thou shalt be fed."

Your affct father
A Wylie

Bloomington July 6th 1846

Dear Son.

I am happy to find that you have good sense enough to shew you the propriety of writing home without having been particularly charged to do so;—& that you seem to have managed other little affairs with a "quantum suff." of discretion.

I shall have your books and things sent by Woodwards waggon to care of B. O. Davis. It starts on monday next.

I am in a hurry preparing to go to convention[7] John goes with me to Indianapolis (where it meets) & thence on to Richmond. He seems to be still getting better: but his constitution has received a severe shock and it will be long yet before he recovers—if ever.

You will be in danger of a thousand things from which no care of mine—nor your own, nor any other mortal can preserve you. Think of this.

As to health: you must exercise every day & keep the pores clean by *sweeating* washing is good; but it acts on the end of the tube: whereas the *sweat* goes through and cleanses out the whole channel.

But health is not the chief thing, important as it is. You may rise early—take the morning air, avoid late hours & hard eating & drinking and all other things which tend to disease & yet you may get into ways which are not good, as to the health of the Soul. Put it down in your inmost thoughts that all those things are evil and will prove so in the end which tend to make one forget God.

You will do well to remember that you are poor; have no fortune in prospect and that the people among [whom] you live being wealthy you may not safely imitate their expensive habits. Be plain & decent in your dress: this is enough to please sensible people, and the less you follow such as are not so the better.

What remains of the price of the mare—having paid for the Corn-Sheller—consider as yours: but the other is yours only *to use* till you come home. Being in a slave-state I suppose you cannot readily get the privilege of working enough for exercise. If so, you must ride

God bless & guide you in the right way

Your affct father

Mr S. Wylie A Wylie

Bloomington Feb. 21th, 1847

Dear Sam.

Lest you should think yourself forgotten, I fill up an interval by writing to you. Your mother is still in bad—very bad health—chills and fever with regular irregularity sometimes very violent. We have no girl. Poor 'Liz is our only dependence. She is a heroine. But I am sorry she is so oppressed. We have two boarders Charles West & Chris. Graham good boys enough: but in a month or so they will leave, & then no more of that.—New Years night Dodds had a party the Faculty all at it but myself. I was sick. Williams & Trimble members of the Senior class & leaders of the Philomathian Society organized the Society that night as a band of Chivareers—they blacked themselves &c and cut up capers round Dodd's house, in short the Faculty, finding Williams & Trimble to have been in the affair called them to account.[8] They brought the rest—Some twenty—

to share their fate. The Faculty demanded an apology. It was given such as it was. That of Williams & Trimble was *hardly* an apology. But the Faculty agreed to accept it with the rest & ordered me to dispose of the case with remarks on the impropriety of such conduct. I did so. Williams & Trimble, offended because the remarks were not postponed till some distant period when they might not be thought of in connexion with said remarks, demanded an honorable dismission. It was not granted. They, aided by Millan & others of the Law Department, threw the Philomaths into a phrenzy. They passed certain resolutions censuring the Faculty & giving Diplomas to Williams & Trimble who went out of town with the mob shouting for Greencastle! So the thing ended. But the end is not yet. Of cour[s]e I will be made the butt, at which shafts from all who for any reason may think it the time to join in, will be aimed. Of course, too, the sectarian opposition will take advantage of it and at the next meeting of the Legislature I expect a scheme for some time in agitation will be pushed into execution if possible to divide the funds of the University among the leading sects.[9]—There is no telling what the event may be. The students are quiet now: but there is in some of them a bad spirit.

From 'Mag. & 'Rene I hear almost every week Margaret thinks she can learn nothing, & of course will not learn much. Irene learns well: but has gone to balls: a think [of?] which I do not approve

From John I hear nothing lately.

The rest join in love to you. You like not your present occupation. I'd rather clean streets like a scavenger than be a dirty pettifogging puppy such as some of these in our Law School will be if they live.

Be an honest man at any rate: be a Christian and then in the end you will find what in this world you will not find—peace & happiness

Your affct father
A Wylie

FOOTNOTES

* Acknowledgement is made to Mrs. Thana Wylie, Bloomington, Indiana, for making xerox copies of these letters available for publication. Mrs. Wylie, whose husband was a grandson of President Wylie, has generously made other xerox copies of these letters available to the Lilly Library, Indiana University, and also to the Indiana University Archives. They, along with a number of similar letters already in the archives, are an important source of information concerning Andrew Wylie and the beginnings of Indiana University.

1 The biographical material in this introduction largely follows James Albert Woodburn, *History of Indiana University, 1820–1902* (Vol. I; Chicago, 1940), 204–207 and Herman B Wells, "The Early History of Indiana University as Reflected in the Administration of Andrew Wylie, 1829–1851," *The Filson Club History Quarterly*, XXXVI (April, 1962), 113–27. The editor thanks Mrs. Mary B. Craig, archivist, Indiana University, for her assistance concerning illustrations. Thanks also are due to Mrs. Karen Tannenbaum, former assistant editor of the *Indiana Magazine of History*, for doing much of the research for this document.

2 In the preparation of these letters for publication, every attempt has been made to transcribe President Wylie's handwriting accurately. However, both his writing and the condition of some of the letters have forced the editor to use some discretion in interpreting certain words or phrases. In those instances where a word or part of a word was unclear, the most likely correct choice has been inserted in brackets. In a few cases, a blank indicates complete illegibility of the word omitted. As was common in his day, Wylie did not always use standard capitalization or punctuation; his style has not been corrected. Likewise, abbreviations and obvious misspelling remain untouched. Raised letters and numerals have been brought down to the line.

3 Jacob Ammen, a graduate of West Point, was a professor of mathematics at Indiana

University, 1840–1843. He also directed the students in military drill; but this practice, begun under him, was discontinued upon his departure from the university. James Albert Woodburn, *History of Indiana University 1820–1920* (Vol. I; Chicago, 1940), 166–68, 257, 284.

4 John I. Morrison was professor of languages at Indiana University, 1840–1843. In the latter year he resigned to become principal of a seminary at Salem, Indiana. As a member of the Indiana Constitutional Convention, 1850–1851, and in other ways as well, Morrison made significant contributions to the university. Woodburn, *History of Indiana University*, I, 121, 173–74, 257.

5 The persistent and vigorous opposition of Dr. William C. Foster, a Bloomington physician, to Dr. Wylie is noted in Woodburn, *History of Indiana University*, I, 119–20. The remarks about Foster are from an historical sketch of the university by Judge David D. Banta which constitutes the first several chapters of the Woodburn history.

6 Nothing about this invitation has been found in Woodburn.

7 This convention was probably an educational or religious meeting, many of which Wylie attended.

8 The Philomathean Society was one of various literary societies which played an important part in the early decades of the university's development. As here indicated, however, not all of their activities were literary. Woodburn, *History of Indiana University*, I, 77, 201–202, 230–31, 303–304, 316–17.

9 Continued charges claimed that Indiana University was sectarian, often insisting that Presbyterian influence was dominant. Woodburn, *History of Indiana University*, I, 21, 29–30, 32, 33, 73–76, 112–16, 211, 251–52, 265, 363, 374. As these references indicate, both David D. Banta and James Albert Woodburn defended—perhaps more vigorously than warranted—the university against the charge of sectarianism.

"Family letters of Andrew Wylie, President of Indiana University," ed. by Donald Carmony, December, 1968.

Document 38

Realizing the Great Commitment

In an eloquent statement of a sense of deep obligation, the Board of Trustees opened the new era of the University's history with a report and a promise to the public. They said they could not fill the classrooms with students, but they could see to it that they were worthy to be filled. With prophetic vision the trustees reviewed the aspirations of the framers of the Constitution and legislators and assured the public, "The full attainment of these great Soul-stirring objects may yet be afar off."

*　　*　　*

"Address by a Committee of the Trustees of Indiana University, to the
People of Indiana"
(Indianapolis, printed by Stacy & Williams, 1840).

The undersigned were appointed, at the last meeting of the Board of Trustees of Indiana University, a Committee to address the Citizens of the State, on the subjects of the conditions and prospects of that Institution.

We approach the duty thus assigned to us impressed with a deep sense of its importance. The Institution of which we, in conjunction with our fellow Trustees, are the executive guardians, is an essential portion of that extended and liberal System of Public Instruction, which, a quarter of a century since, the wise and good men who framed for Indiana her Constitution, incorporated in that excellent instrument. The constitutional provision under which the Indiana University was established, may be usefully recalled to notice. It is contained in the Ninth Article of the Constitution, and reads as follows:

"It shall be the duty of the General Assembly, as soon as circumstances will permit, to provide by law for a General System of Education, ascending in a regular gradation from Township Schools to a STATE UNIVERSITY, wherein tuition shall be gratis and equally open to all."

No Single provision in the Charter of our State Liberties exceeds, if indeed any equals, in importance, that which we have just quoted. It contemplates, though in the distant future perhaps, a scheme of moral and intellectual improvement, such as has been seldom conceived by a legislative Convention, and such as was never yet executed in any nation; a scheme co-extensive at once with the limits of the State and the wants of the people.

When "circumstances permit" Indiana to carry out the bold and enlightened views, to which, by her Delegates in Convention assembled, she was thus solemnly pledged, she will have laid, deep in the immovable rock of Human Improvement, the foundations of Public Peace, of Social Order and of National Happiness. When to all, without distinction of rank, of sect or of party, the elevating and ennobling influences of Education shall be thus made free; when every citizen shall feel, that, let his lot have fallen as it may, his children shall share with the richest and most favored, that cultivation of the mind and heart which raises man, far more than wealth or titled distinction, among his fellow men; then may Indiana boast, that her liberties and her prosperity are safe, beyond the reach almost of Fate itself. Then shall Equality rest, not upon Sumptuary laws or agrarian restrictions, but upon the stable and peaceful basis of equal education. Then shall the doubts, if such still linger in our Republic, of the capability of the People wisely to govern themselves, be dispelled for ever; since those who already by law have the power of self-government, shall then be universally confessed to have, by education, the intelligence also.

The full attainment of these great and Soul-stirring objects may be yet afar off. Our State has already engaged in public expenditures of a different character, which limit the resources she might otherwise, in accordance with her Constitution, even now have appropriated to Public Instruction. She is deeply in debt; and prudence warns her to lessen her present liabilities, instead of involving herself yet deeper. But though the complete execution of the intentions of our Constitution is thus unfortunately retarded, the duty is but the more imperative, to employ, with sedulous care, the resources at our command, and to profit, to the utmost of our power, by the opportunities which still remain to us.

Of these resources, the proceeds of the grant, by Act of Congress in the year 1816, of two townships, to our State, "for the use of a Seminary of learning," form no inconsiderable item. These two reserved townships, now nearly all sold, have yielded a fund of upwards of One Hundred Thousand Dollars; the present endowment of Indiana University.

This fund, a small portion of which was employed to establish the original "State Seminary" at Bloomington, while the remainder afterwards served to endow the "Indiana College," is, now that the Institution has reached its highest grade and has become, as the Constitution contemplated, a "State University," vested in the Trustees of that University and their successors in office; and it is declared that the said fund shall "be and for ever remain a permanent fund for the support of said University."

Thus Congress and our own State have done what Government can do, to render this Institution prosperous and permanent. It devolves upon the Managers of the Institution and upon the People of the State to do the rest.

As the Institution ascended from the grade of a Seminary to that of a State College, its reputation and the number of its Students gradually increased. So that, at the time when it became a University and during the succeeding session the number exceeded one hundred. From that period, however, until last session, the number had gradually decreased, until *fifty-four* Students only were found in the classes; and although it appears, to judge from the number already entered, that the present session-roll will show and increase, still this falling off in the prosperity of the Institution demands from us to the People of the State, an explanation of what we consider the chief causes of the decline. The Indiana University is emphatically their own Institution; created by their law, endowed with their funds; directed by the Trustees of their choice. It is, not their right only, but their bounden duty, to investigates its conduct, to care for its prospects and to take measures for its advancement and success.

The causes which have cast a temporary cloud over the prosperity of this Institution, are such as very commonly affect Seminaries of learning, at some period of their existence; especially such as are endowed by public funds; and are thus placed under the supervision of a State Legislature. Unhallowed ambition, to subserve its own private ends, has sought to excite, both within and without the Halls of Legislation, dissentions, heart-burnings, and prejudices against the University.

[outlines case of Dr. Wm. Foster vs. Dr. Wylie and conclusions—2.5 pp.]

. . . .

The Board, under-estimating, it may be, the effects which the tongue and pen of detraction, however false they be, often produce, by iteration, upon the public mind, did not publish the evidence adduced before them, nor even take measures to lay before the People of the State, whose ears the injurious reports had reached, the verdict of full and unanimous acquittal. To the neglect so to do,— a neglect not intentional certainly on their part—may possibly be traced a portion of the evils which have resulted from these unprincipled proceedings. The records of the Institution were indeed open to all; but how few ever inspect, or have opportunity of inspecting, documents of that description?

[Details several other publicity schemes vs. univ. 1 p.]

. . . .

We turn with pleasure from this brief glance at these crooked doings, to a review of the present position and resources of the University itself; and we present these with confidence to the Public.

All the buildings which form the necessary appendage to the University are now completed and ready for occupation. These include a Boarding House of spacious dimensions, where students who cannot find comfortable boarding in town, may be accommodated, and where private rooms for study can be furnished, at a moderate rate, to such young gentlemen as desire them.

Another building has been erected containing a Laboratory, chemical lecture room and museum, with the necessary furnaces and apparatus. It furnishes, for the illustration of that important branch of collegiate instruction, chemical science, facilities not equalled in any Public Institution in the State.

The University Library has been recently augmented by a purchase of about two thousand dollars' worth of books, some of them rare and valuable. Among them we may incidentally enumerate the "Thesaurus," of Ugolinus, in itself an encyclopedea or complete storehouse of Biblical learning, valuable editions of the Ancient Classics, the folio editions of the works of Milton, Bayle, Selden, Dupin, Bochart and of the Pandects of Justinian; the French Classics, and the best standard works on history, biography and the sciences; together with a selected variety of miscellaneous literature.

The faculty of the University, in which, during the two last sessions, several vacancies have existed, is now filled to the entire satisfaction of the Trustees, with the single exception of the Chair of languages, which, though vacant for the moment, the Board has made arrangements to fill within a few months, and, as they hope, within a few *weeks*, from this date. In the meantime, by some extra exertion on the part of the other Professors, Students in that branch receive regular and ample instruction.

[Follow descriptions of A. Wylie, Ammen, T. A. Wylie, J. I. Morrison, M. Campbell]

. . . .

After this brief statement of the names and qualifications of the Faculty of the University, it is unnecessary for us to say, that we consider them eminently entitled to the confidence of the People of Indiana. We may add, without any intention to depreciate the merits and resources of other institutions similar to our own, that we believe the Faculty we have at length succeeded in assembling, will compare advantageously, for learning, private worth and professional reputation, with that of any other public institution to be found west of the mountains.

The location of the University is universally admitted to be one of the healthiest in the State; and the surrounding scenery is romantic and attractive.

In closing the enumeration of the advantages now possessed by Indiana university, we may allude to its pecuniary resources. These ensure its permanency. It is endowed beyond the reach of temporary reverse, or accidental contingence. Its productive fund, the whole of which will, in the course of a few years, be in the hands of the Treasurer of State, netting to the Institution an interest of eight per cent., exceeds Ninety Thousand Dollars; while the University Campus and Buildings thereon, including the Old and New College Buildings, the Boarding House, the Laboratory and a Private Residence, are worth from Twenty to Twenty Five Thousand Dollars.

These ample funds enable the University, not indeed to fulfil the ultimate intentions of the Constitution, and make instruction *gratis*, but to reduce the tuition fees much below what are usually demanded in similar institutions, and thus place instruction within the reach of means the most moderate. The fees are *eight dollars and a half* a session, or *seventeen dollars* a year; little more than is demanded for schooling in many of the Common Schools of our State. The real cost of the instruction offered at this price, is, if we suppose an average of One Hundred Students, upwards of *Sixty Dollars* each; and this amount, instead of the yearly fee of seventeen dollars, would have to be paid by each student to sustain the Institution, but for its liberal endowment. Are the citizens of Indiana generally aware of the vast difference between the tuition fee demanded and the cost (may we not add the *value?*) of the tuition received? If they were so, we think it cannot be doubted, that the classes of the University would be full, even to overflowing.

As it is, the advantages enjoyed by the comparatively small number, who at present avail themselves of the opportunities offered, are the greater, on account of the moderate size of the classes. The care and attention of the Professor can be more particularly directed to each individual, so as to combine, in a measure, the advantages of private with public tuition. Thus, if the list of graduates be not numerous, we may expect it to be distinguished; and if the University does not turn out many scholars, she will at least have the credit of turning out good ones.

This, in the course of time, will fill her ranks up to and beyond the number they have ever yet received; and will establish her good name, on a permanent basis, even if the present communication should fail to produce that effect. Still we should deeply regret the delay; since it is the evident intention of the Constitution, and should be the earnest endeavor of all who appreciate the value of education, to diffuse as widely and as rapidly as possible, the benefits of such an Institution as this.

But, be the results as they may, the course which duty points out to the Trustees is evident and plain before them. They cannot command success, but they can deserve it. They cannot control prejudice or silence detraction; but they have faithfully endeavored to meet and disarm both. It rests not with them to fill the classes of the Indiana University, but they have bestirred themselves—they trust successfully—in rendering them worthy to be filled.

And they feel assured, that already the tide has turned, and will soon rapidly set in, in favor of Indiana's State Institution. The fact, that even in the present season of pecuniary embarrassment and commercial depression, the class-rolls should show an increase of students, while, in the great majority of other Seminaries of learning, the pressure of the times is marked by a falling off, affords encouraging earnest, that the cloud is passing away and the sun is about to shine out once more.

The Trustees rely, with undoubting confidence, on the decision of their fellow-citizens, to be made when all the facts be plainly before them. And as it is a general and reasonable desire, when opinions on any matter in dispute are expressed, to examine the evidence upon which these are based, they have decided to publish, in the shape of an appendix to this communication, the entire testimony given on the trial to which reference has been made [Foster vs. Wylie], copied from the official record on the books of the University. They are aware, that much of the testimony is wholly irrelevant; but had they extracted the essential portions only, it would have been difficult to escape the imputation of a desire to garble or an intention to conceal. They are aware, too, that men of sense, on reviewing the document, may pronounce the whole matter too frivolous and insignificant to deserve either notice or publication. To such men their apology is, that a small insect may inflict a poisonous wound; that the frivolity of a charge does not always ensure for it the contempt it merits; and that there is a point beyond which even imputations the most insignificant, cannot, with safety, be wholly disregarded or silently passed by.

D. H. MAXWELL, *Ch'm.*
ROBERT DALE OWEN.
C. P. HESTER.
WILLIAM HENDRICKS.
NATHANIEL WEST.

Bloomington, May 14, 1840.

Postscript by the Trustees. Since the above Circular was placed in the Printer's hands, the Committee appointed by the Legislature to investigate the affairs of the University have commenced their investigation. As that Committee has very properly decided to publish, in connexion with Report to be made next winter to the Legislature, the Testimony, which the Trustees, as above stated, proposed to incorporate in an Appendix, and as that testimony will thus come, in the most official form, before the Public, the Trustees are relieved from the necessity of appending it to the present communication.

Bloomington, May 27, 1840.

Printed report pasted on pp. 77–83, *Board Minutes,* 1838–1859.

Document 39

The Weight of the Public Hand

In spite of all the favorable predictions made in special reports, trustee minutes, and even presidential comments, Indiana University went into an immediate decline after it was created a university. There seems to have been no reason why this was true, except there was a sore lack of money for its support. Too, Hoosiers seemed not enthusiastic about collegiate education, and especially that of a public variety. There crept into the legislative part of this report the suggestion that the University should be moved away from Bloomington, a threat which persisted well into the future. Andrew Wylie's statement is an excellent delineation of educational philosophy for the time. His cynical observation that "It is an appalling fact that no Literary Institution has ever yet flourished under legislative management" was almost self-defeating. Wylie might have added, as the central part of this report reveals, that petty politics and personal dissensions were poisonous to the operation of a public university.

*   *   *

REPORT
FROM THE
COMMITTEE APPOINTED AT THE LAST SESSION OF THE
LEGISLATURE TO INVESTIGATE THE AFFAIRS OF
INDIANA UNIVERSITY.
Read, laid on the table, and five hundred copies ordered to be printed

---

TO THE HON. SAMUEL JUDAH,

Speaker of the House of Representatives:

The legislative committee appointed by a resolution of the General Assembly, adopted 21st day of Feb. A. D. 1840, to inquire into the condition of the State University, and the causes of its decline, as also to inquire into the proper means to be adopted to secure its prosperity, and also to inquire into the expediency of establishing an agricultural professorship, report as follows to-wit:

That a majority of said committee met for the purpose of discharging the duties imposed on them by said resolution, at the University Chapel in Bloom-

ington, on the 19th day of May, 1840, and commenced the investigations necessary to meet the requisitions of said resolution. These efforts of the committee
were materially assisted by the action of the board of trustees of said University,
who appointed a committee consisting of five gentlemen of their body, to meet
the legislative committee, and furnish them with such information in their
possession as might be found useful in the course of the investigation then proposed. This commitee consisted of Messrs. Hendricks, Owen, West, Hester and
Maxwell, and the committee deem it an act of justice to these gentlemen, to state
they co-operated efficiently by promptly answering the calls made on them for
information by the legislative committee, during the whole of its session. At the
request of the committee of investigation, they were furnished by the committee
on behalf of the board of trustees, with a condensed historical account of the
institution, as also a tabular statement of the funds of the institution.

These documents herewith submitted, (and marked No. 1 & 2) are sufficiently
explicit on the subjects of which they treat, and in the opinion of the committee
need but little comment. By these documents it appears that the total of the
funds of the college, arising from donated lands amounted to $117,821.84. In
addition to other information in relation to the available funds of the University, and the amount of unsold lands belonging to it, these documents contain
a valuable and interesting abstract of the early enactments of the Territory in
relation to this institution. Your committee accord fully with the deductions
drawn by the committee appointed on behalf of the trustees of the University
from these enactments, and cannot express too strongly their approbation of
the liberal and enlarged views of the *then* Governor, and Legislature (1807) in
relation to education. Many of the provisions of those enactments are worthy
of imitation at the present day.

The investigating committee next directed their attention to the causes of the
decline of the University in public favor. The conduct of the President of the
University, has been on more than one occasion the subject of severe criticism
in the public prints and elsewhere, and the committee soon after their meeting,
instituted an inquiry into the justice of these complaints. This inquiry was
conducted openly, and in such a manner as to afford every legitimate means of
accusation and defence. The committee were induced to take a wider range in
their investigations into this matter, than they would otherwise have deemed
necessary or proper, from the fact that a previous investigation into the conduct
of Doct. Wylie had been had, and complaints had been made by persons inim-
ical to him, that sufficient latitude had not been allowed the accusers in making
and sustaining their charges against him.

After the most patient investigation of the evidence adduced, the committee
unanimously concur in the acquittal of Doct. Wylie of all the charges preferred
against him, and see no reason whatever to suppose that any conduct of his
has been prejudicial to the institution. On the contrary they believe him to be
eminently qualified for the station which he occupies, and find from the investigation that he has discharged the high trusts committed to him with an ability
and fidelity worthy of all commendation; although surrounded with almost
insurmountable difficulties and embarrassments. The committee in the course
of their investigations called upon the petitioners, who preferred those complaints to the legislature, which caused the passage of the resolution under which
the committee of investigation acted, and none of them (except one) made any
statements calculated to throw the slightest suspicion of blame on the accused.
On the contrary some of those petitioners who had entertained suspicions
injurious to Doct. Wylie became in the progress of the investigation so well

satisfied of the injustice of those suspicions, as to be induced voluntarily to furnish your committee with written statements expressive of their approbation of his conduct.

The only one of the petitioners who gave it as his opinion that Doct. Wylie had been to blame in the management of the institution, did not support that opinion by any testimony. Your committee entered into a minute inquiry as to the causes of the decline of the University in the number of its students. Your committee refer to document No. 3, as containing the opinions of the President of the instittuion in relation to its decline. On the same subject your committee also refer to document No. 4, being a memorial of the citizens of Bloomington and of the county of Monroe, remonstrating against the removal of the University, stating their opinion of the causes of the decline of the institution, and exempting the *present* faculty from the censure of producing it. In the opinion of your committee the causes which have produced the decline of the University may be divided into two classes. 1st. Such as operate injuriously on most of the institutions of the country; and 2dly, Such as are peculiar to the circumstances of this institution and its peculiar organization and management. Under the first head the most prominent of those causes is the indulgence which the parents of the students have been disposed to grant to them in supplies of more money than is sufficient for their reasonable wants during the sessions of the university. This practice always induces extravagance and excesses amongst the students, the odium of which is by the community thrown on the institution. To remedy this evil, the committee would suggest a legal provision requiring the pocket money furnished by the parents to the students, to be paid at the opening of each session of the University into the hands of some officer, appointed by the faculty, to be by him paid out for such outlays as might appear in his discretion to be reasonable and proper, and in connection with this to make it penal for the shop-keepers and other dealers in goods or groceries to sell to the students on credit. Under the present head may also be stated those jealousies and prejudices existing in every community against institutions of learning which in the neighborhood of universities assume a personal character and are directed against the persons who have charge of the institution.

The Indiana University and its professors have suffered in no small degree, from the operations of this cause.

Under the second head, the most prominant one is in the number of the board of trustees, (21.) In order to avoid the influences of sectarianism, it was thought best to have a large number of trustees. In the choosing these trustees, men of different religious prejudices were thrown together in such a manner as to combine all the elements of religious discord. This method of choice has resulted in petty bickerings and discontents, which have operated very injuriously on this institution and the reputation of the professors. To remedy this evil, the committee propose a reduction in the number of the board.

Your committee found on investigation, that this institution had been injured to some extent, by several rival colleges and theological seminaries, the management of which had been placed in the hands of persons belonging to some of the religious sects of the country.

While the committee approve of allowing the fullest latitude to the various religious sects of the community in educating their children in their own way, they believe it right for the public to sustain at least one college in which the sciences are taught and the morality of the bible inculcated, without any reference to the peculiar tenets of any sect of christians; and they therefore recommend to the guardian care of the legislature our present State University. After a full examination of the subject, your committee can see no good reason at present for the removal either of the University or the President. Your committee believe the reasoning in reference to the removal of the institution, in the document (No. 5) herewith submitted, to be conclusive, and are indisposed to weaken those arguments by attempting to expand them.

The present faculty have been selected with a view to their high moral character and scientific acquirements, and the committee have every reaosn to believe that the institution under their superintendence, will be well and ably managed. We deem it unnecessary at this time to form an agricultural professorship in the Indiana University. The public mind is already aroused on that subject, and societies are springing up over the State, which will doubtless accomplish the objects of such a professorship in an effectual manner.

Your committee herewith submit a bill emphasizing such provisions as they deem necessary for the benefit of the institution, and recommend its adoption.

Respectfully submitted,
JAS. H CRAVENS, *Chairman.*
JOHNSON WATTS,
JOS. S. JENCKES.

HON. JAMES H. CRAVENS,
CHAIRMAN OF LEGISLATIVE COMMITTEE.

SIR:

The committee appointed by the board of trustees of Indiana University, to meet and receive your committee, having received from your Secretary a resolution requesting that they would furnish to you a condensed history of the institution from its origin, have had that subject under consideration, and now submit to you the result, in the following

REPORT:

The reservation of land by Congress, whence the present endowment of the Indiana University is derived, consists of two townships, one in Gibson county, the other in Monroe county, both in this state.

The reservation of the Gibson county township, and its original appropriation for the support of a University, are contained in some act of Congress, not to be found among the documents prefixed to our revised code, nor in any other work of reference now within the reach of the committee of trustees. The exact date of that act of Congress is unknown to the committee; but it is dated before the 17th September 1807.

For, among the "laws of Indiana Territory" published by authority in 1807, occurs an "act to incorporate an University in the Indiana Territory," approved September 17, 1807; the second section of which commences as follows: "And whereas Congress has appropriated a township of land of twenty-three thousand and forty acres, for the use and support of the University or a public school in the district of Vincennes, and whereas the township is now located and the boundaries designated &c."

The preamble and provisions of the act above referred to, to "incorporate an University in the Indiana Territory," afford striking proof how liberal and enlightened, even in these early days, nine years before Indiana became a state or obtained a constitution, were the views of her legislators, on the subject of education; and are well worthy of preservation and remembrance.

The close of the preamble reads thus: "and for as much as literature and philosophy furnish the most useful and pleasing occupations, improving and varying the enjoyments of prosperity, affording relief under the pressure of misfortune, and hope and consolation in the hour of death, and considering that in a commonwealth where the humblest citizen may be elected to the highest public offices, and where the heaven-born privilege of the right to elect and reject, is retained and secured to the citizens; the knowledge which is requisite for a magistrate and elector should be widely diffused," therefore be it enacted &c.

The further provisions of the act are in accordance with this noble exordium. The sixth section provides, "That the trustees shall, as speedily as may be, establish and erect an University, within the limits of the borough of Vincennes, and shall appoint to preside over, and govern the said University, a President and not exceeding four Professors, for the instruction of youth in the Latin, Greek, French and English languages, Mathematics, Natural Philosophy, Ancient and Modern History, Moral Philosophy, Logic, Rhetoric, and the law of Nature and of Nations."

The same principal which is still incorporated in our present charter, guarding against sectarianism, is set forth in the tenth section of the above act, in the following words: "Be it further enacted, that no particular tests of religion shall be taught in the said University, by the President and Professors mentioned in the sixth section of this act."

The next section provides, that the trustees shall "use their utmost endeavors to induce the Aborigines to send their children to the University, for education, who when sent shall be maintained, clothed and educated at the expense of the institution." And further, "that the students, when-even the funds of the institution shall, in the opinion of the trustees, permit it, be educated gratis at the said University, in all or any of the branches of education which they may require."

Again, in the thirteenth section, is a provision of acknowledged importance, yet, to judge by the charter of our University, beyond the immediate views of our Legislature, even at the present day. In that section, it is enacted, "that the said trustees, as soon as in their opinion, the funds of the institution will admit, are hereby required to establish an institution for the education of females, and to make such by-laws and ordinances for the said institution, and the government thereof, as they may think proper."

Finally, in further evidence of the extended views of those days, we find, in the 15th section, the enactment, "That for the purpose of procuring a library and the necessary philosophical and experimental apparatus, agreeably to the eighth section of this law, there shall be raised a sum not exceeding twenty thousand dollars." The means by which this sum was to be raised, were less praiseworthy than the object in raising it. It was to be "by a lottery."

As regards the amount of land which, by the above act, the trustees were authorized to sell; the second section provides, that the Trustees may dispose of "any quantity not exceeding four thousand acres."

By subsequent acts of Congress, to which the committee of trustees cannot, at this moment, refer, the further sale of these lands to the amount of *thirteen sections* (including the above 4000 acres) was authorized: and they were sold and the proceeds expended for the use of the university.

So that, when by act of Congress, approved April 19th, 1816, "to enable the people of Indiana territory to form a constitution and state government" it was enacted "that one entire township which shall be designated by the President of the United States, in addition to the one heretofore reserved for that purpose, shall be preserved for the use of a seminary of learning, and vested in the legislature of the said state, to be appropriated solely to the use of such seminary by the said legislature;" the total quantity of land thus appropriated, was two townships, less thirteen sections; or fifty nine sections; or thirty-seven thousand seven hundred and sixty acres.

This land, with the exception of about 4,800 acres, has all been sold and the proceeds appropriated for the use and support of the present institution, at first under the name of the "State Seminary," afterwards as the "Indiana College," and now as the "Indiana University." The above 4,800 acres, still unsold, are estimated by the Treasurer of State as worth 2,500 dollars.

It appears by "an act to provide for the sale of the Seminary township in Gibson county, and for other purposes, approved January 2d, 1822," that, at some time previously, the board of trustees of the Vincennes University had ceased to exist. The preamble to the seventh section of the above act reads thus: "Whereas it is stated to this General Assembly, that the former board of trustees of the Vincennes University has expired by the negligence of its members," &c.

At what precise date this board expired, the committee have not been able to discover: but it may be presumed to have been previously to the year 1820; for by an "act to establish a State Seminary and for other purposes, approved January 20, 1820," this institution was established at Bloomington and the trustees of the said State Seminary were empowered to sell any quantity of land in the reserved township in Monroe county, not exceeding in all one section.

The act referred to is very brief, and provides for little else except the sale of the above lands, and the erection, out of the proceeds thereof, of "a suitable building for a State Seminary and also a suitable and commodious house for a Professor." Its tone and the limited character of its provisions form a striking contrast to the liberal views incorporated in the charter of the Vincennes university, granted thirteen years before, in the very infancy of Indiana territory.

Various supplementary acts were passed, from time to time augmenting the number of the trustees of the said State Seminary, permitting them to loan money, and authorizing the renting and sale of additional lands.

Of these the most important is an act approved January 25th, 1827, appointing James Smith Commissioner to sell the Gibson county township, and James Borland Commissioner to sell the Monroe county township, and fixing the minimum price of said land, if first rate at three dollars and fifty cents: if second rate at two dollars and twenty-five cents; and if third rate at one dollar and twenty-five cents per acre. The same act, by its tenth section, provides that three sections of the Seminary lands in Monroe county contiguous to the section heretofore sold shall be reserved from sale.

About the same time an act was passed, approved January 26th, 1827, appointing a board of visiters to the State Seminary at Bloomington.

By an act approved January 24th, 1828, the State Seminary was superseded by the "Indiana College," established "for the education of youth in the American, learned and foreign languages, the useful arts, sciences and literature."

By that act it was provided (section 12) that "all moneys arising from the sale of the seminary townships in the counties of Monroe and Gibson, shall be, and forever remain, a permanent fund for the support of said college, and the interest arising from the amount of said sales, together with the three reserved sections in the seminary townships situated in the county of Monroe, and all the buildings which have been erected adjacent to the town of Bloomington, in said county of Monroe, for the use of the State Seminary, with all the real and personal property of every description belonging to or connected with said State Seminary, as the property of the State, and all gifts, grants and donations, which have been or hereafter may be made, for the support of the college, shall be and hereby forever are vested in the aforesaid trustees and their successors."

By the same act, a board of Visiters consisting of five members, was appointed; and it was made their duty annually to visit the college, inspect the course pursued by the trustees and faculty, examine the books of the college, and make a report of their examinations, inspections and inquiries, to the Governor, to be by him laid before the General Assembly. Of these visiters three were to constitute a quorum; but during the ten years' existence of the college, a quorum was present but once; and during the latter half of the period referred to, to wit: during the last five years of the existence of the college, none of the board officially visited the college, or reported in connexion therewith.

Finally, by an "act to establish a University in the State of Indiana," approved February 15, 1838, the institution reached its highest grade, and all the estate, funds, property, rights and demands, formerly vested in the trustees of the college, were transferred to the trustees of the university, in whom they still remain vested.

This act incorporating the "Indiana University," is, in its general provisions, a transcript of the charter of "Indiana College," with this difference, that no board of visiters is appointed, and that the number of trustees of the University is increased to twenty-two, from the number of fifteen, appointed under the college charter. Also, by the charter of the university, the power of conferring degrees in law and medicine is added to the power formerly vested in the college, of granting degrees in the liberal arts and sciences.

The total funds of the university, originally derived from the reserved lands, as above explained, are estimated by the trustees as follows:

Productive lands, including moneys at interest,
moneys due or in hand, and a small amount of lands
for sale, (say $2,500 worth, not actually productive
at this time,) $98,471 84
Deduct debts due by the University, chiefly to
the Branch at Bedford of the State Bank of
Indiana, ... $3,650

                                                                94,821 84
Unproductive property, chiefly real estate, in-
cluding the University Campus and buildings
thereon; including also the library and
apparatus, ...   23,000 00
    Total, ... $117,821 84

For the separate items which make up the above amount and exhibit in detail the resources of the University, your committee is referred to document F, spread on the records of the Board of Trustees, at pages 66, 67, and 68, with its accompanying documents D, C, and B; of which accompanying documents the former marked D, is recorded on the said records at pages 72 and 63; and of the two latter, the first is recorded in the book entitled "Treasurer's Reports;" all of which books and reports have already been placed by the committee of trustees In-the hands of your committee.

The committee of trustees further begs to refer your committee to document G, on pages 70 and 71 of the records of the University, as exhibiting in full the probable expenses and available means of the institution, for the ensuing year.

Any further information on these or other subjects which is within the reach of the committee of trustees, they will cheerfully furnish. In the meantime the above is respectfully submitted.

D. H. MAXWELL, *Chairman.*
WILLIAM HENDRICKS,
C. P. HESTER,
ROBERT DALE OWEN,
NATHAN'L WEST,
Committee of Trustees.

Bloomington, May 20, 1840.

To THE INVESTIGATING COMMITTEE.

GENTLEMEN:—By virtue of certain resolutions passed by you, the undersigned has been laid under the obligation of stating to you his opinion, as to what have been the "causes of the decline of the University in the number of the students," and as to what legislative action he may think necessary "to secure and promote its prosperity:"—and by another resolution it is made his duty to submit to you "a brief account of the paternal system" of government.

In compliance with the will of the committee, as expressed in those resolutions, the undersigned respectfully submits the following statement:

First, as to the decline of the University in regard to the number of students:

In the sessions of 1837–8, there were students in actual attendance, ...	105
In the ensuing winter session of 1839, there were in actual attendance, .	78
Shewing a decrease of, ...	27

This diminution was, I think, owing to the following causes:

1. In the year preceding the diminution, several students had indulged themselves in idle and extravagant habits, by which their parents were put to a great deal of unnecessary expense and the institution itself brought, to a considerable extent, into disrepute.

About all places to which youth resort, *who have money to spend,* persons will be found who hesitate not to make use of dishonorable methods to possess themselves of it:—sharks, that prey upon the indiscretion of the generous, the confiding, the inexperienced. And, afterwards, when the natural consequence of their short-sighted selfishness takes place, in the diminution of the number of their victims, *these very persons* are first and loudest in their clamors and complaints, attributing of course, the matter which is the subject of their complaints to any other than the true cause.

2. About the time when the cause just referred to was secretly preying upon the root of the institution's prosperity, dissatisfaction, jealousy and discord began to take place in a certain portion of the faculty, which, as it covertly sent forth its influence among the students, had a tendency to diminish, and did, to my certain knowledge, diminish their number.

3. Simultaneously with the operation of these causes there rose up other institutions within that region to which the Indiana University naturally looks for

a supply of students;—one at Crawfordsville, one at Greencastle, one at Hanover, and one at Vincennes,—three of them colleges, the fourth a University;—besides, these, another institution, designed I believe to become a college, situated at Franklin, still less remote from the seat of the Indiana University than any of the others; though all of them are within a circle of not more than about an hundred miles in diameter.

The agents employed by some of these institutions have presented their claims, not unsuccessfully, even in Bloomington itself, and among the students of the University. The sectarian spirit, on the strength of which these rival institutions depend, in part, for their support, began, about the time to which this part of my narrative refers, to direct a fervid and unkind influence upon the Indiana University: and with what ultimate design this was done may be inferred from the fact, that from statements made before the board of trustees at their last meeting, it appears the proposition is openly made to destroy the Indiana University at once, by taking away its charter and dividing its funds among the other institutions just referred to.

The undersigned simply mentions these things as historical facts, and without any intention of reflecting censure upon the friends of these other institutions, whose zeal in their favor and in opposition to the Indiana University, proceeds, it may be charitably supposed, from an honest conviction that no State institution can be made to prosper, or at least, that there is "a more excellent way" for conducting the interests of education, than that which is prescribed by the charter of the Indiana University.

Many good people think their children can be preserved from those influences which they consider dangerous to their moral and religious character, only by placing them in institutions which they, as a religious sect, can guard and manage as they think best. Such is their honest belief; and they have acted and will act according to it. It is their right; and the undersigned, although he thinks he has had some reason to complain of the manner in which it has been exercised, has no disposition to say a word in opposition to the right itself. It is one which he hold to himself most dear, and which he most cheerfully allows in its legitimate exercise, to all others.

He might mention other co-operating causes, but it is unnecessary. The above mentioned are, he thinks, of themselves sufficient to account for the diminution in the number of students which, to the amount of twenty-five or twenty-six, had taken place in the winter of 1839.

There was, indeed, another cause which had been operating in the board of trustees, to retard the growth of the institution while it was a college, and which had done more than all others to produce the diminution in question. But it deserves a distinct notice by itself; because it has continued to exert, and still exerts at this moment, a power influence in opposition to the best interests of the University, and has produced a still further reduction in the number of its pupils.

The progress of your investigations, gentlemen, will, I trust, show the following train of facts to have sprung from the agency of the man who now stands before you in the character of an accuser.

That he had repeated quarrels with students;—that he was a turbulent member of the board;—that his violence towards Mr. E. N. Elliott drove from the institution that gentleman, who took with him Mr. D. Maxwell, superintendent of the Preparatory Department;—that when, by extraordinary efforts to meet the emergency thus brought upon the institution, Mr. Ruter and Mr. Dodds were induced to enter into the Faculty and give their aid in carrying forward the business of instruction in the departments assigned them, he contrived to invade the province of the Faculty and disturb the harmony of their operations, by a resolution assigning a part of the duties belonging to one of these professors to another who was was less competent to perform them;—that by interfering with the office of Janitor, he, in concert with certain other individuals, members of the board, so managed, that though the Janitor's salary was doubled, the duties of the office were very imperfectly performed, leaving the Faculty and students to suffer great inconvenience in consequence;—that he contrived to produce further difficulty and embarrassment to the Faculty, by usurping the power of making laws for the government of the institution,—that he exerted himself to prevent the undersigned from carrying into effect the known will of the President of the board, in particular, and of the whole board collectively, in regard to the purchase of books and apparatus which were essential to the very existence of the institution;—and finally that when, for pursuing this course of conduct, he was left out of the Board of Trustees, upon the occasion of its re-organization by the Legislature, he adopted the resolution of being either reinstated in his former place or "tearing down" the institution, he did, to carry out and accomplish said resolution, exhibit before the Legislature in the winter of 1838–9, certain false and scandalous charges against the Board of Trustees and against the undersigned.

What must necessarily result from such a course of conduct on the part of a Trustee of the institution is sufficiently manifest. I shall call your attention particularly to one fact in the series: I refer to the fact that the aforesaid charges were presented before the Legislature, by one who had been a Trustee, and *purporting* to be endorsed by two others, who were still Trustees, and acting, therefore, under the most solemn obligation to promote the interests of the institution committed to their care.

The news of a fact, so novel and extraordinary, flew, as on the wings of the wind, all over the country. It was published in the newspapers in the city of New York, not long after it happened, and was speedily spread all over the Union. It produced, of course, different impressions on different minds: but whatever might be the precise character of the impression in each particular case—it could not fail to operate, for a time, to the detriment of the institution. The friends of the undersigned would regard the charges as malicious and un-founded: and they, of course, would have their faith in the institution shaken, because, being a State institution, it is exposed to such attacks. His enemies would, of course, consider them true, and be confirmed and encouraged in their hostility. Others would not know what to think; and they, of course, while in this state of suspense, would give the preference to any other institution which might present any thing like equal claims to their regard. Others again who are governed not by reason, but by promise, would shake their wise heads and exclaim "Where there is so much smoke there must be some fire:" they would condemn the undersigned, as did a certain member of the Legislature, simply because "there should be no disturbance in a literary institution." These charges, it is true, were afterwards investigated by the board, and pronounced false and unfounded. But what of that? The mischief had been done. The poison was diffusing itself and had been working, for months, in the public mind, before the antidote could be applied.

The board, on investigation of the charges, though they pronounced the undersigned not guilty, found, in the course of their investigation, cause for removing three out of the five professors then in the institution. The chairs thus vacated have but just been filled. The fact of their having been vacated could have produced, in no conceivable circumstances, any other *immediate* effect than that which actually followed it,—a further reduction in the number of students.

As to the act of the board itself, the undersigned has nothing to say. Right or wrong, expedient or inexpedient, such as has been stated, was its inevitable consequence.

Another cause to which it may be proper just to advert is the fact that the Department of Natural Philosophy and Chemistry has not been, till very recently, that is, only two weeks since, furnished with a Laboratory; the Professor being under the necessity of performing his experiments at the fire of a common stove. Students coming hither from abroad, and finding the institution—though nominally a University—deficient in so essential a part of its organization, would naturally feel disappointed, and communicate their feelings, by letter, to their friends: so that, if they should not go away, others, at least, would be prevented from coming. So deeply has this consideration, with others of a like nature, pressed on the mind of the undersigned himself, anxious though he is to increase the number of students, that he never has made any special effort for this purpose. Till now, it would have been premature: for, not till now has our organization, even as a college, been complete.

And here the undersigned may be permitted to suggest a thought, as to the principle assumed in the representations that have been made to the legislature and the public, in regard to the number of our students. It has been stated to be *less*—at one time by twenty-five; at another, by fourteen than it actually was. But on this I make no comment. I advert to the *principle* which assumes that the number of students actually at a college, is a sure indication of its character and prospects, *at the time*. Numbers however, taken alone, afford no such indication. The causes which affect numbers, either in the way of increase or diminution, operate slowly and often most effectually, when, as yet, they are *latent* from the pubic eye. Our own history affords a recent instance of this. In 1837, when our number was the greatest, causes were at work which diminished it rapidly: and now, on the other hand, when our number is reduced to about half of what it was, it requires not the eye of divination to see in the condition of the University the prognostics of a certain and a steady increase. The institution has not indeed passed the crisis: but it has reached that point in it, at which adverse influences having exhausted their force—"vitamque in vulnere ponunt"—those of an opposite character will begin to exert themselves.

4. To proceed, gentlemen, to the next question that, namely, which respects the action of the Legislature—three things, it seems to the undersigned, ought to be regarded, as the elements of prosperity to any literary institution—the character of the board and faculty, the character of the sphere within which the powers of the institution are to operate, and the furniture of means with which it is supplied to effect its objects.

By the "prosperity" of the Institution, it is taken for granted that more than the mere number of students is intended. Institutions may be so conducted as to attract numbers, and to keep up a succession of numbers too, and yet generate nothing but pestilence and moral death for the community. The moral capacities, as well as the intellectual powers of the pupils must be educated. Their weaknesses must not be flattered: nor their indolence soothed. Modesty of deportment and deference to superiority in knowledge, virtue, and experience must be inculcated. Honesty and simplicity of character and purpose must be taught; as well as literature and science. That method which will best effect these ends will not, at first, attract numbers. In the long run it may. What is morally wrong grasps at present advantages, which TIME, deified in ancient mythology, destroys. The poisonous mushroom springs up in a night: the growth of the oak is marked by the lapse of ages. The good are content to sow, that others who are to come after them may reap the harvest.

To insure that kind of prosperity which is really desirable for a literary Institution, the Faculty in the first place, should be composed of men whose characters are neither feeble through intellectual imbecility, nor marked with moral turpitude. By the way, it should be remarked, that when raised to a place above its proper level, intellectual imbecility too frequently becomes moral turpitude: for to sustain itself it is constantly tempted to resort to dishonest and time-serving expedients.

Such as cannot succeed in other professions are sometimes represented, as *falling* into that of a pedagogue. To you, gentlemen, I need not say that the state of things should not be such any where in *our* country as to justify such a mode of speaking as this.

Of the character of a Board of Trustees the same remarks will hold; though, perhaps, not with equal force.

As to the population in the immediate vicinity, of the University it should be such as to generate and maintain such a tone of moral sentiment as to keep in check those tendencies to corruption from which no society on earth is altogether free.

As to the more remote parts of the sphere, from which the University must derive its supply of students, it should be kept in mind, that the larger religious sects occupy, with their influence, the greater portions. The smaller sects, who either because they are not able to sustain institutions of their own, or because they are liberal enough to unite in common in favor of an Institution whose advantages were intended for all, have not thought it necessary or expedient to provide the means of educating their sons apart by themselves: these, added to those more insignificant portions of society which are indifferent as to sect, are the people who may be expected to send their sons to our University. A few of the more liberal and enlightened of all sects may also be expected to regard it with favor. The University may be so managed as not to offend the prejudices of any liberal-minded good man. But that it should suit itself to the peculiar views of any sect or any party, is neither to be expected nor desired. Whatever influence it exerts should be calculated to bring all good people, of all denominations, into closer union. The spirit of the religion which Jesus taught should live and breathe in its halls, or it will not prosper—it should not. As to the furniture of means &c., viz.: Books, Apparatus, buildings—It is sufficient merely to name them on this occasion.

We are prepared, now, to ask, on which of these sources, whence prosperity is to be derived to the Institution, can the Legislature exert an improving influence? Should the Legislature undertake to improve the Faculty, on what would the question of appointment or removal turn? On the qualifications of the individual? Or his creed? Or would it depend on the amount of misrepresentation which at the time might, by *confidential letters,* be injected into the Legislative counsels?

It is an appalling fact that no Literary Institution has ever yet flourished under Legislative management. This Institution, when the undersigned took charge of it, ten years ago, was a mere Grammar School, without a Library, without Apparatus, and with but two Professors, having a strong tide of prejudice and opposition to stem. In these circumstances, *"none was so poor to do it reverence."* It was with difficulty a quorum of the Board could be got together once a year. Yet under all difficulties, it grew; till, in 1837, it numbered one hundred and five students, and a place in its Board of Trustees was thought to be an honor worth all that mighty agitation which the accuser has, by moving heaven and earth, excited on the subject. Yet the Legislature no sooner began to be moved about it, than it sank at once. And this is now cited, all over the land as another proof that no Literary Institution *can* prosper, which is even *liable* to Legislative influences.

But, for his part, the undersigned is not yet prepared to give in to, or give up to, this opinion. He yet believes that this University, though subject to Legislative interference, can be made to prosper. He believes further, that the Legislative interference, in this very instance will prove most salutary. The manner in which this interference was invoked and all the circumstances connected with it, show who is the person struck at, at why he has been struck at,—struck at, now the third time. You, gentlemen, when you have patiently examined into every alleged cause of complaint, will say whether he is guilty, and OF WHAT; and he will remove himself forthwith, from your Institution and from the state which contains it—and *all will be well*—will it? Or on the contrary, should your report be favorable—will not all be well? There is some doubt. For the accuser, in his letter to Mr. Berry, says he will renew his efforts every year till his object be accomplished: and should he be able to excite *another* such commotion and tempest, his object will be accomplished. And, gentlemen, should he *have* this power, the Legislature, with all the resources of the State at their command, cannot save the University from prostration and ruin.

The undersigned does not feel himself competent to suggest, with any degree of confidence, any preventive, which it is thought, the Legislature would feel themselves authorized to apply. He has heard it suggested, by some honest and good men of great experience, that if any person undertaking to prosecute charges against the State University were to render himself liable for the costs of prosecution, in case he failed to establish his charges, it would prevent the recurrence of a case similar to that which has, in this instance, put the State and the University to so much cost and trouble.

So far as the prosperity of the institution may depend upon the board of trustees, the undersigned has nothing to propose. The history of all literary institutions goes to establish the principle, that a board of trustees having been appointed by the Legislature, should be left, in all ordinary cases, to manage the trust committed to their stands, unless the interference of the Legislature should be invoked by the Board themselves, acting in their joint and corporate capacity.

In reference to the wants of the state, it has long been the conviction of the undersigned that a department of Didactics, such as is sketched in his letters to Mr. Dunning, and such as corresponds in most respects to the Normal Schools of Europe, is greatly needed in the University. It would enable Farmers in moderate circumstances to fit their sons for those positions and occasions, in which the interests and views of that highly useful and respectable class of the community need to be represented and advocated.

In obedience to the resolution requiring the undersigned to lay before you a brief account of the paternal system of college government, he begs leave to submit to the committee the following brief extract from the annual catalogue for the year 1837–8, page 11, and an extract on the same subject from a discourse delivered before the Legislature; and were it not for fear of trespassing too far on the patience of the committee, he would be gratified to submit to their inspection a still more expanded view of the same subject, contained in a discourse delivered before the college of professional teachers, and published in the 5th vol. of their transactions.

"The government is paternal, the reason and moral sense of the student are called into exercise by frequent appeals in relation to the matter and manner of his conduct; and he is thus taught to govern himself." This I consider the fundamental principle of the Paternal System. It is expanded in the following remarks, extracted from my "Discourse on Education, delivered before the Legislature of the State of Indiana, at the request of the joint committee of education, and published in pursuance of a vote of the House of Representatives Jan. 17, 1830." They are found on pages 20 and 21. "In the remarks which I have to offer, as to the methods proper to be adopted for the purpose of guarding against the formation of evil habits, I can not be particular. I may be allowed to specify one thing which, if I am not utterly mistaken, has had a most pernicious influence, and must have, whenever it is adopted. I allude to the practice of governing students by a multiplicity of written laws, supported as they must be, by a system of espionage. The laws of a state differ essentially from those of a school. The former have for their object the protection of individuals in their just rights: that of the latter is the formation of character. Young men should be formed in character and habit, so as not merely to shun vice, and to practice virtue, but to love the latter and detest the former. And this is what mere law and authority can not do. No one becomes good by constraint. Besides, laws often provoke to their own violation. A generous youth does not like to be commanded to do what he knows he ought to do, and would do if left to himself. What he does by constraint, or under the appearance of constraint, he loses the credit of doing. Further; the formation of character contemplates, a thousand things, which change their nature, if enforced by authority. If you go about to make people religious by compulsion, you make them hoypocrites. Who would think of teaching politeness by rules and penalties? Further still; if you lay down a law, it must be invariable. But the dispositions of the young are different, and demand a different treatment. Yet again: watch a body, and you do him an injury: you treat him as a slave; and such treatment will gradually generate a base and servile spirit, which will need to be watched. Too much government is always injurious, a maxim which rulers are sure to learn. There is but one law in heaven, the law of love; and the Author of our salvation has proposed no other for the government of those whom He is forming for an eternal residence in that happy place. The society of a college ought to be a family in which the faculty is the parent and the pupils the children—of different tempers and attainments, and therefore to be treated differently, but all under the same kind and paternal government. And those who cannot be governed in this way, it would be wrong to educated, if it were possible."

It will be observed from these extracts that the Paternal System stands opposed not to all laws whatever, but only to such "a multiplicity" of them as would, in carrying them into effect, render necessary a system of espionage. For instance, in some Institutions, letters sent home by the pupils must first be inspected by the Faculty.—Let each professor be strict in requiring *the performance of the duties of the recitation room,* and he will soon find out who do not behave well out of it. And, let such, after sufficient trial, be dismissed, that they may, before the season of youth be past, be set to some other employment, in which they may be useful in future life, to themselves and others.

All which is respectfully submitted,

A. WYLIE.

Bloomington Sept. 25th 1840.

Indiana *Documentary Journal,* 1840, House Doc. No. 31.

Document 40

The Public Face of the University

The University Catalog for 1840–1841 presented a formal outline of the workaday university's operations. Historically this interesting document presents a clear summary of an institution struggling to achieve high objectives with severely limited faculty and student body.

*   *   *

Board of Trustees.

DAVID H. MAXWELL, M. D., *of the County of* MONROE,
PRESIDENT OF THE BOARD
MILES C. EGGLESTON, *of the County of* JEFFERSON.
WILLIAM T. S. CORNET, *of the County of* RIPLEY.
ROBERT DALE OWEN, *of the County of* POSEY.
NATHANIEL WEST, *of the County of* MARION.
JOHN LAW, *of the County of* KNOX.
JOSEPH S. JENCKES, *of the County of* VIGO.
LOT BLOOMFIELD, *of the County of* WAYNE.
JAMES SCOTT, *of the County of* CLARK.

JAMES D. MAXWELL,
Secretary of the Board.

FACULTY.

REV. ANDREW WYLIE, D. D.,
PRESIDENT,
and Professor of Moral and Mental Philosophy, and Belles Lettres.

REV. THEOPHILUS A. WYLIE, A. M.,
Professor of Natural Philosophy and Chemistry.

JACOB AMMEN,
Professor of Mathematics and Civil Engineering.

J. I. MORRISON, A. M.,
Professor of Languages.

MATTHEW M. CAMPBELL, A. M.,
Principal of the Preparatory Department.

JOSEPH M. HOWE,
Treasurer of the University.

CATALOGUE OF STUDENTS.

RESIDENT GRADUATES.

John A. Clement,	*Princeton, Indiana.*
John R. Cravens,	*Madison, Indiana.*
John W. Dunbar,	*Natchez, Mississippi.*

RESIDENT GRADUATES, 3.

SENIORS.

Richard T. Allison,	*Jefferson County, Kentucky.*
John F. Dodds,	*Monroe County, Indiana.*
Hugh A. McKelvy,	*Randolph County, Illinois.*
Albert R. Shannon,	*Carmi, Illinois.*
Charles B. Thomas,	*Lexington, Kentucky.*
John H. Wylie,	*Bloomington, Indiana.*

SENIORS, 6.

JUNIORS.

Wm. Borden,	*Providence, Indiana.*
Isaac B. Gwathmey,	*Louisville, Kentucky.*
James F. Hester,	*Bloomington, Indiana.*
Samuel Millen,	do. do.
David W. Stormont,	*Princeton, Indiana.*
Henry Tanner,	*Washington County, Indiana.*
James Woodburn,	*Monroe County, Indiana.*

JUNIORS, 7.

SOPHOMORES.

John Borden,	*Providence, Indiana.*
Robert B. Campbell,	*Bloomington, Indiana.*
Richard A. Gwathmey,	*Louisville, Kentucky.*
William H. Head,	*Louisville, Mississippi.*
John A. Hendricks,	*Madison, Indiana.*
Levi Hughes,	*Bloomington, Indiana.*
James Hughes,	do. do.
Orrick Metcalfe,	*Adams County, Mississippi.*
George H. Monson,	*Bedford, Indiana.*
Samuel T. Wylie,	*Bloomington, Indiana.*

SOPHOMORES, 10.

FRESHMEN.

Wm. H. Jones,	*Louisville, Kentucky.*
Hiram Moyer,	*Orleans, Indiana.*
G. M. Overstreet,	*Johnson County, Indiana.*
Elijah M. Parks,	*Monroe County, Indiana.*
Joseph D. Ray,	do. do. do.
Paul S. Seig,	*Harrison County, Indiana.*
Beverly Ratcliff,	*Washington County, Indiana.*

FRESHMEN, 7.

IRREGULARS.

Preston Beck,	*Bolivar, Missouri.*
James W. Metcalfe	*Adams County, Mississippi.*
James M. Rawlins,	*Bedford, Indiana.*
Daniel H. Sessions,	*Adams County, Mississippi.*
Nelson G. Coffin,	*Vermillion County, Indiana.*
J. F. Kelso,	*Dubois County, Indiana.*
Davis Batterton,	*Bloomington, Indiana.*
Robert Clark,	*Monroe County, Indiana.*
Edward Cannon,	*Louisville, Kentucky.*
Clarendon Davisson,	*Monroe County, Indiana.*
Thomas J. Edmonson,	do. do. do.
James M. Mathes,	*Gosport, Indiana.*
Milton Hight,	*Monroe County, Indiana.*
John Moore,	do. do. do.
William Ruddick,	*Columbus, Indiana.*
J. S. Speed,	*Louisville, Kentucky.*
John O. McKinney,	*Livonia, Indiana.*

IRREGULARS, 17.

PREPARATORY DEPARTMENT.

Jesse J. Alexander,	*Gosport, Indiana.*
Granville Batterton,	*Bloomington, Indiana.*
A. H. Baldwin,	*Harrison County, Indiana.*
E. F. M. Blair,	*Bloomington, Indiana.*
William Blair,	*Monroe County, Indiana.*
Issac M. Brown,	do. do. do.
George Butler,	*Bloomington, Indiana.*
James Carter,	do. do.
John Campbell,	do. do.
Shadrach Chandler,	*Brown County, Indiana.*
Richard Denton,	*Bloomington, Indiana.*
William T. Downs,	*Woodville, Mississippi.*
John A Farmer,	*Monroe County, Indiana.*
R. N. Fee,	do. do. do.
James Green,	*Bloomington, Indiana.*
Addison Hill,	do. do.
John H. Killough,	*Monroe County, Indiana.*
Gabriel Laberteaux,	*Bloomington, Indiana.*
Armwell Lockwood,	*Washington County, Indiana.*
David H. Maxwell,	*Bloomington, Indiana.*
William McMahan,	*Harrison County, Indiana.*
Alexander McCaughan,	*Monroe County, Indiana.*
John A. Millen,	*Bloomington, Indiana.*
Robert Morris,	*Washington County, Indiana.*
James H. Nield,	*Monroe County, Indiana.*
Alexander Owens,	*Bloomington, Indiana.*
James Seward,	do. do.
William Stone,	*Monroe County, Indiana.*
John Stone,	do. do. do.

William Stewart,   *Indianapolis, Indiana.*
Henry Wright,   *Washington County, Indiana.*
PREPARATORY
DEPARTMENT, 31.

RECAPITULATION.

Resident Graduates, ...	3
Seniors, ...	6
Juniors, ...	7
Sophomores, ...	10
Freshmen, ...	7
Irregulars	17
Preparatory Department	31
Total, ...	81

A STATEMENT
OF THE
COURSE OF INSTRUCTION, EXPENSES, &c.
IN
INDIANA UNIVERSITY.

Terms of Admission.

CANDIDATES for admission to the FRESHMAN CLASS are examined in Arithmetic, English Grammar, the Grammars of the Latin and Greek Languages, Caesar's Commentaries, Sallust, Cicero's Select Orations, Ovid, (first three books and thirteenth), six books of Virgil's Æneid, and the first course of Jacob's Greek Reader. These studies are attended to in the PREPARATORY DEPARTMENT, in which instructions are also given in Orthography, Reading, Writing and English Composition.

A candidate for an advanced standing, whether from another College or not, in addition to the preparatory studies, is examined in the various branches to which the class he proposes to enter has attended.

Testimonials of good moral character in all cases are required; and those who are admitted from other Colleges must produce certificates of dismission in good standing.

Course of Instruction.

The whole course of study, in the University proper, occupies four years. In each year, there are two terms or sessions.

By a recent arrangement adopted by the Faculty, an opportunity is given to the JUNIOR CLASS to enjoy the advantage of instruction by the President, along with their other studies in those of his Department.

The method pursued by the President in regard to the higher branches which fall under his care, it may be proper here to state. Daily lectures are given, and dissertations are each day required of the student, on the basis of notes taken by him of the preceding lecture. The substance of these is condensed into the form of a syllabus; and afterwards opportunity is given for free discussion, in a thorough catechetical examination of the whole.

Each of the four classes attends three recitations or lectures in a day.

The following scheme gives a general view of the authors recited by the several classes in each term:

FRESHMAN CLASS.

I.
- Horace's Odes and Epistles.
- Jacob's Greek Reader.
- Fiske's Classical Manual, Part I.
- Grammatical Exercises and Written Translations.
- Davies' Bourdon's Algebra.

II.
- Horace's Satires and Art of Poetry.
- Xenophon's Anabasis.
- Fiske's Classical Manual, Part II.
- Grammatical Exercises and Written Translations.
- Davies's Legendre's Geometry and Trigonometry.

A recitation in the Greek Testament, every Monday morning during the year.

SOPHOMORE CLASS.

I.
- Folsom's Livy.
- Homer's Iliad, commenced.
- Classical Manual, Part III. and IV.
- Anthon's Greek Prosody, with Scanning.
- Davies' Surveying and Analytical Geometry.
- Natural Philosophy, preparatory course commenced.

II.
- Virgil's Georgics and Cicero de Officiis.
- Homer's Iliad, finished.
- Classical Manual, Part V. with Ancient Geography.
- Anthon's Greek Prosody, with Scanning.
- Davies' Differential and Integral Calculus.
- Natural Philosophy, preparatory course finished.

Part of the Greek Testament are read during the year.

JUNIOR CLASS.

I.
- Cicero de Oratore.
- Xenophon's Memorabilia of Socrates.
- Davies' Descriptive Geometry.
- Cambridge Mechanics, Statics and Dynamics.
- Turner's Chemistry. Heat and Electricity.
- Blair's and Campbell's Rhetoric, with Lectures.

II.
- Juvenal and Persius, or Cicero de Sensctute and Cicero de Amictia.
- Demosthenes' Select Orations.
- Cambridge Mechanics, completed.
- Optics. Bache's Brewster.
- Inorganic Chemistry.
- Whateley's Logic. Lectures by the President.

SENIOR CLASS.

I.
- Tacitus: the History.
- Longinus.
- Astronomy, Gummere.
- Moral Philosophy, and Evidences of Christianity, with Lectures by the President.

II. $\left\{ \begin{array}{l} \text{Tacitus: Manners of the Germans and Agricola.} \\ \text{Woolsey's Greek Plays.} \\ \text{Chemistry Completed.} \\ \text{Say's Political Economy; Reid's and Stewart's Mental} \\ \qquad \text{Philosophy, with Lectures; and Constitution of the} \\ \qquad \text{United States.} \end{array} \right.$

Declamations, Essays and Rhetorical Reading, by all the Classes, on every Saturday during the whole course.

In addition to the regular course of instruction here given, such as desire it may receive instruction in Hebrew, French, Civil Engineering and Book-Keeping. And to those who wish to accomplish themselves in Civil Engineering, an opportunity is afforded, during the summer session, of exercising under the direction of the Professor, in practical operations with the Theodolite, Compass and Level; and in making maps and draughts for bridges, railroads and other public works.

The Chemical lectures, as well as those on Natural Philosophy, are illustrated by a course of experiments. A Laboratory and Lecture Room have recently been erected on the University campus, entirely separate from the principal building, for the express accommodation of this department. It offers to young gentlemen, who intend ultimately to devote themselves to the Medical Profession, great advantages.

A course of Lectures on History will be delivered by the President of the University, once a week, to the Freshman and Sophomore Classes.

Specimens of English Composition are exhibited at least once a fortnight by all the Classes. Written translations from Latin and Greek authors are presented weekly by the Freshman, Sophomore and Junior Classes. These Classes are also instructed in Latin and Greek Composition. The Senior and Junior Classes have occasional disputations before their instructors.

The object of the course of instruction given to the under graduates in this Institution, is to commence a thorough course, and continue the same, so far as the time of the students' residence at the University will permit. The course prescribed embraces those subjects only which ought to be understood by every one who aims at a liberal education. The principles of science and literature are the common basis of all high intellectual attainments. They supply that furniture, and discipline, and elevation to the mind, which are the best aids in the study of any profession. The student, in further prosecution of his professional career, may enter a school of Law, or Medicine, or Theology. With these the under graduate course is not intended to interfere. The object is, not to teach what is peculiar to any of the professions, but to lay a foundation which is common to all.

Arrangements are now in progress by which a separate LAW SCHOOL, in connection with the University, will be established under the care of a distinguished member of the Profession. There, one branch of those higher studies which more immediately qualify the student for the actual duties of life, will be completed.

There are two public examinations in a year; one in March, and the other in September.

A semi-annual session of the Board of Trustees begins on the Monday before Commencement. On Commencement, which takes place on the last Wednesday in September, the candidates for degrees each deliver in public a thesis on some subject selected by themselves.

There are two vacations in a year, each of a month; the one beginning at

Commencement, the other at the close of the Winter Session. No student is allowed to be absent without leave, except in vacation. The absence of a student, even for a few days, in term time, exerts on his progress an evil influence which is seldom fully appreciated by parents and guardians. For a similar reason, no apology but that of sickness or other unavoidable accident is suffered to excuse a student from regular attendance at recitation.

Discipline.

In the government of the University, the leading principle is to procure strict discipline by mild means. It is considered a more effectual mode of forming the character, to call into exercise the reason and moral sense of the student by parental appeals, than merely to coerce an outward form of obedience by forcing his will. The ultimate endeavor is, to enable and induce him to govern himself.

For minor offences or neglect of collegiate duties, students are admonished or reprimanded, in private or in public, by the Professor, or by the President on behalf of the Faculty. For graver delinquencies or obstinate insubordination, suspension is the ultimate punishment.

Public Worship.

Prayers are held in the chapel every morning before the recitations commence; and all the students are required to attend, unless excused by the President.

In accordance with the provision of the University Charter, that no exclusive privilege shall be accorded to any particular sect, the Chapel of the University is open to the reception of the ministers of every denomination of Christians for purposes of Public Worship, under the direction of the Faculty, giving no preference to any, but securing to each who may desire it, an equal participation in the use of the Chapel for that object.

In obedience to the same principle, the following is one of the bye-laws of the Institution:

"It is recommended, that each student attend Public Worship every Sabbath day in the University Chapel, or such other place of worship as his parents or guardians may designate, or his conscience approve."

Literary Societies

There are two Literary Societies connected with the University, nearly equal in number of members, and both in a flourishing condition; the PHILOMATHEAN and the ATHENIAN Societies. Each has a well selected Library of several hundred volumes; and each occupies a room in the principal University building, handsomely fitted up by the gradual contributions of the members.

Such Societies are of high value in a Collegiate Institution. They teach young men to think and act for themselves, preparatory to their entrance upon the great drama of life. They tend also to initiate the students in the art of public speaking, useful in all countries—indispensable in our own.

Library.

The Collegiate Library is open to all the students, on paying a subscription of *fifty cents* per session. Each subscriber is permitted to take out a volume every Saturday.

This library has recently been augmented by a purchase of about two thousand dollars worth of books, some of them rare and valuable. It embraces a choice collection of Greek, Latin, French and English Classics; the best standard works on History, Biography and the Sciences; together with a selected variety of Miscellaneous Literature.

Military Exercises.

At such seasons as the weather permits, a portion of the students are instructed by the Professor of Civil Engineering (himself a graduate, and formerly an Assistant Professor, at West Point,) in Military Exercises. The hour of drill is after recitation hours; and attendance, on the part of students, is voluntary. Arms have been furnished by the Government.

Expenses.

The fees in the College Proper are *Twelve Dollars* a session; in the Preparatory Department *eight and a half dollars* a session.

Students can board and lodge in private families at from *a dollar and a half* to *two dollars* a week. Boarding and lodging may be had in the Boarding House belonging to the University, recently erected on the campus, at *a dollar and seventy-five cents* a week. Washing will cost about *five dollars* a session.

With regard to apparel and pocket money, it is earnestly recommended to all parents sending their children to this Institution, no matter how wealthy they may be, not to furnish them with extravagant means. The character and scholarship of the students are often grievously injured by a free indulgence in the use of money. Whatever is furnished beyond a moderate supply for ordinary expenses, exposes the student to numerous temptations; and endangers, rather than increases, his happiness and respectability.

As a precaution against extravagance, it is suggested that parents at a distance may deposite funds with some one residing in the vicinity of the Institution, and in whom they have confidence; who, in that case, may pay particular attention to the pecuniary concerns of the student, settle his bills and correspond with the parent, transmitting an account of the expenditure, &c.

Or, if a parent or guardian prefer trusting to the honor and self-command of his son or ward, he may entrust him with the funds necessary to bear his expenses for a quarter or for a session, exacting from him an account, containing every item of expenditure, to be sent home at stated periods.

The utmost vigilance will, on all suitable occasions, be exerted by the faculty, to prevent the indulgence, by any student, in habits of extravagance and dissipation. Yet it must be borne in mind by those in whose sons, before they reach this Institution, such habits have become inveterate, that the indirect influence which can alone be exerted by the Faculty on the private conduct of students residing without the walls of the University, may sometimes fail to correct the vices of years; and that, where reproof and remonstrance fail, it may become necessary, in order to protect others from the influence of evil example, to resort to the ultimate remedy of dismission, suspension, or—acting in conjunction with the Board of Trustees—expulsion from the University.

APPENDIX

BY THE BOARD OF TRUSTEES.

A law, which originated in the Report of an Examining Committee of the Legislature of Indiana, charged to investigate the affairs of Indiana University, was passed at the last session. That law re-organized the Board of Trustees, reduced their number to nine, and required them to meet on the third Monday in July, at Bloomington, and then and there to enter on the discharge of their supervisory duties as guardians of the State Institution over which they have been called to preside.

They found the result of the recent measures which have been adopted by the Legislature, in conjunction with the efforts of the former Board and present Faculty, to be most satisfactory. Undisturbed harmony now reigns, not only within the walls of the Institution itself, but in all its relations with the citizens of the adjoining town and surrounding country. The increased industry and accelerated progress of the students, give evidence how much has been gained to the Institution by liberation from the distracting influence of local jealousies and petty jarrings from without, and by the recent accession of two members of high reputation to her Faculty.

In regard to the entire under graduate course of the University, the Board have found little to amend; and they feel assured, that nothing now is wanting to the full prosperity of this portion of the Institution, except to persevere, firmly and quietly, in the good work thus successfully begun.

Commencement Week.

In addition to the usual exercises on Commencement occasion, an address is expected from ROBT. DALE OWENS, to the Monroe County Lyceum; and also an address from JOHN WILSON, Esq., to the Philomathean Society.

Catalogue of the Officers and Students in Indiana University, 1840–41.

Document 41

A Nine-Man Board of Trustees

The number of trustees was reduced from twenty-one to nine by this act of the General Assembly, February 15, 1841. The powers of the Board were broadly outlined, and their jurisdiction over student affairs was established in at least two specific areas. The new law amended that of 1838.

*   *   *

CHAPTER XXVII.

An Act to provide for a better regulation of the Indiana University.
[APPROVED, FEBRUARY 15, 1841.]

SEC. 1. *Be it enacted by the General Assembly of the State of Indiana,* That the board of trustees of the Indiana University is hereby reduced to the number of nine, a majority of whom shall constitute a quorum, and the following named persons shall constitute said board, to-wit: Miles C. Eggleston, of the county of Jefferson, William T. S. Cornet, of the county of Ripley, Robert Dale Owen, of the county of Posey, Nathaniel West, of the county of Marion, John Law, of the county of Knox, David H. Maxwell, of the county of Monroe, Elisha M. Huntington, of the county of Vigo, Lot Bloomfield, of the county of Wayne, and James Scott, of the county of Clark.

SEC. 2. Said board shall have full power to fill the vacancies in their own body and to fix the times of their semi-annual meetings after their first meeting which is hereby directed to commence on the third Monday of July next: *Provided,* That there shall not be two trustees from the same county at any one time.

SEC. 3. The civil courts of the state shall have no jurisdiction to punish trivial breaches of the peace committed by the students of said university within the college campus.

SEC. 4. Said students are hereby exempted from militia duty and road taxes during their continuance at the university.

SEC. 5. If any trustee shall fail to attend two consecutive regular meetings of the board without satisfactory excuse in writing, his seat shall be *ipso facto* vacant. The members of the board shall each have the same *per diem* and mileage as members of the legislature, to be paid out of the college fund.

SEC. 6. It shall be the duty of the secretary of state to forward to the president of the university a certified copy of this act within ten days after its passage. And it shall be the duty of said president to inform the trustees created by this act of their appointment within ten days after he shall receive said certified copy.

SEC. 7. So much of the act entitled "an act to establish a university in the state of Indiana," approved February 15, 1838, as comes within the purview of this act, be, and the same is hereby repealed.

Laws of Indiana, 1840–41 (general), pp. 110–111.

Document 42

The Jacksonian Surplus Funds

All across the country in the late 1830s and 1840s, legislators, state officials, and crusading educational leaders sought to procure and use the surplus funds distributed by the United States Government. Indiana University had shared in this windfall, and the Board of Trustees, July 28, 1841, wished to have these funds secured through the responsibility of the state treasurer and to draw on them through the legislature, thus establishing the greatest possible protection.

*　　*　　*

Copy of a letter from D. K. MAXWELL, *President Board of Trustees of Indiana State University.*

BLOOMINGTON, *July* 28, 1841.

GEORGE H. DUNN, ESQ.

Treasurer of Indiana.

SIR:—At the late meeting of the Board of Trustees of Indiana University the following resolutions were adopted viz:

Resolved, That in the opinion of this Board the 10th section of the act of February 1841 entitled "an act to amend an act approved February 6th 1837" entitled an act to provide for distributing so much of the surplus revenue of the United States as the State of Indiana may be entitled to, and receive by virtue of an act of Congress approved January 23d 1836, and which provides that the funds of the Indiana University, which it was generally intended should be secured by the Treasurer of State by mortgages upon real estate, be for the future invested in the stock of the State Bank of Indiana, is deemed by this Board an impolitic change of the investment of said funds and having by possibility a tendency to render the same hereafter less secure and certain than they would be, if secured as they were before the passage of said act, by mortgages on real estate.

Resolved 2d, That it is our earnest desire, that the original plan of permanent security, which has heretofore worked *admirably well,* should be continued, and that the President of the Board communicate this resolution to the Treasurer of State, expressing to him the very great advantages to the best interests of the University which the Board conceives would result, if he the said Treasurer, could consistently with his duty as a State officer, delay to place any of said funds in Bank until the ensuing session of the Legislature, and the Board have an opportunity of memorializing the said Legislature on the subject,

Resolved 3d, That the President of the Board present to the next Legislature, a memorial setting forth their wishes upon this subject, and requesting the repeal of so much of said 10th section of the act of February 5th, 1841 as relates to the funds of Indiana University.

Indiana *Documentary Journal,* 1841, House Doc. # 5, p. 61.

Document 43

Free Tuition

Although the Indiana General Assembly made no direct appropriation to the support of the University, its members were quick to examine its financial conditions and to take advantage of the constitutional provisions establishing the institution. This free tuition issue was to dog the progress of the institution for years and reflected more of a desire to hold down costs than to advance the University into the rising scientific fields.

*   *   *

CHAPTER CLXXI.
A Joint Resolution of the Legislature of the State of Indiana in
relation to Indiana University.
[APPROVED, JANUARY 27, 1842.]

Whereas, It is made the duty of the General Assembly of the State of Indiana, by the second section of the 9th article of the constitution of the aforesaid State, so soon as circumstances will permit, to provide by law for a general system of education, ascending in a regular gradation from township schools to a State University, wherein tuition shall be gratis and open to all: Therefore,

Be it resolved by the General Assembly of the State of Indiana, That the trustees of Indiana University be, and are hereby required, at the next regular meeting of said board, to examine into the resources of said University and make full and complete report of the same to the next Legislature, together with the amount of salaries paid to professors, and all other expenses of said institution; and also, whether in their opinion the resources of said University are sufficient to enable the Legislature to pass a law making tuition gratis, in compliance with the constitution of the State above referred to.

Laws of Indiana (general), 1841–42, pp. 174–175.

Document 44

Gubernatorial Rhetoric

Governor Bigger's description of the state of the University was more glowing than was the actual condition of the institution. In a message to the General Assembly on December 6, 1842, he called for a large order to at once conserve its funds and to extend its reputation.

* * *

. . . .

It affords me great pleasure to communicate to the Legislature, that the affairs of the Indiana University present a more prosperous appearance than they have exhibited for several years. The recent efforts to give efficiency to its organization, promise to be eminently successful, and to secure to the State the full benefits of its ample endowments. In the supervision of this institution, the Legislature has a most important trust. To make it extensively useful; to preserve its funds, and render them productive, and to extend its reputation, constitute the prominent duties of this trust, which, if faithfully executed must add to the character and dignity of the State.

. . . .

Indiana *Senate Journal,* 1842–43, pp. 14-24.

Document 45

Beginnings of the Law School

This was the University's first real adventure beyond the narrow pale of the liberal arts and was to become a major division of the instructional program in the future.

* * *

LAW SCHOOL
PROFESSOR HON. DAVID M'DONALD.

In establishing this department, it is the design of the Board of Trustees to build up a Law School that will furnish to gentlemen intended for the bar, a complete course of legal education. But as time and experience are necessary in order to establish such an institution upon a firm basis, and to give it such a character as will insure its success, it has been deemed advisable to adopt a merely temporary arrangement for the present year. Accordingly the next session of the Law School will commence on the first Monday of December, and will continue for three months; after which time, the Board will establish such permanent regulations, as the success and utility of the department may seem to require.

It is intended that the course of study shall occupy four sessions. The students will be divided into two classes—the Junior and the Senior. It is desirable that all students commence with the Junior Class. Those, however, who have elsewhere made sufficient progress in the study of the law, may, if they prefer it, be at once admitted to the Senior Class, And gentlemen, not wishing to study law as a profession, may enter the Junior Class for instruction in that part of the course, which relates to International, Constitutional and Commercial law.

The text-books of the Junior Class are Blackstone's Commentaries, Story's Commentaries on the Constitution, Chitty on Contracts, Stephen on Pleading, and Kent's Commentaries; those of the Senior Class are Kent's Commentaries, Chitty on Bills, Chitty's Pleading, Starkie's Evidence, Story's Equity Jurisprudence, and Story's Equity Pleading. Students must furnish themselves with text-books; but those who enter the Junior Class will not need the books of the Senior, till the end of the first year.

Besides daily examinations on the text-books, the Professor will deliver a course of lectures embracing the various branches of International and Constitutional law, Common law, and Equity Jurisprudence. He will hold a moot court once a week, in which the students will be exercised in drawing pleadings, and arguing legal questions and law cases previously given out; and on each of which he will afterwards deliver an opinion, as well on the questions of law involved, as on the manner of the arguments.

Persons applying for admission into the department must produce satisfactory testimonials of good moral character.

Students, when deemed qualified for graduation, will receive diplomas, under the direction of the Board of Trustees.

Number of Students in the University.

For 1839–40	64
" 1840–41	81
" 1841–42	89
" 1842–43	115

At a Public Commencement held in September, 1842, the following gentlemen received the Degree of Bachelor of Arts:

ISAAC B. GWATHMEY,	*Louisville,*	Kentucky
SAMUEL MILLEN,	*Bloomington,*	Indiana
GEORGE H. MONSON,	*Bedford,*	do.
DAVID W. STORMONT,	*Princeton,*	do.
HENRY TANNER,	*Salem,*	do.
JAMES WOODBURN,	*Bloomington,*	do.

Catalogue of the Trustees, Officers, and Students of Indiana University, 1842–3 (Bloomington, 1843), pp. 17–18.

Document 46

John Borden's Report

Free of the rhetoric of politicians and the sometimes vague formalities of trustees, professors, and the president, John Borden viewed Blooming-ton and Indiana University at freshman-eye level. Certainly his views did not have the endorsement of the Presbyterian minister or of "Mr. Orchard the money-grubber."

*   *   *

Bloomington May 19th 1843

Dear Mother,—

. . . .

If you want to know what I am going to do this session, I can tell you, that I am going to do my best. And, by the bye that's about as much as can be asked of any body.

As [to] the folks they all live by eating and drinking as usual—especially myself. They have about as much t[a]ste as [?],—which is about [fit] that of hogs in a pigpen. If any of them were taken through their criticism and asked what is man's chief end: there is no doubt that they would answer making money. Mr Orchard would answ[er] man's chief end is to make all he can and cheat all he can. And he is not alone in that particular. There is certainly less taste, less sense, higher prices and more rascality in this place than exists on [a]ny other spot of ground of its size in United States, except some choice spots on Salt creek. In short this place would never be heard of, except on account of it mud and counterfeiters if it was not for the college down at the lower end of it. In common language it is about [10]0 miles from every other place, & 200 to w[h]ere any body lives. It is [n]o wonder then that [nothing] of importance is to [be] told of this place or its people, and it is no wonder then that short letters find their way out of here.

The trustees me[et] [som]e time in June. It is then expected that Morrison [and Ammen] will resign their seats. This is no rumor it is . . . understood that Ammen has or is going to reccommend [*sic*] a graduate of West Point as a proper person to supply his . . .

If you have gotten any thing to send out to me you need not send it by the stage if you do, I don't expect ever to see it. I left my trunk at Orleans when I came up, and not withstanding I told them to be sure and take it out it came near going on a trip to Indianapolis.

. . . .

Your son
J. Borden

Indiana Division, Mss. State Library.

Document 47

The Boarding House Club—the Beginnings of a Bloomington Tradition

Bloomington was too small a town fully to accommodate even a small university student body with proper lodging and boarding facilities. Too, students were as frugal as governors and state legislators, and they sought to reduce costs for themselves. This was a forerunner of the campus dormitory, and was also an attempt to by-pass the abuses mentioned by John Borden in the previous document.

*   *   *

The following resolutions were unanimously adopted.

Resolved That the request of the applicants, viz. Messrs Irwin, Simler, McBride, Wells Lhuck, J. Love T. Love Wood Fravel, Bates and Roberts; that the New Boarding House be granted to them for their use and the use of such as may hereafter associate with them, be acceded [*sic*] to, on the following conditions

The above students are to be considered the nucleus of an association to which the above boarding house is granted, for the purpose of aiding them in self boarding; possession to be given so soon as the said students shall have made out for themselves, and sighned, a code of laws and regulations for the preservation of domestic order; which code shall meet the approval of Professor Campbell, who, in token of such approval, shall thereto append his signature, and shall *ex officio*, have a seat in all meetings of the association.

In the above code shall be incorporated a provision that each bed room, except that in which the stairs ascend shall be occupied as the association is filled up, by two students

And also, that each student pay one dollar per session as rent; which rent shall be placed in the hands of a committee of three, namely two students selected by the association and Profr Campbell, and shall be appropriated every session under the direction of said Committee in current repairs of said boarding house

When the said Boarding House is entirely filled up as above the old building adjoining shall be granted upon the same terms. The right is reserved to the trustees and faculty or any member of either body, to visit and inspect, at any time, the said houses; and it is made the special duty of Professor Campbell to see to it, that the code of regulations adopted by the above students is strictly enforced by them. A failure in the association to enforce their regulations shall work a forfeiture of this grant The garden lying east of said boarding house, and the lot east of the garden, extending to the east line of the campus, is granted free of rent to the association, they keeping at all times the fences of said garden and lot in good repair, except the fence common to said lot and the campus. The repair of the board fence around the houses, to be paid for out of the fund for current repairs as above provided for.

Board Minutes, 29 September 1843, pp. 158–159.

Document 48

*State of the University in the Cardinal
Year of National Expansion*

James Knox Polk was still President of the United States, and the nation had just concluded the Mexican War and had negotiated the Treaty of Guadeloupe-di-Hidalgo with Mexico which added a vast new area to the republic. Gold had already been discovered in California, and within a month of this report there would begin the feverish gold rush activity to the Far West. Internally the nation enjoyed a certain degree of prosperity, and there was an increasing consciousness of the cultural and practical educational responsibilities of the American people. This Annual Report reflects both Indiana and the University's situation in this moment of national excitement.

*   *   *

HON. PARIS C. DUNNING,
> *President of the Senate:*

Please lay before the Senate over which you have the honor to preside, the accompanying Annual Report of the "Trustees of the Indiana University."
> Respectfully,
>> DAVID H. MAXWELL,
>>> *President of the Board of Trustees of Indiana University.*

BLOOMINGTON, INDIANA, Dec. 12, 1848.

In Senate, 16*th December* 1848, read and laid on the table, and 500 copies ordered to be printed for the use of the Senate.

CHARLES H. TEST,
Secretary of the Senate

HON. GEO. W. CARR,
> *Speaker of the House of Representatives:*

Please lay before the House of Representatives, over which you preside, the accompanying Annual Report of the Board of Trustees of the Indiana University.
> Respectfully,
>> D. H. MAXWELL,
>> *President of the Board of
>> Trustees.*

BLOOMINGTON, Dec. 12, 1848.

HALL OF THE HOUSE OF
REPRESENTATIVES,
December 18th, 1848.

Read and laid on the table, and one thousand copies ordered to be printed for the use of the House.

J. W. DODD, *Clerk.*

REPORT.

To the General Assembly of the State of Indiana:

In compliance with a resolution of the Legislature of Indiana, passed January 15th, 1848, the Trustees of the Indiana University, respectfully submit the following Report, showing the progress and condition of the University.

OFFICERS OF THE UNIVERSITY.

By the Charter, the following State Officers constitute a Board of Visitors, viz: the Governor of the State, the Lieutenant Governor, the Speaker of the House of Representatives, the Judges of the Supreme Court, the Judge of the Monroe Circuit, and the Superintendent of Common Schools.

While individual members of this Board have frequently been present at the public exercises of the University, they have never officially organized themselves as a Board.

The Board of Trustees at the close of the College year consisted of the following members, viz:

David H. Maxwell, of the county of Monroe.

James Scott, of the county of Clark.

Miles C. Eggleston, of the county of Jefferson.

William T. S. Cornet, of the county of Ripley.

Joseph S. Jenckes, of the county of Vigo.

James Morrison, of the county of Marion.

John W. Davis, of the county of Sullivan.

John I. Morrison, of the county of Washington.

Albert S. White, of the county of Tippecanoe.

At the late meeting of the Board, letters of resignation of two members, viz: of Miles C. Eggleston and John W. Davis, were presented and accepted.

Robert Dale Owen, of the county of Posey, and Joseph L. Jernegan, of the county of St. Joseph, were elected to fill these vacancies. The Board of Trustees meet each year, and for several years past there has been no failure of a quorum for business. A committee of three from the Board, is also appointed to be present at the annual and semi-annual examinations of the classes in the University.

The provision of the Charter requiring the Trustees to be chosen from different counties, effectually guards against merely local and neighborhood influences.

THE FACULTY.

The Board of Trustees in the selection of the Faculty of Instruction, has been governed by the single motive of securing the best qualification and experience which their means would command. The following are the number of this body, as exhibited in the Catalogue of this year:

Andrew Wylie, President, and Professor of Moral Philosophy.

Daniel Read, Professor of Languages.

Theophilus A. Wylie, Professor of Natural Philosophy.

Alfred Ryors, Professor of Mathematics.

David McDonald, }
William T. Otto, } Professors of Law.

M. M. Campbell, Principal of the Preparatory Department.

Professor Ryors, in consequence of a call to a University which was able to offer higher inducements for his services, resigned his connection with this University, near the close of the last College session. At the late meeting of the Board, Washington McCartney, Esq., a distinguished Mathematician, and author of a text book on the application of the Differential and Integral Calculus to Geometry, was elected to supply this important chair. But, unfortunately, he had previously entered into engagements with another Institution, which prevented his acceptance. The duties of the chair are, for the present, distributed among the other Professors.

Since this Report was made, a letter has been received by the President of the Board from Professor McCartney, notifying him of his acceptance of the Professorship in the University, which had been previously tendered to him.

STUDENTS.

The number of Students for each year, from 1840, has been as follows, viz:

1840 64
1841 81
1842 89
1843 115
1844 160
1845 174
1846 198
1847 163

The number of Students for the year closing in September last, was 177. Arranged according to the following classification:

Seniors 6
Juniors 12
Sophomores 21
Freshmen 20
Scientific and Irregular 39
Preparatory 50
Law 29

The number of Students in attendance upon the several Departments of Instruction for the past year, not including those in the Preparatory Classes, is as follows:

Moral Philosophy, &c., ...24
Natural Philosophy and Chemistry, ...43
Languages, ...64
Mathematics, ...66
Law, ...29

The highest number which the University has at any time had, from other States than Indiana, is *thirty-one*. The number for the present year, from other States, is *nineteen*. For the more specific residence of Students, reference is made to the annual Catalogue, copies of which have been forwarded for the use of the Legislature. A register of the ages of Students was at one time kept, but it was found that those somewhat advanced in years, felt much delicacy in giving their ages, but the practice of making enquiry was abandoned. It may, however, be remarked, that the Students are in general of more mature years, than those of Colleges in the older States.

It is not unfrequent that Ministers of the Gospel are found in the classes of the University.

Since the passage of the law, authorizing two Students from each county in the State, to be taught gratuitously, the average number in attendance of those who have availed themselves of the privilege, has been about *sixty.*

The County Provision, and the Boarding Club, hereafter to be mentioned, so reduce the expenses of Education, as to bring it within the attainment of most young men of enterprise. The entire expenses of the Student, availing himself of these privileges are considerably less than the tuition alone, in many of our American Colleges. Indeed, not more zeal, industry, self-denial, and energy of character, are requisite to secure to the most indigent, the advantages of the State University, than are necessary to enable a young man to rise in his profession after he has acquired an education.

The Board by no means present either *cheapness,* or *number* of *Students,* as the chief tests of the merits of an Institution of higher education. The late President Dew declares in regard to William and Mary College, that when that time-honored Institution was sending forth those distinguished men, which caused Virginia to be hailed as the mother of great men, there was at no time within the walls of the College, a number of Students exceeding sixty. It is the spirit of a College, its thorough scholarship, its influence in elevating and purifying the sentiments of community, which entitle it to public confidence and support.

COURSE OF STUDY.

The whole course of study in the College proper, occupies four years. There are four classes, each attending three recitations in a day. It is the design of the University to maintain the highest standard of education which the state of the country will admit.

It is an evil, incident to a new state of society, that young men, from want of means, from haste to enter professional life, and other causes, take only a partial course of study. But whatever studies the student undertakes, he is required to pursue in a rigorously accurate and thorough manner. None are permitted to graduate unless they have completed the prescribed course, which is as extensive as usual in our oldest and best regulated Colleges.

Students, however, completing the course of any one Department, are entitled to Diplomas, certifying that fact. The scheme of study pursued by each of the classes is given in the Catalogue. The following statement in regard to the several Departments will exhibit the course of instruction as pursued in each.

PREPARATORY DEPARTMENT.

Connected with the Institution is a flourishing Grammar School, which serves the double purpose of a Normal School and a Preparatory Department. In this the studies are arranged by the session, while in College they are arranged by the year. Besides thorough drilling in the elements of Latin and Greek, (including Virgil in Latin, and the Greek Reader, as the most advanced studies,) preparatory to the Freshman Class, a full course of instruction is given each session in English Grammar, Geography and Arithmetic. This is often attended by Teachers, who sometimes bear strong testimony to the superior advantages they enjoy here over any school they ever attended.

This arises in part, at least, from the superior classification and concentration of effort. All who are engaged in the same study, are classed together, and an hour is usually spent at the recitation, partly in oral instruction, but chiefly in a close examination of the class, on the lesson assigned, and in a more general examination by way of review of preceding lessons. Most of the students in this department, as in the regular classes of the University, are young men, consequently most of them have previously made some progress in their English studies, and those who have made the most derive most benefit from the instruction here given. The Latin and Greek languages, however, are commenced each session, and no preparation for admission is necessary beyond that, which every son needs upon leaving the paternal roof; good moral principles and habits of application.

THE MATHEMATICAL DEPARTMENT.

The first subject to which the attention of the student is directed in this department is Algebra, the study of which is continued for about one-half of the year. Geometry and Trigonometry, sometimes Geometry alone, are studied during the remainder of the year. The studies of the second or Sophomore year, are Trigonometry, plane and spherical, if not completed, during the preceding year; Surveying, Analytical Geometry, and the Differential Calculus; and of the following or Junior year, the Integral Calculus and Descriptive Geometry.

Peirce's course of Mathematics was lately introduced, but notwithstanding the general excellence of that course, it, particularly, in that part which treats of the higher branches of Mathematics, was not found so well adapted to the capacities of the students as Davie's course, which was formerly used, and has now been re-adopted.

DEPARTMENT OF ANCIENT LANGUAGES.

The number of students in this Department during the last year was *sixty-four*. When it is remembered that a considerable amount of preparation is requisite for admission to the department, the fact of so large a number of young men entering it, evinces the high estimate, on the part of parents and pupils, of the classical studies as a part of a scheme of liberal education. The department is so conducted as to open before the students, as far as possible, the whole field of literature. It is a constant practice to present to the classes in connection with the authors read in the Latin and Greek languages, the cognate literature of our own languages. Thus, when the class reads Juvenal's *tenth* Satire, Johnson's admirable imitation, the Vanity of human Wishes, is read and compared with it. In common with the third Satire of the same author, Johnson's London is made the subject of examination and comment. So also, with the reading of Virgil's Pastorals, or those of Theocritus in Greek, reference is made to the Pastorals of Pope and Shenstone, and also the Pastoral poetry of the Hebrews as found in the Bible. The same course is, as far as practicable, pursued with all the authors read. In this manner the connection between ancient and modern literature is exhibited, and how far our literature has grown out of that of Greece and Rome. The examination of particular words is made a practical exercise in philology. The student is required to give the primary and secondary meaning of words, to trace derivations, the principles upon which made, &c. A single example will illustrate the process. Suppose the word under examination is *pontific*—the student gives its composition, comparing it with other words formed in the same way, its etomylogical meaning, which is *bridge-maker,* its secondary and usual signification, which is *priest,* how the word came to have its secondary meaning, its English derivative *pontiff,* &c. He is then shown that Milton uses the word in its primative sense, as in the lines—

"Now had they brought the work by wonderous art
Pontifical, a ridge of pendent rock
Over the vexed abyss.

He at the brink of chaos, near the foot
Of the new wondrous *pontifice* unhoped,
Met his offspring dear."
In this manner the uses of the classical languages, in their bearing upon our own language and literature, are constantly presented, The actual work of the department will be best exhibited by a statement of the course of study pursued by each of the four classes during the past year. The Freshman class entered with less preparation than usual. Their reading in Latin was five books of the Æneid, the Pastorals of Virgil, first book of Livy. In Greek select Diologues of Lucian, selections from Anacreon, first book of Xenophon's Cyropedia. Exercises in Grammar and Prosody were carefully attended to throughout the year.

SOPHOMORE CLASS.

In Latin, Satires and Epistles of Horace, including *De arte* poetical references of Pope's imitations of Horace and his art Criticism, the Andrian and Adelphi of Terence. Familiar illustrations of the differences between the ancient and modern drama, Cicero de Senectuti. In Greek, select portions of Isocrates and Demosthenes, three books of the Iliad.

JUNIOR CLASS.

First and second book of the history of Tacitus, and the account of the siege of Jerusalem by Titus, as given in the fifth book, eight Satires of Juvenal. In Greek, the Medea of Euripides, the Œdipus Tyrannus of Sophocles.

SENIOR CLASS.

In Latin, Cicero de Oratore, with lecture on the differences between ancient and modern eloquence. Tacitus on the manners of the Germans—modern institutions, supposed to have had their origin with the ancient Germans, pointed out.
In Greek, portions of the Odyssey and Pindar's Olympiad.

DEPARTMENT OF NATURAL PHILOSOPHY AND CHEMISTRY.

By the time the student has nearly completed his course of pure Mathematics, he enters this Department, where he sees the practical application of many of those principles already taught. The first subject which engages his attention is *Mechanics,* comprising *Statics* and Dynamics; the former teaching the equilibrium the latter of the motion of the bodies. After this, the subjects Heat and Electricity are taken up, which form an introduction to, and prepare the way for, the chemical course, which course is nearly completed during the Junior year.

On entering the Senior class, Hydrestatics and Hydredynamics—the application of the principles of Mechanics to fluids, Optics, Astronomy, and Organic Chemistry are taken up in succession. There are several subjects, which properly belong to this Department, such as Military and Civil Engineering, Scientific Agriculture, Minerology, and Geology, which are not formally taught, it being thought better to lay a solid foundation in those departments. It being thought better to lay a solid foundation in branches of science, on which these most wholly depend, and without which, these as well as many useful arts cannot be well understood. The progress of the students is tested by daily examinations, and his studies are pursued principally by using approved text books, and partly by attending lectures, illustrated by numerous experiments for the exhibition of which a Labratory provided with suitable arrangements and apparatus, has been erected apart from the other buildings of the University.

The cost of the apparatus, belonging to the University, was originally about nine hundred dollars, and though by no means so complete as could be desired, still there is enough for the elucidation of the general principles, and many of the most interesting phenomena of physical science.

LAW DEPARTMENT.

This Department was organized in the year 1842. It had its origin in the desire of the Board, to afford gentlemen, who are preparing for the Bar, all the conceded advantages, which such an institution well conducted, confers in the acquisition of professional knowledge.

It was committed to the charge of the Hon. David MacDonald, whose ability as a lecturer and teacher, has fully met the high expectations which his acknowledged reputation as a jurist created. The growing prosperity of this branch of the University, and the increased labor thereby devolving upon the law faculty have induced the Board to appoint an additional Professor. Hon. William T. Otto, was elected a Professor at the annual meeting of the Board 1847. The course of instruction consists of lectures, on the various titles of the law, and in recitations by the students, from text books of established authority. A moot court has been organized, and two sessions are holden in each week.

Cases are prepared, and counsel designated by the Professors, for the plaintiff and for the defendant. Suits are instituted by the students, who prepare the pleadings and conduct the cases in conformity with the usages of courts of record. The Professors preside over the deliberations, and decide the points which the case stated involves. The exercises of the moot court, are regarded as furnishing the most efficient means of instruction.

They enable the students to apply practically, the information acquired in the lecture and recitation rooms, familiarize them with the forms of pleading and the details of practice, and cultivate the faculty of public speaking, which performs so conspicious a part of the duties of professional life. The course of instruction in the law department, is, it is believed, well adapted to secure its intended object. A high standard of proficiency is required from the candidates for its honors, and the Board can most cheerfully recommend it to the public, as furnishing advantages to such as are seeking instruction in the science of the law, equal to those afforded by any similar institution. It may be proper to add, that no portion of the funds of the University, is applied to the maintainance of the Law Department.

The compensation of the Professors is derived solely from the tuition fees of the students.

DEPARTMENT OF MORAL SCIENCE.

In this Department, which is under the care of the President, are taught, Moral and Mental Philosophy, Rhetoric, Logic, and Evidences of Christianity, Political Economy, and the Constitution of the United States. The course of instruction on the principal of the Branches, is intended to be as thorough and extensive as possible. Moral Philosophy, for instance, embraces Natural Religion, Ethics, the Doctrine of Special Obligations, in its application to the various domestic, social and civil relations. The science of government, and International law, and Rhetoric is so treated, as to include Philology and Criticism; and under the head of Mental Philosophy, the Fine Arts, and the Laws of Human Nature in general are introduced.

The method of instruction on these subjects combines with Lectures, the advantage of dissertation and catechetical examination, thus: A lecture is given, of which the class take notes at the time; these notes are worked up by the student into the form of a dissertation, which is read the next day, the members of the class reading each a dissertation in turn. And when a whole subject is gone over in this way, it is renewed catechetically.

Irregular, that is students who do not feel it convenient, to take the whole course necessary for a Diploma are admitted, along with the Junior and Senior classes, to share in the benefit of these instructions, so far as they can.

The full benefit of them, will, of course, be received by such only as have been prepared for it, by the previous studies. Exercises in Composition, Declamation, Argumentation, and original speaking, are performed on the forenoon of every Saturday by the classes in this Department.

DISCIPLINE.

The discipline is intended to be strictly parental, and to accomplish its effect, by appealing to the better principles of the heart, avoiding, if possible, severe and disgraceful punishments; students are treated as reasonable beings and as gentlemen. If it should appear that a student is not susceptible of the influence of such discipline, he is returned to his friends in the hope, that under other circumstances he may form an estimable character.

Immoral, disorderly, or dishonorable conduct, or habitual negligence of duty, or want of preparation, is always sufficient reason for directing a student to leave the University. There has been little occasion during the past year for punishment of any kind, further than caution and admonition before the Faculty: and, in a single case, writing to a parent, to take away his son in consequence of neglect of study.

There are among the students no College *tricks,* as they are denominated, which produce whenever existing, great waste of time, and a blunting effect on the moral sensibilities.

BOARDING CLUB.

The University Board House is occupied by a boarding club of 30 or 40 students, who under the supervision of the Faculty, make their own regulations, furnish their own table, and employ their own cook. The members of this club board themselves, at from 50 to 75 cents per week.

Other than the boarding club there is no system of *College Commons.* The students for the most part, board in private families; and thus are brought under family supervision and restraint. It is impossible under any system to bring together a large number of young men, within the same walls, without great danger to their manners and morals. Hence, it is not a part of the plan of the Board, even had they abundant means, to erect dormitories on the College grounds for the use of the students. Boarding and lodging in private families are had from $1 00 to $1 50 per week.

PROPERTY.

This consists of the permanent fund, the campus, and buildings of the University, and the Library and apparatus. The amount of funds in the loan office is given by the Auditor of State, in his annual report to the Legislature. As the Trustees are wholly dependent on this report for information, in regard to the condition of the fund, placed in the hands of the Treasurer of State, to be loaned at an interest for the use of the University, they respectfully refer to the Auditor's report to the present General Assembly, for the only correct information, which can be given on the subject. The average annual amount of interest which has been drawn from the State Treasury since the year 1843, up to the present time, is (say) $3,688 29, which, with the tuition fees of about $1200 a year, has constituted the fund for the payment of the President and Professors.

The amount of principal and interest remaining due and unpaid, for seminary lots on reserve sections around the University buildings is, as reported by John M. Berry, Commissioner of the reserve township of land, in Monroe county $3,669 00.

This fund is by law placed under the control and management of the Board of Trustees, to be applied to the erection of buildings, increase of Library, and other necessary purposes, connected with the interests of the Institution. The campus on which the University Buildings are, containing ten acres, is estimated to be worth $750 00.

The Buildings are the main College edifice, 75 by 50, three stories high, in which are the Chapel, Recitation Rooms, Library Rooms, Society Halls, estimated value, ...	$12,500 00
The "Old College" 60 by 31, two stories high, estimated at	2,000 00
Labratory 48 by 32, valued at	2,000 00
Boarding House 88 by 30, two stories high, with small dwelling attached, ...	3,000 00
Library estimated at	2,500 00
Chemical and Philosophical apparatus and Cabinet of Minerals, ...	800 00
Making the total valuation of these items of property, ...	$23,550 00

CLAIM OF THE STATE UPON CONGRESS.

The Board beg to call the attention of the Legislature to the fact, that the State has a claim of the most undoubted validity upon Congress for four thousand acres of land for the benefit of the University. The grounds of the claim are the following:—Congress by their Act of April 19th, 1816, vested in the State of Indiana, for the use of a Seminary of learning two "ENTIRE" townships of land —that in Gibson county and that in Monroe. Previous to that time, certain persons claiming to be the President and Trustees of the Vincennes University, and, without any color of right, seized upon, and sold four thousand acres of the township in Gibson county. The purchasers finding the title, conveyed to them, by said President and Trustees, to be of no effect, applied to Congress, to confirm their title; and Congress by a strange inadvertence, AFTER having thus vested the said Gibson township, in this State, confirmed the title to said purchasers by a SUBSEQUENT act of April 22d, 1816—eight days after the grant to the State, thereby assuming legislative power over lands already by them expressly granted. The Board cannot doubt, that, upon a proper representation of the subject, by the Legislature, to Congress, the deficit of four thousand acres, less than the two "ENTIRE" townships of land, will be immediately made up by Congress to the Legislature.

Upon a review of the condition of the University, the Board of Trustees congratulate their fellow-citizens on the increasing usefulness of the State University, and its establishment, as they trust, upon a firm and permanent basis. The fund placed at the disposal of the Board for the support of the University, is less than that of any of the other State Institutions; while it is believed that no other College or University in the West, resting upon a similar foundation, is at this time, in a condition of higher prosperity than our own State University, either in regard to the number of students or extent and thoroughness of the course of instruction.

The extreme economy of expenditure to which the Board is limited, will be seen by a comparison with that of some of the best known Colleges in our country.

For example, near a half million was expended on the Virginia University, before a student was admitted within its walls, and $15,000 per annum is permanently appropriated to its benefit by the Legislature. The cost of tuition, to each student taking a full course, is $75 a year, which is paid the Professors. The total amount of tuition is from $12,000 to $15,000, making a total annual expenditure of near $30,000. The number of students for 1847, was less than that of our own University. The annual expenditure of Union College, N. Y., besides its expenditure to aid indigent students, is about $20,000. The present number of students is 299. The annual expenditure of Columbia College is near $25,000. The number of students is 134.

Were a larger fund at the disposal of the Board, its expenditure for Library, for apparatus, for the establishment of additional Professorship, would place the University upon much higher grounds of usefulness and respectibility. In the U. S. Military Academy at West Point, where the system of instruction is designed to be as nearly perfect as possible, the Academical Staff or Faculty of instructors, consists of thirty-two members; and in that institution the course of instruction is more circumscribed than in our University, and the students but slightly more numerous. In Harvard and Yale, the system of instruction is perfected by a subdivision almost equally minute. In addition to Professorships sufficiently numerous to afford the highest order of instruction, and an extensive Library; cabinets of minerals, models in the arts, an astronomical observatory, and many other improvements, are requisite for an institution that shall stand with the first in the nation and form a just subject of State pride.

These advantages, if they are ever possessed by the Indiana University, must be the work and accumulation of many years, and the result of individual and State munificence. In the present condition of the finances of the State, the Board do not feel at liberty to call upon the Legislature for aid in building up an institution of learning which shall be in all respects, worthy this great State.

A judicious liberality is, however, in many cases the wisest economy. It is supposed that near one hundred youth from Indiana, at an expense annually, of from $200 to $500, are pursuing their studies without the limits of the State, while our University makes reprisals upon other States of only from 20 to 30. Other Institutions in the State without doubt, still further reduce the balance. Still there is a balance against us. It may be of comparatively little moment to our most wealthy citizens, whether there is a College at all in Indiana, or what its character shall be. They can, and will send their sons, where the best advantages are to be had. There is no opinion more incorrect than that Colleges are institutions for the *rich* alone. The truth is, the larger proportion of students in our American Colleges, are aspiring young men from the middling, and even from the very humble walks of life; many of them having by their own efforts procured the means of their education, and not a few of them, for the sake of learning, denying themselves, what most would consider the necessaries of life. To this class, it is of the utmost importance, that there should be in our midst, provision for the highest instruction, in every department of human knowledge. To the great body of our people it is important. The Indiana University, in the opinion of the Board, in a good degree makes this provision. But it is their wish to render it, in a still more ample manner, worthy the design of the framers of our Constitution, who contemplated a State University as standing at the head of a system of public instruction in Indiana. Not only have these wise and good men given their sanction to the value of College education, by the very organic law of our State, but it is a remarkable fact, that Colleges have the most emphatic commendation possible to be given, of the three names best known and most venerated among the American people,—those of WASHINGTON, JEFFERSON and FRANKLIN.

Washington himself endowed a College with lands, the proceeds of which yield a larger annual revenue than that of the Indiana University. Jefferson gave the last seventeen years of his life to founding the University of Virginia, and desired no other memorial with posterity than as author of the Declaration of Independence, and Founder of the Virginia University. Franklin was the founder of the University of Pennsylvania. The framers of the Constitution, were wise in uniting in the same scheme of instructions, Commons Schools and the University. Common Schools and Colleges go together. They are mutual friends and helpers.

They flourish in the same soil and harmonize in the same system. The Common School furnishes the College, the well trained student, it calls forth the first germ of talent, it directs attention to the College. In turn, the College furnishes the teacher to the Academy, and the Academy to the Common School. Thus the College elevates the general standard of teaching and the qualifications of teachers, and is an essential part in every well directed system of public instruction.

In conclusion, the Indiana University has no rivalry with any other Institution in the State. She sends kind and cordial greeting to every Institution of sound learning belonging to whatsoever party or sect. There is room for all, and work for all. While she herself stands alone, belonging peculiarly to no sub-division of the people, having no special advocates or defenders, she commends herself to a wise and liberal policy of the State Legislature, and to the fostering care and patronage of the whole people of Indiana.

> By order of the Board,
> Respectfully submitted,
> D. H MAXWELL, President
> *Of the Board of Trustees*
> *Ind. U.*

Indiana *Documentary Journal,* 1848.

Document 49

A Landmark in the Redirection of the University

A constitutional convention had drafted a new state constitution in 1851, but this document did little more than take cursory notice of the existence of the University. In 1852 a combination of several forces resulted in a complete restructuring of the University in an omnibus legislative act. The new law, without saying so specifically, provided for the eight-member Board of Trustees, restated the purposes of the University, provided for expanding the curriculum, outlined the Board of Trustees' authority, and made new fiscal provisions for the management of the school's investments and financial affairs. It likewise continued, but with marked reduction in membership, the Board of Visitors. This was indeed a fundamental document in the history of Indiana University.

*　　　*　　　*

CHAPTER 114.

AN ACT providing for the government of the State University, the management of its Funds, and for the disposition of the Lands thereof.

[APPROVED JUNE 17, 1852.]

SECTION 1. *Be it enacted by the General Assembly of the State of Indiana,* The institution established by an act entitled "an act to establish a college in the State of Indiana," approved January 28, 1828, is hereby recognized as the University of the State.

SEC. 2. The present trustees, three of whom shall reside in the county of Monroe, and their successors, shall be a body politic, with the style of "The Trustees of Indiana University;" in that name to sue and be sued; to elect one of their number president; to elect a treasurer, secretary, and such other officers as they may deem necessary; to prescribe the duties and fix the compensation of such officers; to fill all vacancies in such board; which appointment shall continue until the next meeting of the General Assembly, at which time the General Assembly shall fill all such vacancies; to possess all the real and personal property of such university for its benefit; to take and hold in their corporate name any real or personal property, for the benefit of such institution; to expend the income of the university for its benefit; to declare vacant the seat of any trustee who shall absent himself from two successive meetings of the board, or be guilty of any gross immorality, or breach of the by-laws of the institution; to elect a president, such professors and other officers for such university as shall be necessary, and prescribe their duties and salaries; to prescribe the course of study and discipline, and price of tuition in such university; and to make all by-laws necessary to carry into effect the powers hereby conferred.

SEC. 3. Said trustees shall annually meet at the town of Bloomington, at least three days preceding the annual commencement of the university.

SEC. 4. Five of such trustees shall constitute a quorum; and, in case an emergency is declared by the faculty, after there shall have been a called session, at which the other members failed to attend, the three trustees residing in the county of Monroe may fill vacancies in the faculty of the university, and board of trustees; and, in case there should not be three trustees in attendance upon such emergency, then those that are in attendance, together with such members of the faculty as may be in attendance, shall fill such vacancies; but appointments thus made shall expire at the next meeting of the board.

SEC. 5. The trustees of said university shall receive the proceeds of the sales and rents of the three reserved sections in the seminary township in Monroe county, and the same shall be paid to the treasurer of said trustees, on their order.

SEC. 6. The interest arising from loans of the State university fund shall, as received at the State Treasury, be paid on the warrants of the Auditor of State; such warrants to be granted on allowances made to the persons entitled thereto, by the board of trustees, and duly certified by their secretary.

SEC. 7. The president, professors and instructors shall be styled "The Faculty" of said university, and shall have power:

First. To enforce the regulations adopted by the trustees for the government of the students.

Second. To which end they may reward and censure, and may suspend those who continue refractory, until a determination of the board of trustees can be had thereon.

Third. To confer, with the consent of the trustees, such literary degrees as are usually conferred in other universities, and in testimony thereof to give suitable diplomas, under the seal of the university and signature of the faculty.

SEC. 8. No religious qualification shall be required for any student, trustee, president, professor, or other officer of such university, or as a condition for admission to any privilege in the same.

SEC. 9. No sectarian tenets shall be inculcated by any professors at such university.

SEC. 10. The trustees shall provide for the tuition, free of charge, of two students from each county in this State, to be selected by the board of county commissioners.

SEC. 11. The secretary of the board shall notify the county auditor of each county of the State, whenever there shall not be in attendance at the university, the number of students which such county is entitled to send free of tuition, of which such auditor shall notify the board of commissioners of such county, at their next meeting.

SEC. 12. The treasurer of the university shall give bond in a penalty, and with surety to be approved by such board, payable to the State, conditioned for the faithful discharge of his duties, which bond shall be filed with the Auditor of State.

SEC. 13. The Governor, Lieutenant Governor, Speaker of the House of Representatives, Judges of the Supreme Court, and Superintendent of Common Schools, shall constitute a board of visiters of the university and any three thereof a quorum.

SEC. 14. In case the members of such board of visiters fail to attend the annual commencement exercises of the university, the president of the board of trustees shall report such of them as are absent to the next General Assembly in their annual report.

SEC. 15. Such board of visiters shall examine the property, the course of study and discipline, and the state of the finances of the university, and recommend such amendments as they may deem proper, the books and accounts of the institution being open to their inspection, and they shall make report of their examination to the Governor, to be by him laid before the next General Assembly.

SEC. 16. The secretary of the board of trustees shall keep a true reccord of all the proceedings of said board and certify copies thereof. He shall also keep an account of the students of the university according to their classes, stating their respective ages and places of residence, and a list of all graduates.

SEC. 17. The treasurer of said university shall,

First. Keep true accounts of all money received into the treasury of said university, and of the expenditure thereof.

Second. Pay out the same on the order of the board of trustees, certified by their secretary.

Third. Collect the tuition fees due the same.

Fourth. Make semi-annual settlements with the board of trustees.

Fifth. Submit a full statement of the finances of the university his receipts and payments, at each meeting of the board of trustees.

Sixth. Submit his books and papers to the inspection of the trustees and visiters.

SEC. 18. The board of trustees, their secretary and treasurer, shall report to the superintendent of common schools, all matters relating to the university, when by him required.

SEC. 19. One member of the faculty, to be designated by a majority thereof, of which the secretary of the board shall be informed, shall by himself or competent substitute, deliver a public lecture on the principles and organization of the university, its educational facilities, (being careful not to disparage the claims of other institutions of learning in the State,) in at least fifteen different counties of the State, of which he shall give due notice; and in a vacation of less duration than one month, a member of the faculty to be designated as aforesaid, shall deliver such lecture in at least three different counties; a brief statement of which lectures shall, by the persons delivering them, be reported to the board of trustees annually, to be by them incorporated in the annual report to the General Assembly; but no two such lectures shall be delivered in the same county, until all the counties of the State have been lectured in.

SEC. 20. Such Lecturers shall make such geological examinations, and collect such mineralogical specimens as they may be able to make and procure, a report whereof they shall make to the board of trustees to be by them incorporated in their annual report to the General Assembly; and such specimens [together with those] they may procure by voluntary donations, they shall deposit in a suitable room in the university buildings, to be fitted up for that purpose.

SEC. 21. The Governor of the State shall order the printing annually of five thousand copies of the annual report of the board of trustees, twenty-five hundred of which shall be for the use of the members of the General Assembly, and twenty-five hundred for the faculty.

SEC. 22. Such report shall contain what is now included in the annual catalogue, with such other matters as may be deemed useful to the cause of education, connected with the university.

SEC. 23. The board of trustees through its president shall give at least one month's notice of the commencement of each session of the university, in at least one newspaper in the cities of Indianapolis, Louisville in the State of Kentucky, and in New Orleans in the State of Louisiana.

SEC. 24. The board of trustees shall annually appoint a committee of their body to examine the university buildings and grounds adjacent, who shall report the kind and cost of repairs, if any are needed, and one of the number of the faculty shall be appointed to take care of such buildings and grounds.

SEC. 25. Such trustees shall establish a normal department for instruction in the theory and practice of teaching, free of charge, of such young persons, [male and female,] residents of the State, as may desire to qualify themselves as teachers of common schools within the State, under such regulations as such board of trustees may make, in regard to admitting [to], kind, and time of delivery of lectures in such department, and the granting of diplomas therein; and such regulations shall be incorporated in the annual report of the trustees to the General Assembly.

SEC. 26. Such trustees shall also appoint [establish] an agricultural department in such university, under proper regulations, which shall likewise be set forth in their annual report.

SEC. 27. All laws and parts of laws coming in conflict with this act are hereby repealed.

SEC. 28. The university fund shall consist of the lands in Monroe and Gibson counties, and proceeds of sales thereof, and all donations for the use of such university, where the same is expressly mentioned in the grant, or where in such grant the term university only is used, the principal of which fund, when paid into the State Treasury, shall be loaned, and the annual interest thereon applied to the current expenses of the university, upon warrants drawn on the Treasurer of State by the Auditor of State, on the requisition of the board of trustees, signed by the president and attested by the secretary thereof.

SEC. 29. It shall be the duty of the Auditor of State to loan out such fund upon real estate security, and he shall duly inform himself of the value of all real estate offered in pledge, and shall be judge of the validity of the title thereof; and all persons applying for a loan shall produce to said auditor, the title papers to such real estate, showing title in fee simple, without incumbrance, and not derived through any executor's or administrator's sale, or sale on execution.

SEC. 30. The mortgage to be taken may be in the following form in substance, to-wit:

"I, A.B., of the county of ———, in the State of Indiana, do assign over and transfer to the State of Indiana, all (here describe the land,) which I declare to be mortgaged for the payment of ——— dollars, with interest at the rate of seven per cent. per annum, payable in advance, according to the conditions of the note hereunto annexed."

SEC. 31. The note accompanying the same may be in substance as follows, to-wit:

I, A.B., promise to pay the State of Indiana, on or before the —— day of——— the sum of ——— with interest thereon at the rate of seven per cent. per annum, in advance, commencing on the ——— day of ———, 18–, and do agree that in case of failure to pay any instalment of said interest, the said principal shall become due and collectable, together with all arrears of interest; and on any such failure to pay principal or interest when due, five per cent. damages on the whole sum shall be collected with costs, and the premises mortgaged may be forthwith sold by the auditor of public accounts, for the payment of such principal sum, interests, damages and costs.

SEC. 32. No greater sum than five hundred dollars shall be loaned to any one person out of such fund; nor shall the loan be for a longer period than five years, and the sum loaned shall not exceed one half of the appraised value of the premises to be mortgaged, clear of all perishable improvements, and the auditor may reduce the amount to be loaned on any such valuation, when, for any cause, he may have reason to believe the same was not in proportion to the prices of similar property selling in the vicinity; such valuation to be made from the valuation of the same property, in the assessment of the State revenue.

SEC. 33. The rate of interest required shall be seven per cent. in advance, payable annually; and on failure to pay any instalment of interest when due, the principal shall forthwith become due; and the note and mortgage may be collected.

SEC. 34. Such mortgages shall be considered as of record, from the date thereof, and shall have priority of all mortgages or conveyances not previously recorded, and of all other liens not previously incurred, in the county where the land lies.

SEC. 35. It shall be the duty of the auditor to have such mortgages recorded with due diligence; the expense whereof shall be borne by the mortgagor, and may be retained out of the money borrowed.

SEC. 36. The person applying for a loan, shall file with the auditor the certificate of the clerk and recorder of the county in which the land lies, showing that there is no conveyance of, or incumbrance on said land, in either of their offices.

SEC. 37. Such person shall also, before he receives the money to be loaned, make oath to the truth of an abstract of the title to his said land, and that there is no incumbrance, or better claim, as he believes, upon said land.

SEC. 38. On making any loan of such fund, the auditor shall draw his warrant on the treasurer, in favor of the borrower; and the treasurer shall pay the same, and charge it to the proper fund.

SEC. 39. All loans refunded, and all interest, shall be paid into the State Treasury, and the treasurer's receipt shall be filed with the Auditor of State, who shall give the payer a quietus for the amount thereof, and make the proper entries upon his books.

SEC. 40. Whenever the amount due on any mortgage shall be fully paid, and the treasurer's receipt filed therfor, the auditor shall endorse on the note and mortgage, that the same has been fully satisfied, and surrender them to the person entitled thereto; and on the production of the same, with such endorsement thereon, the recorder of the proper county shall enter satisfaction upon the record thereof.

SEC. 41. When the interest or principal of any such loan shall become due and remain unpaid, the auditor shall proceed to collect the same by a suit on the note, or by sale of the mortgaged premises, or both, as to him may seem most advisable; he may also, by proper action, obtain possession of the mortgaged premises.

SEC. 42. In case of suit on such note, and judgment theron, no stay of execution or appraisement of property shall be allowed.

SEC. 43. On failure to pay any interest or principal when due on any such mortgage, the auditor shall advertise the mortgaged property for sale in one or more of the newspapers printed in this State, for sixty days; such sale to take place at the court house door in Indianapolis.

SEC. 44. At the time appointed for such sale, the Auditor and Treasurer of State shall attend, and the Auditor shall make sale of so much of the mortgaged premises, to the highest bidder, for cash, as will pay the amount due for principal, interest, damages and costs of advertising and selling the same; and such sales may be in parcels so that the whole amount required be realized.

SEC. 45. In case no one will bid the full amount due as aforesaid, the Auditor shall bid on the same, on account of the proper fund; and as soon thereafter as may be, shall sell the same to the highest bidder for cash, or on a credit of five years, interest being payable annually in advance.

SEC. 46. The sale authorized in the preceding section, shall not be for less than the amount chargeable on such land; and if for more, the overplus shall be paid to the mortgagor, his heirs or assigns.

SEC. 47. The Treasurer shall attend and make a statement of such sales, which shall be signed by the Auditor and Treasurer, and after being duly recorded in the Auditor's office, shall be filed in the Treasurer's office; and such record, or a copy thereof, authenticated by the Auditor's or Treasurer's certificate, shall be received as evidence of the matters therein contained.

SEC. 48. When any land is bid off by the State at such sale, no deed need be made therefor to the State; but the statement of such sale, and the record thereof made, as in the preceding section required, shall vest the title in the State for the use of the fund.

SEC. 49. In case of a sale of any such lands to any person for cash, on the production of the Treasurer's receipt for the purchase money, the Auditor shall give to the purchaser a certificate, which shall entitle him to a deed for said land, to be executed by the Governor of this State, and recorded in the office of the Secretary of State.

SEC. 50. In like manner, when any tract bid off by the State is sold on a credit, on the execution and delivery of a note and mortgage for the proper amount, as in other cases required, the purchaser shall be entitled to a deed for the same, to be made as prescribed in the preceding section; and the transaction shall be entered, and appear upon the Auditor's and Treasurer's books as a payment of the sum bid, and a re-loan of the same to the purchaser, and the proper receipts and warrants shall pass therefor.

SEC. 51. For the services of the auditor and treasurer in conducting such sales they shall be entitled to receive five per cent. damages chargeable on such sales.

SEC. 52. The auditor and treasurer shall keep fair and regular entries of the sums received, and paid out on account of said fund, and shall include the same in their annual reports.

SEC. 53. In addition thereto, the auditor shall keep fair and regular accounts with the borrowers of said fund, and shall report the names of borrowers with his annual report.

SEC. 54. Should any interest remain on hand not wanted for the use of the university, the same may be loaned as other funds.

SEC. 55. The care and disposition of the lands belonging to and for the use of said university, remaining unsold or unpaid for, shall be vested in the present commissioners of the reserved townships, in the counties in which such lands may lie, who shall sell such as remain unsold, and such as are forfeited for non-payment on such terms and under such regulations as the board of trustees of such university may provide, except that in every instance the interest on the purchase money must be paid in advance, and no purchaser, his heirs or assigns, shall have the right to cut down or destroy timber standing upon such land other than for the erection of fences and buildings thereon, or for fire-wood to be used on the premises and in fairly improving it for cultivation.

SEC. 56. On the first payment for any such land being made, the proper commissioner shall execute to the purchaser a certificate therefor, and on final payment the original certificate shall be surrendered to the commissioner, and by him filed away; and he shall give to the purchaser two final certificates stating the whole amount of principal and the whole amount of interest paid; one of which certificates shall be forwarded to the Auditor of State, if in all things correct, he shall countersign the same, which shall entitle the owner to a patent, to be issued by the Governor for the land so paid for.

SEC. 57. Such commissioners may, from time to time, lease any such unsold improved land for terms not exceeding one year, until the same can be sold; and such leases shall be guarded against trespass and waste by proper covenants.

SEC. 58. Such commissioners shall make an annual report to the board of trustees of the lands remaining unsold; such as are forfeited; such as are not fully paid for; the amount due; and money collected from sale, as interest or principal; which report shall be subscribed and sworn to by such commissioners, respectively, and be incorporated in the annual report of such board to the General Assembly.

SEC. 59. Money collected by such commissioners shall be paid over to the treasurer of the board, who shall execute to said commissioner two receipts therefor, each specifying the persons from whom such money was collected, and the amount thereof, whether for interest or principal; one of which receipts shall be immediately forwarded to the Auditor of State to be by him used in his settlement with such treasurer.

SEC. 60. Such board shall regulate the compensation of such commissioners.

SEC. 61. Patents for lands sold shall be made by the Governor, and recorded in the office of the Secretary of State.

Indiana *Revised Statutes*, 1852, Vol. I, pp. 504–512.

Document 50

The Death of Andrew Wylie

Perhaps Andrew Wylie never felt completely at home in Indiana, nor did the Hoosiers always feel at ease with him. He nevertheless made a major contribution to the establishment of the University in its very important transitional years. President Wylie had two hobbies, riding horseback and chopping wood. On November 1, 1851, he cut his foot and ten days later died from the resulting infection. For two decades he had been a great personal force in Bloomington, and he was, in the context of the day, a scholar and a good administrator with well developed notions of what a university should be. Governor Wright was correct in looking ahead to Wylie's successor because the fortunes of the University depended upon him.

*   *   *

In pursuance of law, I attended the commencement exercises of the State University at Bloomington, in August last. This Institution, then under the immediate control of the late distinguished President, Rev. Andrew Wylie, and an able corps of Professors, I found admirable conducted, and in a flourishing condition. The wholesome rules are strictly enforced: the system of instruction is of the most permanent and thorough character. It is understood that application will be made to the Legislature, by the Board of Trustees, for new powers, in order to enlarge its capacity for future usefulness. The high character of the gentlemen composing that Board, and others interested in its management, is a sure guaranty that you will give them a favorable hearing.

Little did I then think, it would be my melancholy duty to record the death of the late President Wylie! This event, which has so suddenly deprived a family of its honored and beloved head; a church, of one of her most talented ministers; our State, of one of its brightest ornaments, and the University of its learned President, took place on the 11th day of November, 1851, at his late residence! Truly, a great and good man has fallen. The question forces itself unbidden upon us, which way shall we turn, to whom shall we look to repair the loss the University has so lately sustained? As an Educator, in the opinion of those who knew him best, the late President stood unrivalled. A residence among us of more than twenty years, most laboriously spent in the cause of education, had secured for him a reputation, to attain which, must be well considered enough to satisfy the aspirations of the most ambitious of men. May his mantle descend upon some one worthy to bear it!

Indiana *House Journal,* 1851–52, Vol. 1, pp. 18–19.

Document 51

State of the University in 1851

This report was in essence a factual memorial to Andrew Wylie. It looked to the future and an expansion of the curriculum and the services of the University. The Board announced the appointment of John H. Lathrop of the University of Wisconsin as successor to Wylie. Lathrop was an up-state New Yorker who was trained at Hamilton College and Yale University. He taught mathematics and natural philosophy. He had also served as president of the infant University of Missouri. The trustees, however, were too quick to announce Lathrop's appointment because he turned them down, and Alfred Ryors, a Presbyterian minister, was elected instead.

*   *   *

REPORT.

To the General Assembly of the State of Indiana:

The Board of Trustees of the Indiana University, through their committee, respectfully submit the following report, supplemental to the annual report made to the General Assembly in December last:

In accordance with the act passed on the third day of March, 1852, reorganizing the Board of Trustees of Indiana University and defining their powers and duties, the Board met in the University Chapel, on the 10th day of April.

The following Trustees were present, viz:

Thomas M. Adams, of the county of Brown;
N. C. Browning, of the county of Monroe;
George Evans, of the county of Henry;
Michael A. Malott, of the county of Lawrence;
Johnson McCullough, of the county of Monroe;
John I. Morrison, of the county of Washington;
Patrick Joseph R. Murphy, of the county of Daviess;
Joseph G. McPheeters, of the county of Monroe.

The Board elected as President of their body, JOSEPH G. McPHEETERS, M. D.; JAMES D. MAXWELL, M. D., Secretary; and JOSEPH M. HOWE, Esq., Treasurer of the University.

The Board of Trustees desire to express their deep sense of the irreparable loss sustained by the University, in the sudden death of its late distinguished President, the Rev. ANDREW WYLIE, D. D., which was communicated to the General Assembly in the last annual report; and in testimony of their high appreciation of his great talents, profound learning, and eminent piety, the Board have ordered the following resolutions, adopted unanimously, to be spread upon their records. [See appendix, marked A.]

A delicate and difficult duty devolved upon the Board, in selecting officers to fill the vacant chairs in the Faculty of instruction. This duty was rendered still more perplexing by the fact, that the Trustees were required by law to proceed, at their first meeting, to the election both of a President of the University, and a Professor of Mathematics, without having had the opportunity of conference or correspondence with literary men throughout the country.

JOHN H. LATHROP, LL. D., now Chancellor of the University of Wisconsin, was elected President and Professor of Moral and Mental Science and Belles Lettres; and ROBERT MILLIGAN, now a Professor in Washington College, Pa., Professor of Mathematics and Civil Engineering.

Dr. Lathrop has an experience of nearly thirty years as a College officer, and is recommended to the Board by those well knowing him, as eminently qualified to succeed the late distinguished President of this University.

Prof. Milligan is recommended by high testimonials from the most eminent sources. The Board have great reason to believe, that in both these gentlemen they have found worthy associates of the present learned and accomplished Professors; and that the Faculty, as now organized, will meet the just expectations of the people of Indiana and their representatives.

The Board cannot forbear an expression of their gratification, that by extraordinary labors on the part of the existing Faculty, the course of instruction was fully kept up in all departments of the University, after the lamented death of Dr. Wylie. The committee appointed to be present at the examinations, closing during the first week of April, made a most satisfactory report, which is herewith submitted in the appendix, marked B, as exhibiting the course and manner of instruction now pursued in the University.

It is proper to say, that the Law School, connected with the University, maintains its high reputation, and that the following gentlemen were graduated as bachelors of law at the Law Commencement, on the 20th day of February, viz: Samuel A. Bonner, of Greensburg; John P. Baird, of Terre Haute; William M. Connelly, of Spencer; Joseph T. Draper, of Scipio; James T. Embree, of Princeton; Stephen C. Taber, of Logansport; Henry D. Wise, of Vincennes; and Wm. H. Green, of Mt. Vernon, Illinois.

The Board of Trustees, aided by consultation with the Faculty, have given much consideration to the means of extending the usefulness of the University, and of rendering it more acceptable to all classes of the people of Indiana who may, for themselves or their children, desire to enjoy the advantages of such an institution. The difficulty and embarrassment which the Board experience in their plans of enlarging the course of instruction, and in adding new departments to those already existing in the University, are found in the limited means placed at their disposal. It is their most earnest desire to adapt the University to the educational wants of the State, and to make it an instrument in carrying out the constitutional obligation of the General Assembly, to encourage, by all suitable means, moral, intellectual, scientific, and agricultural improvement.

In pursuance of these designs, the Board of Trustees, at the recent meeting, resolved upon the four following measures, and have adopted plans for carrying these measures into immediate execution:

1. *The Establishment of a course of Agricultural Chemistry.*

Lectures and experiments in this course, it is intended, shall commence on Thursday, the 23d day of September—the first day of the first term of the collegiate year. Other departments of study will also be open to young men, who may resort to the University with special reference to this subject. It can hardly be doubted, that this provision will be highly acceptable to the most numerous class of our citizens, and that many, designed for agricultural pursuits, will avail themselves of its benefits. The Board entertain the hope that through the proposed department, the State University may be made a valuable auxiliary in promoting a species of knowledge of great importance in that branch of industry which is the great source of wealth and prosperity of the State; and they confidently trust that at this period, when so much interest is awakened on the subject of scientific agriculture, many may be disposed to avail themselves of the advantages now proffered in the University.

The Board are happy to state, that this important improvement will be attended with little additional expense, as the University already has a very excellent Laboratory and apparatus, adequate to all required experiments. The

University is also most fortunate in having at the head of this department, Prof. T. A. Wylie, who, by early training, (under the celebrated Dr. Hare, of the University of Pennsylvania,) and ample experience, is eminently fitted for the new duties which will devolve upon him.

2. *The Establishment of a Normal Seminary, under the Direction of the Resident Trustees and the Faculty, having two Departments, one designed for Males and the other for Females.*

The design is, to bring the State University, through these departments, into more immediate connection with the system of common schools, required by the State Constitution; and to render it useful in training a class of professional teachers, who will be prepared and qualified to take charge of union and district schools; and to diffuse, wherever they may be, educational knowledge, and make known the best methods of teaching and school government. The subject of training professional teachers in normal seminaries, is one which attracts much attention throughout the United States; and is beginning to awaken attention and inquiry in Indiana, as a means of elevating the general standard of qualification for the great work of teaching.

The plan of the seminary, as designed by the board, is the following: One of the professors, in addition to other duties, will be constituted Professor of Didactics, or of the Theory and Art of Teaching. A regular course of studies for this department will be prescribed by the Faculty; and those who complete it and pass a creditable examination, will be entitled to a certificate or diploma, signed by the Faculty. The several departments of the University will, likewise, be open to the members of this class; and they will have the opportunity of reviewing and perfecting themselves, without additional cost, in any branch of knowledge taught in the University.

But as auxiliary to the instruction of this class, a *model* school is required, in order to present to the eye of the learner, a common school, as nearly perfect as possible in its order, arrangement, furniture, classification, and methods of teaching; and also as a school of practice, in which to exercise and test the young teacher's ability and tact. The Board have resolved to fit up rooms in one of the present buildings on the College Campus, for a boys' model school; and to procure a teacher, who has been trained in a normal school, as its superintendent.

Inasmuch as it is known, that a large proportion of all the teachers in those States, where the common school system is brought to the highest perfection, are females, amounting in some States, it is believed, to five-sixths of the total number; and as it is exceedingly desirable, on every consideration, to increase the proportion of female teachers in Indiana, the Board of Trustees have felt, that without provision for a normal department for females, they would have accomplished less than half their work. They have, therefore, made provision for a normal department for females, to be organized and controlled as the male department.

In this design, the Board are exceedingly favored by circumstances now existing in the town of Bloomington, which, it is hoped, will enable them to carry the measure into early execution. The Monroe County Seminary, distant over half a mile from the University, is by law a female seminary. This seminary has been conducted in such a manner as to secure universal favor in the community where it exists, and a widely extended reputation. It is considered by the best judges to be, in its present organization, a model seminary for females. The accomplished Principal has extensively visited normal schools and institutions of female education, with a view of acquiring a knowledge of the best systems of education; and in tact, talent, and capacity for influencing her pupils, possesses remarkable power. It is believed that the Board will be able to secure the services of this lady, together with her accomplished corps of teachers; and in a few weeks, to organize the school under the direction of the resident Trustees and the Faculty, as the female department of the Normal Seminary.

It is the wish of the Board to place this department upon the most elevated grounds; and to make it subservient both to general education and to the elevation of the female sex. It is certainly just and proper, that while so much is done to prepare our sons for the business of life, by numerous institutions designed for their benefit, that some public effort and expenditure should be made to fit our daughters, not merely for a business by which they may gain for themselves an honorable livelihood, but render most important service in the general education of the State. The Board trust, that by wise and prudent management, the department now established, under the most favorable circumstances for success, will become an ornament and a blessing to the State. The department will derive great benefit from its connection with the University, through the lectures and experiments of the Professors.

The Board of Trustees respectfully represent to the General Assembly, that in order to carry out their plans in regard to this department, in as ample a manner as is desirable for its success, they will be subjected to a considerable expenditure; and pray that the General Assembly will grant, in furtherance of this object, such pecuniary aid as they make think wise and expedient. The Board believe that such aid would be consistent with justice and sound policy; would be eminently honorable to the State, and would be fully sustained by public approval.

Finally, in regard to the whole subject of a Normal Seminary in both its departments, the Board do not hesitate to express the conviction that with very slight additional means, obtained through State or private munificence, the Seminary, by its connection with the University, will be more efficient, more likely to secure public confidence, will possess more ample means of instruction, than were the entire University fund converted to the sole purpose of a Normal Seminary.

3. *The establishment of a School of Theoretic and Practical Engineering, in connection with the Mathematical Department.*

The numerous public works now in process of construction, render civil engineering a most important branch of University education; and it cannot be doubted that instruction by an able and accomplished mathematician, in this important branch, together with practical illustrations in the field, will meet one of the present demands of public education in Indiana, and add a new and valuable class of students to the University.

4. *The establishment of a Scientific Department.*

It has long been a subject of complaint, that proper provision has not been made by our colleges to encourage that class of students who do not complete a full course of classical reading. The degree of Bachelor of Science will, hereafter, be conferred upon all who have completed the full course prescribed for this department; and diplomas will be granted, and the same formalities observed, as in conferring the regular degrees now known in the University. This arrangement will be highly satisfactory to a large class of students, hitherto designated in the catalogues as irregulars; and, it is hoped, will induce many, by having a definite object in view, to continue connected with the University, until they shall have finished a full scientific course.

The Board, at their late meeting, restored the former order and number of sessions and vacations, and established the rates of tuition, as follows:

The collegiate year is now divided into three sessions. The first begins on Thursday, the 23d of September, and continues until the 24th of December, and is followed by a recess of one week. The second begins on the first Monday of January, and ends on the first Wednesday of April, and is followed by a vacation of four weeks. The third (being the ensuing session,) begins on Thursday, the 6th of May, and terminates on Wednesday, the 4th of August, which is commencement day.

TUITION.—In college proper, eight dollars per session; in preparatory department, six dollars per session. County students are required to pay a fee of one dollar per session for contingencies.

In conclusion, the Board have endeavored to add new facilities of public education, without destroying any of the advantages now existing in the University. All the branches heretofore taught will still be taught. New duties and responsibilities have been thrown upon the Faculty, which, it is due to them to say, they have manifested no reluctance to undertake. The State University, with enlarged means of usefulness, with a Faculty of able and earnest Professors, opens her doors to the youth of the country, and commends herself with renewed confidence to the fostering care of the General Assembly.

Respectfully submitted, on behalf of the Board of Trustees:

JOHN I. MORRISON, PATRICK JOSEPH R. MURPHY, JOSEPH G. MCPHEETERS, *Committee.*

APPENDIX (A.)

Resolutions of condolence, occasioned by the death of the Rev. Andrew Wylie, D. D., late President of Indiana University, unanimously adopted by the Board of Trustees, at their recent meeting.

WHEREAS, It has pleased Almighty God, since the last meeting of the Board of Trustees of this University, to remove by death the Rev. ANDREW WYLIE, D. D., its late distinguished President;

Resolved, That it is due the exalted worth and eminent services of this great and good man, as well as his official position in this University, that the Board should record an expression of their sense of the loss, which in his death, has befallen not only our University, but the cause of education and the interests of literature in our State and country.

Resolved, That the death of him who has so long been a tower of strength to the State University, and whose very name has given character to our Institution, is an event most deeply deplored by the Trustees, individually and as a body; and that, while we lament his removal as a public calamity, we tender to his widow and bereaved family our heartfelt sympathies and condolence, and commend them to the grace and keeping of that Almighty Being, who is the widow's God, and the father of the fatherless.

Resolved, That a just regard to the memory of the first President of our University, who had labored so long and earnestly to build up an institution of learning worthy of our State, imposes new and greatly increased responsibilities upon all connected with the University; and that the best and most permanent monument to his name is the Indiana University, made such as he, for a series of years, was striving to make it—the pride and ornament of Indiana.

Resolved, That the Secretary be directed to send a copy of these resolutions of the Board to the widow of the deceased.

APPENDIX (B.)

A Report of Examination, by a Committee of the Board of Trustees of Indiana University.

In compliance with an order, made by the former Board of Trustees of Indiana University, the undersigned attended the examinations of the several classes connected with the University, which commenced on Saturday, the 3d, and closed on Wednesday, the 7th day of April, 1852, and beg leave respectfully to submit, as the result of their labors, the following

REPORT.

The examination was opened on Saturday, with the classes in the Preparatory Department, under the charge of Prof. M. M. Campbell.

The examinations in this department were confined, as we think, very properly, to the grammars of the Latin and Greek languages, together with such exercises in translation as were deemed necessary for practical purposes. With every portion of the grammars, the familiarity of the classes was alike creditable to their own diligence, and to the assiduity and fidelity of their instructor.

In the Mathematical Department, under the charge of Prof. Marshall, the classes in College proper were examined on Monday, in pure Mathematics, commencing with Algebra, and extending over Analytical Geometry, Descriptive Geometry, Trigonometry, and the Differential Calculus. Upon all these subjects, the classes were subjected to a severe and searching examination. The admirable proficiency and accuracy in this department reflected the highest credit upon the students and the Professor.

On Tuesday, in Professor T. A. Wylie's department, the Junior and Senior classes were examined in the several branches of Natural Philosophy; and the Freshman class, in Latin and Greek. In the demonstrations of some of the most difficult propositions in Mechanics and Optics, the young gentlemen evinced a degree of knowledge seldom found in under-graduates, and well sustained the high reputation of their Professor.

In the department of Languages, in charge of Professor Read, the examinations were, for want of time, necessarily brief, but highly satisfactory to the committee. Since the lamented death of Dr. Wylie, late President of the University and Professor of Moral and Mental Sciences, &c., the duties of this chair have, for the most part, been discharged by the Professor of Languages. In the President's department, the subjects of examination, in the Junior and Senior classes, were Rhetoric, Logic,. and International and Constitutional Law. Upon these subjects the examinations were very full and rigorous. In addition to the usual questions proposed on such occasions, the young gentlemen were required to exhibit on the blackboard a complete analysis of each topic. This afforded the committee a favorable opportunity to ascertain how far and how profoundly the subjects had been studied; and they feel constrained to say, in behalf of the students, and in justice to the distinguished Professor, who has with such signal ability and success conducted their studies, that the examinations in this department have not been surpassed by any every witnessed by them, in this or any other similar institution.

In general terms, the committee represent to the Board, that the examinations throughout the different departments have been conducted to their high gratification and entire satisfaction.

Respectfully submitted:

JOHN I. MORRISON, ⎱ *Com.*
D. H. MAXWELL,   ⎰

[IV]

A World in Travail
1852–1870

Consistently throughout the history of Indiana University the question has been raised of moving the institution away from Bloomington. The Monroe County seat was criticised for many reasons, ranging from its isolation to the "litigious, quarrelsome, tricky character of a great many of the people there." Some of this criticism with the University's location no doubt was serious but ridiculous, and some of it was based upon sound reasoning because of transportation difficulties. Most of it, however, was petulant and politically selfish.

As indicated in the introduction to the previous chapter the search for presidential leadership went on with frustrating results. If every other condition of the institution had been normal, this problem alone would have delayed expansion of the internal university program. There occurred, however, a devastating blow which almost destroyed the University. When the main building was destroyed by fire in 1854, future prospects for the school were darkened. Not only was the key building reduced to ashes, but so was most of the educational apparatus of the institution. The magnificent Owen Cabinet or archaeological and geological collection was destroyed. The library was burned, and so were student literary society collections.

In order to restore the building the University had to seek financial resources far beyond its present capacity to produce funds. This necessitated an attempt to sell bonds on the public market, an effort which resulted in utter failure. In a desperate drive to produce capital in a moment of dire need, the Board of Trustees made one of the most astounding mistakes that could have been imagined. It authorized the sale of perpetual scholarships which were improperly conceived and safeguarded against future abuses. This blunder was to haunt the University for at least a half century.

Remarkably the University went through the Civil War without an appreciable amount of actual disruption. The records of the institution

151

are almost silent on the subject of the conflict. Occasionally mention was made of a professor or a student who was engaged in the war in some way, but there were no military activities on or near the campus, and remarkably little bitterness seems to have been expressed in the university community. In Bloomington there were debates and rallies about the village square, but these remained away from the west end of College Street. Actually the university enrollment was so small in 1860–1865, few boys were caught in the military draft.

Cyrus Nutt, although not a strong administrator, did pull the University together in its adversities and in the face of national crisis. He brought it through the hard times of war with a fairly clearcut notion of what it should become in the changing times of the post-war era. Nutt and his colleagues had a concept how important it was for Indiana University to encourage the Indiana Legislature to turn it into a land grant college with major emphasis in the field of the mechanical arts and agriculture. Nutt's pleas in this field were impressive as indicated in Document 65 of this section.

Document 52

The Perennial Issue of Removal of the University from Bloomington

For almost a century this issue of the location of the University in a small southern Indiana town plagued trustees, presidents, professors, and legislators.

*   *   *

Editor Locomotive:—I notice among the late appoinments of the Governor, an agent to select lands for the State University. This calls up the subject, and renders it a proper time to consider the location of that Institution. I think every consideration is in favor of its being removed to some other locality.

1st. It has done nothing in its present location. As was well remarked by the late "Indiana *Statesman,*" in noticing its last commencement, it showed more professors under pay, at the expense of the State, than graduates who had received instruction.

2nd. It is located in an out-of-the-way place, to which no one can get with any convenience, and where no man well qualified for the station of teacher will live. No railroad or stage route passes it. A mud hack is the only conveyance to it. Look at the refusal of the late gentlemen, Messrs. Lathrop and Barnard, to take the presidency of the University. If it was removed to Franklin, Columbus, Noblesville, or Greenfield, it would be somewhere in the world.

3d. Those who have an acquaintance with the place object to sending their children there on account of the litigous, quarrelsome, tricky character of a great many of the people there. The students become contaminated. I have often heard men remark, that they never knew a politician educated at Bloomington who was not a Janus-faced political gouger. This objection, whether well founded or not

I pretend not to say or know, but I do know that it is believed in the community to be well founded, and hence, it operates against the institution as though it were true. For these, and other reasons, I think the State should waste no more money on the institution where it is, but remove it. I should like to hear from you on the subject.

LOVER OF LEARNING.

[We cheerfully give place to the above communication, and hope the subject will receive the consideration of all interested in our State Institutions. It is a notorious fact that but little good has or ever will be done by the University until it is placed in a position accessible from all parts of the State, and where the citizens will take interest to make the benefits and advantages known. We believe every county in the State is entitled to send two students to the University free of charge for tuition, and yet so little is known of it that but few counties avail themselves of this privilege. If it was in a location where its advantages could be known, there would be as much strife to get students from the different counties to it, as there is now to get appointments to West Point. We hope the incoming Legislature will take this matter under consideration, and if the University is continued, that it will be removed to some point where its benefits can be better understood and appreciated.—ED.]

Indianapolis, *The Locomotive,* December 11, 1852.

Document 53

On the Eve of Crisis

The Board of Trustees in 1851 had attempted to hire Dr. Henry Barnard, the great American scientist, to be President of Indiana University, and then provided that if he declined Reverend Alfred Ryors would become President. This action placed Ryors in office almost by default. The report for 1852 seemed to indicate a growing and expanding institution, but this was not to be because a disastrous fire almost destroyed the institution.

* * *

HIS EXCELLENCY, JOSEPH A. WRIGHT,
            Governor of the State of Indiana:
SIR:—I have the honor to present to you, and through you to the General Assembly, the annual report of the Board of Trustees of the University of Indiana.

Respectfully your ob't. serv't
JOS. G. MCPHEETERS,
INDIANAPOLIS, Jan. 29, 1853   *President of the Board.*

REPORT.

The Board of Trustees of the Indiana University respectfully submit the following report:

By the 13th section of an act approved June 17, 1852, providing for the government of the State University, the management of its funds, and for the disposition of the lands thereof, the following State officers constitute the Board of visitors of the University, viz:

His Excellency, Joseph A. Wright, Governor of the State;
Hon. Ashbel P. Willard, Lieutenant Governor:
Hon O. B. Torbert, Speaker of the House of Representatives;

Hon. William Z. Stuart,
Hon Andrew Davison,
Hon. Samuel E. Perkins,   ——————————— Judges of the Supreme Court;
Hon. Addison L. Roache,

Prof. William C. Larrabee, Superintendent of Public Instruction.

At the late annual commencement, a quorum of the Board of Visitors was not in attendance; his Excellency, the Governor of the State, being the only member present.

THE BOARD OF TRUSTEES.

William McKee Dunn, of Jefferson county.

George Evans, of Henry county.

Jacob Helwig, of DeKalb county.

Rev. John Benoit, of Allen county.

Michael Malott, of Lawrence county.

Rev. Patrick J. R. Murphy, of Martin county.

Thomas M. Adams, of Brown county.

Johnson McCullough, of Monroe county.

Nathaniel C. Browning, of Monroe county.

Joseph G. McPheeters, of Monroe county.

Jos. G. McPheeters, President; James D. Maxwell, Secretary; Jos. M. Howe, Treasurer.

At a meeting of the Board of Trustees held in Bloomington on the 3d day of June last, and called in consequence of Dr. Lathrop's declining the Presidency of the University previously tendered to him, the Hon. Henry Barnard, of Connecticut, was elected President; and to provide against the necessity of another called meeting of the Board, in case of his declining, the Rev. A. Ryors, President of the Ohio University, was elected alternate, at the same meeting.

Mr. Barnard having declined on account of "injuries received from being thrown out of a carriage," the Presidency was accordingly tendered to Rev. A. Ryors, and accepted.

The Faculty of the University is, therefore, now constituted as follows, viz:

Rev. Alfred Ryors, D. D., President, and Professor of Moral and Intellectual Philosophy and Belles-Lettres.

Daniel Read, A. M., Professor of Languages.

————— —————, Professor of Natural Philosophy and Chemistry.

Rev. Robert A. Milligan, A. M., Professor of Mathematics and Civil Engineering.

Hon. David McDonald, Professor of Law.

Matthew M. Campbell, A. M., Adjunct Professor of Languages, and Principal of the Preparatory Department.

Professor Theophilus A. Wylie, who for fifteen years has occupied the chair of Natural Philosophy and Chemistry in the University, resigned his place near the close of the late term, in consequence of his election to the chair of Mathematics in Miami University, at Oxford, Ohio. The ability and fidelity with which Professor Wylie discharged the duties of his department during his long connection with the University, have secured for him a high reputation throughout the State. For the immediate present, the duties of the vacant chair are distributed among the other Professors. It is hoped, however, the Board will be able to make provision for the vacancy at the meeting called for that purpose, on the 9th of February.

STUDENTS.

The number of students in attendance during the University year closing with the commencement in August last, was one hundred and sixty-seven. These were arranged according to the following classification, as may be seen by an examination of the accompanying catalogue, to which the Board respectfully beg leave to refer.

Seniors 7, juniors 5, sophomores 9, freshmen 16, scientific and irregular 50, preparatory 62, law 18. Notwithstanding the circumstances which during the past year especially tended to diminish the number of students, a greater number have been in attendance in the several departments, since the close of the last collegiate year, up to the present time, than during any corresponding period for years past. This is a fact which the Board are happy to present to the friends of the institution, as evidence of its flourishing condition and future prospects. And as the causes of depression have been transient, the hope may reasonably be indulged, that hereafter a constant and regular increase may be attained, and that the University of Indiana, with a faculty composed of men in the prime of life, unsurpassed in literary and scientific attainments, and ability to impart instruction, is yet destined to a brighter and more prosperous future.

COURSE OF STUDY.

The course of study in the college proper, occupies four years. It is the design of the University to maintain the highest standard of education which the state of the country will admit. None are permitted to graduate, unless they have completed the prescribed course, which they are required to pursue in an accurate and thorough manner.

Students, however, completing the course in any one department, are entitled to diplomas certifying that fact.

Candidates for admission to the Freshman class are examined in Arithmetic, English Grammar, Latin Grammar, Caesar's Commentaries, six books of Virgil's Aeneid, and Bullion's Greek Reader. These studies are attended to in the Preparatory Department, the design of which is to prepare students for entering the Collegiate department.

A candidate for an advanced standing, whether from another college or not, in addition to the preparatory studies, is examined in the various branches to which the class, that he proposes to enter has attended. Those who are admitted from other colleges, must produce certificates of dismission in good standing.

The following scheme gives a general view of the authors and subjects studied by the several college classes in each term.

FRESHMAN CLASS.

First Term.—Livy, Graeca Majora, Grecian and Roman Antiquities (Bojesin,) Algebra (Davies' Bourdon,) History (Taylor's Manual.)

Second Term.—Livy, Graeca Majora, Grecian and Roman Antiquities, Algebra completed, Geometry commenced (Davies' Legendre,) History.

Third Term.—Horace, Odes, Graeca Majora, Geometry completed, History.

SOPHOMORE CLASS.

First Term.—Horace, Satires and Epistles, Graeca Majora, Plane Spherical Trigonometry (Davies' Legendre,) Surveying commenced (Davies',) History continued.

Second Term.—Horace, Graeca Majora, Survey completed, Descriptive Geometry (Davies') Analytical Geometry commenced (Davies',) History.

Third Term.—Terence, Iliad and Odyssey, Analytical Geometry continued, History.

JUNIOR CLASS.

First Term.—Tacitus, Greek Drama, Euripides, Mechanics of solids (Bartlett's,) Chemistry, Heat and Electricity, Analytical Geometry completed, Differential Calculus commenced (Davies',) Rhetoric, Intellectual Philosophy (Reid.)

Second Term.—Juvenal, Greek Drama, Mechanics continued, Differential Calculus completed, Rhetoric completed, Logic commenced (Whateley's,) Moral Philosophy (Stewart.)

Third Term.—Juvenal, Greek Drama, Sophocles, Mechanics of solids completed, Integral Calculus (Davies') Inorganic Chemistry, Logic completed, Evidences of Christianity (Paley's.)

SENIOR CLASS.

First Term.—Cicero de Oratore, Pindar, Olympic and Pythian Odes, Mechanics of Fluids, The Analogy of Religion to the constitution and course of Nature (Butler's.)

Second Term.—Latin and Greek Classics, as selected by the Professor, Optics (Bache's Brewster,) Political Economy (Say's.)

Third Term.—Latin and Greek as selected, Astronomy (Gummere's,) Organic Chemistry, International and Constitutional Law (Kent.)

Declamations and Essays are required of all the classes every Saturday during the whole course. Written translations from Latin and Greek authors, are presented weekly by the Freshman, Sophomore and Junior Classes. These classes are also instructed in Latin and Greek composition.

NORMAL SCHOOL.

In pursuance of a resolution of the Board, Professor Daniel Read was appointed by the Faculty and Resident Trustees, to give lectures on Didactics in the Normal Department. The number of the class attending these lectures during the late term, was thirty-four, of whom twenty-two were males, and twelve females. The course of lectures on Didactics, and the principal subjects of study in this school, will hereafter be attended to during the summer term; this arrangement being thought more convenient to persons now engaged as teachers in the State, or designing to become so engaged. A course of weekly lectures, however, will be continued through the present term in this department.

The following course of studies has been prescribed for the Normal School, viz:

Reading, elocution, writing, linear drawing, mental and written arithmetic, book keeping, geography, with outline maps and the use of the globes, English grammar and composition, algebra, geometry, mensuration, surveying, natural philosophy, chemistry, human physiology, history—United States, and general—history of English literature, vocal music, Didactics. Those who complete the foregoing course, and pass a creditable examination thereon, will be entitled to a certificate or diploma, signed by the Faculty.

Auxiliary to the Normal department, the Board of Trustees have fitted up rooms in one of the buildings on the College campus, for a boys' model school, which they have placed under the general superintendence of the Faculty, and under the immediate instruction of Mr. John C. Smith, a graduate of the University in the class of 1851, and who, by a personal inspection of the most popular schools of this character in the Eastern States, had made himself well acquainted with the most approved modes of conducting them.

The Board have effected an arrangement with the accomplished principal (Mrs. E. J. McPherson,) of the Monroe County Female Seminary, by which this Seminary is placed under the direction of the Resident Trustees and the Faculty of the University, as the female department of the normal school. This arrangement most happily secures for this department the advantage of an admirable female model school, and the services of a lady possessing great capacity and tact as an instructor of youth. The Board trust the General Assembly of the State will grant some additional pecuniary aid to meet the increased expenditure necessarily incurred, and to enable them so to extend the department now established, as to furnish the most ample provision for the thorough training of the increasing numbers which our State school system will, every year, invite into the profession of teaching.

Agricultural Department.

In this department are embraced natural philosophy and chemistry, both organic and inorganic, including an account of nutrition, growth and respiration, in the vegetable and animal economy, and analysis of soils and manures, ores, marls, &c., as connected with agriculture. The course also includes mineralogy, geology and botany.

School of Theoretical and Practical Engineering.

This school is connected with the mathematical and chemical departments. It proposes, besides the collegiate course in mathematics and natural philosophy, to afford instruction in the theory of roads, railroads, canals, and bridges, the laws of heat and steam, theory and construction of the steam engine, and topographical surveying.

Law School.

In this department the students are divided into two classes, the Junior and senior.

The text books of the Junior class are, Blackstone's Commentaries, Kent's Commentaries, Smith on Contracts, and Stephen on Pleading. Those of the Senior class as Kent's Commentaries, Chitty on Pleading, Greenleaf on Evidence, and Mitford's Equity.

The course of instruction embraces all the branches of legal science. The classes are examined every day on their lessons in the text books; and lectures are delivered daily on the various subjects embraced in the study of jurisprudence. A moot court is held every Saturday, in which all the students are exercised in preparing, pleading and arguing legal questions and cases previously given out, on each of which an opinion is given by the presiding Professor.

A good law library is provided for the use of the students, but they must furnish their own text books. Members of the junior class will not, during the first session, need the text books of the Senior class.

Students who shall have attended the law school for two sessions will, in the discretion of the Law Faculty and Board of Trustees receive diplomas. None but practising attorney will be entitled to them in less than that time. The present session will end on the first Wednesday of April. The graduation fee is five dollars.

Commencement and Examinations.

The public commencement takes place on the first Wednesday of August. There are three public examinations, one at the close of each session.

General College Calendar.

The College year is divided into three terms. The first term begins seven weeks after the first Wednesday of August and ends on the 24th of December.

The second term begins on the second of January, unless that day fall on Sunday, in which case it begins on the third of January, and ends on the first Wednesday of April.

The third term begins four weeks after the first Wednesday of April, and ends on the first Wednesday of August, the day of commencement.

DISCIPLINE.

The government is intended to be strictly moral and paternal, avoiding, if possible, severe and disgraceful punishment. Students are treated as reasonable beings, and gentlemen. At the opening of each session, a lecture is given by the President, in which the course of conduct they are expected to pursue is pointed out, and such cautions and instructions are not only given by him, but by the Professors in their respective departments, from time to time, as occasion may require. By this means students are encouraged to think, to reason, to reflect, so that at length they may be expected to become "a law to themselves," and act with propriety in whatever circumstances they may be placed.

PUBLIC WORSHIP.

A portion of sacred Scripture is read, and prayer is offered every morning in the chapel at the calling of the roll; and the students are required to attend. Students are recommended to attend public worship on the Sabbath, either in the chapel of the University, or in some other place of worship in town. It is expected that parents will direct in this matter.

LITERARY SOCIETIES.

There are two Literary Societies, the Athenian and Philomathean, connected with the University, nearly equal in numbers, and both in a flourishing condition. Each has a well selected library of several hundred volumes; and each occupies a room in the principal University building, handsomely fitted up by its members.

LIBRARY.

The University Library is open to all the students on paying a subscription of fifty cents per session. Each subscriber is permitted to take out a volume every Saturday. The Library contains a choice collection of Greek, Latin, French and English classics; the best standard works on History, Biography, and the Sciences; together with a well selected variety of Miscellaneous Literature.

EXPENSES.

Tuition fees are in the College proper, eight dollars per term, in the law department, thirty dollars, and in the preparatory department, six dollars per term. In the model school, pupils are charged three dollars and fifty cents per term.

By an act of the Legislature of the State, two students from each county of the State, to be selected by the Board of County Commissioners, are admitted to any department of the University free of charge for tuition. County students are, however, charged one dollar per term for contingencies, as other students.

Students can board and lodge in private families at from $1 50 to $2 00 per week. The boarding club occupying the College boarding house, employ a cook and furnish their table, at a cost of $1 00 per week to each member.

COUNTY LECTURES.

In accordance with the requisition of the law, the Faculty appointed one of its members, the President, to visit three counties of the State, and in each "*deliver* a public lecture on the principles and organization of the University, and its educational facilities," during the recent vacation of one week. In compliance with this appointment, the President gave due notice of such lectures, to be delivered in the counties of Lawrence, Washington and Floyd, but the prevalence of high waters prevented him from reaching the places designated in time.

FINANCES.

For statement of the amount and condition of the University Fund, reference is respectfully made to the report of the Auditor of State, and also, to the report of Finance Committee, made at the last annual meeting of the Board, which is hereto appended.

SITE.

The town of Bloomington, the seat of the University is pleasantly situated in an elevated and well watered limestone region, upon the line of the New Albany and Michigan Railroad. From Gosport, situated on White River and sixteen miles distant, a branch of the road is in progress of construction, and promises an early completion to Indianapolis, the City of Railroads, thus making Bloomington easy of access in all directions.

In point of cheapness of living, healthful situation, and in many other respects, no place in the State is more suitable for the purposes of education.

Respectfully submitted on behalf of the Board,

Jos. G. McPheeters,
President of the Board.

APPENDIX

Report of Committee on Finance to the Board of Trustees, August, 1852.

MR. PRESIDENT:—The Committee on Finance to whom was referred the report of the treasurer, (Joseph M. Howe,) of the Indiana University, together with the duties generally of inquiring into the financial affairs of the University, have had the same under consideration, and directed the following report:

The committee, after careful examination and inquiry into the finances of the Institution with all the lights at command, find the amount of funds for which it mainly depends for existence and support (the interest of which being applicable only,) to be as follows:

Amount as reported by Auditor of State, Feb., 1852	$67,608 70
On loan in J. M. Howe's office	2,681 91
Probable amount in Commissioner Berry's outstanding	2,109 39
Total amount principal and interest	$72,400 00

The committee would urge upon the Board the propriety of keeping the principal up to the above sum, and if possible, to increase it. There is a portion of the "University Fund" in the hands of the Auditor of State under suspension, but what amount the committee is not advised. There is a large amount of interest unpaid on notes in Commissioner Berry's hands, for sales of land, the immediate collection of which is recommended.

The reliable income for the ensuing year may be estimated as follows, viz:

From interest receivable at the State Treasury	$4,000 00
From interest on funds in J. M. Howe's hands	160 00
From interest on funds in Jno. M. Berry's hands	800 00
From interest on funds in J. M. Howe's hands, due	660 00

Document 54

A New Helmsman

Alfred Ryors could hardly be considered a successful president, or to have had any real personal impact upon the institution. He resigned the presidency in 1852, after having served in the position only six months. He was succeeded by William M. Daily, a noisy camp-meeting Methodist orator, and a graduate of Indiana University. Governor Joseph Wright was an ardent Methodist and Democrat and he looked to a man of the faith to save the school. Daily's Inaugural ranged widely over the world and the past, but his generalities indicated little knowledge of what a university should be on August 2, 1853.

*   *   *

INAUGURAL.

Here, in these academic groves, we meet for a literary festival. You come to enjoy the classic associations of the hour, and, by your presence and your smiles, to say "God speed" to the cause of liberal learning. Your speaker comes to assume the responsibilities of the high trust committed to his care in the eloquent and impressive charge, just delivered by our worthy Executive. To him, therefore, this hour is one of far more than ordinary interest. The magnitude of the trust, so vividly brought before the mind, would make any man, not wholly insensible, tremble, and he could only be sustained by the hope of being able to discharge its duties with fidelity, and to meet the responsibilities connected with it, in such a way as to show himself in some good degree worthy of the confidence reposed by the honorable Board of Trustees.

Long established custom has made it obligatory upon me, in assuming this trust, to deliver an address on some subject appropriate to the occasion.

An adventurer in Central America, after climbing over range after range of volcanic hills, rising one above another, at length stood upon the dividing summit, from which he could see both oceans at once. On the one hand he beheld the blue Atlantic with its storms and its islands of tropical beauty, while on the other lay the dark heaving Pacific, rolling away to those elysian climes, where the dreams of the west have placed the paradise of earth. So, after the struggle of ages, man has reached a lofty eminence,—an almost sky-piercing pinnacle—which commands a view of the ancient and modern world at the same time. On the one hand are the fairy isles of the ancient civilization, science and literature; on the other, is, another part of the ocean of eternity, on which may be traced the courses of richly freighted argosies, ploughing their way towards a destiny known only to that God whose eye can pierce the clouds and darkness which rest upon the unknown deep.

We, of the present generation, have reached this lofty eminence in arts, science, civilization and religion; still we should not forget that we have a rich inheritance in the past. Rob us of this inheritance, and we are left in abject penury both in literature and science. It is true, we can see a little farther than those who have gone before us, but it is only because we stand upon a mental pyramid which has been reared up for us by the labors of countless generations.

Now, instead of looking down with scorn, as some are wont to do, upon the mighty achievements of our predecessors, it should be our ambition to carry this pyramid still farther towards heaven, and not make ourselves little, in the contemplation of our greatness.

There is rife among us, at this day, what may, appropriately, be styled an *anti*-historical philosophy, which we can but regard as being at once "the root and the offspring" of a shallow scepticism. The disciples of this school would have us look upon the whole past as an inextricable maze of the weakest self-delusions, or a kind of wholesale jugglery. They are unwilling to undergo the labor, if indeed they have the mental capacity for so doing, of separating the pure bullion of truth from the alloy of error and delusion; hence, they hastily consign the whole to the tomb of explored chimeras'. According to their philosophy, nature is a machine, life the motion of particles, and history a tissue of folly, selfishness and priestcraft. Every great nature full of fiery earnestness about matters with which they happen to have no sympathy, or for which they have no capacity, is denounced as a hypocrite, an imposter, or a fanatic. And every lofty manifestation of the better part of man's nature in ages gone by, is sneered at as an outburst of silly enthusiasm, or a trick of selfish ambition.

All this contempt for the past, under the specious pretext of *progress,* I regard as literary, moral and political desolation. To exclude God and his Providence from the history of the past, is not only to sap the foundation of religion, but to bring into doubt almost everything which exalts and embellishes the nature of man. And in relation to civil affairs, contempt for the past is an error to which American Society is peculiarly exposed, and, therefore, the duty of combating it, is especially enjoined upon every American Scholar. We are in little or no danger of falling into the opposite extreme, as is the case in some parts of Europe. Toryism can never take deep root in American soil; hence it would be idle in us to aim our blows at a mere imaginary foe, while there is a real tendency, threatening the very extinction of all reverence for the learning and civilization of the past, with all the ennobling emotions allied to such reverence. That groveling demagogueism which is ever ready to sap the very foundations of our learning and civilization, by fostering this tendency, should be regarded as a moral pestilence, more to be dreaded than the greatest physical calamities.

We have met with a popular sycophancy which would fain make us believe that all learning of *utility,* political wisdom, and the great principles of liberty, are, like *potatoes* and *tobacco,* indigenous to American soil. And some of these Goths and Vandals have gone so far as absurdly to contend for what they are pleased to call an *"American Education."* By which they mean, an education that shall effectually cut us off from all connection with the past, and forever cancel all our obligations to the wisdom and learning of the old world. Most suicidal policy! No nation ever did, or ever will become learned, polished, or great, by such a process. There are nations of the earth where they have still some remnants of old abuses to demolish; but ours is not the task to destroy, but to build up. We have nothing to spare from the rich lore of the past: in it we have a priceless inheritance.

In speaking of the progressive development of man's destinies upon earth, we would borrow a figure from the Scandinavian Poetry, and represent it as a mighty tree. Now, you may, nay, even should prune off all the surplus branches and remove all injurious excrescences, but you should never forget that the most beautiful flowers of modern civilization and learning, and the richest fruits which have ripened in the sunshine of modern science, have drawn their vital sap from the broad and buried roots of antiquity, which has been carried up through a mighty trunk, the growth of ages.

To the barbarian, you may apply Plato's definition of man, "a two-legged animal without feathers." Barbarianism is unmitigated animalism, a sort of slumber from which man never awakes until some stimulus is applied. He seems to be subject to a moral gravitation that weighs him down to the "vile dust from which he sprang." Everything which ennobles and exalts him, is in opposition to this gravitation. It is true he has eagle wings, yet he is ever prone to fold them at his side, and content himself with feeding upon the mere garbage of earth. It certainly requires either external, or divine culture, to raise his eyes heavenward and plume his pinions for the mountain top, and the upper skies. However, the very moment he is thoroughly aroused from his moral and mental stupidity, by the appliances of religion and learning, and thus rendered sensible of the advantages of civilization, the internal change in his nature manifests itself in a thousand forms of external improvement, and the definition of Plato will no longer apply. He now rises above mere animalism, and seeks the lofty embellishments of his nature.

Still, nothing that we know of the primitive seats of the human race, gives the least countenance to the theory that barbarism was the primeval state of man. It is rather the state into which he falls, from a total neglect of external culture, and a rejection of Divine teachings. The theory of a gradual rise of man, from the stupidity of barbarism into civilization and refinement, is almost as absurd as the old Egyptian notion that men originally grew like mushrooms from the mud of the Nile, or the more modern infidel notion, that they were *monkeys,* and have gradually ascended to the grade of men, which means that we are a race of monkeys, slightly modified. We do not marvel that infidels, who reject the light of revealed truth, as well as the light of history, should ascribe the origin of man to some monstrous absurdity, such as an unnatural excitation of material bodies, or that they should look for *their projenitors among monkeys,* or brutes; as there is certainly something congruous and seemly, in fixing the origin of man, in the same state to which they are sure to conduct him by their boasted philosophy. Man may fall from his primeval state into barbarism, and from this state he can only be raised by the stimulus of external or Divine culture—in a word, by *Education.*

From our mount of observation, we may trace the streams of art and knowledge, through Greece, Asia Minor, and Phoenicia to the valleys of the Nile and the plains of Chaldea. Here the lights of profane history go out, and without the Hebrew Scriptures, we would be left in utter darkness. The traveler in the silent deserts of Upper Egypt, in the "marble wilderness of Syria," the jungles of India, and the cyclopean ruins of Greece and Italy, is often startled at the time-defying relics of an almost unparalleled civilization, which belonged to those mighty ages, of which all that is known is comprised in a few chapters of Genesis. What is known, therefore, must bear a small proportion to what has forever perished, if ever chronicled.

When we trace the streams of population towards their sources, they invariably lead to the banks of the Euphrates; so that we may fairly infer that the country lying between the Euphrates and the Indus, was the primitive seat of our race. And in all probability the Ark rested upon one of the lofty summits of the Indian Caucasus, parts of that mighty chain, extending from the frontier of China, to the Black Sea. This forms the northern boundary of that region which was the cradle of Art, Religion, Science, and civilization—that great zone of light, which gleaming westward, across Europe and America, will soon have encircled the globe.

The foundations of the modern world, with all her civilization and refinement, were laid by a few small tribes around the Mediterranean. There were the Hebrews, the Greeks, and the Romans. To the Hebrews was allotted the custody of moral and religious truth; to the Greeks, the empire of reason and imagination; to the iron Romans, the power of arms, by which, with their own civil institutions, and the arts, literature and religion of the other two nations, they laid a deep and broad foundation for what we call the Christian civilization. Upon this foundation, the free Germanic nations, have built the modern world. Hence, we can no more dispense with the learning of the past than the edifice can dispense with the foundation.

The influence of the Greek Language and Literature, upon the destinies of man, cannot well be over-rated. Athens is still endeared to us as the *Alma Mater* of the literary world. The Greeks followed the Roman arms to the ends of the earth. Wherever the eagle perched, there the master-pieces of Grecian genius soon found an entrance; to awaken the powers of the mind, or to stimulate a generous emulation. Erasmus said, in presenting a copy of the Greek Testament to a friend, "If you would drink deep of the well-springs of wisdom, apply to the Greek. The Latins have only shallow rivulets: The Greeks copious rivers, running over sands of gold. Read Plato; he wrote on marble with a diamond; but above all read the New Testament, 'Tis the key to the kingdom of heaven.' "

Intellectually, the Greeks were the masters of the Romans, though politically their subjects. It was the emulation of the fine Grecian models, that caused the Latin Literature to make its rapid advances. Though it never reached the perfection of its prototype, it ranks next to Christianity itself as an element of modern civilization.

In the development of the Divine plan, link after link, in a continuous chain, for the education and elevation of mankind, the introduction of Christianity,— the Gospel of the Lord Jesus Christ—forms the culminating point, the summit level of the line of communication opened between earth and heaven. It sheds light upon the past, and pours its healing streams through the desolate wastes of humanity, causing the moral desert "to rejoice and blossom as the rose." In its origin, it was quiet and unobtrusive. Not until it came in contact with the upper crust of custom, prejudices, and old institutions, hardened by time into stone, did it begin to shake the world. It steadily gained ground, however, in its onward course, overthrowing the proud temples and altars of Paganism, until even the eagle of imperial Rome, veiled his eye of fire before the Cross of Jesus.

In our very rapid survey of the past, we can only pass from one mountain top to another, and take a mere summary glance, at the almost boundless regions of Philosophy and Literature, leaving for those of more leisure or learning, to explore the richer valleys.

The progress of *Language,* and that of *Intellect* are so nearly concurrent, that the one may generally be taken as the measure of the other. *Language* has been called "the vesture of thought;" more properly, it might be called *"the body* of which thought is *the soul."* They generally grow together, and exercise a reciprocal influence. If we carefully watch the process of thought in our own minds, we will find that *we think in words.* Indeed we cannot carry on a train of thought, without words. It is often said, that such a man has good ideas, but has not words to express them. We would reverse this statement, and say, the man does not think clearly on any given subject, because he has not words to fix the fugitive thought in his memory, until the whole matter has passed under review. Poverty of language is usually connected with poverty of intellect; and the connection is so intimate, that it is difficult to say, in any given case, which is the *cause,* and which the *effect*. But to enrich the language of men, is, certainly, to enlarge the range of their ideas. And here, again, we see our obligation to the past. Modern literature was under no necessity of inventing a language. The iron Romans not only imposed their laws, but also their language upon all conquered provinces. Everywhere the Latin language became the language of civil and ecclesiastical proceedings, of learned men, and of the most cultivated classes of society.

The *English Language* was introduced into the island of Great Britain in the year 450 by two rude tribes—the Angles and Saxons—from Hanover in Germany,—and their combination produced the Anglo-Saxons. The lineal elements of the English Language, are, the Anglo-Saxon, Celtic, Gothic, and Classic. The Anglo-Saxon is the base, and consisted at first of but *one thousand,* or *fifteen hundred,* words;—an exceedingly meager language. But it has gone on absorbing the other elements, until it has swelled into a language of more than *eighty thousand* words, including its scientific terms. After the conquest of Great Britain, by William the Conqueror, the classic element, composed of Latin and Greek, began to be introduced; but this element has been incorporated principally since the Revival of Literature, and the Reformation. Each lineal element of the language has its practical value, and appropriate scope of thought. Hence, the English Language should be studied by its lineal elements. Our literature is founded upon the literature of the past; hence, to absolve ourselves from all allegiance to the literature of the ancients, is to sweep away the very foundations of modern learning.

In our hasty sketch we pass over the long night of the Dark Ages, during which the fountains of knowledge were sealed up, and come to the age, called the revival of Literature.

The first glimmer of returning light, disclosed the dove of Christianity, which had survived the general ruin. In her mouth she bore the olive branch, and from her plumage shook the seeds of a mightier civilization. We can but rapidly sketch the mighty changes which, almost immediately, followed.

The revival of literature thoroughly awakened the intellect of the modern world, and stimulated every species of inquiry. The first drafts from the unsealed fountains, seemed to produce a kind of intoxication. In all ages the love of knowledge is an unquenchable passion of the human soul, and is, perhaps, destined to survive all others, and live on with the immortality of man. But there is probably, nothing in our times that will enable us to form a proper conception of the enthusiastic reverence for wisdom and learning, which, after the revival of letters, and the consequent establishment of the Universities, drew around the celebrated teachers, such throngs of eager and devoted students. In the fourteenth century, there were in the University of Oxford alone, no less than thirty thousand students. Some, modern would-be lights of the world, have thought proper to sneer at the literary enthusiasm of those times; because, forsooth, *in their opinion,* the pursuits of the multitude of students were *unprofitable*. It is true, some of the questions of the schoolmen appear to us exceedingly puerile; yet we must remember that the human mind had then but fairly waked up, after the slumber of ages. And furthermore, an undying interest in those deep matters, chastened by an experimental knowledge of the limits of human knowledge, in our present state of being, lies at the bottom of every philosophic mind.

The question is often asked, in this *ultra-utilitarian age,* of what use are enquiries, or researchers, that can yield no certain result? This question certainly betrays very narrow views of the real objects of intellectual culture. Science may make contributions to wealth, comfort and luxury, but we must never lose sight of this great fact, that one of the prime objects of education, is, the development of the mental and moral faculties themselves. The expansive mind will despise no species of research which will lift the soul above the paltry concerns of earth-born selfishness, and spread it abroad where it may exercise its own mighty power in wide and lofty regions. The scholastic Philosophy was a sort of *intellectual gymnastics,* which accustomed the mind to the exercise of its own powers, and thus prepared the way for the inductive system of Bacon. This great philosopher was under obligations to the very men whose authority he demolished forever. It is thus the half enlightened labors of one age, may become a part of the culture of the next.

We often hear it said that most discoveries in science have been the result of accident. But we forget that the same accident might have happened a thousand times, had no philosophic mind been present to improve it, without producing any such result. Before the eyes of the uncultivated, Phenomena pass unheeded, while to the Philosopher, they furnish ample scope for disciplined powers of research. Millions of apples had fallen, long before that simple circumstance became to the disciplined mind of Newton, the first link of a chain that encircled the universe. His mighty mind had been borne upward by the ever rising surges of a mysterious tide, of which, the scholastic philosophy had been a tributary, until he reached a point from which his eye could sweep the universe of God.

It might be well for us to remark in this connection, that the aspirations and attainments of man, are usually on a level with his views of his own nature and destiny. Hence, we turn to the Bible as the great source of truth, and as the best guide to the highest style of man. It presents the most ennobling views of the origin, nature, and destiny of man. Such views as will lead to the greatest mental effort and scientific research. The Bible, then, should be regarded as the great patron, or foster mother, of the arts and sciences. All great thoughts and lofty aspirations, claim kindred with immortality and infinity. A Newton could be happy, in picking up shells and pebbles on the shore of the vast ocean of truth, because he believed in the immortality of man, and that he should one day launch forth into the ocean itself, and spend an eternity in exploring its mighty secrets. Only convince a man that when his eyes shall close in death, that the lights of mind must go out in everlasting night, and that he never again will look out upon this wondrous universe, and you quench forever, his lofty aspirations. It may be said that some who have professed this dismal creed, have been ardent in the pursuit of knowledge. True, but men often act unconsciously upon principles which they discard in theory. The common belief of the immortality of man, is so deeply implanted in the human soul, that some fibres of it will live on, in spite of a sceptical philosophy. And it must not be forgotten that the Atheistical philosophers lived in times when knowledge was not only reputable, but also a source of wealth and position in society; and these may have been the motives that awakened their ardor in the pursuit of knowledge.

We have seen, in our rapid sketch of the past, that the first vigorous shoots of the civilization of the modern world, sprung up from the ruins of the Roman empire. These were sheltered by Christianity from the northern tempests, experienced the fostering care of monarchy, in the persons of Charlemagne and Alfred, and bloomed under the culturing hand of a chivalrous aristocracy. As the tender germ, which in summer, is to expand into a flower, and in autumn, mature into a wholesome fruit, is wrapped up in fold after fold, the outer one being the roughest and most capable of withstanding the bleakness of early spring, so the germs of modern improvement have been sheltered from the storms of the world's spring, by the strong outer coats of these institutions. The germ and the inner folds expanded, and the outer ones, as their purposes were completed, burst open, and fell off; so that now, we enjoy the flowers and fruits of the modern civilization.

We are all wont to look upon the Anglo-Saxons as the vanguard of the hosts of freedom; but they have still another great mission entrusted to their hands. Divine Providence has partitioned off the greater part of the world between the two great branches of this dominent race of men, as a vast field for *the diffusion of their Language and Literature,* as well as their political institutions. The empire of Great Britain has pushed forward the outposts of civilization, to the shores of New Zealand, in the south, and to the very verge of the polar ice, in the north. The off-shoots of this wonderful race, which were planted on the Atlantic coast of North America, only two centuries ago, have already grown into a mighty nation, upon a territorial foundation extending from ocean to ocean. Already our civil, literary, and religious institutions are attracting the gaze of surrounding nations. The Anglo-Saxons are everywhere regarded as the torch-bearers of religion, science, and liberty. They are kindling their lights on every hill-top through all the ancient realms of darkness; and when these shall flash on high, and run together, the earth will be encircled with a brilliant illumination.

When we see with what accelerated velocity, the English Language, Laws, and Literature, are being diffused to the farthest bounds of earth, we are almost tempted to imagine that Divine Providence has given to the Anglo-Saxon race a fee simple conveyance of this planet, "with the appurtenances thereunto belonging."

American society is *the net product of the whole past,* eliminated from those terms, which, though useful in working out the problem, must be cancelled to obtain the result. At one time, to be called a Roman citizen, was an honor greater than royalty itself; but still greater honor and responsibility, should attach to the citizen of the Anglo-American Republic! If we are only true to ourselves, and true to the cause of *liberal education* we cannot doubt, that, here, human intelligence is destined to reach its loftiest earthly manifestations, and civilization attain its most glorious triumphs: But to insure this, we must give to genius, wisdom and learning their due regard, place virtue and intelligence above wealth and office, preserve that true liberty which is consistent with a lofty morality, and above all, cling with holy veneration to that most precious of all legacies, THE BIBLE—the Revelation of God to man. Much, very much, has been given us, and much, very much, will be required.

This nation has a deeper and more living interest in the cause of Education, than any other nation that now exists, or, that ever has existed. The genius of our government, our lofty position, our manifest destiny, and the great mission entrusted to us by Divine Providence, all combine to make it necessary that we should regard Education, in the broadest sense of the term; of paramount importance. The man who is a zealous patron of liberal learning, in the country, is a world's benefactor.

That COLLEGES are needed in this country, is a point unnecessary to argue before an audience like this. We need, nay, *we must have Colleges.* Colleges amply supplied with all the material and personal conditions for realizing the true and noble idea of such institutions. The College holds an indispensable, as well as a most important place, in every perfect system of Public Instruction. And it is certainly the duty of the State, according to our organic law; to provide a complete and perfect system of Public Instruction. The obligation is already partially recognized by the Legislature of this Commonwealth. To establish and organize the University and the College, in connection with the primary and secondary institutions, so as to constitute one great system, such as the wants of the State demand, and as the idea of a complete system of Public Instruction implies, is a *Public* work, and can be *well done,* only, by the Public power.

The State of Indiana has her University. And we intend it shall be a place to obtain a really *"liberal education"* in the good old scholarly meaning of the term,—the course of studies shall be *"liberal"* studies. In a college course, as we humbly conceive, the object should not be the acquisition of special knowledge for this or that particular destination in life. These should always come afterwards, as any one may choose. The College course of under-graduate studies, should be mainly a discipline for the mind. It should afford ample scope, and means, for the fullest and most harmonious development and culture of the mental faculties, and for acquisitions of knowledge and accomplishments of taste, which form the *true liberally educated man.* To accomplish all this, there is no conceivable organization of studies so well adapted, as, the good old-fashioned *curriculum,* of classical, mathematical, logical, and rhetorical studies. These studies, properly proportioned, and thoroughly pursued, will secure the very best possible training for the mind. The course of studies at the Institutions of Europe, and of this country, is the same, and has been adopted only after the most mature reflection, by the literary, the wise and the good. To resist this, will be to oppose your judgment against the opinion of men most distinguished for learning, wisdom and piety. This would certainly be irrational, and contrary to sound discretion.

In all reason, the four years of under-graduate study is time short enough, for accomplishing to any real good purpose, the course above referred to. And yet there is a disposition in some Colleges, to crowd into this four years an additional number of studies; so that the course of classical and mathematical learning is compressed, or hurried through with, in order to make time for the modern additional courses; and these, in their turn, are of necessity compressed into mere meager and fruitless compends. It is thus, sometimes, that by attempting to do too much, we do nothing thoroughly. We would very much prefer making a thorough mastery, not only a possibility, but a reality; that we may inspire that true love of learning, which *thorough learning* always inspires, and thus impart that high discipline, and fine mental culture, which will be a source or real pleasure and power through life.

We do not object to courses of practical instruction in the modern languages, in physics, in the application of science to the useful arts, or anything which the spirit of the age, and the wants of the times demands. These should all be connected with our Universities, too, provided they are either *literary,* or *scientific,* and that they be not crowded into the four years under-graduate course; but come after, or on one side of it. The regular College course is needful for the pure interests of science and good letters, needful to make scholars; and nothing should be allowed to impair its proper functions.

It is not my purpose, neither does it comport with my views, to magnify the studies in one part of the course at the expense of those in another; but I must say, classical and mathematical studies are the two great pillars upon which rest the whole edifice of human learning. The sciences rest upon Mathematics, and literature upon the Classics. The vast temple, of literature and science, with all its beautiful proportions, its spacious halls, and almost endless corridors, can only stand on the sure foundation of mathematics and the classics. Let any daring Samson, in his blindness, destroy either of these pillars, and his only glory will be to perish in the wreck of human learning.

But, it is said there are some whose circumstances will not permit them to take this extensive course—they wish merely to prepare for teaching the elementary schools, or for business pursuits. To all such we say, our classes in this University are most cheerfully opened. We will only ask that what you study, you study well. But the most earnest advice, to all young men, whose circumstances will at all permit, is, to pursue the entire College course, taking the studies in the regular order; believing this course the best calculated to develop the mind, and make the scholar.

But all this does not comprise the whole of education: There is a part of human existence to which this life is but the vestibule. *Intellectual power,* to be a blessing to the world and its possessor, must be combined with *moral goodness.* Hence, while we would carefully avoid a narrow, illiberal, or, merely partizan religious instruction, in this University, we announce to the world, that it shall be our aim to have this Institution under the hallowing influences of the Gospel of God. It is our design that the waters of the Pierean stream, should mingle with those of "Siloa's fount, that flows fast by the Oracle of God;" and that the evergreens of Parnassus should grow with the living vine which clusters on Mount Zion. We will look to the Bible, as the great text book of human duty; and endeavor to form a high character of moral excellence, by an appeal to the sense of religious obligation, and principles drawn from this book alone. In this country we have no Penates, or household gods, but books. Of these "there is no end." But we could ever remind the student, that above, and beyond all others, proudly pre-eminent, is that "Book of Books," the Bible; and that it should stand among his other books, like Jupiter among the gods,—*supreme.* And we would say to him, from this book you may gather a rich lore, far surpassing that of Greek or Roman story; be led to the highest eminence of moral excellence, and secure the enjoyment of supreme felicity.

We intend that *the government* of our University shall be *parental.* Instead of relying upon a long code of arbitrary rules, to secure order, we expect simply to appeal to the judgment and moral sense of the student. We will treat him as a friend, and teach him to properly appreciate his relations to the Faculty, and his obligations to the University. It is true, that, in some things, College government is *sui generis,* and while it is parental, we intend that it shall be, at the same time firm and strict, sufficiently so, at least, as to secure the most perfect order, and complete subordination.

I stand before you under circumstances, which, as I trust, justify a word of personal reference.

Eighteen years ago I went forth from this Institution with my first College honors; bestowed by him who sleeps on yonder's slope, in an honored grave. Peace to the memory of my old, and much revered Preceptor! One year ago, at the call of this honorable Board of Trustees, I returned to enter on the duties of my present office. And a year's experience has only increased my deep sense of the responsibilities I have assumed, in accepting the Presidency of this University. But I bring to the service of my ALMA MATER, a deep devotion to her interests, a high sense of her honor, and a consecration of all my energies.

Gentlemen of the Board of Trustees: To you we look for direction, for sympathy, and for support. By your resolute and persevering efforts, we confidently expect this Institution to become a glory, and a blessing to the State, to the nation, and to the world of letters. For this we will live and labor.

This has been to your Faculty a year of extraordinary care, anxiety, and toil. Indeed it has been an eventful year in the history of the University. Our main building has been swept from us in a night. Our University Library, in some respects beyond price—rich in learned lore, comprising some volumes of very rare merit, and such as cannot be replaced if ever, for many years to come:—this, too, has perished in the flames. Our beautiful Society Halls, endeared to our students by so many hallowed associations, with all their tasteful furniture, and valuable Libraries—all, all gone!

For a time, these things sickened and saddened our hearts. And when we saw Athenians and Philomatheans, going "to and fro," in search of suitable Halls as temporary homes, we thought of Noah's dove, when driven from the Ark, "without a place for the sole of her foot;" of Abraham when "he went out, not knowing wither he went;" and of Hagar, in the wilderness, when "she lifted up her voice and wept!"

But in the midst of all this, our students, with a devotion to their Alma Mater, almost unparalleled, have rallied around us, and, in the day of adversity, have adhered to us like noble Spartans, with the greatest fidelity. So much so, that our classes have even increased in strength. We have had ample opportunity to demonstrate to the world, that *Indiana University is competent to an emergency;* and that her reputation does not depend on "brick and mortar," on architectural display, or even on extensive and valuable libraries. It is for you to say how far we have succeeded.

Fortunately, we still have our Laboratory and apparatus,—our "Old College" building, for recitation rooms, and our morning prayers;—and also these sacred groves of Academus, hallowed by a thousand pleasant associations, to many now before me. These constitute "our vine and fig tree" under which we expect to dwell, until by your zeal and enterprize, a new University Building, Phoenix-like, shall rise from the ashes of the old, more spacious and beautiful, furnishing us and our Literary Societies, permanently, with ample homes and Halls. We confidently look forward to the day when it shall be said, "The glory of the latter house, is greater than the glory of the former." May Indiana University live forever! the pride of her Alumni, the glory of our beloved State, and a blessing to the land!

Gentlemen of the Faculty: We are brethren. Like Jonathan and David, our hearts are "knit together," in the arduous and incessant labors of Academic life. Let us labor on, while the day lasts. Ours is a great work. We are forming the character of immortal intellects. Verily, we "paint for eternity." Our work will be inspected in the gallery of eternity. Let us, then, find in our labors their own exceeding great reward.

Young gentlemen of the University: We call upon you to second all our efforts for your advancement. We have tried to do your minds and your hearts good. We have every reason to believe that you think so, in the fidelity with which you have adhered to the University in the day of her calamity. We will still live and labor for your good. And now, we ask, that, as you go out into the world, you go to reflect honor upon your Alma Mater. Cherish her memory. And may the world learn from you the great advantages of science and letters, brought under the influence of Christian principle.

Inaugural of William M. Daily, August 2, 1853.

Document 55

Disaster

Whatever William Daily may have envisioned for Indiana University in the future, that promise went up in smoke. On April 9, 1854 at 2:00 a.m., the University building and its precious collections were consumed by fire. To restore the building and to begin operation of the University all over was the most serious challenge the institution ever faced in its long history.

*   *   *

REPORT.
To the General Assembly of the State of Indiana:

The Board of Trustees of Indiana University respectfully present the following Report, supplemental to their regular Annual Report which has already been made, in accordance with the provisions of law.

The Annual Report presents a full and detailed statement of the condition of the University, so far as relates to the several departments of instruction, the course of studies therein, the officers, students, and the ordinary operations of the Institution.

There are facts and circumstances not immediately connected with the regular progress and work of the University, which it is proper should be brought to the cognizance of the General Assembly, for such action as they may deem expedient in the premises.

It is generally known that the main University edifice, containing the chapel, the principal recitation rooms, and the halls of the two literary societies—fitted up by those societies at a large expense—together with the college and law libraries, and the libraries of the two societies, was, on the night of April 9th, last, consumed by fire. The burning occurred near the beginning of the spring vacation, when there was no fire in or about the college buildings for any lawful purpose, nor had there been for more than three days—breaking out about two o' clock at night. It is generally supposed to have been the work of an incendiary.

The grand jury of the county of Monroe have spent much time in attempting to ferret out the perpetrator of the crime; and at the late term of the circuit court, and individual was indicted for arson in burning the college.

The loss of many volumes of rare and curious books, collected by the late Dr. Wylie, and a monument of his learning, is one which money cannot repair. Some of those volumes could not be furnished in the United States, and some of them could not now be had in any book market of the world; so that their destruction is justly regarded as an irreparable calamity to the State.

On the 27th of April, a special meeting of the Board of Trustees was called, to take into consideration the course necessary to be adopted, in consequence of the destruction of so much property of the University. The Board deemed it expedient and indeed necessary, to take immediate steps for the erection of a new University edifice. With this view, Wm. Tinsley, Esq., an architect well recommended to the Board of Trustees, was employed to prepare a design, according to a specification of accommodation furnished him, and with a limitation of costs to $18,000. The outline of the plan which was submitted by the architect, and adopted by the Board, is herewith communicated in the paper, marked A.

In order to raise the means for this extraórdinary expenditure, a subscription was proposed to the citizens of Bloomington and vicinity; and as the result, the sum of $10,000 was subscribed. The Board further resolved to apply for a loan of $6,000 from the Sinking Fund. The commissioners of this fund consented to the loan, in case legal security could be given. Members of the Board, in their individual capacity, and private citizens proffered their names, upon the agreement and understanding that application should be made to the Legislature, at the present session, to discharge them by law from personal liability, and in their stead to charge the lands granted by Congress to the State, for the use of the University, with the liabilities incurred by this loan. In this manner the loan was effected. As the State has in trust for the University full control of these lands, amounting to 23,040 acres, and of all the funds which may arise from the sale thereof, as well as all the other funds of the University, with undoubted legal power to apply these means, beneficially, for the use of the Institution, there is more than ten-fold security under the control of the State. To individuals, the security which they have cheerfully tendered is an embarrassment upon their property, and in justice to them ought clearly to be transferred to the property of the University and charged thereon.

The Board of Trustees respectfully ask that this transfer be made by act of the General Assembly.

Immediately after the Board resolved to commence rebuilding, a contract was entered into for the necessary quantity of brick; but from uncertainty in procuring funds, and from other causes, the work of construction could not [be] begun before the middle of September. A strong force was then applied, and building operations were diligently prosecuted, until further progress was arrested by cold weather. A substantial foundation of stone work has been made, and the walls have been carried up to the third story, and carefully protected from the action of the whether [sic], until the work can be resumed in the spring. This is the present condition of the building. Unless the Board shall be embarrassed by the want of funds, it can be completed during the ensuing summer and fall.

The subscription in aid of the building was made prior to the present general pecuniary embarrassment of the country, and before the indications of suffering from drought; and it is feared the intervention of these causes will produce delay and difficulty, if not loss, in the collection of subscriptions. The fear of the diversion of a large portion of the endowment fund, in consequence of the late decision of the Supreme Court of Indiana, has also operated unfavorably to the collection of subscriptions, and will continue to do so, until all doubt on this subject is removed.

The suit brought against the State by the Vincennes University, after various decisions by different courts, has been finally decided against the State, by the Supreme Court of the State. The decree against the State in that suit is for above sixty thousand dollars; and the court orders the decree to be discharged by the Auditor and Treasurer of State, and a certain commissioner, out of a fund in charge of the State, and which is designated in the State Treasury as the *University Fund*. The greater portion of that fund has arisen from the sales of land in the college township, in Monroe county, and belongs exclusively to the State University at Bloomington; and it is certain that the offices of the Auditor and Treasurer of State furnish no evidence of any moneys or securities, out of which the decree can be legally discharged.

It is impossible, in the opinion of the Board, that the aforesaid funds can be made liable to the said decree, which is rendered against the State alone, in a suit against the State, and to which suit the State University was not a party.

The Vincennes University has, however, moved the circuit court for a mandate to compel the Auditor and Treasurer of State and said commissioner, to discharge the said decree out of the said University fund, and that motion is now pending in that court.

The Trustees of the State University have filed a bill in chancery in the proper court, praying a decree to enjoin the Auditor and Treasurer of State and said Commissioner, from discharging the decree against the State, by the payment or transfer of any of the moneys or securities in the State Treasury or elsewhere belonging to the State University. And, as that University was no party to the suit or to the decree, the Board have every reason to expect, that the injunction will be granted and be made perpetual.

These are the facts with respect to the decree against the State, in favor of the Vincennes University. They are respectfully submitted with the hope, that the Legislature will, by law, make such disposition of the said decree, as will forever prevent it from having any effect upon the funds of the State University. These funds are held by the State, in trust, for the State University; and they must in the language of the State Constitution, *"remain inviolate, and be faithfully and exclusively applied to the purposes for which the trust was created."*

However favorably for the State University, the questions involved in the pending controversy may, in the end, be settled, it is well known that the Institution cannot be carried on successfully, while the use of its funds is suspended or withheld by injunctions or decrees of court, unless the General Assembly shall interpose and direct, by law, that an amount, not exceeding the annual proceeds of the University fund, shall as heretofore, be paid upon the warrant of the proper University officer; or unless other aid, such as the General Assembly may in its wisdom devise, shall be extended to meet the present emergency of the Institution. In the existing condition of the suit, there are no means without legislative action, at the command of the Board to meet the salaries of the Professors, which, for the current quarter, fall due the last of this month. The liabilities of the Board for the current year, will more fully appear from the report of the committee of Finance in the accompanying paper, marked B.

The Board confidently appeal to the General Assembly for aid, in enabling them to fulfil the obligations of honor into which they have entered; and they make the appeal with greater confidence, inasmuch as the present condition of the fund is the result of legislative action, in which the Board was not a party. They also feel great confidence, that the funds of the University will, by course of judicial decision, be relieved in such manner, that advances made for the University to meet the existing exigency, may be repaid from its own means. If the aid as asked for, shall not be granted by the General Assembly, the suspension of the University, which has been so long in successful existence, affording the means of literary and scientific education to hundreds of young men, and dispensing to many of them gratuitous instruction, would seem inevitable; and all experience shows, that the resusci[ta]tion of an institution of learning, which has been permitted once to go down, is more difficult than the building up of one upon foundations entirely new.

The lands recently granted by Congress to the State for the use of the University, ought, in the opinion of the Board, to be made productive at as early a date as practicable. As these lands were selected at a late period, when but little public land remained unsold from which selections could be made, their value cannot be placed at a high figure. In order that the most may be realized from them, the Board would propose that they be sold, on easy terms to the purchasers. The Board respectfully ask, that an act of the Legislature be passed, authorizing their sale in the following manner and upon the following conditions, viz: That the lands be sold through the Auditor and Treasurer of State, on a credit of ten years—one-fourth of the purchase money to be paid down; interest paid in advance on the residue; and the interest paid annually, in advance, with a portion of the principal, until the whole is paid. The lands to be placed in two classes; the first class to be sold at not less than three dollars and fifty cents per acre; and the second class at not less than two dollars per acre—none of said lands to be subject to entry at these prices, until after a public sale, of which due notice shall be given.

In conclusion, the Board of Trustees commend the State University to the fostering care and protection of the Legislature, asking in its behalf, such action as shall continue it an integral part of the educational system, early adopted by the founders of our State government; and which, under the existing constitution, is required to complete that system of public instruction, which the State has nobly undertaken to furnish the rising generation of this great commonwealth.

Respectfully submitted on behalf the Board of Trustees of Indiana University.

JOHN I. MORRISON,
President of the Board.

Indiana *Documentary Journal,* 1854, pp. 781–785.

Document 56

Assuming a Central Educational Responsibility

The training of teachers to carry out the mandate of the first Indiana Constitution and the subsequent laws enacted by the General Assembly became a major challenege to Indiana University. In 1855 the faculty began to approach the task in a professional way by creating a Normal Department.

*   *   *

NORMAL DEPARTMENT.

This department is designed to prepare young men for the profession of teaching. Through it, the University designs to afford its aid in carrying forward the great scheme of public education, thus making itself an ally of the general school system of the State.

Lectures are given embracing the following subjects: education, its nature and design; physical education; intellectual education; moral education; aesthetical education; the history of education; an examination of the powers of the mind, especially with reference to receiving and communicating knowledge; school house architecture, including school furniture, grounds, &c; organization and classification of schools; graded schools the proper incentives for the school; rewards and punishments; modes of teaching different subjects; the office of teacher; his duties to himself, his school, and the public; duty of the State, in reference to educating its citizens; the educational policy of Indiana.

It is intended, in this course of lectures, to present, as nearly as may be, the whole duty of the teacher, and to point out such modes of school discipline and management as shall assist the young teacher in preparing for his great work. The members of this department are also required to write on various topics connected with education, and to discuss, in form of debate, such subjects as may be assigned by the professor.

As auxiliary to the training of the Normal Class, the Board of Trustees have fitted up a room in one of the college buildings, and established a *model school*, under a teacher who has been trained in a Normal School, in order to present to the eye of the learner a common school, as nearly perfect as possible, in its order, arrangement, and modes of teaching; and also as a school of practice, in which to exercise and test the young teacher's ability and tact.

The course of lectures on the theory and practice of teaching commences on the first day of May, and continues during the summer term of the University. The student designing to qualify himself for teaching is, however, permitted to pursue any of the studies of the literary or scientific course, and may with profit enter the University at the opening of any term, as may suit his convenience.

In addition to the course of lectures on didactics, the student must pass an examination on the following subjects, in order to entitle him to a diploma from the University, as a qualified professional teacher, viz: reading, writing, linear drawing, mental and written arithmetic, book-keeping, geography, with outline maps, and the use of the globes, English grammar and composition, algebra, geometry, mensuration, surveying, natural philosophy, chemistry, human physiology, history, United States and general, history of English literature, Constitution of the United States and of Indiana, and vocal music.

AGRICULTURAL DEPARTMENT.

In this department are embraced Natural Philosophy and Chemistry both organic and inorganic, including an acount of nutrition, growth, and respiration, in the vegetable and animal economy, and analyses of soils and manures, ores, marks, &c., as connected with agriculture. The course also includes Geology.

ENGINEERING.

This school is connected with the Mathematical and Chemical Departments. It proposes, besides the collegiate course in Mathematics and Natural Philosophy, to afford instruction in the theory of roads, railroads, canals, and bridges, the laws of heat and steam, theory and construction of the steam engine, and topographical surveying.

DISCIPLINE.

The discipline of the Indiana University is intended to be strictly *parental*, and to accomplish its effect by appealing to the better principles of the heart, avoiding, if possible, severe and disgraceful punishment. It is designed to be *preventive*, rather than *penal*. But, if it should appear that the student is not susceptible of the influence of such discipline, he will be returned to his friends, in the hope that under other circumstances he may yet form an estimable character.

Immoral, disorderly, or dishonorable conduct, habitual negligence of duty, or want of preparation, is always sufficient reason for directing a student to leave the University.

The Faculty will not, except in extraordinary cases, grant letters of dismission, or give leave of absence, until the close of the session, nor until the student applying for such letter, or for leave of absence, shall have sustained his examination with his class.

The absence of a student, even for a few days, in term-time, exerts on his progress an evil influence, which is seldom fully appreciated by parents or guardians; hence no apology but that of sickness, or other unavoidable accident, is sufficient to excuse a student from a regular attendance at recitation.

As *teachers* and *scholars* come together in a University with objects and interests which are identical, we hold that they should always regard themselves as *co-workers* and *endeared friends.*

It is our cherished desire that the *Faculty* and *students* of this University should *always*, as at present constitute an undivided, harmonious *family*, among whom the feelings most appropriate to *parents* and *children* shall constitute the paramount and characteristic relation.

Our system of government may be understood by its name: *"The Parental."*

Annual Report of the Indiana University, Including the Catalogue, for the Academic Year, MDCCCLIV–V (Bloomington, 1855), pp. 22–24.

Document 57

The Threat of Insolvency

This report by William M. French of Jeffersonville on his inability to sell Indiana University bonds anywhere in the country produced a day of stern reckoning. Someone had to produce some capital funds quickly or Indiana University faced the tragedy of insolvency.

*   *   *

To the Board of Trustees of the Indiana University,
Gentlemen,

At a former meeting of the Board the undersigned W M French & John I Morrison were appointed a Committee to negotiate a loan with which the Board might be able to complete the College edifice now in course of erection It was thought by the Board at the time of the creation of the Committee that the loan could be effected some where in this state or vicinity. In view of the pressing wants of and urgent demands against the building committee, your committee proceeded without delay to correspond with the leading monied men of Cincinnati, Indianapolis, and Louisville. Not receiving a favorable & satisfactory answers as we desired at the instance of my colleague Mr Morrison I visited those places in person and made diligent enquiry in regard to the sale of University Bonds or the procurement of a loan by other means.

The result of my investigation clearly satisfied me, that the money could not be borrowed in this State or in any of the adjoining cities above named upon the terms proposed, not finding any one who had the amount of Money we required, who would loan upon our time and security, I immediately communicated this fact to President Daily and made with him an appointment by which we could confer freely upon the subject of the proposed loan. Dr Daily advised that I proceeded immediately to confer with Prof Morrison and if he approve of the course, that the bonds necessary papers &c, be gotten up with a view of their sale in the city of New York. The suggestion of Dr Daily was at once acceded to by Prof Morrison, when I at once entered upon the duty of looking into the legality of the claim of the State University against the lands held and claimed by said Institution on a consultation with Judge McDonald, Prof Morrison & others it was thought best—indeed it was deemed imperative that in order to secure the loan desired it would be necessary to mortgage more land that what the committee were authorized by the Board hence the reason and necessity of anothe[r] called Meeting, the proceedings and particulars of which we refer you to the record.

We state in brief to the Board that in order to ascertain all the facts and to procure the necessary evidence and documents to insure the sale of the Bonds in New York or any Eastern Market it required our whole time and personal attention for three Months. We commenced the above work on the 22nd day of April and labored until the 14th day of May during the most of which time we were either in Indianapolis preparing the bonds and procuring a description of the lands or travelling to see the commissioners who located the same whose location is in this (Monroe) and White counties On the 14th day of May 1855, we started for New York after laboring there for two or three weeks in order to effect a sale of the bonds, without success, we determined to alter their character, so as to make the time of their final liquidation three instead of Ten Years. We made the change because we were imp[r]essed with the idea that the Board, had passed, a resolution authorizing the committee to make such alterations in the character of the Bonds which they might deem essential to their speedy sale, but on an examination of the record, it proved that no such resolution had been passed which prevented Prof Morrison from making the desired change. The Bonds were returned to me at New York with but one alteration. That change required the Interest to be paid Semi-Annually which change was important and enabled me to find a purchaser It is unnecessary here to state to the Board our troubles and to recount the many difficulties we were compelled to encounter in the sale of the Bonds, no man except he who has had a schooling in the sale of a New Bond can form any conception of the work and time necessary to establish the credit of a bond when first offered for sale among Wall Street shavers and Bond speculation.

At this period in our negotiations it became necessary in view of the repeated and urgent letters received from Bloomington to effect a temporary loan, which we did, to the Amount of $3,000, on our own *personal* & *individual* responsibility & at the time, with but little hope of a sale of the Bonds, out of which we might be re-imbursed. We were told that winter was coming on a pace—that the college edifice had only been reared to the second story, and that without funds the whole unfinished building would be exposed to inclement winter—the workman would abandon the work and the contractors sue for and probably obtain heavy damages. In view of this extreme emergency we not only involved ourself but obtained the endorsement of friends, rather than have the work cease. This temporary loan, at once relieved the building committee and gave us additional time to obtain a price for the Bonds. The item of expense in the bill of particulars marked (10) was considerably increased in consequence of a negotiation which we had pending in New England for several weeks, and which place was visited once in person and twice by pr[o]xy. We had every reason to believe for several weeks that we would obtain 83 cents for the bonds—indeed we had them sold for that price to the Savings Bank at Norwich Conneticut, but when the day arrived that the Bonds were to have been discounted after all the arrangements had been made—the kind of money we were to receive in payment of the bonds &c agreed upon we were informed by the directory of the Bank that they declined taking such a small loan and therefore refused to ratify one of their own bargains. It was probably our intense anxiety to procure a fair price for the Bonds, that kept us so long in the Market our patience finally became exhausted & in view of other Bonds being offered and sold for sixty and as low as fifty cents, the securities of which were considered to be nearly as good as ours, we closed a sale for Eight Bonds at 70 cents, subsequently we sold two others to the same purchaser at the same price. John M Lord N 27 Wall Street, New York, being the purchaser of all the Bonds, Nos 6, 7, 8, 9, 10, 11, 12, 13, 14 & 15. In accordance with a resolution of the Board your com— has handed over to the President of the Board, the remaining unsold Bonds, Nos 1, 2, 3, 4 & 5.

In accordance with a resolution of the Board passed at the last meeting, I herewith present the expenses of the above negotiations as per mileage and per diem allowance including all monies expended, the particulars of which will be found in the accompanying papers.

Indiana University In Acct with WM French

To expenses as per bill rendered	$1149.94
" " in procuring library	95.00
	$1244.95 [*sic*]

The following nominal credit of Fifteen hundred dollars, which was the cost of the library donated presents a balance in favor of the University of one hundred and fifty-six dollars' and 94 cents. The donation covers the entire expenditure incurred by your committee with the above balance which presents the Bonds *net* at 70 cents. Since the last meeting I have gone to Indianapolis twice in order to procure the unsold Bonds and to return them in accordance with your instructions to the President of the Board. I have also gone to Cincinnati O. twice on business connected with the above named donation from H W Derby, travelling the four trips 1000 miles, and expending some fifteen days time for which I make no charge. By a referance to the annual catalogue it will be seen that the Faculty have selected the Amount of Books above named making 800 volumes, and they are now the very necessary appendage to our new buildings scarcely could fifteen hundred have been expended to a better purpose, or where it could have yielded a larger percentage and although it was made as a free donation by the enterprising Book Publishers of the West and to him the friends and patrons of the Unive[r]sity should feel grateful yet the donation was not obtained without a special effort & a great sacrifice of time on the part of your committee. I am free to admit that from the expensive trip East, the effort on our part to procure the donation would not have been made. It was commenced, prosecuted and urged with no other view upon our part, than to cover the expense of the negotiation and thereby secure a valuable addition to the College Library. In addition to the above your Committee has corresponded with Hon Thos H Hendricks Commissioner of the general Land Office at Washington City on the subject of the deficit of seven hundred acres of Land, yet due the University, which correspondence has resulted in a Commission and order to Gov Wright authorizing him by an agent to locate lands sufficient to supply said deficit Said papers were referred to Gov Wright, to which he responded by saying that he had commissioned Benjamin Reynolds of White County, to make the selections authorized by the commissioner of the Genl Land Office.

All of Which is respectfully submitted
W. M. FRENCH

(Doc. A)
Indiana University
1855   To W M French Dr

Oct 15 To travelling expenses to Indianapolis, attend college Library	$15.00
Oct 15 To 8 days service employed	24.00
Nov 2 To expenses to Indianapolis via Bloomington to attend to sale	
Nov 2 Bonds to Fund Commissioners	16.00
Nov 2 To 5 days	15.00
Nov 10 To Expenses to Cincin attend to College Library	10.00
Nov 10 To 5 days	15.00
	$95.00

(Doc B)
Indiana University
1855   To W M French Dr

April 12 To Mileage Cincin	300.
April 16 To Mileage Indianapolis twice	432.
April 22 To Mileage White County & Bloomington	880.
April 22 To Mileage Indianapolis twice	400.
May 14 To Mileage New York & Back via Springfield Mass	2100
	4112
Milege at 12 cents per M	$493.44
May 20 to Cash copying deed	5.00
May 20 to Cash paid Express	1.00
May 20 to Com on Bonds (No 10)	200.00
May 20 to Interest & Indorsing for loan	112.00
May 20 to Cash paid printing bonds	15.00
May 20 to Postage	1.50
July 20 to Cash paid Tarkington	4800.00
July 20 to Interest on bond (Dec)	350.00
Augt 20 to Expense Indianapolis to obtain proceeds	
bonds No 14 & 15	11.00
Augt 20 to 3 days	9.00
Sept 2 to Expense to Bloomington & 3 days	17.00
Sept 2 to Paid (Akin)	1050.00
Sept 2 to 95 days service 3$	285.00
	7349 94.

Cr

By Proceeds of Bonds, 6, 7, 8, 9, 10, 11, 12.		
By Proceeds of Bonds, 13, 14, 15 at 70 cents		$7000.00
By Cash of Board		180.00
By Interest & Premium	15.00	7195.00
Bal due W M French.		154.94

Board Minutes, August 8, 1856, pp. 375–380.

Document 58

Land Sales

After a disheartening failure to sell university bonds, the Board of
Trustees had only one recourse left and that was to dispose of some uni-

versity lands. The Board faced a demand for payment for the construction of the new building, and this was now the only way it could meet that obligation short of being sued by the contractor.

* * *

To the Board of Trustees of the Indiana University,
Gentlemen:

You have been called together to consider the prudential interests of the University and to devise the ways and means of discharging her indebtedness. In consequence of the expense that would be incured, this call, under the circumstances, has been made with due deliberation.

It is important, that the usual annual report, to accompany the Catalogue should be made and published, before the next annual meeting, setting forth among other things of general interest and for information, an accurate Statement of the financial condition of the University. To the Trustees elected to fill the vacancies occasioned by the experation of the terms of service of Messrs Akin, McFarland and Evans, it is due and it is alike due to the University that the benefit of their views Should, after consultation with the trustees, holding over, be obtained and represented in that report.

At your last annual meeting, it was determined, that the General Assembly should be asked to provide for the Sale of the lands donated by Congress, that the interest that might arise on the purchase money, might be realized, and by means of which the indebtedness of the University should be met and discharged. For that purpose and in accordance your instructions, the following report was Submitted on your behalf to the General Assembly in January last, Supplementary to the Annual report and Catalogue for the Academical year 1856:

To the General Assembly of the State of Indiana:

The Board of Trustees of the Indiana University respectfully report that, when the present Board commenced its administration of the affairs of the University, their predecessors had already made contracts for the construction of the new building, in place of the one which had been destroyed by fire. By the sixth Section of the act of the 3rd of March 1855, these contracts were legalized and made binding upon the Trustees, and they found themselves charged with the construction of the building, liable to Suits from contractors, for damages in case of any default on the part of the Board, and destitute of means to meet the extraordinary expenditure. The only available means was the University Fund proper, the interest of which was barely Sufficient to meet the ordinary current expenditure of the University. The United States had made to the University a generous donation in lands, but no provisions had been made for the Sale of them, and the realization of the interest might arise upon the purchase money. The unexpended interest of the University Fund had from time to time been invested as principal, and could not be withdrawn So as to meet the exigency. Under these embarrassing circumstances, liable to vexations and expensive Suits from contractors, and to injury of the unfinished building by a failure to progress with it, the Board was compelled to borrow money for the purpose of completing it. It was the only alternative left, and reluctantly adopted. The building is now completed at a cost of $22,135.00, for a considerable portion of which Sum the Board has to provide. The citizens of Monroe County, with a liberality worthy of all praise, had made a generous donation towards the rebuilding of the University, and this donation, paid in at intervals in money and material, was really the only fund at the command of the Board for that purpose. They ask, therefore, the enactment of a law to bring the unsold University lands into market, So that the interest of the purchase money may be made available, and the payment of the principal ultimately be Secured, and the lands themselves be protected from waste; and as the interest only of this fund can be applied, it is reccommended that the credit to be given upon the Sales may be Sufficiently long to ensure the bidding of a full price for them. These lands do not lie in a body, but are made up of Selections in different parts of the State, and it might not be advisable to throw all of them into market at once. In one Section of the State it might be advisable to dispose of them from time to time, in another to withhold them as circumstances might require, a matter which might very properly be left to the Sound discretion of the Board a member of which should be required to attend each public Sale to prevent combinations injurious to the interests of the University. It is believed that the Sale might very properly be conducted by the County Officers of the Counties where the lands lie, who are already charged with the duty of selling the lands belonging to common Schools. The Trustees are desirous, in addition to the discharge of their debt, to make the University Still more efficient in the cause of public education in the State. It was designed, and ought to be the head of the educational System of the State. In view of this, a Normal Department, with a model School attached, has already been established, the details of which may be found at page 24 of the annual report and Catalogue. But the University can do still more when its means are made available. The great want of the common Schools of the State, is well educated and efficient teachers. Attempts have been made to supply this deficiency by bringing into our State teachers from other Sections of the Union, but although many excellent and estimable teachers have thus been introduced, the increase is Scarcely felt. We must rely upon ourselves and Supply our own people. This can be done. At present but a very small Sum is realized from tuition fees; the whole amount received during the year ending July 31, 1856 was but $676.00, a Sum not equal to the Salary of a Single professor. The great mass of Students is composed of those who are selected by the county commissioners of the various counties of the State, and who receive gratuitous instruction, and it is very gratifying to the Trustees to be able to Say that these Students, in point of Scholarship and attainments, will favorably compare with those of any collegiate institution in the State. Their number is limited to two from each county, and no reciprocal Service is exacted by the State in return for the instruction which they receive. It is believed that the limitation might advantageously be abolished, and that they might very reasonably be required, after completing their course of instruction, to teach a certain number of terms in the common Schools of the State. This plan was adopted Successfully in the State Normal School of the State of New York, and would give us the opportunity of Sending annually into the common Schools of the State an additional Supply of well trained teachers, and would remove the obligation which some high-minded young men feel in taking the appointment of the Board of County Commissioners by enabling them to give the State, in their Services as teachers in the common Schools, an equivalent for the education which they receive.

The University has already accomplished much. It has its graduates in many honorable and useful public positions—it has a corps of instructors unrivalled in the State. If it has not accomplished more, it is because its means have been limited, and an inspection of these would silence the cavils of projectors of Utopian Schemes who complain that the University has done no more. The institution must be progressive, its usefulness must be Steadily increasing, and its progress must always depend upon its means. It is unfortunate that one of man's frailties is impatience. No great design is Suddenly accomplished, and it would be as wise to find fault with the sun because he does not suddenly dart to the meridian, as to complain that the University has not already accomplished, with very limited means, all the great results which the friends of education expect from it.

Of the Board of Visitors, the Govenor [*sic*] alone attended the commencement exercises of 1856, which fact is communicated to the General Assembly in obedience to the law.

All of which is respectfully Submitted:

W. K. EDWARDS, President

In accordance with Said report and in pursuance to your instructions at the last meeting, Col. Bryant proposed and caused to be Submitted to the General Assembly, a bill providing for the Sale of the lands donated by Congress to the University. That bill failed to become a law. It is unfortunate that Such was the result, as it would afford the best means of relieving the pecuniary embarrassment of the University. The University fund proper is barely Sufficient to meet the current expenditures, and to use the accruing or accrued interest of that fund to pay the indebtedness, would necessarily suspend the operations of the University.

At the time the call was issued for this meeting, I believed, judging from the exegency of public affairs, that a session of the General Assembly would be called, for an early day. In that event, your application for provision to sell the University lands, should be renewed

Respectfully Submitted
W. K. EDWARDS, President

Board Minutes, June 2, 1857, pp. 392–396.

Document 59

Perpetual Scholarships

In short-sighted desperation, the Board of Trustees sought in 1854 to raise funds by selling perpetual scholarships for $100.00 each. Perhaps no other American university involved itself in a more impractical scheme than this one. The trustees, in their moment of dejection, no doubt were incapable of looking ahead when claimants in perpetuity would come to Bloomington with their offspring, asking that they be made beneficiaries of their grandfather's investment.

*   *   *

The Committee to whom was refered this afternoon, the propriety and expediency of establishing Scholarships in the State University, have had the subject under consideration and authorised me [Mr. Jenckes] to report the following resolution

That Scholarships be established in the University upon the following plan viz.

All those who pay One Hundred dollars to the Treasurer of the College receive from him a certificate of the fact, authorising them to keep one student each in the Preparatory and Academical Departments perpetually and without the payment of tuition

Resolved further that the following shall be the form of Certificate given by the Board sighned by the President & countersighned by the Secretary viz

No

Know All Men by these Presents

That _____ of the County of _____ and State of Indiana, has by the payment of One Hundred dollars into the Treasury of Indiana University, purchased a perpetual scholarship in said University, containing provisions and limitations as follows viz

1st One scholar at a time, may be kept forever, free from Tuition Fees in any of the Classes of the Academical or Literary Departments of the University in such studies as are or may be necessary to Graduation

2nd The scholarship shall not be assighnable or transferable.

3rd Only one Student during the same session, can, under any circumstances, be kept on said scholarship.

4th During the life of the purchaser, no student, (except as specified below) can receive tuition on said scholarship, unless he be the purchaser himself, or his son or his grandson

5 After the death of the purchaser, the right of tuition for himself, his son or his grandson, shall descend by perpetuity to such descendant or other person as may be specified in the will of the purchaser, and the right shall descend from generation to generation by Will, and not otherwise

6 Should the purchaser die intestate, then the right of personal tuition shall descend to any or all of his sons or grandsons, who may claim such tuition, one at a time in succession

7 It is further agreed, as a modification of the above articles that the purchaser aforesaid, shall have the additional right of keeping in the Institution as aforesaid, any young man whom he may select to educate and who shall bring with him a certificate from said purchaser, that he is sent by him without any compensation received or expected from the student or his friends, Provided also, that but one student at a time shall be received on said scholarship

8 Nothing in the above is to be construed as giving any right, to any Student, to remain in the Institution, who is guilty of immorality or disobedience to the rules and regulations of the University, as established from time to time by the Trustees or Faculty of the University

In testimony whereof The Trustees of the Said University have issued to the said _____ this *scholarship* sighned by the President and Secretary of said Board and dated this _____ day of _____ AD 18____

  Secty.

                                   President

which report with accompanying resolutions were concurred in

Board Minutes [1838–1859], April 28, 1854, pp. 290–291.

Document 60

The Limit of Perpetuity

On November 10, 1890, the Board of Trustees rescinded the action of the Board in 1854 and invalidated the perpetual scholarships. This involved a contractual issue which the Trustees could not resolve, but they specified limitations under which university officials would accept scholarship claims.

*   *   *

University Perpetual Scholarships

On motion the following report was adopted.

Mr. President:

The undersigned, a majority of your Committee on legal affairs to whom was referred the matter of outstanding perpetual scholarships, would respectfully report—That the only evidence as to the number of perpetual scholarships ever issued by the Board, and as to whom issued, is the list of such scholarship which appears in the report made by R. W. Akin August 7– 1856, and recorded in Old Trustees' record on pages 366 and 367, and the supplemental list purporting to be made by R. C. Foster, Secretary of the Board, which appears on the next to the last fly-leaf of said "Old Record". From said lists it would seem that altogether between 50 and 60 of such scholarships were issued. From the best data obtainable it appears that all said scholarships were probably paid for by their purchasers prior to the year 1857 although the written certificates evidencing some of said scholarships were dated some what later. Your committee further report that by the express terms and conditions of all of said scholarships, it was provided and so set forth therein, that such scholarship entitles its purchaser to keep (1) one scholar in the academical (not law) department of the University free of tuition fees, provided that during the life of such purchaser, such scholar must be the said purchaser himself or his son or his grandson, or some student selected by the purchaser, to educate free of charge (and no one else) and after death of said purchaser the only persons who were entitled to the use of such scholarship were:—

1st In case he died testate, the person specified in his will and upon the death of such specified person, then the person designated in such one's will, and so on from generation to generation but in each case by will but not otherwise.

2nd In case such original purchaser died intestate, then the right of tuition under such scholarship should descend in succession to said purchasers sons and grandsons from generation to generation.

Said scholarships were expressly made non-assignable or transferable. That all said scholarships were made out upon printed blanks or forms reading as follows:—

No. _____ Know all men by these presents that

_____of the County of _____ State of _____

has, by the payment of one hundred dollars into the treasury of the Indiana University, purchased a perpetual scholarship in said University containing provisions and limitations as follows, viz:

1. One scholar at a time may be kept forever free from Tuition fees, in any of the Academical or Literary Departments of the University in such studies as are or may be essential to graduation.

2. The scholarship shall not be assignable or transferable.

3. Only one student during the same session can under any circumstances be kept on said scholarship.

4. During the life of the purchaser, no student (except as specified below) can receive tuition or scholarship unless he be the purchaser himself or his son or his grandson.

5. After the death of the purchaser the right of tuition for himself, his son or

grandson shall descend in perpetuity to such descendant or other person, as may be specified in the will of the purchaser and the right shall descend from generation to generation by will and not otherwise.

6. Should the purchaser die intestate then the right of personal tuition shall descend to any or all of this sons, or grandsons, who may claim such Tuition, one at a time in succession.

7. It is further agreed as a modification of the above articles that the purchaser aforesaid shall have the additional right of keeping in the institution as aforesaid any young man whom he may select to educate, and who shall bring with him a certificate from said purchaser that he is sent by him without any compensation received or expected from the student or his friends, Provided also that but one student at a time shall be received on such scholarship.

8. Nothing in the above is to be construed as giving any right to any student to remain in the Institution, who is guilty of immorality or disobedience to the rules and regulations of the University, as established from time to time by the Trustees or Faculty of the university.

In Testimony Whereof, the Trustees of said University have issued to the said _____ this scholarship signed by the President and Secretary of said Board and dated this _____ day of _____ A.D. 18_____

_____ Secretary.   _____ President.

That one of the said printed forms is attached to this report. That in the year 1857 and after the said scholarships had been issued the legislature of this State passed a law. (See Sec. 4591 Rev. Stat. 1881) providing that said scholarships might be sold or transfered by the holder thereof, and afterwards in the year 1861 passed a law (See Sec. 4592, Rev. Stat. 1881) limiting the contingent fee upon and providing that the Trustees might extinguish said scholarships by purchase.

It will be readily conceeded that such a scholarship constituted a valid and binding contract between the University in its corporate capacity on the one side and such purchaser on the other, and this being so, it must be admitted that no law could or can be passed to alter the terms or impair the obligations of such contract. The scholarship very explicitly specifies who shall be entitled to its use. It is stipulated that it shall not be sold or transferred.

The law above referred to attempts to nullify these express stipulations of the contract, and by making such scholarship assignable attempts to enlarge the contract so as to embrace persons who by its terms were excluded. Your Committee therefore, are of the opinion that the above laws are unconstitutional, and that said scholarships impose no greater obligations by reason of said laws, and that those persons and only those are entitled to use such scholarships as are so specified therein. Hence, that the only person entitled to their use are:

1st Students being gratuously educated by the original purchaser, and then only by presenting a certificate from such original purchaser as required in the 7th paragraph of said scholarship.

2d. Such original purchaser himself, or his children or grandchildren.

3d. In case the original purchaser died leaving a will, then such person who can trace their right to use the scholarship through the will of said purchaser, and in order to trace through a will, the will must in effect bequeath the scholarship to the person so claiming.

4th. In case the original purchaser died without a will then the lineal descendants (that is children, grandchildren, &c.) of said original purchaser. Under no circumstances can any person be entitled to admission to the University upon a scholarship unless he or she belongs to one of the four classes above enumerated.

Your Committee is informed that a large number of students are now attending the University upon such scholarships who are not entitled, and your committee therefore reccommends that after the present term said scholarships be recognized and honored only when presented by persons entitled to their benefits as herein above set forth, and that the Secretary of the Board so inform the Treasurer of the University and all students now in the University, and also that the Secretary report to the Board at its next regular meeting the names of all the scholarship students, upon what scholarship each is accredited and by what rights each of such students is entitled to the scholarship

G. W. YOUCHE, Ch'm'
R. S. ROBERTSON,
Com. Legal Affairs.

Board Minutes [1883–1897], November 10, 1890, pp. 369–372.

Document 61

Rebuilding the Library and Scientific Collection

The great fire of 1854 wiped out the library holdings of the University and destroyed the very fine Owens physiological and archaeological collections. From 1854 until 1860, the institution operated with the meagerest resources in the library and museum areas. The Indiana General Assembly undertook to correct this shortcoming in a parsimonious and inexpensive way by transferring public documents to the University.

*   *   *

AN ACT to authorize the Trustees of the State University to appropriate a certain amount of the University Funds for the enlargement of its Cabinet and Library, and directing the State Librarian to transfer certain documents and books herein named to the Library of the State University; also making the State Geologist a member of the Faculty of the University and requiring him to deposit specimens in mineralogy and geology in the Cabinet of the same.

[APPROVED MAY 11, 1861.]

SECTION 1. *Be it enacted by the General Assembly of the State of Indiana,* That the Trustees of the Indiana University shall be authorized to appropriate one thousand dollars out of the proceeds of the sales of the University lands for the purpose of enlarging the Cabinet of the University, and that Professor T. A. Wylie, or such other person as the Trustees may designate, be appointed to take charge of the above appropriation and expend the same in the purchase of specimens.

SEC. 2. That the State Librarian be directed to transfer from the State Library to the Library of the Indiana University a complete set of journals of both houses of the Legislature a copy of all laws enacted since the organization of the State, and of all reports from the several departments of State and of those received from other States and from the General Government, together with all other books and documents of which there are duplicates now in the State Library or shall be hereafter received: *Provided,* That such books and documents can be spared without injury to the State Library, and that such transfer be made without expense to the State.

SEC. 3 The State Geologist, while he holds his office, shall be regarded as a member of the Faculty of the University; and he is hereby directed in his reconnoisance to collect duplicate specimens of mineralogy and geology, and to deposit one set of the same in the cabinet of the State University.

Laws of Indiana (special session), 1861, pp. 88–89.

Document 62

Lathrop's Dream

William Daily resigned the presidency of Indiana University, January 26, 1859. The Trustees once again turned to John H. Lathrop. In a board meeting, July 12–14, 1859, by a vote of four to two, Lathrop was again chosen. He was then a professor in the University of Wisconsin, and a messenger was sent posthaste to seek his acceptance. He did accept and was in Bloomington by mid-spring. His inaugural address, like those of his predecessors, was filled with high moral thoughts, idealistic platitudes which envisioned what might be, and not what was in Bloomington.

*   *   *

PRESIDENT J. H. LATHROP'S ADDRESS.

Governor Willard:

The grateful acknowledgments of a distinguished pupil, thus publicly rendered, are among the most pleasing incidents of the literary life. They will be garnered up with the treasures of memory. They are, too, suggestive of recollections of other, and earlier days. Well do I remember the omens which hovered around your student life; prophetic of civic honors. Right early have you redeemed the promise of your halcyon days.—Scarcely past the dew of youth, you have harvested the laurels which engage the life-long struggles of less gifted men.

It is graceful that this life, in the public eye, has not been expulsive of the scholarly sentiment; that the dignity of the State is, this day, present in her halls of learning, participating in the solemnities which inaugurate a new educational administration.

In her darkest hour, the University of Indiana found in you a steadfast friend. Long may you live to witness the glories of her risen day.

Gentlemen of the Board of Trustees:

My thanks are profoundly due to you for the rare distinction of having been twice called, by your suffrages, to the responsible duties of the Presidency of this seat of learning, entrusted to your care by the constituted authorities of the State. In accepting your sober second call, I have committed to your hands, one of the most delicate trusts, which man can repose in his fellow-man. My professional character is, measurably, in your keeping. The success of my administration demands your steady support, your cordial co-operation, your indulgent consideration.

For thirty years, and more, you have, as a corporate body, exercised a formative and guardian care over this exalted public trust. You have contended successfully, with the ordinary difficulties which beset new institutions of learning in a new country. The assaults of the demagogue have been repelled; the ignorance and malice which would level down, and not level up, has grown weary of its unholy work, or has been converted to a better temper. The University has passed successfully through perils by party, and perils by sect. Its revolutionary period is over and gone. Once ruined in its finances, good men came to its rescue—consumed by fire, a noble pile has risen from its ashes, a fitting temple for an exalted worship.

But *Fellow citizens:* What means this structure in which we are assembled? What the purpose of this edifice, and these surroundings? What else, than to subserve the great cause of popular cultivation and advancement; to exalt mind to its true position; to secure to the intelligent principle, its rightful dominion over the earthly and the sensual; to train it up to habits of patient and independent thought; to lofty aspirations after the spiritual and the divine; to assure to it that knowledge and that discipline, which shall be available to the great purposes of its being; to convert the creature of time into the denizen of immortality; in fine, to do its appropriate work, in preparing the whole man for his whole destiny.

A temple of truth and of reason, then, like that in which we are assembled, should be the home of thought; the seat of intelligence; the palace of the soul; the heart of an intellectual and moral influence, extending its pulsations throughout every limb of the body social, and contributing from year to year and from age to age, to the great end of human culture—the consequent advancement of our christian civilization, with its benign and saving influences, with its practical out-growth into those arts which render the powers of nature subservient to the well being of man.

It is with a just view to the accomplishment of these great objects, within and beyond the limits of our commonwealth, that the University of Indiana has been founded and organized; and it is not irrelevant to the solemnities of this day, that I should give expression to some of the judgments I have been able to form, relative to the proper conduct of institutions of learning, and the principles which must govern our action here, in order that the University of the State of Indiana may accomplish the high ends of its establishment, in dispensing intellectual and moral good, and in contributing to the essential dignity of the State, whose institution it is, whose name it bears, and with whose credit and character, at home and abroad, it is indissolubly connected.

In providing, then, for the uses to which a temple is consecrated, our attention is very naturally drawn to the constitution of its priesthood, their position, and their official functions. It is, therefore, pertinent to the place, and to the occasion, to raise the inquiry—what should be the composition, and what the relations of that body of men, to whom the immediate ministrations of this temple of science are now, and are hereafer to be committed.

It is a fact, fellow-citizens, about which there should be no debate, that the essential element, in an institution of education, is the LIVING INSTRUCTION which it extends to the pupil.

A splendid and commodious edifice is, in itself, well. Furnished and varied apparatus; chosen collections in the several departments of natural science, and the fine arts; a well selected library, the great treasure house of the recorded thoughts of the mighty past; touch still more nearly, than the edifice, the great objects for which seminaries of learning are founded. These are all important, in their several degrees. But they are important, mainly, as aids to the LIVING INSTRUCTOR. They are valuable appliances, available, in his hands, to his professional uses. He can do much, however, without them; they can do nothing without him.

It is not in my mind to abate the tithe of a hair, from the just estimation of any one of the means of education. Nor do I do this by the averment, that the character of an institution of learning must depend, especially, on the fullness and the ability of the board of instruction and discipline. Buildings, apparatus, books, and cabinets, are all subordinate means, and valuable chiefly, because they are thus subordinate, and subordinary to the living instructor.

All this is true and manifest; and yet, the practice of those who shape the destinies of our literary institutions, has been greatly at variance with this idea. Look through the length and breadth of our land, and count, if you can, the literary incorporations which have, in the beginning, mistaken the BUILDING for the University; exhausting their funds, and incurring debt, in the erection of costly edifices; leaving nothing for books and apparatus, and less than nothing for the living instructor. How many of these splendid temples may be found in our land, almost without a priest, and without a worshipper—all beautiful and attractive without; while all within, is vacancy and silence; still as the habitation of the dead; or if tenanted at all, perchance it is, by the gaunt forms of literary mendicants, heart-sick with promises, "made to the ear, but broken to the hope"— luckless candidates for a speedy immortality.

The maxim then, which commends itself to the understanding of men, is this, that in the inception of a literary institution, ample funds should be reserved— first, for the support of an able board of instruction; secondly, for the collection of books, and apparatus, for the uses of the several departments; and thirdly, and lastly, the residue, if any, may be properly applied to the erection of commodious and tasteful edifices, for their reception and accommodation. Few institutions in our country, have the ability to provide well for the first two classes of objects; and surely, no perversion of literary funds can be more palpable, and more suicidal than to expend on a physical structure, those means which may be essential to the perfect action of the intellectual portion of the machinery of education.

Having ascertained the position of the living instructor in the educational process, let us proceed to examine his place in the arrangements of human society; his relation to the other agencies which are concerned in human civilization.

"In the sweat of thy face, shalt thou eat thy bread," is the scriptural announcement of the great law of humanity, that labor is necessary to the acquisition, and enjoyment, of physical, intellectual or moral good. The resulting good, however, in its quantity and its quality, is greatly dependant on the degree of wisdom, with which human industry is directed.

The earth is capable of sustaining but a sparse population, and that at a low standard of physical comfort, and without intellectual and moral advancements, where the labor of each individual is directed to the production of precisely those commodities, and those only, which meet his own wants. This is the condition of *savageism*, the world over. In the aspects of civilization, on the other hand, nothing is more characteristic, than the very dense population which the earth is able to sustain, at a vastly more exalted standard of physical comfort, and a still more elevated standard of intellectual and moral cultivation. And nothing is more essential to the introduction of these invaluable results than the DIVISION OF LABOR and EMPLOYMENTS, which we observe to obtain in all civilized communities, with a minuteness, and distinctness, corresponding with the type, and the degree of the civilization which prevails. By conforming skilled labor, in each department, to its habitual and well known processes, the aggregate product of human wants, is increased beyond calculation; and time is saved to the individual, for the purposes of intellectual and moral improvement.

But again, the separation of production employments begets the necessity of exchange; and if each producer were bound to effect his own exchange, a large portion of his time would be withdrawn from production, and a large amount be thus subtracted from the produced values—the physical wealth of the community. By setting up, then, the class of merchants, to do the exchanges for the producers, the latter are no longer withdrawn from the creation of values; and so, the *increase* of the volume of production pays for the skilled labor of the mercantile profession, and leaves a balance in the hands of producers far exceeding their *whole* production, provided they act the merchant for themselves; the physical wants of the entire community are better supplied; time and means are thus furnished for an advanced stage of intellectual and moral cultivation.

But our economical argument may be carried still further. In order to the greatest possible production of physical values, the health of the producing, and the exchanging classes must be provided for; and thus a demand springs up for skilled labor in the healing art. But if each producer were bound to acquire this skill for himself, and to seek out and compound his own simples, production must be suspended the while; the skill comes too late; the race is dying out, not of disease, but of starvation. It is sound economy, therefore, to sustain a medical profession as a distinct class; for the consequent enlargement of the wealth of the community will pay, many times over, the charges of the profession, leaving the producer and the merchant with ampler means and sounder health, to provide, not only for their physical wants, but also, for the more exalted purposes of their being.

But again, it is essential to human progress, that the rights of men, in the civil State, should be ascertained, defended, and vindicated. The calls for skilled labor, in this department, must be met, or the law of the strongest prevails; violence takes the place of social order, and civilization is at an end. Shall this call for skilled labor be met by each producer for himself, or, is it sound economy, that he shall meet it by attorney—that a profession of those learned in the law shall be feed and fed, to do that service, which the individual can not do for himself, without ruinous neglect of the processes of production and exchange? Civilization and economy return their united answer that the bar must be sustained, as a distinct and independent profession.

Again, that "righteousness exalteth a nation," is the scriptural annunciation of the general principle, that the sentiments of reciprocity and benevolence, pervading and controling the popular mind, constitute the broad and deep foundation on which reposes the structure of civil society, and on which alone, it can repose in safety. The sentiment of justice, controling the common mind, gives to beneficent legislation its strength and vitality; it lies at the foundation of the right of property; without it, production and accumulation are at an end, and civilization is but an empty name. How divinely is the pulpit adapted to imbue the common mind with that righteousness which exalteth a nation. The pulpit inculcates a perfect rule of life, the germinating principle of all just legislation; and what is vastly more important, it enforces that rule, not like the human law-giver, by sanctions drawn from this present life only, but by those transcendent considerations, which respect our immortal being, our relations to God, the judge of all, and to the community of spiritual intelligences, throughout eternal ages—the sanctions, namely, of the christian faith, without which, as the experience of man, in all ages, has shown the best constituted, and most perfectly balanced, social structures have tended uniformly to decay and dissolution. These unspeakably important ministrations of the pulpit demand skilled labor. The most exalted interests of man require that these ministrations should be committed to the clergy, as a distinct and independent profession. "Give thyself wholly to these things," is the apostolic injunction.

Such is a very brief analysis of the economy of civilized society, as we now see it.

The producing classes, throughout the various subdivisions of the agricultural and mechanic arts, create all the values, destined to supply the physical wants, and to gratify the tastes of the whole community. The mercantile classes produce nothing; but, by transfer and exchange, make such a dispostion of existing products, as to facilitate the division of labor, to enlarge the volume of production, and thus to minister to the well-being of all. The professions, strictly so called, terminate their industrial processes, not on physical products, but on those CON-DITIONS, in human society, which give to the producing and exchanging agents the disposition, and the power, to execute their several functions most effectively and beneficently. The specific results of professional industry, are the HEALTH, the ORDER, and the MORALITY of the community.

The question now returns upon us—what is the position of the educator in the mechanisms of civilized society? I answer that his industrial agency terminates not on physical products, nor yet on social conditions, but directly upon the MAN. His raw material is the young mind, the unformed intellect. His resulting product is the finished MAN; prepared by varied knowledge, by thorough discipline, to act well his part, as an agriculturist, as an artizan, as a merchant, as a physician, as a lawyer, as a divine; to be useful in the civil state, useful in those more extended relations, which concern him as a member of the human family, and as a subject of the universal empire of God.

It is quite obvious, then, that the educator stands at the point of power, and applies the moving and guiding force to the mechanism of human society. For, to the successful action of this mechanism, INTELLIGENCE is valuable at every point—on the farm, in the manufactory, in the counting-house, in the practice of the healing art, at the bar, and in the sacred desk. There is not a single employment within the scope of our economical analysis of society, whose results would not be rendered, by an increase of intelligence, more beneficial to society, and more honorable and profitable, to the industrial agents concerned in it. It is a safe judgment, that the communities which are the better educated at *every point,* must be the more wealthy, and the more powerful, as well as the more respectable. The experience of the civilized world abundantly confirms the fact.

How deeply, then, does it concern industrial agents, of every class, how profoundly does it interest our civilization, that the educational processes should be the action of skilled labor. How pre-eminently is the business of education, imparting to all, borrowing from none, entitled to rank as a distinct and independent profession. How greatly does it interest the civil state, to secure to the educator, emoluments enough, and distinction enough, to fill the ambition of the honorable and the high minded; to call into the ranks of the profession the highest order of talent, the brightest intellects, the ablest men of the community.

It is by realizing this great idea—I mean the distinctness and independence of the educational profession—that the whole economical and social mechanism will be made to work best at every point, and to contribute, most largely, to the higher development, and culture of man, individual and universal.

All this is true and manifest—and yet, the sentiment has very generally prevailed, almost down to the present time, that the business of education has, of itself, no distinct substantive existance, as a department of *industrial,* or, if you please, of *professional* agency; and, especially that the high places, in our higher seats of learning, belong of right, to the eminent in the clerical profession. This sentiment, having at its root, no living social principle, must wither and die.

But like many other traditionary articles of popular belief, it has continued active and influential, after the causes that gave it birth, have passed away; like plants, which continue to exhibit their characteristic energies, long after they have been separated from the parent stock. The sentiment has come down to us, from the period when the clergy were the only learned men of the age. Gratitude is due to them, from the men of every generation, that, in the ages emphatically called dark, they kept the lights of science burning, and became the EDUCATORS of the race. They were the STATESMEN, too, of the time. But at this period of advancing civilization, there is no shadow of reason why they should, by virtue of their profession, be the one, or the other. The tendency now is, in all our social arrangements, to the more perfect distinctness of the various arts and professions, in order to the application of more disciplined intellect, and greater practical skill, at every point.

Society is, most of all, interested, as I have before remarked, that the profession of education should have the benefit of this principle. To this end, it is of vital importance that the most exalted honors and emoluments, within the gift of our literary incoporations, should be bestowed on eminence *in* the profession of education, and not on eminence *out* of it.

Let us suppose, by way of illustration, that a young man of acknowledged ability, and elevated character, at the completion of his University course, has voluntarily withdrawn himself from those avenues to distinction, which usually allure the footsteps of the young, the ardent, the honorably ambitious. He has chosen, on mature reflection, the path which leads on to literary eminence; not in the sequestered walks of authorship, but on the more public, and thorny course, which he must tread, who devotes his life, his energies, to the business of instruction.

He has engaged in the great and good cause, in the love of it; he has, by abundant and varied labor, earned distinction as an educator. By a long series of approved professional service, it has come to be generally admitted, that he possesses, in an eminent degree, those qualities of mind and of heart, which fit him to preside over, perhaps, the destinies of an institution of learning of the highest grade. And now it may well be asked, on what principle, respectable in the eye of God or man, is he to be shut out from the highest honors within the walks of his profession? What is the crowning qualification which he lacks, without which, all the endowments of heaven, and all the accomplishments of earth, are to avail him nothing toward his advancement in his own chosen profession? Is it the laying on the hands of the presbytery? Is it a preparation for another, and a different profession?

The absurdity of all this is patent; and yet, the constitution of a large proportion of the educational institutions of our land, involves this very absurdity. The sentiment is indeed passing away; already do we find the presidency of several of our older seats of learning, holding the first rank among American colleges, occupied otherwise than by clergymen.

But it is incident to the progress of reform, that one error is often abandoned, to make room for the introduction of another, which experience will compel us to abandon, in its turn. Innovations, especially those which concern great social interests, should be made with judgment. Literary incorporations, by ceasing to confer the appropriate rewards of educational merit on the eminent in the clerical profession, have done wisely. But instead of conferring these rewards on the distinguished educator as the principle directs, they have taken these same literary honors, and laid them at the feet of eminent lawyers and civilians, begging them to condescend to wear them, for the sake of the extrinsic dignity which may accrue to the cause of education.

Now adopt if you please, the eulogistic language of Burke, and pronounce the law to be the first and the noblest of human sciences; a science which does more to quicken and invigorate the understanding, than all other kinds of learning put together. As Burke did not regard this minute, pointed, and accurate discipline, as the best training for exalted and comprehensive statesmanship, so it is pertinent that we should enquire what analogies there are, between the processes, habits, and functions of the legal profession, and the processes, habits, and functions of the educational profession, that can entitle the skilled labor of the former, to the appropriate rewards of the skilled labor of the latter. It is just as philosophically absurd to take a distinguished lawyer, and place him at the head of a literary institution, as to take a distinguished educator, and place him centrally on the bench of the supreme court.

The truth is, that literary incorporations, in parting from the clergy, have mistaken their direction, in this matter. If Moses' seat, in our literary synagogues, is to be occupied, not by those who enter in at the door, but by those who climb up some other way; if it be so, that the priest in the temple of science, must be chosen from among those who are strangers to its mysteries, let us go back again to the clerical profession; for it is manifestly and distinctly true, that the ministrations and the discipline of the pulpit, are far more germane to the processes of education, than are those of the bar.

In fine, the true doctrine, on this subject, is, that the educational profession should be regarded as distinct, and as close a division of social service, as any other—that, as a profession, it should vindicate to itself its own appropriate rewards, both of honor and emolument—that if gentlemen in the other departments of the social economy, choose to abandon their professions and become educators, they should fall gracefully into the rear, and abide their time for preferment; and not, with a questionable modesty, complacently suffer themselves to be placed in the van of those who have borne the heat and burden of the day, who have seen service, and, by a regular and successful experience, have learned the duties and the discipline of the profession.

The true doctrine thus stated and illustrated, commends itself to the understandings of men, and, if properly trusted and applied, will be available to the solution of questions of policy, involved in the practical management of institutions of learning.

It is, for example, a matter of doubt, with literary incorporations, whether, in making appointments to the several chairs of instruction, regard should not be had to securing the interest of some man, or clique, or party, or sect, and to catching the various knots of influence, scattered here and there, over the surface of human society. The good will of the community, at every point is doubtless to be desired; but if run after, the little thus gained will be sure to cost more than it is worth. A literary institution, which acts upon the coaxing principle, makes itself the sport and the mockery of those very interests it so anxiously courts. The decisive consideration in literary appointments, respects the ABILITY of the candidate to discharge by skilled labor, the precise duties of the vacant department. This question of ability, being once clearly settled, all extraneous considerations may be very safely left out of the account. Graduates of the highest promise, constitute the material for tutors. The approved tutor ripens up into the permanent professor; and the professor who has fairly earned the character of an able educator, who has served his institution well, is a very proper man to preside, in his turn over its destinies. Whether he be a minister, or a barrister, whether he be a favorite with this or that interest, whether he can catch this or that vulgar prejudice, are questions unworthy of the consideration of the appointing power.

A mistake, just here, may foist into literary position, a man of impure life and unscholarly attainment, to the offence and the opprobrium of the Republic of Letters. Unclean birds may wade the Castalian fount; asses may brouse, and bray, and breed, on the summit of Parnassus; but not without a dereliction of duty, on the part of the Custodians of the hallowed precincts of virtue and of learning, which no outside pressure, no lure of ephemeral advantage can for a moment excuse.

An institution of learning, ably manned and skillfully conducted, will command the favor and the patronage, it would not stoop to buy; like the proud ocean steamer, it has a self-propelling power, and holds gallantly on its way, unheeding the storm and the surges which hurry by, to sport with, and engulf the unlucky barque which has been instinctively busy the while, trimming its sails, to catch a favoring breeze.

There is, my fellow-citizens, no prejudice which has been more common, or more respectably entertained, than that the fortunes of a literary institution are made at once, if some man of distinguished name can be induced, at any price, to stand at its head. If the distinguished name has been gained in some other department of the social economy, as the fact usually is, the arrangement is liable to the theoretic objections, which have already come under review, and abundant experience demonstrates that the objections have been well taken.

The magic of a name is not a permanent enchantment. After he is fairly in his seat, and the nine day's wonder is over, the officer thus chosen, must be judged of by the same sober rule, which is applied to other men. The question which concerns pupils and patrons, is not what he has been, heretofore, and elsewhere, but, simply, whether he has the qualifications, the discipline of mind and of heart, the experience, the skill, which can make him useful as a PRACTICAL EDUCATOR. Does he, in the discharge of the precise duties of his present office, bring skilled labor to the working point? This is the question. The skilled labor is every thing; the name is—*vox et preterea nihil.*

Perhaps the officer, chosen on the false principle I am exposing, deems it derogatory to his dignity to labor at all. The record of his appointment, is documentary evidence of his estimation among men. He has come down from his appropriate field of labor, and taken a position, not to gather new laurels, but to repose on his old ones. He lives on his acquired reputation as so much accumulated capital; and need I say that he will, assuredly, become a bankrupt before he dies, involving in damage and dishonor, the institution which has been the subject of the experiment.

But, possibly, the eminent officer in question, may be of a more mercurial spirit. His genius may lead him rather to the exhibition of a splendid character, than of a useful one. He makes entry upon his new stage—takes his attitude—turns all eyes upon himself. He identifies not himself with the institution, but the institution with himself. His career is brilliant and meteor-like. The vital energies of the institution are exhausted in feeding the flame—the light goes out in mid heaven, and darkness broods over the present and future. The illusion is gone—endowments are gone—and what men fondly deemed the light of science, was nothing but the exhibition of a splendid man. The pageant cost more than it was worth.

But again, it is a possible case, that the man has brought the distinctions of his appropriate profession into his educational position, with a cherished and ever present desire to make himself useful in this new vocation. If so, he will soon make the discovery, that he has every thing to learn. He will be grateful for the skilled advice and instruction of those over whom he has been, strangely, called to preside. If he is happily born, he will, in process of time, get through his apprenticeship, master his profession, and render service, to the cause of education. But if less apt, and too tenacious to retire from his position, he will extend his noviciate to gray hairs, and "totter on, in blunders, to the last." There have been cases under this head.

I make these several points, in illustration of the true rule of the University appointments. The doctrine is, that the priest in the temple of science, should have been EARLY consecrated to the service of the altar. Each case of departure from this sound principle, is an expensive and hazardous experiment to the institution which makes it—a wrong to the educational profession, and a damage to civilization.

But again, it is sometimes made a question of policy, whether instruction may not be cheapened, by appointing men to educational departments, who may have other professional or business pursuits, from which they derive a portion of their support. This policy is so manifestly opposed to the great principle of the separation of employments, that the matter need not be re-argued here. The educator should have a department broad enough, and deep enough, to fill his mind and engage his time; and then, he should give ALL his industrial power to the perfection of his department.

Where endowments are scant, indeed, and boards of trust are ambitious, it is customary to eke out the instructional body, by a chance employment of men in other avocations, on small pay, with the implication that the living is still to be made by the prosecution of outside duties. It is, however, in these cases, well understood that the institution obtains but a meager and profitless service; save that, a lengthened array of honorable and reverend names, with a doubtful honesty, adorn the pictured page of the annual catalogue.

But not so, when a man has consecrated his energies to the educational profession, and enlisted in the service of an institution of learning on full and adequate pay. Such a man does not belong to himself; he has been bought with a price. His time, his talents, his very spirit, his true allegiance, constitute the precise consideration which he has contracted to render, for the honors and the emoluments of his position. He owes to the institution, not merely his daily routine of instruction; he owes hours of preparation, by day and by night. His reading, and his thought, in their widest range, should, with entire singleness of purpose, be made tributary to the treasures of the lecture-room. He owes to the institution even his vacations. For what is the philosophy and what the justification of the vacation, save that it is needed, both by instructor and pupil, to restore the tone of the system, exhausted by the over drafts of the literary life. It is quite impossible that a man, thus situated, and thus obligated, can be found on the political arena; can stray away into the walks of authorship; can engage in mercantile pursuits; can be employed at the bar, or at the sacred desk; without substracting from the value of his services as an educator. The principle I understand to be, that the professional educator be precisely what he professes to be; and withdraw himself from any and every field of labor and profit which is foreign to his art. The principle is sound and valuable.

But, if it be sound policy to confine the industrial agency of the educator to his professional processes, it is equally so, that his profession be made to yield him EMOLUMENTS adjusted to the value of his services. Society is deeply interested, that minds of the very highest order should enter the educational profession, as a separate and exclusive field of labor. But talent, like capital, will be attracted toward the best market. In order, therefore, to secure the desired end, men must be addressed in the educational profession, precisely as they are in every other honorable and useful art or calling. The educational profession must vindicate to itself its own appropriate honors and emoluments; and skilled labor in the educational profession, is clearly entitled to the same measure of emolument, which, under the arrangements of civilized society, accrues to the same grade of talent and skill, in the other learned professions. The highest places in the University, should be on the same general level with the highest places at the bar, in the pulpit, in the practice of the healing art, and in the services of the civil state.

Some institutions make these emoluments, in part, certain, and, in part, contingent on the success of the professional labors of the instructional body; either jointly, or in their several departments. It is proper that men should be addressed in this profession, as in all others. If, by extraordinary devotion and skill, the instructional body have extended the usefulness and fame of their institution, and have disseminated more largely among the many just appreciations of the value of liberal culture, and a disposition to acquire it—it is right—it is due to them—that they should reap where they have sown. That the more abundant harvest of patronage and revenue, rendered more abundant by their labor, should yield, to them, their proper portion of the increase. On the other hand, if a general apathy characterize the members of the instructional body; if the soul of the profession has departed; if its interesting processes have degenerated into a heartless and barren routine; there is small reason why they should, in the enjoyment of liberal and sure emoluments, feed and fatten on the life-blood of the institution. "If any man will not work, neither should he eat."

It is proper too that discriminations should be made between members of the same instructional body, in order that a due relation may be preserved, between the revenues of the Chair, and the value of the services of the incumbent. Give, for example, to the youthful professor, a fair support in the beginning; assure him that his emoluments shall be adjusted, from year to year, to the increasing value of his services, until he arrives at the manhood of his professional skill, and you appeal to principles which will make him an abler and better man, than if you had distanced his hopes, and palsied his energies, by gilding his infant labors with the same ample rewards which are due to the skilled agency of the practiced educator.

I would fain hope, that the mercenary odor of these sentiments, touching emoluments, will offend no delicate nostril here present. I desire to see no man in any chair in this University, nor indeed, within the walks of the educational profession, who is insensible to the desire of accumulating about him physical comforts, and refinements after the fashion of civilized men; of gathering the means of social respectability, for himself and family; of providing amply for the support, the education and the usefulness of those whom God has committed to his care. The man who has, by study and drill, converted himself into an intellectual machine; who, if you supply parchments and porridge, forgets that there are men, and women, and children, in the world; who is dead to the amenities of social life; who knows not of the pleasures of hospitality, and of fellowship with his kind; who appreciates not the glorious privilege of being independent, of having the ability to discharge his public and private duties, according to his judgment and without constraint, is not the man to occupy any post in a literary institution as the guide and the exemplar of the young mind. The educator should not be a man of one idea, or of that one class of ideas within the daily routine of his instructions; but a man of varied and extended knowledge. He should not only know books, but things and men; he should be, in fine, a man of the world, in an unexceptionable sense of the phrase; in a sense which implies GOLDEN RETURNS into his own bosom, for the priceless services he is rendering to society and to civilization.

Again it happens not unfrequently that some man of fair intellect, has failed of success in the pulpit, or at the bar. He has put out on the voyage of life, but does not hold on his way; his barque lies stranded on the beach, not far from the point of embarkation. The man has, possibly, been broken up by the storms and the labors of his professional career; perhaps, through physical inactivity, he has become acid and hypochondriac; perhaps again, he is of too feeble a spirit to succeed at any thing; he has tried one experiment, and another, and another, and has failed in them all. Persons of this class are often found lying around the doors of the temple of science. It would doubtless contribute to their comfort to be placed in some quiet seat within and be fed from the altar. Family interest and the sympathy of friends, combine to create an influence in their favor, which it is often difficult for literary incorporations to withstand. And yet, it is their solemn duty to withstand them. The business of education is of right a distinct and independent profession, and distinguished places are here, as elsewhere, due to distinguished ability and professional skill. The helpless are doubtless to be provided for, as objects of christian benevolence, according to their several characters and wants. Not, however, by bestowing on them the emoluments of a position, whose duties can be discharged by those alone, who have the strength and the will to labor. If any University is to accomplish the ends of its establishment; if it is to hold a respectable rank among the institutions of the land, it has its distinction to achieve, and to preserve, by the skill and the hard labor of the instructional body. It can not afford to convert its halls into a hospital for invalids, a retreat for decayed gentlemen, a house of refuge for the lame and the lazy, a hive for the drones of society.

Once more, it is worthy of the consideration of the appointing power, that the ablest and the most laborious corps of instructors will disappoint the hopes of the friends of an institution, unless they are so homogeneous in their material, so loyal in temper and in habit, as to act heartily and harmoniously together; laboring for the common cause; rivaling each other only in their devotion to the interests of the institution with which they are connected. Faculties should be made up of able men, or representative men; men who will, with singleness of purpose, address themselves to the precise work assigned them by the appointing power; each with an unselfish ambition, intent on that measure of revolution and reform which lies through the renovating influence of a bright and shining example; provoking colleagues through a generous emulation to a like devotion, each in his department, to the common cause.

It is the distinct duty of the trustees of the University of Indiana, to select and maintain in this seat of learning, a Faculty of this exalted character. The power of appointment has been executed by the Board. And in reference to my esteemed and honored colleagues, I deem it but just and proper to say, even in this presence, that the delicate and responsible duty of selection, has been discharged with perfect discrimination and judgment. Indiana has abundant reason to repose entire confidence in the wisdom, the loyalty, the scholarly and christian character, and the professional skill, of our instructional body and to concede to it all that permanence, and freedom, which is consistent with a just responsibility on the one hand, and essential on the other, to the intelligent, harmonious, and successful performance of the sacred duties of their unspeakably important trust.

Many, perhaps most of the Universities of our land, have, in their early career, disappointed the hopes of the generation which founded them, chiefly because appointments have been made without system, on interested recommendations, and without personal knowledge of candidates. Discordant material has been brought into juxtaposition; unseemly broils have profaned the ministrations of the temple of science, to the scandal of the cause of sound learning, and to the deep and lasting disparagement of the institutions thus unhappily manned.

Without looking too narrowly into the myths which garnish the early story of our own institution, we are admonished by an abundant general experience, of the importance of developing and adopting a rule of appointment, which will secure, through an able, united, and permanent instructional body, the vigorous and uninterrupted growth of our University, from this day onward. Surely no line of policy can be more safe, more thoroughly conservative, than that to which the experience of our most successful literary institutions has brought them; namely, to impose upon the instructional body, the duty and the responsibility of naming to the board of direction, those whom they deem best qualified to fill vacancies, as they occur in the several departments of instruction.

This doctrine is not only the dictate of experience, but is plainly founded in the reason of things. If the instructional body have been wisely chosen, for the sensible reason that they have been able and successful educators, they will bring a professional judgment to the selection of their associates; and their professional acquaintance with literary men will present a wide field of choice. If their connection with the institution has been wisely arranged so that their fortune and their character are connected with its prosperity, there is little ground for the apprehension, that their judgment will be swayed by any undue bias. The power properly reserved to the board of direction, to accept or reject these recommendations, to fix salaries, to remove incumbents at pleasure, would still constitute a supreme and final control over the whole matter. Such is the policy which, in my judgment, will not fail to secure to this University, from this time onward, that element, without which it would be worse than idle to expect success; I mean a harmonious and co-operative board of instruction and discipline.

And now, fellow-citizens, I need hardly say, in conclusion, that such a priesthood as I have described, thus chosen, and thus constituted, is to be charged with a service which will call out all its strength, its zeal, its skill, and its fidelity. This service is nothing less, than to unfold the mysteries of the temple of science; to preserve order and decorum within its sacred precincts; to return ready and true responses to those who ask counsel and guidance at the shrine; and to provide that no young and devout worshipper shall go away unsatisfied and unblest.

Inquiries into the proper instructions and discipline of the University; its relations to the subordinate departments of public instruction; to the professions, and to the industrial arts; the distinct functions of the State and of the church as educational agencies, open inviting fields of discussion, on which I do not now propose to enter. It lies in my way only to observe, that when literary incorporations have invested wisely the funds with which they are intrusted; have provided suitable buildings, books, and apparatus; and have accomplished the crowning work of inducting into office an able and devoted band of instructors, subject to removal for non-feasance or mal-feasance, they have discharged their responsibilities. At this point, begin the responsibilities of the educators thus chosen. The instruction and discipline of the University is their trust. They are, morally speaking, the professional agents, not of the appointing power, but of those for whose benefit the trust was created; and should discharge these responsibilities with the same independence, the same freedom from external constraint, as does the Judge the duties of the bench. Within the whole range of these responsibilities, there has been no instance in which the delicate hand of professional skill has been pushed aside by the unpracticed touch of naked power, without damage to the institution which has been the subject of the experiment.

With an instructional body thus chosen, thus sustained, and thus trusted, it is safe to rely, under God, on the healthful growth and the permanent prosperity of our University. The instructions and the discipline of this temple of science, administered by those who feel that they have abated nought of their personal independence, by assuming their respective positions in it, will be ever such as become the most exalted educational organ of this our honored Commonwealth; such as the sons of Indiana have a right to enjoy, at the hands of the Republic. Its teachings uncommitted to any sectional or selfish end, unpledged to the dogmas of party or of sect, shall rise and expand into sympathy with pure truth; its investigations, unsatisfied with barren abstractions, resting not even in the attractive field of physical observation, shall successfully aspire by the study of MAN, social, rational, immortal, to dispel the illusions of the past, and scatter light in the path of the political and the moral reformer. Thus shall the University of the State of Indiana fulfill its glorious destiny, by ministering to every valuable patriotic end, till love of country shall be merged in universal philanthropy; till even the memorials of our national growth, shall be commemorative only of the triumphs of civilization, and the pride of the American citizen be lost in the dignity of the man.

And now, gentlemen of the Faculty, while we thank God for the occasion of these solemnities, and are cheered by the omens of good which surround us, let us, conscious of the impotence of human effort, and the fraility of human counsel, make out earnest supplication, that He who has brought us hitherto, and has made us priests in this temple of science, may deign to bless our ministrations with His hallowing presence and His choicest influences. And while we dedicate our best services to truth and to reason, we humbly pray the God of truth, and the God of reason, to accept the dedication.

Document 63

The Exigencies of War

One reads the official records of Indiana University for this period and can be left almost unaware of the fact that the nation was engaged in a bloody fratricidal war. This petition to Oliver P. Morton does indicate, however, that the war reached out and dragged in students and graduates. John Hood was fortunate; he had not long to wait before Sherman's Army invaded Columbia, South Carolina, a fact far more influential than the intervention of Oliver P. Morton.

*   *   *

Bloomington Ind.
Dec. 24th 1864

His Excellency,
Gov. O. P. Morton L. L. D.
Dear Sir.

Lieu't, John Hood, 80 Reg't. Ills. Vol. was captured by the Rebels, in Col. Straight's raid 1862; and has been held a prisoner of War ever since, suffering all the hardships which Rebel inhumanity and atrocity inflict. We earnestly desire, that you would use your influence with the proper authorities to secure a special exchange for him. His friends are able and would willingly pay any necessary expenses incurred in obtaining his release.

Lieu't. John Hood graduated at the State University in 1862 and soon after enlisted in the Union Army. He was one of our best students, a good young man, and a noble soldier. He was much esteemed by the Faculty, students, and the citizens of this Community. He is now at Columbia S. C. Your efforts to obtain his exchange, will be most greatfully [*sic*] remembered, by him and his many relatives and friends, and will be regarded as a great personal favor by your

Very O'b't s.

CYRUS NUTT, Pres. Ind. Uni-
T. A. WYLIE Prof. Ind. Univy
DANIEL KIRKWOOD, Prof. of Math.
JAMES WOODBURN, Prof. Ind. Univy

P. S.

Mr Hoods address is as follows.
Lieut. John Hood
80th Regt. Ill. Vols
Prisoner of war
  Columbia S. C.
Via Hilton Head.
In care of Lieut. Col. J. E. Mulford
        Agent of Exchange

Governor Morton Papers, Archives Division, Indiana State Library.

Document 64

The Library

The drive to recreate the library had met with some success. Besides books gathered from miscellaneous sources, the University still had only limited library facilities. Mention is made in this document of the Derby Collection which was, in time, to form the foundation stone of the present University's special collections.

*   *   *

GRADUATION AND DEGREES.

The Degree of Bachelor of Arts, in accordance with general usage, will be conferred on students who complete the Classical Course, and pass the examination in the same.

The degree of Bachelor of Sciences will be conferred on students who complete the Scientific Course, and pass the examination in the same.

The Degree of Master of Arts will be conferred upon such graduates of three years' standing, as have in the meantime pursued professional or general scientific studies.

By a resolution of the Board of Trustees the Valedictorian is elected by the class. The student standing highest on the merit roll during the whole course, is appointed by the Faculty to deliver the Latin Salutatory.

APPARATUS AND CABINET.

The apparatus for chemical and philosophical illustrations has had several important additions made to it recently, and a large telescope, purchased in Boston, is daily expected.

To aid in the lectures on Natural Science, Prof. Owen has brought an extensive collection of minerals, fossils, and zoological specimens, as well as of illustrative charts, diagrams, and maps.

Besides the general collection, one room will be fitted up especially to facilitate an intimate acquaintance with the geology of Indiana, by exhibiting the various rocks of the State, in their correct relative position, on a large table, which will allow about a foot and a half square to each county.

The study of phytopaleoutology is aided by a hortus sciepus, particularly of the ferns, conifers and leaves of forest trees, such as are found fossil; also by a large diagram exhibiting a comparative synopsis of ancient and modern vegetation.

For Physiology, besides the usual charts to illustrate Cutter's textbook, there are papier-mache models of full size, and a fine skeleton just received from Philadelphia.

Besides the usual adjuncts for geological surveys, such as dinometer, compasses, Locke's levels, and the like, there are Aneroid barometers and a sextant with horizon.

For the illustration of physical geography, the excellent maps of Prof. Guyot have recently been purchased.

LIBRARY.

The Derby Donation, and contributions from other sources, form a considerable portion of the present Library. Early measures will be taken by the Board to establish a Library Fund, and to replace the original collection lost by fire. The Library contains many valuable works, and is accessible to the students on payment of a small fee.

About a thousand volumes, brought by Prof. Owen, have been placed in the Library, to be used by the students, under the same regulations which apply to the books owned by the University.

Annual Report of Indiana University, Including the Catalogue, 1863–64 (Indianapolis, 1864), pp. 28–29.

Document 65

Cyrus Nutt's Plea for the Organization of an Agricultural College

Cyrus Nutt was elected President of Indiana University on July 27, 1860 and served the institution in that capacity until his death, August 23, 1875. He campaigned heavily for the location of the Agricultural and Mechanical College in Bloomington. In his annual report for 1865-1866, he abstracted his lecture on the subject and this was reprinted in the Catalogue for that academic year.

*   *   *

Every citizen of Indiana has a life interest, for himself and his descendents, in the State University. It belongs to the whole people. The financial value of this Institution is at least two hundred thousand dollars, all of which is devoted to the education of the youth of the commonwealth. It furnishes a college edifice, large, commodious and bountiful; an excellent Faculty; a Laboratory and Museum well supplied with all that can facilitate illustrations in the natural sciences. These, with the society halls, libraries, cheapness of boarding at Bloomington, with its social, moral and religious advantages, afford facilities for education elsewhere rarely to be found.

Besides, in your State University, TUITION IS FREE TO ALL who may choose to attend. Formerly, two students from each county were admitted free of charge for tuition, on the certificate of the County Commissioners. But in July, 1860, this arrangement was modified so as to admit all without charge for tuition in the literary and scientific departments. Thus, through the noble and generous policy of the State, every one is presented with a perpetual scholarship in the State University. The privileges purchased at other Institutions for a hundred dollars, or a still larger sum, are granted without money and without price, to all the citizens of Indiana. Why should they not avail themselves of these means of education, so munificently furnished?

The State University, also, presents great facilities to young men of limited means who are educating themselves; examples of what can be done by those possessed of energy and perserverance, were presented.

Some of the advantages of education:

1. It promotes individual happiness, affording intellectual and moral pleasures of the purest and highest order alloted to humanity.

2. It imparts power over matter and the elements. It gives power its possessor in society—in the State.

3. Its value and blessings are imperishable, lasting as the mind itself.

4. It promotes national greatness and happiness.

5. It is the safeguard of civil liberty.

The State Agricultural College should be located in connection with the Indiana University.

No more important subject can claim the attention of the citizens of Indiana, than the disposal of the munificent grant made by Congress, for the endowment of Agricultural Colleges in each of the States. It vitally concerns every man, woman and child in the Commonwealth. It is the question of subsistence—of how many human beings can be provided with the necessaries and comforts of life in the State of Indiana. It was said by a great man, "that whoever causes one blade of grass to grow which otherwise would not have grown, becomes a benefactor of his race." But this is an enterprise designed to increase the productions of all the industrial classes. It contemplates the means by which the greatest results may be obtained by the least possible expenditure of labor and capital. Should the General Assembly fail to dispose of this grant in the best manner, the loss will be felt by the present and all future generations.

As the grant has already been accepted, the important question remains, "In what manner shall it be appropriated, in order to secure the greatest good to the greatest number?"

The conditions on which the grant is made must be complied with or the grant ceases, and the immense advantages which it might have afforded are lost. This fact cannot be overlooked. Such an error would at be fatal. Some of these conditions are the following:

1st. "At least one College must be organized where the leading object shall be, without excluding other scientific and classical studies, and including military tactics, to teach such branches of learning as are related to Agriculture and the Mechanic Arts."

2d. "If any portion of the fund, principal or interest, shall be lost, it shall be replaced by the State."

3d. "No portion of said fund, nor the interest thereon, shall be applied, directly or indirectly, under any pretense whatever, to the purchase, erection, preservations, or repair of any building or buildings."

4th. "The State shall provide, WITHIN FIVE YEARS, not less than one College as described above."

5th. "Land of no higher value than a dollar and a quarter can be taken. If lands of greater value are selected, than a less quantity is to be taken, so as to make it equal to the above value."

These are the most important restrictions, and all that are necessary to be considered.

For the disposition of this important trust, three plans have been proposed:

First. The endowment of Agricultural Departments in some five of the leading Colleges of the State, including a central institution of research at Indianapolis.

Secondly. The founding of a separate Agricultural College.

Thirdly. The establishment of an Indiana State Agricultural College in connection with the Indiana State University.

The objection to the first plan, which looks to the endowment of one or more professorships in several leading Institutions of the State, and the establishment of a College of research to be located at Indianapolis, is its impracticability. It is impracticable, because the fund which will be realized from the sale of land scrip, will not be sufficiently large to carry out such a scheme. As none of the principal can be appropriated, except ten per centum for the purchase of an experimental farm, the interest only can be used for the salaries of Professors and Instructors. The State is prohibited from locating the land scrip, but must place it in the market. The price at which it can be sold, will not be higher than that of land warrants, which are not worth at present more than fifty cents per acre. At this price the grant of 390,000 acres would net only $195,000. Mr. Fletcher, who is a good financier, estimates the amount at not more than $200,000. But suppose the State to be most fortunate, and to realize $300,000, and that ten per centum of this sum be appropriated for the purchase of an experimental farm, there would remain $270,000 to be invested in State or United States bonds, which, bearing interest at five per cent., would yield only $13,500 per annum. This would be all the means available to pay all the salaries of the Professors appointed by the Board of Regents to the five Colleges selected, and the salaries also of those eminent men employed in the great central Institution devoted to the "Department of Research," at Indianapolis. According to the *first* condition named above, in each of these Colleges there must be taught, at least, these three branches: The sciences which relate to Agriculture, the Mechanic Arts, and Military Tactics. On the lowest possible scale, there must be at least one Professor in each of these chairs, or the instruction, which the law making the grant requires, can not be imparted, and the grant will cease. In truth, the Department of Agriculture would employ all the time of two Professors; one in agricultural chemistry, and another in practical farming and gardening. This would give twenty Professors for the five Colleges, paid at the rate of $670 per annum each, while nothing would be left to pay those employed in the central Institution.

But there is no justice or propriety in limiting the number of Colleges which shall be recipients of this bounty, to five. Five more at least must be added, which are equally entitled to the fostering case and patronage of the State with Hanover, Wabash, Greencastle, and North-Western Christian Colleges. These represent only four of the religious denominations. For the State University, which the advocates of this plan have courteously included in the favored five, does not belong to any sect, but to them all, and to all the citizens of the commonwealth. Why should not Franklin, Merom, Notre Dame, the Lutheran College at Fort Wayne, and Earlham College at Richmond, also be included? Shall this favor be monopolized by the Presbyterians, Methodists, and Reformers alone? Why are Baptists, Christians, Catholics, Lutherans and Friends left out in the cold? It would scarcely be thought that a man who has a heart in the right place, would tolerate for a moment such exclusiveness. We may, then, legitimately conclude that if distribution is to prevail, and some of the sectarian Colleges shall receive this contribution, that all will be embraced. The whole number of Professors would then be forty, and their salaries would be the enormous sum of $335 per annum! No competent man can be obtained for so paltry a sum.

It might also be inquired, how are the laboratories and apparatus, requisite for illustration, to be provided? How are the machine shops, with engines, gearing and tools, to be furnished in these ten Institutions? These Institutions must furnish them, or the State must make an appropriation to each of them for this purpose. It will take years for these Colleges to raise the means, if they can do it at all. For the State to furnish it, would require a heavy expenditure which must be met by taxation.

It is impracticable, also, from the fact that there are too many different elements and diverse interests to be harmonized and made to work in unison. All these institutions, with the exception of the State University, are under the control of independent Boards of Trustees, elected by conferences, synods, or associations. They are not responsible to the State, nor subject to its control. And it is only by courtesy or consent of these Trustees, that the State can use any of their rooms for recitation, or any of their apparatus or fixtures, and the professors whom she may appoint are mere "tenants at will," liable to be ejected at any moment. One of these institutions might, after a short trial, find it inconvenient to receive such professor, and then that Agricultural College would expire; and another might follow the example, until the last should cease, and the grant be forfeited. No wise Legislator would be willing to embark the State in an enterprise involving such uncertainties; or render her dependent for success upon sectarian Boards of Trustees.

But were success possible, the instruction imparted at these several institutions would be much less perfect than it would be were the departments divided among a greater number of professors, and each more thorough in the field allotted him, as would be the case if the State should establish only one institution. Then eight or ten professors might be employed, and the student attending this College would have the advantages of these ten instructors at no more cost than would be necessary at these separate institutions, in which but two or three were engaged in imparting instruction. The expense of the student would be about the same for boarding, &c., at whatever college he might attend, but the benefits which he would enjoy would be vastly greater at an institution having a full corps of professors, whose researches and lectures were all accessible, than at one where there was but one or two.

Hitherto we have said nothing of the Department of Research, which the advocates of this plan propose to found at Indianapolis. How is the Agricultural Farm to be obtained! The buildings, the laboratory, the cabinet, apparatus, library, the observatory, the telescope and astronomical instruments requisite for making astronomical observations, to be provided? And where are the funds to pay the men of learning and skill competent to fill these various chairs? To establish such an institution would require an outlay of five hundred thousand dollars. Will the Legislature make the appropriation? or will the citizens of Indianapolis make a donation of that sum? Neither is at present probable. The scheme may be a beautiful conception, but unfortunately it cannot be realized. It is a bubble, glancing in the sunbeams, and presenting the varied colorings of the rainbow, but the moment you touch it it bursts and dissolves in air.

II. The fund, then, should by all means, be kept together. To distribute it would be to throw it away. All schemes, contemplating this, must end in utter failure. Only one institution should be established. The remaining question, is, where shall be located? As no part of the principal or interest of the Agricultural Fund can be appropriated for the purchase, erection, or repair of any buildings, and the College must go into operation within five years from the time the grant was made, of which there are but one year and eight months still remaining, it is necessary that the Legislature should establish the College during its coming session; for after the commencement of the next, in 1867, there will be only six months left before the grant will cease. The buildings and fixtures necessary for opening the College must also be provided. There is no time to be lost. Now, three modes of accomplishing this result will doubtless claim attention. First, voluntary suscriptions by different localities. Secondly, direct appropriations from the Treasury of the State. Thirdly, occupying the buildings and grounds of the State University for opening and conducting the College. If the first plan be adopted, notice must be given and agents appointed to receive the subscriptions, and compare them and determine which competing locality furnishes the largest amount available. This operation will require much time. It will also be difficult to determine what amount can be collected; for there is always a great contraction when the subscriptions are collected, and the whole process is slow and uncertain. Then, when the collections have been made, the buildings are to be erected and the apparatus to be purchased, the machinery put into operations, and all this must be done in one year and eight months. Should the subscription prove inadequate, or unlooked for delay occur, the grant is imperiled. Besides, what locality will likely contribute more than the value of the State University, which is the property of the State, and worth at least, at present prices, three hundred thousand dollars? Will Indianapolis, or any town of Indiana, contribute more than that sum?

It may be admitted that according to the second mode, by an appropriation sufficiently large, the Legislature could found a splendid Agricultural College, that would be an honor to the State, separate from all other institutions. But it would require a heavy tax upon the people, who are at present already heavily burdened with State and United States taxes. The amount which must be paid out of the State Treasury this year, for all purposes, interest on the State debt, military claims, and other State purposes, will scarcely be less than $1,400,000. When we add to this the internal revenue tax, the bounties to volunteers in the several counties, the support of soldiers' families, it is doubtful whether their burdens should be increased. It is doubtful whether the Legislature should levy a heavy tax to raise a hundred and fifty thousand dollars to erect buildings for an Agricultural College. Judging from the past, our legislators will not make that appropriation now, and the people will thank them for it. In a few years, when the clouds which now overshadow our country have passed away, appropriations will be made for this purpose, and then a higher tax will be levied for the support of common schools. But should this additional burden be laid upon the people just now? No, if it can be avoided and yet save the grant.

This is possible by locating the said College at Bloomington, in connection with the State University. Over this institution the State has complete control, except to divert its funds to other objects than those of education. It is the child of the commonwealth, and should be an object of interest to every resident of the State. One would naturally suppose that the proper location for the State Agricultural College would be in connection with the State University. Some of the advantages of this arrangement are: *First.* The whole property of the University becomes subsidiary to the State Agricultural College. This, at the lowest estimate, is worth three hundred thousand dollars. The building is the largest and best adapted to college purposes of any in the State. This is said without any disparagement to other literary institutions. It is one hundred and forty-seven feet in length, consisting of a main building and two wings, all three stories high and finished after the Collegiate Gothic style, and presents a very beautiful and tasteful appearance. The Campus contains twelve acres, and is planted with trees and shrubbery. The cabinet is one of the largest and best in the West. Recently many interesting portions of the cabinet of the late Dr. David Dale Owen, of New Harmony, have been transferred to the State University, and now fill an entire wing of the building. In the basement of that wing is the laboratory, the chemical and philosophical apparatus; on the first floor are the mineralogical and geological specimens; on the second floor the cabinet is continued; and in the centre of the room is placed a large table, on which is traced a map of Indiana, with her rivers, towns, roads and counties. And on each county is placed a specimen of the rocks and soil of that county; so that the student has before him at one glance the whole resources of the Commonwealth, mineralogical, geological and agricultural. Every one must perceive the facilities which such an arrangement affords for instruction. On the third floor is the Department of Paleontology in two divisions, embracing animal and vegetable remains. The vegetable are arranged in the form of a dry garden, just as they used to grow on this earth during those vast geological epochs which rolled away while the crust of our earth was forming. The animal remains are scientifically classified and arranged, by species, genera, orders and classes, beginning with the lowest forms of animated nature, the zoophites, or animal plants, thence rising to the highest—man—the crowning glory of this world. The apparatus, libraries, and literary halls will compare favorably with those of any other institution in the State. All these are at the services of the Agricultural College, and afford a good foundation for a commencement. The endowment of the University is $80,000, invested by the State at seven per cent., which is equal to $112,000 at five per cent. There have been realized from the sale of lands of the last appropriation by Congress to the University, $22,000, bearing interest at seven per cent. This, added to the old endowment, makes $102,000. Besides this, there are more than eleven thousand acres of land belonging to the University yet unsold, valued at $50,000. The buildings are worth at least $50,000, making altogether $200,000. This, united with the $300,000 of the Agricultural Fund, would make $500,000, a handsome endowment, forming a University of which our State might justly be proud.

The above estimates are made upon the gold basis, as prices ranged three years ago. At the present rates, the value of the University would exceed three thousand dollars.

The citizens of Monroe county tender to the State, on condition that the State Agricultural College is located there, an experimental farm, equal in value to any that may be tendered by any other locality; also, the entire cabinet of the late Dr. David Dale Owen, worth at least fifty thousand dollars. This includes his apparatus for the analysis of soils and vegetables, which cannot be duplicated without visiting Europe and importing many of the articles of which it is composed, which would require a vast expenditure of time and money. Such another cabinet and apparatus could not now be collected for seventy-five thousand dollars. This, and the Agricultural Farm, added to the above, would amount to four hundred thousand dollars, all subservient to the Agricultural and Industrial College.

Whatever else may be needed can be furnished as easily at Bloomington as anywhere else. The teacher, in military tactics, is already on the ground, in the person of Professor Owen, than whom none better qualified can be found in the country. He is a regular graduate of a military college in Europe, was a Captain in the Mexican war, Colonel of the Sixtieth Indiana Volunteers, and commanded a brigade for more than a year in the late war.

Secondly. This disposition of the grant is the cheapest method of establishing the State Agricultural College. As no part of the principal or interest of this fund can be taken to pay an agent or officers employed by the State in collecting, investing or managing it, the Trustees of this College must be paid by the State. Now, this expense the University proposes to defray, paying them from its own funds in the same manner that her own Trustees are paid. It will cost the State nothing to manage the affairs of the Institution. But with a separate College, not only must the agent employed to sell the land scrip, and the commissioners appointed to invest the funds, be paid from the State Treasury, but, also, the Trustees. This will amount to a considerable sum. On the ground of economy, this plan has the advantage of combining efficiency with the least expenditure.

Thirdly. Tuition is now free to all, in the State University. Formerly, two students from each county were admitted free of charge, upon the certificate of the County Commissioners. In 1850 this arrangement was changed, and the Trustees provided that *no tuition fee* should be charged against any student. Hence, the State Universtiy offers a perpetual scholarship to all who will accept it, without money or price. The doors of our University are freely open to all! Now this will harmonize perfectly with the plan for free tuition in the State Agricultural College. Students attending the Agricultural College will have all the advantages of recitations and lectures, in any department of the University they may choose to attend, without any additional expense. The benefits of such an arrangement cannot be easily over estimated. The libraries, museums and reading rooms are, also, available. In a separate Institution equal facilities could be furnished only at an immense expenditure, and the establishment of several professorships, the same as those now in the State University. Indiana would thus present the singular spectacle of a sovereign State, at double the expense necessary, establishing two Institutions, duplicating and competing with each other, to the great injury of both. This would be an instance of folly exceedingly humiliating.

Fourthly. This arrangement makes the Agricultural College a certainty. There will be no discount on the property and funds furnished by the State University. It is not dependent upon future contingencies of subscription and collection. It is already *there* at the disposal of the Legislature. The whole machinery is provided for a commencement of operations, without any immediate appropriation from the Treasury of the State. In a separate foundation, all the buildings, laboratory, and preparations for analyses of soils, cabinets, and means of illustration, must be collected, and with the risk of delay, which would imperil the original grant. But on the plan here advocated, success is sure.

Fifthly. The location in connection with the State University, will enable the Agricultural College to go into operation immediately, and secure to the State the benefits intended by Congress, without the possibility of failure. On any other plan considerable time must elapse before the means can be furnished, and the arrangements made for opening the Institution, involving more or less uncertainty.

It will be objected probably, that Bloomington is not the place. That it should be located at Indianapolis, the center of the State, and a point most accessible. Indianapolis has many advantages doubtless, and hence in many respects would be a desirable location. But this would involve the outlay of funds from the Treasury of the State, and an increase of taxation. Another insuperable objection is the fact that Indianapolis is a great commercial metropolis, and will soon become one of the great cities of the land. Great cities are no places for institutions of learning, and least of all, for an agricultural one. The great Universities of the world are not located in cities. Oxford and Cambridge, the two great Universities of England, are not in London nor any other of the great cities of the British Empire. The towns of Oxford and Cambridge are made up of the fifteen or twenty Colleges of which the Universities are composed. So of all the Agricultural Colleges of Europe, not one of them is located in a large city. The impression *there,* is that large cities are unfavorable as the location of Institutions of learning. The same is true in the United States. Our most successful Colleges and Universities are located in comparatively small towns and villages. Harvard is at Cambridge, some six miles from Boston. Yale College has made what there is of the town of New Haven. Thomas Jefferson never displayed more wisdom than when he located the Virginia University, not in Richmond, but at Charlottsville, an insignificant village. Franklin located that of Pennsylvania in Philadelphia, and it has proved a comparative failure.

The allurements which Indianapolis presents to draw off the attention of students from their appropriate work, are an objection. The temptations to vice are too strong, and the facilities for escaping detection too great, to make it a favorable location for a literary institution. Besides, the expense of living would be too great, and only the sons of the wealthy could enjoy the privileges of your Agricultural College. Of the cost of boarding at the capital, the members of the present General Assembly may have some personal experience, and of it they may retain, in a diminished purse, hereafter some unpleasant remembrances.

Bloomington is on the L. N. & C. R. R., and is as accessible as any other place, except the railroad centers. Boarding can be obtained as cheap as at any other place in the State. It is one of the most healthy points in Indiana. The State Institution has been in operation over forty years, and not more than three graves of students can be found in her cemetery. The same cannot be said of other locations of the Colleges of Indiana. There are few opportunities and few temptations to vice and dissipation. In its quiet retreat, far removed from the throng and bustle of the great emporiums of trade, the student can pursue undisturbed his studies and investigations.

But it may be said, "Why hitch it on to the State University? Why suffer it to be absorbed in this institution?" The Act making the grant requires a College with independent "powers." Now instead of saying that the Agricultural College is hitched on to the State University, it may with more propriety be said that the University is hitched on to the Agricultural College. It will not make the Agricultural College less prominent as an institution, but it will add to that prominence which it would have in any other locality, all the importance and prestige of the State University, which will contribute all its resources for its benefit. The bills introduced by the Hon. P. C. Dunning, in the Senate, and the Hon. S. W. Buskirk, in the House, provide for a separate Board of Directors with a distinct corporate seal and Faculty from that of the University, so that all the requirements of the Act of Congress, making the grant, are met.

"But why should the State University be the only Institution favored? Are there not other Colleges and Universities equally deserving of public favor?" True, there are several Institutions founded and conducted by the enterprise of different religious denominations, of which we may be justly proud. They are an honor to the State. But the relation which the government of the Commonwealth sustains to the State University, is very different from that which it sustains to these sectarian Colleges. These belong to and are under the exclusive control of the denominations founding them. They have never, with one exception, received any aid from the State, except their charters, nor have they asked it, for should the aid be granted, it would furnish an excuse, at least, for interfering in their management. This they do not desire.

It is otherwise with the State University, though, by many, this fact is overlooked, and an effort is made to ignore it and class it as one of mere local and sectional interests, like the rest, while, in fact, the State has but one University, and this is under its exclusive control. It cannot ignore its offspring, without a crime, any more than the parent can abandon its helpless child. Many have tried to persuade the State to act the unnatural part of step-dame, and to discard and neglect it. But she must, unless she is willing to be false to herself, perform her duty in recognizing and fostering her own Institution. She has another charge now committed to her care, in this grant of Congress. These children can be cherished and nurtured together cheaper and better than when apart, for they would have, then, the advantages of mutual help, while the same house and furniture would answer for both. Why, then, unnaturally tear them asunder? The divorce must be strange and unaccountable.

Again, it has been asked, "Why has the State University just waked up to the interests of Agriculture, to which she has heretofore paid no attention, although her organic law requires her Trustees to establish Agricultural and Normal Departments? Now, this failure is not the fault of the Trustees or Faculty. Both these Departments would have been established, long since, had there been the necessary funds. These departments could not be carried on without means. These means have not been furnished by the State, and the Trustees could not accomplish impossibilities.

Lastly. An Agricultural and Industrial College cannot succeed by itself; it must be connected with some other institution of learning, or it must have provisions for teaching those branches usually taught in literary institutions. Agricultural science and mechanics cannot be pursued, except by those who have a high degree of scientific and literary culture. To study with success "Analytic Chemistry," requires a thorough knowledge of the elements of the science of chemistry and philosophy. So, also, mechanics requires a knowledge of Algebra, Geometry, Trigonometry, Analytical Geometry, and Calculus. Where, then, shall the students of your Agricultural College be prepared? Is it proposed to take boys without previous training, and put them in this College? You might just as well require them to speak Greek without ever having studied that language, as to expect them to succeed. Will you receive only those who have been prepared in other institutions? If so, the number will be small; for young men who have spent four or five years in accomplishing their literary course, will not likely spend three or four years more at an Agricultural College. This would require eight years instead of four, the usual term, and double the expenditure. But if located in connection with the State University, both courses can be accomplished together, with little or no additional cost of time and means.

This view is confirmed by experience. New York established such an institution some years ago, in a spot most advantageously located in the interior of the State. She purchased a thousand acres, overlooking some of the most beautiful of her lakes; and erected, at great expense, suitable buildings; a corps of Professors and instructors were placed in charge, and the institution was opened for the reception of students. At first, a number of students attended; but they soon became dissatisfied, and the number diminished. It never had any prosperity, and to-day that College has neither a Professor nor student. It proved a perfect failure. Michigan has made three failures in her efforts to establish an Agricultural and Industrial College, without the literary and scientific departments attached. She provided a farm and shops, and put the institution in operation. It continued by a short time, closing for want of students. The Legislature made additional appropriations and revived the College. To induce students to attend, tuition was made free; but still it languished. It was again reorganized; and the price of boarding was also placed at the lowest figure, and the young men were not compelled to engage in manual labor, while the highest prices were paid those who chose to labor, for every hour they were thus employed. And yet, it proved a failure. Some years ago, a similar institution was established by a gentleman of wealth in Kentucky. He soon found that it could not succeed, and abandoned the enterprise. Such institutions in Europe have, with one exception, proved failures. This one, which seemed to be a success, was kept up by the indomitable energy of its founder, but at his death it expired.

Annual Report of Indiana University Including the Catalogue, 1865–66 (Indianapolis, 1866), pp. 31–42.

Document 66

The Farmer's Needs

Indiana University began a drive to secure the Morrill Land Grant Funds for the purpose of enlarging its struggling agricultural program. Richard Owen, speaking in his southern Indiana homeland, undertook to make an intellectual case for the establishment of an agricultural college in Bloomington.

*　　*　　*

SYNOPSIS OF LECTURE ON EDUCATION.
DELIVERED DURING VACATION OF 1864, IN THE SOUTHERN COUNTIES OF INDIANA, BY PROFESSOR R. OWEN.

The law was first read (Sec. 19,) by which the Legislature of Indiana makes it the duty, each year, for one of the Professors to lecture on the principles and organization of the University, and its educational facilities. The lecturer stated that he proposed, in accordance with the above instructions, to give some account of the advantages of the State University, and then to show in what way the Agricultural College, if organized by accepting the grant from the General Government, could be most favorably connected with the State University.

He then went on to show that the Indiana University has recently had buildings erected at a cost of $30,000, and has endowment enough to pay a corps of five or six Professors, besides lands yet unsold, the interest of which would create a yet larger salary fund.

The students are consequently received without any charge, except a small fee for the Janitor, who has the care of the building. That fee amounts only to $11 per annum. The additional expenses are boarding, lodging, traveling to and from home, and the necessary text-books. The present (1864) rate of boarding and lodging in the forty weeks of the session, or academic year, would be about $140, and including books and traveling, even from distant parts of the State, would not exceed $175 each year. The clothing need not cost more than at home. Thus parents, by a total expenditure of four time $175, or $700, can give a son all the advantage of a full collegiate course, and thereby benefit him infinitely more than by presenting him, at the age when he would leave College, four or five times that sum. Some parents may prefer, for economy of time and money, to give only a scientific course. Full provision is made to meet also that demand. Others may contend that they are unable to expend even the three or four hundred dollars necessary for that purpose. Let them not say so until they have calculated how much some of their little luxuries cost them each year, and have balanced the self-denial necessary to leave off a bad or useless habit, as compared with the pleasure of having a son morally and intellectually worthy.

Some may ask, what advantages the State Institution possesses over denominational colleges? The reply is, that it is considered highly advantageous for all young persons to have the highest grade of morality and religion inculcated, as it is at Bloomington, amid a strictly religious community of all sects, yet with careful provision that no sectarian influence should prevail, until the mind is capable of judging from dispassionate examination.

And the same may be said of political party spirit. The effort is to inculcate the highest tone of patriotism, with a spirit of toleration, and a sense of justice, which will concede to others all we claim for ourselves, and insure acquiescence in the fully ascertained will of the majority of the qualified voters.

In addition to the above, it is claimed in the Department of Natural Science, that their valuable museum enables them to educate, through the eye, in half the time required on the exclusively oral system.

To illustrate the above, that branch of natural history, termed zoology, was selected, and a small portable cabinet was presented to the audience, showing the types of the various departments, classes and orders. The facility was then pointed out with which any one of the 500,000 species of different animals might be assigned to its department, class and order, and then ultimately to its genus and species; just as a soldier might be traced to his geographical department, army corps, division, brigade, regiment and company.

The lecturer then proceeded to the second subject, the Agricultural College, and endeavored to show that this is the most favorable form of college for the education of the masses, in fact for all, because it develops equally the physical, mental and moral faculties.

The professions being overfilled, and agriculture and manufactures being the chief means by which the resources of a country are developed, it becomes important to induce young men of talent to qualify themselves for disseminating, practising and originating valuable improvements in the cultivation of the soil, in practical science, and in mechanic arts; so as to make the earth produce more than ever formerly, yet without deteriorating its strength and capabilities; also, so as to keep pace with other nations, or even outstrip them in mechanical inventions and improvements, calculated to diminish the evils of over-work in certain classes, and promote by labor-saving machinery the products and comforts.

Having dwelt, at some length, on the advantages of industrial colleges, the lecturer concluded by appealing to his hearers to avail themselves of the advantages in the State University for the education of their sons; and by urging that legislators should be instructed to vote so as to secure for Indiana all the advantages to be derived from a State Agricultural College.

Annual Report of Indiana University, Including the Catalogue, 1864–65 (Indianapolis, 1865), pp. 32–33.

Document 67

The University in Limbo

Failure to secure the Agricultural and Mechanical College in Bloomington placed Indiana University squarely back on its liberal arts bases. The needs of the institution were great. Actually the institution had made only limited progress in touching directly the lives of any considerable number of Hoosiers. Bravely the Board of Trustees and the faculty reported the year just closing as the most successful in the University's history but then outlined its needs if it were to keep pace with other state universities.

* * *

THE CONDITIONS AND WANTS OF THE UNIVERSITY.

All must acknowledge that the educational interests of a State are, to her, of the utmost importance commercially and morally. Immigration cannot be expected unless good educational facilities, at moderate prices, are offered to those seeking new locations; and the better the school system, the better will be the class of citizens who will there seek to make their homes.

The common school system of Indiana, now compares favorably with that of any other State in the West. It is also exceedingly gratifying to the friends of higher education to know that the State University, the head of the common school system, is in a most flourishing condition. The year now closing has been the most successful in its past history. The largest number of students has been in attendance, and the greatest progress has been achieved. The whole number for the present year is 279, of whom 236 are in the four College Chapels and Law Department. This is the result of the liberal policy recently inaugurated by the State toward this Institution, and that the same liberal policy by the State should be continued is of the highest importance to its educational interests.

As a justification of this protecting care on the part of the State let us glance a moment at the past history of the Indiana University. Though crippled from its commencement, for the want of funds, until the recent appropriation, the annual income averaging scarcely five thousand dollars, yet she has 568 alumni, graduates who have completed their course. And besides these, more than five thousand young men have received a partial course of instruction in the University, and thereby been better qualified for the discharge of life's duties. A large number of these have devoted themselves as teachers to the diffusion of knowledge among the youth. Many of them have attained the highest distinction, as lawyers, judges, legislators, physicians and ministers of the gospel, in our own and adjoining States; and some as missionaries in heathen lands.

In the recent terrible struggle for national existence, the roll of honor from her alumni and students is long and bright. They filled, with distinction, every grade from that of private to general officers, and they are represented among the honored dead upon every battle-field. Many have won high honors in Congress, as Governors of States, and as ministers to foreign courts. Truly Indiana has just reason to be proud of the past history and present condition of her University.

As the interest of the State, material, intellectual and moral, are best promoted by general and higher education, could the Legislature expend a part of her resources to any greater advantage than to add a few thousand dollars per annum to the amount now appropriated to the University? Every enlightened and well disposed citizen will undoubtedly be willing to increase these appropriations, knowing that education is the cheapest and best preventive of vice and crime, which now require vast expenditures from the public treasury to restrain and punish. Besides Christianity, morality and the advancement of civilization make it the sacred duty of the State to support the University, the head of her school system.

Every good citizen rejoices in the success of the benevolent institutions of the State—the asylums, for the insane, the blind and the deaf mutes; and the liberal provisions she has made for their maintenance. These constitute no small part of the glory of our commonwealth. The State University presents equal claims to her fostering care, as one of the grand agencies by which humanity is elevated, and the greatest prosperity of the State is secured.

Should the inquiry be made "For what purposes are additional funds needed?" we would say that, with the funds placed at the disposal of the Trustees, by the recent appropriations of the Legislature, they have established four additional chairs in the Literary and Scientific Departments, which were essential to their complete success. They have also founded a Law School, with two Professors, in which tuition is free, as well as in all the other departments. This has been a great success; upwards of fifty young men, from every section of the State, and a number from other States have been in attendance during its first term. Nearly three thousand volumes have been added to the Library. They have also purchased the extensive mineralogical, geological and philosophical cabinet of the late Dr. David Dale Owen, the best to be found west of the Allegheny Mountains, and scarcely inferior to any in the United States.

But in order to keep pace with the continued and increasing prosperity of the University, it is indispensable that another building should be erected. The present college edifice, though one of the largest and most commodious in the State, has been filled to overflowing. There must be more room provided. The Trustees will be under the necessity of renting a hall for the Law Department at the opening of the coming session. The cabinet, too, is now boxed up for the want of a suitable room in which to display it, and so it must remain, a useless expense to the Trustees for warehouse room, a sealed book of nature for the expectant student. To supply these wants, another large building should be erected upon the college campus, at least one hundred and fifty feet in length, sixty in breadth and thirty-five in hight from the first floor. Such an edifice would furnish room for the cabinet, laboratory and recitation rooms for the department of Natural Science and recitation and library rooms for the Law Department.

A Gymnasium is also greatly needed. The military feature recently added to the University under the superintendence of an officer of the army of the United States, works well, and thus is made some provision for the physical training of the student, which the Faculty have long felt deserved special attention. In a gymnasium this great desideratum would be furnished. Opportunities for healthful exercise would thus always be secured, even in weather unsuitable for drill.

Another professional department should be established, that of Medicine. A first-class Medical College should be provided, connected with the University, in which tuition shall be free for all. Then Indiana, with her excellent common schools, her graded and high schools, her Normal College, at Terre Haute, her Agricultural and Mechanical College, at Lafayette, and her State University, embracing the College of Science and Arts, the College of Law, the College of Medicine, and that of Military Science, would have her system of education complete, and equal to that of any other State in the Union. Then no young men or women need leave their own State in order to secure the best, liberal and professional educations in any vocation they may select. Indiana owes this to herself and her sons and daughters. Her children should not be dependent upon other commonwealths for what she, herself, is abundantly able to furnish.

There is one point more to which the attention of the Legislature is earnestly called. Gambling tables, and the traffic in intoxicating liquors and gaming tables should be prohibited by law within the distance of two miles of all higher educational institutions belonging to the State. These are found to be the great drawbacks to good government, and wholesome moral and religious influence over the students. We earnestly crave this aid from the Legislature at their coming session.

Annual Report of Indiana University Including the Catalogue, 1869–70 (Indianapolis, 1870), pp. 35–36.

[V]

In Search of New Directions and New Support 1871–1882

The loss of an opportunity to expand Indiana University into broader fields of educational and public endeavor through the creation of Purdue University was a serious blow. The America of the 1870s and 1880s was a booming, materialistic one in which money, machines, production, and armies of labor characterized the age. The demands on educational institutions for services became increasingly greater, especially as the Morrill or land grant institutions came into existence. They could serve the demand for engineers, trained farmers, and scientists of all sorts. Too, by the very nature and intent of the Morrill Act with its land grants, the new universities could go down into the ranks of work-a-day Americans and translate education into terms of practical accomplishment. This was an area that Indiana University had to invade if it was to capitalize on its position as head of the state's educational system. It was ill-prepared to do this in the two decades under consideration.

Wedded to the liberal arts tradition, or more especially to the old classical curriculum, it was hard to lower barriers of academic proprietary interests. Too, it had been difficult to break away from the tradition of preacher-presidents, of which Cyrus Nutt perhaps was the ablest. He gave evidence of being a realist who understood the potential for the future in the addition of the sciences to the Indiana curriculum. He and his colleagues fought for the Morrill support and lost. Now Indiana had to find new directions for itself. It is in this search that these documents become a vital source of history of the transitions of the University.

The Board of Trustees gave evidence of being practical men who dedicated themselves to the advancement of the University, but they were unable to read aright the need for competent non-sectarian administration of campus affairs. In contrast to Cyrus Nutt, Lemuel Moss was pompous and pontifical, translating higher education in terms of sermons on higher ideals. Amazingly, the University had shown little growth in this age of American expansion. It was well enough for the preachers to speak in the

214

esoteric phrases of the "higher ideals," but it was an altogether different thing to extract money from the Indiana General Assembly.

Moss's social indiscretion was perhaps no more than a minor setback, if a hindrance at all. It may well have been that the discharge of Lemuel Moss by the Trustees was indeed a step forward for the University. It broke once and for all the theological bondage. The loss by fire of the University building in 1883 was indeed tragedy. Loss of building and materials robbed the institution of precious possessions, but—even more—it came as a heavy blow to morale at the moment efforts were being made to gain better financial support for a far-too-meager program of instruction. It may well be reasoned that the fire, viewed from a longer perspective of future developments, was not entirely tragic. The purchase of the Dunn lands gave the University room in which to expand. Too, the institution made a fresh beginning with new buildings in a graceful setting under a new, imaginative administration which gave it a new sense of purpose and security.

The very essence of these documents has to be considered as lack of financial support. With the monotonous cry of the raven, presidents and trustees appealed to the governors and the legislators to be more generous with appropriations. The miracle of this age is not that Indiana University made some real progress in maintaining and even adding to its education status, but that it continued to exist at all. These were the courageous years in which professors and trustees persevered far beyond the normal call of duty. Their dedication, and even their optimism, was monumental.

Document 68

The Beginnings of a Long Fiscal Road

This brief presidential letter from Cyrus Nutt to Governor Conrad Baker marks the beginning of an era in which the Indiana General Assembly was asked to take serious steps to finance the kind of university the people of the commonwealth deserved. No longer in this age of expanding America would the pittance of endowment allotted to Indiana University accomplish any substantial educational purpose.

*   *   *

Inda. State University
Bloomington Indiana
9th Jan. 1871

His Excellency
Conrad Baker
Governor of Indiana
Dear Sir

The Faculty of the Indiana University, remembering the lively interest, which you have always manifested in its welfare, have directed us to address you on the subject of its present financial crisis. With the amount which the liberality of the Legislature added to the former endowment, you will see how much has already been effected, (when you read the semi-annual Report of the Trustees) and how much remains to be accomplished, all of which absolutely fails of success, unless the same liberality be continued.

We cannot for a moment doubt that your sympathy with the great cause of education, and your State pride, as her chief Executive, will render you desirous to see the State University of Indiana placed on as liberal and independent a basis as that of our Sister States, such as Michigan.

But the history of all Universities shows that the high point of success cannot be attained without a large fund, whose annual interest shall be sufficient, when faithfully & judiciously expended, to maintain a large corps of able professors, and to keep up the necessary buildings, museum, apparatus & other adjunctive aids, so essential to a liberal collegiate system.

In addition to the kind mention already made, in your message, regarding the Inda. University, we look with confidence to your further earnest recommendations to the Legislature, regarding the appropriation of such funds as the repayment of the State Debt, or other means, may place at their disposal, for such permanent and efficient endowment as shall render all subsequent legislative aid unnecessary, and place the Indiana University in the foremost rank of colleges.

With profound respect & esteem,

We are, Governor,

Very respectfully & truly yours

CYRUS NUTT President
Inda. Univ.

Richard Owen
Sec. of Faculty

―――――

Indiana Division Mss., State Library.

Document 69

Apex of the Indiana Educational Pyramid

A half-century after the framers of Indiana's first constitution designated the University as the head of the state's educational system, the trustees, faculty, and the superintendent of public instruction faced the problem of shaping a new curriculum and new requirements to achieve this objective. This particular document is even more important because it outlines a program by which the University and the public school offerings could be co-ordinated so as to direct students toward achieving full educational accomplishment. Too, the document contains a substantial germ of liberal arts training.

*   *   *

CIRCULAR.

―――――

The Trustees of Indiana University, having introduced essential modifications in the course of instruction, deem that an explanation is due to the other colleges and universities of the West, and to the citizens of Indiana. They, therefore, present the following reasons for those modifications, and most cordially invite the co-operation of the other institutions of higher education in this effort, thus to unify and harmonize the educational system of the State. These changes affect merely the order in which the different branches will be pursued, but do not detract, in the least, from their number or extent, nor from the high standard of scholarship which the University has hitherto required.

THE RELATIONS OF THE UNIVERSITY TO THE SCHOOL SYSTEM OF INDIANA.

It has been long admitted as a fundamental truth, that a general diffusion of knowledge among the people is essential to the preservation of liberty, and the maintenance of Republican institutions, so the founders of the Commonwealth believed; and they incorporated the following truthful sentiments and noble provisions in the first Constitution:

"Knowledge and learning generally diffused throughout a community, being essential to the preservaton of a free government; and spreading the advantages and opportunities of education through the various parts of a country being highly conducive to that end, it shall be the duty of the General Assembly to provide by law for the improvement of such lands as are or hereafter may be granted by the United States to this State for the use of schools, and apply any funds which may be raised from such lands, or from any other quarter to the accomplishment of the grand object for which they are, or may be intended. * * * The General Assembly shall, from time to time, pass such laws as shall be calculated to encourage agriculture, scientific and intellectual improvements, by allowing rewards and immunities for the promotion and improvement of arts, sciences, commerce, manufactories, and natural history; and to countenance and encourage the principles of humanity, honesty, industry and moralty."*

"It shall be the duty of the General Assembly, as soon as circumstances will permit, to provide by law for a general system of education, ascending in regular gradation from townships schools to a State University, wherein tuition shall be gratis and equally open to all."†

The second Constitution, adopted in 1851, provides for carrying out the same system of general education, and recognizes, the Indiana University at Bloomington, Monroe county, as the State University. The Indiana University is, therefore, an essential part of the educational system of the State, and is designed to complete and crown the work of the Common High schools, by furnishing the means of the highest culture to her youth, and providing the most ample facilities for extensive and thorough instruction in the learned and scientific professions.

The want of a proper adjustment of the High school and Collegiate courses of study has been long and deeply felt. This want of unity, has been, for years, the subject of earnest and protracted discussions in State Teachers' and Collegiate Associations, in State Institutes, Educational Conventions and the State Board of Education. The much desired union has at length been reached; and the method by which it has been attained will be explained by the following documents, together with the reasons of the change in the *curriculum* of the University. The authorities of the University rejoice in this happy adjustment of the whole course of instruction in the educational system of Indiana, by which the student can pass without interruption or delay through all the grades, from

* Cons. Ind., Art. 9, Sec. 1.
† Cons. Ind., Art. 9, Sec. 2.

the Primary, through the Intermediate, High School, Collegiate and University courses of instruction, and thus thoroughly equip himself for life's duties. The hearty support and active co-operation of teachers, principals of High schools, county superintendents, and all the friends of education, in these new arrangements are earnestly desired.

OFFICE OF STATE SUP'T OF PUBLIC INSTRUCTION,
INDIANAPOLIS, INDIANA.

Gentlemen of the Faculty and Board of Trustees of the Indiana State University:

The subject of a continuous course of study in the Public Schools, from the Primary Grade to the University has occupied the attention of the educators of the State for years, but no satisfactory results have been attained. The State Board of Education would respectfully request that the consideration of the subject be renewed.

It is the desire of the Board to promote the welfare of every child in the State by affording him the best facilities for education, at the least expense of his time and money. In order to accomplish this, every grade of our system of State schools should be brought to the highest degree of efficiency, and each should be adapted to the wants of the student until he arrives at the termination of the University course. We regret that this chain of gradation is not complete, so that students who finish the studies usually taught in the High school may immediately enter the Collegiate Department of the University.

"The problem we present is, "How shall we harmonize these two grades of the Public School System that the best interests of both shall be secured?

"*Second*—The University is the highest educational institution in the State. It should be second to no institution in the country, and while we respectfully ask the re-arrangement of its course of study, we emphatically demand that there shall be no abatement, either in the number or the character, of the studies required to complete the Collegiate curriculum as now prescribed. It is supported by the people, and should be so organized, in connection with the other parts of the school system of the State, as to do the greatest good to the greatest number that can be induced to accept its advantages.

"We, therefore, respectfully propose, on behalf of the High School, to establish a *minimum course of study*, which, when completed, shall entitle the student to admission to the Collegiate Department of the University. This shall consist of "Orthography, Arithmetic, Geography, English Grammar, Physiology, United States History, Algebra, Geometry, Latin Grammar, Caesar and Virgil." In indicating this course, it is not intended to limit the number of studies that may be pursued in any school; on the contrary, it will be a special gratification to the Board of Education to know that every High School is able and willing to offer a more advanced course to its students, including a preparation in the Greek Language.

"To find the correct solution of the problem, it is necessary to understand the relations of both institutions to ascertain what changes can be wisely made in each to bring them more closely together.

"*First*—The Public High School is an institution of comparatively recent growth. It has almost entirely superseded the Academy, because it is more economical, and is better adapted to the wants of the people. Being supported by taxation, its usefulness is best attained when it gives to the community that support it, the highest culture for the greatest number of youth that can be induced to accept its advantages. Each community determines for itself the degree to which this culture may be extended; the people may enlarge it, or abolish it, as they think best. Comparatively few pupils, in any of our cities enter the High School, and of these a very small per cent. complete the prescribed course of study. It appears, therefore, unreasonable that its course shall be arranged with reference to the very small number of students who may ultimately attend the University, rather than to the majority who do not desire further advancement. The almost unanimous voice of those who control the High Schools declares that they can not afford to give the preparation in Greek, which the University requires, while they are able and willing to give more than an equivalent in other branches, for which there is a popular demand.

"We also respectfully propose, on part of the University that, in consideration of instruction given by the High School in Physiology, Algebra, and Geometry, the students may be admitted, and the course so modified that the study of Greek shall be commenced in the Freshman class.

"By such an arrangement, it will be observed there is no abatement or abridgment of any study which is now required, but only a transposition of the studies of your present curriculum.

Very respectfully,
ALEX M. GOW,
Com. of B'd of Education."
"INDIANAPOLIS, May 7. 1873.

"At a meeting of the Superintendents and Principals of schools, having an enrollment of four hundred or more pupils, held in the city of Indianapolis for the consideration of matters pertaining to the welfare of the schools, the question 'How to harmonize the High School and University courses of instruction,' elicited considerable discussion.

"The following resolutions were unanimously adopted:

"*Resolved,* That we, the members of the Convention of Superintendents of the High Schools of the State, respectfully represent that we fully approve the plan of uniting the High Schools with the University by the method proposed, viz.: That the High Schools shall prepare pupils in Orthography, Arithmetic, English Grammar, Geography, Physiology, United States History, Algebra, Geometry, Latin Grammar, Caesar and Virgil, which shall admit them to the Freshman class without the necessity of preparing them in the study of Greek; and that the study of the advanced Mathematics be considered an equivalent for the additional amount of Greek now required for admission.

"*Resolved,* That Mr. Gow present the above resolution to the Trustees of the University, at their meeting in June, as the expression of our views."

Prof. A. M. Gow came before the Faculty and Trustees, and presented the above documents, and explained their purport and objects; whereupon the following action was taken by the Board of Trustees:

FRESHMAN CLASS.

"Ordered by the Board of Trustees of Indiana University, that the minimum standard of admission to the Freshman class in the University, shall be a creditable examination in Orthography, Reading, Geography, English Grammar, United States History, Composition, Word Analysis, Physiology, Algebra, Geometry, Latin Grammar, Latin Prose Composition, Caesar and Virgil, or their equivalents."

"*Second,* In order to bring the University into closer connection with the High Schools of the State, we recommend the following plan, viz.: A Certificate from certain High Schools (the schools to be hereafter named by the State Board of Education) of a satisfactory examination sustained in the Preparatory

Course, will entitle the bearer to admittance to our Freshman class. And no one will be admitted as a student in the University, (except those admitted to select studies) without such certificate from the authorities of the High Schools, the High School of Bloomington being named among the number."

The State Board of Education have taken action with a view to carry out this order of the Trustees of the University, and will name the High Schools whose certificates shall entitle the bearers to admission to the Freshman class, so soon as they can obtain the necessary information in regard to their standing and qualification for this important trust. So also any High School of the State, though not at first numbered in this class, will be designated as soon as it shall have attained the requisite standard of excellence.

PRESENT CONDITION OF UNIVERSITY.

The whole number of the Faculty is 26; the whole number of students in attendance the past year, 382; number of volumes in libraries, 7,000; number of specimens in the museum, 200,000; number of graduates for the year, 92. Whole number of Alumni, 864. The State University justly ranks among the very best Universities in the land.

NOTE TO OTHER COLLEGES AND UNIVERSITIES.
DEPARTMENT OF GREEK.

An important change has been made in the Department of Greek. Hereafter no preparation in Greek will be necessary for admission to classic Freshman standing at the beginning of the year. Those who take the classical course will begin in the Greek Grammar at that time. But let it be noted that *the amount of time devoted to Greek will be the same as before.* And as the students will be further advanced in Latin and other studies, and habits of study and general mental discipline, they will, it is hoped, make even greater progress in the Greek in the same time than their predecessors, who took it up at an earlier part of their course. The cause of Greek learning, therefore, so important to wide and thorough mental culture, will not lose but gain by the change.

The new arrangement was made necessary by the very general lack of the means of studying the elements of Greek throughout the State. Moreover, the policy has been recommended by the State Convention of Teachers, and has been adopted by the State Board of Education, to exclude Greek from the course of study in the Public High Schools of the State. For all elementary instruction in Greek, therefore, our youth will have to look to private opportunities, to the few existing Academies, and to the Preparatory Departments connected with the various Colleges and Universities. The consequence will be, as heretofore, that most of the youth who come to us ready, in other branches of study to enter the University, will have made no beginning in Greek, and they will have to be admitted as irregular, or held back, until they make up the deficiency, or else a change must be made in the course. But it is the policy of the State Board of Education, approved also by the Trustees of the University, to bring the Public High Schools and the State University into nearer and harmonious relationship, by adjusting the course of study in each, with reference to each other; so that a student who has passed through the High School course with approbation, may be admitted at once to Freshman standing in the University. The change now made in regard to Greek will secure that so desirable end; and it was the only method, in the present state of things, by which this could be done.

Supplemental Report of Indiana University, 1872–73 (Indianapolis, 1873), pp. 19–24.

Document 70

Jefferson v. *Boisen*

Mr. J. W. Jefferson learned the hard way that the professor, and especially, Hermann B. Boisen, was master of his classroom. This is a particularly interesting document because it not only reveals the disciplinary process in faculty-student relations, but also reflects the seriousness with which the faculty regarded a breach of behavior. The student was still regarded as the "receiver" and not the "giver" of instruction and advice.

*   *   *

[Prof. Boisen charges Mr. J. W. Jefferson on 10 Jan. 1872 with "gross disrespect, disorder, and disobedience" in Latin recitation (p. 204). Had meetings with witness over a period of four days. Concluded trial on 13 Jan. (excerpt from that meeting's minutes):]

On motion it was agreed to hear what Prof. Boisen and Mr. Jefferson might wish to say in concluding the trial. Each then made brief remarks reviewing the case after which they retired. The charges were then taken up, and the following decision was reached.

1st That Mr. Jefferson was guilty of too persistent criticism in Latin recitation on the 10th inst.

2nd That the 2d Specification, That he approached his Prof demanding apology is *not* sustained by the testimony, The Faculty deeming that a misapprehension of language was possible.

3d That the 3d Specification—that of disobedience in not leaving the room when ordered, is sustained.

4th That the 4th Specification—that of disrespectful language toward his Prof. is sustained

From these Specifications Mr Jefferson is proved guilty of disobedience, disrespect, and disorder. It being after twelve Oclock Faculty Adjourned.

A. ATWATER, Sec'y.

Faculty met at 3 P.M. Prof Boisen absent.

After a discussion of the resolutions of punishment in the case of Mr. Jefferson, it was resolved to invite Prof. Boisen to be present before the resolutions should be passed After he had come in the following resolutions were adopted.

Resolved 1st. That Mr. Jefferson be reproved in the presence of the Faculty for disobedience in not leaving the room when directed to do so by his professor, and for using disrespectful language toward him. And that he be further admonished that in general he should avoid wasting the time of class with unnecessary questions, and that he should also be more careful to avoid factious criticisms in future. The Faculty are thus lenient in view of the fact that Mr. J—. has avowed that, at the time, he was not aware that a professor has the right of sending a student from his room, and had he known this he would have obeyed.

And since there was entire absence of testimony in regard to the words used by Mr. Jefferson at the stand, the Faculty—while sustaining the Professor—give to the student the benefit of a possible misapprehension of language.

Resolved further, That Mr. Jefferson be required to give satisfactory assurances to the Faculty of future respect to the rules of recitation room and the instructions of his Professor.

On motion it was determined that the foregoing resolutions of censure should be read in Chapel.

The following resolution was unanimously adopted by a rising vote, Resolution. In reference to the late unhappy occurrence in Prof. Boisen's room and the decisions reached by the Faculty respecting Mr. Jefferson we wish also to say that we appreciate highly Prof. Boisen's qualification, zeal, and success, and know well his popularity as a teacher, and we hope he will not permit these occurrences to discourage him, that he will continue to maintain the discipline of his class room with all interest and good nature, and endeavor to receive Mr. Jefferson, reproved and admonished as he has been, with all kindness and treat him with all forbearance.

On motion at a late hour Fac. adjourned.

A. ATWATER Sec'y.

Faculty Minutes, October, 1865—June, 1872, pp. 209–212.

Document 71

Off Limits—Way Off Limits—The Ladies' Room

Indiana University may have been co-educational in fact, but it was still Victorian in the management of feminine affairs in the institution. The ladies' room (not the "rest room") was a place of retreat, not one of social tryst or zoological exhibit. The ladies' president was to see to it that these confines were kept free of masculine invasion either physically or by sound of voice.

*   *   *

. . . Committee informally appointed to consider the subject of disorder in the Ladie's room reported as follows.

1st That one of the ladies be appointed by the Pres. of the University as presiding officer for the hour, making four presidents in all each of whom shall hold her office for one week.

2d That no talking aloud, disturbing noise or movements that would interrupt study be permitted.

3d It shall be the duty of the president of the hour to call to order in case of any violation of the rule and report to Dr. Nutt on a slip of paper next morning, "No violation during the —— hour," or "Violation of the rule by the following persons." Report adopted. . . .

Faculty Minutes, September, 1872—June, 1887, p. 10.

Document 72

God Help Mr. Huitt and Mr. Rose

There was a "rude knocking at the door" with evident intention of subversion. This was a matter for grave censure. These students might as well have knocked on the Pearly Gates. Nevertheless, some of the ladies did not share faculty views of the matter.

* * *

Faculty met at 10 A.M. after Sat. public literary exercises. The case of Mr. Huitt charged with being found in the Ladie's room, and Mr. Rose and Mr. Henly being implicated in such violation was stated as being the subject for consideration. The gentlemen being called, each acknowledged his participation in the affair. The following was adopted the last clause of the resolution being appended by the faculty at a subsequent called meeting on the 15th inst. Resolved that the deportment of certain students on Tues. last in loitering in the hall making boisterous noises, entering the ladie's room in violation of well known rules, knocking with evident rude intent at the door of a recitation room is subversive of good order and therefore highly reprehensible and worthy of grave censure And that the young ladies who engaged in conversation with the young gentlemen at the window, and who invited them to enter the room are also included in this censure.

After general discussion upon certain students bringing up modern languages adjourned.

A. ATWATER, Secy.

Faculty Minutes, September, 1872—June, 1887, p. 32.

Document 73

The First Step beyond Undergraduate Status

This was a landmark proposal which obviously did not achieve its objective, but nevertheless was the first step in trying to take the half-century-old liberal arts university onto a loftier level of academic training.

* * *

Fac. met at 3. P.M. Prof. Boisen absent. Faculty reviewed and emended their recommendations to the Board of Trustees. The committee appointed on the recommendation of a Post-Graduate Course reported the following which was adopted.

1st We recommend that the Board take steps at its coming session for the establishment of a Post-Graduate Course.

2d The following is submitted as an outline of studies to be provided for in this course I Eng. Literature, 1. Principles and Practice in public speaking, 2 Philosophy of Rhetoric 1 term and Theses 1 term.

3. Analysis and Criticism of Eng. Classics 1 term.

II Modern Languages. 1, German Lang, & Lit. 2 terms,

2. Anglo Saxon	3 terms
III Ancient Languages, 1 Latin Lang & Lit	2 terms
2 Greek Language and Literature	" " "
3 Hebrew	5 " "
IV Engineering	
Mining engineering. Bridge building and Mechanics	2 " "

V Physical Sciences
1. Analyt. Chem. & Labratory Practice   3 terms,
2 Geology   2 "   "
3 Comparative Anatomy, & Physiology   " "   "
4 Zoology   " "   "
VI Mathematics, Astronomy   " "   "
VII. Metaphysical and Empyrical Sciences.
1. Political Economy and International Law.   2 terms.
2. Social Science   " "   "
3 History of Civilization & Philosophy of History   3 "   "

Appropriate degrees will be conferred on the completion of all, or certain portions of the above studies. Respectfully submitted

GEO. W. HASS ⎫
AMZI ATWATER ⎬ Com.
RICHARD OWEN ⎭

After some discussion on the subject of the College Calender, Faculty adjourned to meet at 8½ A.M. tomorrow. A. Atwater, Sec'y.

Faculty Minutes, September, 1872—June, 1887, pp. 55–56.

Document 74

The Status of the University in 1875

The previous report revealed a desire to move the University into a new and more highly specialized area of education. This one with its covering letter from President Cyrus Nutt to Governor Thomas A. Hendricks reveals in fairly clear fashion not only the condition of the University, both academically and status-wise, but in its almost silent manner makes an appeal for additional public support. This report came soon after the Commonwealth of Indiana extended limited financial support to the institution.

*   *   *

Indiana State University
Bloomington, Ind.,
Feb. 20th 1875.

His Excellency,
Thomas A. Hendricks,
Gov. of State of Ind.
Dear Sir.

Please find enclosed, a statement of the aims, Plans and present condition of Indiana state University. I shall be exceedingly gratified, if you will give our programme and arrangements your careful attention; and give us any suggestions in regard to the plans and administration of its affairs. Knowing the deep interest you feel in the University, and all matters of education, leads me to present this report. I believe it also to be due to you, personally, and to your office, as chief magistrate of Indiana, that the Faculty of the state University should report their doings to you.

Please accept assurances of my highest esteem; and gratitutes [*sic*] for the influence, you are wielding for the preservation, intact, of the present income of the University.

Your devoted friend, & most ob'e't s'v't.

Cyrus Nutt

Indiana State University.

The Results of the Recent Modifications in the Administration and Management of the University—Report of the Faculty to the State Board of Education.

The want of a proper adjustment of the High Schools of the State to the Colleges has been long and deeply felt. After much discussion in State, Collegiate and High School Associations, upon the recommendation of the Convention of Superintendents of Public Schools, held in the City of Indianapolis in the spring of 1873, the State Board of Education recommended and the Trustees of Indiana State University adopted a modification in the Collegiate course of study. This change was made for the purpose of uniting, harmonizing and completing the school system of Indiana. Middle education is the problem of the age. Where shall students be prepared for college? This is the real question. It is proposed to make the High Schools the middle schools of Indiana, and thus filling the vacuum before existing between the district schools and the University. To perfect this union, it was determined that the study of Greek should be commenced in the Freshman year, and continued through the four years of the college course, thus making the whole amount of Greek equal to that of both the preparatory and collegiate Greek taught in the best institutions in the land. To compensate for this preparatory Greek, transferred to the collegiate course, Higher Algebra, Geometry, Sentential Analysis and Physiology were placed in the preparatory course, and made requisites for admission to the University. This change, while it abates nothing from the extent and thoroughness of the usual curriculum, both preparatory and collegiate, is of the greatest importance, as it unites together and harmonizes all the sections of the public schools of the State into one complete system. The student can now pass directly from the primary, through the intermediate grades and high schools, to the University, without delay or interruption. He is not now required, after completing his High School course, to spend, as heretofore, two years in some preparatory school or Academy, in order to bring up his Greek, and fit himself for the Freshman class.

Initiatory Examinations.

As this modification aimed to make the High Schools of the State preparatory schools for the State University, it was also provided that the work done in the High Schools, which had attained the proper grade, should be recognized and credited by the University. Hence, applicants presenting certificates from the Superintendents of those High Schools, which are commissioned by the State Board of Education, certifying that they had completed the preparatory studies, should be admitted to the Freshman class, without further examination. All applicants, not thus furnished with certificates, were to be examined by the Superintendent and principal of the High School of Bloomington.

These examinations are conducted in writing, and are very thorough. They embrace ten questions upon each of the studies in the preparatory course; and a high grade in each is required for admission.

RESULTS.

The time has been too short, only eighteen months have elapsed since its adoption, to test fully the wisdom and feasibility of the present plan. Thus far, however, the results have been favorable. In 1873, one hundred and nine applied for admission to the University; of whom, fifty passed satisfactory examinations, and were admitted on the certificate of the Superintendent and Principal of the High School of Bloomington. Fifty-nine having failed to pass satisfactory examinations, were rejected. In 1847, there were fewer rejections; as the term of admission and the high grade of scholarship required, had become more generally known.

Of the twenty-one High Schools commissioned by the State Board of Education to prepare and examine students for the State University, only a very few have sent students. Greensburgh has sent three; Evansville, two; New Albany, two; Princeton, one; Peru, one, and Bloomington twenty-six. The larger part of these twenty-six, had come from other sections of the State to Bloomington, to prepare for college. All the others, who have been admitted to the Freshman class, have been examined by the Superintendent and Principal of the High School of Bloomington.

The effect upon the High Schools of the State has been very beneficial. They have been inspired with greater zeal and energy in the work of education, and the standard of scholarship has been elevated. The most of the High Schools which have not already been commissioned to prepare students for the University, are striving to reach that grade which will entitle them to that honor. The failure to send students to the University was not for the want of a disposition to do so, on the part of the officers of the High schools. These have generally regarded it an honor to receive a commission from the State Board, and have cordially co-operated to make the plan a success.

THE EFFECT UPON THE STANDARD OF SCHOLARSHIP IN THE UNIVERSITY.

The grade of scholarship of the students of the University has been greatly advanced. In accuracy, thoroughness, comprehensiveness, and maturity of mind and culture, the Freshman class is nearly equal to the Sophomore of former years; and the same may be said of the higher vigor of thought and breadth of information, with which they grapple with subjects presented for their investigation. Their command of the English language and its resources is also of a high order.

CLASSICAL COURSE.

Since the change has been made by which Greek is begun in the Freshman year, the number of students taking the classical course has greatly increased. Formerly one-half of the Freshman class were scientific; now nine-tenths are classical. Such, according to present indications, will continue to be the result of the present arrangements. Instead of lowering the standard of education, the present plan has greatly elevated it; and instead of the ancient classics being dishonored and ignored, they are now better taught, made popular, and greatly honored. Nor do we deem it too much to say, that classical education has been greatly benefitted by the recent arrangements.

THE NUMBER OF STUDENTS.

While there has been no diminution in the number of students, but on the contrary, a steady increase; yet the number in attendance, is less by one hundred per cent. probably, than it would have been under the old *regime,* several causes having combined to produce this result:

1. The complete separation of the preparatory from the collegiate department has diminished the aggregate number of students. No student, in the preparatory department, is permitted to recite in any of the college classes, and no student in the select course in college is allowed to recite in classes belonging to the preparatory department. This complete isolation of the two departments cuts off a considerable number of irregulars, who desire to recite in preparatory and collegiate studies at the same time. This was allowed in this University some years ago, and is still in vogue in most of the colleges in the West.

2. This arrangement tends to diminish numbers, in the second place, since the preparatory students do not meet in the University chapel, for prayers each morning with the students of the collegiate and professional grade; nor do the two departments intermingle, as they do in most Western institutions, in which students of the preparatory course mingle indiscriminately with those of collegiate grade, and recite to the same professors. Many prefer institutions where such irregularity prevails.

3. The rigidness of the iniatory examinations, and the thoroughness of scholarship required for admission to the University tends also to lessen the number of students. The sifting process is now applied at the door of admission to the University, instead of being postponed, and too charitably applied, during the collegiate course. The custom of most of the colleges in the State has been to admit students upon an oral and very superficial examination, leaving their subsequent standing to be determined by their success in their studies. This course of necessity, produces irregularity, lowers the grade of scholarship, and leads to many difficulties.

The State University now admits only those who pass satisfactory examinations, and are up in all their studies. This arrangement, while it has introduced order, regularity and system, and elevated the standard of scholarship, has diminished the number, which otherwise would have attended the University. Nearly one hundred applicants for admission to the Freshman class, in the last two years have been rejected.

4. The elevation of the standard of scholarship leads some to prefer other institutions where college honors are more easily won. The grade of recitations requisite for graduation from one class to another higher, is seventy per cent. on the general average, and in no one study must the student fall below fifty per cent. A student who fails to reach this standard falls back into the next lower class. Some who have thus failed, have gone to other colleges, rather than to go back into the lower classes; as they could there go on with their class, and graduate a year sooner than at the State University. As, therefore, it might have been reasonably expected, the number of students in attendance is probably one hundred per cent. less than it would have been, had the old order and regulations continued. But, what is lost in quantity, is more than made up in quality. Yet there has been no decrease in the number of students, as has been incorrectly stated, but on the contrary, the increase has been regular, as the catalogues of the last five years will show:

In the year 1870-1—Aggregate No. 301
In the year 1871-2—Aggregate No. 358

In the year 1872-3—Aggregate No. 368
In the year 1873-4—Aggregate No. 371
In the year 1874-5—thus far in the year 389

The number of students at Bloomington, not counting those of the Medical Department is as follows:

1870-1—(Including Normal Class) 301
1871-2—(Including Normal Class Abolished) 268
1872-3—Aggregate Number 264
1873-4—Aggregate Number 264
1874-5—Aggregate Number 282

It is the aim of the Faculty and Trustees to do work of the highest grade and order, making thorough scholars and elevating the standard of scholarship, and when this is secured, numbers will not be wanting; but the popular sentiment, has from the beginning, judged the merits of institutions of learning, by the size of the crowd, that attends them, not taking into account, discipline, thoroughness of scholarship, and training; as if it were the sole business of a college to gain numbers and to graduate a crowd instead of scholars.

The present plan, we believe to be working well for the interests of education in Indiana, and, if it were comprehended, it would not only be approved, but highly commended by the people. It rests with the educators and friends of education in Indiana, whether the new measures adopted by the University shall prove a success or a failure. With their co-operation, the State University will soon become what it aspires to be, the head and crown of the public school system; a University not only in name, but in reality, ranking among the very first in the land, an honor to the State, and a source of pride to all her citizens.

> CYRUS NUTT, President
> T. A. WYLIE, Prof. Nat.
>   Philosophy.
> R. OWEN, Prof. Nat. Science.
> D. KIRKWOOD, Prof.
>   Mathematics.
> E. BALLANTINE, Prof. Greek.
> J. THOMPSON, Prof. Civil
>   Engineering.
> A. ATWATER, Prof. Latin.
> G. W. HOSS, Prof. Eng.
>   Literature.
> S. P. MORRISON, Ass't. Prof.
>   E. L.
> T. C. VANNUYS, Prof.
>   Chemistry.

Indiana State University.

TUITION FREE TO ALL.

CIRCULAR OF THE FACULTY.

To the Superintendents of the Public Schools, and County Superintendents:

The founders of this Commonwealth, in the original Constitution of Indiana, provided for a system of *Free Public* Schools, to include in regular gradation, the district and intermediate schools and a State University. The same wise and liberal provision is sanctioned in the present constitution, while the laws of the State recognize the Institution at Bloomington, Monroe county, as the State University.

Although the State University, and the Graded Schools, by the above Constitutional and Legislative provisions, form one and the same system of Public Instruction, they have not, until recently, harmoniously co-operated. A plan for adjusting the University course of study to that of the High Schools was very maturely considered by the State Board of Education, by a convention of Superintendents of Public Schools, and by the Trustees and Faculty of the State University; and, as the result, the classical course was enlarged to include all Preparatory Greek, and the Mathematical and Scientific courses correspondingly diminished; the Preparatory Latin and the excluded Mathematics and Science being incorporated in the High School Course; which is as follows, viz: Orthography, Arithmetic, Geography, English Grammar, Algebra, (both Elementary and Higher,) Geometry, four books, Physiology, History of United States, Latin Grammar, Latin Reader, Latin Prose Composition, two Books of Caesar, and two books of Virgil, or their equivalents in Latin.

All High Schools in the State which are prepared to teach the above named branches, and possess the other qualifications prescribed by the State Board of Education, are entitled to a commission to prepare students for the State University, and to grant certificates of proficiency in the above studies, which shall entitle the holder to admission to the Freshman Class of the University, without further examination. This commission also authorizes the Superintendent to examine any person who may apply, and to grant a certificate, if the applicant is found thoroughly proficient in all the studies of the Preparatory Course. The trouble and expense of a journey to Bloomington may, thereby, be, in some cases, avoided.

It is earnestly requested that notice be given throughout the section of the State in the vicinity of each designated High School, at what time applications may be made for examination, and that the President of the University be duly notified of the results of these examinations.

This system may not be wholly satisfactory to all of the friends of the Public Schools in Indiana, but it certainly has great merit; and shall it not be faithfully sustained and its provisions executed, until an opportune moment for its amendment shall arrive?

The State University, chief public School of the State, may not be free from defects, but it is progressive, and it will seek to know the demands of popular education in Indiana and to meet and satisfy them fully, expecting in return to be cordially sustained and liberally supported.

Cyrus Nutt, President of the Faculty.

A. Atwater, Secretary.
Bloomington, Indiana, April 15th, 1875.

Annual Report of Indiana University Including the Catalogue, 1874–75 (Indianapolis, 1875), pp. 52–58.

Document 75

How to Manage on $47,583.50

The university budget for 1875 has more than a touch of unreality about it. A century later one can scarcely visualize the operation of an institution of any sort on so little money. Yet there is a thread of optimism running through the narrative part of this report. Lemuel Moss had become president, and the institution was making plans to join in the celebration of the nation's first century of existence.

*   *   *

REPORT.

To THE HON. THOS. A. HENDRICKS,
            Governor of the State of Indiana:
    The undersigned, in behalf of the Board of Trustees of Indiana University, submit the following report for the year A. D. 1875:

RECEIPTS.

There was received during the year, from all sources, $47,583.50, as follows:

Legislative appropriation	$23,000 00
Endowment	8,925 00
Janitor's fees	1,205 00
Loans	12,500 00
Miscellaneous	2 50
Balance in treasury	1,186 85
Interest on lands	764 15
Total receipts	$47,583 50

DISBURSEMENTS.

The disbursements were as follows:

Professors' salary	$21,300 00
Trustees' salaries	601 80
Examiner's salary	301 00
Secretary's salary	132 00
Treasurer's salary	100 00
Librarian's salary	150 00
Janitor's salary	634 58
Fuel	225 94
Advertising	369 44
Insurance	150 00
Contingent	578 32
Meteorological observations	99 97
Department Natural Science	400 00
Department Natural Philosophy	293 20
Department Chemistry	1,352 43
Department Law	684 50
Civil Engineering	370 00
Buildings and repairs	2,197 95
Postage	116 80
Owen cabinet, sixth payment	2,541 00
Same, cases	1,593 78
Library	174 99
Loans paid	12,500 00
Interest	303 76
Total expenditures	$47,171 46
Balance in treasury	412 04
Total	$47,583 50

The Committee on Finance, at its last meeting, recommended the following specific appropriations, which were adopted by the Board of Trustees, and the several amounts recommended were appropriated:

Chair of Natural Philosophy	$ 300 00
Chair of Civil Engineering	300 00
Chair of Latin	150 00
Chair of Chemistry	1,000 00
Library	150 00

The estimated receipts by the Committee on Finance was as follows:

Legislative appropriations	$23,000 00
Endowment fund	8,000 00
Janitor's fee	1,200 00
Interest on lands	800 00
Total	$33,000 00

Estimated expenses, including the above specific appropriations, payment on Owen cabinet, salaries, and other expenses, $32,000, leaving an unexpended balance of $1,000.

All the improvements recommended have been made, but the limited means at the disposal of the Board rendered it impossible to make any appropriations for increasing the library, or making any additional improvements in the museum. This is deeply to be regretted, for there are thousands of specimens yet boxed up which can not be exhibited till additional cases are provided for their accommodation. The chemical laboratory is now one of the most complete in the west. It is capable of accommodating forty-seven students, and is furnished with gas, water, atmospheric filters, reagents, balances of the finest and most delicate character, and all other necessary apparatus for making qualitative and quantitative analyses. Fifteen students, who are aiming to take a thorough course in chemistry, are now under instruction in this department. This is a very encouraging attendance, considering the fact that this is only the second year since this department was established. Specimens of minerals and mineral waters have been sent to this department from many parts of the State for analysis, and thus far all demands of this kind have been promptly responded to, either by the professor in charge, or by the advanced students under his direction. There is no longer any necessity of sending Indiana minerals, earths, and soils out of the State for analysis.

The Owen cabinet, (although not completely exhibited, as herein-before indicated,) is displayed with such fullness that the students in geology and mineralogy have nearly all the facilities for instruction in these important studies which they could desire.

The department of civil engineering is completely organized, and is furnished with the best apparatus that could be found in the country.

The practical work of this department is done in the field, where the students, with compass, level and chain, are required to do the work of the surveyor and engineer.

The vacancy in the office of president was filled by the election of Lemuel Moss, D. D., of Chicago, who entered upon the duties of the presidency at the beginning of the present college year. The choice of President Moss seems to have been wise and politic, for he has impressed upon trustees, faculty and students, and generally upon those who have come in contact with him, the belief that he is peculiarly fitted for his work.

The Preparatory Department is accomplishing a great work for the State, and gives great promise of accomplishing much more. It furnishes thorough and systematic training to those who there prepare to enter the freshman class, and insures a uniform degree of culture and attainment. The large attendance at this department furnishes a guarantee that the college classes will always be well filled.

The arrangement made, at the suggestion of the State Board of Education, to admit students into the freshmen class from the many high schools of the State, which have provided the same or a higher course of study as that provided by the preparatory department, has worked satisfactorily. Those who enter the freshman class under this arrangement, graduate with as high scholastic and scientific attainments as those who graduated under the old regime. While, therefore, there has been no falling off in actual scholarship by the change, but, on the contrary, an improvement in that respect, one marked and most encouraging effect thereof has been the fact, that more than nine-tenths of those who have entered the freshman class since the change was made, have entered upon the regular course of study. Those who have entered the University thus far, under this regulation, have generally been persons of limited means, but have proved themselves to be persevering, energetic and ambitious.

This alliance between the common schools and the University is to be fostered by the State, as the course from which shall come her best citizens and most accomplished scholars. Application, up to the present time, has been made by twenty-five high-schools for admission to the privileges of the University, upon the terms agreed upon by the Board of Trustees and the State Board of Education, as hereinbefore stated, and the number of applications are increasing every year.

NUMBER OF STUDENTS IN THE SEVERAL DEPARTMENTS.

Preparatory 128
Literature and Science 140
Law 50
Medicine 107
Total 425

Arrangements have been recently made, by which the University will be represented in the Centennial.

In behalf of the Board,
ROBERT C. FOSTER,
Secretary.

INDIANA UNIVERSITY, Jan. 11, 1876.

Documentary Journal, 1875.

Document 76

A Bright New Torch

The preacher-president Lemuel Moss addressed the Board of Trustees in a sermonette on university education in Indiana. Higher education viewed through Moss's eyes was to be cast in proverbs of inspiration and superior human accomplishments. The thoughts were high in 1876 when the nation was congratulating itself on a century of achievement, but the budget in Bloomington was low.

*   *   *

INDIANA UNIVERSITY.

BLOOMINGTON, Dec. 23, 1876.

To the Board of Trustees:

GENTLEMEN:—I have thought that you would not take it amiss if I should address you somewhat freely upon what I conceive to be the aims and wants of our University. Your knowledge of our present condition is such that I do not now need to dwell upon it. Our numbers are encouraging, and are steadily increasing, but they ought to be speedily doubled or quadrupled, and would be if the work here done were thoroughly understood and appreciated thoughout the State. Our Faculty is sufficiently large, perhaps—at most it needs but one or two more men—for the present number of students. In its ability, its senior members are readily recognized as holding high rank among scholars in their several departments of study and teaching. In apparatus and appliances we are comparatively well supplied, except that our Library, of which I shall have more to say further on, is miserably inadequate. It is true that in all respects the University could be very materially advanced, if the means were furnished for so doing, and it would undoubtedly be a wise economy for the State to supply the means; but the Institution is in a healthy, hopeful and growing condition, and its friends may well feel encouraged about it.

As you are well aware, the central and chief factor in our University is its

COLLEGIATE DEPARTMENT.

At this point I will ask your permission to quote from a paper of my own, already published, some thoughts upon the purposes and aims to be kept in view in such an institution as the one committed to your care:

"The fundamental idea of an American college is obviously this, that it is a training school, having much more reference to the student than to the course of study. Its aim is to train the intellectual and moral faculties of man, to strengthen and develop all his inherent powers, so that he may know himself, and may know how to use and handle himself. We can not be far astray if we say that the powers, or the groups of powers, to be trained and developed are these four:

"1. The faculty of observation. The student must be taught to see truly, exactly, accurately, whatever may be the object observed. The ability to do this in one sphere of thought and knowledge helps toward the ability to do it in all spheres. The objects of observation are facts, which are of almost infinite variety in their forms and relationships. There are facts of external nature, facts of physical law, facts of the phenomena of consciousness, facts of mathematical and of logical sequence, facts of historical events and characters, facts of the ideas and construction and interpretation of languages, facts of artistic and ethical feeling. Upon these and a multitude of other forms of facts the student is to be trained in his power of mental vision, until he can see clearly, correctly, completely, just that, wholly that, and only that which is contained in the particular fact before him. Defective mental vision comes from an inherent weakness of an organ, or an immaturity of its powers, or ignorance, or prejudice. Of course, no collegiate training can remove organic weakness, but it ought to leave no excuse for some degree of maturity and accuracy and moral clearness.

"2. The faculty of judgment. By this is meant the ability to estimate the relative importance of facts. Of two things equally true, both may not be equally valuable or equally pertinent. We must learn to recognize and seize upon the capital facts of a science, the first principles of a philosophy, the vital points of a theory. Many of the errors of speculation, as well as of practical life, come from an inability to discover what is primary and what subordinate. To know and occupy and hold the key of the position is quite as essential to an argument as to a battle, and we must be able to arrange our mental resources in the order that will yield the largest mutual support and make the whole most effective. He has made no small attainment in mental training who can discriminate facts with accuracy and assign to them their relative value and importance.

"3. The faculty of thought. Here we pass from the seen to the unseen. Here we seek to look upon the mysterious mechanism of the mind itself, as it elaborates materials supplied by sense and understanding, by perception and judgment, for purposes of inference, invention and discovery. To think is to compare facts, and to reveal the deeper facts which they enclose. To think is to reason—to rise from perceived phenomena to their causes, and from recognized causes to prophesy their effects. The region of thought, of reasoning, of inference, is and must be the great arena of strife in science, in politics, in law, in religion. Men may agree as to their primary facts, and yet differ widely in their conclusions. Still there are laws of thought just as true, universal, resistless, infallible, as the law of things. Man is made for thought—for intercourse of the human reason with the divine. No word can overstate the importance of the training which secures it.

"4. The faculty of utterance. Speech is to thought what coinage is to gold— fixing its form, naming its value, and fitting it for circulation. All culture ought to assist in cultivating the power of speech. It has been said that the ability to express his thoughts and feelings is the highest energy in man, for by this he transfers his feelings and thoughts to other minds, and thus becomes almost creative. God created all things by His world, and by his word man became the author of momentous changes in his neighbor, in his nation, in the world. We know that practically there is no limit to the influence of this power, and no limit to the degree of its development.

"If this, in outline, is the aim of college training, it is further obvious that much more depends upon the training-master than upon the method. The first and absolutely vital requisite in a college is men—men who can themselves see and judge and think and speak, and who can therefore assist others somewhat in attaining these incommunicable arts. A true college is mainly a company of competent instructors, with such auxiliary appartaus and instruments as they may need—instructors who can draw out all that is in the student, and thus make him as large-minded as his native capacities will permit."

If it be borne in mind that in all steps of training constant regard must be had to moral purity and vigor, in a word, that character is the chief end of all true culture, then perhaps the foregoing brief sketch will be accepted as suggesting our work here. It will also be seen that these various elements are contributed in each department of study. Whether the subject in hand be language or mathematics, physics or metaphysics, ethics or political economy or history, the student is taught to observe, to discriminate, to reason, to put his thoughts into articulate form. This view will thoroughly justify the emphasis we give to the demand for

COMPETENT INSTRUCTORS.

No man should be placed in charge of a professorship here whose ability as a teacher has not been tried and demonstrated. Knowledge, though of prime importance, is not the only quality requisite in a teacher. It is indispensable that he should understand what he proposes to impart; but aptness to teach—that indefinable sympathy with the student which sees difficulties as the student sees them, and that intelligent enthusiasm which carries both teacher and student through the difficulty, are equally indispensable. It is justly recognized that a position here is for life, and the list of Professors, past and present, in the University, not large for its years, contains many illustrious names. The State is entitled to the best men that can be obtained, and wise economy will spare no expense in securing and caring for them.

Teachers' salaries are small, and always will be small, as compared with corresponding positions in other callings. A railroad president's salary would support an entire faculty. If rumor be true, head cooks in our city hotels are better paid than the best teachers. I have no wish to see our college professors receive the salaries paid to railroad and bank officers; but they should be so compensated that they can live comfortably, look toward the future with reasonable confidence, and have a fair margin for books and similar facilities for professional work, as also for needed recreation. Nor should our professors be unduly burdened with teachings. They have more to do than to prepare daily for the day's work. Every field of thought is now actively occupied with eager investigators and explorers, and the teacher must at least keep not too far in the rear of those who are widening the bounds of his own science. The student has a right to know the last valid word, if not the last theory, in the subject brought before him. Hence the teacher must be incited to push his own inquiries up to the limits of present knowledge, if not beyond them; and he should therefore, have the facilities and opportunities for so doing. The number of students which any teacher can profitably instruct at one time is small. Especially is this true of the earlier years of the college course, when the elements of the languages, the sciences, and the mathematics occupy chief attention, and when the main endeavor is to ground and drill the student thoroughly in these elements. Such a class probably should not exceed twenty-five, or at most thirty. As some of our classes now number fifty or more, the question is already upon us: In what way can our teaching force be most efficiently and most economically increased? It would seem a wise policy to adopt, as a policy, to introduce young men as assistant professors, subordinate to the principal professors, and on smaller salaries, selecting for these positions men who give certain evidence of the true aptness and enthusiasm in acquiring and imparting knowledge, and who might thus be in training for full professorships as vacancies occur. I am well aware that we are now living up to the limit of our income, and that any increase in our teaching force, or in our present salaries, will require a corresponding increase in our resources; but I am confident that our State, upon a proper understanding of the case, can hardly fail to provide for the urgent needs and desirable development of this University. It is scarcely an exaggeration to say that there is not an acre of ground nor a household in the commonwealth that is not powerfully affected, directly and indirectly, by such a school as this. Wealth, enterprise, virtue, are attracted and promoted by intelligence. The invigoration and advancement of our schools will not of themselves insure the perpetuity and power of the State, but they are surely essential to these ends.

OCCASIONAL LECTURES.

It has seemed to me that increased attractiveness and very great profit might be secured at a small expense, by supplementing our regular college work with courses of lectures by specialists in the various departments of literature, science and art. If even $1,500 or $2,000 a year were expended for this purpose, under the direction of our Faculty, we could call to our aid some of the eminent inquirers in mental, moral, political, historical, physical science, who would bring to us the latest results from their fields of research. That such communications should be made by strangers to the students, in fresh and novel forms, would itself be of no slight advantage, in that it would widen their acquaintanceship with men, stimulate their curiosity, augment their sympathy with intellectual pursuits and strengthen their interest. While such lectures should be free to the students, a small fee might be charged, if thought best, to citizens and others who desired to attend them.

OUR LIBRARY

Doubtless our greatest need at the present time is the enlargement of our Library. If our students are to get the highest benefit from their studies here, they must learn how to handle books, to consult them constantly and bring together the results of their examinations. To this end the Library must be kept supplied with the latest and best works in all departments, and must be at all times accessible to the students. Our Library is good as a foundation and beginning, but it is sadly lacking in many of the earlier, and in almost all of the later standard publications, nor have we any means of supplying ourselves with that which is indispensable in current literature. I would most earnestly recommend that the Legislature be now asked, even if they must deny us every other request, to appropriate a sum sufficient to replenish our Library, and make it less inadequate to our pressing needs. Six thousand dollars is the least sum that should be thus appropriated; ten thousand dollars could be wisely expended, and then leave our necessities far from satisfied, for our wants include costly and numerous books in every department of literature. And then, that we may at least partly provide for current needs, without calling directly upon the Legislature or the people, I would respectfully suggest that the contingent fee for students be increased from three dollars per term to five dollars per term, and that of this sum three dollars per term be applied to the Library for constant additions. This would give us an annual library fund of about one thousand dollars, more or less, specially burdensome to no one, contributed by the students, and expended for their immediate benefit. This would be a small sum for such an object, but it woud be vastly better than nothing, and would enable us to buy some of the works most necessary for us. If this advance in the contingent fee is made, the library should be free to all students; and I would further urge that arrangements be adopted whereby the Library can be open every day for consultation and reading.

In regard to this matter, it can not be too strongly stated that books are a necessity to the teacher and student. They are not a luxury, not a convenience merely; they are indispensable. What tools are to a mechanic, or raw material to a manufacturer, or seed to a farmer, such are books to a scholar. I do not here discuss the question whether bookish men are superior or inferior to so called "practical" men, nor whether original thought is better or worse than borrowed thought. I should as soon think of discussing the comparative merits of fire and water, or ask whether nitrogen or oxygen is the more important constituent of the air we breathe. I simply insist that, next to good teachers, good books are the necessity of the student; and that without this auxiliary even good teachers are shorn of half their power; the attempt to teach, therefore, without a serviceable library, is like being compelled to fight or to swim with the left hand. The elements, then, for constructing a college are, first, men; secondly, books; thirdly, buildings; and when the buildings come, let them be adapted to the men and the books, rather than to the architect's notion of what is fit and fine looking. Lest I should be misunderstood, I must add that with books I include all other apparatus and appliances needful for efficient teaching.

Let it be further noted that in pleading for good books I do not mean rare and curious books only or chiefly. Such works are certainly not out of place in a college library. Whatever is enriched by exceptional skill, or excellence in art, or historical associations, may surely be treasured where the taste, the imagination, the reason, the conscience of successive generations of our most talented and aspiring youth are being trained, not only by the living and enthusiastic teacher, but by all the unconscious influence which flows in though ear and eye. But I now am pleading for the very bread of life, without much reference to more luxuriant viands, or to the form of chiselling of the platter upon which the bread is served. We want a working library, for daily use and daily food, the best editions of the best books of the best writers in all departments of thought and knowledge. To this end I urge the appropriations asked for above.

HISTORICAL PROFESSORSHIP.

Our different lines of study are, for the most part, very satisfactorily arranged. We can do the work in ancient languages, modern languages, mathematics, physical science, philosophy, etc., for which our students are prepared. As our secondary and high schools are improved, we can gradually advance our requirements here, and thus elevate our course; but this is a work which will, as it were, take care of itself, through the diligence and earnestness and growing power of the teachers of all grades. The University, as I understand it, is part of the common school system of the State, and I shall endeavor so to administer it. The improvement and advancement of one part of the system is therefore the benefit of all parts.

I may mention, incidentally, that we wish to give our students an historical and philosophical knowledge of their own language, as well of other modern and the ancient tongues. Our education, like our social, political and religious life, strikes its roots down into the fertile and exhaustless soil of ancient languages and literatures; but for this very reason our own language and literature, because they inherit all antecedent civilizations and cultures, deserve the prominent place and careful study which we here strive to give them. Our English speech has a history, an etymology, a philosophy, which, together with other very practical considerations, commend it to the most thorough and conscientious investigation. In this matter we need the careful co-operation of all our preparatory schools.

But I wish especially to commend to you, in this connection, the enlargement of our course in history. The Freshman Class have a daily recitation through the year in general history, which is of very great value. If upon this, and their previous historical study as a basis, a daily recitation were assigned (say) to the Junior Class, in modern constitutional and political history, the benefit could not fail to be manifest and permanent. It is evident that our country holds very different relations to the rest of the world than those which obtained so recently as a generation ago. The nations especially of Christendom, are much nearer each other, and in many respects are almost like provinces of one kingdom, governed by a common public opinion. Personal intercourse, and the interchange of intelligence, have vastly increased, and are still rapidly increasing. The scholars, statesmen, diplomatists, rulers, of the several nations are seeking each other's sympathy and co-operation. The same social and political questions are pressing upon all, and the combined wisdom and virtue of all will be found none too great to solve them. If we, as a people, have felt comparatively free from international disputes and international responsibilities, the day of our isolation and exemption is swiftly moving to its close. In every important political sense we are much nearer to Europe than to Mexico, and England effects us more intimately and more powerfully than she did a century ago. Considerations of this kind, and others that might be urged, make it obligatory upon us to understand the political history of modern Europe, that our politics may be aided by all the light that comes from this accumulated experience. We have no monopoly of practical wisdom. Finance, taxation, pauperism, public education, commerce, penal administration, are not matters that can be dealt with offhand. The light of the past is the only light we have, and we shall be very unwise if we do not walk by it, though we may happily find it possible to improve upon past methods. We can not go far in such studies here, it is true, but we can give the student a start, enabling him to get an outline of the great subject, and the bearings by which he may direct his future reading. If our educated citizens are to take the part they should in public affairs, the line of study thus suggested becomes of prime importance. Should your judgment approve the views I have briefly presented, there will be needed at the earliest practicable moment a professorship of history, to which a competent man can devote his whole strength and time.

PROFESSIONAL SCHOOLS.

We recognize, as component parts of what has been called the "university system" of the State, the Normal School at Terre Haute and the Purdue University at Lafayette, and we certainly desire to do our full part in co-operating with these worthy institutions. We have no wish to trench upon the special provence of either. If the Purdue University shall develop into a number of special schools of applied science, where specialists and experts may be trained, it will, I think, be the consummation most to be desired. And the training of teachers at Terre Haute is a work which deserves all suitable maintenance and encouragement. It is not for me at this time, if at all, to enter into an argument for their defense; suffice it to say that they must, in their several aims and methods, commend themselves to the cordial and liberal support of the State. But I wish further to say that it seems entirely proper and desirable for the State to establish professional schools, as of law and medicine, or to aid in their establishment. There is no reason why the State should not, under proper regulations, teach the elements of these sciences as well as of other liberal and practical sciences. Only they should be so taught as to promote the highest intellectual and moral culture. Our law and medical schools ought to be strictly post graduate schools—that is, they should require the collegiate course, by way of preparation, and be based upon it. That men should be passed through these professional schools with little or no preliminary training, and little or no preliminary examination—ignorant of language, of literature, of history, of mathematics, of science, of philosophy, and almost wholly destitute of intellectual discipline—is to the disadvantage alike of good morals, good learning and good professional ability. You will agree with me that there is no present necessity for swelling the ranks of untrained and incompetent lawyers, and physicians, and clergymen. It is with me a grave question whether the State has a right to incorporate a private institution for doing such imperfect and superfluous work; there can scarcely be a doubt that it is unwise and inexpedient for the State to do such work directly and with its own funds. Not, as I have said, that the State should abstain from supporting professional and special schools, but that it should insist upon their being so organized and conducted as to be a constant incentive and aid to general and liberal education. The number of men sent forth from such schools is a very minor matter; their quality and character, whether as specialists and experts or as citizens and leaders in the purification and elevation of public sentiment, is a matter of the very highest importance. It may not be practicable for you at once to require the degree of preparation I have indicated as the condition of admission to a professional school, but surely some requirement may be made, so that persons who would fail in an examination for entrance into an ordinary grammar school may not readily pass, under the patronage of the State, to the study of medicine or law. I would recommend, as the minimum requisition, to be increased as soon as practicable, that any person who wishes to enter any professional school which is or may hereafter be under the control of your board, should pass a preliminary examination equivalent to that required for entrance into the Junior Class in college. This would be a considerable and very much needed step in advance, and would, in the circumstances, be the most difficult step to take. It is always the first step that costs; but the first step must be taken first, and it often counts most as well as costs most. Were this once done it would soon be found feasible to make the professional courses strictly post-graduate courses, and to require the whole college course as their antecedent.

These are some of the topics upon which I wished to speak frankly, reserving others perhaps equally important for future consideration. I close with an expression of my hearty interest in the great school work of the State. I rejoice in what has been done since I left the commonwealth in my boyhood. It is but sixty years since Indiana ceased to be a territory, and her citizens have many reasons to be proud of her advance during these years, and to be incited to higher endeavor. I rejoice in what is now doing in educational affairs. Our educational exhibit at Philadelphia was a very great gratification and encouragement, and we may well labor with hope for increased unity, co-operation and efficiency. The denominational colleges of the State, with their growing endowments and influence, deserve our gratitude and congratulations. They are doing an important part of the immense and urgent work which appeals to the sympathy and activity of all, and are aids to the State not less than to the churches. The friends of higher education everywhere may well stand together, with mutual courtesy and assistance, counseling and endeavoring the moral and intellectual advancement of our own commonwealth.

LEMUEL MOSS, *President.*

Annual Report of Indiana University Including the Catalogue, 1876–77 (Indianapolis, 1877), pp. 37–45.

Document 77

Growth, but not Staggering Expansion

With 159 students enrolled in 1878, President Moss could report perceptible growth to the trustees. That, however, was not enough; the trustees were given another dose of Moss's educational philosophy cast in the lofty terms of the pulpit. There is in the report one realistic note,

"Cheap teachers can undoubtedly be had, but they are liable to prove themselves very expensive, even if their services were gratuitous."

*   *   *

PRESIDENT'S REPORT.

The following is the Report of the President of the University to the Board of Trustees, at their meeting in November, 1878:

To THE BOARD OF TRUSTEES,

Indiana University:

GENTLEMEN—The Institution under your care and direction shows a larger attendance than a year ago. The whole number in the College classes is now 159. The several classes, if we assign the conditioned or irregular ("select") students to the classes in which their studies mostly fall, or which they are striving to gain, will number as follows: Seniors, 17; Juniors, 33; Sophomores, 42; Freshmen, 67; total, 159. In the Preparatory Department there are 148. The whole number in both Departments, therefore, is 307. The range and quality of work being done will be shown by the reports of the several instructors and officers herewith submitted, and by your own inspection and observation in the various rooms.

THE UNIVERSITY.

It seems to me not unfitting that I should at this time ask your attention to the aims of this University, and to the results which the people of the Commonwealth have a right to expect from it, if it be wisely and generously cherished and supported. While the professional schools are in suspension, our attention is here wholly given to collegiate education, and our desire is to make this as complete and thorough as possible. The courses put before the public in our Catalogue are courses of general, liberal discipline, and not of special or professional training. Whether as the result of accident or policy, the highest educational institutions maintained by the State are located at different points, under separate boards of control, instead of being gathered at a common centre and under one management. There are undoubtedly advantages as well as disadvantages in this arrangement, but wisdom and efficiency require that each of these institutions regards itself as a part of a State system, whether there be any formal bond of union or not, and that each keeps itself to its appointed sphere, while giving appreciation, sympathy and co-operation to the others. Leaving, therefore, the special professional training of teachers to the Normal School at Terre Haute, and the development of separate technical schools to the Purdue University at Lafayette, our business is to seek that discipline of all the mental and moral powers of those who come to us, which is necessary to the highest effectiveness in all the leading pursuits of life. We thus endeavor to carry on and complete the work begun in the public schools of the Commonwealth, and to vindicate our place as an integral part of the general educational system of the State. Our graduates may not be ready at once to enter, with advantage and as leaders, upon the practical activities of life, but they should be pre-eminently qualified to receive that special training that will fit them for any of the great duties and honorable pursuits to which inclination, the needs of their fellow-men, or the providence of God may call them.

COURSES AND STUDIES.

Centuries of experiment and use have pretty well settled throughout Christendom, and for all time, the chief materials and methods of higher education.

There may be great improvements in details and better facilities for the work, as these are constantly changing and growing, but there can never be much change in the prominent and characteristic features of the scheme. Our intellectual and spiritual powers are to be developed and trained by the acquisition of truth, for which undoubtedly the human soul was made. Truth is the harmony between our thoughts or conceptions and the facts of existence. These facts are displayed in the soul within us; in the human race of which we are members; in the universe of objects, animate and inanimate, around us; and in the eternal, almighty, all-holy, and all-loving God above us. These facts it is the duty and privilege of man to investigate; and the ability to do this, in part at least, with accuracy and interest and earnestness, is the one great aim of a liberal education.

This aim of true education determines what must be our main lines of study and teaching. We study language and literature, because in these man and mankind, the individual and the race, have left their truest, clearest and most permanent records. We study mathematics, pure and applied, because the whole universe of matter and force in its masses and motions is constructed upon mathematical principles and laws, from the infinitesimal atoms that unite in the tiniest molecule of the lightest gas to the largest suns and systems of suns which occupy the most remote stellar spaces. We study the natural sciences, because these describe for us, in an orderly and systematic and intelligible way, the objects which constitute the material creation. We study metaphysics, and logic, and ethics, and politics, because these discuss for us the nature of man considered in itself and as seen in our multitudinous relations to those about us and above us. We study history, because this reveals to us the combinations and conflicts and conquests of the great race to which we belong, whose empire is the earth, and with whose destiny our own is vitally identified. And in all this round of study we strive to cultivate reverence and obedience toward Him whose presence shines through every fact in the universe, and whose providence is manifest in every movement of every living thing, from the microscopic insect to microcosmic man.

These studies might be logically divided into two great classes—the science of nature and the science of man. Man and nature are thus seen to be parts of one great whole, hemispheres of the one globe of truth and knowledge, each vitally related to the other, and both of them revelations of energies and laws which are higher than either. The sciences of nature are rooted in mathematics and physics; the sciences of man are rooted in language and philosophy. In the first great division of studies we train the mind to observe external facts and phenomena, and to move forward along the lines of demonstration and unalterable certainty. In the second great division we train the mind to observe its own processes, internal facts and phenomena, to school itself in processes of reasoning inductive and less than demonstrative, where the conclusions at best are only highly probable and not absolutely certain. Probability is the guide of life; and hence one reason why the burden of educational discipline must be borne by the sciences of man, while a very important subordinate part is borne by the sciences of nature. Even experts in the latter need familiarity with the former; but the great majority of our students will not be scientific experts, nor experts of any kind; they will have to do with practical affairs, and need the training which will fit them for such a life.

When from these general principles we try to pass to more specific statements about the particular subjects which shall be included in our courses of study, and the extent to which they shall be prosecuted, we meet with greater difficulty. No two College Faculties, probably, would settle this matter in precisely the same way, and no two teachers, perhaps, in the same Faculty, would be in absolute agreement. The reasons for such divergence of opinion are obvious. But it is quite as easy to exaggerate these differences as to overlook them. Many things are important which are not in all cases essential. Things desirable, and even obligatory in a Faculty of forty members with five hundred students, would be unwise, if not impossible, with ten professors and one hundred and fifty students. And yet, the principles of growth and preparation for it should be manifest in the organization of every living institution.

One guiding thought here deserves a moment's notice. I would advocate the provision of elective courses rather than of elective studies; and in harmony with this thought, our schedule of work is now drawn up. We do not deny all option in regard to particular subjects, and the range of this freedom may be somewhat extended as number and facilities increase; but we limit such selections to the junior and senior years, and then make them subservient to some well-defined plan. A student may often be able to tell, in consultation with his teachers, what general course of study will best develop his capabilities and fit him for his future purposes; but he is rarely qualified to decide what special subjects he should pursue; and temptation to "easy" and "attractive" studies is usually so strong—a desire for "high marks" rather than for sound scholarship and vigorous discipline—that few students can be safely subjected to it.

Taking, then, our courses as well adapted to the ends in view, how shall we vindicate the selection and arrangement of details?

1. Pure Mathematics goes far enough to prepare the students for the elementary discussions of mechanics and physics, including theoretical astronomy, while these latter enable them to understand something of the mechanism of the physical universe—its molecules and masses and forces and motions—so that from the start here given they may pursue these subjects as far as taste may incline or duty require. A less amount of mathematics, pure and applied, would be insufficient for purposes of general culture; a greater amount is perhaps not necessary except for special students.

2. In the Natural Sciences, including Chemistry, we must teach the leading facts and great theories and settled principles, so that the student may not be ignorant of the wonderful creation about him, nor unmoved by it, nor incapable, with the alphabet here given him, or learning its higher lessons and uses.

3. General and Political History should be so taught that the learner may understand existing nations and governments, the influences that have made them what they are, their political and social organizations, their relations to each other, and their present tendencies. As has been said, history is philosophy, especially moral philosophy, teaching by examples. In the probation of practical life, we have no guide but experience, and in our national development we have a growing need of the illumination of this historic light. The historic spirit also, cultivated and strengthened into a habit by this study, may well be regarded as indispensable in all other lines of inquiry.

4. Philosophy proper is the analysis of human nature. What man is, in his constituent capacities and faculties, in his mental and moral processes and feelings and activities, in his relations to the universe, to society, and to God, cannot be overlooked or slighted in a course of liberal training. Philosophy is at once the method of right study, the guarantee of correct thinking, and the condition of intelligent and efficient action. We cannot here go very far in

exploring this vast and important field. But we can survey and map the main outlines, secure the most important regulative principles, and direct the student to the main positions which should be conquered and retained by his own explorations and independent thought. No student is taught that he can complete his work with us in any department. He is taught, in the contrary, that he gains but a beginning,—a partial outfit and equipment and a sketch map of his journey,—and that he is born to the inspiring heritage of an endless career.

5. The indispensable discipline supplied by linguistic studies is shared by five great languages and their literatures,—Latin and Greek from among ancient tongues; French and German, from modern foreign languages—all converging and culminating in our own supreme vernacular. Other ancient and modern languages are important and valuable, and no one who makes language his special study would be long content without pushing far beyond our narrow limits; but the tongues enumerated have no substitutes in our courses of liberal study, and cannot be excluded from them. The reason for this is not far to seek. These languages are the keys to the mightiest civilizations and literatures the world has ever known. They not only open the past, but they alone furnish an explanation of the present. They show man in his highest creative moods and controlling activities. All that is venerable and effective in religion, art, poetry, eloquence, statesmanship, law, social organization, science, comes to us through these great tongues, and no one can tell which is the more fitly called living or which makes the more necessary contributions. Whoever may neglect these humanizing and quickening studies, the American student must not. He is to be the true cosmopolitan, gathering wisdom and inspiration from all time and all peoples, that he may build strongly and durably his own political and social structure of true Democracy. Large and broad scholarship and culture are desirable under any form of national life; in a republic which invites and assimilates all races, they are vital.

The scientific and philosophic knowledge of our own speech fitly crown the entire educational edifice. To observe clearly, to think accurately, and to speak correctly and forcibly, in English, is the chief goal of all liberal training with us, —the outward form with us of that disciplined mind and spirit which is the one great end of education every where. All our studies aid in this result, beside those which are expressly directed to it. Whether solving a problem, analyzing a compound, or describing a fossil, or discussing a linguistic construction, or translating a sentence, or examining a movement of consciousness, there is constant exercise in exactness of thought, and precision of speech. Our own language, in its history and composition, and in its masterpieces, as richly merits minute and critical study as any language every spoken by men, and will as largely repay it.

THE PROFESSORS.

Some of your Professors have more teaching required of them than they can properly do, with the demands you should make upon them for investigation and study beyond the routine of their daily work. Three recitations a day, with the special preparation for them is quite as much as the best teacher can attend to, and he will then have a scanty margin of time and strength for original research and incidental reading. In the departments of experimental science two recitations a day are enough for one man; and in the department of English, where much time must be given to the students individually, in suggesting, analyzing and correcting their themes, for various class-room and public exercises, two daily recitations are certainly sufficient. It must be remembered that we are aiming for the highest and best results, and are not simply seeking to compete with institutions of inferior purposes and attainments. Your Professors of the ancient and the modern languages are liable to have four recitations each daily. It is accidental rather than otherwise if they do not have this number every term. This is more than they can do, without risk alike to health and the quality of their work. I do not recommend the establishment of another full professorship at present, but I would approve the appointment of assistants,—one for the departments of Latin and Greek, one for the modern languages and English, and perhaps one for the experimental sciences. Such provision would be wise, economical and efficient. It must be borne in mind also that our classes are now quite as large as is compatible with faithful and profitable teaching, and the experience of all our best institutions shows that for every increase of from fifteen to eighteen students an additional instructor is required.

SALARIES.

Permit me to emphasize the need for an increase of the salaries of the Professors. It is unwise and ruinous to expect to secure or retain such men as are required for our work while offering an insufficient compensation. Cheap teachers can undoubtedly be had, but they are liable to prove themselves very expensive, even if their services were gratuitous. Two thousand dollars are certainly a very moderate salary, and outside of the pulpit and the school room no one who trains himself for a profession is expected to serve for such a sum; yet for this salary, with perhaps a few additional hundreds in the case of exceptional ability or experience, we can find excellent teachers, who would prize the careers here presented to them.

RELATION TO THE PUBLIC SCHOOLS.

This University is part of the public school system of the State. The high schools, on certain conditions, can graduate their pupils into our Freshman class. We have, and can have, no other preparatory department. This relation must be maintained and improved, so that we may find our enlargement in the growth of the public schools. Especially do I urge the importance of our relations to the High School of this city, where students from all parts of the State, and from other States, who can get no fit preparation at home, may be properly prepared for our courses. The Bloomington High School has done, and is doing, excellent work. They sorely need more time, however, for the requisite thoroughness and fullness of training. Their course should be at once extended from two years to three, and I would respectfully and earnestly ask that you will do whatever is found practicable in encouraging and aiding them to attain this improvement.

I would also suggest that as we are part of the public school system of the State, we should be so related to the school income of the State that its constant increase would work as constant a growth in our resources and facilities.

LIBRARY AND APPARATUS.

Your attention will be invited to the need of illustrative apparatus for several departments of study. The library also appeals for any enlargement you can give it. I would recommend that a considerable part of any sum you can appropriate might be profitably expended for dictionaries, atlases, and other similar standard works of reference.

MISCELLANEOUS.

According to your authorization, Prof. O. B. Clark, of Antioch College, Ohio, was invited to take charge of the chair of Greek, made vacant by the resignation of Prof. Ballantine. He accepted the position, and is now in charge of its duties. His appointment will be formally confirmed by you and should be dated from August 1, 1878.

Professor John C. Freeman, of Chicago, whom you invited to the Chair of History, at your last meeting, accepts the invitation on condition that you will permit him to assume its duties at the opening of the next college year. I recommend to you the granting of his request. In the meantime, in order to relieve Professor Atwater, Professor Houghton was asked to take the class in general history, during the current college year, in addition to his duties in the High School. I ask that this appointment be confirmed, and that Professor Houghton be granted such extra compensation as in your judgment may seem appropriate.

In my own department of instruction the Senior Class has daily recitations during this term, four days in each week, in Moral Philosophy, using Professor Calderwood's text-book. On Mondays they recite in Schwegler's History of Philosophy. The Junior Class recites daily in Psychology, using Dr. Mark Hopkins's "Outline Study of Man." On Saturday morning I meet the Freshman Class for a conversational lecture on some of the elements of Practical Ethics.

According to previous arrangement and announcement, as provided for by you at your last meeting, President Angell, of the University of Michigan, will deliver a course of six lectures before this University in February next. His subject is "International Law as Illustrated by American History."

Finally, I herewith lay before you a memoir of the Mexican Calender Stone and Sacrificial Stone, prepared by Hon. Thomas H. Nelson, of Terre Haute, to accompany his gift of the plaster models of these most interesting relics of Aztec civilization. I trust that his thoughtful generosity will stimulate many others to a similar remembrance of us in their liberality.

> Respectfully submitted,
> LEMUEL MOSS,
> President.

INDIANA UNIVERSITY, November 5, 1878.

All of which is respectfully submitted in behalf of the Board of Trustees of Indiana University.

> ROBERT C. FOSTER,
> Secretary.

Documentary Journal, 1878.

Document 78

Catalogue Woes

These were sweet uncomplicated days when President Lemuel Moss could appeal directly to Governor A. G. Porter to give the state printer a nudge to print the University Catalogue. Perhaps this is more reflective of the day when the public printer fed at the trough of state patronage, and Governor Porter was his master.

*   *   *

The Indiana University,
President's Room.   Bloomington, Monroe Co.,
                                              Ind.
                                              Mar. 17th 1881.

My Dear Sir—
   Our Annual Report & Catalogue will be ready for the printer about April 10.
It is very desirable that we get it as soon as practicable after the "copy" is
furnished. We have been frequently delayed by the fact that the state printer
was not supplied with the requisite paper, &c, for the work. It will be a great
favor if the Commissioner of the Printing Bureau is instructed to see that the
necessary arrangements are made for the speedy prosecution of our work, & I
venture to ask (as I do not know who the Commissioner now is) that this request
may reach him through you. The size of the Catalogue will be about as usual; the
number called for by statute is 5,000.
                                              Very Sincerely,
                                              LEMUEL MOSS, Prest.

Hon. A. G. Porter, Governor.

                                              The Indiana University,
President's Room.   Bloomington, Monroe Co.,
                                              Ind.
                                              April 11- 1881

Hon. A G. Porter—
My Dear Sir—
   By express today I send you the "copy" for our Annual Catalogue. Thank
you for the assurance that it shall be "pushed" by the printer. I saw Mr. Hastings last week, when I was in the city, & he said that every arrangement had
been made for putting it in hand at once. I will be obliged, if Mr. Hastings will
drop me a Postal card, saying that the copy has been received.
                                              Very Sincerely—
                                              LEMUEL MOSS

Lemuel Moss to Gov. A. G. Porter, March 17, 1881; April 11, 1881.

Document 79

The Second Flame of Disaster

   The fire which swept the new College Building in July 1883 in many
ways burned the University into another era of its development. The fire
was disastrous in that it burned materials which could not be replaced,
but removal from the original site meant that the University was to begin
all over again with some new perspective on the future of its role in
Indiana public education.

                         *   *   *

   The Board of Trustees of the Indiana University met in special session called
in consequence of the loss by fire of the new College Building with all the

chemical and philosophical apparatus the Owen cabinet and museum, and the entire library of the University, which fire occurred on the night of the (12th) twelfth day of July A. D. 1883.

There were present the following members of the Board, to wit; D. D. Banta Prest., Dr. J. D. Maxwell, H. L. Stetson, Robt. W. Miers and Robert D. Richardson. Absent:—Isaac Jenkinson, Robert S. Robertson, James S. Mitchell. There being a quorum present the Board was called to order by the Prest. D. D. Banta, and the Secretary of the Board, W. W. Spangler, being absent, Robt. D. Richardson was chosen secretary *pro tem.*

Letters of regard and sympathy for the great loss sustained by the University were read, from the following persons:—

> Jas. B. Angell, Prest. of Michigan University. Jos.
> F. Tuttle, Prest. of Wabash College. W. T. Shott,
> President of Franklin College. Jno. M. Coulter,
> Prof. in Wabash College. Jas. S. Rollins, the
> oldest graduate of this Univ. and now Prest. of
> the Bd. of Regents of the Univ. of Mo. Amos W.
> Butler, Brookville, Indiana, A. C. Hamil,
> Chicago, Ill. and Sarah Morrison, Knightstown,
> Ind., the first lady student of this university,
> who kindly enclosed five dollars as an expression
> of her kind regard for the University, and which
> contribution it was resolved to appropriate
> to the purchasing of a Record and Minute Book
> for the Trustees of the University, the Minute
> Book having been destroyed by the fire.

Upon motion of Mr. Stetson, the following resolution was adopted:—
Resolved:—That the local Board be and is hereby instructed to have the debris of the burned College Building cleared away, and such materials as may be fit put in shape for use in a new building.

Upon motion of Mr. Stetson, the following resolution was adopted,
Resolved:—That, it is the sense of the Board of Trustees, that immediate steps be taken for rebuilding the building destroyed by fire, and to this end, that the Local Board proceed, at once, to mature and prepare a plan of a building for the use of the Scientific Departments of the University, and that said Board be instructed to consult with Profs. Wylie, Van Nuys, Jordan, and Gilbert, touching the size, plans, etc. of the proposed building, and that said Board have power to procure any additional aid necessary to obtain suitable plans for such building, said plans to be submitted to the Board of Trustees at their next meeting.

It was further ordered that the Local Board be authorized to make all necessary arrangements for recitation rooms &c. for the use of the University at ensuing college term, and that immediate notice be given by the Prest. of the Board of Trustees and the President of the Faculty, that the University will open September the 6th, 1883, for work in all its departments.

* * * * * * * *

Attest: D. D. Banta Prest.

Board Minutes, 1883–1897, pp. 29–30.

Bloomington, Aug. 29, 1883.

Board met at the National House at 8 o'clock a.m.

Dr. Moss read the following declaration which on motion of Mr. Jenkinson, was unanimously adopted:—

In view of the recent disaster to the Indiana University in the burning of the Scientific building, with the Library, museums, laboratories, and apparatus, we, the Trustees of the University desire to put on record the following declarations; viz:—

-1.- In this calamity we reverently recognize the hand of God, and we regard it also as a summons to advance the University toward the position of effectiveness and influence that it ought to occupy.

-2.- The history of the University with all the associations that gather about its work of more than fifty years makes it eminently desirable that the institution should remain in Bloomington, where it was first established and where has been passed its long period of trial and of worthy achievement.

-3.- The present campus is wholly inadequate and unsuitable for the proper development and enlargement of the University, and should now be exchanged for a site that will fully meet all present and prospective requirements.

-4.- The insurance companies have promptly met their obligations in the payment of losses, but our means from this source are small; the Legislature will not convene in regular session until sixteen months hence; many interests are imperilled by delay, while we are powerless, through lack of money, to secure the university against these perils; we will therefore gladly welcome any cooperation and aid that may come to us from the County of Monroe and the City of Bloomington, while we confidently rely upon the generous sentiment of the people of the State and the liberality of its General Assembly.

. . . .

Board Minutes, 1883–1897, pp. 32–33.

The Fire 1883

On the night of Thursday July 12, 1883 a little after 10 O'clock, the new College building was found to be on fire and the alarm was given. As the crowds gathered, the flames were seen bursting out from the second story from the room used for storing apparatus and as a work room on the east side. The Fire Dept. of the town with its new steam fire engine, and its smaller engine, did its best to extinguish the flames. In this attempt it failed but succeeded by energetic work in saving the old building by keeping the roof and end adjacent to the burning structure soaked with water. Within two hours from the discovery of the fire, the entire roof had fallen in and only the walls with a few clinging timbers remained. The building thus distroyed was three stories in hight and was built in 1873 at a cost of $33,000 It contained the Library of 14000 volumes the Museum in which was the Owen Cabinet of 85000 specimens carefully labeled and displayed in suitable cases. The Ward Casts of Extinct Animals and many other valuable collections. In the third story was Prof. Jordan's collection of fishes.

In the department of Physick there was much costly apparatus and the Chemical Labratory in the 1st & 2d stories was well equipped for its work. A few cases of minerals from the museum alone were saved. The following estimate of the loss has been made. Building $33,000, Museum $30,000 Library $40,000, Labratory $8,000 Total loss $111,000, Total insurance $27,454.50.

Faculty Minutes, September, 1887–June, 1909, p. 248.

TRUSTEES' REPORT

To His Excellency, The Hon. Albert G. Porter, Governor of the State of Indiana:

Herewith is submitted the annual report of the Trustees of the Indiana University, showing receipts and expenditures for the fiscal year ending October 31, 1883.

The calamitous loss the University sustained by fire during the year and the steps taken to repair that loss, seem to furnish a sufficient excuse for a more extended prefatory statement than has heretofore been the custom to make on submitting these reports.

On the evening of the 12th day of July last, one of the principal University buildings, and which contained the Library, Museum and Chemical, Philosophical, and Natural History Departments, was destroyed by fire, together with all that it contained, save about one-fourth in value of the Museum. It is difficult to arrive at correct estimates in such cases, and especially so in this, inasmuch as all the recent University records, containing inventories and values, were likewise destroyed; but the following general estimate of losses incurred it is believed is a reasonably fair approximation:

The building, finished in 1873, cost	$ 46,000 00
Museum and cases (less one-fourth) estimated loss	15,000 00
Library, containing 12,000 volumes and 3,000 pamphlets, estimated loss	30,000 00
Apparatus, fixtures, etc., Chemical Department, estimated loss	8,000 00
Apparatus, fixtures, etc., in Philosophical Department, estimated	4,000 00
Apparatus, specimens, etc., in Natural History Department, estimated	1,200 00
Total estimated loss	$104,200 00

This great loss, representing the accumulations of years, meant more to the University, than the mere dollars and cents of estimated values, though that of itself, was a severe blow. It came at a time when there was a greater demand than ever before for all the facilities and appliances necessary to carry on scholarly and technical work and also when the friends of the institution, encouraged by the beneficent action of the last Legislature, were indulging the hope that it was on a better foundation than ever before.

As soon as practicable after the fire, the Board set about the work of preparation for the accommodation of students at the Fall term. By procuring other quarters for the janitor and his family, and cutting down the society halls somewhat, additional recitation rooms were fitted up in the "old building;" and when the term opened the management was gratified to learn that the number of students matriculating was but little less than the year before. The Board did what it could with the limited means at hand, and with the confined quarters afforded by the "old building," to furnish the room and appliances necessary for carrying on collegiate work; and in all it did, it was cheerfully seconded by both the professors and students.

The messages of good will and offers of assistance that came on the heels of the fire, from sister colleges, learned societies and sympathizing friends were highly encouraging, and the substantial aid that has since followed, in the shape of valuable specimens contributed, has put the Natural History Department on as good a foundation, as regards number, variety and value of specimens, as it was before the fire. Of the contributors, may be mentioned, Harvard College, through Prof. Alexander Agassiz; Yale College, through Prof. A. E. Verrill; Wabash College, through Prof. John M. Coulter; United States National Museum, through Prof. Spencer F. Baird, Dr. Tarleton, H. Bean and Robert Ridgway; California Academy of Sciences, through W. G. W. Harford; Illinois State Laboratory of Natural History, through Prof. S. A. Forbes; United States Fish Commission, through Prof. D. S. Jordan; Brookville Natural History Society, through A. W. Butler; J. W. Byrkitt, Michigan City; Charles C. Leslie, Charleston, S. C.; Rosa Smith, San Francisco, and H. C. Ford, Santa Barbara, Cal.; Leonel Plasencia and Felipe Poey, Cuba; A. Bettelina, Cedar Keys, and Silas Stearns, Pensacola; Isaac M. Gwinn; William Stout, and Profs. Jordan and Gilbert, of the University.

It affords us great pleasure to state that Monroe county came forward with a magnificent donation of fifty thousand dollars to the University, to be used in erecting necessary buildings. This sum, together with twenty-five thousand dollars of the money received from the insurance companies, has been set apart as a building fund, and with it we hope to defray the expense of the erection of two buildings, in lieu of the one destroyed, and purchase additional college grounds. Plans of two fire proof buildings—one designed with special reference to the wants of the Chemical and Philosophical Departments, and the other to the wants of the Natural History Department—have been approved by the Board, and it is expected that the contracts for erecting these buildings will be let in time for the contractors to begin work in the spring.

The present campus, containing about eleven acres, and more than half of which, by reason of its being low land, is unfitted for college building purposes, the Board deemed unsuitable as a site for the buildings to be erected the ensuing season, and for such other buildings as the expansion and growth of the institution in the future will demand. The Board therefore, made arrangements for the purchase of twenty acres of high, rolling woodland, adjoining Bloomington, on which the contemplated buildings will be erected. These buildings we hope to have completed in time for occupancy at the beginning of the next Fall term, or very soon thereafter.

Respectfully submitted,
D. D. BANTA,
Pres. Board Trustees,
Indiana University.

Attested, July 1, 1884.
WM. W. SPANGLER,
Sec. Indiana University.

Documentary Journal, 1883.

Document 80

Monroe County's Response to the Fire

Before any unsympathetic soul could get a head start with the perennial argument that Indiana University should be removed to a more central location in the state, the Board of Commissioners proposed aid to the extent of $50,000 to help rebuild the university plant. There was a string tied to the offer: the sum would be returned to the county if the University was moved.

*   *   *

Bloomington, Indiana.
September 8, 1883.

. . . .

The Board of Trustees were waited upon by the Board of Commissioners of Monroe County, Ind., and the following certified copy of the record and action taken by said Board of Commissioners, was presented, and upon motion ordered spread upon the minutes, which is now here done:—

In the matter of the
Indiana University,

Come now Jno. Waldron, W. J. Allen, and other taxpayers of Monroe County and petition the Board of Commissioners to assist the Trustees of the Indiana University in erecting new buildings for said University, and in making other improvements. And the Board having duly considered the matter, it is ordered that there be and hereby is donated to the Trustees of the Indiana University, out of any money in the County Treasury, the sum of fifty Thousand ($50,000.00) Dollars, to be by them, [the] said Trustees, used in erecting new buildings for said University and in making other improvements,—said sum is donated upon the express condition and if accepted, is to be accepted subject to the condition that said University be and remain in the county of Monroe and State of Indiana, and in case of removal of said University at anytime hereafter from said County of Monroe, said buildings and improvements made by said fund are to revert to said County of Monroe.

And the Auditor of said County is hereby directed to draw a warrant on the Treasurer of said County in favor of the Trustees of said Indiana University for said sum of Fifty Thousand ($50,000.00) Dollars, and deliver the same to the Trustees of said University, when said Trustees shall have entered on the margin of the record of this order, their receipt, accepting said donation upon the conditions herein expressed.

Whereupon, on motion of Mr. Robertson, the following was unanimously adopted by the Board of Trustees,—Whereas;—The Board of Commissioners of Monroe County have tendered to this Board of Trustees of the Indiana University the sum of Fifty-Thousand ($50,000.00) Dollars to be used in the erection of buildings for the use of the Indiana University, as appears by their action and record now presented to this Board,—Therefore; be it Resolved;— That said donation be accepted and said sum be ordered paid to the Treasurer of this Board for the purposes expressed in said record and action of said Board of Commissioners.

Board Minutes, 1883–1897, pp. 36–37.

Document 81

The Cold Facts of University Needs

Lemuel Moss was gone, the victim of an indiscretion which the Board of Trustees, in a puritanical age, could not forgive. David Starr Jordan had not yet come on the scene. Nevertheless, the Board of Trustees laid before Governor A. G. Porter an austere report of the financial needs of the University. There was none of Lemuel Moss's pontificating in this report—it was to the point: Indiana University needed funds, and it needed them badly.

*   *   *

INDIANA UNIVERSITY.

TRUSTEES' REPORT TO GOVERNOR.

To his Excellency, HON. A. G. PORTER,

Governor of Indiana:

In transmitting the annual report of the Board of Trustees of the Indiana University, the committee delegated by the board to present to you some of the urgent needs of the institution, begs leave to submit the following:

The State University, through its career of more than half a century, has been left to the meager appropriations which each Legislature has deemed sufficient to carry on its actual work at as low a cost as could be estimated, and has thus been compelled to economize to the verge of penuriousness, instead of being able to reach out with liberality to grasp the new ideas and developments of modern science, and the actual necessities of modern education.

Notwithstanding this fact, it has assumed a position of more than local celebrity, and has been a source of incalculable benefit to the State.

It has produced among its graduates and faculty, names renowned in literature, science and politics, not only in the nation, but among the great nations of the world.

Only of late has there been the beginning of a policy which will lay its foundations broad and deep—the act of the last Legislature making provision for an endowment which will be permanent. But that endowment fund is not yet available, and will not supply necessities for some years to come.

We feel that we have a right to ask of the State that she provide for her children as becomes a great State, rich in agricultural, mineral, and manufacturing wealth.

If one citizen of our State, moved by generous impulses and noble aims, can endow a denominational college with a gift between a quarter and a half million dollars in value, the mere interest of which amounts to more than has been appropriated annually to the necessities of the State University, what could not, and should not, the State do, to make of its University one of the great Universities of the world?

We do not appear in the character of mendicants asking for alms, but in the character of stewards of a trust, who report on the condition of the trust, and ask for means to carry out the orders and instructions which the State has given us in regard to one of its greatest and dearest interests.

We hope the time will soon come when we shall not be compelled at every session, to stand before the Legislature, like Oliver Twist before his master, crying for more.

The University suffered a great loss by fire during the past year, yet notwithstanding the fact that no appropriation has been made to meet it, the work of the institution has been kept up to its former high standing, and, cramped as we have been, the loss we have sustained has been the less felt on account of the increased zeal of the faculty and students.

The financial loss resulting from the fire of July 12, 1883, may be stated as follows:

The burned building, comparatively new, having been erected
in 1873, cost ....$ 46,000
Museum and cases 15,000
Library of 12,000 vols. and 3,000 pamphlets 30,000
Apparatus, fixtures, etc., Chemical Department 8,000
Same in Philosophical Department 4,000
Same and specimens, Natural History Department 1,200

Total estimated loss $104,200

By the generous and magnificent liberality of Monroe county, which at once donated to the Trustees the sum of $50,000, and the proceeds of Insurance policies paid, we were enabled to set apart $75,000 as a building fund.

Upon careful consideration, deeming the low ground and limited capacity of the present campus a sufficient reason for not erecting there the new buildings, which are absolutely a necessity for the growing wants of a State University, we purchased twenty acres additional, securing a site unsurpassed in the State for its natural beauty and fitness for the purpose, upon which we have erected two buildings, one for the Chemical and Philosophical, and the other for the Natural History Department, whose solidity, stability, architectural beauty, and adaptability to the purpose for which they are erected, command the admiration of all who have seen them.

The land cost ....$ 6,000 00
The buildings cost about 60,000 00

Total $66,000 00

Incidentals connected with their completion will exhaust the $75,000.00 available.

We have estimated that there will be required from the State to complete the work thus begun and nearly completed, the sum of $50,000.00 Surely the State can well afford to give as much to its own work, as has been so generously and willingly given by the not over wealthy citizens of the good county of Monroe.

This will be expended for heating apparatus and plumbing, furniture, fencing and improving the grounds, fitting up a gymnasium, supplying the library, for museum and apparatus for it, and the different departments; lighting the buildings and erecting an engine house.

With the $50,000.00 donated and the $50,000.00 we ask the State to appropriate, in all $100,000.00, together with the generous gifts of specimens which have been showered upon us by other institutions, we can now make a better exhibit in all but the library, than before the loss. In other words, we more than make up the loss of $104,000.00 by an appropriation of $50,000.00.

Certainly the State can well afford to replace its loss of upwards of $100,000.00 by new and better buildings and contents, at a cost of only $50,000.00.

We especially desire to call attention to the wants of the library. A well selected library is one of the most necessary elements in the working departments of any University. Our funds have been so limited, and our necessities so great, that only such a sum as would supply immediate necessities in the working departments was set apart for books. We only expended $1,512.83 for books, and $128.92 for periodicals during the fiscal year since the fire, and the selections were made with special reference to the wants of the classes as designated by the faculty. These books are of the first-class, but the library is almost entirely deficient in all but the departments of history, political economy and *belles lettres.*

With a few thousand dollars we can supply enough to make a good working library, leaving the growth of the future to make it better.

But there is one suggestion we consider worthy of the careful consideration of yourself and the Legislature. The State has a library which for years has been of doubtful utility to the people of the State. Situated as it is, with changing control, subject only as to its increase to the ideas of those who have, from time to time, been chosen to oversee its affairs, without a catalogue which would indicate to students where they could find their specialities in research, it is probably fair to say, without casting any reflection upon its management in the past, that it has not been, is not now, and will not become of sufficient use to the people of the State to pay for the cost of its maintenance.

Why not give it to the State University, and thus utilize it to the best advantage by opening its unused pages to students who will hereafter become the bulwarks of the State? We urge candid and careful consideration of this question on the grounds given, including the ground of wholesome economy.

There is not and should not be any antagonism between us and the legislators. The University is the child of the State, and the trustees its guardian. There is no selfish end in view in making these recommendations. It is our earnest desire that the glorious school system, of which Indiana is so justly proud, may be augmented and bound together in one harmonious whole; that the common schools, as a base to the pyramid, may contribute to the support of a great, comprehensive university, broad enough in its aims and ideas to be of the highest use to the State, to fulfill the highest aspirations of all who love the cause of education, and become an institution second to none upon the continent. Respectfully submitted,

R. S. ROBERTSON,
Chairman Committee,

Adopted by the Board of Trustees, December 17, 1884.

D. D. BANTA,
President Board of Trustees.

WM W. SPANGLER,
Secretary Ind. Univ.

Documentary Journal, 1884.

Document 82

Out of the Ashes

When the ashes of disaster had cooled, and Professor Joseph Swain had had an opportunity to take inventory, it was found that quite an astonishing amount of material had been saved. Also, contributors were generous in making gifts to the University.

*   *   *

MUSEUM

JOSEPH SWAIN, ACTING CURATOR.

Since the fire of July 12, 1883, in which the old Museum, including the famous Owen cabinet, was almost totally destroyed, the growth of the Museum has been very rapid.

In the department of Vertebrate Zoölogy, especially, it is already very rich. The collection of fishes is already the third in size in America, and tenth in the world, while additions are frequently received from various quarters in America and Europe. The collection of birds is also, thanks to the generous interest of the Smithsonian Institution, very extensive and valuable.

A considerable sum of money has been recently appropriated for the increase of the University Museum. This sum will, when expended, more than double the present bulk of collections. The following is an outline of the chief contents of the Museum at present:

BIRDS.

One thousand three hundred mounted birds and bird-skins, part of them (700) presented by the United States National Museum, through Mr. Robert Ridgway, curator of birds, the rest from the collections of Professors Jordan and Gilbert. About 200 skins of birds and mammals, collected in the Amazon region by Mr. Edward M. Brigham, have been recently added to the Museum.

FISHES

About 12,000 specimens, representing 1,100 species. The bulk of these have come from the explorations made by Professors Jordan, Gilbert, and Swain as assistants to the United States Fish Commission, in Cuba, the Southern States, Massachusetts and Italy. Many more have been presented by the United States National Museum, through Dr. Tarleton H. Bean, curator of fishes in that Institution. Large and valuable collections have also been received from Mr. W. G. W. Harford, curator of the California Academy of Sciences; from Mr. Silas Stearns, of Pensacola, Florida; from Miss Rosa Smith, San Diego, California; from Leonel Plasencia, of the University of Havana; from Mr. Charles C. Leslie, of Charleston; from Mr. W. P. Shannon, of Greensburg, Indiana; from Mr. Henry S. Bates, of Bloomington, and from various others interested in the study of fishes. Collections have also been received from the Museum of Comparative Anatomy (Harvard), through Professors Alexander Agassiz and Samuel Garman; from Yale College, through Professor A. E. Verrill, and from the Illinois State Laboratory of Natural History, through Professor S. A. Forbes.

INVERTEBRATES.

Of Invertebrates, the University has about 1,000 specimens, representing some 290 species, mostly marine. Many of them were presented by the United States National Museum, through Mr. Richard Rathbun, curator of that department. A collection of marine shells has been received from Wabash College, through Professor John M. Coulter, in exchange for fishes. A large and valuable collection of corals from the Island of St. Thomas has lately been added to the Museum.

PLANTS.

In the department of Botany, the collections are scanty. A collection of Marine Algae ("sea mosses") of California has been presented by Mr. H. C. Ford, of Santa Barbara. The herbarium of the late Professor H. B. Boisen has been given to the University by Mrs. Boisen.

FOSSILS.

Of the Owen collection, four cases of fossils, comprising some 700 specimens, were saved from the fire. Among these are many of the types of new species described by Professor David Dale Owen, and, therefore, among the most valuable objects in the Owen collection. The skeleton of *Megalonyx Jeffersoni*, from Hendersonville, Kentucky, perhaps the most important specimen in the old Museum, was also saved. This specimen, the most complete of the species in existence, has been described by Professor E. D. Cope for the report of the Indiana Geological Survey.

A considerable series of fossils has been received from Wabash College.

MINERALS.

Four cases, comprising the finest crystals in the Owen collection, some 600 specimens in all, were saved from the fire. A few other specimens have been received as donations.

Fifty-Fifth Annual Report of the Indiana University, Including the Catalogue, 1884–85 (Indianapolis, 1885), pp. 53–55.

Document 83

University Park

This cession from the Dunn family ceded an unspecified number of acres in a boundary deed to the University. In this woodland the new campus of the University was to be located; today, it is the heartland of the greatly enlarged campus tracts. Here a new beginning was to be made, with modernized buildings and a bright young president who brought a spark of progress to Bloomington, such as had never existed there before.

*   *   *

"University Park." (Deed.)

Hon. Moses F. Dunn of Bedford was present and closed sale of "University Park" and, on payment of Six Thousand Dollars ($6,000.00), purchase mony [*sic*] in full, delivered deed for same to the Board, which deed was ordered to be recorded in these minutes and also in the recorder's office of Monroe county.

The said deed is in words and figures as follows:—

This Indenture Witnesseth; That Moses F. Dunn (unmarried) and George G. Dunn, and Euphemia Dunn his wife, of Lawrence County in the State of Indiana, convey, and the said Moses F. Dunn conveys and Warrants to the Trustees of the Indiana University, and to their successors in office forever, for the sum of Six Thousand Dollars ($6,000.00) the following real estate in Monroe County in the State of Indiana, to-wit:—

A part of the South East quarter of Section Thirty-Three (33) in Township Nine (9) North, Range One (1) West, bounded and described as follows, to-wit: —Commencing at a point Twenty (20) feet north of the south side of said quarter section and four hundred and thirty-five (435) feet east of the south-east corner of Lot Number five (5) in Dunn's Addition to the city of Bloomington, thence east parallel with said Section and township line Eleven and Eighty hundredths (11.80) chains—thence north Sixteen and ninety-five hundredths (16.95) chains—thence west Eleven and Eighty hundredths (11.80) chains— thence souuth [*sic*] Sixteen and ninety-five hundredths (16.95) chains to the place of beginning; also the said grantors convey without Warrant a strip along the south side thereof and extending south to the center of the turn-pike road, and east and west to the east and west lines of said tract.

And the said Grantor, Moses F. Dunn, reserves all fences now on and around said tract and grants for the use of said University a right of way from the end of Kirkwood avenue east to the tract of land herein conveyed, of the full width of said avenue, and whenever the land lying between Gamble Street in said city and the said tract herein conveyed shall be platted, laid out, or sold, said grantor will extend said avenue to the west line of said tract and will throw open and dedicate to the public a street sixty feet in width running north and south on and along the west side of said tract, the west line of said tract to the east line of said street.

In witness whereof, the said grantors have hereunto set their hands and seals this 5 day of November 1885, to relate back and take effect from the 4th day of February 1884.

Seal
Seal
Seal

State of Indiana }
Lawrence County } SS.

Before me, a Notary Public in and for said County personally appeared the above named Moses F. Dunn, George G. Dunn and Euphemia Dunn, and each acknowledged the execution of the foregoing deed. Witness my hand and notarial seal this 5 day of November 1885.

Seal

Board Minutes, 1883–1897, pp. 175–176.

Document 84

The Rebuilding on the Dunn Acres

Removal of the University to a new campus and the receipt of numerous gifts, including the local Monroe County aid, in no way eased Indiana University's financial plight. In this brief but pointed report, the Board of Trustees made clear to Governor Isaac P. Gray the facts of life in the University in 1887–1888.

*   *   *

TRUSTEES' REPORT.

To His Excellency Isaac P. Gray, Governor of Indiana:

I have the honor of transmitting to you herewith the biennial report of the Board of Trustees of the Indiana University for the fiscal years ending October 31, 1887, and October 31, 1888.

And accompanying the same I beg leave, on behalf of the Board, to call attention to the most pressing wants of the University at this time. During the past few years the attendance of students has steadily increased, until the institution has outgrown its quarters. In four years the increase of attendance in the college classes has been more than one hundred per cent. When, after the disastrous fire of July, 1883, the three new buildings known as Wylie Hall, Owen Hall, and Maxwell Hall, were completed, it was supposed that these, with the old college building, would afford room enough to answer all demands upon the University for some years to come; but already, by reason of the greatly increased numbers of students and the multiplying of the various departments of learning to meet the requirements of the times, we find the University hampered for want of a room to such an extent that we feel it an imperative duty to call attention to the fact.

Succeeding the disastrous fire above referred to, the Board of Trustees, as soon as circumstances would permit, began to supply the loss of the library by the purchase of books for a new one, and annually since then have books been added, until there are now on the shelves something more than 9,000 volumes, besides a large number of periodicals and miscellaneous documents, all useful and of great pecuniary value. For want of a better place, one of the rooms in Wylie Hall, which was designed for a recitation room, was utilized as a library room, and for a time it answered the purpose fairly well; but by reason of the library's growth it is no longer large enough for library purposes. But we have no better place for our books.

The immediate erection of a suitable library building would seem to be an imperative necessity, and it is believed that for the present at least it would fairly solve the problem of more room. Such a building, planned on a scale commensurate with the wants of a growing University, should be of proportions much beyond the necessity of the library for the present. It could be so constructed as to contain a number of rooms suitable for recitation rooms, which, with the room now occupied as a library, would, it is believed, afford the room imperatively necessary for recitation and laboratory purposes for some years to come.

Other plans could be suggested whereby the present evils could be remedied, but we believe the plan named could be carried out at the least expense to the State, and we are content with its suggestion in this place.

Very respectfully,
D. D. BANTA,
President Board of
Trustees.

Documentary Journal, 1888.

Document 85

Beautifying University Park

Symbolic of the enthusiasm and change of the Jordan years in Indiana University, efforts were being made to preserve and improve the beautiful sylvan setting of the new university buildings. Olaf Bensen's landscape plan was taking form, and some of the improvements are still visible.

*   *   *

Mr. Maxwell submitted *Report* of the *Local Executive Committee* as follows which was adopted on motion of Mr. Miers:—

To Hon. Bd Trustees, Ind. U.

The undersigned Executive Com. of Board would respectfully submit the following report.

At the last meeting of Board, your committee were authorized to take steps at once toward improving the grounds in University Park. To this end they opened a correspondence with Mr. Olaf Bensen, landscape gardener, who has had the laying out and ornamentation of Lincoln Park, Chicago. As a result of this correspondence, Mr. Benson came to Bloomington and spent over a week in mapping off the ground and making a rough sketch of improvements, which afterward were reduced to the sketch or plan herewith submitted, with the necessary specifications as to work. The work was somewhat delayed in its commencement, by reason of landscape gardener not completing and forwarding details as soon as was expected, and have been more seriously delayed since by reason of bad weather. A few days of good weather would enable your committee to complete both drive and walk-ways to Owen and Wylie Halls, which will close the work for the season. The drive is sixteen feet wide, including gutters, which can be driven upon by vehicles in passing each other—is to be covered with six inches of small broken limestone—packed by rolling with heavy iron roller—and this covered again with two inches of gravel, also made compact by rolling. The gutters have outlets by means of catch basins at proper intervals for getting clear of surplus water, through vitrified tiling laid in cement. The walk-way or pavement of hard burnt brick is 7 feet 4 inches wide, laid upon a four inch bed of gravel or coal cinders well tamped, on top of which is a bed of sand two inches thick. The edging or curbing is of brick tiling 8 inches deep 12 to 16 inches long and 2 inches thick—

This improvement, to make it both useful and sightly, involved a large amount of earth excavation and grading, especially in front, where the whole width of the street or sixty feet was a cut—

The approximate cost of work when completed to College buildings which will be about 800 feet from front to buildings, will be—

Allowance to landscape gardener—	$150.00
Assistance in laying off grounds	5.00
Excavation of ground 2000 yds & grading @12¢	240.00
Construction of 800 x 16 ft. driveway including guttering @4½¢	580.00
Construction of 800 ft. walkway @60¢ per sq. yd. & 3¢ per lineal foot curbing	420.00
City surveyor expense	19.90
Making a total when finished of about—	$1414.90

There are some small incidental expenses connected with moving of plank walk-way &c. that are not included in this estimate and which have come more properly under the head of contingencies—There remains unpaid of this sum and until the work is completed—

To Adams and Denton (walk-way) —	$290.00
To Robertson and Meadows	580.00
(Driveway) —	$870.00

. . . .

(*Supplemental* Report—)

Your committee would take the liberty of urging upon the Board the necessity of some action at an early day with reference to the purchase of additional ground for University Park— The improvements which are being made at entrance to campus will greatly enhance the value of Mr. Dunn's grounds for building purposes, as in fact will all the improvements which the Board may make—
Your committee feel that it would be one of the greatest misfortunes which could happen to us to have rows of cottages built up along the line of our drive-

and walk-way on either side, thereby obstructing the beautiful landscape view and encumbering the ground—

The chairman of your committee had a proposition two years ago for the sale of all the front on the west to Dunn Street, on the north to brink of hill near the creek and on the east sufficient ground to make twenty acres, at the same price paid for the first twenty, that is $300.00 per acre—

What Mr. Dunn would do now, since his return, from his tour, is unknown to your committee—

       Respectfully submitted—
           JAS. D. MAXWELL
           R. W. MIERS—
           Executive Committee—

Board Minutes, 1883–97, pp. 274–277.

[VI]

From Jordan to Bryan, Years of Fighting for Status 1889–1913

Tragically, much of Indiana University's history has to be written in terms of struggling for financial support in order to meet the challenges of the various periods of its existence. From a modern perspective, it appears that a slightly greater amount of public assistance in the years that David Starr Jordan was helping to bring about changes in the academic organization would have enabled the University to assume equal status with its more aggressive neighbors. The fact that this support was not forthcoming makes the accomplishments of the academically transitional years all the more significant.

Perhaps it is obligatory that incoming university presidents should make statements of faith in their inaugural addresses. If so, the Indiana presidents were no exception to this rule. A historian can only speculate on how much the presidents believed what they said or how much they hoped to inspire citizens and state officials to set high ideals and then live up to them. Four presidents in this era outlined the future for the institution, stated their educational philosophies, and indicated something of their approaches to fulfilling the responsibilities of the office.

In more mundane terms, Isaac Jenkinson recited annually the urgent needs of the University. His reports were clear and specific. No governor or legislator could have pleaded ignorance of Indiana's educational plight if he took time to read the Jenkinson reports. In a general, backward glance at American public educational history, one is amazed at the amount of inertia present in an age when the Republic was surging forward with such vigor and enthusiasm in so many areas of its growth. It is not enough to lay the responsibility entirely at the doors of a reluctant agrarian society in Indiana for failing to recognize and meet the challenges of the times. There were other forces, of course, one being a lack of sufficiently informed leadership at the head of both Indiana capital and political power structures. Too, the vision which was clear in the minds of

261

the Indiana University administration and the Board of Trustees was almost impossible of translation in non-partisan terms to the people of the state. The public mind was fractured by many conflicting institutional loyalties which actually encouraged costly conflict in the field of education. For most Americans in the latter decade of the nineteenth century, the efficacy of higher education had not been demonstrated. Excepting education, not a single area of direct human need had been developed in Indiana.

This latter fact was nowhere more clearly revealed than in the traumatic struggle to clarify the medical school issue. It is impossible, of course, to present here all of the materials extant on this subject. Revealed by it, however, are several cardinal facts. There was clearly lacking a sense of the serious need for a high degree of professionalism in all that this term implies in venturing out into so vital an area as the human sciences. Too long the state had shirked its responsibility for the care of the physical well-being of its people. Now, in a modern age of advancing medical science, it had to begin catching up by first deciding which state institution would be permitted to establish and develop a medical school. The documents included in this section are the concluding ones in the making of this important decision. By 1908 Indiana University was advanced a second long step into the broadening of its professional curriculum, but more than this, it was advanced to a new point where it had to concern itself deeply with catching up with the accomplishment of other American universities.

Of all of the Indiana University presidents, William Lowe Bryan faced the most staggering challenge to date. It was not enough in his era to talk and write eloquently about excellence, or to state starry-eyed ideals; the University had to set out actively to achieve competence in the professional areas which were being accredited, and where standards were being harshly compared with general national achievements. Not clearly stated in any single document in this section was a keen sense of destiny; nevertheless, this was in the minds of all responsible university leadership. With severely limiting material support, Indiana had to break the restricting shell of geographical and intellectual provinciality and turn itself into a university in the truest professional sense—a challenge which provoked many a cry of anguish in the process.

Document 86

Three-Quarters of a Century

Near the middle of the Jordan administration, Judge David D. Banta prepared a historical essay of three-quarters of a century of the University's growth. It was this essay which formed the basis for informational material which was carried in future catalogues. Also, it constituted a main source of information for speakers who discussed the University before the public. Two historical facts are of interest: despite its misfortunes, Indiana University never lost a day in its operation during sixty-six years; second, it had granted in these years only 902 bachelor's degrees.

* * *

HISTORICAL SKETCH OF THE INDIANA UNIVERSITY.

BY JUDGE DAVID S. BANTA.

On the 18th day of April, 1816, the Congress of the United States passed an act providing for the admission of Indiana into the Union. In this act certain propositions were tendered to the people "for their free acceptance or rejection." Two of these related to education, the one proposing to donate every sixteenth section of land in aid of common schools, the other to give a township of land "for the use of a seminary of learning."

The wisdom of the acceptance of both these propositions by the people of the new State through their agents, composing the Constitutional Convention of 1816, has been attested by the experiences of seventy-three years. Out of the township of land thus given by the United States "for the use of a seminary of learning," has grown the Indiana University, a brief sketch of the history of which is here given.

Eleven days after the acceptance of the propositions had been made known, President Madison designated for seminary purposes a Congressional township, which, on the organization of Monroe County, became a part thereof under the name of Perry Township. On the 20th day of January, 1820, the Legislature of the State passed an act establishing the "State Seminary," and appointed a Board of Trustees with power to locate its site on the reserved township, to sell a part of the land, to erect the necessary buildings, and to open the school.

In 1824 two buildings had been completed, the one for school purposes, the other for the residence of a professor. On the first day of May in that year, a school was opened under the care of Rev. Baynard R. Hall. Since that time every school day of each year has witnessed the assembling of teachers and students for recitation and drill in the class-room.

Three years later, a second professor, John M. Harney, subsequently distinguished as an editor, was elected, and in the fall of 1828 the school had taken such rank, as to the general character of its work and the number of pupils in attendance, that the General Assembly of the State gave it a new charter under the name of Indiana College.

A new Board of Trustees was named in the charter. The first act of this body after organizing was the election of Rev. Andrew Wylie, D. D., as President.

Dr. Wylie was at that time President of Washington College in Western Pennsylvania, and it was a year before he was able to enter on his new field of labor. In 1829 he took his seat, and for a number of years the work of the schools was carried on with efficiency, with Rev. Baynard R. Hall as Professor of Languages, and John M. Harney as Professor of Mathematics and the Sciences.

Later, however, the efficiency of the school became impaired by lack of harmony among the teachers. This led to a reorganization of the faculty in 1832, after which, till the death of Dr. Wylie in 1851, the growth of the institution kept pace with the development of the State. Early in Dr. Wylie's administration a new college building was built at a cost of $11,000. This was a structure of three stories, the lower occupied by the chapel, the second by the recitation rooms, the third by the halls of the Athenian and Philomathean literary societies. This building, with all its contents, was destroyed by fire in the spring of 1854.

In 1838 the growing importance of the Indiana College led the Legislature to grant it a third charter, this time raising it to the dignity of a "University," with the name and style of "The Indiana University." Under this charter its existence is still maintained.

In 1843, in response to a general demand, a Law School was established at Bloomington in connection with the University. This department was successfully continued until the year 1877, when adverse legislation compelled the Trustees to suspend its operation.

During the administration of Dr. Wylie the institution became widely and favorably known. He was a man of signal ability and aptitude for teaching, and he was supported by a body of professors, all of whom were scholarly and earnest men. Students from remote States were drawn to the institution, and in all respects of thoroughness and efficiency, it stood in the front rank of the Western colleges of the day.

After the death of Dr. Wylie, Rev. Alfred Ryors, D. D., was elected to the Presidency, an office which he retained for a single year. He was succeeded by Rev. William M. Daily, D. D., LL. D., who remained President until 1859.

In Dr. Daily's administration a series of calamities befell the University, by which it was greatly crippled. The main college building was destroyed by fire on the night of the 8th day of April, 1854, together with the college library of 1,200 volumes, and the furniture and library of the two literary societies. Still more disastrous consequences came from a litigation prosecuted against the State in behalf of the Vincennes University, in the result of which the Indiana University became vitally interested.

While Indiana was still a territory, a township of land in Gibson County was set apart in pursuance of an act of Congress for the use of an institution of learning, to be located in the Vincennes land district. Subsequently, in 1807 the Territorial Legislature passed an act to incorporate "The Vincennes University," and appointed for it a Board of Trustees. The site for the proposed institution was selected at Vincennes, then the capital of the Territory, and about 4,000 acres of the Gibson County reservation was sold, the proceeds being applied to the erection of "a large and commodious brick building in Vincennes." Here the matter rested. The State was organized, the capital had been removed to Corydon, the Board of Trustees ceased to act, and no school was opened under its auspices. This was the condition of things in 1820, when the State Seminary was established at Bloomington.

It was even then believed by many that the charter of the Vincennes University had been forfeited by non-user. In that year, the State for the first time assumed control of the Gibson County lands. Two years later was passed the first of a series of acts providing for the sale of the remainder of these lands, and the appropriation of the proceeds to the State Seminary. Thus the matter rested until 1846, when the Legislature authorized the bringing of an action in behalf of the Vincennes University for the recovery from the State the money realized from the sale of the Gibson County lands. The long and tedious litigation which followed, resulted, in 1852, in a judgment for $60,000 in favor of the plaintiff.

Meanwhile this amount had become part of the endowment fund of the Indiana University, and after its supposed loss came the most discouraging period in the history of the institution. For nearly two years its life trembled in the balance, until in 1854 when the State finally assumed the debt to the institution at Vincennes, and the sum in question was kept to the credit of the University.

Soon after the fire of 1854 the Board of Trustees made arrangements for the erection of a new and more imposing college building. The citizens of Monroe County lent a helping hand with a subscription of about $10,000, and with this aid was built the substantial building on the old campus now used by the Preparatory School.

After Dr. Daily's resignation, in 1859, Rev. Theophilus A. Wylie, D. D., was appointed acting President for one year, and until the election and inauguration of John Lathrop, LL. D. After one year, in the fall of 1860, Dr. Lathrop was succeeded by Rev. Cyrus Nutt, D. D., who remained at the head of the institution until 1875.

During all these years the income was inadequate to the wants of the University. There was always need of scrimping and pinching to make both ends meet. The library destroyed in 1854, which it had taken twenty-seven years to collect, did not exceed 1,200 volumes. After the fire, not a dollar could be spared for the purchase of a single book. Soon after, however, Mr. H. W. Derby, a bookseller in Cincinnati, gave from his stock in trade $1,500 worth of books. For more than twenty years the "Derby Donation" formed a considerable part of the University Library.

For many years the scope of the work done in the University, which differed in no essential respect from that done in most contemporary colleges, was adapted to a small income. Mathematics, Ancient Languages and Philosophical studies constituted the chief part of the course of study, while the Modern Languages, Science, Literature and History received but scanty notice. Expensive apparatus of any sort was scarcely thought of, much less provided. For nearly forty years one professor was deemed quite enough for all the teaching of the Sciences which was done in the institution. The text-book was made the basis of instruction, and no matter how large the class might be, a division into sections was rarely expected.

But in time something more was demanded. This demand was not peculiar to Indiana, but it was felt more or less by all the colleges of the country. In response to it, there was in all institutions a disposition toward the broadening of the College Curriculum. One of the consequences of this tendency was a gradual increase in the necessary cost of maintaining a college. In the Indiana University, this increase was met in 1867 by a legislative act appropriating to its use the sum of $8,000 annually. This beneficent act of the State, the first of its kind in the history of the institution, was followed by such an increase in the attendance that in 1873 it was found necessary to make an annual appropriation of the additional sum of $15,000.

Dr. Nutt's administration of fifteen years was in the main a period of growth and progress. The facilities for instruction were much enlarged, and with this the number of students steadily increased. In 1867, the wall of partition was broken down and women were admitted to the College Classes on the same footing with men.

In 1872, the very extensive collection of minerals and fossils collected by

David Dale Owen and Richard Owen, known as the "Owen Cabinet," was purchased at a cost of $20,000, and in the following year a large building was erected at a cost of $24,000 to contain the Museum, the Library and the Laboratories. In the same year an arrangement was made by which the graduates of the High Schools commisisoned by the State Board of Education, were admitted without examination to the Freshman Class in the University. This arrangement has been of great benefit to the High Schools as well as to the University.

After the resignation of Dr. Nutt, in 1875, Rev. Lemuel Moss, D. D., was called to the presidency, which office he retained until 1884. In his administration the work of the University went on with a steady advance in breadth and thoroughness. The Law Department was suspended in 1877, on account of adverse action of the General Assembly, and the purely nominal connection which had existed between the Indiana University and the Indiana Medical College of Indianapolis, was also broken.

The departments of Chemistry and Physics were, however, equipped and provided with expensive material and apparatus. The Library also became a special object of care, 12,000 well-selected volumes being upon its shelves. In 1880, extensive collections in zoölogy were obtained largely through the aid of the United States Fish Commission.

All these collections, the Owen cabinet, the library and the laboratories were in the new Science Building, and the whole went up in flame and smoke during a heavy thunder storm on the night of the 12th of July, 1883.

Nothing could have been more discouraging. It seemed impossible to carry on University work without books, material or apparatus, and without even the necessary recitation rooms. And there was no money with which to buy or to build, for the only fund available was the ordinary income, for the most part already appropriated for the salaries of the professors.

The Board of Trustees met at once and decided to begin the work of rebuilding and refurnishing without delay. The remaining building was refitted as well as was possible, and word was sent forth that the work would begin as usual in September; for this fire, like the one nineteen years before, had come in vacation.

It was decided to abandon the old campus, too small for future expansion, and so near the railroad that the noise of the trains interfered with the work. The Board selected as the future University campus that high, rolling tract of woodland on the east side of town known to twenty student generations as "Dunn's Woods."

A donation of $50,000 was made by Monroe County, and with this and some $20,000 received as insurance money, two buildings of brick and stone, "Wylie Hall" and "Owen Hall," were built on the new grounds. A less pretentious wooden building, "Maxwell Hall," was built for the reception of those classes which could not find room in Owen Hall, and in the fall of 1885 all the collegiate work was removed to the new grounds. Afterward, the General Assembly of 1886 appropriated the sum of $43,000 for the purpose of providing books, specimens, apparatus and the furniture needed in the new buildings.

Dr. Moss resigned the presidency in November, 1884, and Rev. Elisha Ballantine, D.D., was made acting president until his successor was elected. The most important event in the administration of Dr. Moss was the securing of the University Endowment Fund. The friends of the institution had long felt the importance of some permanent provision for its maintenance. As early as 1828, Governor Ray had pressed upon the General Assembly the propriety of providing an endowment, but over half a century passed before anything was done in this regard.

In the fall of 1882 the Board of Trustees, thinking that the time was propitious for legislative action, caused the preparation of a bill for the permanent endowment of the University.

The Alumni all over the State gave the measure the weight of their influence, while those of their number who were members of that Fifty-third Assembly were active in its support.

This act, which became a law on the 3d of March, 1883, provides that "in the year 1883, and in each of the next succeeding twelve years, there shall be collected a half-mill tax, which shall be placed to the credit of a fund to be known as the 'Permanent Endowment Fund of the Indiana University.'" It was hoped by the projectors of this scheme that this fund would amount, in thirteen years, to half a million dollars, but it is likely to fall considerably below this sum.

The resignation of Dr. Moss was followed, January 1, 1885, by the election of David Starr Jordan as president. Dr. Jordan has held for five years the Chair of Biology in the University. The chief change in his administration has been in the direction of the specialization of the work of the different departments, and in the great extension of the elective work in the different courses of study. That this change was met with popular approval is evident from the fact that the attendance in the college classes has more than doubled with the introduction of greater freedom of choice. Still more marked is the improvement in the general character and thoroughness of the work done in the different departments.

The increase in the number of students and the increase in the number of professors rendered imperative the demand for more room. This need was laid before the last General Assembly, and an act was passed appropriating $60,000 for the erection and equipment for a fire-proof Library building.

Besides this, an additional sum of $7,000 per year for the next two years was granted. In view of this, the Board of Trustees, in response to what seems to be a general demand, have restored the Department of Law.

This institution, as Seminary, Collge and University, has been in active operation for sixty-six years—the oldest college in the State, and one of the oldest in the West. Notwithstanding the misfortunes it has from time to time encountered, it has never been closed to students for a single school day in all that time. The entire course of its history has been marked by a steady purpose to promote the welfare of the State through the education of its youth.

From first to last about 4,000 students have been trained in its hall, of which number 902 have been honored by its bachelor's degree.

This number, 4,000, is exclusive of the Seminary students, of whom no record exists. It also excludes the students in the Preparatory School (1,581 in number before 1888) who did not enter college, and the law students, 603 in number, of whom 384 obtained the diploma of LL. B. The aggregate total of different names from the date of the first catalogue to 1888 is 5,860, to which the past two years add about 400 more.

Who can estimate its influence in the past? Who can forecast it for the future?

Annual Catalogue of the Indiana University for the Sixty-Sixth College Year, 1889–1890, pp. 76–81.

Document 87

The Jordan Stewardship

This annual report of Isaac Jenkinson is an important one. It is in essence a report on the administration of David Starr Jordan. Despite the outline of needs of the University there is a note of optimism in the report. The number of students had increased, and so had the number of faculty members. The preparatory school had been discontinued, a fact which indicated material improvement in the Indiana system of public education. Reflecting the pressures put on the University by the private institutions, the President of the Board emphasized that it was a school for Hoosiers of limited means and of good moral character.

*   *   *

PRESIDENT'S REPORT

INDIANAPOLIS, IND., December 11, 1890.

To the Honorable, ALVIN P. HOVEY,

Governor of Indiana:

DEAR SIR—I have the honor of transmitting to you herewith the biennial report of the Board of Trustees of the Indiana University for the fiscal years ending October 31, 1889, and October 31, 1890.

And accompanying this report permit me to make a brief statement of the present condition of the University and of its most pressing needs.

The growth of the University within the last five years has been very rapid. Contrasting the present condition of the University with that of five years ago we find that the number of students has increased 150 per cent., the number of teachers employed 90 percent., the number of different classes taught 250 per cent., and amount paid yearly in salaries by about 85 per cent. In 1885 the total number of students in attendance in the college classes was 156, there being twenty-six members in the graduating class. For the present year the total enrollment will not be less than 360 (exclusive of about twenty-five persons taking studies in law only), and the graduating class in the "liberal arts" numbers seventy. In considering these numbers it should be borne in mind that the Indiana University now maintains no preparatory school. None of the work of the high schools or of other parts of the public school system is now duplicated in the University. As its instruction begins where the work of the high school leaves off, its lowest class is composed of those who have successfully completed the course of the high school or a fair equivalent. There are but two or three other colleges in the West which have as large a number of students in the college proper, as distinguished from preparatory and professional schools.

The various sections of the State are all well represented in the University. Students are now in attendance from seventy-five of the ninety-two counties. The counties of the State which have sent no students within the past three years are eight in number, as follows:

Lake, Porter, Starke, Steuben, Newton, Parke, Tipton, Ohio.

In the same period the counties best represented have been: Monroe, Wayne,

Marion, Madison, Morgan, Decatur, Carroll, Lawrence, Bartholomew and Posey.

The matter of numbers is in itself no test of the value or the success of any institution of learning, for the most advanced students in any department of study are few. It can, however, be said that the best students will go where the best work is done, and the Indiana University will never lack for numbers as long as its instruction is thorough, and its work is abreast of modern thought and modern methods.

More important than the fact of the increase of numbers is the fact of the steady improvement in the quality of the work done by the professors and students. The reputation of the University, both within and without the State, has been constantly rising. No well informed person now speaks with disrespect of the work done in the University, while among college men throughout the country, the Indiana University is regarded as one of the most progressive and most promising schools in the United States. It may be further said that the Indiana University is especially a school for persons of limited means. Expenses are lower in Bloomington than in any other town in the West which is the seat of a State University. The great majority of the students are not rich, and fully three-fourths of them have earned, by their own work, much or all of the money spent on their education. Connected with this lack of money for lavish expenditure is the fact that in no institution are the students, as a body, more earnest, or their moral tone higher, than in the State University.

The chief immediate needs of the University may be briefly summed up as follows:

1. A public hall and chapel building. The University has no room suitable for general lectures or for its own public exercises. The little temporary chapel in Maxwell Hall, with seats for 225, has been wholly outgrown, and there is imperative need of a new building which shall contain a commodious hall and a number of office and recitation rooms.

2. Equally pressing is the need of suitable accommodations for the large and growing Department of Physics. While technical training is not given in the University, the demand for thorough instruction in General Physics on the part of teachers and others is very great. The Physical Laboratory must be in a building free from iron girders, and constructed especially to meet the needs of the department. Such a building need not be large or costly, but it must be fitted for its purpose.

3. The University has pressing need of a gymnasium for the work of physical culture.

Very respectfully yours,
ISAAC JENKINSON,
President of the Board of
Trustees of the Indiana
University.

Indiana *Documentary Journal,* 1890.

Document 88

"Uncle Joe" Swain's Perspective

President Joseph Swain, a native Hoosier of Quaker persuasion, succeeded John Coulter as President of the University in 1893. During the preceding eight years the institution had definitely gained momentum. All of its "life" statistics had gained, and for the first time it could take some satisfaction in the fact that it was beginning to achieve elementary university status at least. The challenge was great in the 1890s, not only to continue the forward thrust generated by Jordan, but to overcome the historical inertia created by the state of Indiana itself. Swain's inaugural address is a common-sense document, neither dreaming too romantically nor peddling too much negativism. It was a blueprint which the new president undertook in the next decade to develop. Few inaugural addresses have reflected so clearly the personality and philosophy of a president.

*   *   *

ADDRESS

I am sensible of the great honor bestowed upon me by our honorable Trustees in electing me to the presidency of Indiana University. I should never have sought the position to which I come to-day. I may well shrink from the responsibilities it imposes, but if it is right that I should be here, and if all the friends of the University give the institution their sympathetic co-operation, with divine guidance, I trust there will come that strength which the work demands.

To return to my native state in which I have a just pride; to my *Alma Mater,* an institution which I have loved with a filial devotion; to the faculty which I have known and honored; to the alumni which each year are increasing in number and influence; to the students for whom the University exists; to the city of Bloomington, for twelve years my home; to the people who have treated me with uniform kindness and whose friendship I cherish; and to all the friends of the University; this is indeed a pleasure. Nevertheless, I now accept the trust which you give into my keeping, with an even keener appreciation of the duties it imposes, than of the honor you bestow, or of the pleasures which I feel on my return. But with the determination and inspiration which come from a sense of this "high calling," be my stay long or short, I shall work as if I were to remain for a lifetime, and I ask you all to give me your hearty, undivided, and continued support.

A state university is indeed a public trust, and sooner or later the people of the state will see to it that this University is built "higher and broader and deeper" than any ideal which we may now contemplate. It is well that Leland Stanford and John D. Rockefeller devote their millions to the building of great universities, but were there such an endowed institution in every state in the Union, it would only strengthen and not retard the growth of the State University. The efficiency of the University of California has increased more within the past two years than within any other period of the same length in its history. This is not only manifest in the increased number of its students, but in the improvement and breadth of its work. Thus, the establishment of Stanford University has not only given California a new institution, but it has at the same time been of great service to the State University. In turn the State University is necessary to the highest development of the newer institution, and the efficient work of the former has made the latter possible. Likewise in this state every seat of learning is strengthened by the growth of the State University. Besides, the dignity and self-respect of a state is lost when it depends wholly upon denominational institutions, or upon institutions endowed by private munificence, however, excellent in character they may be. In time to come the people of the state will feel that this University is their own in a yet more special sense, and they will provide for it more abundantly. In contributing to the maintenance and growth of the State University we not only make better every high school in the state, and therefore the common schools, but every step of the University in advance compels like steps in the other colleges and private schools of the state. The good results of the changes in the curriculum in this University, which were made eight years ago, are evident not only in the higher institutions of learning in this state, and consequently in the lower schools, but these changes have had a beneficial effect on other institutions of learning outside the state, as well. In like manner every advance made in other universities or colleges is helpful to us. Let denominational and private seats of learning rise and flourish. Each has its purpose and results. In most states, however, we shall expect most from a university endowed by two millions of people, and especially in a state such as this where its wealth is almost equally distributed.

While a state university is peculiarly the child of the state and must be watched and guarded and fostered by it, its immediate guardians must be its trustees. And who are these trustees? These are its Board, its Faculty, its Alumni, its students, and such citizens of the state and friends of the University as acquaint themselves with its highest purposes and aims.

The Board and the Faculty are by their relation to the University pledged to do everything in their power to promote the growth of the institution until it shall meet every demand of a growing state. In no other institution which I know has there been more self-sacrifice on the part of these bodies, and so much done with the same means, as in this. No great institution can be built if men stop to ask, "What will be my reward for this work?"

I feel sure that however deserving and loyal other men may have been it will not be unfitting to mention two—one of the Board of Trustees who a year ago passed to his reward, with the love of a grateful community. Dr. James D. Maxwell, in his fidelity, his unswerving self-sacrifice day after day for a long and useful lifetime, is a type of such men as have made Indiana University possible. The other to whom I refer is Daniel Kirkwood. The learning, the wisdom, the manhood, the unselfish devotion to an ideal in life as well as in scholarship, of this beloved and great man, now far advanced in years—these are a heritage of the institution, the magnificence and proportions of which words can merely suggest. Here and now our Board and Faculty may well dedicate themselves anew to the further achievement of those high ends for which these men have spent their lives.

The Alumni are in a special sense trustees of this University. In half a century the institution has sent out many of the strongest men which the state possesses. Our graduates are found engaged in every worthy pursuit. "By their achievements they are commending their dear mother, not only for the mental discipline she gave them, but for the brave, earnest, manly spirit which by her free methods and by the character of her teachers she has nourished in them." [Angel.] Fellow Alumni, the University must be judged by the work it does. As its debtors, as its product and as men who stand for the welfare of the state, we must not be content to rest on past achievements and present laurels, but we must see to it that means are provided by which this, our *Alma Mater,* may become the ideal, the "People's University." We by our past and present knowledge are not only in touch with the University, but by our widely diverging pursuits and by our geographical distribution, are acquainted with the needs and wants of the state. It is ours to keep alive a love of the arts and sciences among the masses; to see that the University keeps pace with the needs of the state; to do all in our power to give the University that substantial support which shall insure to her the best library, the best laboratories, the best men. We can afford nothing but the *best*, in our *Alma Mater.*

Students of the University, but for you none of us would be here. It is for your needs, and it is to develop the possibilities within you that the University exists. In affording you the advantages of higher education the state is in no sense making you a gift. It invests its capital in you as the cheapest and best means of protecting itself. The nations of the earth have in the past spent their hard earned millions in support of standing armies, but we in the United States are beginning to see that our millions must be spent in making men and women. If this institution equips you as you should be, and gives you the armor which fits you to battle with life, we recognize that "you will cultivate this public sentiment in favor of the University which will find its expression in ample endowments and crowded halls."

It has been well said that this University is as the "apple of its eye" to the city of Bloomington. Its citizens are in an important sense trustees of the University. To them is entrusted for four years the care of the young men and young women who take a course in this institution. It is for us to see that our city is the best place in the world for these young men and women, a place where those exalted principles of life, which are the possession of every really educated man and women, are *known* and *lived* up to. As another has well said: "To use the phrase which the lips of Lincoln have made commonplace, the University is of the people, for the people, by the people. Of the people, in its establishment, in its recognized place through legislation. They are its organizers and upholders. For the people in its very existence; it is originated, built up, maintained, for them. By the people, in its administration." [Kellog.] The people elect the legislature, the legislature provides means for the appointment of the Board, the Board selects the faculty. As that portion of the people nearest the University and who have the best opportunity to know its condition and needs, the citizens of Bloomington have a special and an emphatic trust. Let us continue to stand for all that is good and true in the life of the University.

To all the friends of the University everywhere, let me say: come join hands and make this what it should be, the ideal university, the University of the state.

"I would found," said Ezra Cornell, "an institution where any person can find instruction in any study." Make this the *best* instruction in any study and we have the ideal university. "Its courses of study would be so broad, so thorough and complete, that no young man or woman of Indiana would need to leave the state to secure the best education the world affords." [Jordan.] Such a university must be modern, democratic, human, and in its instruction must be largely individual.

The modern university is the product of modern life. All subjects which can be reduced to a science should have equal attention in its curriculum, and every branch of human inquiry should command its share of the time and attention of university men. While it must sacredly "preserve all the treasures of the past, and must not neglect the spirit and refinement of the old-time scholars," it must most of all recognize the demands of the living present, and extend the boundaries of human knowledge by countless pathways into the infinite creations and thoughts of God, in whom these pathways meet.

The State University exists for the state and must therefore be democratic. The young man from the farm, from behind the counter, stands side by side with the son of the minister, the doctor, and the lawyer. In a people's university there can be no aristocracy of trade, profession, or wealth. The only road to high regard and distinction is through the avenue of superior excellence. This avenue is one through which the poor man's son is more likely to pass than the son of the rich man. Poverty in itself has no virtue; but the qualities of mind and heart which have grown while overcoming poverty, and have led the young man to consecrate himself to the highest things are, "more to be desired than gold, yea than much fine gold."

A university must recognize its environment. Yet an institution of learning would be foolish indeed should it accept and promulgate any current theory simply because it is current. To teach either free trade or protection because either is the theory of the party in power, would be unworthy of and wholly contrary to the ideals of the scholar. It should be the duty of the university to examine into every question, industrial, historical, philosophical, political, scientific, which is of present or future interest to the people of the state. To gather together all the facts of experience and the thoughts of the profoundest thinkers on these questions and place before the students and people a scientific treatment of the subject, is of the utmost importance. The safety and progress of the state demand it.

Dr. Jordan once said: "If our work is successful, our ideals will appear in the daily life of the school. In a school as in a fortress, it is not the form of the building, but the strength of the materials, which determines its effectiveness. With a garrison of hearts of oak, it may not even matter whether there be a fortress. Whatever its form, or its organization, or its pretension, the character of the university is fixed by the men who teach. 'Have a university in shanties, nay, in tents,' Cardinal Newman has said, 'but have great teachers in it.' The university spirit flows out from these teachers, and its organization serves mainly to bring them together. 'The University,' to use Emerson's words, 'should bring every ray of light to its hospitable walls, that their combined influence may set the heart of the youth in flame.' Strong men make universities strong. A great man never fails to leave a great mark on every youth with whom he comes in contact. Too much emphasis can not be laid on this, that the real purpose of the university organization is to produce a university atmosphere, such an atmosphere as gathered itself around Arnold at Rugby, around Döllinger at Munich, around Linnaeus at Upsala, around Mark Hopkins at Williamstown, around White at Ithaca, around all great teachers everywhere."

"The university should be the great refuge hut on the ultimate boundaries of knowledge, from which daily and weekly adventurous bands set out on voyages of discovery. It should be the Upernavik from which polar travelers draw their supplies, and, as the shoreless sea of the unknown meets us on every side, the same house of refuge and supply will serve for a thousand different exploring parties, moving out in every direction into the infinite ocean. This is the university ideal of the future."

Indiana University is not yet the ideal university, but she has the spirit of modern progress. She was one of the first to recognize the equal rights of the sexes, and men have always been upon equal footing within her walls. The fact that nine years ago there were but 156 students in this institution, while this present year there are five hundred and seventy-two, twenty-two of whom are graduate students, but feebly indicates the difference between the old conditions and the freedom and growth which have come with modern spirit. The adoption of the seminary and laboratory methods in nearly all the departments of the University; the extension of the elective system, enabling a student to select those studies for which nature has given him aptitude, and which are in some way related to his future life; the increased earnestness and greater ambition on the part of our students; the tendency of students to continue for a lifetime work begun in college; the universal desire on the part of teachers and students to extend the boundaries of human knowledge and to send out to the world in some published form the results of their work; the popularization of the University by University Extension and other means; the growing tendency to consider degrees, if given at all, as arbitrary landmarks in one's journey, and nothing for which one should turn aside; the fact that the university student is amenable to the laws of the state and has no privileges which the best citizen would not claim for himself; that it is as much the duty of the student as of the professor to see that no one shall do aught to bring the university into discredit—these facts and tendencies are much more important in the usefulness of the institution than mere numbers. This work is not so much the result of the efforts of any man or set of men as it is the product of the age.

The fact that we in our university life have already reached a high plane makes it possible for us not only to see distinctly the winding valley through which we have passed, but compels us to look up and beyond to the great ridge of the mountain which lies before us, inviting us to its ascent. Our present vantage ground gives us an intimation of the possibilities before us, and having ascended the foot-hills and gained the first ridge of the mountain we can never rest content until we have scaled to yet more and more exalted heights this mountain of university progress.

The needs of the University are appearing on every side. While she stands in the front rank among state universities her needs are manifold and imperative, if we are to retain the vantage ground which we now have. That $50,000 were given by our last legislature for a new building and our annual appropriation increased by $10,000, notwithstanding adverse circumstances, shows a friendly relation to and a faith in the University on the part of the state. With an income of about $80,000 we can do more next year than during any previous year in our history, but when we remember that Cornell University, the State University of New York, has an annual income of more than $500,000, the University of California about $350,000, the University of Michigan over $300,000, the University of Wisconsin about $275,000, and each of these institutions, except Cornell, located in a state of less wealth and smaller population than Indiana, we find that we do not yet provide as well for the wants of the State University as do our sister states. No institution anywhere of equal means stands so high among scholars as this. She is always compared with those of much greater wealth. In no university has the income been more wisely expended. Every dollar spent in equipping Indiana University has counted for much more than a dollar in the promotion of civilization in Indiana.

The encouraging lesson from our sister states is this: the greater the development of the higher institutions of learning, the more determination there seems to be on the part of the states to provide still more ample means for their expansion and for increasing their efficiency. In general the growth of this University must first be in the direction of still greater efficiency, and expansion will follow as a consequence. Our teachers now, in common with the teachers of other schools in the state, give too many hours to instruction. No university teacher with modern demands can do his best for three or four consecutive hours in different topics, especially with the more advanced students. If a lawyer should be required to speak three or four hours every day before a jury, his client would soon find it to his interest to go elsewhere and obtain counsel having the time to acquaint himself with the facts bearing on the individual case in hand, then to examine the law in the case and to arrange his arguments. But it is said the teacher should know what he is going to teach before he begins his work. This is not more true in the case of the teachers than in the case of the lawyer. The possibilities of any subject are infinite and it is the duty of the teacher to open up these possibilities to the student. He who presents this year the same matter in exactly the same manner in which he presented it last year is by so much behind the times. A multitude of workers in every department of inquiry are adding new material and methods of work, and the teacher needs more time to master these and to make excursions of his own. If our instruction is to be the best, the work of the teacher must be largely individual, and this means a reduction in the size of the classes. The lecture has its place, but it is introductory or collateral and not the chief thing. Both the reduction of the number of teaching hours and the reduction of the size of the class, implies additions to our force of instructors. Harvard has to-day a teacher for every nine students.

It is becoming well known that Indiana University is a "training school" for professors of more wealthy and larger institutions. No better encomium could be paid to the men who have selected her faculty. It is now recognized that a succession of the best equipped young men is to be preferred to a more permanent corps of instructors who have reached their level at $1,500 a year. Even with our increased income we must still depend on rising young men, but we can at once hold them up to a higher level than the one at which they have been taken from us in the past.

There are general needs of the institution which I may mention here. We need funds to vastly increase at once the facilities of our library. While it is the best working library of its size in the state, it is yet far short of our needs. Anything short of all the available books on any topic is unsatisfactory. No teacher or student can be sure that he is abreast of the times unless he has access to or is familiar with all that has been published in his line of investigation. We need more room and equipment and consequently a greater teaching force for physical training. Systematic instruction and training in the gymnasium is now recognized to be the natural and necessary accompaniment of the modern university. Athletics should be under the direction of a medical director who is an expert in medical science, who knows the laws of the development of the human body, and who can seize upon and direct the best instincts of college men. In general a sound body is the condition of a sound mind, and physical training is now the outlet for the animal energies of the college man. Wisely directed athletics in the modern university, by giving a legitimate outlet to the student's God-given animal spirits, has done more than any other one thing to eliminate class rows, hazing, vandalism, and other forms of time-worn traditional rowdyism.

When I leave the general needs of the University and turn to the departments I find urgent demands in every direction. While I recognize the perfect equality of departments, it will not be unfitting to illustrate our needs by citing the needs of one. In the department of Physics we need a new laboratory building, additional equipment, and consequently additional instructors. The fact that there is great demand on the part of the High Schools of the state for teachers in physics is reason enough that the University should equip herself for preparing these teachers in the best possible way. But this is only one reason. The training obtained through the use of the best instruments and methods in the modern physical laboratory, carrying delicate experiments to the utmost refinement of accuracy, is inestimable in value in the subsequent work of the student, it matters not in what field it may be. Its wide application to the wants of modern life makes it apply in a special way to the immediate needs of the state.

What I have just said concerning the needs of the department of physics, may, with slight modifications, be justly said concerning many departments now in the University and those that are yet to come. It is for us, the trustees, to make known these wants to the state, and we may depend upon the impetus of every institution of higher learning and upon the spirit of the age to help us gain one more ledge of the mountain.

It is as true of institutions as of individuals that the world will help those who have first learned to help themselves. I have already called attention to the devotion of its friends to the University. They have done all in the past that they could. The University must be chiefly maintained by the state, but has not the time come, when we, as do the universities of other states, should receive something from private sources? Cornell University, the State University of New York, owes the greater part of its wealth to private munificence. Henry W. Sage alone gave $1,500,000. There is not only the fortune of Ezra Cornell, but also the magnificent library building, the Young Men's Christian Association building, Sibley College, Sage College, beside other buildings. The endowed department of Philosophy, scholarships and other gifts, are the substantial recognitions by private capital of the worth of that institution. To the University of California was given the Lick Observatory. The gift of a citizen built the assembly hall and endowed the chair of Philosophy, and numerous fellowships testify to the loyalty of friends.

The doctrine that the state universities are to be supported from the treasury of the state is well established, but that it should receive help from every possible source should also be evident. There is ample opportunity in the University for persons of small or large means to do something for higher education in Indiana. A book to the library, a scholarship to help some struggling student, a building in honor of some persons, the endowment of a department, while benefiting the coming ages, each would have its place and would not be lost to the individual giving it, in the larger fame of the University. The University would welcome assistance from any quarter in any department whatever. We should do the thing which, in view of all the conditions, we can do best.

And now to our departing President I would say: You with your associates have kept the light burning; you have added fuel to its flame; you have carried it nearer to the top of the mountain. From its greater elevation it commands a larger horizon. From its intenser brilliancy it shines with a greater luster. Indiana University would have been fortunate indeed to have had you continue to bear her colors from ledge to ledge, but other possibilities and other duties open out before you. May that brilliant success which you have here achieved be even more marked in your new positions. We congratulate the university to which you go; you have our friendship and our highest hopes. The prayers of this community are with you. When you come to another milestone in life's journey, may all about you say, as they do here, well done, well done.

Inaugural address of Joseph Swain, June 14, 1893; Annual Commencement of Indiana University.

Document 89

A Rising Reputation, and Lagging Support

Isaac Jenkinson's Report for 1893–1894 described a university which had almost doubled its student enrollment, but had done so without adequate building and library facilities. There was the cheering note that "No well informed person now speaks with disrespect of the work done in the University. . . ." Also, Jenkinson reflected the sobering effects of Jordan's raiding the Indiana faculty, and the loss of professors to other institutions.

* * *

PRESIDENT'S REPORT

INDIANAPOLIS, IND., Dec. 1, 1894.

To the HON. CLAUDE MATTHEWS, *Governor of Indiana:*

DEAR SIR—I have the honor of herewith transmitting to you the biennial report of the Board of Trustees of the Indiana University for the fiscal years ending October 31, 1893, and October 31, 1894.

The progress of the University during the past two years has been gratifying to all friends of higher education. This progress has been not chiefly in the number of students, but much more in the increasing favorable recognition of the University among the educators of the country. The University is known to be one of the most progressive of our institutions, and its peculiar organization of work has attracted wide attention and imitation.

The matter of numbers is in itself not test of the value or the success of an institution of learning, for the most advanced students in any department of study are few. It can however, be said that the best students will go where the best work is done, and the Indiana University will never lack for numbers so long as its instruction is thorough, and its work is abreast of modern thought and modern methods.

More important than the fact of the increase of numbers is the fact of steady improvement in the quality of the work done by professors and students. The reputation of the University, both within and without the State, has been constantly rising. No well informed person now speaks with disrespect of the work done in the University, while among college men throughout the country, the Indiana University is regarded as one of the most promising schools in the United States. It may be further said that the Indiana University is especially a school for persons of limited means. The great majority of the students are not rich, and full three-fourths of them have earned, by their own work much or all of the money spent on their education. Connected with this lack of money for lavish expenditures is the fact that in no institution are the students, as a body, more earnest, or their moral tone higher, than in the State University.

Seventeen departments of work are now organized, each department representing some great subject in which three or four years of work are offered. The scope of these subjects, as illustrating the great fields of knowledge open to the young men and women of Indiana, is indicated by the following enumeration: (1) Greek, (2) Latin, (3) Romance Languages, (4) Germanic Languages, (5) English, (6) European History, (7) American History, (8) Economics and Social Science, (9) Philosophy, (10) Pedagogics, (11) Pure Mathematics, (12)

Physics, (13) Chemistry, (14) Geology, (15) Zoology, (16) Botany, (17) Law. With this presentation of subjects it is evident that our young people can have a very wide range of choice in training. It is considered no longer a tenable proposition that all kinds of minds demand the same kind of training. There is the greatest diversity of gifts, and this must be provided for in any rational system of education.

The only purpose of education is to develop power, and this can be developed by the proper study of any subject, but it is much aided if that subject has the consent of the pupil's taste. The widest liberty, is, therefore, given by the University in the selection of subjects. However, there are groups of subjects which prominently stand for culture, and a certain amount of selection from these groups is required.

It is shown that distorted courses are practically unknown; that the proportion among subjects is practically what it was under prescription; that German among languages holds the first place in numbers of students, but the Greek shows the most graduates; that such studies as language, history and economics attract a far larger student body than do either the physical or biological sciences; that very few students graduate with only the minimum requirement. Better results than these which have been tabulated are those which show that this policy has improved the whole student body, by developing self-reliance and that interest which comes from responsibility, and has wonderfully improved teaching through the stimulus of interested learners.

It is these methods and results which have called attention to the University. It will be remembered that Indiana University no longer maintains any preparatory department, none of the work of the high schools or of other parts of the public school system being now duplicated in the University. Its work begins where that of the commissioned high school ends and it is constantly becoming more intimately connected with these schools. That this relationship is becoming more widely recognized throughout the State is testified by the fact that during the present year eighty-one of our ninety-two counties have sent pupils from their schools to the University.

In comparing the attendance at the University with that of other institutions it must be remembered that the University maintains no preparatory or professional schools of any kind, excepting that of law, and that in these various schools will be found the largest part of the attendance of the universities that maintain them.

A tabulated view of the attendance for the last twelve years will show the development of the University within recent years:

Year	Attendance	
1884	144	21
1885	156	26
1886	202	20
1887	263	22
1888	275	39
1889	300	41
1890	321	47
1891	394	75
1892	497	70
1893	576	68
1894	633	76
1895	*740	85

* Estimated from those now in attendance.

It will be noticed that the attendance has been nearly doubled within the last four years, and this has necessitated a large increase in the force of instruction and an overwhelming demand for room.

In everything that goes to make a university, such as numbers in college classes, variety of subjects presented, method of work, opportunities for advanced and original work, Indiana University stands very high among the universities of neighboring States; but in the matter of material, equipment and income, it stands very low. A study of the following table will show that the State of Indiana can show more for every dollar it has invested in its University than any neighboring State; and it will also indicate what results the State may hope for when it takes a financial interest in the University commensurate with its own resources. The following is the showing: [table omitted]

I desire to call careful attention also to the following extracts from the President's report to the Board of Regents of the University of Michigan for 1891. President Angell by his long service is more competent than any other man to speak of the position of State Universities in the west:

"While we can not but be gratified by the growth of this University during the last twenty years, we also observe with great satisfaction that there has been rapid development of the State Universities generally throughout the west. Their progress, and we may say in the case of almost every one, their assured success, are proofs that the principle on which this Institution was founded is sound, and makes it reasonably certain that the great universities of the west and southwest are, as a rule, to be those established and supported by the State. They have all frequently and gratefully testified to the helpful influence of this University upon their life. They have, in a large degree, followed our methods. In their success and in their promise we can heartily rejoice. From their increasing strength we also draw strength. Every State from Ohio to California and from North Dakota to Texas now has its State University. Some of these institutions have encountered great difficulties and bitter opposition. But in almost every State of the west, the State university is the best endowed, the best equipped and the most universally attended institution of higher education in the State. The objections raised to them at the outset have proved to be in the main groundless. The States are committed to their support by the large expenditures already made upon them and by the power of public sentiment, which naturally looks with favor on the universities that offer the best type of higher education in arts, in technology and in the professions, almost without money and without price, to every young man and every young woman. While in the east, the higher education will continue to be furnished by institutions resting on private endowments, in the west and southwest, though similarly endowed colleges will flourish and do a useful work, the great universities will almost exclusively be those sustained by the States."

The pressing needs of Indiana University are as follows:

1. ADDITIONAL BUILDINGS.—With the completion of Kirkwood Hall, two of the departments will still be in basements never designed for class-room work. Four of the professors will have their rooms in an attic, and six of the teachers will still have their classes in the libary. No adequate assembly room is to be found on the grounds of the University, there being no provision for large assemblies. The University needs an assembly room, a science building, a gymnasium, a building for history and political science and English and a general heating plant. These should cost not less than $250,000.

2. ADDITIONAL INCOME.—It goes without saying that the increase of thirty per cent. on the number of students since the last meeting of the Legislature

makes an increase in our appropriation for professors' salaries necessary. Not only is the additional appropriation for additional teachers necessary, but the great demand for our teachers in other institutions makes it necessary that we should pay some of our faculty more money. The best men are the cheapest men in the long run. During the past four years Indiana University has lost fifteen professors who are now getting outside the State $1,000 more than twice the salaries received in Indiana University.

3. ADDITIONAL LIBRARY FUNDS.—The entire work of the Uversity depends upon its library more than upon any other one kind of equipment. It will be remembered that the library was completely destroyed in 1883. Since that time the attempt has been made to keep up with current publications, and to complete a few sets of periodical publications. Special provision, however, should be made that will at once enable the library to somewhat extensively complete valuable sets of periodicals. It would, therefore, be a very wise measure to secure at once for the libary of the University, by a special appropriation, a sufficient equipment of books and periodicals to make it useful and attractive to advanced students and investigators. Very respectfully yours,

ISAAC JENKINSON,
President Board of Trustees.

Indiana *Documentary Journal*, 1894.

Document 90

The "Golden Nineties"

The Committee on Salaries no doubt took the golden age of William McKinley seriously. The Board of Trustees adopted this salary scale, and it was to serve as a basic one for a long time to come.

*   *   *

"Gentlemen of the Board:—
Your committee on salaries recommend the following scale of salaries:—
Professors:—$2000 to $2500.
Associate Professors:—$1500 to $2000.
Assistant Professors:—$1000 to $1500.
Instructors:—$500 to $1000.
Laboratory Assistants:—$100 to $500.

The basis for determination within these limits shall be value of servies to the University from length of service, special preparation, amount of work, and power to inspire pupils and to represent the University in a public way.

R A OGG
R I HAMILTON } Committee
NAT U HILL

Board Minutes, 1897–1910, p. 38.

Document 91

Building Self-Esteem

Many times throughout the years down to 1900, Indiana professors, the presidents, and the Board of Trustees almost seem to question the validity of their institution. In 1898–1899 the University reached one objective at least: every county in the state was represented in the student enrollment. Included in this statement of faith and objectives are the testimonials of friends of the University from outside Indiana. Of all of these Jacob C. Schurman's was undoubtedly the most heartening.

*   *   *

THE GROWTH OF INDIANA UNIVERSITY.
[From the Indiana School Journal, August, 1899]

The Enrollment this Year Exceeds One Thousand. For the second time in its history, the annual enrollment of students in Indiana University exceeds one thousand. The catalogue for the year just closed was issued in June, 1899, and the figures given therein are pleasing to every friend of higher education in Indiana. Old students have frequently said they hoped to see the day when Indiana University would have a thousand students. This hope has been more than realized, and the future is filled with even greater promises.

The exact enrollment for the present year is one thousand and fifty. Of these, seven hundred and thirty-two are men and three hundred and eighteen are women. During the year 1898-99 *every County in Indiana was represented.*

The present institution began its existence at Bloomington, as the Indiana Seminary, in 1820, was made a college by act of Legislature in 1828, and a university in name in 1838. The annual attendance prior to 1850 ranged from thirty-eight in 1841 to one hundred and fifteen in 1846. From 1850 to 1884 the smallest attendance in the University was forty-eight in 1853, one hundred and ninety in 1881. The remarkable growth since that time is best told by the figures:

YEAR.	TOTAL.	GRADUATES.
1884	144	21
1885	156	26
1886	202	20
1887	263	22
1888	275	39
1889	300	41
1890	321	51
1891	394	76
1892	497	66
1893	572	81
1894	638	96
1895	771	91

1896...........................879...........................115
1897...........................944...........................130
1898..........................1049...........................119
1899..........................1050...........................126

Thus for sixteen years each year has shown a substantial increase over the preceding one. The growth began under the administration of President David Starr Jordan, continued under the administration of President John Merle Coulter, and under the administration of President Swain (1893–1899) the attendance has increased from five hundred and seventy-two to one thousand and fifty.

In view of the fact that the University does not have a preparatory department, that the standard of admission is being constantly raised, and the classroom work being made more thorough, the enormous attendance, as shown in the above figures, indicates that the people of Indiana are loyal to the head of the State's great educational system.

THE INDIANA UNIVERSITY SUBMITS THE FOLLOWING OPINIONS IN THE BELIEF THAT MANY PERSONS AT THE PRESENT TIME ARE INTERESTED IN THE STANDING OF THE INSTITUTION.

From William R. Harper, President of Chicago University.

Deserves the Support of the State.

"The Indiana University has won a high standing through the reputation of the men who have served in its faculty, and from those who have been called elsewhere, as well as through the character of the graduates whom it has sent to other institutions. I believe most heartily that it fully deserves the support of the State which it represents."

From Benjamin Ide Wheeler, Professor of Greek in Cornell University,
Ithaca, N.Y.

Vigorous and Promising.

"The faculty of Indiana University has contained within the past ten years some of the most vigorous and promising men in the country. I believe the tone of the University has been aggressive and earnest, and the character of the graduates whom I have met here particularly confirms that belief."

From John M. Coulter, Ex-President of Lake Forest University, now
Professor of Botany in the University of Chicago.

Does More with Less Money.

"I am glad to say now, as I have always said, that Indiana University does more with less money than any institution I know of. It is thoroughly permeated by the right spirit, and has little of that ancient rubbish to impede it which clings about some of our universities. Contentions as to educational methods have been going on vigorously for years, but the observant student can note that there is an annual march of curricula toward the Indiana plan. Of all the interests which come under the Legislature's care none brings a greater reputation to the State than Indiana University, none generates as much force to be used in the State."

From Edward A. Ross, Professor of Economics in Leland Stanford, Jr.,
University, Palo Alto, California.

Plain, Practical, Effective Kind of University Education.

"I know of no institution in the country of same pay and opportunities that has been able to enjoy the services of a body of men equal in ability and training to those that have worked in Indiana University. Selection and care, progressiveness and reputation have done for Indiana University all that they can do in the way of getting and holding able men.

"As regards the students from Indiana University, I find them to be sober, earnest, painstaking, diligent and unpretentious. The Indiana University men are free from the pretention and caste of spirit of higher education, but exhibit in the highest degree its solidity, worth and availability for usefulness in every walk of life. There is no other institution in Indiana that is doing anything like the service of Indiana University in leading the way toward a plain, practical, modest, effective and earnest kind of university education."

Fr. J. McK. Cattell, Professor of Experimental Psychology in the Columbia
University, New York City, and Editor of "Science."

Contributes
Greatly to
Educational
Advancement

"In my own department the work done at Indiana University has been of a very high order, equaling that of any other university. As far as I am competent to form an opinion, the work accomplished by the faculty of Indiana University has contributed greatly to the advancement of science and educational methods in America."

From Jacob G. Schurman, President of Cornell University,
Ithaca, New York.

Assures any
Scholar of the
High Standing
of the Faculty.

"Reference to a score of professors who have taught at Indiana University and have been called to higher positions in institutions scattered throughout the United States would assure any scholar of the high standing of the faculty that has included these names.

"As to the character of the graduate students who have come to Cornell University from Indiana University, my impression is that they have been an unusually fine class. I know that they have proved themselves worthy of confidence, on account of the large number of fellowships which they have secured at Cornell University. I remember several instances in which Indiana University students have taken the highest honors here."

From Stephen A. Forbes, Director Illinois State Laboratory of
Natural History, Champaign, Illinois.

Its Career
Phenomenally
Brilliant, Brings
Distinguished
Honor to the
State.

"The recent career of Indiana University has been phenomenally brilliant; a fact which, so far as I can judge, is due solely to the exceptional ability and training of its faculty combined with the genius for administration which its presiding officers have exhibited. It seems to me to have done more than any other agency to bring distinguished honor to the State which it represents, in the field of higher education. It has certainly richly earned the strong and cordial support of the people of Indiana and their efficient aid in its upbuilding and development."

From J. M. Stillman, Professor of Chemistry in the Leland Stanford, Jr.,
University, Palo Alto, California.

More than Its
Share of
Distinguished
Men.

"I consider that Indiana University has had more than its average share of distinguished men in its faculty during the past ten years. In so far as I have had to do with its graduate students, I have found them of good ability and of careful training."

From T. C. Mendenhall, President Worcester Polytechnic Institute, Mass.

Its Standing in
Scholarship and
Reputation
Exceptionally
High.

"During the last ten years I have had a tolerably intimate acquaintance with the Indiana University, its faculty and its work, and with some of the members of its faculty, I have had very pleasant personal relations; I am, therefore, able to declare with confidence that the standing of the institution, both as to scholarship and general reputation of its faculty, and as to the character of the work done, has always been high. Indeed, I may say that when considered in the relation of other institutions, in the great Mississippi Valley, its standing has been exceptionally high. I know of few, if any other institutions of learning west of the Alleghanies that can make a better showing, particularly in the way of maintenance of high standard of scholarship and the production, from time to time, of valuable results from original investigations carried on by members of its faculty, than the University of Indiana. I do know that many scientific men, coming from eastern institutions and incidentally becoming acquainted with the work of this institution, have expressed their surprise and gratification at its quantity and superior character."

From Stanley Hall, President of Clark University, Worcester, Mass.

Its Atmosphere Tends to Develop Manliness. "From all these gentlemen, I have formed, as every one must, a very high opinion of the standing of the faculty and the quality of the work done at Indiana University. I think that I can safely say that on the whole the gradutes of no other University whom we have had here outrank, in either ability or training, those from Indiana. The impression the University makes upon one can perhaps be described a little more specifically as of an institution that has maintained its perspective and distinguishes clearly between essentials and nonessentials in its work, and secondly, as animated by a commendable spirit of co-operation, loyalty, and general interest in studies, and as having an 'atmosphere' that tends to develop those qualities for which I know no better name than manliness.

"Large as its usefulness has been and is, it would be a matter of congratulation to every friend of higher education to see its sphere of usefulness greatly enlarged."

From W. G. Hale, Professor of Latin in Chicago University.

Influences the Thought of the Times. "If my impression corresponds to general opinion, the standing of the faculty of Indiana University in the last ten years is very high. The graduate students whom I have known have been of exceptionally high character.

"Those of us who believe in what is called the 'State University' as well as in the University privately endowed, greatly desire to see such institutions as the Indiana University strongly supported by the State. I doubt very much if any State University in the Country has produced as much original work—that is, has done so much to influence the thought of the time—as the University of Indiana."

From Charles D. Marx, Professor of Civil Engineering in the
Leland Stanford, Jr., University, Palo Alto, California.

Graduates are Earnest, Practical Men and Women. "Every institution must be measured by the quality of its graduates. I have had the pleasure of a personal acquaintance with a number of graduates of Indiana University. I have found them earnest, working men and women, ready to take upon themselves the practical problems of every-day life."

Pamphlet inserted in Indiana University Catalogue, Seventy-Fifth College Year, 1898–99; *Indiana School Journal*, August, 1899 (Vol. XLIV, No. 8), p. 529.

Document 92

The Seventieth-Mile Mark

Professor James A. Woodburn prepared a new historical sketch of the University to be included in the Catalogue for 1894. It revises Banta's statement in that Woodburn had a better perspective of Indiana University in relationship to the history of the state and the nation. While the Woodburn essay is less than objective in many of its insights, it has high validity because the highly competent author was able to insert his own judgments.

*　　*　　*

INDIANA UNIVERSITY.

HISTORICAL SKETCH
BY JAMES A. WOODBURN.

"Religion, morality and knowledge being necessary to good government and the happiness of mankind, schools and the means of education shall be forever encouraged."

This is the language of the ordinance of 1787. It is, therefore, part of the fundamental law of every State in the old Northwest Territory. Indiana is one of these States, and the first complete act which provided a civil government for the territory, from which the State was carved, guaranteed a system of free education. The great ordinance which organized a civil government for the Northwest Territory, passed by the Congress of the Confederation before the adoption of the United States' Constitution, guaranteed to the people who were destined to inhabit this territory, free soil, free schools, a free church, and free men, with civil rights, privileges and immunities. This is the first and greatest landmark in the history of education in Indiana, and therefore, it is the first in the history of Indiana University.

Jefferson's ordinance of 1784 was a precedent for much of this great enactment, but it contained none of the notable articles of compact afterwards incorporated in the ordinance of 1787, and it contained no provisions for schools and academies. Timothy Pickering in a letter to Rufus King, first called prominent attention to this omission, and on May 20, 1785, a new ordinance was adopted. In this act of 1785 occurs this notable clause relating to education:

"There shall be reserved from sale the lot No. 16 of every township for the maintenance of public schools within the said township."

This was the first law of Congress relating to education within the present territory of Indiana. It marks the beginning of a policy which, observed ever since by the United States, has set aside one-thirty-sixth of the land in each new State for the uses of education.

The ordinance of 1787 guaranteed a continuance and enlargement of this liberal policy. It was passed July 13, 1787. After its passage Congress still hesitated to offer satisfactory terms of land sales to intending settlers in the Northwest. The reservation for school purposes of section 16 in every township according to the terms of the law of 1785 was easily secured. But this was not satisfactory, especially to Dr. Manasseh Cutler, who was negotiating the land purchase for the Ohio company. Through Dr. Cutler's insistence the law of July 23, 1787, reserved the whole of two additional townships in the proposed new State of Ohio for the perpetual support of a university. This act for Ohio became a precedent for similar treatment of Indiana. On March 26, 1804, Congress, in making provision for the sale of public lands in the "districts of Detroit, Kaskaskia and Vincennes," reserved the 16th section in each township for schools and "one entire township in each of the three districts for the use of a seminary of learning." In 1805 the Detroit district became the Territory of Michigan; in 1809 Kaskaskia became Illinois. Another seminary township was reserved for Indiana when she came into the Union in 1816.

These two seminary or university townships for Indiana were located, the one in Gibson County, October 10, 1806, by Albert Gallatin, then Secretary of the Treasury; the other by President Madison, in 1816, in Monroe County. [This was Perry Township. The south end of Bloomington is in this township.] These townships became the basis for the earliest university funds. The consideration of this early land endowment brings us subsequently to consider the relation between the State University and Vincennes University, and to the litigation between Vincennes University and the State over the appropriation of the proceeds from the land sales.

The first Legislature of the Territory, "begun and held at the borough of Vincennes," passed "an act to incorporate an university in the Indiana Territory." This act was approved by Governor William Henry Harrison November 29, 1806. This school afterwards became the "Vincennes University." This was the first institution for higher learning established by the public act of Indiana, and it was the first institution of the kind within the present limits of the State. It was given the seminary township in Gibson County, with power to sell 4,000 acres and to hold not exceeding 100,000 acres of land.

The Territorial University at Vincennes was not fully open for instruction until 1810. Rev. Samuel Scott was its first President. Mr. Scott is reported to have preached the first Protestant sermon in Indiana, and he founded the first Protestant church in the State, the "Indiana Church" (Presbyterian), as it was called. He opened a private school in Vincennes in 1808, and the school became the nucleus of the proposed university.

The Vincennes school was in continuous existences, in some capacity, until it was converted into the "Knox County Seminary" in 1825, an act which was afterwards declared to be illegal. But during these years from 1810 to 1825, while it was nominally a public institution, it received no support from State taxation. The State acted upon the assumption that the trustees had allowed their organization to lapse, and the Legislature withdrew all care and attention from the affairs of the school. In 1822 an act was passed by the General Assembly for the practical confiscation of its lands for the support of the new "State Seminary" at Bloomington, and in 1824 the State formally declared the Vincennes institution extinct. This act of 1822 recited the fact that the Trustees of Vincennes University "had sold portions of such lands, and had negligently permitted the corporation to die without having executed deeds to purchasers," and the act provided for the sale of the balance of the seminary township in Gibson County, and for the use of the money as a productive fund for the benefit of the State Seminary. Subsequent acts, in 1825 and 1827, were passed further providing for the sale of the seminary townships in Gibson and Monroe counties, on the assumption that the lands granted to Vincennes University in 1806 were still the property of the State. Out of these acts, under which 17,000 acres of the Gibson County lands were sold, and the proceeds returned to the State Treasury for the benefit of the seminary and college funds, came the subsequent litigation between Vincennes University and the State, to which we have referred.

This litigation is of interest in this connection, since it shows one of the embarrassments surrounding the material foundation of the State University.

After the school at Vincennes had continued for some years as the "Knox County Seminary," the old corporation was resuscitated by an act of the Legislature in 1838, making provision for supplying vacancies in the Board of Trustees. A clause, however, was inserted in this act intended to prevent the renewal of any claim to the seminary township taken from it in 1822. But in 1845 the Trustees of Vincennes University, thus revived, laid claim to the Gibson County lands, and to the proceeds of previous sales made by the State, which had been transferred to the Indiana University, formerly the State Seminary, and suit was brought to test the question of title. On January 17, 1846, in order to make legal a suit against a State, and to relieve the occupants of the lands of responsibility and litigation, an act was passed by the State Legislature authorizing "the Trustees of Vincennes University to bring suit against the State of Indiana, and for other purposes." This suit, in the Marion County Circuit Court, resulted in a decree in favor of the Trustees in the amount of $30,099.66 as the proceeds of previous sales. On an appeal to the Supreme Court of the State, this decision was reversed, the court holding that the act of the Territorial Legislature of 1806 granting the lands to the Vincennes University was nugatory, because no such power was vested in it by an act of Congress, and that they were not, at the time of this sale and disposal, in existence as a corporation, having allowed their corporation to lapse. In this suit Mr. Samuel Judah appeared for the trustees of Vincennes University and Mr. O. H. Smith and Mr. Geo. G. Dunn for the State.

The Trustees of the Vincennes University were not satisfied with this decision, and they sued over a writ of error from the Supreme Court of the United States, which, at the December term, 1852, reversed the decision of the Supreme Court of the State, holding that when the Territorial Legislature of 1806 incorporated a "Board of Trustees of the Vincennes University," the grant of a township in the Vincennes district by the Congress of 1804, and which was located by the Secretary of the Treasury in 1806, attached to this board, although for the two preceding years there had been no grantee in existence; and holding further that, if the Board of Trustees, by a failure to elect when vacancies occurred, or through any other means, became reduced to a less number than was authorized to act by the charter, the corporation was not thereby dissolved, but its franchises were suspended until restored by legislative action. By this decision the State restored to the Vincennes University the sum of $66,585, one-fourth of which was retained as attorney's fees.

After this recovery of more than $40,000 of its land endowment, the Vincennes University again opened for academic instruction in 1853, and has since continued as an institution independent of State support and control.

We return now to the early beginnings of the "Indiana Academy," which became the Indiana University.

Indiana was admitted to the Union December 11, 1816. At that time the settled parts of the State were confined to narrow strips of territory along the Ohio border from Fort Wayne to the Ohio River, along that river to the Wabash, and up the Wabash to Vincennes. The great interior part of the State was a wilderness. The total white population was 63,837, less than half of the present population of Indianapolis. Monroe County was then part of Orange County, and was not laid off as a separate county until 1818.

The first Constitution of the State, adopted in 1816, recognized the importance of education; it provided for the improvement of the school lands of the State, forbade the sale of such lands prior to the year 1820, and decreed that it should "be the duty of the General Assembly, as soon as circumstances will permit, to provide by law for a general system of education, ascending in regular gradation from township schools to a State University, where tuition shall be gratis and equally open to all." This was the first formal action of the State toward the establishment of the State University. On January 20, 1820— our "Foundation Day"—as soon as the four years during which the Constitution required the lands to be withheld from sale had expired, the Legislature, in session at Corydon, established a "State Seminary" at Bloomington. At that time Bloomginton contained about three hundred people, and the town was considerably north of the center of population. Among those who came to Bloomington on account of the location there of the Seminary township by President Madison in 1816, was Dr. David H. Maxwell. Dr. Maxwell came to Bloomington in 1819. He was full of zeal and energy in behalf of education. He had been a member from Jefferson County, his former home, of the first Constitutional convention of the State, in 1816. It was chiefly through his influence with members of the Legislature at Corydon in 1819 and 1820 that Bloomington was chosen as the seat of the new Seminary. Dr. Maxwell became a member of the first Board of Trustees, and he served in this capacity almost continuously until his death, thirty years later.

In 1825 the new Seminary was opened to the public. Prof. Baynard R. Hall was the first teacher, and for the first few years he was the "faculty" of the seminary. He was a man of excellent classical attainments, and while the General Assembly of the State was legislating the seminary into existence he was finishing his course at Union College under the tuition of the celebrated Dr. Nott. In his book, entitled "The New Purchase, or Seven and a Half Years in the Far West," he gives a vivid idea of the primitive habits of the time. This new school was a State Seminary, therefore it belonged to the "people;" instruction was to be "free" in all branches, including the most elementary. The consequence was a perfect stampede from the private schools of the town, and the principal was under the necessity of sending the pupils back to their schools. In sifting the applicants only ten were found qualified for entrance. As the warm weather approached, the "ten boys and young gentlemen" came to recitations without coats, and "as the thermometer arose, they came without shoes." After the manner of the time, the Judge on the bench sat in court "without coat and cravat, with his feet modestly reposed on the upper rostrum, showing his boot soles to the bystanders and lawyers." The lawyers were in their shirt sleeves, and the Governor of the State, when he appeared on the "stump," had the same careless dress and manner. In the election of the second teacher, the "people" proposed to have a voice. A mass meeting, with a local politician in front as spokesman, marched to where the Board of Trustees were in session and made known their demands. But the trustees, who had received intimation of their coming, speedily determined the election, whereupon the opposers, moved partly by sectarian motives, and partly by the spirit of pure democracy, carried their complaint to the State Legislature. They objected to a "foreigner" in their college, though the accepted candidate was recognized as a scholarly gentleman, the best qualified of all the applicants, and lived no farther away than the neighboring State of Kentucky. But it was suspected by the men who opposed his election that he "smelled of Presbyterianism."

Prof. John H. Harney was the second professor elected, at the time of this "democratic episode." He was made "professor of mathematics and natural and mechanical philosophy and chemistry." These two professors were allowed a salary at first of $250 each, which was soon afterwards increased to $400, with fees which might increase it to $650. The fees of the students were $10 per year, and when the trustees raised this to $15, the opponents of the college, always ready for an occasion to arouse opposition, complained that "poor persons" were thus debarred from the privileges of the institution.

This complaint led to a legislative investigation, and Dr. Maxwell was called upon for a full report of the work of the seminary. From that report we learn that thirteen students attended the seminary the first year, fifteen the second, and twenty-one the third. Professor Hall's salary of $250 as originally fixed was continued at that sum for three and one-half years, during which he "preached to the Presbyterian Church of Bloomington, for which service they paid him $150 in articles of trade." At the end of the three and one-half years the trustees forbade the preaching and advanced his salary to $400.

By an act of the General Assembly, January 24, 1828, the "Indiana Seminary" was converted into the "Indiana College." Rev. Andrew Wylie, D. D., President of Washington College, in Pennsylvania, was elected the first President. Mr. Hall and Mr. Harney were continued as professors, and Mr. W. H. Stockwell was appointed as principal of the preparatory department. Dr. Wylie did not begin his labors in Bloomington until the fall of 1829. In addition to being President he was also professor of moral and mental philosophy, political economy and polite literature. President Wylie was a man of very positive character, an excellent scholar and a successful teacher. Many young men who had studied under him in the East followed him to his new field of labor in the far West. He continued as President of the new college during its formative period until his death in 1851. In 1832 a difficulty arose between the President and the members of the faculty, which resulted in the resignation of Professors Hall and Harney and the withdrawal of a number of students. The vacancies in the faculty were supplied by the election of Ebenezer N. Elliott, a graduate of Miami University, as professor of natural philosophy and chemistry, and of Beaumont Parks, a graduate of Dartmouth College, as professor of languages. Mr. James D. Maxwell, a young graduate of the Indiana College, and who was subsequently so honorably associated a long time with the university as a member of the Board of Trustees, succeeded Mr. Stockwell in the preparatory department. Most of the students in these early days were boys of poor families, who were making their own way through college. In many cases they could attend school but for a year at a time, teaching or engaging in some work in alternate years, to pay their way. In the early records it is stated that "Joseph A. Wright was allowed for ringing the bell, making fires, etc., during the last session of 1828, the sum of $16.25, and $1 for repairing the top of one of the chimneys." Joseph A. Wright was afterwards twice elected Governor of the State, and subsequently became the United States Minister to Berlin. Many of the early alumni worked their way through college as young Wright did. The State University has never ceased to be a college for poor boys, and its worthiest alumni have been its self-made men.

In 1836 a new college building was erected at a cost of about $11,000. It was not of educational architecture, but resembled rather an "old-fashion New England factory." During the first decade of the college, from 1828 to 1838, there was much annoyance and loss in efficiency from quarrels and discord and local petty opposition. Some of this arose from the bitter sectarian strife of the time, some from personal jealousies, some from local prejudice and ignorance, from a desire of the "people" of the community to have a hand in electing the teachers and in the management of the institution. In 1838 one of the members of the board, who had failed of re-election, brought charges against the president of maladministration. Dr. Wylie was charged with "duplicity," with "refusing to obey the by-laws of the college," with "arbitrary and ungentlemanly conduct," and with "misrepresentation and falsehood." The authorities considered the matter of sufficient importance to institute a thorough investigation which completely exonerated President Wylie, and on behalf of the Board of Trustees the Hon. Robert Dale Owen prepared an address to the people setting forth the facts in the case. It was merely a case of petty annoyance. By act of February 15, 1838, the Indiana College was changed to the "Indiana University." The act provided for a board of twenty-one trustees. Among the first trustees under this act, were Governor William Hendricks, Jesse L. Holman, Robert Dale Owen, and Richard W. Thompson. In 1841 a law school was opened in connection with the university. Judge David McDonald was elected to the Professorship of Law. This was continued until 1877, when it was suspended on account of adverse influences in the Legislature. The law school was resumed in 1889, and with Judge D. D. Banta, as Dean, is in prosperous operation.

At the time the statute changed the "college" into a "university," in 1839, the faculty had been reduced to three, the president and two professors. In 1840 the number of students was sixty-four. By 1843 the students had increased to one hundred and fifteen, and by 1850 there were one hundred and sixty students enrolled. This was the last year of Dr. Wylie's presidency, and during the last ten years of his regime he had seen the university prospering, with harmony in the faculty, peace in the community, and growing favor in the State.

After the death of President Wylie, in 1851, Henry Barnard, LL. D., of Connecticut, was elected president, but owing to bodily injuries received by being thrown from a carriage, Dr. Barnard was unable to accept. Rev. Alfred Ryors, D. D., President of Ohio State University, was then chosen. Dr. Ryors held the position but for one year. After his resignation, the trustees called to the presidency, April 10, 1852, John H. Lathrop, LL. D., then the Chancellor of the Wisconsin University. Dr. Lathrop declined. Professor T. A. Wylie had been made superintendent of buildings by the trustees, and acting president by election of the faculty. The few professors generously assumed the additional teaching which had theretofore fallen to the president, whose office was now vacant.

Upon the resignation of Dr. Ryors, in August, 1853, William Daily, D. D., was appointed as successor. Dr. Daily was a member of the Board of Trustees immediately before his election as President, and resigned apparently for the purpose of being elected to succeed Dr. Ryors. The administration of Dr. Daily was notable for the loss by the State of the suit with Vincennes University, which resulted in a surrender of $66,000 of the land endowment of the University. This, however, was assumed by the State, and the loss was made good to the university. This loss for awhile seriously threatened the institution. These were gloomy years for the university, between 1851 and 1854. Some of its most hopeful friends expected to see it forced to close its doors. Another serious loss was that of the main college building by fire on the night of April 8, 1854. The fire destroyed the library of 1,200 volumes; also the libraries of the Athenian and Philomathean Literary Societies. To repair this loss the citizens of Monroe County donated $10,000, and, with an appropriation by the State, a new and very substantial building was erected—the one now standing in the old college campus.

When Dr. Daily resigned in 1859, Rev. T. A. Wylie, who had been a professor in the university since 1837, became again acting President. Dr. Wylie served in this capacity for one year, when he was succeeded for a short time by Dr. Lathrop, of Wisconsin, who was induced, this time, to accept the call extended him. Dr. Lathrop resigned within a year to accept the presidency of the University of Missouri, whose first President he had been from 1842 to 1849.

Rev. Cyrus Nutt, D. D., then became President of Indiana University, and served in this capacity from 1860 to 1875. H was followed by Rev. Lemuel Moss, D. D., from 1875 to 1884.

On the resignation of Dr. Moss in the fall of 1884, Rev. Elisha Ballantine became the acting President until the election, a few months later, of Professor David Starr Jordan, Ph. D., at that time Professor of Zoology. Under Dr. Jordan's regency the university made a radical change in its academic administration and literary, or internal, constitution. Its curriculum took on the form in which it now appears.

But before turning from the mere external history of the university to consider the internal changes in its academic policies, a few words will be in order as to the financial support of the institution. This was very meagre for the first fifty years. No regular appropriation was made by the State for the current expenses until 1867. The reliance was on the land endowment. Michigan held all of her university lands for thirty years, and some still longer. The land values appreciated and Michigan realized a good land endowment for her university from her congressional lands. Indiana sold her land early and at a great sacrifice. Most of the land was authorized to be sold within four years of the admission of the State. The land brought altogether something over $100,000. The regular income from this was about $8,000. This was increased by fees and some incidental resources to about $11,000. In 1867 the State recognized that the income from the permanent endowment was insufficient and made an annual appropriation of $8,000. This was increased in 1873 to $23,000, and in 1889 to $30,000. At the last session of the Legislature $10,000 additional was given to the annual appropriation, making the regular income from the State Treasury $40,000.

This, together with the incomes from the original and permanent endowment gives the university a total income of about $78,000. This is increasing year by year.

The most notable advance in the financial history of the university was made in 1883. On March 8, of that year, an act passed the General Assembly providing for a larger permanent endowment. This act assesses for the benefit of the university one-half of one cent on each $100 of taxable property in the State. The tax is to run for twelve years, and "when collected and paid into the State treasury shall be placed to the credit of a fund to be known as the Permanent Endowment Fund of the Indiana University." It was estimated that in twelve years this fund would amount to about $800,000, but it is now seen that it will fall much short of what was anticipated. The weight of the tax, or its lightness, will be appreciated from the statement that a citizen assessed for $5,000 worth of property will pay but 25 cents a year to the University Endowment Fund. The alumni were very active and influential in securing from the State the recognition of some fixed and permanent plan like this in caring for the growing needs of the university.

Very unfortunately the summer after the permanent endowment was secured, on the night of July 12, 1883, one of the main buildings of the university was destroyed by fire. This building had been erected in 1874 at a cost of $24,000, and contained the museum, the literary and law libraries, and the laboratories.

The museum had been collected chiefly by Richard Owen and David Dale Owen, and was known as the "Owen Cabinet." It was purchased by the university in 1872, at a cost of $20,000. This fire was very discouraging; books, material, apparatus were all gone, and there were not sufficient recitation rooms for the classes. As in 1854, at the former fire, the student body stood by the university, they returned in September as usual, upon the announcement that the work would be continued as usual, though under temporary embarrassments.

The Monroe County Commissioners made a donation of $50,000 for new buildings, and with this and $20,000 received as insurance money, two substantial brick buildings were erected ("Wylie Hall" and "Owen Hall"), in the new campus east of Bloomington in the grove known to many generations of students as "Dunn's Woods." At the same time a small frame building was built for chapel and recitation purposes. For the improvement of the new grounds and for apparatus, the Legislature appropriated $43,000. Thus the university found itself in a better condition and in better quarters than before. Since 1883 special appropriations have been made by the State of $60,000 for a new library building in 1889, and $50,000 for a new building in 1893. The latter building is now in process of construction.

From the time of its foundation as the "Indiana Seminary," January 20, 1820, the Indiana University has been open to the public for seventy-four years. In this time the institution has changed from an academy with one teacher and fourteen students to a well-equipped university with forty professors and instructors, and a body of six hundred and twenty-eight students. This statement indicates growth and change. The change has been masked in the way of buildings and appliances. But the most important changes have been those in the curriculum of the institution; and the most interesting history of the university to one interested in the progress of higher education would be a satisfactory account of the various important changes in the college curriculum, the reasons for those changes and the educational principles on which they were based. This might be called the internal, or *structural*, history of the university. Such a history would reveal the change of ideas and policies which have determined the real character of the institution, which has modified the educational life and ideals of the State, and which, in later instances, have made Indiana University known and respected abroad. Such a history would be very valuable but it can not be accomplished in this brief sketch. Some of the more notable changes, however, should be briefly indicated.

A recent article in the Harper's Weekly [October, 1893.] on the celebration of the twenty-fifth anniversary of Cornell University quotes a Columbia professor as recently saying, when asked what college has the best course: "If you mean the curriculum it is probably the Indiana University." When Senator Stanford and his educational aids visited the universities of the East they decided that the new university on the Pacific Slope should be laid out on lines already indicated in Indiana, and for this reason President Jordan, of Indiana University, was called to the presidency of Leland Stanford. It was under President Jordan's administration that the curriculum which distinguished Indiana University had been instituted.

In the first catalogue of this institution, published in 1831, we find that the Freshman year of the course was given up chiefly to the study of Greek and Latin;

the Sophomore year was devoted to the completion of the course in Greek and the beginnings of the higher mathematics; in the Junior year "mathematics was finished," and the attention of the student was then given to mechanics, astronomy, physics and physical geography; in the Senior year the course involved mental and moral philosophy, evidences of Christianity "in connection with natural religion," rhetoric, logic, political economy, the Constitution of the United States, with a review of Greek, Latin and English classics. The idea of President Wylie seems to have been that of *concentration*. His course involved a kind of specialization by rotation, without any idea of election. The student should complete his languages (meaning Latin and Greek) , then his mathematics, then his philosophy. "The studies," we read in the first catalogue, "are so conducted that each student gives his undivided attention to one principal subject till it is completed. This method has been adopted by the President under the full conviction, founded on twenty years' observation and experience, that it possesses many and decided advantages over that which is pursued in most colleges, of blending together a variety of studies. During the whole course, however, special attention is given to rhetorical reading, composition, elocution and English grammar." Dr. Wylie called attention to the fact that "in some of the older States, where colleges have been multiplied to an injurious degree, the desire to attract numbers has operated to depress the standard of education; and the emulation, in too many cases, seems to have been which institution should surpass the rest in shortening the way to a diploma. It is the ambition, and will be the aim, of those intrusted with the affairs of this institution to pursue an opposite course, one which, should it meet with encouragement from the community, will render their diploma, in every case, a *true document*."

This course continued during President Wylie's administration without material change. In 1837 French was introduced, "taught as a separate study." By 1840 such students as desired might receive, "in addition to the regular course of instruction, lessons in Hebrew, French, civil engineering and book-keeping; and a course of lectures on history were delivered by the President to the Sophomore and Freshmen once a week." During this period each class was required to attend three recitations a day, and none were graduated except those who had completed the prescribed course. The college year was divided into two sessions: The winter session began on the first Monday in November and lasted till March; the summer session began in May and closed in September. The commencement season was at the first of September or the last of August.

In 1850 about one-fifth of the students—29 out of 135—were classified as "Scientific and Irregular," and the proportion of these students began to increase. In April, 1852, the trustees established a *Normal Department,* with a Model School for practice in teaching. Both girls and boys were to be admitted to this school. In 1854 a *Scientific Course* was arranged, providing for the graduation of the students pursuing the course, with the Degree of Bachelor of Science. The course embraced certain preparatory studies, with some "history, rhetoric, mathematics, chemistry, mental and moral philosophy, surveying evidences of Christianity, international laws, astronomy, Constitutions of the United States, and Butler's Analogy." It omitted all Greek and Latin, and no modern language is mentioned.

These continued to be the courses of instruction without much varying until in 1877, under Dr. Moss' administration, three courses were allowed:

1. *The Course in Ancient Classics,* containing the usual subjects leading to the B. A. degree.

2. *The Course in Modern Classics,* differing from the preceding by substitut-

ing French and German for Greek. This course led to the degree of B. L. (Bachelor of Letters) .

3. *The Course in Science,* in which, in the department of languages, the student might choose between the modern languages and the Greek, and it gave the student, also, by means of elective studies, during the Junior and Senior years, the opportunity of paying special attention to the principles of Physical Science.

These three courses were regarded as the same in extent and value, requiring four years for completion. The "Scientific Course" formerly required only three years, and it had done much to lower the academic standard of the institution.

David Starr Jordan, a graduate of Cornell University, in the Class of 1872, became president of Indiana University, in the fall of 1884. He continued in this capacity till called to Leland Stanford University, in June, 1891. During the second year of his administration the list of electives was enlarged, and eight courses were established, as follows:
1. Ancient Classics; 2. Modern Classics; 3. English Literature; 4. History and Political Science; 5. Philosophy; 6. Mathematics and Physics; 7. Biology and Geology; 8. Chemistry.

The eight courses were the same in extent and value, and each required the same preparation for admission. The first two courses led to the degree of A. B.; the 3d, 4th and 5th to the degree of Ph.B.; the 6th, 7th and 8th, to that of B. S. It was intended that every graduate of the university should have a thorough drill in some department of human knowledge, while breadth of culture was encouraged by means of wide electives.

The following year, 1886-7, it was determined that the A. B. degree should be the only baccalaureate degree conferred by the university, and the distinct special courses were increased to fourteen. All of the fourteen courses led to the A. B. degree. The candidate for the degree was required to complete the following work:

General. English, one year daily; Mathematics, one year daily; some one Science, one year daily; one Language, two years, or two Languages each two years daily; Prose Composition, once a week throughout the course.

Special. Every student must select for a speciality a subject in which a four years' course is offered, the first year of which is identical with the required work in the general course.

Collateral. The head of each department may lay out, in connection with his course, work in related subjects, such required collateral work not to exceed six terms of daily recitations.

Elective. The remainder of the work the student may elect from any department of the university.

This scheme involves the basis of the present curriculum. Other departments have been added, so that now the university has seventeen separate departments. The field of election has been enlarged and certain requirements have been transferred to the fitting school. The candidate for graduation is still required to pursue the languages, the mathematics, and some of the natural sciences for fifteen terms out of thirty-six. For these fifteen terms he has freedom of choice within defined limits. For the other twenty-one terms he is left to his own election under the guidance of his advisor, the head of the department where his speciality lies. It is believed that this scheme involves the merits of the *group* system, at the same time making provision for elasticity in a wider range of choice. Under competent advice the student will make the group best adapted to his needs and his inclination. This elective system involves the two ideas of a more thorough preparatory course including some subjects now usually taught in Freshman and Sophomore classes in most of western colleges, and the placing of all college subjects on an equality so far as the honors of the course are concerned. In harmony with these ideas the requirements for admission have already been increased.

The theory on which this system is based has best been stated by President Jordan in his "Evolution of the College Curriculum." No two students require exactly the same line of work in order that their time in college may be spent to the best advantage. The college student is the best judge of his own needs, or at any rate he can arrange his work for himself better than it can be done beforehand by any committee, or by an consensus of educational philosophers. The student may make mistakes in this, as he may elsewhere in much more important things in life; but here, as elsewhere, he must bear the responsibility of these mistakes. The development of this sense of responsibility is one of the most effective agencies the college has to promote the moral culture of the student. It is better for the student himself that he should sometimes make mistakes than that he should throughout his work be arbitrarily directly by others. Freedom is as essential to scholarship as to manhood. "Free should the scholar be—free and brave."

When Dr. Jordan was called to California in 1891, Professor John Merle Coulter, of Wabash College, was elected to the presidency of Indiana University, in which position he served for two years, when he accepted a call to the presidency of Lake Forest University. Dr. Coulter had been for a long time the associate, in educational and scientific work, of President Jordan, and he had an appreciation of the university ideas which were here being worked out; and with these ideas he was in entire sympathy. The growth of the university was greatly promoted by the energy and ability and untiring work which Dr. Coulter brought to the presidency.

Upon Dr. Coulter's resignation in 1893, the trustees elected as President Professor Joseph Swain, at the time professor of mathematics in Leland Stanford Jr., University. President Swain had been Professor of Applied Mathematics in Indiana University at the time of Dr. Jordan's call to Leland Stanford, and he was one of the first chosen counsellors of Dr. Jordan in the establishment of the new university in the west. He has a complete understanding of, and is in full sympathy with the changes in the Indiana University in its new age. In the first year of his administration the university has continued its growth in a very remarkable way, and to-day it has a larger corps of teachers and a greater number of students, with better equipments for their accommodation, than ever before in its history.

Annual Catalogue of the Indiana University for the Seventieth College Year, 1893–94, pp. 102–116.

Document 93

Turn of the Century

The opening of the twentieth century, by the mere turn of the calendar, all but began a new age in America. Indiana was entering that age in many respects. The redoubtable Isaac Jenkinson recited the University progress in one part of his report, and with monotonous refrain told Governor James A. Mount of the needs of the institution—and they were urgent. The student enrollment had now exceeded 1,000; more space was mandatory if the enlarged student body was to be properly cared for and instructed.

*   *   *

PRESIDENT'S REPORT.

BLOOMINGTON, IND., December 3, 1900
To the HON. JAMES A. MOUNT, *Governor of Indiana:*

Dear Sir—I have the honor of herewith transmitting to you the biennial report of the Board of Trustees of the Indiana University for the fiscal years ending October 31, 1899, and October 31, 1900.

The growth of our State universities in the past fifteen years has been one of the most remarkable facts in the educational history of the United States. Within this period the people have come to realize more and more that the State university is an essential part of the great public school system, and have from time to time increased the appropriations in order to better care for the great number of students who are flocking to these institutions.

The growth in attendance in Indiana University is shown by the following:

Year.	Students.	Graduates.
1885	156	26
1890	321	47
1895	771	85
1900	1,017	123

Of the 1,017 students in attendance in 1900, 960 were from Indiana. There were students from every county in the State. These were distributed as follows:

Adams	2	Franklin	3
Allen	23	Fulton	2
Bartholomew	12	Gibson	17
Benton	2	Grant	13
Blackford	6	Greene	26
Boone	27	Hamilton	20
Brown	2	Hancock	15
Carroll	13	Harrison	5
Cass	12	Hendricks	9
Clark	5	Henry	15
Clay	8	Howard	9
Clinton	11	Huntington	18
Crawford	1	Jackson	12
Daviess	15	Jasper	12
Dearborn	5	Jay	14
Decatur	9	Jefferson	5
Dekalb	11	Jennings	7
Delaware	27	Johnson	9
Dubois	13	Knox	9
Elkhart	12	Kosciusko	10
Fayette	3	Lagrange	2
Floyd	6	Lake	1
Fountain	6	Laporte	5

Lawrence	12	Rush	7
Madison	26	St. Joseph	6
Marion	37	Scott	4
Marshall	3	Shelby	4
Martin	13	Spencer	12
Miami	21	Starke	1
Monroe	85	Steuben	1
Montgomery	5	Sullivan	5
Morgan	7	Switzerland	9
Newton	5	Tippecanoe	5
Noble	4	Tipton	6
Ohio	8	Union	4
Orange	10	Vanderburgh	25
Owen	17	Vermillion	5
Parke	14	Vigo	17
Perry	3	Wabash	9
Pike	4	Warren	4
Porter	7	Warrick	10
Posey	9	Washington	20
Pulaski	1	Wayne	9
Putnam	2	Wells	8
Randolph	11	White	10
Ripley	6	Whitley	1

A study of this table shows that Indiana University draws its students from all parts of the State of Indiana. It is in no sense a local institution. The attendance from the six counties surrounding Monroe County is as follows: Brown, 2; Morgan, 7; Lawrence, 12; Jackson, 12; Greene, 26; Owen, 17. There are seventy-six in all, or an average of thirteen students to the county. This is but slightly above the average attendance of the counties for the whole State. While Monroe is accredited with 85 students, a very large number of these persons have gone to Bloomington for educational advantages, and therefore make that city their temporary home.

The progress of the University during the past two years has been gratifying to all friends of higher education. This progress has not been chiefly in the number of students, but much more in the increasing favorable recognition of the University among the educators of the country. The University is known to be one of the most progressive of our institutions, and its peculiar organization of work has attracted wide attention and imitation.

The matter of numbers is in itself no test of the value or the success of an institution of learning, for the most advanced students in any department of study are few. It can, however, be said that the best students will go where the best work is done, and Indiana University will never lack for numbers so long as its instruction is thorough, and its work is abreast of modern thought and modern methods.

More important than the fact of the increase of numbers is the fact of the steady improvement in the quality of work done by professors and students. The reputation of the University, both within and without the State, has been constantly rising. Among college men throughout the country, Indiana University is regarded as one of the promising schools in the United States. It may be further said that Indiana University is especially a school for persons of limited means. The great majority of the students are not rich, and fully three-fourths of them have earned, by their own work, much or all of the money spent on their education. Connected with this lack of money for lavish expenditures is the fact that in no institution are the students, as a body, more earnest, or the moral tone higher, than in the State University.

The faculty of Indiana University is selected from the best men that can be secured anywhere for the salaries the University can pay. They have received their post-graduate instruction at the best institutions in this country and Europe. The wide range of their training is shown by the fact that the different members of the faculty have studied at forty of the best institutions of higher learning. In this country, Harvard, Princeton, Yale, Columbia, Johns Hopkins, Cornell, Chicago, and Stanford Universities have all contributed to the faculty of our State University. Continued demand for the professors of Indiana University in much wealthier institutions is significant. In the past few years fourteen teachers have been called to Stanford, three to Harvard, one to Yale, two to Cornell, one to Johns Hopkins, two to Northwestern, one to Columbia, one to the University of California, two to Chicago University, and one to Syracuse University, and one to the presidency of Michigan State Normal. There is nothing that better indicates the strength of a faculty than the demand for its services in the larger and wealthier institutions.

Dr. T. C. Mendenhall, formerly of Rose Polytechnic, now President of Worcester Polytechnic Institute, Massachusetts, says:

"During the last ten years I have had a tolerably intimate acquaintance with the Indiana University, its faculty and its work, and with some of the members of the faculty I have had very pleasant personal relations; I am, therefore, able to declare with confidence that the standing of the institution, both as to scholarship and general reputation of its faculty, and as to the character of the work done, has always been high. Indeed, I may say that when considered in the relation to other institutions in the great Mississippi Valley, its standing has been exceptionally high. I know of few, if any, other institutions of learning west of the Alleghenies that can make a better showing, particularly in the way of maintenance of high standing of scholarship and the production, from time to time, of valuable results from original investigations carried on by members of its faculty, than the University of Indiana. I do know that many scientific men, coming from eastern institutions and incidentally becoming acquainted with the work of this institution, have expressed their surprise and gratification at its quantity and superior character."

The following statement from Dr. John M. Coulter, head professor of botany in the University of Chicago, and so well and favorably known in Indiana, is of interest:

"I am glad to say now, as I have always said, that Indiana University does more with less money than any institution I know of. It is thoroughly permeated by the right spirit, and has little of that ancient rubbish to impede it which clings about some of our universities. Contentions as to educational methods have been going on vigorously for years, but the observant student can note that there is an annual march of curricula toward the Indiana plan. Of all the interests which come under the Legislature's care, none brings a greater reputation to the State than Indiana University, none generates as much force to be used in the State."

The requirement for entrance is four years of high school work of at least eight months each or their equivalent. The entrance requirements are three years of mathematics, three years of English, three years of language, one year of history, one year of science, and five years of elective work. These conform to the requirements of the State Board of Education for commissioned high schools.

There were 69 graduate students the past year. This is encouraging. Much of the strength of the institution comes from its most advanced work.

Eighteen departments of work are now organized, each department representing some great subject in which three or four or more years of work are offered. The scope of these subjects, as illustrating the great fields of knowledge open to young men and women of Indiana, is indicated by the following enumeration: Greek, Latin, Romance Languages, Germanic Languages, English, History and Political Science, Economics and Social Science, Philosophy, Pedagogy, Mathematics, Mechanics and Astronomy, Physics, Chemistry, Geology and Geography, Zoology, Botany, Fine Arts, Law. With this presentation of the subjects it is evident that our young people can have a very wide range of choice in training. It is considered no longer a tenable proposition that all kinds of minds demand the same kind of training. There is the greatest diversity of gifts, and this must be provided for in any rational system of education.

The purpose of education is to develop power, and this can be developed by the proper study of any subject, but it is much aided if that subject has the consent of the pupil's taste. The widest liberty is, therefore, given by the University in the selection of subjects. However, there are groups of subjects which pre-eminently stand for culture, and a certain amount of selection from these groups is required.

It is shown that distorted courses are practically unknown; that the proportion among subjects is practically what it was under prescription; that such subjects as English, language, history, and economics attract a far larger student body than do either the physical or biological sciences; that very few students graduate with only the minimum requirement. Better results than these which have been tabulated are those which show that this policy has improved the whole student body, by developing self-reliance and that interest which comes from responsibility, and has wonderfully improved teaching through the stimulus of interested learners.

It is these methods and results which have called attention to the University. It will be remembered that the University no longer maintains any preparatory department. The work begins where that of the commissioned high schools ends, and it is constantly becoming more intimately connected with these schools. That this relationship is becoming more widely recognized throughout the State is testified by the fact that during the present year every county in Indiana has sent pupils from their schools to the University.

In comparing the attendance at the University with that of other institutions, it must be remembered that the University maintains no preparatory or professional schools of any kind, except that of law, and that in these various schools will be found the largest part of the attendance of the universities that maintain them.

In everything that goes to make a university, such as numbers in college classes, variety of subjects presented, method of work, opportunities for advanced and original work, Indiana University stands very high among the universities of the neighboring States; but in the matter of income it stands very low.

In 1898-9 the total income of the University of Michigan was $533,524; of the University of Wisconsin, $426,663; of the University of Minnesota, $398,177; of the University of Illinois, $379,294; of the University of Nebraska, $287,000; of the University of Ohio, $277,593; of the University of Missouri, $176,821. There are not fewer than forty-five colleges and universities supported by the State. A study of the statistics will show that the State of Indiana can show more for every dollar invested in its University than any neighboring State; and it will also indicate what results the State may hope for when it takes a financial interest in the University commensurate with its own resources.

In 1883 the Legislature provided a tax of one-twentieth of a mill on the taxable property of Indiana, to run for thirteen years, to promote a permanent endowment fund for the University. This fund, together with the interest of the township land fund, yields about $33,000 annually. With an appreciation of the growth of the University and greater understanding of its needs, together with a better realization on the part of the people that the University is the head of the public school system—a fact that has been repeatedly recognized by the Legislature—the Legislature increased the annual appropriation from time to time until, in lieu of the annual appropriation for maintenance, the Legislature of 1896 passed a tax of one-fifteenth of a mill on the taxable property in the State. This yields about $85,000 annually. This is what the people of the State are now contributing for the support of the University—less than four cents per capita. In other words, the average voter pays less than fifteen cents annually for the support of the University.

Indiana University, in common with other State universities of the West and Northwest, has had free tuition. There has been, however, a contingent fee of five dollars per term in addition to small charges for the use of the library, laboratories, and gymnasiums.

The Trustees for several years have desired to abolish the contingent fees in the departments of liberal arts as soon as they could do so. They have felt that instruction should be absolutely free in all parts of the public school system of which Indiana University is an essential part. Never until now have they seen their way to do so. The income of about $10,000 per year from these fees is much needed for the proper equipment of the University, but notwithstanding these needs, they have thought best to pass the following resolution which explains itself:

"Whereas, It is desirable that admission and attendance at Indiana University be absolutely free to the people of the State.

"Resolved, That from and after January 1, 1901, all contingent fees be abolished, except in the School of Law: Provided, however, That this resolution shall not be construed to do away with a reasonable charge for the use of the gymnasiums, library, and the equipment and supplies in the laboratories."

On February 7, 1900, Wylie Hall was partially burned. The fire originated from chemical explosion. It was purely an accident and no one was at fault in the matter. Every effort was made to extinguish the flames, but the upper story, excepting the brick walls, was consumed before the fire could be put out. Both the building and contents were fully insured. The insurance companies paid $19,404.90. This would have been sufficient to rebuild and refit the building before the fire. The Trustees decided, however, that it was economy to place a third story on the building, which was done at a cost of about $10,000. The whole building is now fireproof.

A stone observatory building and a telescope of 12-inch aperture have been completed on the campus. The total cost of the equipped observatory was about $12,000. All these contracts were advertised in State papers and trade journals and let to the lowest bidders in each case.

The University has grown much more rapidly in attendance than in the addition of buildings. As a result, all departments are very greatly crowded. Every foot of space in all the buildings, including basements and attics, is utilized. In order to provide more room for students, classes are running all day, morning and afternoon. Seven departments are wholly or in part in basements and attics. The administrative offices and the classes of eight teachers are in the building used for a library. All this space is needed for other purposes. No assembly room is provided. The chapel services and other gatherings are held in the men's gymnasium. The laboratories are very much crowded. No museum is provided. The demand for library facilities is greatly in excess of the supply.

The Trustees respectfully call the attention of His Excellency, the Governor, and through him the attention of the Legislature, to the overwhelming demand for room in Indiana University. They shall express the belief also that every additional dollar given by the State for the support of the State University will count for better citizenship. The State receives no better return than from money expended in all grades of the public schools.

ISAAC JENKINSON,
President Trustees, Indiana
University.

Indiana *Documentary Journal,* 1900.

Document 94

The Seventy-Seventh Year

Within a decade, three separate histories of Indiana University appeared in essay form: one by Trustee David D. Banta, one by James A. Woodburn, and the following documentary statement by an unidentified compiler. All three of them make contributions. This one was particularly concerned about Indiana University's relation to the state. It draws together the various statutory provisions which established and governed the institution. Especially significant is the inclusion of the law of March 8, 1895, which provided for the levy of a millage tax on assessed real property for the support of Indiana, Purdue, and the Indiana State Normal School.

*   *   *

THE UNIVERSITY

ITS HISTORY

The legislation which led to the founding of Indiana University begins with two acts of Congress setting aside portions of the public domain, within the limits of the present State of Indiana, for the endowment of an institution of higher learning. The first of these is an act, approved March 26, 1804, for the disposal of the public lands in the Indiana Territory; in it provision is made for the reservation "of an entire township in each of the three described tracts of country or districts [Detroit, Kaskaskia, and Vincennes], to be located by the Secretary of the Treasury, for the use of a seminary of learning." The second is the act of April 16, 1816, which provides for the admission into the Union of the district of Vincennes as the State of Indiana; in this an additional township is set aside "for the use of a seminary of learning and vested in the legislature of said State, to be appropriated solely to the uses of such seminary by the said legislature." These two seminary townships for Indiana were located, the one in what is now Gibson county, October 10, 1806, by Albert Gallatin as Secretary of the Treasury; the other by President Madison, in 1816, in what is now Monroe county.

The first act of local legislation looking toward a university in Indiana is the act of the Territorial Legislature, approved November 9, 1806, establishing the borough of Vincennes "an university . . . to be known by the name and style of The Vincennes University," and appropriating to its use the township of land reserved by the act of Congress of 1804. Owing to a number of circumstances the institution thus established did not prosper, and when the Indiana Seminary, which was later to become the Indiana University, was established, the General Assembly turned over to it the Gibson county lands, together with the township of land in Monroe county. This action led to a long and tedious litigation, which finally resulted in a verdict of the Supreme Court of the United States, in 1853, in favor of Vincennes University. To compensate the University for the loss of endowment thus sustained, Congress granted to the State 19,040 acres of public land in Indiana "for the use of the Indiana University" (Acto of February 23, 1854).

In the constitution of the State, adopted in 1816, upon its admission to the Union, the following provisions occur with respect to education:

ARTICLE IX.

SECTION 1. Knowledge and learning, generally diffused through a community, being essential to the preservation of a free government, and spreading the opportunities and advantages of education through the various parts of the country, being highly conducive to this end, it shall be the duty of the General Assembly to provide by law, for the improvement of such lands as are, or hereafter may be granted by the United States to this state for the use of schools, and to apply any funds which may be raised from such lands, or from any other quarter, to the accomplishment of the grand object for which they are or may be intended: But no lands granted for the use of schools or seminaries of learning, shall be sold by authority of this state, prior to the year eighteen hundred and twenty; and the monies which may be raised out of the sale of any such lands, or otherwise obtained for the purposes aforesaid, shall be and remain a fund for the exclusive purpose of promoting the interest of literature and the sciences, and for the support of seminaries and public schools. The general assembly shall, from time to time, pass such laws as shall be calculated to encourage intellectual, scientifical, and agricultural improvement, by allowing rewards and immunities for the promotion and improvement of arts, sciences, commerce, manufactures, and natural history; and to countenance and encourage the principles of humanity, industry, and morality.

SEC. 2. It shall be the duty of the general assembly, as soon as circumstances will permit, to provide by law, for a general system of education, ascending in a regular gradation from township schools to a state university, wherein tuition shall be gratis, and equally open to all.

In accordance with this last provision of the Constitution, the General Assembly, by an act passed and approved January 20, 1820, took the first definite step toward the establishment of the Indiana University. The act is as follows:

AN ACT *to establish a State Seminary, and for other purposes.*
[APPROVED JANUARY 20, 1820.]
SECTION 1. *Be it enacted by the General Assembly of the State of Indiana,* That Charles Dewey, Jonathan Lindley, David H. Maxwell, John M. Jenkins,

Jonathan Nichols, and William Lowe, be, and they are hereby appointed trustees of the state seminary, for the state of Indiana, and shall be known by the name and style of the trustees of the state seminary, of the state of Indiana, and they, and their successors in office, shall have perpetual succession, and by the name and style aforesaid, shall be able and capable in law, to sue, and be sued, plead, and be impleaded, answer, and be answered unto, as a body corporate and politic, in any court of justice; and the trustees hereby appointed, shall continue in office, until the first day of January, one thousand eight hundred and twenty-one, and until their successors are chosen and qualified.

SECTION 2. The trustees aforesaid, or a majority of them, shall meet at Bloomington, in the county of Monroe, on the first Monday in June next, or so soon thereafter as may be convenient, and being first duly sworn to discharge the duties of their office, shall repair to the reserved township of land in said county, which was granted by Congress to this state for the use of a seminary of learning, and proceed to select an eligible and convenient site for a state seminary.

SECTION 3. It shall be lawful for the trustees hereby appointed to appoint an agent, who shall give bond with security to be approved of by the trustees aforesaid, payable to the Governor and his successors in office, for the use of the state seminary aforesaid, in the sum of twenty thousand dollars, conditioned for the faithful performance of the duties of his office; and it shall be the duty of the agent aforesaid, after taking an oath of office, to proceed to lay off, and expose to sale, under the sanction of the trustees aforesaid, any number of lots, or quantity of land, within the reserved township, aforesaid, and contiguous to Bloomington, not exceeding one section, or six hundred and forty acres thereof.

SECTION 4. It shall be the duty of the agent aforesaid, first to expose to sale, such lots as may be selected most contiguous to the site which may be selected for the seminary aforesaid, and take of the purchasers of any lots or lands which he may sell, under the provisions of this act, such payments and security therefor as may be directed by the trustees aforesaid.

SECTION 5. The trustees aforesaid, shall so soon as they deem it expedient, proceed to the erection of a suitable building for a state seminary, as also a suitable and commodious house for a Professor, on the site which may be selected by them for that purpose.

SECTION 6. The trustees aforesaid, shall within ten days after the meeting of the next General Assembly, lay before them a true and perfect statement of their proceedings so far as they have progressed under the provisions of this act, and a plat of the lots or lands laid off and sold, and the amount of the proceeds of such sales, and also a plan of buildings, by them erected, or proposed to be erected.

SECTION 7. The trustees hereby appointed, shall, before they enter upon the duties of their office, give bond and security, to be approved of by the Governor, in the sum of five thousand dollars, payable to the Governor and his successors in office, for the use of the state seminary, conditioned for the faithful performance of the duties of their office; and if any vacancy, by an appointment which shall expire on the first day of January next.

As a result of this legislation the new seminary was opened in May, 1824. Within three years it had made such progress in number of students and the general character of its work that a Board of Visitors, appointed by the General Assembly in 1827, recommended that the Indiana Seminary be raised to the dignity of a college. This recommendation, indorsed by Governor Ray in his annual message, induced the General Assembly to pass the following act:

AN ACT *to establish a College in the State of Indiana.*
[APPROVED JANUARY 24, 1828.]

SECTION 1. *Be it enacted by the General Assembly of the State of Indiana,*
That there shall be, and hereby is created and established a college, adjacent to
the town of Bloomington, in the county of Monroe, for the education of youth
in the American, learned, and foreign languages, the useful arts, sciences, and
literature, to be known by the name and style of the Indiana college, and to be
governed and regulated as hereinafter directed.

SECTION 2. There shall be a board of trustees appointed, consisting of fifteen
persons, residents of this state, who shall be, and hereby are constituted a body
corporate and politic, by the name of "The trustees of the Indiana college,"
and in their said corporate name and capacity may sue and be sued, plead and
be impleaded, in any court of record, and by that name shall have perpetual
succession.

SECTION 3. The said trustees shall fill all vacancies which may happen in their
own body, elect a president of the board, secretary, treasurer, and such other
officers as may be necessary for the good order and government of said corporation, and shall be competent at law and in equity to take to themselves and
their successors, in their said corporate name, any estate, real, personal or mixed,
by the gift, grant, bargain, sale, conveyance, will, devise, or bequest of any person
or persons whomsoever, and the same estate, whether real or personal, to grant,
bargain, sell, convey, demise, let, place out on interest, or otherwise dispose of,
for the use of said College, in such manner as to them shall seem most beneficial to the institution, and to receive the rents, issues, profits, income and
interest thereon, and apply the same to the proper use and support of the said
College, and generally, in their said corporate name, shall have full power to
do and transact all and every the business touching or concerning the premises,
or which shall be incidentally necessary thereto, as fully and effectually as any
natural person, body politic or corporate may or can do, in the management of
their own concerns, and to hold, enjoy, exercise and use the rights, powers and
privileges incident to bodies politic or corporate, in law and in equity.

SECTION 4. The said trustees shall cause to be made for their use, one common
seal, with such devices and inscriptions thereon as they shall think proper,
under and by which all deeds, diplomas, certificates and acts of the said corporation shall pass and be authenticated.

. . . .

SECTION 7. The said board of trustees shall, from time to time, as the interests
of the institution may require, elect a president of said college, and such professors, tutors, instructors and other officers of the same, as they may judge
necessary for the interests thereof, and shall determine the duties, salaries,
emoluments, responsibilities and tenures of their several offices, and designate
the course of instruction in said college.

. . . .

SECTION 9. The president, professors, and tutors, shall be styled the faculty of
said college; which faculty shall have the power of enforcing the rules and
regulations adopted by the said trustees for the government of the students,
by rewarding or censuring them, and finally by suspending such as, after
repeated admonition, shall continue refractory, until a determination of a
quorum of the trustees can be had thereon; and of granting and conferring, by
and with the approbation and consent of the board of trustees, such degrees
in the liberal arts and sciences as are usually granted and conferred in other

colleges in America, to the students of the college, or others who by their proficiency in learning or other meritorious distinction may be entitled to the same, and to grant unto such graduates, diplomas, or certificates, under their common seal, and signed by the faculty to authenticate and perpetuate the memory of such graduations.

SECTION 10. No president, professor, or other officer of the College, shall, whilst acting in that capacity, be a trustee, nor shall any president, professor, tutor, instructor, or other officer of the College ever be required by the trustees to profess any particular religious opinions, and no student shall be denied admission, or refused any of the privileges, honors, or degrees of the College, on account of the religious opinions he may entertain, nor shall any sectarian tenets or principles be taught, instructed or inculcated at said College by any president, professor, tutor or instructor thereof.

. . . .

SECTION 12. That all monies arising from the sale of the Seminary townships, in the counties of Monroe and Gibson, shall be and forever remain a permanent fund, for the support of said College, and the interest arising from the amount of said sale, together with the three reserved sections in the Seminary townships, situated in the county of Monroe, and all the buildings which have been erected adjacent to the town of Bloomington in the said county of Monroe, for the use of the State Seminary, with all the real and personal property of every description belonging to or connected with said State Seminary, as the property of the State, and all gifts, grants and donations which have been or hereafter may be made, for the support of the College, shall be, and hereby are forever vested in the aforesaid trustees and their successors, to be controlled, regulated and appropriated by them in such manner as they shall deem most conducive to the best interest and prosperity of the institution: *Provided,* That the said trustees shall conform to the will of any donor or donors in the application of any estate which may be given, devised or bequeathed for any particular object connected with the institution, and that the real estate hereby vested in the said trustees and their successors, shall be by them held forever for the use of said College, and shall not be sold or converted by them to any other use whatsoever.

. . . .

SECTION 16. That the constitution of the said College herein and hereby declared and established, shall remain the inviolable constitution of said College, and the same shall not be changed, altered or amended by any law or ordinance of the said trustees, nor in any other manner than by the legislature of this State. . . .

The continued growth and increasing importance of the institution led the General Assembly, in 1838, to confer upon it the name and style of the Indiana University. The material portions of this, the third charter of the University, are as follows:

AN ACT *to establish a University in the State of Indiana.*
[APPROVED FEBRUARY 15, 1838.]

SECTION 1. *Be it enacted by the General Assembly of the State of Indiana,* That there shall be, and hereby is created and established a University adjacent to the town of Bloomington, in the county of Monroe, for the education of youth in the American, learned and foreign languages, the useful arts, sciences (including law and medicine) and literature, to be known by the name and style of the "Indiana University," and to be governed and directed as hereinafter directed.

SECTION 2. There shall be a board of trustees appointed, consisting of twenty-one persons, residents of the State, who shall be, and hereby are constituted a body corporate and politic, by the name of "the trustees of the Indiana University," and in their corporate name and capacity, may sue and be sued, plead and be impleaded, in any court of record, and by that name shall have perpetual succession.

. . . .

SECTION 12. That all moneys which have heretofore or which may hereafter arise from the sales of the seminary townships of land in the counties of Monroe and Gibson, shall be and forever remain a permanent fund for the support of said University, and the interest arising from the amount of said sales, together with the amount of the sales of the three reserved sections in the seminary township, situated in the county of Monroe, the residue of the unsold sections aforesaid, and all the buildings which have been erected adjacent to the town of Bloomington, in the said county of Monroe, and which are now used by and belong to the Indiana College, together with all the estate, whether real, personal, or of any description whatever, belonging to, or in any wise connected with the Indiana College, as the property of the state, and all gifts, grants, and donations which have been or may hereafter be made, previous to the taking effect of this act, for the support of the Indiana College, shall be and hereby are forever vested in the aforesaid trustees and their successors, to be controlled, regulated, and appropriated by them in such manner as they shall deem most conducive to the best interest and prosperity of the institution: *Provided,* That the said trustees shall conform to the will of any donor or donors in the application of any estate which may be given, devised or bequeathed for any particular object connected with the institution, and that the real estate hereby vested in the said trustees and their successors, shall be by them held forever for the use of said university, and shall not be sold or converted by them to any other use whatsoever.

. . . .

SECTION 16. That the power and authority of the present trustees of the Indiana College, over and concerning the said institution, the funds, estate, property, rights and demands thereof shall forever cease and determine, from and after the organization of the board of trustees of [the] Indiana University named in this act; and all the funds, estate, property, rights, demands, privileges and immunities, of what kind or nature soever belonging or any wise pertaining to said Indiana College, shall be and the same are hereby invested in the Trustees of [the] Indiana University appointed by this act, and their successors in office, for the uses and purposes only of said university, and the said trustees and their successors in office shall have, hold, possess, and exercise all the powers and authority over the said institution and the estate and concerns thereof in the manner hereinbefore prescribed.

Between the years 1838 and 1851, a number of acts relating to the University were passed by the General Assembly. Of these most are concerned with the sale of the Seminary lands and with similar matters; but one, the act of February 15, 1841, reduces the number of Trustees to nine, exempts students at the University from militia duty and road taxes, and denies to the civil courts of the State jurisdiction of "trivial breaches of the peace committed by the students of said university within the college campus."

In 1851 the present constitution of the State was adopted, and in it the following provision with respect to education occurs:

ARTICLE VIII.

SECTION 1. Knowledge and learning, generally diffused throughout a community, being essential to the preservation of a free government; it shall be the duty of the General Assembly to encourage, by all suitable means, moral, intellectual, scientific, and agricultural improvement; and to provide, by law, for a general and uniform system of Common Schools, wherein tuition shall be without charge and equally open to all.

. . . .

SECTION 7. All trust fund, held by the State, shall remain inviolate, and be faithfully and exclusively applied to the purposes for which the trust was created.

In the convention which adopted the constitution, the question of the relation of the State to the Indiana University had arisen, but no explicit statement was incorporated in the constitution. At the first session of the General Assembly after the adjournment of the convention, it was therefore thought desirable to have an explicit statement on the subject; and to this end the act which may be regarded as the fourth charter of the University, and the one by which in the main the University is still governed, was adopted. Its material provisions are given below:

AN ACT *providing for the government of the State University, the management of its Fund, and for the disposition of the Lands thereof.*
[APPROVED JUNE 17, 1853.]

SECTION 1. *Be it enacted by the General Assembly of the State of Indiana,* The institution established by an act entitled "an act to establish a college in the State of Indiana," approved January 28, 1828, is hereby recognized as the University of the State.

. . . .

SECTION 5. The trustees of said university shall receive the proceeds of the sales and rents of the three reserved sections in the seminary township in Monroe county, and the same shall be paid to the treasurer of said trustees, on their order.

. . . .

SECTION 7. The president, professors and instructors shall be styled "The Faculty" of said university, and shall have power:

First. To enforce the regulations adopted by the trustees for the government of the students.

Second. To which end they may reward and censure, and may suspend those who continue refractory, until a determination of the board of trustees can be had thereon.

Third. To confer, with the consent of the trustees, such literary degrees as are usually conferred in other universities, and in testimony thereof to give suitable diplomas, under the seal of the university and signature of the faculty.

SECTION 8. No religious qualification shall be required for any student, trustee, president, professor, or other officer of such university, or as a condition for admission to any privilege in the same.

. . . .

SECTION 13. The Governor, Lieutenant Governor, Speaker of the House of Representatives, Judges of the Supreme Court, and Superintendent of Common Schools, shall constitute a board of visitors of the university, and any three thereof a quorum.

SECTION 14. In case the members of such board of visitors fail to attend the annual commencement exercises of the university, the president of the board of trustees shall report such of them as are absent to the next General Assembly in their annual report.

SECTION 15. Such board of visitors shall examine the property, the course of study and discipline, and the state of the finances of the university, and recommend such amendments as they may deem proper, the books and accounts of the institution being open to their inspection, and they shall make report of their examination to the Governor, to be by him laid before the next General Assembly.

SECTION 16. The secretary of the board of trustees shall keep a true record of all the proceedings of said board and certify copies thereof. He shall also keep an account of the students in the university according to their classes, stating their respective ages and places of residence, and a list of all graduates.

. . . .

SECTION 18. The board of trustees, their secretary and treasurer, shall report to the superintendent of common schools all matters relating to the university, when by him required.

The second section of the above act deals with the composition and duties of the Board of Trustees. This section has been modified by an act approved March 3, 1855, and still more recently by an act of March 3, 1891. The provisions of this latter act are so important that they are given practically in full:

AN ACT *prescribing the number of Trustees of the Indiana University and the manner of their election, and declaring an emergency.*
[APPROVED MARCH 3, 1891.]

SECTION 1. *Be it enacted by the General Assembly of the State of Indiana,* That the Trustees of Indiana University shall hereafter be elected for such terms of service, and in such manner as is herein provided, and the terms of service of the Trustees now in office, and of those hereafter elected, shall expire on the first day of July of the year in which such terms are to end.

SECTION 2. Successors to three Trustees whose terms of service expire in the year eighteen hundred and ninety-one (1891) shall be elected by the Alumni of the University at the College Commencement of the year 1891; one of the Trustees so elected shall serve for one year, one for two years, and one for three years. At the first meeting of the Board of Trustees after July 1, 1891, the several terms of service of such three Trustees shall be determined by lot. At the annual commencement of the year in which their terms expire, successors to such three Trustees shall be elected by the Alumni of the University, each to serve for three years. When vacancies in the Board of Trustees arise from death, resignation, removal from the State, expiration of term of service, or otherwise, of any of the three Trustees to be elected in 1891, or of any of their successors, such vacancies shall be filled by the Alumni.

SECTION 3. Successors to the two Trustees whose terms of service expire in 1893 shall be elected by the State Board of Education, and one of such two successors shall be elected for a term of two years, and the other for a term of three years. Successors to the three Trustees whose terms expire in 1894 shall be elected by the State Board of Education, one for a term of two years, and the other two Trustees for a term of three years. Successors to the five Trustees herein provided to be elected by the State Board of Education, shall be elected by the said State Board of Education, each Trustees so elected to serve for three years: *Provided,* That Trustees elected by the Alumni or the State Board of Education, to fill vacancies caused otherwise than by expiration of terms of service, shall be elected for such unexpired terms only. When vacancies in the Board of Trustees arise from death, resignation, removal from the State, expiration of term of service, or otherwise, of any of the five Trustees or their successors herein provided to be elected by the State Board of Education, such vacancies shall be filled by said State Board of Education.

SECTION 4. A registry of the name and address of each Alumnus of Indiana University residing in the State of Indiana shall be kept by the Librarian of said University, who shall correct such addresses when notified by the Alumni so to do. The Alumni of the University shall be those persons who have been awarded and on whom have been conferred any of the following degrees: Bachelor of Arts (A.B.), Bachelor of Letters (B.L.), Bachelor of Science (B.S.), Bachelor of Philosophy (B.Ph.), Bachelor of Laws (LL.B.), Master of Arts (A.M.), Master of Science (M.S.), Doctor of Philosophy (Ph.D.).

SECTION 5. Any ten or more Alumni may file with the Librarian of the University, on or before the first day of April in each year, a written nomination for the Trustee or Trustees to be elected by the Alumni at the next college commencement. Forthwith after such first day of April, a list of such candidates shall be mailed by said Librarian to each Alumnus at his address.

SECTION 6. The annual meeting of the Alumni for the election of Trustees shall be held at the University on the Tuesday before the annual commencement day of said University, at the hour of nine o'clock a.m., at which meeting a Trustee shall be elected to serve for three years from the first day of July of such year, and any Trustee or Trustees which the Alumni may be entitled to elect to complete any unexpired term or terms.

SECTION 7. Each Alumnus resident in the State of Indiana may send to said Librarian, over his signature, at any time before the meeting of the Alumni for the election of such Trustee or Trustees, the vote for such Trustee or Trustees which he would be entitled to cast if personally present at such meeting, which vote such Librarian shall deliver to such meeting to be opened and counted at said election, together with the votes of those who are personally present; but no person shall have more than one vote. The person or persons having the highest number of votes upon the first ballot shall be declared the Trustee or Trustees according as there may be one or more than one Trustee to be elected: *Provided,* The votes received by said persons, or by each of said persons, [are] at least fifty per cent. of all the votes cast. Otherwise, the Alumni personally present at said meeting shall, from the two having the highest pluralities, elect a Trustee, unless their pluralities shall aggregate less than fifty per cent. of the votes cast, in which case there shall be included in the number of those to be voted for, so many of those coming after such two highest in order of pluralities as will bring the aggregate of such pluralities of those to be voted for to fifty per cent. of the votes cast. . . .

The funds of the University, in its earlier days, were derived almost wholly from the proceeds of the Seminary lands, from gifts, and from fees paid by students. In 1867, by an act approved March 8, the General Assembly provided for the increase of these funds by an annual appropriation. "Whereas," the act read, "the endowment fund of the State University, located at Bloomington, Monroe county, is no longer sufficient to meet the growing wants of education and make said University efficient and useful; and whereas, it should be the pride of every citizen of Indiana to place the State University in the highest condition of usefulness and make it the crowning glory of our present great common school system, where education shall be free," therefore eight thousand dollars annually were appropriated out of the State treasury to the use of the University. This amount was found to be insufficient, and from time to time the amount of the annual appropriation was increased. In 1883, by an act approved March 8, provision was made for a permanent endowment fund to be raised by the levy for thirteen years of a tax of "one-half of one cent on each one hundred dollars' worth of taxable property in this State," to be paid into the State treasury to the credit of the Indiana University. Finally, in 1895, the following act was passed:

AN ACT *to provide funds for the benefit of the Indiana University, Purdue University and the Indiana State Normal School, and declaring an emergency, and repealing all laws and parts of laws in conflict therewith.*
[APPROVED MARCH 8, 1895.]

SECTION 1. *Be it enacted by the General Assembly of the State of Indiana,* That there shall be assessed and levied upon the taxable property of the State of Indiana, in the year one thousand eight hundred and ninety-five (1895), and in each year thereafter, for the use and benefit of the Indiana University, Purdue University and the Indiana State Normal School, to be apportioned and distributed as hereinafter in this act provided, a tax of one-sixth (1/6) of one mill on every dollar of taxable property in Indiana, to be levied, assessed, collected and paid into the treasury of the State of Indiana, in like manner as other State taxes are levied, assessed, collected and paid. And so much of the proceeds of said levy as may be in the State treasury on the first day of July and the first day of January of each year, shall be immediately thereafter paid over to the Boards of Trustees of the respective institutions for which the tax was levied, to be distributed and apportioned among them severally upon the basis as follows, viz: To the said Trustees of Indiana University upon the basis of one-fifteenth (1/15) of one mill; to the Trustees of Purdue University upon the basis of one-twentieth (1/20) of one mill, and to the Trustees of the Indiana State Normal School upon the basis of one-twentieth (1/20) of one mill on every dollar of taxable property in Indiana, and the Auditor of State of the State of Indiana is hereby directed to draw a proper warrant therefor.

SECTION 2. All moneys due said institutions respectively, in accordance with any State law heretofore enacted, or that may hereafter be enacted, making annual appropriations thereto for maintenance, shall be paid to the respective institutions for the fiscal year 1895–6 and not thereafter, it being the intent that the moneys appropriated by the first section of this act shall from and after the date of the first payment thereof be paid in lieu of the moneys described in this section: *Provided,* That nothing in this act shall affect in any way any permanent fund that may belong to or may have been appropriated for either the Indiana University or Purdue University, named in this act, and that the proceeds of this tax accruing to Indiana University shall be used for maintenance.

Admission to the University was, until the college year 1868–69, restricted to men; but by a resolution of the Board of Trustees the doors of the University were at the beginning of that year opened to women on the same terms as to men. Since 1869, therefore, the University has been co-educational in all its departments.

At the November meeting of the Board of Trustees, 1900, a resolution was adopted declaring all contingent fees (excepting those in the School of Law) abolished from and after January 1, 1901. This does not, however, do away with "reasonable charges for the use of the gymnasium, library, and equipments and supplies for the laboratories."

RELATION TO THE STATE

By virtue of the State constitutions of 1816 and 1851, and the acts of the General Assembly thereunder, the Indiana University is the State University of Indiana, and the head of the public school system of the state. In order that there might be no doubt of the special relationship of the University to the State under the new constitution of 1851, the General Assembly in 1852 enacted that "the institution established by an act entitled 'an act to establish a college in the State of Indiana,' approved January 28, 1828, is hereby recognized as the University of the State" (act approved June 17, 1852; see p. 30) ; and again in 1867 the General Assembly characterized it as the "crowning glory of our present great common school system" (act approved March 8, 1867; see p. 33) .

Cognate schools, connected with the public school system, are Purdue University, at Lafayette, established under the Morrill Act of Congress as the State School of Agriculture and Mechanic Arts, and the State Normal School at Terre Haute, founded for the training of teachers. The Board of Trustees of the Indiana University is required to report biennially to the Governor of the State, and to the Superintendent of Public Instruction whenever by him requested, on all matters relating to the University. The whole administration of the University is likewise open to the inspection of a Board of Visitors, composed ex-officio of the chief executive, legislative; and judicial officers of the State; and all accounts of the University are regularly audited by the Auditor of State. The President of the University, also, is ex-officio a member of the State Board of Education, a body which has general supervision of public education within the State. The law, as amended March 4, 1899, provides that this board shall be composed as follows: "The Governor of the State, the State Superintendent of Public Instruction, the president of the State University, the president of Purdue University, the president of the State Normal School, the superintendent of common schools of the three largest cities in the State, and three citizens of prominence actively engaged in educational work in the State, appointed by the Governor, at least one of whom shall be a county superintendent, none of whom shall be appointed from any county in which any other member of the State Board of Education resides, or from which any other member was appointed." The State Board, as thus constituted, consists at present of the following members: Frank L. Jones, Superintendent of Public Instruction (ex-officio President) ; Winfield T. Durbin, Governor of Indiana; Joseph Swain, President of the Indiana University, Winthrop E. Stone, President of Purdue University; William W. Parsons, Secretary, President of the State Normal School; Calvin N. Kendall, Superintendent of the Indianapolis schools; W. A. Hester, Superintendent of the Evansville schools; J. N. Study, Superintend–University; William W. Parsons (Secretary) , President of Earlham College; W. T. Stott, President of Franklin College, and Enoch G. Machan, Superintendent of the Lagrange County schools.

The Indiana University Catalogue, Seventy-Seventh College Year (Bloomington, 1901), pp. 22–37, 37–38.

Document 95

"Plain Beyond the Necessity of Argument"

Isaac Jenkinson must have grown weary reporting to one governor after another that Indiana University had substantial needs far beyond the state's willingness to support it. The table of income from 1891 to 1902 included in this document gives a good view of the University's fiscal situation. There were 1,334 students—a record—but there was neither adequate staff nor space to offer the kind of program the administration and faculty deemed necessary. The meager library was housed in the basement of Maxwell Hall, the books stored on wooden shelves. Even the completion of Science Hall made almost unmanageable demands on the services necessary to operate it.

*   *   *

REPORT OF THE INDIANA UNIVERSITY.

BLOOMINGTON, IND., December 12, 1902
To the HON. WINFIELD T. DURBIN, *Governor of Indiana:*
Dear Sir—I have the honor to transmit to you the biennial report of the Board of Trustees of Indiana University for the fiscal years ending October 31, 1901, and October 31, 1902.
On June 24, 1902, the Supreme Court of Indiana, in the case of Fisher vs. Brower, rendered a decision, without a dissenting opinion, that "the Indiana University is an integral part of our free school system;" "that it was the special creation of the Constitution," and that "the University as well as its endowment has always been under the supervision of the State."
This decision may be regarded as the final act in the long struggle for a complete system of free schools maintained by the State.
The Constitution of 1816 required such a system "ascending in regular gradation from township schools to a State university wherein tuition shall be gratis and equally open to all." But no part of the school system required by the Constitution has been established without a struggle.
In 1848, out of a total vote of 140,410 on the establishment of free common schools, 61,887 (about 44 per cent.) votes were cast in the negative. In the half century since that time the whole people have come to be of one mind in favor of the common schools maintained by the State.
The free public high school (replacing the old private academy) established itself gradually in custom before it was adequately recognized in law. The strength of the original opposition to the high school is indicated by the fact that that opposition is not yet wholly dead. There still survives, here and there, a man who would have the State school system close with the eighth grade. The extreme rarity of these men shows how thoroughly the people of the State have been converted to belief in education.
Like the State common schools and the State high school, the State University has had to struggle for its life. But, as the decision cited above recites in detail, the State of Indiana has at all times by repeated legislative acts maintained the University as "an integral part of our free school system." And as in the case

of the common and high schools, the opposition once so strong is disappearing, and is practically a thing of the past.

At the present time the "free school system ascending in regular gradation from the township schools to the State University" is finally established in fact, in law, and in the convictions and affections of the people of Indiana.

Two main questions confront the University, as they do the school system as a whole. First, the question of maintenance. Second, the question of adaptation to the needs of the people. The two questions belong together, for the needs can be met only if means for maintenance be provided.

What the people need and demand is that their children shall have a chance—as good a chance as any other children in the world—to make the most of themselves, to rise into any and every occupation, including those occupations which require the most thorough training. What people want is *open paths* from every corner of the State through the schools to the highest and best things which men can achieve. To make such paths, to make them open to the poorest and to make them lead to the highest, is the mission of democracy.

In this work the State University has an essential part to perform. It has to meet in fact and in full measure the promises of the common schools. It has to make accessible to the people the highest learning in many fields and it has to open the way to the highest levels in many great occupations. The University comes, without an apology, asking that the State shall make adequate Financial provision for the fulfillment of this great mission.

Enrollment. The following table shows the annual attendance the past ten years:

1891–2	497
1892–3	572
1893–4	633
1894–5	771
1895–6	879
1896–7	944
1897–8	1,049
1898–9	1,050
1899–00	1,016
1900–01	1,137
1901–02	1,334
1902–03	1,500*

* Estimated.

The enrollment to date for the present year is 1,183, an increase of 190 over the corresponding date last year. At this rate of increase the attendance for the year will exceed 1,500. For the past five years every county in the State has been represented annually.

The total attendance last year at the time the catalogue went to press was 1,285. Later forty-nine students enrolled, making a total for the year of 1,334. One-half of the students of last year came from north of a line drawn east and west through Indianapolis.

Income. The following table shows the income of the University for each year since 1891–2 (omitting balance carried over from year to year):

1891–2	$ 64,728 85
1892–3	63,766 32
1893–4	117,791 18

1894–5	105,767 07
1895–6	111,289 69
1896–7	139,788 83
1897–8	131,943 64
1898–9	137,797 02
1899–00	153,849 63*
1900–01	142,527 00
1901–02	129,961 01

* This includes $19,904.90 fire insurance on Wylie Hall.

The following chart shows in one view the total enrollment and the total income for each year since 1891–2: [CHART OMITTED HERE]

The vastly larger body of students, the necessarily larger teaching force, and the necessarily greater cost of maintaining the plant, taken in connection with the abolition of tuition fees, have made the problem of maintenance extremely difficult during the past two years.

The appropriations for the laboratories have been cut to a point below which their efficiency would be seriously impaired. Yet each year the increasing attendance makes the demands upon the laboratories greater.

The appropriations for library purposes have been cut to such a point that the departments can not buy the representative current books in their several lines.

Additional instructors, much needed in overcrowded departments, could not be employed on account of lack of funds.

Six heads of departments have received offers of higher salaries elsewhere within the year.

Twelve thousand books and pamphlets are placed on wooden shelves in the basement of Maxwell Hall, where they are subject to deterioration from dampness, and where they, with the shelves, increase the danger from fire. The Legislative Committee of four years ago called special attention in its report (page 43) to this fact. The University has not had and does not have money to buy the metal stacks for these books, even when it shall have the room for them up stairs.

Science Hall, which is now about completed, is a very much needed addition to our plant, but also of course involves extra expense for heat, light, water, janitor service, etc. We have not the money to meet this expense.

Next year, $60,000, the gift of students, alumni and friends of the University, will be spent for two buildings to be used by the students for social and religious purposes. These buildings will become the property of the State and will be of great service to the University. But they will involve additional expense for heat, light, water, janitor service, etc., and this expense we have no means of meeting.

In a word, the University's need of greater income is plain beyond the necessity of argument. We are in the position of a city whose school enrollment has nearly doubled while its funds for school purposes have not increased. Each year, in spite of more rigid entrance requirements, an increasing number of young people from every corner of the State are crowding in upon us. This is the decisive annual vote of the people of the State that they want the opportunities offered here. The University comes—as in law, and in fact—as an integral part of the common school system of the State, to ask that the State provide for its own children.

We ask that the fraction of a mill tax for the maintenance of the State University be increased from one-fifteenth (1/15) of a mill to one-tenth (1/10) of a mill. We feel that no smaller increase than this one-thirtieth (1/30) of a mill should be considered. It makes only a minimum provision for the maintenance of the University on a strictly economical basis. In proof of this, we invite and urge the most thorough-going investigation of all the facts of the situation.

The Completion and Equipment of Science Hall. Notwithstanding the great increase in the cost of material and labor, the Trustees have been able to build and equip the new science building as a fire proof structure within the appropriation of $100,000.00 made therefor by the last Legislature, and now have it ready for occupancy.

In order to heat the building in the most economical way, it has been necessary to make additions to the small central heating plant amounting to $8,120.00, which additions can all be utilized to advantage in the construction of the new heating and light plant hereafter referred to. The furniture and laboratory equipment of the building will cost $3,897.00. These two items, aggregating $12,017.00, should be provided for by a special appropriation.

The Heating and Lighting Plant. The heating and lighting plant of the University is quite inadequate and is not economical from the point of view of coal consumption. From the standpoint of the State the erection and maintenance of such a plant is not good business. From the standpoint of the University it has been a matter of necessity. We have submitted to the Legislative Committee estimates by competent engineers as to the cost of reorganizing the heating and lighting plant upon a moderate basis. Their estimate is $33,850.00. They estimate a saving in fuel of 20 to 25 per cent.

The Library. Four years ago the Legislative Committee called attention to the inadequacy of existing library facilities. There is not room enough for the books nor for those who use them. One-fourth of the books are in a damp basement, on wooden shelves. We have submitted to the Legislative Committee an architect's estimate for an addition to the library to cost $35,280.00

In conclusion, we desire to call attention to the fact that friends of the University have given precisely one-half as much for the erection of buildings on the campus as the State has appropriated for that purpose.

All buildings, by whomsoever given, are the property of the State.

Respectuflly submitted,
ISAAC JENKINSON,
President Board of Trustees.

Indiana *Documentary Journal*, 1902.

Document 96

Flee Like Elijah to Horeb

President Joseph Swain left Indiana University to accept the presidency of Swarthmore. His presidency in Bloomington had been diligent and faithful without being flamboyant. His successor, William Lowe Bryan, was in most respects an altogether different personality. Bryan, if not a patrician, was then a man of high personal moral and religious standards. His ideals were those of the scholarly philosopher. The intellectual perspective of the new president was set forth in his inaugural address. He declared that the salvation of the common man was also the salvation of society.

*   *   *

FAITH IN EDUCATION

Inaugural Address, January 21, 1903

I WISH to speak for a very few minutes of that faith of the people in education of which this University is one product.

The faith of a people, says Professor Tarde, the real faith, which determines what they want and work at and achieve, is indicated by their most important building—pyramid, temple, fortress, what not. And the building which shows what we believe in most, he says, is the railway depot. This is a witty expression of the fear that no faith has any longer a deep and general hold upon our society except the faith in money. In other times, it is said, in the days of Moses, of Pericles, of Washington, noble passions touched the people and made them forget everything else in their service. But now, it is said, the great historic ideals and faiths are dying. Art, religion, learning, morality—each is indeed cherished by a faithful remnant. But society, it is said, in its passion for money, forgets them all and the few who have not forgotten must presently choose between social exile and standing as lackeys in the courts of the rich.

This is the indictment of our age and especially of our country. If it is true, we should know it. We should face the fact. And then each of us could choose for himself whether to make terms with a life which is not worth living or to flee like Elijah to Horeb where the still, small voice shall promise some far-off victory of the Spirit.

But this indictment is not true, or rather it is only a fragment of the truth. Let us recall a wider circle of facts which should be commonplace but which are often forgotten. In general, we should not forget that all men of all times are in many essential ways alike. We share with all the fundamental instincts and many of the habits good and bad which grow out of them.

Hunger, for example, and kindred instincts are of course common to all. In most men they give rise to the desire for wealth, with its comfort, luxury, and power. In many men they give rise to that passion for wealth which the Bible declares to be the root of all evil. And finally, in all the dominant races those instincts give rise to habits of economy, industry, and thrift, and to industrial institutions,—which habits and institutions together lay the foundation for all the higher forms of civilization. In all those particulars, good and bad, we differ from our ancestors of the earliest and historic time less than we are like them. For the strenuous life was here before its first historian.

Moreover, we share with men generally a great number of so-called *higher* instincts. Curiosity, for example, which shows itself in animals, babies, and savages, in the village gossip, in the daily newspaper, but which shows itself also in the insatiable interest of theology, philosophy, and science to know everything in the universe, utterly regardless of its practical utility. Or again the play instinct, which appears in all the higher animals, and which is universal among children, youth, and indeed among men, partly training them for their life work, partly keeping them young and plastic in spite of their life work, and which blooms out at last into the high and noble forms which we call art. For art, as Schiller and many since his time have shown us, is simply the highest of human plays. Or finally there is fear, almost universal among animals and men in its lower forms, but rising and refining through innumerable stages into a sense of the sublime and the holy.

These higher instincts and their higher manifestation in science, art, and religion are indestructible as hunger. When we cry out in panic that these higher hungers are about to be stifled and to perish, and when we hurry together for a last desperate struggle in their defense, we should be quieted by learning where their true defense lies. It is not simply in the surface resolution of a few men who are called good, but also in the constitution of all men. It is in the Prodigal who flees from his home to feed with swine but who can never be satisfied with husks,—because he is the son of his father. It is written that man doth not live by bread alone, but by every word that proceedeth out of the mouth of God.

I would say then that our people are like every other in the possession of certain instincts and habits, lower and higher; but I would then go on to say that, rising out of these, we have developed along with much other good and evil two salient characteristics. One of them is that strenuous practicality with which all the world gives us credit. The other is less obvious, is often overlooked, often denied, but has always quite surely been here, fighting with or fighting against practical interests,—in either case always effective and never more so than at present. This characteristic is devotion to ideals which lie quite above the world of money.

Andrew D. White, ex-president of Cornell University, in his farewell address as ambassador to Germany last October [1902], says that it is a fact not sufficiently recognized that "the people of the United States, while on a superficial view the most materialistic of nations, are at the same time among those most powerfully swayed by beliefs, ideals, and sentiments. . . . In no country can the action of these two forces, apparently so antagonistic, making on the one side for the practical and on the other for the ideal, be seen more vigorously acting and reacting on each other." He cites our political literature and affirms that "there are utterances appealing to ideal considerations in the Declaration of Independence, in Washington's Farewell Address, in Webster's Reply to Hayne, in Jackson's declaration regarding the Union, and in Lincoln's speech at Gettysburg which millions of Americans regard as oracles, as inspired commands compared to which all material advantage is as nothing." He cites also the case of our Civil War, when the commercial and industrial interests were in the outset in favor of subordinating moral considerations and our national ideal to the financial interests. "But suddenly," he says, "all this fabric of material interests was whiffed away in a moment. The cannon shot fired at the American flag on Fort Sumter gave a united continent to the American people which swept away all materialistic considerations. . . . This sentiment was not a mere sudden flash of anger. It was a conviction and a devotion as real and as permanent as that which seized Saul of Tarsus on his way to Damascus. This it was which against all disappointments and defeats kept up the courage and the energy of the loyal part of the Union during the four terrible years which led to the triumph of nationality and the destruction of slavery."

There is another illustration to which President White alludes and which no one has more right than he to cite in proof of the alliance in our people between practical sense and higher faith, and that is the attitude of the people toward education.

The sober truth is that the faith in education is the dominant faith of our time. It pervades our society with a compelling power like that which sent Christendom again and again upon crusades for the possession of the Holy Sepulchre. It has taken possession of the rich,—the very men who are said to have made this the age of money,—Johns Hopkins, Clark, Stanford, Rockefeller, Carnegie, Armour,—men who were for the most part poor and without liberal education, but who have faced the commercial situation of our time and in one way or another wrested from it great fortunes,—these men come bringing their surplus millions to the service of education.

It is a significant fact that these hard-headed men have thought it practical to give their money not solely or even mainly to foster strictly money-making occupations, but also for fine art, for research in pure science, and for the study of the ancient classics. The common sense of giving, as these men see, is to give so that men shall be set to work. And the statesmanship of giving is to give so that men everywhere shall be set to work at what they can do best. The individual motives of these men doubtless vary widely, but one and all they are caught up by the power of a social faith which is wiser and stronger than any man.

There is yet stronger proof of the dominance of this faith in the conversion to it of the whole people. They have no surplus millions. Their strength must go to provide the necessities of life. But it is a fact which heartens us when we think of the history of our race, that most people are willing to sacrifice material necessities to a spiritual one if they believe in it. The people of Athens in the days of Pericles lived in mean houses and covered the Acropolis with temples. They did not do this as a luxury, but because they believed that the protection of the gods, and especially of their patron goddess of wisdom, was as necessary to the city as its walls.

In that sense and in that measure our people have come to believe in education. And the building which represents our strongest faith is not the railway depot, but the schoolhouse. This campus is an Acropolis. And the people know that they have here a defense that is stronger than a battleship.

This is no idle figure of speech. The meaning of democracy is opportunity,—not the opportunity for every Jack Cade to become king, but the opportunity for every Jack Cade to enter as far as he can and will into all that belongs to a man,—it may be at last to show that he is king by the highest right. Democracy means that society at its best, in every worthy art, craft, and calling shall set lessons for the children of the people, shall make paths for the children of the people which lead to society at its best.

Let me say this again: What the people need and demand is that their children shall have a chance—as good a chance as any other children in the world —to make the most of themselves, to rise in any and every occupation, including those occupations which require the most thorough training. What the people want is *open* paths from every corner of the State through the schools to the highest and best things which men can achieve. To make such paths, to make them open to the poorest and make them lead to the highest, is the mission of democracy.

We have here indicated, as I think, the inevitable program of our democratic educational system. It provides for teaching the A B C's, but it does not condemn the poor to stop with that. It provides for the dissemination of culture and does this far more effectively than if it tried to do nothing else. The school which does nothing but disseminate culture broadly and thinly over the country has this vice in it, that it is not self-perpetuating. It is a borrower and not a producer, and it will die like a plucked flower. The only condition on which culture of any value is ever kept alive in a country is when it is there as a living occupation.

Finally this program provides training for the strictly money-making occupations, but it is far too practical to stop with that. It goes further and trains a due share of the population to earn their living in arts and sciences and professions which are as essential as the handicrafts. It lifts these thousands out of competition on a low plane into cooperation on a high plane. It does the most practical thing possible, for in training men for every occupation it develops the whole potential capacity of the people into the whole circle of human efficiencies. The democracy which educates in this fashion is indeed the hope of the common man. It does not come to him as it did a hundred years ago with enchanting promises of unearned happiness. It comes to him stern as the voice of God. It comes to him with tasks, with years of strenuous apprenticeship. It leads him by a straight and narrow path. But this is the path by which, if he will, the common man may go up into the seats of the mighty.

And the salvation of the common man is also the salvation of society. Society at its best cannot live in temples made with hands. It cannot live apart from the touch of the living multitude. It lives by being born again and again in the children of every generation.

William Lowe Bryan, inaugural address.

Document 97

The Bottom Rail

Isaac Jenkinson early developed a format for his annual reports to the succeeding governors of Indiana. This particular report has more vitality than some of the crises-laden documents from the president of the Board of Trustees in the past. This one gives some comparative notion of Indiana University's support from the state as compared with that of neighboring universities. It would not have been profane, even in the views of the strict religionist William Lowe Bryan, for Jenkinson to have cried in anguish, "Thank God for Kentucky!"

*   *   *

REPORT OF THE INDIANA UNIVERSITY

BLOOMINGTON, IND., February 8, 1905.

To the HON. J. FRANK HANLY, *Governor of Indiana:*

Dear Sir—I have the honor to transmit to you the biennial report of the Board of Trustees of Indiana University for the fiscal years ending October 31, 1903, and October 31, 1904.

The financial reports from the Universities of the States which were formed from the Northwest Territory (Ohio, Indiana, Illinois, Michigan, Wisconsin) show that Indiana is far behind all of the others in the appropriation which it makes for higher education.

The reports from New York, Minnesota, Iowa, Nebraska, Missouri, Kansas, California, and Texas show that Indiana is in all cases behind the others and in most cases far behind them.

The reports of the United States Commissioner of Education show that the total amount spent for higher education by State and non-State colleges and

universities combined is much less for Indiana than for any of the other surrounding States except Kentucky.

The catalogues of twenty-five leading institutions outside of Indiana, for 1903–
1904, show that they had enrolled 973 students from this State. Of these 632
were enrolled in the Universities of Ohio, Michigan and Illinois. The cost of
tuition and living expenses at the twenty-five institutions concerned ranges
from $500 to $1,000 per student. Ths means that between one-half million and
a million dollars of Indiana money went out of the State last year for higher
education demanded by our people. On the same scale the amount of Indiana
money going into Illinois, Ohio and Michigan last year ranges between $316,000
and $632,000. The total amount of money sent out of the State for higher edu-
cation is much greater than the total amount spent by the State for higher education within the State. It is an interesting fact that only 172 of the 973 students
attend the great universities of the Atlantic States. The West is providing
magnificently for higher education, but Indiana, although it has done much, is
behind her sister States and is not providing for her own people.

Our common school system, though it requires improvements and the expenditure of more money, is regarded by every one as one of the best in the
country. Our high school system is everywhere looked upon as a model. No
youth can better himself by leaving Indiana for an elementary or high school
education. But when it comes to higher education we must confess that we
have not in Indiana the bare room to receive all the young people of the State
who wish to go to college, and still less have in adequate measure the facilities
required by the demands of modern civilization.

The whole scale of our expenditures is necessarily far below what it is in
the States mentioned. It is a fact which can be shown item by item that we
spend less for buildings, for equipment, for books and for men than the States
which are about us, excepting those to the south and not excepting all of those.
I wish here to record the warning that if these conditions do not change decidedly in the right direction, they will infallibly change more and more in
the wrong direction, and that Indiana will presently send the bulk of the money
which it has to spend for higher education out of the State, and at the same
time have the reproach of being a State that will not adequately support higher
education.

THE LIBRARY AND ADMINISTRATION BUILDING

The present building was erected fifteen years ago. It was suited in size to the
needs of the institution at that time. Since that time the enrollment has increased approximately five hundred per cent. The result is that our library has
long been far from adequate. Six years ago the Legislative Committee recognized
the inadequacy of the library and so stated in its official report (page 43) . Since
that time the enrollment has increased by a half. Two years ago the Legislative
Committee again officially recognized in its report the need of a larger and
better library.

To meet immediate needs, without taking any account of the future, the
building should be twice as large as the present one. It is a plain business
proposition that we should erect a building which would be large enough at least
to last one generation. It should contain space for the offices of administration.
It should be absolutely fireproof.

LAND

In 1884 the University purchased part of the present site, paying $6,000.00 for
20 acres. In March, 1897, an additional tract of 9 acres was bought for $12,000.00.

In June, 1897, a tract of 20 acres was bought for $6,963.00. The forty-nine acres in the present campus cost $24,953.00, or an average of $509.25 per acre.

Meanwhile the city has grown rapidly, extending about and beyond the campus, and the price of land has greatly increased. The Trustees have long realized the danger of having the campus hemmed in with no possibility of enlargement except at prohibitive prices, but they have had no funds available for the purchase of adjacent land.

THE HEAT, LIGHT AND POWER PLANT

This is another extreme necessity. It is not necessary to repeat from past reports the history of the old plant. The situation of two years ago plainly demanded an adequate modern plant with every appliance for economy of coal and service. We were given $20,000. It was extremely difficult to know how to make a wise use of such a sum. The problem was to do something to meet immediate necessities and at the same time waste nothing on temporary appliances. After long consideration and consultation with the Governor, we decided to have plans and specifications made for a complete plant, and then build as much of that plant as we could afford.

We have accordingly a new building, one boiler, one engine and generator, with space and with plans for a completed plant.

Meanwhile we must run the old plant and the one boiler in the new plant together. We have no mechanical stokers. We must have extra service for the two plants.

OWEN HALL AND WYLIE HALL

These two buildings were built in 1884 from funds donated by Monroe County. Both require enlargement. Owen Hall requires to be made fireproof. For two years students have been turned away from classes in Owen Hall for lack of space, though all space is utilized, including the basement. The overcrowded Department of Chemistry in Wylie Hall also urgently requires more space. The Department will be compelled to do part of its work in the old power house until proper provision can be made.

Detailed estimates of the amount necessary to meet these needs have already been submitted to you in the report of the President of the University.

Members of former Legislative Committees have stated, after careful investigation, that the State has more property here in proportion to the amount invested than anywhere else in the State. Approximately one-third of the amount invested in buildings has been donated to the State.

Respectfully submitted,
ISAAC JENKINSON,
President of the Board
of Trustees.

Indiana *Documentary Journal,* 1904.

Document 98

The Library Era

The hand of Isaac Jenkinson had grown cramped and shaky in the years he communicated his annual wails of poverty to the governors of

Indiana. He had kept himself surprisingly well informed about affairs in the University, and without fear or hedging he stated the school's urgent fiscal needs. In 1907, Benjamin F. Shively made his first report as president of the Board of Trustees. This document concerned itself centrally with the matter of completing a new library and placing the collection of 58, 941 volumes and a sizable pamphlet collection on new shelves. Likewise, the Student Building was on the verge of being completed.

*   *   *

REPORT OF THE INDIANA UNIVERSITY

BLOOMINGTON, IND., January 9, 1907.

To the HONORABLE J. FRANK HANLY, *Governor of Indiana:*

Dear Sir—I have the honor to transmit to you the biennial report of the Board of Trustees of Indiana University for the fiscal years ending October 31, 1905 and October 31, 1906.

1. A BRIEF HISTORY AND DESCRIPTION OF THE UNIVERSITY

By virtue of the State Constitutions of 1816 and 1851, and the Acts of the General Assembly thereunder, the Indiana University is the State University of Indiana and is the head of the public school system of the State. The institution was founded by an Act of the Legislature, approved January 20th, 1820, establishing "the State Seminary" at Bloomington and appropriating to its use certain lands granted by Congress to the State for that purpose. Its doors were opened for the reception of students in 1824. By an Act of January 24, 1828, its name was changed to that of the "Indiana College;" and by an Act of February 15, 1838, to "the Indiana University." After the adoption of the present Constitution in 1851, the Legislature passed a bill (approved June 17, 1852) enacting that "the institution established by 'an Act to establish a college in the State of Indiana,' approved January 28, 1828, is hereby recognized as the University of the State." On June 24, 1902, the Supreme Court of Indiana, in the case of Fisher v. Brower, rendered a decision, without a dissenting opinion, that "the Indiana University is an integral part of our free school system;" "that it was the special creation of the constitution;" and that "the University, as well as its endowment, has always been under the supervision of the State."

The first graduating exercises were held in 1830. The University was made co-educational in 1868. The School of Law was established in 1842, and the School of Medicine in 1903.

2. GROWTH OF THE UNIVERSITY—ATTENDANCE BY TERMS DURING THE
   PAST TEN YEARS

[CHART OMITTED HERE]

3. NEEDS OF THE INSTITUTION

I beg to submit the following statement of our most urgent and immediate necessities.

HEATING AND LIGHTING PLANTS

Two years ago the condition of our heating and lighting plant was reported to the Legislative Committee as follows:

"It is not necessary to repeat from past reports the history of the old plant. The situation of two years ago [1902] plainly demanded an adequate modern plant with every appliance for economy of coal and service. We were given $20,000. It was extremely difficult to know how to make a wise use of such a sum. The problem was to do something to meet the immediate necessities, and at the same time waste nothing on temporary appliances. After long consideration and consultation with the Governor, we decided to have plans and specifications made for a complete plant, and then to build as much of that plant as we could afford.

"We have accordingly a new building, one boiler, one engine and generator, with space and with plans for a completed plant.

"Meanwhile we must run the old plant and the one boiler in the new plant together. We have no mechanical stokers. We must have extra service for the two plants."

Since that time two new conditions have arisen:

1. The boiler capacity of the old and new plants combined is not sufficient when the new buildings are added.

2. The old steam mains have given out in various places. We have been obliged to put down a temporary high pressure main to supply the Student Building, because we could not afford to buy the larger, but, in the long run, the more economical low pressure main. We are in urgent and immediate need of an entire new system of mains, properly laid in tunnels where they will be accessible.

THE EQUIPMENT OF THE NEW LIBRARY

I submit plans and estimates for the equipment of the New Library. An appropriation for the purpose is of equal importance with that for the heating and lighting system, and the appropriation therefor should be made immediately available.

Stacks—The University has at present 58,941 volumes on its accession book, 859 volumes bought and not "accessioned," 3,000 volumes of bound duplicates, and 6,000 pamphlets. To house this material will require all of two stack stories, and to provide for eight years of growth at the present rate will require another story. The plan of our stack house, with the main floor on the level of the third stack story, necessitates the installation of three stories to make the stacks usable. The plan finds its justification in the fact that by its employment the books are at once close to the seminar rooms in the basement, and to the delivery desk on the main floor.

ADDITION TO LIBRARY AND ADMINISTRATION BUILDING

Two years ago we were granted an appropriation of $100,000 for a library and administration building. It was impossible, for that sum, to erect a building which would provide for these purposes at the present time, without consideration of the future. It was therefore vitally important that the building should be so constructed that it could easily enlarged when the Legislature should see fit to provide for the same. Accordingly, after consultation with the Governor, plans were made for a building which could be built for $100,000, and which could be added to in a natural and convenient manner. The architect of the building has designed the proposed addition. We are in great and immediate need of this addition, especially for the use of the administrative offices. Our present office space is entirely inadequate. The offices are used by the entire body of students and faculty more than any other department of the University. We have a vast quantity of public record but no fire proof vaults. We very earnestly urge that this pressing need of the University shall be met.

ADDITION TO MAXWELL HALL

Maxwell Hall, now used as a library, is to be used for the Law School. Unfortunately the building does not provide enough space for the law classes even with the present enrollment. We have, therefore, planned an addition which can be made in a convenient manner. The plan is submitted.

CHEMISTRY BUILDING

The science departments in Owen and Wylie Halls are all over-crowded. Students are every term turned away from some of these departments for lack of space. We are of the opinion that the best mode of immediate relief would be the erection of a separate building for the department of Chemistry. It is particularly desirable that this department should have a separate building, because of the gases, which are offensive and injurious to apparatus in other departments. The plan is submitted.

ADDITION TO STUDENT BUILDING

The Student Building is the gift of about two thousand alumni, students, and other friends of Indiana University. The building contains the following accommodations: Rooms for social and religious purposes for women; Women's Gymnasium; lecture room (50x80, capacity 600 seats) for smaller assemblies, lectures, etc.; rooms for social and religious purposes for men; offices for various student organizations, etc. The building should be completed by the addition of an East wing (140x80, corresponding to the West wing already built) which can be used as a Men's Gymnasium, and also in the absence of a University Auditorium as a hall for larger University assemblies. The plan is submitted.

LAND

The University has not received an appropriation to purchase any part of the present campus. In consequence, the Trustees have been obliged to purchase small additions at prices which increase as the city extends about the campus. We have repeatedly urged that an appropriation be made to buy land which is adjacent to the campus and which is not yet built upon by private parties. We urge this again in the hope that the purchase may be made before we are hemmed in on every side.

Respectfully submitted,
BENJAMIN F. SHIVELY,
President of the Board
of Trustees.

Indiana *Documentary Journal,* 1906.

Document 99

A Treaty of Peace for the Medical School

It seems almost sacriligious to present the subject of the Medical School fight between Indiana and Purdue universities in so brief a space as this joint Stone-Bryan statement. Behind this document are literally hundreds of pages of board minutes, communications, newspaper stories, speeches, and angry conversations in board rooms. The volume of this material would constitute a large compilation indeed. This agreement and the two documents which follow give the essence of the matter. No single chapter in the history of Indiana University had greater meaning than the gaining of the right to establish and maintain a medical school. So William Lowe Bryan and the Board of Trustees must have believed.

* * *

The following statement concerning the consolidation of the Indiana University School of Medicine and the Indiana Medical College was agreed upon by Presidents Bryan and Stone and ordered given to the public:

"The efforts of Indiana University and of Purdue University to promote medical education in the State, through cooperation with the members of the profession and with existing proprietary medical schools have been undertaken in good faith and with the one aim of establishing this important branch of professional training upon a sound educational basis.

"Indiana University has sought for many years to establish and develop such a department in which efforts it has encountered many obstacles, but has made continuous progress. Purdue University entered this field only when convinced that a service could be rendered to the profession and the State by the tender of offices in consolidating existing forces and aiding in the evolution of a single, strong medical school at Indianapolis, under the auspices of the State and with the cooperation of other educational interests, a task which was undertaken only after it seemed that other efforts in this direction had failed.

"Out of these efforts by the two institutions had grown an unfortunate controversy which operated to confuse the situation and becloud in the minds of the public the true relations of the Universities. In the belief that the present conditions are delaying the educational progress and interfering with the highest functions of the two Universities the logical conclusion follows that the two medical schools now in operation in Indianapolis under the direction of the two Universities should be united into one school and that this should be under the exclusive control of one or the other of these institutions.

"Since Purdue University has at no time regarded a department of medicine as an essential part of its program and on the other hand Indiana University believes that it has been especially charged with the responsibility for such instruction, the latter institution has been selected to proceed in the matter and the Trustees of the two universities have this day mutually agreed to the following conditions to which the faculties of their respective medical schools assent, namely: to a union of the two medical schools under the direction of Indiana University; to a selection of the faculty of the new school with due regard to the members of the present faculties; and to the maintenance of a complete medical course in Indianapolis as well as the two year course in medicine at Bloomington.

"Only in this way does it seem feasible to accomplish the ultimate purpose of developing for the State a sound system of medical education which has been the aim of both parties in their efforts in the field, as well as to promote those harmonious and friendly relations so essential to the proper discharge of the functions of both institutions.

"It is hoped, therefore, that the citizens of the State, whether remotely or intimately interested in this question will accept the above decision as evidence of the disinterested motives of these institutions, and their desire to serve the State with undiminished energies.

(signed) W. L. BRYAN
Pres. Indiana University
W. E. STONE
Pres. Purdue University

April 4, 1908.

Trustee Minutes, 1897–1910, pp. 402–403.

Document 100

Accepting the Medical School

Like the foregoing document, this one seems tame and matter-of-fact when compared with the bitter struggle which culminated in this simple resolution. This was the first official step in the establishment of the Indiana University Medical School under the control of the Board of Trustees.

*   *   *

On motion of Mr. Shea the following resolution was adopted:

"Whereas, The Trustees of Indiana University, in April, 1908, entered into conditional agreements, with the Trustees of the Medical College of Indiana, the Medical School of Purdue University and with the Trustees of the State College of Physicians and Surgeons to take over the medical schools, directed by them, including their faculties, students, good will and all tangible property subject to bona fide indebtedness, for the purpose of uniting these schools into one under the direction of the Trustees of Indiana University, all subject to the approval of the Legislature at its ensuing session, and

"Whereas, The Legislature, by an act dated March 2, 1909, gave the Trustees of Indiana University the authority to carry out the said agreements,

"Therefore, The Trustees of said Indiana University hereby make formal record of their acceptance of said medical schools, including their faculties, students, good will and all tangible property subject to their bona fide indebtedness as itemized below

. . . .

Trustee Minutes, 1897–1910, p. 502.

Document 101

Setting in Operation a Medical School
Plan of Administration

This resolution outlined the organization of a central committee and the line of communication necessary to the organization of the Medical School.

*   *   *

On motion of Mr. Rose the duties of the Executive Committee of the Indiana University School of Medicine, appointed by President Bryan and ratified by the Trustees of the University were defined as follows:

First. To act as a central committee in touch with all others, referring questions to the various committees, receiving reports from them, and, in cooperation with other committees, giving consideration to all questions affecting the School of Medicine.

Second, To take executive action on all matters referred to them for that purpose by the Faculty or Board of Trustees and to take the initiative in such matters as seem to urgently or immediately require action.

On motion of Mr. Shea the following resolution was adopted:

Be it resolved by the Board of Trustees of the Indiana University as follows:

First, That there be and is hereby constituted a Finance Committee to be appointed by the Board of Trustees from the members of the faculty of the Indiana University School of Medicine, resident at Indianapolis, Indiana.

Second. That said committee be composed of three members whose duty shall be to receive all moneys of the University arising from that part of the said School of Medicine of the University conducted in Indianapolis, Indiana, and to disburse such moneys of the University, in carrying on said department of the University at Indianapolis, as shall be appropriated for that purpose, subject to the directions and orders of the Board of Trustees and Executive Committee thereof and to their right to make disbursements therefrom.

Third. That all moneys received by said committee, as such, shall be forthwith paid over to the Treasurer of the University and receipts taken therefore.

Fourth. That said committee be composed of the following members of said faculty until further ordered by said Board of Trustees to wit: Dr. John F. Barnhill, Dr. F. F. Hutchins and Dr. E. D. Clark.

Fifth. That one member of said committee be appointed Treasurer thereof, by the Board of Trustees, who shall actually receive such moneys arising from that part of the said School of Medicine of the University conducted at Indianapolis, Indiana.

Sixth, That all moneys paid from such appropriations in carrying on said department of the University at Indianapolis shall be paid on warrants signed by the President or Secretary of the Board of Trustees or by the Treasurer of said committee.

Seventh. That such Treasurer execute to said Board of Trustees a bond in the penal sum of Five Thousand Dollars ($5,000.00) to the approval of said Board or the Executive Committee thereof conditioned for the faithful performance of his duties, as such, and to honestly account for all moneys which may come into his hands belonging to the University.

Eighth. That Dr. John F. Barnhill be and is hereby appointed Treasurer of said committee until further orders of the Board of Trustees.

Trustee Minutes, 1897–1910, pp. 502–504.

Document 102

The Medical School Plan in Brief

In a resolution of March 1910, the Board of Trustees outlined the history of the fight to gain the Medical School for Indiana University, and then the skeleton plan for its operation. The plan expressed high ideals which in the future were often challenged.

*   *   *

On motion of Mr. Batman the following memorandum was adopted as the policy of the Board in relation to the School of Medicine:

"The Trustees of Indiana University formally established the School of Medicine at Bloomington in 1903. From time to time before and after that date they were solicited to enter into affiliation with one or another School of Medicine at Indianapolis. As the records of this Board show, these solicitations were repeatedly declined, on the ground that the Trustees could not then see their way to the maintenance at Indianapolis of a Medical School upon a university basis. When finally it appeared feasible to undertake the large work the Trustees officially announced that any such School of Medicine must be an integral part of the University wholly under its control and supported financially by the State as liberally as any other part of the University. These positions were maintained throughout the troubled period which ended with the union of all the medical schools in the State (except that at Valparaiso) under the direction of the University. Where for example in 1907 the Legislature was urged to establish a School of Medicine under other auspices with the guarantee that no money would then or afterwards be asked from the State, the Trustees of the University, by their representations, at a public legislative hearing and otherwise, declared that they would not undertake to maintain a Medical School to be conducted without adequate financial support from the State. Having made this official declaration at the time when it was most perilous to do so, the Trustees have no reason to take a backward step at this time when there is nothing to fear.

"In view of the present backward state of the medical department at Indianapolis, the needs of that department will be especially urged at the coming session of the Legislature. The Trustees will not rest from the efforts which have occupied them so largely throughout the past six years until they have established in the State a Medical School in which every department, whether at Indianapolis or at Bloomington has been placed upon a thoroughly good University basis. In determining the details of this development the Trustees will seek as in all other departments, the best obtainable men as teachers and the counsel of the best authorities in medical education throughout the country. Meanwhile the best assurance of the convictions and plans of the Trustees is to be found in those parts of the Medical School which they have fully established.

"The plans of the Trustees include the following details:

1. Daily supervision of the work at Indianapolis by the Dean.

2. The whole time of competent men as directors of the dispensary clinics and of the hospital clinics.

3. Competent and prompt service for clinicians from the clinical laboratory courses.

4. Thoroughly modern equipment and instruction in all the laboratory courses.

5. A selection of the best available men for clinical positions as rapidly as we judge the situation will permit."

Trustee Minutes, 1897–1910, pp. 514–516.

Document 103

The Gift of Mr. and Mrs. Robert W. Long of a Hospital

The Long gift of the central hospital for use by the Medical School was of tremendous importance in the operation of the school. The resolution of acceptance was couched in cold, formal language, but the feelings of trustees and university administration were warm and deep. This gift meant the availability of facilities which might have been a long time coming under public appropriations.

*   *   *

"To the President, and Trustees of Indiana University.

Gentlemen:

Your Committee to whom was referred the gift of a University hospital by Mr. and Mrs. Robert W. Long, for appropriate action by the Trustees, report as follows:

Whereas, Dr. and Mrs. Robert W. Long, of Indianapolis, Indiana, have given and transferred to the State of Indiana, on behalf of the State University, property in the City of Indianapolis, to an approximate value of Two Hundred Thousand Dollars ($200,000.00) for the purpose of establishing and maintaining a hospital under the control and management of the Trustees of Indiana University, and

Whereas, By an act of the last Legislature of Indiana, said gift of Dr. and Mrs. Robert W. Long was formally accepted under the terms and conditions of the donors, and made provisions for the location and, in part, for the maintenance of such hospital, therefore be it

Resolved, That the Trustees recognize the philanthropic purpose of this gift, intended as it is, to provide proper medical care and attention for worthy people of limited means in all parts of the State, and at the same time to advance the cause of medical education in Indiana. Be it further

Resolved, That the Trustees accept the trust and duties imposed upon them in said donation and hereby express to Dr. and Mrs. Long their high appreciation of this most generous gift.

We further recommend that this preamble and resolution be spread of record and copy thereof be sent to Dr. and Mrs. Long.

Committee {
Respectfully submitted
T. F. ROSE
JOSEPH H. SHEA
J. W. FESLER

Board Minutes, 1910–1913, p. 64.

[VII]

The Widening Span of the Bryan Years 1910-1939

With the elevation of William Lowe Bryan to the presidency of Indiana University in 1902 the institution at last had leadership which remained with it for thirty-five years. This long span was reminiscent of the administration of Andrew Wylie. Bryan in these decades left a deep personal impress on the University. A man of high intellectual standards, of rigid moral rectitude, and personal dedication to the institution, he set precedents which are still discernible. There was hardly a moment between 1902 and 1937 when Indiana University did not face need of greater financial support. In the same manner, these three-and-a-half decades were years in which herculean efforts were made to break the stifling strictures of the purely arts and sciences traditional curriculum.

The step into professionalism was a long one which involved deep emotions and a bitter rivalry with the sister institution, Purdue. At no time in his administration did President William Lowe Bryan exert a greater influence than in the extended contest with Purdue over the location of the Medical School in Indiana's system of higher education. Despite the bitterness generated in this contest, the end result left remarkably few permanent bruises. Both President Bryan and President Stone of Purdue proved to be reasonable men in the end, and their institutions profited from this fact.

When the Board of Trustees paid tribute to William Lowe Bryan for his quarter of a century of service in 1927, they singled out the management of the medical school contest as the highlight of his career. There were, however, many other areas in which Bryan was a powerful personal force. He held a reasonably strong faculty together, improved course offerings, made a modest expansion of the physical plant, and—most of all—helped the University to reach a much larger number of Hoosiers with its programs.

In the midst of his administration Bryan was faced with the unsettling experiences generated by World War I. Some of the documents included in this section reveal the great moral and political uncertainties which Americans had about the European war. In Bloomington, the Indiana faculty for the most part looked upon war as a crime against humanity, and militarism as a force to be resisted at all cost. Remarkably, the war years changed much of this point of view. Where the Indiana State National Guard appeared to be an insidious element to be kept out of the University in 1915, the Reserve Officers Training Corps seemed to be a desirable adjunct of the University's program at the end of the war.

Indiana University eased through the expansive years of the roaring 'twenties with some degree of equanimity; nevertheless, the hand of change rested heavily upon it. The expansion of enrollment and the stubborness of legislators to appropriate building funds presented an all-but-insoluble problem. There is no doubt that the cause of the University was presented with intelligence and fervor in Indianapolis, but the state made remarkably limited response to pleas for funds.

It was not until the onset of the Great Depression that Indiana began a significant era of expansion. The institution was able to secure federal funds on a matching basis and to use an appreciable amount of local unskilled labor, with the result that new buildings, including the Bryan Administration Building, the Music Building, the Memorial Building, and the Stadium, were added.

William Lowe Bryan "resigned" from the presidency on March 15, 1937. Although this move came as a surprise, the way was prepared for such action. After considerable investigation and discussion, the University was able to institute a pension plan which prevented the retirement of professors without the guarantee of a source of livelihood. Few incidents in Indiana University history were to have a more immediate bearing on its future than the retirement of over-age faculty members. This transition took place at the time when a young president came into office and began immediately to rebuild the faculty with able professors who, in subsequent years, were to bring the University fine reputations in several fields.

The elevation of Herman B Wells to the presidency of Indiana University was a moment of promise. Judge Ora L. Wildermuth's charge to the youthful executive is one of high expectations indeed. The plan to make a complete self-study of the University and to point new directions was no doubt of as far-reaching importance. The pension plan enabling the University to retire old professors and hire new ones, plus the opportunity to realign the entire University structure, marked the beginning of a revolution.

Document 104

Who's Who on the Staff

Indiana University's staff, like that of every other state university, grew by accretion. In 1912 it became necessary to sort out staff members and give them titles, and by doing so the trustees specified the duties of the various categories. These staff members enjoyed the distinction of being listed in the catalogue.

*   *   *

The definitions of minor positions in the University, as proposed by the Faculty, were approved, which definitions are as follows:

"*Assistants* are (usually) undergraduate students who assist, directly or indirectly, in instruction by the care of apparatus, collections, departmental libraries, etc., whether paid by the hour or term. Those whose work is mainly clerical, or that of janitors, laborers, etc., or who serve as pianists in the gymnasiums, etc., should be excluded from this class, and their names ought not be given in University publications.

"*Teaching Fellows* are members of the Graduate School who assist in instruction. They are appointed for the college year, and must give approximately two-thirds of their time to study in the Graduate School.

"*State Fellows* are graduates of other Indiana colleges who hold fellowships established for this class of students, and are doing an equivalent of not less than fifteen hours' study in the Graduate School.

"*Research Fellows* are graduates of this or other colleges who are appointed on account of special fitness to carry on specific lines of research work.

"*Tutors.* It is recommended that the grade tutor be revived to designate officers of instruction who conduct classes, giving the whole or part of their time to this work, but who are not appointed to one of the higher grades of the instructional staff. Inasmuch as the statute governing the University (Act approved, June 17, 1852) says: "The president, professors, and instructors shall be styled The Faculty of said University, and shall have power" etc., it is submitted that persons who may now be styled Tutors will not be members of the Faculty, and the duties and responsibilities of University government should not be shared with them."

Trustee Minutes, 1910–1913, pp. 134–135.

Document 105

Disseminate the Truth, even if it does cost Money

Benjamin F. Shively's report to Governor Tom Marshall in 1912 is a revealing document. It contains the continuing theme of need for funds to expand the institution. This report, however, informs the Governor that "Indiana does not belong to the group of states which have adequately supported a university, either by public or private funds." Unhappily, said the President of the Board, trained Hoosiers were leaving their home state to find specialized employment. Too, Indiana University was now being called upon to make better provisions for the training of the women of the state. One item in this request was for a woman's dormitory, which—as Memorial Hall—did not materialize until much later.

*   *   *

REPORT OF THE INDIANA UNIVERSITY

BLOOMINGTON, IN., December 19, 1912

To the HONORABLE THOMAS R. MARSHALL, *Governor of Indiana:*

Dear Sir—I have the honor to transmit to you the biennial report of the Board of Trustees of Indiana University for the fiscal years ending September 30, 1911, and September 30, 1912.

The University has two chief reasons for being. The first is the discovery of truth. The second is the dissemination of truth. Society requires both. As population thickens, the necessity for both becomes more and more apparent.

As the easily available natural resources become scarce, we are compelled to look for hidden resources for food, fuel, and everything that we need in order to live. This means that we are driven by necessity to science—to the technical sciences, back of them to the pure sciences, to the social sciences which marshal human experience concerning the conduct of human affairs. As this necessity becomes apparent, society sees itself compelled to establish in the universities a corps of men who are there, not to teach the elements of science to young people, but who are there to find out as thoroughly and as rapidly as possible what society must know for its own preservation and well-being.

The second duty of the University is to disseminate the truth. It does this, first, through the young people who attend it. But this is not enough. The millions who do not go to the University require now all that the University can now give. The farmer of today requires what the agricultural college has to teach. The man who is sick today needs the benefit of the latest discovery of the University school of medicine, the most certain diagnosis from the University laboratory of pathology. Our American democracy is engaged now in a vast struggle to establish wise and just laws suited to our complex economic and social life. We can not succeed in this by guess work any more than we can succeed in farming by guess work. The whole people (since it is the whole people that vote and decide upon the laws to be established) need to study these questions with all the help possible from those who have studied them most. Beyond the purely physical and economic necessities of the people, there are higher necessities which the people do not fail to recognize. The people need, and know that they need, the great literature, the great art, the great upper life for which the lower life exists. It is the highest office of the University to minister to the spiritual hunger of men. The American university glories in its modern task of teaching the farmer who has never visited it to raise more corn in a row; but it glories, also, in its ancient task of teaching him some Shakesperean idea which will hearten him to hoe to the end of his row.

In sum, what society requires is the truth. It requires that the truth shall be found. It requires that the truth shall be made known and applied and made to bring food, health, justice, beauty and joy to all mankind. Toward all these ends the University is able and willing to serve as minister.

There is a group of States where the people show their faith in the university as a social necessity. They show this by private gifts or by State appropriations, or by both. Consider the following statistics:

ANNUAL INCOMES.

Privately Endowed Institutions—	*1910.*	*1912.*
Harvard	$2,421,221	
Yale	1,453,811	
Columbia	3,172,686	
Pennsylvania	1,087,226	
Cornell	1,769,669	
Chicago	1,980,668	
Johns Hopkins	755,826	
Northwestern	714,373	

States Having One State University—

Wisconsin	$1,854,910	$2,189,056
Illinois	1,560,040	2,305,211
Minnesota	1,806,800	2,344,455
Missouri	690,468	1,854,743
Nebraska	799,054	911,840

States Having More Than One State University—

Iowa State University	$ 649,328	$ 806,902
Iowa State College		871,474
Total		$1,678,376
Kansas University		$ 567,417
Kansas Agricultural College		718,152
Total		$1,285,569
Ohio State University	$ 924,611	$1,029,958
Ohio University	200,338	324,346
Miami	109,000	236,447
Total	$1,233,949	$1,590,641
Michigan University	$1,431,064	$1,472,838
Michigan Agricultural College	450,000	463,407
Total	$1,881,064	$1,936,245
Texas University	$ 583,098	
Texas Agricultural College	290,005	
Total	$ 873,103	

Indiana does not belong to the group of States given above. Indiana belongs to another group of States which have not adequately supported a university, either by public or by private funds. Indiana is one of the States which has compelled most of its young men and women seeking the most advanced university training to go outside the State for it. Indiana is one of the States which has allowed most of the eminent scholars who were born in it, or who have lived temporarily in it, to find their life work in other States. *Of the thousand leading American scientists, Indiana was the birthplace of twenty-eight and is the residence of twelve. (Seven of the twelve are at Indiana University, nearly every science department having at least one of them.) The other four Northwestern States have one hundred and forty-seven of these eminent scientists. No State can pursue such a policy without paying a heavy penalty. No State can continuously impoverish itself in the number of its great scholars without corresponding impoverishment of its entire civilization. Nor will the false economy which drives away these scholars make the State rich. It will, instead, make the State poor. The best population and the greatest wealth flow to the States which are most enlightened.*

We, therefore, plead for a revolutionary change of policy toward the two State Universities. We ask that Indiana be taken out of the wrong group of States and placed in the right group of States. We ask that we be given a chance to have in Indiana at least as many eminent scholars as are born here. We ask that the vast and essential social service of the University be recognized at its true value and that we be given a chance to do in Indiana what the great universities in the adjoining States are doing for their people.

STATEMENT OF NEEDS.

Income—

Our greatest need is for a larger income. We ask:

(a) That the mill tax for maintenance be doubled. There has been no increase in this tax since 1903. Within that time the enrollment has been increased from 1,469 to 2,448, and the cost of general maintenance correspondingly increased.

(b) That there be levied for the support of research in the graduate school and medical school a graduated collateral inheritance tax. It is to be noted that there is an inheritance tax in thirty-eight States, that a collateral inheritance tax is one to which there is a minimum of objection on the part of those who pay it, that its returns vary widely from year to year so that it is not suited for the support of any work which requires a steady support, and that it is for this reason specially adapted to the support of research which may expand or contract from year to year.

(c) That until the above mentioned taxes become available, specific appropriations be made as follows:

For general maintenance, annually $65,000
For the graduate school and extension division, annually 35,000

Buildings—

(a) Education Building.—We place first the request for an education building to house the School of Education, which last year had 17 teachers and 506 students. We note that the School of Education hereafter should provide instruction in domestic economy, and that this is made specially necessary by the large number of women students (enrollment of women students this year, 900). We note further that the School of Education must hereafter train teachers and supervisors in industrial education, and that provision for such training must be made if industrial education is to be made compulsory throughout the State, as recommended by the State Commission on Industrial Education.

(b) Administration Building.—Every legislative committee for years has recognized our pressing need for an administration building. The trustees, the faculty and its committees, the president, five deans, the registrar, and the bursar, and their clerical assistants carry on their business, which brings to these offices all the students of the University, in six rooms, of which five are very small. All the University records are kept in the same rooms, which are not fire-proof.

(c) Auditorium.—The University has no adequate auditorium. We sometimes use the old gymnasium for men. The student organizations sometimes rent a theater up town. Sometimes, when the weather permits, we hold our larger gatherings upon the campus.

(d) Men's Gymnasium.—We have no proper gymnasium for men. In view of the fact that private donors have given to the University one hundred thousand dollars for a student building, we believe it would be a fitting thing for the State to supplement this gift by providing an adequate men's gymnasium.

(e) Women's Dormitories.—We believe that the time is at hand when the State should provide proper housing for the women students by a system of women's dormitories.

Water Works.—Two years ago doubt was expressed whether the plans proposed by our engineers for a water supply would work. It was doubted whether there would be enough water within the drainage area, and also whether the bottom and sides of the reservoir and the dam would hold. These doubts have been cleared up. There is abundance of water to be caught and the reservoir and dam hold. For lack of means, however, we were not able to guard properly the purity of the supply. There are about two hundred acres of the drainage area which the State does not own. Cattle, hogs, and sheep are fed upon the area and the water is polluted thereby. Our experts have asked for the counsel of the Secretary of the State Board of Health, who sent us Dr. Cravens, and of Professor Sackett of Purdue University. These authorities have united upon the following recommendations:

Increase in height of dam	$18,000
Duplicate machinery	2,500
Land and improvements	12,000
Filtration plant	8,000

It is is further recommended that the drainage area be conducted as a State forest preserve.

Street Improvement.—There is assessed against the State, for the improvement of Third Street, $5,549.58 and interest thereon from July 19, 1912, at 6 per cent.

Miscellaneous Items.—Besides the above, there are a number of pressing minor needs, which are listed below:

Power Plant—

Pump and heater	$ 2,000 00
Tunnel to Biology Hall	4,800 00
Greenhouse heating ....$150 to	600 00
Campus lights	360 00
Vacuum cleaning apparatus	5,000 00
Renovating and repairing of buildings	19,500 00

Cement Walks—

Walk around Biology Hall, with steps and connections, arch foot bridge, and walk from Biology Hall to Library	1,990 00
Walk from Biology Hall to Fourth street entrance	810 00

Driveways—

New walk from Fourth street entrance to Science Hall and south to Third street, with wagon bridge	3,610 00
Widening old drive from Science Hall to Kirkwood avenue entrance	1,975 00

In support of the foregoing, we shall submit separate reports showing in detail the present and proposed work of the University including especially the work of the graduate and professional schools, the extension division, and of the historical survey.

SUMMARY OF REQUESTS.

Income—

1. Doubling of mill tax for maintenance.
2. Graduated collateral inheritance tax for the maintenance of research in the Graduate School and Medical School.
3. Until the above taxes become available, specific appropriations as follows:

Maintenance, annually	$ 65,000 00
Graduate School and extension division, annually	35,000 00

Buildings—

1. Education Building, including provision for instruction in domestic economy and the training of teachers in industrial education 150,000 00
   Equipment of same 35,000 00
2. Administration building 100,000 00

Water Works: (Estimate by Professor Foley, Dr. Cravens, of the State Board of Health, and Professor Sackett, of Purdue)—

Increase in height of dam	$18,000 00	
Duplicate machinery	2,500 00	
Land and improvements	12,000 00	
Filtration plant	8,000 00	
		$ 40,500 00

Street Improvement—

Third street improvement	5,549 58
Interest on same at 6 per cent. from July 19, 1912	....

Miscellaneous Items.

Power Plant (estimate by Professor Foley)—

Pump and heater	$ 2,000 00	
Tunnel to Biology Hall	4,800 00	
Greenhouse heating ....$150.00 to	600 00	
Campus lights	360 00	
		$ 7,760 00

Renovation and Repairs on Buildings (Estimate by Professor Foley and Mr. Kerr)—

Total	24,500 00

Walks and drives (Estimate by Professor Mottier)—

Total	8,385 00

Respectfully submitted,
BENJAMIN F. SHIVELY,
President of the Board of
Trustees.

Indiana *Documentary Journal,* 1912.

Document 106

The Old, Old Story

President William Lowe Bryan presented to Governor Samuel M. Ralston the hard facts of university operation. Operation of the Medical School had involved a tremendous cost which the legislature had not fully recognized.

*   *   *

Bloomington, Indiana,
December 29, 1913.

My dear Governor Ralston:

Responding to your kind suggestion that I write you in regard to the matters affecting our income, I beg to say:

I do not now grasp the situation. I do not know how much of the appropriations made for the current year by the last Legislature is to be regarded as terminated. I understood you to say that the Fifty Thousand Dollars for land for the Long Hospital would be ordered paid. Beyond this, I do not know what is intended.

In general I would say that if the old appropriations are cut off before the new are actually available, we shall not be able to meet our obligations either here or at the Medical School without borrowing money, and if money is in any manner borrowed for this purpose, it means, as far as I can see, that the maintenance for this year and the next year must both come out of next year's income.

So far as I can understand the situation, our worst difficulty will be with the Long Hospital. We had a meeting last week to study the financing of the Long Hospital. We were afraid to open at once for fear we should not have money enough to run the Hospital with an appropriation which we have from the last Legislature. We adjourned the meeting until this week for a further study of the situation. If now the appropriation made by the Legislature is to be withdrawn, I can not see how it will be possible for us to open the Hospital at all at this time. It seems to me certain that even if money could be borrowed, we are not justified in borrowing so much for this year's maintenance from next year's income.

I realize in part the difficulties of your situation and I appreciate profoundly the genuine friendship which you have shown to the University. I know that you will deal with the matter as the primary trustee of the University and will do what you decide to be just and right.

Very respectfully yours,
WILLIAM L. BRYAN.

MG
Governor Samuel M. Ralston,
          Indianapolis, Indiana.

Ralston #23, Archives Division, Indiana State Library.

Document 107

One Solution to the Housing Problem

Janitor Frank Everman's living quarters must have dramatized the University's need for housing. It is a wonder that some legislator did not suggest tents for the student body.

* * *

March 24, 1914

It was ordered that Frank Everman, who is a janitor in one of the buildings, be allowed the privilege of erecting and using a tent for living purposes on the back campus of the University. This privilege is given on condition that Mr. Everman shall, under the direction of University authorities, devote a part of his time to watching and guarding the campus and orchard in the vicinity of his tent.

Trustee Minutes, January, 1914—March, 1920, p. 9.

Document 108

Water, Water!

Water in sufficient and pure supply was almost as grave a problem for Indiana University as financial support from the state. This was a perennial problem, except that it had grown more serious by 1914, and the city fathers of Bloomington were vague about their plans to supply the institution. Otherwise, the University was faced with closure.

* * *

Bloomington, Indiana
May 13, 1914.

Gentlemen:

I beg to ask that the Trustees of Indiana University may meet you for a conference on the water situation in Bloomington on Wednesday, May 20th. We should prefer the hour of 1:30 P. M. so that all the Trustees may be able to arrive and so that they may be able to go away at 4:00.

The authorities of the University have no desire to interfere in local matters. On the other hand, they feel a heavy responsibility for the health and well being of the young people from all parts of the state who are under their charge. The University has been gravely injured three times by water famines. Last Fall the University could not have opened at all except for the fact that the University had provided a supply of water for its own use, which, however, did not make provision for the students at their places of residence. Those who are charged by the state with the responsibility for the University wish to know definitely what the prospects are for an immediate water supply during the coming Summer and Fall, and what assurances can be given to the State for an adequate supply in the future. They wish to inform themselves as fully as possible with regard to the situation for their own guidance, and in order, also, to report the facts to the Governor of Indiana.

Very truly yours,
[WILLIAM LOWE BRYAN]

The Mayor and Common Council,
    City of Bloomington, Indiana.

Ralston #23, Archives Division, Indiana State Library.

Document 109

Locating a National Guard Unit on the Campus

Although this is a brief and not altogether explanatory document, it resulted from the move to solve the problem of building a gymnasium on the campus by asking the state to locate a unit of the National Guard there in an armory that could be used for dual purposes. There was some strong faculty feeling against this plan.

*   *   *

[This was read and upon questions re meaning of some statements the minority report was substituted and adopted.]
"A majority of the Committee recommend that in view of the fact that it is uncertain to what extent the signers of this petition were influenced by the desire for a new gymnasium, and in view of the recent decision of the Trustees to build a gymnasium out of the first funds available, the Faculty approve the principle of a battalion at the University, but decide that the matter be dropped for the present and action postponed till such a time as it may be decided on its merits."

(Signed) W. A. COGSHALL
F. T. STOCKTON
J. L. BAKER

Faculty Minutes, 1913–1915, p. 129.

Document 110

The Shadow of War was upon the Land

The same day that three faculty members presented a brief petition objecting to the location of a national guard armory on the campus, a faculty group petitioned the University to pursue a course of peace.

*   *   *

[Made a matter of record at March 13, 1915 faculty meeting (p. 129).
Petition with 292 student signatures attached p. 131.]
The present condition of Europe would seem to show that armaments and battalions lead not to national security, but to war and destruction. Since our

American universities are the source of our nation's ideals, they should lead the way toward the establishment of international peace, and should discourage militarism in all its forms.

We, the undersigned, therefore respectfully petition the President and Faculty of Indiana University not to sanction the establishment of a battalion in this University.

Faculty Minutes, 1913–1915, p. 131.

Document 111

A Plea for Ending a Rowdy Tradition

While the faculty was resolving against war and the rumors of war it took time out to seek the end of the famous victory parades down Indiana Avenue after games. They had come to be blackmailing ventures forcing merchants into supporting victory celebrations in order to protect their property. In faculty eyes this practice brought discredit to the University.

*   *   *

[Recommended by Student Affairs Committee and adopted by faculty on May 31, 1915 (p. 146)]

It is the sense of the Faculty that the method of celebrating athletic victories by students entering places of business or amusement in a body, and in effect, coercing the proprietors or managers to contribute goods or furnish amusement without price is unlawful, unjust to the business men, and unworthy of students. This practice tends to dull the student's sense of the personal and property rights of individuals, and if unrestrained, may lead to violence and disorder. If students desire to rejoice over a victory they ought to be willing to pay for the celebration themselves and ought not to force merchants to foot the bill. The Faculty are constrained to believe that most students who have participated in this practice in the past have done so out of pure thoughtlessness and that a little straight thinking would lead them to see that such conduct is clearly unlawful.

Be it resolved, therefore, by the Faculty, that any student found guilty of particing in such disorder shall be subject to such penalty as may be deemed fitting.

Further, it is recommended that a committee of students, such as the "Boosters Club," assume the direction of all student celebrations and conduct them in a manner which will not bring discredit upon the student body or upon the University.

Faculty Minutes, 1913–1915, p. 145.

Document 112

In Plain Words, These were the Needs

In the midst of war time the Indiana University Board of Trustees set out in plain tabular form the needs of the institution. This document was in fact a review of the cumulative needs of the University which had never been satisfied.

*   *   *

On motion of Dr. Smith, the recommendations to the Legislature, as set forth in President Bryan's Report, were adopted, including Vocational Needs and an appropriation of Three Hundred Thousand Dollars ($300,000.00) for Medical Building, Power House and Laundry. Following is a statement of the needs of the University which have been considered by the Trustees at former meetings:

I Buildings:
1. Building for Education, Vocational Education and Home Economics.
2. Auditorium.
3. Administration Building.
4. Nurses' Home, Power Plant and Laundry at Robert W. Long Hospital.
5. New Medical Building. (The cost of this would be met in large part if the present medical building were sold.)
6. New Power Plant
Estimated Cost $1,000,000.00 to $1,250,000.00

II Additions to Buildings Asked For:
1. Additions to Wylie Hall.
2. Additions to Owen Hall and Animal House.
3. Addition to Printing Plant.
4. Wing to Library.
5. Completion of Men's Gymnasium.
6. Modification of Student Building
Auditorium to cure its acoustic defects.
Estimated Cost $182,000.00

III Other Improvements.
1. Better Seats in Auditorium.
2. Grading for New Athletic Field and Tennis Courts.
3. Telephone System.
4. Equipment of Cottage for Home Economics.
5. Commons.
Estimated Cost $16,000.00

IV Expansions Asked For:
1. School of Commerce or Professor of Commerce.
2. Professor of Orthogenics.
3. Professor of Economic Geology.
4. Expansion of Social Service at Indianapolis.
5. Expansion of Extension Division.
6. Expansion of Summer School Budget.
7. Expansion of Stenographic Service.
8. Increase of Library Funds.
9. Expansion of Medical Service for Students.
Estimated Cost per Year $43,500.00

V Requested Increases of Salaries:
Estimated at $23,600.00 plus some requests for increases without specified amounts.

Trustee Minutes, 1914–1920, pp. 174–176.

Document 113

The Plague of War on the Homefront

The deadly threat of war came to the Indiana campus, and President Bryan proposed to meet it by the following procedure. Perhaps this bulletin, as much as anything else, brings back the fright of World War I.

*   *   *

President Bryan read to the Board the notice which was recently prepared by the health authorities of the University. This notice was read before the classes and was placed in printed form upon the bulletin boards and published in the Indiana Student. After full discussion the Board approved this notice with the following additions:

"The University physician is authorized to receive acceptable certificates of vaccination by outside physicians." The notice with this addition reads as follows:

"Influenza has reappeared in the student body, especially among the girls. This condition calls for the individual effort and the support of every member of the University.

"The student health authorities have adopted the following regulations:

1. All students not already vaccinated against pneumonia are required to be vaccinated before January 10th with the U. S. Army hypo-vaccine. This is given to students without charge at the campus office of the University Physician beginning January 7th:

    Girls: 10:30-11:30 a.m.; 1:00-2:00 p.m.
    Men: 2:00-4:00 p.m.

2. Unessential gatherings of students either on or off the campus are forbidden. This includes convocations, movies, dances and all gatherings except scheduled classes.

3. Students are permitted to go into the town only for the prompt transaction of necessary business. Attendance at movies, the theatres and loafing in the Book Nook, pool rooms and similar places is forbidden.

4. Students are not permitted to leave Bloomington for week end visits except on consent of the deans.

5. Students having increased temperature (fever), cough, sore throat and headache are to be regarded as influenza suspects and must report at once for examination at the office of the University Physician, or consult a local physician of their choice.

6. The University Physician is authorized to receive acceptable certificates of vaccination by outside physicians."

It was ordered that any student who refused to be vaccinated or who did not present a satisfactory certificate of vaccination to the University physician should be denied the right to remain in the University.

Trustee Minutes, 1914–1920, pp. 323–325.

Document 114

A Reversal in Attitudes

After the end of the war the faculty sought the location of a Reserve Officers' Training Corps on the campus because it was thought it would better prepare men students to meet the exigencies of a world torn assunder by martial violence. This was quite a change in attitude from that expressed in March, 1915.

*   *   *

Whereas, the preparation of its students for the performance of their duties as citizens of the State and of the Nation is one of the leading functions of a State University, and whereas the performance of these duties may require of any able bodied male citizen of the United States between the ages of 18 and 45 years military service in the defense of the Nation; therefore, be it

Resolved, by the Faculty of Indiana University, that we recommend to the Trustees of the University:

1. That an adequate opportunity be given the male students of Indiana University for instruction in military science and tactics.

2. That to this end, an application be made promptly by Indiana University to the Federal Government for the detail of an officer of the Army of the United State as professor of Military Science and Tactics in Indiana University and for the establishment and maintenance therein of a Senior Division of a Reserve Officers' Training Corps, under the terms and conditions of the Act of Congress of June 3, 1916.

3. That the Secretary of War be requested to prescribe standard courses of theoretical and practical military training for such Reserve Officers' Training Corps to be established in Indiana University and that these prescribed courses be adopted into the curriculum of the University.

4. That attendance upon these courses be compulsory for first and second year students for at least three hours per week per academic year.

5. That attendance for third and fourth year students be optional, under the regulations of the statute of June 3, 1916, as to members of the senior division of the Reserve Officers' Training Corps who have completed two academic years of service in that division.

6. That a specific application be made to the Secretary of War for the necessary arms, uniforms and equipment for a Senior Division of a Reserve Officers' Training Corps at Indiana University, with such public animals and their forage, as may be needed.

7. That a specific application also be made to the Secretary of War for participation by members of the Indiana University Reserve Officers' Training Corps in a Summer Camp of Military Instruction maintained by the United States Government during a period not longer than six weeks in one year, for the transportation of the members of the Corps to and from the Camp and for their subsistence in travelling to and from such Camp and while remaining therein.

8. That a Committee of three be appointed by the President to consider, in conjunction with a committee from the Board of Trustees and the Professor of Military Science, the Rules and Regulations which should apply to the said

course in Military Science and Tactics at Indiana University, and report thereon to the President, with a view to the inauguration of the course in the fall of this year.

Faculty Minutes, 1919–1925, pp. 16–17.

Document 115

Winona Lake Biological Station

This is an announcement of the opening of the Winona Lake Biological Station by Indiana University in 1923. In time this institution was to become popular with both mature biological research scientists and teachers from the general area. This document explains the mode of operation of the Station.

* * *

Biological Station

Location. The Indiana University Biological Station is located on Winona Lake, Kosciusko county, Indiana, in the grounds of the Winona Assembly. The post-office is Winona Lake, Indiana.

Advantages. The summer session at Winona Lake offers the opportunity not only for the best of work, but for wholesome recreation. There are several factors which contribute to the pleasure of working at the Station. The conventionalities of the University are left behind and, as the number of students is not large, all become acqainted and associate much as a large family. Work begins at eight o'clock in the morning and closes at four in the afternoon and is so planned that the student, by working intensively, can do it in this time. In addition to the natural outdoor attractions of Winona Lake, there is the Winona Assembly, which offers an excellent program each evening for six weeks of the term.

Outfit for the Student. For the students taking the course in general zoology, it will be advantageous to have some old clothes, a comfortable pair of shoes, a sweater, and a bathing suit. A field glass is desirable but not a necessity.

Equipment. The Station owns two buildings located on the lake front at the mouth of Cherry Creek, and the necessary equipment for teaching the courses offered and for research in cytology, limnology, and certain lines of genetics.

Plan of Work.* The Biological Station is a field laboratory. Emphasis will be laid on field work, and on such lines of work as can be given to better advantage at the Station than with the equipment of the University laboratories and under the restrictions imposed by a recitation schedule during the regular University sessions. In general the work will be adapted to the needs of medical students, teachers, and investigators in lines of zoology, physiology, and botany. Each course offered will be planned to occupy the full time of the students taking it.

---

* A limited number of research tables are open to investigators. Applications for these should be made as early as possible to the Director, Professor Will Scott, Indiana University, Bloomington, Indiana.

Each class will go to the field or lake as often as may be desirable, daily if necessary. A number of general excursions are taken to familiarize the students with the lake and the neighboring region.

An important service that the Station is rendering is the studies that are being made upon the lake. These studies are believed to be fundamental to the development of our aquatic resources.

University Credit. The requirements for admission to the work at the Biological Station are the same as those for entrance to the College of Arts and Sciences. The courses in general zoology (1, 2, and 3) are open to all students. The courses in embryology (20) and limnology (24) are open to students who have passed in general zoology. A maximum of ten hours of credit will be given to students who remain in attendance during the entire session.

Fees and Expenses. The laboratory fee for each half-term is $15, or $30 for the whole term. No reduction will be made for partial terms or partial work.

The widest choice is open to students for their mode of living. Many parties tent and cook their own meals. Rooms may be rented at from $2 to $4 per week, and good board has been furnished at from $5 a week upward. There are three hotels available, with rates varying from $10 a week upward. There is every facility for securing provisions on the grounds.

Boats for private use can be rented for $10 for the summer. The Winona Assembly will charge each student a fee of $3, which will entitle him to attend all the popular lectures given during the summer, and to bathing privileges. For all information concerning cottages, address the Secretary of Winona Assembly, Winona Lake, Indiana.

Session of 1923. The session of 1923 will be the twenty-ninth annual session of the Station. Registration will take place on Saturday, June 9. Work will begin on Monday, June 11, at 8 a.m. The Station will close on Friday, August 17, at noon. The work will consist of one lecture and six hours of laboratory or field work, with supplementary reading, or of two lectures and five hours of lab-
[pages missing]

Announcement of Session of 1923, pp. 1–8.

Document 116

Bryan's Silver Anniversary

The Board of Trustees, June 6, 1927, took cognizance of the fact William Lowe Bryan had served Indiana University a quarter of a century as president. It is significant that the trustees picked out the untangling of the Medical School mess to praise him for his educational statesmanship. Both student body and faculty had quadrupled under his stewardship.

*　　*　　*

On motion of Judge Batman, seconded by Judge Wildermuth, the following resolution was adopted:

"On the occasion of the silver anniversary of the unanimous election of Dr. William Lowe Bryan as president of Indiana University, the Board of Trustees desire to extend to him and the institution their congratulations on the wonderful success that has come under his administration to the head of the state's educational system.

"Under the leadership of President Bryan, Indiana University has increased from 1334 to 1902 to 5742 this year; the faculty has increased from 65 to 310; new buildings have gone up here and at Indianapolis and others will rapidly follow. The campus has grown, and on every side are evidences of substantial growth. While he has stood steadfastly for the College of Liberal Arts and has added many departments thereto, he has wisely enlarged the university's sphere of service by the additions of graduate and professional schools. Scholarship and research have at all times been encouraged and emphasized.

"The part that President Bryan had in uniting all the medical interests in the state into one outstanding institution was preeminent. His wise counsel in the work of the University's interests at Indianapolis—the Medical School, the James Whitcomb Riley Hospital, the Robert W. Long Hospital, the School of Dentistry, and the Extension Division—has aided in the establishment of harmonious organizations that are making these institutions of education and service favorably known throughout the entire country.

"The confidence that the people of the state have in President Bryan has caused an ever-increasing interest in the University. His friendship for the other educational institutions of Indiana has been one of the chief characteristics of his administration.

"In the manifold problems that have come to our Board we have found in President Bryan a leader to whom we have always looked with confidence. As great as are his abilities as an administrator, we prize still more his high ideals of life, that bring to him the admiration and affection of all those with whom he comes in contact. In all his work President Bryan has had the active cooperation of Mrs. Bryan whose wisdom and fidelity to the highest ideals have ever been an important force in the success of the University.

"Indiana University under President Bryan's administration has gone forward along all lines that make an educational institution strong and great and on this, his silver anniversary, we express the hope that he will continue in his present position for many years to guide and direct the university in its onward march of achivement [*sic*] and service."

Trustee Minutes, 1924–1930, p. 269.

Document 117

The Ten-Year Plan

The University Council on May 3, 1932, outlined a ten-year plan by which Indiana University might progress toward the future. This was actually the beginning of a series of suggested plans which would make a rather significant break with the institution's traditional academic past. It also reflected the tremendous influence the other Big Ten universities had on Indiana.

*　　*　　*

REPORT OF THE UNIVERSITY COUNCIL TO THE FACULTY:
(Tuesday, May 3, 1932, Science 32, 4:00 p.m.)

During this school year the University Council has studied the following subjects:

1. Postgraduate High School Work. Its relation to the work of the University: (a) University credit for work done in high school after graduation; (b) postgraduate work in high school which enables students to take advantage of achievement tests at the time of their admission to the University. These problems were considered important at this time because of the large number of students who return for a fifth year of high school work. It was the general opinion of the Council that high schools be reminded of the achievement tests in foreign language and in English so that they might encourage students to spend a fifth year in better preparing themselves to pass these tests. This has been done.

2. The Ten Year Program.

This matter has not been reported upon by the committee in charge.

3. The Relations of the North Central Association of Schools and Colleges to the Different Schools of the University. This discussion dealt largely with the accrediting standards by which the Association is guided.

4. Means of Making the Library a More Active and Potent Factor in the Work of the University. Council discussions of this question have dealt largely with conditions in the corridors of the Library. The treatment of this subject has been left to the Library Committee of the faculty.

5. A Report by Prof. R. E. Lyons on a Meeting of the Presidents of State Universities. This meeting was devoted to a discussion of the effects of the depression upon the work of different state schools.

6. Placement of Students After Graduation. Present methods of aiding students in finding employment were discussed by those most actively engaged in such work. Modifications and extensions of such agencies were also discussed.

7. The following motion was passed by the Council on April 5, 1932: that the University initiate some effort to enlist the support of all state colleges in (1) giving information to the people of the state concerning the work and services of the colleges, and (2) in administering college aptitude tests and in securing other information relative to the probable success of high school graduates in college. This was to be referred to the President and faculty. [this last sentence is marked out in pencil]

8. The following motion was approved and recommended to the faculty on April 5, 1932: that each department (or school) definitely appoint some member or members of its staff as counselor or counselors to consult with students concerning their problems, and that said counselor or counselors announce definite office hours and that students be notified of the opportunity provided for conferences. This motion resulted from one of the discussions on undergraduate standards. [last sentence marked out]

9. Undergraduate Standards. The following phases of this problem have been discussed.

10. Admission requirements. Specifically, these questions have been considered: Should the University attempt to exclude *any* student? Should the present catalogue statement concerning requirements for admission be retained since it is not followed in passing upon qualifications for admission?

(b) An extension of the present placement and achievement tests. This was looked upon with general favor by the Council.

(c) The appointment of a field agent, or field agents, to interview prospective students with a view toward selection and for the purpose of checking upon the success of graduates in their employment in various parts of the State.

(d) The Wisconsin plan which requires a student to have a grade point average of 1.3 in his work for the first two years before admission to Junior standing. If his standing falls between 1.1 and 1.3 his case is decided by a special committee. If it is below 1.1 the student may be granted a certificate entitling him to the rank of Junior Graduate in Liberal Studies. The Council was of the general opinion that our present system accomplished about the same results as the Wisconsin plan.

(e) The supervision of freshman class instruction. It was the general impression that much good might result from more careful supervision of all instruction in freshman classes by heads of departments.

(f) Vocational and Education Counselors for Students.

(g) Wider interest of students in current social, economic, political, and cultural problems and events.

(h) More frequent reports on standing of students, particularly of freshmen. The suggestion was made that freshman instructors give an examination at the end of the first four weeks of the semester and that these examination papers should be graded and returned to the student as soon as possible, so that he may discover his standing as early as possible in the semester and before wrong and wasteful habits of work become too firmly fixed. It was suggested that the freshman is not acquainted with how much is expected of him, and that early recognition of the fact that he is not devoting sufficient time to studies, or perhaps is not studying efficiently, might be important in the development of his whole attitude toward college.

(i) More definite objectives for students. Instructors should provide students with definite objectives; the student should know what the instructor expects of him.

(j) An orientation course for freshmen. Such a course might deal with how to study, what the college has to offer, requirements of the different professions, etc.

(k) The adjustment of an instructor to classes of different orders of intelligence. One member of the Council for example has one group with a psychological test average of 63.7 and another of 27. It was suggested that courses given to students of different scholastic groups should be conducted by instructors who teach one group or groups which are comparable to it and that students of different groups should not be thrown into the same class.

(l) Improvement in the working and living conditions of students. Participation in too many trivial activities. It was suggested that the University cooperate with the students in bringing about an improvement in the conditions of group life on the campus. The question of the amount of time which a student should spend in earning expenses was also considered. The deans were asked to supervise such matters very carefully.

(m) Examination and grading procedure: More examinations should be given; a more complete and inclusive final examination; provide proper time for examinations; departmental examinations for large classes; supervision of examinations by deans and heads of departments; more uniformity in grading methods.

(n) Improvements of class schedules; convocation schedule; Saturday A. M. Classes; week-end work of the University and absences of students from Bloomington.

(o) Extension of facilities for more complete analysis of psychological test results.

10. The work of the Extension Center at Gary and the Gary Junior College.

With the exception of paragraphs 7 and 8 the above report is offered without recommendations by the Council.

W. L. BRYAN, chairman
H. T. BRISCOE, secretary.

Faculty Minutes, November, 1931—May, 1940, Vol. I.

Document 118

The Bookstore and the Faculty

The Bookstore became a matter of prime interest to the faculty in the depression year 1932. This report by the special faculty committee reveals a moment of need for change in another unit of the University's operation. This committee report lays bare the operation of a functional part of the university which had its up and downs since its founding.

*   *   *

REPORT OF SPECIAL BOOKSTORE COMMITTEE

June 3, 1932

To the Deans and Heads of Departments of Indiana University who joined in the appointment of this Special Bookstore Committee:

The special committee on the Indiana University Book Store respectfully submits the following report:

1. The committee was appointed by you on May 12, 1932, and has held 5 meetings. At its first meeting the Committee elected its Chairman. Its members discussed the purposes for which the committee was appointed, and the possible methods by which it might conduct its work.

2. The committee formulated its objectives as follows:

(1) To consider in general the desirability and legality of having a bookstore connected with a state university, and operated as one of its departments;

(2) To investigate the situation and activities, past and present of the Indiana University bookstore;

(3) To report its findings and its recommendations, if any, to the body by which it was appointed.

3. The committee decided upon the following procedure for carrying on its work:

(1) To ask other members of the Faculty for specific information and personal opinions of these subjects;

(2) To examine official records in regard to the Indiana University Bookstore, subsequent to its financial failure in 1910, which resulted in its being taken over as a department of the University in that year.

4. In addition to examining the records, the committee requested the manager of the Bookstore to meet with it, and to assist it in getting some of the facts required for its report. The committee thereupon received the assistance of the manager, and of other members of the staff of the Bookstore.

5. With such assistance and under its own direction and control, the com-

mittee has formulated the following summary statements of fact about the operations of the Bookstore.

The Bookstore was established by students and faculty as a co-operative association in 1890, flourished for a time under good management, and then, after getting into campus politics, it failed in 1910.

It was taken over by the University in 1910 and has since been thus maintained.

This department is under the direct supervision of the Board of Trustees, the same as other departments of the University. The manager is appointed by the Board of Trustees. The manager appoints the clerks. All employees work on a straight salary. No commissions are allowed. This is done so as to keep prices at the lowest possible figure. It avoids the temptation of raising prices so as to increase commissions.

Since the present manager has had charge, 1923, on each August 1 a detailed report has been made annually to the President and Board of Trustees. Reports were also made by the present manager's predecessor, but in a much less complete form. These reports are on file in the President's office, Bursar's office, and in the Bookstore. These are open for inspection by students and faculty who may be interested.

The store aims to make a net profit of 5¢ on each dollar. This it has not been able to do the last two years. The sales of the current year in keeping with the general depression do not promise much, if anything, in the way of profits.

The publishers grant to the bookstore a uniform discount of 20% on all textbooks, 10% is allowed the student and the remaining 10% is used to cover transportation, overhead, loss on account of left overs and new editions. The loss on new textbooks is never less than $3500 each year.

Old textbooks, when they are used again the next year, are bought at 50% of cost price and sold at ⅓ off list. This allows a slightly better margin of profit.

On all other items when the stationary discount is allowed, from 25 to 33⅓% discount is allowed the student.

No profit is made on sales to the University departments and to the Library. Because of the bookstore's agency connections, advantageous discounts are obtained, thus, saving the University hundreds of dollars.

The average sales for the past 8 years was $113,965.96. The best year was 1929-30 with $124,306.40. The average annual profits and interests was $6,535, representing 5.7%.

As an illustration the details of the 1930-31 transactions may be taken.

Sales

a. Sales to students, faculty and alumni		$ 93,034.29
b. Sales to University departments		21,392.50
	Total Sales	114,426.79

Cost

Cost of books		$ 57,691.26
Cost of supplies		32,796.37
Freight and express		1,608.42
Salaries and payroll (7 permanent employees, including the manager and 12 student clerks)		13,995.01
Other expenses		3,880.70
Depreciation on building		400.00
	Total	110,371.76
	Net Profit	4,055.03

Approximately 60% of total sales is on texts
  Overhead
    The itemized overhead for the year 1930-31 is as follows:

Salaries—7 permanent employees, including the manager	10,710.00
Salaries—12 student clerks	3,285.01
Freight, express and drayage	1,608.42
Stationery and postage	208.24
Mail order expense	277.01
Insurance and fidelity bonds	356.77
Advertising	862.11
Telephone and telegrams	177.86
Office supplies	220.42
Janitor's supplies and laundry	26.10
Miscellaneous	594.17
Repairs	85.15
Total	18,411.26

This represents about 16%. During the last four years the overhead has been practically the same. At the time of removal from the library to their former wooden structure the overhead was increased in order to render more efficient service for the rather large volume of business done. In the present new quarters there had to be added one permanent man due to the post office being on a separate floor. It is also proposed to employ another employee to care for the proposed rental library on the mezzanine floor. This salary is, however, to come from earnings of this new department. If it proves not to be self-supporting it will be abandoned.

Two surveys of the overhead of college bookstores in the country reveal that the average is 26% and 31%. This speaks well for our own store.

It has been the hope of the two successful managers since 1910 that the department might at some time own its own building, adequate for the proper development into a first class bookstore. To this end it has accumulated its profits from year to year until these, under the present management, amout to $67,682.25. Of this sum $25,394.42 was earned by interest on these accumulations.

From this sum, since 1923, the following contributions have been made: (1) $699.50 for hospital expenses for students, (2) $1,476.05 for miscellaneous items; (3) $67,500.00 toward the Union Building. This represents all of the earnings since 1923. There remain approximately $12,000 cash, a little less than the cash accumulations prior to 1923.

Comparing our bookstore prices with the prices of privately owned stores in college towns where the college does not maintain its own store, we estimate, conservatively, that the Indiana Bookstore has in the last 8 years saved the students at least $126,000.00, an average of nearly $16,000.00 a year. This is in addition to the $67,000.00 profits previously set out. This last named sum has been turned into donations of one sort or another to the direct or indirect benefit of the students.

Besides this, it has been the policy of the management throughout the career of the store to employ student help. In recent years from 9 to 12 students have been thus employed for most of the year. The larger university bookstores are not doing this, believing it is not satisfactory. During the past 8 years $27,963.93 has been paid to students for this service.

Out of a list of 188 college bookstores belonging to the National Association of

College Stores, over half are college or university owned. On the west coast all of the universities own their stores. In Indiana, the Ball State Teachers College and the Terre Haute State College own their stores. Purdue is agitating for this. The senior class of last year left their memorial money for that purpose. An incomplete list of other state supported schools in our own and contiguous territory is as follows: Ohio State, Engineering School of the University of Minnesota, Kentucky, Missouri, Nebraska, Michigan State College, Tennessee, Utah.

6. The committee submits the following findings and recommendations:

(1) That the operation of a bookstore as a department of Indiana University, by the Board of Trustees of Indiana University, is well within the scope of the legal powers and duties of the Board of Trustees, as defined by the constitution and statutes of the State of Indiana. The committee, however, commends the policy of the Bookstore in restricting the scope of its operation more narrowly than is customary in many university bookstores, thereby leaving the fullest possible scope to private enterprise.

(2) That a university bookstore is both desirable and necessary. No privately managed bookstore could be expected, according to accepted business methods, to provide as promptly, accurately, and economically, the books that are necessary for the work of the faculty and students of the University.

(3) Because of the actual loss sustained in the sale of textbooks, the limited margin of profit realized upon the total sales could easily be wiped out under unfavorable conditions. The committee therefore is convinced that the store is dependent for its existence upon the full cooperation of the individual members of the faculty and of the student body.

(4) That more of the actual facts in regard to the operation of the Bookstore, as shown in the annual reports, be placed before the student body and members of the faculty in accessible form. The committee makes this recommendation because it is satisfied, not only that there is nothing to conceal about the operation of the Bookstore, but also because the committee is convinced that each faculty member and each student who knows these facts will thereby be able to increase the goodwill of the Bookstore and to make it still more successful in serving the interests of the faculty, the student body and the friends of the University.

Faculty Minutes, November, 1931–May, 1940, I. U. Archives.

Document 119

The Depression's Hand of Woe

This is a fascinating document. Perhaps President William Lowe Bryan was never more candid with his faculty than in this discussion of a possible cut in salaries and, certainly, a cut in most of the University's services. There was a ray of hope that the state's Budget Committee might be more generous with personnel than with services. This scene between president and faculty could be duplicated many times throughout the country during these bitter years of retrenchment.

*   *   *

The Faculty of the University met at 4 p.m., on Wednesday, August 3, 1932, in Science 32, President Bryan presiding.

. . . .

The President stated that at the time of the previous meeting of the Faculty, June 10, 1932, the Governor was positive that no extra session of the Legislature would be held, but that he later called a meeting because of irresistible pressure for such a meeting, coming from both political parties and all classes of citizens.

The President stated that it had been the hope of those interested in the welfare of the state educational institutions that they might give up the building tax and keep the rest down to a 10% cut. This proved impossible. In the House the legislators were divided between those who wished a cut of 15% and those who wished a cut of 20% or more. By a small majority the House passed a bill cutting the University appropriation 15%. This bill is coming before the Senate tomorrow morning at 10 o'clock. The indications are that the 15% bill will go through. The building tax is being cut off, either entirely or by a moratorium to extend two or three years.

. . . .

Information received within the hour from Indianapolis includes the following item: A bill is now before the Senate to prevent state institutions from belonging to associations having members outside the state, such associations as medical schools, and of law schools, and the North Central Association.

. . . .

An effort was made to include educational salaries in a bill reducing all state salaries by a proportional or percentage reduction.

Legislators from Gary, Evansville, Fort Wayne, and other localities, although eager to go home to care for personal affairs, have stayed in Indianapolis in an effort to help the situation.

Our appropriation at Bloomington is $1,325,000. 15% would be $198,750, or about $200,000 to be cut off.

Upon my appearance before the Ways and Means Committee, one question directed to me was, "Will you cut salaries?" My answer was, "There seems to be no way to avoid it." The reply from members of the Committee was, "Well, if you do not cut salaries, we will get to the salaries in January."

A movement is now under way to put the fixing of all salaries in the hands of the Budget Committee appointed by the Governor.

What we must do is to go through all the general things that money is spent for, and then cut; not because such action is wise, but because such action is necessary. All departments will have to do the same thing.

The President of Purdue University says that he is already making a 20% cut in his budget for the coming year.

. . . .

One bill proposed to do away with the State Board of Education. This would place the selection of texts in the hands of the Governor of the state. My observation over many years has been that the present system has been reasonably honest and efficient.

Another bill would limit travelling expenses, to a specified amount for lodging and meals. It seems clear that if the 15% cut goes through, the University will have to reduce travelling expenditures. I do not know what effect this will have on Extension work.

Some of the most influential leaders have tried hard to control the situation. Official leaders of the two parties wrote a bill to provide that the reduction should be 10%, but they were unable to maintain it.

In former years we have all been well represented by our friends in the Legislature, but this year many of them have suffered heavy financial losses and are not in a position to help as they have formerly done. (In answer to a question from the floor) the most powerful organization in the state seems to be the organization of township trustees.

It seems probable that the 15% bill will go through tomorrow. Senator Hoadley and others say that Representative Biddle has made the best fight possible against it. But he is looked upon this year as one especially interested in University matters, so that his influence is weakened.

. . . .

The immediate necessity seems to be that all those who have to make budgets shall cut out everything possible whether possible or not. If this is not done, it will be necessary for the Trustees of the University to do it.

Faculty Minutes, 1931–1940.

Document 120

More Depression

There remained in August, 1932, uncertainty about the plight of the University faculty's salaries. President Bryan, in the face of certain cuts, outlined procedures. He added the note that enrollment would be off in the fall if projections were to be trusted.

*   *   *

The Faculty of the University met at 4 p.m., August 10, 1932, in Science 32, President Bryan presiding.

. . . .

The President discussed the present situation of the University budget. If the bill limiting tax levies to $1.50 is permitted to stand, the situation seems grave. It seems that some proponents of these severe changes recognize that the proposals are revolutionary. It seems further that such proponents believe that, before the state tax system can be improved, the present system will have to be wrecked.

It is reported that the bill regarding the membership of state educational institutions in national associations will be withdrawn.

The bill in regard to the state budget committee has not passed the House and it is reasonable to suppose that it will not pass the House. It seems that a special committee recently appointed may present important suggestions.

It is essential that someone be in the engrossing room checking on paragraphs dealing with Indiana University. This has been customary and will be done this year.

The financial situation in regard to the University will be uncertain until the Legislature adjourns. It will then be necessary to have a meeting of the Board of Trustees. It seems that the effect of new legislation may be that the University cannot lawfully pay out any money prior to such meeting. As far as the Faculty is concerned, it will not be possible to pay amounts due in August to Faculty members.

For all members of the Faculty who are charged with the responsibility of making out budgets, the following steps are immediately necessary. It is requested that those who make out budgets for schools and departments shall make an itemized list of everything for which money has been spent in such school or department, except for salaries of Faculty members, for the years 1931–32, 1928–29, and 1926–27. These columns will be for the fiscal years, extending from September 30 to September 30. It will be convenient to have these years arranged in parallel columns for comparison. We want to see what has cost the extra money, if any extra money has been spent, other than salaries. These amounts are to include all personal service, except for members of the Faculty.

. . . .

The applications for admission for the fall of 1932 now total 581. At this time last year, the applications were 672. A very forceful argument in presenting the University's interests to members of the Legislature has been in the fact that attendance for 1931–32 was not below the usual attendance.

. . . .

Faculty Minutes, 1931–1940, I. U. Archives.

Document 121

More Depression

The Indiana General Assembly remained in session for the full forty days, and like the forty days of biblical fame, it produced a severe dampening of hopes. John W. Cravens, registrar and master political observer, reported to the faculty as to what might happen. The Budget Committee would not pass upon salaries until the session of 1933. This placed some burden upon faculty members to agree to cuts voluntarily.

*   *   *

The Faculty of the University met at 4 p.m., August 17, 1932, in Science 32, President Bryan presiding.

The President announced that the financial situation of the University seems to be almost the same as it was a week ago. An invitation was extended for questions and discussion.

. . . .

Registrar Cravens discussed the recent session of the Legislature. He pointed out that the session ran its full forty days. At the middle of the session it looked like the cut in the University's appropriation would be at least 20%; many said it would be 25%, and a few advocated 50%. A leading member of the House said on the floor of the House that the reduction in the salaries at Indiana University should be reduced 50% and that no one would resign as the result of such reductions. We have never before seen conditions like they were at this session. They struck out to lower taxes and educational institutions stood out as opportunities for reductions. Many unkind things were said about the University, but there was not the ill feeling which was shown in the session of 1899, when sectarian schools fought the universities. At this session the attitude of sectarian schools was friendly.

On the forenoon of the last day, it seemed that the general salary bill would be applied to all county and state offices and to university faculty members. The House favored leaving university salaries out of the operation of the bill; the Senate favored leaving university salaries within the provisions of the bill. The Conference Committee was deadlocked for a long time. Finally an amendment was agreed upon to the effect that the Budget Committee would not pass upon present university salaries, either to raise them or to lower them, but that it would be necessary that university authorities go before the Budget Committee in order to raise any salaries or to make any new appointments.

Professor Book states that he thinks the University is morally bound to reduce salaries, and that by so doing the University will be better off when the Legislature meets in January, 1933.

. . . .

It was moved, seconded, and carried unanimously that the thanks of the University be extended to the gentlemen who supported the interests of the University in the Legislature.

The President commended this action and stated that the thanks of the University were properly due to many individuals, including Representative Biddle who served as the point of a flying wedge. Mr. Cravens, Mr. U. H. Smith, Senator Hoadley, and others were commended. Among political leaders exercising an active influence in favor of the University were Mr. Ball, in the Republican Party, and Mr. McNutt and active legislative representatives in the Democratic Party. The powerful support of Governor Leslie likewise was acknowledged. Without this support it seems that the University's interests might have been seriously injured.

The Faculty of the University then adjourned.

JAMES J. ROBINSON
Secretary of the Faculty.

Faculty Minutes, 1931–1940, I. U. Archives.

Document 122

A Fundamental Discussion of University Restructuring

In 1935 Indiana University faced the realities of realigning its whole instructional program to meet expanded and modern needs of a Midwestern university. This particular report concerned itself with student relations and the instructional program. These Council reports were actually forerunners of the general self-study which was made in 1938–1939.

*   *   *

To Members of the Faculty:

At its meeting on October 29 the University Council approved the following series of programs for the year:

November and January—Topics related to the improvement of the work of students and methods by which the University may help students in achieving success.

February—The quarter vs. the semester system.

March—Pensions and retirement.

April and May—Topics related to the improvement of the work of the faculty. These topics are to center about research.

Committees are at present engaged in the study of these problems.

At its meeting on November 26 the Council heard reports from Professors Yeager and Eaton on the subject, "What can the University do to increase the efficiency of the student body in college work?" The following is a summary of the recommendations made by Professor Yeager:

1. Extension of the use of placement and proficiency examinations, especially in required courses for freshmen and sophomores.

2. An extension of facilities for students, especially freshmen and sophomores, to consider with some one as a counsellor the fields of study, and the subjects to be studied during the following semester(s).

3. More detailed mid-semester reports on the work of freshmen and sophomores who are regarded by their respective instructors as doing work below the level of the general average (e.g., below C).

4. Counselling with students who, on the basis of evidence readily obtainable by the end of the first month at least, might be considered to be likely not to do a very high grade of working their first semester in college.

5. The provision of a curriculum for the freshman and sophomore years which will have a maximum of appeal and interest to the student; and which will provide opportunity for either (a) continuing study on a more advanced level of study during the junior and senior years, or (b) leaving at the end of one or two years of collegiate study with more of a general education.

After consideration of these points the Council voted to make the following recommendations to the faculty:

1. Mid-term reports should be made at least two weeks earlier than at present.

2. More detailed mid-semester reports should be made on the work of freshmen and sophomores who are regarded by their respective instructors as doing work below the level of the general average (e.g., below C).

3. Some system should be found by which reports on students can be made to faculty members. The following was one suggestion of how this might be done. Much good might come from having a small committee selected from among instructors of freshmen to consider the mid-term and final reports on freshmen students. This committee, by bringing together several opinions concerning the work of each student and reporting its findings to the individual instructors, might serve better than any other agency in meeting the problems of the failing students.

Following the report of Professor Eaton, who dealt with the "failing student," the Council asked Professor Holmstedt to report at the next meeting on whatever findings he may be able to make concerning the following questions:

1. What is the mortality rate among our students?

2. What kind of students fail? To what classes or groups do they belong?

The Council also expressed considerable interest in the earlier publication of the schedule of classes. The general feeling was that the schedule for the second semester should appear shortly after Christmas and for the fall semester not later than the beginning of the final examinations in the spring. A report will later be made to the Council on the feasibility of this proposal.

———————

Since its inauguration, the University Council has considered the following subjects. Wherever any definite action has been taken, or any recommendation has been made, the action or recommendation is indicated.

1. Faculty advisors for students.

A report on this subject was approved by the Council and considered by the faculty. Certain parts of this report were adopted by the faculty.

2. On several occasions, reports from the Curriculum Committee of the College of Arts and Sciences were made and considered.

3. Campus elections.

The discussion on this topic was informal and resulted in no action.

4. A ten year program for the University.

The report on this subject has been summarized and presented to the faculty on different occasions, including one open meeting of the Council.

5. The quarter vs. the semester system.

Reports on this subject have been made to the Council, but this body has never formulated any recommendation.

6. Examination schedule.

A report on this subject was approved by the Council and later by the faculty.

7. Matriculation, registration, and enrollment.

A committee reported in favor of pre-enrollment. This was approved and submitted to the faculty and the plan was later tried for a short time.

8. Convocations.

The report of the committee on this subject was approved by the Council and later by the faculty.

9. Awarding of county scholarships.

10. Improvement of work in the Graduate School.

11. Teaching load.

The report of this committee on this topic was accepted and placed on record without recommendation.

12. Establishment of a Graduate School faculty.

13. Training of University teachers. Dean Payne's report was referred to the faculty for further discussion.

14. Distribution of appropriations for research, supplies, and equipment.

The report of the committee on this topic was approved and submitted to the faculty.

15. A course in bacteriology on the University campus.

16. Housing situation for girls.

17. Library. Methods of increasing its usefulness to students and faculty.

18. History and various phases of the work of the North Central Association.

19. Undergraduate standards.

A committee on this topic made one recommendation which was referred to the faculty: That each department definitely appoint some member or members of its staff as counselor or counselors to consult with students concerning their probelms, and that said counselor or counselors announce definite office hours and that students be notified of the opportunity provided for conferences.

20. Service of the University to the state.

21. Placement of students after graduation.

22. Relation of the University to the High School and Junior Colleges.

Upon the recommendation of a committee a letter was sent to the high schools calling attention to the work which post-graduate students in high schools may do to prepare themselves for University admission and credit.

23. Relation of the University to the North Central Association of schools and colleges.

24. Cooperation between the graduate school and other units of the University. Cooperation between departments within the college of Arts and Sciences.

25. The plans and objectives of the School of Business Administration.

26. The plans and objectives of the School of Education.

27. Work of the School of Music.

28. Operation of a new curriculum in the College of Arts and Sciences.

29. Current trends and experiments in education.

30. Current trend and experiments in Business Administration.

31. Establishment of a Two Year Elective course.

The Council spent almost one year in formulating recommendations which were adopted, with modifications, by the faculty.

32. Stimulation of students before their enrollment.

33. Stimulation of students of superior and mediocre ability.

34. Improvement in instruction.

35. Ways in which the University Council may be made more useful.

36. Research in problems of higher education.

37. Retirement annuities.

38. Personnel movement in education.

39. Work of Indiana University School of Medicine and the relationship of this school to the other parts of the University.

40. Occupational trends in the United States.

41. Underlying problems of educational guidance.

Faculty Minutes, November, 1931—May, 1940, Vol. I.

Document 123

The School of Music

The School of Music in these New Deal years had outgrown the facilities of Mitchell Hall. Federal funds were now available for the construction of a building and the dean of the School lost no time in beginning the pursuit of W. P. A. funds.

*   *   *

TO THE PATRONS AND FRIENDS OF INDIANA UNIVERSITY SCHOOL OF MUSIC

The business of music, which the United States Bureau of Statistics shows to be under only that of steel and oil, can hardly be passed by as unimportant. The manufacture of radio sets, phonographs, organs, pianos and small instruments; concert companies and orchestras; broadcasting and movie business; church music, and music publishing, and the great teaching profession—the millions of Indiana's music business is astounding. And the foundation of all this is the school of music: without teachers there would be no music business.

There are six economic reasons for a School of Music building at your State University at this time:

1. The cost would be less than at any time in the future, due to the availability of Federal funds.

2. It would keep much of the tax-payer's money in Indiana, which now goes to other states, a substantial loss to business. Letters from schools of music outside of Indiana show that approximately 2,000 of our most talented students are taking about $4,000,000.00 of our money out of the state annually. Is this business worth bidding for? Even ten per cent of it would circulate thousands of dollars in the state.

3. The overhead now is relatively much higher than it would be were the classes of our teachers normally filled, in which case some of them would cost the state nothing.

4. Practice facilities are extremely meager. We cannot supply rooms, and students are obliged to take what they can get, scattered all over town, resulting also in enormous loss of time and practice supervision.

5. This fifty-year old firetrap, with its oil-soaked floors should be condemned as unsanitary and unsafe. Less impressive than the carpenter shop, it is a disgrace as representing an important school of the university. It contains $40,000.00 worth of valuable and unreplaceable instruments, books, scores, records and other equipment upon which no adequate insurance can be placed except at prohibitive rates, not to speak of the ravages of rats and mice and the rapid deterioration of costly pianos and other instruments through dampness, heat and cold.

6. Indiana University School of Music has never and is not now sending out its graduates to swell the ranks of unemployment.

McNutt Drawer 95, Archives Div., ISL.

Document 124

Co-operative Programs with Purdue University

Indiana and Purdue universities were constantly involved in areas where the lines of domain were not clearly drawn. This particular incident involved an extension course offered jointly by the two schools in the field of criminal law and criminology, but obviously the bigger question of cooperation was involved. This is a rather forceful statement of policy. An interesting note is that relating to pharmacy, which was definitely in Purdue's domain.

*　　*　　*

February 10, 1936

My dear Governor McNutt:

I enclose with this a letter from Professor Sutherland and Professor James J. Robinson concerning the position of Indiana University in relation to criminal law and criminology. I enclose also a memorandum which I have prepared in regard to this matter to submit to the Trustees of Indiana University at their meeting on February 11th.

It is my view that the Trustees of Indiana University should adopt this or some such memorandum on the subject and transmit the same to the Trustees of Purdue University in order to state our position in the matter.

Professor Sutherland and Professor Robinson made an engagement to meet representatives of Purdue together with the head of the State Police at Indianapolis on Thursday evening. It is my wish that the position of Indiana University be stated at that time to those participating in the conference.

Very truly yours,

WILLIAM LOWE BRYAN.

Governor Paul V. McNutt,
State House,
Indianapolis, Indiana.
MC

Copy

THE INSTITUTE
Of Criminal Law and Criminology
Indiana University

February 10, 1936

Dear President Bryan:

It has become necessary to place before you a situation which has arisen in connection with the work of the University in police training. Our work in this field and in related fields, as you know, has been going on for more than ten years. Over eight years ago several members of the faculty entered into definate plans which have been gradually leading up to professional courses for police officers. Those engaged in these conferences have included Dean Myers and Dean Gatch of the Medical School, Dean Payne of the Graduate School, Professors Book and Yeager of the Department of Psychology, Professor Robinson of the Law School, and representatives of the Department of Sociology.

On December 6, 1930, the University held a "Regional Conference on the Observance and Enforcement of Law." On August 5th and 6th, 1932, the University held "The First Statewide Conference of Sheriffs, Chiefs of Police, and the Other Peace Officers of Indiana." On June 15, 1935, the Board of Trustees established the Institute of Criminal Law and Criminology in order to organize and to extend the work of the University in this field. For many years, of course, the University has been assisting the administration of criminal law in this state by conducting investigations, supplying expert witnesses, and drafting improved statutory provisions for enactment by the legislature.

The Institute is now engaged in preparations for a conference on criminal law problems to be held here on March 31. This conference is to be followed by a series of regional conferences on police training to be held in selected cities of the state during April and May. It has been our plan to announce at the conference on March 31st, the Regional Conferences. We have planned also to announce details at that time, in addition to those already published by the University during the past year, in regard to two professional police training courses, requiring two years and four years, respectively, of residence work here at the University. In fact, our past experience and the information to be gained at these regional conferences will be used in preparing the details of the professional courses.

In carrying forward these plans, we desire, of course, to cooperate with the Indiana State Police. We are informed, however, by the Superintendent of the Indiana State Police, that he has received a tentative request for cooperation in a proposed four-weeks training school for police at Purdue University. The Superintendent states that he is willing to assist to the limit of his resources, but that such effort seems likely to suffer by duplication and resuling confusion.

We do not know that Superintendent Stiver is accurately informed about the situation at Purdue. It is obvious, however, that the continued progress of our plans for police training requires that this question be settled.

Sincerely yours,
J. J. Robinson
E. H. Sutherland

Indiana University and Purdue University have had less duplication of work than exists in any of the other states in which there are two universities supported by the State. A certain amount of work which is judged to be necessary at all universities is provided both at Indiana and at Purdue. But each of the two institutions in our state has developed important fields of work which the other does not undertake. The division of work thus developed does not always appear logical. Thus it would seem that pharmacy should be associated with medicine. But pharmacy having been established at Purdue is left there undisturbed. Other examples will readily suggest themselves. The essential principle has been that so far as possible work, especially professional work, established at one of the institutions should not be duplicated at the other. We have accordingly Schools of Agriculture, Engineering, Pharmacy, etc. at Purdue; Schools of Medicine, Law, Education, Business Administration, etc. at Indiana without, as in other states, duplicating these schools at the two universities.

Indiana University has an Institute of Criminal Law and Criminology. This Institute is simply a formal organization of schools and departments long established here and long active cooperatively in dealing with problems of crime. For illustration: Through a period of years Dr. Weatherly, head of the department of Sociology, a specialist in criminology, directed an investigation of more than 1500 individuals at Indiana and West Virginia belonging to an interrelated group of derelicts. The School of Medicine made Wasserman tests; the psychologists made mental tests; the economists investigated the economic status of the derelicts, etc. The School of Education is now directing an investigation of derelict children in this country.

Adequate dealing with the problems of crime requires the cooperation of several schools and departments. Basic and not to be dispensed with are:

The Department of Criminology (a branch of
general sociology)
The School of Law
The School of Medicine.

Other departments whose cooperation is important and in some problems necessary are psychology, government, economics, education, besides the departments of physical science that may be called upon to make necessary scientific tests.

It is not now possible to provide these essential facilities for dealing with the problems of crime in this state except at Indiana University. It is accordingly obvious that, under the policy of avoiding the duplication by one institution of work competently established at the other, the field of criminology should be left to Indiana, as the field of agriculture is left to Purdue.

It may be noted that Indiana University has on a number of occasions withdrawn courses which Purdue University viewed as properly belonging to that institution. As an example on the other side I note in 1922 the Trustees of Purdue University, without suggestion from Indiana University, passed the following resolution:

"PURDUE UNIVERSITY
Lafayette, Indiana

January 9, 1922

*** Resolved, that the Board of Trustees decline to sanction any adjunct or extension work or the giving directly of University credits which would violate in letter or spirit the agreement now existing between the late Dr. Stone and Dr. Bryan, that the institutions should not engage in extension work which would constitute duplication of work or trespass upon the proper field of work of each other. ***

Sincerely yours,
(signed)   Henry W. Marshall
Vice-President and Acting President."

Our attention has been called to a suggestion from Dean Skinner of Purdue University that committees from Purdue and from the School of Business Administration of Indiana confer on the practicability of a plan for a combined course in agriculture and business. Dean Wells and his faculty will be glad to go into such a conference in the interest of the policy of cooperation without duplication.

WLB.

McNutt 1936 (#99), Archives Division, Indiana State Library.

Document 125

A Faculty Retirement Plan

Internally, no greater barrier confronted Indiana University than its aged faculty, which could not and would not be retired because the University had no retirement plan. This committee report of April 21, 1936, is a revealing document. Ultimately a retirement plan similar to the one suggested in this report was adopted, and there was a tremendous turnover in university personnel, including the retirement of William Lowe Bryan himself.

*   *   *

REPORT OF THE COMMITTEE ON RETIREMENT

The report on a retirement plan for Indiana University is presented in four parts:
1. Recommendations of the committee
2. Estimated cost of the proposed retirement system
3. Some pertinent facts concerning the faculty of Indiana University
4. A brief summary of retirement plans now in operation in colleges and universities in the United States and Canada.

W. S. BITTNER
B. D. MYERS
B. C. GAVIT
H. L. SMITH
R. W. HOLMSTEDT, Chr.

RECOMMENDATIONS FOR A RETIREMENT PLAN FOR INDIANA UNIVERSITY

There are several factors favorable to the establishment of a retirement system at Indiana University at the present time:

a. The situation of those members of the faculty who are not eligible for Carnegie pensions is extremely uncertain unless the university makes some definite provisions for them. Fifty-nine members of the faculty are over sixty years of age. Of these, thirty-three are eligible for Carnegie pensions; twenty-six are not.

b. The fact that a large proportion of those members of the faculty who are near retirement age are eligible for Carnegie pensions would reduce the immediate cost to the University. Postponing the establishment of a definite retirement system will greatly decrease the advantages to the university accruing through the Carnegie pensions.

c. A retirement system benefits not only the instructor but the university as well in that definite provisions are made for those who no longer can render effective service.

d. There are more than 150 colleges and universities in the United States and Canada in which retirement plans have been adopted. Due to economic insecurity at the present time university faculty members have become increasingly cognizant of the advantages of definite provisions for retirement. Without a retirement system Indiana University may expect to experience increasing difficulty in securing and retaining outstanding individuals for its faculty.

Your committee is of the opinion that the establishment of a retirement system should be one of the first adjustments to be made in faculty compensation. The following outline of a desirable retirement plan for Indiana University is submitted for your consideration:

(1) That a compulsory retirement plan be established to include those who have completed at least 3 years of service as an instructor or as an administrative officer, excluding the part-time instructors on the medical, dental and other professional faculties. Membership should be optional after a person otherwise eligible had completed one year of service.

(2) Retirement age at the beginning should be fixed at 70 years. Provision should be made by the Board of Trustees when the plan is established to scale down the retirement age to sixty-five years as soon as feasible. It is suggested that the retirement age might be reduced one year every two years so that at the end of ten years retirement would be at sixty-five. Provision should be made for optional retirement before normal retirement age with adjusted compensation. Provision should also be made for extension of service beyond normal retirement age. Extensions of one year should be granted by special vote of the Board of Trustees only upon the recommendation of the head of the department of instruction or administration and with the approval of the President. Such extensions should not exceed five years.

(3) Each faculty member and administrative officer should have deducted 5% of each salary payment for a retirement annuity. The University should allocate an equal amount. Payment should be forwarded to the Teacher's Insurance and Annuity Association for the purchase of deferred annuity contracts on the life of each member.

(4) The retirement annuity should equal the amount purchased by the joint contributions, provided that the annuities so purchased, together with any amount received as a Carnegie pension, shall not exceed one-half of the final salary or $2,400. The normal retirement annuity should approximate 50% of the

average salary of those who will have served the university 30 years or more. Provisions should be made so that the University's payment would not exceed its share of an annuity equal to one-half of the salary or $2,400. Payment by the University should cease when the annuity has been built up to this amount.

(5) Provision should be made for supplementing the annuities purchased through joint contributions for those members of the faculty who are now near retirement age. There are several methods for providing such supplements.

a. The most desirable plan would be for the University to provide a supplement which, when added to the purchased annuity and the Carnegie pension, would provide a total retirement annuity equal to 2% of the salary on the effective date of retirement for each year of service at the University. The total sum should not exceed 50% of the salary or a maximum of $2,400 per year.

b. In the event that such supplements can not be financed those eligible for Carnegie pensions may be eliminated and only those not on the Carnegie pension list made eligible for supplementary pensions. For these non-Carnegie members the purchased annuity plus the supplement should not exceed $1,500 per year or one half the salary received at retirement. Since the normal Carnegie pension is $1,500 per year at age 70, this plan would provide a maximum pension equal to that received by those on the Carnegie pension list.

c. The least desirable alternative would be to let the retirement annuity be just that purchased by the joint contributions. Such a plan would make no provision for those at or near retirement age who are not eligible for Carnegie pensions.

The committee recommends the adoption of plan (a) which provides a total annuity equal to 2% of the salary for each year of service with the maximums suggested. In the event that retirement age is reduced to age 65, adjustments could be made in the supplement so that the total retirement annuity would not exceed the amount which would have been purchased through joint contributions during a similar period of service.

(6) Those already having an annuity contract with the Teacher's Insurance and Annuity Association started at another institution should enter the system at Indiana University, receiving full credit for the payments made by the former institution. Those already having their own contracts with the Association should be allowed to continue with them and have the payments herewith provided for applied upon them.

(7) In the event that there is no possibility of establishing a joint-contributory system at this time, a definite retirement age should be established and pension provisions made for those not eligible for Carnegie pensions. The possibilities of membership in the Indiana State Teacher's Retirement System should be considered. Such provisions, however, should be considered as only temporary until such time as the University should be able to adopt a joint-contributory plan.

ESTIMATED COST OF THE PROPOSED RETIREMENT PLAN

The annual cost to the University of a joint-contributory retirement plan would equal 5% of the annual salaries of those eligible plus whatever amount is provided for supplementary pensions. The total of the annual salaries of the Bloomington faculty, the administrative staff, the library staff and the Indianapolis faculties is approximately $780,000. Five per cent of this amount equals $39,000. Since some of those included on the payroll may not be eligible for membership in the retirement system, the basic cost would probably be some what less than $39,000. Future adjustments in salaries would necessarily cause variations in the annual cost of the retirement plan.

The cost of pension supplements would depend on the plan adopted. Two sets of estimates are submitted in the following table. The first column shows the estimated cost of supplements to provide a total annuity equal to 2% of the salary for each year of service as suggested in plan (a) above. The second column shows the estimated cost of supplementary pensions for those not eligible for Carnegie pensions as suggested in plan (b) above. Both estimates are limited to those faculty members over 60 years of age. These estimates may be considered as maximum amounts in as much as no allowance was made for possible deaths during the ten year period and no extension of service beyond the age of 70 was assumed.

ESTIMATED ANNUAL COST OF SUPPLEMENTARY
PENSIONS FOR FACULTY MEMBERS OVER SIXTY YEARS OF AGE.*

Year	Plan (a)	Plan (b)
1937	$ 5,340	$ 2,600
1938	8,060	3,550
1939	10,150	5,000
1940	13,000	6,300
1941	18,600	10,000
1942	20,200	10,000
1943	24,700	13,800
1944	27,500	16,500
1945	33,200	19,600
1946	39,700	23,400

* Plan (a) provides a total annuity equal to 2% of the salary at retirement for each year of service with a maximum of $2,400. Plan (b) provides only for those not eligible to Carnegie pensions, the pension not to exceed $1,500 per year or one half of the salary at retirement.

It may be safely assumed that the maximum cost of supplementary pensions will be reached in ten years. The normal life expectancy at age 70 is eight years and it is reasonable to assume that decreases in pensions due to deaths after ten years will offset the increases for new annuitants. Further decreases may be secured by the retention of men over seventy on a part or full time basis.

Summarizing the above estimates, the total cost to the University of the proposed retirement system would be approximately $40,000–$45,000 per year at the beginning and would increase to approximately $70,000–$80,000 per year within the next ten years.

THE STATUS OF THE INDIANA UNIVERSITY FACULTY

The age status of those eligible to membership in a retirement system is an important factor to be considered. The following table shows the age distribution of the Indiana University faculty. The number eligible to Carnegie pensions is also indicated. It should be noted that only 23 faculty members under 65 years of age are eligible for Carnegie pensions, while 24 of the 32 members over 65 years of age are on the Carnegie list. Postponement of the adoption of a retirement system will result in loss of the advantages of including the Carnegie pensions in the retirement annuities and in the meantime, the number of faculty members without retirement expectations will increase.

AGE DISTRIBUTION OF INDIANA UNIVERSITY FACULTY

AGE	NUMBER	CARNEGIE PENSIONS
70	12	10
65-69	20	14
60-64	28	9
55-59	23	6
50-54	34	7
45-49	19	1
40-44	39	
35-39	32	
Under 35	47	
Total	254	47

. . . .

Faculty Minutes, 1931–1940, I. U. Archives.

Document 126

A Look Backward—A Look Forward

The speeches of Governor Paul McNutt and President William Lowe Bryan on the occasion of the dedication of Bryan Administration Building followed the usual pattern. Bryan took occasion to look back to the old days and to enunciate a bit of personal administrative philosophy. The building itself, however, symbolized the opening of a new age of physical expansion. The University had found its way to Washington and the fount of federal matching funds. The Bryan Building was a product of the new fiscal era.

*　　*　　*

Governor Paul V. McNutt was next called upon. He said:

We are here to participate in a corner stone laying by remote control. Visualize the new building and the stone we are about to place. I wish to bring greetings on behalf of the people of Indiana. This stone is a foundation stone of progress for I. U. Tangible symbols are now placed; the foundation stones were laid in 1816 by the framers of the first constitution who made provision that the state should provide a system of public education "ascending in a regular gradation from township schools to a state university, wherein tuition shall be gratis and equally open to all." This was a declaration of faith of the people of Indiana. The citizens of Indiana have kept this faith. The buildings now rising fill long-felt wants. Buildings are not the University. The University is found in men and women members, found in a man, William Lowe Bryan. His name will be upon this building, a tangible symbol to remind future generations of the greatness and goodness of this man. He typifies the institution. It, through him, has played a full part in education; it has risen to a place of leadership. Whatever we can build will not replace the gratitude and affection we find in our hearts. The children of Indiana University appreciate all he has done and will do for I. U.

He has brought to us the freedom of live and let live. No freedom can exist long which feeds upon others. Aristotle said that the good man, the educated man, and the free man are one and the same. Virtue is just intelligent behavior. There are two kinds of men; men who govern themselves by reason and virtue, and those who govern themselves by desire and prejudice. Only those who govern themselves by reason and virtue are free. Would you be free? Then first become civilized. We have been free here from the beginning. For this priceless heritage I place this stone, a symbol of a building we have within our hearts, a true memorial to the man who has given us the freedom we now enjoy. Honor I. U.; repay her with service; remain loyal to the institution; thank him for the things he has given us; to him we bring sincere affection and deep admiration.

President Bryan responded:

I remember when the first corner stone on this campus (Wylie Hall) was laid in 1884. It rained. That stone also was laid by remote control, in the Methodist Church down town. Your Excellency, I wish to express appreciation of your words. When overwhelmed with tributes I think of what President Lord said he did under similar circumstances. "I send them to my mother; she believes them." I wish I could do that—to the mother who left us so long ago.

Your Excellency, you do us honor by laying the foundation stone of this Administration Building as part of the educational plant of which you are by law the chief administrator. You have earned the right to lay this stone. Through the years when many children and youth of our country have been denied the schooling which is their dearest right you have seen to it that none in Indiana have been denied that right. Whatever any friend or foe of yours may say of you none can deny you the title of Protector of the School.

A friend of mine, an alumnus, wrote me criticizing the use of money for an administration building when the money should have been used for things of the spirit. I welcome every such straight-from-the-shoulder criticism. But I wish to state a different view. As I think, there is no stone in any schoolhouse which may not contribute to the things of the spirit. And there is no building on any campus more essential to things of the spirit than the building which houses the administration. Whatever goes on elsewhere on the campus that which goes on here must be right if the life of the school as a whole is to be right.

The teaching of truth, the inspirations of art, the incarnations of morality within those who teach—all are essential parts of what makes the University live as it should within the commonwealth. But these necessary and precious things are never enough unless there is justice in this workaday house where the business of the University is done. Unless what is done here with a dollar is every way right, nothing within the University can be entirely right. Unless what is done here in dealing with men is just, the whole structure of moralizing influences within the school is undermined.

I wish to say a word concerning that part of the administrative system which underlies all the rest—the Board of Trustees. I can speak freely on this subject because it is a part of the University for which I am in no way responsible and because for many years I have known intimately the deeds and spirit of the Trustees of this University. I have another qualification. I have never asked the Trustees for anything for myself. In the year of my graduation, on the day when the corner stone of the first building on this campus (Wylie Hall) was laid, I was astonished and electrified by notice of my election as instructor in Greek at a salary of $250 a year. In fact, I made a speech that day at the laying of that corner stone. Somehow the text has survived. I wrote it on the first typewriter ever brought to this town, picking out the letters with my forefinger. I understand that there have been developed since other methods of typing of diabolical ingenuity. But I stick to the good old forefinger method of the horse and buggy days. What I wish to say is that from that day to this I have never directly or indirectly asked the Trustees for anything whatever for myself and I never shall until the day rolls around when I ask them to accept my resignation. I shall say now only what I have many a time said to them to myself. In the darkest hours I have kept myself in heart by my knowledge of the integrity and the devotion of the Board of Trustees to the interests of this University. I was never more sure of that than now as this foundation stone is laid. Members of the Board are not subservient to one another or to friend or to foe. Each one carries his judgment and conscience under his own hat. They are free to agree or to disagree. Whether they agree or disagree, they agree or disagree as free men. Once in a long time there is a majority-minority vote as happens in the Supreme Court of the United States. Nearly always our Trustees talk out their differences and get together on what is finally decided to be most wise and just. Such individual independence with such cooperation is the soul of democracy.

Here I wish to name two men who should be named when the corner stone of the Administration is laid, in remembrance of their years of unexcelled devotion to the administration of the University—John William Cravens and James William Fesler.

Now, let us take a look at our corner stone. When Emerson climbed Monadnoc, the mountain said to him:

> "Gentle pilgrim, . . .
> If thou trowest
> How the chemic eddies play,
> Pole to pole and what they say;
> And that these gray crags
> Not on crags are hung,
> But beads are of a rosary
> On prayer and music strung;
> And, credulous, through the granite seeming,
> Seest the smile of Reason beaming; . . .
> Knowest thou this?
> O pilgrim, wandering not amiss!
> Already my rocks lie light,
> And soon my cone will spin.
> For the world was built in order,
> And the atoms march in tune."

So, champions of the spirit, look at this stone as the poet looked at the mountain. See with the eyes of exact science that it is not a dead lump but a universe of whirling electrons. The scientist measures them. Milton would hear them sing as he heard the planets sing on the morning of Christ's nativity. The planets may seem dead lumps of matter. But not to Milton on that morning. They were crystal spheres that sang—you remember:

> "Ring out, ye crystal spheres!
> Once bless our human ears,
> If ye have power to touch our senses so"

Indiana University Alumni Quarterly, Vol. XXIII, No. 3 (Summer, 1936), pp. 282–285.

Document 127

Labor Strife and the Music Building

Leslie Colvin, general contractor and builder from Indianapolis, was confronted by a strike which threatened violence on the job in both Bloomington and Indianapolis. The trouble in Bloomington was lack of skilled laborers of local origin, and the importation of union workmen caused trouble in the mixture of union and non-union skilled workmen. The workers supplied by the government relief employment agencies struck, and this stopped work on the entire contract. This was the first time the University faced this kind of problem with the intensity of violence and interference with work.

*   *   *

July 16, 1936

Board of Trustees,
Indiana University.
Mr. Forest Logan,
State Director, P. W. A.
Hon. Paul V. McNutt,
Governor of Indiana.
Gentlemen:

This is to formally advise you with reference to certain facts and occurrences in connection with my contracts for the erection of the New Medical Building and School of Music Building for Indiana University.

I wish first to state that the work on the Medical Building has been entirely stopped and that the work on the School of Music Building is practically stopped. due to a strike of common laborers and hod carriers which was called on Monday, the 6th day of July, 1936.

The strikers have not only refused to work but have maintained a large gang of picketers along Third Street, fronting the building sites, and they have threatened and intimidated others who desired to work to the end that all the mechanics on the Medical Building have been forced to quit work. They have not only threatened but have committed acts of violence. We have appealed to the local authorities and are told that they can do nothing.

The Baker Forms Company, of Indianapolis, have a sub-contract for the erection of forms on the Medical Building and have been working about twenty-five men on this job. These men have been forced to quit work by threats and acts of violence. Mr. McClintock, foreman for the Baker Forms Company, was assaulted by these men who were armed with clubs. The strikers have intercepted trucks bringing materials to these buildings and refused them permission to enter the premises by threatening and intimidating the drivers of the trucks. They have also threatened that they will come to the homes of these workmen at night and will beat them up unless they quit work.

Under my contract with Indiana University, I am required to use workers from the relief rolls as assigned to me by various Government agencies in the performance of this work. It is clearly understood and clearly provided that I am allowed to build these buildings with either union or non-union men. It has been the custom and our practice in the past, to depend on union labor for the skilled trades and non-union labor for the unskilled trades or common labor. It is upon this basis that work has been done in Indianapolis for many years and that was the basis upon which I expected to do the work in Bloomington, Indiana, insofar as that plan was consistent with P. W. A. regulations. It was necessary that some union labor be imported by the Government Employment agencies because of a shortage of skilled workmen in the Bloomington area to perform the work. These union workmen, when once on the job, insisted that their union rules were of more importance than the P. W. A. regulations and they required that all the men in any craft be union men, with the result that such skilled workers as had been assigned by the United States Employment Agencies had to be dismissed and their places filled with union men. With several union men of the various crafts working on the job, they then insisted that all the branches of the work be done by union labor, insofar as there was an organization of these workers from which to draw men. The unions were again successful in enforcing this step in their program.

There is no recognized organization of common laborers in Indianapolis or in Bloomington. This is a new organization for the purpose of collecting initiation fees and dues from the workers during the life of these particular jobs, in my opinion. This common laborers union is not now recognized and does not have the support of the other union crafts on the buildings. In all our requisitions we have asked for non-union unskilled labor through the USES and so far as we know, were supplied with relief workers through the USES.

These relief workers assigned to us are now on strike and are committing acts of violence to the end that they have stopped the jobs, causing a loss to all concerned including the owners, the contractors, and the workmen who are willing to work.

As I view this situation, my hands are tied and I am powerless to do anything about it. I have a contract which prevents me from employing men in the regular way. I must requisition these men through the Government agencies. The men who have been supplied to me have struck. I am advised that the Government will not supply me other men in their place. I request, since I am powerless to act in this matter, that you take such steps as are necessary to permit this work to proceed. These steps, as I see it, include the following:

First,—To furnish protection to those men who wish to work on the job.

Second,—To require the relief workers to resume work or that you furnish men in their place.

Third,—That if step two is impractical and impossible, I be given permission under my contract, to employ men from any other source to complete the work.

I have complied with all the P. W. A. regulations and all the stipulations of my contract and the delay in this work is from causes beyond my control. I request, therefore, that the time for the completion of my contract for both the Music School and the Medical Building be extended for a period equal to the time lost on account of this strike.

Yours very respectfully,
LESLIE COLVIN

LC:FM

McNutt 1936 (#99), Archives Division, Indiana State Library.

Document 128

William Lowe Bryan's Resignation

On March 15, 1937, William Lowe Bryan sent the letter below up to the head of the Board of Trustees table to George Ball, President of the Board. It was read to the trustees by Judge Ora L. Wildermuth. Apparently no one knew before hand that the president would resign at this meeting. The Board of Trustees had adopted a pension plan for retired professors, and the legislature had approved it. Now President Bryan could lead the procession of over-age professors in retiring from the university staff without being threatened with a state of penury in old age. This is an important document. It opened the way for new leadership, and a new day in the University.

*　　*　　*

The following communication was presented:

"March 15, 1937

To the Honorable, the Board of Trustees of
  Indiana University
Mr. President, Mrs. Teter, Gentlemen:

I present herewith my resignation as president of Indiana University with the request that my service may close at the early convenience of the Board of Trustees.

I take this occasion to express my grateful appreciation for the unfailing friendliness and support which the Board of Trustees has given me. I have deeper cause for satisfaction as I retire from this office because of my assurance that the control of the University is in the best of hands. I have served as president under twenty-six trustees. Throughout these changes nothing has changed the disinterested devotion of the Board of Trustees to the highest interests of Indiana University.

Respectfully submitted,
WILLIAM LOWE BRYAN."

Judge Wildermuth moved, with great regret, that the resignation of President William Lowe Bryan be accepted to take effect at a date to be determined later, but upon condition that the President and Mrs. Bryan continue to occupy the president's house which their generous contributions helped to build, and that Dr. Bryan be given the title of President Emeritus of Indiana University, and that his present salary be continued during his life. The motion was seconded by all the other trustees present, and was unani[m]ously carried.

Board Minutes, September, 1936—April, 1938, p. 62.

Document 129

Self-Appraisal

The retirement of William Lowe Bryan raised many rather urgent issues in the University. The most important of these was a thorough-going self-study of the institution, a thing the faculty had advocated earlier. This resolution was to bring about the organization of a committee and the publication of a searching survey of the University. As indicated in the final paragraph, it was to have the partial oversight at least by the acting president. This was in fact the authorization for the outlining of a new approach to the future for the University.

*   *   *

RESOLUTIONS

BE IT RESOLVED by The Trustees of Indiana University that the recommendation of the deans of the University (at Bloomington) asking that provision be made for a survey of the University be approved and that the Acting President of the University is directed to appoint a committee of three from the University faculty to conduct such a survey.

BE IT FURTHER RESOLVED that the committee so appointed is hereby empowered and directed to conduct a survey of the University and to report the results and the recommendations and the suggestions of the committee to The Trustees.

BE IT FURTHER RESOLVED that the extent of the survey shall be left to the judgment of the committee.

BE IT FURTHER RESOLVED that The Trustees now makes available to the committee all pertinent records and data controlled by the University and directs the officers and faculty of the University to give full cooperation to the Committee.

BE IT FURTHER RESOLVED that the committee is empowered to employ necessary secretarial assistance subject to the approval of the Executive Committee and to publish in mimeograph form its reports, all of which reports are to be published confidentially for the benefit of the administration and the faculty of the University, unless a wider publication is expressly authorized by The Trustees.

BE IT FURTHER RESOLVED that if thought desirable by the Acting President the teaching load of the members of the committee be reduced or cancelled.

Board Minutes, September, 1936–April, 1938, pp. 182–183.

Document 130

A New Helmsman

Judge Wildermuth's charge to Herman B Wells hardly sounds like instructions to an acting president with brief expectations of remaining in the office for more than a year. Wells had served well indeed in the interim period between Bryan's departure from office and his election to the position of president. The president of the Board of Trustees left no doubt in anybody's mind that they expected the young president to equal, and even surpass, the records of his predecessors. This was both a serious and onerous charge. The trustees admonished their new appointee in rather dramatic fashion to demonstrate "practical wisdom, admirable temperament, and high ideals." Thus, a new age was begun.

*   *   *

[HBW unanimously elected.]

President Wildermuth then made the following remarks to President Wells:

"The Trustees of Indiana University have come to a decision on the most monentous [sic] question that has come before the Board in thirty-five years. We have by unanimous ballot elected you President of Indiana University. In so doing we have brought very great honor to you. But, we have also given you equally great responsibilities.

"Your responsibilities are great because of the footprints that have been made by the giants whom you succeed. Remember that you follow in the steps of Dr. David Starr Jordan, Dr. Joseph Swain, and Dr. William Lowe Bryan, three of the greatest educational administrators of this country. They made Indiana University a great university respected and revered by her sister schools and educators everywhere. These colossal figures who marched across this campus have cut a pattern that will not be easy to fill.

"No university in America ever had three succeeding presidents that stood higher in their fields than these three men. So your responsibility is great,— greater, perhaps, than if you were to become the president of most any other university. It seems to us that you have the qualifications to carry on the important functions of this office. You have youth, ambition, courage, ability, and intelligence of a high order, and with these qualities you cannot fail. You must, you will succeed.

"The members of the Board have interviewed in the last year the leading educators of the country, from Maine to California, in an effort to find the very best man possible to be found to assume the leadership of this great University. We have interviewed a great many men who have been recommended to us, some of them repeatedly. We have made a study of their fitness, character, ability, and qualifications. This election of your did not come by default, but came as the result of an extensive study. After having examined all of these men from everywhere in the country, and after comparing their qualifications with yours, we were satisfied with your superiority. We have picked one of our own sons, a native Hoosier, in whom we place our trust and hopes.

"I am sure that you will have the cooperation of the Board. I know that you will have mine to the fullest extent in carrying on these responsibilities and upholding the University, and keeping it in that high place which it achieved under these three great men, and making it still an ever greater University.

"We pledge to you our entire support, feeble though it may be. I stand ready to do everything I can to help you succeed in this important position."

President Wells then replied as follows:

"Judge, and members of the Board:

"I deeply appreciate the compliment you have paid me. I think I am more impressed, however, by a realization of the responsibility of the position than by any other feeling. In fact, to be altogether frank, I feel wholly inadequate to undertake this important task. I told Dr. Bryan as much when I talked with him in my office this morning. He assured me, however, that he was frightened by the responsibility when he was called upon thirty-five years ago to accept the office. I hope the decision made here today will prove in the years to come to be at least in a small part as wise as was the decision made by that earlier Board. There is a great opportunity here. To meet it, I shall need your cooperation very much. I shall do my best—I shall give all of my thought and energy to this work. And I pray that that will be enough."

On motion of Mr. Rabb, seconded by Mr. Nolan, the Board approved the issuance of the following statement under the name of "The Trustees of Indiana University":

"Herman B Wells is this day elected President of Indiana University.

"With great expectations, we invite him to great responsibilities. His observed experience, practical wisdom, admirable temperament, and high ideals give conspicuous assurance of enduring achievement. With trust in him, we have confidence in the future."

Board Minutes, September, 1936—April, 1938, pp. 226–227.

Document 131

Before the Mountain

On December 1, 1938, Herman B Wells had occupied the president's chair for more than a year. He had gone through with one budgetary request, had gone in search for new faculty members, had dealt with disgruntled retiring professors and their wives, had a keen appreciation of the conditions of the times, and had seen in fairly clear perspective the needs of Hoosiers themselves. Never the flowery orator climbing his own Mount Olympus, Wells had the faculty of stating needs and challenges in the plain words of his people. His inaugural address viewed the needs of Indiana University in terms of the tremendous burden of making of education at all levels an instrument of democracy. His challenge to his colleagues and to Hoosiers in general was issued in calm language, but with assurances that however great they were, they could be met.

*   *   *

The Inaugural Address
Delivered by President Herman B Wells at His Inauguration
on December 1, 1938

The formal beginning of a new administration inevitably marks the close of the old. Dr. Bryan's administration is unique in the annals of our University, both in length of service and in record of achievement. Under his leadership, the institution has had its greatest growth in physical and intellectual resources. Dr. Bryan, those of us who have been fortunate enough to experience the strength of your leadership are keenly aware of the extent of your contribution to Indiana University. You have won the genuine gratitude, the unqualified admiration, and the deep affection of all the sons and daughters of Indiana. For your many kindnesses, your wise counsel, and your steadfast support since I assumed the headship of the University, I offer you my deepest personal gratitude.

Indiana University is a dynamic institution in a dynamic world. The brilliant chapter in the history of our University written during President Bryan's administration has been completed. We must of necessity begin the writing of another. It is appropriate, therefore, for us to look toward the future this morning. I shall speak of some of the factors which may condition that future.

Faith in education has been a dominant feature of our society since the beginning of the republic—a faith so strong that through private philanthropy and public taxation a school system has been built unparalleled elsewhere in the world. Throughout the history of our nation, there has been a deep-rooted conviction that a democratic form of government could be made operative only by educated men and women.

This faith in education was manifested in early days by the zeal with which the pioneers developed school systems in the new territories. The first president of Indiana University, Dr. Andrew Wylie, in his inaugural address gave expression to that faith, to its profound depth and breadth, in this sentence: "I am a believer in the omnipotence of education." And well did he need the sustaining power of his faith, for Indiana College, as the University was then called, stood at the very edge of the wilderness, piercing farther into the great unexplored North-west Territory than any other institution of higher learning. The difficulties faced by that tiny institution must have seemed insurmountable: few resources, meagre equipment, a faculty of only three—yet the responsibility of training the leadership needed to develop in a trackless forest a busy, stable, organized society.

Today as we look toward the future, the conviction grows upon us that the task of the University is even bigger now than it was in the beginning. It is true that much has been accomplished by society. It is true that the University's physical and intellectual resources are now great. But the problems which the University's students must be trained to meet are even greater, arising as they do out of changed economic and social conditions. The physical frontier, which for generations has exerted a profound influence upon the progress of society, has disappeared. The mighty stream of immigration which flowed from Europe has been stopped. Restricted immigration and a declining birthrate indicate a stationary population to be reached during this century. A larger and larger proportion of our total population tends to lead an urban life. Society has not yet fully adapted itself to the far-reaching economic effects of the Industrial Revolution, including the minute division of labor separating the worker from control of the finished product, with the resulting insecurities of employment. The social adjustments made necessary by industrial progress are in a large measure yet to be achieved.

Just as challenging are developments in present-day political thinking. For the first time in several generations, the trend toward democracy throughout the world has been arrested. Some peoples not deeply rooted in democratic government have been seduced by the grandiose promises of unscrupulous leaders. They have traded their precious guaranties of liberty for the quick and transitory gains of a dictatorship. Totalitarian government, with communism comprising its left boundary and facism its right, runs amuck in the world today.

Even more disturbing has been the recent outbreak in Germany of the mass persecution of a minority group the like of which the world has not known for centuries. This display of barbarism might cause timid souls to doubt the reality of human progress.

In addition, there are new and significant developments in the educational system of the country that affect our responsibility. I shall mention one development which concerns us particularly: the emergence of the state university as a dominant factor in higher education in America. Lest there be those who believe the wish father to the thought, I quote the views of the president of Harvard University. In an address at Cornell University last year, as reported in the press, President Conant said: "When I examine the history of higher education in America in the last fifty years and note the growth of the publicly supported institutions—the increase in student body, in plant, and in capacity for scholarly and professional work of the highest order—I can arrive at only one conclusion. During the next century of academic history, university education in this republic will be largely in the hands of the tax supported institutions. As they fare, so fares the cultural and intellectual life of the American people."

Here, then, at Indiana University we find that, because our future activities must be carried on in a disturbed and rapidly changing world, and because of the nature of our institution, we shall be called upon to bear increasing responsibility. It is appropriate, therefore, that we re-examine the functions of a university.

It would be generally agreed, I believe, that publicly supported education from the kindergarten through the graduate school has for its objective the fitting of the student to play his role effectively in a society of free men. At the university level, this purpose is best accomplished when the primary energies of the institution are devoted to the promotion of the intellectual life. It may seem strange that it is necessary to reaffirm *this* function of the University. But the fact is that the University, like other large and complex institutions, may easily become involved in all types of programs that, while superficially attractive and important, absorb its resources to the detriment of the basic work.

In our garden of the years the intellectual objective must dominate the design, and its welfare must be the first concern of the cultivators. Other plantings must be studied with relationship to the central plant, lest they destroy its dominance in the design or sap the nourishment needed for its roots.

The University cannot discharge *any* of its obligations to society unless it is first and foremost an institution dedicated to scholarship and scholarly objectives: a place where students learn the slow and arduous processes of mental discipline by which knowledge is acquired and wisdom won; a place where the frontiers of new truth are pushed back by the research explorer and old truth is subjected to critical analysis until it assumes new significance; a place where reason is exalted over emotion and force. Unless the University is such a place, it cannot develop in each succeeding generation of students that "tough-mindedness" which is essential for effective living in a complex society. Unless it is such a place, it cannot continue to be a reservoir of truth, old and new, upon which youth and adults can draw in charting the course of society.

I do not mean that the University's work should be carried on in a cloistered unawareness of the busy, practical world. There can be no effective teaching without illustrative material drawn from an understanding of current affairs. The physical scientist in the university laboratory must keep constantly abreast of the problems of industry and of the experimental efforts to solve them; likewise, the social scientist finds the raw materials for his work in the frenzied atmosphere of the exchange, the squalor of the slums, the uncomfortable hovel of the sharecropper—in fact, any place in this wide land where social problems exist. But knowledge of current affairs is not sufficient for an understanding of fundamental principles. Universities must be maintained as watch towers of human progress, from which men may gain a view of life in its entirety, and in which there will be maintained the calm and quiet necessary for objectivity and comprehension.

In addition to promoting the intellectual life, the University must help students develop sound bodies and habits that affect constructively not only their physical well-being while on the campus, but also their health throughout life. This latter phase has become increasingly important because the large majority of our students now come from and return to urban communities. It is important that they acquire an interest and skill in those forms of sport which may be continued throughout maturity. The University must provide year-round facilities for these activities.

With the development of mind and body, the University also has responsibility for the development of character. Never was that responsibility of greater significance than at the present hour. If the rising tide of intolerance and hatred is to be arrested before it engulfs the world, there must be, in the words of a group of eminent Englishmen, "moral re-armament" of all people. This is no mere abstraction. On all sides there is a general appreciation of the growing importance of moral values in modern life. For the regeneration of the individual is the key to the moral regeneration of the city, state, and nation, and, consequently, the solution of many of our most pressing contemporary problems. In this important work of character development Indiana University, though secular in organization and affiliation, has had the whole-hearted and necessary co-operation of the churches of this community, many of which have made special provision for service to the student body. This vital co-operative relationship must be continued and strengthened wherever possible.

The University also has a vocational function. Those who entirely disavow this function must of necessity be unaware of the reasons for the founding of most of our institutions of higher learning, both public and private. History has preserved for us evidence of the vocational interest of the founders of these institutions, both in the content of their charters and in the statements of policy made by early leaders.

Personally, I find no fault with the vocational motive being prominent in the University's organization and activity if the particular training offered is compatible with university standards. Our vocational efforts should emphasize fundamental principles rather than technical skills better learned in the business or profession itself. We should give proper recognition to the social obligations and implications of each vocation, and diligently strive for the development of new truth through scholarly research. Vocational training of this nature conflicts in no way with the intellectual ideal of the University.

But the responsibilities do not cease with the training of youth. Universities are also called upon to supply educational opportunities for adults. These include forums, extension classes off the campus in the evening hours, short courses on the campus, instruction by correspondence, and popular lectures. This demand is altogether proper. Multitudes of college seniors have been assured in numberless commencement speeches that graduation marks the beginning, not the end, of education. Knowledge increases so rapidly in most professional fields that frequent return to the classroom and laboratory for at least short periods of time is desirable. Not so obvious, but none the less real, is the desire of adults everywhere to extend their cultural background. Indiana University, through its Extension Division, has been and must continue to be a leader in adult education.

In late years, publicly supported universities, in particular, have been called upon to supply direct services to citizens of the state. Justification of the demand for these services is based upon the thesis that the institution belongs to the state and therefore should furnish advice and assistance in the solution of difficult technological and social problems with which the government and its citizens are faced. That such services are desirable all will agree. Indiana University has in the past always been ready to provide them.

A reasonable amount of direct service can be offered without affecting adversely the classroom and laboratory work of the institution. But when the demand becomes so great that it can be satisfied only at the expense of other functions of the University, the conclusion is inescapable that this service either should be provided for by special appropriation or should be paid for by the person, firm, or department of government receiving the benefits. An illustration of what I have in mind may be found in our great Medical Center at Indianapolis. In the beginning, a limited amount of hospital and clinical facilities was required for laboratory purposes in the training of physicians and nurses. Throughout the years, the demand for medical attention and hospitalization on the part of those without means to pay has developed very rapidly, and the University has tried to meet the demand. The result has been that the cost of meeting this demand has now absorbed so large a proportion of the appropriation made to the School of Medicine that the facilities for training physicians and nurses are seriously affected.

As I review the statement of fundamental policy just expressed, I am struck with the realization that it adds little or nothing new to the concepts and ideas which have so long guided the work of this institution, and that is a reassuring thought. Nevertheless, even though the basic concepts change little, new problems constantly arise which must be analyzed and met in a manner consistent with the University's fundamental pattern. I wish to mention a few of these that I see immediately ahead.

The first has to do with the faculty. A university can be distinguished only as its faculty is distinguished. Throughout the years, we have been fortunate in being able to retain on our campus some of the nation's leading scholars largely because of their intense loyalty to the institution. To replace such outstanding men as they retire, to attract and hold promising young men, is our major problem. So keen is the competition everywhere for outstanding men that they are difficult to secure, even for institutions with adequate resources; but for institutions such as ours, with limited revenues, the problem is unusually acute.

This problem is of concern to all of the institutions of higher learning and to all of the citizens of this state. The star rating in the volumes of *American Men of Science* is the universally recognized mark of distinction in the physical and biological sciences. Of the twelve men born and educated in Indiana to receive this coveted award during the past ten years, none today remain to do their work in this state. Only two born and educated in other states have been brought to Indiana. Therefore, we have suffered a net loss of ten. Evidence equally startling with reference to the loss of scholars in other fields is available. We must conclude, accordingly, that year after year the state loses a large portion of its most talented men. Loss of men such as these constitutes a reduction in human resources not less serious than the loss of physical wealth caused by the erosion which yearly washes the productive top-soil from our denuded hill land.

Great teachers beget great men. The minds of scores of the next generation's leaders may be moulded by a single teacher. Moreover, every new step in technological or human progress must first be conceived in the mind of a man. In fact, civilization moves forward only by the efforts of the intellectual giants of each generation. Any state that wishes to remain in the vanguard of progress must have within its borders men with original and superior minds. It has been said that "There is only one thing more powerful than armies, and that is an idea whose hour has arrived." We must keep, within our borders and on this campus, the mighty constructive force of the ideas of renowned scientists and scholars.

Indiana University has occupied a prominent position in research activity since the days of David Starr Jordan. In recent years, however, that position has been jeopardized by lack of funds. The reduction in the University's appropriations at the bottom of the depression, combined with rapidly increasing enrollments, has left few funds available for research. Without financial aid this work suffers. Tanks of chemicals, cages of white mice, musty monographs, computing machinery, and hundreds of other materials are the unspectacular but necessary essentials of research activity. Graduate research assistants are necessary in order that the valuable time of the senior men may be efficiently utilized—a procedure universally recognized in industry as "good business." As soon as possible, adequate provision must be made for the expansion of our research program. All society will benefit through the new wealth created by the discoveries of the scientist, and our students will receive the stimulation of intellectual enthusiasm which is imparted by the teacher flushed with the ardor of discovery.

Obsolescence is a prominent feature of university life, and that is as it should be. An institution dedicated to a search for the new and a re-interpretation of the old by the very nature of its activity, if successful, accelerates the rate of change beyond that to be expected in other areas of human endeavor. It is necessary, therefore, that our administrative machinery and pedagogical procedure keep pace with the procession, with the changing tempo of new ideas in the arts, the sciences, and the professions.

We have recognized this need. A committee of the faculty has been engaged for several months in a thorough analysis of administrative and teaching methods. It is hoped that its recommendations will furnish the basis for changes in University organization and policy to facilitate the work of teachers and students, either by application of that which has been tried elsewhere and has been found successful, or of methods entirely new. A preliminary report calls attention to changes which have sufficient promise of rich educational rewards to warrant very serious consideration by both faculty and trustees. Among these are comprehensive examinations; survey courses for the first two years; the divisional as distinct from the departmental form of organization; and the general college plan both as a program for achieving better orientation of the student and as a method of providing a course of training with a two-year terminal.

Although the University must continually modify its own procedures and techniques, it must at the same time guard against fads and panaceas with only the novelty of the moment to recommend them. Changes should be made only upon the basis of adequate information. Therefore, I believe that at the conclusion of the present self-survey, either a new standing committee should be appointed or a bureau of university research organized to provide an administrative fact-finding facility.

At the present time, the University finds itself concerned anew with the place ascribed to education by society. The social necessity which caused our people to erect a great public school system during the past century still exists today. The importance which they assigned to education, making it the first responsibility of the state after the maintenance of peace and the protection of its citizens, has not lessened. Dr. Wylie, in that address to which I have already referred, said, "An ignorant people cannot long be free." An ignorant people fall easy prey to the blandishments of the demagogue, who promises all without thought of performance. Realization of this simple fact has caused our people always to rally in support of our schools when their existence has been threatened by the selfish desires of unthinking or unscrupulous groups.

We are now entering a period in our national existence when this traditional position of importance assigned to education may be challenged. Many new demands are being made and will be made upon the public purse. Economic and social conditions are now such that many of the demands will be motivated by the very commendable desire to increase the security of our people during youth and old age, and in their jobs. Educators certainly are in sympathy with the desire for security. Their lives are spent in helping students develop their fullest capacities and abilities for adjustment to modern living, which in turn open for them the doors of opportunity leading toward individual security. The efforts of scholars in the laboratory and in the library are aimed toward developing new discoveries and processes which add to the job and earning opportunities of all. Thus it would be foolhardy to relegate education to secondary position in public responsibility, since that very action would cripple an instrumentality making for security.

Our public school system also is our great bulwark of liberty; action which would weaken it in all probability would imperil our liberty. Without liberty, there can be no security worthy of the name. A slave may have the security of food and shelter for transitory periods, but always his very existence is subject to the whim of some master. *That* is not the security for which the American people strive.

The public school system is not only the bulwark of democracy, but also its noblest work. The state university is the crown of the public school system, and as *such* should both by precept and by example vitalize the democratic way of life. It is the duty of the University to ensure that every student understand the fundamental philosophies underlying democracy. I choose my words advisedly. I would not suggest that the student be indoctrinated with a given set of principles, but rather that he understand the philosophical basis for democracy—an understanding that encompasses not only its benefits, but its weaknesses as well. Democracy need not depend for acceptance upon a bureau of propaganda, which uses evasion, half-truths, and distortion. It is the one system of government about which the truth can be told to win the support of men, for it is the only form of government compatible with the dignity of men.

There has been a little too much tendency on the part of our people to accept democracy as a priceless possession won by our ancestors, to be handed to members of the present generation on a silver platter without effort or thought on their part. Nothing could be farther from the truth. As John Dewey has said, "Democracy has to be born anew every generation, and education is the mid-wife."

Life on a state university campus can offer students unusual lessons in democracy, quite apart from classroom work. It is important, therefore, that we retain on this campus the wholesome tradition of genuine democracy that has always characterized the social relationships of our student body.

But the responsibility of a state university for democracy does not end with the intelligent presentation of doctrine in the classroom and the assurance of democracy within the student body. In its own organization and operation it must set a dramatic example of democracy in action inspiring to all citizens of the state. Authority must derive from reason, not from position. There must be clear demarcation of authority and responsibility among trustees, administrative officers, faculty, and students, arrived at by the democratic processes of investigation and discussion. Each of these four groups must be interested, *not* in personal prerogatives or in selfish desires, but in the good of the institution as a whole, and in its service to society. There must be sincerity, devotion, and loyalty, and, above all else, determination to further the fundamental work of the University.

The University and the state alike have limited resources with which to meet unlimited demands. Only by diligent husbanding and efficient utilization of all financial and human resources can University and state discharge their obligations. In this effort, the University again should become be a model of democracy in action, achieving a record of fiscal integrity and efficiency that will furnish an inspiring refutation to those critics who attack representative government on the grounds of fiscal ineptitude.

In the past few months, I have been presented with numerous programs, both academic and administrative, almost all of which, when considered alone, were commendable and would serve a desirable end. Frequently, sponsors maintain as a part of their argument in support of their proposal that "X" school, "Y" school, or "Z" school has it, and that, if we are to compete, we must have it. But academic "keeping up with the Joneses" is likely to result only in extravagant and unnecessary expenditures. Competition among schools is a healthy, wholesome thing when that competition takes the form of efforts to raise academic standards, but quite another when it takes the form of elaboration and multiplication of courses, man power, and equipment without regard to the needs of the institution's clientele. Many of the proposals are in the nature of educational and administrative gadgets, desirable and pleasant to have, but not essential to the furtherance of the fundamental work of the University. I am inclined to place my faith in an educational program which considers the essentials first and the gadgets second. The resources of our institution are too slender, and the work to be done too great, to countenance any improper drains on the available funds.

It is incumbent upon the University not only to husband its own resources, but also to participate in any plan which would husband the total resources for higher education in Indiana. State and regional coordination and co-operation of effort have been much discussed by educational leaders recently, both in this state and elsewhere. The opportunity for the successful development of a program of this nature is excellent here because there has long existed the friendliest spirit among all of our institutions, both public and private. Distances are not great, and communication and transportation facilities are unexcelled. It seems to me, therefore, that there is no reason why the institutions in this state might not assume a position of national leadership in developing co-operatively a plan for higher education which would ensure the elimination of unnecessary overlapping and duplication and allow each institution to draw upon the specialized facilities of the others. More important, the successful operation of the plan would mobilize the resources for higher education, and in so doing would provide the maximum benefit for our youth and for society. In the development of such a plan, Indiana University should be ready to make any necessary adjustments in its own program, deterred neither by tradition nor by institutional pride.

Democracy in education implies equal opportunity for all who are capable of learning. In our grade schools this ideal has been achieved. We have made substantial progress toward achieving this ideal in high school; not many youth with capacity to learn at this level find it necessary to quit because of limited financial resources. At the college level, however, equality of opportunity is not yet realized. Notwithstanding the fact that the state has generously developed great tuition-free educational institutions, the cost of attending, together with the loss of income which might otherwise be earned, presents a problem of great difficulty to youth in our lower economic strata.

Only one out of ten persons of college age attends an institution of higher learning. Most persons familiar with college students would agree that there are some in that group who do not belong there, but attend principally because their families have the means to send them and it is the popular and pleasant thing to do. I think it would likewise be agreed that some of the ninety per cent who are *not* in college *should* be, but are denied that opportunity for pecuniary reasons. The present selective process, therefore, fails to ensure the attendance of all those who would profit from college training or whose further education would yield great returns to society.

Some states, in seeking a solution to this problem, have been thinking in terms of more institutions. It seems to me that a better solution, and one of less cost, would be an enlarged system of scholarships on the basis of need and superior ability, provided for either by the state or by private donors. I do not make any plea for the attendance of all youth in college or university. But I am convinced that new selective processes must be developed to determine which young persons should continue their education, and that adequate financial provision must be made for the attendance of the persons so selected.

Many of our noisiest reformers are greatly concerned with the rigidities established in our society by economic power. The social significance of economic stratification will, in my opinion, be minimized if society determinedly keeps the door of educational opportunity open to the boy and girl of superior ability.

In this statement of contemporary problems challenging our attention, my treatment, as is apparent, has been selective rather than exhaustive. Other problems could be included—problems inherent in the development of our great professional schools, both on this campus and in Indianapolis; problems that must be solved in order to enrich student social and recreational life; difficulties that must be overcome in effecting an even closer relationship between the University and its alumni; relationships that must be determined between the University and the community both here and at Indianapolis. Opportunity has already presented itself for the discussion of some of these, and other opportunities will be available in the future. Moreover, my remarks are not intended to constitute a declaration of policy to serve as a platform or all-inclusive guide for future action. Such an attitude would imply that the function of institutional planning was the responsibility solely of the executive, an implication with which I cannot agree. Mention of these matters today, however, will, I hope, serve to expose my thinking on matters of importance, and will form the basis for future discussions on the part of interested persons, which will aid in the formulation of sound policies.

Though the problems be many and grave, they need not discourage us. The resources available for their solution are vast. Not the least of these are the friendship of community and state as evidenced by the presence here today of high state officials and friends from every walk of life, and the co-operative spirit of the institutions of higher learning as indicated by the presence here of so many of their leaders. Within the institution itself, elements of incalculable strength are to be found: the competence and loyalty of the student body; the generous devotion and keen foresight of the Board of Trustees.

Cognizant of the rich resources which are ours to command, heartened by the achievements already won in more than a century of distinguished service to state and nation, we face the future with confidence.

Indiana University Newsletter, pp. 3–12.

Document 132

Steambent, Birch, or Plywood

There were some Hoosiers who looked upon Indiana University through the mundane eyes of trade. In this case the furniture manufacturers were concerned that Hoosiers be seated in Hoosier chairs, that they sleep in Hoosier beds, and that these be made from sturdy Hoosier maple. They expected Governor Cliff Townsend to aid them in their aspirations.

*   *   *

June 23
1939

Mr. Albert Rabb
1350 Consolidated Building
Indianapolis, Indiana

Dear Al:

A group of Indiana furniture manufacturers was in my office today seriously complaining about the specifications for furniture to be purchased at Indiana University.

They have three complaints: first, that a P.W.A. building at the University of Michigan specified "birch" furniture, which is manufactured principally in Michigan. This, of course, protected the Michigan manufacturers. Indiana University specifications specified "birch only" until a complaint was made and then it was modified to include maple.

Second, Indiana is the center of ply wood furniture manufacturers and ply wood with a modern glue is conceded to be better than solid furniture. Yet, these specifications eliminate ply wood furniture.

Third, steam bent furniture is specified, which will very likely result in imported furniture being bought.

While we all know that there are a few factories in Indiana making a cheap grade of furniture; yet some of the best furniture in the world is made in Indiana. I am opposed to trade barriers and I know the Federal government prohibits specifications that contain trade barriers; yet we should frown upon specifications that eliminate Indiana made products as that would be a trade barrier to us most obnoxious.

I am calling this to your attention with the hope that when the bids are open, Indiana manufacturers will be given very sympathetic consideration if they bid.

Very truly yours,
Governor.

MCT:LM

Townsend 1939 (#127), Archives Division, Indiana State Library.

[VIII]

A Frantic Decade of Displacement and Revolution 1940–1950

Indiana University in the decade 1940 to 1950 underwent tremendous pressures, internal and external. This was the first decade of the Wells presidency, and had times been normal or peaceful there still would have been phenomenal changes. Before World War II was to have its overwhelming impact on the world, the young President and his administrative associates were searching for faculty replacements who would lift the institution onto a new scholarly and productive plane. This drive was disrupted at its inception, and after the war it had to be re-opened, but this time in a much more highly competitive professional "sellers" market.

Mixed in with all of the emergency measures which were necessary to prepare the University for tremendously increased student enrollment was the internal matter of readjusting almost all procedures to expanded teaching and research programs. Every division of the University had to be reexamined, and its functions adapted to the new era. This was a moment when the administration and faculty struggled so hard to bring about reorganization of graduate work. Almost unbelievably this area of university instruction had been allowed to grow up around various divisions of the school, and without much central control over it. With the rising demand for graduate instruction, it was necessary to undertake major unification of the program. Closely associated with this issue was that of granting faculty leaves on an established sabbatical plan. Never in any formal document did anyone, Faculty Council, Graduate Division, or colleges and departments, put into the record a specific policy of "publish or perish," but in the requests for annual faculty reports, and in promotional procedures this policy was unspoken but understood. The sabbatical plan was designed largely to encourage scholarly growth in the building of a new faculty.

It is almost trite to say that during this decade Indiana University struggled to enter a new age of development without sufficient legislative support. Perhaps it was never possible for American universities to secure all the funds which the faculties and administrations deemed necessary for institutional growth. Certainly Indiana was never in this fortunate position. In discussing the 1949–1950 budget with the Faculty Council, there is an almost defiant note in President Wells' statement that Indiana University would become a great university despite the fact that the legislature had reduced its operating capital. These were years when faculty members had to be employed on a "sellers' market," when inflation made the raising of salaries mandatory, building costs had tripled and were still rising, supplies, maintenance, and services costs reflected war time increases, and there was general public sentiment for retrenchment from war time costs.

No problem which Indiana University faced in the latter half of this decade was greater than the emergency need for student and faculty housing, and for the construction of capital buildings to serve classroom and laboratory demands. In a statement to the Faculty Council, President Herman B Wells reflected this fact in his reference to the construction of a large classroom building, which, in time, became Ballantine Hall. The University no doubt suffered from the fact that it was not located in a town of sufficient size to supply a fair amount of public housing to students and faculty. The need for housing was acute, and meeting the need required a near miracle. Few, if any, universities were confronted with a graver problem. Indiana had to build housing facilities almost from the ground up in a remarkably short period of time. It had to do this with only limited financial support from the state.

Ordinarily the minutes of faculty bodies are rather dull and unexciting documents, and those of Indiana University are no exception. These, however, do give a keen insight into the day-to-day operation of the University, and more particularly the approaches to problems and revelations of the processes by which they were solved. In the report of professorial questioning is revealed at once the lack of knowledge of the average professor about many university matters, and the degree of professorial caution in trying to devise policies indicates how fundamentally conservative the faculty really was in these years. The Faculty Constitution is within itself revealing of the degree of impersonalization which was coming to Indiana University in this decade of war and university reorganization. Added to this problem was the organization of a rather large faculty body in the off-campus centers which had to be given a voice in decision making, but which was separated from many of the processes of arriving at answers to issues.

The Indiana University faculty was ever responsive to the national currents. In the discussion of physical fitness it was being sensitized by the current wave of criticism of American physical "softness" which was a popular topic in current news and commentaries of the times. On the surface it seemed that the University could help to correct a small part of the national problem by requiring its students, men and women, to condition themselves for active physical lives. In devising a program, however, provisions had to be made for exceptional cases. As Dean Fernandus Payne observed, the problem of determining the validity of the exceptions might be greater than putting muscle on the physically able but "lazy" Americans. The Student Council had differing views.

The faculty raised the question of grading. It would have been a shame to have let so exciting a decade as this one pass without injecting this issue into the general discussion of changes. Perhaps few of the professors who engaged so seriously in the discussions of grades and their fractional values realized that their predecessors had gone over this subject many times, saying almost the same things on the subject. Grades brought under the light of Faculty Council discussion appeared in one perspective, but viewed from a long siege of reading blue books they appeared to instructors in a more uncertain light. This was an era when grades began to assume a new status because so much of social and personal progress through the University depended upon them.

Standing out in bold outline, even in the most prosaic of documents, was the fact that Indiana University was moving well beyond its traditional lines in seeking to become an institution of broader scope and of more scintillating programs in at least a half dozen areas of innovative testing. The personalities who made material contributions to the University's accomplishing its new objectives stand out in many of the documents included in this section. They produced the reports and special findings, raised the questions, served in the classrooms, and were quick to perceive the possibilities of the decade. Always a formal documentary of this sort was little more than a blue print. The real historical significance lay in the application of the new rules and plans. There was involved in all of this an enormous amount of human emotions which evaporated with time, but which comprised the tremendously important ingredient of humanity which liberalized and lubricated the machinery of education no matter the size of the institution or mass of professors and students.

Document 133

The Governor's Dedicatory Remarks on the Opening of the Auditorium

To date, nothing in Indiana University's history had brought more genuine happiness or more pride than the dedication of the great Auditorium in 1941. Governor Henry F. Schricker's prediction was correct; the building has stood through several generations of students and faculty members, a monument to the finer things of Hoosier life.

*   *   *

PRESIDENT WELLS, DR. BRYAN, MEMBERS OF THE FACULTY, STUDENTS AND FRIENDS OF INDIANA UNIVERSITY:

It is with sincere pleasure that I come to this great university on this historic occasion. Having a daughter who was graduated from Indiana, and a son who is now a sophomore here, our visits to Bloomington have been both frequent and delightful. Always your welcome has been most gracious and always you have made us feel very much at home.

This is a momentous event in the history of Indiana University. We are assembled to dedicate this beautiful Auditorium—this veritable architectural masterpiece—which is the latest addition on the campus of this institution of learning.

You must have been inspired, as I have been, by the grandeur of this magnificent building. It is so much more than stone and steel. As we thrill at its splendor, we are reminded that it provides physical facilities for the presentation of music, art, drama and the lecture—all cultural values which mean so much to the life of any student body, and to any community.

We know, you and I, that this Auditorium will stand for generations, and through these years, thousands of our good citizens will assemble here from time to time to enjoy the finer things of life. Within these walls our sons and daughters will be trained in the cultural arts, and when they leave the college halls, they will be better prepared for positions of importance and responsibility in our nation. The culture they acquire here will not only enrich their individual lives, but will, in a large measure, train them to solve the problems of a troubled world.

Never before in the 121 years of the University's existence has it enjoyed adequate facilities, devoted solely to the artistic side of education. Recorded history takes us back to those early days when the University chapel was utilized for public assembly and class room purposes. In 1896 Assembly Hall was erected. This was then believed to be large enough to meet the needs of that generation, and to provide adequate facilities for all cultural and athletic programs.

Within two years after its completion, however, its capacity no longer served the needs of the growing student body. Yet Assembly Hall, for more than a third of a century continued to be the only auditorium on the campus where the best in music and dramatic art could be presented. It was in this historic building that the Garrick Club thrived and prospered, and where all social and cultural events were conducted.

Old Assembly Hall, with its precious memories, has also passed into history and in its place stands this magnificent edifice, which we are privileged to dedicate tonight. A cherished dream of the venerable Dr. Bryan, and those associated with him, has become a reality indeed, and Indiana University has reached another milestone in its steady growth of cultural attainment.

The first step toward the fulfillment of this dream was taken by the General Assembly of Indiana in July, 1938, when, at a Special Session, $300,000 was wisely appropriated for this building. This original appropriation was supplemented by a grant of $526,500 from the Public Works Administration, $305,000 from a University bond issue, and $38,500 from other University funds, making a grand total of $1,170,000.00. It is to be noted that of the total cost of the Auditorium only 25.8% came directly from the State Treasury.

To many of us here assembled $1,170,000 may seem to be a tremendous sum of money, but we are proud tonight that every dollar of it was expended in the erection of a permanent structure dedicated to the purposes of peace and suited to the needs of this and succeeding generations.

We have expended these monies to promote the cultural, the artistic and the spiritual side of life, and these elements when molded into the lives and character of our youth will continue to pay rich dividends as long as life shall last.

In such a noble enterprise the amount here invested should give us small concern in comparison with other contemporary human endeavors. Let me remind you that the cost of this structure would build only two modern air-bombers. Sixty times this amount would be needed in the structure of one modern battleship, and it is estimated that this sum of $1,170,000 would finance the war raging in Europe for less time than this program will consume this evening. In the light of these comparisons who would venture to say that the cost of this beautiful structure has been unwisely spent? This building not only embraces a large auditorium capable of seating approximately 4,000 persons, but also includes a modern theater, radio broadcasting studio, band rehearsal room, class rooms and laboratories for speech and drama. Here the major activities of the University will be carried on throughout the year, and this marvelous auditorium will provide ample facilities for convocation, commencements and cultural entertainment in the future.

In the main lobby the famous Chicago World Fair Murals, painted by Thomas Hart Benton, have found a permanent home and it is anticipated that thousands of Americans will come each year to enjoy the pictorial history of our state.

As Chief Executive of Indiana, I take unstinted pride in the completion of this building, and I know that every loyal Hoosier shares this feeling with me. I can not refrain from emphasising our common pride in this great commonwealth. Indiana is constantly moving forward on all fronts of human endeavor. We are truly the cross roads of America. Within the confines of our borders the Federal Government has seen fit to locate many of its National Defense Projects. We are proud of this recognition and mindful of the responsibilities it entails.

We believe our people to be typical of things American. Here is found the typical American home. It is not in the home of the rich or the poor, but rather the man who loves his fireside and educates his children in the schools and universities of his state. It is for his children that this magnificent structure has been fashioned and erected on this campus. Let us hope and believe that its majestic beauty will inspire a greater love for home and state in the hearts of those who are privileged to enjoy it.

It is not only a pleasure, but a very high privilege to speak for more than three and one half millions of Hoosier citizens on this occasion. Their heart throbs and devotion to the processes of free government have made this marvelous structure possible. In their name and by their authority I now present to you, President Wells, and to the Trustees of Indiana University, this beautiful Auditorium, to the end that its constant use and enjoyment may add to the glory and achievements of our people.

March 22, 1941; Xerox of carbon copy, Archives Division, Indiana State Library.

Document 134

The University's War Plan

President Wells outlined for Governor Schricker the war program of the University. By the beginning of 1942, the institution had pretty well adapted its program to serving the country's cause by considerably replanning the curriculum and revising the entire university calendar. There was no doubt in President Wells' mind that his institution was going to be called upon for major instructional and personnel services.

*   *   *

February 23, 1942

The Honorable Henry F. Schricker
Governor of Indiana
Indianapolis, Indiana
Dear Governor Schricker:

I am sending you herewith a complete statement of Indiana University's War Service Plan, the principal features of which are the inauguration of a year-round, three-semester schedule, the establishment of a Lower Division to deal more adequately with the problems of the adjustment of high school students to the first year of college, and the requirement of a program of mental and physical conditioning for the entire student body.

Our new war plan was instituted at the request of Federal officials who met with a group of college and university presidents in Baltimore on January 3 and 4, 1942, to consider resolutions and recommendations as approved by the Committee on Military Affairs of the National Committee on Education and Defense and the Divisional Committee on Higher Education of the U. S. Office of Education Wartime Commission. These Federal officials impressed upon the group the importance of accelerating the flow of trained college personnel into society for the benefit of both the armed forces and war production.

The new schedule adopted by Indiana University affords the maximum acceleration possible. Our students may take a traditional four-year course in two and two-thirds calendar years. Three complete semesters' work is offered during each calendar year, yet the academic calendar has been arranged so that students will have the same number of recitations and approximately the same examination periods which they had in each of the former long semesters. This arrangement has been effected for the most part by the utilization of Saturdays, including Saturday afternoons until five o'clock, and by the elimination of vacations during each semester.

The new plan requires full-scale operation of the entire University throughout the year, where formerly its operation was confined to approximately nine months plus a small, nearly self-supporting summer school. (No academic work was offered at the Medical Center during the summer under the old plan, and the new one involves, therefore, the summer operation of the academic portion of that plant for the first time.) As a consequence, it is apparent that it will be impossible for us to operate under the new schedule with the same amount of money that the old one required.

I have presented, through the Wartime Commission of the U. S. Office of

Education, a statement of the cost involved in our new program. It is my under-standing that the Wartime Commission contemplates asking Congress for an appropriation to meet the cost of acceleration here and in other institutions, and it is to be hoped that Congress will respond favorably. If its response is un-favorable, however, the program for the current year will absorb all of our working balances. In addition, it will be necessary for our faculty to teach the third semester with very little additional pay—certainly for much less than they formerly were paid for a shorter period in the summer. For many individuals it will mean an actual dollar decline in annual income at a time when living expenses are rising rapidly.

The members of our faculty are willing to make this sacrifice if it becomes necessary, and the University is willing to use its entire surplus supplies and working balance. Even with these measures, it will be impossible for us to pro-ceed for more than one year under the new plan unless extra funds are provided by the state.

I present this background to you, as the responsible head of the state govern-ment, for your information at this time, and I solicit your judgment and counsel to assist us in charting our course and in making wise decisions.

Very truly yours,
H. B WELLS

Schricker #150, Archives Division, Indiana State Library.

Document 135

The Administrative War Council

The Administrative War Council reported to the faculty its proposed program. This voluminous report indicated the extent to which the Uni-versity believed it would eventually be involved in the war effort. The Indiana program was in conformity with that outlined by the National Conference of College and University Presidents. A copy of that report is included in this document. As in World War I, there was an almost sud-den change in the general faculty and administrative attitude toward the University's wartime position.

*   *   *

GENERAL FACULTY MEETING
INDIANA UNIVERSITY
2:30 P.M.

January 15, 1942

The Faculty of the University met on Thursday, January 15, 1942 in the Little Theater. President Wells presided. The reading of the minutes of the last meeting was postponed.

President Wells stated that the Administrative War Council, of which he had spoken at the last meeting had prepared a report for presentation to the Faculty. He called upon Dr. Kohlmeier, chairman of the Committee on Style of the Ad-ministrative War Council to read the report, a complete copy of which is made a part of the minutes.

Dr. Kohlmeier read to the conclusion of Article I, at which time President Wells made a statement concerning the financing of the proposed program. A copy of President Wells' statement is attached to the minutes. After these remarks, Dr. Kohlmeier completed the reading of the report and then moved that the rules be suspended and that the report be adopted. The motion was seconded by Dean Gavit.

President Wells then called upon Dean Briscoe to make a general statement concerning the proposed program. Following this, Dean Stout spoke upon the three semester program in reference to the calendar. Dr. Cleland was then called upon for remarks on the physical fitness portion of the proposal. President Wells then called upon Professor Hall for a statement on the Junior Division and finally Dean Payne was asked to make a statement concerning the probable effect of the program upon the graduate school and graduate work. The substance of the remarks by all of these men is made a part of the minutes.

After a brief discussion, the question was asked for and the motion was adopted by a unanimous vote of the Faculty.

President Wells then stated that he was sure that the members of the War Council would want him to pledge the Faculty that should any material changes be made in the plan as adopted, the new plan would be brought back to the Faculty for action.

The Faculty adjourned at 4:30 P.M.

EUGENE W. KANNING
Secretary of the Faculty

President Wells' Report on the Financing of the Proposed Report of the Administrative Council.

These war days create grave financial problems for all colleges and universities. Enrollments have already decreased, and if the war continues, far more drastic reductions are certain in the future. In addition, rising prices contribute to the budgetary problems of institutions just as they do to those of staff members. As a result, academic budgets of many institutions were slashed this year, and larger reductions will have to be made in the coming year.

Fortunately, we are in good position to meet the impact of these war conditions. Our financial program has been careful and conservative. It has been skillfully administered by Mr. Biddle and his associates, who have enjoyed the co-operation of our deans, department heads, faculty, and staff members.

As a consequence, no horizontal salary reduction is necessary now, nor is one contemplated during the present biennium. Moreover, there is nothing in the plan of operation recommended by the Administrative Council that would require any reduction in our regular academic salaries.

Most institutions have already launched, or will soon be forced to launch, some type of accelerated program. In some universities, staff members have been asked to contribute both the extra effort and the extra time required, without additional compensation.

The recommendation of the Administrative Council contemplates that this year each member of the faculty will be expected, if needed, to teach two- and one-half semesters, approximately forty weeks. During the following year the plan proposes a uniform period of service of two- and one-half semesters. Only in exceptional cases will an additional eight weeks of teaching be necessary or be allowed.

Legally, there is no question that the members of our faculty are employed for ten months' service. Ten calendar months total forty three and one-third weeks. Notwithstanding the legal form of the contract, you and I know that in practice the University has expected of the faculty nine calendar months of service, or thirty-nine weeks. The University also has expected, in addition to teaching, research, public service, and a fair share of committee work during this period. If all of these activities are maintained in equal measure throughout forty weeks, members of the faculty will work harder than formerly. The full-time administrative staff likewise will be affected. Customary vacations will probably be impossible and harder work required throughout the year.

In at least one large midwestern university, the members of the faculty, through a committee, have volunteered their services for an accelerated program. Several members of our group have made informally and as individuals a similar offer.

Fortunately, it appears that some additional compensation will be possible here. The amount cannot be determined at this time. It depends upon three variables:

1. The enrollment and the resulting income from fees.
2. The amount of saving effected by the committee on replacements, staff utilization and scheduling.
3. Possible Federal or State aid in defraying the cost of acceleration.

Members of this body can influence two of these items. By counseling with students you can persuade a large number to remain in school throughout the year. By co-operation with the committee on staff utilization and scheduling, you can increase the effectiveness of its work.

The third variable is beyond our control. I can pledge you, however, that we will make an immediate and vigorous presentation of our case to the proper Federal authorities and to the State authorities as well, if the opportunity offers.

The cost of the extra semester must be met, therefore, from these sources plus the small subsidy in the budget for our present summer school. An additional overhead for supplies will be needed, but the remainder will be available for salaries, which will constitute the principal item of cost. Every available dollar will be used for salary additions. We can go no further. We cannot spend money which we do not have.

Advice and opinion will be widely sought and used in developing the method and basis of distribution. I pledge you that the plan will be as fair and as equitable as our collective wisdom and effort can make it.

I wish that I might be able to suggest that large increases for this additional service are probable. Unfortunately, I can not do so. Unless we receive an additional appropriation to defray the costs of acceleration, I believe the percentage of increase will be small.

There is one matter of especial interest to those members of the faculty who have previously taught in summer school. The plan recommended abolishes our traditional summer school. Our third semester will be a regular semester, with the same type of schedules, the normal winter teaching load, and the same administrative organization as in the other two semesters. However, the best available forecasts indicate an enrollment of only a few hundred students in our summer session, if it is run in its traditional manner. Since summer salaries always have been contingent upon enrollment in classes, salary prospects on the present summer school basis would not be bright.

To summarize:

1. There is no intention or expectation that basic salaries will be decreased this year or next year.

2. All members of the faculty this year wil be expected to teach an additional one-half semester, additional compensation will be given in an amount not yet determined.
3. If there are those whose services are not needed in the third semester, their term of service for this year will terminate June 2, 1942.
4. For next year, a uniform term of service of two and one-half semesters is planned. Compensation for this term of service would consist of the present base salary plus an additional percentage.
5. Teaching loads and administrative control will be comparable in each of the three semesters.
6. The amount of additional salary available can be increased by the efforts of the members of the faculty.
7. The administration will be vigilant in search for additional sources of revenue to defray the costs of acceleration.

The substance of Dean Briscoe's remarks:

"I shall confine my remarks to general statements which seem to be pertinent. I shall point out a few important considerations we should keep in mind in thinking about this program.

"First, we must be convinced that it is the result of certain conditions and demands that cannot be denied or disregarded. The three most important are the following:

(a) The insistent request of the government that more trained men and women be supplied for essential needs in less time.
(b) The demands of students and parents that men be allowed to complete as much training as possible before they reach the age at which they must be inducted into the military service.
(c) The protection of the interests of the faculty, the students, and the whole University during this unusual situation.

"Second, I should like to impress upon you that we feel that this program is not the result of any hysterical thinking or action. This plan, or some other, might have been worked out during Christmas vacation or during a few hours following the attack on December 7. It was, however, only after all of the possible information had been gathered that one person or a group of persons could sit down and make the program. I believe that the actual time in which this was considered is as great as it would have been had it been spread over a semester, or even a year.

"Third, this program and its success, or any other program that we adopted in this period, calls especially for unity of purpose and action. It isn't a program that anyone can consider as having been designed for his own benefit. The divisions that work the most must be protected by those who work the least. Here as never before, the University has an opportunity to work together. Through our efforts, we hope that there will come standing contributions.

"Fourth, the program has for its objective acceleration. It is centered around three semesters. All of the other parts of the program are necessary for the successful operation of the whole. It has been stripped of all unessentials.

"Fifth, this program involves some uncertainties. Those who have worked with it in the Council meetings believe that it involves fewer and less hazardous uncertainties than any other program we were able to devise. We could proceed as usual, without any changes. To do so, the Council believes, would certainly be hazardous to all of us and to the objectives of the University. We could continue just as we have been. But we feel that whatever we do must be done now. It must be done before the students leave. It must be done at this time, so that the students in high school may plan their programs and so that the plan of the University during the summer may be completed. All of this must be done now to insure us that if the worst happens and the emergency continues, we shall still have a University and shall make our maximum contribution to the war effort."

The substance of Dean Stout's remarks:

"My chief interest in the three-semester plan was the question of whether we could do our work on the standard basis with a shortened semester. The registrar went through past calendars to learn how many days the semesters included, and planned the calendars proposed on a comparable basis.

"We hope to be able to get the teachers that come from the small town and township high schools during the first part of the third semester. We must say 'third semester' because we want people to think of this semester as a semester and not as two eight-week sessions. But we do want to meet the needs of teachers, and we think we are making adequate provision for them. It is our plan to offer two and one-half hour courses continuing throughout the semester, making a total of five hours, just as economics is now offered."

The substance of Dr. Cleland's remarks:

"This is the sort of thing which has been in operation in many institutions for some time. Where I went to school, they had a four-year required program in physical education. I believe it was one of the features of the curriculum which was of the greatest value. What we have proposed is not an ideal program, but a compromise between what we think the faculty would accept and what the army and navy want."

The substance of Professor Hall's remarks:

"I presume there is a question in some of your minds as to why this plan is being presented at this time. We have been at work at it some time, however. When the War Council was called, the Committee was asked to submit a report, because it was thought that such a report would be helpful. I believe I should give you a little history of the work of the Committee.

"When the Survey Report was voted upon, it was voted to ask the President to appoint a committee on a Lower Division. He did so last spring. The committee met and prepared a list of the problems it encountered and sent it to the members of the faculty this fall. The answers came back, and we again worked. Last summer, Dean Bengtson of the University of Nebraska, who is in charge of the lower division there, was on the campus, and we had an opportunity to talk with him. The plan in operation in that institution seemed successful. Later, a subcommittee of our committe visited the University of Nebraska—Professors Starr and Ittner and I. There we studied the plan in operation and got faculty reaction. We were greatly impressed and found practically no objections to it. Upon our return we presented our report to the full committee, and the committee asked that it be sent to the faculty. It was in the course of these deliberations following that the War Council called upon us.

"There are three things which the War Council thought would be particularly helpful to the war-time program:

(1) The establishment of uniform entrance requirements;

(2) The offering of terminal courses for men called into government service; and

(3) The counselling and guidance program, which seemed to be especially helpful in this emergency.

"The committee was eager to find a plan which had been in operation and

therefore would not be so likely to have features which would need changing."
The substance of Dean Payne's remarks:

"Many of you came here and have remained here because of opportunities for research. The administration is very much interested in seeing that these opportunities are continued. I believe also that the Federal government would like to see us continue with our research program.

"I see, in fact, certain advantages in this program. Those who have taught in the summer session have given their whole time to teaching, with no assistance. Those who teach in the third semester will have time for research, as in the regular year.

"The graduate and research program depends more upon each one of you than upon the administration. So we need your help, as you need ours."

REPORT OF THE ADMINISTRATIVE WAR COUNCIL
TO THE FACULTY OF INDIANA UNIVERSITY, JANUARY 15, 1942, 2:30 P.M.

In view of the request of our government that higher institutions of learning introduce acceleration programs to make it possible to graduate students before they reach the age for military or other wartime service [Exhibit A] and because of the unmistakable evidence that unless adjustments are made at once by our own University to render this service to her present and prospective students she would fail to live up to her historic role and would allow unnecessarily large numbers of young men and women to face the present emergency and the post war period without the benefits of a college education [Exhibit B], the President of Indiana University called together an Administrative War Council to prepare proposals for meeting this emergency. This Council submits the following recommendations to the University faculty for consideration and for recommendation to the Board of Trustees:

ARTICLE I
Calendar

Section 1. The University shall go on a three-semester basis (except the Normal College of the American Gymnastic Union, the Extension Division, and the Training Course for Social Work), each semester including seventy-seven teaching days and six days for examinations, and making use of enough Saturdays to make the plan workable.

Section 2. The first semester shall normally begin in the first week in September and end before Christmas. The second semester shall begin early in January and end in the latter part of April. The third semester shall begin in the second week in May and end after the middle of August. In 1942 the second semester shall begin on January 24 and end on May 10.

Section 3. The third semester shall be divided into two approximately equal parts.

Section 4. The three semesters shall be considered on the same basis with respect to teaching load of individual members of the staff, quality of instruction, content of courses, facilities for research, etc.

Section 5. During the present University year, members of the teaching staff shall consider it to be their duty to teach two full semesters and, if their services are needed, one-half of a third semester.

Section 6. During the present University year, faculty members not teaching in the third semester will receive their basic salary by remaining in the service of the University until June 2, 1942.

Section 7. If the three semester plan continues after the present University year, the normal annual period of service to the University for each member of the faculty shall be two and one-half semesters.

(The substance of Article I may be adopted by the approval of the calendar submitted) [Exhibit C].

ARTICLE II
Faculty

Section 1. Leaves of Absence.

(a) Leaves of absence for the period of emergency and for an additional period of six months thereafter will be granted the members of the staff having permanent tenure who are inducted into or who enlist in the military forces of the country. During such leaves, replacements and adjustments, if made, will be made on a temporary basis for not more than one year at a time.

(b) A member of the staff granted leave under these conditions may resume his position at the end of any period for which a temporary appointment or adjustment has been made during his absence, subject to the same adjustments in salary, service and tenure as prove to be necessary for members of the staff who continue regular service during his leave.

(c) Applications for all other leaves of absence during the emergency shall be considered as individual cases arise by a University committee appointed by and responsible to the president of the University.

(d) During the emergency, members of the staff on a temporary basis will be granted leave of absence for a period of not longer than one year at a time for military service or for other reasons approved by the University committee referred to above. Such leaves shall not extend, unless renewed, beyond the period of appointment. The renewal of a leave of absence will be considered on the same basis as a renewal of appointment would have been considered if the person concerned had continued regular service for the full period of his appointment.

Section 2. Additions and Replacements. Additions to the staff and replacements of members of the staff whose services are discontinued for any reason during the period of the emergency, will be made only after the necessity for the addition or replacement has been proved by the school or department making the recommendation. Such proof should include evidence that the school or department has made every reasonable effort to meet the need by elimination or combination of courses, by shifting the teaching staff within the department, by borrowing temporarily teaching time from other departments, and by other emergency measures.

Section 3. Budget. In making budgetary and staff adjustments during the period of the emergency, the University recognizes that changes, both expansions and contractions, may be necessary at later dates. Budget changes and staff adjustments made during the emergency will not necessarily be permanent and will not be considered as prejudicial to the normal future development of schools and departments.

ARTICLE III
Student Body

Section 1. Admissions and Advanced Standing.

(a) During the emergency, second semester resident and non-resident high school seniors who give promise of success in college, and who have minor University entrance deficiencies or deficiencies preventing graduation from high school, and high school graduates who give promise of success in college and who have minor University entrance deficiencies may be admitted to the University if done by the unanimous consent of a committee consisting of the Director of Admissions as chairman, the Dean of the Faculties, and the dean of the college or school concerned.

(b) During the emergency, such modifications in the rules and regulations governing the advanced standing of transfer students as are deemed necessary may be made by the committees on admissions for several colleges and schools.

Section 2. Military Credit.

(a) A student ordered to report for military service after the completion of at least six and not more than ten weeks of a semester will receive credit to the extent of one-half of the hours for which he is enrolled, subject to his standing in each class at the time of leaving. If withdrawal for the same reason occurs after the completion of at least ten weeks of a semester, the student will receive full credit for the courses in which he is enrolled, subject to his standing in each class at the time of leaving.

(b) If a student is not satisfied with the grade earned up to the time of leaving the University, he may have the opportunity of taking a special examination without payment of the special examination fee.

(c) A student who has met all the requirements for graduation except those which he would fulfill by completing the courses for which he is registered at the time he is ordered to report for military service, will be recommended for his degree provided he has completed at least seven weeks of that semester for which he is registered, and provided that he has a standing in the courses for which he is enrolled which if maintained to the end of the semester would satisfy the requirements for graduation. Cases demanding special consideration will be acted upon individually by the Committee on Graduation. The same regulations will apply to students who normally would have completed the requirements for graduation at the end of the first semester of 1941-42.

(d) The application of a student asking that academic credit be granted for honorable military service will be considered and acted upon by the proper authorities of the University after his military service has been completed.

(e) These regulations will be applied to students who enlist and to those who are inducted under the Selective Service System.

Section 3. Entrance of Students from High School at the Beginning of the Third Semester.

(a) Request shall be made to the State Board of Education by President Wells and Dean Briscoe to co-operate in the war emergency by authorizing secondary school officials to waive minor graduation requirements, such as permitting seniors to withdraw in May, enter college, and receive their diplomas from high school.

(b) Information shall be sent to school superintendents, principals, and guidance officers by President Wells acquainting them with our War Program and request shall be made for their co-operation, by sending the University mailing lists of their seniors and by making recommendations for the admission of seniors who may be slightly deficient in meeting normal entrance requirements.

(c) Letters and bulletins shall be sent to prospective students and parents acquainting them with the newly designed opportunities.

(d) Contacts shall be made with other colleges for the facilitating of transfers.

(e) Personal contacts shall be made so far as possible with prospective new students and with high school officials in explaining the war program.

Section 4. Student Emergency War Council.

The Council shall be appointed by the President of the University and shall have the following functions:

(a) Rescheduling and reorganizing the social program.

(b) Promoting for defense purposes certain financial drives, as the sale of Defense bonds and stamps, contributions to the Red Cross and other war causes approved by the University Committee on Campus Financial Drives.

(c) Developing a system of voluntary clerical help for offices overburdened by their part in the Defense program.

(d) Promoting the student interest in and attendance of special courses: First Aid, Home Nursing, Background and Progress of the War, etc.

(e) Promoting enthusiasm for the new health program.

(f) Co-operating with the University for the care of its property and for conservation in general.

Section 5. Social Organization.

In view of this all-out program for the national emergency in which all individuals and organizations are asked to play a part, the faculty urges and recommends that every fraternity and sorority do its part by operating on a year-round basis and that students, alumni advisers, faculty advisers, alumni groups and local and national pan-hellenic and inter-fraternity organizations be encouraged to further this policy.

Section 6. Student Aid.

There shall be established a number of War Service scholarships in which students may render War-time service to the University in return for their compensations. The number and character of these scholarships shall depend upon the need of individual students and the ability of the University to finance them.

ARTICLE IV
Curriculum

Section 1. Departments and schools shall study their curricula from the following points of view:

(a) Elimination of courses and small classes.

(b) Condensation into fewer courses or sections.

(c) Alternating courses.

Section 2. A schedule of courses for the next four semesters shall be prepared and submitted by each school and department by 5 p.m. January 22, 1942. These schedules shall show how course offerings and staff can be distributed to take care of these four semesters.

Section 3. A committee of three, of which the Dean of the Faculty is chairman, shall be appointed to administer this program.

Section 4. For the maximum degree of protection of the interests of the faculty and of the University during the emergency, all the talent and ability of the staff shall be used where it can best serve in taking care of needs that arise from vacancies and from expansions made necessary by the unusual situation. A survey of the preparation and special abilities of the staff is now being made. Questionnaires will soon be mailed to members of the faculty for the purpose of securing this information.

ARTICLE V
Special War Effort

Section 1. War Aims Courses and Lectures on the Campus.

(a) General convocations in which lectures and audio-visual materials on War Aims and American Institutions and Culture shall be presented to the entire student body. (This may require the installation of equipment now being contemplated in the Hall of Music.)

(b) A special lecture series on the backgrounds of the war and the current progress of the war shall be available to all students. Special attention of upperclassmen should be directed to the lectures on these subjects to prospective officers in the Military Department which may be opened to them.

(c) A series of week-day exhibitions of films and other materials dealing with governmental problems and war aims shall be held in Alumni Hall and available to all students during the noon hour and through the middle of the afternoon, in order that students may have an opportunity to see the 16 mm. materials being prepared by duly authorized agencies of the government. (This will require the installation of equipment at a cost of about $700.)

(d) The student forum program shall be expanded to reach organizations and dormitories more directly.

(e) A reading shelf on American Institutions and Culture shall be established in every organization, dormitory, the larger divisional libraries, and in the general Library, to contain the basic materials of American Institutions and Culture, so as to bring within the easy reach of as many students as possible the fundamental principles of the American Faith and Constitutional Government.

(f) The University's program of work in the Good Neighbor Policy shall be correlated and emphasized.

Section 2. Courses in Special Training Areas.

(a) In setting up the program of special courses which have to do with national defense, precaution should be taken to see that the program put into effect does not interfere seriously with the regular work of the University.

(b) New courses of an intensive nature which are proposed to meet the needs as they arise shall be considered and approved by a general University committee. This committee shall also study carefully all requests for special courses received by the University from outside sources and shall make recommendations to the schools and departments concerned. During the period of the emergency, publications and news releases shall emphasize possibilities of special training related to the war effort. Descriptions shall cover these three types of courses:

1. Regular courses of the University which provide specialized training needed by the armed forces and the various civilian agencies supporting them.

2. Intensive short courses both with and without University credit, which may from time to time be scheduled.

3. Courses required or strongly recommended for enlistment in special branches of the military service.

Section 3. The Extension Division shall undertake to direct the preparation of teaching materials for ten fields of the civilian defense program, and the faculty of the University shall support the Extension division in this program.

Section 4. Intensified Health and Physical Fitness Program.

(a) Courses for Men. In compliance with urgent requests from naval and Military authorities and in harmony with resolutions passed by representatives of the Association of American Colleges and by the Presidents representing approximately 800 American universities and colleges at Baltimore Indiana University shall require, beginning January 24, 1942, that every undergraduate man student, unless excused by the Director of Health Service, pursue a course in physical education each semester. During the second semester of 1942, this program shall be required of all men who shall have reached the age of twenty on or before May 8 and shall be an elective for all others. The outstanding emphasis in this course shall be the physical and mental fitness of Indiana University men students. The program for all students, and especially those with physical defects who have been or who may be rejected as unfit for military service, shall be developed by the Department of Physical Education for Men with the collaboration of the Bureau of Health Service. The classes shall meet for one period on alternate days of a six-day week. In addition, students enrolled will be required to participate each week in the intramural and recreational sports program for two periods of approximately two hours each. One credit hour per semester shall be granted for each semester's work if satisfactorily passed. Such credit hours shall be in addition to present requirements for graduation.

(b) Courses for Women. Every undergraduate woman student shall be required to pursue a course in physical education each semester, with option in the junior and senior years of substituting courses such as first aid, home nursing, safety training, or nutrition which may be approved. One credit hour per semester shall be granted for each semester's work, if satisfactorily passed. Such credit hours for the junior and senior years shall be in addition to present requirements for graduation. During the second semester of 1942 this program shall be optional for juniors and seniors.

(c) Military Courses. The faculties of the individual schools shall give consideration to the giving of academic credit for the Basic Course in Military Science and Tactics.

ARTICLE VI
Economies

Section 1. In Operation of Physical Plant.

(a) Additional efforts by faculty, staff and students of the University are recommended to conserve the University's expenditures for utility services, namely, electricity, heat, water, and maintenance, both as a patriotic duty during the war period and as a means of effecting economies in University expenditures.

(b) Classrooms and offices should be lighted only when in use and temperatures maintained only at the minimum degree of general comfort. The University power plant now is being operated at maximum capacity and only through cooperative conservation of its product will it be possible to avoid expensive additions.

(c) Conservation of man-power in the services of the buildings and grounds staff can be effected through greater cooperation in lightening the work of that staff.

Section 2. In Use of Faculty and Staff. Every effort shall be made to make the economies that can be secured by the proper use of the instructional staff and the proper scheduling of courses as indicated under Article II, Section 2, and Article IV.

ARTICLE VII
Junior Division

The present emergency plan provides the framework into which a number of desirable details may be fitted if the faculty accepts the plan and works together wholeheartedly for its improvement in details. Some details need to be settled at once if the larger program is to operate successfully. The Administrative War

Council concluded that the report of the Committee on Junior Division dealt with so many problems of this nature, such as admissions, guidance, terminal courses, etc., that it should be submitted to the faculty at this time as highly conducive to the success of the program as a whole. The report is therefore included and recommended.

Proposed Plan for a Junior Division At Indiana University

In order to serve new students more adequately, the faculty of Indiana University recommends to the President and Board of Trustees the creation of a Junior Division.

The purposes of creating such a Junior Division are as follows:

1. To improve and enlarge the guidance and testing program for first year students.

2. To plan more adequate curricula for students who expect to remain in the University only one or two years.

3. To assist students to make up deficiencies.

4. To provide uniform entrance requirements to the University.

5. To act as a clearing house for information which might lead to improving the teaching of first year students.

6. To study curricula and academic problems of freshman students and make recommendations.

Organization of the Junior Division

The Junior Division shall be administered by a dean who shall rank on a par with the deans of the schools. He shall be assisted by such technical and clerical staff as may be necessary, and by an advisory board and group of student counsellors as hereinafter provided.

The Dean of the Junior Division shall be assisted by an advisory board which shall consist of ten members. This board shall act as an advisory body to the dean. In addition to his duties as an adviser to the dean, each member of the board shall act as director to a group of student counsellors. He shall perform such other duties as are hereinafter designated or deemed necessary by the dean.

Four members of the advisory board shall be representatives one from each school which now registers freshmen, namely the College of Arts and Sciences, the School of Business, the School of Education, and the School of Music. Each such representative shall be nominated by the dean of his school and appointed by the President and Board of Trustees upon recommendation of the Dean of the Junior Division.

The other six members of the advisory board shall be selected by the Dean of the Junior Division in accordance with what he believes to be the needs or interests of the Junior Division and of the various groups of the University, and recommended to the President and Board of Trustees for appointment.

Each member of the advisory board shall be appointed for one year and shall receive appropriate compensation for his services.

The Dean of the Junior Division and the advisory board shall be assisted by a group of student counselors. It shall be the duty of each counselor to advise students in accordance with the regulations laid down by the Dean of the Junior Division.

Student counsellors shall be recommended for appointment to the President and Board of Trustees by the Dean of the Junior Division after consultation with the dean and chairman or head of the department and the members of the advisory board from the school of which the counsellor is a member. Each counsellor shall act as adviser to a group of students, the number to be determined by the Dean of the Junior Division. He shall be appointed for one year and shall receive appropriate compensation for his services.

Functions of the Junior Division
The functions of the University Junior Division shall be:
1. To matriculate all freshmen and other students not matriculating in any other school.
2. To assemble information pertinent to the guidance of new students.
3. To counsel and guide new students.
4. To classify all new students into groups as follows:

> Group A shall consist of those students who have chosen a school and who appear to be fully qualified to pursue the work of that school. Each of these students shall be advised by a counsellor who represents the school which the student intends to enter.
>
> Group B shall consist of students who have chosen a school but who have deficiencies which must be removed before they may enter the school of their choice. Each of these students shall be advised by a counsellor who represents the school which the student intends to enter.
>
> Group C shall consist of students who wish to pursue terminal curricula offered by the Junior Division of the University. Such students shall be assigned to counsellors especially designated for this service by the Dean of the Junior Division.
>
> Group D shall consist of students who are designated as adult special students. Such students shall be advised by counsellors especially appointed for that group.
>
> Group E shall consist of students who have not made a choice of school. Such students shall be designated as unclassified students and shall be advised by special counsellors selected for that purpose.

5. To discover defects and deficiencies in students which impede their progress, and to provide means of removing these as speedily as possible.
6. To arrange with the various schools for one and two year curricula (terminal courses) which meet the needs of students who are unable or who do not wish to work for a degree.
7. To assist in the placement of students at the proper instructional levels and to facilitate the offering to exceptionally well-qualified and well-prepared students of opportunities to demonstrate by examination that they have mastery of certain subjects and thereby enable them to earn credit or be excused from taking courses which otherwise would be required.
8. To arrange examinations to test students' interests and aptitudes and to encourage students to take such tests.
9. To cooperate with the schools in improving the teaching of first year students and in developing courses which are designed for freshman students.
10. To cooperate with the schools in studying critically the requirements for entrance into the University, and the requirements which schools may establish for admission into their sophomore classes.

Entrance Requirements
The power to fix the entrance to the *University* shall be vested in the Dean of the Junior Division and the advisory board subject to the approval of the President and Board of Trustees.

The requirements for admission to the Junior Division shall in no way affect the powers of the several schools to fix entrance requirements to their respective schools.

> Members of the Lower
> Division Committee
> Herman T. Briscoe, ex officio
> Samuel T. Burns
> Robert Cavanaugh
> Frank Edmondson
> Oliver P. Field
> Cora B. Hennel
> Frank Horack
> Robert T. Ittner
> James E. Moffat
> Russell Noyes
> George W. Starr
> Paul Weatherwax
> Arthur M. Weimer
> Wendell W. Wright
> Ford P. Hall, Chairman

Article VIII
Publication of University War Program

Complete understanding of "The Indiana University Plan" by students, faculty, alumni and the general public is essential to its success. To that end, the outstanding features of the Plan shall be carefully explained and widely publicized. This publicity shall include:

Section 1. Announcements in Newspapers.

(a) Announcement of the principal features of the Plan immediately upon its approval by the Board of Trustees, this announcement being furnished through correspondents to Indianapolis, Louisville, Chicago and New York newspapers and directly to the three press associations.

(b) Announcement for the particular benefit of students and faculty through a special complete free distribution edition of the Daily Student which would present not only a summary of the Plan in news form but the report of the Administrative Council as approved by the faculty and trustees (type used in printing the report in the Student should be held for use in printing a booklet).

(c) Communication of the Plan either in mimeographed form or through the proposed booklet, provided it can be off the press in time, to newspaper editorial writers in Indiana and several of the larger cities outside the state, such as New York, Chicago, Louisville, Cincinnati and St. Louis.

(d) Continuing publicity on the Plan and its details and workings through newspapers following the initial announcement, in fact centering all University publicity so far as possible about the Plan and various developments resulting from it.

Section 2. Special Booklets.

(a) Immediate preparation and publication of a booklet somewhat similar to that of Princeton University, setting forth the Plan in clear, concise language, this booklet to be so designed as to be used for circulation among students, faculty, parents of students, public and parochial school administrators, alumni, other colleges and universities, members of the state legislature and state officials, and on request to the public.

(b) Preparation and publication immediately of an insert, four or six pages in length, for the booklet "Invitation to Learning," presenting the high-lights of the Plan and making corrections.

(c) Preparation and publication as early as possible, certainly not later than March 1, of a bulletin devoted to the offerings of the third semester.

(d) Abandonment of the preliminary Summer Session booklet for which type has been set and the substitution for the preliminary Summer Session booklet of a special self-mailing piece particularly designed and sent to all teachers in Indiana as given in the official directory.

Section 3. Presidential Letters.

(a) A letter over the signature of the President to each student of the University setting forth the advantages to the student of the Plan and enclosing a copy of the explanatory booklet.

(b) A letter over the President's signature to the parents or guardian of each student now in the University pointing out the advantages of the Plan from the standpoint of both student and parent and enclosing a copy of the ex-planatory booklet.

(c) A letter over the President's signature to presidents of city and town boards of education, county and city superintendents and high school principals advising them of the Plan with particular reference to the Plan's provisions for admission of high school graduates.

(d) A letter to officers and councillors of the Alumni Association advising of the Plan and enclosing several booklets describing the Plan which they would be urged to distribute to advantage.

Section 4. Student Convocation Monday, January 19, from seven until eight o'clock, at which advantages accruing to students under the Plan would be set forth briefly with a portion of the period devoted to student questions.

Section 5. Arrangements through Student War Council for members of the Administrative Council upon invitation to visit during the second semester fraternity and sorority houses and dormitories to present the Plan and its advantages to students.

Section 6. Presentation of Plan at all alumni meetings held during winter and spring months.

Exhibit A

RESOLUTIONS AND RECOMMENDATIONS

adopted by the

NATIONAL CONFERENCE OF COLLEGE AND UNIVERSITY PRESIDENTS

ON HIGHER EDUCATION AND THE WAR

held in Baltimore, Maryland, January 3-4, 1942

under the sponsorship of the

Committee on Military Affairs

of the

National Committee on Education and Defense

and the

United States Office of Education

Preamble

In the present supreme national crisis we pledge to the President of the United States, Commander-in-Chief of our nation, the total strength of our colleges and universities—our faculties, our students, our administrative organizations, and our physical facilities. The institutions of higher education of the United States are organized for action, and they offer their united power for decisive military victory, and for the ultimate and even more difficult task of establishing a just and lasting peace.

Not all the needs to win a total war can be accurately defined now. Nor can total present and future resources of trained man power be fully appraised. New areas of need and of potential service will develop as the months pass. We pledge our unstinted effort to meet these needs as they arise.

For the immediate and more effective prosecution of our varied tasks in the service of the nation, the National Conference of College and University Presidents proposes the following resolutions and makes the following recommendations:

A. *Allocation of Total Man Power*

The surest and quickest route to victory is the full, energetic, and planned use of all our resources and materials. Where shortages may develop, both efficiency and the principles of equality require that the government take steps in advance to allocate resources to meet total needs, with a fair distribution of sacrifice. This is at present being done with materials such as rubber, aluminum, and tin. It is clear that productive man power is also an area in which critical shortages are already evident. Therefore, it is recommended that:

1. Institutions of higher education cooperate to the fullest extent with the National Resources Planning Board and other federal agencies responsible for surveys (a) to determine the immediate needs of man power and woman power for the essential branches of national service—military, industrial, and civilian, (b) to determine the available facilities of colleges and universities to prepare students to meet these needs, and (c) to appraise the ultimate needs in professional personnel for long-term conflict and for the post-war period, in order that a continuous and adequate supply of men and women trained in technical and professional skills and in leadership to meet both immediate and long-range needs shall be maintained;

2. There be brought to the attention of the President the necessity of issuing a statement of national policy which will avoid competitive bidding for faculty and students by government agencies and by industry and will conserve adequate personnel on all levels of education to assure the effective instruction of youth and adults, in order to provide a continuous supply of trained men and women;

3. The United States Office of Education Wartime Commission be requested to study and develop appropriate plans for the solution of the problems of (a) how to meet the teacher shortage in elementary and secondary schools and the shortage of workers for community programs, and (b) how to supplement the training of present and potentially available teachers and other workers for new and changing responsibilities;

4. The United States Office of Education Wartime Commission offer its services for cooperation with the United States Department of Agriculture, the Executive Committee of the Association of Land-Grant Colleges and Universities, and the Conference of Negro Land-Grant Colleges to assure an adequate supply of county agents, 4-H club leaders, home demonstration agents, and other leaders in rural life.

B. Acceleration of Educational Programs

It is important to retain as far as practicable a degree of uniformity among colleges and universities in such matters as calendar changes and credits, while making adjustments in the interests of acceleration. Recognizing the increasing demand for men and women trained in technical skills and in professions essential to total war and the consequent need for preparing them for such service at the earliest possible time, and further recognizing that basic education should be completed prior to induction through Selective Service at the age of 20, we recommend that:

5. All institutions of higher education give immediate consideration to ways and means for accelerating the progress of students through such extension of the annual period of instruction and such adjustments of curricula as may be consistent with national needs and with educational standards, and as may be possible with available resources.

6. Desirable acceleration of programs of higher education should be accomplished without lowering of established standards of admission to college.

*7. An immediate study be made by the National Committee on Education and Defense and the United States Office of Education Wartime Commission of desirable articulation in the academic calendars of the secondary schools and the colleges to facilitate acceleration of total educational progress.

The preliminary evidence indicates the possible need of financial assistance to higher educational institutions and to students in order to carry out comprehensive accelerated programs of study. It is therefore recommended that:

8. An immediate study be made by the National Committee on Education and Defense and the United States Office of Education Wartime Commission as to the needs for and bases of federal financial assistance to higher education (including junior colleges), for the duration of the emergency, in order that the training of students for national service may be accelerated.

C. Exchange of Information

Since it is of primary importance that there be the fullest possible clearance of information concerning proposals and practices relating to institutional adjustments during the war emergency, it is recommended that:

9. The National Committee on Education and Defense and the United States Office of Education Wartime Commission be requested to assemble and publish accounts of changes made by educational institutions in the interest of war service.

D. Credit for Military Service

In recognizing the significance of military service, some colleges and universities are adopting a policy of granting credit to students who leave college to serve with the armed forces. In order to establish some degree of uniformity of practice, it is recommended that:

10. Credit be awarded only to individuals, upon the completion of their service, who shall apply to the institution for this credit and who shall

---

* Unanimously approved by the Resolutions Committee; inadvertently omitted from the final report to the conference.

meet such tests as the institution may prescribe. In cases in which degrees are of distinct advantage to students in the service, it is recognized that some departure from this practice, on an individual basis, may be justified.

E. Health

Individual health is essential to national efficiency and to maximum war effort. Almost one million young men have been rejected for military service because of inability to meet minimum military standards of physical fitness. Therefore, it is recommended that:

11. All colleges and universities take such steps as will be necessary to bring each individual student to his highest possible level of physical fitness.

F. Military Service

The experiences of the United States in the last world war, and of England in the early months of the present conflict, offer abundant evidence that volunteer enlistment for military service is a threat to the total allocation of man power for its most effective utilization. In their eagerness to serve the nation, many of our most capable youth enter the armed forces despite the fact that they may now be serving or preparing to serve the nation in ways even more vital to total war and more in keeping with their training and ability. Therefore the Conference records its belief that:

12. The general application of the principle of selective service promises the most effective means for the placement of the individual in accordance with his capacity to serve national needs and with the least disturbance of basic social institutions.

The wartime health needs of our armed forces and of our civilian population and the inevitable post-war strains upon physical and mental health make it necessary to assure an ample number of adequately prepared candidates for admission to medical and dental schools. Therefore, be it resolved that:

13. The Selective Service System be requested to make adequate provisions for the deferment of bona fide *premedical* students in colleges whose tentative admission to an approved dental school has already been assured on the basis of the completion of not less than two years of college.

14. The Selective Service System be requested to make similar provisions for the deferment of bona fide *predental* students in colleges whose tentative admission to an approved dental school has already been assured on the basis of the completion of not less than two years of college.

The demand for trained and experienced chaplains in the armed forces, and the contribution of religion to the civilian morale of the nation, make desirable the maintenance of an adequate supply of candidates for the priesthood and the ministry. Therefore it is recommended that:

15. The Selective Service System be requested to make provision for the deferment of bona fide *pretheological* students in colleges or universities who have been approved by their appropriate ecclesiastical authority.

The increasing demand for highly trained men requires that selected students be permitted to continue their graduate study in such fields as are now or may be covered by directives for undergraduate students. Therefore, it is recommended that:

16. The Selective Service System be urged to issue a directive calling attention of state directors and local selective service boards to this need and the

consequent necessity of providing occupational deferment for selected individuals pursuing graduate work.

Exhibit B
REPORT OF ADMISSIONS & INQUIRIES
JANUARY 1, 1942

Admissions Granted During Period October 1-December 31, 1941 40
Comparisons:

  October 1-December 31, 1937...........................47
  October 1-December 31, 1938...........................78
  October 1-December 31, 1939...........................60
  October 1-December 31, 1940...........................35
  October 1-December 31, 1941...........................40

Inquiries. Comparison for periods October 1-December 31, 1939, 1940, 1941

Period	Pieces of Mail Received	Mailings Sent Out	Individuals Represented
1939	2578	4174	1774
1940	3223	5004	2265
1941	2297	3684	1378

 This report does not include 44 new students who have been granted admission under the rule that an Extension student enrolling for as many as seven hours of work is automatically expected to apply for admission to the University.

Summary of Admissions Granted.

Calendar Period	1938	1939	1940	1941	1942
Oct. 1 to Jan. 1	47	78	60	35	40
Matriculants for Year	1938	1939	1940	1941	
Ending October 1	2266	2034	2028	1868	

Additional Extension Admissions		1940	1941	1942
Oct. 1 to Jan. 1		207	109	44

CALENDAR
1942

		Saturdays Used
Enrollment	Jan. 24, Sat.	Jan. 31—Monday classes
Classes begin	Jan. 26, Mon.	Feb. 7—Tuesday ″
Exams. begin	May 4, Mon.	21—Wednesday ″
Semester ends	May 9, Sat.	Mar. 7—Thursday ″
Commencement	May 10, Sunday	14—Friday ″
		21—Monday ″
		28—Tuesday ″
		Apr. 11—Wednesday ″
		18—Thursday ″

Holidays

Apr. 3—Good Friday

Schedule of Graduation of Different Classes
According to Different Plans

	2 semesters +12 wks summer	4-12 wk. terms beginning June '42	3-16 wk semesters beginning May '42	3-16 wk. semesters beginning Sept. '42 and 12 wks. summer '42	Present Plan
Present Juniors	*February 1943	March 1943	December 1943	*December 1943	June 1943
Present Sophomores	February 1944	December 1943	August 1943	August 1943	February 1944
Present Freshmen	August 1944	August 1944	April 1944	April 1944	February 1945
New Freshmen June 1942	June 1945	April 1945	December 1944	December 1944	September 1945
New Freshmen September 1942	June 1945	June 1945	April 1945	April 1945	September 1945

* One hour short of required number
In some instances, the hours earned are in excess of number required for graduation
Dates are on basis of maximum load of 11-12 hours for 12 weeks summer session; 8 hours for 8 weeks summer session; 11 hours for 12 weeks term; 16 hours for a semester.

CALENDARS

12 week Summer Session—June to August
4 terms: October to December; January to March; April to June; July to September
3 semesters: September to December; January to April; May to August

Saturdays Used

Registration	May 7, Thurs.	May 16—Monday classes
Enrollment	May 11, Mon.	23—Tuesday "
Classes begin	May 12, Tues.	June 6—Wednesday "
First Half ends	June 27, Sat.	13—Thursday "
Exams. begin	Aug. 17, Mon.	20—Friday "
Semester ends	Aug. 22, Sat.	27—Monday "
		July 11—Tuesday "
		July 18—Wednesday "
		July 25—Thursday "

Holidays

July 3—Friday

Saturdays Used

Orientation	Sept. 3-5, Th.-Sat.	Sept. 12—Monday classes
Registration	Sept. 3-5, Th.-Sat.	19—Tuesday "
Enrollment	Sept. 5, Sat.	Oct. 3—Wednesday "
Classes begin	Sept. 7, Mon.	10—Thursday "
Exams. begin	Dec. 17, Thurs.	31—Friday "
Semester ends	Dec. 23, Wed.	Nov. 28—Monday "

Holidays

Nov. 26—Thurs.—
Thanksgiving

Heretofore, we have maintained a semester average of 77 class days, 1 reading day (except in School of Business, 3 days), and 8 examination days.

The new calendar provides either 77 or 78 class days and 6 examination days. The average length of a semester is 15½ calendar weeks. We get the 77 or 78 class days in about 14 weeks by using regular school days and from 6 to 9 designated Saturdays each semester.

CALENDAR
1943

Registration	Jan. 4-6, Mon.-Wed.	Jan. 9—Monday classes
Enrollment	Jan. 6, Wed.	23—Tuesday "
Classes begin	Jan. 7, Thurs.	Feb. 13—Wednesday "
Exams. begin	Apr. 16, Fri.	27—Thursday "
Semester ends	Apr. 22, Thurs.	Mar. 20—Friday "
		27—Monday "

Saturdays Used

Registration	May 7, Thurs.	May 15—Monday classes
Enrollment	May 10, Mon.	22—Tuesday "
Classes begin	May 11, Tues.	June 5—Wednesday "
First Half ends	June 26, Sat.	12—Thursday "
Exams. begin	Aug. 16, Mon.	19—Friday "
Semester ends	Aug. 21, Sat.	26—Monday "
		July 10—Tuesday "
		17—Wednesday "
		24—Thursday "

Holidays

May 31—Mon.—
　　　　Memorial Day
July 5—Mon.—Inde-
　　　　pendence Day

		Saturdays Used
Orientation	Sept. 2-4, Th.-Sat.	Sept. 11—Monday classes
Registration	Sept. 2-4, Th.-Sat.	18—Tuesday "
Enrollment	Sept. 4, Sat.	25—Wednesday "
Classes begin	Sept. 6, Mon.	Oct. 9—Thursday "
Exams. begin	Dec. 16, Thurs.	16—Friday "
Semester ends	Dec. 22, Wed.	Nov. 27—Monday "

Holidays

Nov. 25—Thurs.—
　　　　Thanksgiving

Heretofore, we have maintained a semester average of 77 class days, 1 reading day (except in School of Business, 3 days), and 8 examination days.

The new calendar provides either 77 or 78 class days and 6 examination days. The average length of a semester is 15′ calendar weeks. We get the 77 or 78 class days in about 14 weeks by using regular school days and from 6 to 9 designated Saturdays each semester.

Faculty Minutes, May 23, 1940—June 24, 1942, pp. 113, 115, and inserts following.

Document 136

The Cost of War was Indeed Dear

In his second informational letter to Governor Henry F. Schricker, President Wells outlined some of the disturbing economic facts of war. The University was losing personnel, and replacements cost much more. Material costs were not only up, but many materials were becoming hard to obtain. Wells informed the Governor that he and his administration were now forced to use all their powers of persuasion to retain an operating staff.

*　　*　　*

February 23, 1942

The Honorable Henry F. Schricker
Governor of Indiana
Indianapolis, Indiana

Dear Governor Schricker:

By way of report upon a serious problem which is now developing at Indiana University, I should like to give you a few facts concerning the rate of turnover in our non-academic personnel.

Between October 18, 1941 and January 20, 1942 we have lost 104 non-academic employees at the Indianapolis campus out of a total of approximately 710. This represents an annual turnover rate of approximately 60%. According to the best information which we have, these 104 persons received an average increase in salary of nearly 30% in their new positions.

The annual turnover rate on the Bloomington campus is about 30%. We have lost 74 members of our non-academic staff, out of a total of 550, in the period from July 1, 1941 to January 1, 1942. According to our information these persons averaged an even greater increase in salary in their new positions, and in many instances they have doubled their salaries. Many have gone to some Federal agency where the salary range appears to be much higher than ours. A few specific instances will help to describe the situation. A secretary receiving $1300.00 a year here accepted a Government post at a beginning salary of $1620.00, with a raise to $1800.00 in forty-five days and a top salary of $2600.00 if she proved satisfactory within the trial period. A stenographer who was being paid $75.00 a month here accepted a position with an Indiana law firm at $150.00 a month. Another stenographer whom we paid $900.00 accepted Government employment at $1742.00 a year and has since received a raise; a stenographer at $858.00 accepted a $1300.00 a year job, and so on.

I am confident that the rate of turnover on the Bloomington campus soon will begin to accelerate, because of the demand for laborers at nearby Camp Atterbury. Moreover, I think both campuses will be affected in an increasing degree by the demand of the war industries for employees, as soon as that demand really begins to make itself felt in this state.

Naturally, such a situation greatly impairs operating efficiency. We are losing our first-rate employees and are having to replace them with individuals with much less training and experience. As you know, inexperienced stenographers make more mistakes and require longer time in which to write letters; inexperienced laboratory technicians ruin equipment and waste chemicals; second-rate power plant employees not only tend to endanger expensive machinery but also make for waste in coal and electricity; inferior laundry workers ruin uniforms and linens.

We are using all of our powers of persuasion in an attempt to hold our employees. We point out to them the permanency of their positions here as well as other attractive features of the position in each individual case. Such argument has little effect in most instances.

In view of the ever-increasing demand for war workers by industry and by the Federal Government, at rates of pay much higher than we can offer, I am of the opinion that the University's rate of loss will be materially accelerated with a corresponding decline in efficiency of operation.

Very truly yours,

mc   H. B WELLS

Schricker #150, Archives Division, Indiana State Library.

Document 137

*Looking Ahead to the Return of Peace and
an Influx of Students*

Almost from the outset of the Wells administration, the formulation of an active student government was a matter of deep concern. Year after year this debate dragged on largely because it seemed impossible to satisfy important segments of the student body, the administration, and the faculty. In 1944 President Wells could address himself to the problem in terms of reconversion of the University to a peacetime program. This proposed constitutional guarantee reflects the nature of the continuing debate.

*   *   *

Office of the Coordinator

January 27, 1944

TO: President Wells

RE: Statutory bases for student government

Primary authority for establishment of a system of student government is placed in the Trustees of Indiana University. The faculty is charged with the responsibility of enforcing the regulations adopted by the Trustees. The pertinent provisions of the law are as follows:

Burns' Statutes, Sec. 28-5302. The Board of Trustees . . . (shall have power) . . .

(10) to prescribe the course of study and discipline and price of tuition in such University; and,

(11) make all by-laws necessary to carry in effect the power herein conferred.

Burns' Statutes, Sec. 28-5313. The President, professors and instructors, shall be styled "The Faculty" of said University, and shall have power:

First.   To enforce the regulations adopted by the trustees for the government of the students.

Second. To which end they may reward and censure and may suspend those who continue refractory, until the determination of the board of trustees can be had thereon.

INTERPRETATIONS OF PROPOSED CONSTITUTION
APPROVED BY THE FACULTY
Article II
Organization

2. ELECTION

Candidates for the Student Council shall be nominated and members of the Council elected annually at a mass meeting of all students, the election to be supervised by the Registrar of the University. Nominations shall be made from the floor. The mass meeting shall be held the Tuesday of the fourth week before the beginning of final examinations of the Spring semester. Each student present at said mass meeting may vote for not more than eight nominees. His vote shall be so distributed that he votes for not more than two independent women, not more than two independent men, not more than two organized women, and not more than two organized men. There shall be no ex officio members on the Student Council.

Article IV
POWERS

The Student Council shall have the power:

1. to initiate and enact all legislation on extra-curricular matters which concern the entire student body and on all such other matters as are consistent with the stated purpose of the Constitution and agreeable to the President of the University.

4. to recommend to the President faculty members for committees which deal particularly with problems of student affairs.

5. to name student representatives, the number of whom shall be decided by the President of the University, to sit on such faculty committees established by the President as in the opinion of the Student Council directly affect the student body.

Article V
PROCEDURE

All actions of the Student Council must be approved by the President of the University before they become effective.

PROPOSED CONSTITUTION
for
STUDENT SELF-GOVERNMENT

Article I
PURPOSE

We, the students of Indiana University, in order to govern ourselves more effectively, to formulate and enforce rules and regulations concerning the student body, to work with the administrative officials of the University in all affairs that affect the students, and to integrate and co-ordinate the activities of all other existing campus organizations do hereby ordain and establish this Student Council of Indiana University, which is the highest student legislative and judicial organization on the campus responsible only to the President and Board of Trustees of the University.

Article II
ORGANIZATION

1. MEMBERSHIP

The Student Council shall consist of twelve students; three organized men, three organized women, three independent men, and three independent women. All officers of the Student Council shall be elected by the said Council and from the membership of the Council and shall have only such duties and power as the Council may see fit to vest in them from time to time.

2. ELECTION

Candidates for the Student Council shall be nominated and members of the Council elected annually at a mass meeting of all students. Nominations shall be made from the floor. The mass meeting shall be held the Tuesday of the fourth week before the beginning of final examinations of the Spring semester. Each student present at said mass meeting may vote for not more than eight nominees. His vote shall be so distributed that he votes for not more than two independent women, not more than two independent men, not more than two organized women, and not more than two organized men. There shall be no ex officio members on the Student Council.

3. VACANCIES

Any vacancy that occurs on the Council shall be filled by the candidate of the group represented by the one whose position is vacant who in the previous election polled the next highest number of votes. If a member of the Council changes from the independent group to the organized group or vice versa he loses his position on the Council.

Article III
MEETINGS

The first meeting of the Student Council shall be called by the chairman of the preceding Student Council; and thereafter the Council shall meet at least twice a month and at such other times as it may deem necessary. The chairman of the Council shall call all the extraordinary meetings and shall notify the other members of the Council beforehand about them. A quorum shall be enough to transact all business except amendments to the Constitution.

Article IV
POWERS

The Student Council shall have the power:

1. to initiate and enact all legislation on extra-curricular matters which concern the entire student body and on all such other matters as are consistent with the stated purpose of the Constitution and agreeable to the President of the University.
2. to represent the student body on all questions concerning it.
3. to co-ordinate and integrate the activities of all other existing student governing bodies.
4. to recommend to the President faculty members for committees which deal particularly with problems of student affairs.
5. to name student representatives to sit on such faculty committees established by the President as in the opinion of the Student Council directly affect the student body.

Article V
PROCEDURE

All actions of student council must be approved by the President of the University before they become effective.

Article VI
ENFORCEMENT OF REGULATIONS

The Student Council shall organize a body to serve as the enforcer of its rules and regulations and to punish all violators thereof.

Article VII
AMENDMENTS

An amendment to this Constitution may be made by a two-thirds majority vote of all members of the Council and with the approval of the President of the University.

GENERAL FACULTY MEETING
INDIANA UNIVERSITY

February 10, 1944

The Faculty of the University met on Thursday, February 10, 1944, in the Social Sciences Auditorium. President Wells called the meeting to order at 4:10 p.m.

The secretary read the minutes of the meeting of October 28, 1943. The minutes were approved as read.

President Wells called for the presentation of lists of candidates for degrees in December, 1943. The Faculty voted to recommend to the Board of Trustees the candidates from the College of Arts and Sciences, the Graduate School, the

Schools of Education, Business, Law, Music, and Medicine. There were no candidates for degrees from the School of Dentistry.

At Dean Briscoe's suggestion, President Wells presented a report, previously given to the Board of Trustees, of the work of the University in this war period. Our previous high enrollment figure had been 6486, in the fall of 1940–41. In September 1943–44 it was 6583. The respective figures for January 1941 and January 1944 were 5855 and 6059. In terms of credit hours taught, the figure for the regular year 1940–41 was 163,500 and that for 1943–44 will be approximately 262,270.

The problem of securing and maintaining a staff of high quality for this greatly increased effort has been great. Many faculty members have been drafted and many have enlisted, and others are engaged in non-military vital war work. Excellent reports have been received on the activities of these men and women on leave. Sixty-two members of the faculty are on leave from the Bloomington campus. Sixty-nine are on leave from the School of Medicine. Ten faculty members of the School of Dentistry have left to join the armed services. Forty-six of the non-academic staff on the Bloomington campus are on leave.

In order to carry on the increased task of the University one hundred and fifty-seven individuals have been added to the teaching staff. In addition nineteen individuals have taken on teaching duties in a field new to them. This retraining has been made possible by a reduction in the number of courses and sections offered in schools and departments where a decline in enrollment occurred. Comparing the offerings in the fall of 1941 with those in the fall of 1943, it is noted that courses were reduced from 501 to 431 and that courses and sections together were reduced from 883 to 604.

As a part of our war time program a few new courses were added; many, naturally, were changed in their orientation.

Special and secret government research projects have been carried on in three departments; contracts for this work total $146,000.

The housing and boarding situation is also characterized by a tremendous change. While in the first semester of 1941–42 the University furnished board and room to 936 and room to 144 additional, in the first semester of 1943–44, it furnished board and room to 3,612 and room to 58 additional. The dollar volume of business in the Commons this year will be double that of the fiscal year 1941–42.

Other war time activities of the University include the teaching of ESMWT courses throughout the state, which gave instruction to 2300 individuals last fall; special services to the public schools of the state; industrial personnel work and research under the direction of Mr. Yeager; and the work on the War History Commission of the state.

President Wells also paid tribute to the fine spirit and energy of the faculty in retraining for other teaching, for revamping course materials, for year-'round teaching loads, for complete or partial shift from teaching to administrative duties; he also commended the non-academic, business, and general administrative staffs for the way they have carried out new and increased responsibilities. He expressed his happiness over the excellent relations the University was enjoying with the Navy staff assigned here and with Colonel Shoemaker and his staff.

President Wells then discussed briefly the problems of reconversion facing the University. New demands of a complex student body and of society would have to be met. Without doubt, four years of education or training, on any level for which the student is fitted, would be made available to ex-service personnel. Greatly increased numbers would be only a part of our problem; the current experiences of these students would necessitate a great deal of individual attention and guidance.

. . . .

Dean Thornbury, chairman of the Student Affairs Committee, presented the Proposed Constitution for Student Self-Government to the Faculty. That Committee, having agreed with the provisional Student Council on the interpretation of Articles IV and V, recommends the Constitution as so interpreted, to the Faculty. President Wells pointed out that the Board of Trustees was responsible for student activities and conduct, but that it would naturally wish the approval of the Faculty for any change in the policy of administration.

Professor Artin asked what besides social affairs might be involved in measures proposed by the Student Council. Dean Thornbury explained that the constitution would probably make possible student representation on committees charged with discipline, convocations, class schedules, examination schedules, the calendar, the auditorium series, and perhaps others.

Professor Willis pointed out the close relationship between curricular and extra-curricular activities, and wondered whether the faculty would have any power at all over extra-curricular activities.

Professor Benns questioned the wisdom of the Constitution in permitting an amendment to the Constitution by a two-thirds majority vote of all the members of the Student Council.

Professor Larson, replying to Professor Willis' question, stated that Article V answered Professor Willis' question on faculty power over extra-curricular affairs.

Professor Willis asserted that Article V gave no legislative power to the Faculty; it merely gave to the President veto power over legislation enacted by the Student Council.

Professor Patty wondered what the definition of extra-curricular activity might be, since in some institutions the student body had considerable control over intercollegiate athletics.

Professor Switzer, referring to Article III, asked what constituted a quorum. Dean Thornbury stated that according to Roberts' "Rules of Order", a quorum was a majority unless specifically stated otherwise.

Professor Stempel stated his approval of the proposed Constitution, pointing out that it, as a constitution, was only the general framework within which student government could develop. The proposal was a great step forward in that the provision of a Student Council was a distinct improvement over the arrangement by which four bodies, the A. W. S., Mortar Board, Board of Aeons, and Union Board—, dealt separately with student activities.

Professor Strayer suggested that, if in Article IV, Section 1, the fifth word, "all", be eliminated, then all objection to the proposed Constitution would be removed.

Dean Gavit stated his full agreement with Professor Stempel's remarks. He pointed out also that even though the Board of Trustees approved this Constitution, it could at any time recall this delegation of power to the students.

Professor Benns asked what the Faculty was being asked to vote upon, pointing out that it had no right to make an amendment to the Constitution.

Dean Hall pointed out that the Faculty can accept the Constitution as interpreted and that the student body would then vote on these interpretations at the same time it elects officers.

Professor Morgan asked four questions: One, why disturb the present machinery for dealing with student activities? Two, why are freshmen not as much concerned in this matter of student self-government as upperclassmen? Three, what else will members of the Student Council have time to do, if they carry out all the duties prescribed and allowed them? Fourth, will it not make a great deal more work for the President?

President Wells assured Professor Morgan that he would delegate a large part of the repsonsibilities placed upon him by the proposed Constitution.

Professor Stempel pointed out that many of the responsibilities and duties would be taken care of as at present. He said that, after all, this was just the Constitution, in the framework of which a body of By-Laws would in time be enacted.

President Wells suggested that the Faculty again meet at 4:00 p.m. Tuesday, February 15, to continue the study of the proposed Constitution, providing that the Faculty By-Laws did not necessitate a longer interval between meetings.

The Faculty adjourned at 5:25 p.m.

> Respectfully submitted,
> ROBERT T. ITTNER
> Secretary

GENERAL FACULTY MEETING
INDIANA UNIVERSITY

February 15, 1944

The Faculty of the University met on Tuesday, February 15, 1944, in the Social Sciences Auditorium. President Wells called the meeting to order at 4:05 p.m.

The secretary read the minutes of the meeting of February 10, 1944. The minutes were approved as read.

Dean Thornbury moved the approval by the Faculty of the Proposed Constitution for Student Self-Government as interpreted. Mr. Janssen seconded the motion.

Professor Williams asked whether student representatives on University committees would have the right to vote. There was considerable discussion which led to another point, the power of the Student Council. With regard to this point, Professor Davis moved that Article V be interpreted to read: "All actions of the Student Council must be approved by the President of the University before they become effective." Motion seconded by Professor Kime. Motion passed.

Discussion on Professor Williams' question was resumed. He moved that Article IV, section 5, be clarified by the addition of the sentence: "Such representatives shall not have the power to vote." Seconded by Professor Davidson. There was further discussion. Professor Williams with the consent of Professor Davidson withdrew his motion. Professor Williams then moved that Article IV, section 5, be clarified by the change "to name a student representative." Professor Kime seconded the motion. Professor Edmondson moved an amendment to Professor Williams' motion so that this section would read: "to name student representatives, the number of whom shall be decided by the President of the University, to sit on such faculty committees—etc." Seconded by Professor Davidson. Amendment passed. Motion as amended passed.

Professor Hennel asked for a report on the meeting, held earlier in the day, of the Student Affairs Committee and any students opposed to the proposed Constitution. Dean Thornbury reported that the protests were based on objections to certain details, not to the idea of Student self-government. Dean Mueller added that some students felt the provisions of the Constitution were not clear.

President Wells pointed out that changes in the Constitution could be made fairly easily. He assumed that candidates for membership on the Student Council would run on platforms advocating certain specific changes and clarifications of the Constitution. He added, in response to a question by Professor Benns, that the students wanted the elections supervised by the Registrar's Office.

Professor Kime moved the clarification of Article II, section 2, by the addition to the first sentence of: "the election to be supervised by the Registrar of the University". Professor Field seconded the motion. Passed.

There was further general discussion. In response to a question from Professor Field, President Wells stated his belief in the principle of student self-government, largely because of its value as an educational influence for later responsibilities. He felt this was the proper time to begin the procedure because so many students wanted it, and he felt the system might help greatly in solving post-war student problems.

After further general discussion there was call for the question. Motion was passed unanimously.

Dean Gavit reported that 35 A. S. T. cadets in Term III of the Basic Phase had just been called out. The Army regarded them as graduates of Basic Phase. He moved that the University grant full term credit in a subject to any cadet called out for reassignment, if he has a passing grade, and if he has completed at least eight weeks of the work of the term. This is in line with our practice with civilian students called to service. Motion seconded.

On another matter, Dean Gavit pointed out that present Army regulations prevented the graduation of a cadet with a grade of "F" on his record. Some cadets have very good general records even though they have failed in a course. Dean Gavit moved that the Faculty authorize the various departments to grant a cadet in the A. S. T. P. who has a failure but who nevertheless has a sufficiently good record to be promoted the opportunity to take a special examination in that subject, and that if he passes the examination the Registrar be authorized to change the record. Motion seconded.

The Faculty adjourned at 5:40 p.m.

Respectfully submitted,
ROBERT T. ITTNER, Secretary

Faculty Minutes, 1942–45, pp. 152–153, 154–156, 157–158.

Document 138

The Roaring Herd of GI's

Almost instantly, Indiana University, like every other university in the land, had to shift directions in its programs. Not only did it have to redirect its programs to peacetime operations, but several new dimensions had been added to higher education: the return of the veterans, the enormous changes which had come about in American society in the past four years, and the necessity to revive Indiana's general program of catching-up. There was clear recognition of the fact that certain unusual conditions had to be met to serve the GI's. There was debate how best to meet the demands—even including consideration of instituting a special veteran's program.

*   *   *

PROPOSED ORGANIZATION OF THE VETERANS PROGRAM AT INDIANA UNIVERSITY

Ex-servicemen enrolling in the University during the next few years will present peculiar problems which the University should be prepared to handle adequately. Such problems will involve admission, the evaluation of credits and of special training, refresher courses, programing and special curricula, etc. Three possible modes of action suggest themselves. These are (1) to set up no new organization; (2) to establish a new division of the University, co-ordinate with existing divisions and colleges; (3) to establish a temporary organization administered by an all-university committee chosen in such a way as to represent the various subdivisions of the University concerned with the veterans' problems.

I. The first possibility would require no special organization and would force the individual schools or divisions to work out their plans for returning veterans in their own way. We consider this possibility to be definitely undesirable for the following reasons:

(a) It would probably result in a chaotic condition in which different schools might adopt different policies in relation to the various aspects of the Veterans' problem.

(b) It would not make evident the University's concern for the special problems of returning veterans.

(c) It would be difficult to establish satisfactory University liaison relations with the government agency in charge of Veterans' affairs.

II. The second possibility is the one adopted by certain other universities such as Illinois and Yale, namely, the establishment of a new and separate division of the University coordinate with existing colleges and empowered to confer degrees. We consider this possibility to be also undesirable for the following reasons:

It would deprive existing schools and divisions of the University of control over the programs of the ex-servicemen who would be enrolled in their classes. Veterans whose programs were aberrant would register in the new division rather than in one of the colleges and would work for its degree or degrees, although they would attend classes listed in the various schools of the University.

Furthermore, there is danger that such a new division might be more difficult to eliminate than to initiate.

III. The third possibility is the establishment of an Office of Veterans' Affairs to be supervised by an all-university committee. This office would work with existing colleges and divisions in an endeavor to coordinate the program for returning veterans and provide for their needs so far as feasible.

The features of this organization as suggested are listed below.

1. Organized for a limited period under the Dean of the Faculties (and responsible through him to President).

2. *Suggested composition of committee.*

(a) A representative of each of the undergraduate schools or divisions: *College of Arts & Sciences, School of Business, School of Education, School of Music, Junior Division.*

In the case of certain schools, this representative might well be the Dean himself. In other cases the Dean might not be able to give sufficient time to the work of the committee and might prefer to delegate authority to some other person. In this event, the Dean would nominate the representative of his division subject to the approval of the President. In any case, the representative should have the power to act in behalf of the school or divisions which he represents.

(b) Director of Admissions.

(c) Dean of Men and Dean of Women.

(d) Head of Extension Division.

(e) Director, who shall act as chairman of the committee, appointed for a limited period by the President.

3. *Duties of the Committee*

(a) To formulate procedure and policies subject to approval of the President, or (on occasion) the General Faculty.

(b) To administer the various aspects of the program for ex-servicemen as follows:

    i. Evaluate and transfer credits from other institutions, credits for military service, and credits for courses of the Armed Forces Institute and for special training received in military service; supervise examinations where these are necessary to make possible such evaluation; determine special admission to the University.

    ii. Aid in providing for housing and satisfactory living conditions.

    iii. Provide preliminary guidance service to determine type of academic program needed.

    iv. Administer placement examinations.

    v. Furnish guidance in order to work out a satisfactory program with the student, and secure the cooperation of the schools concerned in the acceptance of this program, when proposed programs cut across college boundary lines or do not fall within the province of a single college or division, or when the individual wishes to enroll as a special student or to pursue special or unusual terminal or refresher programs. The Committee will insist that all such programs shall be logical and justifiable from the educational point of view and that no concessions shall be made which will in any way lower the standards of the various schools or divisions. In return it will expect from the various schools every reasonable effort to provide for the specialized needs of returning ex-service men.

    vi. Where programs seem to be normal, to refer students for detailed advice and guidance to the proper college or division.

    It is anticipated that the great majority will wish to follow more or less conventional programs. It will be an important function of the committee, however, to serve the small minority who will wish to pursue special programs, and to work out the needs of these individuals according to a uniform, university-wide plan and policy. It is visualized that all students, no matter how irregular their programs, will be from the first enrolled in one of the existing divisions of the University, either as regular students, or if their programs are sufficiently irregular, as special students.

    vii. Maintain personal relations with all veterans enrolled in the University. Keep them informed of all developments within and without the University which will be of concern to them and thereby serve as the successor to the Office of Military Information.

viii. Act as liaison between students and the government agency dealing with Veterans' Affairs.

It is suggested that the Committee as a whole might function largely as a policy-making body but that for administrative purposes it might be subdivided into subcommittees. Thus, there might be a subcommittee on special programs, to be known as the Committee on Special Programs, composed perhaps of those members of the committee who represent the respective colleges or divisions together with the Director. This Committee might function in behalf not only of veterans but also of other students who have specialized needs. Similarly most of the work of evaluation of credits might be performed by the Director of the Office of Veterans' Affairs and the Director of Admissions, acting within a framework developed by the committee as a whole. These and other administrative details could probably be left to the committee itself to work out.

The Committee would probably wish to have attached to its office a few part-time counselors, chosen possibly from ex-service men on the faculty, who would specialize in their guidance work on the problems of veterans.

The proposed plan is similar to that adopted by Ohio State University, the chief difference being that the ex-servicemen would enroll from the start in some school or division of the University rather than in a new special division.

The plan proposed above has certain important advantages.

(a) It recognizes the University's special responsibilities to ex-servicemen.

(b) It is a simple and relatively inexpensive form of organization, easy to set up and easy to terminate.

(c) It should ensure a unified and coordinated program for the veteran, making maximum use of existing facilities throughout the entire University.

(d) Existing colleges and divisions will not be deprived of a full share in administering the veterans' program, since (1) the Committee will include representatives of each of the undergraduate schools and divisions, (2) all students desiring more or less normal programs will be turned over to the individual divisions for guidance, and (3) all students will be enrolled in one of the existing divisions. The Committee will furnish the machinery which will ensure joint action on the part of the schools and divisions in behalf of the veterans. It will not take the handling of these problems out of the hands of the divisions, but will ensure that they will work together in a coordinated fashion.

For the above reasons, we advocate the establishment of an Office of Veteran's Affairs as outlined above. The success of this type of organization will depend upon securing a pledge from the administrations of existing colleges and divisions to work with it in a spirit of wholehearted cooperation. The only alternative which the Post War Planning Committee could recommend would be the establishment of a separate division in which veterans would be enrolled who could not fit successfully into one of the existing colleges or divisions.

Dean Wright moved the adoption of the plan for recommendation to the Board, seconded by Prof. Lewis, passed, without dissenting vote, on March 21, 1944.

The following amendment was moved by Prof. Benns, seconded by Prof. Locke and passed by the faculty:

"Nothing in the plan shall deprive the individual school or college of the right to formulate entrance requirements and conditions for the granting of degrees."

Faculty Minutes, 1942–45, following p. 164.

Document 139

Indiana University's Naval School

Indiana University had done well indeed with its special services programs, and President Wells wanted Governor Schricker to know about it. The University had consistently ranked at the top of the Navy's 200 specialists college programs.

*   *   *

May 26, 1944

The Honorable Henry F. Schricker
Governor, State of Indiana
State House
Indianapolis, Indiana
Dear Governor Schricker:

We at Indiana University wish you as a state official to have a share in the pride which we have in the accomplishments and record of the United States Naval Training School established at the University nearly two years ago by the Navy Department.

This School, one of many contributions made by your University to the war effort, was commissioned in June, 1942, one of the first special training programs instituted by the Navy at any college or university. It was established for and has continued to give training in the business branch of the naval service, the Navy Department thereby recognizing the high standing of the University's School of Business.

The Indiana University Naval School has been one of relatively few training programs in which the instruction has been given by and under the direction of the educational institution. To provide this instruction the University used so far as possible members of its own staff and brought in experts in the fields covered by the training program.

The nearly two years of operation of the School has given the University the privilege of training for the Navy Department 5,008 yeomen and storekeepers, both women and men, for service in the Navy, Coast Guard and Marine Corps. These men and women now are serving in naval establishments and stations throughout the world with honor to the School.

Now that the training needs of the Navy have diminished the specialized schools throughout the country are being de-commissioned. The Indiana School is one of these and its last class is being graduated on May 29th. This we, naturally, regret but we have a feeling, which we hope you share, that we have done a good job. In support of this feeling, we have the statement of the Navy Department that the Indiana School has consistently ranked at the top of the list of the 200 specialized schools operated by the Navy, by the fact that its graduates have been eagerly sought by the Navy's stations, and by the testimony of the trainees themselves. It is our belief that a number of the men and women who were graduated from the School will return after the war to obtain training at the University.

In order that you may be informed as to the type of instruction given at the School, we are sending to you herewith a booklet on the storekeeping courses which recently was published jointly by the Navy and the University.

Cordially,
H. B WELLS
President

Schricker, #150, Archives Division, Indiana State Library.

Document 140

War on the "Soft" American Youth

The Indiana University War Council responded to the charges that American youth had grown soft. It proposed a rather extensive revision of the university calendar with special emphasis upon the physical fitness curriculum. As indicated in "Section 4," there was not unanimous approval of this spartan suggestion.

*   *   *

The following material is being sent members of the faculty, in accordance with the request made at the March 7, 1945, meeting.

ROBERT T. ITTNER
Secretary

The Administrative War Council recommends to the faculty and the Board of Trustees a calendar based on the considerations stated below. The date on which the calendar is to be put into effect is to be determined by the Board of Trustees.

1. The academic calendar is to be based upon two normal semesters and a summer session nine weeks in length.
2. Students will register for the fall semester late in September, usually around September 25.
3. There are to be three weeks of classes between the end of Christmas vacation and the beginning of the first semester's final examination period.
4. The second semester will end about June 12.
5. The summer session will be held from about June 20 to about August 15. (If needed, a special session of 3, 4, or 5 weeks can be arranged between the end of the Summer Session and the beginning of the Fall Semester.)

The Administrative War Council recommends to the faculty and the Board of Trustees the following program and requirements of physical fitness:

I. All students at Indiana University unless prohibited by the University Physician or exempted by the Dean of the Faculties because of age, because they are part-time students, or because of other reasons deemed sufficient by the Dean, shall be required to take physical education two hours per week, during their Freshman, Sophomore, Junior, and Senior years.

II. The kind of physical education required shall be dependent upon their physical needs. Provision should be made for three classes of students:
   A. Those who are organically sound shall be required to take such work as shall be prescribed by the Department of Physical Education. (The

committee strongly recommends that as much emphasis as possible be placed on recreational aspects of physical education, especially during the sophomore, junior, and senior years, and that every effort be made by the Departments of Physical Education to widen the scope and variety of the recreational activity available to students taking required physical education.)

B. Those who, although organically sound, are in need of physical development shall be required to take a program much like the present developmental program.

C. Those who have some physical or organic disability but who are recommended by the University Physician to take some physical exercise, shall be required to take such work as shall be prescribed by the University Physician after consultation with the Department of Physical Education.

III. Upon admission to Indiana University, all students shall be given physical examinations by the University Physician. Thereafter, all undergraduate students shall be given annual physical examinations.

IV. All students unless they have been exempted by the Dean of the Faculties, shall be required for graduation to have completed one credit in physical education for each semester of full-time residence on the Bloomington campus over and above the 120 hours required for graduation.

Minority Report of the Postwar Planning Committee to the Administrative War Council.

The report deals with the topic of student health, and I shall therefore include recommendations concerning health in addition to those concerning physical education. The following recommendations apply equally to men and to women.

I. The University should make fuller provision of medical care for students.

II. There should be instituted a required course in hygiene which treats of human physiology and gives a little elementary information in the fields of diagnosis and pathology. To eliminate the factors which have vitiated such courses in the past, three requirements must be met.

A. The courses should be given by instructors whose primary interest is the teaching of physiology and hygiene, rather than by the staff of the University Medical Center.

B. The students should receive academic credit for the course, possibly in the field of biological science.

C. The examinations should be administered like those in other courses, so that students who shirk the work fail the courses, and those who apply themselves receive commensurate recognition.

III. There should be an annual physical examination of every undergraduate student. This should be the basis for medical treatment and also for the classification of students described in IV.

IV. For the purposes of physical education, students shall be divided into three groups.

A. Those, who because of the precarious nature of their health, are forbidden to take part in officially sponsored exercise.

B. Those who have some physical deficiency which will respond to corrective exercise. These will be required to take prescribed exercise until the conditioned disappears.

C. The largest group, the students of normal health and physical development. The University should provide recreational facilities for these students, but not oblige them to take supervised exercise. I am opposed to a program of required exercise for these students for several reasons.

1. In most cases, it would merely displace recreational exercise which the students spontaneously engage in, and would not increase the total period of exercise. This is probably more true of men than women.

2. In the case of students for whom the required exercises would be an added activity, I doubt that it would have a significant effect on their health. I believe that college boys and girls are in such a state of physical vigor that two or three hours of exercise a week would effect no appreciable improvement.

3. Exercise cannot be stored. An advantage gained will be lost when the exercise ceases. A program of exercise, therefore, will not have a significant effect on the health of the student after he leaves school.

4. The proposal of the majority deviates from the established policy of the University. We content ourselves with minimum standards of intellectual development, but the program of the majority sets optimum standards of physical development. I propose that we fix in the field of health the minimum standards of normal health and physical development.

5. The proposal of the Committee will involve a considerable expansion of the physical facilities and staff of the University, an expense which will in my opinion bring very meagre returns.

6. I do not believe that competitive games instill the moral values sometimes attributed to them.

7. It is not my observation that the physical training program for women teaches grace and poise, as it is sometimes said to do. These objectives, if valid, should be separated from the problem of health, and attacked directly.

Faculty Minutes, 1942–45, following p. 176.

Document 141

More Spartan Spirit

The faculty adopted the physical fitness program by a considerable majority, but there was sharp disagreement as to whether it would work when the University attempted to implement it.

*   *   *

GENERAL FACULTY MEETING
INDIANA UNIVERSITY

March 27, 1945

The Faculty of the University met on Tuesday, March 27, 1945, in the auditorium of the Social Sciences Building. President Wells called the meeting to order at 4:05 p.m.

The Secretary read the minutes of the meeting of March 22, 1945, and they were approved as read.

Professor Ford Hall moved the adoption of the Administrative War Council's recommendations on the future physical education program, and added that his motion included the provision that the program go into effect September, 1945. Motion was seconded. He stated that the recommendations were, in part at least, motivated by the feeling that the present program should be reduced, by the hope that students would carry on after graduation some of the habits formed through the program, and by the desirability of having the students take an annual physical examination.

Dean Payne felt that the Dean of the Faculties was too busy to pass on the applications for being excused, and he also pointed out that these recommendations involved the only requirement for graduation imposed on the various schools of the University. Professor Hall stated that it was assumed that the Dean of the Faculties would delegate his authority, so as to relieve himself of the routine work involved.

Dr. Edith Schuman reviewed briefly the work of the Student Health Center, as partial background for her support of the recommendations, and added that the students who would be benefitted most by the requirement were the ones who would not take part in a voluntary program.

Professor Silverstein asked whether there was any evidence that the physical education program was beneficial to health. Professor Harmon stated that in his view young people came to the University to be students and that he doubted the value of such a program as a means to helping them as students. He added, however, that there was no evidence on the other side.

Professor Christenson moved the adoption of a substitute motion, which was seconded:

I move the adoption of the following resolution by the General Faculty of Indiana University for transmission to the Board of Trustees:

Resolved that:

1. All entering students at Indiana University shall be given a physical examination by the University Physician. Thereafter all students shall be encouraged to have an annual physical examination which shall be provided by the University Health Service without payment of special fee. Recommendations for proper therapeutic treatment should, of course, be made on the basis of these examinations.

2. Effective September 1945, or as soon thereafter as is practicable, the entire program of physical education for professional, graduate, and undergraduate students at Indiana University shall be placed on an elective basis.

3. The Faculty looks with favor upon the evolution of a genuine recreational program on an elective basis which shall include broad offerings of intramural sports, training in various recreational skills, hobbies and handcrafts, as well as physical education in the more traditional sense.

4. Credit for any and all phases of this program shall be left to the determination of the faculties of the individual schools of the University.

Professor Patty pointed out that college students were not normal persons as far as the period of their physical development was concerned. While physical activity might or might not be beneficial to older persons, our students were at the immediately post-adolescent age and would be benefitted by the recommended program.

Dr. Dane corrected an earlier statement to the effect that the outlined program would involve much more than two hours a week, by stating that actually the student spent only 32 minutes of his assigned time at physical activity and that remainder of the hour was taken up by changing clothes and bathing.

Professor Horack felt that our principal objective was academic training and stated that the proposed program gave physical education precedence over all the rest of the student's program.

Professor Clevenger pointed out that the present staff for men's physical education could take care of from two to three times as many men as were at present enrolled. He also pointed out that these two major wars have shown the low physical health of our young men. He stated that in colleges where intramural programs were purely voluntary, there was less than 50% participation.

Professor Mathers felt that students spent too much time on physical education and stated, in answer to Professor Clevenger's remarks, that the war was being won primarily by scientists. He also stated that there would be a required military program in colleges after the war.

Dr. Schuman said that her conception of health had various aspects—mental and social, as well as physical, and that participation in recreational sports would benefit in all these respects.

Mr. Dane gave the results of a questionnaire sent to 70 state-supported colleges and universities. Of these, about 21% reported that their postwar plans for physical education had not been determined, 14% were planning a smaller program than the present, 35% the same, and 28% more.

Miss Munro stated that the present program for women had increased intramural participation greatly. Mr. Schlafer reported that intra-mural participation by eligible men had increased from 30% to 80% since the adoption of the four year physical fitness program.

Question was called for on the substitute motion. It was passed, 95-66.

The meeting recessed at 5:30 p.m.

> Respectfully submitted,
> ROBERT T. ITTNER
> Secretary

Faculty Minutes, 1942–45, pp. 179–181.

Document 142

A Year of Triumph—a Future of Challenge

The Presidents' report to the faculty reviewed Indiana University's accomplishments in four trying years of its history, but more particularly the accomplishments of the immediately previous year. By October 1944, Wells could clearly see that an even bigger challenge awaited the institution. The time had come for consideration in depth of the University's future.

*   *   *

REMARKS AT THE GENERAL FACULTY MEETING
Social Science Auditorium   October 10, 1944

Our first faculty meeting of the year has traditionally been a time of review of the past year and discussion of some of the problems of the year ahead.

The Past Year
The past year has been one of the most interesting in the University's history. We have reason to be proud of our accomplishments. More students were

taught in a greater variety and complexity of subject matter than ever before in our history. Significant research programs for the Federal government were conducted. Students were fitted for specific assignments in the armed services, and at the same time provision was made for the continuance by civilian students of a normal academic program, though at an accelerated rate. Specifically, we taught during the past fiscal year in all divisions of the University 28 per cent more student credit hours than in 1938–39, our previous high.

The most interesting aspect of the year was the teaching assignment for the Army. This assignment was not easy. Many adjustments were required in existing subject-matter fields, and it was necessary, as we all know, to develop entire new courses in order to meet the needs of the Area and Language students. Nevertheless, our teaching efforts were successful. Those in authority in the Army have been generous in their praise of our Area and Language program.

Our record in the A. S. T. basic program is likewise impressive. In February of this year, shortly before the basic Army Specialized Training Program was discontinued, standardized achievement tests were administered to the cadets of all 48 training units throughout the country. At Indiana University 1465 cadets took these examinations, in physics, mathematics, chemistry, English, history, geography, and engineering drawing. The results have been compiled and compared with the scores made by the cadets on the Army General Classification Test administered to the cadets as they entered the Army. Although the specific figures are "restricted" and so cannot be published, it is possible for me to report that our AST students achieved results about 25% higher than was expected, on the basis of the classification tests. Such results could not have been attained without the skillful and unselfish efforts of the members of our teaching staff. Many persons taught especially heavy schedules, shifted from their own fields of specialization to other fields, or assumed new administrative or other duties growing out of these wartime programs.

I wish to mention specifically the problem faced by our Medical and Dental Schools. Many members of their faculties are in the armed forces. Notwithstanding this fact, both Schools have managed to maintain capacity operation of high quality. Much of the teaching in these Schools is done by active practitioners, and those men, as we all know, have been overworked in their private practices because of the shortage of physicians and dentists. Yet, they have been scrupulous in the discharge of their teaching duties.

The activities of the past year give renewed evidence of the superior quality and devotion of the members of our staff in all of the divisions of the University.

The Year Ahead

The year ahead promises to be less arduous so far as student load is concerned in all divisions except Medicine and Dentistry. Our enrollment as of the beginning of the fall term in all divisions of the University was 4356. This relief should enable the members of the faculty to resume research projects, some of which have had to be deferred, and still to have considerable time for the rather arduous task of making plans for conversion to peacetime operation.

The problems of conversion will not be easy. Note that I have used the term conversion rather than reconversion, for I believe conversion is the better word for changes in the University program. We do not necessarily need to go back to what we had before. The postwar period may demand considerably more than we have done in the past.

You have all received a copy of a resolution recently adopted by the Board of Trustees evidencing an active interest in and pledging support for the postwar program. This resolution took cognizance of the necessity to plan in the fields of plant, recruitment of staff, and curricula. It urged early reports by all faculty committees concerned with these matters.

Our two major all-University postwar planning committees have been making progress. These committees are headed by Mr. Biddle and Mr. Hall. Mr. Biddle's committee is concerned with the problems of postwar building and the self-supporting enterprises. This committee has already prepared a preliminary report which was considered by the State Budget Committee in the course of its special postwar building tour during August. At the time of the Budget Committee's visit we were not far enough advanced to be able to indicate any order of priority. The order of priority for these buildings on the Bloomington campus is now receiving the consideration of the Administrative Council. A committee of the Medical School faculty has already made a recommendation for the Medical School. The members of the Board of Trustees will, of course, have to make the final decision as to priority in light of the requirements of all divisions of the University and of other factors.

Building Needs

The need for new buildings has been determined in the most democratic fashion. All divisions and departments were asked by Mr. Biddle's committee to submit their requests to Mr. Rice, the co-ordinator of postwar building. The information thus collected has been adjusted to the estimate of our postwar enrollment.

A large amount of new construction is needed on the Indianapolis campus to provide for a variety of new services. Increased facilities for training in psychiatry, for postgraduate teaching of physicians and dentists, for retraining physicians and dentists who have been in the service for a number of years, and for laboratory facilities for the expansion of research, illustrate the types of new programs for which space is required.

On the Bloomington campus we were already short of space prior to the war—a shortage which will become acute soon after the close of the war, when veterans and others whose education has been interrupted begin to return. Experience has proven, and administrators generally recognize, that not less than 225 square feet of space per student, excluding living quarters, is required for satisfactory work on a campus of the Bloomington type. Such a figure is of course far below that used by the richer institutions and so represents only the acceptable minimum, not a desirable figure. The Army, accustomed to the most efficient utilization of space, adopted the 225 square foot standard in securing facilities satisfactory for the A. S. T. P.

In 1917, on the Bloomington campus, we had 219 square feet per student. In 1918, because of the wartime decline in enrollment, we had 265; but in the very next year we again had only 218 square feet available—less than the acceptable minimum. Since 1919 we have never come up to the figure of 225, despite the building program of the 1930s. In 1927 we reached the low of 133 square feet per student. In 1937, after we had nearly doubled our floor space compared with 1917, we still had only 159 square feet per student. During the past year we had but 192, despite a further increase over 1937 of about 25 per cent in total floor space. In a few words the situation is this: in the past twenty-seven years the number of square feet of floor space per students has declined from 219 in 1917 to 192 in 1943.

A special committee consisting of Mr. Bartley, Mr. Cookson, Mr. Elliott, Mr.

Starr, and Mr. Wright has estimated our postwar enrollment on the Bloomington campus as follows:

Year	Freshmen	Sophomores	Juniors	Seniors	Graduate Students	Total
1945–46	4026	1400	900	855	359	7539
1946–47	3000	3006	1380	998	420	8798
1947–48	2500	2210	2786	1406	580	9482
1948–49	1600	1625	1938	2639	1108	8810
1949–50	1750	1040	1995	2862	1202	8849

If this enrollment materializes, I think we all know without any statistics that it will be impossible to accommodate any such number of students in our present buildings. We must either have additional structures or turn away large numbers of students, including veterans.

It has ben estimated that approximately one million square feet of space, exclusive of housing, will be needed to accommodate the expected student enrollment on the Bloomington campus. As we build for space, careful planning does make it possible, of course, to meet unsatisfied needs for specialized facilities. Such unsatisfied needs will have all been incorporated in the program. Housing for students, single and married, is acutely needed on both campuses. This problem is receiving careful and active consideration.

But all space needs are not confined to the Bloomington and Indianapolis campuses. Our Extension system is destined to have a rapid development in the postwar period as the adult education movement increases. Consequently, the needs of our Extension Centers must be met. A new building in Indianapolis and additions in East Chicago and Fort Wayne are immediate requirements.

Personnel Problems

The resolution of the Board of Trustees to which I have already referred mentions our need for staff in the postwar period. Many department heads and several of the deans are actively considering this matter. A number of deanship vacancies exist in the Arts College, and Dean Payne has been especially active in finding prospects for those positions. In recent weeks, Dean Briscoe and I have spent a substantial portion of our time in a study of personnel problems. We have devoted careful thought to the Arts College deanship and to the other deanships which must be filled in the course of the next few years. In some quarters there are near-hysterical predictions as to staff shortages in the immediate postwar period. None can deny that there will probably be a keen demand for staff following the war, but personnally I do not believe the most extreme predictions are justified. Enormous numbers of trained teachers are now in government or military service. Notwithstanding careful paper plans for gradual demobilization, I predict that when the war is over, demobilization will become precipitant and the number of good men then looking for jobs will be large.

The Postwar Calendar

The Postwar Planning Committee, headed by Mr. Hall and until recently headed by Mr. Wright, has been studying many curricular and academic aspects of postwar operation. Special attention has been given to the needs of veterans and only recently, as you are aware, the Committee has recommended a postwar calendar. Our present accelerated calendar is the very heart of our War Service

Program. The transition to this calendar that we made after Pearl Harbor was not easy, for any change in calendar affects curricula, students and parents, budget, methods of paying faculty and staff, etc. I believe that we made this transition with as little difficulty as any other school anywhere experienced in adopting a wartime calendar. Our change was successful in part because of the method we used in making our plans. It would seem to me, therefore, that we might benefit from our past experience as it becomes necessary to plan for a new calendar.

Our Postwar Planning Committee has recommended the broad outlines of a postwar calendar without undertaking to deal with any of the complex detailed problems which must be answered before any change can be made. Even though many of the problems have not yet received consideration, the Committee felt, and I think wisely so, that the faculty should now begin to think about the subject. Additional time must be spent upon the proposal before a complete plan can be brought before the general faculty for consideration.

Legislative bodies—academic or political—the world over, use subcommittees and committees for preparing measures for debate. In view of our past successful experience, and in view of the seriousness of the problems involved in making the transition to a new calendar, it would seem to be wise for us to reconstitute our Administrative War Council to begin active consideration of this matter. Therefore, after consultation with the members of the Administrative Council and with individual members of the faculty, I wish to announce the appointment of a reconstituted War Council to consist of the following persons:

President	H. B Wells
Vice President and Treasurer	W. G. Biddle
Registrar	Thomas A. Cookson
Vice President and Dean of Faculties	H. T. Briscoe
Dean, School of Education	H. L. Smith
Dean, College of Arts and Sciences, and of Graduate School	Fernandus Payne
Dean, School of Medicine	W. D. Gatch
Dean, School of Law	B. C. Gavit
Dean, School of Music	R. L. Sanders
Dean, School of Business	A. L. Prickett
Dean, School of Dentistry	William H. Crawford
Dean, Junior Division	W. W. Wright
Assoc. Dean, School of Law, Evening Division	Henry B. Witham
Director of Extension	R. E. Cavanaugh
Director of News Bureau	E. Ross Bartley
Assistant Dean of Men	W. D. Thornbury
Dean of Women	Kate H. Mueller
Director of Admissions	Frank R. Elliott
Director of Normal College of American Gymnastic Union	W. W. Patty
Assistant Treasurer	J. A. Franklin
Librarian	R. A. Miller
Historian of University's War Record	O. P. Field
Commandant of ROTC and ASTP	Major F. T. Reed

Director of Athletics	Zora G. Clevenger
Assistant to the President and Secretary of Committee on Administrative Research	Robert T. Ittner
Co-ordinator of War Service Programs	F. E. Horack
Chairman, Postwar Planning Committee	Ford P. Hall
Representatives of Faculty At Large	A. L. Kohlmeier R. E. Cleland E. H. Sutherland P. H. Harmon George W. Starr
Chairman, Program Committee of University Council	Harold F. Lusk
Alumni Secretary	George F. Heighway

All of those who served before have been included, and a few persons have been added. The membership is widely representative yet small enough for efficient work.

While the Administrative War Council is working, perhaps other bodies of the faculty will wish to consider the subject: the University Council, the A. A.-U. P., or others. Some weeks hence, it should be possible for the Administrative War Council to present a report to the general faculty. That report should include a carefully detailed plan for the inauguration of the quarter-system calendar, with a statement of all its implications. It is entirely possible, of course, that the War Council might also present careful alternative proposals. The procedure just outlined will bring this subject before the general faculty in such a way as to insure the most thorough and intelligent debate. Deliberation on the part of the general faculty should continue until a crystallization of opinion has been reached. Fortunately it will not be necessary, so far as we can now see, to hurry as we did following Pearl Harbor.

Postwar Curricular Programs

The calendar and its related problems are only a part of the subject matter of debate and study required during this year. We need to give special attention, of course, to the matter of adequate programs and facilities for returning servicemen, to the matter of improving our teaching efficiency which I fear has suffered in some respects as a result of the many changes forced upon us, and to the matter of better guidance and adaptation of our curricula to the student. I would like to see us give serious consideration to the matter of opportunities for the superior student. We have a high enough ratio of faculty to students to enable us to give special attention to the superior student and to make a good undergraduate teaching program possible. Further personnel could be made available through the elimination of duplication of course material and of unnecessary courses. This subject is receiving attention in many institutions at the present time. It is a major problem in American higher education and one we have some chance of solving with less trouble than many others because of our relatively favorable faculty-student ratio, which I have already mentioned.

Above all else, however, we must give our attention to plans for the graduate and advanced professional schools. The people of the State are wholly dependent upon us for teaching and research in medicine, dentistry, and social service, and, for the most part, in law. If the people of Indiana are to have available first-rate programs of research and graduate teaching in most other fields, they must be furnished by Indiana University. In the graduate and advanced professional schools, therefore, lies our greatest responsibility and our greatest opportunity. Outstanding success in these fields will depend in no small measure upon the attitude of the senior members of our staff. Scholars can work with maximum efficiency only in a favorable "climate." The senior members of the staff must stand at all times for the scholarly ideals of the University. They must encourage junior men to go forward with their research and writing, and must support title and salary recognition for those men who make the sacrifices necessary to achieve distinction.

This incomplete survey is sufficient to indicate that the year before us should prove to be interesting. Many important decisions must be made, and if they are made wisely they will do much to insure the success of future years. Widespread participation in discussion of these matters by all members of the faculty and wholehearted co-operation and consideration on the part of all members of the University family will do much to insure the wisdom of our decisions.

Faculty Minutes, 1942–45, following p. 174.

Document 143

From Those Whose Backs were Bent

It might have been an interesting experiment if the faculty had voted a regimen of physical fitness for itself. It learned, however, that the Student Council was in disagreement with its new policies. The Council suggested a rather substantial reduction in physical educational requirements.

*   *   *

Dr. Robert T. Ittner
Secretary of the Faculty
Administration Building

Dear Dr. Ittner:

Student Council, through the authority vested in it as the representatives of the students, wishes to make the recommendation that physical education be put on a completely voluntary basis. As a second choice, we make the following recommendations:

Pertaining to men,

1. That all compulsory courses in physical education be given only three days days per week;
2. That physical education be compulsory for four (4) semesters only;
3. That one hour of academic credit be given for each semester of physical education completed and that academic credit consist of grades of X or F respectively;
4. That the inclusion of credit hours in physical education shall in no way result in an increase in the number of credit hours required for the bestowing of a degree.

Pertaining to women,

1. That all compulsory courses in physical education be given two days per week;
2. That physical education be compulsory for four (4) semesters only;
3. That one hour of academic credit be given for each semester of physical education completed and that academic credit consist of grades of X or F respectively;
4. That the inclusion of credit hours in physical education shall in no way result in an increase in the number of credit hours required for the bestowing of a degree.

These recommendations are supported by the Interfraternity Council, Panhellenic Council, I. S. A., the Student Council House of Representatives, and other representative bodies which we feel give an accurate cross section of student opinion. With the return to normalcy, which is evident throughout the university, we feel that the wartime physical education curriculum is in need of revision. Realizing the importance of physical education it is our opinion academic credit be granted in a manner similar to that followed by other schools in this university. In the event that the complete abolishment appeal fails to materialize, we offer our recommendations as the next best plan.

We trust you will give this matter as much consideration as have students and their representatives.

Sincerely,
Student Council
s/ Lois Tabbert
Corresponding Secretary

Faculty Minutes, 1942–45, preceding p. 183.

Document 144

In an Age of Expansion an Old Problem—the Budget

In all the stir and fermentation which took place immediately after the end of World War II it almost seemed that Indiana University had entered an easier age of financial support. The University's financial condition was made more stringent by its increased enrollment, demands for classrooms and housing, the employment of new professors in a competitive market, and the fact the Indiana General Assembly had not been called into extraordinary session to make budgetary adjustments. Nevertheless, as President Wells explained in his report on the various activities taking place on the campus, the University was moving forward.

*   *   *

President Wells discussed briefly some of the problems faced by the University and the attempts at their solution. Because there did not seem to be full understanding of the new budget, he said, he wished to point out that the University would be operating on a close budget for the next year or at least a part thereof. While most States have had regular or special sessions of the Legislature since the war ended to adjust budgets, Indiana has had none. He stressed that this was a statement of fact and not a complaint. It meant, however, that all increase in operating costs must come from increases in student fees.

The general policy adopted, he continued, was to avoid increases in staff as far as possible and to put every available cent into salaries. There was only one dissenting vote in the Administration Council, he continued, to the proposal adopted, which provided for a horizontal increase of $500 for all members of the academic staff who had been at the University more than a year except in cases where there had been changes in duties; $200 for all who had been here for one year, and none for those who had been here only a semester. Further, promotion from instructor to assistant professor carried an additional $100, from assistant professor to associate professor, $150, and from associate professor to professor, $200.

The clerical staff, he said, had received some prior adjustment, so the increase was not so marked, but amounted to $10 a month. Junior administrative officers received $200 to $250 more, and senior administrative officers received the same increases as the faculty except that there were no increases in the top salaries.

President Wells mentioned two comparative studies on faculty salaries. The University of North Carolina survey, he said, gave returns from twenty-four of the thirty-three members of the Association of American Universities, including all the larger ones, and from nine southern universities. Even before the increases for next year, Indiana ranked in fourth place in the average pay of instructors, in seventh place in the average for assistant professors, in fifth place in the average for associate professors, and in ninth place in the average for professors.

A similar survey by DePauw University, he said, included all the universities and colleges in Indiana and some of the better known liberal arts colleges outside the state. Indiana's scale was the highest in this list, higher even than Purdue's.

A study of salaries at Indiana University, recently completed, he said, showed that all those who were instructors here in 1940–41 and were still on the staff as instructors had received increases averaging 48.2 per cent; those who were instructors in 1940–41 and had been promoted have received increases of 55.2 percent; those who were assistant professors in 1940–41 and still are assistant professors have received increases of 41.4 per cent, and those who were assistant professors in that year and have been promoted, 48.3 per cent.

Turning to the question of Fall enrollment, President Wells praised the work of the Indiana Conference of Higher Education, guided largely by Dean Wright, which has all Indiana schools working together in an attempt to care for all Hoosier youth who desire to take college or university work and to prevent closing Indiana institutions to out-of-state students. The schools are agreed, he said, to accept the same ratio of out-of-state students as they had before the war, which in the case of Indiana was 15 per cent.

The University's interpretation of this plan includes acceptances of all Indiana residents who stand in the upper half of their high school classes, to require those in the lower half to come to Bloomington for interviews and tests to determine their fitness for college work, to accept out-of-state students who stand in the upper third of their classes or who have specific sponsorship of some member of the faculty (703 have been refused admission under this ruling), and to accept out-of-state students not in excess of 15 per cent of the total enrollment (186 have been refused admission for this cause).

The best estimate, he continued, is that there will be between 8,500 and 9,500 students on this campus next Fall, depending on the provisions of the draft law, the job situation, etc.

Concerning housing President Wells said that fluctuations in enrollment, uncertainty of Federal allotments, labor and material shortage, uncertainty as to surplus properties, and money had been factors delaying progress. Furthermore, those handling the housing situation found it necessary to obtain accord from nine Federal agencies. They also faced the problem of approaching maximum capacity of the heating and power plant. Final stages of solution became possible with approval of a Federal allotment on May 10.

By Fall, the President reported, the University expects to have added 288 temporary two-bedroom apartments for married students and junior faculty members; spaces for 1,008 in permanent dormitories; spaces for 1,940 men and women in temporary construction; a borrowed heating plant; 35 houses and 15 apartments for senior faculty members on the Bloomington campus, and 35 apartments and 150 rooms on the Indianapolis campus. The faculty housing and 2,100 single spaces for students will be financed by 2¼ million dollars in bank loans.

Decrying the term barracks, President Wells said that the temporary housing, with the exception of Hoosier Halls, are not barracks and never were. These temporary structures, the most recent of which were obtained from Bunker Hill Naval Air Station, will provide single and double rooms, baths, and carpeted floors similar in every respect to those in the permanent dormitories except that they will be in frame structures.

The 288 temporary apartments will go on the tract the University owns immediately north of the railroad track behind Fee Woods.

The new permanent dormatories to be built this summer, he continued, will be on the rise east of the temporary housing on East Tenth Street. The buildings will be an experiment in which Ed James, Indianapolis architect, will seek to build a permanent structure of available materials that can be converted to other uses after the crisis is over. Mr. James proposed concrete block and brick construction with precast concrete floors for the seven two-story dormitories, which will be connected by one-story lounge units. A central dining hall will be provided. Rooms will be the size of present double rooms in the dormitories and will be used as double rooms for students at present. Eventually these may be converted to single rooms for graduate students and junior faculty men.

The borrowed heating unit will service the east group of dormitories.

For faculty housing the University had expected to begin construction of two large apartment buildings in January on East Third Street. Slowness of reconversion did not permit this, but by midsummer it is hoped to begin construction of these buildings to house 225 families.

The thirty-five houses are to be prefabricated two- and three-bedroom units, to be erected on lots scattered through the residential section. The last lot was optioned last week, and the first of the prefabricated units will arrive in about two weeks.

Several large houses the University owns will be converted from student dormitories to apartments, providing 15 to 17 apartments for faculty members.

President Wells reported that as of the end of May, 46 houses were under construction east of Walnut street, and that a large additional number had been begun in June.

A faculty committee will handle allocation of the new University units for faculty members.

In 1939–40 the University had 1,030 housing spaces for students, the President said, and for next year it will have 5,095 housing spaces. He paid tribute to the business staff of the University and especially to Mr. Franklin, Dean Wright, and Dean Weimer for the accomplishment of this development. In addition, he continued, the F.H.A. has agreed to build 50,000 trailers for allocation to educational institutions, and Indiana may obtain a share of these if necessary.

Asserting that what the University had done in housing, salary adjustment, and meeting enrollment problems for next year compared favorably with what was being done in any other institution, the President said that discussion of and action on the recommendations of the University's Postwar Planning Committee would be of first importance during the coming year.

Faculty Minutes, June 11, 1946, pp. 204–206.

Document 145

A Faculty Constitution

Just as students sought to define their rights and privileges on the campus in the form of a constitution for student government, the faculty proposed this constitution which defined the position of its members in this era of expansion and change.

*   *   *

To the members of the faculty:

Your committee on rules and business submits for your consideration a proposed faculty constitution. The proposal will be a subject for discussion at the next meeting of the general faculty. Please bring your copy of the proposal to the meeting.

> The Committee on Rules
> and Business
> F. LEE BENNS
> CARROLL L. CHRISTENSON
> FRANK E. HORACK, JR.
> PAUL WEATHERWAX,
> Chairman

A Proposed
Constitution of the Faculty of Indiana University
Article I

Sec. 1. Source of Powers. Subject to the limitations imposed by the laws of the State of Indiana, this constitution confirms and establishes in the faculty the powers and duties herein specified.

Sec. 2. "The Faculty": Title. The president, professors and instructors shall constitute "The Faculty" of Indiana University.

Sec. 3. Voting Members. The president, dean of faculties, the academic deans and persons holding appointments to the academic rank of instructor or professor, as full-time instructional or research members of a regularly established college, school, or academic division of the University, shall be voting members of the faculty.

Sec. 4. Associate Members. Persons listed as "administrative officers" in the official bulletin of the University who do not hold academic rank, and all persons holding academic appointment but who do not qualify as voting members, shall be associate members of the faculty. An associate member shall have all membership privileges except those of voting.

Sec. 5. Emeritus Members. An emeritus member of the faculty shall have the same privileges as an associate member.

Sec. 6. Certification of Members. The vice president and dean of faculties shall certify to the secretary of the faculty the names of all academic appointees and their membership classification. The certification shall be made within two weeks after the opening of the school year, 1947–48, and thereafter as appointments by the board of trustees occur.

Article II
Officers

Sec. 7. Presiding Officer. The president of the University shall be the presiding officer of the faculty. In his absence, the vice president and dean of faculties shall preside. In the absence of the vice president and dean of faculties, the senior academic dean present at the meeting shall preside. Seniority shall be determined by the order of the establishment of schools and colleges.

Sec. 8. The Secretary. The secretary shall be elected annually from the voting members of the faculty. He shall assume his office at the first regular meeting of each academic year.

Sec. 9. The Parliamentarian. The parliamentarian shall be elected annually from the voting members of the faculty. He shall assume his office at the first regular meeting of each academic year.

Sec. 10. Manner of Election. The elective officers of the faculty shall be elected as follows:

1. The president shall annually appoint an election committee of three voting members.
2. The committee shall mail to each voting member a nomination ballot at least six weeks before the end of the academic year.
3. Each voting member shall submit a nomination for each elective office.
4. From the result of this ballot the committee shall submit by mail a second ballot containing the names of the three nominees for each office receiving the largest number of votes.
5. The candidate receiving the highest number of votes on the second ballot shall be declared elected and the committee shall report the results to the faculty and to the president. In case of a tie the selection shall be determined by lot.

Article III
Meetings

Sec. 11. Regular Meeting. The faculty shall hold one regular meeting during each academic year, at which time the president shall report in detail on the state of the University, summarizing the academic, public service, and fiscal operations of the preceding academic year. He may make such recommendations to the faculty and call such problems to their attention as he deems pertinent to their responsibility as a faculty. The date of this regular meeting shall be fixed by the president and shall be during the first three weeks of the first semester of each academic year.

Sec. 12. Special Meetings. Special meetings of the faculty may be called by the president, or in his absence by the vice president and dean of faculties, or by a petition of twenty-five voting members.

Sec. 13. Notice of Meetings. Except in the case of an emergency declared by the president or in his absence by the dean of faculties, the secretary of the faculty shall notify by mail each voting member of the faculty at least one week in advance of the date of a regular or special meeting.

Sec. 14. Quorum. Twenty-five voting members shall constitute a quorum for the conferring of degrees and for the receiving of reports; for all other business fifty voting members shall constitute a quorum.

Sec. 15. Record of Meetings. The secretary shall prepare, in triplicate, minutes of all faculty action. He shall retain the original in his own office and file one copy with the president and one copy with the faculty council.

Article IV
Legislative Authority of the Faculty

Sec. 16. Legislative Authority. The faculty shall exercise the legislative authority, of the University, on all matters relating to:

1. The conferring of degrees.
2. The curriculum.
3. Student conduct and discipline.
4. Faculty conduct, tenure and discipline.

Sec. 17. Resolving Authority. The faculty may express, by formal resolution, their opinion on any question relating to the policy or administration of the University.

Sec. 18. Exercise of Authority. The legislative authority of the faculty may be exercised by the faculty in regular or special meeting, by mail vote, or, subject to the limitations of this constitution, by the faculty council.

Article V
Faculty Council

Sec. 19 Faculty Council. The faculty council shall be composed of fifteen members elected at large, the president, the dean of faculties and the deans of the:

College of Arts and Science
School of Law
School of Medicine
Graduate School
School of Education
School of Business
School of Music
School of Dentistry
School of Adult Education
School of Health, Physical Education, and Recreation

In addition there shall be the following ex officio members: the dean of the Junior Division, the dean of students, the treasurer, the registrar, and the director of libraries. The ex officio members shall have the privilege of the floor but shall not vote.

Sec. 20. Election of Members at Large. The members to be selected at large shall be selected from the voting members of the faculty who have acquired tenure. The election shall be according to the procedure prescribed in Section 10.

Sec. 21. Term of Office. The term of office of all elected members of the faculty council shall be for one year from the first regular faculty meeting of the academic year following their election.

Sec. 22. Officers. The president shall be the presiding officer. In his absence the vice president and dean of faculties shall preside. In his absence, the senior academic dean shall preside.

The council shall select its own secretary.

Sec. 23. Quorum. A majority of the voting members of the faculty council shall constitute a quorum.

Sec. 24. Faculty Council: Legislative Jurisdiction. All matters appropriate for faculty action may be submitted to the faculty council, but no action of the council shall be binding upon the faculty unless concurred in by two-thirds of its total membership.

Sec. 25. Faculty Council: Reports. The faculty council shall report to the members of the faculty all its proceedings. Reports shall be sent to the members of the faculty at such times as are appropriate to inform them of the action taken.

Sec. 26. Faculty Council: Mail Vote. When a proposal receives a majority vote of the faculty council but less than a two-thirds majority, the president may request the secretary of the faculty to prepare a ballot to submit the question to faculty vote. A majority of the council may, on its own motion, request the secretary to submit a question to a mail vote.

The ballot shall include a brief statement of reasons in support of and in opposition to the proposal. The ballot shall provide for a vote of "for," "against," and "proposal should be presented to a faculty meeting for discussion." The selection of more than one of the choices shall invalidate the ballot. The ballot shall be returnable to the secretary who shall count the ballots, preserve them for future inspection, and report the results to the faculty council, to the president, and to the faculty.

A mail ballot on a matter previously rejected by the council shall require a two-thirds majority of those voting to constitute binding faculty action.

Sec. 27. Faculty Council: Administrative Jurisdiction. The faculty council may:

1. Prepare by-laws to this constitution to be submitted to the faculty for approval.
2. Prepare the agenda for meetings of the general faculty.
3. Circularize the members of the faculty for the recommendation of matters to be placed on the agenda.
4. Appoint committees.
5. Present, on its own initiative, proposals for consideration at a faculty meeting.
6. Present proposals for faculty vote by mail ballot.
7. Fill for the unexpired terms vacancies which occur in the office of secretary or parliamentarian or in any committee, except that it shall not fill vacancies in its own membership but shall order an election according to the provisions of section 19 and 20.

Sec. 28. Meetings. Within two weeks after the beginning of the school year the president shall call a meeting of the faculty council. At this meeting it shall organize; and thereafter it shall meet upon the call of the president.

Sec. 29. Additional Representation on Faculty Council. Whenever a new college or school is established with an independent faculty of at least eight voting members, the vice president and dean of faculties shall certify the fact to the secretary of the faculty. The new unit thereupon shall be entitled to be represented on the faculty council by its dean.

Article VI
Judicial Authority of the Faculty

Sec. 30. Judicial Authority. The faculty shall have judicial authority, on all matters pertaining to the enforcement of regulations adopted by the trustees for the government of students, "to which end they may reward and censure, and may suspend those who continue refractory, until a determination of the board of trustees can be had thereon."

Sec. 31. Advisory Judicial Authority. The faculty shall have advisory judicial jurisdiction on any case presented to the faculty raising an issue of academic freedom and tenure.

Sec. 32. The Faculty Board of Review. The advisory judicial authority shall be exercised by a faculty board of review. The elected representatives on the faculty council shall select five voting members of the faculty as the faculty board of review and shall designate one of them as the presiding member. The members shall hold office for one year and shall be eligible for reappointment.

Sec. 33. Faculty Board of Review: Jurisdiction. A case may be brought before the faculty board of review when:

1. A member asserts that his appointment has been terminated or action has been taken recommending the termination of his appointment in violation of the principles of academic tenure.

2. A member charges interference or an attempt to interfere with his academic freedom.

Sec. 34. Procedure in Tenure Cases. When a violation of academic tenure is charged, the faculty board of review may fix a date for a hearing, permit all parties involved the right of counsel, and the privilege of cross examination, and upon the evidence presented make a written report to the president and to the complaining member of the faculty.

Sec. 35. Procedure in Academic Freedom Cases. When a violation of academic freedom is charged, the faculty board of review shall investigate the case without holding a public hearing or affording the complainant the right of cross examination and shall determine on the basis of its investigation whether there is probable cause to support the charge. If it determines that probable cause exists, it shall order a hearing according to the procedure set forth in section 34. If it determines that probable cause does not exist, it shall dismiss the complaint with a formal report to the president and a copy thereof to the complainant.

Sec. 36. Disqualification. If a member of the faculty board of review is involved in a case before the board, or is a member of a department (or college which is not departmentalized) from which a case arises, he shall be disqualified to hear or investigate the case.

Sec. 37. Personal Disqualification. A member of the faculty board of review shall disqualify himself from hearing or investigating a case whenever he believes he cannot render an impartial judgment.

Sec. 38. Appointment of Temporary Member. Whenever a person is disqualified by the terms of section 36 or disqualifies himself as provided by section 37, the faculty council shall appoint a member to fill the vacancy for the particular case pending before the board.

Sec. 39. Continuation of Powers. All action taken prior to the adoption of this constitution and not in conflict with it is hereby specifically confirmed until changed by formal action taken under the terms of this Constitution.

Sec. 40. University Council. The existence, powers and duties of the university council are hereby terminated.

Article VII
Amendments

Sec. 41. Method of Amendment. When an amendment to the constitution is proposed the procedure shall be as follows: A motion which identifies the proposal as an amendment to the constitution shall be presented in either a general or special meeting of the faculty. Debate on the proposed amendment shall be a special order of business at a special or regular meeting at least one week after the introduction of the amendment. Consideration of the amendment shall take precedence over all other business. The vote on the proposal shall be by mail ballot within one week after the faculty has voted in special or regular meeting that discussion on the proposal is closed. A two-thirds majority of those voting by mail shall be necessary for the adoption of an amendment.

Faculty Minutes, 1945–1964, supplement following p. 218.

Document 146

Wells Reported to the Faculty

The President of Indiana University after 1938 reported annually to the faculty on the state of the institution. This voluminous report for 1947 is an especially full and interesting one. It gives a rather searching insight into the University which had survived World War II and was now pointing itself in new directions in a post-war world which was astir with both optimism and uncertainty.

*　　*　　*

THE STATE OF THE UNIVERSITY

Article III, Section 11 of the constitution adopted by the Bloomington faculty last year provides that the Faculty shall hold a meeting at the beginning of each academic year at which time, and I quote, "the President shall report in detail on the state of the University, summarizing the academic, public service, and fiscal operations of the preceding academic year. He may make such recommendations to the Faculty and call such problems to their attention as he deems pertinent to their responsibility as a Faculty. The date of this regular meeting shall be fixed by the President and shall be during the first three weeks of the first semester of each academic year."

Literal compliance with this provision is, in my judgment, impossible. The published annual reports of the President and Treasurer of the University ordinarily contain from two to four hundred printed pages. Even so they include only summarized versions of the activity of the various divisions of the University. In the past several years these reports have been appearing from twelve to eighteen months after the close of the academic year. There have been a number of reasons for this tardiness; one has been difficulty with printing, but another has been the slowness with which the various divisions of the University have submitted their reports.

I believe that those who take the time to read these reports have a right to expect them to appear promptly. Consequently, the report for the year ending July 1 will be in your hands sometime during this semester. To do this it will be necessary to go to press without waiting for the tardy reports. We hope that by thus being arbitrary this year we will have better cooperation from reporting officers in succeeding years.

Since you will have detailed information within the next month or two, it seemed to me that today I should merely highlight a few of the achievements of the last year and indicate some of the problems which need our attention during the coming year. It is my guess that the framers of our faculty constitution had some such type of statement in mind rather than that which is described by the section I quoted. Moreover, the University is an extraordinarily complex organization with a range of interests and problems nearly as wide as life itself. To keep my remarks within the bounds of endurance it is necessary to omit even a reference to many important subjects. If the material presented today does not meet your expectations, and it is unlikely that it will do so in all respects, your suggestions can serve as the guide for improvement in future years.

This group scarcely needs be reminded that the past year was an extremely busy one. Rapid increase of enrollment brought unparalleled problems. These problems were dramatically illustrated by our enforced delay in opening which further complicated the problems of the year. In view of the enormity of our task the most remarkable feature of the year is not that we had difficulties, but that we had so few. We achieved so much that credit is due all who participated—faculty, non-academic staff, students, administrative officers, and trustees.

Happily I believe the reconversion period is nearly finished. The smoothness with which we opened this year is evidence of that fact as well as of accurate and effective planning and organization on the part of a number of officers for which they deserve praise. Another bit of evidence is the new spirit everywhere on the campus, which is a welcome change from the past two years.

Finance

The adoption of a budget is a necessary preliminary step to planning for any year. It is logical therefore to begin our discussion with a description of the budget. Our budget for the current year, exclusive of self-supporting enterprise, is summarized as follows:

Income:

From state appropriation for operation	$4,530,000
Student fees	2,350,000
Hospital income, including payments by counties for ward patient care	1,981,000
Dental clinic fees	25,000
Tuition payments by the Bloomington City Schools	77,000
Endowments, research grants, and miscellaneous	112,500
Total	$9,075,500
Expenditures	9,019,914
Balance	$ 55,586

More than ninety-nine percent of our estimated income has been obligated and our budget is too close for comfort in this time of rapidly fluctuating prices.

Certain income items deserve discussion. The hospitals are operated to provide teaching laboratories for the medical and dental schools and their approximately two million dollar income is, of course, immediately offset by comparable hospital expenditures. With their income eliminated, the bulk of our income comes from the State appropriation of $4,530,000 and student fees of $2,350,000. It may surprise some of you that our income from student fees is roughly half as much now as our State appropriation. This is due to two causes: first, increase in number of students; and second, increase in fee rate. The increased fee rate does not apply to Indiana non-veteran resident students. There has been, however, a substantial increase in fees for out-of-state students, although the total revenue from this source is small. The largest student fee income comes from the Federal

Government's payment for veteran students. If our present student body were all non-veteran, it would pay only $1,200,000 in fees as contrasted with the $2,350,000 which we shall receive. The higher fees paid by the Federal Government are in accord with a policy established by the Congress and the Veterans Administration to protect taxpayers in the states which have adequate public systems of higher education.

Six of the Eastern states, as is well known, have practically no state-supported systems of higher education. Consequently, nearly all of the college students in those states are enrolled in privately supported institutions having high tuition fees. The Federal Government must pay the regularly established fees of private institutions up to $500. Thus the Federal Government is paying in six of our Eastern states, approximately $500 per year for each veteran enrolled in those states. It is easy to see the injustice had the Federal Government limited its payments to public institutions in the other 42 states to the normal fees. Hoosier taxpayers would have had to increase still more their appropriations to this institution and at the same time pay their share of the high cost to the Federal Government in the states without state university systems. It was determined, therefore, by the Congress and the Veterans Administration that equity for all taxpayers required a payment higher than the established fee to the public institutions, municipal, state, and so on throughout the entire United States. Even under this system Indiana taxpayers do not fare relatively as well as do those in New York or New Jersey.

I think it important that our faculty be fully informed on this point. One student organization last year alleged that the University was profiteering at the expense of the Federal Government and the taxpayers. Such a point of view is naive because all monies received by this institution or any other educational institution must be spent on its program, therefore on behalf of the students; and moreover, in determining our appropriations our State legislature scrutinizes income, including that from the Veterans Administration, quite as carefully as it does proposed expenditures. The fact that this agitation was instigated principally by a young veteran who is a resident of one of the states without a state-supported system of higher education seemed to me to add insult to the attempted injury to the good reputation of the University.

In arriving at our expenditure budget this year all possible funds were applied to faculty salaries. Instructors were raised an average of 17.19 per cent, assistant professors and associate professors 16 per cent plus, and full professors 11.8 per cent.

In order to make these increases and add new staff members as requested by the departments, it was necessary to reduce the appropriations for library and scientific equipment. Although such reductions were undesirable, they seemed to me justified in view of the rapid rise in the cost of living.

Average comparable increases for non-academic staff are somewhat higher than faculty increases. Percentages, higher than those for the faculty, are I am sure you will agree, justified, since the rise of prices works a special hardship on those in the lower wage groups.

The budget I have just described provides only for the Bloomington and Indianapolis campuses. In addition the Extension Division is expected to have an income of $1,074,671, with a corresponding amount of expenditure.

Self-Supporting Enterprises

The income of the self-supporting enterprises is estimated to be $4,500,000 with an equal expenditure. This budget, of course, must remain somewhat flexible because it varies with the volume of business and cannot be predicted in advance as accurately as the income for the academic departments. It is hardly necessary for me to remind the faculty that there are no profits from the operation of self-supporting enterprises in the usual sense, that is, there are no profits to individuals. Such profits as there are, and they are surprisingly small, are always used either for the development and amplification of service offered or for other student and faculty welfare. Since there are many new members of the faculty, it may be well to say that the State of Indiana makes no appropriation for the construction of dormitories, Union buildings, athletic plants, and so on. Consequently, such facilities must be developed as self-supporting enterprises. Our Union Building was built by the contribution of faculty, students, and alumni, and by the issuance of bonds to be retired from student fees. Since the students who gave generously to build the Union Building never had the direct benefit of the building, it was thought that succeeding generations of students should also share in that cost by payment of a special fee. Our stadium and fieldhouse have somewhat similar financial history. The State has made no appropriations for dormitories with the exception of a small amount for site improvement. Even our Auditorium had to be built in part from a bond issue to be repaid by student fees. Some disapprove of this policy of the State which makes a large amount of self-financing necessary, but there has been no indication that the legislature will change its position in the near future.

In general, the past year was a difficult one for the self-supporting enterprises. Many extraordinary costs were incurred by the influx of students, the late opening, and the shifting during the early months of large numbers of students from one type of eating facility to another. Our enterprises felt the general rapid rise in cost of food and other commodities and, in addition, suffered seriously from the inefficiency of the staff—particularly, I regret to say, the inefficiency of student help. I think I can make graphic my statement of these difficulties by giving you some significant figures.

The volume of business done in the Union Building during 1946–47 was $1,211,478. After allocating cost of utilities, the net result of operations from the three units housed in the Union Building are as follows:

Bookstore	profit of	$29,942
Union Food Department	loss of	17,117
Union Building	loss of	17,738

Combining these figures the operation of the Union Building resulted in a net loss of $4,913.

The Bookstore handled 441,335 customers; the Union Food Department served 1,369,862 customers; the Union Building served 751,767 persons for movies, dances, meetings, hotel accommodations, lounges, and so on, making the total use of the Union Building 2,562,964 persons.

The margin on Bookstore sales amounted to five per cent. The largest single item of bookstore sales was for textbooks of which all students received a 10 per cent reduction in retail price. Ninety per cent of the college bookstores in this country sell at the regular retail price. The reduction granted by our Bookstore represented a saving of $54,000 to all students—approximately five dollars per student. The textbook section of the Bookstore operated at a slight loss. The profit was derived from the other departments and from the exceptional volume of business. Typical past years have shown profits of two or three thousand dollars.

A disappointing postwar feature of the cafeteria operation has been the large-scale theft of utensils during the past year as follows:

28 iced tea spoons
375 ash trays
1,016 knives
2,105 forks
2,105 soup spoons
4,673 teaspoons

This loss seems to be increasing. Since the close of the fiscal year, from July 1 to August 12, 65½ cases of milk bottles, or 1,965, were lost.

This fall to help us all meet the high cost of living, the cafeteria is serving a 45 cent luncheon and dinner each day consisting of properly balanced 1,400 calorie menus complete with dessert and beverage. This innovation represents a triumph of careful planning, for these meals have no equal as to price in town. Moreover, the Union Food Department continues to serve only government-inspected meats and to observe the sanitation instructions of the State Board of Health, all of which costs. Few other eating establishments take similar precautions.

Travel

The sum spent in travel has been growing at an alarming rate during the past several years. Part of this growth can be attributed to an increase in the size of the University and part to a slightly larger allowance for travel reimbursement, but the major portion of the increase can be attributed to the greater number of meetings at which the different faculties or the administration believe we should be represented. For the past year we spent in excess of $35,000 for travel, *exclusive* of the cost of travel for extension teaching.

Perhaps there are those with a somewhat lively imagination who might think my own travel bill constituted a major portion of this. It is true, of course, that the work of a president of any institution involves a certain amount of travel in order to represent the institution at various academic functions, and in the case of our institution a certain amount of regular travel is necessary between the Bloomington and Indianapolis campuses. Travel over the State to extension centers and to meet with various groups is likewise essential. In addition, last year was a legislative year which required many trips to the Statehouse. Notwithstanding that the University reimbursed me only $1,040.59. And in the first half of the year a portion of this was for reimbursement at five cents a mile for my personally owned car. For several years my personal car had been used as an all-university vehicle whenever a car was needed for some general purpose even though I was not directly involved. I am grateful that this is no longer necessary, since the University recently purchased a station wagon and a passenger car. Formerly there were no university-owned passenger vehicles.

I have long felt that if possible we should help defray under certain circumstances the cost of travel to scholarly meetings for members of the faculty. It seems to me therefore that this is one of the matters which might well go upon the agenda of the Faculty Council for consideration this year. Perhaps it will be impossible to develop any kind of comprehensive faculty travel plan which will be within our means, but we cannot be sure without thorough exploration.

Retirement and Annuity

I am happy to announce an important action taken by the Board of Trustees during the summer with reference to retirement for members of the faculty who were 45 or more in 1937. Our present retirement program, set up in 1937, guaranteed these persons supplemental benefits to a maximum of $1,500 annually (The Carnegie Foundation allowance) upon retirement at age 70. Board action this summer allows these persons to retire at 65 if they wish with the same supplemental benefit they would have received at 70. This is of special significance to our colleagues who have the least time in which to build a retirement annuity.

The decreasing yield on securities and the general inflation may require in the near future reconsideration of the percentage of contribution in our pension plan. A number of institutions have been studying this matter and it seems to me that our Faculty Council might well do likewise.

Only a few years ago a Group Hospital and Surgical Benefit Insurance program was inaugurated, yet in some respects the coverage is inadequate; consequently, Mr. Franklin in conjunction with a faculty committee has already begun a study of this matter. Personally, I hope a way will be found to make the plan attractive enough to enlist the support of the non-academic staff and to provide maternity benefits for the wives of all university employees. Mr. Franklin is likewise studying our Group Life and Accidental Death Insurance program in the hope that a way may be found to increase the amounts of insurance available. Modernization of these two programs together with our plan, unique among American institutions, for total disability coverage and the University's generous sick leave policy will provide members of the staff an unusual degree of security against illness and disability.

Land and Property Acquisition

During the past year the University has continued to purchase land needed for present or future expansion so far as the funds and properties were available. In these purchases two are of special interest.

The first, the purchase of the property at 1515 East Tenth Street is to serve as a corridor between the housing units in that area and the athletic fields to be developed on the vacant property across the railroad. In the future when the intercollegiate plant is moved to the area beyond the IC Railroad this lot perhaps will also become an important vehicular entrance to that portion of the campus.

The second purchase of special interest was that of the Wylie house built by the first president of the University in the 1830's. This house was purchased many years ago from the Wylie family by Mrs. A. S. Hershey, widow of one of our distinguished faculty members. The Wylie house is the one physical link that we have with the University's pioneer days. Mrs. Hershey has long felt that the property should be restored and owned by the University. Its purchase now precludes the possibility of sale of the property to commercial interests for substantial alteration or wrecking. The house is a handsome example of pioneer architecture, and I am sure that those who have an affectionate interest in the history of the University and its early struggles will agree that the house is worthy of preservation and restoration. In this purchase we acquired also an apartment building to be used for staff apartments. Perhaps of greatest immediate interest, we acquired vacant lots adjacent to the University on Jordan Avenue providing space for a vehicular driveway from the Auditorium to Jordan Avenue thus relieving much of the congestion that now occurs when the Auditorium is filled.

Our expenditures for physical development come from funds appropriated by the legislature for that purpose only. They cannot be used for the payment of salaries or for other operating expenses.

Recreation

The recreation facilities on the campus for students and faculty have been encroached upon by the additional housing and temporary classroom buildings.

Plans are under way and approval has been given by the Board of Trustees for development of four new areas for tennis courts. The present tennis courts have received an all-weather service to permit more constant use. Also areas adjacent to the new housing projects are being developed for other types of play such as aerial darts, volley ball, softball, touch football, and so on. An additional football practice field is being built which will release another field for intramural play.

New Construction

No major classroom or academic building projects have been launched or are about to be launched out of funds appropriated by the last legislature. It is hoped that building conditions will stabilize a little more before it is necessary to begin this type of construction. We have started, however, a dormitory to accommodate 1,000 men and women and two apartment buildings for married students and faculty to contain 236 apartments. Work is progressing on these structures satisfactorily. These structures are to be built with borrowed money, and money at this time is relatively cheap. There are two combinations possible in the construction of self-liquidating projects of this type: (1) cheap materials and high-priced money, or (2) high-priced materials and cheap money. As building costs go down it is certain that money rates will go up, so we decided that we might as well proceed with these structures now when favorable money rates are available. To illustrate, we have in the past built and financed dormitories issuing bonds with rates as high as 4¾ per cent. The bonds for these new structures have been floated at an average rate of 2.38 per cent. The addition of one per cent to this average rate for the money necessary to build these structures would increase the cost of the money by a little more than a million dollars during the life of the loan.

Our dormitory projects will proceed deliberately without the use of overtime payments or exorbitant numbers of men. Whereas it was necessary to use up to 1,400 men at a time during our construction last year, the present projects will require an average of only 200 to 250 men. Thus, the construction of these buildings will *not* monopolize the local labor supply. There will be plenty of labor for home construction and other building.

Housing of Faculty and Students

At the present time there are housed in University facilities 6,200 persons (not including children). However, present permanent housing facilities, including the semi-permanent Smithwood units, will accommodate only 2,509 persons with normal occupancy. Permanent units under construction will house an additional 1,257, or a total of 3,766. Under the terms of the Federal statute granting temporary housing structures at government expense, we are required to dismantle the temporary housing units within two years after the formal declaration of the conclusion of the war. This declaration was made as of July 25, this year. The only exception allowed is in case we can show critical need for their continued use. Structures of this type on our campus are the 400 trailers, 300 apartments north of the I.C. Railroad, and Rogers #1 unit housing 700 men. Although not legally in the same category, Hoosier Halls and Town House with a capacity of 500 are so temporary in nature that they can be used for only a brief time. A combination of new construction and a shrinkage of enrollment will, it is hoped, make it possible for us to begin the elimination of these structures as required by law and reduce all permanent structures to a normal occupancy basis within the next few years.

One hundred sixty-one full time and 188 part time staff members are housed in University properties at the present time. This number is far larger than any one would have predicted two years ago.

Safety

As the University grows the problems of safety increase. The Safety Division has been entirely reorganized under the able leadership of Captain Kooken, nationally known teacher and practitioner in the field. He and his colleagues, under the direction of the Safety Committee, are developing a comprehensive program copies of which will soon be sent to members of the faculty. It provides sufficient personnel for 24-hour coverage of the entire campus, including all University housing areas. Quarter hour inspection of temporary dormitories at night reduces the possibility of serious fire loss. Regular fire drills will be held. A motor patrol of the entire campus is to be instituted as soon as equipment is delivered. Perhaps the most helpful step of all is the provision of regular inspection of all campus buildings to discover all types of needed preventive maintenance. Finally, a 24-hour telephone service through Safety Division headquarters in the Health Center will be available as soon as equipment can be installed.

The Growth of the University

The growth of the University student body has been rapid and has brought increased responsibilities. However, the faculty has increased proportionately even a little more than the student body has. (The figures refer only to the Bloomington campus.) In 1940–41 we had 311 full time faculty members; this year we have 608. In 1940–41 we had 150 part time staff members; this year we have 388. The full time staff has not quite doubled (it would exactly double if there were 14 additions); but the part time staff has more than doubled. The student body has increased from approximately 5,500 to approximately 11,000. I assume that due to peculiar situations certain departments are as yet understaffed, but on the average we have a ratio of faculty to students comparable to our pre-war ratio which we then considered adequate. In fact, our ratio then was higher than that of most like institutions and compared favorably with many of the best liberal arts colleges. The effect of this faculty is demonstrated by the size of freshman classes in the humanities and social sciences. In 1940, such classes averaged 31 students. Last year that figure was 41½. This year our schedule provided for an average of 27.

Before leaving the discussion of the number of faculty members, it may be of interest to you to know the number of faculty members in divisions of the University away from Bloomington. The Schools of Medicine, Dentistry, Law, Nursing, Social Service, and Health, Physical Education, and Recreation in Indianapolis have 77 full time and 329 part time teachers. The Extension Centers in Indianapolis and throughout the state have 70 full time and 282 part time faculty members.

To return now to the Bloomington campus, our space has not expanded as satisfactorily as has our staff. In 1940–41 we had about 650,000 square feet of classroom and office space. This year we have added 81,000 square feet, or a little less than 13 per cent. As I have stated, both our faculty and student body have doubled. Much of this new space, however, has been devoted to faculty offices. Only 18 classrooms have been added to the 94 which we had in 1940–41 bringing the number at the present time to 112 or an increase of 19 per cent. We have, however, provided many additional laboratory, clinical research, and other special areas so that departments such as Fine Arts, Nursing Education, and Speech Correction are better equipped than they were prewar. The number of faculty offices, moreover, has increased from 203 to 383 since 1940–41. Thus office space has increased almost seven times more than classroom space and has, in fact, almost kept pace with the increase in the size of the faculty. It was felt that as satisfactory working conditions as possible should be provided for the faculty even though it would be necessary to conduct regular classes during a full 10-hour day. I hope, however, we can eliminate the late afternoon classes in the near future. Although we are not quite as well off for faculty offices as we were in 1940–41, we are substantially better off than we were in 1939–40. In 1939–40 the Bloomington faculty numbered 297 and there were 167 offices. Today our faculty has increased 104.7 per cent, but our faculty offices have increased 129.3 per cent.

As temporary academic buildings have been moved to the campus almost every department has gained office or laboratory space. For instance, the location of the electron microscope in Biology Hall necessitated the assignment of two small laboratories to Botany in Science Hall. Zoology has a new teaching laboratory and several research areas in the same building. Psychology has also secured additional teaching and research laboratory space there. The increased program and personnel of Military Science and Tactics have required more space. Government has overflowed to Science from Social Science. In Kirkwood and the adjacent quonset huts to the north additional office space has been allocated to the French, German, Russian, and Spanish teaching staffs.

The construction of the Business and Economics annex has, peculiarly enough, not benefitted those departments a great deal, except that they have the part-time use of the additional classrooms. However, this building does provide expanded and improved quarters for the Speech and Hearing Clinic, the Psychological Clinic, and the Reading Clinic. The rooms in Alpha Hall vacated by these Clinics give the School of Education much needed offices and a laboratory for Library Science. The entire Mottier House is now available for the School of Health, Physical Education, and Recreation. The new English Building gives that department an attractive and efficient office and classroom arrangement, locating the entire staff under one roof. Fine Arts has four new studios and four laboratories in the structures just added to the Art Center. In addition, a well-designed lecture room of 200 student capacity and a classroom seating 50 are available for general purposes in a portion of the campus where they will be most useful. The Music Annex provides nine additional much-needed teaching studios. East of Jordan, in the center of student housing, the Library Annex gives an additional reading room and distribution point for reserve books. This building also houses the offices and a classroom for Nursing Education. The space in the Health Center vacated by Nursing Education will be occupied in part by the Institute of Criminal Law Administration and in part by the Safety Department.

A temporary building on the medical campus will give additional space for the Department of Public Health, for business offices, for the Bookstore, and more classrooms.

We regret that these new buildings could not be equipped fully before the opening of school. Even though some details are unfinished, I think that we will all agree that Mr. Franklin and his colleagues on the business staff have accomplished wonders in view of the size of the task and enormous difficulty of carrying on any kind of construction in a hurry.

Student Development

As the University grows larger we must not forget the individual student. An individual student might be just as neglected in a student body of 500 where there was no special machinery responsible for student growth as in an institution of 10,000. But larger institutions must place emphasis on counseling and advising machinery.

Counseling can be most effective only when all available knowledge concerning the student is assembled for the counselor. The instructor's impression of the student can be a helpful source of information. Accordingly, it is hoped that the faculty will cooperate more actively in the submission of the student rating charts. It is not expected that each instructor report on each of his students, but rather on only those students needing special attention or worthy of special interest.

Students needing help for any reason should be referred to the Counseling Office or the Dean of Student's Office. We have had students who were markedly inferior, or whose health was critical, or who otherwise were in great difficulty, drift on for some time before anyone encouraged them to seek aid from the various University agencies established to serve them. Students who have continuous or excessive absences, or who seem to be carrying too much outside work, can be aided by proper counseling.

Cheating in examinations and other written work is one of the more common causes of disciplinary action. A student seems to cheat for one of three reasons. First, he may be habitually dishonest and try to get away with anything he can; second, he may not be aware he is being dishonest due to lack of ethical maturity; third, he may give way to sudden temptation, knowing that his actions are wrong but not having enough strength of character to refrain. While the evidence may well look alike for all three types of cases, in the final analysis it is generally agreed that most more nearly parallel the sudden temptation class. The faculty can do much to remove the temptation. Too many instances have come to the attention of the office of the Dean of Students during the past year indicating lack of forethought in administering examinations. For example, giving an identical examination to different sections throughout the periods in one day or after a lapse of several days gives the later sections an advantage. The general knowledge among students that adequate safeguards are not always taken to protect examination questions has lead to several efforts, some successful, to break into offices and secure this material. Permitting untried clerical help to have access to examinations prior to scheduled periods offers a source of temptation to the clerical help as well as to interested students. There seems to be considerable evidence that a certain percentage of students are engaging in organized cheating and substituting for each other in examinations. In every case of *flagrant cheating lack of administration at examinations has been a factor.*

It is suggested that the faculty study the possibility of attempting uniform regulations which could be applied to the grading system. At present, in general, each school has its own system. For example, while it is generally understood that upon the removal of an "E" (condition) a final grade cannot be higher than a "D", some schools award a grade commensurate with the work done for the removal. In some schools the grade of "F" once received cannot thereafter be removed. In other schools the grade of "F" is automatically removed from all records when the course has been satisfactorily completed. This lack of uniformity is not conducive to the best morale among the students and works a hardship in many cases.

The members of the faculty should devote at least a part of one of the early class periods in the semester to explaining clearly the policy with regard to absence from class, assigned work, relative weight to be given class work, written tests, final examinations, etc. It is frequently an alibi of students that such policies are not clear; however, general confusion can only result from inadequate explanations of policies. There were many instances of this situation during the past year.

We should all refrain from making off-hand or flippant comments about the intention of the University to "get rid of" or "weed out" as many students as possible because "we have too many now", or in general, giving the unintentional impression that the individual student is unwanted.

It is urged that those instructors who do not have a policy of daily attendance checks at least occasionally make such a check and that all instructors report to the Office of the Dean of Students those students with excessive absences. Such reports aid in proper counseling and discipline.

The Veterans Administration pays the cost of fees, books, and supplies needed by students authorized for government benefits under P.L. 16 and P.L. 346. The veteran, under the federal statute, is entitled *only* to those books and supplies required in his courses. This regulation has been interpreted wrongly to refer to quality as well as quantity. Some few veterans have attempted, by appealing to instructors, to obtain supplementary and collateral reading materials or supplies of much better quality than those considered adequate for their course. We will appreciate cooperation in certifying a veteran for only those books and supplies definitely required of all students in the course. The University's obligation is not only to help the veterans gain all the benefits provided by law but also to help prevent abuse in the granting of benefits.

Finally, all of our activities and policies for students should be designed to develop men and women trained for positions of leadership and responsibility. This obligation means nothing less than the deepest concern with all aspects of the growth of the individual including not only intellectual progress and achievement but also emotional make-up, physical condition, social relationships, vocational aptitude, moral and religious values, leadership training, and an appreciation of gracious living.

Enrollment

The latest figures on enrollment indicate that we have 14,176 full time students in all divisions. In addition, we have 7,191 part-time extension students and 3,965 correspondence students. On the Bloomington campus alone we had 3,218 new students this semester compared with 4,055 in the first semester last year. These new students are distributed among the various classes as follows:

	1st Sem. 1946–47	1st Sem. 1947–48
Freshmen	3,241	2,118
Sophomore	295	386
Junior	213	304
Senior	35	40
Graduate	179	250
Professional	92	120
Total	4,055	3,218

We have 5,797 veteran students on this campus compared with 5,961 a year ago. The data for the other divisons of the University are not as yet available.

The first semester of the academic year 1939–40, we had 1,898 women on this campus and this fall we have 3,388. In the entire University in 1939–40, we had 2,239 compared with 4,078 women this year. This sensational upturn in the enrollment of women is, in my judgment, directly attributable to the increasing acceptance of women by the professions and by business. Education of women, therefore, offers to us one of our greatest opportunities and deserves increasingly careful study of our program and facilities. There might be profit in considering the desirability of a special college of the University organized somewhat along the lines of the Junior Division devoted solely to the promotion of programs of study for women. Such a division would be in a position to mobilize our existing curricular offerings for the needs of women's education and to cut across departmental and school lines when flexibility is needed in making this adjustment. I would recommend study by our Council of this subject.

I should like to direct your attention to another significant comparison. In the fall of 1939–40, we had on this campus 388 graduate students. This fall we have 898. They are distributed as follows:

Graduate School	526
Graduate Business	85
Graduate Music	25
Graduate Education	150
Graduate HPER	56
Total	898

In addition, our law, medical, and dental schools here and at Indianapolis have 452 students holding baccalaureate degrees. These data give impressive evidence of the desirability of continuing our policy of emphasizing the development of facilities and staff for graduate studies.

Teacher Preparation

Higher salaries are stimulating a much larger number of our students to prepare for public school teaching. The need for additional teachers is not uniform in all subject matter fields. In fact, there is no longer *any* shortage of teachers of physical education for boys, social studies, or English. I wish to urge, therefore, that all divisions maintain close contact with our bureau of teacher recommendations in order that counseling of prospective teachers may be based upon the latest and most accurate information concering the positions available in the public school system.

The Freshman Student

Our Junior Division students constitute a special responsibility. They have all the problems of making transition from high school to college and therefore deserve extra attention. The Junior Division reports that the number of entering students with low reading skills seems to be increasing. This may reflect poor preparation either in grade or high school or in the home. Many naturally talented students have this deficiency. The first semester last year about 3,200 freshmen took the mental maturity and reading tests during orientation week. One thousand eighty of these showed at least a 50 per cent deficiency in reading skills in comparison with their mental maturity scores.

An interesting observation is that many parents recognize this defect in their youngsters. In some cases, often with justification, they blame the small township schools for the situation. Our rule requiring those students in the lower half of their high school classes to take pre-admission tests and counseling has helped to point up some of the worst reading deficiency cases. In view of this situation it would be helpful if all instructors of all reading courses would spend some time in showing students how to study, how to take notes, etc.

The Junior Division receives complaints and commendations from parents which reflect the attitude of students toward instructors. Poor teaching and untactful conduct on the part of instructors are likely to bring reverberations from parents. It is true that complaints are often made on baseless rumors. But on the other hand, it is apparent that there may sometimes be justification for complaints. No doubt it would surprise some instructors to hear parents whom they had never seen or who had never seen them reiterate the good or bad points of the classroom teaching or conduct of the instructors almost as if the parents themselves had been in attendance. I cannot emphasize too strongly the fact that you in the final analysis are the University's ambassadors to the people of the State.

Student Health

I am happy to report that the addition to our Health Center has been completed and we now have an infirmary with a hundred beds which is adequate for all needs except in case of an epidemic. Epidemics must be dealt with by special measures in any event, plans for which our medical staff keeps constantly revised and up to date. In addition, our staff has been increased in keeping with the increase in the student body.

The completion of the addition to the Bloomington Hospital further strengthens the health facilities of the community so that now, for the first time since the war, I feel that our staff and facilities and those of the community are adequate. It is impossible to praise too highly the work of Dr. Schuman and her colleagues who, notwithstanding many handicaps, have carried on this all-important phase of the University's work with brilliant success.

Library

During the past year, we added 41,367 volumes to our library. A total of $158,250 was spent for purchases and for binding.

During the year we received the final two installments of the distinguished collection of Western Americana, assembled by Robert S. Ellison of 1900 and presented to us by his widow, Vida F. Ellison. This collection consists of 3,413 books, many of them rare, and 5,148 manuscripts; also, 96 maps, approximately 40 prints and three broadsides. We have just received from Mr. George A. Ball his remarkable collection of Lafayette materials. The Lafayette Collection comprises some 1,700 original letters and documents, 1,100 photostats and facsimiles of letters and documents, 1,800 portraits, 1,600 engravings, prints and pictures, 325 pamphlets, 200 maps, etc., illustrating the history of Colonial America, the United States, England, and France from the year of Washington's birth to the year of Lafayette's death, 1732–1834. Outstanding purchases during the year include the Renton collection on drama and stage and a substantial number of manuscripts. Although we have been emphasizing the development of the library in recent years, our need is still so great that there can be no relaxation of this effort. It is a source, therefore, of regret that the library requests for this year had to be reduced, as I have mentioned elsewhere.

New Programs

In spite of the influx of students during the past year there has been time to devise and launch some major changes in our policy and programs. Certainly this report would be incomplete without mention of the formation of the Division of Adult Education and Public Services and the School of Health, Physical Education, and Recreation. These new divisions afford the structural basis for a rapid and distinguished advance in their respective areas. The accomplishments of each during this past year and their future promise might well occupy a statement of considerable length if time permitted. In addition to these two organizational developments most of the schools of the University have studied their curricula and made changes in their courses of study and the requirements for degrees in line with their objectives and plans for the future. This is especially true of Business, Law, Music, and Education. Medicine and Dentistry have also taken steps to revise the work of some of their departments, and a committee of the Medical School is now at work on possible future changes in the curriculum of that school.

Because of the large enrollment many departments have found it necessary to teach certain courses that were previously taught in small recitation groups in large lecture sections. This experience has called for new techniques and teaching methods, including experimentation with new types of examinations, tests, visual material, etc. On the whole, the reports indicate that results are satisfactory. There are indications, however, from the comments of students and from statements made in the annual reports of members of the faculty, that improvements are possible and desirable in the handling of large classes in certain subjects. It must be evident to all of us that the work offered to a large group by the lecture method must be carefully planned. This is especially true when the lectures are accompanied by quiz sections in charge of several instructors. A frequent student complaint is that standards and procedures in various sections of the same course differ radically. It is especially important in such courses that *the entire teaching staff* agree upon and follow closely the same objectives, and that the lectures, quizzes, and examinations emphasize the same material.

The Optimum Size of the University

We have followed a policy much more conservative than most state institutions with reference to admission of students during this period of rapidly increasing enrollments. So far as I have been able to learn we are the only state school that puts substantial barriers in the way of the in-state student who graduates in the lower half of his high school class. Moreover, our restrictions on out-state students have been rigid. Notwithstanding these policies we have grown rapidly just as was predicted several years ago by Dean Wright, Dean Sikes, Dr. Ittner, and Assistant Registrar Strain. I was certain that their predictions were correct at that time, and I am certain that their predictions that the student body will decrease a few years hence are likewise correct. All of our general administrative planning is being done on the basis of a shrinkage of approximately 30 per cent from our present level. I trust the shrinkage will not be greater, and that we will so conduct ourselves during this period of large enrollment that we will earn a reputation for efficiency and interest in the individual students which will encourage students to come to us in slightly larger numbers than we had prewar. The secular trend of our enrollment prewar was upward at the rate of about 300 a year, and there is every reason to believe that that trend was normal and healthy. I believe that we should be able to absorb our share of the high school graduates in Indiana who wish to enter college for many years to come without having an institution too large to be managed efficiently or to give to the individual student that which he deserves to get from his college experience. I know of only one institution in America that has been able to achieve scholarly distinction in a substantial number of departments and yet remain relatively small. Knowledge has become so specialized that departments must have a diversity of specialists in order to encompass the whole of their field. Without this range of specialties, as represented by a number of men, departments cannot attract the best students either undergraduate or graduate or hold their own in rigorous competition for research eminence. So size itself is not to be feared if proper provisions are made to reach the individual, but rather offers additional opportunity for distinction both for faculty and for students.

Foreign Students

The American university has a special responsibility to scholarship at the present time. Our institutions are the only ones in all the world able to function in a reasonably normal manner and with facilities that can be stretched to care for students from abroad. As a consequence students from every corner of the globe are flocking to America either on their own resources or on government subsidies. We must take care of our share of these students.

This year we have 103 students from 32 countries. Many of these are graduate students, some of them scholars and teachers of distinction in their native land. It seems to me that it is essential that we offer them not only the hospitality of our classrooms and libraries but also the hospitality of our homes. I know that food is high and help is scarce, but these men and women from other lands will be grateful merely to share with you a simple family meal. All of you who have spent time abroad know how generously the scholars of other lands receive us when we visit their institutions. I hope that the quality of our hospitality will not suffer by comparison.

You will soon receive a list from the Dean of Students Office of all foreign students who are enrolled together with their Bloomington addresses. Will you please make contact with these students and invite them into your homes. Moreover, Mr. Leo Dowling, advisor to foreign students, in the Dean of Students Office, asks that you feel free to confer with him at any time.

Faculty Council

The Faculty Council created by the Bloomington faculty last year will have its first meeting next week. The Council deserves the wholehearted support of members of the faculty and of administrative officers during its formative period. Only by a fair and thorough trial can we measure the usefulness of our new system.

I have already suggested certain subjects which I believe need discussion by the Council. I trust that members of the faculty will suggest others. Although many of the recommendations of the faculty postwar planning committee have already received favorable consideration there are others which could well receive study by the Council. A tremendous amount of work by many members of the faculty went into the preparation of this report, and we should fully utilize this material.

Public Service

The modern American university has a three-fold responsibility—teaching, research, and public service. In some future statement to the faculty, I shall deal with our public service program in some detail. I wish to mention today, however, that certain divisions have had active and successful public service programs during the past year. Among these are Dentistry, Medicine, Social Service, School of Education, Business, School of Health, Physical Education, and Recreation, Department of Speech, and the Department of Radio. Last week the Radio department launched a new public school program over a statewide network of 12 stations which will be carried on throughout this year. This is the most important effort that we have made in the use of radio for public education, and our department deserves the support of all divisions of the University.

New Extension Centers

During the past year there has been expansion of our extension centers. A new center has been added at Gary in cooperation with Gary College. The Southeastern Center at Jeffersonville has augmented its facilities by the opening of a branch at Charlestown. We leased from the Federal Government handsome permanent brick and concrete buildings that were constructed as laboratory buildings for the Charlestown Ordnance plant. These buildings are not only adequate for the use of the Jeffersonville Center but also have plenty of space for any other departments such as Geology that might have field operations in that part of the State. Moreover, there is within easy walking distance of these buildings a large public housing unit containing both furnished and unfurnished houses and apartments, and our students and staff have first called upon these facilities.

We have joined with Evansville College and Purdue University to furnish certain graduate and professional work in the Evansville community. The Kokomo Center building is being remodeled to provide, in addition to other facilities, modern science laboratories for freshman and sophomore work. One of our newer centers, namely, that at Richmond in conjunction with Earlham College, has had a surprisingly healthy growth. All the centers are in a flourishing condition as to enrollment, morale, and program.

Research

Perhaps the most notable feature of the past year was the national and international recognition received by an unusual number of our research scholars. Men from many departments were recognized, but the biological science departments were outstanding both in the number of men honored and in the significance of their awards. Of pre-eminent importance was the Nobel award to Dr. Muller of the Department of Zoology.

It is hoped that the past year's record may be repeated this year and in succeeding years. If we are to attain that goal it will be necessary for us to be ever alert to provide proper research facilities and working conditions, to encourage the development of our younger men of promise, and to continue to emphasize the importance of graduate studies.

Literary Quarterly and University Press

I am one of those who believe that we should have a literary quarterly and a university press, so it is a source of regret to me that we have been unable to launch these projects. The problems involved are complex and the solutions proposed by various persons and groups have failed to win widespread support. It is my hope that someone will soon come forward with an attractive and practical plan of action which will enable us to go forward with these enterprises.

Riley Centennial

The Centennial of the birth of James Whitcomb Riley will be celebrated in two years. In view of the many associations with this institution during his life and of the importance of the James Whitcomb Riley Memorial Hospital on our Medical Campus I believe that we should begin to plan soon either to take the lead in or participate with other agencies in adequate observation of this anniversary. This occasion will need the support not only of the School of Medicine but also the Departments of English, Folklore, Drama, Music, Journalism, and so on. To that end it is my hope that we may make contact soon with other agencies and begin to develop our plans.

Committee on the Role of the University in a Democratic Society

At a meeting of the faculty last year Professor Jerome Hall asked if we were making any effort to inform the people of the state as to the real function of the University in a democratic society. Promptly thereafter I asked him if he would head a committee to prepare a statement which might be used as the basis of a broad educational campaign throughout the state. Professor Hall accepted the assignment and Professors Oliver Field, Fernandus Payne, A. M. Weimer, Sam Yellen, Ralph Fuchs, Carl Franzen, H. H. Carter, and Oscar Winther were asked to serve with him.

These men have been hard at work for several months and expect to be able to report soon. This report will be presented for discussion to the faculty, to the Faculty Council, and to the Board of Trustees. The program committee of the Indiana Conference on Higher Education has invited me to discuss the subject before that body on November 6, 1947. Officers and faculty representatives from all Indiana Colleges and universities are members, and for this particular session representatives from the boards of trustees are invited.

In the course of my remarks I shall present the report of our committee and recommend that it or some modification of it be adopted by the group as a document to be presented to the people of the State. I shall suggest that many types of organized citizen groups be asked to help us stimulate this discussion, for example, Farm Bureau, State Chamber of Commerce, A. F. of L., C. I. O., Parent Teachers Association, Indiana State Teachers Associations, American Legion, State Federation of Womens Clubs, Hoosier State Press Association, and so on.

Such a program will not be completed in a few months, yet it seems to me important enough to be worth the expenditure of considerable time and energy during the next few years.

Possibility of Leave this Year

Newspapers have mentioned recently that the War Department has requested the Board of Trustees to release me for the position of cultural advisor to General Clay, in charge of the American occupation zone in Germany. The cultural advisor will be one of the four cabinet advisors to General Clay. These four men, with the General, will have the task of formulating American occupational policy. The cultural advisor generally will be responsible for education, religion, newspapers, magazines, theaters, music, museums, and so on. The task will involve not only tasks in Germany but also mobilization of education, cultural, library, and scientific forces in this country in support of the occupational policies. General Clay proposed this post to me in the course of a brief educational mission in Germany this summer. I replied that his request could be acted upon only by the Board of Trustees, that if the Board wished me to undertake the work I would be willing to do so but that I preferred to have no part in the negotiations. These negotiations are now in process, but I am not informed as to when a decision is to be made or as to what its nature is likely to be.

The opportunities for service in Germany are great, and if I am assigned to that task I shall undertake it willingly but at the same time with some regret. In my judgment the present year will be one of fulfillment, and we shall reap the rewards of the hard work and planning by the members of the staff which have gone into our reconversion. It is only human to want to savor some of the satisfaction we will all feel as the year unfolds.

Conclusion

As I suggested in the beginning, I believe that the events of the coming year will prove that we have nearly finished the reconversion process with its attendant problems and grief. I predict that we will have a quiet, normal year—the first since 1939–40.

I hope that this is so for it will give us an opportunity to devote all of our energy to the restoration and improvement of our prewar standards of teaching and research. After the strange new tasks and responsibilities of the war years it will be good to concentrate on the traditional work of the University.

In such a period we are reminded of the power and influence of the University and of our heavy responsibility to the people of the State. A thoughtful and experienced member of the staff wrote to me recently as follows:

"Many times it has occurred to me, as it has to many of our colleagues, that when you say you are on the staff of Indiana University a magic door opens to you. You find it with people on the buses and on the trains and in the hotel lobbies and with the people you go to see on business. So many times the person to whom you are talking is eager to claim some kinship with Indiana University. It is a magic thing which this University has created in the minds and hearts of the people of the State. It is, and can continue to be, a great power if we keep it that way. We can lose it more quickly than we have gained it."

I am certain that our staff has the will, the scholarship, and the character to serve our constituency in a manner that will merit continued confidence and respect. The days of this year present us with opportunity for fruitful achievement. United in wholehearted cooperative effort we can realize their full potentialities.

Faculty Minutes, 1945–1964, following p. 242.

Document 147

The Faculty Council in Action

This is a work-a-day report by the Faculty Council, but it reflects the kinds of questions which came before it and the actions taken.

*   *   *

FACULTY COUNCIL
SUMMARY FOR OCTOBER, 1947—APRIL, 1948

Organization of the Faculty Council.

The membership of the Faculty Council for the academic year 1947–1948 consisted of the following:

President Wells and Deans Briscoe, Ashton, Gavit, VanNuys, Thompson, Wright, Weimer, Bain, Hine, Hall, and Patty;

Professors W. P. Breneman, C.G.F. Franzen, W.H. Fox, P.M. Harmon, N.H. Long, P. Weatherwax, O. O. Winther, S. Yellen, F. L. Benns, E. H. Buehrig, C. L. Christenson, R. L. Collins, F. E. Horack, C. L. Lundin, H. F. Lusk, and E. D. Seeber;

Ex officio (non-voting) members—Deans Sikes and Shoemaker, Mr. Franklin, Mr. Cookson, and Dr. Miller.

It was agreed to meet regularly on the first and third Tuesdays of each month, from 3:30 to 5 p.m.; and to leave the preparation of the agenda to the presiding officer, with the understanding that the Council would feel free to suggest changes at any time. Professor Yellen was elected secretary for the current year.

The following Faculty Board of Review was selected for 1947-1948: Professors Mabel M. Harlan, Velorus Martz, James E. Moffat, Harry Sauvain, and Harry L. Wallace (chairman).

An amendment to the Constitution of the Faculty to provide for the filling of vacancies on the Council was submitted to the Faculty.

Calendar, Examinations, Absences, etc.

The Council spent a good deal of its time clarifying and modifying the rules governing such matters as examinations, absences, admission to classes, etc. During the current year, rules were formulated to govern the following matters:

Absences before and after vacations (November 4 and 18) ;

Night examinations (November 4) ;

Late admission to classes (January 20) ;

Final examinations (January 20) ;

Final examinations for seniors (February 3, March 2, 16, and 23) ;

Hour examinations during the week preceding final examinations (February 3, March 23).

In addition, the Council had to deal with a number of routine matters. It adopted the calendar for the academic year 1948-49 (October 14), and shortened the academic day for the second semester of 1947-48 (November 18). It acted on a series of minor and miscellaneous matters: appointment of necrologist (November 18) ; denial of request to lengthen Christmas vacation (December 16) ; change in R.O.T.C. requirements (January 20) ; appointment of secretary of the Faculty *pro tem* (March 16) ; denial of request for earlier final examinations for students in Nursing Education (March 16) ; excusing of R.O.T.C. students from classes to permit them to take part in the annual Federal Inspection (April 6) ; dismissal of classes on the morning of Foundation Day (April 6) ; maintenance of Library services on Foundation Day (April 20) ; and agreement to cooperate with the Inter-Fraternity Council in providing information concerning pledges' scholarship standings (April 20).

While many of these matters were not important, they required action, and sometimes considerable discussion, by the Council. However, the Council devoted most of its time during the current year to help solve some pressing problems of larger scope.

Housing

The immediate problem in housing was to settle on a system of priorities for University housing during academic year 1948-1949. A committee consisting of Dean Ashton (chairman), Professor D. L. Dieterle, and Mr. H. W. Jordan brought in a series of recommendations concerning priorities, which the Council adopted. (October 21, November 18, December 2 and 16.)

The Council realized that there are long-range problems concerning housing which must be solved. It, therefore, set up a committee to consider ways and means of providing housing through private means or otherwise for both permanent and temporary members of the staff. This committee, consisting of Dean Weimer (chairman), Mr. Franklin, and Professor E. E. Edwards, brought in a preliminary report and a series of recommendations, which the Council adopted. The committee is still active, and is to report back to the Council as soon as it has further recommendations. (December 16, January 20, March 2 and 16.)

Insurance

Two important changes were made in the University insurance provisions, at the recommendation of the University Committee on Insurance and Retirement (Professor R. W. Holmstedt, chairman). The first had to do with hospitalization insurance; and the principal recommendation was to make the Blue Cross hospital and surgical service plans available to all fulltime regular employees of the University, while the present plan carried by the John Hancock Insurance Company was to be continued for those now participating in it or others who are eligible. (February 17, March 16.)

The second change, approved by the Board of Trustees on December 16, 1947, provides for a greater amount of insurance available under the Group Life and Accident plan. (March 16.)

Salary Policy

The Council has spent many meetings considering the question of establishing a salary policy for the Faculty. It studied the proposals of the A.A.U.P., Post-War Planning Committee, and Teachers' Union. A committee was then appointed to draw up a set of proposals for the Council to act on. That committee, consisting of Professors Buehrig (chairman), Breneman, and J. F. Mee, brought in a report on March 23. The Council has not yet completed its consideration of that report. (November 18, December 16, January 6, March 23, April 6, and 20.)

Parking

The Council devoted the greater part of the meeting on February 3 to a discussion of the seemingly insoluble problem of parking on the campus. The difficulty, it learned, lies in the fact that there are 900 cars with permits to park on the campus and only 200 proper parking places. It asked the University Parking Committee (Professor J. F. Mee, chairman *pro tem*) to study the possibilities and make recommendations to the Council. The report of the University Parking Committee was presented to the Council on March 8, but consideration of it has been postponed during the deliberations on salary policy.

Other unfinished business

Bookstore. At its meeting on February 17, the Council discussed the possibility of improving the University Bookstore, particularly in the quality of books and magazines exhibited and sold there. A committee was appointed—Dean Ashton (chairman), Dr. Miller, and Professor Yellen—but it has not yet reported back to the Council.

Course numbering. The Curriculum Committee of the College of Arts and Sciences (Professor Winther, chairman) proposed in February that the Council consider the possibility of devising a uniform and logical course numbering system for all schools in the University. Action on this proposal has been postponed during the deliberations on salary policy.

Faculty Council Minutes, 1947–1950, pp. 50–52.

Document 148

Salaries

In 1948, Indiana University was caught in a somewhat precarious situation. First, its budget never reflected the real demands being made on the University. Second, it had never established what might be considered a "salary structure." This report to the Faculty Council is a full and revealing document. It divulges not only prevailing salaries on the campus, but also gives a glimpse of some of types of pressures which bore upon the institution.

*   *   *

The Faculty Council met in the Board of Trustees Room at 3:30 on Tuesday, May 18, 1948, with Dean Briscoe presiding. Those absent were Deans VanNuys and Hine, Mr. Franklin, Dr. Miller, and Professor Christenson. The following alternates were present: Professor R. F. Fuchs for Dean Gavit, Professor R. W. Holmstedt for Dean Wright, Professor J. F. Mee for Dean Weimer, Professor M. C. Wakefield for Professor Franzen, and Professor L. H. Wallace for Professor Horack. The minutes of the last meeting were approved as corrected.

The Council devoted the first part of the meeting to a final consideration of the report of the Committee for the Study of Salary Policy. (The original report is attached to these minutes.) The recommendations in the original report were modified during the preliminary discussions of the Council (meetings on March 23, April 6 and 20, and May 4) to read as follows:

The Faculty Council presents for the consideration of the President and the Board of Trustees the following recommended policies on salary and related problems:

I. That—

(a) immediate and continuing action to be taken to establish a salary structure with the ultimate objective of achieving commensurate salaries on a university wide basis;

(b) as a first step, fixed salary minima be established for the respective academic ranks within each school of the University;

(c) with reference to the administrative question of procedure, consideration be given to the advisability of engaging administrative experts to perform the necessary groundwork.

II. That—

(a) a base minimum salary for instructors be established on a university wide basis with the proviso that only qualified candidates be appointed to this rank;

(b) the practice be continued of employing the category of teaching fellow for those persons employed on a temporary or substitute basis.

III. That a Review Committee be established consisting of five members representative of all academic ranks, members to be selected by the elected members of the Faculty Council. The Review Committee would have authority to review any case brought to its attention by a member of the Faculty who might wish to have an independent examination of his own or another's claim for salary increase and/or promotion, or of the nature and conditions of his work. It would have the authority to confer with heads of departments, deans, and the Dean of Faculties to determine what recommendations have been made and what actions have been taken, and, after such consideration, to recommend to the Dean of Faculties either that an adjustment be made or that the original determination be affirmed. A copy of the findings of the Committee should be furnished to the interested parties.

A motion was made by Professor Buehrig that the following statement be added and approved as Part IV of the recommendation on salary policy:

That, in the event of the approval of the above recommendation by the Board of Trustees, a progress report be made by the administration to the Faculty Council twelve months after such approval.

Seconded by Professor Lundin. Passed unanimously.

A discussion followed concerning procedure for dealing with the report. Professor Benns pointed out that two of the recommendations in the original report of the Committee for the Study of Salary Policy had been modified or eliminated against considerable opposition during the preliminary discussions in the Council. On one of the issues—the change from "fixed salary ranges" in the original I, A (2) to "fixed salary minima" in the final I (b)—the vote for the modification had been 11 to 7, a majority in favor, but not quite a two-thirds majority, as required in the Constitution. On the other issue—the elimination of recommendation for automatic salary increases in the original II (1) and (2)—a proposal by Professor Christenson to adopt the recommendation of the Post-War Planning Committee that minimum yearly increases be given instructors until tenure is reached was defeated by a vote of 12 to 8. Professor Benns suggested that the controversial issues might be sent back to the general faculty for a vote. The council considered various means of putting this suggestion into effect.

A motion was made by Professor Weatherwax that the report on salary policy, as finally modified in the Council discussion, be approved. Seconded by Professor Fox.

A motion to amend was made by Professor Yellen that the two controversial issues—that in I (b) of the final recommendation and that in Professor Christenson's proposal—be submitted to the faculty for a mail vote, and that the Council again consider these issues next Fall in the light of the results of that vote. Seconded by Professor Lundin.

Dean Ashton objected to linking the two controversial issues, since the second involved the defeat of a proposal, whereas the first involved the approval of a proposal though not by a two-thirds majority. He pointed out that the Constitution did provide for returning issues to the faculty for a mail vote when the Council gave approval though not by a two-thirds majority; but that sending a defeated proposal back to the faculty for a mail vote might set the precedent for sending all defeated proposals back for such a vote.

A motion was made by Professor Benns to amend the amendment proposed by Professor Yellen so as to remove Professor Christenson's proposal. Seconded by Professor Long. Passed, with two dissenting votes.

Professor Yellen's motion to amend, as now amended, was then passed unanimously.

A motion to amend Professor Weatherwax's original motion was made by Professor Lundin to provide that Professor Christenson's proposal, even though it had not received a majority vote in the Council discussion, be submitted to the faculty for a mail vote, and that the Council again consider this issue next Fall in the light of the results of that vote. Seconded by Professor Yellen. Passed 14 to 7.

The original motion by Professor Weatherwax, as amended, was then passed unanimously.

The secretary asked for instruction as to how to report the deliberations on salary policy in the minutes.

A motion was made by Dean Thompson that the original report of the Committee for the Study of Salary Policy, as well as the recommendations as modified by the Council, be included in the minutes. Seconded by Professor Long. Passed unanimously.

At the conclusion of the consideration of salary policy, Dean Briscoe reminded the Council that it still had to deal with a proposal by the Curriculum Committee of the College of Arts and Sciences (Professor Winther, chairman) that the Faculty Council "consider the possibility of devising a uniform and logical course numbering system for all schools in the University." (Quotation from letter to the Council by Professor Winther, February 4, 1948.) It was taken by consent that Dean Briscoe should appoint a committee to consider this proposal during the Summer and to report back to the Council.

Dean Briscoe then spoke of the difficulties of preparing the budget at the present time when income is reduced while enrollment and the needs of the University are not being reduced. H said that requests for new developments and expansions have been trimmed down, and that staff additions in new positions are being held at a minimum. He pointed out that while less staff would be needed at the freshman and sophomore levels, more would be needed at the junior, senior, and graduate levels next year. He concluded by saying that the budget is so close that any raise at one place must come out of a reduction at another place.

Adjournment at 5:00 p.m.

REPORT AND RECOMMENDATIONS TO THE FACULTY COUNCIL
OF ITS COMMITTEE FOR THE STUDY OF SALARY POLICY

The Committee for the study of salary policy, in accordance with the instructions of the Faculty Council, has taken as the basis for its work the studies of the salary and related problems which have been made by the local chapter of the A.A.U.P., the Post-War Planning Committee, and the Indiana University Teachers' Union. The proposals of these bodies were presented to the Council at its meetings of December 16, 1947, and January 6, 1948; the proposals of each body and the ensuing discussion in the Council may be found in the minutes.

The consideration which has previously been given to this problem has been of great assistance to the Committee. The present report focuses on the issues which the reports of the A.A.U.P., the P.W.P.C., and the Teachers Union have served to identify as the relevant points of departure; in addition the appended charts set forth the most recent data on salary structure and information on promotion procedure at Indiana. The issues fall into five categories, as follows:

    I. Policy on Salary Structure
    II. Policy on In-Grade Salary Increases
    III. Policy on Promotions
    IV. Policy on Contracts
    V. Policy on Review of Grievances.

The Committee is aware that the problem of the general salary level will be a continuing one both from the standpoint of the individual teacher, who is interested in an income permitting freedom of action and a dignified standard of living, and of the University, which is confronted with the necessity of keeping and attracting a superior faculty in the face of a highly competitive national situation which seems likely to prevail indefinitely. Although it is not in the province of the Committee to make recommendations with respect to this problem, the Committee wishes to point out in passing that the administration has shown itself to be fully aware of the existence of the problem. The Committee is properly concerned with the other aspects of salary policy, which, however, also have a direct bearing on the large objectives of good morale and the progress of the University.

I. POLICY ON SALARY STRUCTURE

In order to provide the basic information for study and analysis of the problem of salary structure, the Committee has obtained from the Office of the Dean of Faculties and the Treasurer's Office the salary data set forth in Charts I, II, III, and IV, which are appended to this report. It will be noted that these data and the report itself are concerned only with the salary structure at Indiana University, and not with the question of comparative salaries at other institutions.

The problem of salary structure is an internal one concerned with relative remuneration within a given organization. The central problem is to attain a situation in which there is comparable remuneration for comparable proficiency and work, and to attain the still more difficult objective of a state of mind which is relatively satisfied that such a situation prevails.

One answer to this problem is the use of ranks, of which there are customarily four in American universities. The Committee considers some such hierarchy to be a rudimentary requirement and does not favor the suggestion that the ranks of assistant and associate professor be abolished, leaving only those of instructor and professor. In the opinion of the Committee such an action would result in more inequalities than may now exist for it would make still more amorphous the problem of commensurate salary for equal services.

A. *Fixed Salary Ranges*

As a general proposition, the Committee takes the view that a fixed salary range within each rank would be a desirable step in the direction of rationalizing the salary structure. The administration has been striving to establish such a relationship. However, as the data appended to this report show, overlaps in salary for the various ranks occur. The Committee finds that for the most part these overlaps are as between schools and departments and reflect the different competitive situations in the various areas covered by the University. It can be expected that this situation has resulted in instances in which individuals with similar requirements of preparation and similar levels of performance in skill and work are receiving unequal remuneration.

The Committee wishes to bring forcibly to the attention of the Faculty Council the existence of these inequalities. The problem is not one, however, which can be quickly solved by arbitrarily imposing a rigid, uniform salary structure for the entire University. The reason for this is that as a practical matter the salary level in any given area of the University has its most significant comparison not with other areas within the University but with similar areas in other universities. Purely practical considerations, however, should not be permitted to obscure the inequities, even though many of these are long standing and not the result of the new conditions which have developed in the last few years.

Keeping in view comparable remuneration for comparable proficiency and work as the ultimately desirable goal, the Committee believes that the first step in a systematic solution of the problem must be the establishment within schools* of a fixed salary range in accordance with rank. The ground would then be prepared for the second step, to be taken by degrees and as opportunity presented, of adjusting the salary structure on a university wide basis.

In wrestling with this problem the Committee has become aware that the recommendation of a principle is incomplete without taking cognizance of the requirements for its implementation. The Committee recognizes that the rationalizing of salary structure by schools, and the setting up of proper relationships between schools, would involve time-consuming and tedious labor. The Committee, therefore, can appreciate the position taken by the Post-War Planning Committee in its reaction to the A.A.U.P. proposal for fixed salary ranges, namely that the institution of such a policy would require an administrative survey of the University. The Committee is not convinced, however, that such a survey need include an analysis of all academic positions in the University and does not believe, therefore, that the type of technical job analysis undertaken in government and business is called for.

The Committee anticipates that any attempt to classify individual academic positions would encounter the difficulty of making relevant distinctions because an academic organization does not involve gradations of authority in like degree or kind with that found in business and governmental organizations. In the view of the Committee, the establishment of a salary structure involves the following factors: (1) the selection of criteria which could serve as a guide for appointment and promotion, which would take into account the different circumstances appertaining to different areas of the University; (2) the analysis of differentials in salary levels in various parts of the University; (3) a comparative study by areas of salaries at other selected universities; and, (4) the drawing up finally of a salary structure for as many different areas of the University as seem indicated.

The problem of procedure in this matter is essentially one for the administration to deal with; moreover, the Committee is not persuaded that outside experts would bring to the task skill and judgment which is unavailable among University administrators. However, the Committee does see two advantages in such expert assistance: the task would perhaps be too time-consuming for the administrative staff to undertake, and, perhaps more important, outsiders would have a greater objectivity of viewpoint.

The Committee proposes that the Faculty Council recommend to the President and the Board of Trustees that:

(1) immediate and continuing action be taken to establish a salary structure with the ultimate objective of achieving commensurate salaries on a university wide basis;

(2) as a first step, fixed salary ranges be established within the respective academic ranks (with no upper limit on full professors) within each school of the University;

(3) with reference to the administrative question of procedure, consideration be given to the advisability of engaging administrative experts to perform the necessary groundwork.

---

* As used in this report "schools" include the College of Arts and Sciences.

B. *A Basic Minimum Salary for Instructors*

The A.A.U.P. proposes that a basic minimum salary of $2500 be established for all instructors. Although the Post-War Planning Committee has reservations about the adoption of a university wide minimum salary, this position seems inconsistent with their advocacy of automatic increases for staff members at the instructional level: the automatic increase would largely lose its force and justification if there were not a base line from which to measure such increases.

An aspect of the present problem is the hiring of individuals with sub-standard qualifications to perform instructoral duties on a temporary or substitute basis. This problem has now been solved by the setting up of the category of teaching fellow.

The Committee takes the view strongly emphasized by both the A.A.U.P. and the Post-War Planning Committee that it is a matter of the highest importance that the University place itself in a position to attract capable and highly qualified instructors. This is a subject to which the Committee returns in the following section of its report.

The Committee proposes that the Faculty Council recommend to the President and the Board of Trustees that:

(1) a base minimum salary of $2800 for instructors be established on a university wide basis with the proviso that only qualified candidates be appointed to this rank; and

(2) the practice be continued of employing the category of teaching fellow for those persons employed on a temporary or substitute basis.

C. *Tying Salaries to the Cost of Living Index*

The A.A.U.P. proposes a five percent salary increase for each five point rise in the cost of living index as determined by the Bureau of Labor Statistics. The question of tying salaries to decreases in the index is not raised. The Post-War Planning Committee makes no references to the relating of salaries to the cost of living.

Without passing judgment on the principle involved, the Committee notes that two cost of living increases have been made since 1946 to the extent of budgetary allowance and takes the view that, since the faculty has already experienced a lag in salary adjustments in relationship to price levels, no presumption should be created that salaries should decline in direct proportion to any downward trend in price levels.

D. *Salary Policy Committee*

The A.A.U.P. proposes the establishment of an all-university salary policy committee which would be advisory in character to the administration on matters of salary adjustment, departmental expenses, and general budget policy. The committee would also be charged with a "study of the entire salary structure and the formation of a detailed salary plan."

The Committee agrees with the judgment of the Post-War Planning Committee that such a faculty body would find itself burdened with essentially an administrative function. The Faculty Council, which has meanwhile been established, is the proper faculty organ to make periodic inquiry into the problem of general salary policy.

II. POLICY ON IN-GRADE SALARY INCREASES

The Teachers Union favors a policy of automatic $200 increases for each of the first three years in any rank. The proposal would not bar larger increases based on merit during this three year period or subsequent additional increases within the rank.

The A.A.U.P. proposes a policy of "periodic salary increases" to be given "each individual upon reasonable demonstration of merit and achievement in the type of work performed by the individual." The A.A.U.P. approves of the practice of requiring annual reports from each member of the faculty and recognizes that these have been made a substantial element in salary decisions. It proposes, however, in order to achieve fully the desired psychological effect, that there be a regular biennial review of salaries and that increases should in no case be less than $200. Thus the effect of the A.A.U.P. proposal, while not making automatic in-grade increases obligatory, would be to create a presumption favorable to periodical, minimum increases: "Within the salary ranges established for a particular rank, an individual faculty member should be able to assume that once having established tenure and therefore presumption of competence, he could expect on the proof of merit regular biennial salary advances until he reached the maximum salary for his rank and grade."

The Post-War Planning Committee takes issue with the A.A.U.P. report on the question of salary increases. The P.W.P.C. recommends that individuals in any of the three professorial ranks (i.e. excepting the instructoral rank) should be granted salary increases (except for cost of living adjustments) "on the basis of outstanding performance and not on the basis of merely satisfactory or acceptable devotion to duty."

With reference to the instructoral rank, however, the P.W.P.C. would go further than the A.A.U.P. and institute a policy of automatic salary increases, in the amount of $100 annually "until the assistant-professorship is reached or until a stated maximum has been attained." The reasons for this recommendation are given as: (1) the advantage the University would gain in ability to attract superior individuals at the beginning level; (2) the lessening of the danger of too early evaluation of new recruits and the injustices and the sense of injustice which result from judgments based on too little evidence; and (3) the discouragement of hasty preparation of publishable articles on topics chosen because they promise sure, though perhaps meager, returns rather than topics chosen for their importance.

Although less directly, the question of in-grade salary increases is related to the problem of comparative equity raised in the foregoing discussion of salary structure. While it may be expected that major inequities would be eliminated by placing an individual within the appropriate rank, which, in turn, is fixed as to salary range, there is still an area in which irrelevant influences might operate. The proposals of both the A.A.U.P. and the Teachers Union are designed to minimize such factors. On the other hand, the Post-War Planning Committee is prepared, with respect to all ranks above instructor, to place full reliance on administrative judgment (which, of course, cannot in any event be dispensed with or mechanized) and, moreover, to base increases in salary on "outstanding performance."

In formulating a judgment on in-grade salary increases, the Committee became aware of two aspects of the problem which it feels should be clearly separated: the question of principle and the question of practicability. The latter question involves a decision of administrative character which the Committee feels it is not in a position to make with confidence. For example, an obligatory and automatic increase within ranks at all levels would constitute a fixed charge against the budget which might be viewed as involving too much inflexibility, since legislative appropriations are a variable factor. While the Committee is of the opinion that relatively small automatic increases would not add up to a total sum of significant size, it recognizes that, especially in the event of any marked decline in the income of the University, budgetary difficulties might be encountered. In the view of the Committee the crucial test from the practical standpoint would come in periods of budgetary stringency when automatic increases might be expected to hamper the making of merit increases.

The Committee suggests that the Faculty Council confine itself to passing judgment on the question of principle, and with respect to this aspect of the problem the Committee is of the opinion that the crucial judgment on merit is more appropriately made in connection with promotion to higher ranks than with salary increases in a given rank. The Committee feels that if an individual has merited promotion there is implied a confidence in him, which, roughly speaking, might be expected to carry him over a period of time halfway into the next salary bracket. At the same time it is important to guard against a situation in which the incentive deriving from merit increases would be rendered inoperative, and the Committee recognizes that there are those who would take the position as a matter of principle that the best results can be expected from a policy of granting only merit increases. While the Committee recommends a policy of automatic increases, it points out that its suggested policy is designed to avoid endangering the effectiveness of the merit increase. At the same time the faculty member would gain in peace of mind, and the administration would be relieved from many small decisions and could give more undivided attention to making judgments on outstanding performance.

The Committee proposes that the Faculty Council recommend to the President and the Board of Trustees that:

(1) a policy of automatic salary increases above the base minimum, in the amount of $125 for each of the first three years, be adopted at the instructoral level;

(2) with respect to the professorial ranks, the policy of regular in-grade salary increases up to $500 above the base minimum in each rank be adopted, budgetary considerations in any given year permitting, and that this progression be spread over four years in any individual case.

(It should be noted that merit increases would not be excluded at any point on the scale, and that after mid-point had been reached in any bracket merit would be the sole basis for further increase.)

III. POLICY ON PROMOTIONS

Apart from the setting up of a faculty review committee which would include within its jurisdiction the question of promotion in individual cases, a proposal which is made under Part V of this report, the Committee has no recommendations to make concerning the procedures employed for determining promotions.

With the exception of the suggestion made in Part I-A of this report pointing out the desirability of refining and differentiating the criteria for appointment and promotion in the various areas of the University, the Committee does not feel that it is called upon to reiterate the various suggestions made by the P.W.P.C. with reference to promotion policy, which have for the most part been incorporated into the subsequent practice of administration. Like the P.W.P.C. the present Committee is very favorably impressed with the discussion of "Criteria for Appointment and Promotion" to be found in the Harvard faculty report appended to the P.W.P.C. recommendations on promotion policy.

Believing that it would be a matter of general interest, the Committee has gathered information on the procedures now employed at Indiana University to pass on promotions and salary increases.

Present Salary and Promotion Procedure

There is considerable variation among the different schools of the University in the procedure employed to initiate promotions and salary increases. The methods which are practiced in the different schools are summarized in Chart V, which is appended to this report.

It will be noted that, with the exception of the School of Dentistry, each school has a committee which advises with the dean concerning promotions. Dean Briscoe's statement quoted in the minutes of the Council for January 6, 1948, is an accurate account of the procedure which is followed:

"Recommendations for promotion originate in the departments. They then go to the dean of the school or college of which the department is a part. They are usually reviewed by a faculty committee, which acts in an advisory capacity to the dean. This committee suggests other names for consideration, if it feels that worthy persons have been overlooked; it also considers names suggested by other members of the faculty. All the recommendations, with or without approval, are then sent to Dean Briscoe. They are then studied and reviewed by a general faculty committee, appointed by Dean Briscoe, a committee composed of six full professors, one associate professor, and one assistant professor. This committee may also suggest further names for consideration. The original recommendations of the departments, together with all the recommendations of the college committee and the general faculty committee, whether approved or not, go to the promotions committee of deans for study and review. Again further names may be suggested. The recommendations then proceed to the president for his approval; if he disagrees with the promotions committee of deans, he presents his reasons and usually arrives at some agreement with that committee. The recommendations then go to the Board of Trustees for final approval."

It should be noted that in addition the Department of English has a committee which advises with its Chairman on both promotion and salary.

The pattern followed for salary increases is much less standardized than that for promotions. The departmental chairmen present their recommendations for salary increases directly to the deans of five of the schools: Arts and Sciences, Business, Dentistry, Education, and Music.

In three of the schools—Health, Physical Education, and Recreation; Law; and Medicine—the advisory committees consider both salaries and promotions. The decision of the dean is then relayed to the administration.

The administration maintains a current file on each member of the faculty which contains the annual report of the faculty member and all other available information concerning his professional activity. These files may be studied by the advisory committees and are considered by the general faculty committee on promotions and by the administration. Weight is given the following factors in determining promotion and salary: degrees held, length of service, research contributions, committee work, public service, and effectiveness of teaching. It would appear that the intent of the general instructions for comparative evaluation of the faculty given in Appendix A, page 91, of the Post-War Planning Committee report is being followed very closely by the administration.

IV. POLICY ON CONTRACTS

The Teachers Union, alone among the three groups which have formulated recommendations on salary policy, raises the question of "legally binding" contracts "with tenure, salary, and responsibilities specified."

The Committee is of the opinion that this proposal is in part based on the mistaken asumption that the letters of appointment given by the University do not have contractual force. Moreover, in the Committee's opinion a more formal document could in no substantial way enhance the security which may be predicted on the general tenure and academic freedom policies which have been formally enunciated by the University. The present tenure rules of the University have been declared by the national offices of the A.A.U.P. to be exceptionally good. With reference to those members of the staff at the in-structoral level, the Committee is not persuaded, on the basis of the data set forth in the last column of Chart V, that there is any justification for a feeling of insecurity in any significant degree.

Only as regards the question of defining responsibilities of a faculty member so as to forestall unreasonable work loads does the proposal have, in the opinion of the Committee, a measure of justification. In the judgment of the Committee, however, this particular problem can best be handled through the device of a review committee, which is recommended below.

V. POLICY ON REVIEW OF GRIEVANCES

The A.A.U.P. recommends the establishment of a "Salary Review Committee," which would have the power of independent review of any case brought to its attention by a complaining faculty member. The P.W.P.C. "heartily supports" the setting up of such a body. The Teachers Union, in proposing the establish-ment of a similar body, approaches the question from the side of promotions rather than of salary.

Since salary and promotion are inseparable elements in many situations, the more so if a rationalized salary structure is adopted, the Committee takes the view that any grievance committee should have jurisdiction over both types of cases. Moreover, the Committee believes that such a body should have jurisdic-tion over any question relating to the conditions of employment, it being un-derstood, of course, that it would in no way impinge on the Faculty Board of Review, which has responsibility as regards academic freedom and tenure cases.

The Committee proposes that the Faculty Council recommend to the President and the Board of Trustees that a Review Committee be established consisting of five members representative of all academic ranks, members to be selected by the elected members of the Faculty Council. The Review Committee would have authority to review any case brought to its attention by a member of the faculty who might wish to have an independent exami-nation of his claim for salary increases and/or promotion, or of the nature and conditions of his work. It would have the authority to confer with heads of departments, deans, and the Dean of Faculties to determine what recommendations have been made and what actions have been taken, and, after such consideration, to recommend to the Dean of Faculties either that an adjustment be made or that the original determination be affirmed. The complaining staff member should receive a copy of the Committee.

WILLIAM R. BRENEMAN
JOHN F. MEE
EDWARD H. BUEHRIG
(Chairman)

SALARY STRUCTURE OF ACADEMIC STAFF
INDIANA UNIVERSITY CAMPUS
1947-1948

Rank	No.	Salary Range		Average Salary	Salary Deviation		Remarks	Rank Overlap*
		Upper	Lower		Above	Below		
Professor	73	8150	4450	6339 X / 6053	35	38		
Associate Professor	73	5950	3900	5197 X / 4805	33	35	4 on the average	1500
Assistant Professor	116	5150	3350	4272 X / 4090	52	64		1250
Instructor	140	4150	2550	3176 X / 3160	55	69	16 at 3150-3160 23 below 2900 10 below 2800 0 below 2550	800

Salary Range connecting differences (arrows):
Professor–Associate: Upper 2200, Lower 550, diagonal 4250.
Associate–Assistant: Upper 800, Lower 600, diagonal 2600.
Assistant–Instructor: Upper 1000, Lower 800, diagonal 2600.

All of the following classifications have been eliminated from the study:
1. Persons who hold administrative spots in addition to academic rank.
2. Persons on athletic coaching staff.
3. Persons paid on 12 month basis.
4. University School teachers, counselors, etc.

*–Difference between top salary for each rank and lowest salary for next higher rank.
X–Figures underlined show salary averages for each rank with administrative personnel included.

CHART I

SALARY STRUCTURE OF ACADEMIC STAFF
INDIANA UNIVERSITY CAMPUS
1946-1947

Rank	No.	Salary Range		Average Salary	Salary Deviation		Remarks	Rank Overlap*
		Upper	Lower		Above	Below		
Professor	91	8000	4300	5805				
Associate Professor	65	5500	3400	4438				1200
Assistant Professor	107	5000	3000	3647				1600
Instructor	122	3400	2100	2868				400

Upper differences: 2500, 500, 1600. Lower differences: 900, 400, 900. Diagonal differences: 4600, 2500, 2900.

The above classifications include all personnel who hold academic rank.

* Difference between top salary for each rank and lowest salary for next higher rank.

CHART II

SALARY STRUCTURE OF ACADEMIC STAFF
INDIANA UNIVERSITY CAMPUS
1945-1946

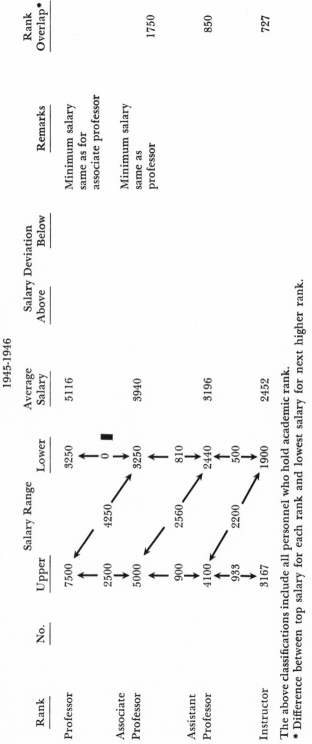

Rank	No.	Salary Range		Average Salary	Salary Deviation		Remarks	Rank Overlap*
		Upper	Lower		Above	Below		
Professor		7500	3250	5116			Minimum salary same as for associate professor	
Associate Professor		5000	3250	3940			Minimum salary same as professor	1750
Assistant Professor		4100	2440	3196				850
Instructor		3167	1900	2452				727

Upper differences: 2500, 900, 933
Lower differences: 0, 810, 500
Diagonal: 4250, 2560, 2200

The above classifications include all personnel who hold academic rank.
* Difference between top salary for each rank and lowest salary for next higher rank.

CHART III

SALARY RANGE IN ACCORDANCE WITH RANK

Rank	Minimum Salaries			Maximum Salaries			Average Salaries			Overlap between Rank		
	1945-46	1946-47	1947-48*	1945-46	1946-47	1947-48*	1945-46	1946-47	1947-48*	1945-46	1946-47	1947-48*
Professor	3250	4300	4450	7500	8000	8150	5116	5805	6053			
Range	0	900	550	2500	2500	2200	1176	1367	1248			
Associate Professor	3250	3400	3900	5000	5500	5950	3940	4438	4805	1750	1200	1500
Range	810	400	600	900	500	800	744	791	715			
Assistant Professor	2440	3000	3350	4100	5000	5150	3196	3647	4090	850	1600	1250
Range	500	900	800	933	1600	1000	744	779	930			
Instructor	1900	2100	2550	3167	3400	4150	2452	2868	3160	727	400	800

CHART IV

* Personnel with Administrative Positions eliminated

OUTLINE OF PROMOTION AND SALARY PROCEDURE
(Bloomington Campus)

School	Promotion	Salary	Instructors Released 1945-46 and 1946-47
Arts and Sciences	Chairman of Department originates, except in English Department where Chairman consults with Advisory Committee. College Promotions Committee recommends to Dean.	Chairman and Dean originate, except in English Department where chairman consults with Advisory Committee.	7
Business	"Planning Committee" advisory to the Dean.	Chairman and Dean	0
Dentistry	Dean recommends.	Same as Promotion	0
Education	Senior Staff advisory to the Dean	Chairman and Dean	0
Health, Physical Education, and Recreation	Committee advisory to the Dean	Same as Promotion	0
Law	"Advisory Committee" to the Dean	Same as Promotion	0
Medicine	Committee from Indianapolis Campus with Drs. Harmon and Kime	Same as Promotion	0
Music	"Advisory Committee" to the Dean	Dean	2

CHART V

479

Document 149

State of the University

In this voluminous document the President of the University not only gave a full accounting of what had happened during the past year within the institution, but he reviewed plans and activities which were then taking place in the expansion of the campus, the fact of rising enrollments, and matters of direct concern to the faculty. As in all the Wells reports, this one contains the strongest suggestive element.

*   *   *

REMARKS TO THE FACULTY

Social Science Auditorium
Indiana University

4:30 p.m.

December 9, 1948

STATE OF THE UNIVERSITY
1948-49

My report to the faculty concerning the state of the University has been delayed, as you know, until complete budget data could be prepared. Permission to delay beyond the statutory time set in the Constitution was given at the First Faculty meeting. The figures for the operating budget were completed about three weeks ago. The capital portion of the budget request could not be completed, however, until the past week, and my statement today is being made the first day following available for a general Faculty meeting.

(No publicity on capital items.)

The time needed for preparing the biennial budget request is difficult to anticipate accurately. Unknown factors frequently change the situation on short notice. The interests and wishes of several bodies, including Faculty, Board of Trustees, Faculty Council, State Budget Director, Governor, and Governor-elect, all influence the situation. Consequently, it is my judgment that two years from now, even at the expense of having two meetings of the general faculty, it will be desirable to make a statement at the beginning of the semester dealing with academic problems followed by a second statement after the completion of the budget request.

Past Year

The past year was one of constructive activity. The detailed reports of the schools and divisions of the University record the year's achievements. These reports will be published in the President's Annual Report and are worthy of a careful reading by each member of the faculty. I cannot even summarize them in the space of this statement. I will mention certain developments, but only as they relate to problems ahead of us. Failure to mention many others in no way suggests they are unimportant.

Enrollment for the Fall of 1948

Enrollment increased slightly this fall in conformity with the trend in most institutions of higher learning throughout the country. Enrollment is as follows:

	First Semester 1946–47	First Semester 1948–49
Full-Time Students	13,110	14,414
Part-Time Students	5,558	8,717
Total Students	18,668	23,131

The increasing concentration of the full-time student enrollment in the junior and senior years and in graduate study is shown as follows:

	First Semester 1946–47	First Semester 1948–49
Juniors	1,601	2,752
Seniors	1,041	2,341
Graduate	703	1,226
Professional	463	634
Totals	3,808	6,953
Percentage of Total Bloomington Campus Enrollment	41	60.5

According to the United States Office of Education we rank ninth in over-all enrollment in the country. All of the Big Ten schools were in the first 20 in size except Iowa and Purdue.

All surveys and analyses, both on the basis of national estimates and the University's carefully worked out forecasts, indicate a continuing full-time enrollment at approximately the present 14,000 level. The passing of the veteran enrollment began this year and will be accentuated greatly in 1949–50 and 1950–51. However, the current enrollment increased as compared with a year ago despite the drop in veterans from 7,521 in the first semester of 1947 to 6,731 in the present semester. This clearly indicates that the places of the veterans are more than being taken by recent high school graduates and students who transfer from other colleges. Factors which will hold the enrollment at 14,000 or more are: (1) the larger percentage of each high school graduating class going to college, (2) the state's nearly 500,000 increase in population since 1940, (3) the attainment of college age by children whose parents went to college after World War I, (4) the increased number of alumni having children of college age, and (5) the greatly increased number of Indiana students transferring to the University for junior, senior, and graduate work.

Finally, the number of this year's entering class is the most significant index of all. It is the first normal postwar entering class and has few veterans in it who are here as the result of the stimulation of the G. I. Bill of Rights. As you know, the entering class in the long run determines the over-all size of the institution. Our entering class this year of 4,547 is in contrast to 2,100 in the last prewar year. An entering class of 2,000 to 2,100 sustained a total prewar enrollment of six to seven thousand. Therefore, a class of 4,500 should sustain a postwar enrollment of approximately 14,000.

Last Year's Budget

In my remarks last fall I pointed out that more than 99 per cent of our estimated income had been obligated and our budget was too close for comfort in a time of rapidly fluctuating prices. The apprehension suggested in that statement was well founded. Due to rising prices our expenditures exceeded our income for the past year by $860,103. This was not a paper deficit but a real deficit, and required a special appropriation from the cigarette tax fund by the Budget Committee with the approval of the Governor.

Budget for 1948–49

Our budget for this year contains an even more serious deficit. The budget for the current year, exclusive of self-supporting enterprises, is as follows:

Income:

From state appropriation for operation		$4,500,000
Student fees		2,450,000
Hospital income, including payments by counties for ward patient care		2,469,000
Dental clinic fees		35,000
Tuition payments by the Bloomington City Schools		85,000
Endowments and Miscellaneous		172,000
Adult Education Income		1,240,803
	Total Income	$10,951,803
Expenditures:		12,364,792
Deficit		$ 1,412,989

You will note that there is a deficit here of $1,412,989. This again is not a paper deficit. There is no surplus fund to take care of it and our first legislative task will be to ask the legislature to make an emergency appropriation to meet this deficit.

Our sister institution, Purdue, likewise has an operating deficit this year of approximately $1,200,000. Purdue will not have to request a deficiency appropriation since she can absorb the operating deficit out of operating balances. This has already given rise to question in some quarters as to why one institution should require a deficiency appropriation and the other require none. There are several fiscal differences between the two institutions that more than account for this difference in operating costs. Some of these differences are as follows:

1. Indiana University has to operate on two campuses.

2. Our Medical Center, while providing instruction for approximately five per cent of our students, takes close to 33⅓ per cent of the budget. This School has to provide a wide variety of special services that are in addition to its strictly teaching functions.

3. We have a substantially larger student body.

4. We have a substantially larger extension organization and enrollment.

5. A higher percentage of students at Purdue are men because it is an engineering school. Because there are more men there are more veterans. More veterans mean more extra G.I. fee income from the Federal Government.

6. Purdue takes a relatively high percentage of out-of-state students and benefits from the out-of-state fee, again meaning Purdue collects a larger amount in fee income although having fewer students than we have to serve. This alone practically accounts for the difference between the two institutions.

7. Purdue receives something more than a million dollars a year from the Federal Government for a variety of state and campus programs as the result of being a land grant institution. Moreover she receives approximately $100,000 per year in operating funds from the state as an offset against our allowance for general obligation bonds.

Let no one assume from this comparison that I believe Purdue has more money than she needs. Quite the contrary, I believe that she needs a large additional amount to carry on her work.

Self-Supporting Enterprises

Since I dealt with self-supporting enterprises in my statement last year, and since we need to discuss at considerable length our legislative request, I shall omit detailed information on the budget of the self-supporting enterprises. There is little in their situation that differs from last year except that in the case of all the housing operations it is becoming increasingly difficult to stay solvent due to the fact that neither room nor board rates were raised for this semester, although food prices and staff salaries have both increased. The management is exerting every effort to stay in the black, and I hope that they will be able to do so.

Budget Request for Biennium Ending June 30, 1951

Our budget request covers a period which will not be ended for thirty months, consequently it can at best be only an estimate and estimates must be based upon certain assumptions. The two basic assumptions in arriving at our costs of operating are these:

1. That the present level of prices will remain approximately the same. Our Bureau of Business Research predicts that we have reached a plateau for the present. The Bureau predicts that any decline in the cost of food and clothing next year will probably be offset by increases in other classifications.

2. That our load of student teaching and services for the biennium will be approximately the same as at present.

The budget request compared to the present year:

	Estimated 1948–1949	Requested for 1949–1950	1950–1951
Expenditures	$12,364,792	$15,645,904	$15,550,167
Income	6,451,803	6,624,281	6,324,841
Request from State—Appropriation	$ 4,500,000	$ 9,021,623	$ 9,225,326
—Deficiency	1,412,989		
One half total Biennium Request		$ 9,123,474	
Deduct Present Annual Appropriation and Deficiency		−5,912,989	
Deduct ½ Loss of Income for Biennium		−970,422	
Net Annual Increase		$ 2,240,063	

In addition to the operating request we are making these special requests:

	1949–1950	1950–1951
Retirement	$ 182,500	$ 188,500
Medical School Expansion (2 year program)	68,385	75,990
Repairs to Old Buildings	345,150	345,150
Public Health	51,340	66,015
Bond Retirement and Interest	101,732	102,337
	$ 749,107	$ 777,992

The increased operating request will provide for:

Personal Service—	
Present Staff	$ 923,546
Staff Additions	505,276
Supplies, Expenses, Repairs and Equipment	342,156
Medical Center Increase	469,085
	$ 2,240,063

The operating budget of $9,123,474 plus $6,474,561 is divided geographically as follows:

	Expenditure	Income
Bloomington campus and general administration including insurance, annuity, etc.	$ 8,523,146	$ 2,077,225
Indianapolis campus	5,186,727	3,462,180
Extension Division	1,888,162	935,156
Total	$15,598,035	$ 6,474,561

How did we arrive at these budget requests? In early September the individual departments and schools of the University were asked to submit an estimate of their needs. These requests were compiled and presented to a group consisting of the heads of the spending divisions of the University, three elected members of the Council, and certain individuals who will bear the burden of presenting this year's request to the legislature. These men spent two full days and two full evenings in earnest discussion of the requests and finally came to unanimous agreement as to the sums to be asked and their allocation. The detailed estimates were prepared in accordance with these conclusions.

A Comparison With Other Institutions of Our Operating Request

There is one other comparison which I think will be of special interest to you, namely, the comparison of our operating request with that of other institutions in our territory.

COMPARATIVE LEGISLATIVE BUDGET REQUESTS
FOR BIENNIUM 1949–1951
OTHER SCHOOLS

	Estimated Enrollment Annually	Annual Request	Request per Year Per Student	1948 Enrollment	State Appropriation	1949 Average per Student
Uni. A	23,538	$30,199,985	$1,283	25,955	$22,223,120	$856
Uni. B	9,175	8,160,409	890	10,886	3,896,000	358
Uni. C	23,178	14,786,731	637	25,343	9,797,709	386
Uni. D	21,000	12,815,000	610	21,195	9,750,000	460
Uni. E	19,365	14,306,599	739	22,324	10,310,451	462
Total	96,256	$80,268,724	$ 834	105,703	$55,977,280	$530
Indiana U.	17,476	$ 9,123,474	$ 522	17,476	$ 5,912,989	$338

You will note that if we are given our entire request this year, we shall receive $8 less than the average received by the others for the past biennium.

I would like also especially to call your attention to the fact that this deals only with legislative appropriations. Wisconsin has substantial income from its patents. Minnesota has an 18 million dollar endowment; Michigan a 40 to 50 million dollar endowment. Our supplemental income is minor compared with these and the disparity becomes all the greater. I think these figures prove conclusively that the financial and academic administration of this institution is extremely conservative and economical.

Capital Request

We are now ready to make the following request for capital structures:
New Buildings most urgently needed during the Biennium 1949–51.

Bloomington Campus (in suggested order of priority)

(1) General Classroom and School of Education Office Building (addition to University School) (793,000 cu. ft.)

(2) Life Science Laboratory Building for Bacteriology, Botany and Zoology Departments (North of Alpha Hall on 3rd & Forest) (2,282,820 cu. ft.)

(3) First Unit of New Power Plant and Utilities distribution system on I.C.R.R. (2000 KW generator) (60,000 lbs. boiler)

(4) New Library Building (near center of campus) (1,000,000 volumes) (2,500,000 cu. ft.) (present structure needed for School of Law and other departments)

(5) Addition to Swain Hall (for departments of Astronomy, Mathematics and Physics) (335,000 cu. ft.)

(6) Addition to Chemistry Building (Completion of 4th floor and two wings extending south on each end of present structure) (400,000 cu. ft.)

(7) New Stores and Service Building (on I.C.R.R.) (700,000 cu. ft.) and remodeling of present structure for Journalism.

(8) Acquisition of Real Estate adjacent to campus (Fielders Addition)

(9) Extension of Walks and Drives

Indianapolis Campus

(1) Power Plant Expansion (to care for new State Board of Health Building, Carter Hospital and Veterans Hospital and New University buildings) (2-3000 KW Turbines and 3-50,000 lbs. boilers) The portion needed to serve other State and Federal structures should not be charged to Indiana University's allocation.

(2) Food Service, Housing and Physical Education facilities to serve students and staff. University will be unable to provide food service for the new State Board of Health and Carter Hospital unless this building can be provided. Present facilities in Riley Hospital cannot be expanded. Living space for nursing staff, students, continuation study groups, etc.

(3) Remodeling and Rehabilitation State Board of Health Building (for Medical Center Administration and Research use)

(4) Laundry and Service Shops Building now poorly housed in Riley Hospital and to permit serving of new State units and Veterans Hospital (600,000 cu. ft.) Paint and carpenter shops, creating a serious fire hazard, must be moved from Riley Hospital.

(5) First Unit New Medical School Building (to meet modern teaching and research requirements) (1,250,000 cu. ft.)

In arriving at our capital request we have tried to balance practicality and need. We have listed some of the buildings most urgently needed and those which from the standpoint of plans and available supplies might be started effectively during this biennium. We recognize that this list does not include many structures needed on this campus, on the Indianapolis campus, and in the Extension Centers. It would be easy to justify a list nearly twice this length if immediate need were the only consideration.

The priority of requests for buildings is essentially that stated in our postwar building program formulated by the deans and members of the faculty three years ago. The size and contents of some of the structures have been modified after more detailed studies by architects, but changes have not been major.

Plans and specifications are complete for the general classroom building. Architects are in the midst of working drawings for the life science building, and preliminary plans have been drawn for the power plant on the Bloomington campus. On the Indianapolis campus preliminary plans have been drawn for the power plant and floor plans drawn for the central dining room, kitchen, and continuation housing center unit. Planning will continue on these structures in the hope that we will be able to start building immediately when funds become available. Architects' offices are jammed with business these days and it takes a long time to get detailed workings for large complicated buildings.

The general administrative officers feel cumulative pressure from many departments for space. We know the need is acute and almost daily we receive new requests. Not a single available inch of space remains on the Bloomington campus for any new development. We have been ten years without any new permanent classroom structures. During this period enrollment tripled. To accommodate this increase the University is using 30 temporary buildings, most of them of frame construction, obtained from the Federal government by which they had been used as temporary barracks, storage space, etc. The government determined the buildings given the University, selecting structures generally which had deteriorated to a point no longer usable for the original purposes, and moved and re-erected the buildings on the campus. In contrast, temporary structures obtained for housing were selected by the University and were moved and re-erected by the University—a procedure which gave us far better buildings even though temporary in nature. In further contrast, the temporary buildings now used for classrooms were not designed for that purpose and their structural limitations were such as to make it impossible to adapt them for satisfactory classroom use. In ceiling height, lighting, noise potential, and ventilation they are ill suited for their present use, as well as being very costly to maintain and operate. Even with the most careful maintenance they will not stand up long under present usage.

Twenty-five per cent of the University's teaching faculty have their desks for grading, counseling, and study in temporary structures. For instance, 20 faculty members have desks in one such building with no partitions, poor lighting, and little ventilation other than doors opened at each end. Similar conditions exist in most of these structures.

Twenty-two per cent of the hours taught by the faculty and spent by students in class are in temporary structures—the total of student class hours (one for each student) is 13,104 per day in temporary structures. In addition, 17 classrooms, in which 4,200 class hours are taught daily, and desk spaces for 204 faculty and staff members are situated in attics, basements, one condemned building, and other quarters not designed for classrooms and offices. Lighting is poor, ventilation bad, and fire hazard great.

On the Indianapolis campus the space situation is critical but for a different reason. We are involved in changing somewhat the character of the Medical School program to bring it into conformity with modern professional trends and the needs of the State. It is of the utmost importance that we complete this transition, but this program cannot be executed without additional space.

This problem has been brought to the attention of the Budget Committee repeatedly. The Committee has been sympathetic with our need but has been unable to give us substantial help. Our funds for construction come from a special tax on alcoholic beverages levied to finance institutional building. This fund has proved inadequate because revenues have not been as great as expected and because contracts which have been let have been much higher than was anticipated. The tax is now yielding $5,700,000 per year. The situation is made all the more acute by the fact that other Midwestern institutions have had substantial building programs actually in progress during this biennium. Relatively we are losing ground so far as plant is concerned. A statement of this comparison, I think, will interest you.

FUNDS FOR NEW BUILDINGS IN MIDWESTERN STATE UNIVERSITIES

	1947–49 Biennium			Requested for 1949–51 Biennium
Institution	State	Other	Total	from State
U. of Ill.	$13,244,732	$ 1,800,000	$15,044,732	$63,065,000
Iowa State	3,713,500	3,580,000	7,293,500	11,700,000
U. of Iowa	3,773,000	480,000	4,253,000	16,165,000
Mich. State	13,239,000	15,450,000	28,689,000	8,320,000
U. of Minn.	9,752,000	5,964,000	15,716,000	12,437,700
U. of Wisc.	11,470,000	4,700,000	16,170,000	13,986,608
Ohio St. U.	19,604,900	541,100	20,146,000	——
U. of Mich.	11,969,500	10,625,000	22,594,500	8,855,000
	$10,844,580			$19,218,472

I shall not enumerate the arguments to be used in presenting our budget to the legislature and the public since those will be contained in a printed pamphlet soon to be placed in your hands. In presenting our budget this year we shall follow a somewhat different procedure than in the past several years. In the recent past we have told our story only to the Budget Committee and officers of the legislature. This year we shall attempt to supplement those efforts by a campaign of public education to acquaint all of the people of the State with our needs. We know that the legislature will wish to meet our request if possible. General public understanding will assist the legislature in its desire to aid us. You have already seen considerable newspaper publicity which begins that process. Students, parents, and alumni will be supplied with a considerable amount of information. On next Saturday we shall have a meeting here of all alumni members of the legislature and of representative alumni at which time we will present our case. Throughout the session we shall continue to keep our alumni informed and do all in our power to bring the seriousness of this situation to the general public. Naturally, in this educational effort, members of the Faculty can be of great help and I would urge you to read the printed material which will be supplied you, ask questions today or at any time so you will have the facts clearly in your mind.

Our legislative effort will be centralized in a committee consisting of Mr. C. Walter McCarty and Mr. Alexander Campbell of the Board of Trustees, Mr. Ross Bartley, Mr. Claude Rich, Mr. Pressley Sikes, Mr. William H. Snyder, and Mr. H. B. Allman.

A number of members of the faculty will be in close contact with the legislature as consultants, technicians, bill drafters, etc. They can all be of great help in presenting the University case if they work in active cooperation with our committee. It is requested that all members of the faculty who will participate in presenting programs of any nature to the legislature inform Mr. Sikes or Mr. Snyder of that fact. Situations arise in which members of the legislature ask our designated representative concerning interests of faculty members. They wish to know whether a bill is being sponsored by the University officially or by members of the faculty acting in other relationships. It is essential to the success of our budget request that there be coordination of all our legislative activity. This is in no sense a measure designed to restrain members of the faculty from legislative participation. It is protective rather than restrictive. If your individual activities are going to be detrimental to the budget request, our commitee has the right to know of it in advance so they can do all that is possible to minimize the damage. We all owe that much cooperation to each other.

Many members of the faculty will have personal acquaintanceship and other connections with members of the legislature that might be helpful. You are urged likewise to report those facts to our legislative committee.

Travel

I am happy to announce that a modest sum of money has been appropriated by the Board of Trustees to defray the cost of travel of members of the faculty to academic and scholarly meetings. Previously, travel expenses were allowed only to meetings at which it was thought the University as an institution should be represented. The sum available for this year will not be adequate to cover the entire travel expenses of staff members who may wish to attend such meetings. The plan which we are following in the allocation of these funds for the current year is experimental and it may be possible to work out a better plan before the beginning of the next academic year.

Retirement and Annuity

I am happy to announce that the Board of Trustees has recognized that inflation affects most severely our retired faculty members and has made an adjustment for this year resulting in an average increase of $500 per person. This was accomplished by increasing the amount of the supplement which the University pays in addition to the teacher's annuity from two to three per cent for each year of eligible service and increasing the maximum from $1,500 to $2,250.

We are the first institution in the country to make an adjustment for our retired faculty members on the formula basis. While the adjustment was made for this year only, it is hoped that the arrangement can be continued as long as cost of living remains high.

There has been considerable discussion about the fact that many institutions are increasing the retirement contribution from 10 to 15 per cent in order to build up a larger pension at any time of retirement. Investigation with Teacher's Insurance and Annuity Company reveals, however, that in every instance where this change has been made, it has been accompanied by a reduction to 65 for the retirement age. Investigation reveals that a 15 per cent contribution annually will build up nearly exactly the same retirement for a man at age 65 as a 10 per cent contribution will produce for a man at age 70, and the annuitant will likewise have the higher earnings of the last five years of activity in case he desires to remain until 70. Of course there are members of the faculty who do not feel like carrying on past 65 and our Board has already taken one step to protect these persons. As you will recall, last year I announced that members of our staff who were age 45 or more in 1937 were permitted to retire any time between 65 and 70 of their own volition and still receive the same retirement supplement they would have at age 70 without further payments. Personally, I should like to see us explore the further extension of this plan rather than the plan of increasing annuity contributions. TIAA informs us that this proposal which we have already inaugurated for all the older members of our faculty is unique both in form and liberality. We have, as most of you know, a third feature of our pension and retirement program which is unique, namely, that provision which protects income of members of our faculty and staff against *permanent* and total disability after 10 years of service. Such coverage can no longer be purchased commercially. When it could be purchased it was available only after rigid medical examination. The only disability protection that now may be purchased is limited sharply as to age, length of benefits, and amounts. It is available only to those who can pass exceptionally strict medical examinations. These limitations are not present in our plan.

Moreover, during the spring semester, the required percentage of the staff approved a modification of the group insurance program whereby additional life insurance with disability benefits was provided. Most of the faculty now have this added protection at a small increase in cost over the lesser protection of the original plan.

Sabbatical Leaves

From the beginning of our policy of sabbatical leaves until the end of the school year of 1944–45, 31 leaves were granted, most of them previous to the war. Since the Fall of 1945, 37 leaves have been granted, and of these 17 were granted in 1947–48. Applications for leave are now on a steady increase; 17 have already been granted for the current year.

As stated in the original announcement of our policy, sabbatical leave with full salary for one semester or half salary for a full year may be granted to members of the faculty who present a program of study and research that is approved by a special committee. It is expected that the granting of such leaves will ordinarily be made without incurring the additional expense of employing a replacement. In most cases, therefore, the work of persons on leave has been absorbed by other members of the staff or, in some instances, certain courses taught by them have been dropped temporarily from the schedule. It is apparent that, without provision for a considerable increase in the budget, the number of leaves granted cannot be increased indefinitely. It is difficult at present for members of small departments to take leaves of absence. In large departments, schedules can be shifted more easily. For these and other reasons it is desirable to restudy this matter to the end that our policy on sabbaticals may be as equitable as possible to all.

Therefore, I would recommend that the Faculty Council place this matter on its agenda for early consideration.

New Construction—Self-Liquidating

Our two largest construction projects are those financed by borrowed money, namely, the apartment and dormitory structures. The apartments on East Third Street will contain 236 apartments. It is now believed that the first of these will be ready for occupancy by the beginning of the second semester and the second unit by June.

It is expected that the dormitories on East Tenth housing 750 men and 250 women will be ready for occupancy by the fall semester. Portions will be ready long in advance of that time; in fact, certain portions are nearly ready now. I am happy to report that, to date, these buildings are being constructed within their budget and with fine work. An important factor in this achievement has been the scrupulous observance by the labor unions of their agreement to finish the job at rates in force when construction began. We have had also excellent superintendence and construction management.

At the time we began these projects it may have seemed to some that the timing was inopportune. We pointed out in these remarks last year that we were able to borrow money at a very low rate, that the cost of money is a substantial portion of the cost of building with borrowed funds and that the saving in interest would, in part, offset the high cost of the construction. The wisdom of our start last year has been demonstrated by the experience of a neighboring institution which recently attempted to let a contract for a dormitory simpler than ours and discovered that the best bid called for a cost per student of $7,500 in contrast to our cost per student of $4,000. In addition, interest rates are now substantially higher than at the time we sold our bonds.

Although occupancy of the apartment houses should ease the housing situation for married students and faculty to some degree, a shortage will remain. Neither will the occupancy of the new dormitories solve all the problems of housing single students. We do hope, however, to be able to discontinue the use of wooden buildings on each side of the Fieldhouse as dormitories, to eliminate the doubling up in the South, West, and North Halls for men and in the Memorial Hall quadrangle for women. It seems unlikely that we will be able to reduce occupancy in Rogers II to the capacity for which the unit was originally designed or to abandon Rogers I, steps which must come at some future time. These latter two steps are not urgent now, so with the completion of the new units we will have reason to feel satisfied with our progress in housing students.

Construction with State Funds

At the Medical Center substantial remodeling of the Dental School building has been in process to provide more efficient quarters for the School. The change includes excavation and development of a basement for school purposes.

Substantial remodeling is in process in the Medical School instructional building, and contracts have been let for construction of an addition to the Clinical Building to house a cancer clinic at a cost of $280,634.96. We are just completing a fourth floor on the Long Hospital consisting of 22 bedrooms containing 32 beds and other facilities to be used as an isolation ward. This new floor is paid for out of funds left by the Robert W. Long bequest and other gifts to the hospital. Finally, money has been allocated by the State Budget Committee to the Riley Memorial Association for the construction of a research wing to the Riley Hospital to cost approximately $400,000. It is expected that contracts will be let for this work within a few days.

Under construction on the Bloomington campus at the present time are steam and electric distribution lines which will serve the new apartment buildings, the new men's dormitories, East Hall and the classroom building used by Nursing Education. It will be adequate also to serve the proposed women's dormitory. This line serves the further purpose of tying together our two power plants in such a way that the old plant can be relieved of part of its heat and power load. Contracts let on this project to date total $286,124.30 and an estimated $25,000 will be required for completion.

In order to assure adequate water supply for the new apartments, for the future women's dormitory, and for such other buildings as may be constructed east of Jordan in the future, a new 8-inch water line is being run a distance of 2,210 feet from Union Street to Jordan Avenue. The existing line in Third Street is too small to serve these buildings.

A City-owned sewer serving the east part of the City and some University buildings on the east part of the campus had proved inadequate even without the addition of the new apartments and the future women's dormitory. The University is, therefore, running an 18-inch line for a distance of 2,240 feet from Jordan to a point near Jordan Field to provide this service.

The sewer and water lines are being installed at a total contract price of $53,001.81.

Finally, we are also developing a new area for Botany research gardens and are erecting a small greenhouse and research building on the site at a cost of $30,000.

On February 18, 1948, we purchased from the Lumberman's Mutual Insurance Company the stone-fronted office building adjacent to the Indianapolis Extension Center. As no funds were available from the State for this purpose, the Trustees of this University executed a mortgage payable over 15 years. Certain floors of the building have been rented commercially, and from these rents we hope to pay for the building over a ten-year period. The remaining floors of the structure are being remodeled for the use of the Indianapolis Center and will greatly add to the facilities for our work in Adult Education in Indianapolis.

Classroom Utilization on Bloomington Campus

Since there are so many unsatisfied demands for classroom space, it is perhaps worthwhile to review for you the efficiency of our classroom utilization. I think few institutions can claim economy and efficiency of operation of plant equal to ours.

For many years the percentage of classroom use has averaged much higher at Indiana than it has at sister institutions. Percentage of classroom use in one of our neighboring state universities in 1945–46 was 29 per cent. Percentage of use in state-controlled colleges in Maryland prewar ranged from 27 per cent to 77 per cent with only one institution at the 77 per cent figure and no other close to it. Percentage of use of 1,400 rooms in four liberal arts colleges, four engineering schools, eight teachers colleges and six state universities studied by Ray L. Hamon in 1930 averaged 18 per cent. *Percentage of use at Indiana University in 1938–39 was 73.*

Since the war we have increased our class day from seven hours to ten hours, but our percentage of use for ten hours is even higher than it was for seven hours; i.e. first semester 1947–48 use equaled 82.5 per cent.

Such a high percentage of use is not efficient since it requires a schedule so inflexible that sometimes it violates accepted educational practice. For years a percentage of 75 was regarded as absolute maximum.

We are unable to convert any classroom space to other uses even though the educational needs of the institution demand it. For instance, one department in the College of Arts and Sciences requested that a small classroom be converted into a research area so that three new instruments could be used by its ten staff members. This request could not be granted, even though the only other area for the machines is the department chairman's office.

We are using many rooms which are not suitable for instruction; i.e., the kitchen demonstration room in Wylie Hall has assigned to it classes in Linguistics, Education, German, and Music. This lack of flexibility in our classroom program prohibits the utilization of new educational techniques such as audio visual aids.

Percentage of classroom use for first semester 1948–49 will be approximately 88 per cent. With no increase in classrooms this high percentage of use will continue or become even larger because our institution is teaching increasing numbers of students at the junior, senior, and graduate level. Such students can be properly instructed only in classes totaling fifty or less. More students at these levels necessitates more classrooms. I present you with this information so that you may fully understand the difficulties sometimes facing the general administrative officers in providing the facilities that you need.

Instruction

Owing to the continued large enrollment, it is still necessary to use graduate assistants and large classes in certain subjects. However, during the year 1947–48 the average class size for the Bloomington campus was 31.2 as compared with an average of 42.7 in 1946–47 and 28.8 for 1939–40. Despite the conditions forced upon us by the large enrollment following the war, it is gratifying to note that the work of students has not deteriorated. Indeed, as shown by the credit points per credit hour average, student achievement has decidedly improved, and not all the change can be traced to the larger numbers of veterans and older members of the student body, since the average for women has also improved. There is no indication that the better grades are the result of lower standards in grading or in the quality of work required by the faculty. In 1940–41 the credit point per credit hour average for women was 1.487; for 1945–46 the last year before the days of our present large enrollment, it was 1.447; for 1946–47, it was 1.422; and for 1947–48 it was 1.506. For men, the average in 1945–46, the year of small classes and small total enrollment, was 1.19 as compared to 1.34 before the war. In 1946–47 the average rose to 1.351, and in 1947–48 it climbed still higher to 1.406.

Faculty Salaries

In the budget for 1948–49, no general increase in faculty salaries was possible because it was necessary to provide for approximately the same enrollment with a lower income as a result of a decline in the number of veterans. Some increases were made on a merit basis for those whose salaries were below the average for their ranks, and in those cases where the salary was at the very bottom of the general scale. It was not possible to do as much as seemed desirable in many instances. Not all those who deserved at least the average salary for their rank could be brought up to that average, but we moved in this direction as far as we could go in face of the rather unfavorable budgetary situation.

During the last two years the size of the faculty has increased approximately 45 per cent. It has been necessary to add many instructors and some assistant professors on temporary tenure. In addition, many teaching fellows have been appointed in certain areas. It was never the intention that all such appointments should become permanent; and as our enrollment during the next few years finds its normal pattern, it is evident that many persons now employed on a temporary basis cannot be reemployed year after year. Several such persons were not reemployed for the year 1948–49. This condition does not reflect on the merits of members of the staff who are not reappointed, but, rather, it is in keeping with the only possible solution of the problem of shifts in the enrollment which result in smaller numbers of freshmen and sophomores and larger numbers of junior, senior, and graduate students. The large number of staff members still on temporary appointment places a grave responsibility upon the executive officers of the University. The case of each person on temporary tenure must be thoroughly reviewed each year in the light of the University's need for his services, his qualifications, his success, and his promise for the future. We owe this to the individual as well as to the institution.

Faculty Ranks and Promotion

For 1948–49 the distribution of the entire faculty of the University by ranks is as follows: full professor, 143; associate professor, 106; assistant professor, 186; instructor, 258. For the Bloomington campus only there are 115 full professors; 82 associate professors; 134 assistant professors; and 216 instructors. For 1948–49, 34.5 per cent of the entire faculty and 36 per cent of the Bloomington faculty is in the top two ranks. In 1946–47, the percentage was 35 per cent; in 1945–46, 39 per cent; in 1944–45, 40 per cent; and in 1940–41, 42 per cent.

On the whole, this distribution by ranks of the faculty is satisfactory and healthy. We must have a sufficient number of members in the upper ranks to insure adequate instruction in advanced courses and, at the same time, there must always be room at the top for promotion of those who merit it. Thus far, we have been able to consider promotions without placing a limit upon numbers of persons in any rank. I trust that our promotions policy can always recognize merit without undue delay.

The Strengthening of Upperclass Work

The staffs of several departments have been strengthened during the year, especially at the upperclass and graduate levels. Much has also been done during the year to strengthen materially the graduate curriculum and to develop research training facilities in Medicine, Dentistry, German, French, Chemistry, Geology, and other divisions of the University. Although our graduate programs have shown good progress since the war, it is my opinion that they can be further developed and strengthened. When so many men and women are being trained in the colleges, it is highly important, indeed it is essential, that our universities expand their training programs at the most advanced levels to insure a large number of persons trained as college teachers and also a sufficient number to meet the demands and needs of industry, government, and the professions. Graduate work is scattered throughout many divisions and departments, some of these without graduate school affiliation. This results in confusion and, perhaps, in inefficiency. I believe that we should study this problem during the next two years to seek ways of coordinating and integrating the graduate work of different schools, and I would recommend that such a study be reinaugurated by the graduate faculty, by the Council, or under such other auspices as may be prepared to undertake the work.

Research

1947–48 was a productive year in faculty research and publications. The bibliography of publications by the faculty shows almost 800 items as compared to approximately 465 for the preceding year. In these 800 items are many of great importance, and one, the volume published by Professor Kinsey and his colleagues, is already known to scholars throughout the world. This is a splendid record, especially in view of the increased teaching responsibilities which most of you have had to share. In addition to funds for research made available in the University budget, and in addition to many relatively small but important grants in aid of research made by various industrial concerns and groups of citizens, the sum of $361,867.99 was provided for the use of staff members in the form of funds made available by various governmental agencies.

We likewise received a gift of the Link Observatory, which has a cash value of approximately $300,000 but value as a research instrument that is incalculable. This gift is a reflection of the confidence of Dr. Link in the quality and the productivity of our excellent staff in Astronomy.

Faculty Honors

The Faculty, likewise, won extraordinary recognition measured by the number of offices held in professional and learned societies, special awards, invitations to lecture at other institutions, and similar forms of professional recognition. According to the records in our offices, 93 men and women were honored in this manner. I am sure we all take pride in the winning of these significant honors by our colleagues. We hope to publish the entire list in the annual report, and as a consequence we would like to have the record as nearly complete as possible. I am certain the list which we have, though impressive, is not complete, and we urge that you supply us with such information about yourself if it has not already been reported.

Library

On July 1, 1948, the library holdings of the University were reported as 1,075,403 separate items. Of this total 755,000 represents our volume count. Among university libraries in the country we remain firmly established in twentieth position. During the year we added 52,000 volumes and 40,000 pieces of manuscripts.

I should like to emphasize the responsibility of all faculty members with respect to our Library. A great library can be developed only by the constant attention of members of the faculty who make careful suggestions for purchases for building great collections in their own subject matter fields. In many areas our Library is not strong. It can be made better by faculty recommendation. We shall continue to provide as much money as our finances will permit in meeting these recommendations.

A significant development in the library area is the proposal now being considered by a number of groups for the construction of a Midwest storage library for little-used materials. This suggestion has been discussed for the past several years by the presidents of some of the Midwest institutions which have an organization called the Committee of Thirteen. The membership of the committee consists of the presidents of the Big Ten institutions plus Michigan State, Iowa State, and the Illinois Institute of Technology.

A report financed by the Carnegie Corporation, just completed, recommends the immediate erection in Chicago of a storage library to be administered cooperatively by a board representative of the institutions participating. Finally, a committee consisting of Mr. Hutchins and Mr. Colwell of the University of Chicago, Mr. Hancher of Iowa, and myself presented a request of the officers of the Carnegie Corporation last Monday in New York for funds to build and equip the structure. We received from the officers of the Corporation a sympathetic hearing and a promise to give the matter serious consideration.

In all of the discussions concerning this subject we have maintained contact with Dr. Miller, Director of Libraries, and through him with the Library Committee. The matter has now developed to the place where it deserves serious consideration by the Faculty as a whole, and for that purpose I have asked the Council to place the subject on its agenda. It is to be expected that the Council will create appropriate machinery for studying the matter and finally make recommendations as to our participation in the project.

Student Relationships

I cannot emphasize too much or too often the importance of willingness on the part of instructors to confer with students about matters which the students wish to bring to their attention, especially matters concerning their own academic status. We have more unfavorable criticism from parents on this score than any other. This does not necessarily mean the teachers deliberately refuse to talk with students, but it arises, I believe, from the fact that in certain large classes students do not have the opportunity of talking to their principal instructors. The announcement of definite office hours by each faculty member of, say, two to three hours per week, would help greatly in contributing to the friendly relations between teachers and students that are so essential to effective teaching. I know that many of you already follow this practice.

On the administration side we are doing everything we can to make certain that each student receives the attention which his problems demand. For freshmen this is the function of the Junior Division. For upperclasmen, this function belongs to the Counseling Division of the Dean of Students Office, and to the offices of the different deans and department heads. Members of the faculty also play an important part in this work. In my opinion, the work which we do in counseling students pays large dividends in good will as well as in direct and immediate service to the students themselves. That there is a demand for such counseling is indicated by the fact that the counseling division in the Office of the Dean of Students during 1947–48 held 3,358 conferences with students. For the most part these conferences were sought by the students and dealt with a great variety of personal problems.

There are those who object to counseling on the ground that it removes from the student the responsibility of thinking out his own problems. This is not a valid observation so far as our organization is concerned. Our counseling programs are not designed to do a student's thinking for him, but rather to encourage him to find the solution for himself. Indeed, there is great need throughout the University to emphasize the acceptance by the student of responsibility for his own education and discipline. Counseling best serves its purpose and has for its objective a stimulation of interest in the student's own problems and the development of his own capabilities of finding solutions to these problems. The burden of responsibility for success or failure in the University, for choosing careers wisely, for making the total college experience fruitful, must be put more and more upon the individual student, with the counselor guiding the student toward the acceptance of this responsibility.

Our system could be improved by better coordination of the counseling by different advisers who may make contact with students at different times during their college careers. At times some students seem to be confused by the advice which they receive from different persons on academic matters.

It seems to be the general opinion today that a higher percentage of our young people should and will go to college. If this is true, the problem must be faced realistically rather than idealistically. Our young people differ greatly as individuals, and if they are all to go to college it is possible that we should diversify our programs even more than we have. Certainly, in the present trend in enrollment there are many problems to be studied by a university faculty. If larger numbers of young people are to be accepted as college students, what will they do eventually and how should they be trained? Does the traditional college program seem best suited to their needs? Shall we make available more space for them in the professional schools already established in the University? Should additional professional curricula be established, and, if so, in what areas? Shall our objective primarily be to educate towards ways of making a living, or shall it be to educate for better and fuller living? How is the superior student to be challenged to realize his full potentialities when competing with those who are less gifted?

I suggest that it would be profitable and desirable for the Faculty Council to initiate a number of studies seeking to find the answers to these questions for the students at Indiana University.

Within the faculties of the different schools there is need for continuing studies of the adequacy and general effectiveness of curricula. It appears to me that in some parts of the University there is a growing tendency to divide areas of instruction into smaller and smaller highly specialized units. There are dangers in a policy of this kind. It is wasteful of manpower and of the time and energy of the faculty. I ask you, therefore, to consider carefully, as you study the curriculum of your school or department, the possibility of consolidating small units of instruction covering narrow areas of learning into more general, fundamental courses. I believe that for undegraduate students at least such action is sound pedagogically.

Continuing careful coordination between the office of the Dean of Students and members of the faculty is desirable. There are a variety of problems that need consideration at this time such as desirable faculty action when requested to approve books for purchase by veterans, hospitality for foreign students, willingness of members of the faculty to serve as sponsors for student organizations, and also to chaperone student functions, adequate utilization of our counseling remedial clinics and bureaus. I would recommend that the Faculty Council create a committee or series of committees to consider these problems with the Dean of Students for the purpose of making recommendations to the faculty for action.

Extension Students

During 1947–48 the number of full-time students in the extension centers was 3,428. Large numbers of these students will transfer to the campus during 1948–49 and 1949–50. The extension centers, therefore, must be recognized as integral parts of the University, since a significant percentage of our students is now being trained in these centers during their freshman and sophomore years. It is highly important, therefore, that deans, department heads, and faculty members do everything possible to bring about coordination of the work in the centers and on the campus. A great deal has been accomplished along this line, but there is still more to be done. Among other things, the teaching staffs of these centers must be kept in close touch with the work of the various departments on the campus, and ways must be found to incorporate them more intimately into the activities of the general university faculty. It is important that deans and department heads at all times keep in close touch with the work of the staff and with the students in the centers.

Extension Organization

In some future statement I wish to devote a substantial portion of my remarks to our public service and extension activity. Time available today will permit me to report only that our new Division of Adult Education and Public Services has made substantial progress in developing a well-rounded program for the State as a whole and in solving many organizational problems. Of special significance this year was the merging of the Gary Junior College with our Gary Center. Gary Junior College has been in existence as a part of the public school system of Gary for many years, and yet the authorities in charge after careful study concluded that the interests of the community would be better served by an extension center of the University than by their own institution. This in no way reflects upon the excellent program that had been carried on in the Gary College. It has been one of the most successful institutions of its type in the country. But there are certain resources that may be brought to a community by an extension arrangement with a university that are never possible in a high school-connected junior college, even though its management and program are exceptional as at Gary.

Summer Session

It appears that we may expect our summer session enrollment during the next few years to return to a distribution of students somewhat similar to prewar.

There were strong indications of this trend during the summer session of 1948. It will be necessary, therefore, before the summer session of 1949 to plan our schedule of classes well in advance, and to limit our staff to those required to teach the courses of this changed pattern. In certain areas this will mean that only a small proportion of the regular staff will be needed. In other areas it may even be necessary to add staff to take care of increased enrollment during the summer.

Riley Centennial and Riley Research Fund

By proclamation of the Governor the year 1949 has been designated the Riley Centennial year during which time the state will observe the centennial of the birth of the Hoosier poet, James Whitcomb Riley. A state-wide committee is soon to be created to develop a year-long program. The committee will be serviced by a small full-time staff. It will need, however, the active cooperation of the educational institutions of the State and especially of this institution because of the close associations which we have with Mr. Riley.

As another means of observing the Centennial, the Riley Memorial Association will conduct a campaign for a million dollars to be used in support of research at the Riley Hospital. Specifically, it will be used to finance the scientific program in the research wing now being constructed by the State at the Riley Hospital, to which I have already referred. Two weeks ago Monday night a campaign was launched with a dinner at the Riley Hospital at which I spoke for the University as a whole, Dr. Van Nuys for the Medical School, and Mr. Arthur Baxter, chairman of the drive, for the drive committee. The first phase of the campaign is to be conducted without publicity, designed to contact large givers in Indianapolis alone. As soon as this work is completed the sum thus raised will be used as a basis for the announcement of a state-wide campaign, designed to appeal to all of the people of the State.

As soon as this campaign is announced, we should speak well of it on every possible opportunity throughout the State and cooperate in any specific way requested by the campaign committee.

The Faculty Council

The faculty has reason to be proud of the record of the Faculty Council during the first year of its existence. You have already received from the Secretary of the Council a review of the Council's activities during the year. The group met the first and third week of each month, made many important decisions, and studied many problems of general University concern. Problems formerly discussed with the Administrative Council were taken up by the Faculty Council; thus, the faculty through its elected representatives, as well as through the deans, had a voice in administrative affairs as well as in legislation on academic policies. The attendance of your representatives was excellent, and throughout the year all members worked for the general welfare of the institution. This is as it should be; representatives on the Council represent no one division of the University or no one faculty group. They are elected by the entire faculty and, therefore, must represent all parts of the faculty and all parts of the institution.

There are many topics to which the Council can give its attention during this year in addition to those which I have already mentioned. I should like to state once again the need for studying special problems connected with the education of women. There is need, too, for a study of our grading system with the view of attaining greater uniformity in the interpretation of the meaning of the letter-symbols used in reporting grades. The Council should determine some way by which divisions of the University not located on the Bloomington campus can participate in its activities. This matter is urgent and deserves our best thought and a prompt decision.

It is very important, it seems to me, for us to improve our teaching. There is so much activity in so many institutions seeking this objective that this subject may fairly be called a matter of national academic concern. In general it takes two forms: first, effort to devise methods of in-service training and to stimulate effective classroom performance; and secondly, effort to interest the best students in college teaching as a career. I heard one prominent man say recently that the indifference of the teaching profession to the quality of its successors is shocking. Interesting experiments are taking place at the University of Missouri, at Michigan, Chicago, Princeton, and at scores of other institutions. I think we might well organize our consideration of this matter either through a committee of the Council or committees of the individual colleges. If a committee or committees are formed, I shall be happy to place in their hands a considerable amount of information concerning these other experiments and programs.

Conclusion

We have successfully met the emergency problems arising out of the postwar reconversion of the University to peacetime curricula, greater emphasis upon graduate and professional work, and a greatly expanded student body. We can all take pride in the manner in which we have solved these emergency problems. Yet as I review our situation, I am struck by the fact that there remain a large number of fundamental problems of long-range nature all of which are clamoring for thought and attention. We can be grateful that the solution of the emergency problems now gives us opportunity to attack these longer-range issues. This task in itself furnishes a challenge to us sufficient to insure that the work of this year and the years ahead will be stimulating and exciting, demanding the best of our minds and energies.

(The End)

Faculty Minutes, 1945–1964, following p. 250.

Document 150

Grades and Buildings

The Indiana University faculty had not indulged itself in a discussion of that ever-favorite subject—grades—for some time. There was not much that was original in this report, but the fact that it was before the Faculty Council was definite assurance that the subject was still a live and unresolved one. President Wells reviewed the building program. He mentioned the need for the general classroom building; this was finally constructed as Ballantine Hall.

*   *   *

Dean Briscoe, chairman of the Committee on Grading, then presented the following report:

"The Committee recommends that all academic divisions of the University employ the same system of grading symbols in reporting grades. The Committee further recommends that the system of symbols used consist of the letters, A, B, C, D, E, F, Inc., and Def., and that these symbols be regarded as having the same meaning as at present. The Committee recommends discontinuance of the use of the symbol X.

"It is recommended, also, that the use of plus and minus signs be discontinued, and that no attempt be made to equate letter grades in terms of percentages.

"The Committee further recommends the following subjects for consideration of the Council:

(a) Uniform evaluation of grades in terms of credit points.

(b) Means of attaining greater uniformity in the assignment of grades. If this question is studied, it is suggested that consideration be given to the report made by a committee of the Arts College in May, 1948.

(c) The practice of certain schools and departments of requiring, for different purposes, a grade higher than the lowest passing grade accepted by the University."

Discussion of the report followed. Professor Benns suggested that the plus and minus signs helped to measure real differences in student attainment and ought therefore to be retained. Dean Briscoe replied that at present there is no uniformity in the use of such signs, and that many instructors never use them. Professor Weatherwax said that he doubted the validity of the refinement in grades suggested by plus and minus signs. Dean Ashton suggested the possibility of the instructor's using plus and minus signs, but of not including them in the official record. Professor Harmon pointed out the importance of achieving uniformity in grading symbols throughout the University. Professor Yellen asked if the symbol X might not be necessary for such non-credit courses as English 106. Dean Briscoe suggested that even though no credit is allowed, a grade might nevertheless be given; and Dean Ashton added that there are now many noncredit courses in the College in which grades are given. Dean Gavit asked if the recommendations would be applicable to the Indianapolis campus and the other Extension centers. President Wells replied that if the recommendations are approved, it should be understood that the off-campus schools and centers would be given an opportunity to present a rebuttal should they wish to do so.

A motion was made by Dean Bain that the Council approve the recommendations in the first two paragraphs in the report of the Committee on Grading. Seconded by Dean Ashton.

A motion was made by Dean Gavit to amend Dean Bain's motion so that the new recommendations would become effective as of September, 1949. Seconded by Professor Long. Passed unanimously.

A motion was made by Dean Wright that Dean Bain's motion, as amended, be tabled until the next meeting of the Council, in order to provide more time for consideration of the problem. Seconded by Dean Gavit. Defeated by a vote of 11 to 7.

The original motion by Dean Bain, as amended, was then passed by a vote of 17 to 2.

A motion was made by Dean Ashton that the Committee on Grading continue its deliberations of the problems suggested in the third paragraph of its report. Seconded by Dean Wright. Passed unanimously.

President Wells then spoke of the program of new buildings now being recommended to the State Legislature (a list is given in the minutes for December 2, 1948), and read the following letter of transmittal (dated January 3, 1949) to Mr. Roscoe P. Freeman, State Director of the Budget:

"We transmit herewith a summary list of the new buildings most urgently needed by Indiana University in suggested order of priority for each the Bloomington and Indianapolis campuses. Other structures are critically needed and are a part of the University's long term planning but the Board did not deem it necessary to burden the committee with those plans at this time.

"On the Bloomington campus the General Classroom building is needed first and you are familiar with this need as it has been presented previously. However, a short statement covering this need and for all items in the summary is attached. As already reported to you, plans and specifications for this project are completed and ready to advertise for bids. The Federal Government loaned funds for planning. The project could be completed during the coming biennium and is estimated to cost about $1,300,000.00

"The Life Science Laboratory Building is in the planning stage with Federal Government funds also. However, it could not be ready before another six months and construction will require at least 2 years so that this project would probably not be entirely completed with the biennium. Of the total estimated cost of $3,400,000.00, probably $2,500,000.00 to $3,000,000.00 would be needed during the biennium.

"The First Unit of the New Power Plant and Utilities Distribution is through the preliminary planning stage. If the turbine and boiler equipment were ordered in the next six months, it is doubtful if it could be delivered during the next bennium. However, some of the work on site, building and distribution could go forward during the biennium. Expenditure during biennium would be between $1,500,000.00 and $2,000,000.00.

"The Library and other construction projects are only in preliminary planning stage and actual construction will not be possible until late in the biennium or the next biennium of 1951-53. Funds for actual plans should be provided, however, during the coming biennium of 1949-51, at least for Library and Swain Hall and Chemistry additions.

"On the Indianapolis Campus plans for Power Plant Expansion are about ready for ordering of turbines and boilers and The Budget Committee has approved proceeding with the project which is vital to other structures. It should be completed during the coming year at a cost of $1,000,000.00 to $1,500,000.00 depending on whether the Veterans Hospital needs are included.

"The Food-service Unit will be ready for bids in six to nine months. The first draft of preliminary plans is completed. The total cost including equipment will be about $4,500,000.00. The first unit should be completed during the biennium at a cost of about $3,000,000.00

"Remodeling of the State Board of Health building and construction of Laundry, Stores and Shops building should be carried out during the biennium in separate units. The Laundry plans are about completed; other plans are in preliminary stage only. However, it appears all units could be carried out for around $1,000,000.00

"The First unit of the Medical School building is in preliminary planning stage but eighteen months would be required before final plans could be ready. If authorization for proceeding with planning could be given the funds for actual construction cost could be considered later probably about the beginning of the 51-53 biennium.

"If Federal Funds for additional planning or construction should be made available; we would expect to make application therefore keeping the committee advised of our progress and possibly speed up our planning.

"The University desires to proceed on an orderly and well-planned construction program over a period of years."

President Wells suggested that at its next meeting the Council discuss the proposed reorganization of the American Association of Universities.

Adjournment at 5.

Faculty Council Minutes, 1947–1950, pp. 88–89; 89–90.

Document 151

Off-Campus Faculty Relations

This report by the Committee on Off-Campus Faculty Relations to the University deals with a growing and complex subject. Specifically at issue was the question of how a member of the faculty in one of the centers could be fully participating member of the decision-making body. Outlined here was a somewhat complicated process as to how this could be accomplished.

* * *

REPORT OF COMMITTEE ON RELATIONS
OF OFF-CAMPUS FACULTY TO THE UNIVERSITY

Your committee has considered the problem of off-campus representation and wishes to report its tentative proposals to the Council prior to a presentation of the plan to the off-campus representatives for their consideration. It is clear that unless there is general agreement both on objectives and procedures between the Council and committee no plan can be inaugurated in time for the spring elections.

As a basis for preliminary consideration, the committee makes the following proposals:

The Facts. The Constitution of the faculty provides that any member of the staff devoting full time to teaching or research and holding the rank of instructor or above is a "voting member" of the faculty. During the present semester there are 708 such persons in the employ of Indiana University. Of this number 558 are employed on the Bloomington campus and 150 are employed off-campus. In other words, one-fifth or 21% of our full time teaching personnel is resident outside the city of Bloomington. They are distributed as follows:

Indianapolis Faculty Other Than Adult Education

Dentistry	14
Health, Phys.Ed.Recr.	4
Law	7
Medicine	44
Social Science	10
TOTAL	79

Adult Education Faculties

Calumet Center	19
Earlham	1
Fort Wayne	10
Gary	2
Indianapolis	16
Jeffersonville	6
Kokomo	5
South Bend	12
TOTAL	71

TOTAL OFF-CAMPUS 150

Under the Faculty Constitution these 150 persons are entitled to representation on the Faculty Council. They may vote for representation on the Council and it has been customary for them to receive ballots and some have voted in past elections. It is recognized, however, that it is extremely unlikely under existing procedures for them to elect a representative other than a resident on the Bloomington campus. Thus, there is no practical way in which their faculty representatives may report back to them and their only channel of communication is through the administrative officers who represent their Schools and Divisions.

The Problem. 1. How to ensure greater dissemination of information concerning Faculty Council and administrative action among the off-campus faculties.

2. How to insure greater off-campus representation on the Faculty Council.

The Proposals. 1. The dissemination of information is primarily an administrative matter and certainly involves no change in the Faculty Constitution. Two methods seem feasible:

(a) the distribution of so much of the agenda as practicable in advance of Council meetings.

(b) the circulation of the mimeographed minutes of Faculty Council action to all voting members of the faculty, both on and off the campus.

Further, your committee recommends, that the Council appoint a committee to study the feasibility of the establishment of a Faculty Bulletin, similar to that published by the University of Illinois, to be published in 10 issues a year as an official faculty organ for announcements, action, and reporting.

2. For improvement in off-campus representation by the amendment of the Faculty Constitution to permit independent election of representatives of off-campus personnel.

At the present time one-fifth of the voting members of the faculty are employed off the Bloomington campus. Thus, if the present council of sixteen was increased by four off-campus members they would represent the approximate relation that off-campus voting members of the faculty bears to the total faculty. It is therefore recommended that the faculty representation on the Council be increased to twenty members, four to be selected by the off-campus faculties.

Method of Selection. The principle of representation fixed in the present Faculty Constitution is that Council members represent the entire University and therefore should be selected on a University-wide basis. The experience of the Council indicates that University-wide election has resulted in selecting council members with a true feeling of University-wide responsibility. Therefore, it would seem desirable that a similar principle should guide the off-campus system.

Some adjustment in this principle seems advisable, however, because of the divergence in program and problems that exist between the Division of Adult Education and the five Indianapolis professional schools. Thus, it is proposed that the four off-campus representatives be divided equally between these two groups—two to be selected by the five professional schools and two by the eight centers of Adult Education.

Election Procedures. The same election procedure should be followed in the selection of the four representatives as is used on the Bloomington campus, i.e., an election committee of three appointed by the President, a nominating ballot to all voting members from which the top four in each group are selected, a final ballot to select the two representatives from each group.

Eligibility for Council Membership. Although it is assumed that the off-campus faculties will desire to select one of their own members to represent them on the Council, it is also recognized that the inconveniences of schedules and transportation may in certain instances make it desirable to select a person on the Bloomington campus as a member or as an alternate, therefore it is recommended that either off-campus or on-campus voting members be eligible for election as off-campus representatives.

The Proposed Amendments. If the above proposals are agreed upon, then they should be put into effect by amendment to the Faculty Constitution. The Amendments might read as follows:

Sec. 19. Faculty Council. The Faculty Council shall be composed of 16 members elected at large *by the voting members* on the Bloomington campus, *4 members elected at large by the voting members off the Bloomington campus,* the President, the Dean of Faculties, etc.

Sec. 21.1. Election of Off-Campus Members. (1) The voting members of the Indianapolis faculties other than those in the Division of Adult Education shall elect two members to the Council.

(2) The voting members of the Division of Adult Education, other than those resident on the Bloomington campus shall elect two members to the Council.

Sec. 21.2. Election Procedure. The procedure for the election of off-campus members of the Council shall be the same as that prescribed in section 10. Upon holding the first election, one member from each group identified in section 21.1 shall be elected for a term of two years and one from each group shall be elected for a term of one year. Thereafter, all elections shall be for two year terms.

Sec. 21.3. Eligibility. The off-campus voting members may select for their representatives any person who is a voting member of the faculty regardless of whether he is resident on or off the Bloomington campus.

Committee Procedure. The Committee requests that the Council give tentative approval to this proposal. If the Council feels that the proposal is generally satisfactory then the Committee believes that it should circulate a memorandum outlining the history of the organization of the Faculty Council and the background for this proposal to all voting members of the off-campus faculty for their consideration.

After this circularization the Committee will then hold a meeting of all off-campus personnel in Indianapolis to consider the report. When agreement has been reached on a specific proposal the Committee will then report back to the

Council and recommend that the Council propose appropriate amendments to the Constitution to be submitted to the Faculty in accordance with constitutional procedure.

G. BROWNING	H. NORMAN
R. N. HARGER	H. VEATCH
M. HINE	F. E. HORACK JR., Chairman
H. LUSK	

Faculty Council Minutes, 1947–1950, pp. 124–127.

Document 152

"Funds Sufficient to Operate a Great University"

The report President Wells gave the faculty in March 1949 was largely a repetition of an ancient theme. The General Assembly had reasoned, so the report indicates, from a false premise. The University was left with less money to operate in the next biennium than it had been given for the past one. Wells nevertheless told his colleagues, "In my judgment the amount of money we have is a sum sufficient to operate a great university. . . ."

*   *   *

REPORT ON BUDGET
March 15, 1949

It has always been my custom to report to the members of the faculty at the conclusion of each session of the General Assembly. I shall make such a report to you this afternoon and through you to the entire faculty.

It is important first that we understand some of the conditioning factors in this session of the Assembly. They were:

(1) Chief in importance—the bonus which influenced nearly everything that happened.

(2) The rapidly mounting costs in all state institutions and in all other areas of government. Some of this results from the necessary neglect of the war years. An example is to be found in the crumbling highways and in the deplorable condition of the mental institutions. And of course part of these mounting costs always came from inflation.

(3) The dramatic downturn of the economic indeces that produced in the minds of the legislators a conviction that our costs would decline rather than increase.

(4) The strong belief that enrollments would decrease rapidly in the two universities—Indiana and Purdue—that we would not have nearly so large a university as we had asked money for.

(5) The fact that the two houses of the Assembly were divided politically—a Republican Senate and a Democratic House—and that in both branches there were many new, unseasoned members.

(6) The difficulty in convincing the Assembly that increased appropriations did not mean increased operating funds for the University. At our Budget Retreat last fall we anticipated this and knew that it was going to be

extraordinarily difficult to convince the legislature that one type of income was disappearing at the same time our enrollment was staying constant, even increasing.

In passing it should be noted that in contrast with two years ago the private schools this year were friendly to the University.

I wish to pay special tribute to the active members of our legislative committee —Mr. Franklin, Mr. Allman, Mr. Bartley, Dean Sikes, and Mr. Snyder—and to our Board of Trustees committee—Mr. Campbell, Mr. Henley, and Mr. McCarty. All gave of their time and their energies without stint. In the performance of their jobs they made great personal sacrifices. It is something like a nightmare for the men who have to engage in this work, requiring, as it does, eighteen hours a day, even twenty towards the end. Also, I want to express appreciation to our two local representatives, Mr. Rogers and Mr. Evans, both of whom served us with great fidelity and ability in this session, and to the alumni, many of whom responded more than we had a right to expect. Some came to the Assembly personally to assist. We had a fine alumni organization and many friends in both houses. Finally we had a great friend in Governor Schricker, who is deeply interested in Indiana University.

This is the background.

The budget bill was the most important of the several bills in which we were interested, and I shall try to explain its provisions in detail.

First, what did we receive and how does it compare with our request? This can best be given by the following table:

INDIANA UNIVERSITY
LEGISLATIVE BUDGET
1949-1951

	Requested	Approved	Per Cent Reduction
Operation	$18,246,948.	$13,600,000.	29
Medical Center		500,000.	
Deficiency	1,460,458.	1,450,000.	
Retirement	371,000.	300,000.	
Medical School Expansion (2 year)	144,375.	144,375.	
Repairs to Old Buildings	690,300.	550,000.	
Public Health	117,355.	70,000.	
Bond Retirement and Interest	204,069.	204,069.	
Department of Conservation—Geology Division (Indiana University Petroleum Severance Tax)	376,000.	255,000.	
	$21,610,505.	$17,073,444.	26.5
New Construction	11,800,000.	1,300,000.	

The capital allowance, of course, is small, but this item needs some explanation. This allotment for building was from the General Fund rather than from the Postwar Building fund which is derived from the special tax on alcoholic beverages. Since we may be able later to get some money from the ABC fund, the sum stated above is not necessarily the total for the biennial construction program.

What does the operating appropriation of $13,600,000 for the biennium—the

$6,800,000 per year—represent? By taking the $4,500,000 which we were appropriated for the past two years by the General Assembly, adding to it our deficiency, and adding to that our loss in veteran fee income, we arrive at $6,883,411, as the sum required to maintain our present level of expenditure. So the $6,800,000 which was appropriated is $83,411 less than our present basis of operation. This is further described by the following table.

Net Operating Expenditure Budget from State for this year 1948-49		$5,912,999.00
(Regular State Appropriation	$4,500,000)	
(Deficiency reported to Budget Committee	1,412,989)	
Loss of Federal Income because of Veterans Enrollment for each year of next biennium		970,422.00
Necessary to maintain *present level of expenditures*		$6,883,411.00

What had we asked for in addition to our present basis of operation?

Additional needed to *maintain present program*		
Salary Increases		
(Because of cost of living, no general increase last year, retaining present staff, etc.)	$923,546.00	
Staff Additions		
(reduce class sizes, give higher level of instruction, etc.)	505,276.00	
Supplies, Repairs and Equipment		
(Inflation, increase in prices and added needs because of increased enrollment and temporary facilities.)	342,156.00	
Medical Center		
(Increased supplies cost salary adjustments, improve teaching of doctors and nurses—full-time teachers, etc.)	469,035.00	2,240,063.00
		$9,123,474.00

The $6,800,000, although less than we requested and need, is never the less a great deal of money. The question is, "What shall we do with the money we have? Where shall we put our first emphasis? What shall we eliminate? What shall we protect? What shall we develop?"

It seems to me that we should try to evaluate all that we do, determine that which is really important from the standpoint of the University and cut off that which is unimportant—if we can find anything that is unimportant.

Certainly we can all agree that we should protect the scholarly advancement of the University, our graduate studies and research program, and our staff and facilities that are essential to these functions. We should make merited salary increases. And of course we have to take care of fixed expenditures of a general nature that we can't escape.

Moreover, we should provide for such additional programs as may seem desirable, as for example the contemplated University Press for scholarly publications. Of course, a new program like this and all such other new programs must be evaluated in the light of all other needs.

How do we realize these objectives with less money to spend than we are now spending? The answer is not clear at the present, but there are some steps which must be considered. In the first place, we shall have to make all possible economies. We must eliminate unnecessary expenditures and operations wherever we can throughout the entire University—academic, non-academic, administrative, everything we can think of.

This may mean in time a reduction in staff, both academic and non-academic. A little later I shall present some figures on multiplicity of course offerings and on average class size, which are relevant to our thinking about the size of the staff.

There is possibility of an increase in fees, both for students and for services. We may find that we are giving certain kinds of public services which are not needed or for which fees could properly be charged.

There is the possibility of suspension of certain programs or even departments of the University.

To my mind a time like this, while it is trying, may not be altogether a misfortune because it causes us to re-evaluate that which we have done under relatively easy conditions; it makes us put first things first and put them in their proper perspective.

In the cutting of our program we must, as a matter of protection, make the cut in a dramatic way to show what smaller appropriations mean. It must be put in such terms that it can be understood by the public if we are ever to get our appropriations increased to the proper level. In addition to the money for necessary new staff and salary increases, our cut will have to provide for the following items.

Reduction in our present basis of operation		$ 83,411
Present basis of operation requires	$6,883,411	
Legislature has appropriated	6,800,000	
Deficiency in amount required for retirement program per year		35,500
Deficiency in request for repairs to buildings and		
desired departmental remodeling		70,150
Increase in utilities (Bloomington campus)		
Due to increased rates for electricity, telephone,		
water, etc.		200,000
Group health insurance (all divisions)		
A desirable addition to our present coverage which would		
make it possible for the non-academic staff to participate.		50,000

These items will, for the most part, have to be absorbed in whole or in part before we can begin to make salary adjustments.

The medical and dental units, it is true, can absorb their salary increased out of their increased appropriations. However, for salary adjustments and new staff elsewhere you can see that funds will have to come in some fashion from existing budgets. We have discussed having a flat over-all percentage decrease—for the main divisions of the University, both academic and non-academic—and perhaps thus accumulate a sufficient fund to do the required job. From this fund, then allocations can go back to the divisions of the University in accordance with the respective needs for salary adjustments and promotions.

This may not be the way to do it. I suppose no way will be satisfactory to everybody. However, in due course, we will have to arrive at some procedure and follow it.

Now, what has been happening to us, from the beginning of the war years to the present? What percentage of the University budget goes for general administration now as compared with the prewar years? According to the figures that I have today, in 1940-41, 6.1 per cent of the University budget went for general administration, and for this year's budget, the same percentage—6.1 percent.

Salaries have increased from 1939-40 as follows:

	1947-48	1948-49
Administrative	20.0%	24.2%
Deans	24.5	29.4
Professors	36.6	38.8
Associate Professors	50.7	48.0
Assistant Professors	51.0	50.0
Instructors	51.0	54.0

There are those who may say, "These increased rates have been achieved by bringing in new people at high salaries." But the facts prove otherwise, because persons who were with us in 1939-40 and are still with us in 1948-49 have averaged a 60 percent increase.

We have had some very rapid increases in certain types of expenditures, all of which have to be re-examined:

(1) Telephones—both because of increased rates and because of the improved service requiring an increase in instruments.

(2) Traffic policemen—and at nearly every meeting of the Faculty Council there have been requests to further increase the number.

(3) Group expenditures—we are doing more and more all the time in the way of group insurance, annuities, workmen's compensation, and so on. I think it is a justifiable increase, but the increase has been very rapid.

(4) Public service—maybe we have increased more than we should. We will compile figures on this aspect of our problem later and give it careful study.

Then there is the matter of size of the teaching staff in relation to enrollment. For the Bloomington Campus the following figures show the increase in faculty and enrollment from 1939-40 to the present:

	1939-40	1947-48	1948-49
Full-time Faculty (Teaching staff only)	266	511	516
Part-time Instructional Staff	150	398	500
Enrollment	5,367	11,300	11,414

That is, both the enrollment and the faculty have doubled, while the part-time instructional staff has more than tripled.

Now, what has happened to average class enrollments, for obviously this is where our major expenditures are?

Average Class Enrollments
First Semester, Bloomington Campus

1939-40	1946-47	1947-48	1948-49
28.8	42.7	31.2	31.9

What is going to happen to enrollment next year? As best we can predict, the enrollment in 1949-50 on the Bloomington campus will drop about 10 per cent.

		1948-49	1949-50
Bloomington Campus			
Freshmen		2,415	2,300
Sophomore		2,046	1,900
Juniors		2,752	1,800
Seniors		2,341	2,600
Graduate		1,226	1,400
Professional		634	600
	Total	11,414	10,500
Indianapolis and miscellaneous		3,000	3,000
	Total	14,414	13,500
Part-time Extension		8,717	8,000

If this estimate of enrollment figures for next year is correct and if no adjustment is made in staff, then our average class size will sink approximately to what it was in 1939-40, or about 10 per cent. It should shrink even farther if we had the money, but, as we didn't get the money, this is one of the ways by which we can demonstrate to the people of Indiana that we didn't.

According to the catalogue, no division except the School of Education has decreased its number of courses. The number of individual courses has grown from 743 in 1940-41 to 1,051 in 1948-49, an increase of 371 courses. There may be that many divisions of value in human knowledge, but I doubt it. It seems to me that another way of demonstrating to the people of Indiana that we cannot continue to do all that we are now doing is to have three or four hundred courses appear in the catalogue marked in red as "Suspended, 1949-50, for reason of lack of funds."

Since we have begun to talk about this problem, I have heard from various persons many ways to cut departments—that is, departments other than the one to which the proposer belonged. Music, for example. Music, however, is quite an earner of fees and most of the expansion in music has taken place in the applied field, which brings in a surprising amount to pay for the cost of that instruction. The Music School from 1946-47 to 1948-49 has had a sensational increase in course enrollments—from 1,721 to 2,870—and has absorbed this load with a $30,000 increase in budget. This is the smallest increase enjoyed by any school of the University during this period and is smaller than that of many single departments.

I give this information to illustrate the fact that there is no easy or magic way to cut our expenditures. We have always operated conservatively, so economies are not obvious. There will have to be made, a little bit here and a little bit there, without prejudice and so fairly as we can. As we look at what we have to do, the important thing is to remember that each of us has to do some part of it, and the specialist in his own department can best see where the reduction can least damagingly be made.

As to the possibility of getting more money by increasing our student fees, you will note from the following schedule that our regular fee is already fairly high when we compare it with similar fees in other institutions. It is perhaps the highest of the institutions that operate on a semester basis. I think this is an area that must be considered, but it is not perhaps the wisest way to get more money.

Typical Fees for Liberal Arts, Education, etc.
Per Semester, or Per Quarter

		Resident	Non-Resident
Illinois	Semester	$58.00	$ 98.00
Iowa	Semester	65.00	150.00
Michigan	Semester	70.00	175.00
Michigan State	Quarter	47.00	122.00
Minnesota	Quarter	46.45	91.45
Ohio State	Quarter	58.00	133.00
Wisconsin	Semester	75.00	225.00
Purdue	Semester (Includes Athletic Book and Convocation Ticket)	55.00	155.00
Indiana	Semester (Including Athletic and Music Tickets)	65.75*	170.75

* None of the other institutions include these items in their fees, so this is the comparable figure.

In this connection it may be interesting to see what our students received last year in the way of financial help from direct University sources.

Payments to Students
1948-49

	Number	Amount
Scholarships and Fellowships	598	$ 92,175.00
Earnings by Students	2,000	432,000.00
Graduate Assistants	581	566,089.00
	3,179	$1,090,264.00

In student aid of one type or another a respectable amount is paid out of University funds. But again, as economic conditions may be such by next fall that some students will suffer, it seems unwise to increase fees directly or indirectly by reducing our funds in aid.

This entire report, of course, is given without expectation that there is any answer from anybody at this time or that any answer can be arrived at quickly. There hasn't been time since the close of the Assembly to decide what we can do. The Council is asked to share in the thinking and to make suggestions, and out of this combined thinking maybe we can arrive at some solutions.

I should say before concluding that one of the things we have to consider is a more intensive program of interpretation and better coordination of our interpretation to the people of the State. All universities are going to be faced with this task. We coasted through the war years when we didn't have to justify expenditures. But now all types of state services are being re-evaluated and we must protect the function of higher education during this process. Higher education requires a tremendous amount of the biennial budget now. Our figure alone, even with the reduction, is $18,373.000. Add Purdue and the state normal schools, and together we are just behind the highways as a consumer of tax revenues.

Finally, I want to recall some words of Walter Jessup, of the Carnegie Foundation. He once said that all universities can be great when the financial trend is upward. The true test of faculty and administrative abilities comes when the trend of support is downward. Can we be great in the face of a downturn in revenues? We shall have to measure ourselves against this test. In my judgment the amount of money we have is a sum sufficient to operate a great university, and with the wholehearted support of all members of the University family we shall be able to meet the test.

Faculty Council Minutes, 1947–1950, pp. 113–121.

Document 153

Faculty Housing

Bloomington was not large enough, nor did it have sufficient surplus housing available to take care of the influx of faculty during these years of rapid staff expansion. At the same time, the University did not have more than a minimum amount of housing for staff members at its dis-disposal. This report by the Faculty Housing Committee reveals the pinched conditions at Indiana University in 1949. It is likewise an interesting historical landmark by which to gauge how many changes have occurred in the past quarter of a century.

*   *   *

REPORT OF THE FACULTY HOUSING COMMITTEE
March 31, 1949

REASON FOR THIS REPORT:

August 31, 1949, for 34 members of the faculty and staff, is the end of their occupancy period in University-operated housing as provided by the housing policy adopted by the Faculty Council at its meeting on December 16, 1947. A number of those concerned and others interested, have discussed the matter, and at least one organization, the AAUP, has formally communicated with the Faculty Council on behalf of members of the faculty who are affected. The Faculty Housing Committee considered the AAUP letter on December 17, 1948, and reported to the Faculty Council that it was believed there was no basis for a change in the Faculty Council policy at this time. The Faculty Council decided to have a review of the housing situation at its meeting of April 5, 1949, and asked for a report from the Faculty Housing Committee.

HISTORY OF PRESENT POLICY CONCERNING FACULTY HOUSING:

1. Soon after the emergency faculty housing program got underway in the Summer of 1946 it became apparent to the Faculty Housing Committee that some policy regarding the period of occupancy would be necessary. Accordingly, on January 15, 1947, a notice was sent to all occupants at that time which stated in part:

"Any such occupant who finds himself without a place to move after August 31, 1947, will at some time not later than June 30, 1947, be given an opportunity to prove to the Faculty Housing Committee that he has made an extended effort to find something for himself but that he has been unable to locate satisfactory housing. If it can be demonstrated that actual effort has been made to find housing but without result, the Committee will recommend renewal of the housing contract (lease) for not to exceed one additional year from August 31, 1947."

This created a two-year limit on the period of occupancy in emergency housing under the jurisdiction of the Faculty Housing Committee, which consisted of the prefabricated houses, remodeled apartments (Foley, Horner and Martindale), Hoosier Courts (then known as University Apartments) and Cottage Grove apartments, and which would include the Union Club when its use in the emergency faculty housing program was started.

2. The housing occupancy-limitation question appeared on the agenda of the Faculty Council soon after it was organized in the Fall of 1947. The matter was referred for study to a committee consisting of Dean John W. Ashton, D. Lyle Dieterle and Harold W. Jordan. The report of this committee was adopted by the Council on December 16, 1947 and provided the policy under which the Faculty Housing Committee has operated since that time. The policy provides, in general, that faculty on temporary appointment may be given housing for a maximum period of three years, the faculty and staff on permanent appointment may be given housing for a maximum period of one year, that faculty already on the staff may be provided housing under certain conditions, and makes provision for housing of graduate assistants. (A copy of this policy is attached.)

3. In the Spring of 1948, it developed that 14 members of the staff who held academic tenure would be required by application of the policy to vacate their quarters at the end of the Summer. After consideration of the matter, the Faculty Council on March 16, 1948, extended the deadline for one year beyond August 31, 1948, for those of the 14 not living in the prefabricated houses in adopting the following recommendation submitted by a Faculty Council committee:

"In view of the strong probability that the University's new apartments will be ready next fall, it is recommended that those faculty members on permanent appointment who are not living in University housing units other than single family houses and who came to the campus (or returned to the campus) in the fall of 1946 and 1947 be allowed to continue occupying faculty housing of this type for one additional academic year, that is, through the school year 1948-49. The relatively inexpensive housing provided in this manner should help the faculty members involved to save money toward down payments on later house purchases."

PRESENT EXTENT OF FACULTY HOUSING PROGRAM:

At the present time the units in the emergency housing program affected by the policy are Hoosier Courts, the prefabricated houses, and the remodeled apartments. With completion of the first building of the University Apartments, Cottage Grove Apartments were dropped from the emergency housing list, and there has been no reason to limit occupancy of the relatively few faculty who continue to live at the Union Club on a permanent basis.

SURVEY OF OCCUPANTS:

In order to have accurate information on which to base its report to the Faculty Council, the Faculty Housing Committee made its annual survey of occupants a month earlier this year. This survey was designed to reveal which members of the faculty, among those who were eligible for reassignment, wished to be reassigned and which planned to vacate. This information was obtained.

In order that the Committee could know the date on which those who were not eligible for reassignment would vacate a statement intended to produce such information was also included. Generally, however, that information was not obtained, for with a degree of consistency that seemed to be more than coincidental, the blanks from those not eligible for reassignment under the present policy came back marked with a check at the point to indicate that reassignment was requested and with a big question mark by the statement that should have been checked. The Committee presumes that the staff members concerned are waiting for some modifid statement of policy from the Faculty Council, but has for purposes of this report assumed that all will vacate by August 31, 1949. (Those persons affected were notified formally of the deadline on November 22, 1948, in addition to informal notice which was sent at the time copies of the Faculty Council housing policy were sent to all occupants of emergency housing units a year or so ago.)

RESULTS OF THE SURVEY:

The survey produced the following information from the faculty and staff now housed in the various units:

	Hoosier Courts	Remodeled Apartments	Prefabs	Totals
1. Number of faculty and staff housed in emergency units at time of survey	72	12	35	119
2. Number vacating voluntarily during summer	10	0	5	15
3. Number whose housing deadline is August 31, 1949 (None included in Line 2)	17	5	12	34
4. Maximum to be housed in emergency units during 1949-50	60*	12	35	107
5. Number of new assignments which can be made for 1949-50 if present policy is *not* maintained	−2	0	5	3
6. Number of new assignments which can be made for 1949-50 if present policy is maintained	15	5	17	37

* 12 more than faculty quota for 1949-50 are now housed.

At this time there are 5 applications on file for new, eligible faculty members for the Fall, and there are 7 applications on file from faculty and staff members new on the staff who need other quarters.

The survey does not, of course, reveal changes that were not anticipated at the time it was made. It has been the experience of the Committee that 10 to 15 changes in addition to those anticipated occur during the Summer as various members of the staff find other quarters to rent, purchase their own property, or leave the University.

The survey indicates to the Faculty Housing Committee that *insufficient space for new staff members will be produced unless the present policy is followed.*

RECOMMENDATION:

The Faculty Housing Committee recommends that the present policy be maintained for the following reasons:

1. This is probably the last chance to maintain an occupancy-limitation policy. If there are to be three changes of policy of postponements of action, there may as well be no policy. It is unfair to the faculty not to have a policy. Some may have drawn the conclusion that they do not have to worry about housing. If no occupancy-limitation policy is followed, the only way that the emergency program can be reduced as the housing situation improves is to slow down or stop altogether new assignments.

2. Six staff members with tenure were forced out of University housing a year ago as a result of the Faculty Council policy. More than 30 others, anticipating their occupancy deadline, have moved from Faculty Housing units into houses they had bought or built since the emergency program started. In the absence of a definite easing of the housing situation in all types of units, it would appear to be a break of faith with these staff members to permit others to live in University housing indefinitely.

3. Permitting staff members to remain indefinitely in Hoosier Courts results in a discriminatory practice because of the subsidized nature of that housing. Faculty living in town, or those living in other University accommodations are paying for the capital cost of their housing. This is not true at Hoosier Courts project, however, which was erected largely at the expense of the Federal Government. A person who has lived at Hoosier Courts, or for that matter, in one of the remodeled apartments, for a period of three years has had a financial advantage of at least $1,000.00 to $1,200.00 based on rental of $42.50 per month, including utilities and furnishings, as compared with rental for comparable furnished apartments of unfurnished houses of $60.00 or more per month, plus an average of $10.00 per month for utilities and $10.00 per month for fuel.

4. Providing housing for staff members does not necessarily of itself keep staff members. Of some seventy persons who have left University housing since 1946, about half bought or rented other housing, but the other half left the University altogether.

5. The threat of leaving the University if housing is not continued to be provided is not considered too important. The "somewhere that housing is provided" must indeed be an unusual and much sought-after place. In individual cases it is likely that the staff member would be lost anyway.

6. It must be remembered that Hoosier Courts project was provided for student housing. There is still continued pressure for married student housing and this results in an important public relations problem. The University cannot satisfy all demands for some types of married student housing; it can in no way begin to satisfy demands of students who would prefer Hoosier Courts to trailers. Trailers are beginning to wear out, and it is expected that 15 to 20 of them cannot be used next year since they have deteriorated beyond repair. Only students with children are housed at Hoosier Courts, and many students with children are forced to remain in trailers.

7. Priority has been granted graduate assistants in housing quotas for Hoosier Courts and the other units. While this means that space is provided for those who assist directly in the teaching and research load, it also means that in Hoosier Courts half of the 280 apartments are not available for general student assignments.

8. University Apartments units will offer considerable relief to the faculty housing problem. More than 30 faculty and staff are living in the first unit; at

least 22 have already signed up for the second unit. The Faculty Housing Committee has considered that sufficient space is now available in Bloomington for couples without children and will take no more applications from such couples for the emergency housing units. It may be desirable to extend this policy to couples with one small child.

9. We are committed under the present policy to house about a third of our present quotas until 1950 and another third until 1951. In other words, there will be no possibility of eliminating Hoosier Courts from the emergency faculty housing program until 1951 even if new asisgnments were stopped at this time.

REPORT OF THE COMMITTEE ON HOUSING FOR FACULTY
AND ADMINISTRATIVE STAFF WITH DEPENDENTS
November 14, 1947

The Committee makes the following recommendations:

1. Since the University does not now plan to embark upon a definite and long-range policy of permanent housing for faculty and administrative staff, we recommend that all University housing used by faculty and administrative staff be kept on a temporary basis and that it be assigned according to the following pattern. (The term "year" as used here means the period from September 1 to August 31. If a faculty member enters University housing within any such period, later than the beginning of the period, that is to be counted as one year.)

A. *New Appointments*

   I. Faculty on temporary appointment may be given housing for a period of three years as a maximum, unless they go on permanent appointment within that period. In the latter case, they may continue in University housing for a maximum of one year following that in which the change in status takes place, provided always, however, that their total period of occupancy shall not exceed three years.

   II. Faculty and staff on permanent appointment may be given University housing for a maximum of one year, with the proviso, however, that on submission of evidence that a contract to build or buy has been entered into, the individual may be given an extension of time not to exceed one additional year.

B. *Faculty Already on the Staff*

   I. Those without housing on return from Sabbatical or other leave may be given a maximum of one year of University housing.

   II. Those evicted from quarters that they have rented may be given one rental year or such fraction as remains of the year.

   III. Faculty whose domestic status changes (i.e. by the acquisition of dependents) after they have begun their work at the University, may be eligible for housing for one rental year or such fraction as remains of the year, on proof of necessity for such housing.

C. *Graduate Assistants*

   I. It is recommended that housing to be furnished for such appointees for the period of their appointment in such status.

II. It is recommended further that a block of apartments of sufficient size to take care of the expected number of graduate assistants and fellows be set aside and held until August 1 to assure places for such appointees.

2. It is recommended that all contracts run from the date of occupancy to the first of September next following.

3. This statement shall not constitute a guarantee of housing to any faculty member, new or old, temporary or permanent, but only an expression of willingness to assist faculty and staff in an emergency to the extent that facilities are available.

4. These rules shall be applied to present occupants of University housing, except that each such resident may complete the current year even though he thereby runs over the maximum period allowed. In such cases, the period of occupancy shall be deemed to have begun in September, 1946, or September, 1947, whichever is the year of his coming to the University or his return from leave.

D. L. DIETERLE
H. W. JORDAN
J. W. ASHTON

Faculty Council Minutes, 1947–1950, pp. 134–140.

Document 154

Matters of Faculty Concern

As indicated earlier, minutes of the Indiana University Faculty Council are not the most fascinating bit of reading that can be found. Nevertheless it was in this body that most campus issues finally were settled, or sent on their way to higher authority for adjudication. Most important, the issues which came before this body were of vital importance in the daily operation of the institution.

*   *   *

FACULTY COUNCIL
SUMMARY FOR MAY, 1948—APRIL, 1949

Calendar and other routine matters.

As was true last year, the Council had to spend much time considering and ruling on a variety of routine matters. It adopted the calendar for the academic year 1949–50 (November 2, 16), and then later revised the calendar for the Summer of 1950 (January 4, February 1). It formulated rules to govern the following matters:

Establishment of a Dean's honor list for each school and college (November 2);

Absences from class because of activities in other classes or schools (November 16);

Shifting from one section of a class to another on the day preceding or following a vacation period (January 4).

In addition, the Council considered and dealt with a number of problems and suggestions: the shifting of students from one section to another in multiple-section courses (November 2) ; the possibility of eliminating the vacation between semesters (November 16, March 1) ; the absence of veterans from classes (November 16) ; the denial of a request for a February Commencement (January 18) ; the dismissal of classes on the morning of Foundation Day (March 29) ; the excusing of honor students from afternoon classes on Foundation Day (March 29).

The Council also passed on degrees recommended as of October 15 (November 16), took part in a ceremony to receive the bronze Mark of Commendation awarded to Indiana University by the Secretary of the Navy (January 18), decided where this bronze plaque is to be placed (March 1), and met with representatives of the Board of Aeons to learn some of the functions of that organization (March 29).

Salary Policy.

The Council concluded its discussions of the report on salary policy brought in last year (May 4, 18). It adopted several recommendations, chiefly that immediate and continuing action be taken to establish a salary structure with the ultimate objective of achieving commensurate salaries on a university-wide basis, that fixed salary minima be established for the respective academic ranks in each school, that a base minimum salary be set for instructors on a university-wide basis, and that a review committee of five members, to be chosen by the elected members of the Faculty Council, be established to deal with complaints concerning salary, promotion, and the nature or conditions of work (May 18). On two controversial issues, the Faculty supported the decisions of the Council, voting 227 to 57 for the principle of fixed salary minima rather than fixed salary ranges, and 172 to 89 against a proposal for a minimum yearly increase in salary for instructors until tenure is reached. The recommendations were sent to the Board of Trustees in November.

Biennial budget and building program.

Much of the Council's time was given to consideration of the proposed budget and building program for the biennium 1949–1951. Three representatives of the Council—Professors Breneman, Christenson, and Yellen—were invited by President Wells to take part in the preliminary discussions on September 29 and 30 of the proposed budget and building program to be submitted to the State Legislature. The Council considered the proposed building program and gave its approval to the priorities list drawn up by the Administration (December 2, January 4). On March 15, President Wells reported to the Council on the appropriations passed by the Legislature and on the probable effects upon budget and building program during 1949–1951.

Parking.

Again this year the Council dealt with the problem of campus parking and studied reports by the University Parking Committee (October 5, 19, February 15). Approval was given to recommendations providing for a one-dollar fine for faculty members who violate the campus parking regulations, for the denial of parking permits to those delinquent in their fines, and for a committee of three to whom appeals may be made. It was agreed that the fines collected are to go into the Library's Book Fund. These recommendations were approved also by a Faculty vote of 314 to 146 (March 15).

Housing.

The housing problems that came to the attention of the Council were of two sorts—the long-range problem of providing adequate housing for faculty and the immediate problem of tenure in present University-owned housing. The Committee on Long-Term Housing Problems reported on its progress, and informed the Council of the proposed apartment building to be constructed by Mr. A. N. Strauss and also of the proposal to sell some ten University prefabricated houses to faculty members (October 5, March 1, April 5). The immediate problem of tenure was raised chiefly by the A.A.U.P. Standing Committee on Housing. The Council considered a report by that committee along with a report by the Faculty Housing Committee, and decided finally to approve the recommendation of the latter that the present policy concerning University emergency housing be maintained (April 5).

Academic matters.

The Council studied reports by committees proposing uniformity in grading practice and course numbering. On January 4, it adopted recommendations providing that all academic divisions of the University employ the same system of grading symbols—A,B,C,D,E,F, Inc., and Def.; that the symbol X be discontinued; that plus and minus signs be discontinued; and that no attempt be made to equate letter grades in terms of percentages. It was agreed that the Committee on Grading is to continue its study of grading problems. On February 1, the Council adopted a series of recommendations establishing a uniform system of course numbering.

Miscellaneous.

During the current year, the Council considered the following matters and took action wherever it was deemed proper:

Report by the Bookstore Committee concerning the periodical and books carried by the Bookstore (November 2) ;

Approval in principle of a report by the Committee on the Relation of Off-Campus Faculty to the University, proposing amendments to the Faculty Constitution to provide for representation of off-campus faculties on the Council (November 16) ;

Recommendations that Indiana University join the Midwest Inter-Library Corporation, with final action postponed (March 1) ;

Recommendation that the University issue an annual printed directory of the administrative staff and faculty, with the final decision to enlarge the present directory in the back of the Schedule of Lectures and Recitations (January 4, March 29, April 19) ;

Collection of books and periodicals for European libraries (January 4) ;

Approval of a recommendation that faculty promotions be announced to those concerned before being released to the newspapers (March 29).

Other unfinished business.

The Council expects to receive further reports from its committees on grading, on the relation of off-campus faculty to the University, and on long-term housing problems. In addition, its committee on faculty rules is yet to report. Certain topics proposed in the President's "State of the University" speech last December are to be considered by committees still to be appointed—*viz.*, sabbatical leaves, the coordination and integration of graduate work, the improvement of teaching, and education of women. The Council has before it also a suggestion that it consider the role of department chairmen, and it has, furthermore, agreed to discuss the functions of the Junior Division and the recent reorganization of the American Association of Universities.

Faculty Council Minutes, 1947–1950, pp. 146–148.

Document 155

The Mid-West Inter-Library Corporation

By 1949 Indiana University along with its Mid-West neighbors had accumulated a major library problem. The Library, in these years of vast documentary production, had acquired huge volumes of little-used materials. These were too valuable to destroy and yet they were too voluminous and costly to service in the traditional library mode of book management. The Mid-West Inter-Library Corporation was an attempt to solve this problem for a fairly large cluster of institutions. The questions raised in the Faculty Council Discussion were those which confronted all the other potential cooperating institutions.

*   *   *

Dean Thompson presented the report of the Committee on the Midwest Inter-Library Corporation. (A copy of the report is attached to these minutes.) He made several additional remarks. One concerned the difficulty of defining the term "little-used research materials," a difficulty which resulted in the second recommendation of the committee. Another remark dealt with the financing of the proposed storage library. A million dollars for the building itself is to be given by one of the foundations. The cost to Indiana University would be approximately $4,000 per year. Dean Thompson requested that action on the report be postponed until the next meeting of the Council, when both President Wells and Dr. Miller might be present.

Discussion of Dean Thompson's report followed. Dean Briscoe asked if the books and other materials sent to the storage center would remain the property of the original libraries. Dean Thompson replied that they would. Professor Weatherwax expressed some skepticism about the usefulness of such a storage library for research, since it is best to be able to deal with the materials directly rather than through a catalogue; he suggested, furthermore, that materials are not used by one department alone and consequently the decision as to whether or not to store them ought not to rest with any one department. Dean Hall said that in the field of government there would be an advantage in having a storage center where the little-used government documents might be kept. Professor Benns pointed out that there would be an important advantage in having little-used materials catalogued; and Professor Breneman added that many publications might become poor, particularly as the center grew larger. Professor Lundin pointed out some of the difficulties encountered at Harvard in attempting to make use of materials kept in the New England Deposit Library. Dean Thompson suggested that a storage center might ease our own immediate storage problem considerably. Dean Briscoe asked if Chicago and Northwestern are to pay more than other schools for the upkeep of the proposed storage center since it is to be located in Chicago. Dean Thompson replied that they are to pay more, and that the formula for determining the contribution of each university takes into account the distance from Chicago. Dean Patty asked if the plan is to keep the proposed center a storage place for little-used materials or to make it a research center with rare research materials assembled there. Dr. Byrd replied that the plan at present calls for only a storage library, but that perhaps later it will turn into a huge research center with cooperative buying of books and other materials.

Adjournment at 4:40 p.m.

REPORT OF THE COMMITTEE ON THE MIDWEST INTER-LIBRARY CORPORATION

Your local committee appointed to consider Indiana University's participation in a proposed Midwest Inter-Library Corporation, recommends the following:

1. We recommend to the Faculty Council that Indiana University become a participating institution in the Midwest Inter-Library Corporation;
2. That it will be a policy of Indiana University Library not to send to the Inter-Library Center any material without the full consent of the departments interested.

Respectfully submitted,
/s/ STITH THOMPSON
(chairman)
O. O. WINTHER
T. W. TORREY
W. H. FOX
KARL BOOKWALTER
H. C. SAUVAIN
R. A. MILLER
R. C. BULEY

The Midwest Inter-Library Corporation

The Midwest Inter-Library Corporation has as its objective the provision and promotion of cooperative, auxiliary library services for non-profit educational, charitable, or scientific libraries, principally the research libraries of the middle west.

Functions: 1. The Corporation will establish and maintain a Midwest Inter-Library Center for the cooperative custody, organization, housing, servicing (and for some materials, ownership) of little-used research materials. The Center will constitute essentially a collection of little-used materials placed on indefinite loan in its custody, and available on inter-library loan to member institutions under terms established by its Board of Directors.

2. The Corporation will serve as an agency for encouraging, promoting and implementing coordination of collecting policies for specialized fields, among the cooperative libraries. The Corporation through its officers and through the Director of the Inter-Library Center will encourage libraries to define their acquisition policies in special fields, will make known to the cooperating institutions these selections, and will attempt to encourage further selection and definition to the end that midwest libraries may provide more adequately and with less duplication for the research needs of the middle west.

3. The Corporation will serve as an agency to explore the possibilities for cooperative bibliographical services among the member institutions.

Organization: The Corporation will be chartered as a non-profit corporation under the Laws of the State of Illinois, the members of which will be the officially designated representatives of the participating institutions. It will be governed by a Board of Directors, two-thirds of whom will be the member representatives of the participating institutions maintaining the largest research libraries, and one-third to be elected from the remaining members. The actual management of the Inter-Library Center will be the responsibility of a Director of the Center.

Finances: The Corporation will be financed in part by an initial foundation grant and in part by fees for services paid by cooperating libraries. Fees for services will be proportioned according to the size and hence the extent of use made by the participating libraries of the Corporation's services. Separate schedules of charges for service will be set up for: (a) research libraries; (b) college libraries; (c) public libraries; and (d) other libraries which do not fit in the first three categories.

Faculty Council Minutes, 1947–1950, pp. 107–108, 110–111.

Document 156

Sabbatical Leaves

Since the 1880s the question of sabbatical leaves for research and travel for the faculty was an important one. Characteristic of faculty discussions, this one evoked the eternal question of "for what purposes" would leaves be granted. In this document the four acceptable reasons were outlined. This report came at a time when there were not so subtle pressures on faculty members to do research and publishing. There was, always, the problem of granting a leave to a professor, and at the same time trying to carry on the program of departments and colleges with least possible disruption. This plan undertook to reduce the administrative-instructional problem as much as possible.

*   *   *

A Sabbatical Leave Program
FOR
Indiana University

I. *Purpose.* The sabbatical leave program is undertaken by the University to encourage special studies, research, and other creative activities on the part of members of the faculty, in order to increase their capacity for contribution to the whole educational program of the institution. A statement of proposed use of time is required to indicate the manner of conformance to this general objective. Acceptable programs for the use of time may include:
   1. Research on significant problems.
   2. Important creative or descriptive work in any means of expression, for example, writing, painting, and so forth.
   3. Postdoctoral study along a specified line at another institution.
   4. Other projects satisfactory to the Sabbatical Leave Committee.
II. *Terms of Leave.* Sabbatical leave will be for one semester at full salary or for one year at half salary.

III. *Eligibility.* A faculty member is eligible for one sabbatical leave during each period of seven years full time service (including time on sabbatical leave), following the completion of his first six years of full time service. For example, a faculty member may be granted one sabbatical leave in his seventh, eighth, ninth, tenth, eleventh, twelfth, or thirteenth year of service, and one in his fourteenth, fifteenth, sixteenth, seventeenth, eighteenth, nineteenth, or twentieth years of service. Ordinarily, however, a sabbatical leave will not be granted within less than four years following a preceding sabbatical leave. For example, a faculty member who is granted sabbatical leave in his twelfth year would not again be eligible until his seventeenth year.

IV. *Scheduling.* As far as possible, departmental schedules should be arranged so as to permit eligible members of the staff to take leave. In arranging schedules, attempt should be made to minimize the cost of substitute instruction and the disruption of the departmental program. To facilitate this planing, applications for the first semester of a school year normally should be initiated before November 1 of the preceding school year, and for the second semester before March 1 of the preceding school year.

V. *Administration.* Applications for leave will initiate with the eligible faculty members. The application will be routed through successive administrative stages for appropriate action.

    1. Department. The departmental chairman or head, will forward the application to the Dean of the appropriate school. He will attach a statement confined to showing the proposed schedule adjustments to permit the leave, and the additional staff or other expenditure that will be necessary.

    2. Dean of the School or College. The Dean will forward the application to the Sabbatical Leave Committee with any appropriate remarks concerning budget or scheduling.

    3. Sabbatical Leave Committee. The Sabbatical Committee, (consisting of three members of the faculty, appointed by the President, with the Dean of the Graduate School in addition, ex officio) will forward the application to the Dean of the Faculties and the President, with appropriate recommendation for action. In arriving at its recommendation, the Committee may call on the chairman and other members of the applicant's department for an evaluation of the worth of the proposed program. It may also call on the Chairman of the Department and the Dean of the School or College if scheduling problems are the only bar to the leave. If the number of otherwise acceptable applications for one semester or year is so great as to entail excessive expense to the University or an unreasonable increase in the teaching load of resident staff, the Committee will of necessity have to determine a schedule of priorities among the applications. In determining such priorities, the Committee will give due consideration to the apparent relative importance of the programs proposed, the effect of postponement on the timeliness of the activity, the possibility of a permanent loss of a sabbatical leave opportunity, and insofar as possible on the record of accomplishment on previous sabbatical leaves. The applicant shall be given the opportunity to make representation to the Committee, if he considers it advisable, to support his application.

    4. Dean of the Faculties. The Dean of the Faculties, in passing on an application may himself or through an appropriate committee, review with the department concerned the problem of scheduling if the cost

of the leave applied for, or its prospective disruption of schedule, appear excessive.

Faculty Council Minutes, 1947–1950, pp. 159–160.

Document 157

Unfinished Business

The end of the decade, 1940–1950, caught the University in mid-stream of its expansion and program development. This routine set of minutes of the Faculty Council reveals the fact that a university's advancement is a continuous web, and that it never really gets more than a small portion of its problems solved. Yet this decade was an enormously important one. Indiana University underwent some of its most significant expansions in this era. The institution had now moved onto an entirely different plane of operation, and the pending matters before the Faculty Council reflected this fact.

*   *   *

FACULTY COUNCIL
SUMMARY FOR MAY, 1949—MAY, 1950
Organization of the Faculty Council.
The membership of the Faculty Council for the academic year 1949–50 consisted of the following:
President Wells and Deans Briscoe, Ashton, Gavit, VanNuys, Thompson, Wright, Weimer, Bain, Hine, Hall, and Patty;
Professors A. Anderson, F. L. Benns, D. S. Berrett, W. R. Breneman, E. H. Buehrig, C. L. Christenson, H. Frenz, R. F. Fuchs, A R. Lindesmith, C. L. Lundin, N. T. Pratt, N. L. Silverstein, H. B. Veatch, P. Weatherwax, S. Yellen, and J. W. T. Youngs;
Ex officio (non-voting) members—Deans Sikes and Shoemaker, Mr. Franklin, Mr. Harrell, and Dr. Miller.
During the current year Professor R. W. Holmstedt served as alternate for Dean Wright, and Professor P. E. Bergevin served in a like capacity for Professor Pratt. Professor N. P. Stallknecht served as alternate for Professor Veatch during the second semester. Professor Berrett was elected secretary for the year.

Calendar and other routine matters.
Much of the Council's time was given to a variety of routine matters. It adopted the calendar for the academic year 1950–51 (November 1), and then later revised the calendar for the Summer of 1951 (February 7). It approved a February Commencement for 1950 (November 15) and a Monday Commencement for June 1950 (November 15). A Monday Commencement for June 1951 was approved also (December 6). The Council ruled on the following matters:
Special holidays (February 7);
Establishment of Founders' Day as a part of the regular calendar (April 18);
Establishment of Senior Day as a part of the regular calendar (May 2, 1950);
Adoption of rules of procedure for the Faculty Council.

The Council also considered and acted upon a number of problems and suggestions: provision for the circulation with absence reports of pertinent information regarding policy before holidays (April 18); the excusing of students for military inspection (May 3, 1949); student protest against Monday Commencement (April 18); dismissal of classes on the morning of Founders' Day (April 18); the excusing of honor students from afternoon classes on Founders' Day (April 18).

The Council passed on the recommendations for the degree of M. S. in Psychiatry (June 2, 1949), on the degrees recommended as of October 15 (October 18), and on the degrees subject to the record of June 1950 (May 30, 1950). It also approved recommendations for honorary degrees (May 24, 1949 and May 16, 1950).

Salary Policy.

While the Council did not devote as much of its time to matters of salary policy as it had in the first two years of its existence, it did receive a report on general salary changes for 1949–1950 (June 2, 1949), and also a report that a University-wide minimum salary for instructors had been set as well as minimum salaries for individual ranks within the various divisions of the University (November 1). It was also reported that the Board of Trustees in approving the budget for 1949–1950 had approved a budget based upon the Council's recommendations in respect to salary policy. It set up procedure for the election of the standing Review Committee on Salary Policy (November 1) and elected the committee (November 15).

Tenure policy.

On May 3, 1949, the Council re-elected for one year the members of the Faculty Board of Review which deals with problems of tenure. It discussed certain difficulties in the administration of tenure policy (February 7) and made minor changes in the statements of tenure policy which appear in the Faculty Handbook. These changes were designed to bring the statements up to date and to define more exactly the phrase "period of service" (February 21).

Budget and building program.

The Council discussed the budget for the year 1949–1950 (June 2, 1949) and set a procedure for reconsideration of priorities in the building program (January 3).

Academic matters.

The problems occasioned by students' withdrawals from classes were discussed by the Council on October 4 and were referred to its committee on grading (February 7). The matter of enrollment in advanced courses R.O.T.C. was discussed (October 4), and recommendations for a change in the statement in the University catalogue were adopted (October 18). Some time was given to a discussion of the function of the Junior Division (November 1), and the problem was referred to a committee.

The question of the organization of graduate studies raised in the State of the University speech was brought to the attention of the Council (January 3) and was referred to the faculties of the divisions for action (January 17). On May 16, the Council heard a report on the action taken by various divisions with regard to the reorganization of graduate work and approved a recommendation that a committee be appointed by Dean Briscoe to consult with him in matters concerning the general welfare of the graduate program. Implied in the action of the Council was the suggestion that the committee should continue study of possibilities for further reorganization.

Housing.

The question of housing received only brief consideration from the Council. On April 18, the Long-Range Housing Committee reported on various private housing projects under way in the city, and also on the approval by the Board of Trustees on the sale of additional prefabricated houses owned by the University.

Miscellaneous.

During the current year, the Council considered the following matters and took action wherever it was deemed proper:

Approval of the report of the Committee on the Midwest Inter-Library Corporation (May 3, 1949);

Definition of the functions of department chairmen (May 3, 1949);

Recording of votes of Faculty Council members (May 24, 1949 and May 30, 1950);

Discussion of attendance at public lectures (May 24, 1949) and approval of a portion of a committee report dealing with the question (November 15);

Approval of recommendations for hospitalization and surgical insurance (October 18);

Approval of the report of the Committee on Sabbatical Leaves (November 15);

Faculty use of lockers in the Men's Gymnasium (December 6);

Off-campus representation on the Faculty Council (November 15, December 6);

Reporting of student absences (December 6);

Establishment of a file of examinations in the Library (February 7, April 4, 18);

Recommendation that a Senior student be appointed to the Commencement Committee (April 4);

Smoking in the Library (February 7, March 21);

Opportunity for student review of examinations (April 18);

Request by professional librarians for faculty status (March 7, 21; May 30);

Approval of a report of the Committee on the Improvement of Faculty Teaching which recommends a period of orientation for new faculty members and continuing study of the problems of teaching and its evaluation (April 4, 18; May 2, 30, 1950);

Education of women (April 18; May 30, 1950);

Faculty rules (May 30, 1950).

In addition, the Council received several informal reports on matters of interest to the members of the faculty: on the Turkey Run meeting of the Indiana Conference of Higher Education (January 3); on the State School Cost Survey (January 17); on the Conference on Advancement of Teaching (March 7); on the reorganization of the American Association of Universities (January 3); on the planned bi-centennial celebration of the founding of Columbia University (May 30, 1950).

Unfinished business.

Further reports are expected from the Council's committees on grading, on the improvement of faculty teaching, on long-range housing problems, and on faculty-student relations. In addition, its committees on the function of the

Junior Division and general education, on new curricular areas, on extra-curricular offerings, and also on augmentation of outside fellowship grants have yet to report. The Council has agreed to further discussion of certain points of the report of its committee on attendance at public lectures, and calendar of events.

Faculty Council Minutes, 1947–1950, pp. 225–227.

[IX]

Enlarging the University's Sphere
1947–1957

In many respects Indiana University entered its most exciting years in the 1950s. The Wells Administration had vastly matured in the past decade, world conditions had created phenomenal demands, and students were coming to the campus in droves of thousands. Never before had there been so many challenges in so short a time to make adjustments in old plans of operation, and to make new plans in the expanded areas of university concern. First of all, it was necessary for the system of higher education in Indiana to break the parity scheme under which it had operated since the early 1930s. This formula had served the institutions in an era when there was danger of disastrous rivalries for limited state financial support. The 1950s was a period of expansion, and the more fundamental question of specialized functions of the various Indiana universities and colleges required different answers from those of the past. The study which led to the formulation of new types of budgetary requests based upon the objective facts of functions and needs was within itself a revolution in approaches to higher educational support in Indiana. Too, this opened the door for expansion into new areas by each of the four institutions.

Within Indiana University itself there was both a period of self-examination and of planning. At least four major curricular areas were reexamined, and in every case the field of activities was broadened. The statement of the need for expansion in the School of Law was both interesting and revolutionary. The teaching of law in Indiana University under this plan took the institution onto new and higher philosophical planes. For the student and professor alike, study in this discipline acquired a new dimension of universality which lifted it out of its ancient role of serving a purely provincial legal system.

Always Indiana University raised the question of what kind of education, and for what purposes, it offered students. It was easy enough for a professorial committee to state the ideals of the University in this area, but it was difficult to achieve them. There was a re-examination of the program of the Lower Division, and to considerable extent a readjustment of its offerings. In all of the excitement of the war and the great influx of veterans the Lower Division had almost been forgotten. The demands of the 1950s with the pressures of numbers made mandatory an updating.

In another area the university was reaching out to break the bondage of tradition. As a liberal arts university it in some way had to reach into the service field, first to offer greater returns to the people of Indiana, and, second, to counteract the broad influences of Purdue University with its various applied science service functions. Development of the off-campus centers was an achievement which resulted in a rich academic-service return to the university. Also the institution gained appreciable national reputation in this field. There were other services provided by Bloomington, such as the development of a far-reaching audio-visual aids program, the broadcasting of all sorts of academic and artistic programs, and increasing the service features of the School of Business. These various areas had sprung up without much coordination, but in this stirring decade it was necessary to make a much clearer analysis of their places in the university's broader academic and service offerings.

Physically this was an era of vast expansion. The old campus with its 1880s buildings was entirely inadequate, and the university was faced with numerous bothersome questions about future expansion. One concern was to serve history by leaving intact the old Jordanesque plan which had remained largely untouched for so many years. To preserve the past and at the same time serve the future necessitated the devising of a plan for new campus facilities located within an area small enough to accommodate the daily class schedule. The plan included here is a fundamental document which underwent changes, but nevertheless its authors looked ahead to a long-range future. Because of this plan the institution served its practical and sentimental objectives with admirable success.

In the nonacademic area this decade was one of athletic triumphs and disasters. Professor John F. Mee's report to the Faculty Council was comprehensive, but it raised more questions than it settled. There lingered on in university athletic closets the haunting ghost of being a "footpad" in the highly competitive Big Ten Conference. In trying to answer some of the baffling questions, especially in the area of football, Indiana University suffered a decade of grief and disaster. The Mee report outlines the pride, aspiration, and even the uncertainties which confronted the institution.

Finally the University had to carry out an expanding program in an era when rigidly conservative forces ran loose in both the state and the nation. With the American Legion's national offices located in Indianapolis, the university was constantly brought under fire with charges of communism on the campus. Throughout the decade there were hearings, threats of hearings, professors in possible jeopardy, and constant questions about materials coming into the library. On top of this was the national lunacy of the McCarthy era.

In the great masses of incoming students there were individuals of all sorts of moral attitudes. In the breaking off of the old intimate student-professorial relationship there were greater possibilities of cheating and fudging in the day-to-day work of the classroom. The faculty devoted a good amount of time to this problem, again writing into reports a high moral code but never quite working out its practical application. The questions of who was going to catch the cheater, who would prove him guilty, and, finally, what would be the penalty for cheating, were never fully answered.

During this decade the mimeograph machine whirred overtime, and every division of the University produced thousands of pages of reports, plans, questionnaires, correspondence, and notes. University documents grew longer, and the element of caution became more noticeable in the detailed prescriptions which were written into many of them. Selection, almost as a matter of course, has to be arbitrary, always with the realization of the fact that the formal document was but the tip of the broad action which was taken, of the causes for its coming into existence, and of its application. Nevertheless, many of the documents of this section had far-reaching importance in revising both the University's objectives and approaches to modern higher education.

Document 158

A New Field, a New Faculty

In the period of great internal changes in the 1950s, the Library Staff personnel came forth with a request for a definite statement of status in the professional hierarchy of the University. This report sets forth the various questions involved in classifying service personnel in a non-teaching facility.

* * *

FACULTY STATUS
The Indiana University Library staff positions are divided into two groups: professional and clerical.

The Survey Committee recommends that the professional group, whose responsibilities are such that they can be successfully performed only by graduates of library schools or by those with academic qualifications equal to those required for the academic staffs in the University, be accorded faculty status in Indiana University.

The professional staff of the library is directly and actively engaged in the educational and research program of the University. It is upon these librarians that a considerable part of the value of the University as an institution depends. A distinguished library with an efficient and co-operative staff is a natural corollary of a distinguished university.

I. Educational Qualifications

Educational qualifications for the members of the present professional library staff on the Bloomington and Indianapolis campuses are summarized below, as justification for classification with the educational faculty group:

5 staff members have an A.B. or B.S. degree.

1 staff member has a B.S.L.S. degree

12 staff members have an AB. or B.S. degree plus the degree Bachelor of Library Science which represents a year of professional training beyond college graduation. Since 1948 this degree has been granted as an A.M. degree in most schools of Library Science.

10 staff members have an A.M. or M.S. degree in addition to an A.B. or B.S. Degree; this represents a year of professional training beyond college graduation.

2 staff members have Ph.D. degrees.

4 staff members have no degrees.

This list shows that seventy-one percent of our professional library staff has completed five or more years of academic preparation. Five members of the Library staff hold teaching positions in the University at the present time; four of these are teaching courses on the graduate level.

Most of the Library Schools from which the staff have received their degrees are set up on a graduate basis. College graduates are admitted through a process of selection, scholarship and evidence of ability as prospective librarians. The Library Schools of the Universities of Illinois, California, Michigan and Columbia are grouped with the professional schools of Medicine and Law of their respective universities. Undergraduate study of two or three years, however, will give admission to the professional curricula of most professional schools. Type I Library Schools require for admission four years of undergraduate study leading to the A.B. or B.S. degree, with a final average grade of not less than B, and an acquaintance with two foreign languages. Thus, actually a wider background of general education is required for prospective librarians than for most other professional groups. It would appear, then, that:

1. Educational requirements for librarians approach those of the teaching faculty and are above those of the clerical and administrative staffs of Indiana University.

2. The work performed is of recognized professional type.

II. Professional Character

The intellectual character of the work of University librarians warrants that it be termed professional. The University is building up specialized research and teaching collections of materials to supplement direct classroom instruction. To handle these collections, to organize them and to make them available require a special staff skilled in the use of bibliographical and general as well as specialized reference tools.

The interpretation and successful application of the principles of library service for the greatest benefit to the institution require a considerable amount of direct individual responsibility from each staff member. Each renders a service in proportion to his previous background and the ingenuity and judgment which he brings to bear on each problem confronting him.

III. ACADEMIC CHARACTER AND INSTRUCTIONAL FUNCTION

The duties of the librarians are not only professional but academic. Current educational policies emphasize the use of library materials as an aid to instruction as well as to research developments. It is the task of the library to make all known resources available upon request.

The University Libraries serve undergraduates, graduate students, professional students, the faculty, and visiting scholars. Such specialized, comprehensive service as the librarians necessarily render their exacting clientele has given them an active, if auxiliary, part in the instructional and research program of the University. The Librarian not only complements the formal classroom and laboratory courses of the institution, but serves as an educator in his own right as a guide to intellectual stimulation for its own sake.

IV. UNIVERSITY RECOGNITION

Indiana University accords the Director of Libraries the title of Professor and the Associate Director the title of Associate Professor, but has hitherto been satisfied to lump all the rest of the highly trained library staff under the general supervision of the Personnel Department, along with the secretaries, clerical and maintenance workers. That this practice is contrary to the usage of leading colleges and universities of the nation may be seen in the attached chart which shows the status of Librarians in various institutions.

In Indiana, not only do the Purdue University librarians enjoy faculty status, but all public and private school librarians have equal status with teachers, with the accompanying privileges of equal salary schedules, provisions for tenure, vacations, and leaves. The State Department of Public Instruction and the North Central Association of Colleges and Secondary Schools have recognized that a Bachelor's degree from an accredited library school is the equivalent to the A.M. or M.S. degree.

V. SUMMARY

It is the conclusion of the Survey Committee, first, that professional librarians, by the nature of their functions, definitely belong in the instructional and research group; second, by comparative standards of education and preparation, they qualify for inclusion with the teaching staff; and, third, there are numerous tangible and intangible advantages for librarians in holding an academic classification. With reference to the last point, the factor of staff morale is of primary significance. One can expect the best results from any organization only if its place is clearly understood and appreciated.

VI. RECOMMENDATION

It is recommended by the Survey Committee that these members of the professional staff, with five years or more of college or university work, or its equivalent, be granted complete faculty status in Indiana University.
February 24, 1950

> ANITA M. PIGOTT
> PEGGY A. WAGNER
> JOHN R. THOMPSON,
> Chairman

Faculty Council Minutes, 1947–1950, pp. 189–192.

Document 159

Good Teaching

This report of the Faculty Committee on Teaching, April 4, 1950, deals with the central problem of every university. There was little, however, of "Mark Hopkins, the log, and the eager student" in this attempt to evaluate the teaching process. Already the Indiana approaches to basic problems had begun to assume bureaucratic complexions.

*   *   *

THE COMMITTEE ON THE IMPROVEMENT OF FACULTY TEACHING: FIRST REPORT

The present Committee on the Improvement of Faculty Teaching has met frequently since May, 1949, and its members have individually profited from these discussions. The Committee believes, however, that no significant improvement in the quality of University teaching can result from the Committee's drawing up a single report composed solely of generalized suggestions and of principles equally applicable to all of the teaching divisions and units of the University. The improvement of instruction calls for a continuous and vigorous program of study and action on all levels and in all areas of the University.

The Committee has five recommendations to make at this time:

I. *The Recognition of Teaching.*

One basic principle only does the Committee wish to recommend to the Council for its affirmation—that the best way to secure fine teaching is to reward it for its own sake. This principle has been stated in numerous earlier reports; the Committee feels that it is so fundamental in a program of improving teaching that it should not only be reasserted but that measures should also be taken to assure its application.

The Committee therefore recommends that the Faculty Council adopt this basic principle so that all those who have the responsibility for promotions and salary increases will vigorously follow the policy of recommending that salary increases and promotions to all professorial ranks be granted for outstanding teaching, fully and to the same extent as for outstanding research or other service to the University or the State. In putting this principle into effect the Faculty Council should (1) declare it to be the policy of the University that for a faculty member to be eligible for promotions and salary increases solely on the basis of teaching performance, he should normally carry a heavier teaching load than does one who also engages in research or in other activity and (2) ask each Dean to report to it at the beginning of each school year what was accomplished along the lines of this policy within his province during the previous year; that such reports reach the council at its second meeting for the school year; and that the Council pass on to the Committee on Improvement of Teaching the information thus obtained.

II. *A University Committee on the Improvement of Teaching.*

As a result of the all-University representation on the Committee, the Committee has become aware that there are, in one section or another of the University, a number of noteworthy experiments and administrative practices aiming at the improving of teaching. The School of Business, for example, has a very active Committee working on the improvement of teaching standards; various departments in Arts and Sciences have persons or committees charged with the study of teaching methods and in particular with the training of graduate assistants.

In view of the numerous unrelated activities that are now taking place in the University that have the goal of improving teaching, we recommend that the University Committee on the Improvement of Faculty Teaching be made permanent with the function of stimulating and of coordinating efforts to improve teaching in the various schools. It is further recommended that in the future the membership of the University Committee should be limited to ten, that it should change regularly in a manner to be suggested later by the Committee itself, and that the majority of members should be drawn from those most actively concerned with the improvement of teaching in the various schools. In addition to the representatives of the various schools, we recommend that the Office of the Dean of Faculties and of the Junior Division be represented on the Committee.

III. *School Committees.*

Each school of the university which does not yet have a committee actively at work on the problem of improving teaching should create such a standing committee. In order to insure continuity of purpose and programs the members of this Committee should serve for three years, but initially they should be appointed by the deans for one, two and three year terms. Each committee should be actively and continuously engaged in improving the quality of teaching in all the units of its school.

These committees should be charged with the following responsibilities:

a. To cooperate with the permanent university committee on the improvement of faculty teaching by assisting it in the collection of information concerning teaching standards, techniques, administrative devices, student evaluation, training and supervision of graduate assistants, the handling of multiple section courses, etc.

b. To submit to the permanent university committee periodic reports on its activities in the school.

c. To encourage, as far as possible, the voluntary organization of the faculty into discussion groups concerned with the improvement of teaching.

d. To make at least one annual report of its activities and recommendations to the dean and to the faculty of the school.

e. To stimulate experimentation in teaching methods, materials, and approaches.

f. To call in consultants when needed for assistance in the solution of problems that have to do with the improvement of teaching.

g. To collect and distribute materials pertaining to the improvement of instruction to all teaching personnel.

h. To encourage new faculty and especially graduate teaching assistants to visit classes of outstanding teachers in the school.

i. To administer student ratings of instructors from time to time and to interpret the results in general faculty meetings in the light of their implications for the improvement of teaching.

j. To arrange that one or more faculty meetings each year be devoted to the presentation and discussion of problems that have to do with the improvement of teaching.

k. To encourage the development of special programs for supervising and improving the teaching of graduate assistants.

l. To seek greater and more effective use of the guidance and counseling services of the school and the University.

IV. *An Orientation Program for New Staff Members.*

The Committee, recommends that, under the supervision of the Dean of Faculties Office, a series of orientation meetings (not more than three or four) be held for new faculty members, including graduate assistants and teaching fellows. The following general topics—The University and its Schools, the faculty, faculty administrative procedures, and University services to the faculty and to the student body—should be presented by appropriate University officials. This Committee would be glad to cooperate in the planning of such a program.

V. *Proposed Effective Date for These Recommendations.*

It is proposed that recommendations I-IV be put into effect in September, 1950.

VI. *Activities of the Present University Committee.*

The present University Committee proposes to concern itself for the remainder of the 1949-50 academic year with the important problem of the improvement of teaching in multi-section courses.

> H. T. BATCHELDER, Assistant Professor, School of Education
>
> T. R. BOSSORT, JR., Instructor, Management
>
> A. S. CLAYTON, Associate Professor, School of Education
>
> F. H. ELLIS, MRS., Assistant Professor, German
>
> F. C. SCHMIDT, Associate Professor, Chemistry
>
> A. SLATER-HAMEL, Assistant Professor, HPER
>
> J. E. STONER, Associate Professor, Government
>
> H. E. WOLFE, Associate Professor, Mathematics
>
> G. R. WAGGONER, Chairman, Assistant Dean, College of Arts and Sciences

Faculty Council Minutes, 1947–1950, pp. 201–203.

Document 160

The New University Woman

During the decade when Indiana University was deeply involved in World War II, returning veterans, and expanding both internal educational and physical facilities, there came into view an even greater long-range problem. Women were now seeking education at all levels in much larger numbers. They came not as guests of the system, but as a major integral part of the program. This report of the Committee on Women's Education recognizes the fact that fundamental changes had come to both American society and to the Indiana University campus. This committee of campus women staff members is a forceful discussion of the needs of their sex in the future of the University and the country.

*　　*　　*

REPORT OF THE COMMITTEE ON WOMEN'S EDUCATION
To: The President and Dean of the Faculties, March 1950.
Part I. Recommendations.

In these middle decades of the twentieth century, because of the great acceleration in all social processes following two world wars, the change in the opportunities and in the functions of men and especially of women have run far beyond the educational programs available to them. At the same time there has been a shifting in the focus of higher education in general, and an evolution in our economic structure which has resulted in larger numbers of young people seeking higher education and in a shift in the proportion of those who attend state universities rather than private institutions.

In 1948 President Wells therefore reactivated the Committee on Women's Education and asked for a rethinking of all phases of Indiana University's offerings for women, and for a study of the contemporary situation and the needs of women relative to those of men with a view to determining how best the University could serve the student group as future citizens of the state. After a year of work the committee submits the following recommendations:

1. *Establishment of a new unit.* The Committee recommends that there be established in the University, within one of the schools if that seems feasible, a new unit on the departmental level which would accommodate students who can profit from more flexibility and more individualized counseling than is possible in the existing structure.

2. *Purpose of the new unit.*
   A. To attract to the University as many as possible of the high school graduates who are qualified, and especially those of high caliber and serious intent, who will be challenged by the service and facilities which the University offers them in fulfilling their professional aspirations. This is especially important in view of the prohibitive costs of education in private institutions.
   B. To provide for a greater flexibility in the program and to make possible a wider diversity of course offerings than is now available. This is a service which many young women especially need.
   C. To train and stimulate such students in the recognition of their greater responsibility for participation in civic and cultural activities in the community, state, and nation.
   D. To improve the placement opportunities especially for women graduates in positions commensurate with their interests, abilities and competence.
   E. To publicize more extensively, in and out of the state, the ways in which the University is serving the special educational needs of all women.

F. To stimulate by way of offerings an increasingly high enrollment level of women students in the University.

3. *Organization of the new unit.*
   A. Administrative Head:
   The unit would have an administrative head with the authority necessary to carry out all of its functions. The appointment of a woman to the position seems essential in view of the special problems of women which the unit is designed to meet. The head of the unit would be a member of the administrative council.
   B. Policies:
   The unit would have an executive council composed of faculty members with special consideration given to women who serve as heads of departments, or academic administrators (e.g. a woman who may be assistant dean in any college.) Women faculty members should be drawn especially from schools and departments which attract a large proportion of women students.
   The executive council would determine and direct the policies of the new unit. Such policies would be closely coordinated with all other university divisions to which its functions are related. They would be concerned with all the functions mentioned below.
   C. Secretary and Office:
   A full time well qualified secretary and a well equipped centrally located office would be essential to the functioning of the unit.
   D. Budget:
   A separate budget should be needed for the unit. Special consideration should be given to offering stipends or lightening the loads for counselors serving in the division.

4. *Functions of the unit.*
   A. In order to provide the greater flexibility in curriculum which may be required to meet educational needs of students it will be necessary for this division to arrange for a bachelor's degree (probably a Ph.B. or B.S.) free from the requirements of any one of the present undergraduate curricula and allowing the student to make combinations of disciplines and interests which require cutting across the present schools and departments. The number of students in such individual or tailor-made curricula would be small. Their eligibility would be determined by the executive council of the unit according to the following considerations:
      (1) Level of academic achievement.
      (2) Clear statement in writing of purpose and vocational plans.
      (3) Endorsement of one faculty member who is willing to serve as sponsor and advisor.
      (4) Satisfactory preparation in basic areas of general education such as literature, science, social science, fine and applied arts.
   B. There are large numbers of students, (many of them women) who anticipate only one or two college years. If no other division or department assumes the responsibility for these students, the new unit may offer individual counseling based on their backgrounds, needs, and desires. These students should have (1) individually planned curricula and (2) recognition of satisfactory accomplishment which might take the form of a certificate. Programs would be planned with a view to the

academic attainment of the student, the integration of his courses around a central purpose and attention to basic areas of knowledge.

C. In order to provide the necessary understanding of individual and society and of the problems important to women in society, this unit should establish, if they are not already available in the appropriate departments, certain new kinds of courses:

    (1) Integrated courses in the humanities, social sciences, and sciences, each of which will make available in a year's course the significance of our heritage in these fields.

    (2) Two of three courses concerned more specifically with the functions and problems of women. Examples: a course dealing with social, economic and political responsibilities and opportunities as related to women; a course dealing with the changing functions and status of women.

    (3) For students, especially, freshmen, who are undecided on curriculum and life work, a systematic vocational study and orientation course. This would include individual laboratory study and guidance, and would probably carry one hour of credit.

D. One of the most important functions of the new unit is the counseling of students. This function must be coordinated with the individual counseling which is done through faculty counseling in the Junior Division and in the other schools of the University.

The counseling program of this division will consist of:

    (1) Training of the council members and other faculty counselors through group study of (a) techniques of counseling, (b) current courses, (c) curricula offerings, (d) current opportunities and problems of women.

    (2) Individual counseling of (a) students who will earn their degrees under the direction of the unit and (b) students who may be referred by Deans or other faculty members.

E. A continuous program of survey and research on:

    (1) Enrollment trends, curriculum-election trends, and alumnae satisfaction.

    (2) Women's opportunities for participation in professional, business, and political activities.

    (3) The activities and programs of the major professional and cultural organizations for women.

    (4) The trends and currents on higher education, especially new curricula and courses for women.

F. To encourage through a special representative for women in the alumni office.

    (1) More active participation in the work of the alumni association.

    (2) More education of alumnae in the current activities and opportunities for women on the campus.

    (3) More distribution of information, and more systematic recruiting of able and serious high school seniors.

G. To provide for better placement of graduates without specific vocational training through a special placement officer who shall:

    (1) Work in close cooperation with other placement officers on the campus.

    (2) Investigate and develop employment opportunities beyond those

of the more steretotyped professions, especially for students with unusual interests or demands.

(3) Work with departmental advisers to keep them appraised of both the opportunities or limitations of their fields.

(4) Discover and publicize further fellowship, assistantship, and other self-help devices for women qualified for graduate work in all fields.

REPORT OF THE COMMITTEE ON WOMEN'S EDUCATION
TO THE PRESIDENT AND DEAN OF THE FACULTIES, MARCH, 1950
PART II: THE PROBLEMS IN THE EDUCATION OF WOMEN
Differences Between Men and Women

Psychologists and sociologists are now agreed that there are no significant differences between the sexes in intellectual capacity, in personality traits, in citizenship responsibilities or in spiritual and personal needs. It has become obvious that there are much larger differences between groups of individuals within one or the other sex than between sex groups. We must however as educators, look further into this problem and ask ourselves in what ways men and women do differ, and therefore in what ways their education should be adapted to meet these varying needs.

In the one very obvious biological difference, the child bearing function of women, scholars are in quite general agreement that it is the social implications, e.g. enforced absence from the working world, which give significance to this biological function. All family and marriage counseling points to the importance of *both* parents in assuming responsibility for the rearing of the children, from the very earliest age.

Men and women differ not at all in their intellectual capacities, very little in their attitudes and personal traits, (and all of these differences may be traced to social factors) very much in the patterns of their life activities as they grow from adolescence to later maturity in our society, and most of all in opportunities. The differences in the social pattern of the life of men and women are primarily in the shorter length of the working period for women, the limited opportunities which are available to her, and especially in the last two decades, the duplication of effort in which she becomes involved,—homemaking in addition of a job outside the home. These differences of course lead to conspicuous differences in achievement.

One other important difference may be seen as the result of social forces of long standing: women have traditionally assumed more responsibility than men for the cultural values in the home and the immediate community, at least for the appreciative, if not for the creative aspect of the arts. Likewise they have traditionally also created more awareness, sympathy and responsibility in both the spiritual and moral realm. Religious organizations and the general agencies for social welfare are kept alive largely through the responsibilities and efforts assumed by women.

These three kinds of differences between men and women in 1) the biological function, 2) life pattern and opportunities, 3) traditional cultural and social responsibilities cannot fail to be significant differences for educators in planning new courses and curricula for women to meet their individual and changing needs.

The Relation of Women's Education to General Educational Philosophy

The planning for these specific needs however must be integrated with other current changes in the educational philosophy for all men and women students in general. Certain trends designed to shape the thinking of the next generation toward better world conditions, better living standards, better adjustment of individuals are equally necessary for both sexes. These trends are obviously planned to meet the changing economic, social, and political circumstances and ideologies. They assume that the transition from war to peace in both international and civil problems, can be guaranteed and accelerated only through more sound and more widespread education. They recognize further that our spiritual and moral ideologies are also in a transitional state, and that the general shifting from absolute to relative standards in such fields as religion, morals and art, also requires changes in our educational principles and practices.

That we are also in a period of transition in regard to the position and responsibilities of women has not up to this time claimed so much attention from the educators, although it is now emerging and differentiating itself more clearly as the central problem in the education of women. From the longest possible perspective, we may see women as the last unit in the long process of bringing industry out of the home. Gradually the functions of women in preparing and preserving food, in producing and caring for clothing, and finally even in child care and training, have moved outside the home circle and gradually also the security and ego feeling of the women have been damaged, to such an extent that her mental health and that of her children are becoming increasing hazards in our society. Although the ultimate solution cannot be predicted, it is obvious that especially in an era that urges individual responsibility, woman must find new and different functions beyond those dictated by centuries of feminine tradition. She must inevitably be drawn into more of the world's work, in business, the professions and in civic affairs.

Although when we are thinking in terms of another hundred years or more, these trends may seem very clear and inevitable, it is also clear that in thinking of the next ten or twenty years, difficulties and uncertainties loom with formidable importance. We do observe the slowly but certainly rising numbers of women especially of older women, in the labor force. We see also the larger numbers of men who are drawn more and more into the problems and routines of family living. We see also the trend toward greater sharing of tasks and responsibilities in all fields, by men and women, and the greater equalization of the sexes in terms of opportunities, activities, and interests as well as in personality and attitudes. But these are the very long term trends and in the meantime we see also the large differences in individuals, the cultural lag in many groups and areas, and the many different kinds of resistances, whose decelerating effects are difficult to calculate. It is the uncertainty about the rate at which these various trends will unfold and the directions into which current events may turn them which makes current planning difficult. Young women must be educated in the uncertain 1950's for a life to be lived in the still more uncertain 70's and 90's.

Difficulties in Planning a Program for Women

To be more specific, the present dilemmas include the following:

1) The uncertainties of the economic opportunities for women in the next two decades are tied to the economic uncertainties for all workers, but more especially those of both white collar workers, and youthful workers. It has been pointed out that the present trend is toward the education of more youth for white collar jobs than can be absorbed, and the rising age and better health of our population makes a less rapid turnover and therefore keener competition for available jobs. Likewise, the prediction of our economic future in general, the fluctuation of good times and bad times is becoming more uncertain as the

economic and political fabric of the world becomes more complex. "Women are the last to be hired and the first to be fired."

2) It is difficult indeed to introduce any changes in curricula, but slightly more difficult to effect changes for women, because in addition to the usual resistances there is the long feminine tradition which obtains especially with the lay public, and with the parents and the young women themselves. The social prestige of college work is also a more important item with women than with men, and will obscure a more realistic approach to the problem.

3) The place which the institution of the family will continue to take in our society, including the respective roles of the husband and father, and of the wife and mother is not only in a transitional stage, but is claiming unusual attention from social science and educators. In what direction this problem will move, and at what rate, will have an important, but at the moment unpredictable, effect on women's attitudes and functions.

4) While the pioneers among women educators will assume that young women should be educated to take the lead in creating a new position for women in society, and to lead women the more rapidly out of this transitional period toward greater equalization with men, there will be many who will argue that it would be better to educate the present generation of young women primarily for the understanding and acceptance of the world as she finds it, for adjustment and satisfaction in the status quo. This is a problem which involves public relations and could not be successful without a careful and well planned education of the parents, and while it seems clear that an educational institution should always take the lead in any direction to which its scholars point with assurance, it has not always seemed feasible to move too rapidly in that direction. The resistances must also be calculated.

5) The continuing size of our women student body, and the sources from which it will be drawn in the future will be affected of course by the general economic situation, but also by the fate of the private colleges and especially of the women's colleges, and the junior colleges. It is obvious however that a university of our size must plan for many different kinds of students, for those from the different intellectual and economic levels, and for students who will remain either one, two, or four years, and who will come to us with widely different educational objectives.

6) In an era which emphasizes differential and individual treatment of the student, especially in respect to educational guidance, it is obvious that our size and our financial program will force us to devise and perfect techniques for counseling and for teaching in larger and larger groups. Successful group methods can undoubtedly be worked out, but this aspect of educational work often does not serve as a challenge to the teaching faculty. To find good teaching and counseling staff is not easy.

Principles and Programs for Women's Education

In summary, then, we will reiterate two general principles on which a new program for the education of women must be based.

First: The historic roles of men and women, the man as fighter, earner, adventurer, director in the world of affairs, the woman as mother and homemaker, protected in the family circle have been drastically modified and are constantly drawing closer together, and their personalities, interests and attitudes are likewise becoming similar. Although the rate at which these changes will proceed is difficult to predict, there will still be in the next quarter century substantial differences in the life patterns of men and women. Men will still dominate the world of business, professions and politics, and the gains which the women will be making in these fields will be made while they are still assuming the greater share of responsibilities for child rearing and for both the cultural level and the management of the home. All women must therefore be educated to carry a dual role. All women will work, and as the second half of the century unfolds, they will work in larger and larger numbers and for longer and longer periods. They must learn how to manage a successful and spiritually satisfying home and they must learn the new ways in which they can make their contributions to the business or professional or community life of the world.

Second: We recognize that the next 25 to 50 years constitute a transition period in many ways, from war to peace, from nationalistic to global philosophies, from the older to the newer ideologies in business, economic and governmental theories. *All citizens* must be educated to the *understanding* of these changes, and the reorganization and new emphases in curricula for both men and women from kindergarten to graduate school is called for. But since it is also a transition period in respect to the functions, opportunities, and responsibilities of men and women in society and in the home, women, who represent the minority group in these changing functions, must be educated to an understanding of all the aspects of this transition. If she does not know the general outlines of this movement, she will never really understand her own situation and she will lack the best means of coping with her own difficulties and of making the most of the opportunities offered her.

1) All women must not fail to give more attention than does the comparable man student to those cultural or liberal arts courses which teach her an understanding of herself and society and prepare her to assume leadership in the spiritual and artistic fields.

2) This means probably specially devised courses for those women who are undertaking intensive professional training, e.g. Elementary Education or Medicine, a streamlining of the diversified present requirements into one or more unit courses which shall contain the necessary basic elements.

3) It means a greater emphasis than at present on those cultural courses which give understanding of self, society and the arts *during the first two years,* so that those women who do not stay beyond the first or second year will be better prepared for their subsequent responsibilities.

4) It means that emphasis on vocational courses and curricula must always be accompanied by equal emphasis on cultural courses, and curricula, and that while our women students are preparing themselves for positions of greater or less responsibility in the business and professional world, they are also preparing themselves to understand and to undertake the responsibilities of family and community life. This may demand changes in the requirements for major work in the various departments, and greater flexibility in the requirements for the bachelor's degree.

The underlying assumption here is that most women will in the future continue longer in work outside the home, or will return to it after an interval devoted to child rearing, and that the present great interest of students and parents in vocational education will continue. It does not necessarily follow however that vocational studies need occupy the major portion of the curricula. It would seem better to emphasize the dual training for *every* woman, liberal *and* vocational, and with even more emphasis on the liberal, for the following reasons:

   a) Business and professional leaders have long been saying that it is the general well-rounded and versatile woman worker who can be of greatest service to them.

   b) Present practice provides for much of the technical training and learning, especially for the beginning worker, to be acquired on the job. In-service training is a standard procedure in the modern world.

   c) Women need to be opportunistic in their attitudes because of the fact that most of them will be married, not free to move about seeking opportunities which fit their talents and training, but forced to make the best of any opportunities which may be present in the particular geographic area where the husband's work is located.

   d) Emphasis on the values to be found in cultural interests and responsibilities is the best possible preparation for the inevitable difficulties and disappointments which any worker, but especially women workers, will encounter. The woman worker has still prejudice to meet, especially if she is married. The problems and difficulties of carrying her dual role will for many women be most easily solved in the next few decades, by staying in the lower echelons in the working world and acquiring the five star ranking in home and community life. (There is also widespread agreement that the dilemma caused by the increasing number of white collar workers in relation to the opportunities for them, may best be solved through education for satisfactions outside the job as well as in it.)

   5) Women need training in understanding the forces of society as they affect her changing role. Since we are in a transition period in respect to the position of women, she cannot be educated to embrace any one certain role because the nature of the different roles that she may be called on to play may change more rapidly than we can predict. She needs education for understanding the nature and implications and the responsibilities of these changing roles. Men also need this understanding, but it is logical to expect that women, not men, will take the lead in preparing themselves to deal with the problems and trends which are of greater significance to them, so that the evolution will proceed in the most orderly possible fashion and to the greatest benefit of all society.

Respectfully submitted,

KATE HEVNER MUELLER,
   Chairman

AGNES ANDERSON

ESTHER BRASHER

MARY ELIZABETH CAMPBELL

MARY M. CRAWFORD

BEATRICE GEIGER
   (by UNA ROBINSON)

WINIFRED MERRILL

EDNA MUNRO

MARGARET RUFSVOLD

BARBARA SHALUCHA

RUTH STRICKLAND

Faculty Council Minutes, 1947–1950, pp. 209–219.

Document 161

A New Student Awareness

For a century and a quarter Indiana University struggled with the problem of student-university relationships. This, however, was not a unique Indiana problem. Every institution of higher learning in the United States in the 1950s had to reassess student-faculty-university relationships. Pressures of numbers, "publish or perish," outside contracts with government and private industry, the greater mobility of students, and the complexities of housing all contributed to the ancient problems.

*   *   *

REPORT OF THE COMMITTEE ON FACULTY-STUDENT RELATIONS

December 19, 1950

To the President and Faculty:

The Committee on Faculty-Student Relations was appointed in October, 1949, pursuant to the action of the Faculty Council on October 4. It herewith submits its report covering its activities during the intervening period.

Pursuant to its own recommendation, the Committee became a joint committee, including students as well as members of the faculty, in March of this year. Previously, the Committee had met a number of times with a representative group of students designated by the Dean of Students. It was felt that the Committee's work would be advanced if the cooperating students became members by appointment of the President. The President assented and the appointments were made. From among those originally named, Miss Flo First, Mr. Rex Fleener, Mr. Glenn Graves, and Miss Martha Hefler have since graduated from the University. Three new student members have been appointed this fall. The faculty membership has remained unchanged.

In addition to acting as a joint group, the Committee functions through separate faculty and student subcommittees when appropriate. It has had the continued advice and collaboration of the Dean of Students, who regularly meets with it.

Preliminary Discussions Between the Committee
and Representative Students.

During November and December, 1949, the original Committee held several informal meetings with the group of students designated by the Dean of Students, for the purpose of exploring the problems with which the Committee might helpfully concern itself. These discussions were valuable and formed the basis for the Committee's subsequent activities. The problems which emerged most prominently fall into four categories:

(1) Alleged inadequacy of informal personal contact of faculty and students at Indiana University. It is widely believed to be difficult for the general run of students to become personally acquainted with any members of the faculty until they enter advanced work in particular departments, if then. This situation results mainly from the size of the University and the reduced opportunity for meeting faculty members in their offices or visit-

ing faculty homes. Housing conditions contribute, of course, to the factor last mentioned. Informal gatherings in chapter houses and dormitory units occur to only a limited extent. Faculty chaperoning of social affairs often operates unsatisfactorily because of the typically stilted character of the relationship at these functions.

(2) Policies and practices of the University and its faculty with which students become dissatisfied, whether because of lack of understanding on their part or lack of consideration of student viewpoints in formulating these policies.

(3) A deficiency in opportunities for serious intellectual interchange among faculty and students, except for advanced students and faculty in particular curricular areas.

(4) Indifference on the part of large numbers of students to opportunities for contact with faculty members. It is recognized that many students, perhaps a majority, do not take advantage of existing opportunities for personal contact and intellectual exchange with faculty members. Faculty members who go out of their way to create such opportunities are sometimes unsuccessful; attendance at receptions and serious meetings for discussion or lectures often is poor; and advantage frequently is not taken of faculty office hours.

The foregoing problems exist in the setting of a University community which in general is friendly and replete with social and cultural opportunities for both students and faculty.

The students with whom the Committee discussed the foregoing problems tended to urge (a) that additional ways be found for faculty members, as human beings rather than as specialists, to come in contact with students. Joint recreational activity and faculty participation in performances were suggested. The students also tended to urge (b) the correction of allegedly inconsiderate faculty actions, such as assignment of term papers too near the end of a semester, scheduling of numerous tests on the eve of a holiday, and dismissal of a final class before a holiday after a mere calling of the roll. The members of the faculty Committee expressed particular concern with increased use of conferences in faculty offices and the promotion of occasions, in housing units or elsewhere, for faculty and students to engage informally in serious discussion.

The Committee's Subsequent Program.

On the basis of the foregoing discussions, the Committee came to view itself as a body which should, primarily, develop a program of action to reduce existing deficiencies in faculty-student relations and of encouragement to attempts by other groups directed to the same end. The following projects have been undertaken:

(1) A subcommittee, consisting of Professor Meessen, Miss First, and Mr. Fleenor, was established to consider unsatisfactory aspects of the conduct of examination and recommend means of improvement. Upon the recommendation of this subcommittee the Committee on Faculty-Student Relations recommended to the Faculty Council, and the Council adopted, the measures taken at its meetings of April 18, 1950. These requested the University departments to provide files of typical past examinations for consultation by students in the University libraries and requested instructors to provide opportunities for students to review their performance in examinations.

(2) As representatives of the Committee, Professors Breneman, Morrill, and

Waters participated in a panel discussion at the Y.M.C.A.-Y.W.C.A. Freshman Leadership Conference before the opening of the present academic year, which took up problems of faculty-student relations. This discussion was widely appreciated and probably will be repeated in the future orientation of leadership programs.

(3) As the result of a proposal which emerged in the spring of 1950, arrangements were made under the auspices of the Committee, with the aid of the Junior Division, whereby several University divisions undertook to provide social occasions for Freshman students in the fall of this year to meet members of faculties engaged in professional or advanced instruction to which these students looked forward. At a meeting of deans and their representatives in August, the project was approved. President Wells made his entertainment fund available for the purchase of refreshments for these occasions. In addition to similar activities in the School of Business which had been begun in previous years, the following affairs of this nature have been conducted; an entertainment and party given by the Faculty of the School of Music in Recital Hall during the registration period; a reception by the School of Health, Physical Education, and Recreation for its undergraduates in the Student Building, October 25, 1950; and an open-house for Pre-Medical Junior Division students in the Medical Building on the campus, November 17, 1950. The school of Law may have an affair of this nature later in the academic year. No other active planning has been reported. Attendance at each of these affairs is reported to have been approximately 200. Junior Division students are said, however, to have responded poorly to the invitation of the Medical School, perhaps because of conflicting laboratory classes. Their place was taken by medical students who joined the party. Intermingling of faculty and students was uniformly accomplished, and the Schools of Music and Health, Physical Education, and Recreation have expressed a desire to have similar affairs in future years.

(4) At the solicitation of the Indiana Union, the Committee undertook to sponsor and arrange for a faculty variety show at the Union's Fall Carnival following the Notre Dame game. Professor Raymond G. Smith acceded to the Committee's request that he assume active charge of the performance. The Men's Faculty Club and the Women's Faculty Club provided funds to purchase material for the construction of the booth. The Union undertook to construct the booth. Professor Smith secured the participation of the following faculty members in the performance, which took the form of a series of acts that were staged at intervals during the evening: Professors Troy Cauley, Robert L. Hagen, Robert H. Lee (with Mr. George Willeford), W. Richard Lomax, and William E. Ross. The following Deans served as barkers in front of the booth: John W. Ashton, Ralph Collins, Ford P. Hall, Raymond L. Shoemaker, Pressly S. Sikes, and George R. Waggoner. An informal subcommittee of the Committee, composed of Professors Anderson, Merrill, Breneman, Endwright, Richey, and Fuchs, officiated in various capacities during the evening. The project was successful from a financial standpoint, grossing approximately $80.00, and is said to have been much appreciated. Certainly the acts were of admirable quality.

(5) Beginning immediately after the Christmas vacation, the Committee will hold monthly open meetings at which any person connected with the University who may wish to present a matter involving faculty-student

relations for the Committee's consideration will be invited to appear. Publicity will be given to the opportunity to appear at these meetings, and it is hoped that significant problems may be called to the Committee's attention by this means.

Appraisal of the Committee's Progress.

As the foregoing list of accomplishments reveals, the Committee has made only modest progress toward the objectives that it exists to serve. Its projects have made a beginning, however, and the working relationships between faculty members and students within the Committee have been worth while in themselves. No success has been achieved in promoting new forms of serious intellectual discussion among faculty members and students generally, although several projects directed to this end have been under discussion and may materialize before the end of the academic year.

The work of the Committee has received very little publicity so far, and it is hoped that the Committee's usefulness may be increased by improvement in this respect from now on. One encouraging development is the creation by the Union of its own committee on faculty-student relations, which was active in promoting the Fall Carnival participation and has other projects in mind, including at least one of a serious nature.

Suggestions from faculty members for the Committee's future work are especially solicited.

Respectfully submitted,

NANCY COLLIER	JOHN E. SPARKS	HUBERT J. MEESEN
JAMES COLEMAN	JOHN TERHUNE	WINIFRED MERRILL
JEAN GORDON	MARTHA McCULLOUGH,	ROBERT W. RICHEY
GENE HUDSON	Student Chairman	JOHN E. STEMPEL
KEN KRESS	AGNES ANDERSON	LAWRENCE L. WATERS
TED OLSEN	WILLIAM BRENEMAN	RALPH F. FUCHS,
NANCY SCHANLAUB	JOHN R. ENDWRIGHT	Chairman

Faculty Council Minutes, 1950–52, pp. 10–13.

Document 162

Americanism, Subversion, and a Free University

Indiana in the 1950s was a hotbed of "Americanism" stirred afresh by world events, by the unusual activities of the American Legion, patriotic groups in general, and by individuals who searched for a communist under the cover of every book in the university library. At no time was the university's freedom challenged more than in these years. In this particular document, the president and faculty discussed a pending piece of legislation concerning Indiana University which offered an enormous threat to academic and individual freedom in the name of preserving democracy.

*   *   *

President Wells pointed out, by way of introduction, that three subversive activities bills—#72, #183, and #550—had been under consideration in the Committee on Judiciary A of the House. (The three bills are appended to these minutes.) The final decision of the Committee on Judiciary A, President Wells informed the Council, was to recommend amended House Bill #72 to the House for passage.

Professor Horack then read amended House Bill #72. (This bill is attached to these minutes.) Professor Horack pointed out that, unlike House Bill #183, amended House Bill #72 has eliminated the concept of enforcement through an oath; and that amended House Bill #72 applies to all persons in Indiana, not only employees or teachers. He added that Sections 1 and 4 affect the University most directly.

A discussion of amended House Bill #72 followed. Mr. Miller pointed out that the Library might be held in violation of Section 1, subhead 2, and asked if it would be appropriate to ask the General Assembly for interpretation. In reply, Professor Horack suggested that the phrase "for the purpose of" might be substituted for the words "containing or" in Section 1, subhead 2. Professor Frenz asked if the amended bill was sponsored by both parties. President Wells replied that it was, and that it also had the backing of the American Legion. Professor Fuchs asked if there was any real chance that the bill might be defeated in the House or that it might not get to the Senate. President Wells replied that the opinion was that the bill would pass in the House and most likely in the Senate as well. Professor Cleland suggested that the passage of this bill might forestall the passage of something worse in these times of public hysteria. Professor Buehrig added that in general the University has no ground on which it can criticize the bill, except for the phraseology concerning the circulation of books, papers, and documents. Professor Mann pointed out that the idea of outlawing a political party is counter to our tradition, but that despite serious objections to the bill, opposition might produce something worse. Professor Fuchs added that even though the idea behind the bill may be abhorrent, the University as such is not peculiarly affected and the Faculty might not feel it necessary to act. Professor Lundin asked if teaching the facts of the American Revolution might not constitute a violation of the bill. Professor Horack suggested that changing the language in Section 1, subhead 2, as proposed above, would avoid that difficulty. Professor Mann asked if Section 4 would not constitute an invasion of our principles of academic tenure and freedom. Professor Horack replied that the procedure in cases involving academic tenure and freedom would remain the same, but that the grounds for dismissal would be changed. President Wells added that he assumed that the same steps would be followed in dealing with a case of dismissal under the proposed legislation as are now set forth in our tenure rules. Dean Ashton asked if there was any danger of an oath provision being tacked on after the bill reaches the House. President Wells replied that there was some danger, but that the amended bill represents what the sponsors think they can get. Dean Weimer suggested that it might be best to try to get the adjustment in the language of Section 1, subhead 2, as proposed by Professor Horack.

> It was taken by unanimous consent that President Wells would try to get the language of Section 1, subhead 2, changed as proposed by Professor Horack; and that the amended House Bill #72, since it would be less objectionable than #183 or #550, should not be opposed by the University. It was further agreed that President Wells should inform both the Teachers' Union and the local chapter of A.A.U.P. of the decision taken by the Faculty Council.

President Wells then spoke for a few minutes on the progress of the University's budget in the General Assembly.

Adjournment at 4 p.m.

Chapter 226

Approved March 5, 1951

HOUSE ENROLLED ACT No. 72

AN ACT concerning public offenses and declaring an emergency.

Be it enacted by the General Assembly of the State of Indiana:

SECTION 1. It is hereby declared to be the public policy of the State of Indiana and of this Act to protect the peace, domestic tranquility, property rights and interests of the State of Indiana and the people thereof from the tenets of the ideology known as Communism as the same is known and presently exists in the world today.

SECTION 2. It is further declared to be the public policy of the State of Indiana, and of this Act to promote and to enforce the Constitution of the United States of America, the Constitution of the State of Indiana, and all laws passed pursuant thereto guaranteeing and defining the rights of all free Americans and, to that end, to exterminate Communism and Communists, and any or all teachings of the same.

SECTION 3. For the purpose of this Act, the term Communism or Communist as herein defined shall include, but shall not be limited to the Communist political party as it presently exists. The Communist Party for the purpose of this Act is hereby defined as an organization which engages in or advocates, abets, advises, or teaches or has a purpose which is to engage in or advocate, abet, advise, or teach, activities intended to overthrow, destroy or alter, or to assist in the overthrow, destruction, or alteration of, the constitutional form of the Government of the United States, or of the State of Indiana, or of any political subdivision thereof, by revolution, force, or violence.

SECTION 4 (A) It shall be unlawful for any person to be a member of the Communist Party or of any party, group, or organization which advocates in any manner the overthrow, destruction or alteration of the constitutional form of the Government of the United States or of the State of Indiana, or any political subdivision thereof by revolution, force, violence, sedition, or which engages in any un-American activities.

SECTION (B) It shall be unlawful for any person by word of mouth or writing to advocate, advise or teach the duty, necessity, or propriety of overthrowing or overturning the Government of the United States or of the State of Indiana or any political subdivision thereof by force or violence; or print, publish, edit, issue or knowingly circulate, sell, distribute or publicly display any book, paper, document or written or printed matter in any form for the purpose of advocating, advising, or teaching the doctrine that the Government of the United States, or the State of Indiana, shall be overthrown by force, violence or any unlawful means.

SECTION 5. Whenever two or more persons assemble for the purpose of advocating or teaching the doctrine that the Government of the United States, or of the State of Indiana, should be overthrown by force, violence or any unlawful means, such an assembly is unlawful, and every person voluntarily participating therein by his presence, aid or instigation, shall be guilty of a felony.

SECTION 6. Every editor or proprietor of a book, newspaper or circular and every manager of a partnership or incorporated association by which a book, newspaper, or circular, is issued, is chargeable with the publication of any matter contained in such book, newspaper or circular. But in every prosecution therefore the defendant may show in his defense that the matter complained of was published without his knowledge or fault and against his wishes, by another who had no authority from him to make the publication and whose act was disavowed by him as soon as known.

SECTION 7. No person shall hold public office or be employed by any department, board, bureau, commission, institution or agency of the State of Indiana, or any of its political subdivisions, who is a member of the Communist Party or participating in any of the activities declared unlawful by this act or has been convicted under any provisions of Section 1 or 2 of this Act and any person now employed by any department, board, bureau, commission, institution or agency of the State of Indiana or any political subdivisions, who is a member of the Communist Party or who is engaged in any of the activities declared unlawful by this act shall be forthwith discharged. Evidence satisfactory to the head of such department, board, institution or agency of the State of Indiana or any of its political subdivisions shall be sufficient for refusal to employ any person or cause for discharge of any employee for the reasons set forth by this section. Any person discharged or refused employment under the provisions of this section shall have the right to judicial review provided by Chapter 365 of the Acts of 1947, being an act entitled "An Act concerning the proceedings, orders, and determinations of state officers and agencies and judicial review thereof" approved March 14, 1947.

SECTION 8. Any person violating any of the provisions of Section 4 of this Act shall be guilty of a felony and shall, upon conviction, be disenfranchised and rendered incapable of holding any office of profit or trust and shall be imprisoned in the Indiana State Prison for not less than one year nor more than three years.

SECTION 9. No provision of any section of this Act shall be construed to prohibit any right protected by the federal constitution or the constitution of the State of Indiana, including but not limited to rights of freedom of speech, freedom of the press and freedom of religion.

SECTION 10. If any section, paragraph, sentence or clause of this act shall for any reason be held invalid or unconstitutional by any court of competent jurisdiction the same shall not affect the validity of this Act as a whole, or any part thereof other than that portion so held to be invalid or unconstitutional.

HOUSE BILL NO. 72 DIGEST

This bill prohibits any person, firm, or corporation from indulging in any act by any means which in any way advocates the overthrow of the government of the United States or any political subdivision of the United States, specifically enumerating the form that any such act might take, making the committing of any such act a felony, and prescribing the penalty therefor. The bill also prohibits the employment of anyone in any department, board, bureau, institution, or agency of the State of Indiana, who is a Communist or has participated in any Communist activities, provides that the determination of such affiliation or activity by the head of any department, board, bureau, institution, or agency of the State of any of its political subdivisions shall be sufficient grounds for refusal to employ or discharge from employment. This bill contains an emergency clause.

HOUSE BILL NO. 72

A BILL FOR AN ACT concerning public offenses and declaring an emergency.

Be it enacted by the General Assembly of the State of Indiana:

SECTION 1. It shall be unlawful for any person to be a member of the Communist party and all persons who:

1. By word of mouth or writing advocate, advise or teach the duty, necessity, or propriety of overthrowing or overturning the Government of the United States or of the State of Indiana or any political subdivision or either of them by force or violence; or,

2. Print, publish, edit, issue or knowingly circulate, sell, distribute, or publicly display any book, paper, document or written or printed matter in any form containing or advocating, advising or teaching the doctrine that the Government of the United States, or of the State of Indiana, shall be overthrown by force, violence or any unlawful means; or,

3. Organize or help to organize or become a member of or voluntarily assemble with any society, group or assembly of persons formed to teach or advocate the doctrine that the Government of the United States, or the State of Indiana, should be overthrown by force, violence or any unlawful means shall be guilty of a felony.

SECTION 2. Whenever two or more persons assemble for the purpose of advocating or teaching the doctrine that the Government of the United States or of the State of Indiana, should be overthrown by force, violence or any unlawful means, such an assembly is unlawful, and every person voluntarily participating therein by his presence, aid or instigation, shall be guilty of a felony.

SECTION 3. Every editor or proprietor of a book, newspaper or circular and every manager of a partnership or incorporated association by which a book, newspaper, or circular, is issued, is chargeable with the publication of any matter contained in such book, newspaper or circular. But in every prosecution therefor, the defendant may show in his defense that the matter complained of was published without his knowledge or fault and against his wishes, by another who had no authority from him to make the publication and whose act was disavowed by him as soon as known.

SECTION 4. No person shall hold public office or be employed by any department, board, bureau, commission, institution or agency of the State of Indiana, or any of its political subdivisions, who is a member of the Communist Party or participating in any of the activities declared unlawful by this act or has been convicted under any of the provisions of Section 1 or 2 of this Act and any person now employed by any department, board, bureau, commission, institution or agency of the State of Indiana or any political subdivisions, who is a member of the Communist Party or who is engaged in any of the activities declared unlawful by this act shall be forthwith discharged. Evidence satisfactory to the head of such department, board, institution or agency of the State of Indiana or any of its political subdivisions shall be sufficient for refusal to employ any person or cause for discharge of any employee for the reasons set forth by this section. A person discharged or refused employment under the provisions of this section shall have the right within thirty days thereafter to appeal to the circuit court of the county wherein such person may reside for a determination by such courts (with the aid of a jury, if the applicant so elects) as to whether or not the discharge or refusal of employment appealed from was justified under the provisions of this act. The court shall speedily hear and determine such appeals, and from the judgment of the court, there shall be further appeal to the Supreme Court of the State of Indiana as in civil cases.

SECTION 5. Any person violating any of the provisions of sections 1 or 2 of this act shall be guilty of a felony and shall, upon conviction, be imprisoned in the Indiana State Prison not less than one year nor more than three years.

SECTION 6. Whereas an emergency exists for the immediate taking effect of this act, the same shall be in full force and effect from and after its passage.

COMMITTEE REPORT

Mr. Speaker:

Your Committee on Judiciary A, to which was referred House Bill No. 72, has had the same under consideration and begs leave to report the same back to the House with the recommendation that said bill be amended as follows:

By striking out all of said bill after the fiture "1" where the "1" appears in Line 1, of Section 1, and inserting in lieu thereof the following:

It shall be unlawful for any person to be a member of the Communist party and all persons who:

1. By word of mouth or writing advocate, advise or teach the duty, necessity, or propriety of overthrowing or overturning the Government of the United States or of the State of Indiana or any political subdivision or either of them by force or violence; or,

2. Print, publish, edit, isue or knowingly circulate, sell, distribute or publicly display any book, paper, document or written or printed matter in any form containing or advocating advising or teaching the doctrine that the Government of the United States, or of the State of Indiana, shall be overthrown by force, violence or any unlawful means; or,

3. Organize or help to organize or become a member of or voluntarily assemble with any society, group or assembly of persons formed to teach or advocate the doctrine that the Government of the United States, or the State of Indiana, should be overthrown by force, violence or any unlawful means shall be guilty of a felony.

SECTION 2. Whenever two or more persons assemble for the purpose of advocating or teaching the doctrine that the Government of the United States, or of the State of Indiana, should be overthrown by force, violence or any unlawful means, such an assembly is unlawful, and every person voluntarily participating therein by his presence, aid or instigation, shall be guilty of a felony.

SECTION 3. Every editor or proprietor of a book, newspaper or circular and every manager of a partnership or incorporated association by which a book, newspaper, or circular, is issued, is chargeable with the publication of any matter contained in such book, newspaper or circular. But in every prosecution therefor, the defendant may show in his defense that the matter complained of was published without his knowledge or fault and against his wishes, by another who had no authority from him to make the publication and whose act was disavowed by him as soon as known.

SECTION 4. No person shall hold public office or be employed by any department, board, bureau, commission, institution or agency of the State of Indiana, or any of its political subdivisions, who is a member of the Communist Party or participating in any of the activities declared unlawful by this act or has been convicted under any of the provisions of Section 1 or 2 of this Act and any person now employed by any department, board, bureau, commission, institution or agency of the State of Indiana or any political subdivisions, who is a member of the Communist Party or who is engaged in any of the activities declared unlawful by this act shall be forthwith discharged. Evidence satisfactory to the head of such department, board, institution, or agency of the State of Indiana or any of its political subdivisions shall be sufficient of refusal to employ any person or cause for discharge of any employee for the reasons set forth by this section. A person discharged or refused employment under the provisions of this section shall have the right within thirty days thereafter to appeal to the circuit court of the county wherein such person may reside for a determination by such courts (with the aid of a jury, if the applicant so elects) as to whether or not the discharge or refusal of employment appealed from was justified under the provisions of this act. The court shall speedily hear and determine such appeals, and from the judgment of the court, there shall be further appeal to the Supreme Court of the State of Indiana as in civil cases.

SECTION 5. Any person violating any of the provisions of sections 1 or 2 of this act shall be guilty of a felony and shall, upon conviction, be imprisoned in the Indiana State Prison not less than one year nor more than three years.

SECTION 6. Whereas an emergency exists for the immediate taking effect of this act, the same shall be in full force and effect from and after its passage. and when so amended that said bill do pass.

ALLEN.

HB 183
Indiana General Assembly, 1951
Referred to Judiciary A Committee
Introduced by J. Perry Meek (R, Indpls.)
Joseph Klein (D, Lake Co,)

A BILL FOR AN ACT making it a crime to commit acts or advocate acts intended to effect the overthrow of the Government of the United States or the State of Indiana or of any political sub-division thereof by violence or other unlawful means, or to attempt or conspire so to do, relating to subversive organizations generally, to the loyalty of candidates for public office and of officers and employees of the state or of any political sub-division thereof and relating to the policy of the state in giving aid to private institutions which fail to report what procedures have been adopted to determine the loyalty of its officers and employees, providing for the enforcement of the provisions of said act, and providing penalties for the violation thereof.

WHEREAS, there is a World Communist movement under the domination of a foreign power, having as its objective the establishment of a totalitarian dictatorship in all parts of the world under its control; and

WHEREAS, such a dictatorship is characterized by the liquidation of all political parties other than the Communist Party, the abolishment of free speech, free assembly, and freedom of religion, and is the complete antithesis of the American constitutional form of government; and

WHEREAS, the methods used by such a police state include treachery, deceit, infiltration into governmental and other institutions, espionage, sabotage, terrorism and other unlawful means; and

WHEREAS, the World Communist movement is not a political movement, but is a world-wide conspiracy having sections in each country; and

WHEREAS, using the methods above set forth, it has already successfully conquered in recent years a large part of the world and has established spearheads in this country in the form of various conspiratorial organizations, some masquerading under the pretense of being political parties, other infiltrating organizations which they seek to control in order to further the objectives of the World Communist movement; and

WHEREAS, the methods adopted by subversive persons and organizations render it imperative that the loyalty of persons entering the public employment of the State of Indiana or any of its political subdivisions be definitely established, not only for protection of governmental processes but in order to shield employees from unfounded accusations of disloyalty; and

WHEREAS, the Communist movement plainly presents a clear and present danger to the United States Government and to the State of Indiana, Therefore

BE IT ENACTED BY THE GENERAL ASSEMBLY OF THE STATE OF INDIANA:

SECTION 1. For the purposes of this act:

"Organization" means an organization, corporation, company, partnership, association, trust, foundation, fund, club, society, committee, association, political party, or any group of persons, whether or not incorporated, permanently or temporarily associated together for joint action of advancement of views on any group of persons, whether or not incorporated, permanently or temporarily associated together for joint action of advancement of views on any subject or subjects.

"Subversive organization" means any organization which engages in or advocates, abets, advises, or teaches, or a purpose of which is to engage in or advocate, abet, advise, or teach activities intended to overthrow, destroy or alter, or to assist in the overthrow, destruction or alteration of, the constitutional form of the government of the United States, or of the State of Indiana, or of any political subdivision of either of them, by revolution, force or violence.

"Foreign subversive organization" means any organization directed, dominated or controlled directly or indirectly by a foreign government which engages in or advocates, abets, advises, or teaches, or a purpose of which is to engage in or to advocate, abet, advise, or teach, activities intended to overthrow, destroy or alter, or to assist in the overthrow, destruction or alteration of the constitutional form of the government of, the United States, or of the State of Indiana, or of any political subdivision of either of them, and to establish in place thereof any form of government the direction and control of which is to be vested in, or exercised by or under, the domination or control of any foreign government, organization, or individual; but does not and shall not be construed to mean an organization the bona fide purpose of which is to promote world peace by alliances or unions with other governments or world federations, unions or governments to be effected through constitutional means.

"Foreign government" means the government of any country or nation other than the Government of the United States of America or of one of the states thereof.

"Subversive person" means any person who commits, attempts to commit, or aids in the commission, or advocates, abets, advises or teaches by any means any person to commit, attempt to commit, or aid in the commission of any act intended to overthrow, destroy or alter, or to assist in the overthrow, destruction or alteration of, the constitutional form of the government of the United States, or of the State of Indiana, or any political sub-division of either of them, by revolution, force, or violence; or who is a member of a subversive organization or a foreign subversive organization.

SECTION 2. It shall be a felony for any person knowingly and willfully to

(a) commit, attempt to commit, or aid in the commission of any act intended to overthrow, destroy or alter, or to assist in the overthrow, destruction or alteration of, the constitutional form of the government of the United States or of the State of Indiana, or any political sub-division of either of them, by revolution, force, or violence; or

(b) advocate, abet, advise, or teach by any means any person to commit, attempt to commit, or assist in the commission of any such act under such circumstances as to constitute a clear and present danger to the security of the United States, or of the State of Indiana or of any political sub-division of either of them; or

(c) conspire with one or more persons to commit any such act; or

(d) assist in the formation or participate in the management or to contribute to the support of any subversive organization or foreign subversive organization knowing said organization to be a subversive organization or a foreign subversive organization; or

(e) destroy any books, records or files, or secrete any funds in this state of a subversive organization or a foreign subversive organization, knowing said organization to be such.

Any person who shall be convicted by a court of competent jurisdiction of violating any of the provisions of this section shall be fined not more than twenty thousand dollars, or imprisoned for not more than twenty years, or both, at the discretion of the court.

SECTION 3. It shall be a felony for any person after April 1, 1951, to become, or after July 1, 1951 to remain a member of a subversive organization or a foreign subversive organization knowing said organization to be subversive organization or foreign subversive organization. Any person who shall be convicted by a court of competent jurisdiction of violating this section shall be fined not more than five thousand dollars, or imprisoned for not more than five years, or both, at the discretion of the court.

SECTION 4. Any person who shall be convicted by a court of competent jurisdiction of violating any of the provisions of sections 2 and 3 of this act, in addition to all other penalties therein provided, shall from the date of such conviction be barred from

(a) holding any office, elective or appointive, or any other position of profit or trust in or employment by the government of the State of Indiana or of any agency thereof or of any county, municipal corporation or other political subdivision of said state;

(b) filing or standing for election to any public office in the State of Indiana; or

(c) voting in any election held in this state.

SECTION 5. It shall be unlawful for any subversive organization or foreign subversive organization to exist or function in the State of Indiana and any organization which by a court of competent jurisdiction is found to have violated the provisions of this section shall be dissolved and if it be a corporation organized and existing under the laws of the State of Indiana a finding by a court of competent jurisdiction that it has violated the provisions of this section shall constitute legal cause for forfeiture of its charter and its charter shall be forfeited under the laws of this state, and all funds, books, records and files of every kind and all other property of any organization found to have violated the provisions of this section shall be seized by and for the State of Indiana, the funds to be deposited in the state treasury and the books, records, files and other property to be turned over to the attorney general of Indiana.

SECTION 6. The attorney general of Indiana is hereby authorized and directed to appoint an additional assistant to perform the duties of special assistant attorney general in charge of subversive activities whose annual salary shall be provided in the budget, and whose responsibility it shall be, under supervision of the attorney general, to assemble, arrange, and deliver to the prosecuting attorney of any county, together with a list of necessary witnesses, for presentation to the next grand jury to meet in said county, all information and evidence of matters within said county which have come to his attention, relating in any manner to the acts prohibited by this act, and relating generally to the purposes, processes and activities of Communism and any other or related subversive organizations, associations, groups or persons.

SECTION 7. For the collection of any evidence and information referred to in this act, the attorney general is hereby directed to call upon the superintendent of state police, and county and municipal police authorities of the state to furnish to the special assistant herein before provided for, such assistance as may from time to time be required. Such police authorities are directed to furnish information and assistance as may be from time to time so requested. The special assistant attorney general herein provided for may testify before any grand jury as to matters referred to in this act as to which he may have information.

SECTION 8. The attorney general shall require the special assistant herein provided for, to maintain complete records of all information received by him and all matters handled by him under the requirements of this act. Such records as may reflect on the loyalty of any resident of this state, shall not be made public or divulged to any person except with permission of the attorney general to effectuate the purposes of this act. He shall further require the publication, printing and appropriate distribution of all reports of grand juries of this state made as hereinafter provided. The attorney general shall include in his budget estimates, adequate moneys for the printing and distribution of the said reports, and for all other expenses of administering this act. To the extent that his time may not be required in his duties under this act, the special assistant attorney general shall be available for and perform such other duties as may be assigned to him by the attorney general.

SECTION 9. The Judges of the Circuit and Criminal Courts of this state, when in their discretion it appears appropriate, or when informed by the prosecuting attorney that there is information or evidence of the character described in section 6 of this act to be considered by the grand jury, shall charge the grand jury to inquire into violations of this act for the purposes of proper action, and further to inquire generally into the purposes, processes and activities and any other matters affecting Communism or any related or other subversive organizations, associations, groups or persons. Any grand jury charged by the court as provided herein shall not later than the conclusion of its term of service prepare a written report, separate from all other matters considered by said grand jury, of its findings upon the subjects placed before it under the requirement of this act: Provided, however, Such report shall not charge any residents of this state with being disloyal unless they shall have been indicted under the provisions of this act or other provisions of the criminal law of this or some other jurisdiction.

SECTION 10. No subversive person, as defined in this act, shall be eligible for employment in, or appointment to any office, or any position of trust or profit in the government of, or in the administration of the business of this state, or of any county, municipality, or other political sub-division of this state.

SECTION 11. Every person and every board, commission, council, department, court or other agency of the State of Indiana or any political sub-division thereof, who or which appoints or employs or supervises in any manner the appointment or employment of public officials or employees shall establish by rules, regulations, or otherwise, procedures designed to ascertain before any person, including teachers and other employees of any public educational institution in this state, is appointed or employed, that he or she as the case may be is not a subversive person, and there are no reasonable grounds to believe such persons are subversive persons. In the event such reasonable grounds exist, he or she as the case may be shall not be appointed or employed. In securing any facts necessary to ascertain the information herein required, the applicant shall be required to sign a written statement containing answers to such inquiries as may be material, which statement shall contain notice that it is subject to the penalties of perjury.

SECTION 12. The inquiries prescribed in section 11, other than the written statement to be executed by an applicant for employment, shall not be required as a prerequisite to the employment of any persons in the classification of laborers in any case in which the employing authority shall in his or its discretion determine, and by rule or regulation specify the reasons why, the nature of the work to be performed is such that employment of persons as to whom there may be reasonable grounds to believe that they are subversive persons as defined in this act will not be dangerous to the health of the citizens or the security of the governments of the United States, the State of Indiana, or any political sub-division thereof.

SECTION 13. Every person, who in April 1, 1951 shall be in the employ of the State of Indiana or of any political sub-division thereof other than those now holding elective office shall be required on or before July 1, 1951, to make a written statement which shall contain notice that it is subject to the penalties of perjury, that he or she is not a subversive person as defined in this act, namely, any person who commits, attempts to commit, or aids in the commission, or advocates, abets, advises or teaches by any means any person to commit, attempt to commit, or aid in the commission of any act intended to overthrow, destroy or alter, or to assist in the overthrow, destruction or alteration of, the constitutional form of the Government of the United States, or of the State of Indiana, or any political sub-division of either of them, by revolution, force, or violence; or who is a member of a subversive organization or a foreign subversive organization, as more fully defined in this act. Such statement shall be prepared and execution required by the chief examiner of the state board of accounts of every person and every board, commission, council, department, court or other agency of the State of Indiana or any political sub-division thereof responsible for the supervision of other employees, for employees under its jurisdiction. Any such person failing or refusing to execute such a statement or who admits he is a subversive person as defined in this act shall immediately be discharged.

SECTION 14. Reasonable grounds on all the evidence to believe that any person is a subversive person, as defined in this act, shall be cause for discharge from any appointive office or other position of profit or trust in the government of or in the administration of the business of this state, or of any county, municipality or other political sub-divisions of this state, or any agency thereof. The chief examiner of the state board of accounts shall, by appropriate rules or regulations, prescribe that persons charged with being subversive persons, as defined in this act, shall be accorded notice and opportunity to be heard, in accordance with the procedures prescribed by law for discharge for other reasons. Every person and every board, commission, council, department, or other agency of the State of Indiana or any political sub-division thereof having responsibility for the appointment, employment or supervision of public employees not covered by the classified service in this section referred to, shall establish rules or procedures similar to those required herein for classified services for a hearing for any person charged with being a subversive person, as defined in this act, after notice and opportunity to be heard. Every employing authority discharging any person pursuant to any provision of this act shall promptly report to the special assistant attorney general in charge of subversive activities the fact of and the circumstances surrounding such discharge. A person discharged under the provisions of this section shall have the right within thirty days thereafter to appeal to the circuit court of the county wherein such person may reside for a determination by such court (with the aid of a jury, if the appellant so elects) as to whether or not the discharge appealed from was justified under the provisions of this act. The court shall speedily hear and determine such appeals, and from the judgment of the court, there shall be a further appeal to the Supreme Court of the State of Indiana as in civil causes.

SECTION 15. No person shall become a candidate for election to any public office whatsoever in this state, unless he or she shall file with the certificate of nomination required by the foregoing act, an affidavit that he or she is not subversive person as defined in this act; Provided, That in the case of certificates of nomination for President or Vice President of the United States, the affidavit may be made on behalf of such candidates by those persons who file the certificate of nomination for such candidates. No certificate of nomination shall be received for filing by any board of elections or by the secretary of State of Indiana unless accompanied by the affidavit aforesaid, and there shall not be entered upon any ballot or voting machine at any election the name of any person who has failed or refused to make the affidavit aforesaid.

SECTION 16. Before any appropriation of public funds of any character shall be made by the State of Indiana to any private institution of learning, there shall be filed with the Governor, the President of the Senate and the Speaker of the House of Representatives, on behalf of said institution, a written report setting forth what procedures it has adopted to determine whether it has reasonable grounds to believe that any subversive persons are in its employ, and what steps, if any, have been or are being taken to terminate such employment. In the absence of such a report no appropriation shall be included in the state budget or approved by the general assembly.

SECTION 17. Every written statement made pursuant to this act by an applicant for appointment or employment, or by any employee, shall be deemed to have been made under oath if it contains a declaration preceding the signature of the maker to the effect that it is made under the penalties of perjury. Any person who makes a material mis-statement of fact (a) in any such written statement, or (b) in any affidavit made pursuant to the provisions of this act, or (c) under oath in any hearing conducted by any agency of the state, or of any of its political sub-divisions, pursuant to this act, or (d) in any written statement by an applicant for appointment or employment or by an employee in any state aid or public institution of learning in this state, intended to determine whether or not such applicant or employee is a subversive person as defined in this act, which statement contains notice that it is subject to the penalties of perjury, shall be subject to the penalties of perjury as prescribed by law.

SECTION 18. If any provision, phrase, or clause of this act or the application thereof to any person or circumstance is held invalid, such invalidity shall not affect other provisions, phrases, or clauses or applications of this act which can be given effect without the invalid provision, phrase, or clause of application, and to this end the provisions, phrases, and clauses of this act are declared to be severable.

SECTION 19. This act may be cited as the Subversive Activities Act of 1951.

SECTION 20. All laws inconsistent with the provisions of this act be and they are hereby repealed to the extent of such inconsistency.

SECTION 21. Whereas an emergency exists for the immediate taking effect of this act, the same shall be in full force and effect on and after April 1, 1951.

Faculty Council Minutes, December 5, 1950–December 16, 1952, pp. 19–29.

Document 163

A Friendly Legislature, but a Big Budget

In this report to the Faculty Council, President Herman B Wells summarized the current budget request. The University fared well perhaps. The President was of the belief that at last the efforts of the university to maintain a program of excellent quality were beginning to have an impact on both legislators and citizens.

*   *   *

REPORT TO THE FACULTY COUNCIL
March 6, 1951

The Legislature has now finished its work and our appropriations for each year of the next biennium in constrast with our requests are as follows:

	Per Year Request	Per Year Appropriation
Operating	$10,500,000	$9,671,000
Public Health Training	71,865	45,000
New Construction	3,428,571 ⎱	
Repairs and Rehabilitation	500,000 ⎰	1,714,285
Medical Center New Construction	587,500	337,500

In addition our Department of Geology receives for work done for the State $177,350 for the first year and $178,875 for the second year; and it is estimated we shall receive about $10,000 a year from a bill creating a program of training in optometry.

During this session of the Assembly we had to face many special problems. As we all know, these are days of unusual uncertainty, and that uncertainty was reflected in the Assembly. For the past two months newspapers have emphasized daily that colleges were to be denuded of students, that enrollments were already declining, and so forth. Some of these stories emanating from high sources went so far as to indicate that enrollments would be cut to 40 or 50 per cent of their present levels starting next year. Naturally the typical legislator assumed that the universities and colleges would need less money in the future than in the past. A part of our request was for the replacement of lost G.I. fees totaling $1,106,834 per year. It was difficult to explain this request and at the same time ask for more money.

We were faced also with dire statements in the press that construction would be impossible during the next two years, and so it early became apparent that our building requests would be under even heavier pressure than our operating request. The elimination of all capital requests offered an easy "out" for those who wished to cut expenditures.

Other complicating factors worthy of mention are (1) the state's surplus has largely disappeared, (2) the need of the public school teachers for much more state money to pay the state's share of the cost of increased number of teachers required because of the increasing elementary enrollment, (3) the large total now required to operate the four state schools—when our totals were first announced they were so large in comparison with past appropriations that the immediate reaction on the part of many strategic persons and groups was unfavorable and critical, (4) the desire of the private schools that our fees rather than appropriations be increased, (5) the fact that the majority in the Assembly was of a different political party than the Governor which creates difficulty since the recommended budget presented to the Assembly is the Governor's budget, and finally (6) the public reaction against the rapidly increasing tax burden.

Notwithstanding all these difficulties, it is a pleasure to report that we were received in a friendly fashion by the bi-partisan Budget Committee, the Governor, the Lieutenant-Governor, the majority leaders in both houses, the members of the House Ways and Means Committee and Senate Finance Committee, and in fact, by the total membership of the two houses. Our position perhaps was not injured by the fact that we had 36 alumni in the two houses.

We were aided moreover by the fact that all of our budget totals and presentations were made on a quadripartite basis and all of our defense was made on the same basis. In other words, we did not talk about individual institutions except by way of illustration but about the total need of state-supported higher education in Indiana. This method, of course, made it impossible for those who oppose increased appropriations for higher education to break down our position through the technique of appealing to the competitive instincts which are always present in this state.

Quadripartite Research Effort

I think that I have sufficiently described the quadripartite research effort in the State of the University speech of some weeks ago. Without this two-year study the result of this past session would undoubtedly have been less favorable. In my judgment the total appropriation for higher education would have been substantially smaller. I wish to repeat, therefore, that we owe a great deal to Mr. Briscoe, Mr. Franklin, Mr. Sike, Mr. Wright, Mr. Hicks, and all who carried on that effort for us.

The last report of this two-year study was filed on November 15. Two hearings with the Budget Committee followed soon after, the four presidents and the business officers of the institutions appearing for the institutions. We were pleased with the intelligent manner in which our presentations were received by the Budget Director, Mr. Lytle Freehafer, and by the members of the Budget Committee. Their grasp of our problem was a factor essential to success.

Soon after the session opened the presidents and business officers appeared before a joint meeting of the House Ways and Means and Senate Finance committees. Midway in the session when it appeared that we had to meet a determined drive to eliminate the Budget Committee's recommendation of building funds, a committee representing the Boards of Trustees of the four institutions called on the Budget Director, the Governor, and committee members of the Assembly. Our two representatives on that committee were Mr. Hastings and Mr. McCarty, Mr. Hastings acting as spokesman for the group in his usual effective manner. Throughout the fall and throughout the session we likewise received wonderful cooperation from the *Indianapolis News* both editorially and otherwise as a result of Mr. McCarty's interest. We are likewise pleased that while other newspapers did not come to our direct defense, there were few who criticized our requests.

After the first presentation to the Budget Committee, presentations were made by the four presidents jointly to many of the powerful opinion-forming groups in the State such as the State Chamber of Commerce, State Farm Bureau, newspapers, and so forth. Several days were spent in this work meeting with as high as four or five of these groups within a single day.

We were fortunate again this year to have high type representation in the Assembly. Mr. Norman Neely in the House of Representatives, although now in the legislature, soon won the respect of his colleagues and was fortunate enough to be placed on the powerful and essential House Ways and Means Committee. Throughout the session he gave University interests skillful and effective support.

Senator Evans had the advantage of previous experience in the Assembly and is highly respected by his colleagues. He, as in the last session, gave to every University interest strong support rendered with the great skill with which his experience has endowed him. We have every reason to be grateful to these men. As I have mentioned earlier also a friendly, personal interest was displayed by many members of the Assembly including our alumni.

Our active day-by-day work during the session was carried on by Mr. Henley, Mr. Rich, Mr. Snyder, and Mr. Bartley with Mr. Franklin acting as the coordinator of their activities. Mr. Henley was on the job from the beginning to the end as needed. He has an extraordinary knowledge of legislative processes and is highly regarded by the experienced legislators not only for his fine personal qualities but also for his wisdom in legislative matters. His assistance was invaluable. Mr. Rich spent most of his time in Indianapolis throughout the session using to good advantage his wide and favorable acquaintanceship with our alumni not only in the Assembly but also throughout the State. He was assisted in his work by Mr. Snyder during the closing weeks of the Assembly who brings to such activity not only a wide acquaintanceship but rare qualities of personality and enthusiasm. Mr. Bartley, long experienced in public relations work and in newspaper contacts and highly regarded by members of the Assembly, assisted as needed throughout the entire session. Mr. Franklin's wise, calm coordination day by day was an important element in insuring success. Throughout all of the past biennium Mr. Franklin has worked persistently to increase the public understanding of our fiscal problems. It would be difficult to exaggerate the strain, tension, and sheer physical fatigue which results from this type of work. Only those who have actually gone through it can appreciate the demands made by the task. It was necessary to stay on the job until last night. Even after the budget bill had passed both houses there was the threat of a three per cent horizontal decrease and/or the elimination or reduction of capital items.

Strong Financial Base for Postwar University

We are disappointed that our building requests were cut sharply, yet we received a little over $4,000,000 as stated above.

This appropriation should be evaluated in light of the fact that in the previous 130 years the University has only received $11,000,000 for building. Thus, even with the declining value of the dollar, these new appropriations compare favorably with the past record.

Although we were not granted as much as we needed for the coming biennium, it was a successful session in view of all the circumstances. The session was one of the most crucial that we have faced in many years. For the first time the state had to assume the full weight of the postwar University. Prior to this time the Federal government has been carrying much of the load. Thus the state has now obligated itself to a new level of support for the University at about twice its prewar size. It has done so in a period of inflation when the dollar buys less and when there are many new demands on the state treasury. We met all in one session the challenge of inflation, of withdrawal of federal support, and of increased size. It may be decades before we are forced again to face such fundamental adjustment within a single biennium. It would appear that in the immediate future at least we would not have to ask for adjustments other than those that are required by *gradual changes* in number of students, program, or cost of living. Thus this session represents a turning point in the affairs of the University. We now have for the first time since the war a firm financial base for the postwar type University.

University's New Operating Budget

Such money as is available in the new budget will be spent first in making cost of living and merit increases for the non-academic staff, and secondly in cost of living and merit increases for the faculty. Little will be available for new staff or programs.

Notwithstanding the more or less favorable budget picture which we now have, it is still essential that the number and total of our research contracts be increased throughout the University in general with special emphasis on the medical sciences. Because of the large sums available for grants in the medical sciences, they represent our best opportunity for research contracts just as the engineering school represents the best opportunity for contracts at our sister institution.

Research contracts can generally be arranged in such fashion that they finance work which we would probably like to do anyway. They make provision for additional scientific equipment, for additional graduate student financial support, and in rare instances even relieve the overall salary budget by sharing part of the cost of staff salaries. We have made some progress in securing new research contracts this year, but we still lag far behind several other institutions with comparable facilities and staff.

Other Legislation

There were a number of other bills in which we were interested, the principal ones being the so-called anti-communist bills, all of which represented a potential threat to the freedom of thought. The bill that passed was revised in such manner that it was less objectionable and perhaps is in as desirable a form as is possible under existing circumstances. In its adopted form it will not disrupt the freedom of thought or teaching in the universities and colleges. All bills were general in application and were not directed toward us or any other institution or college. In the final revision of the bill the amendment in which we were particularly interested was given excellent support by The Indianapolis Star as a result of the friendly interest of Mr. James A. Stuart.

Other Bills

The optometry bill has been referred to above. Briefly, the provisions of that bill of interest to the University are as follows:

"Sec. 2. There is hereby created a program for the training of optometrists at Indiana University, said program to be established by the trustees of said University and to be effective when adequate funds for the establishment of said program are made available by the optometrists of the State of Indiana through the Indiana Optometric Association, Inc., or otherwise.

"Sec. 3. . . . each registered optometrist at the time of payment of the annual registration fee each year shall pay to the secretary of the board an additional fee of seventeen dollars, which shall be deposited in a optometry school account of the state general fund, and all such fees so deposited on or before April 1 of each year, shall on or before July 1 following be paid to Indiana University to be used by it for the advancement of optometrical research and the maintenance and support of the department in which the science of optometry is taught at the University. A sufficient amount to pay the same is hereby appropriated annually out of such account in the general fund of the state treasury not otherwise appropriated."

At the request of our Medical faculty we took, if I may be permitted to use the vernacular, a "dim view" of the bill as it was presented in the House. The Indiana State Medical Association actively opposed it in the House Committee. However, it passed the House without a dissenting vote, 92 to 0, and, as a consequence, the Medical Association decided to offer no further resistance. Notwithstanding our cooperation with the Medical Association, the optometrists held no ill will against the University, and I am sure that we will be able to work with them in a friendly and cooperative fashion in the development of a sound five-year program for training in optometry. The work will be done on this campus modeled somewhat after curricula now in force at such universities as Columbia University, Ohio State University, and the University of California.

Certain other bills dealing with technical accounting and admission practices in hospitals including our own were passed, but they are not injurious to our operations.

A concurrent resolution was passed by the two houses creating a commission to study the need for and possibilities of enlarging the Medical School. In the form adopted this resolution was not uncomplimentary to the Medical School, and the commission may prove to be helpful in making recommendations for future needed facilities.

There were several other bills introduced which would have been injurious to the various aspects of our operation, but they were all defeated. It is not worthwhile therefore to describe them.

General Observations

Some general observations are perhaps in order. The attitude of the Assembly as a whole was quite friendly to the University. Complaints were fewer than customary and these complaints were for the most part not advanced as threats but rather as suggestions for improvement. Some of these comments are as follows: academic counseling is inefficient, graduate student teaching is poorly supervised and coordinated by older teachers, there is much poor teaching of undergraduates, and finally the assimilation of freshmen is not as efficient as is needed.

In addition we heard complaints from time to time that the extension centers competed unfairly with the private schools, that the extension system had expanded its community services unduly, and that we had done so much building that no more was needed. This last criticism is of course a reflection of the confusion which exists in the public mind as a result of the construction of self-liquidating housing and dormitories.

The Next Session

With the close of one session we must begin preparations for the next session. The present budget bill continues the provision requiring institutions to cooperate in making a cooperative study of their affairs for the purpose of presenting a formula for the distribution of the state monies appropriated for higher education. Our research reports were pleasing to the Budget Director, the Budget Committee, and the members of the Assembly. There was general approval of what we did during the past biennium and agreement that the institutions should continue the procedure. Apparently we are beginning to evolve a technique of cooperative relationship which allows the maximum of individual initiative and development on the part of each institution with a minimum of harmful competition. A similar technique has not previously been perfected elsewhere. It seems to offer greater possibilities than the usual remedy of a single board. Single boards have had very limited success. In most states they have not been able to eliminate inter-institutional bickering. In two or three states where they have eliminated the fighting, they have been unable to secure positive or dynamic cooperation and as a result the total state-supported higher education situation has declined both academically and financially.

The techniques we have employed are already beginning to attract national attention, and I predict that we will be spending more time in this type of activity rather than less in the future. In order to place this kind of work on a solid basis, we think it will be necessary to give the staff officer in charge general administrative rank. We have asked Dean Wright, who performed so magnificently as the principal staff officer in charge during the past two years, to continue this work as a permanent assignment, and he has kindly agreed. He will continue, at his own request, however, as dean of the School of Education.

Conclusion

In conclusion let me say that the state has again reaffirmed its determination to support higher education at a level which permits distinguished scholarship and brilliant service to the state. All of us should be able to approach our task, therefore, with renewed courage and enthusiasm.

Faculty Council Minutes, 1950–52, pp. 38, 40–45.

Document 164

Money to keep the Indiana University Boom Alive

In this case the Wells Administration was deeply concerned with the biting issue of faculty salaries. It did not get the most hospitable reception from the General Assembly because governmental costs frightened agrarian state legislators. The financial mountain to them seemed unscalable.

*   *   *

REMARKS CONCERNING THE 1951-52 BUDGET
PRESENTED BY PRESIDENT WELLS
AT THE MAY 15, 1951 MEETING OF THE FACULTY COUNCIL

The 1951-52 Budget

We have now completed the budget for the coming year subject to a few minor adjustments and revisions, including those that will be required by promotions. In developing this budget we have given priority to increases in salaries for both academic and non-academic staff. It must be remembered that the General Assembly allowed us only an 8% increase on our operating expenses of approximately $15,000,000 per year. Hence it has been unusually difficult to frame a budget which meets the problems arising from inflation.

Non-Academic Salaries

In fixing the rates for the non-academic staff we were guided by the prevailing wage rate in the Bloomington and Indianapolis areas. We not only made our own analysis, but had access to results of studies made by certain industries and particularly to the results of studies made by the Personnel Division of the Crane Naval Ordnance Depot. The new rates adopted are substantially higher in nearly all categories. I believe that they are fair and equitable and will enable us to attract and hold a non-academic staff of good quality.

Academic Salaries

Academic salaries were adjusted on an individual basis taking into account merit, starting rate, and so forth. No flat "across the board" increases were made. We did attempt however to make individual increases sufficient to bring the averages for the ranks of professor, associate professor, and assistant professor up to the 1939-40 purchasing power level. For the instructor rank we exceeded the 1939-40 level.

Let me repeat the above. In fixing academic salaries we took into account the decrease in the purchasing power of the dollar since 1939-40. We attempted to arrive at new salary averages by means of individual adjustments which compensate on the average for this decrease in the value of the dollar for the ranks of professor, associate professor and assistant professor. And for instructors the average not only compensates for the decrease but exceeds it somewhat.

In no case have we taken U.S. Federal Income Tax into account though we recognize for many of the men in the higher brackets these increased taxes represent a real burden. In my judgment it would be unwise to develop salary schedules in conformity with shifting tax policies. In recent years we have had both increases and decreases in the Federal Income Tax rates, a new provision for married couples, a variety of changes and regulations, all of which modify the effect of the tax rates upon individuals. A variety of individual family situations likewise modify the incidence of taxation. Finally, it is the policy of the government to reduce the standard of living of the American people in order to curb inflation and make room in our productive economy for the defense effort. All citizens therefore are certain to feel the weight of increased taxation in the period just ahead.

A discussion of additional salaries in order to offset taxes or any other cost is theoretical so far as this institution is concerned, because our total obligations for the coming year are nearly $300,000 more than our expected income. The difference can be made up in the first year out of accumulated balances. Thereafter this deficit will have to be made up either by a substantial increase in our research contracts or by a reduction in staff. It is my earnest hope that we can close this deficit by increasing our research contract volume, but to do so will require much, much greater success than we have enjoyed to date and a more universal participation on the part of the departments and divisions of the University.

In addition to this operating deficit to which I have just referred, I regret to report that we have not increased the budget for library books, academic equipment, and some other essential types of services. No provision has been made for emergency staff appointments required by unexpected enrollment shifts in the falls. The cost of library books, binding, and equipment is increasing rapidly. Additional money must be found for these purposes. A few emergency appointments are certain to be required. This money must be recovered from unfilled positions, the salaries of persons on leave, and other economies. Under these circumstances it is incumbent upon every division of the University to practice the strictest economy and to cooperate in every way possible in helping to meet this problem.

Notwithstanding this tight budget, we have provided for a number of staff additions in a number of departments which have presented substantial claims that additional manpower was essential to their work. Many institutions are finding it necessary to reduce staff this year. The only justification for a continued increase in our staff grows out of the fact that we have been conservative in adding staff in the past and after next year's additions our student-faculty ratio will not be unbalanced. We will have, however, a student-faculty ratio in keeping with good academic practice, and we should therefore be able to give to our students the finest type of instruction and a substantial amount of personal attention. We should be able to do a superior teaching job and, at the same time, continue the high level of research activity which has characterized the institution for the past several years.

Increase in Retirement Contribution

An inflationary period forces consideration of the adequacy of our retirement plan, and it was hoped that we would be able to meet the recommendations of the University Committee on Insurance for a 5% increase in the University contribution to T.I.A.A. This proved to be unwise for reasons which are apparent from the data presented above. As a consequence, the Board of Trustees has taken action to increase the General Fund contribution $2\frac{1}{2}$% to a total of $7\frac{1}{2}$% of the salary from University sources. This added to the individual's contribution of 5% will provide a total of $12\frac{1}{2}$% for retirement annuity. It is hoped that an additional $2\frac{1}{2}$% can be added soon since, under present-day conditions, a 15% contribution is necessary to provide a satisfactory retiring allowance.

Retirement Minimum

Our Board has authorized one more important change in our retirement program. For those at age 65 or later, a minimum of $60 per year of retiring allowance for each year of service has been fixed with the proviso that in no case shall the allowance be less than $1500 per year. This provision is estimated to cost about $15,000 to $20,000 per year and will take the form of a T.I.A.A. supplement furnished by direct appropriation.

This may seem to you to be too low and I would heartily agree. Yet it will provide several hundred dollars per year additional to many of those who are already in retirement. When our retirement program was inaugurated a few years ago insufficient provision was made for those who retire during the transitional period required to build up individual allowances to an adequate sum. Subsequent inflation has made this problem more acute. This was corrected in part two years ago by action of our Board increasing the University's supplement for prior years of service. This had the effect of increasing the maximum paid to many of those already in retirement. The establishment of this minimum was a logical next step. Of course this provision is of little importance to the present active members of the staff because of the higher salaries now paid, the higher percentage of contribution, and the longer period of accumulation. To make certain that this will be so, the Board has adopted a rule that anyone who joins the staff at the age of 50 or above will be required to agree as part of his employment to a scale of contribution to the T.I.A.A. which will insure a retiring allowance at the minimum or above.

Appreciation

Many members of the faculty and staff, deans, administrative officers, and department heads have contributed time, effort, and thought to the framing of the budget, and Mr. Briscoe, Mr. Franklin, and I wish to take this occasion to thank them all for their generous cooperation and effort.

Finally, on behalf of all of us, I wish to express deep appreciation to our hard-working faithful Trustees who have been determined to provide all possible increases for our staff, and as a consequence, have courageously assumed heavy responsibilities implicit in this budget. Indiana University has many valuable assets. Not the least of these is a Board of Trustees of unusually high caliber, composed of members who are unselfishly devoted to the University, and who build for its future with skill, courage, and great vision.

Faculty Council Minutes, 1950–52, pp. 74–76.

Document 165

Academic Housekeeping

This particular document is not filled with what might be called "human interest," but it does reflect the mode of operation of an administration-faculty body in a university that was growing fast, creating endless problems, and struggling to keep abreast of all these. At the same time efforts were made to allow as broad a personal involvement in the decision-making process as possible. Often this procedure resulted in a tremendous amount of purely parliamentarian minutia.

*   *   *

ANNUAL REPORT OF THE SECRETARY TO THE FACULTY COUNCIL (1951–52)

This report is submitted in compilance with Number 7 of the By-Laws of the Faculty Council, which is stated as follows:

THE SECRETARY OF THE COUNCIL SHALL PREPARE A SUMMARY OF THE ACTIVITIES OF THE COUNCIL EACH YEAR AND CIRCULARIZE IT TO THE FACULTY.

MEMBERSHIP FOR THE YEAR 1951–52

Membership on the Faculty Council is established by Article V, Section 19, of the Faculty Constitution. Two changes took place in the regularly constituted membership during the school year 1951–52. Professor Frank T. Gucker, an elected member, became a permanent member by virtue of having been elevated to the deanship of the College of Arts and Sciences; his elected membership was taken over by Professor Harry C. Sauvain, who had received the next highest number of votes at the time Dean Gucker had been elected. The other change was made necessary by the death of Dean Ford P. Hall, of the Division of Adult Education. This vacancy was filled alternately by Associate Deans Donald E. Carmony and Hugh W. Norman, pending an appointment of a new dean for this Division. The membership list for the year was as follows:

PRESIDENT: Herman B Wells

VICE-PRESIDENT AND DEAN OF FACULTIES: Herman T. Briscoe

DEANS: Frank T. Gucker, Leon H. Wallace, John D. VanNuys, Ralph E.

Cleland, Wendell W. Wright, Arthur M. Weimer, Wilfred C. Bain, Maynard K. Hine, Donald F. Carmony, Hugh W. Norman, and Willard W. Patty

ELECTED FACULTY MEMBERS: Professors Agnes Anderson, Samuel E. Braden, William R. Breneman, Roy W. Feik, Cleon H. Foust, William H. Fox, Carl G. F. Franzen, Horst Frenz, Karl W. Kiger, Newell H. Long, Harold F. Lusk, W. Howard Mann, Norman T. Pratt, Thurman B. Rice, Harry C. Sauvain, Nathan L. Silverstein, John E. Stoner, Henry B. Veatch, Paul Weatherwax, and Samuel Yellen.

EX OFFICIO MEMBERS: Dean Pressley S. Sikes, Dean Raymond L. Shoemaker, Vice President Joseph A. Franklin, Mr. Charles E. Harrell, Dr. Robert A. Miller, Dean Henry B. Witham, and Professor Mary E. Houk

MEMBERSHIP FOR THE SCHOOL YEAR 1952–53

Elected members of the Faculty Council for the school year 1952–53 include those elected at the Faculty Council election held in May, 1952, and those whose terms had one more year to run at that time. The elected membership of the Faculty Council for the school year 1952–53 is as follows: Professors Agnes Anderson, Howard T. Batchelder, Samuel E. Braden, William R. Breneman, Harry G. Day, Roy W. Feik, Cleon H. Foust, William H. Fox, Horst Frenz, Ralph F. Fuchs, Karl W. Kiger, Newell H. Long, W. Howard Mann, Norman T. Pratt, Sid Robinson, Newton P. Stallknecht, Nathan L. Silverstein, Edward W. Snrigley, John E. Stoner, and Paul Weatherwax.

NUMBER OF MEETINGS

The Council met 15 times during the school year. Dates of the meetings were as follows: October 16, November 6, November 20, December 4, December 18, January 15, January 29, February 29, March 4, March 18, April 1, April 22, May 6, May 20, and June 3.

ATTENDANCE

The following table summarizes attendance at the meetings.

Attendance and Absence at Meetings

	Permanent members	Elected members	Ex Officio members	Total
Percentage of actual attendance	54	74	56	64
Percentage of actual attendance plus alternates	77	85	74	81
Percentage of actual absence	46	26	44	36
Percentage of actual absence minus alternates	23	15	26	19

It can be seen from these figures that the elected members had a considerably higher percentage of actual attendance than did either the permanent members or the ex officio members. However, the greater tendency on the part of permanent and ex officio members, compared to elected members, to send alternates when forced to be absent brought the gross attendance records of all three groups fairly well in line with each other.

In setting up a classification of the action of the Council, the Secretary realizes that he has made many decisions on a purely arbitrary basis. Many actions of the Council could be classified under more than one heading, especially those dealing with the Faculty and with the students. In several cases an item may appear in more than one category, mainly when it is involved in a committee report which resulted in some action on the part of the faculty. This report contains only brief comments on action taken. For a fuller account the reader is requested to refer to the minutes of the date listed. In the section in which action of the Council is reported, the first name listed is that of the person who made the motion, and the second name is that of the person who seconded the motion.

COMMITTEES ESTABLISHED

The following committees were established:

1. Law Committee: Professors Cleon H. Foust and W. Howard Mann, Dean Henry B. Witham, and Dean Leon H. Wallace, Chairman.
2. Agenda Committee: Professor Samuel Braden, Dean Ralph E. Cleland, and Professor William H. Fox, Chairman.
3. Nominating Committee for the Faculty Board of Review, and the Review Committee on Salary and Promotions: Professor Harold Lusk, Samuel Yellen, and William Breneman, Chairman.
4. Committee to Study the General Problem of Incomplete Grades: Dean George R. Waggoner, Assistant Dean John H. Porter, Professor Robert W. Richey, Assistant Dean John B. Endwright, Dean Donald F. Carmony, Professor Ralph T. Daniel, Dean Ralph E. Cleland, Dean Leon H. Wallace, Mr. Charles E. Harrell, Chairman.
5. Review Committee on Salary and Promotion: Professor Paul E. Bergevin, Professor Mary Crawford, Professor Cletus J. Burke, Professor Karl Rahdert, and Professor Ralph Fuchs, Chairman.
6. Faculty Board of Review: Professor George Starr, Professor Charles Hire, Professor Ruth G. Strickland, Professor Howard H. Rostorfer, Professor Frank Horack, Chairman.
7. Committee to Study the General Problem of Promotions: Dean Frank T. Gucker, Professor Newell Long, Professor Harold F. Lusk, Dean Leon H. Wallace, Professor William R. Breneman, Chairman.
8. Faculty Elections Committee: Dean Donald F. Carmony, Professor John Stempel, Professor William H. Fox, Chairman.
9. Committee to Study the Feinberg Case: Dean Pressley S. Sikes, Professor Newton Stallknecht, Professor Frank Horack, Professor Turner, Professor Jerome Hall, Chairman.
10. Nominating Committee for Secretary to the Faculty Council: Professor Agnes Anderson, Professor Howard Mann, Professor William Fox, Chairman.
11. Committee to Study the Desirability of Increased Credits for Military Training Courses: Dean Wilfred C. Bain, Professor D. Lyle Dieterle, Professor John R. Endwright, Professor Phillip Peak, Dean George R. Waggoner, Dean Ralph L. Collins, Chairman.
12. Agenda Committee for 1952-53: Dean Ralph E. Cleland, Professor William H. Fox, Professor Samuel E. Braden, Chairman.

COMMITTEE REPORTS

1. Law Committee, Dean Wallace, Chairman: Interpretation of the Constitution with regard to selection of elected members to fill vacancies in the elected membership. It was agreed that the members shall be chosen from the persons receiving the next highest number of votes at the time the vacating member was elected. This report was accepted through motion by Professor Stoner, seconded by Professor Pratt. See also Item 2 of the section in this report on *Action Affecting Operation of the Council.* (Nov. 6)

2. Law Committee, Dean Wallace, Chairman: Report on an amendment to the Faculty Constitution to provide representation on the Council for the new Deanship now held by Dean Ashton. This amendment is a matter for approval or disapproval by the General Faculty, and is not included in the present report. See also Item 3 of the section *Action Affecting Operation of the Council.* (Dec. 4)

3. Commencement Committee, Mr. Claude Rich, Chairman: Presented the following proposals:
   a. That a commencement-baccalaureate type of ceremony be held in February this year for the benefit of seniors who complete the requirements for their degree at the end of the current semester.
   b. That the ceremony be made as elaborate as possible and comparable to the June Commencement, including a reputable speaker and presentation of actual diplomas.
   c. That the ceremonies take place in the University Auditorium at 1:30 p.m. Sunday, February 10.

   A motion to accept the proposals, made by Professor Long and seconded by Professor Mann, was carried unanimously. (Nov. 20)

4. Committee on Faculty-Student Relations, Professor Fuchs, Chairman: Offered the following proposals with regard to the Senior Class:
   a. That the Senior Class Day be removed from the calendar.
   b. That the Dean of Students be authorized to convey notice in advance to the faculty with regard to the date which may be designated as Senior Class Day and that excuses for absences on this day be treated in the same manner as those for members of other organizations which are required to miss classes.
   c. That this action be authorized both for the February and the June classes, with the action applying for the designated date of January 16 for the February, 1952, class.

   See also Item 7 of *Action on Student Affairs* for the acceptance of these proposals. (Jan. 15)

5. Committee to Study the General Problems of Promotions, Professor Breneman, Chairman: The report of this committee was accepted, and suggestions approved with some modifications. See also Items 12 and 13 of *Action on Faculty Matters.* (April 22)

6. Foundation Day Committee, Dean Bain, Spokesman for the Committee: Took no formal action, but generally agreed to cooperate in carrying out request of the committee. (April 22)

7. Committee to Study the Request of Hiroshima University, Professor Strickland, Chairman: The Council approved this report and recommendations. See also Item 14 of *Action on Faculty Matters.* (May 6)

8. Ford Foundation Committee, Professor Waters, Chairman: The report was accepted with recommendations. See also Item 15 of *Action on Faculty Matters.* (May 6)

9. Committee on Faculty-Student Relations, Professor Fuchs, Chairman: The report of this committee was accepted. See also Item 16 of *Action on Faculty Matters.* (May 6)

10. Committee on Honorary Degrees, Dean Cleland, Chairman: The committee recommended five candidates for honorary degrees to be granted at the June Commencement. Later another candidate was recommended. For action on this proposal, see Items 19 and 22 for *Action on Faculty Matters.* (May 20)

11. Insurance Committee, Dean Holmstedt, Chairman: Presented a report on the new College Retirement Equities Fund. The report was accepted through motion of Professor Franzen, seconded by Professor Pratt. The full report appears in the minutes of the Council for May 20.   (May 20)

12. Election Committee, Professor Fox, Chairman: The report of this committee, setting forth the election results for members of the Council and officers of the General Faculty, was accepted. See also Item 24 of *Action on Faculty Matters*.   (June 3)

13. Nominating Committee for Secretary of the Faculty Council, Professor Fox, Chairman: The committee submitted the names of Professor Samuel Braden and Professor Norman Pratt for this position. Professor Braden won in a close election and will serve at Secretary to the Faculty Council for the school year 1952–53.   (June 3)

14. Committee to Study the Desirability of Increased Credits for Military Training Courses, Dean Collins, Chairman: The committee recommmended that no change be made in the number of credits now being given for Military courses. The Council accepted this recommendation. See also item 12 in *Action on Student Affairs*.   (June 3)

ACTION ON FACULTY MATTERS

1. Weatherwax-Breneman: In regard to appointment of a Nominating Committee for the membership on the Faculty Board of Review, and the Review Committee on Salary and Promotions. The President was authorized to appoint the Nominating Committee.   (Nov. 6)

2. Braden-Mann: In regard to the University Calendar for 1952–53. The proposed calendar was adopted. This calendar is attached to the minutes for November 20, 1952.   (Nov. 20)

3. Silverstein-Franzen: In regard to the report on the Cook case, prepared by the Review Committee on Salary and Promotions. The Secretary was authorized to send a copy of the letter, accompanying this report, to members of the Council.   (Nov. 20)

4. Yellen-Breneman: With regard to a plan for changing promotion procedure, drawn up and submitted to the Council by a self-appointed group of Council members. The plan was to be circulated to the General Faculty, and the President was to appoint a committee to study this and other proposals.   (Jan. 15)

5. Silverstein-Yellen: Regarding a proposal to form a committee to study the economic status of the Faculty. The Council rejected this proposal.
                    (Jan. 15)

6. Almost the entire meeting of January 29 was devoted to a discussion of Athletic policy. Stimulation for this discussion had been provided by a communication from Professor Heiser (See minutes of January 29) and by a communication from the Committee on Faculty-Student Relations (See minutes of January 15). No formal action was taken at the meeting, but mention of the discussion is included because it had some bearing on future action. Professor Breneman, past Chairman of the Committee on Athletics, entered freely into the discussion. At the next Council meeting (February 19) Professor Mee, Chairman of the Committee, was present to help with the discussion.   (Jan. 29–Feb. 19)

7. Mann-Weatherwax: With regard to a requested report from the Committee on Athletics. The Committee on Athletics was asked to submit a report

later in the Spring, and to include in the report a discussion of questions which had been raised and discussed by the Council. (Feb. 19)

8. Cleland-Pratt: With regard to Social Security benefits for members of the faculty. The Council requested that the Insurance Committee, Professor Akana, and other interested persons proceed in obtaining further information on this problem, and make a subsequent report to the Council.

(Feb. 19)

9. Anderson-Mann: Regarding the need for a study of the functions of the Junior Division. The Council asked that a committee be appointed to examine the functions of the Junior Division. (March 4)

10. Braden-Silverstein: Proposal for a change in the procedures for amending the Faculty Constitution, suggested by Professor Stempel, Secretary to the General Faculty. The Council requested that a committee be appointed to draw up an amendment which would be based upon the proposal. Professor Stempel's suggestions were as follows:

   a. A proposal for amendment must be submitted by mail to all faculty members at least one week before the faculty meets to consider such amendment.

   b. Debate shall continue until passage of a motion to submit the amendment to a mail vote. Such debate might extend over more than one meeting.

   c. The present stipulation for submitting to a mail vote should provide for naming a committee to count the vote. (March 4)

11. Braden-Anderson: Regarding the decision in the Feinberg case. The Council requested the appointment of a committee to study this decision. (March 18)

12. Mann-Weatherwax: In regard to proposals submitted by the Committee to Study the General Problem of Promotion. The report of the committee was accepted through Section F. (April 22)

   Mann-Cleland: Amending the proposals to eliminate Section E. The amendment failed to pass. (April 1)

   Pratt-Silverstein: Substitution for Section E. The Council approved the substitution. (April 1)

13. Sauvain-Franzen: Regarding criteria for promotions, as suggested in the report of the Committee to Study the General Problem of Promotions. The Council accepted the Criteria listed in the report. (April 22)

   A full account of this part of the report appears in the minutes of April 22, pp. 9 and 10.

14. Mann-Veatch: In regard to the report of the Committee to Study the Request of Hiroshima University. The Council approved the report and also the following recommendations:

   a. That President Wells authorize that the faculty be solicited for contributions.

   b. That contributions be solicited as soon as possible. (May 6)

15. Mann-Frenz: In regard to the report of the Ford Foundation Committee. The Council commended the efforts of this committee, and recommended that the same general line of procedure be continued. (May 6)

16. Mann-Long: In regard to the report of the Committee on Faculty-Student Relations. The Council accepted the report and voted special commendations of the work being carried on by the Committee. (May 6)

17. Resignation of Professor Veatch was accepted by consent. The Council also

offered Professor Veatch congratulations on having been awarded a Ford Foundation fellowship. (May 6)

18. Breneman-Franzen: In regard to the new Procedures and Criteria for Promotion. The Council ordered these procedures and criteria to be published in the next edition of the Faculty Hand Book. (May 6)

19. Cleland-Mann: In regard to recommendation for honorary degrees at the June Commencement, 1952. Degrees were approved as follows: Charles A. Kraus, Doctor of Science; General Lewis B. Hershey, Doctor of Laws, Claude G. Bowers, Doctor of Laws; George E. Armstrong, Doctor of Laws; Fabien Sevitzky, Doctor of Music. (May 20)

20. Veatch-Frenz: Proposal for setting up procedures whereby the Review Committee on Salary and Promotion shall make its report. After some discussion and changes, the Council agreed to the following procedure to replace the former statement in the *Handbook:*

That a Review Committee be established consisting of five members representative of all academic ranks, members to be selected by the elected members of the Faculty Council. The Review Committee would have authority to review any case brought to its attention by a member of the Faculty who might wish to have an independent examination of his own or another's claim for salary increase and/or promotion, or of the nature and conditions of his work. It would have the authority to confer with heads of departments, deans and the Dean of the Faculties to determine what recommendations have been made and what actions have been taken. The Review Committee shall submit its recommendations to the President of the University, who shall make the final decision. He shall state in writing the reasons for his decision, which statement shall be available on request to the Dean of the Faculties, the Review Committee, or the aggrieved person.

21. Breneman-Franzen: Regarding proposed amendments to the Intercollegiate Conference Rules: The Council approved the amendments which are as follows:

(3) In determining whether a candidate has made the progress required above, account shall be taken not only of quantity of credits earned by the candidate, but also of quality. This qualitative element shall be considered satisfied if the credits then earned are substantially such that if the candidate continues at this level for the balance of his undergraduate career, he will qualify for the degree for which he is a candidate. The phrase "substantially such," as used herein means, that, as a prerequisite to eligibility for a second year of competition, a ratio of points earned to credits carried not more than 10% below the average required for graduaation, and as a prerequisite for a third year of competition, a ratio not more than 5% below the average required for graduation. In case the grading plan is not on the basis of weighted points, translations of this rule and application thereof shall be as close to the foregoing as may be possible.

(3) no student shall be eligible to participate in intercollegiate athletics after he has been in resident more than 10 semesters or 15 quarters, exclusive of summer sessions. (May 20)

22. Cleland-Silverstein: In regard to recommendation of Judge Wildermuth for the honorary degree, Doctor of Laws. The Council approved the awarding of this degree. (June 3)

23. Mann-Wallace: In regard to formation of a Guidance Committee on Build-

ing Problems. The Council recommended that both elected and ex officio members be incorporated in a committee to advise with the President this summer on such problems. (June 3)

24. Cleland-Frenz: Regarding the report of the Election Committee. The Council accepted the results of the election, which were as follows:

For Secretary of the General Faculty:
William H. Fox
For Parliamentarian of the General Faculty:
Frank E. Horack, Jr.
For Council members on the Bloomington Campus:
William R. Breneman
Harry G. Day
William H. Fox
Ralph F. Fuchs
Sid Robinson
Newton P. Stallknecht
John E. Stoner
Paul Weatherwax
For Council member from the Indianapolis Faculty:
Edward W. Shrigley
For Council member from the Off-Campus Faculty of the Extension Division:
Roy W. Feik (June 3)

25. Corrections in the report of the AAUP Committee on Pensions and Retirement were allowed to be included in the minutes of the Faculty Council (June 3)

26. Mann-Clelland: Regarding the work of the Secretary during the past school year. The secretary was commended on his efforts during the past school year. (June 3)

27. Frenz-Weatherwax: In regard to a future report by the Committee on Athletics. The Council made a formal request that this committee make a report at an early meeting in the fall, 1952. (June 3)

ACTION ON STUDENT AFFAIRS

1. Gucker-Lusk: Policy with regard to credit for those called into military service. Recommendations were:
   a. That the present policy of allowing half credit for satisfactory completion of six weeks in the semester be eliminated.
   b. That full credit be allowed only upon the satisfactory completion of twelve weeks (ten weeks in the case of second-semester seniors), such satisfactory completion to be subject to final examination at the time of withdrawal.
   c. That a full refund of fees, except building and health, be made to those called into service prior to the day on which they would become eligible for credit. (Oct. 16)

   Wallace-Veatch: Amendment to the above: That acceptance of the new rules be inoperative where previous commitments had been made. (Oct. 16)

2. Silverstein-Yellen: Action with regard to a request from the Board of Aeons to attend Council meetings: Representation at Council meetings was denied, but the organization was informed that the Council welcome them to present anything they wished, through the Committee on Faculty-Student Relations. (Oct. 16)

3. Lusk-Mann: Regarding the established policy of the Committee on Faculty-Student Relations, which would attempt to avoid wild celebrations after notable football victories. The Council approved the action of the Committee. (Nov. 6)

   Cleland-Yellen: Amendment to the above: Left it to the judgment of the Committee to determine whether it should circularize this statement of policy to other agencies on the campus. (Nov. 6)

4. Veatch-Stoner: In regard to establishing a uniform policy for dealing with "incomplete" grades. Authorized the President to appoint a committee to study the problem. (Nov. 6)

5. Pratt-Silverstein: In regard to a request from February graduates for a specifically designated cut day. The request was denied. (Nov. 20)

6. Stoner-Frenz: Presented a motion which outlined changes in the Christmas vacation schedule to meet weather hazards. The proposals were adopted. (Dec. 18)

7. Anderson-Breneman: Regarding proposals for handling the problem of Senior Class Day. Proposals from the Committee on Faculty-Student Relations were accepted. See also Item 4 of *Committee Reports Accepted and Approved*. (Jan. 15)

   Yellen-Mann: Amendment to the above action:
   a. That action be regarded as emergency, with the understanding that Senior Class Day will be moved hereafter to the week before commencement.
   b. That if the recommendations in the original motion are approved, each faculty member will receive a list of those eligible to be excused. (Jan. 15)

8. Gucker-Mann: With regard to student withdrawals. Reopened discussion of a previously tabled motion. (Feb. 19)

   Yellen-Weimer: Same question as above. Established rule that a student wishing to withdraw after a four-week period should be required to show adequate reasons to the Dean of his school; of failing, the recorded grade would be WF, otherwise W. (Feb. 19)

   Holmstedt-Long: Put the new rule in effect immediately. (Feb. 19)

   Weatherwax-Breneman: Reconsidered the Holmstedt-Long motion. (Feb. 19)

   Weatherwax-Lusk: The operation of the new rule was postponed until the beginning of the summer session. (March 4)

   Weimer-Bain: Substitute motion on the same question. Withdrawals, approved by the Dean of the student's school, during the first four weeks of a full length semester and during the first two weeks of a summer session, are arbitrarily marked "W". Withdrawals, approved by the Dean of the student's school, after the first four weeks of a regular semester and after two weeks of summer session, are marked "W" or "WF" according to whether the student is passing or failing in the work of the course at the time of withdrawal. After four weeks in the regular semester and after two weeks in the summer session, the student shall be required to show adequate reasons for withdrawal to the Dean of his school. Students who discontinue class attendance without following the official withdrawal procedure shall receive grades of "F". (March 18)

9. Mann-Pratt: On a proposal from the Student Senate to change the Spring vacation schedule. The petition was denied. (March 4)

10. Anderson-Shoemaker: In regard to the date of Senior Day. The date of May 23, suggested by the Senior Week Committee, was accepted. (May 6)

11. In disposing of a proposal for setting up a new type of orientation program, the Council ordered the secretary to advise the two students who had submitted the proposal to present their proposal to the Committee on Faculty-Student Relations. (June 3)
12. Mann-Frenz: In regard to increasing credits for military courses. The request was denied. See also Item 13 of Committee Reports (June 3)
13. A request from Professor Feik for modification of the procedure in dealing with withdrawals from classes was referred to the Committee on Incomplete Grades, for later consideration. (June 3)
14. Anderson-Frenz: In regard to the Susan Butler Award. The Council approved in advance the candidate to be selected by the Committee of which Professor Kate Mueller is Chairman. This action was necessary in order that announcement could be made at Commencement. (June 3)
15. Mann-Wallace: On approval of graduation lists. The Council approved the granting of degrees to June graduates, subject to the records.
    Weatherwax-Frenz: The Council approved granting of degrees to the August and September graduates, subject to the records. (June 3)

ACTION AFFECTING OPERATION OF THE COUNCIL

1. Donald F. Carmony and Hugh W. Norman were authorized to represent alternately the vacancy on the Council created by the death of Dean Ford P. Hall. (Oct. 16)
2. Professor Harry C. Sauvain was authorized to fill the Council vacancy created when Professor Frank T. Gucker was made Dean of the College of Arts and Sciences. See also this report, Item 1 on *Committee Reports.* (Nov. 6)
3. Mann-Pratt: In regard to representation on the Council of the new deanship now held by Dean John W. Ashton: Extended invitation to Dean Ashton to attend Council meetings. (Nov. 6)
   Yellen-Breneman: Amendment to the above. Authorized the Law Committee to draw up an amendment to the Faculty Constitution, to provide non-voting representation on the Council for this deanship. (Nov. 6)
   Yellen-Weatherwax: The Council recommended that President Wells call a special meeting of the General Faculty to consider an amendment drawn up by the Law Committee. (Dec. 4)
   Braden-Veatch: The Council recommended that the amendment provide for non-voting membership for the Dean of Student and Educational Services. Later the amendment was presented to the General Faculty. It now rests with the General Faculty to discuss this amendment and take action at a future meeting. (Dec. 4)
4. Mann-Silverstein: On the establishment of an Agenda Committee for the Faculty Council. The establishment of this committee was authorized. (Nov. 6)
5. Yellen-Braden: In regard to motions not passed unanimously. Made it mandatory that all divided votes be recorded by name in the minutes. (Dec. 4)
6. Braden-Lusk: Regarding procedures for the Agenda Committee. The Council adopted the proposed procedures. A copy of these procedures was attached to the minutes for December 18. (Dec. 18)

FORMAL AND INFORMAL REPORTS BY THE PRESIDENT

1. The formation of the College Retirement Equities Fund (Oct. 16)
2. Analysis of enrollment data (Dec. 18)
3. Visits with alumni groups (March 18)
4. With Mr. Franklin: Report on the Life Science Building (May 6)

INFORMAL DISCUSSION OF TOPICS SUGGESTED
BY THE VARIOUS MEMBERS OF THE COUNCIL

1. Dean Briscoe: The question of whether the University is affected by the law which requires the teaching of citizenship in public schools prior to public elections. It was generally agreed that the University does not come under the provisions of this act.   (Oct. 16)
2. Professor Silverstein: Proposal to create a committee to study the economic status of the faculty.   (Jan. 15)
3. President Wells: Letter from Mustafa Amer, Rector, Farouk I University.
                                                                  (Jan. 15)
4. Dean Briscoe: The problem of providing greater attention for superior undergraduate students.   (March 4)
5. Dean Ashton: Honesty in examinations.   (March 4)
6. President Wells: University Military Training.   (March 4)
7. President Wells: Possible uses for the Wylie house.   (March 18)
8. Dean Briscoe: Proposal for a faculty news letter.   (April 22)
9. President Wells: Relationship with private colleges.   (May 6)
10. President Wells: Class size in the University.   (May 6)
11. President Wells: Demand for College Graduates.   (May 6)
12. President Wells: Various University problems in general, including
    a. Athletics
    b. International role of American universities
    c. Television as a medium of communication
    d. The formation of state universities into a separate group   (May 6)
13. Dean Collins: The Little 500 Race.

MEMORIAL RESOLUTIONS

Professor Benns, Chairman of the Necrology Committee, submitted during the year Memorial Resolutions on the deaths of three faculty members. These were approved by the Council, and the Secretary of the Faculty was authorized to send copies to the next of kin. The resolutions were on the deaths of Professor Wilbur Adelman Cogshall, Mrs. Myrtle Emmert Stempel, and Professor J. Elmer Switzer.

UNFINISHED BUSINESS

The following agenda items for the school year 1951–52 have not been covered completely by discussion or action. The secretary submits this list to the Agenda Committee for 1952–53, with the suggestion that consideration be given to placing them on subsequent agenda.

1. President Wells: The problem of providing greater attention for superior undergraduate students.
2. Dean Ashton: The question of honesty in examinations.
3. Dean Briscoe: University-wide control of curriculum; and, the establishment of authority for approval of recommended additional courses and curricula.
4. Dean Briscoe: Provision for general educational development of all students. Should special general educational programs for some students be developed?
5. Dean Briscoe: A review and evaluation of our facilities for research, and our needs for further research development.
6. President Wells: Ways and means of bringing members of the Indianapolis divisions of the University into contact with the Bloomington faculty and vice versa.
7. Dean Briscoe: Development and use of teaching techniques which will make students more responsible for their own education.

8. Dean Briscoe: The organization and development of new programs and curricula, e.g. archeology, television, etc.
9. Dean Briscoe: The development of the programs built around areas of study, rather than within single departments and schools.
10. Dean Briscoe: A study of the desirability of consolidating various courses into larger units of hours.

Respectfully submitted
July 8, 1952
WILLIAM H. FOX
Secretary to the Faculty
Council   (1951–52)

Faculty Council Minutes, 1950–52, pp. 219–32.

Document 166

Administrative Restructuring

Further evidence that the University was undergoing fundamental changes is this report of President Herman B Wells to the faculty on the subject of administrative realignments. Historically this document reflects the fact that almost the last vestige of the old administrative procedures were swept away. This was the beginning of an era when internal shiftings of administrative functions were about as frequent as were those in the academic fields.

*   *   *

11. General administrative structure of the University

President Wells read the following explanation of the recent formalizing of general administrative organization of the University. [See attached sheets.]

In further comments, President Wells emphasized that what was being done now was to formalize what had been occurring. For example, Dean Ashton had been making many public appearances during the last few years. Dean Wright had been carrying on negotiations with the other state schools and had been the founder of the Indiana Conference on Higher Education which was the bridge between the University and the private schools of higher education in the state. In this work he had done a marvelous job but it would be advantageous to give him this particular status so that he would come to the job not only as Dean of the School of Education but as one of the general administrative officers of the University.

The President had been directly in charge of the Medical Center but he felt there were four reasons why it was advantageous to transfer it to the jurisdiction of the Dean of Faculties. First, it was bad administration to have it reporting directly to him. Second, the former arrangement had made for lack of uniformity. Third, he had not been able to give sufficient time to the Medical Center, and fourth, Dean Briscoe had more knowledge of the scientific problems as well as of the academic problems of the Medical School. The President expected to continue to help the Medical School with its public relations and also he expected to continue on the Riley Committee.

Would Dean Wright's assignment include coordination of educational matters at the national level (Fuchs)? No, his assignment would be mostly intra state, with the other state and private schools (Wells). Professor Fuchs asked about the School of Letters and Writers Conference. The School of Letters had been at Kenyon College but was being brought here. Its activities and those of the Writers Conference were quite separate. Its length was six weeks and the persons attending it were concerned with criticism as distinguished from the interests of those persons attending the Writers Conference (Ashton). Where is Social Service to be located in the new organization (Miller)? In the Arts College (Briscoe), and in the Graduate School (Anderson); it is just like any other department in the Arts School. It gives work to under-graduates and to graduates (Briscoe).

To the Members of the Faculty Council:

The Trustees have recently acted to reorganize to some extent our general administrative organization in order that all services and activities may be more efficiently and effectively handled by the officers of the University.

Mr. Ashton moves into the central administration with the title of Dean and Director of Student and Educational Services. In this capacity he will help to share with the other officers the heavy load of public appearances both on and off the campus. The following offices and divisions will henceforth be under his general administrative supervision: Defense Projects, Student Affairs, Publications, Radio, Bands, Convocations and Ceremonials, University Press and School of Letters. All these activities will function as they have in the past except that the heads of the different services will report to Mr. Ashton instead of to Mr. Briscoe or Mr. Franklin as they have in the past.

Dean Wendell W. Wright will assume a general administrative position as Director of Administrative Studies and Institutional Relations. He will continue, at his own request, as Dean of the School of Education. In this capacity he will perform duties connected with the University's part in the continuing study requested by the Legislature of the budgetary needs of higher education in the state. He will also be responsible for studies aimed at improving the administrative procedures, for special projects that the University may be called upon to undertake from time to time, and for relations with other institutions of higher education, both within and without the state. He has been carrying on most of these tasks during the past two years but the work is of such importance that it deserves to be recognized by general University administrative status.

The office of Mr. Franklin will continue to function as at present, with the exception of a few sections which are to be transferred to Mr. Ashton.

Mr. Briscoe will be responsible administratively for all the academic divisions including the Library, Records and Admissions, Summer Session, and Adult Education and will serve as Graduate Coordinator. He will also assume administrative duties related to the Schools of Medicine and Dentistry which previously have reported directly to the President.

The News Bureau, Alumni Relations, and Athletics will continue to report as in the past directly to the Office of the President.

The general administrative officers will meet at least once each week to coordinate their different areas and oftener as required. Members of the staff are asked to transmit all questions and recommendations to the proper administrative officer in order that they may receive proper and immediate attention.

This redistribution of duties has been made necessary by the growth in the size of the University, the increasing complexity of our relations with other institutions in the state, the failure of the faculty to approve a central graduate organization, and by the need to maintain closer liaison with the Armed Forces and the various Federal Government Contract and Research granting Departments. Furthermore our Medical Center is having a very healthy and gratifying development and deserves more general administrative time than I have been able to afford it.

In these changes we shall correct several deficiencies in our present structure. Mr. Briscoe will spend time regularly on the Medical campus and will be in active charge of the coordinating committee on graduate studies. Mr. Ashton and I will be able to give some time in support of our departments in their research requests to the Federal Government, and finally we hope to push forward with even greater efficiency the development of data required for the next session of the General Assembly.

If there are any questions concerning this arrangement we shall be happy to answer them.

H. B WELLS

Faculty Council Minutes, 1950–52, pp. 80, 81–82.

Document 167

A New Quadripartite Budget Formula

Since the early 1930s, the four Indiana state universities and colleges had worked under a budgetary formula arrangement which locked each institution into a niche without anyone paying too much attention to what the institutions did specifically. In 1950 a move got underway to break this arrangement and to make an extensive study of the services rendered by each institution in order to arrive at a more intelligent base for making budgets. This required extensive and complicated study which could not be accomplished quickly under any circumstances, but President Fred Hovde of Purdue was reluctant to accept the evaluative formula for his institution. This was all too complicated for the Director of the Budget who threatened some unfavorable cuts. Perhaps no letter President Herman B Wells wrote during his administration was clearer and more to the point than this one addressed to Lytle J. Freehafer, Director of the Budget.

*　　*　　*

October 27, 1952

Mr. Lytle J. Freehafer
Director of the Budget
State of Indiana
Indianapolis, Indiana
Dear Mr. Freehafer:

I have your letter of October 15 and in response to your request I submit for consideration by yourself and the members of the Budget Committee a factual portrayal of the events and negotiations which resulted in the budget request submitted to your office on October 9, 1952.

We are acutely aware of the fact that we have not completed the study on which we had embarked, the objective of which was to arrive at a formula which might be used by your office in arriving at a division of the state's expenditures for higher education. We deeply and profoundly regret that this is so. The completion of this study has been the foremost administrative objective of this institution during the past two years. Failure to complete was not due to any willful neglect but rather to the unforeseen magnitude of the task. Perhaps we attempted too thorough an analysis, but in any event we completely misjudged the amount of time and work that would be required.

Since so much remains to be done, we believe that we should continue the work of the study *at this time* rather than wait until after the conclusion of the legislature as was done two years ago.

You are aware that the plan which we adopted provided for an analysis of each institution, department by department, and the fixing of a desired and efficient standard of operation for each department for its respective function, based upon all information available in our own institutions and in others of similar types in other states. We can assure you that when this process has been completed Indiana University will be willing and ready to accept the result regardless of the dollar relationship with the others that is indicated for our institution. Our Board, our faculties, and our administrative officers are united in a desire to support any scientific program of distribution of the state's appropriations for higher education that will insure efficiency of operation and equality of treatment for students and staff.

Most of the work of analyzing each department of all four institutions has been accomplished. Each department has presented a statement of its needs in light of standards and practices in its field. You have in your hands these departmental analyses. The next step requires the equalization of these needs by a quadripartite committee to arrive at the same level of support for comparable functions. The final step requires the reconciliation of this quadripartite standard with national standards so far as they are available.

The Quadripartite Standards Committee has already started its work and has agreed upon a theoretical scale of salaries for each faculty rank for all four institutions. The harder task of reconciling the desired standard of operation with regard to teaching schedules, student-faculty relationships, requirements for graduation, etc. is ahead. In our judgment, however, this task, though admittedly difficult, is not impossible and could be accomplished by next June if each institution would assign high level personnel to the Quadripartite Standards Committee and give to its representative on the Committee complete and unqualified authority to act.

Let me remind you that we have been able to complete, for all practical purposes, our space study. Two years ago there were those who believed it impossible to achieve that result. To be sure the study will need to be continued, brought up to date, biannually, and refined in light of further study, but it is now a useful and trustworthy document and is so accepted by all four institutions. I for one am unwilling to believe that a similar outcome is impossible with respect to our operating budgets.

The basis for the increase in our appropriation is fully set out in our letter to you of October 9. In the absence of completion of our study we were driven back to the use of our present operations as a base for computing our future needs. As set out in our letter we added to this base a sum sufficient to compensate for the increase in the price index that has occurred since our last request plus a future expected increase. No additional programs were requested except in medicine and agricultural extension. Detailed description of the nature of these will be presented at the time of our budget hearing.

As to the disposition of the appropriation between the four institutions the following paragraphs quoted from that letter briefly state the situation.

"The administrations of the four institutions in considering the respective operating appropriation needs and relationships of the institutions discussed differences in physical plants and plant operations, study programs at differing instructional levels, comparative standards, teaching loads, and faculty and staff salaries. In the absence of reconciled study data and agreed theoretical standards no agreement based on these factors was possible. It was necessary therefore to arrive at an *arbitrary agreement* as to the relationship between the appropriation requests of the four institutions. This agreement does not and can not constitute a precedent for the future after completion of the Inter-Institutional Study.

"The requests which we present are as follows:

Indiana University	\$11,781,819.00	\$11,781,819.00
Purdue University	11,919,322.00	11,919,322.00
Indiana State Teachers College	1,751,940.00	1,751,940.00
Ball State Teachers College	1,911,940.00	1,911,940.00

"Of the above requested appropriations, Purdue University proposes to spend annually \$1,498,012.00 for its Agricultural Experiment Station and Agricultural Extension Service, and Indiana University proposes to spend \$2,421,-514.00 for its Medical Center. The slightly larger request for Ball State represents a differential agreed to because, although the programs of the institutions are identical, there is a difference in their enrollments."

The background of our discussions in arriving at this conclusion is somewhat extended. In our early negotiations we attempted to use the data in the study. These data, as pointed out above, were admitedly incomplete, but we earnestly tried to select certain ones which might be agreed to as an interim basis for a formula pending the conclusion of the study. It appeared for a time that this would be possible, but finally such profound disagreements as to evaluation arose that we had to abandon use of the study until it can be completed and reconciled.

The actual sequence of events following this abandonment of the scientific approach is briefly as follows: The officers of Purdue University stated that they were unwilling to accept anything less than \$250,000 more per year for operation than Indiana, that additional meetings were useless, and that unless Indiana University would agree to this differential, Purdue would withdraw from the quadripartite budget request and submit a unilateral request. It is to be noted that Indiana University had a differential of \$250,000 per year in the request for the present biennium. Notwithstanding this ultimatum two additional meetings were held in the course of which Purdue reduced its demands to the \$137,000 figure which appears in the budget request pending before you and which all four institutions support. No further meetings were possible within the time limit which you had prescribed for the submission of our budgets. In order to preserve unity so that we might continue our study for the present biennium, we accepted the differential as an arbitrary and empirical settlement for this year only. In our final meeting we specifically stated that we were agreeing to the amount only but did not accept in any respect the so-called formula by which

Purdue University had arrived at its demand. The method was unscientific and unacceptable to us. Any method compatible with scientific principles would have yielded substantially different results. We furthermore specifically stated that we made this agreement only as an interim settlement and urgently expressed our desire that the work of completing the study be resumed at once.

In his letter of October 18, copy of which was sent to me, Mr. Hovde presented a computation by which Purdue University justified its request in comparison with ours. This computation was based solely on present operation and did not use scientific or agreed standards of desirable operation.

A formula must start with certain basic assumptions and principles. These assumptions and principles must be applied throughout the entire operation. A formula cannot be based upon a random selection of items for treatment, nor can it change the base of application from item to item, depending upon the convenience or advantage yielded by such changes. Mr. Hovde's computation fails to meet these basic requirements. Furthermore, the formula has other serious inadequacies, as follows:

(1) It makes no distinction whatsoever in teaching load by level of students or type of program. It assigns the same cost to an hour of work given in freshman English as to an hour of credit in constitutional law for a senior law student who is in his seventh year of college work, or to a sophomore course in economics and a graduate course in chemical engineering. This, of course, is in variance with all known practice and places Indiana University at a distinct disadvantage since Purdue's campus volume of freshmen and sophomores is higher than ours, while Indiana University's volume of graduate and professional work is approximately twice Purdue's. Moreover, credit hours is only one basis for arriving at student loads. Institutions differ widely as to the number of hours required for graduation. Purdue University requires 150 to 166 in most of its divisions of the School of Engineering, while equally reputable neighboring institutions require as low as 138-2/3. I am confident that the same subject matter is covered in all of these institutions, the credit hours representing merely a different system of arithmetic used in measuring the student's progress semester by semester. The difference between divisions in the same institution is likewise great. Here undergraduate liberal arts student's semester work is measured in terms of 15 credits, while the advanced law student's semester work is divided into only 12 credits. No one would contend that the law student requires less staff, energy, or teaching cost than the undergraduate.

These differences exist between the two universities with regard to precisely the same work. For instance, Purdue University allows 23-2/3 hours of credit toward a degree for the completion of ROTC work while Indiana University allows only 16 hours toward its degrees. The study indicates that of Purdue's total hours taught for the year 1951-1952, 14,977 hours were military credits compared to Indiana's 7,270 hours. Incidentally, military work is given with very little staff cost to either institution.

Using the above type of unrefined data for teaching loads, Mr. Hovde concludes that the Purdue University campus load is 20.8 per cent higher than the Bloomington campus of Indiana University.

Perhaps a more satisfactory basis for comparing load is the use of full-time student equivalents as a unit of measurement.

Finally, we are not in agreement with the geographical technique used in Mr. Hovde's formula or any other that has been before the quadripartite body. We recognize that geographical divisions must play a part in any analysis which is used, but here again it must not be on a random basis designed to arrive at a preconceived result.

In our thinking, we cannot overlook the fact that Indiana University is one university regardless of the location of its divisions as is the case with Purdue, and that the total institutional responsibility of the two universities is as follows:

Total credit hours for all divisions of the University for the full year 1951-52:

Indiana University	440,904
Purdue University	395,212

Total full-time student equivalents for all divisions of the institutions for the full year 1951-52:

Indiana University	14,681
Purdue University	11,697

Total enrollment (head count) first semester 1951-52 (credit students only):

Indiana University	17,893
Purdue University	12,711

The above offer some of the reasons why we were unable to subscribe to Mr. Hovde's computation even as a basis for an interim agreement. If you wish us to present a point by point analysis of our disagreement, we shall be glad to do so. Moreover, if you would like to have us submit a computation incorporating the changes indicated above in order to present the dollar differences which they make in the result, we shall be glad to do so.

The problem of reconciling the operations of the two teachers colleges is much simpler since they offer the same degrees and, fortunately, require the same number of hours for graduation for each of those degrees. This is true not only of undergraduate work but also of such graduate work as the two institutions now offer.

You inquire concerning the efficiency of our present operations. In my judgment all four institutions are above average in the efficiency and effectiveness of their operations both in teaching and in administration. This is quite clear it seems to me by even a casual comparison of our institutions with others of similar type in terms of amounts of money received from their legislative bodies and in number of students, types of programs, and high quality of degrees granted.

This can likewise be said most emphatically concerning Indiana University. Our general administrative costs are well within the best operating practice with which I am familiar; our personnel costs are, if anything, too low; and our plant operation meets all known standards with exception of the cost of our utilities, a situation for which the present management is not responsible and for which we are asking correction—a fact with which you are fully familiar.

Our academic administration is nationally recognized for its pioneering in cost control of teaching operations. Representatives of other institutions have visited us for the purpose of studying our centralized method of class scheduling, academic staffing, and cost controls in order to receive equitable treatment between divisions. All of this responsibility is centralized in one general administrative officer who has the absolute authority to eliminate duplication between divisions, adjust departmental requests so that each department receives only what it is entitled to rather than what it can get on the basis of eloquence or pressure, and to eliminate unnecessary staff immediately whenever enrollment shifts make it possible. Our visitors express amazement that we are able to accomplish so much in this respect. Without this noteworthy teaching efficiency we would have been unable to care for anything like the present student body with so small a staff and correspondingly low costs.

It is not unreasonable, therefore, to base the budget request of the four institutions on present expenditures plus increases required by the general increase in prices.

I do not mean to imply that our four institutions are perfect nor that improvement is impossible. We continue to make improvements in our operations. I do believe most sincerely, however, that they compare very favorably with similar institutions in efficiency and economy of operations.

Again allow me to express to you our own deep disappointment in our inability to complete this study and to pledge you our sincere determination to move forward with it as rapidly as it is possible to do so.

With kind personal regards, I am,

Sincerely yours,

H. B WELLS

rea

Document 168

Through the Eyes of an Exchange Student

Indiana University received a fairly large enrollment of foreign exchange students. These first came to the campus at a time when there was great excitement over expansion of every phase of university operation. Under ordinary circumstances life no doubt would have proved interesting if not thrilling to them. In this age American life itself almost seemed to be snatching at one last fling with razzle-dazzle. Friedmann Moll, a German exchange student, wrote this letter to the *Indiana Daily Student,* October 21, 1952. It is a rather full view through the youthful eyes of a foreigner.

*   *   *

This letter was written by Friedemann Moll, a German student who spent nine months at I. U. He was a foreign exchange student sponsored by the Institute of International Education in New York.

The Hoosier Campus will hardly imagine how popular its name has become among my friends, relatives, and acquaintances over here in the Black Forest area.

When I returned to my home after one year's stay abroad, they naturally urged me to relate as much of my experience as possible. And so I did. I told them all about the modern equipment and facilities which Indiana University provides for its students and about the instructive lessons in the Department of English where I did most of my work.

My friends were particularly thrilled to hear about American football habits, about the Marching Hundred, the cheerleaders, and the imposing line of Bernie

Crimmins' champions on Cream and Crimson Day. Best wishes to your team this Fall!

I explained to my fellow countrymen what "steady-going" means, the word which we foreigners disliked, because it often crossed our wooing projects. Of course, I could not help reporting about the sensational lingerie raids, the noisy queen elections, and Satchmo's visit in the I. U. Campus.

Likewise, the unforgettable "Parsifal" performance, the concerts of Mr. Hoffman's symphony orchestra, the funny make-up of pledges, the foreign student's tea party given by Sigma Alpha Epsilon and Pi Beta Phi, and our nice dormitory activities in Rogers O found adequate mentioning. By the way, is the "roaring" Jordan River still suffering from chronic dropsy?

When I entered the United States more than a year ago, I was afraid to get "democratized," because in post-war Europe the word "democratization" stood for America's desperate attempts to transfer her own mode of living and thinking to foreign peoples by a propaganda of superlatives without regard for other peoples' historical background.

During my stay in the United States, however, I realized that this term has changed its meaning or rather has disappeared. Instead of delivering rosy propaganda speeches, the Americans now shift over to another, better policy: They invite representatives of numerous foreign nations and give them a chance to see the facts about American life and to form their own judgements on what they see.

This does not mean to imply that these foreigners will Americanize their own countries; but, at least, they will be able to cleanse public opinion of misleading ideas and rumours. This one thing is of the greatest importance, because, in my opinion, rumours and false prejudices do a democracy more harm than Communism or tyrannic systems of the past. So, the student exchanges, sponsored by private institutes and the State Department will certainly pay in the long run.

To state only one example, it is a common prejudice in Europe that the Americans do not have any culture, whatever that word may mean, I found a simple explanation for this basis: Many Europeans consider modern American capitalism to be the same as it was fifty years ago: the greedy, irresponsible, selfish money-making of Wall Street.

How can they believe all of a sudden that Wall Street is dead, that the "new" capitalists do not sit any longer on their money bags, that they rather join private clubs and welfare organizations and generously spend millions of dollars for public projects, hospitals, concert halls, playgrounds, schools, etc? If more Europeans and other foreigners get a chance to see with their own eyes that such a transformation of capitalism is actually taking place in the States, they will soon admit that the Americans do have a culture of their own.

Perhaps you are wondering where I am living now. The beautiful mountains and forests of Swabia are my home, a scenery which I missed a little bit in the flat Hoosier country. Roaming in the intimate, picturesque lanes of my medieval university town I try my best to adjust from vast dimensions to small measures.

But, I shall not conclude this letter without thanking all the professors and students who helped us foreigners to make our stay at the University an agreeable and profitable one; especially in the beginning, when we did not yet know what a blue book, a comic strip, a jukebox, or a stag and drag party was. Indeed I had a high time on the campus of Bloomington: Three cheers for I. U.!"

Indiana Daily Student, October 21, 1952, p. 4.

Document 169

Administrative Complexities and Promotions

Few universities in the early 1950s could say in concrete terms what their promotion policies really were. For at least three decades there had been concern over this issue, and with the tremendous expansion of student bodies and faculties this subject became vital to the instructional wellbeing of institutions. Indiana University in 1952 undertook to clarify its procedures in this vital human area of operation. This document is no different from literally thousands of similar statements generated in the United States, yet it leaves unanswered many of the questions of relativities and intangibles which figure so largely in a human institution.

*   *   *

The following is the introduction to the full report of the Faculty Council Committee on Promotions Policy.

The Faculty Council Committee on Promotions Policy recognized that several important factors contribute to the present dissatisfaction with the University promotion policy. These can be summarized briefly by the following statements:

1. The time at which recommendations for promotions are made is too late in the year to permit careful study and analysis.
2. Inadequate information often is transmitted by the departmental chairmen to the dean of the school or college and to the Dean of the Faculties.
3. Present criteria for determining promotion in rank are inadequate. Such criteria should be defined and published in order that members of the faculty may know the standards for promotions.
4. The consultation and exchange of information between the deans and the departmental chairmen are not always adequate.
5. A faculty member frequently is given no explanation for an adverse decision regarding his promotion.
6. The present complex machinery for recommending promotions obscures the bases of decisions.

The Committee wishes to make recommendations to the Faculty Council on the following matters:

1. Procedure for making recommendations.
2. Criteria for promotions.

> Signed:
> FRANK T. GUCKER, JR.
> LEON H. WALLACE
> NEWELL H. LONG
> HAROLD F. LUSK
> WILLIAM R. BRENEMAN,
> chairman

The following is the *Procedure for Recommendations,* proposed by the Committee and acted upon favorably by the Faculty Council.

PROMOTIONS IN RANK
Procedure for Recommendations

A. The Departmental Chairman shall have the responsibility of submitting to the dean of the school or college the names of those members of his department whom he deems worthy of promotion on the basis of the established criteria. The following responsibilities shall also be assumed by the chairman.

  1. He shall make a continuing study of his staff with respect to:
     a. Teaching performance and development of teaching techniques.
     b. Scholarship and reputation for achievement in his field.
     c. Loyalty and cooperativeness in the department and the University.
     d. Ability to stimulate and direct graduate students.
     e. Administrative work.
     f. Contributions to learned and professional societies.

  2. His recommendations to the dean shall include *specific information* regarding the points outlined above plus any pertinent information regarding:
     a. Character and personality.
     b. Community and other public service.
     c. Contribution to good public relations.

  3. The recommendations for promotion shall be forwarded by the departmental chairman to the dean of the school or college by November the first.

B. It shall be the privilege of any faculty member to submit to the dean of the appropriate school or college or to the Dean of the Faculties a recommendation for the promotion of any faculty member including himself. These recommendations shall be properly documented and submitted.

C. It shall then be the responsibility of the dean of the school or college:

  1. To analyze the information relative to each candidate and to secure any additional information he deems necessary by consulting with the chairman and members of the candidate's department or outside sources.

  2. To suggest the names of additional faculty members he deems worthy of promotion and to consult with the departmental chairman concerning their qualifications. The dean may at his discretion request advice from members of the faculty in the evaluation of any candidate.

  3. To submit to the Dean of the Faculties by December the fifteenth the names of all those considered, together with his recommendations for or against promotion and a complete statement detailing his reasons.

D. The following shall be the responsibilities of the Dean of the Faculties:

  1. To suggest the names of any faculty members he considers worthy of promotion who have not been considered previously and to consult with the dean of the school or college and the chairman of the department of which the candidate is a member in order to compile full information concerning the qualifications of the candidate.

  2. To appoint a University Faculty Advisory Committee on Promotions which shall consider all cases and give advice to the Dean of the Faculties.

  3. To submit to the President by March the fifteenth the names of those considered together with his recommendations and a complete statement detailing his reasons.

  4. To furnish to the dean of the school or college and the appropriate departmental chairman a statement of the action taken including reasons for any adverse action, and to confer upon request with the faculty member involved.

E. It shall be the responsibility of the President to submit to the Board of Trustees in time for consideration at their April meeting the names of those he recommends for promotion. The President shall state in writing to the Dean of the Faculties his reasons for any changes in the recommendations of the Dean of the Faculties.

F. It shall be the obligation of the departmental chairman or dean to review with the candidate who was not promoted the reasons for the failure to promote if such a request is made by the faculty member involved.

Criteria for Promotions

Criteria for promotions in rank include many qualifications, some of which may be regarded as essential, others as less important. A candidate for promotion should be outstanding in at least one essential category and satisfactory in the others. Promotion to any rank is a recognition of past achievement and a sign of confidence that the individual is capable of greater responsibilities and accomplishments.

The initial appointment to instructorship normally requires a pleasant, stable, cooperative personality, outstanding natural ability, and well-rounded intellectual training, represented by the possession of the Ph.D. degree or its equivalent. The University recognized that there are certain fields in its educational program where the Ph.D. degree is not essential and where other evidences of successful study and experience are more important.

Promotion in rank from instructorship to assistant professorship is based primarily on evidences of high quality of teaching, scholarship, and cooperation in the department and the University.

The prime requisites of any effective teacher are intellectual integrity and intellectual independence, a willingness to consider suggestions and to cooperate in all teaching activity, an eagerness to study and adopt improved organization of materials and improved methods of presenting them, and above all, a vital interest in teaching and working with students. The quality of teaching is admittedly difficult to evaluate. This evaluation is so important, however, that it should involve serious consideration of the collective judgement of students, of colleagues who have visited his classes or who have been closely associated with his teaching as supervisor or in some other capacity, or colleagues who have taught the same students in subsequent courses and of student counsellors.

Scholarship may be manifested by a member of the University faculty in many ways. Perhaps it is most clearly demonstrated in his teaching especially in his influence on students over a period of years. It is also manifested by study in his own and related fields, by participation in seminars and other discussion groups with his colleagues and advanced students, and by presentations of papers in state and national meetings. In most of the fields represented in the program of the University, publications in journals of national reputation for scholarship is expected as evidence of scholarly interest pursued independently of supervision and direction. Furthermore, the publication of a Master's or Doctor's thesis or parts of it cannot in general be considered as evidence of independent or even continued scholarly interest, although sometimes the publication of an enlarged and broadened thesis is of greater scholarly value than the publication of the original theses. Quality of publications is considered more important than mere quantity. As to the quantity of publication a single work of considerable importance or a series of studies constituting a general program of worthwhile research can be considered evidence of scholarly merit. The candidate should possess a definite continuing program of studies or investigations. The University recognizes that in certain areas a contribution of a creative nature such as a poem, a picture, a musical composition or a novel may be just as significant or just as deserving as the publication of a scholarly book or article in some other field.

Promotion in rank from an assistant professorship to associate professorship should be based on the continued improvement in the quality of teaching and upon evidence of growth in scholarship beyond the level required for the assistant professorship. The promotion in rank to associate professorship should be considered a significant achievement, and few men reaching this rank should expect to advance beyond it. The candidate should have demonstrated a broad grasp of his own or related fields and should have established a national reputation as a scholar. Definite evidence of independent achievement in the field of scholarship or creative ability should be demonstrated. The candidate must have shown a frank and loyal attitude toward his work, members of the department, and the Institution. Weight may be given to interest in civic and institutional work, particularly that in which the candidate has employed his special skills for the benefit of the community, state, or nation.

Promotion in rank from associate professorship to professorship should be based upon achievement beyond the level required for the associate professorship. The candidate must have demonstrated ability as a distinguished teacher either of undergraduate or graduate students and must stimulate in students a genuine desire for scholarly work. He must have the ability to direct the research of advanced students. The candidate also must have produced creative work rated as first class not only by the head of the department but by authorities in his field. A definite and comprehensive plan of future research covering a number of years should be submitted along with evidence of a fair beginning thereon. Weight may be given to participation in administrative work but such should not be a primary reason for promotion. Consideration also may be given for success in carrying the work of the department or the University to the people of the state. In some instances, special consideration for promotion to a professorship may be given the faculty member whose distinction is that of being a superlative teacher. This consideration, however, should be reserved for the extremely competent and gentle zealot who spends, with supreme patience, an inordinate amount of time with his students, developing in them latent talent, and instilling in them a sense of responsibility and an eagerness to seek learning for themselves.

At this point Dean Briscoe raised a question regarding procedure for the present school year. It would be impossible, of course, to follow all of the new plan this year, but if the Faculty Council were willing, he would try to put into effect as much of the new recommendations as feasible. He recognized that under these new recommendations his own responsibility had been much increased. He would like to assume, as Dean of the Faculties, that he would have the privilege of recommending any person for promotion who has not been recommended through the usual channels.

The consensus of opinion of the Council was favorable to Dean Briscoe's suggestions.

The Council adjourned at 5:05 P.M.

WILLIAM H. FOX
Secretary to the Faculty Council

Faculty Council Minutes, 1950–52, pp. 166–168, 172–173.

Document 170

The World of the Ford Foundation

With the advent of the WPA and the PWA of New Deal days, Indiana University learned the importance of assistance from non-traditional sources of special funds. With the organization of the Ford Foundation a new and, it was hoped, generous source of support for special projects had come into existence. Through the success of the Kinsey sex studies and the work with fluourides in toothpaste, Indiana University saw the importance of extending its activities into the areas financed by the foundations. The Ford Foundation, however, proved to be almost unassailable. As indicated in this report, its procedures were inscrutable.

*   *   *

3. Professor Waters, Chairman of the Ford Foundation Committee, presented the report of that committee. The full report of this committee will be found at the end of these minutes.

Professor Waters pointed out that more than 18,500 projects had been submitted to the Ford Foundation by various colleges and universities. Not a single one of these had received support as yet. Members of the faculty here had sent the committee many fine and worthy projects. The committee had worked diligently in classifying these projects and getting them ready for submission. It was indeed disheartening that, so far, such efforts had not been successful. Professor Waters stated that our projects got a more favorable hearing than did those from most universities. One of the most pointed criticisms was that the Foundation had failed to give out any information regarding the causes for rejection. This places the committee in a position of not being able to evaluate its efforts.

The psychological effect of all this upon the committee was of concern to Professor Mann. He suggested that the committee be encouraged to keep active in case the Ford Foundation has a change of policy. He also thought there might be some opportunity for getting other agencies interested in the various projects. Both President Wells and Dean Cleland supported this viewpoint.

Professor Mann, seconded by Professor Frenz, moved that

THE REPORT OF THE FORD FOUNDATION COMMITTEE BE ACCEPTED WITH COMMENDATION FOR THE WORK OF THE COMMITTEE OVER THE PAST YEAR: A SPECIAL COMMITTEE BE APPOINTED TO STUDY THE WORK NOW BEING DONE BY THE ADMINISTRATIVE OFFICES, SCHOOLS, DEPARTMENTS, AND OTHER DIVISIONS OF THE UNIVERSITY (a) TO STIMULATE RESEARCH PROJECTS; AND (b) TO SECURE OUTSIDE FUNDS IN SUPPORT OF RESEARCH PROJECTS, AND TO REPORT THE RESULTS OF SUCH STUDY TO THE FACULTY COUNCIL AS SOON AS IS FEASIBLE DURING THE ACADEMIC YEAR 1952-1953.

Dean Weimer was of the opinion that the Committee's effort had not been wasted. We now had an excellent list of research projects for an attack through our own facilities and for submission to other foundations. President Wells thought the stimulation of thinking and planning, which the hope for support had engendered, would result ultimately in a greatly increased amount of worthwhile research.

Dean Cleland thought that there were still many latent research projects being formulated and planned by members of the faculty, which would be of interest to various foundations, and such a committee could help bring them to the attention of various agencies. He cited one specific case to show that faculty members do not always recognize such qualities in their projects and do not always know how to solicit such support.

Professor Pratt wanted to know what relationship this proposal for a continuing committee and its attendant responsibilities might bear to activities and responsibilities of Dean Ashton in his new position. President Wells suggested that Dean Ashton might be made the staff officer of such a committee.

Professor Waters pointed out that many of the projects had been kept alive, and that some had been submitted to other foundations. He made the point, also, that it is a big task to develop these projects to workable form. To do so might necessitate freeing a large proportion of the time of the person carrying such responsibility.

Dean Cleland spoke in favor of having the Committee function in studying our policies, and of developing a scheme for getting the projects in order, as well as in aiding the presentation.

Professor Stoner wondered which is the better policy: having a committee or the individual himself present projects to foundations. Dean Weimer thought that both should be involved; the committee could help organize the presentation, but the individual would also have work to do. President Wells pointed out that the committee could contribute in helping supply information for those formulating research projects. Dean Cleland wanted to know whether, in our thinking, we were emphasizing the study function or administrative function of such a committee. The President thought that primarily a study phase might develop into an administrative phase.

The motion was PASSED UNANIMOUSLY.

REPORT OF THE SPECIAL COMMITTEE FOR THE FORD FOUNDATION

On November 4, 1950, in conformance with recommendation of the Faculty Council in session on November 7, you appointed a special committee—"To study the report of the Ford Foundation to inform the different faculties about the availability of the Foundation's support; and to solicit for consideration, projects that various schools and departments may have to propose."

Your committee held organization meetings shortly thereafter and contacted all of the faculty members in the University whose work seemed to fall within the realm to be supported by the Foundation. Great interest was shown by the faculty, and this was subsequently evidenced by the amount of effort which went into the development of interesting and worth-while research proposals. The committee directed its initial efforts along three lines. First, the stimulation of proposals by the faculty; second, the delineation of particular areas in which the Ford Foundation would be especially interested; and third, development of criteria for screening the proposals of the faculty for presentation.

PROJECTS DEVELOPED BY THE FACULTY

1. Collection and Use of Mississippi Valley Historical Records
2. Liaison Between Collegiate Schools of Busines and Business
3. Study of Basic Philosophical Ideas Incorporated in Courses in Literature
4. Study of Civilian and Military Morale
5. A Case Study to Determine Problems and Remedies in Areas of Declining Population: Southern Indiana

6. Proposals for a Central European Program at Indiana University
7. Indiana Studies in Citizen Attitudes Toward Government and Their Expression
8. Learning Theory Applied to Human Behavior
9. American Contributions to the Cultural Life of Occupied Areas (1945-1950)
10. A Tentative Plan for Far Eastern Studies
11. The School of Letters
12. A Clinical Program to Meet the Diagnostic, Therapeutic, and Research Needs of Severely Handicapped Children and Adults Who Have Problems in Communication
13. A Study of Social and Economic Conditions in a Texas County From Which Negroes Have Been Extra-Legally Excluded for 65 Years
14. Prospectus for Adult Education Study
15. Psychological and Sociological Strengths and Vulnerabilities of the German Federal Republic
16. Management Problems of New Enterprises—A Program for Study and Training in the Interest of a Healthy and Expanding Economy
17. National Groups of the Soviet Union
18. Possibilities for Meeting the Revenue Requirements of Increased Defense Expenditures
19. An Experimental Project for an Advanced Interprofessional Seminar in Law, Economics, and Government
20. Government and Business Under the Nazis
21. A Proposal for a Research Project at the Indiana University School of Music

In addition to the above list, fully twice as many proposals were discussed by the faculty with members of the committee in an informal manner. For one reason or another these projects were deemed not feasible for development for the Ford Foundation.

Eleven of the above projects were developed and polished for presentation to the Ford Foundation. Four other projects were presented but were not retained.

The enormity of the work of presentation done by the faculty would be difficult to describe in terms that would do full justice to the persons involved. The proposal on "Southern Indiana," for example, involved a series of meetings of faculty members from five or six departments. The form which the proposal took was so carefully developed that it might have been confused with the final product of the research. This project, if it accomplished nothing else, resulted in a wholesome exchange of ideas among men who had previously had little contact with each other.

ATTEMPT TO DELINEATE PROMISING AREAS OF SUPPORT

The Indiana University committee relied upon the *Report of the Study by the Ford Foundation on Policy and Program* for guidance. This was our bible but our faith seemed to have been somewhat misplaced.

The statement of the Ford Foundation had indicated that almost any undertaking would be within the realm in which support might be given. Universities were encouraged initially to submit projects under the whole of the realm outlined in the report of the *Study Committee*. Members of your local university committee contacted other schools to make certain that our approach was in line with the general understanding. We also endeavored to find out what other schools were doing in order that we could do a better job. The committee came to the conclusion that the Ford Foundation could not possibly have uniform interest in all of the areas outlined in the report. We endeavored, by correspondence, to determine preferred areas and form. Our efforts were not successful as evidenced by the following letter:

This is a belated acknowledgment of your letter of January thirtieth suggesting an informal discussion as a preliminary to the possible submission of certain projects to The Ford Foundation.

I should be very happy to meet with you at your convenience whenever you find it necessary to come to New York. I should advise you, however, that we are not at the present time giving serious consideration to individual grant requests, since we are still in the process of formulating the areas in which the Foundation will give emphasis and support.

On the other hand, if you believe it will be helpful to the development of your own program to have a preliminary discussion, I shall of course be happy to make myself available.

The committee subsequently made arrangements for Professor Harold Moore to visit with officials of the Ford Foundation. This was done in the early Spring of 1951. Professor Moore learned to his dismay that the Ford Foundation had had a change in policy and he reported that the Ford Foundation would initiate its own areas for research and support. He concluded that our proposals should be submitted more as evidence of the University's fitness in the area of research than as specific undertakings which we would carry out as outlined. The committee continued its efforts by personal contact and correspondence to isolate as best it could the areas of interest. Meanwhile other universities submitted projects by the thousands.

SUBMISSION OF PROPOSALS AND THEIR EVALUATION

By the summer of 1951, your committee had seven proposals in substantially final form. These had been screened from more than twice that number. Two or three of the proposals were not believed, by the Committee which your appointed, to blend very well with the objectives of the Ford Foundation, but in view of the difficulty in determining what the Foundation would support, a decision was reached to submit the doubtful ones. The projects were multilithed and bound attractively. The chairman of the committee presented them to the Ford Foundation in August, 1951.

Seven projects had been prepared but the Foundation eliminated a proposal for the *Collection and Use of Mississippi Valley Historical Records.* Because of a change in the policy governing the School of Letters, a project for an enlargement of that instrumentality was not submitted. The five remaining proposals were given an encouraging reception.

The timing for the presentation had been set to coincide with a meeting of staff men and the committee chairman of the Ford Foundation. All of the projects, therefore, that were retained had passed a preliminary screening. At the time of presentation, the Ford Foundation had received 18,000 proposals. some 3,500 were in the realm of business and economics. At that time, August 1951, the Ford Foundation had taken no steps to provide personnel for evaluation of the 3,500 projects. Very little more had been done in other areas. No decisions or information was received and inquiry brought discreet evasion.

Part of the difficulties of the Indiana University committee is implicit in the following two paragraphs taken from a letter by Bernard L. Gladieux, Assistant to Mr. Paul Hoffman.

The individual whom we expected to take leadership in the general field of economics and business for The Ford Foundation has been unable to disengage himself from service in the Federal Government this Fall, as we had hoped. We therefore find that our program in this area must necessarily be deferred for some months again.

Accordingly, the last of November would be too soon to submit projects of this kind since we would have no alternative but to hold them for later consideration. It now looks as though January 1 would be the earliest that we would be in a position to give careful consideration to proposals in the field of economics and business.

In December, the committee prepared four more proposals for submission and they were presented to the Ford Foundation on December 26 and 27. The Ford Foundation made no statements that the policy concerning research projects had been changed but the impression was readily apparent that few, if any, grants would be made unless the Ford Foundation initiated the project. The policy which had invited projects in the beginning had changed to one of initiative on the part of the Ford Foundation. This was superseded in the summer by a willingness to accept university projects primarily because so many had been received as a result of the initial invitation that the Ford Foundation could not reject them all without endangering public relations.

Of the four projects that were submitted in December, one, *Government and Business Under the Nazis,* was rejected. *The Analysis of Difficulties in Launching New Businesses* was accepted although no committee had been appointed by the Foundation to evaluate a project of this nature. It, therefore, was filed with others which had been received by the Foundation over a period of two years. A third project, *An Experimental Project for an Advanced Interprofessional Seminar in Law, Economics, and Government* was referred to the Foundation for the Advancement of Education. A fourth project, *National Groups in the Soviet Union,* was referred to the East European Fund. The division subsequently rejected the proposal. Early in January notice was received that all of the projects submitted in August had been rejected except one. The letter stated that the project (Southern Indiana) had already been rejected in a letter sent from Pasadena, rather than New York. Indiana University is still awaiting the letter from Pasadena.

Only two projects, therefore, are being given any consideration at the present time by the Ford Foundation and the chairman of your committee is most pessimistic about the amount of attention that will be given either project. Other universities received blanket rejections of their projects at approximately the same time as Indiana. No explanations were offered.

Your committee asked the Ford Foundation, in a diplomatic way, to indicate the present policy of the Foundation with respect to projects or to state, at least, why our projects were rejected. The purpose of the latter inquiry was to help us formulate some policies with regard to future relations with the Ford Foundation so that the best approaches and projects would be utilized. The following answer was given February 26, 1952.

Unfortunately, we have no statement regarding policies concerning university grants to which I might refer you for future guidance. By and large, the Foundation, through the Fund for the Advancement of Education, is not considering research proposals as such but is concentrating on certain broad programs dealing with contemporary goals of education and encouraging experimentation.

A review of the operations of the Ford Foundation indicates that Ford Foundation support is going in two directions. First, international relations and activities supplemental to the Point Four program or E.C.A. and second, to undertakings consistent with the philosophy of Education embraced by the Great Books Program.*

In August of 1951 the assistant to the president stated flatly that no money had gone to projects suggested by universities as represented by research proposals such as Indiana University had submitted. The statement might also be true today.

Conclusions

Your committee believes that it has served its functions as well as circumstances permitted. Interest was developed, and good projects were prepared which represented superb effort on the part of the faculty. They were submitted in a manner which had been planned carefully and which should have given Indiana University a favorable chance for success, notwithstanding the amount of competition.

At least one member of the committee feels that under the circumstances there was little or no chance for success. The major function of the committee has been finished and the members should be discharged from their duties. Most of the records have been turned over to Mr. John W. Ashton and your committee recommends that the proposals be submitted to other foundations. Submission would be either by the originator of the project, his Department Chairman, the Dean of the Graduate School, Mr. Ashton, or whoever else is in a position to wield the greatest influence. The chairman of the committee will handle any further relations involving the two projects still in the hands of the Foundation.

HARPER's (December, 1952)
THE FABULOUS FORD FOUNDATION
R. L. Heibroner

(p. 29) But at least it seems significant that of the money which has actually been spent, only a spoonful has found its way into the hands of the established educational and welfare institutions of the country. The large expenditures—the overseas grants, the radio-TV workshop, the faculty scholarships, and the 16½-year-old experiment—have by-passed entirely the plans and the pocketbooks of the great majority of colleges, schools, councils, committees, institutes, and organizations who have spent their lives in the very fields in which the Foundation is supposed to be interested. No wonder there is somewhat less than wholehearted supported for the projects which the Foundation in its greater wisdom has selected.

But while there is of course an element of comedy and a trace of indecorousness in this spectacle of gowned dignitaries tripping on their hems as they scramble for the grab bag, there is a more serious side to the free-for-all. For most of the scramblers are people who have spent their working lives trying to do on a smaller scale what the Foundation now proposes to do in bold and

---

*The appended excerpt from an article "The Fabulous Ford Foundation," in the December issue of *Harper's* indicates that the experience of Indiana was similar to that of other colleges and universities.

massive strokes. It is to be expected that they will scramble—they should scramble. And if they do not happen to be included in the list of donees, at least they should be able to look at the Ford program and admit, however, grudgingly, that it makes sense.

This is just what they don't. And the criticism one hears is not merely a disagreement about the merits of the projects that have made the grade. That sort of criticism, after all, is the occupational disease of all foundation life; every disgruntled donee can call a foundation's pet projects "mere grants of charity" or "ill-coordinated and ineffectual."

But the criticism one does hear is of a different nature and more disturbing. It is a criticism of attitudes rather than projects, and a questioning of whether the Foundation's programs are in line with its objectives. One finds disquieting testimony to a We Know Better attitude at the top of the Foundation which sits ill with outsiders who think they know something of these problems. "And do they know better?" snorted one university official. "They talk peace and support cold-war irritants. They talk education and 'advance' it in ways that would hardly have the support of more than a minority of the nation's educators. They talk of adult education and dribble money away in a garbage-pail program with no real plan behind it. In the meantime there are perfectly good programs under way that are threatened with disaster for lack of funds, good schools which can't make ends meet, deserving but unspectacular work that needs financing. The Foundation doesn't want those. It goes in for the big international splash, the trail-blazing grant that leads God knows where, and for the pet hobby horses of its topkicks. It's all very discouraging."

(p.cl)   Can the Foundation learn to stop, look, and listen.

It did its preliminary planning—decided upon its general objectives—only after long and thoughtful study and wide consultation. But since then there has been an apparent tendency toward something that looks very much like arbitrariness. One has an uneasy feeling that too many of the projects can be identified with the well-known intellecutal predilections of its top officers. This is natural in the early stages of such an enterprise, but it raises many questions about the future. There is a suspicion that ideas which do not happen to fall in line with the Pasadena brand of "contributory thinking" are given short shrift—even when these ideas may be firmly held by a great many quite respectable authorities. There is the impression that the Foundation is sympathetic toward the dramatic gesture, at the expense of many workaday organizations which have been plugging away at some of the Foundation's goals so long that they have lost their glamor.

Item: The Foundation has not yet seen fit to aid any of the excellent civil liberty groups working in the country; none of them quite "fill the bill." Instead it will set up its own.

Item: One of the higher officials of the Foundation sets out on a round-the-world tour to study conditions—and allots, in his plans, only one month for the expedition.

Item: A university president writes to a high official in Pasadena saying that he would like to meet him in New York or elsewhere at his convenience and specifically says that he recognizes that it would be impractical to meet in Pasadena. He receives as answer a note to the effect that it is impossible to meet in Pasadena, period.

Faculty Council Minutes, 1950–52, pp. 175–176, 185–194.

Document 171

Beyond Parity—Financing Indiana's Colleges and Universities

One of the truly significant landmarks in the history of higher education in Indiana was the breaking of the parity arrangement which bound all the institutions in a fiscal formula which failed to take proper consideration of special functions, diversities of programs, and other differences. In this budgetary request in 1954 the four schools outlined their needs in line with the new formula. This request is the result of an intensive study which clarified the diverse functions of each school and also evaluated their respective programs. This request was designed to secure the greatest possible support for higher education in the State, yet keep down costly competition in direct legislative maneuverings.

*   *   *

LEGISLATIVE REQUEST FOR OPERATIONS
INDIANA UNIVERSITY
BLOOMINGTON, INDIANA

September 7, 1954

Mr. Donald Clark
State Budget Director
State House
Indianapolis, Indiana
Dear Mr. Clark:

The four State institutions of higher education unitedly submit herewith their requests for operating appropriations for the coming biennium of 1955–57. The requests are prepared by agreement in materially the same ratio for the two universities. A differential in ratio between the two teachers colleges results from enrollment differences.

The two universities, Purdue and Indiana, were asked during the current biennium by the other Big Ten institutions and the University of California to join with them in an inter-institutional survey and cost study similar to the study already under way in the Indiana institutions. Ford Foundation support to assist in financing the cost of the study has been received. Meetings of representatives of these institutions have been held. Many of the procedures and methods developed by the Indiana group have been incorporated in the plans for the larger study. Additional information to be obtained will make the study more comprehensive and valuable to all participating.

The study involving the Big Ten institutions and the University of California will provide comparisons and standards for comparable educational programs in a number of schools that were not possible when only Indiana institutions were being studied. Indiana state schools are almost unique in lack of duplication of programs, for instance law, medicine, dentistry, music, business, etc. at Indiana University and agriculture, engineering, pharmacy, etc. at Purdue. Thus, in many programs which operate in one institution but not the other, there exists no basis for comparison and measurement until the information on comparable programs is available from other states.

The Appropriation Requests

The appropriation requests of the four institutions are arrived at by agreement, since additional study data are not available for any other basis. The relationship in request between the institutions, therefore, does not constitute a precedent for distribution of the State's dollar for higher education in the future; and it is recommended that any changes from the original request will be made proportionately among the four institutions.

The requests are presented as follows:

	1955–56	1956–57
Indiana University	$13,010,001	$13,649,092
Purdue University	13,161,254	13,807,220
Indiana State Teachers College	1,927,134	2,014,731
Ball State Teachers College	2,303,134	2,398,731

These budget requests are essential to meet the actual needs of the institutions for the coming biennium, assuming there will be no further inflation bringing about a general price increase and that our conservative enrollment estimates are not substantially exceeded.

Basis of Request for Appropriation Increases

A. *Increase in faculty salaries to bring them up to 1939–40 level*

It was pointed out two years ago that our faculties were receiving salaries substantially less in real value than in 1940. This budget request proposes that the first step in faculty salary consideration should be to restore the value of the net income of faculty salaries to those of the period prior to World War II. Certainly the rectifying of this unfortunate situation is justifiable and beyond question.

Although we are not in this budget request seeking anything beyond an adjustment to bring salaries back to the real values of 1939–40, the second step to be undertaken during the 1957–59 biennium is to make it possible for our faculties to share in the national economic advance that has taken place in this country in the past fifteen years. Failure to recognize the justice of and to provide this advance invites a social catastrophe in higher education in our state in the future. Since enrollment increases, inevitable because of the growth in population, will make it necessary to attract large numbers of persons to the teaching profession and since it requires nine to ten years to prepare college teachers, we must begin at once to make teaching in higher education reasonably competitive in salary scales to industrial and other professional occupations.

B. *Increase in staff salaries to enable institutions to approach prevailing wage rates*

The United States Bureau of Labor Statistics shows that wage rates have continued to increase during the past two years. This, in addition to the 3 per cent reduction made by the Legislature, has prevented our institutions from keeping pace with prevailing wage rates in our local communities. In order to continue to keep an efficient, cooperative staff with high morale within our institutions, they must have the assurance that their pay rates and living standards will approach those of their community in similar jobs.

C. *Equipment for laboratories for both teaching and research, also library books and periodicals*

By reason of inadequate operating appropriations in past years, there is a substantial backlog of urgently needed laboratory and scientific equipment and laboratory facilities. With the very rapid advances that are being made in the technological and scientific fields, much of the older equipment has become obsolete to the point that in some cases the lack of modern equipment is impairing the effectiveness of our teaching. Many graduates are finding themselves handicapped when they go into a modern industrial plant after having been trained on equipment that is no longer in use. An educational program must be dynamic and keep abreast of developments if it is to be effective and valuable to the state and nation. In addition to the need for new and additional equipment, there is a very real need for modernization of old scientific equipment and rehabilitation of laboratory facilities that have been deferred because of lack of funds.

Also, our library funds should be increased. During the past three years book and journal publishers have been forced by inflation in both wages and materials costs to raise their prices. Therefore, in order to keep up the present level of acquisition of books and continue scientific journals subscriptions, additional funds are needed.

D. *Special needs for medicine, agriculture and teacher education*

Construction on the new Medical Science Building will begin this fall. Preparation to occupy and use it two years hence means that locating and employing of staff should start now. In addition to an improvement in the teaching program, an orderly expansion in number of students is contemplated. A larger sum should be available the second year of the biennium than is needed for the first year.

In 1920 there were approximately three and one-fourth acres behind each person in the United States. Now, due to the increase in population and the expansion of city limits, there are only about two and one-fourth acres per person producing foods. With population still rising it is necessary to produce more upon a decreasing number of acres. This can only be done by improving and expanding our research effort in agriculture. Such research has, in the past, doubled the corn yield per acre and increased wheat yield by fifty per cent in Indiana and other livestock research has added further millions of dollars to farm income. Thus the further development of research in agriculture is essential to improvement in the economy of the state as well as to assure a growing population that sufficient food will be available.

All citizens of Indiana are well aware of the critical dislocation between supply of and demand for teachers in our public schools. The dislocation can not be immediately removed but increasing enrollments in teacher education programs are encouraging. The number of high school graduates will be increasing by 20,000 each year in Indiana by 1960. Many of these students can be encouraged to complete teacher education programs provided the additional facilities, equipment, and personnel are provided through State funds for the four State institutions of higher education.

E. *Enrollment increase inevitable*

An enrollment increase of 1,144 students for the fall of 1953 alone exceeded our expectations for both years of the biennium. Our most conservative and minimum estimates for the coming fall and the 1955–57 biennium indicate that the four State school enrollments will increase another 4,500 to 4,800 students. This *increase* of 4,500 to 4,800 for our four State schools is approximately equivalent to the enrollment of the largest private school in the state or about four times the average size of all the private schools in the state. Our estimates are calculated on actual high school enrollments and based on the *assumption that the 29 private schools of the state will take their proportion of the increase.* The appropriation will need to be somewhat greater the second year of the biennium than the first year because the number of students will be larger.

Student fees at the four institutions have been increased to a level comparable with the fees charged in public institutions in adjacent midwestern states, even though this increase, or in fact any student fees, is not in accord with the intent of our forefathers as expressed in the Constitution of our State. The request for appropriations has been adjusted to reflect the amount of additional fees students will pay.

F. *Conclusion*

Just as the governing board and administration are responsible at the college or university level for allocation of resources among the several divisions of the institution, so the Budget Committee, Governor, and General Assembly are responsible for allocation of state resources among the departments and divisions of the state in order to assure wise use of funds which will best promote the economic and general welfare of the people of the state. Every allocation to any department or division of the state must be considered in terms of immediate and long range service to the state as well as in terms of total resources of the state.

The state of Indiana has been unusually fortunate in its economic growth and development. New industries have moved into the state, and the population growth is among the highest in the country due to migration into the state in addition to the increased birth rate. The wise provisions contained in its Constitution and statutes, coupled with integrity in administration at the state level, have placed Indiana in an enviable position with respect to a healthy economy and sound financial condition. However, it is recognized that the people of a state are taxed only for the purpose of providing necessary services within the state and the nation and funds which accrue to the state should be distributed to provide the best possible services.

Many years ago the State of Indiana committed itself to the support of four publicly controlled institutions of higher education. These four institutions have served the state and the nation well. They have provided effective educational programs and have included within such programs instruction, research, extension and public service. They have planned and developed facilities for housing, feeding, and recreation for students *at no cost to the State*. They have made substantial contributions directly to the state and national economy through well organized extension programs and public services. They have made further contributions through research programs, which benefits will extend over future years. Finally, they have provided for utilization of the greatest resource still available to the state and nation—the young men and women who, properly trained, will accept major responsibility for the further development of our social and economic welfare.

While the State of Indiana has made progress in the development of its colleges and universities during the past decade or more, it has not provided support for higher education consistent with the total resources available and consistent with support provided for these services in other Big Ten states. (Reference: Council of State Government, *Higher Education in the Forty-eight States,* June, 1952.)

We believe everyone will agree that there is a direct correlation between the educational level of a state and the economic and social welfare of a state. The state of Indiana can have only those services which it is willing to support, and the value of such services will be determined in part by the level of support.

The major problem in state administration involves the determination of which services will provide most constructively for advancement in general and economic welfare, and upon this wise determination of allocating funds in sufficient amount to maintain vigorous development of these services.

This combined budget request reflects the needs of the citizens of the state in the field of higher education. Faculty salaries must be brought up to at least the value level of 1940 if we are to continue to attract to teaching the people of the caliber and in the number needed to teach our growing population. Obsolete equipment below the standards of those our graduates will use in industry must be replaced and new and additional instruments of teaching must be added. Provision must be made for the increased costs of books and periodicals for the libraries. The special needs of our state for expansion of services in the fields of medicine, agriculture and teacher education must be taken into account. Finally, it must be recognized that the growth in population of the state will bring about a large increase of enrollment in all four of the State schools during the coming year and the 1955–57 biennium.

Respectfully submitted,
H. B WELLS
President

This is a joint request of the four State institutions of higher education.

LEGISLATIVE REQUEST FOR CAPITAL
INDIANA UNIVERSITY
July 15, 1954

State Budget Committee
302 State House
Indianapolis 4, Indiana
Attention: Mr. Don Clark, Director of the Budget
Gentlemen:

In accordance with your request, each of the four state universities and colleges is submitting a program for construction, rehabilitation, and repair of its physical plants and facilities. Each program has the complete approval of the respective boards of trustees.

We should like to remind the members of the Budget Committee of the history and background of the current situation in regard to plant development at the universities and colleges. Prior to the 1951 session of the General Assembly the members of the Budget Committee asked each of the educational institutions to submit their projected construction, repair, and rehabilitation program for a ten-year period—or until 1960. Each of the four institutions at that time spent considerable time and effort in working out a conservative ten-year program. The total program for all four institutions amount to some $80,000,000 at 1950 costs. On the basis of that program a request was made to the then current session of the General Assembly for the 1951–53 biennium in the amount of $16,000,000 or one fifth of the total ten-year program. Only $8,000,000 was appropriated. In the 1953 session of the General Assembly a request was made for $16,000,000 plus the $8,000,000 that had not been appropriated in the previous session. In following the same plan for 1955–57 we have set up a request for $16,000,000 plus the $10,700,000 that was not appropriated toward the ten-year building program in the 1951 and 1953 sessions of the General Assembly. The present request, therefore, is $26,700,000 exclusive of the Indiana University Medical Center capital request.

We have repeatedly pointed out to the Governor, the members of the Budget

Committee, and the members of the General Assembly that the $80,000,000 ten-year building program is a minimum program. Since the original program was set up, building costs have increased somewhere in the neighborhood of 15 to 20 per cent, and unless costs should materially drop it will be necessary for us to increase our requests for the last two biennia of the ten-year period in order to compensate for such increases in costs. We should perhaps also caution the members of the Budget Committee that our estimates of enrollment increases and our estimate of the time they would become effective may have been entirely too conservative, with the result that we may need additional construction sooner than was originally anticipated. We definitely need to complete our conservatively conceived ten-year building program on schedule or the State of Indiana will be faced with a speed-up or so-called "crash construction program" which will definitely be an expensive undertaking, because the haste with which it would have to be accomplished would result in a considerably more expensive program than one for which we adequately planned.

During the next five years when we face the next enrollment crisis the Federal Government will not be obligated to rescue the higher education institutions by transferring temporary facilities at Federal expense to meet a short-time burden caused by returning veterans as they did following World War II.

We believe we should again point out to the Budget Committee the salient facts and the fundamental considerations on which the ten-year building program is based:

(a) The universities and colleges in Indiana must be equal to the best *in the field of state supported institutions of higher education*. To accept any lesser goal is to admit that Indiana is a second-class state.

(b) All reasonable and conservative forecasts of enrollment in the institutions of higher education for the decade beginning in 1960 indicate clearly that the four State institutions must prepare to handle and instruct campus enrollments totaling 36,000 students as compared with current campus enrollments of 24,000. This fact alone demands a 50 per cent increase in the total facilities required for the four institutions. Furthermore, this estimate is on the assumption that the private schools in the state will take their share of the enrollment increases.

(c) Temporary facilities and buildings in use on our campuses, built during the postwar years to handle the influx of veteran students, will number 72 at the end of the current biennium. Most of these buildings are rebuilt military barracks, warehouses, and Quonset huts. All should be razed and the space replaced in permanent structures as quickly as possible. Without exception, these temporary buildings are inefficient, unsightly, expensive to operate and maintain, and all of them present fire hazards for our students which cannot be tolerated or justified much longer.

(d) There were 30 permanent buildings on the four campuses which were built prior to 1911. These will be fifty years of age or more by 1960. The 1952 Inter-Institutional Study Committee listed 15 buildings which should be razed and replaced at the earliest practicable date; of these buildings 3 have been razed, leaving 12 still in use. The others must be modernized and rehabilitated if they are to remain useful and safe.

(e) Since the end of World War II the educational institutions have substantially reduced the problems of deferred maintenance that were built up during the war years. There, however, continues to be the usual amount of major rehabilitation and modernization that becomes necessary as the physical plants become older, especially of the structures mentioned in (d) above.

(f) As classroom and laboratory space is expanded to meet increasing enrollments it becomes necessary to increase the number of auxiliary facilities such as power and utility plants, sewer and water systems, roads and parking facilities. Consideration must be given for the expansion of such facilities if the physical plants of the various educational institutions are to remain in balance.

Because the Indiana State Teachers College has developed the current phase of its construction program more rapidly than is the case with the other three institutions (for the current biennium, it needs to complete remaining repair and rehabilitation projects and forward its land acquisition program), we jointly and respectfully request the following distribution of the funds appropriated for the development of the physical plants and facilities of the state-supported universities and colleges:

1. That there be appropriated to the Indiana State Teachers College the sum of $1,000,000.

2. That the remaining $25,700,000 of our current request be appropriated to Ball State Teachers College, Purdue University and Indiana University (for all divisions other than the Medical Center) on a 3:10:12 ratio.

3. That the ratios in 2 above will continue to apply unless or until Ball State Teachers College should be appropriated less than $1,000,000. In such event then the Indiana State Teachers College would be appropriated an amount equal to the appropriation for Ball State Teachers College.

We feel that we will be remiss and fail in our duties as administrators and educators if we do not remind the Governor and the members of the State Budget Committee of the tremendous problem that they as responsible state officials face during the next two years in preparing to meet the demands that the oncoming children in Indiana are going to make on the state's institutions of higher learning in the next few years.

> Respectfully submitted
> H. B WELLS
> President

This letter is a joint presentation of the four institutions of higher education.

Faculty Council Minutes, 1953–55, pp. 223–230.

Document 172

Shades of McCarthyism

By 1953 Indiana University had experienced considerable anxiety over charges made against its program and its faculty. An open hearing of charges of subversion against three faculty members had been held on the campus, and there were rumblings on all sides. The greater threat, however, came from Washington where Senator Joseph McCarthy and his famous investigating team were, Jove-like, hurling thunderbolt charges of communism in all directions. The Fifth Amendment suddenly became a refuge for persons charged with subversive activities who did not wish to incriminate themselves. There was a good chance that Indiana University staff members would be called on the McCarthy carpet, and the Wells' administration was forehanded in stating a policy in such cases.

*   *   *

3. President Wells announced that the A.A.U. statement on rights and duties of universities was released for the morning papers on March 31. He reiterated that the statement comes from the presidents of the thirty-six associated institutions. The A.A.U. is legally an association of the presidents. He thought that the faculty should carefully consider the statement and then decide whether to adopt it, to recommend it to the Board of Trustees, or to take no action. Professors Fuchs and Stoner urged recognition of the fact that the A.A.U. statement emanated from the presidents and not from the institutions as such, and called attention to inaccuracy on this score in local publicity.

4. President Wells directed attention to faculty appearances before investigating committees. This matter is touched on at various places in the A.A.U. statement and is also discussed in the Chafee opinion which is appended to these minutes. Generally speaking, it is the responsibility of testifying faculty members to tell the truth and the whole truth. There may, however, be some individual cases where the protection of the Fifth Amendment should be invoked. The Fifth Amendment should not be used except when advised by competent legal counsel in light of the individual case. There is no general rule that can be laid down with respect to its use. It should not, however, be used as an emotional reaction to a distasteful situation.

President Wells proposed a procedure for faculty members who are called to testify. He suggested that the faculty member might consult with an administrative officer, or some selected colleagues. He proposed that one man should be designated to give advice, for example, by discussing experiences of other faculty members before investigating committees, and the desirability of counsel. He also wondered whether it might be desirable for arrangements to be made with a Washington law firm of distinction to give counsel. He noted that in most cases it is desirable not to use counsel in the actual appearance before such a committee.

President Wells touched on the question about past affiliation with the Communist party. If a question like this is asked, the faculty members should tell the truth. If he has been a member, then he should say so. Such testimony need not necessarily embarrass or endanger the position of the faculty member at Indiana University. It does, however, make it difficult with respect to questions about others as members of the party, and on this point the faculty member may need the help of counsel. Professor Pratt mentioned that at the A.A.U.P. convention last week it was reported that refuge in the Fifth Amendment is usually taken by university administrations as sufficient cause for summary dismissal. The A.A.U.P. opposes this procedure without complete an impartial investigation. President Wells agreed with this position and this is the procedure recommended by the A.A.U. statement.

President Wells then noted that the technique of appearance before investigating committees is of great importance. The willing witness gets along much better than the inflammatory witness. Headlines are wanted by some of the investigators in these hearings. Reference was made to the case of Professor Darling, of Ohio State. Professor Darling was told by a vice president of Ohio State University that prior membership in the Communist party would not endanger his position. However, Professor invoked the First and Fifth Amendments even in his consultation with his own friends and colleagues, and as result he has tended to lose the confidence of many at his own institution.

Professor Fuchs spoke in favor of a procedure of advice on the campus and counsel in Washington, if necessary. He noted that the individual owes candor to his institution. However, he also noted that disclosures to counsel are legally in confidence, but that disclosures to university colleagues are not. President Hogue asked whether the people who are called are selected as representatives of faculties generally or are persons who are being individually investigated. President Wells answered that aside from the professional type of informant, the pople called are likely to be those whose backgrounds involve experience or knowledge of interest to the investigators. President Wells noted that sometimes faculty members are asked by the investigating committee not to talk to anyone before their appearances. Professor Fuchs responded that this is not proper procedure and that a faculty member ought to seek advice on his own campus. *There was general agreement that it is desirable for any faculty member called to testify to talk first to President Wells, to Dean Briscoe, or to Professor Norman Pratt, president of the Indiana University A.A.U.P. chapter, for information concerning such appearances. It was also taken by consent that it should be recognized that the mere fact of being called does not imply that a man is guilty of any offense, nor does it cast suspicion on him.* His appearance may be for information only.

5. The Council adjourned at 5:10 P.M.

SAMUEL E. BRADEN
Secretary to Faculty Council.

Faculty Council Minutes, 1953–55, pp. 37–38.

Document 173

University and Faculty Responsibilities in a Free World

This statement of the role of the university in American life was submitted by President Herman B Wells to the Indiana University faculty as a document of information, but with the strong implication that the position of the Association of American Universities was also the position of Indiana University in the new age when freedom was being threatened.

*   *   *

To MEMBERS OF THE FACULTY COUNCIL:

I am enclosing a copy of the statement on "The Rights and Responsibilities of Universities and their Faculties" prepared by the Association of American Universities. The statement will be released for the Tuesday morning papers of March 31.

At the meeting of the Faculty Council on Tuesday, March 31, I shall ask for consideration of this statement. I am forwarding this copy so that you may have it for study prior to our meeting. I ask you to treat the paper as confidential until the date of official release.

HERMAN B WELLS
President

Release: Tuesday, March 31, 1953.

THE RIGHTS AND RESPONSIBILITIES OF UNIVERSITIES AND THEIR FACULTIES
A STATEMENT
by
THE ASSOCIATION OF AMERICAN UNIVERSITIES
Adopted Tuesday, March 24, 1953

I.
ROLE OF THE UNIVERSITY IN AMERICAN LIFE

For three hundred years higher education has played a leading role in the advancement of American civilization. No country in history so early perceived the importance of that role and none has derived such widespread benefits from it. Colleges moved westward with the frontier and carried with them the seeds of learning. When the university idea was transplanted from Europe, it spread across the nation with extraordinary speed. Today our universities are the standard bearers of our whole system of education. They are the mainstays of the professions. They are the prime source of our competence in science and the arts. The names of their graduates crowd the honor rolls of two world wars and of the nation's peacetime affairs. By every test of war and peace they have proved themselves indispensable instruments of cultural progress and welfare.

In the United States there is a greater degree of equality of opportunity in higher education than anywhere else in the world. A larger proportion of Americans study in universities and colleges than any other people. These universities have shown and continue to show greater responsiveness to the needs of our society than their European counterparts. They have equipped our people with the varied skills and sciences essential to the development of a pioneer country. They have imparted the shape and coherence of the American nation to formless immigrant groups. American ideals have been strengthened, the great cultural tradition of the West has been broadened, and enriched by their teaching and example.

Modern knowledge of ourselves and of our universe has been nurtured in the universities. The scientific, technological, medical, and surgical advances of our time were born in them. They have supplied intellectual capital as essential to our society as financial capital is to our industrial enterprise. They have more than justified the faith of the public in our distinctive system of higher education. They have proved themselves forces of American progress.

II.
THE NATURE OF A UNIVERSITY

A university is the institutional embodiment of an urge for knowledge that is basic in human nature and as old as the human race. It is inherent in every individual. The search that it inspires is an individual affair. Men vary in the intensity of their passion for the search for knowledge as well as in their competence to pursue it. History therefore presents us with a series of scholarly pioneers who advanced our knowledge from age to age and increased our ability to discover new knowledge. Great scholars and teachers drew students to them, and in the Middle Ages a few such groups organized themselves into the first universities.

The modern university which evolved from these is a unique type of organization. For many reasons it must differ from a corporation created for the purpose of producing a salable article for profit. Its internal structure, procedures, and discipline are properly quite different from those of business organizations. It is not so closely integrated and there is no such hierarchy of authority as is appropriate to a business concern; the permanent members of a university are essentially equals.

Like its medieval prototype, the modern American university is an association of individual scholars. Their effectiveness, both as scholars and as teachers, requires the capitalizing of their individual passion for knowledge and their individual competence to pursue it and communicate it to others. They are united in loyalty to the idea of learning, to the moral code, to the country, and to its form of government. They represent diversified fields of knowledge, they express many points of view. Even within the same department of instruction there are not only specialists in various phases of the subject, but men with widely differing interests and outlook.

Free enterprise is as essential to intellectual as to economic progress. A university must therefore be hospitable to an infinite variety of skills and viewpoints, relying upon open competition among them as the surest safeguard of truth. Its whole spirit requires investigation, criticism, and presentation of ideas in an atmosphere of freedom and mutual confidence. This is the real meaning of "academic" freedom. It is essential to the achievement of its ends that the faculty of a university be guaranteed this freedom by its governing board, and that the reasons for the guarantee be understood by the public. To enjoin uniformity of outlook upon a university faculty would put a stop to learning at the source. To censor individual faculty members would put a stop to learning at its outlet.

For these reasons a university does not take an official position of its own either on disputed questions of scholarship or on political questions or matters of public policy. It refrains from so doing not only in its own but in the public interest, to capitalize the search for knowledge for the benefit of society, to give the individuals pursuing that search the freest possible scope and the greatest possible encouragement in their efforts to preserve the learning of the past and advance learning in the present. The scholar who pursues the search on these terms does so at maximum advantage to society. So does the student. To the scholar lie open new discoveries in the whole field of knowledge, to his student the opportunity of sharing in those discoveries and at the same time developing his powers of rational thought, intelligent judgment, and an understanding use of acquired knowledge. Thus essential qualities of learning are combined with essential qualities of citizenship in a free society.

To fulfill their function the members of university faculties must continue to analzye, test, criticize and reassess existing institutions and beliefs, approving when the evidence supports them and disapproving when the weight of evidence is on the other side. Such invstigations cannot be confined to the physical world. The acknowledged fact that moral, social, and political progress have not kept pace with mastery of the physical world shows the need for more intensified research, fresh insights, vigorous criticism, and inventiveness. The scholar's mission requires the study and examination of unpopular ideas, of ideas considered abhorrent and even dangerous. For, just as in the case of deadly disease or the military potential of an enemy, it is only by intense study and research that the nature and extent of the danger can be understood and defenses against it perfected.

Timidity must not lead the scholar to stand silent when he ought to speak, particularly in the field of his competence. In matters of conscience and when he has truth to proclaim the scholar has no obligation to be silent in the face of popular disapproval. Some of the great passages in the history of truth have involved the open challenge of popular prejudice in times of tension such as those in which we live.

What applies to research applies equally to teaching. So long as an instructor's observations are scholarly and germane to his subject, his freedom of expression in his classroom should not be curbed. The university student should be exposed to competing opinions and beliefs in every field, so that he may learn to weigh them and gain maturity of judgment. Honest and skillful exposition of such opinions and beliefs is the duty of every instructor; and it is equally his privilege to express his own critical opinion and the reasons for holding it. In teaching, as in research, he is limited by the requirements of citizenship, of professional competence and good taste. Having met those standards, he is entitled to all the protection the full resources of the university can provide.

Whatever criticism is occasioned by these practices, the universities are committed to them by their very nature. To curb them, in the hope of avoiding criticism, would mean distorting the true process of learning and depriving society of its benefits. It would invite the fate of the German and Italian universities under Fascism and the Russian universities under Communism. It would deny our society one of its most fruitful sources of strength and welfare and represent a sinister change in our ideal of government.

III.
THE OBLIGATIONS AND RESPONSIBILITIES OF UNIVERSITY FACULTIES

We must recognize the fact that honest men hold differing opinions. This fundamental truth underlies the assertion and definition of individual rights and freedom in our Bill of Rights. How does it apply to universities? In the eyes of the law, the university scholar has no more and no less freedom than his fellow citizens outside a university. Nonetheless, because of the vital importance of the university to civilization, membership in its society of scholars enhances the prestige of persons admitted to its fellowship after probation and upon the basis of achievement in research and teaching. The university supplies a distinctive forum and, in so doing, strengthens the scholar's voice. When his opinions challenge existing orthodox points of view, his freedom may be more in need of defense than that of men in other professions. The guarantee of tenure to professors of mature and proven scholarship is one such defense. As in the case of judges, tenure protects the scholar against undue economic or political pressures and ensures the continuity of the scholarly process.

There is a line at which "freedom" or "privilege" beings to be qualified by legal "duty" and "obligation." The determination of the line is the function of the legislature and the courts. The ultimate interpretation and application of the First and Fourteenth Amendments are the function of the United States Supreme Court; but every public official is bound by his oath of office to respect and preserve the liberties guaranteed therein. These are not to be determined arbitrarily or by public outcry. The line thus drawn can be changed by legislative and judicial action; it has varied in the past because of prevailing anxieties as well as by reason of "clear and present" danger. Its location is subject to, and should receive, criticism both popular and judicial. However much the location of the line may be criticized, it cannot be disregarded wtih impunity. Any member of a university who crosses the duly established line is not excused by the fact that he believes the line ill-drawn. When the speech, writing, or other actions of a member of a faculty exceed lawful limits, he is subject to the same penalties as other persons. In addition, he may lose his university status.

Historically the word "university" is a guarantee of standards. It implies endorsement not of its members' views but of their capability and integrity. Every scholar has an obligation to maintain this reputation. By ill-advised, though not illegal, public acts or utterances he may do serious harm to his profession, his university, to education, and to the general welfare. He bears a heavy responsibility to weigh the soundness of his opinions and the manner in which they are expressed. His effectiveness, both as scholar and teacher, is not reduced but enhanced if he has the humility and the wisdom to recognize the fallibility of his own judgment. He should remember that he is as much a layman as anyone else in all fields except those in which he has special competence. Others, both within and without the university, are as free to criticize his opinions as he is free to express them; "academic freedom" does not include freedom from criticism.

As in all acts of association, the professor accepts conventions which become morally binding. Above all, he owes his colleagues in the university complete candor and perfect integrity, precluding any kind of clandestine or conspiratorial activities. He owes equal candor to the public. If he is called upon to answer for his convictions it is his duty as a citizens to speak out. It is even more definitely his duty as a professor. Refusal to do so, on whatever legal grounds, cannot fail to reflect upon a profession that claims for itself the fullest freedom to speak and the maximum protection of that freedom available in our society. In this respect, invocation of the Fifth Amendment places upon a professor a heavy burden of proof of his fitness to hold a teaching position and lays upon his university an obligation to reexamine his qualifications for membership in its society.

In all universities faculties exercise wide authority in internal affairs. The greater their autonomy, the greater their share of responsibility to the public. They must maintain the highest standards and exercise the utmost wisdom in appointments and promotions. They must accept their share of responsibility for the discipline of those who fall short in the discharge of their academic trust.

The universities owe their existence to legislative acts and public charters. A state university exists by constitutional and legislative acts, an endowed university enjoys its independence by franchise from the state and by custom. The state university is supported by public funds. The endowed university is benefited by tax exemptions. Such benefits are conferred upon the universities not as favors but in furtherance of the public interest. They carry with them public obligation of direct concern to the faculties of the universities as well as to the governing boards.

Legislative bodies from time to time may scrutinize these benefits and privileges. It is clearly the duty of universities and their members to cooperate in official inquiries directed to those ends. When the powers of legislative inquiry are abused, the remedy does not lie in non-cooperation or defiance: it is to be sought through the normal channels of informed public opinion.

IV.
THE PRESENT DANGER

We have set forth the nature and function of the university. We have outlined its rights and responsibilities and those of its faculties. What are the implications for current anxiety over Russian Communism and the subversive activities connected with it?

We condemn Russian Communism as we condemn every form of totalitarianism. We share the profound concern of the American people at the existence of an international conspiracy whose goal is the destruction of our cherished institutions. The police state would be the death of our universities, as of our government. Three of its principles in particular are abhorrent to us: the fomenting of world-wide revolution as a step to seizing power; the use of falsehood and deceit as normal means of persuasion; thought control—the dictation of doctrines which must be accepted and taught by all party members. Under these principles, no scholar could adequately disseminate knowledge or pursue investigations in the effort to make further progress toward truth.

Appointment to a university position and retention after appointment require not only professional competence but involve the affirmative obligation of being diligent and loyal in citizenship. Above all, a scholar must have integrity and independence. This renders impossible adherence to such a regime as that of Russia and its satellites. No person who accepts or advocates such principles and methods has any place in a university. Since present membership in the Communist Party requires the acceptance of these principles and methods, such membership extinguishes the right to a university position. Moreover, if an instructor follows communistic practice by becoming a propagandist for one opinion, adopting a "party line", silencing criticism or impairing freedom of thought and expression in his classroom, he forfeits not only all university support but his right to membership in the university.

"Academic freedom" is not a shield for those who break the law. Universities must cooperate fully with law-enforcement officers whose duty requires them to prosecute those charged with offenses. Under a well-established American principle their innocence is to be assumed until they have been convicted, under due process, in a court of proper jurisdiction.

Unless a faculty member violates a law, however, his discipline or discharge is a university responsibility and should not be assumed by political authority. Discipline on the basis of irresponsible accusations or suspicion can never be condoned. It is as damaging to the public welfare as it is to academic integrity. The university is competent to establish a tribunal to determine the facts and fairly judge the nature and degree of any trespass upon academic integrity, as well as to determine the penalty such trespass merits.

As the professor is entitled to no special privileges in law, so also he should be subject to no special discrimination. Universities are bound to deprecate special loyalty tests which are applied to their faculties but to which others are not subjected. Such discrimination does harm to the individual and even greater harm to his university and the whole cause of education by destroying faith in the ideals of university scholarship.

V.
CONCLUSION

Finally, we assert that freedom of thought and speech is vital to the maintenance of the American system and is essential to the general welfare. Condemnation of Communism and its protagonists is not to be interpreted as readiness to curb social, political, or economic investigation and research. To insist upon complete conformity to current beliefs and practices would do infinite harm to the principle of freedom, which is the greatest, the central, American doctrine. Fidelity to that principle has made it possible for the universities of

America to confer great benefits upon our society and our country. Adherence to that principle is the only guarantee that the nation may continue to enjoy those benefits.

Faculty Council Minutes, 1953–55, pp. 41–50.

Document 174

A Letter reflecting Administrative Concern

President Wells's letter to Professor Norman T. Pratt, Jr. contains some of the subtleties of the Wells administrative approaches. The President was ever conscious that he stood between a faculty which sought utmost freedom and a state government which wished to restrict academic freedom. In this case the legislature had taken a stand against the employment of a communist in a public post.

*   *   *

June 15, 1953

Professor Norman T. Pratt, Jr., President
Indiana University Chapter
American Association of University Professors
Department of Classical Languages and Literatures
Indiana University
Dear Professor Pratt:

I thank you for the report of the local chapter of the AAUP on the statement of academic freedom issued by the Association of American Universities. I am glad that the chapter found itself in agreement with most of the statement.

I regret that the Faculty Council agenda was so crowded Tuesday that we were unable to have a discussion of your report. Without prejudice to any future action either the Board of Trustees or the faculty, I feel it is wise to state my own attitudes for the sake of clear understanding in the interim.

I subscribe to the provisions of the AAU statement, including those dealing with the problems arising from the Congressional investigations. As a consequence, should any member of our staff refuse to testify before these committees, I would recommend that he be relieved of his duties while a prompt investigation and hearing of the case is conducted to determine his fitness for future membership on the faculty.

I would like to urge, as I have in past meetings of the Council, that members of our faculty cooperate fully with the Congressional committees; that anyone called upon to testify consult immediately with appropriate University officers for aid in making his presentation; and that any member of the faculty who wishes to refuse to testify do so only after consultation with competent legal counsel. The University will make such counsel available if desired.

Finally, I think it is important that we remind ourselves from time to time that there is an Indiana statute making it illegal to continue a member of the Communist Party in any form of State employment, and that as members of a democratically organized faculty with large opportunity for self-government, we have a responsibility to assist the University in complying fully with this statute.

If the members of our local AAUP chapter would like to have me participate in a discussion of the AAU statement at any time next fall, I shall be glad to do so.

Cordially yours,
H. B WELLS

Faculty Council Minutes, 1953–55, p. 73.

Document 175

Wolves in Sheep's Clothing

Somewhere in the operation of man's first universities there must have been students who posed as such, but sought to make their way by stealth rather than dedication. In the United States in the 1950s with emphasis upon education to secure jobs, grades, and certain social prestige, cheating was inevitable. This prostitution of the educational process was difficult to check and impossible to destroy. The honor system only worked in places where the tradition had become firmly established in smaller student bodies. This is an interesting document in that it so clearly outlines problems and so successfully fails to come to the nub of enforcement of any rule which might be devised.

*   *   *

Report of the Committee on Faculty-Student Relations
Corrected Copy with Reference to the Cheating Problem
April 15, 1953

To the Faculty Council and Student Senate:

The problem of cheating in examinations and in the preparation of student papers at Indiana University has come before the Committee on Faculty-Student Relations through several channels. Dean Ashton originally called attention to the matter in a letter and met with the Committee on one occasion to state the thought which has led to his concern. The Student Senate has considered the problem and has communicated to the Faculty Council with regard to it. The Council, in turn, has referred the problem formally to the Committee and is awaiting a report. After consideration by a subcommittee and discussion at several meetings, some of which have been attended by non-members who were interested or had suggestions to offer, the Committee now presents this report.

Scope of the Problem

It is clear that the problem of cheating at Indiana University has serious proportions. Although there is little evidence that the great bulk of academic work in the University is not carried on honestly, universal testimony is to the effect that much cheating goes on in numerous assembled examinations and that the practice of submitting copies of previous term papers as original work, aided by cooperative arrangements, is all too frequent. In addition, repeated attempts, some of them successful, have been made to obtain copies of examination questions in advance. In the School of Business these attempts have included physical assaults upon the locked door of the room in which examination questions are stored.

At the present time the methods of coping with cheating are limited to general faculty vigilance, the proctoring of assembled examinations, and a disciplinary system which functions only sporadically. The attitude of cynicism is widespread. It quickly infects entering students, and there is more than a little reason to believe that the great majority of students do cheat occasionally in the course of the University work.

Nature and Significance of the Problem

It is not necessary in this report to expand upon the reasons why cheating is harmful to the student who engages in it and to his associates. Obviously it impairs the training the student should be receiving and, insofar as it is successful, it may confer an advantage upon the dishonest student over others, if grading is done "on a curve" or if student work is competitive. Studies are competitive, for example, in relation to entrance into Medical School and in the attainment of class standings which may influence opportunities for employment after graduation. These factors alone create an urgent necessity for eliminating cheating to the greatest extent possible.

In considering possible steps to be taken in dealing with the cheating problem, the Committee has been impressed by its complexity. The matter is as complicated as human behavior in any field, and the means of influencing it are correspondingly numerous. In general it may be said that the factors which bear on student conduct in relation to cheating fall into the following categories: (1) the individual student's personal integrity, (2) the group opinion which surrounds the students, (3) the opportunities for cheating which tempt the student, (4) the degree of respect which students feel for the work they are called upon to do, and (5) the likelihood of disciplinary action if cheating is practiced. The first of these factors is probably beyond reach by means of any formal or organized methods that might be recommended, since it results from the student's whole upbringing; but consideration may usefully be given to ways of influencing each of the other factors. The responsibility for dealing with each of them is distributed among students and faculty in differing degree.

For important reasons, we believe and recommend that the measures to be taken to improve the present situation should emphasize the desirability of increasing reliance upon student honor. The general attitude essential to the success of an honor system relying upon student-operated disciplinary machinery does not exist here at present. There would certainly be difficulty in gathering the evidence necessary for action, due, in part, to the students' reluctance to report specific cases. We do not, therefore, recommend the institution of a campus-wide formal honor system. We have in mind, rather, a series of measures that would endeavor to build up an atmosphere in the University which would encourage each student to be true to the resources of character which he possesses and to assume a share of responsibility for general conditions. That responsibility would be discharged by conduct, by utterance, and by cooperation with procedures he values and respects.

In making this recommendation we have concern for the fundamental importance of strengthening the concepts and the practices which form the basic foundations of democratic society. In a democracy the personal integrity of the great majority of the people is essential; for the operating machinery of a democratic society is based upon trust. The dignity and worth of each individual is recognized and each has a share in the responsibility for effective government. The students on a college campus necessarily will provide much of the leadership of society in the near future. The violation of honorable conduct through cheating, either in an examination or in any other aspect of university life, lessens personal integrity and trustworthiness and thus chips away some of the foundation of freedom. The failure to assume a personal share in matters of common concern weakens the basis upon which democratic government rests.

Recommendations

As immediate means of improving the present situation, we wish to propose specific measures through which (1) the Student Senate and other student agencies may attempt to strengthen the general student attitude and to encourage the assumption of individual and collective student responsibility for maintaining honesty, (2) the Faculty Council may encourage faculty practices which tend to reduce cheating, and (3) the disciplinary system may be rendered more adequate to its task. We now proceed to set forth our several proposals in order:

(1) Action by the Student Senate

We recommend that the Student Senate establish a standard committee on student honor, whose functions it should be: (a) to carry on continuous effort to promote awareness in the student body of the importance of honesty in all forms of academic work and of maintaining a healthy state of affairs on the campus in this regard; (b) to promote the effective use of disciplinary machinery in cases of dishonesty; and (c) to recommend to the Senate, and through it to the University, such measures as in its opinion will strengthen student honor and student responsibility, including treatment of the problem during freshman orientation. The committee should be authorized to invoke the assistance of other student organizations, such as the "Y" and other groups which emphasize the development of character and responsibility. In cooperation with these organizations, it should plan the issuance of literature, the conduct of discussions in housing units and elsewhere, and such other organized effort as may serve to support and strengthen the attitude and the personal conduct of members of the student body in relation to their work. The committee should be required by the Senate to render an annual report each spring, reviewing its efforts and making recommendations for the future.

We can think of no better way in which student government at Indiana University could be rendered more meaningful than by directing its efforts in part to this problem.

(2) Action by the Faculty Council

We recommend to the Faculty Council that it request the University Committee on Improvement in Teaching to prepare and circulate among the faculty a report on faculty practices which bear on the problem of cheating and to report to the Council each year with reference to the effectiveness of the faculty's methods in this regard. While we have no reason to think that examination methods and the conduct of examinations at Indiana University are careless or below standard, we are convinced that a considerable amount of cheating can be prevented by careful faculty attention to the problem. While measures to be taken by the faculty may seem inconsistent with a policy of increased reliance on student responsibility, we do not think there is any real conflict between that policy and steps to reduce temptation or render detection of violators more likely. As is true in civil society, personal integrity is bolstered by methods which are not designed to take its place but, at the same time, to create a healthy environment and give integrity a better chance to succeed.

Faculty attention might helpfully be directed to the following phases of the cheating problem.

(a) The framing of examinations which, so far as possible, avoid reliance upon merely factual answers and require answers which are difficult to anticipate and to copy. We do not suggest the abandonment of objective-type examinations, because of their obvious merit and utility with large classes; but we think it would be desirable to discourage their use with smaller groups.

(b) The methods of duplicating and restoring examination questions prior to their use, so as to guard against premature disclosure. Perhaps each department and school should be requested to review its methods in this regard. The typing and duplication of examinations should obviously be carried on only by limited, trusted personnel as, for the most part, it is at present. Examinations should either be stored in special safeguarded places on the campus or be taken home by members of the faculty, rather than left in their offices.

(c) The administration of examinations. Over-crowding in examination rooms is bad for a number of reasons, aside from the cheating problem itself. As to that problem, we think it would be desirable for instructors to require that students be seated, so far as practicable, with spaces between them while examinations are under way. The measures taken to this end need not be offensive or too rigid. Where a class is crowded in the room originally provided for it, a special request for a larger examination room should be made to the proper administrative authorities. Proctoring, if practiced, should be adequate. Experiments by individual faculty members with honor-system methods, taking the place of proctoring, might well be encouraged. The successful spread of such practices, carefully watched and judged by responsible faculty members, might make a great contribution to the long-run solution of the cheating problem. Such methods, however, should not preclude the submission of cases of actual cheating to the disciplinary authorities.

(d) Reports of cheating. Faculty members should, we think, be required to report to the disciplinary authorities all cases of cheating which come to their attention in their courses and examinations. The regulation on this subject in the present Faculty Handbook provides that "in all cases of cheating in final examinations or any term paper or project, the instructor shall make on the student's report in the course concerned 'Failed for Cheating.' " A rule that would confer discretion upon the faculty member and direct him to consult the disciplinary authorities before acting, would be desirable.

(e) Attention to the cheating problem in class. Instructors should perhaps be urged to consider explicit discussion of the cheating problem in their classes before examinations. Faculty members have more influence with students in matters of conduct than many perhaps realize. Frank discussion of the cheating problem before examinations, which is made the occasion for the instructor to strengthen sound attitudes, might be very helpful. Such discussion is obviously more appropriate with students when they are relatively new in the University than later on, and its advantage in any particular class will diminish as attention is given to the problem elsewhere. Each instructor must probably gauge his course in the light of general practices, his own inclination, and the attitude which he senses in a particular group, but an established custom of not ignoring the subject will necessarily, we think, produce improvement.

(f) Repetition of examinations. Except for objective-type examinations where copies are numbered and carefully accounted for, the repetition of entire examinations which have been given before, or, within examinations, of more than occasional questions which are difficult to answer, should not be practiced. Copies of past examinations are, and should be, on file in the University libraries as well as elsewhere. The re-use of questions is certain to encourage unintelligent study, to increase opportunities for coaching by past students, and to breed disrespect for the examining process and for the instruction as a whole.

(3) The disciplinary system

The regulations in the Faculty Handbook provide that more severe penalties than the grade of Failure for cheating in the individual course "may be assessed by the Faculty or by the committee or office authorized to act for it in such matters." They further provide that "a student found guilty of cheating shall not be allowed to participate in any public exercise of any student, or any University, organization, or to be an officer in any general student organization during the following semester." No published regulations appear to have been issued, covering the disciplinary procedures at present observed. The I.U. Pilot contains no reference at all to the subject. We are informed, however, that the procedure at present prevailing is as follows:

(1) The instructor reports instances of cheating to the Dean of Students' office.

(2) The Dean of Students' office investigates the entire University career of the student involved and calls a conference with him.

(3) After the conference, the Dean of Students' office either recommends academic discipline to the instructor, which is optional with him except for the mandatory grade of Failure, or invokes disciplinary action directly upon the students.

(4) If the student wishes to appeal either action, he may appeal to the Student Affairs Committee, composed one-half of members of the faculty and one-half of members of the Student Supreme Court. The recommendations of the committee have invariably been followed.

It will be observed that under the foregoing outline of procedures, reports by students to the Dean of Students that cheating has occurred are not expected. In fact, however, students have occasionally volunteered information that a particular examination has become available before the time it is scheduled to be given. These reports have not resulted in disciplinary measures, but rather in the substitution of a different examination for the one originally prepared.

This existing disciplinary system is sound enough in its essentials, but it should be overhauled in certain respects and built upon so as to render it a truly effective instrument for control of the cheating problem. We propose that the following steps be taken with regard to it.

(a) We suggest that, for the information of students, a full statement as to the system, together with an explanation of the obligation of students to invoke it when abuses come to their attention, be included in the I.U. Pilot and in the University bulletins.

(b) We recommend that the regulation in the Faculty Handbook as to cheating be revised as previously suggested in this report, and, further, by eliminating the mandatory penalty of non-participation in student activities which the regulation now contains. The regulation should also be expanded to include the composition of the Student Affairs Committee, together with its functions and those of the Dean of Students in relation to cheating.

(c) We urge that campus publicity be given to all actions of the Student Affairs Committee, without inclusion of the names of those involved, and that a report be made and publicized each year, summarizing the work of the Committee and of the Dean of Students in cheating cases.

(d) We suggest that provision be made in the regulation, as revised, for the adoption of special honor systems or other means of controlling cheating in professional schools or other University divisions where such an approach to the problem might be beneficial.

Conclusion

Our suggestions add up to the over-all recommendation that the present *laissez-faire* attitude toward the cheating problem, which characterizes the University community, be replaced by an attitude of active concern, leading to the assumption of responsibility and to the many specific measures that can be taken to improve the situation. Above all, we think it is essential that the matter be kept alive in the minds of students and faculty during the years ahead. We can conceive of no greater contribution to sound relations among all elements in the University than for such a development to take place.

Procedurally, we suggest that the Student Senate take action as soon as feasible with regard to our recommendations addressed to it and communicate its actions to the Faculty Council and that the Council similarly take action on its part. If our recommendations are accepted, the organization of the student honor committee, the drafting of the new cheating regulation, and the preparation of the statements to be published, for which the plan calls, could follow in fairly short order.

Faculty Council Minutes, 1953–55, p. 58–63.

Document 176

The Cheating Rule

This statement of the cheating rule almost incriminates the professor instead of the offending student. No doubt there was wisdom in Vice President Samuel Braden's observation that the mode of reporting was self-defeating. These rules all but make a "Supreme Court" case of student cheating.

*　　　*　　　*

4. Professor Fuchs presented the revised rule with regard to cheating and (seconded by Professor Breneman) moved its adoption.

   Certain amendments in phraseology were approved by the Council.

   Professor Stoner expressed some concern about the possibility that the record of penalties imposed under this act would work to the disadvantage of the student when he later sought employment. Dean Shoemaker stated that records of such penalties are destroyed when the student is graduated from the University. Professor Braden predicted that the amount of reporting required by the rule would reduce the extent of enforcement. Professor Fuchs pointed out the need of procedural rules if the act is adopted. It was generally agreed that, if the rule is adpoted, a study should be made after a year or two to determine its effectiveness.

The question was then called for on the adoption of the rule, amended to read as follows:

It should be the responsibility of each faculty member to maintain the best possible conditions to prevent dishonesty on examinations or other exercises. The student should also understand that it is his duty to avoid the suspicion of cheating, to guard against making it possible for others to cheat, and to do all that he can to induce respect for the examining process and for honesty in carrying out assigned tasks.

The instructor who suspects a student of dishonesty shall initiate the process of determining whether the student is guilty and of assessing, within the course, a penalty in case of guilt. No penalty shall be imposed until the student has been informed of the charge and given opportunity to present his defense. All cases in which the instructor and the student agree upon the guilt of the student and the student accepts the instructor's penalty within the course, which may then be imposed, shall be reported promptly to the Dean of Students (or other agency responsible for handling such cases), who may initiate further disciplinary proceedings if he sees fit.

If the instructor and the student cannot agree on the facts, or if the student wishes to protest the instructor's penalty within the course, or if the case is deemed to require further action, the instructor shall refer the case to the Dean of Students or other agency responsible for handling such cases. After a hearing in a case which has been reported or referred, at which opportunity to present evidence has been given, the Dean of Students or other Agency shall render a decision and, in case of guilt, shall determine the penalty.

A penalty affecting a student's grade may be imposed only through the instructor and with his consent. In any case which cannot be settled before grades are due in the Office of Records and Admissions, a grade of *Incomplete* shall be temporarily recorded.

Any professional or other school at the graduate level may, with the approval of the Faculty, adopt its own rules and set up its own procedures for dealing with cases of cheating.

Faculty Council Minutes, 1953–55, p. 134.

Document 177

The International Outlook

This lengthy document reflects the fact that by 1952 Indiana University was casting its nets far abroad. There is reflected a self-consciousness about the old accusations of isolation charged against the Mid-West. In its recommendations the International Relations Survey Committee suggested that the international outlook be injected into all curricular considerations and that faculty members be actively involved in foreign travel and teaching assignments.

*   *   *

Report of the
International Relations Survey Committee
(Unabridged)

The International Relations Survey Committee was set up by the Faculty Council in the fall of 1952, to cooperate with the Carnegie Endowment for International Peace in a study of the University's role in international affairs. The following report on the University's activity in this field is divided into three parts: Curriculum; Student and General Extra-Curricular Activities; and Faculty Activity.

I. CURRICULUM

In view of the current need for the development of an international outlook and a consequent understanding of the problems of our relations with other nations all over the world, it is extremely important that we take a good look at the offerings of the University in the field of international relations.

The Midwest is probably no longer a breeding ground for isolationism as it once was, but the forces of higher education must constantly meet the new challenge of the need for expert knowledge in the highly critical fields of international relations. This survey attempts to analyze as closely as possible our current activities in this field, to take account of our potential resources and to lay a basis for more effective planning of educational activities in this whole area. It recognizes that the attitudes of our students are formed not only by the course work which they have, but by their associations both on the faculty and in the student body and in the general climate of opinion which exists on the campus.

The Curriculum Subcommittee has attempted to take into account these factors and to base its report on as wide a survey as possible of the materials which are or can be made available.

Survey of Instruction in International Relations

For the purpose of the survey of course offerings at Indiana University in the international field the Curriculum Subcommittee considers instruction in international relations as including:

1) The theoretical, legal, and institutional aspects of the formal relationships among states;
2) The political, economic and cultural foundations of international relations;
3) Studies relating to specific nations or areas;
4) Studies representing a substantial contribution to the orientation and enlightenment of students in respect to international relations and world affairs.

Accordingly the Subcommittee divided the courses into three categories:

A) Courses directly concerned with international affairs;
B) Courses relating to specific nations or world areas;
C) Courses on the periphery of international relations.

These courses are listed in detail at the end of this part of the Report.

General Courses

At Indiana University there is a large number of possibilities for the student to come in contact with an international outlook, and become familiar with some of the problems of international life. This possibility exists for all students in the university, but there is no way to determine the probability of contact.

All students in their Freshman year are enrolled in the Junior Division. Here, their preparation for their academic pursuits is adjusted to their individual needs. The general recommendations made by the College of Arts and Sciences for

Junior Division students include English Composition, foreign language, and one of the physical sciences. From the second year on, students go into the various undergraduate schools of the university.

Students in the College of Arts and Sciences are required to complete 122 hours of academic work. Among the prescribed courses, there are only four in history, and two in anthropology which fit into the classification scheme listed above. Even these few courses are not required, but are part of a group of several from which the student can choose. All students in Arts and Sciences are required to take a foreign language. Aside from this language training (18 hours) it can be assumed that students can go through their entire course of study in the College without any contact with the international world.

However, as was mentioned, there is ample opportunity for a wide and rich educational contact with the variety of human development in the world, and with the specific problems of world life, if the student wants it. There opportunities include:

1) Direct contact through studies of international affairs;
2) Contact with particular outlooks through area studies;
3) General appreciation of the wider world around them through the study of specific aspects of world development.

This generally corresponds to the threefold division of categories undertaken by the subcommittee. The subcommittee realizes that the division is somewhat artificial, for the interrelationship of all three categories in a general understanding of world affairs is apparent.

The problem faced by the Subcommittee should be noted. These can be summed up in two headings:

1) Inadequacy of course descriptions;
2) The impossibility of analysis of programs for students with different majors.

(1) Course descriptions in particular in the third category of courses are often inadequate guides to the suitability of inclusion in this list. Much depends on the way the course is given, and the attitude of the individual instructor. This is especially true in the humanities, and some of the social sciences. Courses in languages, literature, the arts, and philosophy may be expected to give the student some appreciation of the cultural heritage of the western world in general, of other nations in particular, and the heritage of other cultures, and the diversity and sameness of peoples. The same may be said for such fields as anthropology, psychology, and sociology. However, unless these courses are specifically related to the problems of international understanding, the value may be lost to the student.

This is particularly true if it is considered that the greatest problem faced by this committee should be to determine the position of the student who would ordinarily have no interest in or appreciation of other parts of the world. It cannot be expected that these students would by themselves integrate the course content with international understanding.

(2) Without a detailed analysis of the programs of a large sampling of students from each of the departments of the college, it is impossible to tell what utilization is made of the opportunities available. It is safe to assume that a good many students in the social sciences in some way have such contacts. Students in the humanities of necessity at least learn some of the cultural achievements of other peoples. There is no way to determine how well these students balance their education with courses on other aspects of the life of other peoples. In the same way, there is no way to tell whether or not students directly concerned

with international relations and foreign political problems balance their studies with knowledge of the cultural and spiritual aspects of other countries.

Aside from the students of social sciences and humanities, no surmise at all can be made regarding the utilization of these opportunities by other students in Arts and Sciences. This, of course, refers to students of the physical sciences, mathematics, etc.

The survey is mainly concerned with the course offerings in the College of Arts and Sciences. The other schools of the University are of a professional character, and devote most of their interest and time to their particular fields. However, as was mentioned before, all students of the University, and this includes students of education, music and business, must take their freshman year in the Junior Division. Also, in their later years, students of these schools are required to take some courses in the College of Arts and Sciences. Thus, it can be assumed that at least some of them receive instruction related to the problems other than those concerning solely their particular disciplines or the domestic scene.

In addition to this, the professional schools themselves offer a few courses concerning international and general world problems. Thus, in the School of Education there is a course in Comparative Education which discusses the educational systems of other countries. Further, many courses—dealing with the history of education, problems of adult education in democratic society, and with the relationship and responsibility of the educator to society, and similar questions—may be oriented to international society, at least in part. Yet, all depends on the way the courses are given. Also, the School of Music, which includes a department of music history and literature, offers courses contributing to the understanding of the elements of international relations.

The schools which offer only graduate degrees—law, medicine, dentistry, etc.— generally do not have any courses which would fit into the classification for this survey. The one exception is the course in international law offered by the Law School. It should be noted that students of these schools should have received at least some instruction in the field of international relations in their undergraduate work.

With these preliminary remarks, the Subcommittee has considered each of the categories listed above.

(A) *(Courses directly concerned with international affairs)*

In the first category, there is a total of 14 courses, given by the departments of government, economics, history, and geography. Although six of the courses are given on the undergraduate level, the university does not provide for an undergraduate concentration in international relations as such.

There is no general introductory course in international relations which deals with the different basic components of the subject. The Department of Government offers a two semester course in World Politics on the sophomore level. This course is the widest in scope in the field of international affairs, but its emphasis is political. Still, it is the only one to serve the needs of general education in international relations. It is taken by a relatively large number of students, including many from departments other than government. However, especially since the attendance in other, more specialized courses in the field, is smaller, it is obvious that a large proportion of students graduating from Indiana have had no direct study specifically dealing with the subject of international relations.

It has been impossible for the committee to determine the percentage and distribution of students having some contact with the field of international relations as such. The expected small percentage should be modified because of the additional number of students receiving instruction in courses listed in the other two categories which help to give an appreciation of the facts, complexities and problems of international life in its formal aspects.

On the graduate level, courses in international relations are frequently taken as minor or major subjects in the curricula for the M.A. and Ph.D. degrees. The University, however, does not offer a degree in international relations as such, the degrees being taken in one of the regular departments.

Yet, in the Ph.D. program, a heavy concentration in the field is possible, particularly in the departments of government and economics, where the international field may represent (but rarely does) up to four-fifths of the entire study program.

Thus, Indiana University, which has no special school devoted entirely to the study of international relations, offers what might be regarded as a limited graduate specialization in the field. However, its value is somewhat diminished by the lack of coordination—the courses being frequently presented more from the point of view of the individual department than as an integrated study program in the international field. Thus, for instance, the course in international economics—though excellent from the point of view of a student of economics—may appear to be too specialized for a student of international relations. Nevertheless, the international relations program on the graduate level justified the conclusion that Indiana University is adequately equipped for the training both of specialists seeking employment in some branch of the government service, and of those who intend to devote their interests to a scholarly pursuit and teaching of international relations.

Indiana University does not have a special research institute or other study center which would be entrusted with the scientific study of the problems of international relations or its different aspects.

The University has an Institute of Training for the Public Service which is attached to the department of Government, and which devotes considerable attention to students of international relations who may be interested in careers with the federal government. The Institute advises such students in the preparation of their study programs and assists them in finding openings in the public service.

(B)   (*Courses Relating to Specific Nations or World Areas*)

Indiana University offers in its different departments a great number of courses which are concerned with the study of specific nations or world areas. All of them contribute in some fashion to the knowledge of other cultures and peoples and thereby to an understanding of international relations. Their main purpose is to give to the students insight into the history, political institutions, economic systems and civilizations of countries and areas other than the United States.

However, the utility of these courses from the point of view of international relations depends greatly on their organization and on the approach adopted by the lecturer. Also, in order to achieve the aim of orienting the student towards consciousness of the political, economic and cultural interdependence of the world, it would be necessary to provide for the integration of the studies in the different fields.

If history—which offers courses covering the main nations and the principal world areas—is included, there are in all 54 courses belonging to this category.

They are given in the following departments: Geography, Government, History, French, German, Spanish, Classics, Economics, Slavic Studies, and Sociology.

Over two-thirds of the courses are open to advanced undergraduate students who take them on an optional basis, as part, either of their undergraduate major, or, in some cases, of their undergraduate minor. Some courses are both introductory and terminal; others are more specialized and can be taken only by those who have some preparation in the field.

On the graduate level, courses belonging to this category form a part of the major or minor field of concentration for the M.A. or Ph.D. degrees. Indiana University has a graduate program in East European studies, as an area specialization, offering an M.A. degree in East European Studies. The candidates concentrate their work in one of the regular departments, the specialization requiring also the knowledge of Russian and one other area language.

(C) (*Courses on the Periphery of International Relations*)

Third category courses are the most difficult to list. Courses which, while not directly dealing with international relations nor with the more obviously pertinent aspects of particular areas, do have a bearing on the general outlook of the student, providing him with a knowledge of some aspect of the relationships between states, or with an appreciation of the factors that have influenced the development and diversity of different nations.

Courses in literature, the arts, and philosophy,—in general—should be listed here. They must, of necessity, show the student that his own heritage is to a large degree held in common with other nations, but that other nations may have outlooks and values different from our own. However, there must be a specific effort to translate this contact with the works and thoughts of other peoples into terms of world understanding if these sources are to be meaningful for the purposes of instruction in international relations.

Because of the difficulty imposed by the variety of possibility of presentation of such courses, they were not all listed in the appended list.

Instructions in Foreign Languages

The study of foreign languages and literatures is an important supplement to the study of international relations. The mastery of a foreign language and knowledge of a foreign literature are vital to a genuine understanding of the psychology and way of life of other people.

For the specialist in international relations the ability to read foreign texts in the original is indispensable. This is especially true of material published in the Slavic and East European languages, only too little of which is available in translation. Indiana University, recognizing the growing importance of East Europe and the Soviet Union on the international scene, created a Department of Slavic Studies in 1947 and has established an East European Institute, the first of its kind in this country. The foundation of the programs offered by these two institutions is the study of the languages spoken in the area. Similarly, the university offers a full program in the other major foreign languages: German, French, Italian, Spanish, and Portuguese.

Some study of foreign literatures would be of value to the student of international relations, for in many cases a literary work is also a social document. In any event a literary work is the expression of an outstanding representative of a people and thus will reveal certain facets of the national character.

Likewise, the average student, one who completes 18 credit hours or less in a foreign language in fulfillment of the requirements of the College of Arts and

Sciences for the A.B. degree, will increase his understanding of international affairs by means of his work in the field of foreign languages and literatures. He comes in contact with a different cultural heritage, with a different mental outlook, with a different manner of day-to-day living and can thus better appreciate the problems of living in peace and mutual understanding with peoples whose environment and character are quite different from our own. In fact, many elementary language texts are designed as an area study and, as is shown above in our outline of the language problems at Indiana University such texts have been adopted in a number of courses.

Another contribution made by the university's language program toward a better understanding of international relations is the American language and area program offered by the Department of English. Since Indiana University is an important center of study for foreign students this program was organized to introduce our guests from abroad to the American language and the American scene.

. . . .

Production of Materials and Distribution Abroad

Indiana University productions have been receiving some attention—and some orders—from outside the United States. The State Department and the Information Service have a number of prints circulating through their centers, and one print of our industrial safety film, "Plan to Live," is on deposit with the International Labor Organization. Distribution of I.U. films in Canada has been handled through the Agency of the Canadian Film Institute, and similar agencies in other countries are under consideration. Also Indiana University films at U.S. Information Centers in a number of other countries are being televised over local stations.

Worthy of special note is the production of the film on "Wet Mounting," the first in the series on production of inexpensive instructional materials which, it is hoped, will be of significance to various State Department and United Nations agencies concerned with fundamental education and the training of indigenous workers for carrying out the various education campaigns.

Foreign Visitors

Indiana University is on the itinerary of many of the foreign exchanges brought over on the various State Department exchange programs—particularly if these people are interested in audio-visual materials and methods.

Foreign Students

There have been approximately 50 foreign students taking one or more audio-visual courses during the past year, either as regular students, or as short-term exchangees brought in by the State Department.

Perhaps most significant are the half dozen or so foreign students who have been doing graduate work in education, with a considerable emphasis on audio-visual aids.

Staff members frequently receive letters from the students who have returned home asking for help in locating materials, securing information, and suggestions for their work. This present and potential service to audio-visual specialists in several countries is very promising for future professional developments throughout the world and for enriching the I.U. audio-visual program.

Former Staff Members Now Working Abroad

Of comparable significance in stimulating audio-visual developments in other countries is the service of several former staff members now working abroad.

Harold Otwell is in India, Robert Faust is in Puerto Rico, Robert Gobrecht in Iran, Don Williams and Ann Hyer have returned from work in Turkey.

Audio-Visual Center Newsletter Sent Abroad

A final link in our contacts with former students and professional colleagues abroad is the Center Newsletter which reaches a considerable number of key people in various parts of the world.

II. FOREIGN STUDENTS
General Counseling for Foreign Students

The Office of the Foreign Student Advisor in the Dean of Students division is the focal point for the counseling of foreign students. This office passes on the admission of foreign students with the divisions of the university concerned, serves as a liaison between the student and the United States governmental agencies with which he must deal and his own governmental agencies, assists students in dealing with their personal problems, tries to work out adjustments in academic programs where cases seem to warrant a variation from the regular requirements, and looks after the general welfare of the students. The office also provides assistance to the Cosmopolitan Club and various national clubs.

Pamphlets for Foreign Students and Special Application Blank

The University has a special type of application blank for foreign students which covers many points essential to the problem of determining the admissibility of the student but which are not essential from the standpoint of the American student. A special pamphlet is sent to all foreign students inquiring about Indiana University (which emphasizes particularly the differences between education in the United States and other countries and significant points about the University with which the students should be familiar before coming here.) There is also a special pamphlet describing the facilities of the English Language Program for foreign students.

Exchange Policies

The chief agencies that help administer the University's scholarship and maintenance grant programs for foreign students are the Institute of International Education in New York City and the English-Speaking Union. From time to time the University has worked out cooperative exchange plans with a number of foreign governments in a particular year. Presently, plans are being formulated for administering a reciprocal scholarship program with a cultural agency in Spain. Cooperative arrangements already exist with a number of organizations which make fellowship awards to foreign students, notably the Indiana Federation of Womens Clubs, the American Association of University Women, fraternities and sororities on the local campus that provide maintenance for selected foreign students with house guest privileges. Foreign students who have spent at least one year in an American University are permitted to compete for assistantships and fellowships on the same basis as American students. The University has a limited number of maintenance grants with which to assist outstanding but needy foreign students and annually awards in the neighborhood of 50 foreign student fee remission scholarships.

Honorary Degrees to Foreign Graduates

The University has conferred a number of honorary degrees on its distinguished foreign student graduates. At last year's commencement it awarded an honorary degree to Dr. Bocobo of the Philippines.

Foreign Visitors

Every attempt is made to coordinate a foreign visitors program sponsored by a number of governmental agencies and national associations. In all cases a careful consideration is given to providing as broad a view of American life to the visitors as possible in the time allotted for the visiting. The Office of the Dean of Students and the President's Office assist any division or faculty member charged with administering a program for foreign visitors in planning. The success of local programs is due principally to the enthusiastic cooperation of faculty and staff members, fraternities, sororities, and community groups and the contributions they make in the carrying out of these programs.

Foreign Student Directory

A directory containing the names, Bloomington addresses, telephone numbers, and home countries is mimeographed by the Office of the Advisor to Foriegn Students at the beginning of each semester and made available to any faculty members, student and community groups that request them.

Statistics on Foreign Students Enrolled First Semester 1952–53

During the first semester of the academic year 1952–53, there were 223 students from outside continental United States listed in the foreign student directory. Men graduate students numbered 106 and undergraduate 48. Women graduates numbered 54 while undergraduate women numbered 15. Altogether 55 countries were represented in the foreign student enrollment.

Housing

It has been believed desirable from the standpoint of mutual contributions to be obtained that foreign students be housed, at least during their first year of study at the University, in our Halls of Residence. Since there is no problem in the housing of foreign students so far as the matter of color is concerned, it has never been felt desirable to have a specific housing unit set aside for foreign students in a kind of "international house set-up." Placing the foreign students throughout the dormitory system does give them an opportunity to become better acquainted with Americans and does tend to stimulate interest on the part of many American students in persons from other lands. We consider it a most desirable feature to have the foreign student enter into the social activity of the particular hall in which he is placed.

Attention to Health

The University does its utmost to solve health problems posed by its foreign students. For example, a number of them have difficulty in adjusting themselves to American meals and, in consequence, the Health Center has worked out plans with the halls of residence dieticians to prepare special menus for the student with such difficulties.

English for Foreign Students

The University provides courses in English designed to raise the level of proficiency in the language to a point where the foreign student can carry college work for credit. During the present semester there are twenty-five students from twelve foreign countries perfecting their English in classes that employ the most progressive and scientific methods of teaching language and some of the best materials that have been developed in the teaching of English as a foreign language. The army method of using informants is used. Students are divided into small drill groups in order to receive a great deal of individual attention.

American students take charge of the drill groups serving as models of English pronunciation.

Field Trips

During the present year the University has planned a series of field trips designed to give students from abroad an opportunity to see more aspects of life in the United States—especially agricultural, educational, governmental, industrial, and medical developments—outside the University community. Probably one of the most interesting of these field trips worked out to date, and there have been several, was the one in which foreign students went to the senior high school in Newcastle, Indiana, as the guests of the members of the senior English class. They visited classes throughout the day, served on panel discussion groups in the high school classes, were guests in the home of a prominent Newcastle citizen for afternoon tea, were guests in the homes of the American students for dinner, and attended a high school basketball game and dance.

. . . .

Publicity by the News Bureau

Through its News Bureau Indiana University cooperates with the Voice of America in providing materials for broadcast from its foreign students who have been favorably impressed with the American way of life. It also cooperates in furnishing the various cultural offices throughout the world in providing publicity to the home country about students enrolled on the campus here.

Activities in Community

A large number of local organizations, through their efforts, have developed programs designed to open their homes to foreign visitors, not only during the holidays, but throughout the year. To mention a few, the Rotary Club entertains at luncheon between twenty-five and thirty students a year, the Methodist church Men's Class holds a yearly dinner for the foreign students, the League of Women Voters invites large numbers of foreign students to their homes for dinners and social gatherings as do members of the Business and Professional Womens Club and several church organizations.

III. Faculty Activity
1. *Introduction*

An American university is known, judged, and recognized in this country by its athletic teams and by its faculty. Such is not exactly the case when the university's role in world affairs is concerned, because in the eyes of foreign professors and students, even championship basketball or football teams cut no ice. The intellectuals, scholars, and students outside the United States judge a university upon the reputation of its faculty, the honors that its members have received, and the contribution to knowledge that its members have made. Many of those attributes considered of primary importance to Americans when discussing universities not only are relegated to no status at all in the eyes of outsiders, but actually harm American higher education.

For that reason those American scholars who publish in foreign journals, or whose works, no matter what the mode of circulation, have received worldwide recognition do a tremendous service to the cause of international peace and understanding. Such men are especially to be encouraged at a time when a universal smear campaign is being waged to show that American universities and the United States in general are without "culture." Only by real—not pseudo—scholarship can such charges be refuted. The intellectual power of the Indiana

University faculty as represented in its scholarly output and social service gives the lie to propaganda slanted to slander American scholarship, and definitely proves that so far as Indiana University is concerned the Mid-West is not completely isolated from the rest of the world and is not without high cultural standards.

Manners and most ideas travel downward, and consequently it is a primary importance for international understanding that American higher education be viewed in a favorable light by academic colleagues across the oceans. If America is to be understood by all, foreign scholars must first come to realize that the United States is not completely populated with cowboys and Indians, and that its universities have much to offer culturally as well as scientifically to Western and Eastern civilizations. For years European scholars have entertained the most absurd conceptions about America and its cultural vacuums, conceptions which our own faculty by the work of its members in library and laboratory are doing much to dispel—conceptions which many "professional" dispensers of cultural sweetness and light are doing much to confirm.

This survey of the faculty's activities in international relations and the reputation that it enjoys among foreign scholars definitely indicates that Indiana University is playing a most vital role in world education, and international learning. Moreover by keeping their intellectual banners high they are bridging the gaps of petty misunderstandings between peoples. The approach for the most part has been on the highest level. After studying what the Indiana University faculty has accomplished, and after reading some of the literature coming from the Carnegie Foundation, one wonders if that motivating force for academic surveys throughout the United States might not profit greatly by making a survey of its own ideals and perhaps of its basic operating techniques. It would appear that the bulk of this faculty had connections with European scholarship long before surveys were deemed by outsiders to be necessary.

2. Method of Study

The entire faculty was [surveyed] in order to discover what roles various individuals had played in world affairs and in international scholarship. In addition faculty members were invited to submit suggestions as to how international cooperation between American scholars and foreigners might be improved.

As is the normal response to circulars, faculty response was spotty with only 95 of the questionnaires being returned. Yet we feel that a greater response would have only strengthened the final conviction that the faculty, through its normal activity, is doing a splendid job of fostering international understanding. This assumption is based on the fact that many scholars who have accomplished much in international scholarship failed to forward information about themselves to the committee. If they feel slighted that their fields have been overlooked, the fault rests with them and not with this committee. For a few outstanding scholars we studied the yearly reports of faculty publications and the progress reports in the University files. These latter sources of information indicate that considerable information which would have been pertinent to this report never reached the committee's hands. Nevertheless we are of the opinion that such material would have confirmed our general conclusions rather than have contradicted them.

3. Honors

Members of the Indiana University faculty have received honors ranging from a Nobel Prize to election in the most exclusive honorary organizations. Sixty-three foreign elective honorary societies in 22 countries have Indiana

University faculty on their membership roles. As is to be suspected, some of our more distinguished members have been elected to more than one society, but this is compensated by the fact that many societies have honored more than one Indiana professor. In a couple of cases Indiana University had the distinction of having one of its faculty being the only person in the United States so recognized. The following foreign elective honorary societies have at least one of the Indiana University faculty in their membership. The list shows in part the overall spread of honors among the various academic disciplines.

. . . .

Travel

Over 75 members of the faculty have traveled outside the territorial limits of the United States for professional reasons. An even larger number have traveled for pleasure. There is no continent that has not been visited by some member of the Indiana staff on one pretext or another. No attempt has been made in this report to calculate the numbers of persons who have traveled abroad under the auspices of the Armed Services. Many other members of the faculty have gone abroad to serve the nation in civil capacities. Usually, however, the trip is made to widen the horizons of the faculty member and to carry on research. The cost of travel is the greatest deterrent to greater faculty participation.

The University has acted most wisely with a liberal sabbatical leave policy which has made it possible for the faculty to accept Fulbright grants and other types of assistance. Greater encouragement to research abroad might be achieved by allowing professors in the upper academic ranks to be eligible for summer research and travel grants.

Spread of Information by Faculty

Faculty returning from abroad ordinarily give one or two speeches about their travels, and then stop. It is apparent that more along this line could be accomplished in fostering international relations and understanding. It is most unfortunate that returning scholars rarely give a speech outside of Bloomington, and one can be almost sure that one speech will be to a faculty group.

Perhaps the various publicity agencies and speakers' bureaus could do more to line up speeches outside Bloomington. People who have lived abroad could do much to brush away American misunderstandings about the areas of the world wherein the faculty member has been a resident. Such a member of the faculty could do much to correct false statements by the press and by the politicians.

IV. Conclusions and Recommendations

The Committee concludes that interest in international understanding is high at Indiana University, and that much commendable activity is being conducted to increase this understanding. It has indeed been a revelation to the members of the Committee to view the magnitude of the curriculum, campus activity, and faculty effort devoted to subjects that further the cause of international understanding. The following recommendations are offered as a means of further promoting our efficiency in this field.

1. It is recommended that a standing all-university committee be set up to give continuous scrutiny to the problem of training students, broadening scholarship, and fostering understanding in the field of international affairs. This committee might consider: (a) the establishment of a sub-committee to coordinate curriculum so as to provide an inter-departmental specialization in international

relations, at the graduate or undergraduate levels, or both; (b) recommendations to a committee on overall supervision of university curriculum, new curricular developments that might strengthen our offerings in this area; (c) broadening the means of contact between our own staff and foreign scholars and statesmen who visit our campus.

2. It is recommended that consideration be given to the suggestion that university funds might be made available to faculty members on leave with pay in a foreign country to travel to an international professional meeting, on a basis similar to that on which faculty members at home are aided in travel to their professional meetings; and that funds that may be available for summer research and travel be granted to faculty members of all ranks, particularly when foreign study and research are involved.

> MISS JULIA ABEL
> DEAN J. W. ASHTON
> PROFESSOR V. L. BENES
> DEAN L. R. DOWLING
> MR. PHILIP DUNCAN
> PROFESSOR CARL G. F. FRANZEN
> PROFESSOR H. L. JOHNSON
> PROFESSOR JOHN J. MURRAY
> MR. W. G. PINNELL
> PROFESSOR S. E. BRADEN,
> Chairman

4. Mr. Braden presented a report of the International Relations Survey Committee which included the following recommendations and (seconded by Mr. Fuchs) MOVED THAT THE REPORT BE ADOPTED.

(a) It is recommended that a standing all-university committee be set up to give continuous scrutiny to the problem of training students, broadening scholarship, and fostering understanding in the field of international affairs. This committee might consider: (1) the establishment of a subcommittee to coordinate curriculum so as to provide an interdepartmental specialization in international relations, at the graduate or undergraduate levels, or both; (2) recommendations to the University Committee on Curricular Policies and Educational Programs, new curricular developments that might strengthen our offerings in this area; (3) broadening the means of contact between our own staff and foreign scholars and statesmen who visit our campus.

(b) It is recommended that consideration be given to the suggestion that funds might be made available to faculty members on leave with pay in a foreign country to travel to an international professional meeting, on a basis similar to that on which faculty members at home are aided in travel to their professional meetings; and that funds may be available for summer research and travel be granted to faculty members of all ranks, particularly when foreign study and research are involved.

Mr. Braden stated that the report had been circulated to more than 100 institutions which have been making similar studies. The following is a résumé of the questions and comments on the report.

Q., Pratt: To what extent does the average student have contact with the activities discussed in this report?

A., Braden: The committee was made up of representatives of several departments and schools which take part in such activities, and it is presumed that students in those areas have some contact with the problem. All professional fields should be represented.

President Wells: Future studies should give special attention to this aspect of the problem. Steps should be taken to call the attention of students to it and to urge each student to consider taking at least one course bearing on it.

Q., Pratt: How does the University stand with respect to the recommendation that funds be made available for more extended travel for faculty members who are already in foreign countries?

A., Collins: No regular University funds are now available for travel outside the United States. The University Foundation has provided aid for such travel in a few instances, and its literature seeking funds points out this need. It is difficult to convince the public of the propriety of providing funds for travel of this kind.

President Wells: Travel outside the state at state expense is prohibited except on special permission of the Governor. The delegation of this authority by the Governor to the President of the University provides a considerable freedom of action.

Wright: More extensive exchange of faculty members with other countries would be very desirable. Other universities have done this to a certain extent. The visit of several educators from Iran to this University during the first semester of this year has been very profitable. It should be possible for us to send representatives there.

Braden: Mr. Stassen has said that the Foreign Operations Administration intends to sponsor exchanges of faculty and students, but at present the plan seems to apply only to technological fields. The foreign student orientation programs, one of which was held here last summer, are giving good results.

The thoroughness and clarity of the report were highly commended by all who discussed it. A few minor changes in wording were approved, and THE MOTION, AMENDED TO PROVIDE THAT THE REPORT BE DISTRIBUTED TO THE FACULTY, WAS PASSED UNANIMOUSLY.

Faculty Council Minutes, 1953–55, pp. 102–107, 117–119, 122–123, 129–130.

Document 178

The Junior Division, a Reassessment

This extensive review of the functions and achievements of the Junior Division deals with more than mere curricular matters. To a large extent the report reviews the internal relations of faculty and students in a feverish period of university expansion when the ideals expressed so hopefully in 1942 were almost lost sight of in an era of rapid changes.

*   *   *

2. Dean Sikes presented the attached report of the Junior Division and asked for instructions as to further procedure. In conformity with the apparent wishes of the Council, he proceeded to discuss parts of the report orally with the aid of charts and maps. Questions and comments were invited at any appropriate point.

The original purposes and functions of the Junior Division (page 4 of the report) were outlined. In reply to a question (Sauvain) as to which of the purposes had proved to be most important, he said that it was probably the counseling aspect.

Testing and Counseling. The program of testing already in use in 1942 has been expanded by the addition of placement tests in English composition, foreign language, and music theory, and one in mathematics is to be added next year. These tests are strictly for the purpose of guidance. Only the one in English composition results in the requirement of a noncredit course.

Terminal courses. Questions were asked (Norman Batchelder) as to the extent of the program for students who expect to remain in the University for only a year or two.

During the war period many short terminal curricula were set up. Some of these were under the direction of the Junior Division. The heavy enrollments following the war drew attention away from the special curricula and since 1945 little has been done toward developing them. Information distributed to students does, however, make it clear that the Junior Division will assist them in planning such programs. A Student engaging in such a program may remain in the Junior Division for two years. Except for the secretarial training program, probably not more than one percent of the students are involved in the short curricula.

Dean Collins spoke of the additional advisory function of making it clear to the student that if he later wishes to change from one of the special programs to a degree program he may find himself in arrears in certain requirements.

Removing Deficiencies. One example of aid to students in making up deficiencies is the reading clinic. Those who make low scores in the reading test are advised to take the 2-hour credit course in the clinic. A student making a low score in the English composition placement test is required to take a remedial course without credit. Beyond this, deficiencies are made up in such subjects as mathematics or foreign language on the basis of individual counseling.

Dean Waggoner asked if it would not be a good thing to have a University policy as to whether credit be given for courses taken to make up such deficiencies.

Dean Sikes replied that such a policy would be good, but that we do not now have adequate testing machinery for implementing such a policy. It is much easier to persuade a student to begin at a point where he will earn credit than to require him to take a course without credit.

Admission Requirements. The provision made in 1942, admitting to the University any student graduating from an accredited high school, was changed in 1946 to require a student graduating in the lower half of his class to come to the University for preadmission testing and counseling. Students from other states must, in general, be in the upper third of their classes.

In reply to a series of questions by Professor Work, Dean Sikes, said that, in actual practice, in-state students are not refused entrance on the basis of their class standing. The psychological effect of the procedure, however, is good. Some very able students are, for one reason or another, in the lower half of their high school classes. If they are made to see that the opportunity for higher education is a privilege, this is often sufficient incentive to cause them to succeed.

Theoretically a student in the lower half of his class cannot enter the University unless he comes for the preadmission tests and counseling, and most of them comply. In practice, however, some may come without meeting this requirement, but they are placed on a check list for special counseling and warning.

Study of Academic Problems of Freshmen and Improvement of Teaching. The Junior Division acts as a clearing house for information which might lead to the improvement of teaching of first-year students. Information coming from students and parents is passed on to the various departments and divisions. It is difficult to evaluate the effect of this activity except to note the creation of certain new courses, such as those in Physics, Biology, and Literature. Many good ideas about teaching come from the high school principals' conference and from the conferences of teachers of science, home economics, etc.

Q., Batchelder: We have been concerned because we have fewer students attending college in Indiana than have our neighboring states. Is there any evidence that the lack of junior colleges which would provide terminal programs may be partly responsible for this?

A., Sikes: I have no evidence except my own observations, but I think that is perhaps true. Dean Wright's report shows that states with many junior colleges have many students who go to college. I think they are more inclined to set up terminal courses than we are.

Organization. A chart was used to explain the organization of the Junior Division and its relations to other parts of the University. There are about 70 counselors, selected from various divisions. Other details of organization and procedure are given on pages 5 to 11 of the report.

Contacts with High Schools. One of the important functions of the Junior Division is to make high school students, counselors, and principals acquainted with the University. Other divisions make contacts with the high schools, but it is a special responsibility of the Junior Division to see that principals know how to go about approaching the University and what its entrance requirements are. Charts were used to show how this is accomplished.

Career days and college days provide opportunity for visits. Most schools do not welcome visits from college representatives to meet seniors except by appointment. Many arrange for a College Day and invite representatives of all colleges. Sometimes county college days or joint college days of two or more schools are arranged. Our representatives are often invited to college days outside the State. The popularity of college days is increasing, and some principals write for advice on how to plan such activities. When once established, they tend to continue year after year.

Charts and maps were used to show also the extent of visitation by faculty members outside the Junior Division.

In the larger schools we have practically 100% contact with the seniors. In the smaller schools our contacts are less effective. Some reject our offers to send representatives; some do not even reply. Of the students matriculating in 1953, 86% had had opportunity to visit with somone from the University.

High School Football Day, when students are invited to the campus to attend a football game at a reduced admission rate, is arranged cooperatively by the Junior Division, the Department of Athletics, and the News Bureau. On High School Day, in May of each year, juniors and seniors are invited to visit the University. Many groups of students, students and parents, senior classes, etc., add to the total number of visits during the year.

Many principals ask the Junior Division to secure speakers for convocations. Certain departments, Geology, for example, offer their services in supplying speakers for various high school occasions. An information desk is maintained in connection with the annual exhibit at the State Fair.

High School Preparation. Charts were shown giving data on smoke-ups, honor students, certifications, and various tests. There is little evidence to support the statement sometimes made that the less rigid entrance requirements have lowered the quality of our students. In terms of high school subjects taken there is very little difference between the students who entered in 1939 and those who entered in 1953. There is also little difference in pattern of high school program between honor students and failing students. The student most likely to succeed and be certified out of the Junior Division is in the upper half of his high school class and in the upper third of the ACE decile test.

Data on the performance of students entering in 1947 show that the heaviest losses occur before the third semester. These figures, which are near the national norm, are encouraging. The drop-out from college has not been so large as some have thought. Investigation of individual cases have shown that a substantial number of those who have dropped out had good reasons for doing so. Some were interested in courses not given here, some changed to colleges nearer home, some of the girls married, some of the boys were drafted, etc.

Orientation. The activities of orientation week and the purposes of the orientation program were outlined. This program is intended to make the student acquainted with the campus and buildings and to get as much information as possible about him so that the work of counseling can be done efficiently. Tests are given, and the information about the student is assembled so that it will be available to the counselor. There are many activities. The student has opportunity to meet deans and faculty members.

Q., Waggoner: Would it be fair to say that some students are left with the impression that it is rather indecent not to have made up their minds what their eventual vocations will be by the end of the orientation period?

A., Sikes: I think they have that impression when they get here. Maybe we are guilty of intensifying that feeling.

Q., Waggoner: Is it possible to take steps to correct that feeling?

A., Sikes: We have to have some guiding signs. The counselors must be from various divisions of the University and students must be assigned on the basis of their indicated objectives.

Q., Waggoner: Is it assumed that counselors are specialized in only one—their own—field, or do they take some responsibility for knowing the whole University?

A., Sikes: I would say most would be specialized. We take counselors that we can get. I think, on the whole, they are good; but some of them are poor.

Q., Waggoner: Would it be fair to say that, as a result of that system, the student is never exposed to any possibility other than the one that he is brought up with at the time of induction? He has to come to the Junior Division office and make a special demand for non-vocational counseling?

A., Sikes: To the same extent that it is true in talking with teachers. A student talks with his own professors. Counselors are professors doing something else. Frankly, I would like very much to have the best counselor we have to be the only kind of counselor we have.

Bucher: The emphasis on counseling in high school is to get the boy to decide what he wants to do before he graduates. When we talk to them, one third of them are undecided. We start out with sessions on general matters. During the day they speak to various deans. At 2:30 they must make up their minds. We try not to make a boy or girl decide that he must do this, that or the other.

Further questions and answers emphasized the fact that, although it may not be desirable, there is a considerable amount of pressure on the student to decide on his more or less exact objective before he enrolls in classes for the first semester. Certain curricula practically demand it.

Q., Sauvain: Then we are making a mistake in allowing special fields to extend their curricular requirements into the freshman year? Wasn't it the theory that the Junior Division was to have a general program of study where students would not be committed to any specialization?

A., Sikes: I don't see how that could have been if I understand the provisions of the resolution. Maybe that should be incorporated, but you have to plan programs fitted for the different upper divisions, and the resolution provides that the upper divisions will make their own requirements.

Further discussion revealed a considerable amount of dissatisfaction with this aspect of the working of the Junior Division. Dean Wright reminded the Council that the Junior Division was established for the guidance and counseling and not as a curricular division. President Wells also pointed out that the main difference of opinion at the time of the founding of the Junior Division was on this point and that the idea of a common ground for first-year students lost out. Dean Waggoner expressed the opinion that this would be an appropriate time to reopen the question.

By consent, it was agreed that further discussion of the Junior Division be deferred until the next meeting.

PREFACE

In presenting this written report certain explanatory statements should be made in order that it might be better understood. Although the outline is rather complete and detailed, a comprehensive development of it would take more space than we felt we should use for the purpose of the report. We develop, therefore, only certain parts of the outline in the text. These are indicated in the outline by CAPITALS.

Another point is that the report was worked out primarily for oral presentation. Hence some of the material is not available to the reader because it is shown by means of charts, maps, and graphs which do not accompany the text.

We begin this report by summarizing the purposes and functions of the Junior Division, as set forth in the resolution creating it. The burden of the report thereafter is to show to what extent, or in what manner, these purposes and functions have been accomplished.

In order to keep the report within reasonable limits, summary and sampling methods are used. We hope one hearing or reading this report will have a better understanding of the extent and variety of services performed by this division of the University.

April 27, 1954   P. S. SIKES, Dean

REPORT OF THE JUNIOR DIVISION TO THE FACULTY COUNCIL
Outline of purposes, functions, and activities

PREFACE
I PURPOSES AND FUNCTIONS
   A. STATEMENT OF PURPOSES FROM CHARTER
   B. STATEMENT OF FUNCTIONS FROM CHARTER
II ORGANIZATION
   A. ADMINISTRATIVE
      1. DUTIES
   B. CLERICAL
      1. REPRESENTATIVE ACTIVITIES

III ACTIVITIES OF THE JUNIOR DIVISION
   A. High School Relations and Pre-college Counseling
      1. VISITATION AND COLLEGE DAY ACTIVITY
      2. High School—Football Day
      3. High School Day
      4. On campus visits
      5. Pre-admission counseling
      6. Get-Acquainted meeting
      7. Talks to senior classes and convocations
      8. State Fair information desk
   B. Freshman Counseling
      1. Orientation
      2. FACULTY COUNSELING
         a. PROGRAM PLANNING
         b. PROGRESS CONFERENCE
      3. HIGH SCHOOL-JUNIOR DIVISION CONFERENCE
         a. OUTGROWTHS
      4. Probation counseling
      5. SUPERIOR STUDENT COUNSELING
      6. Absence counseling
      7. Interim counseling
         a. Problem counseling
         b. Miscellaneous counseling
      8. TERMINAL AND SPECIAL PROGRAMS
   C. Study and Research
      1. HIGH SCHOOL PREPARATION
         a. ARTS AND SCIENCES STUDENTS
         b. INDIANA UNIVERSITY FRESHMEN
      2. PLACEMENT OF FRESHMEN AT PROPER ACADEMIC LEVEL
         a. ENGLISH COMPOSITION
         b. FOREIGN LANGUAGE
         c. MATHEMATICS
         d. MUSIC THEORY
      3. STUDENT DEFICIENCIES
         a. READING
         b. SPEECH AND HEARING
      4. FACULTY-STUDENT RELATIONS
         a. REPORT ON X COURSE
      5. VISITATION
         a. COVERAGE (see chart)
      6. Pre-admission
      7. CURRICULUM
   D. Publications
      1. *Junior Division Notes*
      2. *Courses Open to Freshmen*
      3. *Junior Division Counselor*
IV PLANS FOR THE FUTURE
   A. IMPROVEMENTS IN COUNSELING
   B. ATTRACTION AND RETENTION OF SUPERIOR STUDENTS
   C. CURRICULUM DEVELOPMENT

I—A PURPOSES

In the resolution creating the Junior Division the following purposes were described:

1. To improve and enlarge the guidance and testing program for first-year students.
2. To plan more adequate curricula for students who expect to remain in the University only one or two years.
3. To assist students to make up deficiencies.
4. To provide uniform entrance requirements to the University.
5. To act as a clearing house for information that might lead to improving the teaching of first-year students.
6. To study curricula and academic problems of freshman students and make recommendations.

I—B FUNCTIONS

Functions in addition to routine matriculation, testing, counseling, etc., mentioned in the resolution were:

1. To discover defects and deficiencies in students that impede their progress, and to provide means of removing these as speedily as possible.
2. To arrange with the various schools for one and two-year curricula which meet the needs of students who are unable or who do not wish to work for a degree.
3. To assist in placement of students at the proper instructional levels and to facilitate the offering, to exceptionally well qualified and well prepared students, of opportunities to demonstrate by examination that they have mastery of certain subjects and thereby enable them to earn credit by such examination or be excused from taking courses that otherwise would be required.
4. To arrange examinations to test students' interests and aptitudes and to encourage students to take such tests.
5. To cooperate with the schools in improving the teaching of first-year students and in developing courses that are designed for freshman students.
6. To cooperate with the schools in studying critically the requirements for entrance into the University, and the requirements that schools may establish for admission into their sophomore classes.

II—A—1 ORGANIZATION

Administrative

As presently organized the division has a dean, assistant dean, four assistants to the dean, an advisory board of ten faculty members, and seventy faculty counselors.

While a listing of all the functions of each of these would require more space than is permitted here, a discussion of some of their principal duties may be informative.

The assistant dean is charged with primary responsibility for orientation, High-School–Junior Division Conference and high school visitation, all of which will be described more fully in later sections. In the last named enterprise he has first call on the services of one of the assistants to the dean who is expected to devote a major portion of his time to high school visitation.

The assistants to the dean serve as liaison agents with the upper divisions, counsel pre-admission students, counsel with prospective students and their parents on visits to the campus, authorize class withdrawals and withdrawals from school. In addition they initiate and carry out research, edit Junior Division publications, assign counselees, and serve as academic counselors for special students and sophomores who fail to certify to an upper division but are eligible to remain in school.

The advisory board is consulted on all matters which relate to the Junior Division at the policy level. They have proved an invaluable aid to the division in its twelve years of existence.

The role of the faculty counselors will be discussed in a later section.

III–C–7

Curriculum

As a measure designed to encourage the work of the superior student and result in an enriched curriculum for the students involved, the Junior Division is supporting research to evolve a plan whereby students may establish credit for college level work satisfactorily completed in high school.

The general pattern up to now has been a four-year under-graduate program for a degree. Only in English composition by rule and in mathematics and foreign languages on the basis of counseling, do many students take courses for which they can get no credit. In the College of Arts and Sciences a superior student with a good high school background might secure as much as thirty hours of exemption but nevertheless would have to do the full four years or 120 hours of work. The Junior Division is now supporting a proposal in the College whereby students can secure credit for certain courses and thus lessen the number of hours required to be taken. We believe that with our experience in English and foreign language testing as much as nineteen hours credit could well be given here.

The development of courses designed for first-year students has been considerable in scope but gradual in its growth.

The High School–Junior Division Conference, office conferences with individual students, especially those with superior students, conference reports of faculty counselors, and direct contacts with deans, department heads, and teaching personnel are some of the sources of ideas for curriculum development. Specific courses such as Physics P100, Biology B100, Geology G100, English W100, and Freshman Literature, are examples of courses developed where there was evidence of a specific need. The change in the regulation for Chemistry C101 as a preparation for C106 was recommended by the Junior Division.

IV.   PLANS FOR THE FUTURE

Improvement of Counseling

In high schools everywhere students are being told by teachers and by representatives of small colleges that the small college is preferable; that in large universities they do not get personal attention. This attitude deprives us of many excellent students. We believe the Junior Division is the best "antidote" for this kind of poison. We further believe that the principal ingredient in this antidote is good counseling and good student-faculty relations. An actual, not just assigned, confidential academic adviser for every freshman student will be our goal for the future. We suggest that in addition to "teaching and research" as measures of the competent teacher "counseling", either formal or informal, should also be more generally recognized. A teacher is justifiably given a lighter class load to allow time for writing and research; in like manner a teacher who is a good counselor might reasonably be allowed time for counseling and also be rewarded for success as a teacher and counselor.

Attraction and Retention of Superior Students

In the final analysis much of the future greatness of Indiana University will derive from the superior students we are able to attract for matriculation and graduation. Accordingly, we set forth for ourselves a fourfold purpose regarding superior students.

Our first aim is to attract the superior high school student to the University. By identifying for him the advantages of the University, indicating to him our special interest in and provision for his individual progress, and encouraging his matriculation by means of scholarship aid, we hope to continue to attract in ever-increasing numbers outstanding high school graduates. Secondly, by methods described in the section on the superior student we plan to identify for the student, for ourselves, and for the faculty those students who are capable of superior academic work. In addition, we think it is highly important that superior students be assigned to recognized superior and challenging teachers. In this way superior teachers would be recognized and encouraged as well. The fourth aim of this program, which is a result of the other three, is to increase the retention of superior students in the University and improve the quality of their work.

Curriculum Development

In this area we plan to continue our research on the development of new courses for freshmen, changes in curriculum and academic requirements, and the granting of credit for college level work successfully completed in high school. In all of these we will, as we have in the past, proceed with caution and in full cooperation with the other divisions of the University each of which is equally concerned with these developments.

In conclusion we should like to raise the question of whether or not we should be satisfied with the education that our graduates receive. Many of us are prone to criticize high schools for graduating and sending to us students unprepared for college, but are we willing to assume that there is a basic education that a person should have to enter college but none for one to have to graduate from college? I have observed that in our most recent graduating group (February 1954) people were awarded A. B. degrees, who, in high school and in college, had never had a course in a physical science. In an atomic and electronics age one may wonder if these graduates have been educated. Perhaps a study should be made of the actual records of graduates to see if there are "gaps" in the training of our final product.

Committee on Faculty-Student Relations
Report for 1952–54

April 8, 1954

To the President, Faculty, and Student Senate:

The Committee on Faculty-Student Relations has submitted two previous summaries of its work covering, respectively, the calendar years 1950 and 1951. This report is designed to bring the record down to date and to furnish a precedent for future reports in the spring of each year.

The first report of the Committee recognized three principal areas in which work might be done to improve faculty-student relations: (1) informal personal contacts between faculty and students; (2) serious intellectual exchange among faculty and students in addition to that for which the curriculum provides; and

(3) policies and practices of the University and its faculty which give rise to student misunderstanding or dissatisfaction. To these areas a fourth might be added in the light of subsequent experience: (4) conditions in the University community which impede satisfactory student-faculty relations.

General Conditions

The general state of affairs with respect to faculty-student relations has altered and probably has improved in significant ways since the Committee was established. These changes have resulted only in part from the Committee's efforts; but it is believed that the Committee has made substantial contributions at various points. If nothing more, the existence of the Committee and publicity concerning its activities have helped to create awareness of faculty-student relations as a significant aspect of University life. As a result, faculty-student panels for the discussion of various issues have become more common; joint student-faculty committees, both official and unofficial, have increased in number; and projects have arisen for bringing students and faculty together informally. Noteworthy among developments in the latter category are the recent practice of the Student Senate and Union Board of inviting members of the faculty to meet with them from time to time. The Committee understands the Indiana University chapter of the American Association of University Professors is initiating a meeting at which its committee on academic freedom will discuss that subject with interested student leaders. The Committee on Faculty-Student Relations of the Union has promoted a series of teas for the faculty of selected University departments and their students during the present academic year. All told, more students are coming in contact with more faculty members on a personal basis now than at any previous time since World War II.

An important development during the present year has been the adoption by the Faculty Council of a policy of having the president of the Student Body and other representatives of the Student Senate participate in its deliberations upon broad categories of subject matter which are deemed important to students. The Committee welcomes this development and recognizes that fundamental changes in the Committee's own functions may come about as a result.

The Committee's Functions

In the past, the Committee has functioned in three principal ways: (1) by conducting certain projects of its own which promised to be helpful in building better student-faculty relations, such as faculty participation in the Fall Carnival, the circulation of a questionnaire to determine the availability of faculty members for various kinds of activities with students, and the conduct of panels to discuss student-faculty relations before incoming freshmen during the orientation period; (2) by considering grievances presented to it and promoting changes in policies and practice on the campus to eliminate causes of dissatisfaction; and (3) by considering problems referred to the Committee from official sources, principally the Faculty Council and the Student Senate. The growing importance of the Student Senate and the collaboration between its president and the Faculty Council may tend to shift some of the matters arising in the last two ways into other channels.

The Committee has met regularly once a month during the academic year and has had additional special meetings when the need has arisen. Subcommittees have handled numerous problems through meetings of their own, as well as otherwise.

Committee Projects

We believe the Committee's Fall Carnival project should now be transferred to other hands, since the Committee lacks funds and personnel with which to carry it on. Accordingly, the Men's and Women's Faculty Clubs have been asked to take over the project, beginning in the fall of 1954. It is hoped that they will consent to do so.

In February of this year the Junior Division incorporated the Committee's faculty-student relations panels into orientation discussions on various aspects of the University, which it presented to incoming students. Although the Committee believes there is danger of formality in sessions of this type which may be inconsistent with the purpose of the panels, it agrees that official provision by the Junior Division for the discussion of faculty-student relations during orientation week is desirable, and it will continue to assist in this project so far as feasible.

The Committee's questionnaire to faculty members was circulated a second time toward the end of the first semester of this year. The response has been gratifying and the Committee at this writing is engaged in promoting the use of the questionnaire by student organizations that may desire faculty participation or assistance in various ways. It is hoped that new methods of promotion now being adopted will be more successful than those that were tried in the past.

Problems Dealt With

   a. *Suggestions for Official Action*

A number of requests for aid in procuring official action desired by students have received Committee consideration and in several instances have led to Committee proposals that have been accepted. As the result of a Committee proposal in 1952, a regular practice of announcing the spring final examination schedule in advance of the spring vacation was inaugurated. Also in 1952, the Committee was able to suggest new arrangements for Senior Class Day, so as to avoid both a "cut day," which had become objectionable to the Faculty, and discrimination in the treatment accorded to February and June classes in this regard. The suggested arrangements were approved by the Faculty Council. During the present academic year, as a result of a Committee suggestion, the University Library adopted a procedure which will enable advanced undergraduate students to gain access to the stacks in proper cases more readily than before.

In early 1953 the Faculty Council referred to the Committee certain suggestions which had been presented by the Student Senate for advancing the date of the June Commencement. The Committee held several meetings with regard to this problem, at which interested students and others appeared. It became evident that the time of Commencement could not be advanced without postponing or abolishing final examinations or withholding degrees until after Commencement. The Committee did not favor abolishing finals for Seniors and no one wanted a Commencement without bestowal of degrees. The Committee therefore recommended that a change be made only as the time needed for recording grades and printing the Commencement program might be shortened. The matter has rested there.

Also in early 1953, the Committee considered objections raised by student groups, including the Student Senate, to a change which the Faculty Council had adopted in the schedule for enrollment. Student objection was directed less to the change itself than to its adoption without prior consultation with students. The Committee suggested that the Council regard the change as experimental, subject to reconsideration in the light of student comment upon the operation of the new plan. This solution proved acceptable, and the Faculty Council took action accordingly. The new arrangement appears to have been successful.

b. *Larger Problems Handled*

Early in 1952, following the resignation of coach Clyde Smith, the Committee took note of campus-wide discussion, accompanied by considerable dissatisfaction, concerning the method of formulating University athletic policy. The Committee concluded that greater student participation in the formulation of policy and more definite assumption of responsibility by the Faculty Council would be desirable. It communicated these views to all of the interested groups. They were considered by the Council and appear to have contributed to the establishment of the present practice of written reports by the Committee on Athletics to the Council.

In the same year the Committee commenced consideration of the problem of cheating in student work at Indiana University, which was referred to it by the Faculty Council. The Council acted both on its own initiative and as a result of suggestions from the Student Senate. Through a subcommittee, the Committee conducted an inquiry which led to a report by the Committee in the spring of 1953. That report recommended steps to be taken by the Faculty Council and the Student Senate to improve the situation, which was found to be greatly in need of betterment. As a result, a new rule for handling cases of cheating has now been adopted by the Council. The Committee will continue to concern itself with this problem and to urge further steps toward its solution. In particular the assumption of greater student responsibility in the matter seems desirable.

c. *Continuing Problems*

Despite frequent attempts, the Committee has made relatively little progress in promoting intellectual exchange among faculty and students outside of the curriculum. Lectures and other discussions on the campus continue to be attended, on the whole, principally by faculty members and limited numbers of students in the sponsoring departments. Convocations and other all-University events, even when more largely attended, are not integrated into further discussions, except occasionally upon the initiative of the instructor in a course. The English Department's weekly readings from literature given in the Union Building, have, however, made a notable contribution to campus life during the past two years. Some housing units conduct early-evening discussions from time to time, with faculty members participating; and a principal purpose of the Committee's faculty questionnaire has been to encourage the use of faculty members in this way. The Committee has not found ways to effectuate suggestions in a report of the Student Senate's culture committee, transmitted to it in the fall of 1952, for relating campus lectures and convocations to the work in credit courses. The YMCA has undertaken to continue its promotion of use of the questionnaires.

Recently, campus interest in public affairs has been heightened, perhaps because of the evident importance of international developments and of dramatic political occurrences within the country. The columns of the Daily Student have been devoted to such matters to a greater degree than before and organized student discussions, with or without faculty participation, have developed. It remains to be seen whether this tendency is more than temporary and whether it can survive in the face of the preoccupation of the University community with specialized studies and, on the part of students, with conventional extra-curricular activities.

The Committee has had under consideration a proposal by one of its present members, Professor J. Albert Robbins, that a seminar for the discussion of current problems, admission to which should be by invitation, be established in the University. So far, difficulty in finding a way to sponsor and administer such a seminar has prevented launching the plan. The Committee favors it, however, and will continue to seek ways to place it in effect.

As a result of a proposal made by two graduating students two years ago, the possibility of an orientation course for incoming freshmen remains under consideration. It clearly would be desirable to increase the student's understanding of his new environment and his place in it, and a subcommittee which has been conducting a study of this matter hopes to consider a specific plan in the near future. Approval of such a plan will be dependent upon a promise of sufficient content for the course to justify requiring the time and effort of entering students for it.

The Committee has considered on two occasions problems created by the three-fold character of the Daily Student as the single printed medium for the continuous exchange of news and opinion on the campus, a laboratory for students of Journalism, and a publication officially sponsored by the University. Student and faculty interest in the freedom and responsibility of the publishers and in the reflection of the University community by the paper have been continuous. A subcommittee which conducted a survey during the summer of 1952 of the arrangements surrounding student newspapers at a number of other institutions rendered a report that suggested the desirability of an advisory committee on general policy, representative of the campus community, with which the publishers might keep in touch. Discussion at a meeting of the Committee with Daily Student personnel early in 1953 brought forth no prospect that an acceptable plan might be evolved, and the Committee took no action upon its subcommittee's report.

For more than two years the Committee has been concerned with the problem of smoking in University buildings, which originally came to it as a result of a request of the Director of Libraries for assistance in enforcing the rule applicable to the Main Library. The Committee has been convinced that a prerequisite to enforcement is the adoption of regulations that make provision for smoking in designated portions of University buildings where pollution of the air is not a problem and the fire hazard can be controlled. Confusion as to the respective responsibilities of the University and the State Fire Marshal in adopting regulations has persisted, and no progress has been made except in the Library through the efforts of the library staff. A subcommittee is now working with the University Committee on Safety on this problem, however, and it is hoped that regulations which the University can adopt on its own responsibility may result. They should be considered by both the Faculty Council and the Student Senate before being placed in effect.

Conclusions

In so large and varied an institution as a major state university the problem of maintaining the most fruitful relations that are feasible between faculty and students will be a continuing one. The existence of such relations is dependent upon the quality of all that is done and said in the University. A committee which is instructed to devote itself to something designated as faculty-student relations can only put in an oar from time to time where there is promise of some progress toward the ultimate goal as a result. No logical basis exists upon which matters appropriate to the concern of such a committee may be distinguished from those that are not appropriate; and shifts will necessarily occur as changes take place elsewhere. The Committee can only continue to use its best judgment as to where it may be helpful and to deal as best it may with problems that are referred to it. This the Committee proposes to do so long as its charge continues.

Respectfully submitted,

JAMES ALLTOP
DAN BAUMAN
MARY BRANSON
BETTY BUCHANAN
DOTTIE EVERDON
CAROL HUDSON
DON DURFEES
KAREN LENTZ
CHARLES RAU
CONSTANCE ROGERS
RODERICK TURNER, Student Chairman

AGNES ANDERSON
W. R. BRENEMAN
J. R. ENDWRIGHT
WINIFRED MERRILL
R. W. RICHEY
J. A. ROBBINS, JR.
EUNICE C. ROBERTS
R. H. SHAFFER
L. L. WATERS
J. A. WORK
RALPH F. FUCHS, Chairman

Faculty Council Minutes, 1953–55, pp. 138–145, 160–161, 161–166.

Document 179

The Junior Division in Extenso

This document comes to grip with the philosophical implications involved in the ideals and curriculum of this more directly personal branch of Indiana University's instructional system. In its final recommendations the committee predicted success for the Division provided it answered several fundamental "ifs."

*   *   *

Report of the Faculty Council's Committee
on the Junior Division

May 4, 1954

The Problem

"To examine the functions of the Junior Division," as we were charged with doing in March 1952, is to see first-hand the huge potentialities and problems of democratic education in the American state university. Our Junior Division is the focal point of an operation which brings hundreds of young people from a variety of domestic and educational backgrounds into the great diversity of academic and other activities provided by Indiana University. This problem—which will become even larger in the years ahead—can be solved only by expert organization which establishes the main lines of procedure in guiding large numbers of students and at the same time allows the maximum of careful attention to individual cases. Obviously all aspects of the University have an immense responsibility here, not only in terms of the welfare of the University and its students, but ultimately in respect to the professional and other needs—that is to day, the future—of our American society.

Our Position

The Committee wishes to make its general attitude clear. The Junior Division is pursuing vigorously its function of developing good working relations with the secondary schools and is also striving to derive the maximum value from its present advising system. Some of its achievements will have appeared from Dean Sikes' report on the division which has been presented to the Faculty Council. The Junior Division's awareness of its problems deserves the fullest possible help from the whole University, and our purpose is to make some contribution to this end.

Background

From the self-survey program initiated by President Wells in 1937, there emerged two main ideas concerning organization for entering students. One was the concept of a two-year Junior College with a core curriculum of several survey courses. The other concept was of a one-year Junior Division with emphasis upon counseling; here the notion of core curriculum was put in the background. Amid various complications, a counseling group was established and a committee appointed to organize the Junior Division. The second concept prevailed, and in 1942 the new division was created, substantially after the pattern of the University of Nebraska. The main purpose of the Junior Division was to be counseling.

Thus the idea of core curriculum virtually disappeared. Only a slight vestige of it is to be found in the document "The Indiana University War Service Plan" announcing the creation of the Junior Division and other measures. Here it is stated (p. 9) that two of the purposes of the new division are "To plan more adequate curricula for students who expect to remain in the University only one or two years" and "To study curricula and academic problems of freshman students and make recommendations."[1] It is also stated in this document that if the student "is not certain of his course, the new Division will make it possible for him to explore different fields so that a wiser, final decision may be made." Another function stated (p. 12) is "To cooperate with the schools (i.e. of the University) in improving the teaching of first-year students and in developing courses that are designed for freshman students."

This is sufficient background to explain why there is a substantial residue of faculty feeling that the nature of the Junior Division from its establishment to the present time has not brought full realization of the original hopes. The Committee is convinced that this is a good time to return to the ideal. The need for giving students a comprehensive education is more pressing than ever. A better climate for discussion and action now exists because of changes in the University, including greatly improved understanding between the liberal-arts college and the rest of the University, and the fact that the professional schools have moved more strongly toward the graduate level.

Our Procedure

The membership of the Committee includes representatives from the School of Business, the School of Education, and the College of Arts and Sciences. We have examined the present functions and problems of the Junior Division freely and critically, and then developed our solutions of what seemed to be the most fundamental problems. Representatives of the School of Music and of the School of Health, Physical Education, and Recreation have met with us for very profit-

---

[1] The first purpose was related to a previous experiment, carried on under the direction of Professor Edgar Yeager, which attempted to provide a two-year elective program for those students who had no intention of staying in college more than a year or two. This program gradually dwindled to insignificance because of lack of support and was then discontinued.

able discussions. There were consultations with Dean Sikes who spoke freely of his dissatisfactions and hopes, and with Mr. Strain, Admissions Director. Also, the members of the Committee brought to bear a substantial amount of experience derived from student-advising, work in general education, and a variety of other educational activities. Rather than spending much time on canvasses or similar problems and solutions found on other campuses, we have concentrated on the conditions and possible solutions at Indiana University. Furthermore, we have not been impressed with attempts to solve problems of this kind by reorganizing the university structurally (*e.g.* the creation of a General College) and agreed early in our discussion that we should think in terms of our present organization.

The Committee has assumed that the basic objectives of the Junior Division are (I) to conduct relations with the secondary schools and to provide a proper initial adjustment of students to the University, (II) to maintain a system of guidance, and (III) to introduce students to the curriculum of the University.

I. *Relations with Secondary Schools, Orientation, and Mechanics*

Relations between secondary schools and the University. At various times, relations conducted by the Junior Division have been disturbed by recruiting of students by other divisions of the University. There is feeling that there has been too much emphasis upon the University as a place for weak students, but here there has been improvement recently through the joint efforts of the Junior Division and th Office of Scholarships and Loans.

Introduction of students to the University. It is obvious that the size and strangeness of the University are initial problems for new students. The orientation period must create an atmosphere of congeniality. However, it is equally important that the first impression convey a sense of the dignity appropriate to the University. Further, more important than the initial adjustment is the need to introduce students to the campus in more fundamental ways. Many students leave the University without any clear understanding of its diversity and its unity. Senior students have expressed themselves in favor of an extended orientation program in preference to the present intensive orientation week which leaves them more confused than enlightened.

Mechanics. Although most courses taken by Freshmen are of multiple sections, serious schedule conflicts do occur, and they are particularly upsetting for new students. Entering students sometimes become entangled in and confused by the registration of other students. Admission records and grade-reports have apparently not always been available to Junior Division Counselors at the right time, partially because of factors beyond the control of the Junior Division. There is confusion in the systems of probation and credit-accounting followed by the Junior Division and other divisions of the University.

Recommendations 1-4

On the basis of the preceding considerations, we recommend that:

1. All other divisions of the University observe the principle that the Junior Division is in charge of relationships between the secondary schools and the University conducted with the purpose of interesting potential undergraduate students in the University, and must be informed of all such activities pursued by other divisions;
2. The Junior Division increase its recent efforts in all dealings with secondary schools to represent the University as a source of educational opportunities for a variety of students, particularly the best;
3. The Junior Division, with the cooperation of other divisions, institute on the

Bloomington campus a series of Freshman orientation lectures given weekly at least throughout the fall semester and designed to instruct students concerning such matters as: the structure of the University; the programs and purposes of the various divisions (including attention to professional training at the graduate level) ; the fundamental purposes of the University as a whole (including its relationships to society, the concept of freedom in learning, teaching, and research, etc.) ; campus ethics in relation to administrative officers, faculty members, staff, and fellow-students; and educational opportunities outside the classroom;

(*Comments.* We are much attracted by the potentiality of this idea, but repelled by the necessary mechanics. We are not in favor of a formal course-structure. Perhaps the best procedure is to make such lectures an extension of the required meetings held during the orientation period. As always in such matters, the most important ingredient is to give a group of about six administrative officers and faculty members the substantial amount of time necessary to develop a plan of excellent lectures supported by audio-visual materials. A sub-committee of the Faculty-Student Relations Committee, under Dean Roberts, is now considering such a plan. We wish to give our strong support to this much-needed feature.)

4. The Junior Division maintain constant attention to such mechanics as: developing machinery to ensure that serious schedule conflicts among courses normally taken by Freshmen do not occur; organizing Freshman registration as a part of the orientation program in such a way that confusion with the registration of other students is avoided; ensuring to the maximum that the necessary records and reports are available to Counselors at the right time; eliminating confusion between its systems of probation and credit-accounting, and procedures followed by other divisions of the University.

II. *Advising*

It would be unjust and false to say that the present system does not produce some good advising; there are faithful and effective advisers who put great effort into the function and produce good results. However, we believe that the system is inadequate for the nature and volume of the work, and is, in some respects, wrongly aimed.

There is overlapping and conflict between academic advising and counseling in such unofficial quarters as the halls of residence. Junior Division Counselors are often inadequately informed concerning academic requirements, procedures, the nature of courses, the proper designation of courses, etc. Pre-admission and subsequent information about individual students is not adequately digested and used. Course loads are not sufficiently adjusted to knowledge about students' abilities, outside-work schedules, etc. The Dean of the Junior Division does not have enough authority over the function of counseling to ensure best results. The system is a hurried one in which, from the beginning, students feel a constant urgency of making decisions concerning course of study and objectives before many of them have any way of knowing what the possibilities are or what their interests may be.

The Advisory Board of the Junior Division meets rarely and does not have time to undertake important considerations of policies and procedures, in which it could be of great service to the Dean of the Junior Division, as a group actively working with the problems involved.

Much of this inadequacy, we feel, can be reduced to the fact that Junior Division advising is now an extra function which commands neither sufficient time nor respect and for which only a small honorarium is paid. One possibility is that compensation be increased substantially. However, we do not recommend this change because we hold that counseling should be done by faculty members genuinely interested in doing it, and should be part of the regular academic function of a faculty member—and a very important part; surely faculty members through counseling can exert a more fundamental influence on students than through most other aspects of their academic function.

In contrast to these dissatisfactions, we have heard Dean Sikes' "dream" of having thirty selected faculty advisers on half-time teaching schedules. We fear that it would be difficult to find this many qualified faculty members willing to devote so much of their schedule to advising, and that this system would contain the danger of developing professional guidance work in the academic sphere. The cost of revising the counseling system in this way or in the way recommended below is large. However, the alternatives seem to be to conclude either that enrollment should be restricted or that we are not in a position to do a better job.

Recommendations 5-6

We recommend that:

5. Faculty members be selected as Junior Division Counselors on the basis of having breadth of educational interests and genuine concern for advising, that they perform this function in lieu of two hours of their regular teaching schedule, and that the Dean of the Junior Division have full charge of directing their activities during the allotted time;

   (*Comments.* The Counselors should not function primarily as specialists in a pre-professional or any other sense; there should be relatively few pre-professional issues involved in advising at this level, and these can be well handled by properly chosen Counselors. It would be expected that an average of at least five hours weekly be devoted to advising, study of students' records, etc. Such expenditure of time is necessitated by the real problems of which the first year on campus is especially full; the primary purpose of leading students to develop responsibility is very time-consuming. It should be normal procedure for some of the Counselors to visit high schools. The Dean should be free, not only to see that the allotted time is well used, but also to appraise and criticize the activities of the Counselors, and to ensure that from year to year he has the best group of advisers available. We are assuming that the present number of 80 Counselors will continue, except as it is modified by expected enrollments, and that the change of system recommended could not be in full effect before September 1955.)

6. The Advisory Board of the Junior Division meet regularly (normally at least once a month), and primarily for the consideration of basic Junior Division policies.

III. *Curriculum*

Section A

The Junior Division document, "Suggested Curricula for Three Semesters," gives a picture of typical Freshman course-schedules on our campus. In most cases, there is a fair distribution of basic liberal-arts courses. It is primarily in the fields of Music and HPER that professional courses dominate curricula from the beginning. We can start, then, with the fact that most programs allow a substantial amount of general education, but that there are areas in which curricular patterns are very largely professional. In areas of the latter kind, it is well-nigh impossible to shift from one school to another after the particular program is started in Freshman year. We recognize, of course, that some professional courses contribute to general education, but our point is that such curricula are controlled by professional objectives. Even where pre-professional programs include a number of general-education courses, the latter are often included because it is thought that they contribute to the specialized training in some particular way, not because they are regarded as significant in themselves.

More generally important is the fact that the non-professional education is not organized according to any plan in all-University terms. If one asks the question, "What work is taken in common by all undergraduate students in the University," the answer is, "Two semesters of English Composition and two semesters of physical education."

The committee believes that there is a clear need *for a basic University curriculum*. There is much current concern about the preparation of our students in the high schools; equal concern about the total education received by our students in the University is long overdue. The University has, it seems to us, the responsibility of making sure that all students acquire a few basic skills and are at least introduced to the main areas of knowledge. There is a voluminous literature on this subject of "general education," but we will state our own ideas briefly.

If we think of the new undergraduate student as moving toward the functions of employee, citizen, and individual, a number of thoughts emerge. For this student as employee-to-be, the University is the hub of a number of vocational roads. The student must discover that the various kinds of training are, in which one he is most interested, to which most suited; any inchoate ideas he has when he comes must be clarified and revised. The process of finding the right niche and of developing the maximum ability for that function has an importance which can hardly be exaggerated, whether considered from the standpoint of social utility or of personal satisfaction. For these purposes the student needs all the time and awareness of various fields that can be made available to him.

Further, even this vocational aspect has much broader implications. The distinction frequently drawn between "general" and "special" education breaks down immediately. The expansion of knowledge in the fields represented by the liberal arts and sciences, and the ever-increasing relevance of this knowledge to industrial, professional, and other activities have intensified the interdependence of the various branches of knowledge, production, and service. As one writer put it, "The time has come when a strictly specialized program of study is not good enough even for the specialist as a specialist." This is one set of reasons why many leaders in the most specialized technological and industrial fields are insisting that the employee must be broadly educated. Another recent quotation states: "The need for technically trained people was probably never greater than it is now. At the same time, we were never more aware that technical training is not enough by itself" (Frank Abrams, board chairman of New Jersey Standard).

Since our initial categories of employee, citizen, and individual have already started to flow together, the latter two can be combined. One way to describe our times is in terms of a conflict which is generally applicable to historical situations, but which has now reached a critical stage, the conflict between the traditional and the new or unknown. As citizens and as individuals we are in the middle of ferment. In terms of tradition, there is a great accumulation of what has happened historically, of the insights and values expressed in literature, religion, philosophy, and the arts, of what has been discovered by science, of what has been described and analyzed in the social sciences. At the center is our western-European cultural tradition, a storehouse of ideas, attitudes, and values which must be known in order to understand our own society and which must be re-examined to determine their present validity.

Although America has its historical roots in this tradition and has been molded by it in fundamental ways, the term "American" has an altogether different reference. The term still conveys—we trust—the notion of a great social experiment growing out of the liberal political tradition, and also denotes a high standard of living. However, in many minds both here and elsewhere the term also implies the dangers of materialism and extreme contemporaneity. We unhappily observe in our students a great ignorance of traditional values or perhaps the vague sense that production has solved everything and that they will merely take their places in a society of machines, over which they have no control. It is a little wonder that they are so minded when education itself has been moving in this direction. We have the obligation to rectify this lack of balance, to make sure that our students are at least aware of the great body of thought and discovery which has been passed on by our predecessors.

There is also a terrible kind of newness facing us in national and international stresses and responsibilities. These problems raise the question, "What combination of traditional and new ideas and procedures will enable us to make our way?" These issues place a huge premium on all the intelligence and vitality which we can muster. We badly need understanding of social forces and institutions, awareness of what humans have achieved, the development of critical sense through contact with the various methods of analysis, and perception of the dangers of provincialism. The Committee believes that the right kind of contact with the basic subject-matter areas can make a substantial contribution to these ends.

Finally, such a curriculum is important for the individual in personal terms. he must acquire certain basic skills for his own use. Simply as an educated person he needs a range of knowledge. If some of the initial obstacles are removed, and interest is aroused, these beginnings can become the source of substantial later satisfactions.

The students themselves have shown concern about curriculum. In a report to the Student Senate dated May 22, 1952, a committee suggested ways of stimulating interest in the cultural opportunities offered by the University. Included was the following statement: "The set-up of the Junior Division was once an excellent idea but lately has been encroached upon by specific schools. It is strongly recommended that the Junior Division general humanities program be more strictly adhered to and that the introductory courses to a specific school be eliminated or delayed to the sophomore year."

Section B

It is something of a let-down to pass from these ambitious theoretical considerations to the question of what we can do about them. After all, college is simply a piece of the process of education. Furthermore, the nature of a large state University makes it difficult to attempt what might be done in a small liberal-arts college. Yet surely we can do something substantial.

The mechanics are difficult. For example, Freshmen headed toward the School of Music take 18-22 hours of Music courses, not to mention the total clock-hours put into musical activities. The Committee recognizes that Freshman curricula cannot be entirely divorced from pre-professional work, and that such complete separation would not be wise in the case of students who are certain of their objectives. At the same time, we wish to recommend a basic University curriculum which is substantial enough to be a real attempt to deal with the problems which we have raised. Therefore we have gone outside our function as a Committee on the Junior Division, so to speak, and have devised a program of approximately 40 hours which obviously will extend beyond the first year. We also think that it is good in itself to distribute such work over several of the undergraduate years. When the program is worked out in detail, there should be allowance for various levels of study.

A quantitative description of the curriculum we propose is as follows:

Skills

Written expression in English: Study to be continued through the level of English W103; exemptions will apply in the usual way (6 hours).

Mathematical Knowledge through the level of high school algebra and geometry. A proficiency test will be given. Students displaying insufficient knowledge will be required to take a course designed for this purpose.

Basic Fields

Introduction to Western civilization: Choice of approved courses in either history of western civilization or world literature or general philosophy (6 hours).

Humanities: a choice of approved course in Art, Literature (American, English, and foreign-language literature in translation), Music, and Theater (6 hours).

Language: study of a foreign language (preferably beginning at the second-year college level); or a course providing an introduction to the field of language through such topics as: the nature and structure of language (illustrated with English and foreign-language material) and the history and distribution of major languages (at least 6 hours).

Analytical Social Sciences: a choice of approved courses in Economics, Government, and Sociology (6 hours).

Physical Sciences: a choice of approved courses in Astronomy, Chemistry, Geology, and Physics (5 hours).

Biological Sciences: a choice of approved courses in Anatomy, Bacteriology, Biology, Botany, Physiology, and Zoology (5 hours).

(We are uncertain about the inclusion in these groups of History as an analytical social science, Anthropology, Geography, and Psychology.)

We favor the principle that this curriculum normally be completed within the first two years. The Junior Division Counselors could project the "basic" schedule for the sophomore year. Since this curriculum would be an all-University feature, the individual schools could administer the completion of the program; a simple balance-sheet could be used for this purpose. The individual school would, of course, continue to control its own policies of certifying students for admission to the school.

Most students would be able to complete this curriculum in two years. We recognize, however, that there will be various degrees of collision with some professional programs; such conflicts will have to be explored, in a manner to be recommended below, and adjustments made. It would not matter particularly if some of this study were carried over into the junior and senior years. Also, progress in the program should be adjusted to the student's personal problems, outside activities, etc.

The Committee has taken the point of view that there should ordinarily be choice of alternatives in a curriculum of this kind, although all the fields must be involved. Such elasticity allows for individual differences among students and objectives, and also spreads among the faculty responsibilities of organization and interest in the program.

The curriculum has been described above in quantitative terms, but we do not conceive of it as simply distribution of fields. The courses must be suited to the general student, free from elements whose only purpose is to prepare for specialization. They must be directed to what is most important for the educated person to know in the field. A number of such introductory courses now exist on campus. Other courses should be revised, some new ones created. There has been considerable attention to the needs of the general student: the introduction of Bacteriology B200, Microbiology in Relation to Man; Biology B100, Man and the Biological World; Geology G100, Geology and Man; experimentation in English L101-L102, Freshman Literature, etc. However, the creation of a framework of general education, as is here recommended, will provide strong incentive for further concern and action.

It is implied in the foregoing that the type of course which cuts across fields is not necessarily the best way to achieve the purposes of general education. The proper answer depends upon the nature of the fields. The test should be whether the combination of material produces obstacles or provides illumination. For example, a sub-committee of the Committee on General Education in the College of Arts and Sciences has under consideration a course-plan for the study of selected social institutions and social systems, emphasizing the interplay of social, political, and economic factors in the domestic and international areas. Here the combination of material shows the nature of the phenomena.

Our ideas have not led us to think of women's education as a separate problem. The freedom of choice among alternatives in the curriculum may provide some answers in this respect.

We also recognize the need of adjusting the basic University curriculum to the training and background of the individual student. The Committee presents no recommendations on this now, since the Policy Committee of the College of Arts and Sciences is developing a plan for dealing with proficiencies and deficiencies of entering students.

Surely, the creation of this all-University plan will stimulate attention to the needs of superior students, and direct its course.

Recommendations 7-9

We recommend that:

7. The Faculty Council approve the principle of adopting a basic University curriculum of the type described above, a curriculum to be required of all students receiving undergraduate degrees from the University;
8. The Committee on Curricular Policies and Educational Programs be asked to confer with the various undergraduate schools concerning the completion of this curriculum as early as possible in undergraduate study;
9. The Committee on Curricular Policies and Educational Programs be asked to recommend to the Faculty Council the courses considered appropriate to be included in the basic curriculum, and to initiate action concerning possible revision of courses and creation of new courses, in accordance with the principles presented in this report.

Conclusion

One interrelationship among our recommendations should be emphasized. If students are helped to know more about the University (recommendation 3), if Counselors can put more time into their advising (recommendation 5), and if both students and counselors are directed by a basic curriculum (recommendation 7), the Committee is convinced that the results be of very substantial value.

Carl G. F. Franzen

John H. Porter

Norman T. Pratt, Jr.,

Chairman

George R. Waggoner

Paul Weatherwax

Faculty Council Minutes, 1953–55, pp. 169–178.

Document 180

The Media

Indiana was a pioneer in the field of educational radio. In the fall of 1954 it was faced with the major challenge of expanding its communication media into the rising and popular field of educational television. The special committee recognized the fact that it created no new purposes or objectives for the University, but it did present problems of internal administration and external relationships. Development of programs for this visual medium presented tremendous and expensive problems. One of the most demanding was the fact that there had to be a good qualitative continuity to the programs.

*   *   *

Television and the University

Foreword

From the moment of its creation last November 6, the University Committee on Curricular Policies and Educational Programs has been confronted with the issue of television as an instrument to be employed by the University. Two considerations brought a decision that this issue should be the object of the Committee's inaugural study. First, television already existed as a force to be reckoned in the University and was exhibiting disturbing signs of chaotic growth; second, the Committee found awaiting it a formal request from the Curriculum Committee of the College of Arts and Sciences that it "study this new area and lay down fundamental policies for the whole University." Inherent to this request was the realization that the world has seen few instruments for molding the minds of men more powerful than television and since the minds of men are the *raison d'etre* of a university, it is paramount that the instrument be employed with fullest wisdom. Accordingly, the Committee initiated a program of interviews, discussions, and readings out of which has evolved the report it now submits to the Faculty Council.

Television and the Objectives of a University

The birth of television has created no new purposes or objectives for a university but has provided, rather, a new instrument whereby the traditional objectives may be attained. So that we may clearly visualize the prospective uses of the instrument, it may be helpful to restate the objectives. They are: (1) acquisition of knowledge; (2) preservation of knowledge; and (3) transmission of knowledge. As a first step in the assessment of the television instrument, certain obvious prospects of television in conjunction with each of these objectives may be stated.

It appears that television is destined to have limited use in the acquisition of knowledge except possibly as a medium through which a mass appeal for data or materials pertinent to a given research project might be made, or for the recruiting and organization of a mass of workers or observers required by a research project. It is true that television has contributed mightily, and will continue to do so, to the creation of a host of problems, social and otherwise, which must become the objects of research. But let there be no confusion between a factor contributing to a situation requiring analysis and the same factor as an instrument for research. The automobile, for example, has been a powerful agent in the development of modern society but serves little purpose as a tool for the solution of the problems it has helped to create. So it is and is likely always to be with television.

Likewise, in the preservation of knowledge, the potential role of television appears to be limited. As a device or technological medium for preservation of data it possesses little in common with a library or museum. There are, however, two by-products of television of some potentiality. One will be found in the stimulus to production of educational films for telecasting purposes and kinescopes of 'live' productions prepared for rebroadcasting. The libraries of such films and kinescopes are in their own way storehouses of knowledge. The other by-product is more subtle but in the long run a dividend of high prospective value. Knowledge preserved only in museums and books is dead stuff; it has meaning and value only in the minds of men. To the extent, then, that television may give knowledge wider currency among people at large, so will knowledge be better preserved.

It is in conjunction with transmission of knowledge that television will make its greatest contribution. In transmitting knowledge, a university deals directly with young people who seek preparation for the professions and for their betterment as citizens in our society, and with adults for whom education is a never ending process. Less directly, a university transmits knowledge by being a constant influence for good in society, by acting with other agencies for the continued improvement of our culture and the accomplishment of our social objectives. In the attainment of these ends television will become one of the more powerful instruments which universities have at their disposal. The conclusions and recommendations presented in the following paragraphs therefore pertain almost entirely to the role that may be played by television in the transmission of knowledge by Indiana University.

Definitions and Principles

It has been stated that of the three traditional objectives with which a university is concerned, television's greatest prospective value is with the transmission of knowledge. For the purpose of this report, the following activities may arbitrarily be grouped under the heading of "transmission of knowledge":

1. Preparation for Careers in Television.
2. Telecasting of Formal Courses for Credit, i.e., "Telecourses."
3. General and Adult Education.
4. Public Relations.

Preparation for Careers in Television

The training of students for careers in television is largely a curricular matter and is not our present concern. As a matter of fact, certain proposals on curriculum have already been passed upon or are under discussion by the Curriculum Committee of the College of Arts and Sciences and the Graduate Council of the Graduate School. There therefore seems no cause for this Committee to enter into this province.

Telecourses

The University is in its first year of telecasting courses for credit. During the fall semester offerings in Linguistics and Art Appreciation were televised; currently, English Composition (W101) and a course in Crafts and Design are available. Modest as this beginning is, it represents a task sufficiently great for the inexperienced, and serves to bring certain administrative problems to the fore. Without reviewing the unconventional manner in which the first two courses were set up, let it be said that governing regulations have gradually evolved. *The Committee believes that rarely, if ever, should a new course be created solely for telecasting; that any course offered via television should be one already present in the conventional curriculum or approved by the proper curriculum agency for both purposes. A decision to offer an established course in "unusual" form, e.g., via television, should be made only in accordance with the usual procedures for listing the course in the first instance, namely with prior approval of the curriculum committees or equivalent agencies of the school or schools concerned.*

It is difficult to set the boundaries beyond which telecourses should not go, for in the minds of some enthusiasts there should be no limits. It has been suggested at Western Reserve University, for example, that education by television be put on the same basis as classroom enterprises with the opportunity to earn degrees via this route. The Committee, however, does not concur with this "freewheeling" vision of the future of television. It feels, first of all, that television should not play any large part in the education of on-campus students. Students will presumably view those telecourses which are available and learn something from them, but only as a segment of a larger public audience which, remote from the campus, has no other opportunity. Surely the telecourse, even with the best of provisions for assigned readings, home or community discussion groups, and reports and examinations through correspondence, is a poor substitute for the personal contact and the give and take of the classroom. The Committee also feels that so far as credits towards a degree may be earned, *definite limits should be imposed on telecourses.* Future policies in this regard will have to be worked out. Finally, the Committee believes that certain courses may not be amenable to telecasting. Any course in which student participation in some activity is at a premium would suffer severely through television treatment. This is not to say that demonstration and illustration on the television screen can never be satisfactorily effective; but there are occasions when the cleverest of showmen demonstrating an experiment or technique is no replacement for first-hand observations, manipulations, or performances by the student himself. *The Committee advises, then, that every course for which telecasting is proposed should be scrutinized from the view of its suitability for this form of presentation.* A specific recommendation on the agency to do the scrutinizing will be presented in the final section of the report.

It has been suggested that university television resources be employed to beam formal courses via "closed circuits" or otherwise to "captive" in-school audiences in elementary and secondary schools. *The Committee feels that generally speaking there should be no invasion of these educational levels by the University. The University's business is university-level instruction.* At the same time, the Committee would not rule out all telecasting to elementary and high school classes, for it recognizes kinds of supplementary values and enrichments of curriculum which may stem from University-sponsored Telecasts.

General and Adult Education

A recent report by the University of Chicago Committee on Educational Television included the following statements. "The broad objectives of educational television are identical with those which should characterize all of the activities of a university. Most distinctively, however, television should be designed and used primarily as an instrument of adult education and broad community improvement. As such it will have powerful impact on both the outside world and the university itself. For the quality of a university is related to and dependent upon the quality of the society of which it is a part. . . . Universities are vast store houses of knowledge which needs to be translated into action. If the things which our professors know are given articulate expression, they will become a part of the stock of ideas which are discussed and acted upon. . . . For those mature members of our society who wish to continue to learn, television presents a great new frontier for . . . education. People will become interested in those reaches of knowledge and art about which they know nothing. And the facts, controversies, and concerns of the various academic disciplines may be presented . . . in such a way that they will all be brought to bear on decisions which individual citizens must make."

The Committee feels that these words express well and adequately its own views as to the objectives and level of adult education via television at Indiana University. They reflect purposes of integrity and high standards of quality in keeping with the dignity of a great university. The Committee holds that these objectives are right and proper, and with this probably few will quarrel. Our greater concern is with the degree of attainment of these objectives, and with the means employed in attaining them.

Television provides a new medium, of unknown but large potentials, whereby the rich resources of Indiana University can be brought to bear upon the problems, the interests, and the needs of countless persons beyond the confines of its own campuses. This means more than simply an opportunity to display a few plays or musical events, air some round-table discussions and debates. It means developing new techniques, new approaches to learning, and new concepts of program content which are made possible by the unique advantages of television. This would include planned group telecasts, often of the "closed circuit" type, which may be provided for special needs and persons such as doctors, dentists, social workers, business executives, or for that matter gatherings of specialists in almost any activity. It would include programs for bringing important economic, social, and governmental processes within the living experience of large numbers of viewers. It would certainly include many creative efforts beyond the competence of this Committee to conceive.

But in developing such programs, our course of action will be determined by two basic assumptions, implicit or explicit, as to their proper character. One pertains to the assumed intellectual level of the viewing audiences; the other pertains to the level of educational experience.

This Committee rejects the assumption that the general public is of low average intelligence which must be catered to by low-level and patronizing programs. We warn against the pitfall of mediocrity all too often stumbled into by commercial radio, television, and motion pictures, and of the monotonous repetition of a formula which having once been successful is thought to have a measure of immortality and thus eliminates the need for further creativeness on the part of the telecaster or new intellectual response on the part of the viewer. Let us not underestimate the intellectual level of the general population. It is better that the viewer be stimulated by a little lifting by his own bootstraps through a high-standard program, than kept in his rut by a steady catering to a modest appetite.

Further, we strongly feel that it is not a proper university activity to engage in transmission of knowledge via television (or any other medium) at an elementary level, or to encourage juvenile "how-to-do-it" hobbyist activities. We realize that there are those who sincerely feel it is a university function and obligation to carry learning opportunity to the state at large and to the mass audience with modest or low educational experience, and in principle the Committee can hardly disagree. But there is a minimum level below which a university should not go, and still retain its dignity as an institution of higher learning. It is difficult to delineate that level, other than to say the limits should probably be defined as the now accepted "normal activity" of the University. It may be added, however, that to the Committee some of the current "normal activity" of the University is below the standards which it, the Committee, would of its own choosing establish.

Public Relations

There can be no doubt that television provides a powerful public relations instrument for a university, if for no other reason than that the mere appearance of its programs on the television screen multiplies awareness of the University's existence. The principal issue is what constitutes a proper display of the University's services and opportunities. Certainly direct promotion of the University's facilities would be unworthy and undignified and no one would seriously suggest that the exhortations of commercial advertising be adopted as a promotional technique. Once again, the best available standard is the current "normal activity" of the University. The University has long displayed its wares through pamphlets, brochures, field representatives, and its news bureau. If this is a proper kind of promotion, then presumably it is still proper if the aid of television can be enlisted in this type of approach. Illustrative is the promotional telecast associated with athletic events and exemplified by the "between halves" programs presented by the University during the past two basketball seasons. (Sports events themselves, of course, provide a kind of advertising. What policies shall be followed by the University in dispensing entertainment and the financial arrangements attendant thereto are not the Committee's concern.)

The Committee feels strongly that such *clearly promotional types of telecasts should be kept at an absolute minimum.* The best interests of the University and the true worth of the University are not going to be furthered and made known in this way. The University's public relations, its advertising, to speak bluntly, should be inextricably blended with its program of telecourses and adult education. It is the personalities, the activities, the opportunities, and services, and the knowledge which collectively *are* the University which should become known to our citizens, for it is from a growing awareness of the existence of and an accompanying utilization of these things that our citizens will derive their greatest values. And the University will reap the benefits of an augmented and improved student body. The ideas which television can carry into the community will promote in parents those insights and incentives which will lead not only to the better upbringing of their children but a desire that they receive a university education.

Operational Procedures

University vs. Commercial Station Ownership. The Committee feels it is hardly its task to explore and report on all the ramifications of the question of station ownership. Nevertheless, certain facts have been revealed in the normal course of the Committee's studies which, along with some tentative conclusions, may be recorded.

The allotment of certain segments in the UHF ranges for educational television has prompted a number of colleges and universities to establish their own stations. Iowa State College was the first, having begun its operations in 1950, followed three years later by the University of Southern California and University of Houston. Since that time others (e.g., Michigan State College, University of Michigan, and University of Wisconsin) have followed, including a number of joint ventures such as the one in Pittsburgh in which the University of Pittsburgh, Pennsylvania College for Women, and Duquesne are participating. Still others are schedules for opening this spring. The alternative to university ownership, of course, is the type of arrangement Indiana University now has whereby it beams its programs through the facilities of a commercial station during certain hours allotted to it. In this instance the station is Bloomington's WTTV.

The principal argument in favor of university ownership and operation of a station is the full freedom of use which is provided. All the hours of the day are available for programming as the university feels fit and the total facilities of the station for student training are likewise at hand. At present Indiana University is limited to the restricted time provided by WTTV; in fact the University's position is in general insecure in that it is largely dependent upon the good will of the station's owner, Mr. Tarzian. Accordingly, ways have been sought to stabilize the situation even to the extent of seeking funds from the Ford Foundation for construction of a University station.

There are, however, strong arguments for operation solely through the outlet provided by a commercial station. First, the construction and operation of a television station is enormously costly and there is, or should be, a real limit to the amount of money this or any other university can divert into this activity. This has led some educators to suggest a kind of compromise wherein an in-institution, owning its own station, seeks to recover some of its operating cost through commercial sponsorship of certain programs. One would predict that any such attempt to use in this way channels ear-marked for educational purposes would bring an immediate howl of protest from commercial operators. Another factor is the relatively limited range of the UHF bands as compared with the VHF bands; thus the square-mile and population coverage now provided by WTTV is enormously greater than would be possible via a station of our own. This coverage could be approached only through some kind of network of related UHF stations. A third factor is that it is difficult to draw an audience away from popular commercial programs. A mass audience must ultimately be attracted if the social objectives of educational television are to be realized and the easier and better way to accomplish this would appear to be to "catch" the audience which is already a follower of a commercial station. Finally, the fully available hours of the day and week which University operation of its own station would provide may be more of a liability than an asset. The difficulty that has already been confronted in filling the modest number of hours now available to us each week makes the prospect of a daily obligation of say eight to fifteen hours frightening indeed. Only by drawing from a multi-institution pool of kinescopes could a university such as Indiana ever hope to maintain all-day, every-day operations of any quality.

It is the judgment of the Committee that a plunge into a full-time UHF operation at this time would be unwise, even if a grant of money sufficient to build a station should become available. *Let the development of the University's television activities be one of steady, carefully planned evolution wherein the financial burden is kept in proper proportion and program standards may be maintained at a high level.* To do otherwise is to invite financial penalties on other university services and to be forced into the production of program hay for the maw of a studio monster.

Manpower and Program Production.

It would be presumptuous of the Committee to attempt to tell those professionally engaged in the production of television programs how to do their jobs. Nevertheless, the committee members have arrived at certain opinions regarding television programming at Indiana University and the production problems attendant thereto.

With regard to telecourses, it is very probably true, as Dean Ashton stated in conversation with the Committee, that in the final analysis only the standard techniques of the classroom are required; that there is no absolute need for special properties, supporting players and the like. Nevertheless the airing of a telecourse is not just a matter of installing a camera in a classroom and letting things go on as they may. Behind a really successful performance lie *two requirements: a principal performer with a flair for the job* and a personality that projects itself from the screen, and a *rigorous period of preparation and rehearsal.* As to the first, it should be *neither desirable nor necessary for the development of a special television faculty.* At the same time it should be recognized that only certain individuals will have the interest in and natural flair for the task. The human implements that will be required should not be under-estimated and there may be special requirements in personnel for telecasting to non-university audiences. As to the second, the smoothness and apparent spontaneity and casualness of the really first-rate performance are in direct proportion to the time spent in rehearsal. It is not alone a matter of compacting a fifty minute lecture into twenty-seven minutes, or even making certain that the right illustrative object is pointed to or picked up at the right time. It is, rather, a matter of careful rehearsal of every movement and gesture which makes for the kind of effective showmanship exemplified, say, by a Bishop Sheen. Regrettably, some recent attempts in our University programming to achieve casualness and informality by performing "off the elbow," so to speak, have succeeded only in being halting and juvenile.

The problems of personnel and production for programs in general and adult education are far more difficult. The telecourse, after all, represents only an adaptation of basic classroom techniques which have a long history of development and perfection. There is no such backlog of experience to guide the framing of programs in general education. True, some may follow the pattern of the conventional telecourse, but more often than not wholly new techniques of production and showmanship must be devised, and in the greatest variety in keeping with the kind of subject matter. Here it would seem that production experts with the necessary "know how" should be recruited and they in turn should then gather about them those faculty members, students, and other persons willing to dedicate themselves to mastering the techniques necessary to the success of such programs. Especially necessary is the "personality" who can "sell" the educational product we wish to market.

The Committee feels strongly that a professional approach and execution is essential. If a mass audience is to be attracted and retained, the programs must present a professional gloss, and this means the production job must be handled by experts, not just well-meaning faculty folk and students learning the ropes. Nothing short of professional execution will wean any sizeable audience from the slick productions of the commercial networks.

In short, then, it must be recognized that the production of topgrade television programs requires a large behind-the-scenes technical staff, a great deal of specialized "know-how", and long hours of preparation by the performers. The amateurish character of some of our current Indiana University programs reflects deficiencies on all these scores. It may be necessary to import a certain amount of the required manpower, but it can be anticipated that members of the present faculty will wish to dedicate themselves in whole or part to educational television. In such instances the work which is displaced by this effort must be done by somebody else. *The job of television production and performance can not be grafted onto the tasks already being borne by the faculty. If the University proposes to engage extensively in educational television, it must recognize what the basic need in manpower is and be prepared to pay for it.*

Administration

The Committee feels strongly that the responsibility for guiding the development of educational television at Indiana University should not rest solely in the hands of the Department of Radio and Television. In our judgment, educational television should be an all-university project and the total resources of the University should be used in its development. Accordingly, *we recommend the creation of a small "Television Council"* consisting of persons derived from the University at large and whose prime qualifications are the capacity for making sound decisions and interest in television as an educational medium. The Council should be appointed by the Dean of Student and Educational Services and should operate in close conjunction with him and his office. The Committee does not care to recommend a more precise administrative pattern than this, preferring rather that the Dean and the Council work out their own pattern as experience and circumstances require. We only suggest that it is not a chain of command which we have in mind; rather we envisage an arrangement whereby the Dean retains power for direct action, but utilizes the judgment and help of the Council and is guided by its recommendations. At the same time the Dean may delegate to the Council any portion of his final responsibilities which he chooses.

The Council, as we see it, should have two principal functions.

1. *It should continually explore the resources of the University and the community in order to develop program ideas which would be sound educationally and which would use the medium of television to the best advantage.* (Actually a special committee with essentially this commission was appointed by Dean Ashton early in the winter.) 2. *It should serve as the clearing house through which all proopsals for television programs, whatever their nature and*

objective, from individuals, departments, or schools are routed. Every such proposal will be scrutinized by the Council, and no program should be aired without the approval of the Dean of Educational Services acting on advice of the Council. However, the Council should have no curricular powers. Proposals for formal telecourses carrying credit, if approved by the Council, must be passed on for final approval to the curriculum committee or corresponding agency of the School or College concerned.

The Committee states, in closing, that it has attempted to lay out certain principles and policies by way of which the Television Council and other agencies and persons concerned with television might be guided in the immediate future. Educational television, however, is a mere infant and no one knows what the future will bring, least of all your Committee. We recognize, therefore, that the blueprinting of policy beyond a certain point is neither possible nor wise; that sooner or later changing circumstances will require new or modified policies. We have attempted to set up a few short-range guide posts, but once over the horizon those responsible for the development of television at Indiana University will be required to blaze their own trail.

The University Committee on Curricular Policies and Educational Programs

> HOWARD T. BATCHELDER
> FRANK E. HORACK, JR.
> PRESSLY S. SIKES
> THEODORE W. TORREY
> (Chairman)
> ROBERT C. TURNER

Faculty Council Minutes, 1953–55, pp. 193–201.

Document 181

The Junior Division in Concrete Outline

This third part of the Junior Division Committee Report was clear in its recommendations as to purposes, curricula, and hopes for the future.

*　　*　　*

ADDENDUM TO MINUTES OF FACULTY
COUNCIL, JANUARY 18, 1955

Recommendations of the Committee on the Junior Division, as amended, adopted by the Faculty Council.

1. All other divisions of the University observe the principle that the Junior Division is in charge of coordinating relationships between the secondary schools and the University conducted with the purpose of interesting potential undergraduate students in the University, and must be informed of all such activities pursued by other divisions;

2. The Junior Division increased its recent efforts in all dealings with secondary schools to represent the University as a source of educational opportunities for a variety of students, particularly the best;

3. The Junior Division maintains constant attention to such mechanics as: developing machinery to insure that serious conflicts among courses normally taken by Freshmen do not occur; organizing Freshman registration

as a part of the orientation program in such a way that confusion with the registration of other students is avoided; insuring to the maximum that the necessary records and reports are available to Counselors at the right time; eliminating confusion between its system of probation and credit-accounting, and procedures followed by other divisions of the University.

4. Faculty members be selected as Junior Division counselors on the basis of having breadth of educational interests and genuine concern for advising, that they perform this function in lieu of two hours of their regular teaching schedule, and that the Dean of the Junior Division have full charge of directing their activities during the alloted time; (approved by the Faculty Council in principle)

5. The Advisory Board of the Junior Division meet regularly (normally at least once a month) , and primarily for the consideration of basic Junior Division policies.

6. The Faculty Council approve the principle of adopting a basic curriculum to be required of all students receiving undergraduate degrees from the University;

7. The various undergraduate schools be asked to confer and work with the Committee on Curricular Policies and Educational Programs for the formulation of a basic curriculum in undergraduate study;

8. The Committee on Curricular Policies and Educational Programs be asked to recommend to the Faculty Council the courses considered appropriate to be included in the basic curriculum, and to initiate action concerning possible revision of courses and creation of new courses, in accordance with the principles presented in this report.

Recommendation of the Committee on the Junior Division referred by the Faculty Council to the Committee on Faculty-Student Relations.

3. The Junior Division, with the cooperation of other divisions, institute on the Bloomington campus a series of Freshman orientation lectures given weekly at least throughout the fall semester and designed to instruct students concerning such matters as: the structure of the University; the programs and purposes of the various divisions (including attention to professional training at the graduate level) ; the fundamental purposes of the University as a whole (including its relationships to society, the concept of freedom in learning, teaching, and research, etc.) ; campus ethics in relation to administrative officers, faculty members, staff, and fellow students; and educational opportunities outside the classroom.

Faculty Council Minutes, 1953–55, pp. 234–235.

Document 182

The Indiana Universities and the State Government

Operating under the new agreement, the presidents of the state universities and colleges went jointly in search of funds. In this case they presented a succinct outline to Governor Handley of needs of the institutions for the immediate future. One of the items was $7,700,000 to finance a 10 percent faculty raise.

*   *   *

Suggested Agenda
Meeting of Governor and State College and University Presidents

1. We are foregoing our requests to meet the universities' and colleges' true needs for libraries, scientific equipment, minimum curricula development, and state sponsored research not because these items are unimportant, but because of our knowledge of the state's financial position and the fact that our priorities must go to meeting larger enrollments and the acute need for faculty salary increases.

2. In the judgment of the Presidents of the four state-supported colleges and universities, an additional $7.7 million should be included in the appropriation for higher education to provide faculty members a 10 per cent increase in salary each year of the coming biennial period. With Indiana institutions already below competitive averages and with the knowledge of what other universities in the Midwest area are planning for salary increases during the next two years, the Presidents cannot assume the responsibility of the lesser amount.

3. Because the state is pressed to secure sufficient funds to operate, it is recommended that $2 million be transferred from the $3 million enrollment contingency reserve already set up in the budget. This would leave only $1 million in the contingency reserve on which the institutions could draw in the event their enrollments were higher than expected. In view of the state's financial position, the four institutions will have to take this risk.

4. An additional $5.7 million would then be required to provide the institutions with adequate funds for the 10 per cent annual salary increase.

5. In order that the 10-year building program, which already has been stretched to a 12-year program, not be further delayed, we strongly urge that the capital request as approved by the Budget Committee remain unchanged.

6. Since by careful planning it was possible to obtain bids to complete the Veterinary Science School of Medicine for approximately $500,000 less than the amount previously estimated and set aside by the Budget Committee, it is recommended that this saving be transferred to Indiana University for their Medical School Construction program.

Your friendly cooperation in setting up this meeting is very much appreciated. It will be a pleasure to meet with you and such others as you designate. You earlier suggested the Budget Committee, including the Budget Director, and the chairman of the Ways and Means and Senate Finance committees. You may well decide that the presence of the presiding officers and the floor leaders of the General Assembly would be desirable.

Handley 1959 file, Archives Div., KSL.

Document 183

Parity Broken at Last

This letter from President Herman B Wells addressed to Donald Clark, Indiana Budget Director, describes the new formula worked out for the four state universities and colleges in the special study of services. As in an earlier letter addressed to Lytle J. Frehafer, Clark's predecessor, this one is direct and its of greater historical significance than the mere detailing of the budgetary needs of the institutions. It reflects the fact that at last there was a recognition of the special work and services which each institution offered. At the same time a financially evaluative formula resulted from the intensive internal study of the inter-institutional relationships.

*   *   *

LEGISLATIVE REQUEST FOR OPERATION
INDIANA UNIVERSITY
BLOOMINGTON, INDIANA

September 7, 1954

Mr. Donald Clark
State Budget Director
State House
Indianapolis, Indiana

Dear Mr. Clark:

The four State institutions of higher education unitedly submit herewith their requests for operating appropriations for the coming biennium of 1955-57. The requests are prepared by agreement in materially the same ratio for the two universities. A differential in ratio between the two teachers colleges results from enrollment differences.

The two universities, Purdue and Indiana, were asked during the current biennium by the other Big Ten institutions and the University of California to join with them in an inter-institutional survey and cost study similar to the study already under way in the Indiana institutions. Ford Foundation support to assist in financing the cost of the study has been received. Meetings of representatives of these institutions have been held. Many of the procedures and methods developed by the Indiana group have been incorporated in the plans for the larger study. Additional information to be obtained will make the study more comprehensive and valuable to all participating.

The study involving the Big Ten institutions and the University of California will provide comparisons and standards for comparable educational programs in a number of schools that were not possible when only Indiana institutions were being studied. Indiana state schools are almost unique in lack of duplication of programs, for instance, law, medicine, dentistry, music, business, etc. at Indiana University and agriculture, engineering, pharmacy, etc. at Purdue. Thus, in many programs which operate in one institution but not the other, there exists no basis for comparison and measurement until the information on comparable programs is available from other states.

The Appropriation Requests

The appropriation requests of the four institutions are arrived at by agreement, since additional study data are not available for any other basis. The relationship in request between the institutions, therefore, does not constitute a precedent for distribution of the State's dollar for higher education in the future; and it is recommended that any changes from the original request will be made proportionately among the four institutions.

The requests are presented as follows:

	1955–56	1956–57
Indiana University	$13,010,001	$13,649,092
Purdue University	13,161,254	13,807,220
Indiana State Teachers College	1,927,134	2,014,731
Ball State Teachers College	2,303,134	2,398,731

These budget requests are essential to meet the actual needs of the institutions for the coming biennium, assuming there will be no further inflation bringing about a general price increase and that our conservative enrollment estimates are not substantially exceeded.

Basis of Request for Appropriation Increases

A. *Increase in faculty salaries to bring them up to 1939–40 level*

It was pointed out two years ago that our faculties were receiving salaries substantially less in real value than in 1940. This budget request proposes that the first step in faculty salary consideration should be to restore the value of the net income of faculty salaries to those of the period prior to World War II. Certainly the rectifying of this unfortunate situation is justifiable and beyond question.

Although we are not in this budget request seeking anything beyond an adjustment to bring salaries back to the real values of 1939–40, the second step to be undertaken during the 1957–59 biennium is to make it possible for our faculties to share in the national economic advance that has taken place in this country in the past fifteen years. Failure to recognize the justice of and to provide this advance invites a social catastrophe in higher education in our state in the future. Since enrollment increases, inevitable because of the growth in population, will make it necessary to attract large numbers of persons to the teaching profession and since it requires nine to ten years to prepare college teachers, we must begin at once to make teaching in higher education reasonably competitive in salary scales to industrial and other professional occupations.

B. *Increase in staff salaries to enable institutions to approach prevailing wage rates*

The United States Bureau of Labor Statistics shows that wage rates have continued to increase during the past two years. This, in addition to the 3 per cent reduction made by the Legislature, has prevented our institutions from keeping pace with prevailing wage rates in our local communities. In order to continue to keep an efficient, cooperative staff with high morale within our institutions, they must have the assurance that their pay rates and living standards will approach those of their community in similar jobs.

C. *Equipment for laboratories for both teaching and research, also library books and periodicals.*

By reason of inadequate operating appropriations in past years, there is a substantial backlog of urgently needed laboratory and scientific equipment and laboratory facilities. With the very rapid advances that are being made in the technological and scientific fields, much of the older equipment has become obsolete to the point that in some cases the lack of modern equipment is impairing the effectiveness of our teaching. Many graduates are finding themselves handicapped when they go into a modern industrial plant after having been trained on equipment that is no longer in use. An educational program must be dynamic and keep abreast of developments if it is to be effective and valuable to the state and nation. In addition to the need for new and additional equipment, there is a very real need for modernization of old scientific equipment and rehabilitation of laboratory facilities that have been deferred because of lack of funds.

Also, our library funds should be increased. During the past three years book and journal publishers have been forced by inflation in both wages and materials costs to raise their prices. Therefore, in order to keep up the present level of acquisition of books and continue scientific journals subscriptions, additional funds are needed.

D. *Special needs for medicine, agriculture and teacher education*

Construction on the new Medical Science Building will begin this fall. Preparation to occupy and use it two years hence means that locating and employing of staff should start now. In addition to an improvement in the teaching program, an orderly expansion in number of students is contemplated. A larger sum should be available the second year of biennium than is needed for the first year.

In 1920 there were approximately three and one-fourth acres behind each person in the United States. Now, due to the increase in population and the expansion of city limits, there are only about two and one-fourth acres per person producing foods. With population still rising it is necessary to produce more upon a decreasing number of acres. This can only be done by improving and expanding our research effort in agriculture. Such research has, in the past, doubled the corn yield per acre and increased wheat yield by fifty per cent in Indiana. Poultry research has produced a hundred million dollar industry in Indiana and other livestock research has added further millions of dollars to farm income. Thus the further development of research in agriculture is essential to improvement in the economy of the state as well as to assure a growing population that sufficient food will be available.

All citizens of Indiana are well aware of the critical dislocation between supply of and demand for teachers in our public schools. The dislocation can not be immediately removed but increasing enrollments in teacher education programs are encouraging. The number of high school graduates will be increasing by 20,000 each year in Indiana by 1960. Many of these students can be encouraged to complete teacher education programs provided the additional facilities, equipment, and personnel are provided through State funds for the four State institutions of higher education.

E. *Enrollment increase inevitable*

An enrollment increase of 1,144 students for the fall of 1953 alone exceeded our expectations for both years of the biennium. Our most conservative and minimum estimates for the coming fall and the 1955–57 biennium indicate that the four State school enrollments will increase another 4,500 to 4,800 students. This *increase* of 4,500 to 4,800 for our four State schools is approximately equivalent to the enrollment of the largest private school in the state or about four times the average size of all the private schools in the state. Our estimates are calculated on actual high school enrollments and based on the *assumption that the 29 private schools of the state will take their proportion of the increase.* The appropriation will need to be somewhat greater the second year of the biennium than the first year because the number of students will be larger.

Student fees at the four institutions have been increased to a level comparable with the fees charges in public institutions in adjacent midwestern states, even though this increase, or in fact any student fees, is not in accord with the intent of our forefathers as expressed in the Constitution of our State. The request for appropriations has been adjusted to reflect the amount of additional fees the students will pay.

F. *Conclusion*

Just as the governing board and administration are responsible at the college or university level for allocation of resources among the several divisions of the institution, so the Budget Committee, Governor, and General Assembly are responsible for allocation of state resources among the departments and divisions of the state in order to assure wise use of funds which will best promote the economic and general welfare of the people of the state. Every allocation to any department or division of the state must be considered in terms of immediate and long range service to the state as well as in terms of total resources of the state.

The state of Indiana has been unusually fortunate in its economic growth and development. New industries have moved into the state, and the population growth is among the highest in the country due to migration into the state in addition to the increased birth rate. The wise provisions contained in its Constitution and statutes, coupled with integrity in administration at the state level, have placed Indiana in an enviable position with respect to a healthy economy and sound financial condition. However, it is recognized that the people of a state are taxed only for the purpose of providing necessary services within the state and the nation and funds which accrue to the state should be distributed to provide the best possible services.

Many years ago the State of Indiana committed itself to the support of four publicly controlled institutions of higher education. These four institutions have served the state and the nation well. They have provided effective educational programs and have included within such programs instruction, research, extension and public service. They have planned and developed facilities for housing, feeding, and recreation for students *at no cost to the State*. They have made substantial contributions directly to the state and national economy through well organized extension programs and public services. They have made further contributions through research programs, which benefits will extend over future years. Finally, they have provided for utilization of the greatest resource still available to the state and nation—the young men and women who, properly trained, will accept major responsibility for the further development of our social and economic welfare.

While the State of Indiana has made progress in the development of its colleges and universities during the past decade or more, it has not provided support for higher education consistent with the total resources available and consistent with support provided for these services in other Big Ten states. (Reference: Council of State Government, *Higher Education in the Forty-eight States,* June, 1952.)

We believe everyone will agree that there is a direct correlation between the educational level of a state and the economic and social welfare of a state. The state of Indiana can have only those services which it is willing to support, and the value of such services will be determined in part by the level of support. The major problem in state administration involves the determination of which services will provide most constructively for advancement in general and economic welfare, and upon this wise determination of allocating funds in sufficient amount to maintain vigorous development of these services.

This combined budget request reflects the needs of the citizens of the state in the field of higher education. Faculty salaries must be brought up to at least the value level of 1940 if we are to continue to attract to teaching the people of the caliber and in the number needed to teach our growing population. Obsolete equipment below the standards of those our graduates will use in industry must be replaced and new and additional instruments of teaching must be added. Provision must be made for the increased costs of books and periodicals for the libraries. The special needs of our state for expansion of services in the fields of medicine, agriculture and teacher education must be taken into account. Finally, it must be recognized that the growth in population of the state will bring about a large increase of enrollment in all four of the State schools during the coming year and the 1955–57 biennium.

Respectfully submitted,
H. B WELLS
President

This is a joint request of the four State institutions of higher education.

FY 1954–55, Arch-File, Budget.

Document 184

Indiana University, the Big Ten Conference, and Eternal Championship Aspirations

This is a full report of Indiana University's athletic posture in the days when Bernie Crimmins was duplicating disastrous seasons in football, and Branch McCracken was leading the Hoosiers to the top of the mount in basketball. John F. Mee was a professorial hero on the Indiana faculty. He was dedicated, thorough, and long-suffering during the decade of the 1950s. In this particular report he presented a full profile of the University, its athletic triumphs, and its frustrations and disappointments. One of the riddles which the Athletic Committee could not solve was whether a winning football team would improve financial support or financial support would improve football.

*   *   *

3. Professor Mee presented the report of the Faculty Committee on Athletics for the academic year 1953–54. In reviewing the report he emphasized that the rules of the Big Ten Conference require full and complete faculty control of athletics and provide rigid standards of eligibility for intercollegiate athletics. He reiterated that intercollegiate athletics at Indiana University is financially self-supporting. He invited comment on the policy for pricing and allocation of faculty, staff, and student season books described on page 12 of the report.

Professor Pratt expressed concern about the need to schedule the better and more advantageous football games away from home in order to realize larger revenues. He said that this seems to make intercollegiate football a commercial enterprise rather than a campus activity and asked whether there is any other way to obtain the required revenues. Professor Mee said that regional television might help, but that we are confronted with a situation in which a major source of revenue for intercollegiate athletics is away-from-home football games.

Professor Shrigley asked whether Indiana is the only school in the Conference with this problem of poor revenues from at-home games. Professor Mee replied that Iowa and Purdue are in much the same situation; that all three schools suffer a locational disadvantage. Professor Robinson thought that the success of football teams has something to do with the size of attendance at games. Professor Mee agreed and said that greater success on the part of I.U. athletic teams is a major objective of the Athletic Committee. He mentioned particularly the need for development of alumni groups to interest prospective students in enrolling at I. U.

Several questions were asked about methods of recruiting athletes. Professor Mee said that it is illegal under Big Ten rules for any member of the Athletic Department or representative of the Alumni Office to contact a prospective athlete off campus. No scholarship may be offered by the Athletics Department or the Alumni office; scholarships for athletes must be handled in the same manner as scholarships for students generally. When a prospective athlete is on campus he may not be entertained beyond a meal and admission to an athletic contest. Visits may be made only on week-ends. Under such rules, prospective athletes must be initially interested in enrollment at I.U. and their visits to the campus arranged by alumni and friends of the University. Such activity is legal under Big Ten rules.

There was discussion of the objective of the intercollegiate athletic program. Professor Mee said that its purpose is to contribute to the educational activities of the University by improving student morale, stimulating alumni loyalty, and developing pride in the University. Professor Veatch suggested that a future report of the Athletics Committee might show how this purpose is accomplished. In this connection Dean Patty pointed out that the intramural sports program of the University is not financed from funds of the Athletics Department, but that certain facilities of the Athletics Department are used for this activity.

A question was asked about the application to the Athletic Director of the University's retirement rules. Dean Collins said that the retirement rules apply only to persons engaged primarily in teaching or supervision of academic work.

Professor Anderson asked whether the inclusion of students in the Athletics Committee is official. Professor Mee said that three student leaders are *ex officio* members of the Committee and participate in its meetings, except for executive sessions.

It was suggested that the Report of the Faculty Committee on Athletics be labeled "Confidential—Only for Information of the Faculty." Without objection, the Chairman directed that the report be so labeled and distributed to the Faculty with these minutes.

(Erratum: There are two typographical errors in the accompanying report. On page 11 the total revenues from home football games in 1953 was $85,697 instead of $95,697. On page 12 in the first sentence of the last paragraph the phrase "pay only two-thirds of this amount . . ." should read "pay only one-third of this amount . . .")

The Council adjourned at 5:00 p.m.

HARRY SAUVAIN, *Secretary*

Report of the Athletics Committee for the Academic Year 1953–54
INTRODUCTION

In accordance with the instructions in the minutes of the Faculty Council meeting on October 5, 1954, the following report from the Athletics Committee is submitted.

(Prior to reading the report of the Athletics Committee for the past academic year, members of) The Faculty Council may be interested in the following background information concerning the Intercollegiate Conference which is known as the Big Ten Conference. This information is extracted from the Handbook of the Intercollegiate Conference of Faculty Representatives.

Although this information was submitted in a previous report, it is repeated here for convenient reference to the members of the Faculty Council.

"At the time of its organization, the Conference was composed of seven members as follows:

University of Chicago
University of Illinois
University of Michigan
University of Minnesota
Northwestern University
Purdue University
University of Wisconsin

"On December 1, 1899, Indiana University and the State University of Iowa were admitted to membership. Ohio State University was admitted on April 6, 1912. The University of Michigan, which withdrew from the Conference on January 14, 1908, was, on June 9, 1917, invited to return, and resumed membership on November 20, 1917. The University of Chicago withdrew from the Conference as of June 30, 1946. Michigan State College was admitted to membership May 20, 1949."

Organization and Procedure
Constitution

"The Conference has no formal constitution, but is governed by precedent and by such resolutions as are passed from time to time."

Membership and Representation

"Only institutions having full and complete faculty control of athletics may hold membership in the Conference. Faculty control at each institution is customarily exercised in one of the following manners:

(a) By the faculty as a whole.
(b) By a committee of faculty members.
(c) By a committee of faculty members, students, and alumni in which the faculty members are in a majority.

"While the Conference recognizes that in the member institutions final authority over all units of the institutions, including the faculties, rests in their governing bodies—trustees or regents—it is to be noted that a member institution becomes ineligible for membership if its governing body fails to respect its delegation of control over intercollegiate athletics to its faculty.

"In keeping with the basic principle of faculty control, it is fundamental that the ultimate authority in the Conference itself resides in the Faculty Representatives. Election to, suspension from and termination of membership in the Conference is exclusively in the control of the Faculty.

"Each of the institutions comprising the Conference is entitled to one Faculty Representative and to one vote. Each Representative must be a faculty member who does not receive pay primarily for services connected with athletics or the department of physical education."

Council of Ten

"The Council of Ten consists of the ten Presidents of the member institutions of the Conference, constituted for the purpose of discussing and acting on matters of mutual concern. The Council of Ten meets annually with the Faculty Representatives or Joint Group in an advisory capacity to review the athletic program of the Conference. The Commissioner of the Conference is elected by the Council of Ten on recommendation of the Faculty Representatives."

LEGISLATION

"Legislative authority over eligibility for competition in intercollegiate athletics is reserved exclusively to the Faculty Representatives."

ADMINISTRATION

"With the exception of the Rules of Eligibility, complete authority over which is exercised by the Faculty Representatives, the administration and enforcement of the Conference legislation are exercised by the Directors, functioning, however, in large measure through the Commissioner."

RULES OF ELIGIBILITY
FOR INTERCOLLEGIATE ATHLETICS
Rule 1. Residence and Curriculum

"Section 1. To become eligible to represent any institution in intercollegiate athletics a student must

(a) have been in residence there in one academic year.

(b) be bona fide matriculated and regularly enrolled as a candidate for a degree and therein have completed one academic year of work.

(c) be doing full work as defined by the regulations of the school or college in which he is enrolled. However, if he is enrolled in a school for coaches, athletic directors, physical education or any similar technical courses he shall not be eligible unless he shall have carried and passed and be carrying at least 12 hours of work in courses which are primarily scholastic in nature and which are credited toward his degree. Primarily activity courses in this field shall not be included in the 12 hours.

(d) In no case shall a student become eligible before the opening day of classes of the corresponding semester or term of the next school year following his matriculation and he shall have registered for that semester or term.

(e) In no case shall a student be eligible for:

(1) a second season of competition in any sport unless he shall have progressed at least forty percent of the way toward completion of the requirements for the degree of which he is enrolled.

(2) a third season of competition in any sport unless he shall have progressed at least sixty percent of the way toward completion of the requirements for such a degree.

(3) in determining whether a candidate has made the progress required above, account shall be taken not only of quantity of credits earned by the candidate, but also of their quality. The qualitative element shall be considered satisfied if his academic record at the time of certification is substantially such that if the candidate continues at that level for the balance of his undergraduate career, he will qualify for the degree for which he is a candidate. The phrase 'substantially such' as used herein means, as a prerequisite to eligibility for a second year of competition, a ratio of points earned to credits carried not more than 10% below the average required for graduation, and as a prerequisite to a third year of competition, a ratio not more than 5% below the average required for graduation. (For example, if the graduation requirement is a grade point average of 2.0, then the requirement for eligibility for a second year of competition would be an average of at least 1.8 and for a third year of competition an average of at least 1.9). In case the grading plan is not on the basis of weighted points, translations of this rule and applications thereof shall be as close to the foregoing as may be possible. (Note: This rule is effective with stu-

dents matriculating on or after May 15, 1952; and applies to whatever work is taken and not to required work only.)

(4) the progress above required shall, in the case of a student who transfers from one curriculum to another, be measured by counting the hours and credits earned in his new course of study as if they were acceptable toward the degree for which he was a candidate before such a transfer. This provision shall be applicable only during the first year following the transfer. In subsequent years of a student's residence the requirement of progress shall be interpreted in terms of the new course of study for which the student is enrolled.

(5) in case of hardship in the application of this rule, the Eligibility Committee is authorized to entertain applications for special indulgence and to grant such relief as the facts warrant."

REPORT OF ATHLETIC EVENTS FOR 1953–54

Highlights of the intercollegiate athletic program at Indiana University for the academic year 1953–54 are presented from the annual report of the Acting Director of Athletics, Dean W. W. Patty, to the President.

Indiana University intercollegiate athletic teams participated officially in twelve different sports during the year 1953–54.

The Program

The intercollegiate sports in which official teams participated were: (1) baseball, (2) basketball, (3) cross-country, (4) football, (5) golf, (6) gymnastics, (7) indoor track, (8) outdoor track and field, (9) rifle, (10) swimming, (11) tennis, and (12) wrestling. During the year these teams represented the University in 124 events.

In addition to the official intercollegiate teams, the Athletic Department provided facilities and a limited amount of financial aid to informal fencing and soccer clubs. They participated in contests, but not as officially sponsored teams and not under the rules of Indiana University and of The Western Conference.

Number Participating

One of the charges sometimes made against the modern intercollegiate athletics program is that it is so strenuous and specialized that few students participate. An answer to this purported weakness has been given at Indiana University by the development of a nineteen sport intramural program with approximately 2,500 different men participating. The intramural program is under the direction of the School of Health, Physical Education, and Recreation.

Our varied intercollegiate athletics program involves a very considerable number of men students. Almost four hundred men participate in the eleven principal intercollegiate sports.

In Table I is shown the number of men students who were members of the varsity and freshman athletic teams at the ends of the respective seasons. Many additional students participate in the early season drills each year, but withdraw when it becomes apparent that they are not quite up to the standard of performance of athletes in this conference. Most of them transfer to intramural teams in similar sports.

In Table I the participation report for indoor track, outdoor track and field, and cross-country are combined since many participants take part in all three. Although an "I" award is now granted for excellence on the rifle team, it is not included in Table I because of the difference in the nature of the performance.

Degree of Success*

When varsity teams win more than sixty percent of intercollegiate athletic contests, the athletic year must be recognized as successful. This is particularly true for teams competing in the Western Conference (Big Ten) since it is recognized as having the highest performance in the United States.

Indiana University teams participated in eleven different sports during 1953–54. They compiled a .617 winning percentage. They won two conference championships and attained second place in two other sports. They placed no worse than ninth in any sport.

Table I
Intercollegiate Sports Participants
Indiana University
1953–54

Sport	Varsity Participants	Freshman Participants
Baseball	25	25
Basketball	22	17
Football	68	60
Golf	10	6
Gymnastics	8	2
Swimming	24	12
Tennis	8	4
Track and Field, Cross Country	32	18
Wrestling	14	3
Totals	211	147
Total Varsity and Freshmen	358	

In addition to the foregoing, it should be recognized that 10 men participated with the informal fencing team, 20 took part in the informal soccer intercollegiate soccer games, and a considerable number in the marksmanship contests of the rifle team.

Aside from winning 61.7 percent of its meets in all sports, a noteworthy achievement in any class of competition and particularly outstanding in the high level of performance of the Western Conference, Indiana won championships in basketball and tennis and was runner-up in Cross Country and Indoor track. Only Illinois and Michigan State surpassed Indiana in the number of Big Ten championships won.

The basketball squad lost only four of 20 games, retaining its conference title for a second consecutive year, and at the end of the season was ranked as high as second and no lower than fourth in the national rating systems.

The tennis team compiled Indiana's first undefeated season and topped off the season by wining a third consecutive Big Ten crown. The cross-country team, only four points away from a conference championship, ranked second in the nation, beating the team to which it had finished second in the conference meet. Brilliant team performances yielded an imposing number of individual honors.

---

* Acknowledgement is made to Mr. Tom Miller, Athletic Publicity Director of Indiana University, for assistance in preparing this summary on the athletic year.

Fall Sports
Football

Although Coach Bernie Crimmins' second Indiana football team posted an identical 2-7 mark as the 1952 team, the Hoosiers moved out of last place in the Big Ten and served notice by their performance that they would be a factor to be reckoned with in 1954. Victory-wise, highlights of the year were a closing rally to down the best Marquette team of the last fifteen years and a decisive triumph over Northwestern, the only team to defeat eastern champion Army. Stirring bids which barely fell short of upsets of Southern California, Iowa, and Minnesota stamped the Hoosiers as a courageous band of fighters which gave of itself to the extent that it nearly overcame obvious and damaging shortcomings in personnel depth and ability. With the most promising group of sophomores in recent years combining forces with a veteran group that retains most of the best of 1953, Indiana expects its football fortunes to take a marked step upward in 1954.

Proof that the slashing aggressive caliber of football taught by Coach Crimmins and his staff was pleasing to football fans and that the Hoosiers were highly-regarded despite their record is reflected in attendance figures. Although the teams of 1952 and 1953 had the same 2-7 records, the 1953 team played to 389,383 spectators, an increase of 76,995 over the 312,388 who witnessed the 1952 season.

Cross-Country

Coach Gordon Fisher's squad had another brilliant season, failing to win both the Big Ten and National titles by the narrowest of margins. Winning all three of its regular meets, which gave Indiana a string of 16 victories without a loss and a fifth consecutive undefeated season since a one-point loss to Illinois in 1948, the Hoosiers won a sixth consecutive Indiana Intercollegiate title. Indiana finished second to Michigan State by only four points in the Big Ten meet, but later bested the Spartans in finishing second in the NCAA meet for the second year in a row, this time by 11 points to Kansas. Lowell Zellers finished 11th in the nation.

Winter Sports
Basketball

Coach Branch McCracken's basketball squad wrote another glowing chapter in I.U. sports history by retaining the undisputed Big Ten championship first won in 1953.

It was denied another possible National Collegiate championship by a one-point loss to Notre Dame in the regional tournament of the NCAA championships, a circumstance which didn't prevent Indiana from being ranked No. 2 nationally by United Press and No. 4 by Associated Press. Overall, Indiana won 20 of 24 games, 12 of 14 in the Big Ten.

Winning a second consecutive championship proved a task of no mean proportion. Indiana was plainly the team to beat and every opponent girded itself for a supreme effort to accomplish it. That Indiana was forced into the final night of the season to win the title should be construed as a tribute to the Hoosiers' ability to react to pressure and a will to win rather than as a short-coming or reflection on their championship caliber.

Best summation was that of President Herman B Wells, who, at season's end, said: "In many respects it is much more difficult to retain a championship than to win it for the first time."

Don Schlundt cornered Big Ten individual records with a new conference scoring record for the 14-game schedule, a new free throw record, a new shooting accuracy record and a new one-game scoring mark of 47 points. He and Guard Bob Leonard were selected for all the recognized All-American teams and Schlundt was picked by Colliers Magazine as the Player of the Year.

Attendance for the season was 241,458, slightly below the 1953 total but compiled without the benefit of two additional games.

Gymnastics

Coach Otto Ryser's gymnasts were never at full strength during the season, a factor partly responsible for a 1-6 record. Indiana placed seventh in the Big Ten meet. Competing in the NCAA, Ron Johnson placed 12th in the nation in two events.

Indoor Track

A largely-sophomore team made an impressive showing in the 1954 indoor season and indicated that Indiana, aided by sophomore additions next season, may end the four-year domination of track by Illinois. The Hoosiers won all three of their regular meets and surprised the Conference by beating out Michigan to finish second to Illinois in the Conference championships. A standout of the season was the mile relay team, which ran seven races, won all and set a new record each time. It won the Big Ten indoor title, establishing a Big Ten record of 3:17.6. Jack Wellman accounted for another crown in winning the two-mile.

Rifle

The Rifle team was again sponsored by the Athletic Department. The Military Department cooperated by coaching and managing the activity. The team had a successful season under the coaching of Lowell Donoho, Captain, Infantry.

Swimming

Although beset by illnesses and injuries, Coach Bob Royer's squad won four of seven meets and broke even in six conference meets. An exceptionally strong field left Indiana in ninth place in the Big Ten meet. The Hoosiers face probably their most promising future in history beginning next season. Bill Woolsey and Richard Tanabe, two 1953 freshmen, are rated among the country's best. Woolsey, competing unattached in the NCAA meet, placed second in both the 220 and 440 free style while Tanabe was a star of the East-West meet early in the year.

Wrestling

Coach Charles McDaniel's wrestling team won four intercollegiate matches, lost five, and tied one. Indiana University defeated Ohio State University, Miami University, Northwestern University, and the University of Wisconsin. The University of Minnesota was tied. This young squad, made up of eight sophomores, one junior and two seniors, gave a good account of itself against strong competition.

Spring Sports
Baseball

Coach Ernie Andres' baseball squad made the big stride out of last place in the Big Ten standings, moving to eighth place, and finishing the season with a highly creditable 12-14 record. In so doing the Hoosiers vacated the bottom spot after a two-year occupancy, along the way breaking a losing string which had extended to 28 games in conference play over three seasons. The manner in which it was accomplished provides ground for much encouragement. The squad was almost entirely sophomore and at times the lineup contained a first-year man in every position. With most of the players available for future seasons and additional help expected from this year's freshmen, the outlook is its brightest in recent years. Individually, Bob Robertson stood out. Playing his first season, although a senior, Robertson finished strong to win the Big Ten batting championship, the first Hoosier to do so since 1949. He also was picked as a member of the All-Big Ten team.

Golf

Coach Owen Cochrane's golfers won four while losing seven meets but established its competitive stature by later upsetting Illinois and Michigan, two of its earlier conquerors. The Hoosiers finished seventh in the Big Ten meet with Captain Elliott Phillips in a tie for second place, the highest individual finish by an Indiana player in many years.

Outdoor Track & Field

In outdoor competition Indiana won three meets while losing a single meet to Illinois by the narrow margin of six points. I.U. won a fourth consecutive Indiana Intercollegiate championships. At the Penn Relays the Hoosier four-mile relay team was victorious, as was High-Jumper Cal Boyd, who set a new all-time Indiana record of 6-7. A 4:09.5 mile time, shared by Lowell Zellers and Jim Lambert, was the second best collegiate time of the year. Six team members won places on the All-Big Ten team. Zellers, running in the National A. A. U. meet, was second by inches in the mile and was picked for an overseas A. A. U. tour. Coach Gordon Fisher's teams had a most successful year.

Tennis

Coach Dale Lewis' squad, one of Indiana's most successful over his five previous seasons, produced its greatest season in 1954. Not only did the Hoosiers win a third consecutive Big Ten championship; the squad marched through a 19-meet schedule to post Indiana's first undefeated season. It boosted I.U.'s record for the last six years to 82 victories in 94 meets. Individual Big Ten championships were won by Bob Martin, Bob Barker, and Carl Dentice, plus a doubles championship by Martin and John Hironimus. That gave Indiana a total of 15 singles and doubles championships over the last four Conference tournaments.

Table II
All-Sports Summary
Indiana University
1953–54

Sport	Season				Big Ten				Conference
	W	L	T	Pct.	W	L	T	Pct.	Rank
Tennis	19	0	0	1.000	8	0	0	1.000	First
Cross-Country	4	0	0	1.000	0	0	0	.000	Second
Indoor Track	3	0	0	1.000	1	0	0	1.000	Second
Basketball	20	4	0	.833	12	2	0	.857	First
Outdoor Track	3	1	0	.750	1	1	0	.500	Fourth
Swimming	4	3	0	.571	3	3	0	.500	Ninth
Baseball	12	14	0	.462	4	9	0	.308	Eighth
Wrestling	4	5	1	.450	3	5	1	.389	Ninth
Golf	4	7	0	.364	2	6	0	.250	Seventh
Football	2	7	0	.222	1	5	0	.167	Ninth
Gymnastics	1	6	0	.143	1	6	0	.143	Seventh
	76	47	1	.617	36	37	1	.493	

The Big Ten Medal, given to a senior "who has maintained an outstanding four-year scholastic rating and who has distinguished himself in one of the fields of athletics" was awarded to E. Duane Gomer of the tennis team.

The Jake Gibel Award, given to a senior at Indiana University "who has distinguished himself in athletics and scholarship and who has displayed an outstanding mental attitude" went to Lowell Zellers of the Track team.

The Balfour Awards are given to "athletes in all sports who bring honor and distinction to Indiana University." For the year 1953–54 the following men were recipients of Balfour awards:

Sport	Recipient
Baseball	Robert Robertson
Basketball	Charles Kraak
Football	R. Jerrold Ellis
Golf	Elliott V. Phillips
Gymnastics	Ronald Johnson
Swimming	Richard Knight
Tennis	E. Duane Gomer
Track	F. Lowell Zellers
Wrestling	Richard James Anthony

Changes in Personnel

July 1953   E. Bryan Quarles, MD, Director of Student Health Services, assumed responsibilities for the medical supervision of athletes in the intercollegiate program as team physician on a part-time basis. He will continue with a major supervisory responsibility for 1954–55, but will delegate some of the duties to John Miller, MD, recently appointed to the University Student Health Center staff.

August 1953   Mrs. Shirley Scott resigned as receptionist in the Athletic Department. She was succeeded by Miss Jacqueline Stiles.

January 1954   Indiana University suffered a real loss in January when Mr. Edward G. Whereatt resigned as head freshman football coach. His advisory work with freshman athletes was especially valuable. His coaching service was highly satisfactory. He left to join the staff of the National Collegiate Athletic Association in Kansas City, Missouri.

Indiana University was fortunate in securing Mr. Howard Brown as a replacement for Mr. Whereatt. Coach Brown came from coaching duties at Arizona State College at Tempe, Arizona.

Miss Jacqueline Stiles resigned as receptionist in January. Mrs. Ruby McCoy was employed as receptionist beginning January 11, 1954.

February 1954   Mr. Paul J. Harrell resigned as Athletic Director at Indiana University February 22, 1954, after approximately twenty-five years of loyal service. His coaching service began in 1929 as assistant coach of freshman football and baseball. Later he served many years as head freshman football coach and head varsity baseball coach. He was Director of Intercollegiate Athletics from 1948 to 1954. He left the directorship in February to assume responsibilities as expeditor for the development program of athletic facilities.

Mr. Harrell was succeeded by Willard W. Patty as acting Athletic Director February 22, 1954.

June 1954 Mr. Joseph Thomas left the Athletic Department in June to accept a position as assistant coach of professional football with the Baltimore Colts. He had served as freshman football, basketball, and baseball coach during the absence of Phil Buck in military service for two years. Mr. Buck will resume his duties as freshman basketball and baseball coach in September.

Mr. George McCoy retired under the policies of Indiana University on June 30, 1954, after many years of faithful service as groundskeeper for the Athletic Department. He was replaced by Mr. Otho Mitchell.

Facilities Improvements

Golf Course

One of the major improvements for facilities for intercollegiate athletics, as well as for physical education and informal recreation of students, to be made at Indiana University during recent years is the new University golf course. An 18 hole course has been under construction for approximately four months on a site north of the baseball fields. It is being constructed in a beautiful natural setting and will be a valuable addition to facilities for intercollegiate golf as well as for use by the students and faculty of Indiana University.

Stadium Football Field Sodded

An improvement on the varsity football field in the stadium was made during the month of May. A major portion of the field was resodded. A Group of all those concerned with repairs and maintenance of playing fields developed a set of policies concerning repairs and maintenance of playing fields.

Field House

Plans for a new field house were advanced during the year. It is planned to have it located near the baseball fields conveniently accessible to state highways, when the bypass is constructed, and with adequate parking space. It is hoped that actual construction will start soon.

FINANCING OF THE INTERCOLLEGIATE ATHLETIC PROGRAM

It has been previously reported to the Faculty Council that the entire intercollegiate athletic program is financed from gate receipts, radio broadcasting, and television contracts. There are also small revenues collected from concession and program contracts.

The expenses for intercollegiate athletic events are paid from revenues described above. These expenses include maintenance costs for the field house, stadium, baseball field, tennis courts, and the like. They also include coaches' salaries, equipment costs, travel expenses, uniforms, and medical service.

Revenues collected from athletic events are collected and administered by the office of the Vice President and Treasurer of the University. Expenses are budgeted and controlled similar to that of other operating divisions of the University by the Vice President and Treasurer.

The major source of revenue for the Indiana athletic program comes from the receipts for football. It may be of interest to the members of the Faculty Council to know the amount of revenue collected from football receipts as well as the attendance records for the 1953 football season. The following presentation shows a comparison of the 1953 home and away attendance and revenue records.

COMPARISON OF 1953 HOME AND AWAY
ATTENDANCE AND REVENUE

Game	Home Attendance	Revenue	Away Attendance	Revenue
Marquette	22,724	$15,147		
Missouri	19,696	19,268		
Northwestern	16,959	15,433		
Purdue	31,235	35,849		
Ohio State			75,898	$ 72,216
Southern California			49,578	36,721
Michigan State			51,698	56,053
Iowa			50,129	45,451
Minnesota			59,486	66,616
Totals	90,614	$85,697	286,689	$277,057
Averages	22,653	21,424	57,357	55,411

In last year's report to the Faculty Council figures were given which disclosed that the football receipts for 1952 from home and away games were $274,939. It is encouraging to report this year that in 1953 the total home and away receipts were $362,754.

Attention is invited to the fact that the majority of revenue from football receipts comes from away-from-home games. Home games in 1953 averaged an attendance of 22,653 persons per game with an average revenue of $21,424 per game. For games Indiana played away from home in 1953 the average attendance was 57,357 persons per game and $55,411 revenue per game. These figures point out quite forcefully the fact that the major portion of Indiana University's revenue is received from games played away from home.

In addition to the revenue from gate receipts of football in 1953, income from the following sources was realized:

$25,000 from Indiana's institutional share of the Rose Bowl receipts

22,067 from Indiana's participation in the NCAA television program

2,414 from broadcast privilege fees

15,000 from basketball TV privileges

3,222 from basketball privilege fees

1,800 from rental of the field house

Income from staff and student year books was $52,000 and the public sale of basketball tickets amounted to $41,000. At the beginning of the 1953–54 fiscal year it was feared that the Department of Athletics might experience a deficit of $140,000; however, unexpected additional income from high attendance at away from home games, participation in the NCAA TV program, and internal administrative economies which reduced costs of operations resulted in a deficit at the end of the fiscal year of only $44,637 of which almost $23,000 consisted of old bills contracted in former years. It is anticipated that the Department of Athletics will operate during the current fiscal year with a similar deficit; however, improved football schedule for away-from-home games during 1955, 1956, and 1957 are expected to more than make up the deficit.

*Policy for Pricing and Allocation of Faculty,
Staff, and Student Season Books*

Two developments prior to the 1954–55 athletic season served to influence the policy of the Athletics Committee pertaining to pricing and allocation of faculty, staff, and student year books. One was the elimination of federal tax on athletic tickets, and the other, the need for additional revenue for the intercollegiate athletic program.

For the football season an experiment was tried with scaled prices of football tickets. Preferred seats between the 35 yard lines, allocated to the public, were priced at $4.00 per game for the Big Ten events and $3.00 per game for the non-Big Ten events. This resulted in a season book price of $14.00 for preferred seats and $10.00 for seats beyond the 35 yard line for public sale. As a result, there was more demand than supply for the preferred seats.

Faculty and staff season books remained at $12.00; student year books were reduced to $11.00. As a result of this pricing and allocation policy it appears that the revenue for home football games for the 1954 season will approximate the same revenue for home games as the 1953 season which is a gain in revenue since Purdue was played away from home in 1954.

Basketball tickets have been raised from $1.50 per game to $2.00 per game with season books priced at $22.00 for the general public.

The present pricing policy realizes $36.00 from the general public for combined football and season year books whereas faculty and staff pay only one-third of this amount or $12.00 for both football and basketball games. In order to maximize revenue from the public sale, a maximum number of seats have been allocated to the public at the price of $22.00 for the basketball season. Although the student seats remain the same as in previous years, the faculty and staff allocation of seats for the 1954-55 basketball season are farther away from the playing floor than in previous years. This was done because of the lower price for faculty and staff season books relative to the public price of the tickets. Although the faculty and staff year books are relatively lower in price this year than in other years, the location of the seats is less desirable. The only justification for this is the need for additional revenue to support the athletic program. An alternative would have been raising the price of faculty and staff year books and giving the faculty and staff seat allocations in the center section of the north side seats.

In summary, the outcome of the present policy has resulted in greater revenue from the public for preferred seats, a relatively lower income from faculty and staff for less desirable seats, and a reduction in price for students with the same allocation of seats as in previous years.

QUALIFICATIONS FOR DIRECTOR OF ATHLETICS

The Indiana University Athletics Committee at the March 1, 1954, meeting agreed upon the following general qualifications as a guide to selecting the candidate for Director of Athletics to be recommended to the President and Board of Trustees.

The candidate should:

1. Have proven executive ability including competency in the functions of planning, organizing, and controlling the activities of an athletic program.
2. Command the respect of the Athletic Department staff coaches as well as other Big Ten conference directors.
3. Have the respect and acceptability of I. U. alumni.
4. Have an athletic background—successful coaching experience desirable but not essential.

5. Be able to properly utilize existing facilities and staff organizational units essential to the athletic program at the University.
6. Have dynamic leadership ability and high personal integrity.
7. Be qualified in the field of sales promotion to administer the ticket sales promotion program.
8. Be interested in and able to organize alumni, friends, and high school coaches in the interests of the athletic program.
9. Be dedicated to a successful football program because of the importance of revenue from that sport.
10. Have ability to properly administer the athletic departmental budget.
11. Be able to plan and effect the new University athletic plant.

A brief report of the activities of the Indiana University Athletic Committee's search for a new Director of Athletics may be of interest.

Since March 1, fifteen possible candidates have been personally interviewed to ascertain their qualifications and interest in the position. Five of them would have been acceptable to the Committee to recommend to the President and the Board of Trustees. However, not one of the five who met the Committee's standards would accept the position, if offered. Obviously, no one has been offered the position, as such could only be done by direction of the Board of Trustees.

The Committee has been in contact with many authoritative sources to solicit recommendations for a qualified candidate. Cooperation with the Committee has been excellent as far as recommendations are concerned. However, it has not been possible to dislodge a candidate acceptable to the Committee from his present position. Reasons given for lack of interest in Indiana were lack of an organization of alumni and friends to legally recruit prospective athletes, lack of housing, and the problems of earning revenue from our football facilities.

It is expected that a recommendation of a suitable candidate for Director of Athletics will be made to the President before the end of the present calendar year. The task facing the new Director becomes somewhat significant when an examination is made of Indiana's all-time conference standing in football since 1896. There follows a presentation of the all-time conference standings of the Big Ten football teams since 1896. (The all-time conference standings are taken from the Big Ten Records Book 1954-55.)

All-Time Conference Standings—Football

	Won	Lost	Tied	Pct.
Michigan State	5	1	0	.833
Michigan	159	63	9	.708
Ohio State	127	75	15	.619
Minnesota	148	99	21	.591
Chicago	123	103	14	.542
Illinois	149	136	18	.521
Wisconsin	129	128	29	.502
Purdue	101	140	20	.425
Northwestern	111	160	16	.415
Iowa	79	140	14	.369
Indiana	69	155	18	.323

It may also be of interest to the Faculty Council to examine the all-time Big Ten Conference standings in basketball. The records are shown as follows.

All-Time Conference Standings—Basketball

	Won	Lost	Pct.
Illinois	363	229	.613
Wisconsin	345	249	.571
Purdue	327	260	.552
Indiana	290	262	.525
Minnesota	295	302	.494
Michigan	217	235	.480
Ohio State	237	263	.464
Iowa	236	282	.456
Michigan State	26	36	.419
Northwestern	222	328	.404
Chicago	185	299	.382

RELATIONSHIP OF ATHLETIC PROGRAM TO GENERAL UNIVERSITY PROGRAM

Although no money from the general University budget has been used to support the Department of Athletics, a brief statement of the contributions of the Department of Athletics to the general University program is presented as follows.

1. In the televising of basketball games from the University, the Department of Athletics contributes seven minutes between the halves of each home game to the University for public relations purposes.

2. Close cooperation is given to the alumni program in such events as Homecoming, Dad's Day, Cream and Crimson Day, and the scheduling of athletic events in areas of alumni concentration throughout the United States.

3. Athletic events on the campus serve to develop mutual interests between the University personnel and citizens of the community. In addition, the athletic facilities are used throughout the year by patriotic and professional organizations in the community such as the Fourth of July celebration of the American Legion, the Monroe County Fair, etc.

4. The high school Semi-Final basketball tournament is held in the Field House each year.

5. High School Day at one of the football games each year encourages the development of high school bands in Indiana and brings many high school students to the campus who are potential students for the University. Between 12,000 and 15,000 high school students visit the campus each year for this event. This number includes around 75 high school bands which participate in the program.

6. Each year the Department of Athletics sponsors the Hoosier Indoor Relay carnival in which over 600 high school athletes from 50 Indiana high schools participate.

7. Members of the Indiana University coaching staff speak at various meetings, high school banquets and convocations, and service groups each year.

8. Films of our athletic contests are sent throughout the state to high schools and alumni groups. These films not only present athletic events but also show residence halls, campus scenes, classroom facilities, student activities, and other portions of the University educational program.

9. Athletic events such as Homecoming, Dad's Day, and Cream and Crimson Day bring parents of the students to the campus each year.

10. Intercollegiate athletic facilities are available to students and faculty of the University at scheduled hours for recreational purposes.

11. The Department of Athletics has been following a policy of paying the expenses of the I. U. band for one out-of-town football game a year.

1. During the past year the following Indiana athletes have been recognized by selection for the Helms Hall of Fame. In addition, the years in which they participated are shown.

Archie Harris	1940-1944
Campbell Kane	1940-1944
Roy Cochrane	1940-1944
Fred Wilt	1944
Don Lash	1940

In addition, Coach Billy Hayes was also selected to the Helms Hall of Fame. This recognition serves to increase the prestige of Indiana's track and field teams.

2. Closer cooperation has been established between the Athletics Committee and the student body by increasing from one to three the number of Ex Officio student members on the Athletics Committee. Student Ex Officio members of the Athletics Committee are appointed by the President upon recommendation of the Student Senate and concurrence of the Dean of Students.

3. Provision has been made for a high school visitor's ticket for all football games at the price of $1.00 per ticket. This practice encourages high school students to visit the campus and acquaint themselves with Indiana's educational facilities.

4. During the past year initiative was taken by the Athletics Committee to effect two changes in the Big Ten rules for the following purposes:
   a. Students who are athletes may now appear on TV providing they are accompanied by their coach or providing the telecast is of an institutional nature.
   b. Indiana University may now schedule athletic contests with the University of Kentucky, a possible natural rival, if mutual agreement can be arranged concerning dates and financial matters.

5. Dean Patty, the Acting Director of Athletics, has investigated and reported on the possibility of a crew for the University. At present the University of Wisconsin has the only crew among the Big Ten schools. Inasmuch as it is estimated that the total initial cost of starting intercollegiate crew activities would be around $39,000 (plus site), further deliberation is necessary because of the present budget condition of the Department of Athletics. No income can be anticipated from crew activities.

6. The Department of Athletics continues to support, on a club basis, the soccer team and the fencing team. Expenses for transportation and appropriate awards come from the budget of the Department of Athletics.

7. The Field House continues to be made available for many general University functions such as high school track meets, the student Fall Carnival, the Monroe County fair, high school basketball events, commencement activities, enrollment activities, ROTC activities, and intramural events. In a similar manner the track is made available for the Little 500 bicycle race. Repairs to the track as a result of the past race was reported at $1,000.

8. Vigorous sales promotion activities were carried on last summer for foot-

ball tickets. Posters were distributed in every city and town of any appreciable size in the State of Indiana. In addition, arrangements were made for free television time over WTTV for this purpose. Because of the need for additional revenue from gate receipts, every means is being taken to promote the sale of tickets for football and basketball events.

9. In order to insure public safety at athletic events, Dean Patty, the Acting Director of Athletics, has this year carried on an intensive program of bleacher inspection, repair, and painting for the comfort and protection of spectators.

FACULTY CONTROL

The present membership of the Indiana University Athletics Committee includes five members of the faculty and three alumni members. They are as follows:

Faculty
Professor W. R. Breneman (Zoology)
Professor E. E. Edwards (Finance)
Professor Ralph Esarey (Geology)
Professor Lee Norvelle (Speech)
Professor John F. Mee (Management)

Alumni
Mr. John Taylor—one year (Sullivan)
Mr. Maurice Bluhm—two years (Chicago)
Mr. James Strickland—three years (Indianapolis)

Mr. Leroy Sanders (Indianapolis) has agreed to assist the Athletics Committee until the new Director of Athletics is appointed.

Faculty members of the Athletics Committee are appointed on a year-to-year basis. Alumni members may only serve for a period of three years and are not eligible to succeed themselves by reappointment.

Respectfully submitted,
JOHN F. MEE, Chairman
Indiana University Athletics
Committee

Faculty Council Minutes, 1953–55.

Document 185

Toward a Unified Graduate Program

For a half century Indiana University struggled to develop and then unify its graduate program. Due to the peculiarities of university departmental and school development over the years, graduate work became the domain of special interests. When Herman B Wells came to the presidency of the University, he began a campaign to unify advanced studies under the administration of a single dean and a unified faculty. This involved a tremendous fight on the part of segments of the faculty to retain their controls. This report in May 1955 by Dean Ralph Cleland is a fundamental document in the history of Indiana University's educational program.

* * *

REPORT OF THE GRADUATE SCHOOL
to
THE FACULTY COUNCIL

May, 1955

HISTORICAL

The Graduate School of Indiana University is essentially an out-growth and extension of the College of Arts and Sciences. Upon the recommendation of a College committee, the Graduate School was formally organized in 1904. When in 1954 the Graduate School celebrated its fiftieth anniversary, it made note of its steady half-century growth, with particular reference to programs leading to graduate degrees, student enrollment increases, and the enlargement and productivity of its faculty.

The programs first offered led to the Master of Arts and the Doctor of Philosophy degrees. In addition to these degrees, the Graduate School now offers the Master of Science, Master of Fine Arts, Master of Laws, and the Master of Arts for Teachers.

In the School's first year, 1904, 30 Master's degrees were conferred. The School awarded its first doctorates in 1908. From this modest beginning, the output of advanced degrees has mushroomed, a total of 974 being conferred by the University in 1953. This included 811 Master's degrees and 163 doctorates. Of the total Master's and Doctor's degrees, 312 were awarded through the Graduate School. Up to June, 1954, the University has conferred a total of 824 Doctor's degrees and 4,617 Master's degrees, for a grand total of 5,441. Indicating the continual growth and increasing emphasis on advanced work, these figures can be broken down to show that only 30 per cent of these degrees were awarded in the first thirty-five years of graduate training at the University, while 70 per cent have been conferred in the past fifteen years. The continuing increase in the percentage of graduate students working toward Doctor's degree is notable. Up to 1930 doctoral students averaged 10 per cent, or less of the total. Since 1930, there has been a steady increase in the percentage of those who go on with doctoral work until in the Graduate School it is, for the second semester of 1954-55, 46.3 per cent.

SCOPE

The Graduate School offers instruction in 48 fields of concentration. Most of these fall within the area of the Arts and Sciences, but certain programs in medicine, dentistry, law, education and music are also included. The Graduate School works, therefore, in close collaboration with other Schools of the University.

Within the area covered by the College of Arts and Sciences, all graduate work is concentrated in the Graduate School. In the other areas, students have the choice between professional degrees or degrees offered by the Graduate School. A student working for a professional degree enrolls in the School which offers that degree; those who desire to work for the Ph.D. or other Graduate School degrees, enroll in that School.

ORGANIZATION

The Graduate School is administered by a Dean and an Associate Dean.

Legislative authority is vested in the Graduate Faculty which is appointed by the Board of Trustees on recommendation of the department or School concerned, and the Dean. The Faculty elects a Council of 9 members, 3 retiring each year, which meets bi-weekly, and to which the Faculty has delegated most of the legislative functions. Minutes of Council meetings are distributed to the Faculty and actions of the Council are subject to review and modification by the Faculty, which can call for a meeting on petition of 5 members.

The members of the Council for 1954-55 are:

Class of 1955—W. Howard Mann, Samuel E. Braden, Tracy M. Sonneborn

Class of 1956—Norman J. G. Pounds, Norman T. Pratt, Charles Vitaliano
(with Dr. John B. Patton substituting during Dr. Vitaliano's absence.)

Class of 1957—John E. Stoner, James A. Work, Paul Weatherwax

The Graduate Faculty at present consists of 343 members, 239, or 70%, of whom are from the College of Arts and Sciences, the others from other Schools or Divisions of the University. The Faculty have received their doctorates from 39 American and 13 foreign universities. The five universities contributing the largest number of doctorates to the Faculty are: Indiana (33), Chicago (31), Harvard (26), Wisconsin (22), Columbia (21).

While most of the instruction is carried on in Bloomington, the Graduate School is also identified with a considerable amount of off-campus instruction. The Department of Microbiology, which offers the Ph.D., is a constituent part of the School of Medicine at Indianapolis. The work leading to a Master of Science (Dentistry) is carried on at the School of Dentistry, also in Indianapolis. The all-graduate Division of Social Service, having the second largest departmental enrollment within the Graduate School, is also located at Indianapolis. Moreover, a limited number of graduate courses may be pursued in the University Extension Centers. Extension courses designated for graduate credit must, in advance of offering, have approval by the chairman of the department involved, the Dean of the Graduate School, the Director of the Center concerned, and the Dean of the Division of Adult Education. These recommendations are based upon the nature of the course and the qualification of the instructor. Work done at the Link Observatory, the Geologic Field Station in Montana, the anthropological diggings at Angel Mounds, the Museum of Northern Arizona at Flagstaff, is likewise an integral part of the Graduate School program.

ENROLLMENTS

In contrast to Graduate Schools in large urban centers, the Indiana University Graduate School enrolls for the most part students who are devoting their entire time to acquiring a graduate education. Of the 897 currently enrolled during the second semester of 1954-55, 841 are working for a degree—only 56 are special, or unclassified students. The percentage working for the Ph.D. continues to increase. In 1947-48, it was only 20.2%, in 1953-54 it had reached 38.1%. During the current semester it is 46.3%.

Beginning with 1951-52, enrollments, which had been growing rapidly since the war, began to decline. Total enrollment for 1953-54 was about 200 under the peak of 1950-51. This year, however, an upward trend is again in evidence. The total enrollment for 1954-55 is a few more than that for 1953-54. The enrollment of 897 for the second semester of 1954-55 compares with 853 for the corresponding semester of last year. Nearly half of our students come from the State of Indiana.

Of those enrolled in 1953-54, 41% came from Indiana, 40.6% from 43 states and 2 territories, and 8.4% from 36 foreign countries; 23.8% held baccalaureate degrees from Indiana University (See *addenda*).

ADMISSION PROCEDURES

The Graduate School handles its own admissions. Applications are submitted to the appropriate School or Department, and acceptance, with or without conditions, or rejections, are based upon recommendations of these divisions and subsequent approval of the deans. Except for the possession of a baccalaureate degree, the Graduate School as a whole has no formal requirements for entrance, such as definitive grade average, attendance at an accredited institution, Graduate Record or other qualifying examination. Some departments, however, require specific tests or have other formal requirements. A high record at a good institution does not entitle a candidate to automatic admission to the Graduate School, nor does attendance at a non-accredited school preclude admission—some of our best students have come from non-accredited institutions.

The Graduate School works closely with Dean Dowling and Mr. Strain in the admission of foreign students.

STUDENT SUBSIDIES

It is becoming increasingly difficult to attract outstanding students unless we are able to offer them a scholarship, fellowship, or assistantship. Of the 1346 students who have been enrolled in the Graduate School during 1954-55, 551, or 41%, are known to the Dean's office to have some subsidization from the University. This figure is probably somewhat less than the actual number. If Indiana is to maintain or improve upon its present high standard of graduate work, it is important to find additional sources of fellowship or assistantship money, not only to increase the number of subsidies, but also to raise their monetary value. Indiana is near the bottom of the universities in the Association of Graduate Schools, with respect to the number of endowed fellowships available. This places the Graduate School at a distinct disadvantage in comparison with other institutions of comparable size and standing.

NEW PROGRAMS

The past five years have witnessed the inauguration of programs in East European Studies, Library Science, Physiological Optics, and School of Letters. More recently, integrated programs in Latin-American Studies and in Social Studies, have been established. Both of the latter are governed by faculty committees made up of representatives from the cooperating departments. Anthropology, Geography, History, and Spanish and Portuguese are represented in the Latin-American set-up. Instructors from the participating departments work together in offering four required basic area courses. The program leads to the Master of Arts and Doctor of Philosophy degrees. The Social Studies program is designed primarily for secondary school teachers and prospective teachers and leads to the M. A. T. degree. It involves work in three of the following social studies departments: Anthropology, Economics, Geography, Government History and Sociology. Students electing this social studies program are required to take six hours of work in Education as well as a six-hour seminar conducted by one or more instructors from a corresponding number of disciplines.

In nearly all instances, graduate teaching is done by the faculties of participating schools. Most members of such faculties offering work leading to graduate degrees are, by virtue of departmental appointment, also members of the Graduate School Faculty. An exception to this general arrangement is the newly-created Graduate Institute for Mathematics and Mechanics. The faculty of this Institute is now identified solely with the Graduate School.

SUPPORT OF RESEARCH

Research is a primary function of the Graduate School. Its responsibility in this direction is two-fold: to the student it has the responsibility of providing training in research at the highest possible level and proper facilities to make it possible for him to do distinguished work; to the faculty it has the responsibility of furthering in every way possible the research and scholarly activities of its staff. A graduate school faculty should include no one who is not energetically contributing to the advancement and development of his field of study. Provision of adequate facilities and support to enable such a faculty member to pursue his research activity should be one of the major concerns of a graduate school administration.

This function is carried out by the Graduate School in a variety of ways, some of them tangible, some more intangible. A goodly proportion of the deans' time is taken up with consultations and discussion with individual members of the staff, helping them so far as possible to develop plans for the presentation of research requests, advising them regarding possible sources of funds, the reinforcing their efforts to secure such support. In addition, however, the Graduate School is able to afford a certain measure of tangible assistance to its faculty in their scholarly work. This takes two principal forms. (1) The Graduate Research Fund amounts to about $45,000 for the current year. This fund is used for two purposes, (a) to provide Summer Faculty Research Fellowships to Instructors and Assistant Professors, which will make it possible for them to devote the summer to research instead of teaching (22 at $500 each have been awarded for the coming summer), (b) to furnish funds for research and technical assistants and for other costs of carrying on research, including travel to and from research libraries, laboratories, etc. Almost 100 members of the faculty receive help from this fund annually. Others receive support from the Research Fund of the Indiana University Foundation. In 1952-53 the members of the Graduate School faculty received from inside or outside the University grants for research in the amount of approximately $1,000,000.

PUBLICATIONS

Since 1910 the Graduate School has sponsored, as well as promoted, scholarly publication of research work done by its faculty. Publications, first entitled *University Studies,* were superseded in 1942 by *Indiana University Publications.* The latter currently appear in the form of four monograph series: social science, science, humanities, and folklore. Altogether, 124 works were issued in the *University Studies,* whereas the following number of volumes has been published in each of the four *Publications* series: social science, 12; science 19; humanities, 33; folklore, 8; total for the four series, 72.

Members of the Graduate School Faculty generously serve as editorial committees. The committees for the 1954-55 academic year are as follows:

Social Science:........Edward Buehrig, Chairman
William C. Cleveland
C. Leonard Lundin

Science: ....Harry G. Day, Chairman
Harold J. Brodie
Theodore J. B. Stier

Humanities: .... Edward D. Seeber, Chairman
Agapito Rey
James A. Robbins
Folklore: .... Stith Thompson, Chairman
W. Edson Richmond
John W. Ashton

Copy-editing, designing, and general processing of all monographs are being done by Mr. Walter Albee; publication distribution through exchanges and sales are managed by the Indiana University Press under the direction of Mr. Bernard Perry.

During the current academic year the following books either have been or are being published; social science—John J. Murray, *An Honest Diplomat at the Hague: Horace Walpole;* humanities—Rudolph B. Gottfried, trans, and ed., Pietro Bembo's *"Gli Asolani";* Robert Champigny, *Portrait of a Symbolist Hero;* Henry W. Hoge. ed., *El Principe Despenado* by Lope de Vega; Richard A. Moody *America Takes the Stage;* A. Lytton Sells, *Animal Poetry in French and English Literature and the Greek Tradition.* Several other manuscripts are now in varying stages of production and still others have been accepted and await publication. The rate of publication is largely limited by the amount of funds allocated each biennium for publication of monographs.

In ways other than those associated with the *Monograph Series,* the Graduate School works in close harmony with the Indiana University Press. The Dean's office is represented on Mr. Perry's press committee; and occasional monographs are, if sales prospects warrant, selected for publication as trade editions under the Press imprint.

PROBLEMS FACING GRADUATE STUDY

Indiana is almost the only state university in which graduate work is not concentrated into a single coordinated Graduate School. Recent suggestions looking toward a closer coordination at Indiana have met with little enthusiasm from several of the professional schools, presumably on the basis that they might thereby lose control of their own graduate programs. The Council of the Graduate School has recently gone on record (*Minutes* of October 12, 1954) in support of the establishment of a confederation in which each graduate division would retain its autonomy with respect to budget, curriculum, faculty, admission, and degrees. It believes that an organization could be effected which would result in close cooperation in matters of recruitment, publicity, and the securing of support, and at the same time preserve to each division independence with respect to its academic program. It is of the opinion that such an organization would greatly strengthen the graduate program of the university.

The needs of the outstanding graduate school are easy to classify but difficult to achieve. They are (1) a faculty composed of outstanding scholars, each a master of his field, each an active contributor to knowledge in his field, each deeply concerned with the fundamental importance of adequate training for the oncoming generation and eager to carry his share of the burden of training them; (2) capable and dedicated students, committed to a life of creative scholarship; (3) ample fellowship and assistantship funds to obtain such a student body; (4) the best equipment and library facilities for advanced teaching and research adequately housed; (5) a climate of public opinion favorable to the training of an ample supply of highly skilled scholars and technicians so that our civilization may keep abreast of the rapidly advancing tide of knowledge and culture. The Graduate School of Indiana University has made great strides in the

past, and it is the determination of everyone concerned with its administration
and activity to ensure even more rapid progress in the near future, so that it may
gain recognition as second to none in the nation in the calibre of its student
output and in the significance of its scholarly contributions.

Faculty Council Minutes, 1955–57, pp. 127–132.

Document 186

The Public Service Challenge

As a liberal arts university, the only possible way that it could reach
out to the Indiana public was through specialized services. The most important areas developed by the University in this field were the off-
campus centers, the correspondence courses, audio-visual aids, business,
and music. By 1955 Indiana University had distinguished itself in several
of these fields. Its extension and off-campus centers programs attracted
national attention. Dean Hugh W. Norman not only reviewed the brief
history of the Division of Adult Education and Public Services, but also
gave a clear summary of what was happening and then ventured optimistic predictions for the next two decades.

*   *   *

THE DIVISION OF ADULT EDUCATION AND PUBLIC SERVICES
A Summary of Developments and Future Plans

Submitted by
Hugh W. Norman, Dean
Division of Adult Education and Public Services
September 28, 1955

The Division of Adult Education and Public Services, like the University as a
whole, had its beginning many years ago. These beginnings were crude and limited. People could not foresee the vast demands for education, research, and
public service which we recognize today. The entire concept of education and a
state university with its obligations to the State, the Nation, and the entire
world has changed.

The future of educational needs—even for fifteen years—is difficult to predict.
It means that there must always be pioneering; the trying out of new plans
and ideas; new and untried ventures; and a willingness to change with the
development of local, national, and world conditions.

The Division of Adult Education and Public Services cannot adopt a set
pattern and say, "This is what we are and this is what we will always be." To
do so would bring stagnation.

The University Centers

Enrollment in credit and non-credit courses off the campus in 1939–40 was
7,825 different students. In 1944–45 the enrollment dropped to 5,868 due to
World War II. In 1949–50 the figure stood at 16,649 due only partly to the
return of veterans. However, in 1954–55 the enrollment rose to 20,565. Of this

last figure, 1,562 were full-time credit students; 9,741 were part-time credit students; and 9,262 individuals were adult education or non-credit students.

Looking ahead to 1970 I can foresee a total of 4,000 full-time students in the Centers. (We had 3,505 full-time in 1947–48 at the height of the veteran boom.) It is quite likely that by 1970 there will be 20,000 part-time credit students. The adults should increase to 26,000, thus making a total of 50,000 different students who will be served annually off campus by the University.

A prediction such as this poses a problem that is startling. Well qualified instructors, both full-time and part-time, must be found. Adequate building facilities including good classrooms, laboratories, libraries, auditoriums, special adult educaton rooms, faculty offices, and attractive lounge and other facilities for young students and adults, must be provided. The University Center of the future cannot be a mere Junior College, but must also serve the citizens as a cultural and adult education center. An ever-increasing portion of the adult population throughout the United States is demanding special training, educational and cultural benefits from all agencies who can effectively provide them. The University should do that which it is best qualified to do, but it should cooperate with other agencies in planning to meet the entire problem.

In our attempt to help solve the problem of building facilities, a new building for the Gary Center, to be financed outside of State funds, is now in the blueprint stage. An addition to the Southeastern Center building as provided by the last Legislature will be started this spring. A new building for the South Bend Center is planned for the near future, and additional classroom space for the Indianapolis Center will be provided yet this year by taking over another floor in our building at 518 North Delaware Street. Provision for building expansion should be made for the Fort Wayne, Calumet, and Kokomo Centers during the next ten to fifteen years.

The Division has had some outstanding accomplishments during the past fifteen years. Notable among these are (1) the addition of qualified fulltime teaching staff; (2) the development of a counseling system; (3) the processing of grades throug the IBM system and the integration of grade records with campus records generally; (4) the improvement in academic standards; (5) improved relations between the campus and the Centers; (6) a marked increase in enrollment; and (7) better support on the part of the University administration and the public generally.

Correspondence Study

Correspondence Study has increased steadily since its beginning in 1912. Enrollments during the past fifteen years (exclusive of enrollments from the Armed Forces) run 1,651 for 1940; 1,611 for 1945; 3,175 for 1950; and 3,376 in 1955.

During the past fifteen years improvement has been made in revision of course outlines and the addition of circulating libraries to serve the individual student. Selection of instructors is now dependent upon approval of the department concerned and the dean of the school. Recent developments in the presentation of television courses jointly with the correspondence study method offer opportunity for developments in the future.

The filming of lectures and laboratory demonstrations which will supplement the orthodox printed lessons and texts will permit the conducting of group-study in cities and towns throughout the State. Kinescopes of Television-Correspondence courses likewise will in the future permit courses to be given over all television stations.

Indiana University has already given fourteen credit courses through the television-correspondence study medium. Results point toward expansion in this field for the next fifteen years.

Not counting an increased enrollment in TV courses, film-correspondence study work, or the large enrollments from the Armed Forces, the regular annual enrollment is expected to be 4,500 in 1960; 5,200 in 1965, and 5,500 by 1970.

The Audio-Visual Center

The developments are summarized by five-year intervals under each of the three major areas of activities: (1) Materials, (2) Production, and (3) Professional Education and Research.

1940–45

Materials Activities:

The circulation of educational motion pictures to school and community groups increased from 18,140 reels in 1940 to 37,414 reels in 1945. Circulation more than doubled during the five-year period in spite of the fact that the War made it impossible for school and adult groups to obtain projection equipment.

During the five-year period, campus bookings increased from 1,082 to 5,670. The increase was due to the expansion of services to schools and community groups and the emphasis on the use of audio-visual materials by the various war-time training programs.

Production Activities:

Photographic activities in 1940 were confined to the taking of a limited number of pictures by staff made up of part-time students. During the five-year period, services of the Photographic Laboratory were expanded greatly with the addition of equipment, physical plant, and the employment of a full-time staff.

Professional Education and Research:

A graduate course in audio-visual education was offered for the first time at Indiana University during the 1940 summer session. Audio-visual courses were offered periodically during the five-year period with in 1945 a total of 33 class enrollments for 77 semesters hours of instruction.

1945–50

Materials Activities:

Off-campus circulation increase from 37,414 reels in 1945 to 90,898 reels in 1950. This increase was made possible by heavy demand for materials from school and community groups and the addition during the period of over $500,000 worth of motion pictures to the library. The addition was paid for by rental income.

Bookings of materials for use by faculty members increased from 5,690 to 8,978.

Production Activities:

There was an expansion in photographic facilities available to schools and departments of the University. Also a recording laboratory was added in 1946, and graphic and motion picture facilities were added in 1947. With the addition of a production planning department in 1948, the production of motion pictures was begun in cooperation with faculty members on a revolving-fund basis. The Audio-Visual Center was able to invest in the production of motion pictures, in cooperation with faculty members on a revolving-fund basis. The Audio-Visual Center was able to invest in the production of motion pictures in cooperation with University departments, the amount of money which could be recovered through sales and rentals within a period of five years.

Work was also begun with Indiana state agencies with the production in 1948 of the motion picture, Your Indiana State Parks.

Professional Education and Research:

Semester hours of credit instruction offered in audio-visual education increased from 77 semester hours in 1945 to 1,188 semester hours in 1950. During 1946 the School of Education faculty approved an integrated program of graduate courses in audio-visual education leading to a minor or major for the doctor's degree.

1950–55

Materials Activities:

The circulation of motion pictures increased from 90,898 reels to 106,936 reels. As of June 30, 1955, the film library contained 24,589 reels of educational motion pictures with a replacement value in excess of one million dollars.

The use of materials on the campus decreased during the period from 8,978 bookings to 8,036 bookings. During the five-year period, the number of projectors was held constant. There was a tendency for instructors to make a better use of educational films by scheduling during any one class period only those films which contributed directly to the topic under discussion. This improvement in the quality of use resulted in a reduction of the number of different titles used.

During 1954 Indiana University entered into a contract with the Educational Television and Radio Center, an agency of the Ford Foundation's Fund for Adult Education with a distribution of selected high quality films produced for television to 16mm audiences, including school and adult groups. The primary objectives of this project are to:

1. Identify adult groups that can profitably employ films and kinescopes produced by the Educational Television and Radio Center
2. Acquaint these groups with the availability of such materials
3. Promote the use of materials produced by the Educational Television and Radio Center by adult groups
4. Maintain a distribution organization that will provide convenient and dependable service to adult groups on a local, regional, and national basis
5. Assist adult groups in improving their selection and utilization of materials produced by the Educational Television and Radio Center
6. Conduct research relating to the selection, promotion, marketing, distribution, utilization, audience acceptance, and influence of films and kinescopes produced by the Educational Television and Radio Center.

Production Activities:

During the five-year period, there was an expansion of production activity in all departments. Part of this was due to an increase in requests from schools and departments of the University. Also there was a great increase in the production of motion pictures for school and community groups under the revolving-fund program and for state agencies. The most important motion picture produced during the period was The Legislative Process which presents detailed information about the various steps through which bills must pass to become laws. During the 1953–54 school year, students in graduate motion picture classes produced films in cooperation with four state agencies—The Mental Hospital Volunteer: Someone Who Cares for the Indiana Association for Mental Health; Your State Trooper for the Indiana State Police Department; The State Beneath Us for the State Geological Survey; and University Air Cadet for Detachment 215, Air Force ROTC.

Since 1946 the Audio-Visual Center has completed production of a total of 243 reels of 16mm motion pictures.

During the period of 1952 to 1955 the Audio-Visual Center presented a weekly series of one-half hour live television programs entitled "Panorama." The purpose of the series was to provide Audio-Visual Center staff and students with the opportunity to utilize still pictures, slides, filmstrips, and motion pictures within TV format.

A number of Indiana University motion picture productions have won important awards. CONSPIRACY IN KYOTO was selected for public exhibition (the highest possible honor) at the 7th International Edinburgh Film Festival and won awards in several festivals in the United States. SPLIT THE RING won the Golden Reel Award, the highest award in the Recreation Category, at the Second 16mm National Film Assembly sponsored by the Film Council of America. THE LEGISLATIVE PROCESS was awarded the George Washington Medal by the Freedom Foundation during its 1955 Washington Birthday ceremonies. THE MENTAL HOSPITAL VOLUNTEER: SOMEONE WHO CARES was awarded a certificate of merit for its functional excellence by the Film Council of Greater Columbus, Ohio. YOUR STATE TROOPER was given an honorable mention by the Screen Producers Guild for its excellence as a student-produced film. SIMPLE MOLDS, the sixth in the Craftsmanship in Clay Series, was awarded a certificate of merit at the Cleveland Film Festival.

The sale of prints of Indiana University motion picture productions increased from 256 in 1950 to 625 in 1955.

Professional Education and Research:

Semester hours of graduate instruction in audio-visual education increased from 1,188 in 1950 to 1,746 in 1955.

There has been a steady increase in the number of students undertaking work in audio-visual education on the doctoral level. Thirty-eight students have completed doctoral studies in audio-visual education. Forty-two students are undertaking work on the doctoral level toward a major in audio-visual education and twenty-five with a minor. Over 75 students are undertaking graduate work in audio-visual education in order to qualify for the audio-visual supervisor's certificate adopted in 1952 by the State Board of Education.

A two-year graduate sequence of four graduate courses was begun in 1951–52. Students in the second year of the sequence produce as one of the requirements of the course films in cooperation with state agencies and non-profit groups.

An effort has been made to employ graduate students wherever possible in all activities of the Audio-Visual Center. That this has been successful is evidenced by the fact that during 1954–55 sixty students held appointments or hourly positions with the Audio-Visual Center with a minimum of employment of twelve hours per week at a rate of $1.00 per hour.

Future Developments

Materials Activities:

The demand by school and community groups for services offered by the Audio-Visual Center will continue to increase during the next fifteen years, and schools will be required to increase substantially expenditures for audio-visual materials according to the Rules and Regulations approved in July 1955, by the Commission on General Education of the Indiana State Board of Education. Circulation during the next fifteen years should increase to an annual minimum of 150,000 reels per year if the size of the library can be increased by 50 per cent to 36,000 reels. This would require an expenditure of another $500,000 for films with a considerable portion of this amount allocated for the addition of films for use by general adult groups and by college and university classes. Here again, the major part of this cost would be covered by income from service fees.

A substantial increase over the next fifteen years can be expected in the use of films by adult groups because of the shortening of the work week, the desire for knowledge and culture by adult groups, and technical developments which will make it possible to use TV receivers for the projection of motion pictures. This demand can best be met by establishing a collection of films in the extension centers, which will make it possible for a program chairman of an adult group to drive to the center and pick up the film the day before its planned use and return it the following day.

The University needs a library of a minimum of 36,000 reels to serve adequately schools and departments of the campus and to meet laboratory demands for a graduate program of education and research in audio-visual education.

The demand is increasing for the use of all types of audio-visual materials by University faculty members. Over the next fifteen years, bookings of materials for faculty use should increase from 8,000 in 1955 to more than 50,000 in 1965.

Production Activities:

Because of the interest of faculty members in the production of motion pictures for use on the campus which will have a wide sale and rental to other universities, public schools, and adult groups, it can be anticipated that there will be over the next fifteen years a substantial increase in production activity. The increase in sales will follow refinements in quality and some increase in quantity with an anticipated sale of 5,000 prints and a gross annual income of over $400,000 within the next fifteen years.

There will be an increasing desire on the part of state agencies to cooperate with Indiana University in the production of films dealing with the human, cultural, industrial, mineral, and agricultural resources of the state. It will be possible to recover production costs through a grant by state agencies and from the income received through the sale and rental of materials to Indiana school and adult groups.

Professional Education and Research:

According to recent Rules and Regulations approved by the Commission on General Education of the Indiana State Board of Education, schools holding a continuous or higher commission must have an audio-visual program in operation and a director of the program who has had at least five semester hours of audio-visual education courses. This ruling affects approximately 1,500 elementary and secondary schools and will result in a heavy demand from a large number of students for audio-visual courses over the next several years.

The increase in the number of students working on audio-visual supervisory certificates will make it possible to recruit from among these outstanding students those who should be encouraged to continue work on the doctoral level.

With the interest of state agencies in the production of all types of audio-visual materials, it will be possible to develop an internship training program with costs covered by grants from state agencies and from income received through the sale and rental of productions in Indiana and neighboring states.

Because of the increasing recognition of the importance of audio-visual materials for the dissemination of ideas, it can be expected that foundations, government agencies, and industry will begin to increase their support of research in mass media. With the continued development of the graduate program in audio-visual education, Indiana University should be in a position to obtain its share of funds for doctoral and faculty research projects.

Bureau of Public Discussion

In 1940 this Bureau was serving a large number of club women and school teachers in the State. No appreciable contact with other types of groups had developed to any large degree. Package libraries including books were loaned on a very wide range of topics.

The Bureau administered four contests, namely the Latin contest, the Mathematics contest, the program of the High School Discussion League, and a Music contest.

Special services were given to such groups as the Indiana Federation of Art Clubs, the Federation of Poetry Clubs, and the Federation of Women's Clubs. For the first two of these organizations the service was chiefly the preparing and mailing of a newsletter to local officers. For the Federation of Women's Clubs a series of club study programs was prepared and sent to officers or members on request.

The service also sent textbooks to the University Centers and to individual correspondence study students. Special collections of art exhibits were loaned to art clubs, schools, and other groups.

A drama loan service was also provided. This service loaned plays to schools and organizations for examination and preview before such groups selected plays for local production. A bulletin *Stage Door* was also released to help schools and other groups in preparing for local play productions.

Home Reading Courses were developed to help individuals select and read good books. Reading courses on various topics were supplied. After completion of the reading and satisfactory reports on the books were submitted, a reading certificate was issued to the individual.

Comparable data is not available to make a comparison with the figures of more recent years. It is reasonable to say, however, that hundreds of schools, organizations, and individuals were served in 1940 and for years prior to this date.

In 1949 the Bureau underwent changes both in administration and program.

The program was studied in the light of its potential for improving the quality of citizenship. It was evident that the intellectual and material resources of the University disseminated by such a Bureau could contribute much to the development of informed citizenship.

The attempt to provide package libraries on literally hundreds of topics was curtailed. The distribution of books was left entirely to the public libraries. Emphasis was placed on briefs, study outlines, and package libraries which informed the public on all views of current local, state, national, and international problems. To this end faculty members and advanced graduate students were used in helping prepare the briefs and study outlines. Cooperation on the part of University departments was excellent. The positions of Package Library Analysts were up-graded, thus making it possible to employ better qualified personnel to spearhead the preparation of briefs, outlines, and the compilation of package library materials.

The revised program served not only club women and teachers but groups such as ministers, county and city officials, labor groups, legislators, and others who play an important part in shaping public opinion and in executing civic improvement.

Among a few of the topics covered by study outlines and package libraries were Indiana State and local government, school building needs, mental health, school and community cooperation, America's law courts, financing tomorrow's highways, religion in the schools, juvenile delinquency, and underdeveloped countries and foreign aid.

Home Reading Courses were continued as a valuable and appreciated service to several hundred people each year who wish to find some purpose and guidance in their reading activities.

The High School Achievement Program was changed to a single program offering as parts of this program competitive examinations in English, Latin, Mathematics, and Spanish. The Indiana High School Forensic League assumed the responsibility for speech contests, and the University School of Music assumed responsibility for the music contests.

The activities of the Bureau for 1955–56 follow the pattern outlined in 1949 and 1950 except for one major change. The study outlines that were originally designed as guides to the study of Package Libraries have seemed to acquire an independent importance beyond what was originally planned. Increasing numbers of the outlines are now being sold outside the State, principally to other colleges and universities and to public libraries, in some cases in large quantities for discussion or study groups. The outlines are supplied free in Indiana. The outlines are now going into many important institutions—the one on law courts to Harvard Law School Library, Kiplinger's magazine CHANGING TIMES has asked permission to list them in their bibliographies. H. W. Wilson is listing them in the VERTICAL FILE INDEX and the Tax Foundation in their LIBRARY BULLETIN; and more than occasionally other publishers or authors make mention of them. It seems that much more in the way of quality and scholarship is now required in these outlines than was in our minds when we first undertook making them.

The High School Achievement Program this year enrolled 2,866 of the best students in many schools throughout the State. About 1,000 of these students and some five or six hundred teachers came to the campus for the final examinations and the selection of the winners in various high school fields of study. This program should be improved and expanded but it cannot be done with the present limited personnel of the Bureau.

During the past year 50,000 briefs were distributed. A total of 5,300 study outlines was supplied and 2,248 package libraries were loaned. A total of 105 persons enrolled in home reading courses, and 230 requests for drama loans were filled.

An informed citizenry is an invaluable asset to the State. The work of this Bureau and all other units of the Division of Adult Education and Public Services lend great service in helping attain this goal. Some of these services such as the Bureau of Public Discussion have little income other than direct budgetary support from the University. Means must be found to permit those non-income producing services that can be administered best by a university to go forward in their work with constant improvement in quality and effectiveness.

Community Services in Adult Education

1947–50

Activities which were developed during this period were of three main kinds: (1) lecture series, leadership training institutes, discussion programs, and campus conferences; (2) the development of an on-campus graduate studies program of adult education—one of the very few in the country; (3) the investigation through research of various kinds of resources specifically aimed at helping adults to help educate themselves in ways which contribute to the maturation of a democratic society. Eight kinds of training, lecture, or discussion series reached over 7,000 people in 90 communities. In addition, adult education councils were established in 11 cities and towns, half a dozen special resources were developed and printed, a newsletter was issued seven times yearly and an adult education library was begun. During part of this period Community Services was also responsible for the Indiana University State Fair exhibits and the coordinating of conferences conducted on the Indiana University campus.

Throughout this period Community Services was feeling its way. Several years were required to clarify the department's function, to discover primary educational needs of the citizens of the state, and to experiment with different methods of meeting those needs. Rather than merely imitating the activities of bureaus of community development carried on by other universities, we were endeavoring to unite the threefold phases of our work—research, service, and graduate teaching—into a program that would permit us to make significant contribution to the broad field of adult education. Our aim was the development and putting to work of a philosophy of education for adults in a free society. To this end were directed the observations, the collection of data, and analysis carried on.

1951–55

In this period several of the above activities continued to receive emphasis while certain others were modified or discontinued in the light of earlier experiment and study. The developing and publishing of resource materials continued to be stressed. The graduate studies program was expanded to the extent that an average of seventy students from 8 to 10 countries were in yearly attendance. The curriculum was approved by both the Graduate School and the School of Education as acceptable for the granting of the doctorate in adult education.

Meanwhile the experience gained in a wide variety of field activities provided the necessary background to develop the institutional approach to adult education in basic institutions like hospitals, churches, and libraries. This latter research-service activity (which now has reached 5,500 persons in 60 communities and has received financial support from four outside organizations) can perhaps be said to have proven itself a unique contribution to the field of adult education. The institutional projects have gained national attention in hospital, religious, and library adult education with one religious denomination already sending persons to the campus from over the nation to be trained to develop similar projects on a nationwide scale.

1955–70

Throughout the state there is growing demand for extension of the institutional adult education projects to religious denominations, public libraries, hospitals, industries, labor unions, etc., that are yet unreached. Before this service can become effective, however, further research is needed to add to the information already obtained in such areas as how adults learn, what are productive methods for adult learning, and how can the coordination of our institutional programs of adult education be effected for community betterment. Of the four community institutions to be studied (industry, hospitals, churches, and libraries) two—hospitals and churches—are now in the final stage of development. The library phase of the study is in the second year and needs an additional year for completion. The industrial phase is just starting the first of a three-year program of research and service.

The final stage of all the separate institutional programs will be in their integration in the community. In several communities we have worked with or are working in all four institutions. The full fruition of the project will be realized only when the 200 to 500 people in the four different institutions in a selected community extend themselves beyond their institution into the whole community.

Each year the demand for service has increased in the area of institutional services, campus clinics, and the graduate program. We anticipate the need for two additional staff members to keep pace with the service demands and one additional research and teaching faculty member. These staff requirements are envisioned despite the fact that an increasingly larger number of graduate students will be used in the development of these projects.

Lecture Bureau

While the offering of special lectures by University faculty members was one of the first forms of extension work dating back to the 1880s, the demand for lectures today is not as great as it was in earlier years.

The advent of radio and television with its many educational programs in the form of lectures, forums, panel discussions, as well as its programs in music, drama, and interpretation of news and world conditions, has overshadowed the individual speaker on the ordinary speaking platform.

In earlier times the University supplied hundreds of lectures to schools, clubs, and civic groups. During the past year slightly more than fifty lectures were supplied through the Lecture Bureau. It is important, however, that the University encourage its faculty to accept lecture engagements when called upon to do so. A faculty member is more valuable to his department and to the University if he gets away from the campus frequently and rubs elbows with citizens of the State.

Bureau of Industrial and Labor Services
Review of Program to Date

Though a few universities have participated on a relatively small scale in worker's education since its inception in this country, it was not until World War II that interest in this area of adult education became widespread. This increased interest resulted, at least in part, from the increased interests of the general field of adult education. It also reflected a recognition of the important role of organized labor in community life, and a growing recognition that individuals associated with the labor movement required specialized training in order to meet their responsibilities more effectively. As distinguished from general adult education, the traditional object of which has been individual improvement, worker's education has been concerned primarily with the needs of the worker in his collective capacity as a member or leader of a trade union, and with labor's collective relationships to management, government, and society as a whole. The underlying assumption of such a program is that it will contribute to better industrial relations.

Increasingly the labor unions are looking to the nation's colleges and universities for educational services which have traditionally been offered to other groups in the community, and the forthcoming merger of the AFL and CIO should give additional stimulus to worker's education activities. Worker's education is becoming an increasingly important function of many American colleges and universities, and labor groups have proposed a national extension bill to increase university services to workers.

In recognition of this trend, Indiana University in 1946 appointed a Coordinator of Industrial Relations to work with labor groups in the planning and development of educational programs. The Coordinator, a specialist in the field of labor relations, was located in Indianapolis and carried a half-time teaching load at the Indianapolis Center in addition to his duties as Coordinator.

Since 1946 educational classes and institutes have been conducted for various labor groups in the state. The United Steelworkers of America have utilized university faculty and facilities for week-long summer institutes each year since 1947, and during the past summer held two such institutes. For several years a similar program was conducted for the United Automobile Workers and the State CIO Industrial Union Council. Occasional week-end conferences and lecture series on particular topics were held in various parts of the state at the request of local groups using Indiana University faculty as instructors. In addition, an effort has been made to acquaint union groups with other services of the university such as those available through the University Centers, correspondence work, package libraries, lecture service, films, etc.

The Coordinator of Industrial Relations since the inception of the program resigned this year in order to devote full time to teaching and research. At this time the service was redesignated as the Bureau of Industrial and Labor Services, and a Director was appointed who is to be located in the Division of Adult Education and Public Services on the Bloomington campus. In addition to his duties as Director of the Bureau of Industrial and Labor Services, he will teach one course at the Indianapolis Center.

Future Development

Though primary emphasis in this report is placed on the continuing development of a program of labor education, it is contemplated that the Bureau will cooperate with other university groups in rendering service to industrial firms and other business groups which may wish university assistance. The first effort along this line will be to work with the University Center directors and the Division's other Service Bureaus to expand the programs which have already been started and to help with developments in other communities as well.

The development of a successful program of worker's education requires the acceptance and active participation of the trade union movement and of those branches of the university which will be called upon to participate in the program. Accordingly it is contemplated that an advisory committee composed of representatives from these groups will be formed, probably after the merger of the AFL and the CIO. This committee will not only be in a position to give valuable advice concerning the development of the program, but will also serve to give to those groups a better knowledge of what the service can offer and how it operates.

An effort will be made to concentrate on quality programs which are within the capabilities of the service as it develops. It will also be the purpose of the service not only to conduct its own programs, but to encourage the development of worker's education activities generally within the state, particularly at the local level. In the past and to a large extent at present the emphasis in worker's education has been on courses designed to meet the practical needs of workers and union leaders such as collective bargaining, parliamentary procedure, labor law, etc. While undoubtedly such topics will continue to be an important part of a program of worker's education, it is toward an increasing use of university "talent" in broader areas of knowledge that future development will probably lie. The future course of development will fall within three general categories: On-campus programs, off-campus programs, and other services.

A. On-Campus Programs
  1. A continuation of the summer institutes during which union members and union leaders come to the campus for a full week of intensive work. Another institute is already being planned for the steelworkers for the summer of 1956. An effort will be made to acquaint other union groups with the advantages of such a program.
  2. During the school year weekend conferences on particular subjects will be held on campus. Plans are now being made for several such conferences for the steelworkers during the coming year.
  3. Regular courses of approximately 12 to 13 weeks duration during the regular school year especially designed for a select group of union leaders have been under consideration. Several problems must be overcome before such a program can be undertaken, particularly that of cost to the union. However it is hoped that eventually such a course can be arranged.

B. Off-Campus Programs
  In order to bring an education program directly to workers in their local communities, extention classes, lecture-forums, and weekend conferences will be made available to local groups. The development of such a program requires the use of instructors from local areas in addition to regular university staff. It is hoped that an adequate number of qualified people in various parts of the state can be persuaded to cooperate in the development of such a program. They could be drawn from various employments, including other colleges, arbitrators, labor attorneys, union officials, government administrators in labor agencies, and labor and industrial consultants.
  In the development of off-campus programs, the Director will work in cooperation with the University Centers whenever possible.

C. Other Services
  Insofar as time and staff permit future development may also include the following services:
  1. Assisting union and management groups in conducting their own programs.
  2. Developing and arranging for the booking of educational movie series for union and management groups.
  3. Providing speakers for management and union-operated programs.
  4. Providing reading lists and reference material to individuals and groups interested in particular subjects.
  5. Supplying materials, suggestions, and advice to local union workers education committees.
  6. Collection of a library of publications which may be loaned to participating groups and be of value to the Bureau in the conduct of its program.
  7. Research and publication on pertinent topics.

State Fair

For several years the administration of the Indiana University exhibit has been under the direction of the Division of Adult Education. About 400,000 people annually view these exhibits of various departments of the University.

The University building at the State Fair grounds contains a large auditorium in which musical events, stage productions, and special lectures are presented. A limited space in the corridors allows facilities for numerous departments to exhibit departmental work and various other phases of University activity. More space for exhibits should be provided, thus allowing the departments to provide better exhibits of an educational nature. By reducing slightly the size of the auditorium additional exhibit space could be provided.

Among the various departments and units which exhibited this year were: Indiana Daily Student, athletics, I.U.'s building program, Adult Education, Medicine, Dentistry, Nurses' Training, speech correction, Medical technology, Fine Arts, I.U. Press, Chemistry, Geology, Botany, Speech and Theatre, Business, Music, English, and the Admissions Office.

A future possibility is to place the State Fair directly in the Division's Audio-Visual Center and to create a year-around department of exhibits. Such a department would not only be responsible for the State Fair but would also serve many other needs as well throughout the year. Graphs, charts, miniatures, and posters could be made for departmental use and for use by campus conferences and institutes. Small educational exhibits, models, and charts could be made in cooperation with University departments and loaned to schools and organizations throughout the State. Such miniature exhibits could be rented to cover a major part of the cost.

Just as the University has a printing plant, a photographic laboratory, a center for motion picture production, a testing bureau, facilities for meeting carpenter, plumbing, and maintenance needs, so should it have a department of exhibits which will fill all-university needs in this field, including the State Fair exhibit.

. . . .

The Division of Adult Education and Public Services has the third largest operating budget in the University. However, due to its student fees and service charges, the Division is 77.1 per cent self supporting. Probably nowhere in the University is so much being done on such a large scale with so little cost to our University appropriations.

It would be ideal for our services throughout the State to be free but the general University budget, without substantial additional funds, cannot offer free this enormous program as it is now developing.

Faculty Council Minutes, 1955–57, pp. 179–192.

Document 187

An Age of the Organization Man

Like every other phase of the growing and complicated new university, the status of student organizations came under constant question. In earlier days it was not difficult to identify the purposes of organizations or to approve their admission to full status on the campus. In the 1950's this task became more complicated. One of the things which stimulated this report was the appearance on the campus of the Green Feather anti-McCarthy organization. Before this issue was settled the Green Feathers had become almost as great ogres as the Wisconsin senator himself.

*   *   *

PROPOSED REGULATIONS PERTAINING TO THE RECOGNITION OF
NEW STUDENT ORGANIZATIONS

I. General Requirements for Recognition

   A. Those organizations whose purposes are consistent with the broad educational objectives of the University and the laws of the United States and the State of Indiana, will be recognized, subject to the regulations which follow. When making application for recognition, the group shall submit a statement explaining how the purposes of the proposed organization are consistent with the educational objectives of Indiana University.

   B. Membership in student organizations shall be restricted to students and employees of Indiana University and their respective spouses.

   C. Recognition will not be granted any organization which prohibits membership in the organization because of race, religion, or national origin. Some of the requirements for recognition may be waived for organizations of religious character.

   D. The group must keep all its funds in a manner acceptable to the Treasurer's Office of Indiana University.

   E. Recognition will not be granted to a petitioning group which duplicates the purposes and functions of a previously recognized group unless it can show in its application the need for an additional group in the area concerned.

II. Meetings for Purpose of Organizing

   Individuals planning to organize a group preparatory to submitting an application for recognition shall notify the Student Activities Office of their intention and arrange for the use of a meeting room for specific organizational purposes. Such notification shall precede any general activities of the group.

III. Procedure for Securing Recognition

   A. To request recognition, the officers of the group shall submit the following to the Student Activities office:

      1. Two copies of the proposed constitution and by-laws.
      2. A list of officers.
      3. A list of prospective members.
      4. The names of any organization with which the petitioning group intends to be affiliated together with a copy of the constitution and by-laws or a complete statement of the purposes of that organization.
      5. A letter from a full-time member of the faculty or administrative staff which indicates his willingness to act as adviser to the organization if recognition is granted. Acceptance of the responsibility of being an adviser to a student organization should evidence genuine interest in the objectives of that organization and of the activities by which it is hoped these objectives will be attained.

   B. Within two weeks, excluding summer sessions and vacations, after receiving the application the Student Activities Office will transmit it and supporting material to the Student Senate with advisory comments.

   C. The Student Senate may vote either to grant or to deny recognition. This vote will be subject to appeal for one week following the date on which it is taken. If the decision of the Student Senate is not appealed within one week, it automatically becomes final. Either the petitioning group or the Student Activities Office may appeal the decision of the Student Senate. If such an appeal is made within the week following the Student Senate vote on the matter, it will be acted on by a committee composed of *a representative of the President of the Student Body, a member of the faculty appointed by the President of the University, and the Dean of Students. The Dean of Students shall serve as chairman of the committee. The action of the committee shall be final.*

D. If final action by the Student Senate is not taken within six school weeks, excluding summer sessions and vacations, from the date the application was referred to the Activities Office, the petitioning group may appeal to the Dean of Students, who will request the appointment of a joint appeal committee as described in III. C. above.

E. While action upon an application is pending, the Student Activities Office may authorize the organization to conduct specific organizational activities upon request.

IV. Requirements for Maintenance of Recognition

A. The organization shall continue to meet the conditions for initial recognition previously listed.

B. The organization shall act in good faith with the spirit of the regulations of the University for recognized organizations.

C. Each organization must register the names of its officers and members with the Student Activities Office at the beginning of each semester or summer session, such a list to be submitted by the end of the third week of the semester (or second week of summer session).

D. Additions to membership must be reported to the Student Activities Office promptly.

E. No student organization may use the name of Indiana University or participate as a group in off-campus affairs. However, where the campus group is a collegiate branch of a larger organization, the campus branch may send delegates to national or regional meetings and participate in the regularly published program of events at such meetings.

F. Groups may have meetings for students and employees of the University, but they may not sponsor meetings open to the public except as co-sponsors with the University. Demonstrations and material distributed by a student organization must be for students and University employees only.

G. Changes in the constitution of a recognized organization or changes in the status or affiliation of a group must be reported to the Student Senate for approval or disapproval within two school weeks excluding summer sessions and vacations. Such changes may cause the recognized status of the groups to be reviewed by the Senate.

V. Withdrawal of Recognition.

Action to withdraw recognition of an organization for violation of the above requirements may be instituted by the Student Senate upon its own discretion and shall be instituted by it upon the request of the Activities Office. Action will be taken only after open hearings at which the officers of the organization may be heard upon their request. This action may be appealed by either the group concerned or by the Student Activities Office by following the procedure for appeal described in III. C. above.

Faculty Council Minutes, 1955–57, pp. 135–137.

Document 188

Planning the New Campus

In this era of constructing new buildings and rushing ahead at break-neck speed in order to provide new classrooms and student housing, it was fortunate that officials took time to draft a campus plan which would serve both functional and aesthetic demands. The campus did not turn out exactly according to this plan; for instance, the library was not located on the site of East Hall. The institution's hundred-year ambitions were outlined in this document.

*   *   *

5. President Wells made an Interim Report on the University's Site Planning Program for the Bloomington Campus. He stated that this is an effort to plan a coordinated building program for the next 75 to 100 years and will require great vision. He requested that Council members hear the report, consider the program carefully, discuss it with other members of the faculty, and make suggestions concerning the program. Faculty members may arrange through Vice-President Franklin's office to see maps showing the locations of present and proposed buildings.

The plan for the campus follows two basic ideas: (1) a compact arrangement of all important class buildings and libraries in a central campus, with student housing and certain nonacademic functions occupying adjacent areas around the central campus, and (2) retention of the present informal wooded areas and the quiet relaxed character of the campus.

To carry out the first of these ideas the Humanities Building, which will be located on Forest Place, will be in the center of the academic area, and no two of the major academic buildings, including the libraries, will be more than 2,000 feet apart. A new library building will be located in the area of East Hall. Buildings for some of the special research institutes not involving large numbers of students may be located outside of the central academic area. Facilities for military classes and playgrounds for use in all class recreational activities will be within the compact central area, i. e., on the fields around the present athletic plant, including Jordan Field. The present field house and gymnasium will be greatly extended to house the School of H.P.E.R. and student physical and recreational activities with separate facilities for men and women. An intercollegiate athletic plant will be built in the region of 17th Street and Fee Lane. Recreational facilities and play areas will be strategically located in all peripheral residential areas. Faculty housing and apartment houses for married students will be developed on lands northeast of the campus. A new University School is planned for the ground just east of the present University School Athletic Field and the present University School Building will be devoted to other academic purposes.

The quiet informal character of the compact campus will be retained by preserving the present wooded quadrangle and the beech grove between the Chemistry and Medical Buildings. Similar wooded sanctuaries will be preserved wherever possible in the housing areas. As an example the woods just east of the new Smithwood Dormitory will be retained. Automobile traffic and parking will be excluded from the central campus and nearby parking lots provided all around its periphery.

In the hundred-year plan the University would plan to acquire all the land between its present holdings and Indiana Avenue in the region between 3rd Street on the south and Matlock Road on the north. In the region of the central academic campus the University would plan to purchase the property facing on 3rd Street from the south and that between Indiana Avenue and Dunn Street on the west, except for present student houses, including fraternity and sorority buildings located in this region.

Buildings being planned for the near future are: (1) the Humanities Building, (2) the Rare Books Library, (3) an addition to Swain Hall, (4) enlargement of the Union Building, (5) Security Training Institute, (6) addition to the Music Building, (7) building for Fine Arts including Radio and T. V., (8) intercollegiate athletic plant, (9) extension of the present field house and gymnasium for H.P.E.R., physical education, and recreation, (10) student housing units for both men and women just east of the Men's Quad, and (11) faculty and married student housing northeast of the campus.

Plan for financing the building program include (1) funds from the State of Indiana for all academic buildings, and (2) self liquidating financing of the Union Building, an intercollegiate athletic plant, and all housing units. State funds have already been appropriated for beginning the Humanities Building and the additions to Music and Swain Halls.

At the next Council meeting Vice-President Franklin will make a brief report on the University's building plan for the Indianapolis campus.

The Council adjourned at 5:05 p.m.

SID ROBINSON
Secretary

Faculty Council Minutes, 1955–57, pp. 139–140.

Document 189

Through the Maze of Athletic Scholarships

Eternally Indiana University struggled with the problem of developing a good athletic program inside the Big Ten or Western Athletic Conference. Its problems stemmed from three sources: lack of money, lack of competitive football talents in the state to supply three major schools, and the complicated and ever-changing rules of the conference. Professor John F. Mee was for many years chairman of the University Committee on Athletics, and in this extensive report he reveals the intricacies, pitfalls, and frustrations of Big Ten athletics.

*   *   *

Action of the Council

3. The Chairman called on Professor John F. Mee, Chairman of the University Committee on Athletics, to present his report. Professor Mee said that some years ago the Faculty Council had requested an annual report from the Committee on Athletics. For several years, the Athletic Committee prepared a voluminous and detailed written report concerning the athletic program. Since there

had been some uncertainty as to the nature of the report desired by the Faculty Council, Professor Mee said that he had decided to present an oral report consisting chiefly of comment on a series of questions submitted to him by the Agenda Committee of the Council. He also said that he would be glad to answer questions raised by Council members.

Professor Mee prefaced his comments by noting that Indiana University was one of the early members of the Big Ten Conference, also known as the Western Conference, or the Intercollegiate Conference. Indiana was an early member of the Conference which was organized before 1900. There has been very little change of membership in its history. From its beginnings, one of the basic principles of the Conference has been Faculty control of athletics. At the level of the member institution, this control may be exercised either by the entire Faculty, by a Faculty Committee, or by a Committee made up of Faculty, alumni, and student representatives. Indiana University operates under the third type of committee, and at the present time the Athletic Committee has as its voting members five Faculty, and three alumni representatives. There are also non-voting advisory members, consisting of designated University officials and representatives of the Student Senate.

The first of the questions suggested to the Athletic Committee concerned the nature and objectives of the recently organized Indiana University Varsity Club. Professor Mee reported that the Varsity Club is Indiana University's official athletic booster organization, and is a part of the University Alumni Association. Its purposes are: (1) To unite, in an organized effort, the friends and alumni of Indiana University who wish to express their interest in the University and a desire to serve it through their particular interest in Indiana University Athletics; (2) To uphold the aims and policies of athletics at Indiana University and of the Big Ten Intercollegiate Conference; (3) To encourage the attendance at Indiana University of outstanding prospective students who may contribute to Indiana University athletics; (4) To contribute, through the Indiana University Foundation, to additional financial opportunities for Indiana University athletes who qualify academically for assistance to be administered by the University Scholarship Committee under Big Ten rules. Any alumnus, former student, or friend of the University is eligible for membership, and the annual membership fee is $5. The Varsity Club last year raised $15,000 for scholarships. The total membership is approximately 1,100-1,200. There are no prerogatives for membership at the present time. As paid-up members of the Alumni Association, members of the Varsity Club are entitled to priority opportunities in the purchase of athletic tickets.

Professor Remak raised a question about the activities of organizations such as the Varsity Club in improperly providing transportation expenses for prospective athletes to visit a campus for interviews. Professor Mee replied that there had been a good deal of concern with this problem, and that the office of the Commissioner of the Big Ten Conference was fully aware of it, and had been undertaking some investigation. One of the sources of difficulty has been activity of this sort on the part of unofficial organizations. Indiana University has not been directly involved in this problem. Funds raised by the Varsity Club have actually been less than sufficient to provide for total scholarships awarded, so that there has been no question of improper use of Varsity Club funds. President Wells reported that the Commissioner of the Western Conference approved of the type of club represented by Indiana's Varsity Club but that he was opposed to the unofficial clubs.

The discussion then turned to consideration of the problem of athletic scholarships, which had been the second question presented to the Athletic Committee. Dean Cleland inquired about the academic standards used by the Scholarship Committee in making awards to athletes, were they the same or different from the academic standards used in making general scholarship awards? Professor Long, a member of the Scholarship Committee, replied that for general scholarships there was actually a higher cut-off point in terms of grade point averages than was the case for either athletic or music scholarships. Several members commented on the desirability of awarding athletic scholarships to those who were also high quality students. Professor Mee expressed complete agreement with this point of view. Under the Western Conference rules he said, an entering freshman must be in the upper third of his high school class in order to receive a scholarship, and must maintain a grade-point average of 1.5 while in the University in order to hold a scholarship. An athletic scholarship may not exceed in amount the highest scholarship granted to non-athletes. In general, the Western Conference schools have faced considerable competition from the Ivy League and the service academies in recruiting athletes who were at the same time outstanding students. The size of the scholarship that can be offered to an athlete is considerably smaller than that offered by certain of the Eastern schools. The solution would appear to lie in a general increase in the level of scholarship awards. President Wells confirmed the loss of high scholarship athletes to the Ivy League schools. Professor Mee said that some misunderstanding of the standards required for athletic scholarships arose because of confusion between the scholarship program, which does not require service, and the work program, for which lower rated students are eligible.

Professor Mee reported that Indiana University had a total of approximately 400 students on all of its varsity squads. This might be compared with a total of 1,535 such students at Ohio State. At Indiana University, 59 of the 400 hold some form of athletic scholarship. The majority of these receive tuition only. Others receive awards over and above tuition. The highest award at the present time is $915 and there are fourteen presently at this amount. There are seven at $594, and others at lesser amounts. In response to a question from Professor Pratt, Professor Mee said that twelve of the recipients of the larger scholarships were on the football squad and two on the basketball squad. There are some freshmen among the recipients of scholarships. President Wells said that there were Ivy League scholarships that ran to $2400-$2800 and that while these were technically not athletic scholarships, athletes with good academic records frequently obtained awards at this level.

In the course of further discussion of athletic scholarship matters, Professor Mee and Dean Patty pointed out that once an athletic scholarship is awarded to a boy, it is paid as long as his academic record is maintained, even if he does not make a team, or should be injured. A student who voluntarily gave up a sport would, however, forfeit his athletic scholarship. Professor Hopper inquired about the Conference scholarship rule which seems to imply that a student with a 1.5 average was a superior student. Professor Mee and Professor Breneman pointed out that this rule was actually an operating rule, and that the language of the rule referred to superior scholarship rather than superior student. The 1.5 average is "superior" in the sense that it is higher than the average required for graduation. Professor Remak inquired about the promise of a full four years of scholarship made to athletes, and asked whether there are similar promises made to nonathletes. Professor Long and Dean Shaffer replied that the general University scholarships are all annual grants, but are usually renewed if the student's scholarship is maintained. Professor Forney inquired as to how many of the 400 members of Indiana's varsity squads received no help at all, either in the form of scholarships or work. Dean Patty and Professor Mee indicated that about half of this group had no financial aid. Professor Mee added that all members of the football and basketball squads are either on scholarships or the work program. Those athletes receiving no financial assistance are mostly in sports other than football or basketball.

Dean Shaffer inquired about the problem of special financial need justifying additional assistance, frequently in the form of loans. Professor Mee said that the Western Conference had recognized the problem of loans and had ruled that loans must come from some official source. Dean Collins then raised the general question as to the control of friendly or unofficial or unauthorized financial aid. Professor Mee said that the Conference rules with respect to loans had actually become so strict as to discriminate against athletes. Dean Gucker inquired about the enforcement of Conference policy with respect to financial assistance. Professor Mee said that the Faculty representatives made the rules and that the office of the Commissioner enforced them. One other enforcement device was the requirement of a signed statement from each athlete that he is not receiving aid from any source other than his parent or guardian or official University aid. President Wells reported that the Big Ten Presidents at their meetings constantly receive reports of violation. He also said that the member institutions in the Conference supplied extensive financial reports of all aid to athletes. The office of the Commissioner maintains a staff of investigators who thoroughly check reported violations. In the majority of cases the rumors of violations are not confirmed by investigation.

As a summary statement on the question of athletic scholarships, Professor Mee said that no State funds were used for this purpose at Indiana University. Athletic scholarship funds are provided entirely by contributions, receipts from television rights, and earnings of the athletic program itself.

Professor Mee then turned to a discussion of the organization and procedures of the Faculty Committee on Athletics at Indiana University. This Committee is appointed by the President of the University and is to be composed of not more than eight members, with a majority being Faculty members. The alumni members serve terms of three years and are not eligible for reappointment until at least one year has intervened after a three-year term of service on the Committee. The President of the University designates one of his appointees as Chairman of the Committee, and has the authority to replace any appointee at any time. Non-voting advisory members include: the Alumni Secretary, the Registrar, the Vice President and Treasurer, Dean of the Faculties, and Director of Athletics, representatives of the Student Senate, and the Director of Buildings and Grounds.

The functions of the Athletic Committee were described as follows: It (1) makes a continuing study of the athletic program and makes recommendations to the Administration concerning matters of policy relative to the conduct of inter-collegiate athletics; (2) votes on Conference and N.C.A.A. legislation and reports to appropriate Faculty legislative bodies; (3) approves selection of Athletic Director, coaches, and all major administrative employees as well as their contracts; (4) approves annual budget of Athletic Department; (5) enforces Conference eligibility rules through Athletic Director, Registrar, and Scholarship Offices; (6) controls ticket-pricing policy, sales promotion, and seating allocations; (7) advises on program of expansion of facilities (with Athletic Director and the University architect); (8) approves television and radio contracts recommended by the Athletic Director; (9) meets with representatives of

Student Senate on matters of special student interest, such as pricing of student tickets, and allocation of student seating; (10) makes complete annual report to the Faculty Council on the athletic program; (11) determines athletic awards policy, varsity letter and numeral awards, approves what sport shall be part of the inter-collegiate program.

The Director of Athletics advises the Committee as to the development of the athletic program. The Faculty representative (in the appropriate Western Conference organization) advises the Athletic Committee as to relationships with other members of the Big Ten and on all matters requiring Faculty action at each regular meeting. The Athletic Committee meets monthly during the school year and at such times as may be necessary.

Professor Remak noted that the University of Iowa chapter of the A.A.U.P. has made certain recommendations on the Faculty control of athletics. He said that it appeared that most of these recommendations had been implemented at Indiana University. He inquired about the question of limited terms of tenure on the Athletic Committee for the Faculty members. Professor Mee replied that this question was presently under consideration. The situation at Indiana University in recent years had seemed to require continuity of membership on the Athletic Committee. Dean Collins pointed out that the Athletic Committee was not unique in this respect and that many of the standing Committees of the University did not operate with limited terms of membership. President Wells said that several of the members of the Athletic Committee had asked to be relieved of their responsibilities but that he too had felt that continuity of membership was important in this case.

Professor Mee then turned to a discussion of the nature of the meetings of the Big Ten Faculty representatives. In general, he said, the Faculty representatives make rules for eligibility of athletes to participate in inter-collegiate contests. They consider and adopt rules dealing with the recruitment and subsidization of athletes. As an example of the type of problem presented to the Faculty representatives, he cited a recent discussion of the problem of recruitment of athletes by certain member schools in the Conference, in Canada, and Great Britain, and even in Australia. Finally he said each Faculty representative works in the interests of his own school and its coaching staff on certain matters. These are generally specific cases of eligibility in which a school may request certain exceptions to the rules in the light of unusual circumstances.

Professor Mee then reported on proposed changes of rules with respect to recruitment and subsidization of athletes. As reported in the press, these rules were adopted by a vote of 6 to 4 at the December meeting of the Faculty representatives. Before becoming effective, however, they must, according to Conference procedure, be confirmed by a second vote, which will be taken at the February meeting.

The rule changes are as follows:

(1) Athletic scholarships are to be on the basis of need. Each scholarship applicant must supply data on financial need to be set forth in a statement by the student's family on a form provided by the Educational Testing Service which reviews it and indicates the dollar amount of need recommended for the individual concerned. Allowance is made for variations in costs at the various Conference schools. An offer of an athletic scholarship limited to the amount recommended by the Educational Testing Service may then be made to the prospective athlete by a Big Ten School. Once the individual accepts an offer, no other member of the Conference may make a competing offer.

(2) No more than one hundred *initial offers* per year may be made by any member of the Conference. Professor Mee said that the purpose of this regulation was to limit the total cost of the program and also to limit the number of scholarships offered by the wealthier schools.

Professor Mee said that as the Indiana representative he had voted against these new rules, not because he disapproved the needs basis for athletic scholarships, but because of the complete omission of any standard of academic performance as a criterion for scholarship awards. The new rule would eliminate the present requirement that a freshman be in the upper third of his high school class and that a grade point average of 1.5 be maintained to retain a scholarship. Dean Cleland and several other Council members expressed approval of the position taken by Professor Mee as Indiana's Faculty representative.

Under the new rules dealing with recruitment and subsidization, a work program is still permissive. Likewise, the University Scholarship Committee will still administer the athletic scholarship program, and the funds for scholarships will still be handled by an official University organization; for example, at Indiana, the Indiana University Foundation.

The last question presented to Professor Mee for comment was "Why does the Athletic Committee feel that a 'big-time' athletic program is important for the welfare of Indiana University?" Professor Mee said that he had no specific answer for this question. The Athletic Committee had reviewed it and had expressed the view that as long as Indiana University remains a member of the Western Conference, the Athletic Committee will continue to work with and cooperate with that organization. The Committee through its Faculty representative will participate in the formation and application of Western Conference athletic policy. Dean Patty pointed out that under Big Ten Rules, athletes in order to be eligible for inter-collegiate competition, must pass every hour of course work in which they have enrolled. He noted that this actually imposed a higher standard of performance than that required of other students. Professor Breneman and Mr. Harrell also commented on the eligibility rules and pointed out that one difficulty was that students participating in athletics are diverted from courses that they desire to take or should take because of their concern for the eligibility rules.

Professor Sauvain (seconded by Professor Work) moved

THAT THE FACULTY COUNCIL EXPRESS ITS APPRECIATION TO PROFFESSOR MEE FOR AN EXCELLENT INFORMATION REPORT.

The motion was passed unanimously.

Faculty Council Minutes, 1955–57, pp. 215–220.

Document 190

Nothing less than an Attorney, a Scholar, and a Gentleman

The Law School was caught up in the exciting fermentation of university expansion. In this report the law faculty outlined a program for the school which took it far beyond the bounds conceived for it up to 1955. The proposed program took the training of lawyers beyond conditioning them for the traditional Hoosier courtrooms. In fact the proposed program looked at the law curriculum as an advance into universality which equipped the student to practice on one of many mature levels. Most important of all it conceived the study of law to be a mature scholarly undertaking.

*   *   *

REPORT OF THE SCHOOL OF LAW
to
THE FACULTY COUNCIL

I. HISTORY AND ORGANIZATION

In 1838, the General Assembly of the State of Indiana changed the name of Indiana College to Indiana University. At the same session, it declared that a School of Law should be established. The School of Law had for its declared purpose, "nothing less than the building up of a law school that shall be inferior to none west of the mountains; *one in which the student will be so well trained that he shall never in the attorney forget the scholar and the gentleman.*" The law faculty was charged with the duty "to furnish a complete course of legal education to gentlemen intended for the bar in any of the United States."

In this tradition the School has operated for more than one hundred years.

In 1842 operation of the School was begun by the appointment as professor of law, of Judge David McDonald, judge of the tenth Indiana judicial circuit. For some years, the School of Law had the unique distinction of having its faculty chosen indirectly by the voters of the tenth judicial circuit, which then consisted of seven south-central Indiana counties. The General Assembly fixed the terms of court so that they would not interfere with the law term of the University.

Since 1902, three academic years of work in law has been required for a law degree. In 1910, a formal requirement of two years' pre-law undergraduate work was imposed. Since 1938, the minimum requirement of three years of pre-law work has been required, with the further condition that the work taken must meet the requirements of the undergraduate school or college to the extent that it will confer its baccalaureate degree upon the successful completion of the first year of law. If this is impossible, an undergraduate degree is required as a prerequisite to admission to the School of Law.

In the summer of 1944 the Indiana University School of Law and the Indiana Law School of Indianapolis were consolidated. The latter school represented earlier consolidations of the following Indianapolis schools: The Indianapolis College of Law, The American Central Law School, The Benjamin Harrison Law School, and the Indiana Law School. As a result of this merger the Indianapolis Division of the School of Law began to function on September 1, 1944.

The Indianapolis Division is operated for the benefit of students who are unable to spend their entire time in the study of law, and who, therefore, can carry only a part of the studies regarded as the normal load for the full time student in the Bloomington Division. The minimum residence requirement for graduation after entrance into the School of Law in the Indianapolis Division is four academic years.

The two Divisions referred to above constitute a single School of Law, and the instructional staffs of the two Divisions constitute the faculty of the School of Law of Indiana University. Consequently, the same standards are maintained in both Divisions, and the same degrees are conferred. The administrative functions of the School of Law are performed by a Dean of the School. The Associate Dean of the School of Law is in charge of the Indianapolis Division and in this capacity performs his duties as the representative of, and with responsibility to, the Dean and faculty of the School of Law.

II. ENROLLMENT

The total enrollment in the Bloomington Division for the first semester of the academic year 1955-56 was 228; in the Indianapolis Division, 220, for a total enrollment of 448. This compares with a total enrollment of 431 in 1954; or 427 in 1953; and 417 in 1952. The ratio between the two Divisions has been about the same.

III. ADMISSION REQUIREMENTS AND PROCEDURES

Except in its graduate program, the School of Law handles its own admissions. Applications are submitted to the appropriate Division, and admission is granted, with or without conditions, or not granted, on the basis of standards worked out by the joint faculty.

Students seeking entrance under one of the combined curricula degree arrangements, at the end of three years of undergraduate college work, must have a scholastic record of 1.6 or better (1 being C). No deviation from this requirement is made. Students with undergraduate degrees must have a scholastic record of 1.2 for unconditional admission. However, if an applicant has not met this requirement, he is given the opportunity of taking aptitude tests administered by the University's bureau of Measurements. If his scores on these tests indicate a probability of his being able to pursue successfully the study of law, he *may* be admitted by faculty action.

Applications of students from without the United States, both for undergraduate and graduate law degrees, are processed with the aid and advice of Dean Dowling and Mr. Strain, and in the case of applicants for a graduate degree, with the further aid and advice of Dean Cleland or Dean Winther.

IV. CURRICULUM

In considering the development and growth of the curriculum of the School of Law during the last fifteen years, it is necessary to remember that during the first five years of that period we were engaged in World War II and during that period all efforts that could be made were made to keep the Bloomington Division in continuing operation and a temporary three semester year was adopted to accelerate the educational process. Indiana University took over the operation of the Indianapolis Division of the School of Law on September 1, 1944 at which time this Division was operated by three full-time teachers and a part-time faculty of eight. Courses were held four nights a week. The course offerings totaled 66 semesters hours and the library was composed of 7400 volumes, many of which were obsolete. In the eleven years since then, the faculty of the Indianapolis Division has increased to nine full-time members and only two or three part-time members are used to fill in for full-time members on leave and in certain specialized areas. The library now contains 44,000 volumes. In 1948 classes were extended to five evenings a week which continued up to the present time. We are now offering 90 hours of work in addition to writing and research and a legal clinic project operated in collaboration with the Indianapolis Legal Aid Society, Inc.

There have been two significant developments in the program of the Bloomington Division in the last ten years. The first development has been the establishment of a first year research program for the purpose of assisting first year students in adapting themselves to the study of law and in learning the techniques of legal research. Two full-time teaching associates are employed to do nothing but work throughout the year with first year students, counseling them, criticising their research efforts, and teaching them the use of books and other materials with which the lawyer must work. Insofar as it is possible, we have attempted a similar program in the Indianapolis Division but not as much can be done, nor in the same way, with part-time students who work five days a week at other jobs as can be done with the full-time students who devote all the days of their week to the study of law.

Students who enter the Bloomington Division of the Indiana University School of Law in September 1956 will have an opportunity to study law in a new building under a new curriculum. In addition to the conventional study of the law, they will have, for the first time, the opportunity to draft such documents as contracts, complaints, deeds, and wills under the guidance and supervision of special tutors. Instead of discussing the art of negotiation, and the method of interviewing clients, they will have an opportunity to participate in negotiation and interviewing. The work in Moot Court will be enlarged. With aid of teaching associates and teaching assistants much more individualized instruction will be provided. Guidance in the revision and improvement of a student's initial drafting efforts will be constant.

The program of preparation of documents and practice in legal techniques will be keyed to the conventional courses, and the program will be carried forward progressively to the second and third years of the student's law school career.

Individual instruction has been regarded as desirable for many years, but such a program is as costly as the laboratory training of physicians and scientists. The program has been made possible for full-time law students at the Indiana University School of Law by an initial grant of $250,000 from Inland Foundation of Indianapolis. These funds will be used to implement special courses in Legal Techniques over a period of five years beginning in September 1956.

Personnel for the laboratory courses in Legal Techniques will consist of teaching associates and teaching assistants under the guidance of a faculty committee. Each of the teaching associates will supervise the work of five assistants, who in turn, will supervise small groups of students. An integral part of the plan is the creation of ten first-year scholarships each year for the five year period.

A. General Background and Reasons Behind the New
Courses in Legal Techniques

The study of the law involves both a knowledge of legal rules and of their application to specific personal, corporate, or governmental problems. For a long time it was assumed, at least so far as legal education was concerned, that these problems could only be solved by litigation. Thus, the "case system" and appellate court advocacy dominated instructional methods. Today, however, a modern law firm gauges its success by its ability to avoid litigation and at the same time insure the legality of its clients' transactions. Recognizing that the practice of law in our fast-moving industrialized society requires many diverse skills, the School of Law as early as 1940 expanded its curriculum. First a required course in Senior Research was introduced; then in 1948, a beginning course in Research was required of all first year students. In the same year, a required seminar program was established. These were attempts to individualize instruction and give proper emphasis to the non-court-room-problems of lawyers. Under these programs, the law school made substantial progress, but lack of curricular time and a shortage of instructional personnel prevented a complete achievement of its objectives. Now, the five year grant from the Inland Foundation will permit inauguration of a modern program of legal education and application of the scientific method to the teaching and practice of law through laboratory exposition and practice of Legal Techniques. Graduates of the School of Law, who have participated in the new program, will be trained not only in traditional legal analysis and appellate court advocacy, but also in legal planning, negotiation, drafting, and trial court advocacy. The primary focus of the laboratory courses will be the translation of legal analysis and policy determinations into documents or action containing sanctions which will insure effectiveness. An attempt will be made, similar to that obtaining in the Medical, Engineering, and Physical Sciences, to develop techniques of practice in law which will have an affirmative effect upon the study, teaching, and practice of law. The inductive method used successfully in those fields will be directed toward law, which has been overwhelmingly subject to the deductive and dialectic methods.

Although many have tried, no law school has been successful in graduating individuals fully competent to apply their knowledge and ability to the solution of a client's problems. The situation in regard to clerical and laboratory instruction is comparable to that which existed in medicine at the time of the Flexner report. It has been assumed by the law schools that these skills and techniques of practice could be learned better after law school training through what amounts to apprenticeship training in law offices. Unfortunately, experience belies this assumption. The more competent the law office, the less time is available for any organized training of recent graduates in the practical application of legal principles. This is the problem about which we propose to do something more than has been done, and to extend our first year research program precisely the principles which the student will remember. We propose to devote four semester hours to these laboratory courses in each of the student's three years in law school. As the students take the courses in the various areas of the law in their laboratory course, they will be drafting documents, memoranda and trial briefs correlated with those courses. *This is frankly an experiment and we hope, with foundation assistance, to institute the program on a five year basis beginning the year 1956 with the first class to enter the new law building on the Bloomington Campus. Planning, negotiation, draftsmanship, and advocacy are well-recognized areas of lawyers' activities. What is not so well known are the consistent values which synthesize all four and make their teaching intellectually productive rather than pure mechanics. These are the things which we hope to bring to our students in the future to supplement the legal analysis which is the core of the present day law curriculum.*

The second significant thing in the development of the curriculum in the last ten years has been the growth of the seminar or small group type of teaching. While we continue to teach the larger areas of law by the course method, we have been steadily expanding our seminar program with small groups in which everyone necessarily participates actively in studying a narrow problem in depth. In the bulletin of the School of Law for 1945-46 no seminars were scheduled at either division. In the bulletin of 1955-56 nineteen seminars are offered in the course of the present three year program at Bloomington and nine are offered in the program at Indianapolis; again the difference between the full-time student and the part-time student who works five days a week has something to do with the extent to which this type of program can be conducted. However, it is the thinking of the law faculty that more and more emphasis will be placed upon the seminar type of training, and with the acquisition of the new building in Bloomington with its four specially designed seminar rooms, the physical facilities will be available to extend and expand this program.

In the field of public service more and more calls are being made upon the School of Law. At present a half dozen of our Indianapolis Division students participate in the legal clinic and we are informed that were it not for the work done by these students in this area, the Indianapolis Legal Aid Society could not perform the public service it now does for indigent persons. At the present time we are participating in the work of instituting a study and recodification of all laws relating to secondary education in Indiana. We are cooperating with two legislative commissions studying the justice of peace system and traffic safety, and we have continued and increasing requests for assistance in drafting various types of legislation, both from public and from private sources.

V. GRADUATE STUDY IN LAW

The Graduate School of Indiana University offers a graduate program in law leading to the degree of Master of Laws.

Admission will be limited to graduates of approved law schools presenting a superior law school record.

In considering applications from foreign students, the difference in academic systems is taken into account, and an effort is made to equate the student's background with the requirements described above. A student whose training has been primarily in a civil law system is generally admitted as a special student, with the possibility of a degree left open if a record of sufficiently high quality is achieved at the school. Foreign students should note that the requirements for a degree include satisfactory completion of written examinations in courses and of research papers in seminars.

The degree of Master of Laws will be conferred upon the successful completion of one academic year of work in residence with at least thirty semester hours of credit. No course for which a grade below C has been given will be counted toward a graduate degree. The candidate shall take such courses and meet such other requirements as may be fixed by the Committee on Graduate Study in the School of Law. In general, the program will include twelve hours of graduate courses in the School of Law; from six to ten hours of courses in the Graduate School or in the School of Business; and from six to ten hours devoted to research and writing a thesis. When, in the opinion of the Committee, the preparation of a thesis would not contribute to the program approved for the candidate, a language requirement may be substituted for the thesis. If a thesis is required, it must represent a scholarly investigation of a legal problem or a social science problem which is directly related to law. The thesis must be typewritten in publishable form. Two copies must be deposited in the Library of the School of Law, and the original deposited in the Graduate School Office fifteen days prior to Commencement. The degree will be conferred only after oral examination by the Committee.

The program will emphasize individual attention and will utilize the various faculties of the University to integrate the studies and research by reference to the particular needs and interests of each student. There will be available to students in this program graduate assistantships carrying a stipend of up to $1,000 a year. A graduate assistant will devote one half of his time to graduate study and one half of his time to assisting the School of Law faculty. The assistantships will normally be renewed for a second year to permit completion of the work required for the degree. Opportunity will be given to obtain classroom and other teaching experience.

Students entering the program will be eligible for scholarship aid offered to students in the Graduate School.

Faculty Council Minutes, 1955–57, pp. 205–210.

Document 191

Getting an Education

Always faculty committees in American universities have wandered on like lonely Ulysses seeking an answer to the basic university question: how to insure that a student gets an education? In no area has professorial rhetoric been uttered more freely and with brighter luster than in trying to say what the educated man should be aware of as a university graduate. This report makes a noble declaration of purposes and faith. In doing so it held on to some of the old verities, but with less positiveness than had been the case with earlier Indiana University faculties.

* * *

A BASIC CURRICULUM FOR INDIANA UNIVERSITY
Section 1—History and Development

Preface

When, on January 18, 1955, the Faculty Council accepted the principle of adopting a basic curriculum to be required of all students receiving undergraduate degrees from the University and went on to instruct the University Committee on Curricular Policies and Educational Programs to recommend the courses considered appropriate to be included in this curriculum, it cast its lot with that movement which is described by the term General Education. In fact, the Council's Committee on the Junior Division, from whose report the decision derived, had also committed itself to this principle and had gone on to propose an implementing curriculum.

With the proposals of the Committee on the Junior Division as a guide, the University Committee initially attempted to come directly to grips with the curriculum itself, but throughout the early discussions the issue of what constitutes General Education persisted in raising itself. That is, it was recognized by the Committee that it could arrive at no final decisions on the constitution of a basic curriculum independently of its own guiding philosophy or "frame of reference." Thus, reluctant as we were to replow the whole acreage of the general education movement, we were obliged to search for common understanding on the frame of reference to be employed.

At the same time, the Committee did not permit itself to lose awareness of the local scene. It felt there was little to be gained from a "glorious blueprint" whose components would be unworkable at Indiana University. Throughout its discussions and in the framing of its recommendations, therefore, the Committee was sensitive to the practical problems of faculty recruitment, composition of our student body, and the nature of existent curricula in the several schools. The analyses and conclusions to follow thus reflect not only what we believe to be sound approaches per se, but reasonable approaches in terms of the local scene.

A Definition of General Education

The difficulty in arriving at a definition of general education is suggested by the near impossibility of identifying a meaning upon which educators at large agree. To some it means education for all in the sense of universal education; to others it carries the diffuse connotation of a sampling of knowledge in general; to still others it is synonymous with liberal education. Or we have the preliminary definition of the Harvard Committee which identified general education as "that part of a student's whole education which looks first of all to his life as a responsible human being and citizen." Appealing to the University Committee by reason of its greater preciseness, however, is the statement found in "Higher Education for American Democracy" (1947, p. 49) wherein general education is identified with "those phases of nonspecialized and non-vocational learning which should be the *common experience* of all educated men and women" and should be concerned with the cultivation of *"common objectives* that can serve as a stimulus and guide to individual decision and action."

It should be noted that the definition encompasses two elements—"common experience" and "common objectives." Experience and objectives are by no means equivalent. Not only is it possible to attain the same objectives by various experiences, but different objectives may be reached by a single type of experience. Accordingly, as one surveys general education programs country-wide, he finds the greatest diversity therein by reason of differences in objectives and the experiences provided to achieve these objectives.

Objectives. Of the ten or more objectives which have been suggested in one form or another by numerous educators, those such as maintenance and improvement of health, attitudes conducive to satisfactory family life, and choice of vocation are not widely held as cogent. Some six others, however, receive widespread endorsement. These, stated briefly, are as follows:

1. An awareness of man's place in nature and the implications of science with respect to human welfare.

2. An awareness of the origins and nature of our social environment and of human institutions in general, so that one may not only achieve a satisfactory relation to his society but be better prepared to participate as an informed and responsible citizen in the solution of social, economic, and political problems whether at the local or international level.

3. An awareness of man in relation to himself, that is to say, in his inner aspirations, his ideals, in his creative ability.

4. The ability to express oneself so as to be understood by others.

5. The ability to think effectively, wherein are included:

   (a) critical thinking—meaning the ability to differentiate between fact and error, between the relevant and irrelevant, to identify the interrelationships among the elements of a complex situation, and to see beyond the obvious and envisage new alternatives;

   (b) abstract thinking—meaning the ability to lift the thought process above the level of immediate, personal experience and to develop valid and meaningful generalizations and abstractions;

   (c) making relevant judgments—meaning the art of applying the abstractions and relationships theoretically arrived at to the actual facts of of a situation and to draw sound conclusions from given premises.

6. Satisfactory personal adjustment to:
   (a) Ideas and institutions.
   (b) Social groups.
   (c) Individuals.
   (d) Oneself.

Experience. As for the educational experience which shall be provided for the attainment of these objectives, it is immediately obvious that the first objective relates to the natural sciences, the second to the social sciences, and the third to the humanities. The fourth is essentially a tool or skill. The fifth and sixth, pertaining as they do to traits of mind, are pervasive objectives related to the totality of educational experience and derive to a greater or lesser extent from all areas of knowledge.

What should be the exact form of experience if these objectives are to be furthered? One answer is that the instruction given by a college or university should be based on a given philosophical system. Historically this was often true and still can be and is done in a totalitarian state and may also be possible in a denominational institution. But for a university to exercise its proper function in our democratic society, its students must be provided with the broadest possible perspective of man's attempts to comprehend the physical universe and shape his own conduct. This in itself is a formidable task, a task augmented by our commitment to "big education" wherein we must deal with masses of students of every conceivable aptitude and goal. It is no wonder that the attempt to provide the answer has induced such a diversity of curricular patterns. They are endless in their variety, but in general may be reduced to approaches along three lines.

The first may be characterized as the "content-oriented" approach. It customarily involves the selection of one or more instructors each from the three areas of knowledge (natural sciences, social sciences, and humanities) who are charged with organizing broad interdepartmental survey courses. Such courses are presumed to be inclusive of what is construed to be the essential knowledge in that area which should be in the possession of every generally educated person. The entire emphasis is upon material content and the function of the course is to expose the student to this survey of accumulated information which he is expected to master. There is usually no concern with or adaptation for individual aptitudes and interests of students; all without exception must ingest their pablum. Nor is there any over concern with issues of relevancy, application of knowledge, attitudes, or any of the rest that might pertain to the cultivation of traits of mind. Mastery of the material of the course becomes an end in itself and all other benefits, if any, are presumed to arise by spontaneous generation.

A second approach accepts more responsibility for the development of capacity to think effectively and to accommodate to new ideas and concepts. While content coverage is still given major attention and community of experience is still emphasized, there is a willingness to sacrifice some coverage in the interest of providing exploratory experiences designed to provide the student with actual practice in attacking and thinking through problems for himself. This approach may then be designated as "intellectually oriented."

The third approach is one which recognizes that different kinds of experience may be of equal value insofar as promoting the development of students. It also recognizes that students are individuals with individual needs, interests, desires, and aptitudes within no two of which will a given experience elicit the same result. Whereas both of the previous two approaches place great emphasis upon the provision of common class-room experience, this "student-oriented" approach, as it may be termed, recognizes that no experience can mean quite the same thing to two different individuals. Accordingly, emphasis is placed on the availability of a number of different courses in given areas and the inclusion of a number of means of individual adaptation such as disposal of requirements by examination, accelerated sections, qualification for advanced standing, and the like.

It will be appreciated, of course, that rarely is any one of these approaches found in its literal form. Individual schools cultivate their own variations of these approaches and within any given school there are commonly found every conceivable compromise and inconsistency. And we must always come back to the individual instructor who tends to be a rugged individualist and orients his teaching as his talents and inclination dictate.

The discussions of our Committee suggest that our sympathies lie with the "student-oriented" approach. In one form or another the view had constantly cropped up that there is no single and absolute formula which should be applied indiscriminately to all students; that one combination of experience may under certain circumstances be as good as another. Nor are the courses which may contribute to the objectives of general education necessarily limited to those offered in the College of Arts and Sciences. In fact, to some degree every course in the University, no matter how special, probably has some general educational value and we reject any system by which general education is sharply segregated from special education. We have also recognized that since the educational process is, or should be, a continuing thing from childhood on, we should insofar as possible capitalize on the experience that the student brings from grammar and high school and build his college program accordingly. This means we must avoid the assumption that all high school training is necessarily bad and must be done over, with the first two or three semesters of university thus being dedicated to remedial work. On the contrary, every effort should be made to evaluate and utilize the student's high school background so that in certain areas he may be encouraged to carry on at moderately advanced level in the beginning of his university days. The extension of this procedure as it is now practiced in the Departments of English and Mathematics and in the languages and other departments would have a salutary effect upon our high schools, through the added responsibility placed upon them, and in the long run strengthen the total educational process.

Our leanings towards diversity rather than community of experience have also been motivated by certain practical considerations. Were we to decide that all students should be required to take a restricted few courses of special design, an enormous problem of faculty recruitment, possibly even the development of a separate faculty for general education, would be posed. The cases for the "content-oriented" and "intellectually-oriented" approaches would have to be exceptionally strong to warrant such a development. But by providing the opportunity for choice among courses in a given area, the burden of large numbers of students may be distributed and most departments would find it possible to absorb the influx with only moderate adjustment. This, then, is our "frame of reference"; six objectives as listed and a "student-oriented" approach to the attainment of these objectives. There follow brief discussions of several segments of educational experiences eligible for inclusion in a basic curriculum and our conclusions regarding each. These in turn are succeeded by a set of specific recommendations.

Section 2—Conclusions

Mathematics

The possible inclusion of mathematics in a program of general education is supported by two lines of argument. First, the natural sciences are concerned with things and events which permit exact definition and measurement, thus yielding description which is numerical and which can be manipulated mathematically. It follows, therefore, that quantitative measurements and their mathematical expression are woven inextricably into the structure of science. In subjects other than the sciences—notably in economics, psychology, sociology, and anthropology—mathematics contributes toward the development of that trait of mind which we have designated as the ability to think effectively. "The ability to analyze a concrete situation into its elements, to synthesize components into a related whole, to isolate and select relevant factors, defining them rigorously; and the ability to combine these factors, often in novel ways, so as to reach a solution, all are important features of mathematical procedure."

Applying these arguments to the actual educational scene, it would appear that the responsibility for the provision of minimum facility in mathematics should fall upon the pre-college years. Every student, no matter what his mathematical aptitude is, should probably acquire reasonable facility in the language of arithmetic and informal geometry by the middle of the ninth grade. Above this point a division must be recognized between students who can derive little profit from further instruction in pure mathematics and those with relatively good mathematical aptitude. Those of the latter group in senior high school should be strongly advised to study both algebra and demonstrative geometry whether they intend to enter college or not. This should probably also be the end of the mathematical line for those college-bound students who have no special interest in science, medicine, technology, or mathematics itself. However, all competent students who do have special interests in these or other fields where mathematics play an important role should take all the secondary school mathematics that is available.

The upshot of this is that we are prepared to accept the position that from the point of view of general education, students will have completed a minimal program in mathematics before entering college and that no additional experience should be required. To institute an all-university requirement would, in the judgment of the Department of Mathematics and this Committee, be a backward step. It would in the first place, pose the enormous practical problem of the administration of a proficiency test to all entering students and the institution of remedial courses for those who fail to measure up to a chosen level. It is very doubtful that such remedial work, necessarily involving much repetition of work already done in secondary school, would result in substantial educational gain. Secondly, it would tend to negate the responsibility of the lower scnools for the provision of this minimal experience. As for those students whose needs and aptitudes call for university training in mathematics, the system of alternative sequences presently operating in the Department of Mathematics appears to be serving adequately.

Foreign Language

The Committee on the Junior Division recommended a requirement of "at least 6 hours" in the study of foreign language, "preferably beginning at the second-year level," or courses concerned with some aspects of linguistics. With regard to foreign language itself, it is not clear what that Committee had in mind if the high school background of the beginning student were less than two years. While it is true that roughly 80% of the entering student body has had two years of language in high school, all of these are by no means prepared to pick up college language at the second-year level. Further, there is commonly a change in language choice between high school and university, particularly if the high school experience has been in Latin rather than a modern language. It follows, then, that for language study to have any value whatsoever, the minimum requirement might have to run as high as 16 hours.

It is the judgment of the University Committee, and this view is shared by many members of the language staffs themselves, that a 6-hour requirement would pay dividends only on the assumption that all students entered the university with two years of solid training in high school language and were willing to continue the study of the same language. But the assumption does not conform to reality; some are ill-prepared even with two years of high school training, others come with less than two years or none at all, and the incidence of change-over in all is high. Faced with this situation, one must choose between a flat, across-the-board 6-hour requirement which for many would provide nothing of worth, or a graduated requirement which might reach a disproportionate amount in the total which can be allotted to general education. Coupled with this is the general feeling in the Committee that even under the best of circumstances it is difficult to make a case for foreign language study which in terms of educational values will stand up beside other types of experience. Accordingly, we do not recommend the institution of a requirement in foreign language for all students in the University. What the separate schools do in this regard is of course another matter. We may add that in our judgment a better approach to "the language problem" is through the strengthening and development of instruction at the elementary and secondary school levels, periods in the total educational process when minds are most receptive to language study.

This decision to exclude a requirement in foreign language from the basic curriculum is extended to the alternatives of courses in the structure and history of languages. It may be pointed out, however, that in recognition of the educational benefits inherent to them, such courses have been included with other choices as satisfactory for the discharge of certain other area requirements.

Communication

The art of communication involves the four related skills of writing, reading, speaking and listening. In recent years certain schools, notably Denver, Illinois, Iowa, and Michigan State, have instituted new programs in "Communication" which have superseded the conventional programs in English Composition. The proponents of such programs speak of the inherent unity of the four aspects of communication and argue for their treatment as a unit. So far it does not seem perfectly clear that communication can be conceived of and taught as an entity, or whether the separate skills must be handled as discrete units. Certainly the results of comparative measurements of improvements in these skills made on students going through both types of programs are not very convincing one way or another. The attempt to handle all four skills in a single program results, in the opinion of some educators, in none being done well and a general superficiality in the whole. Granted that a real oneness may exist, there is also created a serious problem of recruitment of qualified teaching personnel. A talent for developing all the strands in such a course is not easily found in teachers and this becomes an especially serious matter when graduate students must be utilized to fill out a teaching staff. While it might be anticipated that in time a crop of teachers with suitable qualifications and viewpoints might be developed, such persons are certainly in short supply now.

Aside from the actual skills themselves, courses in communication profess to cultivate the objective of effective thinking. This we believe can be accomplished only superficially at best. Besides, this should be one of the objectives of the total university experience, not the province of one course or one area alone.

Since the case for a program in communication does not strike us as being clear-cut, we feel any requirements should be linked to the now-existing programs in English Composition, Speech, and Linguistics. In other words, we cannot feel that the case for "Communication" is strong enough to warrant the scrapping of the presently available offerings and organization with all its attendant disruptions, including the creation of a problem of faculty recruitment. Specifically, then, we are recommending that there shall be a requirement, totalling 6 hours, in a "Communication Group," of which 4 hours shall be in English Composition and 2 hours to be chosen from the third course in English Composition, Speech S121 and Linguistics L103. At the same time we recognize there may be real potential in the unified concept of communication and thus would like to suggest the development of limited experimental sections in communication which may serve as a testing ground out of which there may come a decision as to the desirability of a changeover.

The Social Sciences

No segment of the basic curriculum has given the Committee more difficulty than that concerned with the social sciences. Not that the objective is obscure, for it is not, but how best to attain or at least approach that objective within our frame of reference. How best, that is, to suggest the goals and values, the organizations and processes, the problems and conflicts and the historical roots in our political structure, economic life and social relationships which go to make up our contemporary life. The place to be occupied by experiences in History has induced an especially knotty problem, resolved, for reasons to be stated below, by grouping History in another category.

We have rejected a solution that calls for a block-survey course which would include portions of all the social sciences. Such a survey would make for dilettantism and while probably providing the "jargon" of several disciplines would in its superficiality promote neither knowledge nor understanding of anything in particular. Nor is it sufficient that a student take just any course in the social sciences. A course, even an introductory one, is not necessarily suitable for the purposes of general education simply because it is offered by one of the social science departments. Rather, we have sought to identify those courses presently available in which attempts are made to open the doors to the issues of institutional development, social thought, and human interrelationships. At the same time we should like to suggest that the social science departments give some thought to the development of new courses or modification of extant ones to the end that the aims of general education may be furthered to a greater degree than is presently true for conventional introductory courses.

History and the Humanities

The inclusion of history with the humanities is certainly unconventional but by no means original with the Committee. It is a reflection of the view that history, more than any of the other social sciences in the strict sense, is or should be all-embracing in its scope. History is more than names of dictators and dates of wars; it is a wholeness of the forces, struggles, institutions, ideas and values which have gone into the making of the age in which we live. History is pervasive and in some measure should be a corporate part of every subject taught, whether English Literature or Zoology. The link between history and the humanities per se lies in the record of man's eternal struggle for satisfactory adjustment to himself, society and the physical universe, of his search for a right course of action, of expression of his feelings and desires. Whereas in history, philosophy and literature this struggle is recorded directly, it is given indirect expression of his feelings and desires. Whereas in history, philosophy and literature this struggle is recorded directly, it is given indirect expression in the fine arts and music. The thing is to give to students an awareness of the record of human desires and achievements. For some this awareness may derive from a course in the History of Western European Civilization, for others from Shakespeare, for still others from Greek architecture. This very diversity of human achievement is in itself a clue to man's creative evolution.

The Natural Sciences

The recommendations of the Committee on the Junior Division called for 5 hours in a biological science and 5 hours in a physical science. There are two problems inherent to this recommendation.

The first relates to the objectives we seek. Do we feel that all students should be expected to acquire minimum knowledge in both biological and physical science, or are we more concerned with the development of "traits in mind" which can be served equally well by experience in either? To put it another way, is science any more than a collection of facts, a minimum sampling of which all students should obtain, or is it as well a product of creative imagination? We hold that the facts a student may acquire are evanescent and are incidental to the development of lasting powers of effective thinking which is furthered by an appreciation of scientific method. To this end it appears that experience in either the biological sciences or the physical sciences is suitable, with the proviso that this experience include laboratory study.

The second relates to the practical problem of whether the curricula of the professional schools can absorb 10 hours in science, plus the related issue of the accommodation of thousands of students. Our studies have indicated that for certain curricula 10 hours is unworkable, 5 hours quite feasible. As for the instructional burden, it would be halved and spread by reducing the requirement to 5 hours and allowing for choice in a whole range of offerings in biological and physical science.

In keeping with these practical considerations and the "student-oriented" approach, with the cultivation of effective thinking as the prime objective, we are recommending a requirement of 5 hours and to be selected from the available offerings listed elsewhere.

Supplement

It is expected that ordinarily the requirements of the basic curriculum will be discharged within the first two years or sooner and student counselors are advised to plan programs accordingly. It is recognized, however, that professional requirements or other circumstances may preclude this.

It is suggested that those in charge of certain of the courses in the natural sciences give consideration to a mechanism, such as is now provided in Biology B100, whereby students with aptitude and interest may elect and move on to upper-level courses without penalty. Such an arrangement would seem to be necessary in all disciplines, not just the natural sciences alone, if, among other things, general education is to play its role in assisting the undecided beginner in his choice of an area of specialization. We also recognize that some of the laboratory experience, as presently provided, is making an unsatisfactory contribution to the cultivation of the objective of effective thinking and suggest that individual departments re-appraise their laboratory programs.

In extension of the above, we recommend that every department offering courses presently listed among the options for the basic curriculum survey these offerings with the aim of determining their present suitability for the purposes of general education, and with the further aim of modifying these courses or creating new ones if circumstances call for it.

Section 3—Recommendations

1. All students receiving undergraduate degrees from Indiana University shall complete the requirements of a basic curriculum in accordance with the categories and options described below.

I. Mathematics: no requirement.

II. Foreign Language: no requirement.

III. Communication: 6 hours

4 hours of English Composition (W101 or W111 and W102 or W112) and 2 hours to be chosen from English W103 or W113, Speech S121, or Linguistics L103.

IV. Social Sciences: 5-6 hours.

To be selected from the following:

Anthropology

A103 General Anthropology (3)

A104 General Anthropology (3)

A303 Survey of Anthropology (3)

A304 Survey of Anthropology (3)

Business and Economics

E201 Principles of Economics (3)

E202 Principles of Economics (3)

E300 Economic Principles (5)

W100 Introduction to Business (3)

Geography

G203 Economic Geography (3)

G313 Political Geography (3)

Government

G103 Introduction to American Government (3)

G104 Introduction to American Government (3)

G200 Sophomore Seminar in American Government (2)

G210 Introduction to the Theory of Politics (2)

Sociology

S161 Principles of Sociology (3)

S162 Society and the Individual (3)

S163 Social Problems (3)

S301 Sociological Principles (5)

V. History and Humanities: 5-6 hours.

To be selected from the following:

History

H103 History of Western European Civilization (3)

H104 History of Western European Civilization (3)

H105 American History (3)

H106 American History (3)

Classics
C150 The Greeks through their Literature (3)
C160 The Romans through their Literature (3)
Comparative Literature
C225 Modern Literature and the Arts (2)
English
L101 Freshman Literature (3)
L102 Freshman Literature (3)
Fine Arts
H100 Art Appreciation (2)
Music
M174 Appreciation of Music (2)
M175 Appreciation of Music (2)
Philosophy
P100 Historical Introduction to Philosophy (3)
P200 Problems of Philosophy (3)
P240 Ethics (3)
P250 Logic (3)
Speech and Theatre
S240 Appreciation of the Theatre (2)

VI. Natural Sciences: 5 hours.
    To be selected from the following:

Biological Sciences

Anatomy
A210 Elementary Human Anatomy (5)
Bacteriology
B200 Microbiology in Relation to Man: Lectures (3) } Must be taken
B205 Microbiology in Relation to Man: Laboratory (2) } together
Biology
B100 Man and the Biological World (5)
Botany
B101 Plant Biology (5)
Physiology
P104 Elementary Physiology (5)
P201 General Physiology (5)
Psychology
P101 Introductory Psychology (3) } Must be taken together
P111 Introductory Laboratory Psychology (2) }
Zoology
Z103 Animal Biology (5)

Physical Sciences

Astronomy
A100 The Solar System (3)
A105 Stellar Astronomy (3)
Chemistry
C101 Survey of Chemistry (5)
C105 General Chemistry (5)
Geology
G100 Geology and Man (5)
G101 Physical Geology (5)

Physics
P100 Physics in the Modern World (5)
P201 General Physics (5)

Total: 21-23 hours

2. Certification of the completion of the requirements of the basic curriculum will be the responsibility of the individual schools.

3. New courses may be added to the lists of options only following prior review and approval by the University Committee.

The University Committee on Curricular Policies and Educational Programs
HOWARD T. BATCHELDER
FRANK E. HORACK, JR.
PRESSLY S. SIKES
THEODORE W. TORREY
(Chairman)
ROBERT C. TURNER

Faculty Council Minutes, 1955–57, pp. 238–249.

Document 192

Over and Over Again

No one has reduced to tabular form the hours which the Indiana University faculty and Faculty Council spent discussing the subject of student integrity, trying each time to state clearly what constituted cheating and plagiarism, and to state the penalty for a violation of common human integrity. Likewise, no one has estimated how little basic effect these reports had on remedying the evil of the sly way of getting through a university without getting an honest education. The committees tried hard to create a moral climate.

*   *   *

Report of the Faculty Council Committee to Study the Functions and Procedures of the Student Conduct Committee and the Problems of Cheating and Plagiarism.

The Faculty Council Committee believes that the initial step for the solution of the complex problems of student dishonesty in academic work should be a complete revision of that section of the Faculty Handbook which is concerned with cheating (p. 52). Accordingly, the committee is suggesting extensive revisions as well as certain recommendations for the implementation of the new regulations (see Appendices I and II). The revisions are largely self-explanatory, but the committee is convinced that the following concepts and observations are fundamental to the problem.

A. There is general agreement that if the problem of student dishonesty is to be corrected, vigorous and continuous action must be taken by the faculty. Every effort also must be made to utilize the support and active cooperation of the students and student agencies.

B. It should be the responsibility of each instructor to instill in students a respect for honesty in intellectual pursuits. Furthermore, each instructor should conduct examinations and class exercises in a manner which will minimize dishonesty.

C. A standard procedure should be followed in every case of dishonesty and a report of every case should be placed in the file of the student in the office of the Dean of Students.

D. Clear and comprehensive definitions of cheating and plagiarism should be included in the Faculty Handbook.

E. The rights of both the student and the instructor must be protected by any procedures which are established.

F. Uniform penalties should be established for dishonest acts by students.

G. Provision should be made for progressively more severe penalties for chronic offenders. Likewise, very severe penalties should be imposed for acts such as stealing examinations or altering records.

The committee would like to acknowledge the assistance it has received from Professor Lusk and Dean Shaffer. Also, valuable suggestions were given the committee by two members of the Student Senate, Miss Eakin and Mr. Moss.

STUDENT CONDUCT COMMITTEE

The Faculty Council Committee has reviewed the functions of the Student Conduct Committee and has attempted to evaluate these functions in relation to serious problems of student honesty and good citizenship. The following information provided by Professor Lusk and Dean Shaffer is pertinent for understanding the role of the Student Conduct Committee in disciplinary matters.

A. Composition. The committee is composed of six faculty members, appointed by the President, and the members of the Student Supreme Court. Only six of the latter serve at any meeting of the committee. Two of the faculty members at present represent the Junior Division and the Office of the Dean of Faculties. The Office of the Dean of Students is not represented on the committee.

B. Function. The committee is called upon to render judgment and/or to act on diverse problems of student discipline. Dishonest actions relative to academic pursuits constitute only a small fraction of the cases brought to the attention of the committee.

C. Procedure. Hearings are conducted in accordance with the procedures recommended by the American Civil Liberties Union. The committee conscientiously attempts to preserve the anonymity of the party or parties involved.

D. Authority. No specific reference to the Student Conduct Committee appears in the section of the Faculty Handbook which is concerned with cheating. The committee acts on cases referred to it by the Dean of Students under the Handbook reference "or other agency responsibile for handling such cases."

The fact that a record of this information is not published indicates that the role of the Student Conduct Committee should be clarified and made known to both faculty and students. The committee should be named specifically in the Faculty Handbook as the agency to consider appeals and to act in matters involving serious misdemeanors by students.

APPENDIX I
Proposed Revisions of the Faculty Handbook (p. 52)
CHEATING AND PLAGIARISM

One of the most important objectives of teaching is the development of honesty in students. Throughout their educational program students should be impressed with the fact that cheating and plagiarism are morally degrading and that these practices seriously interfere with learning and intellectual development. It is the responsibility of faculty members to make every effort (1) to inspire in their students an appreciation of and a desire for honesty in academic work; (2) to prevent dishonesty and to protect the honest student, and (3) to take appropriate action in instances of dishonesty.

1. *Undergraduate Students*

Cheating

Dishonesty of any kind with respect to examinations, written assignments in class, alteration of records, or illegal possession of examinations shall be considered cheating.

It is the responsibility of the student not only to abstain from cheating but, in addition, to avoid the appearance of cheating and to guard against making it possible for others to cheat. The student also should do everything possible to induce respect for the examining process and for honesty in the performance of assigned tasks.

It is the responsibility of each faculty member to maintain the best possible conditions to prevent cheating in any manner. Each faculty member shall arrange for vigilant proctering of all examinations and class exercises. He also shall employ every precaution to deny access to class records to examinations to anyone who is not entitled to such information.

Plagiarism

Courtesy and honesty require that any ideas or materials borrowed from another must be fully acknowledged. Offering as one's own work of another is plagiarism. The subject matter or ideas thus taken from another may range from a few sentences or paragraphs to entire articles copied from books, periodicals, or the writing of other students. The offering of materials assembled or collected by others in the form of projects or collections without acknowledgement also is considered plagiarism. Any student who fails to give credit for ideas or materials that he takes from another is guilty of plagiarism.

It shall be the responsibility of each faculty member to define, describe, and explain plagiarism. This shall be recounted in all its aspects whenever the work in his class is of such a nature as to subject his students to the possibility of plagiarim. A student's innocent failure to give credit for sources of ideas or materials because of ignorance of procedures or confusion of assignments may be avoided only by the conscientious and regular effort of each faculty member to discharge this responsibility.

Procedure

A faculty member who has evidence that a student is guilty of cheating or plagiarism shall initiate the process of determining the student's guilt or innocence. No penalty shall be imposed until the student has been informed of the charge and has been given an opportunity to present his defense. If the faculty member finds the student guilty he shall assess a grade penalty with the course *and shall promptly report the case in writing to the Dean of Students* including with this report the names of any other students who may be involved in the incident. The Dean of Students may initiate further disciplinary proceedings if he finds that the severity of the case or other circumstances warrant such action. Otherwise, only a record of the case remains in the student's file in the Dean's office.

Appeal

If the faculty member and the student cannot agree on the facts pertaining to the charge, either the faculty member or the student may request the Dean of Students to review the case and render a decision as to whether or not the student is guilty. If either of the parties is dissatisfied with this decision, the case shall then be referred to the Student Conduct Committee for a hearing.

A hearing of a case referred to the Student Conduct Committee shall be held at which every opportunity to present evidence shall be given. Hearings must be held in the presence of the faculty member concerned (or his representative) and the student involved. Exception to this procedure may be made only when there is outright refusal to attend. After the hearing, the Student Conduct Committee shall render a decision as to guilt or innocence based on the facts of the case irrespective of other circumstances. In the case of guilt, the Student Conduct Committee may determine or recommend a penalty other than that involving the student's grade in the course.

Penalties

A penalty affecting a student's grade in a course may be imposed only by the faculty member.

It is recommended that the following penalties for cheating or plagiarism should be observed:

   a. An F on the particular piece of work should be given for dishonesty on any assignment, examination, or paper which represents only a part of the semester's work; for example, mid-term examinations, short papers, or class assignments.
   b. An F in the course should be given for dishonesty on a final examination, a term paper which constitutes a major part of the course work, or on any major assignment upon which a large part of the course grade depends.
   c. A student who is found guilty a second time of cheating or plagiarism shall be subject to additional penalties such as probation, suspension, or expulsion. These penalties may be imposed or recommended by the Dean of Students or by the Student Conduct Committee.
   d. Students convicted of stealing examinations, altering grades or class records, or any comparable acts shall be subject to suspension or expulsion by action or recommendation of the Dean of Students or the Student Conduct Committee.

A grade of incomplete may be given by the instructor in the event any case cannot be resolved before final grades are due in the Office of Records and Admissions.

2. *Graduate and Professional Students*

Any professional or other school at the graduate level may, with the approval of its faculty, adopt its own rules and set up its own procedures for dealing with cases of cheating and plagiarism.

APPENDIX II

Recommendations for the Implementation of the Regulations
on Cheating and Plagiarism

The committee feels that it is imperative to implement at once the new regulations on cheating and plagiarism and would like to request that the following procedures be practiced:

A. That the section in the *Pilot* relative to student honesty should be rewritten with special emphasis being given to the moral and educational issues involved and should include the revised Faculty Handbook regulations on cheating and plagiarism.

B. That a copy of the revised regulations also should be given to the Student Senate with the request that the Senate assist in presenting to the student body the consequences of dishonesty.

C. That a brief note should be placed in the Faculty News Letter each year directing the attention of the faculty to the section in the Faculty Handbook on cheating and plagiarism.

D. That the announcement from the Office of the Dean of Faculties which explains final examination procedures should also contain a brief statement concerning the responsibilities of faculty members in regard to proper examination practices and to the penalties which may be imposed on the student.

E. That the Junior Division devote a portion of its orientation program for new students to an explanation of the importance of honesty and to the penalties which may follow dishonest action.

F. That a request should be made of the YMCA and YWCA to include a panel discussion of student honesty in their leadership camps.

Faculty Council Minutes, March 1957–May 1957, pp. 277–281.

Document 193

Self-Study of the Faculty Council

At the end of the academic year 1956–1957, a special survey committee reported its findings and recommendations regarding a revision of the organization, procedures, and rules of the Faculty Council. Part of this revision was caused by the rising importance of the off-campus centers, but most of the pressure came from within. As the university became more and more bureaucratic in its operation, it was obvious that one of its most important functional bodies would be caught up in the trend. Administrators and faculty left nothing to chance in formulating new plans and rules. The committee produced a report with marked specificity which left nothing to chance.

* * *

REPORT OF THE FACULTY COUNCIL SELF SURVEY COMMITTEE

The Faculty Council Self Survey Committee, first of all, wishes to acknowledge the assistance which has been given to it by various individuals and especially by the Agenda Committee of the Faculty Council. All suggestions have been carefully considered and many have been incorporated in the appended recommendations. The committee also has studied the minutes of Faculty Council meetings, the annual reports of the Secretaries, and the Faculty Self Survey Committee Report of 1939 in order to acquire background material and information from which to develop this report.

The committee concluded that there are four major areas in which improvement can be made for better Faculty Council performance. The recommendations for the revision of the Faculty Council Handbook, therefore, are designed to accomplish these improvements. The four areas of special concern are the following:

1. *A more precise statement of functions, objectives and responsibilities of the Faculty Council should be formulated.*

The Faculty Council was organized as a result of the recommendation by the Faculty Self Survey Committee that a "University Senate" should be established. The functions of the Faculty Council are outlined in Article V, Sections 24 and 27 of the Faculty Handbook, but these do not adequately reflect the activities which have evolved since the origin of the Faculty Council. It also is the opinion of the committee that certain items now in Article V should be transferred to the by-laws and, conversely, that some statements in the present by-laws would be more appropriately placed in Article V. This is especially important with regards to the clarification of the responsibilities of the Faculty Council to the general faculty. Finally, the committee believes that the central administration should use the Faculty Council more effectively in advisory and consultative capacities.

2. *The Faculty Council should be more efficient in the discharge of its functions.*

It is recommended that the Agenda Committee should assume a more active role in expediting the business of the Faculty Council. Briefly, the Agenda Committee should screen all items presented, make recommendations relative to the preparation of materials to be considered, and draft in final form any new legislation approved by the Faculty Council. It also should be the responsibility of the Agenda Committee to recommend to the Faculty Council that a study be made of the implementation and effect of any past legislation whenever the committee feels that such a study is appropriate.

It is the conviction of the Self Survey Committee that efficiency of action and prompt consideration of items can be accomplished only if the Faculty Council is smaller in size. It has been recommended, therefore, that the Faculty Council should be smaller. The committee recognizes, on the other hand, that invitations to attend Faculty Council meetings must be extended to parties interested in matters which are being considered. The Agenda Committee, accordingly, should assume the responsibility for extending invitations to non-members.

3. *There should be a continuing study of past legislation.*

It appears to the committee that the Faculty Council has been lax in assessing the value of its legislative actions. Considerable expenditure of effort is devoted to the formulation of legislation, but the Faculty Council has seemed to be complacent concerning the effects of its legislation. As was mentioned in the preceding section, the Agenda Committee may ask the Faculty Council to reconsider and assess any of its past actions. The Faculty Council, in the estimation of the Self Survey Committee, should consider this function to be as important as initial action.

4. *The election procedures should be clarified and the terms of the officers and members of the Faculty Council should be stated precisely.*

Aside from the adjustments in procedures necessary for the establishment of a smaller Faculty Council, the recommendations of the committee primarily formalize existing practices with respect to term of office or to succession in membership whenever an elected member must be replaced. One major change is recommended, namely, that no elected member shall be eligible to serve for more than two consecutive terms. He may be reelected, however, after a lapse of one year.

The committee believes that this will assure a better rotation of membership in the Faculty Council among the various Schools and Divisions of the University.

NORMAN T. PRATT JR.
HENRY H. H. REMAK
W. R. BRENEMAN

Specific Recommendations Approved by the Faculty Council, May 31, 1957

ARTICLE V. FACULTY COUNCIL

Section 19. Functions of the Faculty Council

a. Meetings:

The President shall call the first meeting of the Faculty Council within the first two weeks of the Fall Semester.

The Faculty Council shall meet regularly on the first and third Tuesdays of each month and also on the fifth Tuesdays when such days occur during the regular year.

b. Legislative functions:

All matters appropriate for general faculty action under Article IV, Section 16 may be considered by the Faculty Council. The Faculty Council may act or refer such matters with recommendations to the general faculty.

c. Administrative functions:

The Faculty Council shall:

1. Prepare by-laws to this constitution to be submitted to the general faculty for approval.
2. Prepare its own agenda through its Agenda Committee.
3. Initiate proposals for its own and general faculty consideration.
4. Elect committees whenever necessary for the discharge of its functions.
5. Fill vacancies for unexpired terms which occur in the office of Secretary or Parliamentarian or in any elected committee.
6. Make a continuing study of the effects of past legislation.

d. Consultative functions:

The Faculty Council or any members thereof shall be available at all times to act in an advisory or consultative capacity with any members of the central administration on matters of policy.

Section 20. Organization of the Faculty Council

a. Membership:

The Faculty Council shall be composed of sixteen members elected at large by the voting members on the Bloomington campus, four members elected at large by the voting members off the Bloomington campus, the President, the Vice President and Dean of the Faculties, and the Deans of the College of Arts and Sciences, School of Law, School of Medicine, Graduate School, School of Education, School of Business, School of Music, School of Dentistry, Division of Adult Education and Public Services, School of Health, Physical Education, and Recreation, and the Junior Division.

b. Term of office:

The term of office of the elected members of the Faculty Council shall be for two years beginning with the first regular Faculty Council meeting of the next academic year following their election. The elected members of the Faculty Council shall be eligible to serve two consecutive terms but shall then be ineligible for reelection until a period of one year has elapsed.

c. Officers:

The President shall be the presiding officer. In his absence, the Vice President and Dean of the Faculties shall preside. In the absence of both, the senior academic dean present according to Art. II sec. 7 shall preside.

The Faculty Council shall elect its own Secretary (who is also Chairman, Agenda Committee), Parliamentarian, and Agenda Committee. The terms of these officers shall be for one year and shall be from the first of September after their election through August the thirty-first of the following year.

d. Invitations:

The Agenda Committee shall invite general administrative officers, faculty members, members of the student body, members of the university staff, or special visitors to attend whenever matters of particular concern to them are being considered.

e. Additional representation on the Faculty Council:

Whenever a new College, School, or comparable Division is established which has an independent faculty of at least eight voting members, the Vice President and Dean of the Faculties shall certify the fact to the Secretary of the Faculty Council. The new unit thereupon shall be entitled to be represented on the Faculty Council by its Dean. The Faculty Council at such a time shall reassess the balance of representation between the elected members and the deans.

Section 21. Election of Members

a. All members of the Faculty Council to be elected shall be selected from the voting members of the faculty according to the procedure prescribed in Section 10.

b. Election of off-campus members:

1. The voting members of the Indianapolis faculties other than those of the Division of Adult Education and Public Services shall elect two members to the Faculty Council.

2. The voting members of the Division of Adult Education and Public Services other than those resident on the Bloomington campus shall elect two members to the Faculty Council.

3. Eligibility:

The voting members of the Indianapolis faculties, exclusive of the Division of the Adult Education and Public Services, may select for their representatives any persons who are voting members of the faculty either in Indianapolis or Bloomington.

The off-campus voting members of the Division of Adult Education and Public Services shall select as their representatives only members of extension centers outside Bloomington.

c. The election committee shall file with the Secretary of the Faculty Council a record of the votes cast on the final ballot of each election. In the event of a vacancy in the elected membership of the Faculty Council, the nominee who is next in order of votes and who is from the same election unit as that in which the vacancy occurs shall be certified by the Secretary to fill the unexpired terms.

Section 22. Responsibilities of the Faculty Council to the general faculty

a. The Faculty Council shall promptly report to the members of the general faculty all its proceedings.

b. In the event an action of the Faculty Council does not receive unanimous approval, the Secretary shall record and report in his minutes those voting for or against and those not voting on the action.

c. In the event a proposal does not receive a two-thirds concurrence of the members of the Faculty Council who are present, the Faculty Council by a majority vote shall determine whether the action involved is legislative and, therefore, to be submitted to the general faculty as described under item d of this section.

d. A general faculty meeting shall be called to discuss a legislative proposal referred to it by the Faculty Council. After discussion, the Secretary of the Faculty Council shall prepare and circulate to the voting members of the faculty a ballot which shall provide for a vote "for" or "against" the legislative proposal. The ballot shall be returned to the Secretary who shall count the votes, preserve them for future inspection for a reasonable length of time, and report the results to the Faculty Council, the President, and to the general faculty. A majority of those voting shall determine action on a legislative proposal submitted to the general faculty.

Supplementary Recommendations Approved by the Council

ARTICLE II. OFFICERS

Section 10. Manner of Election

b. The committee shall mail to each voting member a nomination ballot during the first week of March.

ARTICLE III. MEETINGS

Section 11. Regular Meetings

The faculty shall hold one regular meeting during each academic year, at which time the President shall report in detail on the state of the University, summarizing the academic, public service, and fiscal operations of the preceding academic year. He may make such recommendations to the faculty and call such problems to their attention as he deems pertinent to their responsibility as a faculty. The date of this regular meeting shall be fixed by the President and shall be during the first six weeks of the first semester of each academic year.

BY-LAWS OF THE FACULTY COUNCIL

1. Roberts Rules of Order shall govern the conduct of the meetings of the Faculty Council except in so far as the by-laws make express provision to the contrary.

2. The meetings of the Faculty Council shall begin at 3:30 p.m. and adjourn at 5:00 p.m. unless a later adjournment is agreed to unanimously. The Faculty Council by concurrence of a simple majority vote may fix a different time for a regular meeting or call a special meeting.

3. Quorum. The presence of a majority of the members of the Faculty Council shall constitute a quorum.

4. The voting for the elected members of the Faculty Council shall be completed before the last meeting of the Faculty Council in April. At this meeting the election committee shall report the results of the voting to the Faculty Council.

5. The Secretary (who is also Chairman, Agenda Committee), the Parliamentarian, and the Agenda Committee shall be elected at the last meeting of the Faculty Council in the Spring Semester. Nominations for these posts shall be

submitted by a nominations committee consisting of members of the Faculty Council. This committee shall be appointed by the President at the last meeting of the Faculty Council in April.

6. The duties of the Secretary shall be as follows:

   a. He shall keep comprehensive minutes of the proceedings and actions of the Faculty Council and circulate these promptly to the general faculty.

   b. He shall prepare a summary of the activities of the Faculty Council each year and distribute it to the general faculty.

   c. He shall serve as chairman of the Agenda Committee.

   d. He shall report in his minutes the absences at Faculty Council meetings and the names of the alternates present.

   e. He shall notify all members and interested persons of the time and place of each meeting of the Faculty Council.

   f. He shall circulate the agenda for meetings of the Council to all Council members and in addition to the Dean of Students, the Treasurer, the Registrar, the Director of Libraries, the Associate Dean of the School of Law in Indianapolis, the Director of the Division of Social Service, the Dean of Student and Educational Services, the Professor of Military Science and Tactics, the Professor of Air Science, the Director of the News Bureau and the Secretary of the Board of Trustees.

7. The Agenda Committee shall be composed of the Secretary, who shall serve as chairman, and two additional members of the Faculty Council. The functions of the Agenda Committee shall be as follows:

   a. The agenda of the Faculty Council shall be determined by the Agenda Committee. All communications requesting Faculty Council action, study, or advice shall be placed on the agenda or be referred to an appropriate body or committee for consideration. In the latter case, the Agenda Committee shall report its action to the Faculty Council which may, with the concurrence of a simple majority vote, request the Agenda Committee to place a referred item on the agenda.

   b. The Agenda Committee shall prepare the final draft of any new legislation approved by the Faculty Council.

   c. Emergency items should be referred to the Agenda Committee before being given precedence on the agenda.

   d. The Agenda Committee at any time may request the Faculty Council to determine the implementation and the effect of any past legislation or action, or to reconsider any past legislation.

   e. It shall be the responsibility of the Agenda Committee to invite non-members to any Faculty Council meetings at which matters of interest to them are being considered.

8. The President may speak "off the record" at any meeting of the Faculty Council.

9. Any member of the Faculty Council may appoint an alternate to serve in his place at any meeting. Any elected member of the Faculty Council who is to be absent for a semester or longer shall be replaced on the Faculty Council for the duration of his absence by the nominee who is next in order of votes and who is from the same election unit.

Faculty Minutes, March 1957 to May 1957, pp. 305–311.

[X]

Challenging the Old Order

The eight documents included in this section obviously are little more than representative of the closing years of the Stahr administration in Indiana University. This was an era when every segment of the institution produced reams of records. The archival files for this period, when finally drawn together and catalogued, will represent a sizable block of the general institutional record. There are all sorts of documents, major and minor, which contain the subtleties and nuances of the age. They reflect the doubts and the uncertainties, the anger and the fears, the emotions and prejudices, and the clouded perspectives.

During the closing years of the 1960s it seemed at times that Indiana University operated in two parts. There was the daily on-going instructional program which was never seriously threatened with disruption, and then there was the external student revolt and administrative activities which seemed central to the whole purpose of the University. Involved in all the commotion of this era were three or four cardinal issues. The first was the guaranteeing of academic freedoms and the rights of honest dissent. To accomplish this purpose required a great deal of sorting out of bona fide complaints and activistic thrusts. Second was the delicate matter of drawing a line between dissent and wanton violence. This was the challenge of making far-reaching racial adjustments in a time when emotions were overwrought for other and often unrelated reasons. Finally there was the matter of formulating official policies for the orderly operation of the University for the benefit of the greatest number of individuals within the context of the greatest possible freedom of thought, expression, and personal decorum.

Both President Elvis J. Stahr's statements and the declaration of policy by the Board of Trustees give highly refined insights into the turmoil and disruptions of the moment. In the background were the protests and evidence of angers, frustrations, and moods which came up from the forums of Dunn Meadow, from the protest marches about the Showalter Fountain before the Auditorium where speakers of every stripe and point of view of the times came to be heard, and from the tidal flow of press and

737

handbill publications. In the background of these documents were the incidents which disrupted the Little 500 Weekend, the truculent march on President Stahr's house, and the even more truculent demands made on the administration for answers to almost endless and at times irrelevant questions. There were the disrupted marches down the streets of Bloomington, the unpleasant incident at the Weir Cook Airport in Indianapolis when President Lyndon B. Johnson landed there to speak.

In these years Indiana University was making full adjustments to greater absorption of Blacks into its student body and faculty. Two of the documents here pertain to the maturing of a social policy which would both in spirit and fact remove every vestige of racial prejudice and discrimination. One of these is a rather deep-searching attempt to ferret out the hidden and subconscious areas of racial discriminations and slights. At times the task of creating a full state of racial harmony and acceptance became confused and frustrating because many of the protestors themselves were unable to state in consistently clear terms what objectives they had in mind.

The document pertaining to the realignment of the University's off-campus centers with the central university in Bloomington is of fundamental importance. The granting of broadly based autonomy to the centers accomplished a basic objective of enabling the liberal arts university to serve a highly diversified and widely dispersed constituency throughout the State of Indiana. Adoption of this plan by the Board of Trustees would seem to indicate a somewhat radical redirection of the University's scope of operation and the increasing breadth of its instructional program.

Elvis J. Stahr's resignation no doubt ushered in a new era of university administration and operation. In a way it ended an era of university history which had a distinct continuity from 1884 down to this date. No one a century and a half before could have visualized a social and political situation in which such loud demands for change would be made from so many segments of American and Indiana society as were made in the troubled decade of the 1960s.

Document 194

The Hope and the Dream

On November 19, 1962, Elvis Jacob Stahr, Jr., was inaugurated President of Indiana University. He came to the position with broad experience. He was a Rhodes Scholar, a practicing attorney, a Dean of the University of Kentucky Law School, a Provost of the University of Pittsburgh, President of the University of West Virginia, and Secretary of the Army under John F. Kennedy. In addition he had served in various advisory capacities in government in Washington. In his speech he pointed the way to the future of the University with the optimism of a young man, emphasizing the role of education and educational research in an open society. He insisted that the University retain its position of leadership and stressed the importance of professional education. In bright terms he visualized Indiana University as a significant part of the greater world of scholarship.

*   *   *

Inaugural Address of President Elvis J. Stahr, Jr.

President Hickam, Governor Welsh, Excellencies of the Diplomatic Corps, Distinguished Delegates and Guests, Colleagues, and Friends of Indiana University:

Let me at the outset affirm most solemnly that this is a very great moment for me personally, that I appreciate deeply the honor just conferred upon me, that I am profoundly grateful for your confidence and support, and that my best efforts are and shall be pledged to the advancement of this University.

But beyond that, and more importantly, this is also a moment of significance for Indiana and for Indiana University, not because it formalizes a change in academic administration, for no change in institutional character, direction, or personality necessarily flows from that, but because it marks, perhaps as well as a single moment can, the beginning of a period in the life of higher education in this State and Nation so momentous, so fraught both with brilliant opportunities and with heavy penalties for failure, that it can without extravagance be termed a new era. It will inevitably be an era of great change, if only, though not only, because of the pace of our times and the impact of forces I shall mention in a moment.

The presence of each of you in this great gathering this morning contributes to both the significance and the enjoyment of this ancient ceremony, and the University is grateful to you all, as am I. You will understand, I know, if I acknowledge with special happiness the presence of my mother and my father. And it is a most delightful thing to me that my Alma Mater, the University of Kentucky, is represented on this platform by her distinguished President and by her noble and beloved President Emeritus, under whom I once served through eight years of rich experience, and that my second Alma Mater, the University of Oxford, is represented by my warm friend, fellow Rhodes Scholar and esteemed colleague, the President of Purdue University.

My feeling of pride in becoming the President of Indiana University is tempered with profound humility each time I reflect, as I often do, that I am succeeding one of the great educational statesmen of the twentieth century, Herman B Wells. Possibly no one but me will ever know fully what a source of continuing strength it is that he is actively with us as Chancellor, inspiration, and friend.

No one should, and I shall not, take lightly the challenge inherent in the leadership of one of the great universities of the greatest nation on earth in the most exciting yet critical period in the history of our planet thus far, for American universities are closer to the heart of state, national, and global concerns than they have ever been.

"*Universitas*—all together, the whole, the universe"—custodian, discoverer, transmitter, interpreter, of all that is known, the university stands at the apex of the educational structure, symbolizing, if not, in fact, embracing, all knowledge, in its diversity and its unity.

In the contemporary surge of creativity and discovery, knowledge doubles and redoubles, each new fact or proposition lighting new paths for exploration and revelation beyond the anticipation or imagination of the most sophisticated. Long established divisions of related knowledge, categorized for convenience and manageability, are stretched beyond the original concepts. Subsequent splinterings into specializations and subspecializations are soon themselves made to seem arbitrary as changed awareness of the grand pattern follows each new discovery and insight.

The function of the university becomes the more important as the accumulation of what we know defies the individual mind to contain it, and frequently challenges the human mind even to classify it so that it may be retrieved with the aid of wondrous new machines and meaningfully interrelated.

Where today, but in the traditional university, can the unity in knowledge be constantly sought and honored whilst the pursuit of new knowledge along all its diverse paths is encouraged and nurtured?

The New Place of the University

These dual responsibilities place an exclusive and unique charge upon our traditional universities, and with the breakthroughs of basic research and the unbelievable pace of technological development, the new place of the university in the total fabric of society begins to unfold.

At the pinnacle of new specializations, new discoveries burst forth, whereupon new relationships suddenly reveal themselves. That which was a research device becomes the heart of a production machine. That which was a theory becomes a fact. The processes of research and development across the whole spectrum of knowledge have pushed universities into a new essentiality to our life and times. Exploring the unknown has always been at the heart of all that education stands for, but the products of its own efforts have placed upon the university of today a mantle of central responsibility for the future of civilization.

Postulate what worthy goals you will for man in this modern world: justice, knowledge, human dignity, economic vitality, international concord, the conquest of space, government by and for the people, the opportunity of every child, every man and woman, to realize the best that God put in him—and ignorance is the bar, education the gate, to each such goal.

The current chapter in the long annals of man's earthly adventure is an unusually dramatic one, with all the elements of high drama focused into an incredibly fast-moving plot. All here present are familiar with the simultaneous bursting upon us of the almost inconceivably powerful forces of what have been called the "explosions" of population, of knowledge, of technology, and of the aspirations of billions of people who for centuries had played but minor roles in the world's affairs. We dare not discount the potentials and rapidly emerging effects of any of these forces—nor the long shadow which intrudes persistently into our contemplation of them and of the future. For looming over every horizon is a deep and seemingly irreconcilable conflict—not a new one, to be sure, but one which in our time has reached heights of danger and suspense never before seen on a global scale. It is at bottom the age-old conflict between slavery and freedom, between deceit and honesty, between aggressive force persistently seeking to invade any vacuum it can find and defensive strength which will move only when there is no answer save a protecting shield.

What a pity that this should be! From the moment victory over fascism was won on the field of battle, this Nation and most of the war-weary peoples of the world turned their backs on armies and conquest. We in America disbanded the greatest military forces ever seen on earth; we offered to every surviving veteran the greatest opportunity our country or any country could offer, the opportunity for higher education; we gathered tens of billions of dollars of our treasure and used them to help friend and foe bind up their wounds and renew their search for a decent life in freedom; we went further and extended a helping hand to hundreds of millions of newly awakening peoples who were yet illiterate and ignorant in the ways of the modern world, but who had legitimate human aspirations. We envisioned and struggled hard, asking all others to join us, to help create a world in which all men might have the opportunity to live in peace, with freedom to pursue their finest goals, each in his own way. And we are still struggling toward those ends.

What a pity, indeed, that the only nation in that post-war world with even the possibility of rivaling America in world leadership should have been one whose own leaders found all of this repugnant, who could not accept the prospect of success of this great effort, this great dream, and who deliberately turned the world into a kind of living hell for country after country, people after people!

Perhaps it was inevitable; I don't know. Maybe we, who ourselves are not free from sin, are doomed on earth to cope with Satan till the day of judgment. Be that as it may, I refuse to believe that we are doomed to surrender to him! We therefore must not succumb to self-pity or to self-righteousness, any more than to the overt challenge of arms.

There are many big and little things we must all do in these anxious years, many day-to-day decisions our elected leaders must make, but, if we are to stay alive, and to keep alive the things that make it worth being alive, there are two overriding tasks confronting America and all free people: the first is to continue to build societies in which man can cultivate the full fruits of freedom, and the other is to maintain military power which will deter the enemies of freedom from attempting to destroy or overrun us.

And education is today indispensable to both!

Military power of the most advanced kind will be essential to protecting freedom so long as the forces of antifreedom themselves have such power and are not content to stay at home. But true education is essential to extending freedom; indeed, it is part of the essence of freedom, and, without it, there can be neither a great deal worth defending nor any means adequate to defend it.

THE ESSENCE OF EDUCATION

I am scarcely saying anything new when I remind all of us that under our American system, from its beginning, the major responsibility for military power has been that of the Nation as a whole through the agency of the federal government, while the major responsibility for the education of our people has been "reserved to the states and to the people." It might be supposed that this indicates that education was thought the less important by the Framers of the Constitution, but I am confident they had quite a different view. They knew full well that no democracy can function without an educated citizenry. They also knew that while military efficiency by its very nature requires strict discipline of large groups of men, centralization of authority, and absolute loyalty to that authority when asserted, education by its very nature requires diversity, decentralization, experimentation, dissent, inquiry. The higher learning in particular is, at its best, a disciplined approach, not to indoctrination, but to the full development of the individual intellect and to the searching out, through many approaches, of the deepest roots of truth, whether about nature, the universe, society, or that wondrous creature, man himself. Therefore, the Framers may well have reasoned, nation-wide responsibility for all of education should not be vested in any single authority. But it should not be overlooked today that education is too vital to the Nation to be permitted for long to be inadequately supported.

All of this presents exceptional challenges to the state of Indiana, for upon each state still falls responsibility under our American system for providing most of the financial resources needed for the work of public education.

Frankly, I doubt one could find more than a handful of citizens of this State who don't want Hoosier children to have opportunity as full and real as is open to any other children of their generation. And I doubt there can be found any instance in history where a high level of educational opportunity failed to make any society more advanced and more prosperous than it was before. But it is enough to recognize that no state or nation can advance without it today!

Many have asked me in recent months how I like it here. It has been clear in every case that they hoped I do like it, that they wanted me to like it, because they like it and are proud of it. My answer was and is unequivocal—I like it wholeheartedly—and so do my wife and our children. This is a beautiful place, conducive to contemplation and learning, as anyone can see, and it is a warm and friendly place, as anyone with good will can feel. It is also an exciting place, a place where more than 17,000 young people, among the brightest of their generation, are striving to complete the process of truly "growing up," are gathered with hundreds of mature and superb scholars in pursuit of answers to all the great questions of the centuries and all the new questions of the age of space and the atom, are trying to digest knowledge which daily probes deeper into the unknown, are trying to prepare for life in a world greatly changed, and still changing, from what their elders have known. These eager students are not data processing machines into which mere information is fed and then regurgitated; they are questioning, debating, impatient, ambitious, sometimes confused, always expectant, never wholly good, rarely really bad, sons and daughters of human kind—and heirs to whatever world we may leave them. This is a very large institution, and I am all the more proud of the living reality of its tradition of active, personalized concern for every individual member of its family, be he student, teacher, or staff member.

The most wonderful thing of all is that this is an intensely vital place: a place of teaching and learning, of searching and finding, of thinking and creating, of high challenge to youth, of profound stimulations and satisfactions for the scholar, the artist, the curious mind, the discriminating taste, and the imaginative spirit. We must keep it that way!

The University itself, though seemingly embodied in lovely acres and impressive buildings, is in truth far more spirit than stone, its beauty but a backdrop for its high endeavors. Dedicated to the pursuit of knowledge for its own sake, it also has a deep sense of mission in the service of both society and of the individual human being. We must keep it that way!

It is even justifiable to say that the entire State, much of the Nation, and most of the world's continents contain part of this great institution. I speak not just of our alumni, who are found throughout this State and all over the world, nor just of our students, who come from every county of the State, every state of the Nation, and eighty-six countries around the world, but also of our direct working relationships with many other institutions, in this State and this Nation, and in Europe, Asia, Africa, and Latin America. In this, as in other ways, we are helping to fulfill that sense of mission of hope of which I spoke. We must keep it that way!

Nearly half of our credit students are enrolled in places other than this Bloomington Campus, mostly in our fine Center for the schools of the health professions in Indianapolis and on our several regional campuses. Together with our sister institutions of higher learning, both private and public, we have provided for Indiana a system which places opportunity for education beyond high school within twenty-five miles of almost every boy, girl, and adult in the state of Indiana. We must work to strengthen all these institutions—and we shall continue to work with them, constructively and cooperatively, for the benefit of the entire State.

What else must we do—particularly we of Indiana University? The list of specific challenges is far too long to be compiled in this address, but I hope that mentioning a few will suggest many of the others.

WE MUST KEEP THE DOOR OPEN

First, we must keep the door of educational opportunity open. In the face of the great upcoming surges in college-age population, we must do every practical thing to insure the continuing vitality of the proposition that ability to learn, not ability to pay, is the key to that door. We must help our fellow citizens understand that the oncoming waves of young people seeking preparation for productive careers should be looked upon not as a problem, but as a blessing.

Second, we must insure that when a youth or an adult enters our door, he will find education of excellence, never of mediocrity. This means that our libraries, our laboratories, our facilities for study and growth, and above all our faculties, must be of the high quality needed to educate for tomorrow—for it is in the complex and demanding world of tomorrow that our students must live their lives and make their contributions. The competition for first-rate faculty nation-wide is becoming so fierce that some institutions may not be able to obtain or retain them. Will our own institution be among these? I pray not. The numbers of bright, ambitious young people who will graduate from high school will increase so vastly and so rapidly, beginning in the middle of the very next biennium, that in some places many will find either closed doors or greatly diluted opportunity inside the doors. Will Indiana be among these? I pray not. Should we at any time be faced with resources inadequate to provide education of high quality to all young Hoosiers who are qualified and determined to pursue it here, then some must be turned away; for it is better truly to educate a few than to defraud many. But we must strive with great energy to prevent such a tragic choice from being forced upon us—for the future of all of us and of our children is bound up with the level and quality of education of our total citizenry.

Third, I would urgently add that we have a heavy obligation within the University to insure in every feasible way that the hard-earned tax dollars entrusted to us are so used as to get every last penny's worth of educational mileage out of every last dollar. This we have done and shall continue to do! Through imagination, ingenuity, sound planning, and determination we can even turn necessities of doing larger tasks into stimulations for doing them better.

Fourth, we must insist that the University retain its leadership in the fields in which it is nationally distinguished. It cannot and will not try to be all things to all people, but it has special obligations in a number of fields in which its contributions to the State and to mankind have been and will be signal. Central among these, and basic to all cultural, technological and professional advancement, must always be the liberal arts and sciences. I was thrilled, as all of you must have been, last month when a graduate of this University received the Nobel Prize in the field in which he had studied here under a very distinguished faculty which itself includes a Nobel Prize winner. I was thrilled again earlier this month when one of our faculty, himself an alumnus, presided at the dedication of the world's largest solar telescope, a joint enterprise of the ten leading universities in the field of astronomy, spanning the nation from Harvard to Indiana to California. There have been other great moments in the life of this institution and there will be again—if we keep our sights on the finest and best. It is worthy of mention now, I think, that we will soon be bringing to this campus the editorial offices of the Mississippi Valley Historical Review, probably the most distinguished periodical in the field of American history. Our distinction in linguistics and in languages, of which we regularly teach more than twenty, and in international studies, is recognized world-wide. Few universities between the Atlantic and Pacific coasts have as many fellows of the National Academy of Sciences and the other great learned societies as do we. Indeed, several of our departments in the academic disciplines clearly rank among the Nation's best, and I am aware of none which is less than excellent.

These vital assets enable us to carry on our largest single function, undergraduate education, with both thoroughness and high standards, in a rich intellectual environment. They also enable us to provide graduate work of demonstrably superior quality. We must keep it that way!

There are two other major concerns of this University: one is professional training; the other is research.

Each of our many professional schools and divisions today is strong; some are among the Nation's leaders; one or two are probably unexcelled. Yet we are determined to improve them all, for complacency is a dangerous enemy of excellence.

The general public is perhaps not fully aware of how important to its own well-being are the professional schools of their State University. Here are the sources of very substantial percentages of the State's physicians, dentists, nurses, lawyers, college teachers, librarians, school teachers and administrators, business managers, scientists, coaches, journalists, artists, musicians, optometrists, medical technicians, public administrators, and others who play key roles in the service of the people. Most professional training is relatively expensive, but it is indispensable to the progress of our society.

Whether in the realms of the natural sciences, the fields of the literary, creative, and performing arts, the study of the affairs of man and nations, or the development of competent and ethical practitioners of the learned professions, both the disciplines and the professions at Indiana, at both the undergraduate and graduate levels, are dedicated to objectivity and creativity, are uncompromising toward mediocrity, are hostile to extreme rigidities of thought. We must keep them that way!

The reference to rigidities of thought may profit from a further word. In the presence of such rigidities on both the extreme left and the extreme right, in a world of terrible tensions, the University's role must be to maintain its even-tempered but relentless search for truth. We shall not stifle, but shall promote, restless seeking and inquiring and debating, so long as it is honest. But we shall insist that there be an atmosphere of basic objectivity. We shall encourage intellectual excitement, but shall firmly suppress both physical violence and efforts to provoke it. We shall be intolerant only of intolerance—and of deceit.

On the Importance of Research

As to research, a symposium of several days' duration would be required to report on the University's accomplishments, activities and aims, covering as they do a wide range—from seeking the causes and cures of cancer and heart disease to probing the secrets of the universe and of life itself, from the motivations of human behavior to ways of making responsible freedom more real to more people, from the management of great enterprises and the administration of justice and government to ways of making education itself more efficient and more fruitful.

There is a further point in this connection. From the basis of two vantage points I have been privileged to occupy in this single calendar year, I am convinced that the economic future of this State and region depends upon intensified efforts in several fields of research. If adequate investment is not made in this area, and in the highest development of our abundant native brainpower, the center of gravity of industrial productivity will move out of the Middle West to the two seacoasts, as it has already begun to do—and an economic wasteland could replace it.

Today, as we have noted, higher education is more directly and significantly involved in technological advancement and economic progress than ever before. Of even private universities is this true; and public universities have felt this responsibility keenly, and with ever-increasing benefits to us all, at least since the inception of the land-grant college movement whose centennial is celebrated this very year.

Both Indiana and Purdue are particularly alert to this challenge, and both stand ready to help. To Purdue's splendid new McClure Park will shortly be added at I.U. a new "Center for Industrial Applications of Aerospace Research," supported in part by the National Aeronautics and Space Administration, in part by Indiana business firms, and in part by the Indiana University Foundation and the University itself. There are other contributions the University can and must make to its own economic base, without which the University itself cannot go forward.

All I have said thus far may help to explain my earlier statement that exceptional challenges are presented in this new era to the state of Indiana. Why "exceptional"? Almost every state faces the exceptional effects of the great "population explosion" which began throughout the country following World War II, and the resulting necessity of educating greatly increased numbers of youth; in this sense, Indiana is no exception, and Indiana University and her sister institutions of Indiana must play greatly expanded roles. Every university faces the exceptional effects of the explosive expansion of knowledge in recent years, and the cumulative, spiraling demands it places upon the functions of organizing, preserving, and transmitting this knowledge, seeking new applications for it, integrating its specialized fields, and, not least, adding to it. In this Indiana University is certainly no exception. But few states will feel quite as acutely as will Indiana the problems resulting from the explosive changes in technology, still only in their infancy. Like an automobile, they are capable of carrying us forward or of running over us. Here, the modern university can play an important, indeed an indispensable, though never an exclusive, role, particularly through research—carried forward vigorously and with the finest talent available.

Alas, there is no magic by which either the State or her colleges and universities can expect to meet these exceptional challenges without a substantial increase in the level of resources invested by the State in higher education. And this decade would be the worst possible time in the history of either our State or Nation for Hoosiers to turn away from the obvious and inevitable facts confronting us. May I bluntly restate just one of these facts, for emphasis? During the next biennium, there will be ten thousand more Hoosier boys and girls, fully qualified, seeking education at the four state colleges and universities of Indiana than during the current biennium—and the numbers will go on up from there, for the foreseeable future!

THE WAY TO A HAPPY ENDING

This part of our story can have a happy ending. Life sometimes, even often, calls for permanent sacrifices for the achievement of worthwhile goals. But not always. Education is one of those wonderful things which is purchased at a profit to the buyer, which only enriches the State which provides it, which returns infinitely more, even in dollars, than it is ever given, which, as in the moral of the parable of the talents, costs only those who will not invest. For Indiana, the needed investment may now appear large, but it will be both small and temporary compared to the enduring richness of the dividends.

In sum, my friends, we at Indiana University are a significant part of the great world of scholarship, and our first allegiance as an institution must always be to that world. Other agencies, other people, have other worthy missions, but ours needs no apology; it is basic to them all. ·

In the years ahead, if God be willing, we shall carry forward with all our strength the great work in which we are engaged, building upon the splendid foundations erected by our predecessors, striving for excellence in all we do, alert to the complex problems, deep conflicts, and tremendous challenges in the world around us, and keeping before us the vision of bringing light to our youth, knowledge to our people, progress to our State, strength to our Nation, and, hopefully, wisdom to ourselves and to our fellows.

Inaugural address, Elvis J. Stahr, Jr., November 19, 1962.

Document 195

Assaulting the Ramparts of Academic Freedom

President Elvis Stahr served Indiana University in an era when academic freedom in its traditional sense came under heavy fire from several quarters. In Bloomington the entire University community was conscious of the stirrings on the American university campus, and the view of academic traditions and freedoms were under severe challenge. No one was certain what might be in store for the institution, or where the various protests and activist upheavals might lead. In order to clarify the University's position on academic freedom President Stahr issued to the public in February 1967 this statement of position.

*   *   *

From:
News Bureau
Indiana University
306 N. Union St.
Bloomington, Ind. (47401)
A.C. 812, 337-3911
Feb. 6, 1967

For Immediate Release
"If anywhere an administration and a faculty can work effectively, it ought to be right here where they have worked together so well for so long," he said.

"But if those bent on disruption can drive a wedge between us, it will be driven, I assure you. If they can alienate the students from either or both of us, they will gleefully do so, I assure you. If those bent on either disruption or control can alienate our public support from us, they will joyously do so, I can assure you."

Dr. Stahr said he was worried about the "referee attitude" of many faculties toward what has been and is taking place on numerous American campuses.

"By that I mean the attitude that the whole business is some sort of feud (annoying to some faculty, perhaps even enjoyable to others) between students and administrations, and that the faculty need have no concern except to see that rules of the game are observed, at least by administrations.

"It is curious to me that there seems to be so little curiosity about the staging of the student tests and protests—that indeed the wohle activity often is viewed merely as a healthful tonic for apathetic students.

"To me, student parroting of propaganda is not educational. Emotional adoption of "lines" is not educational. Repetition of slogans is not educational. Practicing tactics of mass protest may be training of a sort in means, but is scarcely education in substance, and it is ironical, incongruous, and unworthy for the most highly advantaged group of young people anywhere—American college students—to borrow the approaches and methods, such as sit-ins, developed by that long-frustrated segment of our society whose seriously disadvantaged plight has often led to genuine desperation.

"Yet, who has troubled to expose the propaganda? Who has sought to protect the educational processes from forcible disruption? Where is the voice that assures the puzzled student, tyranny is tyranny, whatever the cause masking it? Who points out the mockery of drowning out guest speakers with shouts of 'free speech'?

"Today there are some who almost seem to feel that freedom is automatically abandoned by any refusal to cooperate with those who by preponderant and available evidence have destroyed freedom elsewhere. One wonders most seriously how quick we would have or should have been to condemn a German university in the Weimar Republic which withdrew support from the Hitler Jugend.

"This kind of problem is not new and it is not going to disappear. As universities become more and more important and influential in a society whose survival depends upon the power of knowledge widely dispersed through the citizenry, there will be people of both the far left and the far right who will seek to manipulate or control our institutions. It is important, therefore, that we think carefully about the processes of the institution which minimize the chance of manipulation in whatever guise and particularly under the beguiling mantle of academic virtues cleverly perverted to anti-academic purposes.

"At the same time, it seems to me, university commitment to the search for truth embodies the obligation to protect strongly the processes of the search and the quality of intellectual honesty which should characterize both the searcher and the lay interpreter of truth—above all, when exercising their rights in a publicly supported academic community.

"The battle simply isn't over. It may be only beginning, for as higher education is pushed, whether or not it wants to be, into a more central role in the society, the increased influence, the increased attention and concern of the people will raise more questions and call for more answers.

"Hence, we must think and rethink, affirm and strengthen, but, at the very least, know at all times the meaning of academic integrity—and not just the surface meaning. And, we must be prepared to explain and justify that concept with patience, assurance and candor.

"I fear there is on many campuses not only insufficient faculty acceptance of responsibility but insufficient faculty recognition of the forces at work.

"I abhor the halt to the educational process as a tool of negotiation. Universities are not factories under contract to students. If the partners in a university cannot reason together about differences, where can reason have a forum?

"The tool which blocks the path to the mere Navy recruiter in Berkeley and to the mere President at the University of Chicago can block the path to the classroom door if the teacher—like the recruiter and the administrator—in the performance of his function happens to teach what a few militant students don't want taught.

"Is it not time for a dialog between the faculty referee and the student provoker? Is this not a part of the educational process?

"To me, academic freedom is the freedom to be as objective as human beings of integrity can be. Is its cloak really meant, I question, to cover dogma and conspiracy and deceit? Surely we can deplore the denial of academic freedom to a Galileo without having to insist that his persecutors should have the same defense. Isn't one of the triumphs of academic freedom that it made possible the unmasking of witch doctors?

"Is it wrong, then, not to welcome witch doctors—exploiters of superstition, of prejudice, of emotion, of conflict—in academe? Does academe really have the responsibility to support both freedom and anti-freedom? To question both, objectively, is part of its responsibility—to ignore the findings borders, I should think, on irresponsibility.

"We are fortunate in knowing a good deal about the motives of the leadership of the so-called 'new Left', not alone from inference but from explicit statements of some of its spokesmen which perhaps we weren't intended to know.

"For example, we know from their own words that some are building their strategy currently on the premise that universities in America are national keystones, and therefore the disruption of universities will weaken American society significantly, thus measurably advancing the cause of those who for whatever motives want a general disruption of the American system. Their goal is clear enough, though their means have been thus far highly opportunistic.

"Even though the disruption of campuses is their first goal, I'm not suggesting that we remove the protection of the Bill of Rights from such persons or their puppets, even if we could, but is it an adequate response for the academic community simply to censure people who doubt the wisdom and the necessity of turning the university or its resources to the aid of its would-be disrupters?

"Some of the evidence of their aims is explicit and available. My own notions, at least, on what to do about it are still in the formative state—and I earnestly bespeak your thoughtful assistance in reaching appropriate solutions.

"Let me make one think very plain, however, lest I be badly misunderstood. There has been abundant evidence again during the past year in several parts of the country that threats to freedom and to intellectualism do not originate with one of the extremes alone. Far from it.

"Some criticism comes from thoughtful people who simply fear that we are insufficiently alert to threats from the far left. Some echoes the party lines of leftist extremism. A great deal of attempted pressure, however, comes also from people who are so far to the right that they themselves would, if they could, manipulate and control the educational process: the curricula, the findings of research, the employment of faculty, the handling of student aspirations for greater involvement in campus decision-making, and similar university concerns.

"Such pressures are generally resisted quite successfully, though the assessment of the damage they do is not easy . . . .

"I am by no means suggesting that we should attempt to persuade students that everything is for the best in this best of all possible societies, that American society is utterly without blemish or need of change. We have not practiced our precepts perfectly by a long shot. Witness such problems as civil rights, legislative reapportionment, restricted opportunity, crime, pollution—the list is disturbingly long.

"In short, we know we're not perfect, but we certainly can ill afford to permit those with questionable motives to exploit the vulnerabilities of our imperfect practice. The result could be to diminish or destroy, rather than to enhance, our chances to improve and to correct through democratic processes."

Document 196

A New Order of Statewide University Operation

Indiana University was among the pioneers who organized and offered extension work both by correspondence and at localized centers. Some of the latter evolved into off-campus centers which operated directly under the administrative and instructional supervision of the Bloomington campus. Three of the off-campus centers grew into rather sizable operations. These were Indianapolis, Gary, and Fort Wayne. Then there were those at South Bend, Kokomo, Richmond, and Jeffersonville-New Albany. Demands for instruction outgrew the earlier and narrower concepts of the off-campus objectives. There were even pressures for the awarding of degrees and the offering of graduate studies.

*   *   *

This statement to the Board of Trustees, April 19, 1968, by President Elvis J. Stahr may well be one of the most important organizational documents in the history of Indiana University. It not only outlined the administrative process by which the off-campus centers would become self-contained integrals of the University, but specified the manner in which the whole educational concept of a modern public university could be given broad application in a state. This broadening of the University's base of education and the applied arts had fundamental implications for the ultimate solution of the ancient dilemma of Indiana being a narrowly confined "separate" liberal arts university.

*   *   *

Statement to the Board of Trustees,
Indiana University, by
President Elvis J. Stahr
April 19, 1968

Throughout her 148 years, Indiana University has been dedicated to teaching, research and public service for the benefit of the people of Indiana. She has now become one of the largest and finest of all state universities, but her commitment to the ideal, reflected in the State's first Constitution, of widespread educational opportunity of high quality for those who want it and are capable of benefiting substantially from it led I.U. over a half-century ago on her own initiative to inaugurate a system through which a number of her teaching programs are now conducted in several of the State's largest cities. In recent years these programs have come to enroll well over a third of all the University's students, on campuses other than the oldest one in Bloomington. I.U. degrees may now be earned on five campuses, and that number will grow.

During the 'sixties especially, the University has been adding substantially to the physical facilities and full-time faculties on her urban campuses, and the numbers of full-time students have now begun to grow dramatically. The projections for the future suggest that only a beginning has been made, though a strong one.

Soon after I came to the presidency of the University six of the Extension Centers, as they have been called, were renamed Regional Campuses. Their directors were made assistant deans, and later deans. Campus planning was pushed. Operating and capital appropriations were sought, and in 1967 were formally made. New programs, including several full four-year and some Masters' degree curricula, were developed.

Most academic policy-making, however, and too much of the daily burden of administrative work for the total University, have continued to be centered heavily in faculty bodies and staff offices on the Bloomington Campus, although there have been increasing exceptions. New techniques of communication and ways of making the central academic and service resources available to all other campuses have undoubtedly helped to strengthen those other campuses and to bring them along more rapidly than would once have been possible. At the same time, the close tie-ins of the Bloomington base with both academic and administrative functions throughout the institution are placing tremendous burdens on the understaffed administration in Bloomington and are sometimes causing delays and irritations on our other campuses, which could be avoided if more functions were decentralized.

A major administrative realignment is therefore indicated. This has been under study for more than a year, and indeed every step we have taken since the Report of the Post High School Study Commission in 1962 has been in this direction.

The concept of the new organization I am now ready to propose is basically simple, thought it will take some time to implement all the necessary reassigning of functions and personnel and beefing up of staffs on campuses outside Bloomington.

The concept is similar in many respects to the concepts adopted in recent years by the Universities of Wisconsin and Illinois and Missouri. It also bears some resemblance to the University of California.

Under the concept I am proposing for I.U., the functions and size of central administration, i.e., of the University presidency and all-University staff, will be sharply curtailed. They will be focused in the areas of planning, budget, external relations, University-wide policy and coordination, and those relatively few but important services which can be most economically performed on an all-University basis. I'll give examples of these types of functions a little later.

The operating staff of the University will be divided geographically, into three major groupings initially. These are Bloomington, Indianapolis, and the Regional Campuses. In Bloomington and in Indianapolis, a Chancellor will be appointed who will preside over the Bloomington or Indianapolis faculty, as the case may be, and who will be responsible for the administration of the programs and services which support the schools in his group. All of the University's undergraduate, graduate, and professional schools in Indianapolis—these being at present Medicine, Dentistry, Nursing, Allied Health, Law, Social Service, Downtown Center, Normal College of the American Gymnastic Union, and Herron Art—will compose the group to be known as "I.U.I."—"Indiana University-Indianapolis." A search and screen operation will be launched at once for a Chancellor for I.U.I., who obviously should be a man of outstanding ability and versatility and he will need a well-organized staff. The faculties in Indianapolis will be invited to consider and recommend a form or forms of Faculty organization to consider matters of import to more than one faculty. Administratively, recognition must and will be given to the fact that the Medical Center has important relationships on a Statewide basis, and has also direct academic program tie-ins with Bloomington. The Schools and hospitals of the Medical Center also have, of course, special needs for unusually close interrelation among themselves and for direct involvement in planning and policy making at the level of central University administration and the Board of Trustees—more on this later.

Among the immediate objectives of I.U.I. will be the stepped-up development of physical facilities on a common campus in and around the Medical Center area; the development of graduate, postgraduate and research programs closely tied to the needs and resources of the Indianapolis industrial complex; the continuing improvement of all the existing professional schools; the further development of appropriate four-year undergraduate degree curricula for commuting students and of special programs (where possible in cooperation with others) for the benefit of economically disadvantaged persons in the community and of persons desiring sub-baccalaureate education and training not otherwise available, where such programs fall in areas of I.U.I.'s special competencies. Important groundwork has been laid and moves have been made in each of these directions in recent years, but a major, concentrated effort is now called for and will need the University's full support and that of others. I shall refer to Purdue's part in certain of these developments later on.

A vice President for Regional Campuses will be appointed, and as you know he has now been found as a result of a search and screen operation the past nine months which involved our faculties on all campuses and which has produced for us a man with proven ability and virtually ideal experience for this post. If you approve his appointment today, he will report July 1. His area of responsibility will include besides the Regional Campuses, I.U.'s participation in the unique joint Center in Richmond which Earlham College and I.U. established in 1946 and which last year was reorganized to bring in Purdue and Ball State also.

The five Regional Campuses other than the one in Indianapolis (will become part of Indiana University—Indianapolis) will be renamed and each will have a Chancellor. The present deans of those campuses will each be named Dean and Acting Chancellor, effective July first. The new Vice President for Regional Campuses will provide full-time leadership, working with these Acting Chancellors, to develop administrative machinery of increasing efficiency and autonomy on each campus, under broad policies established by the Trustees; to insure constant access by each campus to the President and his staff and to the Board of Trustees, to all-University services, and to certain key resources of the University such as library, telecommunications, computer centers, etc.; to promote responsiveness to the special needs of each area in which a regional campus is located, and to stimulate arrangements within the total University faculty for increased academic autonomy for each campus. He will also be charged with expediting and helping to arrange the smooth transfer of the Indianapolis Downtown Center from the Regional Campus System to the jurisdiction of I.U.I.

I suggest that certain campuses be re-named as follows; the Northwest Regional Campus would become "Indiana University-Northwest"; The South Bend-Mishawaka Regional Campus would become "Indiana University-South Bend"; the Kokomo Regional Campus would become "Indiana University-Kokomo"; I. U.'s programs on the Indiana-Purdue Regional Campus at Fort Wayne would be known, at least for the internal purposes of I.U., as "Indiana University-Fort Wayne," and the Southeastern Regional Campus would be called "Indiana University-Southeast." The faculty on each campus will be invited to consider with their Acting Chancellor appropriate forms of faculty organization and representation, and to consider with the Vice President for Regional Campuses how the Regional Campus faculties collectively might contribute to the academic standards and policies of each campus. The University Faculty Council is already considering its own reorganization. In addition, the possible structure of a Bloomington faculty, and the responsibilities and relations to each other of faculties in each major administrative group, have been urged by the Faculty Council as matters for immediate study, beginning upon your approval of my proposals today, the principles of which have been endorsed by the Faculty Council as recently as last Tuesday with considerable stress on the urgency of getting on with it.

In sum, what I am recommending is a considerable decentralization of administrative functions on a geographic basis, which will also lead, I am confident, to considerable decentralizing of academic policy-making. The University has reached a level of size and maturity which makes both of these desirable and even necessary. Too many detailed decisions now tend to go to levels higher or broader or more remote than is necessary. This has meant, on the one hand, too little time for centralized planning and well-focused leadership, and, on the other, too little authority in relation to the nature of the responsibilities carried by those "on the ground."

As a prelude to citing key examples of the functions which I propose be retained as responsibilities of the President and his immediate staff, let me say that the Board of Trustees will of course continue to have the same basic responsibilities and powers it has had, but that we shall be able to give you more and better organized facts and more perspective on them, as bases for your principal decisions. There should in time be more opportunity for both you and me to weigh relatively major plans and policy issues because less need for distraction by relatively minor operating problems, and because of a better flow of management information.

It is probably not possible, and it surely would be unwise, at this juncture to identify precisely and to the last detail those responsibilities and functions which would be lodged at the central administrative level and those that would be delegated to the principal operating divisions, or precisely what functions would be assigned to every individual officer. In any major institutional realignment there are more or less significant "grey" areas that can be resolved more sensibly once the foundations of the new structure are reasonably in being. As we move into our own new structure, therefore, we should reserve a degree of flexibility at the edges, so to speak. What we seek is genuine efficiency and effectiveness, not mere theoretical symmetry.

At the outset, however, there are certain functions and responsibilities which pretty clearly would be assigned predominantly to the "worriers" and planners in central administration for consideration together with the Trustees at the policy level, or for coordination where uniformity of implementation is really important.

The following are illustrative; not exhaustive:
1. Financial Policy and Management
    a) Investments
    b) Audits
    c) Financial Reports
    d) Construction financing and capital planning
    e) Purchasing standards
2. Budgeting and Planning
    a) Standards
    b) Procedures
    c) Student Fees
3. Research and Advanced Studies
    a) Grants and Contracts
    b) Scholarships and fellowships
    c) New Programs
    d) Minimum degree requirements
    e) I.U. Press
4. International Activities
5. Undergraduate development
    a) Admission requirements
    b) Minimum degree requirements
    c) Contacts with high schools
    d) Financial aids
    e) Stimulation of curricular innovation
6. External relationships
    a) State government, administrative and legislative
    b) Federal government
    c) Inter-institutional
    d) National organizations (ACE, NASULGC, Foundations)
    e) Alumni and public
7. Academic and general
    a) Academic freedom
    b) Sabbatical leaves
    c) Leaves of absence

    d) Tenure
    e) Outside consulting
    f) Non-discrimination
    g) New programs and degrees
    h) Fringe benefits

University-wide services could include the following:

1. Management information services
    a) Internal Data: collection, classification, and dissemination
    b) Institutional research
2. Payroll and related financial and accounting records Insurance, retirement, etc.
3. Administrative and research computing services
4. Alumni records and services
5. Debt management and services
6. Architectural and construction review and supervision
7. Purchasing services
8. System-wide planning

Of course the policy-making underlying some of the functions would remain either a faculty responsibility or a shared responsibility, and once again I should emphasize the ultimate responsibility of the Trustees obviously cannot be altered. Our goal is simply to differentiate more effectively between policy and administration; to delegate even policy-formulation where appropriate; to delegate administration to the lowest level of competency and efficiency; to keep centralized only those system-wide administrative and service functions that can actually be performed more economically in one place; and to coordinate and monitor only as necessary to insure that the University's objectives and purposes are being achieved in the most effective and efficient manner.

I must stress again that precision in delineating functions, in establishing staff positions, and in assigning or reassignng personnel, will take time, and that all the work of the University must proceed during the transition. There will doubtless be adjustments later in initial organization charts, based on workaday experience or on the special competencies of individuals or on changing needs—and needs do change—but the basic concepts need to be approved and established by this Board and a few beginning steps need to be taken in order that time not be merely wasted.

I have discussed this plan with the president of Purdue University. He reaffirms the desire of Purdue to relocate its Indianapolis program from 38th Street to close proximity to I.U.'s Medical Center and other planned facilities, points out that the 38th Street facilities will by no means be rendered useless for other purposes thereafter and that the State has no investment in them anyway, and agrees with me that the Purdue programs can and should be tied in with I.U.'s for the mutual educational strengthening of each, for the avoidance of unnecessary duplication and for the enrichment and diversification of the opportunities available to the people of central Indiana on a single urban campus. I hope this can become a reality, but regardless of and quite aside from that, the action I am proposing is necessary for the efficiency of I.U. herself and for the realization of the great potential represented by her educational commitments in Indianapolis and throughout Indiana.

I therefore recommend:

    I. That the Trustees of I.U. authorize and establish:
        (a) "Indiana University-Indianapolis";
        (b) Three new administrative offices, one to be headed by a Chancellor

for the Bloomington Campus of Indiana University, one to be headed by the Chancellor of Indiana University-Indianapolis, one to be headed by the Vice President for Regional Campuses.

II. That the Trustees of Indiana University re-name:

    (a) The Northwest Regional Campus of Indiana University as "Indiana University-Northwest";

    (b) The South Bend-Mishawaka Regional Campus of Indiana University as "Indiana University-South Bend";

    (c) The Indiana University programs on the Indiana-Purdue Regional Campus at Fort Wayne as "Indiana University-Fort Wayne";

    (d) The Kokomo Regional Campus of Indiana University as "Indiana University-Kokomo";

    (e) The Southeastern Regional Campus of Indiana University as "Indiana University-Southeast."

III. That the position of Chancellor be established for each campus named in II above, and that the present deans of those campuses each be appointed "Dean and Acting Chancellor."

IV. That the foregoing (I, II and III) be effective July 1, 1968.

I further recommend that the President of the University be authorized and directed to proceed expeditiously to develop further detailed plans for the implementation of the administrative reorganization of the University outlined in proposal presented by him at this meeting, and to bring to this Board from time to time for consideration and approval his further recommendations, as they develop, for assignments of functions and appointments of key personnel, in pursuance of such proposal and such plans.

Document 197

The Little 500 Weekend

The weekend, May 10–14, 1968, was one of the most anxious periods in Indiana University history. It had the possibilities of a bloody racial incident, and only by keeping fairly calm and working almost endlessly was a compromise reached in the incident. Perhaps this was not the most sensible approach that blacks could have made in presenting what they considered to be their grievances. Actually the issue they made against the fraternities was not a viable one. Presented here is President Elvis Stahr's statement of compromise. It consisted of the removal of the Phi Delta Theta contestants from the race because their national convention had not actually voted to remove the color barrier from their charter. As it turned out, the winning team saluted the Phi Delta Theta team, and the blacks lost some esteem.

*   *   *

STAHR TAKES RESPONSIBILITY FOR REMOVING PHI DELTS
STATEMENT

I wish to make crystal clear that the decision to exclude Phi Delta Theta from the "Little 500" race on May 12 was the decision of the University administration and specifically of the President of the University.

At a meeting of a number of faculty members and members of the administration called by me at approximately 6 a.m. on May 12, we examined a Xeroxed copy of the notarized statement submitted the previous evening by the president of Phi Delta Theta to the President of the Student Body, who in turn had submitted it in Memorial Stadium to the spokesman for the Black Students. It was apparent that the statement differed from the statements submitted by other fraternities. There was considerable discussion and some disagreement as to whether it differed in substance as well as form. There finally appeared to be a consensus among those I had called in that Phi Delta Theta should not be permitted to race, and I myself concluded that the statement did not comply with the agreement of the previous afternoon between the Black Students and the President of the Student Body and that a subsequent statement signed by another member of the fraternity had not cured the effect.

I left the meeting and in consultation with several of my administrative colleagues I decided that Phi Delta Theta should be taken out of the race. I called the I.U. Foundation Office and learned that the Executive Director was on his way there from his home. I personally went to his office, told him what I had decided, and he agreed to comply.

Meanwhile, the presidents of all the fraternities were being called together in a nearby room in the Union by the President of IFC, and several of the faculty members and administrators who had been present at the meeting with me were arriving to urge that other teams remain in the race despite the exclusion of Phi Delta Theta. The meeting had not begun, since not all had arrived. The Phi Delta Theta president had arrived, however, and I sought him out to tell him that I had decided that Phi Delta Theta could not race. My purpose was that he would know first hand that it was I who had made the decision, and not the Foundation. I also wanted to be sure, without delay, whether or not he would comply gracefully. It was clear to me that Phi Delta Theta had not withdrawn itself, since he inquired if I were asking him to withdraw his team. I had told him already that I had made a tough decision, and I replied, "Yes" by which I meant that he seemed the most logical person to notify his team that they would not be racing. When I said yes, his response was, "I am prepared to do that for the good of the University."

I then proceeded to Memorial Stadium and told the Black Student group that Phi Delta Theta would not be in the race, that I had made the decision, that I had already notified both the Foundation director and the chapter president, and that both were in the process of complying. I was asked if I would take personal responsibility for what might happen if they should enter the race anyway; I replied that I would take personal responsibility that they would not be in the race at all.

I returned to the Union to see three Trustees whom I knew to be in town for the race. I told them of my decision, and we also talked of other University matters. When I left them, I noticed that the fraternity presidents were still meeting, and I stopped to voice my concurrence with those who were urging that they go ahead with the race. I am told that the president of Phi Delta Theta had already told the other presidents why he had willingly complied and that he had urged them to consider their decision also for the good of the University. Shortly after I arrived, they decided to remain in the race. I then accompanied the president of Phi Delta Theta to their chapter house at his request. He called the members together and announced that he was withdrawing Phi Delta Theta from the race and that the other fraternity teams would race. I realized that he may have interpreted what I had said to him previously as giving him an option of whether to withdraw or not. I immediately spoke up and said that no one should be under the misapprehension that their president was responsible for taking them out of the race, but rather that I myself was responsible, and that I had told him my decision and asked him to proceed to take them out. I stated to them that Phi Delta Theta's written statement the night before had differed from those of the other fraternities and added that I knew my decision was a bitter pill for them to swallow, but I hoped they would take it like men.

(signed) ELVIS J. STAHR
President

Indiana *Daily Student*, May 14, 1968.

Document 198

Aftermath of the "500 Weekend"

Founders Day 1968 follow almost immediately upon the heels of a traumatic racial incident which involved the student activities known as the 500 Weekend in which the University community had traditionally enjoyed a gay carnival while earning scholarship money to be awarded needy students. Some of the blacks on the campus took this occasion to protest the reservation clauses in some of the Greek letter fraternities. They staged a sit-down on the track where the bicycle race was to be run and otherwise threatened disruption of the weekend, if not actual violence. President Stahr's address to the Founder's Day audience on May 1, 1968 was directed to discussing the University's racial policies.

*　　*　　*

It is customary and fitting that Founders Day be a day on which the University looks primarily inward upon itself and especially upon its central missions and obligation: teaching and learning. The world outside quite often reads and talks about many other aspects of the University's life and work—such things as new buildings, enrollments, costs, and extra-curricular activities ranging from a Rose Bowl football team to the incomparable Little 500 Weekend, from student politics and beauty queens to student involvement in national campaigns and issues. Many people, perhaps most, find it difficult to keep *perspective* on universities today. But two things are clear. The members of this University community are proud of their University and want to make it even better; and most are indeed devoted to teaching and to learning—and work hard at it.

Founders Day, the only day of the year on which regular classes are dismissed even for a few hours, reminds us all that what the University prizes most *are* fine teaching and persistent learning. And thus today the main focus once again will be on the best achievers among our students and on representatives of the best of our teaching talent.

Founders Day, being also the one day when faculty, students and parents are substantially represented in a single audience, has long been an annual occasion for important University announcements or special statements on matters of University-wide importance—there has been one such each year for at least the past seven years, to my own knowledge, and this year I have one statement.

The statement I believe is timely. It has to do with the place of race in the University. And let me not keep you in suspense: race should have no place whatever. But if we are to insure that it will not have, we must first face the fact that it does have. Even though most of us here do not wish it so, there has been enough residuum of white racism in America to foster the beginnings of black racism. And there has been enough overflow of attitudes from the general society to make difficult the achievement of the aim of the University society: that every man shall be assessed and assisted and accepted according to his individual qualities and needs, and nothing else. His parentage, his pocketbook, his politics, his physique, his religious faith, the color of his eyes, his hair or his skin—these are simply irrelevant in a university. I believe most of us would agree that what *are* relevant are his intellect, his intellectual honesty, his desire to learn and to work at learning, and his willingness to respect these same things in others. The academic community is a remarkably tolerant one, but it is nonetheless one which has and must have standards if it is to go forward with its own mission. Thus each of its members must somehow be restrained, if he cannot restrain himself, in the indulgence of his own impulses, outrages, whims, animal energies, frustrations, ambitions, reactions, prejudices, rights and privileges sufficiently that there be maintained an environment in which his fellows, whether his roommates or the whole campus family, may teach and learn, and live and work and move about, in peace and dignity, without harassment and without intimidation, real or attempted.

Certainly, then, a continuing concern on every campus is to keep clear the crucial difference between dissent and disruption. Questioning of facts, ideas and theories is an integral part of the process by which students, young and old, learn to think independently and to make rational choices. And it is fundamentally important that they be free to reject and dissent as well as to agree. But dissent that is carried to the point of physical interference with the right of others to inquire, or to express or hear a point of view, or to move peaceably and without fear or hindrance about the campus, is alien to the environment in which knowledge and truth can be pursued and to the spirit without which academic freedom is dead.

I may seem to have digressed from the subject of race, but I think not as far as you may be thinking. For just as the University could not maintain its integrity if its members should have no common defense against physical intimidation, real or attempted, no more can it do so if its members have no common defense against the psychological intimidation, real or attempted, of race prejudice. I said "*common* defense" advisedly in both instances, for it is simply not rational to say there should be no rules, no regulations, no standards, no responsibilities, beyond those imposed on himself by the individual, be he student or teacher or administrator. Individual human beings are just not that perfect, and they do owe something to their fellow man, at least if they wish to enjoy membership in his society. It is for those reasons that rational people concur that rights without responsibilities are not really rights at all.

And one of the primary responsibilities of membership in the University community, I repeat, is to respect the rights of *others,* the rights of the community as a whole and of its diverse members. The community not only expects this, it has the right and responsibility to demand it—and even to exclude those who will not respect it. When the Board of Trustees of this University last year determined that any remaining vestiges of discrimination based on race, religion or national origin shall be eradicated from acceptable standards of recognized activity in this University family, it placed not just an inhibition but a positive responsibility upon all of us. I expect us all to strive to live up to it—for there can be no worthy reason not to do so. Neither white racism nor black racism is a worthy or acceptable objective; each nourishes the other. The vast majority of both races, of all races, on this campus I am convinced find racism abhorrent—although many, particularly whites, may be too complacent to help as much as they could.

I made a more detailed and specific statement on this subject on this campus five weeks ago, which was published in full in the Indiana Daily Student on March 30. I have returned to this subject often in recent weeks, and expect to continue to do so, in speeches, reports and conferences with various of our students and our faculty. They are thinking about it more and more; most really want to help; and I am optimistic that we will attain our goal.

Today what I am saying on this matter is brief and general, but nonetheless earnest, and I hope unmistakable. It is not a threat; it is rather a most serious invitation to all our students, our staff and our faculty to give this objective a very special priority. It deserves it simply because it is the right thing to do. It deserves it also because failure to achieve it will inhibt and corrode all else we may try to do. I ask you to join me, then, *not* in a crusade of violence, or of menace, or of vengeance, or of retribution, or of sanctimonius self-righteousness; I ask you, whether you are white or black, whether you are a prisoner of prejudice or a vicitim of prejudice, whether you are a self-appointed saint with a feeling of disgust for your less fortunate fellows who haven't seen the light or just a man like me who wants to be respected or despised for what he is and does, and not for what he looks like, and who wants all other human beings to have that same opportunity—I ask all of you to join me in a compassionate, honest, determined effort to solve this problem—and to help others who want to help solve it. I ask you to keep high and in plain view the real goal, which is the individual human being and his *genuine* assessment and acceptance *as* an individual. The goal is *not* lip service, nor is it surface compliance with mere deadlines or decrees, or punishment of offenders. It is a positive goal. We have many, many thousands of wonderfully idealistic young men and women in our student body, in our residence halls, in our fraternities and sororities, on our campuses statewide, who really want to help—who are ashamed of the blind and melancholy prejudices or of the simple unconcern which many brought with them to our academic world—who recognize that what they have inherited is a white problem more than a Negro problem—and who want to work with their fellows to help *them* see and free themselves. Let us then work *together* for the *real* objective; let us abjure hate and force and ultimata; let us embrace hard work; persuasion, forgiveness when earned, encouragement, good will even in the face of ill will, and understanding—*understanding*, even of those we scarce can understand at all. After all, understanding those who already agree with us is scarcely a noteworthy accomplishment!

Document 199

"Going from 'Here to There.'"

This extensive document is a revealing statement of attitudes and facts about racial relations at Indiana University. The President of the University recognized the fact that the sensitive issue of race involved so many human nuances and subtleties that the problems of adjusting to the new social order involved the white community more deeply than it did the blacks themselves. In speaking to the Statewide Conference on the Negro in Higher Education on May 17, 1968, Dr. Stahr covered a wide area of university operation as it related to the making of racial adjustments and the erasing of prejudicial barriers. Many of the issues and barriers which now seemed so irritating were actually of almost subconscious origins and did not directly reflect racial animus or intent of discrimination. He related the readjustments which had been made in the university's administrative and instructional programs so as to lower all barriers of prejudice and racial consciousness.

*   *   *

Last March 23rd, in a speech at a Statewide Conference on the Negro in Higher Education, which was held on our Bloomington Campus, I said, among other things, "Now, let me turn again to an issue that presents itself in all discussions of the Negro in higher education: the degree to which special accommodations should be made for the Negro as Negro. I am not speaking of tokenism, if that means making a polite bow in order to be excused to go back to other concerns; I am speaking of *our* concern—actually going on from 'here' to 'there.' How much should we discriminate *for* Negroes when our goal is a campus in which there is *no* racial discrimination? This problem can come up in connection with academic standards, with allocation of scholarships, with tutorial aid, with hiring faculty members, wth administrative appointments, with student offices—in fact, with most areas of the University's work. My own conviction is that extraordinary efforts are in fact necessary and justified until we do get closer to 'there.' "

In subsequent weeks, our Black students have brought out into the open their deeply-felt grievances about what they see as negative aspects of their status at I.U. I share their concern, and have endeavored to make this evident in meetings with them on March 30, April 1, and May 12, and also in numerous meetings with all our deans, with the Faculty Council, with white student leaders, and with various white and Negro faculty members. It should be clearly understood that, while the primary locus of the concerns of both the Black students and myself as Indiana University, the sources of grievances have shameful roots far back in the history of this nation, and the growth from those roots extends throughout the country. In this sense the grievances are not at base against the University but rather against the shortcomings of the academic community in stamping out and remedying the consequences of centuries of discrimination against the Black individual insofar as it is within the province of the University to do.

I have said before and I repeat now that Indiana University has been and is ahead of most institutions in sensitivity to this problem and in taking forward steps. This report will support that statement factually. But this does not imply either satisfaction with or complacency about that progress. I believe that it does indicate that the University has been moving steadily in the direction of eliminating causes for legitimate grievance. It will continue to do so.

I want to stress again that in the past three months I have talked publicly and privately with many individuals and groups, including the University's honor students, Student Government officers, Black students, fraternity and sorority leaders, the Faculty Council, the Deans Council, the Trustees, many of our Negro faculty members, and others, attempting to convey this totality and priority, to learn all I can of facts and feelings, and to stimulate others to help develop positive approaches. Insofar as means are available to me, I shall continue to interpret to our University community a strong feeling that all its members must not only avoid perpetuation of thoughtless discrimination against the Black American student but also must pursue remedial courses of action to place our resources behind righting the prolonged imbalance of opportunity between white and Black men. Our faculty, students, and administrators are seeking and gaining wider and deeper awareness of the total problem and renewing their determination to solve it by a many-faceted attack. Every major address by members of the central administration in recent months has stressed integration as an item of first priority. At the close of this report I shall repeat my Founders Day call to all University people on this point.

So far as I know, however, there has not been, previous to this report, an attempt to isolate in one document the specifics of what Indiana University has done and is doing and planning in this regard. Consequently, no one—Black or white, student, teacher or administrator—has had all the necessary basic information upon which to build further plans. This report itself I am sure is incomplete; indeed, I hope it will stimulate many to let me know of other things the University is doing. It is also not smoothly edited. But it is an honest effort to make known what is being done; and it ranges over both the present and the future, with an occasional item relating to the recent past. I hope it will be widely distributed within the University and also in the State. For ease of later reference, I have numbered items consecutively through the report.

As we push forward, we should remind ourselves of three fundamental things: (a) A University is uniquely a community of scholars where nothing could be more irrelevant than the color of one's skin. (b) The University is complex, operating within the realities of inelastic budgets, limitations on staff sizes, diffused authority, competitive priorities, and designated schedules of time. The steps between identification of a problem and securing its permanent relief are typically not simple, as they might more often be in other types of human organizations. In fact, even the most determined effort to obtain thorough remedy usually takes considerable time. But change does occur, and will. (c) While the University is open to requests from individuals, groups and organizations, not all requests are feasible or in the best interests of the total University. An institution may not serve the interests of a special group to the exclusion of all others' without destroying itself in the process. Nevertheless, its commitment to (a) above remains, despite the realities of (b) and (c).

I.

Now for the report, which I have divided into seven parts. The first relates to specific items discussed in my April 1, 1968, discussion with the Black Student group in Whittenberger Auditorium

1) The Grievance Committee on Discriminatory Practices has been reconstituted as a Joint Committee under the chairmanship of Professor Orlando Taylor (Speech and Theatre). The committee has already investigated several complaints and resolved them. Anyone with a complaint of racial discrimination on any of our campuses could and should present it to the committee.

2) I shall discuss the employment of Black administrators and faculty members in a later section of this report. With regard to the recruitment of Black students, I can report that on May 8 a task force of faculty and Black students from I.U.'s Bloomington and Northwest Campuses visited Roosevelt, Emerson, Tolleston, Edison, Horace Mann and Froebel High Schools in Gary, and Roosevelt and

Washington High Schools in East Chicago, for a "High School Day" program. The purpose of the visit was to learn what these high school students want to know about I.U. in particular and higher education in general, and to establish the University's interest in enrolling graduates of these schools. Visits to high schools in other Hoosier cities by teams of faculty and Black students are now being arranged.

A continuing program of longer standing headed by an assistant dean of the Junior Division assigned to our Indianapolis Regional Campus, Mr. Alvin Bynum (a Negro), has involved not only high schools but direct contacts with large numbers of parents and young Negro high school students at home and work and elsewhere throughout the metropolitan area. This major effort to recruit Negro students includes advising of the availability of substantial financial assistance, and I am asking Dean Bynum to write it up in more detail for later distribution.

Other recruitment plans are described later in this report.

However, it should be mentioned here that the Junior Division is reevaluating the criteria of test results and rank in high school class as valid bases for predicting success in college work. It is pursuing indications that standard test measure aptitudes developed in only certain types of training and background, and are prejudicial to Negro applicants.

I shall defer momentarily the many specifics of curriculum and curricular proposals, and return to them at some length in Part II below and to some extent in still later pages.

3) National officers and local chapter presidents of thirty of the thirty-three fraternities on the Bloomington campus and seventeen of the nineteen sororities have signed the statements I sent them last winter, certifying that their I.U. chapter is completely free to select members without regard to race, religion or national origin. It should be remembered that the deadline for signing these certificates is ninety days after the annual convention of the fraternity or sorority or, even from those with biennial conventions, no later than January 1, 1970.

In addition, this past weekend 30 local fraternity presidents each signed a statement that his chapter will "not recognize and will not honor any total acceptance or other discriminatory clause or practice in its national charter or local bylaws used for the purpose of discriminating on the basis of race, creed or national origin" and "will take active steps to rid the national charter of any discriminatory clauses that may exist." As of the date of this report, another fraternity (Phi Delta Theta) has voted unanimously (on May 13) to request authority, in effect, from its national to sign the same statement, and this is expected shortly; the national has granted this to 45 other chapters and never refused one, and it expects to complete amending its own constitution in August 1968.

The Interfraternity and Panhellenic Councils are working on plans for full and open rushing, to be effective this year, based upon help to individuals who are interested in pledging. This help obligates no one then to pledge but should ensure that bids can and will be made to Black students and those of other minority groups in good faith.

4) The Off-Campus Housing Office has assured me that it does not and will not cooperate with landlords who practice racial and other objectionable discrimination. University housing has been integrated for a number of years.

I should like to make here several other quick points that are important but only indirectly associated with the abovementioned meeting of April 1:

5) University offices, such as Personnel and Physical Plant, are reviewing their

practices and procedures to eliminate any proscribed discrimination. Discrimination in hiring or otherwise, on the basis of race, religion or national origin is proscribed, and this policy was reaffirmed by the Board of Trustees in July, 1967.
6) The Board's resolution itself is worth repeating. It reads as follows:
"BE IT RESOLVED by The Trustees of Indiana University, that the University Administration be directed to take such steps as may be necessary and desirable to accelerate the final elimination of such vestiges of discrimination as may still exist, based on race, creed, or national origin, from all phases of University life including official employment and other personnel policies and participation in campus activities and organizations.
"BE IT FURTHER RESOLVED that the Administration is directed to report from time to time to the Board of Trustees on progress achieved and any problems remaining in this area."
7) All University publications have adopted the policy of including pictures of Black students, as brochures showing only white students were clearly unrepresentative.
8) The Summer Sessions office, through questionnaires soliciting comment at the close of each session, has learned of Black student complaints and has sought when possible to remove the cause of objection. For instance, the circumstance that all operators in the Union Building beauty shop are now specially trained to fashion the preferred coiffures of Black students as well as white is the direct result of action upon such a summer student complaint some time ago.
9) The University now carries identification as an Equal Opportunity Employer on published material, making known to the public what has long been fact. Our placement services now require similar identification of prospective employers seeking to recruit our graduates. Also, the names of all qualified students regardless of race are routinely submitted to would-be employers.

II.

The second part of this report deals with *academic programs.*
10) In many areas, the color of the performer or creator has been considered incidental to the performance or creation. Thus, in Fine Arts, Music, Theatre, Ballet, Creative Writing, and Physical Education there has been little or no attempt to differentiate the Black man's contribution, even though it has been included. However, faculty in these programs are now sensitive to Black students' desire for greater awareness of the heritage that is uniquely Black American. The development of new courses takes time for research and organization, but there is clearly a growing faculty interest in response along these lines, mainly in recognition that a request for separate cultural identification may be justified to engender respect for the contribution the Black man has made.
11) Many regular courses—for example, in Sociology, Literature, Anthropology, Government and History—have always included material by or about the Black American in their content. The present focus on injustice and discrimination will lead many faculty members to review their courses in order to be absolutely certain that the cultural and social influence of the Black people has been appropriately included.
12) Of pertinent curricula already established, the African Studies Center, begun in 1961 with the aid of a Ford Foundation grant, is the outstanding example. Now the third largest African program in the United States, it has an interdisciplinary faculty of 23 members and offered 79 courses in African studies during this year alone. These courses were in the fields of African art, ethnography, history, folklore, literature, geography, economics, linguistics and political science.

13) *Ten* African languages are currently being offered and twelve will be offered in 1968–1969. This probably makes I.U. number one in the country in the teaching of African languages.

14) There are now 95 graduate students at I.U. specializing in African studies.

15) In addition, the African Studies Center is sponsoring the development of a continuing Program on African Culture, History and Development at I.U.'s Indianapolis and Gary Regional Campuses in response to community-wide concern in those cities, by both students and other citizens, for greater knowledge and understanding of the culture of the African continent. The Program will be initiated this month with a film and lecture series on African literature and culture to be presented at the I.U. Medical Center in Indianapolis.

16) In June the University will cooperate with the Children's Museum in Indianapolis in presenting an exhibit of African art, including a number of items collected by Professor Roy Sieber of the Bloomington campus during his recent visit to Ghana.

17) In the fall a credit course on African culture will be offered in Indianapolis and Gary for credit.

18) As for resources, the African collection in the library is being greatly enlarged each year and now numbers approximately 18,000 volumes. It is one of the best in the United States. 19) The African art collection at I.U.'s Art Museum includes several hundred pieces of sculpture, masks, pottery, textiles and beadwork. 20) The Anthropology Museum, as well as the Art Museum, has a fine collection of more than 600 African ethnological objects. 21) The Archives of Folk and Traditional Music has an expanding collection of African oral data and music. 22) The Folklore library has a virtually complete collection of African folklore published since 1963 and is seeking to acquire earlier material. 23) The Audio-Visual Center has more than 125 films dealing specifically with Africa. 24) The map collection in the Department of Geography contains about 20,000 maps of Africa including many topographical sheets. 25) The Human Relations Area Files at I.U. contain extensive data on thirty-five areas and cultural groups of Africa.

Thus, in a relatively few years a sound and vigorous program on Africa, well supplied with research sources, has been made available to students on our Bloomnigton campus and in part will reach students on two of our other campuses soon.

26) In an entirely different area and with the goal of providing trained Negro graduates for high level positions in business and industry, the I.U. School of Business is participating in a consortium project to recruit and train Negro students for the M.B.A. degree. Funded in part by the Ford Foundation with a matching contribution from industry, this program has such features as pregraduate summer study, monthly stipends for participants, and summer intern work on salary. This year twenty-one students are enrolled in the three universities forming the consortium, and forty-five students have been admitted for the program next year. Interest in the project is evidenced not only by the 175 applications received last year, the 260 received this year and the number of unsuccessful applicants who have enrolled nevertheless, but also by the requests of other universities to be allowed to join the consortium.

Numerous additional items of curriculum are in various stages of offering or development. I shall report them by Schools.

27) *The College of Arts and Sciences,* in which many of the African Studies courses are given, also has courses dealing specifically with the American Negro,

such as F484, "Folklore and Culture of the American Negro." Proposals for the introduction of pertinent courses this fall or later including the following:
28) American Studies plans to offer a new 200-level course, "The City Street," which will explore some of the problems of urban America through a program of extensive readings on the life, conflicts and people of the city. 29) American Studies is also currently engaged in the preparation of courses on the Negro, his development and contributions, and their relationship to the fashioning of American literature.

30) The History Department is planning a 300–400 level course in Afro-American History from 1619 to the present which will be taught by four or five of their faculty.

31) The Department of Government will give two senior seminars dealing with the Negro. 32) The departments of Government, Sociology, and Economics are working jointly on the development of a course or courses on public policy with respect to Negro Americans. They will consult with the Afro-American Student Association, and they hope to have one or more courses ready to offer this fall.

33) The College of Arts and Sciences and the School of Education have already agreed at the administrative level that they will prepare a proposal together to seek Federal funds for a program under the Education Professions Development Act designed to train teachers to work in urban areas and particularly among minority groups. Actual preparation of the proposal, involving the necessary faculty, is to begin this summer, with a submission target of June 1, 1969.

34) An ideas is being explored which would involve Student Government and faculty in the establishment of direct work experiences in the Indianapolis ghetto area for our students, possibly with credit awarded for such activity.

35) A number of faculty have proposed the establishment of a minor in "The Negro in America" which would be acceptable as meeting the concentration requirements of the College. Such a proposal may well be made in connection with the teacher-training mentioned above, but the program will be open to other students as well.

The School of Education now has numerous plans and programs under way.
36) Representatives of the School have met with representatives from Indiana's other three state universities and the State Department of Public Instruction to develop a joint proposal for the funding of an urban-situated center in which prospective teachers would receive substantial exposure to the unique culture, values, and educational problems of children in that setting.

37) The Education deans of the four State institutions met to discuss the submission of a proposal under the Education Professions Development Act for June, 1969. This proposal would provide teaching centers in at least two cities in Indiana where prospective teachers could obtain teaching experiences in dealing with the disadvantaged. 38) The Counseling and Guidance Department has established working agreements with the Camp Atterbury Job Corps Program and the Indianapolis Public Schools so that I.U. students can have internship experience with low-income, culturally deprived counselees.

39) The Counseling and Guidance chairman has developed a proposal for training elementary counselors for inner city schools and will shortly submit it to the Indiana Personnel and Guidance Association. The plan calls for a cooperative training effort by the four State universities. The IPGA is expected to agree to support the plan.

40) The Special Education department will request a stimulatory grant from the U. S. Office of Education June 1, 1969 under the Education Professions De-

velopment Act. The grant would focus upon the preparation of teachers to work with gifted children in depressed urban centers. 41) In September, 1968, a teaching minor is expected to be available for teachers who wish to work with urban disadvantaged children. The minor has been developed by two professors in Elementary Education. 42) The Elementary Education departments in Bloomington and at the Northwest Campus are working together to develop a program at Gary for the disadvantaged. The program there would be so arranged that participation experiences for teachers taking their methods courses and student teaching placements are both taken in inner city schools.

43) A representative of the School of Education helped the Indianapolis Regional Campus set up a ten-week in-service training course for neighborhood workers in the Martindale Area Citizens Service Project, Indianapolis. The field workers met at the regional campus once each week for three hours to receive instruction and information. The chairman of that OEO-supported project will be invited to lecture on the Bloomington campus this summer.

44) School of Education personnel initiated conversations with two University Coordinators about the possibility of their using the Social Studies and English course content improvement centers for the preparation of curricular materials for use in elementary and secondary schools; e.g., Negro contributions to American literature, and Negro contributions to American history outside the fields of sports and entertainment. This is to be pursued.

45) The Cincinnati Public Schools were approached by the School of Education earlier and last week expressed interest in setting aside $90,000 to support the development of an *Anthology of Ethnic Minorities*.

46) Last fall, a School-wide effort was made to develop summer programs especially relevant to societal needs. Among proposals which were forthcoming were ones for (a) a summer exchange of advanced doctoral students in higher education administration with administrators in Negro universities in the South, and (b) a series of lectures at the regional campuses by an international visiting professor who would discuss differences between national culture and relate them to the differences the regional campus faculty will discover within the areas they serve. Funding for the programs is being sought currently.

47) Last summer, a workshop was conducted on the Bloomington campus for thirty to thirty-five teachers of urban disadvantaged. Opportunity was provided for them to improve their skill in working with disadvantaged children.

48) Also, during the summer an Education professor directed the Upward-bound program on the Bloomington campus after he had personally prepared and negotiated the grant which supported it. Students in this program are primarily Negro high school juniors. Their study is designed to help them become better prepared for entrance into a university and especially to extend their horizons so that they begin to think of higher education as one of the realistic alternatives open to them after high school. A similar program will be conducted this summer. 49) Another member of the Education faculty has served for two years as Regional Director of the Head Start program. The School of Education, additionally, has trained substantial numbers of teachers for Head Start programs across the nation.

50) *The School of Health, Physical Education and Recreation* is reorganizing its course in the History of Physical Education for next year to incorporate increased emphasis on the role of the Negro. 51) It has also been working with the Division of General and Technical Studies in the development of a two-year program for recreation directors which would have as part of its content interracial relationships.

52) *The Junior Division* conducted a course designated J-100 during the summer of 1967, designed to equip students marginally prepared for admission so that they could better cope with the regular freshman academic program in the fall. This effort seems to have been significantly helpful, and study and evaluation of the course continue.

53) The Indianapolis Regional Campus will also offer J-100 this summer, and a videotape of J-100 is to be made for use all over the State thereafter.

54) Incidentally, the Junior Division is cooperating in and facilitating a tutorial project initiated and conducted by Black students, both graduate and undergraduate. The project has had substantial progress and support during the last few weeks. From a handful of tutors in the beginning, the number has grown to twenty-nine. Twelve are presently rendering tutorial help in the following areas: English, Biology, Economics, French, Government, History, Mathematics, Sociology, Spanish, Statistics, and Anatomy. Fourteen students are now receiving tutoring, some in more than one area. In academic areas where Black tutors are not available, the services of white students will now be accepted. One white student is presently on call to tutor.

55) *The Graduate Library School* will offer for the first time this summer a course entitled "Librarianship and Bibliography of Africa, South of the Sahara." The materials for this course obviously could be of interest to many people interested in Africa.

56) *The Graduate School of Social Service* is in the process of extensive curriculum revisions. While most of the content which the faculty teaches is more class-related than race-related, much of it is nonetheless relevant to the problems of many Negroes, and special attention will be given to the introduction of materials which aid the School's students in coming to a better understanding of the Negro situation in our present society. 57) Many of our Social Service students of both races are regularly assigned to field experiences in agencies which serve Negro clientele, and six of our field instructors are Negroes.

It should be emphasized that courses which contribute to the Negro student's knowledge of and pride in his heritage are equally valuable for the white student's education in understanding and appreciation of the Negro's social and cultural influence in America.

III.

In a number of instances, University personnel sensitive to the changing needs of society have taken the initiative in experimental or cooperative programs.

58) For instance, faculty members at the Northwest Campus had a major part in preparing the Model Cities proposal for Gary and when the requested funds for a pilot program were granted, the I.U. Foundation brought key men in the project to the Bloomington campus for discussion with faculty specialists in problems of urban areas. 59) Mayor Hatcher himself (a Negro and an I.U. alumnus) was President Stahr's guest last winter for a day of conferences with such faculty specialists and to make a convocation address in the Auditorium. The Northwest Campus faculty members are continuing to make available to the City of Gary their talents and services as needed in the pilot program, and 60) Indianapolis faculty members similarly stand ready to aid in any Model Cities project development there.

61) In 1967, throughout the second semester which was called "The Urban Semester" on the Bloomington campus, a series of conferences, seminars, guest speeches and special programs were carried on, involving a large number of experts and interested persons in the University and from outside, built around

the theme, "Focus: the City." Considerable attention was devoted to the problems of urban ghettos.

On another front, Indiana University has been working closely with two predominantly Negro institutions in the strengthening of their programs. 62) Personnel of the School of Business have counseled with their counterparts at Texas Southern University and have shared with them the satisfaction of developing Texas Southern's School to the point where it recently became the first predominantly Negro School of Business in the nation to become fully accredited. 63) The Dean of that School (a Negro) will come to Indiana University in early 1969 for the spring semester as a Visiting Professor and also will aid in the plan to raise scholarships for ten I.U. Business School Negro undergraduates. 64) I.U.'s Business School has helped Texas Southern's School obtain grants of more than three-quarters of a million dollars from the Ford Foundation. 65) The alliance with Stillman College in Alabama has been more extensive, involving the exchange of dramatic performances by student groups, student and faculty exchanges, and the introduction of experimental courses at Stillman College. These same courses may well be employed at I.U. for students whose backgrounds of environment and training have been limited. 66) The Stillman-I.U. alliance was financed initially by a grant from the I.U. Foundation, and I.U. has helped Stillman obtain grants totaling $450,000 from the U.S. Office of Education.

67) Various academic units of the University are well along with plans for an Institute for the Study of the Negro American. Included in the planning are the Schools of Music, Education, Business, and several departments of the College of Arts and Sciences (Linguistics, American Studies, and others).

68) The first and second summer institutes ever held for English professors on the faculties of predominantly Negro colleges were held at I.U., and planned and largely staffed by I.U. faculty, in 1964 and 1965, under the direction of Professors Michael Wolff and William A. Madden.

69) Dean Joseph Taylor of the Indianapolis Regional Campus has introduced a Guided Study Program for new students who do not fully meet the University's admissions requirements but who have the potential for success in college work. The program concentrates on teaching effective study habits. Through weekly lectures on such topics as reading and notetaking, the art of listening, budgeting of time and similar counsel, and through individual conferences it is hoped that the thirty-one freshmen enrolled for the program's first trial this semester may adjust thoroughly to college life and work even while completing the formal requirements for regular admission. Only a few of the current group are Negroes, but efforts will continue to increase their numbers in this Program. 70) Another approach to the problem of interesting Negro youth in continuing their education beyond high school with the assurance of supervisory aid toward their adjustment to college-level work is being worked on by the office for Undergraduate Development. Under this plan, high school students with potential, but insufficient motivation to go beyond the eleventh grade, would be brought to the University for their twelfth grade studies. Here, with careful supervision and attention from both high school teachers and college staff, they would be prepared for college study, would be provided a work-experience in an industry, and then would enter the University, still carefully counseled until their academic feet are solidly on the ground.

71) Another excellent idea recently suggested is that the same techniques used in the urban semester focus of last year be concentrated on the subject of the Negro American. I should like to see this implemented.

IV.

One of the sources of grievance for Black Americans is the difficulty which many of their well-qualified members have experienced in the past in obtaining positions commensurate with their abilities. So long as comparatively few of them occupy professional and executive positions, an impression of unequal opportunity acts to discourage youthful application and ambition and to inhibit the Black person's development of self-respect. Thus, one of our goals is the addition of Black faculty and administrators to our staff.

72) Since faculty and administrators have been employed by the University solely on the basis of their qualifications, it was impossible to state without an inquiry how many Black faculty members are on our staff. The list may still be incomplete but it indicates that in addition to an as yet uncounted number of teaching assistants, research assistants, and graduate assistants and associates, there are at least nine Negro faculty with the rank of Lecturer or higher on the Bloomington campus, six in the School of Medicine, four in the School of Dentistry, six in the School of Nursing, two on the Indianapolis Regional Campus faculty, two at Kokomo, five on the Northwest Campus, one on the Southeastern Campus, and one on the South Bend-Mishawaka Campus. The faculty total of thirty-six or more is thought to be one of the highest in the nation, outside of predominantly Negro institutions.

73) In April a Negro professor was elected to the Faculty Council for the first time. 74) Moreover, our administrative counseling staff includes a Negro dean of a regional campus, a new assistant dean, and, in Bloomington, three Negro counselors in the Dean of Students Office, and a Negro Assistant Head Counselor and nine Negro Resident Assistants in the residence halls.

75) The Athletic Department is actively seeking a Negro football coach, and the Junior Division is seeking an additional Negro assistant or associate dean. Currently the Office of Undergraduate Development is also trying to recruit a Negro administrator for a new position already authorized by the Trustees, and other divisions of the University are seeking other Negro faculty and administrators.

76) The School of Education has now employed two Negro faculty members, one for the South Bend campus beginning in September and one for the Summer Session in Bloomington, and two other Negro candidates are soon to be interviewed. 77) A number of Negro staff members, as well as white, have regularly been employed by I.U.'s summer high school institute programs. 78) Last summer a faculty member from Hampton Institute conducted a highly successful workshop in the School of Education on the problems of the disadvantaged which was attended by teachers who work with minority groups. 79) It should be noted as well that of the four major lectures presented in the high-enrollment introductory Education course (F100) this year, two were given by Negroes.

V.

I have already mentioned several activities and proposals related to the recruiting of Black students. 80) The University also participates in the TUTEOR program, sponsored by the State Scholarship Commission, through which disadvantaged high school students are brought to the campus for visits and discussions about college work and life.

81) The Dean of the School of Business at Texas Southern University, who will be on the Bloomingotn campus next spring, as already noted, will direct part of his attention to aiding the I.U. Business School recruit Black students.

82) Certain divisions of the University other than the Junior Division—the Summer Sessions office and the Adult Education Department, for instance—have made concerted efforts to recruit Black students and continue to do so.

83) The University has established a Division of General and Technical Studies which offers certificate programs in practical training and general college studies. It is designed to attract and aid students who might not otherwise be interested in continuing study after high school. Its first programs have been in Fort Wayne; appropriations will be sought to expand them to other centers.

84) In addition, programs such as the Opportunity Lecture Series at Broadripple High School and the Faculty Emissaries at North Central High School in Indianapolis, and lectures scheduled at other Indianapolis high schools, are directed toward representing to all youth the desirability and possibility of education beyond high school.

VI.

85) Three years ago the University allocated $10,000 for Equal Opportunity scholarships for Negroes, administered by the University Committee on Equality of Higher Educational Opportunity (an important all-University group which works along a variety of lines for the improvement of the overall situation of Negro members of the I.U. family). Last year the amount was increased to $20,000 and a similar total was made available to the Committee this year.

86) While the above sums provide special scholarships for Black students only, Black as well as white students may apply for the Work-Study Program, supported for 1968–1969 by a $1,064,000 grant, or for an Equal Opportunity scholarship under the Federal program for which Indiana University has been allocated $957,000 for 1968–1969.

87) Because no record of a student's race is available in University records, it is impossible to total the full amount of financial aid extended by the University and the I.U. Foundation to Black students, but it is large; and our Office of Scholarships and Financial Aids has extended help to every Black student who has needed and requested it for as far back as the present staff can remember.

University administrators and faculty members have been preparing new proposals for specific financial aid to Black students, such as the already-mentioned plan developed by the School of Business to award ten undergraduate scholarships specifically in Business. The proposers in most of these instances are undertaking to obtain the necessary funding, not being content just to present a plan.

VII.

There are quite a few University endeavors beyond the above categories, and I list them for the record.

88) The Indiana University Press has published the following books, most of which were either commissioned or solicited. The total is thought to be one of the greatest, if not the greatest, number of books about the Negro published by any University in the world.

Melville J. Herskovits: THE AMERICAN NEGRO

Sheila Patterson: DARK STRANGERS

Stanley P. Hirshon: FAREWELL TO THE BLOODY SHIRT: *Northern Republicans and the Southern Negro, 1877–1893*.

Webster Smalley, ed.: FIVE PLAYS BY LANGSTON HUGHES.

Erwin K. Welsch: THE NEGRO IN THE UNITED STATES: *A Research Guide*.

Langston Hughes, ed.: NEW NEGRO POETS: *USA*

Melville J. Herskovits: THE NEW WORLD NEGRO: *Selected Papers in Afro-American Studies.*

Langston Hughes, ed.: POEMS FROM BLACK AFRICA.

Langston Hughes, tr.: SELECTED POEMS OF GABRIELA MISTRAL.

James Meredith: THREE YEARS IN MISSISSIPPI.

89) The following serials are on subscription in Indiana University libraries:

Crisis (National Association for the Advancement of Colored People)
Ebony
Freedomways: Quarterly Review of the Negro Movement (New York)
Integrated Education
Journal of Human Relations
Journal of Inter-group Relations
Journal of Negro Education (Howard University)
Journal of Negro History
Liberation
Negro Heritage
Negro History Bulletin
Negro in Print
New South
Phylon; Atlanta University Review of Race and Culture
Southern Education Report

The library has recently placed subscriptions for the *Harvard Journal of Negro Affairs, Negro Digest,* the *Quarterly Review of Higher Education among Negroes, The Southern Christian Leadership Conference Newsletter,* the *Chicago Daily Defender* and the *Pittsburgh Courier.*

Other newspapers, not on subscription, but available in the I.U. libraries include:

California	Los Angeles Sentinel
Georgia	Atlanta World
Illinois	Chicago Defender
	Chicago Jet
Maryland	Baltimore Afro-American
Michigan	Michigan Chronicle
New York	Amsterdam News
North Carolina	Star of Zion (Charlotte)
Pennsylvania	Philadelphia Tribune
Virginia	Norfolk Journal and Guide

90) Whitney Young, James Farmer, Dick Gregory and Mayor Richard Hatcher of Gary have spoken on the campus this academic year.

91) Among the Negro artists who have appeared in the University Auditorium in the last two years are the entire "Porgy and Bess" cast, Erroll Garner, Johnny Mathis, Nancy Wilson, the Supremes, Leontyne Price, and our Music School graduate in whom we take great pride, Felicia Weathers. The most recent were The Four Step Brothers and The 5th Dimension, last Saturday evening.

92) A representative of Tougaloo College this year sought and received aid from I.U. in attempting to recruit faculty from among our Negro graduate students.

93) Questions about race were removed from admissions and housing applications five years ago. Thus the number of Negro students enrolled is not known. However, careful estimates indicate that over forty percent of the total number

of Negro college students in all of the colleges and universities in the State of Indiana are on the campuses of Indiana University.

94) Negro students have held high elective office in the University, among them Student Body President, Class President, football captain, and golf captain. Also, a Negro girl was selected as Miss Indiana University a few years ago.

95) The Summer Sessions administration has been sensitive to the need for training Negro students and teachers of Negro students. Schedules and announcements have been sent throughout the country, including the South. The film, "Equal Protection of the Laws," will be shown on July 31. Two similar films were shown last summer.

96) The Policy Council of the School of Education, which includes *ex officio* representation from the Undergraduate and Graduate Student Advisory Boards, has been holding a series of meetings to consider steps to be initiated by the faculty and students of the School toward greater responsibility in the area of minorities and the Negro student at Indiana University. Twenty years ago the School established throughout Indiana the principle that I.U. would not be a party to discrimination in student teaching placement on the basis of race. A new check will be made to see whether school systems which assign student teachers have adhered to the principle. Attention will also be given to the placement of practice teachers in predominantly Negro schools and to the placement opportunities afforded Negro graduates.

97) Members of the Indianapolis Regional Campus staff are exploring the possibility of a workshop on the Report of the Commission on Civil Disorders, possibly to take place this summer.

98) A proposal has been developed at Bloomington which involves the recruitment of discharged Negro veterans.

While this report is certanly not exhaustive, it does show that a great many members of the University community are thinking and working constructively toward full recognition of the Black people as co-fashioners of American history and culture, and of Indiana University's Black students and faculty as fully welcome participants and partners in the work of the University.

I should like to close this initial report by calling upon every member of the Indiana University family: faculty, students, staff, and alumni, to join with me in helping to go foward with the blotting out of all negative racial discrimination on all our campuses. We must enlarge our list of accomplishments, and we must also endeavor to ensure that all know of what we have done as well as our intent. I ask that we work together in trust and good will, in determination and in patience, to make absolutely sure that Indiana University leads the country in making equality a fact.

To repeat for emphasis a passage from my 1968 Founders Day address: "I ask you to join me, then, not in a crusade of violence, or of menace, or of vengeance, or of retribution, or of sanctimonious self-righteousness; I ask you, whether you are white or black, whether you are a prisoner of prejudice or a victim of prejudice, whether you are a self-appointed saint with a feeling of disgust for your less fortunate fellows who haven't seen the light or just a man like me who wants to be respected or despised for what he is and does, and not for what he looks like, and who wants all other human beings to have that same opportunity— I ask all of you to join with me in a compassionate, honest, determined effort to solve this problem—and to help others who want to help solve it. I ask you to keep high and in plain view the real goal, which is the individual human being and his genuine assessment and acceptance as an individual. The goal is not lip service, nor it is surface compliance with mere deadlines or decrees, or punishment of offenders. It is a positive goal. We have many, many thousanuds of wonderfully idealistic young men and women in our student body, in our residence halls, in our fraternities and sororities, on our campuses statewide, who really want to help—who are ashamed of the blind and melancholy prejudices or of the simple unconcern which many brought with them to our academic world— who recognize that what they have inherited is a white problem more than a Negro problem—and who want to work with their follows to help them see and free themselves. Let us then work together for the real objecitve; let us abjure hate and force and ultimata; let us embrace hard work, persuasion, forgiveness when earned, encouragement, good will even in the face of ill will, and *understanding.*"

Document 200

Freedom versus Intimidation

In the heat of turmoil and confusion during the troubled spring of 1968 President Elvis Stahr perceived that the ramparts of academic freedom were being assailed by alien forces. There could be no compromises or surrenders on the central spirit of academic rights and privileges. This statement was issued on the day the Board of Trustees formulated and published its statement of policy on the same subject.

* * *

STATEMENT OF PRESIDENT ELVIS J. STAHR TO BOARD OF TRUSTEES
RE: DISSENT VS. DISRUPTION
MAY 24, 1968

Some of the events of this year on campuses across the nation have suggested some searching reflection upon the principles which undergird the academic community. The very soul of the environment for scholars is complete freedom for each to inquire, to debate and to criticize, a freedom that must be preserved against attack from within the University as well as from the outside.

Inherent in such a position is the repudiation of every form of physical pressure or force. Truth is simply not reached by methods of intimidation or destruction. It may be that nowhere else in society can reason, stripped of emotion, be expected to have its unfettered say as it can in universities; in any case, it is crucial that this refuge so remain.

We recognize each individual's right to disagreement, even dissension, but the University and its members must be protected from threat and intimidation. Once means are sanctioned for moral ends, they may as easily be used for immoral ones.

We believe it is vitally important to this nation and to every member of the University itself that the academic freedom of the University be sustained and that the University's activities be subjected to modification only through rational means. Impairment of these principles must never meet reward. We of the administration, and I believe I speak also for the faculty and most, I hope all, of the students, in reasserting our intent to keep the University's campuses free from interference by any with the rights of others, from interference with free inquiry and expression of opinion and from disruption of the University's functioning by menacing or coercive means.

Document 201

Trustee Policy Statement on Academic Freedom and the Right of Dissent

In response to President Elivs Stahr's statement to the Board of Trustees, the board issued this statement of policy which not only clarified the institution's attitude toward academic freedom and the right of dissent but also descried rowdiness and violence. The trustees prescribed the conditions under which disciplinary actions would be taken in cases where individuals and groups sought to disrupt the orderly course of free discussion and the freedom of access to all academic sources.

*   *   *

STATEMENT OF TRUSTEES OF INDIANA UNIVERSITY

The Trustees of Indiana University consider it both timely and appropriate to reaffirm the long-standing commitment of the University to provide maximum educational opportunity for all her students and to make explicit that an essential part of that commitment and of such opportunity is the necessity to maintain genuine academic freedom and to preserve the right of *all* members of the University community to question, debate, criticize and dissent peaceably.

In keeping with these traditional policies, the trustees recognize that educational opportunity, academic freedom and the right to dissent peaceably cannot be preserved in an environment of force and violence or the threat of force and violence which interferes with, or disrupts or obstructs the work and activities of the University or the members of the University community. Such a climate is created by the unauthorized seizure and occupation of University facilities so as to deprive members of the University community of the full use of such facilities for their intended purpose, and of like effect are the use of intimidation, coercion, or the physical restraint or threatening of persons.

In the light of the fact that such events have occurred in a number of academic communities in recent weeks, the Trustees of Indiana University are constrained to make plain their support of the officials of the University in the firm enforcement of University policies and rules relating to picketing, demonstrating and related matters, and we recognize and affirm the necessity to take immediate steps to expel, under established procedures, any student who (1), actively engages in any conduct which includes violence or the threat of violence and which obstructs or disrupts University work or activity or (2), who engages in conduct which usurps University property or facilities; and, further, we reaffirm the necessity to take immediate steps to impose appropriate discipline, including expulsion, under established procedures, upon any student who engages in conduct which unreasonably interferes with the freedom of movement of persons on any campus of the University.

Adopted by the Trustees May 24, 1968.

Document 202

Stahr's Resignation

Elvis J. Stahr served Indiana University six years as president. The last year of his administration was highly disturbed by forces almost beyond his control and not of his making. He and his colleagues were victimized by widespread student dissatisfaction and unrest of the 1960s. Sitting in the very eye of the storm, President Stahr had little opportunity to gain a full-range perspective of events which unsettled the campus. Threats against the safety of his family in one or two of the student commotions seem, on a backward look, to have been more dramatic than real. Efforts to protect the central freedoms of the University and at the same time maintain peace and order in the student body became a physically and emotionally draining ordeal. His letter of resignation came as a surprise to everybody, and is an eloquent statement of his reasons for leaving an office which he had so gallantly assumed just six years before.

*   *   *

STATEMENT

By: Elvis J. Stahr, Prseident, Indiana University
To: Trustees of Indiana University in Regular Meeting
Re: Resignation from the Presidency of the University
Date: July 6, 1968

For at least two years I have been increasingly aware that the heavy and growing pressures of the University presidency were levying a great toll. By the end of the past academic year, I had to face the plain fact that I have succumbed to what one resigning president aptly called "presidential fatigue."

After considering this difficult decision over an extended period and from every angle, including the best interests of the University, my family, and my future health and pursuit of happiness, I have notified the members of the Board of Trustees that I am giving up the presidency on September first. Though I have done this with a feeling of immense relief, I have also done it with genuine regret, because my six years in this office have brought many enduring satisfactions to me and, happily, have been years in which the University has made tremendous progress. I am deeply devoted to the University and hope to remain on her faculty, so that our family can stay in this fine community and this friendly State and I can continue to serve I. U. in a useful even though very different way.

I am happy in the knowledge that I have given the University the very best that is in me every hour of these six long and busy years. I am deeply gratified, too, that all of the Trustees wanted me to continue as president and urged me simply to take a leave of absence and return to the job refreshed. I considered that for some days, but in the end concluded that the decision I have made is the best one to make.

One of my closest friends, when I told him a few days ago that I was going to give up the presidency, interrupted before I could explain further and asked, "What has gone wrong?" My answer to him is my answer to any others who may wonder similarly. Nothing has "gone wrong"; the University is sound and strong, and my own relationships with the Trustees, the faculty, the students and my administrative colleagues are warm and deeply satisfying. I simply have "presidential fatigue," the result of 24 straight years of working unusually long hours in unusually demanding jobs, the last ten years of which have been in positions I can only describe as involving "super-pressure." I think it far better for both the University and me that I step out of that pressure before, rather than after, it renders me seriously ineffective. I also look forward to seeing far more of my young children.

> ELVIS J. STAHR
> President
> Indiana University

RESOLUTION
ADOPTED BY THE TRUSTEES OF INDIANA UNIVERSITY, July 6, 1968

WHEREAS, Dr. Elvis J. Stahr came to Indiana University as its President in July, 1962, after having served with distinction and honor in key positions in the fields of education and government, and

WHEREAS, under his leadership Indiana University has continued to progress, expand, and enhance its position of great distinction in the educational world, and

WHEREAS, during his tenure as President Dr. Stahr has unstintingly given of his time, talent and energies to the successful solution of many of the complex problems confronting Indiana University as well as institutions of higher education generally, and

WHEREAS, the Board recognizes the signal loss to the students, faculty, and alumni of Indiana University and to the State of Indiana which will be sustained as a result of President Stahr's resignation, the Board further recognizes and is grateful that this loss is lessened by the fact that President Stahr will continue to contribute to the University, the State of Indiana, and to higher education as a member of the faculty.

THEREFORE, BE IT RESOLVED that the Board of Trustees of Indiana University hereby expresses its appreciation to Dr. Elvis J. Stahr for the devoted and outstanding service he has rendered and commends him for the outstanding leadership given and the remarkable achievements accomplished during his tenure as President.

AND BE IT FURTHER RESOLVED, that it is with deep regret that the Board reluctantly accepts his resignation as President; however, the Board looks forward to his continued service to the University and the State of Indiana as a member of the University family.

Document 203

The Waning of Student Activism

In the fall of 1968 Herman B Wells was temporarily back in the office of the President of the University as an interim President. One of the major problems he faced was that of bringing some kind of harmony to the campus in this era of emotional upheaval. In this brief statement he gave evidence of some serious re-examination of the ancient concepts by which Indiana University had related itself to its student body. There is also a brief blueprint for future relationships between the institution and its clientele.

*   *   *

Here at Indiana University, particularly on the Bloomington campus, the last few years have seen the rising, insistent claim of student activism. I should have been apprehensive had this not occurred, for on small campuses as well as large throughout the nation, students have found vigorous spokesmen. Without taking the time now to analyze this I might point out the difficulty of decisions that rest on the thin lines between request and demand, between consensus and represented opinion, between felt needs and desired goals. One of the easiest things in the world is to say no to change; one of the hardest to provide for its reasoned and orderly occurrence.

In the perspective of time, I believe that the management of change affecting students at Indiana University will be heralded as a signal characteristic of the Stahr era. I might note in passing that Jordan upon his assumption of the presidency in 1885, revoked all student regulations except two; namely that the students should not set fire to buildings nor shoot their professors. In the last six years, the number of all-University committees with student representation on them jumped from 9 to 37 or more; the Student Affairs Committee was formed to recommend policy on student matters; a bicameral system for presentation of regulations concerning student conduct to the Board was instituted; a pass-fail option came into being; a student evalution of teaching was published for the first time in recent years; and the regulations concerning student life were liberalized.

I tend to agree with Jordan that universities should never have undertaken to use their resources for a role which is not their unique business, the assumption of "in loco Parentis" responsibilities. Those responsibilities have been assumed for only a portion of our undergraduate student body and are generally disciplinary in nature rather than educationally-motivated or fashioned to individual need. Perhaps the best educational service we can render students in this regard is to reenforce principles of self-discipline. To this end, our residence halls should be adapted as rapidly as possible to support a more academic atmosphere. Academic counseling, clinics and seminars ought to be regular features of each hall. Students should find the halls inviting places for study, and the lifting of the requirement that some of our students must live in the halls will contribute to this long-held goal. An outstanding characteristic of the six-year period just completed has been the increasing reliance placed on students to govern and discipline themselves, with gradual withdrawal of the University as an instrument of extended parental control.

Indiana *Daily Student*, October 10, 1968.

Document 204

The Indiana University Position, 1968

President Elvis J. Stahr, Jr. was confronted in the spring and summer of 1968 with militant demands from various groups. The most vocal were the blacks and the opponets of military cooperation on the part of the University. When Herman B Wells returned to the presidency in an interim capacity, he was confronted with the same peremptory demands. These he refused to discuss with student militants who wanted to give him a third-degree excoriation. Instead he chose his time, place, and the conditions under which he would discuss university affairs with students. This document is a report of that discussion. In large measure this meeting with students ended the most militant of campus disturbances which had so sorely troubled the last months of the Stahr Administration. It did not, of course, end student protests against the Vietnam War.

*   *   *

MESSAGE OF PRESIDENT HERMAN B WELLS,
INDIANA UNIVERSITY
TO THE UNIVERSITY COMMUNITY

When I agreed to talk to interested students on the subjects of recruiting in our recreational facilities, "learning how to kill in our classrooms," and performing military research in our laboratories, I felt that the University community had a right to know my views and my information on these topics.

Six days after that agreement, I was presented a list of points described as demands, supported by the Young Socialist Alliance but mentioning repeatedly and prominently "S.D.S.," the initials of an organization known as Students for a Democratic Society. Spokesmen requesting the original meeting were members of the delegation presenting the demands. Through a letter to "Mr. King et al," I explained that the original invitation tendered to me to speak to these issues had been qualified by conditions which made it apparent that my views and information were of minimal interest to those students who had requested a meeting. Therefore, I would present my statement instead to the *Indiana Daily Student* and would have copies available for anyone interested.

The questions raised by the S.D.S., I wish to emphasize, do not concern extra-curricular activities or regulations affecting student life as have issues raised earlier by students. The S.D.S. demands invade the area of academic programs and the scholar's freedom to pursue his research interests.

The impropriety of "demands" as a form of questioning policy and practice in an academic community should be evident to every member of the community. Nevertheless, I shall respond to them specifically in giving my views and the information I have, in order to keep the record as clear as possible.

I believe that any community of scholars would agree that *no* special interest group, internal or external, should be allowed to impose its particular point of view upon the university. This does not imply any restriction on questioning, making suggestions, seeking information or peaceful and orderly advocacy—although usually there are more direct sources of information than the President of the University. It does mean that the policy of an open campus in which freedom of inquiry is protected is of highest importance to the university community. Indiana University has an unblemished tradition of preserving an open campus.

In times of national stress, when public opinion is divided, pressures are invariably brought to bear upon the University to support the views of one or the other side by excluding controversial speakers, activities or programs. The sharp cleavage of opinion about the national involvement in Vietnam has produced such pressures. This background of the open campus and the pressures to restrict it should be kept in mind throughout my disscussion of the nine points raised by the S.D.S.

The S.D.S. document delivered to me through my assistant began: "SDS rejects Indiana University's role as a subserviant, uncritical flunky of the military establishment and of the agencies formulating American policy. We reject this university's commitment to the objectives of American foreign policy and its commitment to train armies and police forces and their spies. Consequently SDS demands that President Wells immediately sever Indiana University's ties to all military and paramilitary organizations and specifically that:

"1. All ROTC programs be eliminated. In other words, that Indiana cease supplying academic credit for ROTC courses, academic personnel to teach these courses, and classroom and office space for ROTC programs. And that Indiana University cease to have any direct or indirect military presence on campus."

My response: Indiana University offered military training sporadically from 1841 to 1874. Its R.O.T.C. program was established in 1917 and military training has been part of the undergraduate curricula ever since then. The program was compulsory for most male undergraduates until September, 1965, when, by action of the Board of Trustees, it was made voluntary. The inclusion of military training in the curricula was instituted on each occasion at the urgent request of students.

Land-grant institutions such as Purdue University are required to provide military training by the Morrill Act of 1862 which established them. Students desiring to come to I.U. but who are intent upon taking R.O.T.C. should not be limited in their choice to land-grant institutions. Furthermore, as a result of R.O.T.C. programs at civilian institutions, the large majority of the men in officer ranks are R.O.T.C.-trained college men and partly because of this, the United States fortunately has not developed a narrow professional group with a stake in militarism.

R.O.T.C. continues to be offered at I.U. because many of our students desire officer training in conjunction with their college education to prepare either for military careers or for a period of military service. The presence of an R.O.T.C. unit on campus in no way interferes with conscientious objectors any more than, for example, the existence of our School of Medicine interferes with students who are Christian Scientists. R.O.T.C. is included as an integral part of the accepted academic program at the Ivy League universities and at all the major state universities.

The University's R.O.T.C. program has been reviewed many times and at least three times in the last seven years by the Curriculum Committee of the College of Arts and Sciences. These reexaminations and one now in progress reflect the fact that the faculty of the College, like the faculties of the other Schools with undergraduate divisions, establishes the number of credit hours in military science applicable to the satisfaction of its degree requirements. Originally, military training at I.U. was associated with a program in civil engineering. Its availability now as an option for students in each of the undergraduate schools is indicative of the variety of duty assignments in the armed services.

The University's agreement with the Department of Defense with respect to the R.O.T.C. program commits the University to granting appropriate academic credit applicable toward graduation for successful completion of courses offered in military science. The University provides classroom and office space as it does for other programs in which courses are taught for credit; the Department of Defense furnishes instructors, equipment, clothing and student retainer pay.

In recent years there has been some experimentation with the R.O.T.C. curriculum. At I.U., students in Army R.O.T.C. may satisfy one of its requirements by taking a course in American History which is open to all interested students and a course in Government is offered under similar conditions to students in Air Force R.O.T.C. and others. The possibility of including additional University courses as part of the R.O.T.C. program can be further explored. This, of course, is not a question of supplying academic personnel to teach R.O.T.C. courses, but rather of permitting course work in various departments to be counted toward satisfaction of R.O.T.C. program requirements.

As a credit program, R.O.T.C. grades are figured in the overall accumulative average of a student in any of the undergraduate colleges except the College of Arts and Sciences, which includes grades of advanced R.O.T.C. work only.

The chairman of the Committee to End the War in Vietnam, Grant Williams, has asked me to respond to several questions about R.O.T.C. which I am including in this discussion. He asked whether such nonacademic factors as appearance, obedience and political beliefs count in R.O.T.C. grades. Factors which contribute to such grades vary as they would in any professional-type training program. For example, appearance, uniforms and obedience are essential factors in the I.U. Marching Hundred and other factors are crucial to HPER courses. Political beliefs, in the sense of a choice among alternatives available to any citizen of a democracy, provide criteria for neither exclusion from nor inclusion in R.O.T.C. If such beliefs as conscientious objection to war are meant by the question, the fact that R.O.T.C. is voluntary makes such a point irrelevant.

Mr. Williams also asked whether admission to advanced R.O.T.C. was limited by such factors as sex and physical qualifications, and if so, was this policy consistent with academic requirements As a matter of fact, female students may enroll for credit in Army and Air Force R.O.T.C. with the approval of appropriate military authorities. Driver Training, Physical Education for Men, Dentistry, and numerous other areas of study have limiting factors for enrollment, including sex or physical qualifications.

Credentials of officers nominated for positions in the Department of Military Science and Air Science are transmitted through the Dean for Undergraduate Development to the University President for appointment. The President need not approve an appointment and he can request relief of an officer for cause.

The CEWV chairman has suggested that R.O.T.C. could be made a voluntary student group, such as the Chess Club. In 1861 military training was provided through an organization called the University Cadets. However, such an approach would not only be in violation of our agreements with the Department of Defense but would place professional preparation for military service at an unwarranted disadvantage in relation to other professional programs.

Mr. Williams further suggested the establishment of a Department of Peace with an equal status to the R.O.T.C. program. Peace, given its broadest meaning, undoubtedly embraces a large number of courses already offered. The rationale for instituting a Department of Peace apparently is that this would be a positive approach to achieving peace. It should be remembered that many people have long held that an important way to achieve peace is through the deterrent of adequate military preparation. Moreover, all who now decry defense should recognize that the nation faces many problems in this area in addition to Vietnam.

I might point out that in 1918, when students became enlisted soldiers while in residence, classes in War Aims were instituted which dealt with the immediate causes of the war and the underlying conflicts of points of view as expressed in the governments, philosophies and literatures of the warring countries on each side of the struggle.

Before concluding my discussion of R.O.T.C., I wish to make two points. If in this time of war hysteria we should be persuaded to cancel out the R.O.T.C. program for political reasons, we would in effect be yielding to precisely the same kind of pressures which from time to time have demanded that we cease teaching anything about Karl Marx, Russian history, and Slavic languages and literature. There is little practical difference to the University whether those demands come from inside or outside the University community. Secondly, while it is understandable that many people who bear the terrible brunt of war should be opposed to war, our national involvement in Vietnam is nonetheless a fact, as is the draft. The likelihood that many of your fellow students will be called upon for military service still remains unfortunately strong. In your zeal to end the war and promote peace, consider the effect of your attack upon R.O.T.C. Its existence is less essential to the war effort than to fellow students who wish to have the advantage of preparation in the skills that will equip them for a better chance of survival in the performance of their mandatory military service. Opposing R.O.T.C. may satisfy your hunger for action but its crucial effect will be to remove the option of valued training for many of your classmates.

S.D.S. demand: "2. Cease actively channeling students into military and military-related agencies (*i.e.,* the Defense Department, State Department, CIA, FBI, Army, etc.) by allowing their recruiters to use University facilities."

My response: The University is not engaged in "actively channeling" students into anything other than its instructional programs. (I mean by this that students are assisted through the University's counseling program to be aware of fields of study for which their scholastic aptitudes and interests fit them.) But, as all students know, they are completely free to choose their courses of study, their fields of concentration and their careers, within the limitations of their capabilities. No one is pressured into accepting any job. Everyone is a free agent, free to accept, reject or ignore recruitment efforts.

Historically, the University began to furnish placement services as a convenience and aid to graduating students in their search for jobs. In recent years, as more jobs became available than graduates to fill them, employer representatives have come to the campus for interviews, a development which again was to the advantage of students.

After a group of students objected to the presence on campus of employer representatives associated with Dow Chemical Company, the Faculty Council elected a Steering Committee to Study Policies Governing Picketing and Demonstrations and added student representatives. One of the first recommendations of that committee was as follows:

"The Faculty Council reaffirms the present policy of providing student placement services and allowing any employer to interview any student for the purpose of lawful employment, subject to the non-discrimination policy established by the Board of Trustees, July, 1967."

This recommendation, in the form of a motion, was passed unanimously at the Faculty Council meeting of February 20, 1968.

At the Faculty Council's meeting on March 12, 1968, the committee submitted a more comprehensive resolution on this subject which was passed after lengthly discussion.

The resolution reads:
"The Faculty Council hereby resolves:
1) THAT IT IS THE SENSE OF THE COUNCIL:
THAT PUBLICIZING EMPLOYMENT AND CAREER OPPORTUNITIES AND RECRUITING FOR
SUCH OPPORTUNITIES SHALL BE GOVERNED BY RULES AND REGULATIONS THAT ACCORD
NO PREFERENTIAL TREATMENT FOR ANY TYPE OF EMPLOYMENT OR SERVICE;
THAT ANY ORGANIZATION, PUBLIC OR PRIVATE, BE PROVIDED UNIVERSITY FACILITIES
FOR RECRUITMENT ONLY WHEN ONE OR MORE STUDENTS HAVE INDICATED AN IN-
TEREST IN BEING INTERVIEWED BY THAT AGENCY;
THAT RECRUITMENT INTERVIEWS OR THE PUBLICIZING OF EMPLOYMENT OPPOR-
TUNITIES, PUBLIC OR PRIVATE, SHALL BE CONDUCTED IN PRIVATE, EXCEPT THAT
CAREER INFORMATION MEETINGS, AS DISTINGUISHED FROM RECRUITMENT INTER-
VIEWS, MAY BE HELD IN DESIGNATED ROOMS, AND THAT REASONABLE PUBLICITY
BY NOTICES PLACED ON BULLETIN BOARDS OR BY LITERATURE DEPOSITED FOR PICK-
UP AT DESIGNATED LOCATIONS, MAY BE PERMITTED;
2) THE OFFICE OF THE PRESIDENT, THE BOARD OF DIRECTORS OF THE INDIANA
MEMORIAL UNION, AND THE DIRECTORS OF UNIVERSITY PLACEMENT SERVICES ARE
REQUESTED TO TAKE ANY NECESSARY STEPS TO BRING CAMPUS RECRUITING PRACTICES
INTO CONFORMITY WITH THIS RESOLUTION."

It should be pointed out that the Indiana Memorial Union is a student building, financed by student fees. Every student officially enrolled on the Bloomington
campus of I.U. is an active member of the Indiana Memorial Union. The legal
title to all funds and property of the Indiana Memorial Union is vested in and
subject to the control of the Trustees of Indiana University. However, The
Board of Directors of IMU, comprised of twelve students and five representatives
of the faculty and administration, is "empowered to promulgate and administer
such bylaws and house rules as may be needed to govern the activities and conduct of members, guests, visitors and organizations in, on, or about the premises
of the Union Building."

By long-standing policy, the Union Board's regulations permit representatives
of the armed services as well as of other organizations to reserve tables in the
Commons Lobby for three days in a five-week period as an informational service
to students.

At present, the policy committee of the Union Board is conducting interviews
to ascertain the opinions of key people on the campus concerning this policy.
The Board will hold an open hearing on this subject Monday afternoon, November 4.

Although the Faculty Council and the Union Board differ in respect to the
locations in which recruiters may provide information and conduct interviews,
both support the "open campus" policy I discussed in my opening comments.

The argument has been advanced from time to time that to allow recruitment
is to approve of the agency doing recruitment. The reverse is more cogent: refusal
to permit recruitment by a particular agency means condemnation of that agency.

Now, placement services and recruitment are admittedly adjuncts to the educational process. They need not take place on the campus except as a matter of
convenience for students. But for the University to select from among the agencies
of government, business, industry, etc., which ones should be permitted to recruit
would place it in the untenable position of passing judgment on an agency.

Those who wish to ban military recruitment on campus either because of their
pacifist views or as a means of protesting governmental policy have an obligation
to consider the full and long-term effect of using the University for promotion of
their own position on war generally or the Vietnam War in particular. Pressure

to use the University for promotion of any group's particular position on an issue constitutes an assault upon the integrity of the University. Yielding to that pressure would make the University vulnerable to any and every special plea. The plain fact is that those who are objecting to military recruitment simply wish to use the University as a means of protesting or even coercing governmental policy. This is an ineffective and even reprehensible use of the University.

S.D.S. demand: "3. All military-financed research be immediately terminated and the University cease to accept contracts and grants from any military or military-related agency."

My response: The University has no contracts or grants which provide for faculty members to engage in military research, if by "military research" one means research directed toward the production and use of military weapons such as tanks, guns or bombs, or to engage in research on chemical or bacterial warfare methods.

Indiana University received $1,281,145 from the Department of Defense agencies last year to support basic scientific research. This represented about 4.4% of our total research support from outside sources. It should be emphasized that these projects are *basic* research and *in every case the project was initiated by the faculty member himself.* Each project represented a research interest of the faculty member, frequently pursued for a long period of time prior to the submission of a proposal. There are no restrictions on publication of the results; that is, *none of the research is classified.*

The history of the discussion leading to the decision of the government to support basic scientific research through DOD (Department of Defense) agencies is pertinent. After World War II with its disruption of fundamental research, the scientific community urged the Federal Government to support basic research. Since there was neither a National Science Foundation (established 1950) nor an Atomic Energy Commission (established 1946) the government turned to the Office of Naval Research and similar DOD agencies and granted them funds specifically to support basic scientific research. These agencies have continued to administer funds of this nature. DOD agencies have *not* asked our faculty to do specific research for the government. To the contrary, our faculty have made their own proposals in their own fields of interest. They seek support wherever available. The DOD agencies use panels of distinguished, non-agency scientists to evaluate the scientific merit of these proposals and to select those to be funded with the monies available. May I repeat, *no* restrictions are placed on publication of results.

In order to avoid too much overlapping of effort, each agency has established certain areas of specialization but these are not necessarily exclusive. It is desirable to have more than one source of possible support, should one agency not have funds available or should some review panels or administrators become biased against a particular area of science.

A special word about the Themis project which is funded by the Air Force. Our faculty proposed three projects which they wanted to pursue under this program and which they felt were within the areas outlined for support with the original funds available to the DOD. One of these was selected by the agency for support and was funded. This project, directed by Dr. Bullard of our Department of Anatomy and Physiology, is entitled "Environmental Hazards to Biologic Systems" and continues work he and others in his department have been engaged in for a lengthy period. The project has to do with physiological adjustments of men to heat, cold, work and altitude, in relation to the effects of aging, physical condition and status of physiological adaptation. It also is concerned with X-irradiation effects, oxygen, sound and light on the nervous system, biological rhythms in amphibians and the regulation of sweating. These are obviously of interest to athletes and space travelers among others. It is good, basic, fundamental research; such research has in the past and will continue in the future to save lives of persons whose conditions of stress do not relate to military activities in any regard, as well as the lives of some who are in military service. It has been prominent among the special areas of research of our Department of Anatomy and Physiology.

Let me reaffirm in the strongest terms our intention to defend the right of every faculty member to carry on without fear of censure or disruption the research in which he is interested. We will seek support for him from any and all legal sources. I need only mention the Kinsey research to illustrate that the University has braved heavy criticism to prevent the subjects of research and of classroom instruction from proscription by external or internal pressure groups.

S.D.S. demand: "4. All special training programs for police forces, foreign or domestic, be ended."

My response: I confess to some bafflement here, having understood that widespread agreement exists on the desirability of the best possible training for police forces everywhere. Consistent with *that* understanding, we have a Department of Police Administration in the College of Arts and Sciences. The University has recognized police administration as a profession since the establishment of the Institute of Criminology in June, 1935. The department exists for students who wish to pursue professional careers in this field. Its faculty perform research to increase knowledge of the field and to improve methods of professional practice. Instruction and research are appropriate university functions. Determination of the curricula is, by statute, a faculty responsibility. Over the nearly century and a half of Indiana University's existence, a narrow classical curriculum has evolved into diverse curricula with many specializations. In general, the developments have represented a response to student interest and needs of our state and society. Within this framework, the existence of a Department of Police Administration asserts the social desirability of University-trained individuals in positions of responsibility for community and state police forces, and evidences a continuing choice by I. U. students to pursue careers in this field. Foreign students enrolled at I. U. naturally have that same option.

Also, as a service to the State of Indiana we have entered into annual contracts with the State for the use of classroom and housing facilities by the Indiana State Police Department in its training program. This is, of course, always subject to the availability of the facilities.

Indiana University, as an agency of the State, is sensitive to the areas of cooperation and service which it can provide when requested to do so. The use of its facilities for another State agency's training program is not inconsistent with the purposes of the University.

S.D.S. demand: "5. The University cease all special training programs for military and intelligence of any kind."

My response: Since I cannot find that we have a single program of this kind, we can hardly *cease* having what we do not have.

S.D.S. demand: "6. The University cease intimidation of student political activity by:

"a. removing all plainclothes and secret police from the campus;"

My response: I do not accept the premise that the University intimidates student political activity. This "when did you stop beating your wife" type of trap need not confuse the discussion.

I want to remind you also that the abandonment of registration procedures for student organizations makes identificaiton of a student with any political organization impossible, except as the student himself establishes that identity. But I do not condone intimidation of students, faculty or administrators who are engaging in lawful pursuits by police *or* by student groups, for that matter.

Now, to the question of plainclothes and secret police. I know of no secret police on the campus. The University quite naturally cooperates with law enforcement agencies, except when a request conflicts with a University policy such as the confidentiality of personal records.

We will not protect illegal activity on the campus and will cooperate with the efforts of law enforcement officers to detect violations and enforce the law in the legitimate performance of their duties.

We do have three investigators on the Safety Department staff at Bloomington in addition to Director Spannuth who customarily do not wear uniforms. There is nothing either sinister or secret about their presence. They are here to protect the University community, its property and the University's property.

S.D.S. demand: "6.b. The University cease intimidation of student political activity by: sending only clearly labeled administrative observers to political events;"

My response: I do not know what useful purpose labeling of individuals would serve, but if that is generally desired, I suggest that everyone be labeled—students and faculty members as well as administrators. Faculty observers and administrative observers are present at demonstrations and for the same purpose: to obtain first-hand information about the event. In earlier incidents, claims and counterclaims by the parties involved produced a confusing picture of the actual sequence of events and of the conduct of the participants. The presence of observers helps guarantee as accurate a report as possible, which is certainly in the interest of students participating. The University is concerned that no wrongful complaints be made against any of its students.

S.D.S. demand: "6.c. The University cease intimidation of student political activity by: ending intimidation of students through the use of cameras and recording devices at such events;"

My response: Again, the University is interested in accurate reports of events. It is not apparent to me why the recording of what is actually said or done could be anything but helpful to students who are not guilty of any violation. Students themselves bring these "devices" to "such events."

S.D.S. demand: "6.d. The University cease intimidation of student political activity by: removing from the campus all implements of political repression such as tear gas, chemical mace and riot clubs, whose only use could be against students."

My response: There is a sly appeal in the picture of the campus as a tranquil place which has no need for a safety division. By implication, the existence of such a division with its supply of deterrent tools must surely be for some questionable purpose. The S.D.S. would have students believe that the division exists to intimidate student political activity. What are the facts?

During the month of September, 1968, the Bloomington campus Safety Division was called upon to investigate 134 reports of incidents, *viz.:*

92 larcenies
20 acts of vandalism
5 assaults
5 vehicle thefts
3 breaking and entering
3 minor sex offenses
2 trespasses
1 suicide
1 attempted suicide
1 attempted rape
1 impersonation of a police officer

The monetary losses reported amounted to $8,872.80.

Clearly the campus is not a crime-free environment and the campus residents need protection. A majority of the suspects involved are outsiders, rings of thieves, etc., who operate out of large cities. It is patently absurd to charge that provisions for protection are disguises for intimidation of student political activity. Campus elections, Dunn Meadow political gatherings, marches around Showalter Fountain, discussions in the area south of Woodburn Hall have always been carried on without Safety Department interference with legitimate activity. The presence of Safety Department personnel at large assemblies, whether for an Auditorium Series event, an athletic contest or a student political rally signifies primarily a recognition of the accident potential in crowds. Quite honestly, there is an additional factor of concern, however, when an emotionally-charged issue is to have partisan presentation before a student gathering; namely, that representatives of the opposing side will lose their constraint.

In either event, the presence of Safety Department personnel is for protection in cases of emergencies and loss of equanimity. Moderate subduers for crowd control have prevented accidents resulting from hysteria and have permitted the resolution of differences to occur in a less emotionally-charged atmosphere.

However, the entire question of Safety is under study by a faculty committee and its report will undoubtedly deal with some of these matters.

Finally, I wish to exercise the prerogative of speaking to one subject of my own choosing. That is our foreign contracts. I do this to correct the impressions left by various assertions made in publications circulated on campus that the University is engaged in supporting reactionary governments abroad.

The facts are:

1) I.U.'s relationships in every case are with universities, not governments;

2) All of the contracts are connected with development—that is, with advising universities on their training programs in order to assist in the development of progressive professional leadership; and

3) Only two of the projects, in Afghanistan and Chile, are funded by an agency other than the Ford Foundation; these two are AID-supported.

Our present contracts are with universities in Afghanistan, Chili, Indonesia, Pakistan, Peru, the Philippines, Thailand and Yugoslavia. Through this aid we hope not only to further the educational progress of newly developing nations but also to discharge our debt to the world of scholarship which we and other American universities incurred when older universities in Europe gave us invaluable assistance during our early years. Happily, the repayment of our intellectual and scholarly debt is financed by the Ford Foundation and AID, without cost to the Hoosier taxpayer. Dean Merritt or I will be pleased to discuss the nature and details of these projects with any of you who are really interested in the facts about our overseas projects.

I thank you for your interest in my views and information on these several topics. May I add that, while I am sensitive to the strong pacifist sentiment among some of our students and faculty members and the depth of their convictions about the United States' involvement in the Vietnam War, I am even more sensitive to the vital necessity of preserving the principle of the open campus. I strongly oppose the exclusion of recruiters and the banning of R.O.T.C., just as I have successfully opposed efforts to have the University oust individuals active in anti-military and other controversial causes. I fully support the discussion and study of issues involved in the Vietnam War, in war itself, and in the presence of the military on campus. I would support as well thorough, objective, unbiased research into the history, development and nature of the military arm of government and its role in enabling American citizens to live according to their Constitutionally-determined choices.

Each of us has a crucial stake in seeing to it that Indiana University enters the post-war period, which will come, still invulnerable to the pressures that would erode its strength and violate its cherished principles: freedom to teach, to learn, to seek new knowledge and to serve society.

Index